The Dictionary of
HUMAN GEOGRAPHY
Third Edition

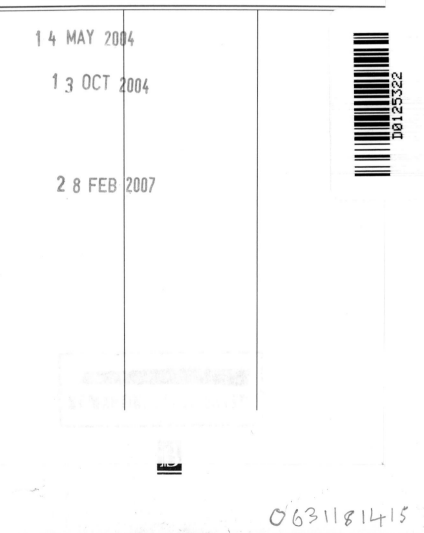

The Dictionary of
HUMAN GEOGRAPHY
Third Edition

Edited by
R. J. Johnston
Derek Gregory and David M. Smith

Copyright © Blackwell Publishers Ltd 1994
Editorial organization © R. J. Johnston, Derek Gregory and David M. Smith 1994

First published 1981
First paperback edition 1983
Reprinted 1985, 1996

Second edition 1986
Reprinted 1988
Second paperback edition 1988
Reprinted 1989, 1990, 1991

Third edition, revised and updated, 1994
Third paperback edition 1994
Reprinted in paperback 1994 (twice), 1995, 1996

Blackwell Publishers Ltd
108 Cowley Road, Oxford OX4 1JF, UK

Blackwell Publishers Inc.
238 Main Street
Cambridge, Massachusetts 02141, USA

British Library Cataloguing in Publication Data
A CIP catalogue record for this book is available from the British Library.

Library of Congress Cataloging-in-Publication Data
The Dictionary of human geography / edited by R. J. Johnston, Derek
Gregory, and David M. Smith. - 3rd ed.
p.   cm.
Includes bibliographical references and index.
ISBN 0-631-18142-3 (pbk. : alk. paper)
1. Human geography-Dictionaries.   I. Johnston, R. J. (Ronald John)
II. Gregory, Derek, 1951–. III. Smith, David Marshall, 1936–.
GF4.D52   1993
304.2'03–dc20
92–44285
CIP

Typeset in 9 on 10pt Plantin
by TecSet Ltd, Wallington, Surrey.
Printed and bound in Great Britain by Hartnolls Ltd, Bodmin, Cornwall

This book is printed on acid-free paper

CONTENTS

PREFACE TO THE THIRD EDITION

Geographical dictionaries have a long history. A number were published during the seventeenth and eighteenth centuries: a few – mostly those with greater pretensions to providing conceptual order – were described as 'Geographical Grammars'. The majority were compendia of geographical information, or gazetteers, some of which were truly astonishing in their scope. For example, Laurence Echard noted with some asperity in his 1691 *Compendium of Geography* that the geographer was by then more or less required to be 'an *Entomologist,* an *Astronomer,* a *Geometrician,* a *Natural Philosopher,* a *Husbandman,* an *Herbalist,* a *Mechanick,* a *Physician,* a *Merchant,* an *Architect,* a *Linguist,* a *Divine,* a *Politician,* one that understands the *Laws* and *Military Affairs,* an *Herald* [and] an *Historian'.* Marguerita Bowen, commenting in 1981 on what she took to be geography's isolation from the scientific mainstream in Echard's time, suggested that 'the prospect of adding epistemology and the skills of the philosopher' to such a list might well have precipitated its Cambridge author into the Cam!

Three centuries later it was in large measure the addition of those skills to the necessary accomplishments of a human geographer which prompted the first edition (1981) of *The Dictionary of Human Geography.* We noted then that the changes in human geography since the Second World War had generated a 'linguistic explosion' within the discipline. Part of our purpose – then as now – was to provide students and others with a general series of philosophical and theoretical frameworks for situating, understanding and interrogating the modern lexicon.

The pace of change within human geography and associated disciplines did not slacken during the 1980s. This stimulated the production of a second edition of the *Dictionary* only five years after the first, with substantial rewriting and a considerable number of new entries. A few years further on, preparation of this third edition has involved yet more extensive revisions and substantial additions to the text, to take account of important recent developments. The first edition had over 500 entries, written by 18 separate contributors, whereas the present volume has over 700, penned by 45 different authors. Over 100 entries appear for the first time in this third edition, and with them we have charted the emergence of new themes, approaches and concerns within the discipline; we have also sought to anticipate fresh avenues of inquiry and new links with other disciplines.

Many of the changes we have introduced are far-reaching. *The Dictionary of Human Geography* is concerned almost entirely with English-language words, terms and practices, but this represents neither parochialism nor imperialism on the part of editors and authors. Of the eighteen contributors to the original edition, fifteen were working in England; our first major change is reflected by the fact that this edition includes 16 authors domiciled in Canada and the United States. In addition, we have taken into account contemporary concerns about ethnocentrism and racism, plus the emergence of a postcolonial critique – all vitally important issues to a discipline like geography. Secondly, and in marked contrast to earlier editions, we have paid particular attention to the importance of feminist perspectives, as reflected in the language used (the only sexist writing appears in quotations).

Thirdly, the original edition was planned at the height of the critique of spatial science, and for that reason most of the entries were concerned with either analytical methods and formal models or with alternative concepts and approaches drawn from other social sciences. We have taken new developments in analytical methods into account in this edition, by no means all of them uniquely associated with spatial science and the emergence of new technical skills and capabilities. Considerable attention has also been paid to developments in the humanities as well as the social sciences – the former have greatly influenced the creation of a theoretically-informed cultural geography, with its interests in power, knowledge and representation, for example. In addition, focus has also been placed on the examination of modernism and postmodernism within human geography, the continued vitality of political geography and the revival of the history of geography and exploration.

None of these changes is a purely intellectual matter, of course, for they have not occurred in a vacuum: the world has changed dramatically over the last decade, and this is reflected in both the concerns addressed by human geographers and their approaches to understanding. New entries cover shifts in the structure of the capitalist world-economy, including key debates over the supposed transition from Fordism to flexible accumulation; they register the dramatic geopolitical shifts, including the dissolution of the former Soviet Union and the rise of nationalisms throughout the world; and they take account of heightened ecological concerns at global and local scales.

In these various ways, the third edition of *The Dictionary of Human Geography* is a report from a crowded and complicated landscape. Like its predecessors, it will surely prove as indispensable as an atlas to all human geographers exploring this vibrant discipline, as various and vital today as it was when Laurence Echard wrote.

Ron Johnston
Derek Gregory
David Smith

ACKNOWLEDGEMENTS

In the production of this edition we have been extremely fortunate in having the strong support and encouragement of John Davey, friend as well as publisher: his unrivalled contribution to the geographical publishing over some thirty years was deservingly honoured in 1992 by the Association of American Geographers. Our thanks are also due to Judith Harvey and Halina Boniszewska for their management of the project, Geoffrey Palmer for superb copy-editing, and Ann Barham for an excellent index.

Production of a multi-authored work is inevitably something of a tense activity. Contributors are encouraged to participate, cajoled to produce the wanted material, prompted to meet deadlines, and subjected to editorial whims: they then have to sit and wait, for what may seem an age, while all of the entries are collected, collated, edited and prepared for publication. To all of those who agreed to undergo these tribulations, our heartfelt thanks: we are delighted with what they have delivered, and hope that they are as pleased with the final product – noting that, in good geographical tradition, the quality of the whole is even greater than that of the many excellent parts.

The authors and publishers wish to thank the following for permission to use copyright material.

Aldine de Gruyter for fig. **reciprocity** from Marshall Sahlins, *Stone Age Economics*, 1972. Copyright © 1972 by Marshall Sahlins;

Basil Blackwell Ltd. for fig. 4, **critical theory** based on Jurgen Habermas, *The Theory of Communicative Action*, Vol. 2, Polity Press; fig. **spatiality**, **production of space**, figs. 1 and 2 and **crisis** from D. Gregory, *Geographical Imaginations*, 1993; fig. **human agency** from A. Giddens, *The Constitution of Society*, Polity Press, 1984; and with the University of Chicago Press for fig. **capitalism** from D. Harvey, *The Limits to Capital*, 1982;

Basil Blackwell Inc. for fig. **time-space convergence** from D. G. Janelle, 'Central Place Development in a Time-Space Framework', *Professional Geographer*, 20, 1968;

Cambridge University Press and The University of Chicago Press for fig. **multiple nuclei model** from Harris and Ullman in H. M. Mayer and C. F. Kohn, eds., *Readings in Urban Geography*, 1959;

Edinburgh University Press for fig. **urban origins**, figs. 1 and 2, from P. Wheatley, *The Pivot of the Quarters*, 1971;

ACKNOWLEDGEMENTS

The Geographical Association for fig. **ontology** from D. Gregory, in Russell King, ed., *Geographical Futures*, 1985;

HarperCollins Publishers for fig. **demographic transition** from P. Haggett, *Geography: A Modern Synthesis*, Harper & Row, 1975;

Hodder & Stoughton Publishers Ltd. for fig. **locational analysis** from P. Haggett, A. D. Cliff and A. Frey, *Locational Analysis in Human Geography*, 1977; and fig. **krondratieff cycle** based on Marshall, 1987, from P. Knox and J. Agnew, *Geography of the World-Economy*, 1989; and fig. **feedback** from J. Langton, Potentialities and problems of adopting a systems approach to the study of change in human geography', *Progress in Geography*, 4, 1972;

The Institute of British Geographers for fig. **cost surface** from D. M. Smith, 'On throwing Weber out with the bath water: a note on industrial location and linkage', *Area*, (1), 1970;

Institut National d'Etudes Demographiques for fig. **population pyramid** from *Population et Sociétés*, INED, 255, March, 1991;

John Libbey Eurotext Ltd. for fig. **mortality** from J. L. Rullu and A. Blum, eds., *European Population: I Country Analysis*, 1991;

Macmillan Publishers Ltd. for figs. **law of the sea** from A. Couper, *Geography and Law of the Sea*, 1978; fig. **locale** and **time-space distanciation** from A. Giddens, *Power Property and the State*, Vol. I, 1981; fig. **resource** from J. Rees, and **layers of investment** and **space economy** from D. Gregory, in D. Gregory and R. Walford, eds., *Horizons in Human Geography*, 1989; with St. Martin's Press for fig. **krondratieff cycle** from Knox and Agnew, adapted from M. Marshall, *Long Waves of Regional Development*, 1987;

Prentice Hall Inc. for fig. **Alonso model** from Martin T. Cadwallader, *Analytical Urban Geography: Spatial Patterns and Theories*, 1985;

Ohio State University Press for fig. **distance decay** from Peter J. Taylor, 'Distance transformation and Distance Decay Functions', *Geographical Analysis*, Vol. 3, 3 July, 1971. Copyright © 1971 by Ohio State University Press;

Routledge for fig. **mode of development** from D. Gregory in Richard Peet and Nigel Thrift, eds., *New Models in Geography*, Vol. 2, 1989, Unwin Hyman; figs. **intensive research**, **internal relations** and **ontology** from Andrew Sayer, *Method in Social Sciences: A Realist Approach*, 1992, 1984, Hutchinson; fig. **cycle of poverty** from R. J. Johnston, *City and Society: An Outline of Urban Geography*, 1984, Hutchinson; with St. Martin's Press for fig. **behavioural environment** from D. Gregory, *Idealogy, Science and Human Geography*, 1978, Hutchinson; figs. 1, 2 & 3, **catastrophe theory** from C. A. Isnard and E. C. Zeeman in L. Collins, ed., *The Use of Models in the Social Sciences*, 1976, Tavistock; fig. **dual economy** from M. Santos, *The Shared Space*, 1979, Methuen & Co.; fig. **stages of growth** from D. E. Keble in R. J. Chorley and P. Haggett, eds., *New Models in Geography*, Methuen & Co.;

Royal Dutch Geographical Society, KNAG, for fig. **applied geography** from M. Pacione, 'Conceptual issues in applied urban geography', *Tijdschrift voor Economische en Sociale Geografie*, 81, 1990;

University of California Press for fig. **cultural landscape** from Carl O. Sauer, *The Morphology of Landscape*, 1925. Copyright © 1925 The Regents of the University of California;

The University of Chicago Press for fig. **zonal model** from R. E. Park, E. N. Burgess and R. D. McKenzie, *The City*, 1925; fig. **structural functionalism** from N. Smelser, *Social Change in the Industrial Revolution*, 1959;

The University of New Mexico Press for fig. **form of economic integration** from P. Wheatley in J. A. Sabloff and C. Lamberg-Karlovsky, eds., *Ancient Civilisation and Trade*, 1973;

The University of North Carolina Press for fig. **indices of segregation** from F. Lancaster Jones, 'Ethnic Concentration and Assimilation: An Australian Case Study', *Social Forces*, 45 (3) 1967. Copyright © The University of North Carolina Press;

John Urry for fig. **civil society** from J. Urry, *The Anatomy of Capitalist Societies*, 1981;

Every effort has been made to trace all the copyright holders, but if any have been inadvertently overlooked the publishers will be pleased to make the necessary arrangement at the first opportunity

CONTRIBUTORS

AGH Tony Hoare
University of Bristol

AMH Alan Hay
University of Sheffield

CWJW Charles Withers
*Cheltenham and Gloucester College
of Higher Education*

DBG David Grigg
University of Sheffield

DEC Denis Cosgrove
*Royal Holloway College,
London*

DG Derek Gregory
University of British Columbia

DH Daniel Hiebert
University of British Columbia

DL David Ley
University of British Columbia

DMS David M. Smith
*Queen Mary and Westfield
College, London*

DNL David Livingstone
The Queen's University, Belfast

GES Graham Smith
University of Cambridge

GML Malcolm Lewis
University of Sheffield

GP Geraldine Pratt
University of British Columbia

IGS Ian Simmons
University of Durham

JAA John Agnew
Syracuse University

JAR Judith Rees
University of Hull

JD James Duncan
Syracuse University

JE John Eyles
McMaster University

JEm Jody Emel
Clark University

JP Joe Painter
University of Durham

JRJ John Jensen
University of South Carolina

LWH Les Hepple
University of Bristol

MB Mark Blacksell
University of Exeter

MDB Mark Billinge
University of Cambridge

MG Mike Goodchild
*University of California,
Santa Barbara*

MJB Michael Blakemore
University of Durham

MJD Michael Dear
University of Southern California

MO Mark Overton
University of Newcastle upon Tyne

MSG Meric Gertler
University of Toronto

MW Michael Watts
University of California, Berkeley

NB Nick Blomley
Simon Fraser University

NJT Nigel Thrift
University of Bristol

NS Neil Smith
Rutgers University

PEO Philip Ogden
Queen Mary and Westfield College, London

PEW Paul White
University of Sheffield

PG Paul Glennie
University of Bristol

PH Peter Haggett
University of Bristol

PAJ Peter Jackson
University of Sheffield

PJC Paul Cloke
University of Bristol

PJT Peter Taylor
University of Newcastle upon Tyne

RJJ Ron Johnston
University of Essex

RL Roger Lee
Queen Mary and Westfield College, London

SC Sarah Curtis
Queen Mary and Westfield College, London

SJS Susan Smith
University of Edinburgh

TJB Trevor Barnes
University of British Columbia

ABBREVIATIONS IN HUMAN GEOGRAPHY

Ever since the Roman inscription 'SPQR' was carved as a short form for 'Senatus Populusque Romanus' (Senate and people of Rome) the invention of abbreviations and acronyms has grown apace. The first volume of a reference work from 1978 (E. T. Crowley, ed., *Acronyms, initials, and abbreviations dictionary*, Gale, Detroit, 1978) contained 178,000 entries. This accelerating trend towards abbreviating and producing acronyms in the place of full titles may well be justified by reason of space saving. At the same time, the failure of all authors and editors to record at least once the full meaning of any abbreviation can make identification tiresome for the reader. Since the number of abbreviations in current use is now so large this brief list gives only those terms most commonly encountered in the literature of human geography in the early 1990s and others used in this *Dictionary*. The standard abbreviations of leading geographical journals are given in italics and follow the recommendations of the *World list of scientific periodicals*. The abbreviation of organizations follows that of the *World guide to abbreviations of organizations* (fifth edition ed. F. A. Buttress, London, Leonard Hill, 1974).

AAG	Association of American Geographers
ABS	*American Behavioral Scientist*, Beverly Hills and London, 1957–
ACSM	American Congress on Surveying and Mapping
Acta Sociol.	*Acta Sociologica*, Oslo, 1955–
Afric. Stud. R	*African Studies Review*, Los Angeles, 1958–
Ag. Hist.	*Agricultural History*, California, 1927–
Ag. hist. R.	*Agricultural History Review*, Reading, 1953–
AGS	American Geographical Society
Am. Anthr.	*American Anthropologist*, Washington, 1888–
Am. behav. Scient.	*American Behavioral Scientist*
Am. Cartogr.	*American Cartographer*, Falls Church, Virginia, 1974–
Am. hist. Rev.	*American Historical Review*, Washington, DC, 1895–
Am. J. Soc.	*American Journal of Sociology*, Chicago, 1895–
Am. pol. Sc. Rev.	*American Political Science Review*, Baltimore, 1906–
Am. Scient.	*American Scientist*

Am. Soc. R.	*American Sociological Review*, Washington, DC, 1936–
AMTRACK	American Track (US National Railroad Passenger Corporation)
Ann. Am. Acad. Pol.Soc.Sci.	*Annals of the American Academy of Political and Social Science*, Beverly Hills, 1891–
Ann. Ass. Am. Geogr.	*Annals of the Association of American Geographers*, Washington, DC, 1911–
Annls dem. Hist.	*Annales de Démographie Historique*, Paris 1965–
Annls Géogr.	*Annales de Géographie*, Paris, 1891–
ANOVA	analysis of variance (statistics)
AONB	area of outstanding natural beauty (UK)
Appl. Geogr.	*Applied Geography*, London, 1981–
Aust. Geogr.	*Australian Geographer*, Sydney, 1928–
Aust. geogr. Stud.	*Australian Geographical Studies*, Sydney, 1963–
Aust. and NZ J. Sociol.	*Australian and New Zealand Journal of Sociology*, St Lucia, Queensland, 1965–
BMD	biomedical computer programs (developed at the University of California at Los Angeles)
Brit. J. Polit. Sci.	*British Journal of Political Science*, Cambridge, 1971–
Br. J. Soc.	*British Journal of Sociology*, London 1950–
CACM	Central American Common Market
CAG	Canadian Association of Geographers
Camb. J. Econ.	*Cambridge Journal of Economics*
CARIFTA	Caribbean Free Trade Agreement
Can. Cartogr.	*Canadian Cartographer*, Toronto, 1964–
Can. Geogr.	*Canadian Geographer*, Montreal, 1951–
Can. hist. Rev.	*Canadian Historical Review*
Can. J. Econ. pol. Sci.	*Canadian Journal of Economics and Political Science*
Can. J. soc. pol. Theory	*Canadian Journal of Social and Political Theory*
Can. Rev. Sociol. Anthropol.	*Canadian Review of Sociology and Anthropology*
Cartogr. geogr. Inform. Sys.	*Cartography and Geographic Information Systems*
Cartog. J.	*Cartographic Journal*, London, 1964–
CBD	central business district
COMECON	Council for Mutual Economic Aid
Comp. Stud. Soc. Hist.	*Comparative Studies in Society and History*
DUS	daily urban system
ECA	United Nations Economic Commission for Africa
Ec. Dev. cult. Ch.	*Economic Development and Cultural Change*, Chicago, 1952–
ECE	United Nations Economic Commission for Europe

ECLA	United Nations Economic Commission for Latin America
Ecol.	*Ecology,* Durham, North Carolina, 1920–
Econ. Develop. Cult. Change	*Economic Development and Cultural Change*
Econ. Geogr.	*Economic Geography,* Worcester, Massachusetts, 1925–
Econ. Hist. R.	*Economic History Review,* London, 1927–
Econ. Societ.	*Economy and Society,* London, 1927–
ECSC	European Coal and Steel Community
EEC	European Economic Community
EFTA	European Free Trade Association
EIA	Environmental Impact Assessment
Environ. Behav.	*Environment and Behavior,* 1969–
Environ. Conserv.	*Environmental Conservation*
Environ. Plann.	*Environment and Planning,* London, 1969–
EPNS	English Place-Name Society
ERDF	European Regional Development Fund
Erdkunde	*Erdkunde: Archiv für wissenschaftliche Geographie,* Bonn, 1947–
ESCAP	United Nations Economic and Social Commission for Asia and the Pacific
ESRC	Economic and Social Research Council (UK)
Europ. J. Marketing	*European Journal of Marketing*
Europ. J. pol. Res.	*European Journal of Political Research*
Eur. J. Sociol.	*European Journal of Sociology,* Cambridge, 1960–
FAO	United Nations Food and Agriculture Organization
GATT	General Agreement on Tariffs and Trade
GENSTAT	general statistics computer programs (developed at Rothamsted Experimental Station)
Geogr.	*Geography,* Sheffield, 1901–
Geogr. Abs.	*Geographical Abstracts,* Norwich, 1966–
Geogr. Anal.	*Geographical Analysis,* Columbus, Ohio, 1969–
Geogr. Annlr.	*Geografiska Annaler,* Stockholm, 1919–
Geogr. Pol.	*Geographica Polonica*
Geogr. Res. Forum	*Geography Research Forum*
Geographica helv.	*Geographica Helvetica,* Zurich, 1946–
Geogrl. J.	*Geographical Journal,* London, 1893–
Geogrl. Mag.	*Geographical Magazine,* London, 1935–
Geogrl. Rev.	*Geographical Review,* New York, 1916–
Geogrl. Stud.	*Geographical Studies,* London, 1954–59
Geogr. Z(s).	*Geographische Zeitschrift,* Wiesbaden, 1963–
GLIM	general linear interactive modelling (computer software package)
GNP	gross national product

Hist. J.	*Historical Journal*, Cambridge, 1958–
Hist. Sci.	*History of Science*
Hist. Theor.	*History and Theory*, Connecticut, 1960–
Hist. Workshop J.	*History Workshop Journal*, Oxford, 1976–
IBG	Institute of British Geographers
IBGE	Instituto Brasileiro de Geografia e Estatistica
ICA	International Cartographic Association
ICC	US Interstate Commerce Commission
IGN	Institut Géographique National
IGU	International Geographical Union
IIASA	International Institute for Applied Systems Analysis
Int. Aff.	*International Affairs*, Moscow, 1955–
Int. J. Man-M.	*International Journal of Man-Machine Studies*, London 1969–
Int. J. urban and reg. Res.	*International Journal of Urban and Regional Research*, Oxford, 1977–
Int. reg. Sci. Rev.	*International Regional Science Review*, Philadelphia, 1975–
Int. Soc. Sci. J.	*International Social Science Journal*
Int. Yearbook Cartogr.	*International Yearbook of Cartography*, Bonn-Bad Godesberg, 1961–
ITC	International Training Centre, Delft, Netherlands
Izv. ser. geogr.	*Izvestiia: Seriia geograficheskaia*, Moscow, 1951–
J. agric. Econ.	*Journal of Agricultural Economics*, Reading, 1954–
J. Am. Plann. Assoc.	*Journal of the American Planners Association*
J. Br. Stud.	*Journal of British Studies*
J. Commun.	*Journal of Communication*
J. contemp. Hist.	*Journal of Contemporary History*, London, 1966–
J. econ. Hist.	*Journal of Economic History*, New York, 1941–
J. Eur. econ. Hist.	*Journal of European Economic History*, Rome, 1972–
J. Forest.	*Journal of Forestry*, Bethesda, Maryland, 1902–
J. Geogr.	*Journal of Geography*, Chicago, 1902–
J. Hist. behav. Sci.	*Journal of the History of the Behavioral Sciences*
J. Hist. Biol.	*Journal of the History of Biology*
J. hist. Geogr.	*Journal of Historical Geography*, London, 1975–
J. Law Soc.	*Journal of Law and Society*
Jnl. Polit. Econ.	*Journal of Political Economy*, Chicago, 1892–
J. Op. Res. Soc.	*Journal of the Operational Research Society*
J. R. Statist. Soc., Ser. A	*Journal of the Royal Statistical Society, Series A*
J. reg. Sci.	*Journal of Regional Science*, Philadelphia, 1958–
J. Rural Stud.	*Journal of Rural Studies*
J. soc. Hist.	*Journal of Social History*, Pittsburgh, 1967–
J. soc. Policy	*Journal of Social Policy*

J. trop. Geogr.	*Journal of Tropical Geography*, Singapore, 1958–80
J. T. S. Behav.	*Journal for the Theory of Social Behaviour*, Oxford 1971–
J. Wash. Acad. Sci.	*Journal of the Washington Academy of Sciences*
LAFTA	Latin American Free Trade Association
Landsat	land satellite – launched by NASA for imaging the Earth's surface
Landscape Res.	*Landscape Research*
LDC	less developed country
L'espace géogr.	*L'espace géographique*, Paris, 1972–
L. Soc.	*Language in Society*, Cambridge, 1972–
Local Pop. Stud.	*Local Population Studies*
MAB	UN programme on Man and the Biosphere
Manchester Sch. Econ. Soc. Stud	*Manchester School of Economics and Social Studies*, Manchester, 1930–
MDS	multidimensional scaling (statistics)
MELA	Metropolitan Economic Labour Area
MIF	mean information field
MINITAB	minicomputer tabulation (a computer program package)
MPC	marginal propensity to consume (economics)
MPS	marginal propensity to save (economics)
MSY	maximum sustained yield (biology)
NASA	US National Aeronautics and Space Administration
NATO	North Atlantic Treaty Organization
NERC	Natural Environment Research Council (UK)
NGS	National Geographical Society (New York)
New Left. Rev.	*New Left Review*
New Soc.	*New Society*, London, 1962–
NIDL	New International Division of Labour
NIMBY	not in my back yard
NNP	net national product (economics)
NORDEK	Nordic Economic Community
NPP	net primary production (biology)
N.Z. Geogr.	*New Zealand Geographer*, Christchurch, 1945–
ODECA	Organization of Central American States
OECD	Organization for Economic Co-operation and Development
OLS	ordinary least squares (statistics)
OPCS	UK Office of Population Censuses and Surveys
OPEC	Organization of Petroleum Exporting Countries

Pap. Mich. Acad. Sci.	*Papers of the Michigan Academy of Science, Arts and Letters*, Ann Arbor
Pap. reg. Sci. Assoc.	*Papers [and Proceedings] of the Regional Science Association*, Philadelphia, 1955–
Past and Present	*Past and Present: A Journal of Historical Studies*, Oxford, 1952–
Petermanns geogr. Mitt.	*Petermanns geographische Mitteilungen*, Gotha, 1855–
Phil. Soc. Sci.	*Philosophy of the Social Sciences*, Waterloo, Ontario, 1971–
Philipp. Stud.	*Philippine Studies*, Manila, 1953–
Photogramm. Engng Remote Sensing	*Photogrammetric Engineering and Remote Sensing*
Pol. Geogr. Q.	*Political Geography Quarterly*, London, 1982–
Pol. Soc.	*Politics and Society*
Pol. Stud.	*Political Studies*
Pop. Stud.	*Population Studies*
Proc. Amer. Phil. Soc.	*Proceedings of the American Philosophical Society*, Philadelphia, 1838–
Proc. Ass. Am. Geogr.	*Proceedings of the Association of American Geographers*
Proc. roy. Geogr. Soc.	*Proceedings of the Royal Geographical Society*, London, 1855–1892
Prof. Geogr.	*Professional Geographer*, Washington, DC, 1949–
Prof. Statist.	*The Professional Statistician*
Prog. Geog.	*Progress in Geography*, London, 1969–76
Progr. hum. Geogr.	*Progress in Human Geography*, London, 1977–
Progr. phys. Geogr.	*Progress in Physical Geography*, London, 1977–
Progr. Plann.	*Progress in Planning*, Oxford, 1973–
Psychol. Rev.	*Psychological Review*
Publ. Admin. Rev.	*Public Administration Review*
Publ. Am. Sociol. Soc.	*Publications of the American Sociological Society*
Q. J. Econ.	*Quarterly Journal of Economics*, New York, 1886–
Q. J. soc. Aff.	*Quarterly Journal of Social Affairs*
Reg. Sci. Urban Econ.	*Regional Science and Urban Economics*
Reg. Stud.	*Regional Studies*, Cambridge, 1967–
Rev. Econ. St.	*Review of Economics and Statistics*, Cambridge, Massachusetts, 1976–
Rev. Fr. Soc.	*Revue Française de Sociologie*, Paris, 1960–
Rev. int. Stud.	*Review of International Studies*
RGS	Royal Geographical Society
RSA	Regional Science Association
Rural Sociol.	*Rural Sociology*, New York, 1958–
S. Afr. geogr. J.	*South African Geographical Journal*, Braamfontein, 1917–

Sci.	*Science*, Washington, DC, 1883–
Sci. Soc.	*Science and Society*, New York, 1936–
Sci. Stud.	*Science Studies*, Texas, 1920–
Scient. Am.	*Scientific American*
Scott. geogr. Mag.	*Scottish Geographical Magazine*, Edinburgh, 1885–
SEATO	Southeast Asia Treaty Organization
SMLA	Standard Metropolitan Labour Area
SMSA	Standard Metropolitan Statistical Area (US)
Soc. Hist.	*Social History*, London, 1976–
Soc. Rev.	*Sociological Review*, Keele, 1953–
Soc. Sci. Med.	*Social Science and Medicine*
Soc. Sci. Q.	*Social Science Quarterly*, Texas, 1920–
Social Res.	*Social Research*
Social. Rur.	*Sociologica Ruralis*, Assen, 1960–
Soviet Geogr.	*Soviet Geography: Review and Translation*, New York, 1966–
SPSS	statistical package for the social sciences (computer programs)
SSRC	Social Science Research Council (UK)
Svensk Geogr. Arsbok	*Svensk Geografisk Arsbok*, Lund, 1925–
SYMAP	computer mapping program using line printer originally developed at Harvard University
Tech. R.	*Technology Review*, Cambridge, Massachusetts, 1899–
Tijdschr. econ. soc. Geogr.	*Tijdschrift voor Economische en Sociale Geografie*, Rotterdam, 1910–
Town Plan. Rev.	*Town Planning Review*, Liverpool, 1910–
Trans. Inst. Br. Geogr.	*Transactions, Institute of British Geographers*, London, 1935–
Trans. roy. Hist. Soc.	*Transactions of the Royal Historical Society*, London, 1872–
Transport. Res.	*Transportation Research*
TVA	Tennessee Valley Authority
UNESCO	United Nations Educational Scientific and Cultural Organization
Urban Geogr.	*Urban Geography*
Urban Stud.	*Urban Studies*, Edinburgh, 1964–
Welsh H. R.	*Welsh History Review*, Cardiff, 1960–
WEU	Western European Union
WHO	United Nations World Health Organization
Wld. Cartogr.	*World Cartography*, New York, 1951–
World Pol.	*World Politics*, Princeton, 1948–

A

---

abstraction Conceptual isolation of (a partial aspect of) an object. For those geographies which are committed to POSITIVISM, abstraction represents the startingpoint of conventional model building. Chorley (1964) emphasized both its basic importance and its peculiar difficulty: 'In developing a simplified but appropriate model for a given object system or segment of the real world . . . huge amounts of available information are being discarded . . . and therefore much noise is being potentially introduced'. In consequence, Chorley believed that 'in geography most attempts at model-building by abstraction have met with minimal success'. Those which have fared best have 'exposed fundamental symmetries and relationships' while avoiding 'excessive simplification'. But he was unable to offer very precise guidelines for their construction, appealing to the 'creative ability and vision of the model-builder'.

For those geographies which are committed to various forms of IDEALISM, and particularly those whose procedures draw upon Max Weber's interpretive sociology, abstraction usually involves the construction of so-called IDEAL TYPES: 'onesided' idealizations of reality seen from particular points of view. There is nothing especially 'scientific' about them, Weber claimed, because this kind of selective structuring is something that we all do all the time. But since it is perfectly possible to construct quite different ideal types of the same phenomenon, depending on one's point of view, the critical moment comes when the ideal type is compared with 'empirical reality'. Even so, commentators differ on just how, precisely, such comparisons are to be made and on how revealing

they are likely to be (see Parkin, 1982, pp. 28–32).

For those geographies committed to REALISM, however, both of these versions of abstraction are inadequate because they are supposed to be based on 'an arbitrary attitude to ONTOLOGY' (Sayer, 1984, p. 216). According to Sayer, abstractions should identify *essential* characteristics of objects and should be concerned with 'substantial' relations of connection rather than merely 'formal' relations of similarity. It is especially important to identify those INTERNAL RELATIONS which *necessarily* enter into the constitution of structures. Hence, Sayer distinguishes a 'rational abstraction', i.e. 'one which isolates a significant element of the world which has some unity and autonomous force', from what Marx called a 'CHAOTIC CONCEPTION', i.e. one whose definition is more or less arbitrary because it rests on relations of similarity. So, for example, Allen (1983) provides a careful typology of landlords within the housing market, whose classifications 'bestow a degree of coherence upon certain groupings, that is, a structure which enables them to act . . . in [distinctive] ways depending upon the spatial and temporal circumstances' and which exemplifies this approach. From this perspective, it is equally important to recognize the existence of different *levels of abstraction*. Marx's own writings are usually cited here because they move from the general to the historically specific (see Johnson, 1982) and a number of workers have sought to elucidate, and indeed to refine, the connections between them (see Gibson and Horvath, 1983; Cox and Mair, 1989). DG

1

References

Allen, J. 1983: Property relations and land-lordism – a realist approach. *Environ. Plann. D: Society and Space* 1, pp. 191–203.

Chorley, R. J. 1964: Geography and analogue production. *Environ. Plann. D: Society and Space* 1, pp. 121–38.

Cox, K. and Mair, A. 1989: Levels of abstraction in locality studies. *Antipode* 21, pp. 121–32.

Johnson, R. 1982: Reading for the best Marx: history-writing and abstraction. In Centre for Contemporary Cultural Studies, *Making histories: studies in history-writing and politics*. London: Hutchinson, pp. 153–201.

Parkin, M. 1982: *Max Weber*. London: Tavistock.

Sayer, A. 1984: *Method in social science: a realist approach*. London: Hutchinson. (Second edition 1992. London: Routledge.)

Suggested Reading

Allen (1983).

Sayer (1992), pp. 85–92 and 138–40.

accessibility At its simplest, the ease with which one place can be reached from another. It may be measured in terms of geodetic distance, topological distance (see GRAPH THEORY), journey distance, journey time or monetary cost. The concept has been broadened in a number of ways. First, general accessibility may be calculated from a single point to all other points or areas in a study region. Second, accessibility may be related to the geographical content of other areas in the study region: access to employment opportunities, access to population, access to educational or health facilities etc. Third, some authors have recognized that access to certain activities and facilities may be made less easy by barriers other than physical distance (e.g. the effects of income and social class) and attempt to incorporate these in measures of accessibility. In all of these applications accessibility is seen to combine at least three elements: the location of a place within a study region (in general, centrally located places are more accessible); the form of the transport system; and the location within the study area of the activities to which access is being measured. AMH

Suggested Reading

Zakaria, T. 1974: Urban transportation accessibility measures: modifications and uses. *Traffic Quarterly* 28(3), pp. 467–79.

accumulation The process by which CAPITAL is reproduced at an ever-increasing scale through continued reinvestment of surplus value. In Marx's words: 'Employing surplus value as capital, reconverting it into capital, is called the accumulation of capital' (1987 edn, p. 543).

Accumulation is a definitive condition of CAPITALISM. To remain in business, the ordinary capitalist must at least preserve the value of capital advanced ('simple reproduction'), but to continue as a *capitalist* he or she must continually augment the value of invested capital ('expanded reproduction', or accumulation). Capital accumulation becomes a central driving force in capitalist society, influencing broader political, social, demographic and cultural change. More than anything else, Marx attributed the dynamism of capitalist society to the imperative of accumulation (see also MARXIAN ECONOMICS).

The imperative of accumulation presupposes capitalist relations of production; on the one side a class of capitalists who own the means of production, and on the other side a class of workers who are 'freed' from ownership of the means of production and who are also free to perform labour for the capitalist. The survival of the individual capitalist is dependent on the ability to sell commodities profitably in the market, and this has the effect of institutionalizing technological change as a means of competition between individual capitals. The imperative for accumulation at the individual level thereby translates into the social imperative for economic growth and technological change. In his 'general law of capitalist accumulation', Marx argued that the imperative of accumulation implied a second imperative, the relative immiseration of the working class that produces the expanding wealth – a fundamental social relation of capitalism (Marx, 1987 edn, ch. 25).

The social relations of capitalism are themselves the result of an historical process whereby workers are separated from the land and from the means of production, largely agricultural. This process, known as *primitive accumulation*, forces workers to sell their labour power for a monetary wage, and is best exemplified by the history of the ENCLOSURES in England and the subsequent privatization of land ownership.

The geography of capitalist accumulation (Harvey, 1977) is central to the fortunes of the capitalist mode of production (Harvey, 1982) and results in specific patterns of UNEVEN DEVELOPMENT at different spatial scales (Smith, 1990). The REGULATION SCHOOL attempts to identify specific stages and forms of capitalist development according to different REGIMES OF ACCUMULATION. Following the early insights of Gramsci (1971), one can distinguish two separate regimes of accumulation: (1) FORDISM, characterized by mass production, mass consumption and state regulation; and (2) POST-FORDISM, which now partially displaces fordism and is characterized by flexible and differentiated production, consumption and accumulation (Aglietta, 1979).   NS

References

Aglietta, M. 1979: *A theory of capitalist regulation.* London: New Left Books.

Gramsci, A. 1971: *Selections from the prison notebooks* (edited and translated by Q. Hoare and G. Nowell Smith). London: Lawrence and Wishart/New York: International Publishers, pp. 277–316.

Harvey, D. 1977: The geography of capitalist accumulation: a reconstruction of the Marxian theory. In Peet, R., ed., *Radical geography.* Chicago: Maaroufa, pp. 263–92.

Harvey, D. 1982: *The limits to capital.* Oxford: Blackwell.

Marx, K. 1987 edn: *Capital*, volume I. New York: International Publishers.

Smith, N. 1990: *Uneven development: nature, capital and the production of space.* Oxford: Blackwell, second edition.

Suggested Reading

Marx (1987 edn) esp. Part VII, 'The accumulation of capital' and Part VIII, 'The so-called primitive accumulation'.

acid rain   The terrestrial deposition of sulphuric and nitric acids formed in the atmosphere from compounds released by fossil-fuel and biomass burning. The British chemist R. A. Smith introduced the term in 1859, although only in the past few decades has it gained wide currency. Specialists distinguish acid rain from dry deposition of acidifying compounds, two processes that are conflated in popular usage. Both have been linked to severe damage to forests and wildlife through ecosystem acidification and the mobilization of toxic metals. They can also damage the built environment. As acid deposition may occur several hundred kilometres downwind from the source, the process frequently crosses national boundaries, and it has aroused international controversy in North America and Western Europe.   JEM

action space   The area within which an individual makes locational decisions, such as where to shop, which house to purchase, and which church to attend. The relevant locations within that space are evaluated and assigned PLACE UTILITIES; if none of the utility values is high enough, then the action space within which SEARCH BEHAVIOUR takes place may be extended. (See also ACTIVITY SPACE; MENTAL MAP.)   RJJ

activity allocation models   Planning models that are used to decide where activities will be located in a region.

In URBAN AND REGIONAL PLANNING prediction is often carried out in stages: the first uses either temporal extrapolation or more sophisticated methods (see ECONOMIC BASE THEORY; INPUT–OUTPUT; MULTIPLIERS) to predict the future aggregate population, industrial, commercial and retail employment, housing needs etc.; the second stage determines where within the region these various activities will be located. Some such models, e.g. LOWRY MODELS, are entirely predictive – they attempt to foresee future patterns in the absence of planning intervention – but some activity allocation models may be normative (see NORMATIVE THEORY) in attempting to use OPTIMIZATION MODELS to locate these activities. Yet others may be evaluative (looking at a number of alternative patterns of development).

The easiest method of activity allocation involves the construction of separate sub-models for industry, retail trade, residential location etc. in which the GRAVITY MODEL often plays a significant role, but the interactions between these submodels often require repeated iterations to ensure that the total results are consistent, e.g. that total journey-to-work trips into a zone equal the number of employment opportunities in that zone. There may also be difficulties in ensuring that the sums of zonal activities equal the aggregate predictions at the first stage. This latter difficulty is not simply a matter of computation: it identifies a flaw in the predictive logic because regional totals may themselves be aggregates arising from processes at zonal level rather than vice versa.   AMH

Suggested Reading
Batty, M. 1970: An activity allocation model for the Nottinghamshire–Derbyshire subregion. *Reg. Stud.* 4, pp. 307–32.

activity space   The space within which the majority of an individual's activities are carried out: it contains the ACTION SPACE within which particular locational decisions are made. Chombart de Lauwe (1952) suggested a hierarchy of activity spaces – familial, NEIGHBOURHOOD, economic and urban sector – within which different activities are conducted. Many of them, especially those at the larger spatial scales, may be discontinuous, comprising points linked by known routes but separated by areas that are virtually *terra incognita* to the individuals concerned. (See also MENTAL MAP.)   RJJ

Reference
Chombart de Lauwe, P. H. 1952: *Paris et l'agglomeratione parisienne.* Paris: Presses Universitaires de France.

age and sex structure   The composition of a population according to age and/or sex. These universal characteristics of human populations are fundamental to understanding demographic processes of FERTILITY, MORTALITY and MIGRATION. Age composition may be summarized in terms of age groups, e.g. 0–15 years, 15–64 years and 65 years or over: the sex ratio is most commonly expressed as the number

of males per 100 females. Characteristics of both age and sex may be expressed in the POPULATION PYRAMID.   PEO

Suggested Reading
Petersen, W. 1975: *Population,* third edition. New York and London: Collier-Macmillan, ch. 3.

agglomeration   The association of productive activities in close proximity to one another, as in a major specialized industrial region or in a large town or city. Agglomeration typically gives rise to EXTERNAL ECONOMIES associated with the collective use of the INFRASTRUCTURE of transportation, communication facilities and other services. Historically, there is a tendency for economic activity in general to concentrate in major agglomerations, the large market associated with metropolitan areas adding to the external cost advantages. Agglomeration also facilitates the rapid circulation of capital, commodities and labour. In some circumstances, DE-CENTRALIZATION within or beyond the metropolis may counter agglomerative tendencies; for example, if land costs and those associated with congestion in the central area are very high. (See also CONCENTRATION AND CENTRALIZATION.)
                                                          DMS

aggregate travel model   A device for estimating the total coverage of distance involved in serving the market from alternative locations. In its more general form this model can be applied to any situation in which it is necessary to aggregate all the trips made by individual participants in some activity, but the most common context is industrial location.

The aggregate travel model is related to the MARKET POTENTIAL MODEL, in that they both compare the advantage of alternative locations with respect to the market, but under different assumptions. The aggregate travel model assumes a market of varying size in different places, but one that is not sensitive to delivered price or distance from the production location. The model seeks the point of minimum coverage of distance, given by

$$A_i = \sum_{j=1}^{n} Q_j T_{ij}$$

where A_i is the aggregate distance travelled to serve the market from plant location i, Q_j is the sales volume expected in market j, and T_{ij} is the distance or transport cost between i and j. The market size Q may be assumed to be proportional to some alternative measure, such as per capita income or retail sales, as in the market potential model. Similarly, T_{ij} may be linear distance, actual cost, or distance raised to some power to reflect the actual cost–distance relationship in the prevailing freight rates (see DISTANCE DECAY; TRANSPORT COSTS).

The aggregate travel model usually provides figures for the relative advantage of alternative locations. Only if Q actually represents the volume of sales and T the real transport cost will the calculation of A give total transport costs for serving the market. As with the market potential concept, figures for aggregate travel can be mapped in the form of a surface (see COST SURFACE). Comparison with a market potential surface derived from the same data reveals differences between the spatial patterns of advantage with respect to serving the market, arising from alternative assumptions as to the nature of the demand situation.   DMS

Suggested Reading
Smith, D. M. 1981: *Industrial location: an economic geographical analysis*, second edition. New York: John Wiley, pp. 272–4.

agribusiness A form of farming organization in which a company owns and directs a factory that processes raw materials produced on a farm that is also owned and managed by the company. Modern management techniques are applied in the factory and the field, and the technology is the most advanced available. In some cases the company also controls much of the distribution of the finished product. The term 'agribusiness' was first applied to joint stock companies based in North America and Western Europe in the late nineteenth century, which grew, processed and transported tropical products. Since then it has been extended to cover many other farming

organizations or trends in the agricultural economy in the developed countries. It has thus been used to describe: (1) large, highly mechanized farms in Western Europe and North America that are efficiently managed and highly capitalized, and may grow some crops, e.g. sugar beet and peas, under contract for food processors, but are not controlled by the processing companies; (2) the whole of the food producing system in a modern economy; and (3) in temperate areas, corporate food processors that – like the original tropical agribusiness – own and manage the land that produces their raw materials (these are almost unknown in Western Europe, and are rare in the United States, where, however, contracting is more important than in Europe). Additionally, (4) some users of the term appear to confine it to the providers of inputs such as fertilizers, pesticides, seeds and machinery.   DBG

Suggested Reading
Burbach, R. 1980: *Agribusiness in the Americas*. New York and London: Monthly Review Press.
Dinham, B. and Hines, C. 1983: *Agribusiness in Africa*. London: Earthscan.
Wallace, I. 1985: Toward a geography of agribusiness. *Progr. hum. Geogr.* 9, pp. 491–514.

agricultural geography The study of spatial variations in agricultural activity. It was a leading subfield within ECONOMIC GEOGRAPHY until the 1950s, partly because it lent itself to prevailing geographical methods such as field mapping and regional delimitation, and in part because the then current belief in ENVIRONMENTAL DETERMINISM was not as inappropriate as in other fields of human geography. As the significance of agriculture in the economy has declined, so has the interest of geographers. Traditionally, the field has dealt with production on the farm and less commonly with trade. It has been argued that agriculture geographers should also concern themselves with *food production systems*, by including the agricultural input and food processing industries, which have become more closely integrated with farm production since the 1930s.

The *description* of agricultural variations has been subject to changes in emphasis. However, the study of crop and livestock distributions, whether singly (Robertson, 1930; Coppock, 1976) or in combinations, has always been prominent, and in the inter-war period land-use mapping was a major research activity in Great Britain (Stamp, 1948); since then the loss of agricultural land to urban expansion has received attention (Best, 1981). There have been numerous attempts to delimit agricultural regions, both at the world scale (Whittlesey, 1936) and for much smaller areas. Recently, the type of farming area approach (FARMING, TYPE OF) has been favoured.

However, it is generally agreed that characteristics other than land use are important and should be considered in both the construction of agricultural typologies and any systematic agricultural geography of an area. A primary distinction can be made between farmers who produce mainly for their own needs – subsistence farmers – and those who produce mainly for the market – commercial farmers (see SUBSISTENCE AGRICULTURE). In the past 30 years commercialization has proceeded rapidly in the developing countries. Many anthropologists and economists have argued that subsistence farmers have different aims from commercial farmers, and are necessarily less influenced by changing prices for inputs and products. Commercialization has conventionally been measured by the proportion of produce sold off the farm, although there are remarkably few spatial or historical studies of its extent. Many writers would also distinguish between those commercial farmers who, although profits are important, aim at the preservation of the family farm and value their way of life (PEASANTS) and those large capitalist farmers for whom profit is all. LAND TENURE is of prime significance, for the differences between tenancy, owner-occupation and communal tenure profoundly affect a farmer's choice of crops, management and PRODUCTIVITY, while the collective and state farms of the former socialist countries and the communes of China require special treatment. The reform of land tenure systems has been regarded as an important prerequisite for agricultural improvement (land reform). Farm size also justifies further inquiry for

it is a basic determinant of a farmer's welfare; the survival of too many small farms is at the heart of the European Community's current farm crisis. In the developed countries many farmers have sought to supplement falling incomes by taking a second job (PART-TIME FARMING).

Farm size, can, through ECONOMIES OF SCALE, influence EFFICIENCY. In the developed countries there has been a continuous decline in the number of small farms over the past 30 years, although in many developing countries rapid population growth has led to subdivision and an increase in the number of small farms. The *layout* of farms has received considerable attention, for many of the world's farms consist not of one block of land but of plots intermixed with other farmers' land (FARM FRAGMENTATION), and this generates inefficiencies. Although most of the world's farms are owned or rented by individuals who work the land – except in socialist countries – there has been an increase in corporate farming in the United States, and particularly by European- and American-owned corporations in Latin America and Africa (AGRIBUSINESS).

The geography of *agricultural labour* has received little attention from geographers, although there are great spatial differences in its density and composition. In Europe, Asia and Africa the family provides most of the labour, but PLANTATIONS, communes and COLLECTIVES have large landless labour forces, paid in wages or sometimes in kind, while in parts of Latin America serf-like labour existed until recently. There are also great variations in seasonal labour, and in the role of women in farm work.

Perhaps the major international differences in farming practice today are in the geography of *inputs*. Variations in the degree of mechanization are well known, yet more has been written upon the historical geography of farm mechanization than on the present pattern. The substitution of power and machines for human and animal labour clearly differentiates modern from traditional agriculture, and leads to great differences in *labour productivity*. But there are equally striking differences in land PRODUCTIVITY, related to the use of fertilisers, pesticides and modern crop varieties. The adoption of these inputs in the developing world has received much attention (GREEN REVOLUTION). In the developed world the use of fertilisers and pesticides has led to much criticism because of their adverse effects on flora, fauna and the water supply. Indeed, although the modernization or industrialization of agriculture in the developed world has massively increased output and productivity, its effects upon the environment, the creation of farm surpluses and the rise of large capitalist farms at the expense of family farming, have led to much criticism and to calls for a return to organic farming (see FARMING, TYPE OF).

Until the 1950s most *explanation* in agricultural geography emphasized the role of the physical environment; the limits of crop distributions were attributed to temperature and moisture variables and, on the microscale, slope, aspect and soil type were regarded as important. But with the rejection of environmental determinism and the adoption of model building in the 1960s this approach has been less common, although important contributions continue to be made. One recent way of looking at farming systems is to regard them as agro-ecosystems. Two aspects are of interest. First, in any ECOSYSTEM there is a food chain in which herbivores feed on the primary plant cover, and herbivores are preyed upon by carnivores; and there is a loss of energy through the system, as there is in agriculture – fewer acres are needed to provide a given supply of food from plants than from livestock. Second, natural ecosystems are maintained in balance over time by the recycling of nutrients; this cannot be in agriculture, where the natural vegetation is removed, but the means by which fertility is maintained – by fallowing, manuring, digging in legumes or using fertilisers – is an important differentiant of the world's agriculture (Bayliss-Smith, 1982; Tivy, 1990).

New approaches were triggered by the translation of J. H. Von Thünen's book (VON THÜNEN MODEL), which led to a large number of studies of the influence of either distance from the market or of fields

from the farmstead, on land use and farming intensity (INTENSIVE AGRICULTURE; EXTENSIVE AGRICULTURE). However, the decline of transport costs and the spread of refrigeration and canning has reduced the significance of this factor, except possibly on the continental and farm scale. There has been a great increase in the empirical study of farming on the urban fringe (Bryant et al., 1982). Two stimulating hypotheses by agricultural economists have prompted inquiries into the relationship between population density and farming. Ester Boserup (1965) argued that in subsistence societies population growth causes an increase in farming intensity – by which she meant a reduction in fallow and an increase in labour inputs – and this has been used to explain spatial differences in farming in developing countries (BOSERUP THESIS).

The theory of induced innovation put forward by Hayami and Ruttan (1985) has been equally stimulating. They argued that agricultural development over the past century has been determined by the original resource endowment. In countries with a low population density, an abundance of land but a shortage of labour, farmers will aim to maximize the use of labour, and hence farming will be highly mechanized but few yield-increasing inputs will be used. Output per labour unit will be high, but output per hectare low. Conversely, in densely populated countries land will be in short supply and expensive, and labour will be abundant and cheap, and so farmers will maximize the use of land by adopting yield-increasing inputs such as fertilisers, irrigation, pesticides and improved crop varieties. Clearly, such an interpretation has spatial implications.

One approach to the adoption of new techniques in agriculture is by the study of DIFFUSION. There are two aspects to this. The first, long-run interpretation is that plants and animals were domesticated originally in a specific region, but then spread to many other parts of the world. This process has taken some ten thousand years, although it was greatly accelerated by European expansion from the fifteenth century onwards, when American plants were brought to Eurasia, and European crops and livestock were taken to the Americas. Investigation has been undertaken largely by prehistorians, anthropologists and botanists, although geographers have made some notable contributions (Sauer, 1952). A more short-run interpretation deals with the present: farmers differ in their willingness to adopt agricultural innovations, and this is often related to factors such as their age and education and the size of their farms (Jones, 1967). There is also a spatial aspect of DIFFUSION, for innovation may spread out from a core region rather like the ripples that result from dropping a pebble in a pond (Hägerstrand, 1967). Geographers and others have made studies of spatial diffusion, although not all find this a satisfactory method of explanation (Blaikie, 1978).

Most geographers have regarded agricultural activity as primarily an economic activity; the principles of COMPARATIVE ADVANTAGE and RENT underlie most of the models of agricultural spatial activity. However, it is very clear that the laws of supply and demand have not operated in much of the world for much of the postwar period. In the market economies of Western Europe, the United States and Japan, farmers have been protected from changes in prices by a variety of methods; the STATE has become a dominant factor in determining agricultural activity by maintaining prices, subsidizing farm improvements and exports, and paying farmers not to grow crops. Although the Common Agricultural Policy of the EC is the best known and most abused, the United States and Japan have given at least equal protection to their farmers (Bowler, 1985). In the developing countries, governments have favoured the consumer rather than the farmer, but have intervened to promote irrigation, encourage the adoption of new techniques, reclaim land for the landless and change land ownership.

Not all differences in farming can be attributed to ecological or economic factors; a variety of cultural attributes may influence differences in crop and animal production, such as the Islamic restrictions on the consumption of alcohol and pigmeat, Hindu reluctance to slaughter cattle, and the difficulties that some Asian and African people have in digesting milk (Simoons, 1961).

In recent years a number of writers have commented upon the increasing industrialization of agriculture (Troughton, 1982; Healey and Ilbery, 1985; Gregor, 1982). Many of the inputs that were once provided upon the farm, such as manure and seed, are now derived from manufacturing industry, and power from humans and animals has been replaced by purchased electricity and petroleum. Similarly, farm produce is increasingly processed by food manufacturers. The raw materials that were once processed on the farm – such as milk into cheese and butter – have long been produced in factories, and farm products that were once processed locally, in industries such as flour milling and brewing, are processed by distant and larger firms. There is therefore a case for arguing that agricultural geographers, who have confined their attentions to production on the farm, should in future incorporate the study of input producers and food processors. To this should perhaps be added the geography of food consumption which, unlike the former, has received some attention; there has been particular interest in the study of the underconsumption of food (Dando, 1980; Grigg, 1985).   DBG

References

Bayliss-Smith, T. P. 1982: *The ecology of agricultural systems.* Cambridge: Cambridge University Press.

Best, R. H. 1981: *Land use and living space.* London: Methuen.

Blaikie, P. 1978: The theory of the spatial diffusion of agricultural innovations; a spacious cul-de-sac. *Progr. hum. Geogr.* 2, pp. 268–95.

Boserup, E. 1965: *The conditions of agricultural change: the economics of agrarian change under population pressure.* London: Allen and Unwin.

Bowler, I. R. 1985: *Agriculture under the Common Agricultural Policy.* Manchester: Manchester University Press.

Bryant, C. R., Russworm, L. H. and McLellan, A. G. 1982: *The city's countryside, land and its management in the rural–urban fringe.* London: Longman.

Coppock, J. T. 1976: *An agricultural atlas of England and Wales,* second edition, London: Faber and Faber.

Dando, W. A. 1980: *The geography of famine.* London: Edward Arnold/New York: Halstead Press.

Gregor, H. F. 1982: *Industrialization of US agriculture: an interpretive atlas.* Boulder, Co.: Westview Press.

Grigg, D. 1985: *The world food problem 1950–1980.* Oxford: Blackwell.

Hägerstrand, T. 1967: *Innovation diffusion as a spatial process.* Chicago: Chicago University Press.

Hayami, Y. and Ruttan, V. W. 1985: *Agricultural development: an international perspective,* second edition. Baltimore and London: Johns Hopkins University Press.

Healey, M. J. and Ilbery, B. W. 1985: *The industrialization of the countryside.* Norwich: Geobooks.

Jones, G. E. 1967: The adoption and diffusion of agricultural practices. *World Agricultural Economics and Rural Sociology Abstracts* 9, pp. 1–35.

Robertson, C. J. 1930: *World sugar production and consumption: an economic geographical survey.* London: John Bale.

Sauer, C. 1952: *Agricultural origins and dispersal.* New York: American Geographical Society.

Simoons, F. J. 1961: *Eat not this flesh: food avoidances in the Old World.* Madison: University of Wisconsin Press.

Stamp, L. D. 1948: *The land of Britain: its use and misuse.* London: Longman, Green and Co. and Geographical Publications.

Tivy, J. 1990: *Agricultural ecology.* Harlow: Longman.

Troughton, M. 1982: Process and response in the industrialization of agriculture. In Enyedi, G. and Volgyes, I., eds, *The effect of modern agriculture on rural development.* New York: Pergamon, pp. 213–28.

Whittlesey, D. 1936: Agricultural regions of the world. *Ann. Ass. Am. Geogr.* 26, pp. 198–240.

Further Reading

Andreae, B. 1981: *Farming development and space.* Berlin and New York: de Gruyter.

Grigg, D. B. 1984: *An introduction to agricultural geography.* London and Dover, NH: Hutchinson.

Ilbery, B. W. 1985: *Agricultural geography: a social and economic analysis.* Oxford: Oxford University Press.

agricultural involution A term coined by Geertz (1963) to describe the over-elaboration of labour-intensive methods of agricultural production. Under conditions of population pressure, agricultural output is maintained by increasing the input of labour, so that while output per hectare rises output per capita remains the same. No new methods are introduced, as known methods of production are endlessly elaborated and intensified, while social and economic structures also remain unchanged. This leads to a vicious circle, since there is little incentive for technological innovation in the agricultural sector which could raise output per capita.

Geertz developed his model in a study of the impact of COLONIALISM on Java where he identified a DUAL ECONOMY: an agricultural sector impoverished through agricultural involution, while in the industrial sector labour productivity continued to grow in response to capital investment. He found a 'sharing of poverty' in the agricultural sector, in that access to land and the opportunities for wage work were shared out, whereas inequality increased in the industrial sector.

Although White (1982) has argued that 'there is room for doubt whether involution and shared poverty as Geertz defined them were ever adequate characterizations of the political economy of Javanese village life', the generalized notion of agricultural involution is a useful ecological model which counters the more optimistic BOSERUP THESIS on the relationship between population growth and agrarian change. (See also the use of involution in writings on PROTOINDUSTRIALIZATION.)   MO

References

Geertz, C. 1963: *Agricultural involution: the process of ecological change in Indonesia.* Berkeley and Los Angeles: University of California Press.

White, B. 1982: Population, involution and employment in rural Java. In Harriss, J., ed., *Rural development: theories of peasant economy and agrarian change.* London: Hutchinson University Library for Africa.

Suggested Reading

Geertz (1963).

Harriss, J., ed. 1982: *Rural development: theories of peasant economy and agrarian change.* London: Hutchinson University Library for Africa.

agricultural revolution A term applied to a period of agricultural change held to be significant in some sense: that 'sense' varies widely from author to author, period to period and place to place (see, for example, GREEN REVOLUTION). Without qualification the term is usually taken to apply to the institutional and technological changes in English agriculture which took place during the century after 1750. Technological changes involved the spread of mixed farming systems which incorporated fodder crops into arable rotations. These new crops, such as turnips and clover, provided fodder to support additional livestock and also made a direct contribution towards improving the fertility of arable land. Clover and other legumes were particularly important, since they converted atmospheric nitrogen into soil nitrogen and thus made a net addition to the supply of the most important nutrient for arable crops (Campbell and Overton, 1991).

Institutional changes included ENCLOSURE by Parliamentary Act, whereby the subdivided arable fields of the English Midlands were replaced by smaller regular fields, while in many northern and western areas rough pasture or waste was physically enclosed for the first time. Private property rights replaced common property rights; thus removing the right to use a tract of land, e.g. for grazing animals, from those not actually owning it. Other institutional changes included the establishment of large farms, usually rented from a landlord by a capitalist tenant farmer who would be employing proletarianized labour. Conspicuous technological innovation for improving labour productivity was a phenomenon of the nineteenth century and included changes in hand-tool technology and, more especially, the introduction of machines for harvesting and threshing grain (Walton, 1979).

This orthodox view of an agricultural revolution (which is particularly associated with the work of Chambers and Mingay, 1966) has been challenged by a number of authors. Kerridge (1967) argues that the agricultural revolution took place between 1560 and 1767, with most achieved before 1673; Jones (1974) avoids the term 'agricultural revolution' but nevertheless considers the century after 1650 as particularly significant for agricultural advance. Claims have been advanced for 'agricultural revolutions' in the nineteenth century based on the underdraining of heavy land (Phillips, 1989) and on the import of feedstuffs and fertilizers from abroad (Thompson, 1968). Apparently reversing his earlier view, Mingay's more recent verdict (1989) on the agricultural changes of the century after 1750 is that 'It could hardly be said that they amounted to an agricultural revolution'.

With so many definitions, the phrase 'agricultural revolution' is in danger of losing its meaning altogether (Overton, 1984). Measuring agricultural performance before national statistics were collected in 1866 is difficult, but recent work tends to re-emphasize the century after 1750 as the period of most decisive and rapid change (Campbell and Overton, 1992; Overton, 1993). From the mid-eighteenth century English agriculture was able to feed an unprecedented rise in population, partly through extensions to the cultivated area but mainly through unprecedented increases in land productivity (see MALTHUSIAN MODEL). Labour productivity was also rising at an unprecedented rate during the eighteenth century, before the spread of machinery in the nineteenth century, thus enabling both INDUSTRIALIZATION and URBANIZATION to take place during the INDUSTRIAL REVOLUTION. The eighteenth century also witnessed fundamental changes in the social relations of agricultural production and the fully fledged development of agrarian capitalism (Tribe, 1981; see CAPITALISM).   MO

References

Campbell, B. M. S. and Overton, M., eds 1991: *Land, labour and livestock: historical studies in European agricultural productivity.* Manchester: Manchester University Press.

Campbell, B. M. S. and Overton, M. 1992: A new perspective on medieval and early modern agriculture: six centuries of Norfolk farming, *c.*1250–*c.*1850. *Past and Present.*

Chambers, J. D. and Mingay, G. E. 1966: *The agricultural revolution, 1750–1880.* London: Batsford/New York: Schocken.

Jones, E. L. 1974: *Agriculture and the industrial revolution:* Oxford: Blackwell/New York: Halsted.

Kerridge, E. 1967: *The agricultural revolution.* London: Allen & Unwin.

Mingay, G. E., ed. 1989: *The agrarian history of England and Wales,* volume VI, *1750–1850.* Cambridge: Cambridge University Press.

Overton, M. 1984: Agricultural revolution? Development of the agrarian economy in early modern England. In Baker, A. R. H. and Gregory, D., eds, *Explorations in historical geography: interpretative essays.* Cambridge: Cambridge University Press, pp. 118–39.

Overton, M. 1993: *Agricultural revolution in England: the transformation of the rural economy 1500–1830.* Cambridge: Cambridge University Press.

Phillips, A. D. M. 1989: *The underdraining of farmland in England during the nineteenth century.* Cambridge: Cambridge University Press.

Thompson, F. M. L. 1968: The second agricultural revolution, 1815–1880. *Econ. Hist. R. 2nd series* 21, pp. 62–77.

Tribe, K. 1981: *Genealogies of capitalism.* London: Macmillan/Atlantic Highlands, NJ: Humanities Press, pp. 35–100.

Walton, J. R. 1979: Mechanisation in agriculture: a study of the adoption process. In Fox, H. S. A. and Butlin, R. A., eds, *Change in the countryside: essays on rural England 1500–1900.* London: Institute of British Geographers Special Publication 10, pp. 23–42.

Suggested Reading

Beckett, J. V. 1990: *The agricultural revolution,* Oxford: Blackwell.

Overton, M. 1989: Agricultural revolution? England, 1540–1850. In Digby, A. and Feinstein, C., eds, *New directions in economic and social history.* Basingstoke: Macmillan, pp. 9–21.

Overton (1993).

agriculture See EXTENSIVE AGRICULTURE; INTENSIVE AGRICULTURE; SUBSISTENCE AGRICULTURE: TRANSHUMANCE.

aid A limited and conditional flow of resources from developed to underdeveloped economies. Aid may be arranged on *bilateral* terms and flow directly between two countries. Flows of resources (capital, technology and expertise), food, export credits, educational and training scholarships and government-to-government lending may be generated in this way. In addition, *multilateral* agencies may coordinate aid. Such agencies may include semi-official bodies, such as the agencies of the UN; commercial institutions, such as the European Bank for Reconstruction and Development (EBRD) set up to aid the process of social and economic transformation in eastern Europe after the events of 1989, and the Inter-American, African and Asian Development Banks; and worldwide institutions of economic regulation and control, such as the World Bank and the International Monetary Fund. Regional programmes of aid are exemplified by the Lomé Conventions of the European Community. In addition, charitable organizations, such as Oxfam, War on Want and Live Aid, also collect and distribute aid.

In 1989, of the OECD countries, only Norway committed more than 1 per cent of donor GNP to official development assistance; at 0.15 per cent of GNP, the USA committed less than any other OECD country. (The UN target figure is 0.7 per cent of GNP.) Norway and Denmark top the list of bilateral donors, both contributing 0.4 per cent of GNP, with the USA again at the bottom of the list at 0.02 per cent. In all low- and middle-income countries taken together, official development assistance amounts to 1.1 per cent of GNP – a figure which hides the range from 7.9 per cent in sub-Saharan Africa to 0.4 per cent in Latin America and the Caribbean. Official development assistance accounts for almost 60 per cent of Mozambique's GNP.

The ideological justification for aid is that it promotes DEVELOPMENT. A number of criteria might be used to assess the quality of aid: Does it reach the most needy, and does it contribute to their basic needs? Does it help to promote human rights and democracy? Does it promote SUSTAINABLE DEVELOPMENT? Does it enable autonomous development or increase DEPENDENCE?

Not only is aid limited in amount, but it extracts a price which may be met directly – to service interest payments on debt, for example – or indirectly, in the form of markets for the exports of donors and access to the resources of the receiver. Aid may also facilitate an extension of the donor's global economic and strategic influence – in a very direct way, in the case of military aid – or purchase the support of sympathetic political regimes or economic policies. In such ways, aid may intensify relations of economic dependence upon the donor economy, shape local elites through educational assistance and, in the case of food aid, disrupt local prices and supply systems. The flow of aid is also highly selective. It is directed mainly towards the 'middle-income' or THIRD WORLD countries rather than towards the poorest countries of the so-called fourth or fifth worlds. The weighted average of receipts in low-income countries amounts to $7.3 per capita, compared to $12.0 in middle-income countries.

It is difficult to resist the conclusion that the geography of the flow of aid is directed by the economic ability rather than the social need of the recipients, and so serves as a means of maintaining and strengthening current relations of political and economic power in the world economy.   RL

Suggested Reading

Conroy, C. and Litvinoff, M. 1988: *The greening of aid*. London: Earthscan.

Corbridge, S. 1986: *Capitalist world development*. London: Macmillan, ch. 5.

Knox, P. and Agnew, J. 1989: *The geography of the world economy*. London: Edward Arnold/New York: Routledge, Chapman and Hall, ch. 2.

alienation   To be estranged from oneself, others or the product of one's labour. Originally used in philosophical and theological discourse, the sociological origins of the term date back to Rousseau (1712–1778) and Hegel (1770–1831). Rousseau believed that individuals give up (alienate) their individual liberty in order to participate in CIVIL SOCIETY. Hegel deployed the term differently, asserting that human consciousness is naturally estranged from the physical world surrounding it, and that this alienation can be overcome only when people recognize that external reality is a projection of human consciousness. Resonances of both definitions can be found in the early work of Marx (which many characterize as humanist rather than materialist), and it is his use of the term that motivates much contemporary thought on the subject.

For Marx, alienation is not an intrinsic aspect of the human condition but is a specific result of capitalist social relations. In notes in which he first outlined his approach to the study of CAPITALISM, Marx (1844) began with the assumption that humans 'objectify' their creativity through labour as they transform the natural world into valued products. Within most social systems this process is straightforward, and one can discern connections between workers and the objects they produce (e.g. artisans produce goods that incorporate their individual character and talent). Under capitalism, however, workers are disconnected, or alienated, from the products of their labour. This disconnection occurs for two principal reasons. First, workers in a capitalist system do not choose when to work, what to produce, how to organize production, or what to do with the products of their labour – these decisions are made by capitalists. Second, workers are paid only a portion of the value they add to the goods they produce. Workers therefore cannot recognize themselves in the objects they make. For capitalists, the distinction between worker and product is blurred: workers are seen as 'input costs' in precisely the same way as raw materials, and both are viewed as interchangeable elements in the rational calculus of commodity prices and profit rates. Moreover, the worth of individual workers is determined by the output they are capable of producing, not by their personal characteristics. To obtain employment, workers must demonstrate their 'value' through productivity, and relations between individual workers become competitive rather than cooperative. Using this logic, Marx concluded that workers, not the products of their labour, are 'objectified' under capitalism. In so doing he attempted to show the relationship between the structural features of capitalism and the subjective feelings of exploited workers.

Since Marx, the concept of alienation has taken on a host of different meanings as it has been redefined by other authors, notably Durkheim (see ANOMIE), Simmel, Freud, Lucács, Sartre, Marcuse and Habermas. Increasingly, with some exceptions, the subjective aspects of alienation have been emphasized. In North America, the radical political content of the term was largely purged as it entered the mainstream of American sociology. Blauner (1964), for example, sought to quantify the degree of alienation experienced by workers in different jobs in an effort to formulate new shopfloor policies and ease capital-labour CONFLICT. Obviously, such research was far removed from Marx's ideas. Human geographers began to incorporate a Marxist definition of alienation into their work in the 1970s (cf. Harvey, 1973), and the concept was particularly helpful during the late 1970s and early 1980s when geographers following HUMANISTIC and Marxist traditions attempted to discover common ground. However, the term is now infrequently used, indicating the profound shift in the terrain of debate in recent years as various issues raised within feminism, post-structuralism, post-colonialism and cultural theory have come to the fore. In particular, the turn towards seeing individual subjects as decentred, as situated within a web of multiple and overlapping relations of power (Smith, 1988), renders the concept of alienation (arising from a single source – the workplace) problematic.   DH

References

Blauner, B. 1964: *Alienation and freedom: the factory worker and his industry.* Chicago: University of Chicago Press.

Harvey, D. 1973: *Social justice and the city.* Baltimore: Johns Hopkins University Press.

Marx, K. 1844: Economic and philosophical manuscripts. In *Karl Marx: Early writings.* New York: Vintage Books (1975).

Smith, P. 1988: *Discerning the subject.* Minneapolis: University of Minnesota Press.

Suggested Reading

Giddens, A. 1971: *Capitalism and modern social theory.* Cambridge: Cambridge University Press.

Ollman, B. 1971: *Alienation: Marx's conception of man in capitalist society.* Cambridge: Cambridge University Press.

Rinehart, J. W. 1987: *The tyranny of work: alienation and the labour process,* second edition. Toronto: Harcourt Brace Jovanovich.

alliance   See REGIONAL ALLIANCE; REGIONAL CLASS ALLIANCE.

allocation   See ACTIVITY ALLOCATION MODELS; LOCATION-ALLOCATION MODELS.

Alonso model   A model developed by William Alonso (1964) to account for intra-urban variations in land values, land use and land-use intensity. It builds on the VON THÜNEN MODEL of agricultural land-use patterns.

The model's key components are ACCESSIBILITY and its relationship to TRANSPORT COSTS. In its simplest form it assumes that all journeys from residential to non-residential areas focus on the city centre. Thus, assuming that households have fixed budgets, the further that a household lives from the city centre the more it will have to spend on COMMUTING and other journeys (notably to shops) and the less it will be able to spend on land and property.

All land users benefit from increased accessibility, according to the model, and thus bid to be in the most accessible locations at or close to the city centre. With commercial and industrial users, for example, the closer they are to the city centre the nearer they are to their suppliers and customers, the lower their transport costs and the greater their profit margins – all other things being equal. In general, these users benefit more from greater accessibility than do households (with commercial users benefiting more than industrial); this means that they can afford to bid more for city-centre land, which produces a zonal distribution of land uses around the centre (as shown in the figure).

In that zonal distribution, the closer that a household or firm locates to the central point the higher the rent that must be paid. Away from the centre, there is a DISTANCE DECAY relationship in the pattern of locational rents (see RENT). For each land use there is an INDIFFERENCE CURVE which represents the relative priority given to accessibility over travel costs: at the centre, accessibility has the greatest priority and travel costs the least, so rents are highest; further out, as travel costs increase rents fall to compensate for the greater costs of movement. According to Alonso, all individual location decision-makers will

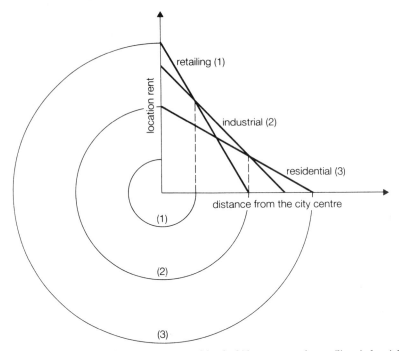

Alonso model *Concentric land-use zones generated by the bid-rent curves for retailing, industrial and residential land use* (Cadwallader, 1985).

have their own BID–RENT CURVES which indicate their relative priorities for rent and travel costs: the point at which each curve touches the indifference curve identifies that individual's preferred location.

Alonso's model of a unicentric city is readily modified to accommodate more than one centre (several shopping centres, for example) and differential patterns of accessibility (perhaps reflecting fast and slow routes from the centres). Its hypotheses of declining land rents and values and land-use intensities away from the defined centres have been largely validated in a substantial number of empirical studies although, as a classic study of Boston illustrated (Firey, 1947), such a model cannot account for the high prices that some people will pay for locations on the basis of such criteria as 'sentiment and symbolism'.

Alonso's model provides an economic rationale for the ZONAL MODEL of urban land uses identified by American sociologists in the 1920s. It also shows why those with higher incomes will tend to favour suburban locations within the residential portion of the city, leaving the INNER CITY to be occupied by lower-income groups at higher densities (thereby maximizing the returns on expensive land): this implies that the higher-income groups have different indifference curves from the less well off, although GENTRIFICATION processes emerge where the richer residents prefer inner-city accessibility to the lower densities of the suburbs.   RJJ

References

Alonso, W. 1964: *Location and land use: toward a general theory of land rent.* Cambridge, MA: Harvard University Press.

Cadwallader, M. 1985: *Analytical urban geography: spatial patterns and theories.* Englewood Cliffs, NJ: Prentice-Hall.

Firey, W. 1947: *Land use in central Boston.* Cambridge, MA: Harvard University Press.

analysis of variance (ANOVA) A parametric statistical test in which the dependent variable has either interval or ratio MEASUREMENT and the independent variables are measured at the nominal scale. The sample of individuals is divided into categories and ANOVA tests whether there are significant differences among the means for those categories on the dependent variable.   RJJ

Suggested Reading
Johnston, R. J. 1978: *Multivariate statistical analysis in geography*. London: Longman.

analytical Marxism, geography and

A school of POLITICAL ECONOMY and social theory that originated during the 1980s, concerned with sorting Marxism into a distinct set of claims that are then analytically scrutinized for their meaning, coherence, plausibility and truth. More generally, the school eschews any form of dogmatic or even exegetical Marxism. Marx is treated as an innovative thinker, but one whose ideas require careful examination and development in the light of intervening history and with the analytical tools available in contemporary philosophy and the social sciences.

Analytical Marxism (or *rational-choice Marxism*) has proponents across a wide range of disciplines, and as a consequence the type of analytical methods employed vary. In economics the favoured method is the assumption of NEOCLASSICAL microeconomic behaviour (Roemer, 1981); in philosophy it is the inexorability of the deductive syllogism (Cohen, 1978; Elster, 1985); and in sociology it is the rigour of multivariate statistics (Wright, 1985). In each case, analytical Marxists strive to be pellucid and logically impeccable in their writings, for the principal task is always to cleanse and purify Marx's frequent obscurantism so that the usefulness of his ideas can be critically assessed in understanding the issues of our own time and place.

The antecedents of the movement are with the Canadian philosopher Gerald Cohen and his book *Karl Marx's theory of history: a defence* (1978); a work that is painstaking in its logic, and ' . . . chock-a-block with nice distinctions other people hadn't dreamt were there' (Carling, 1986, p. 25). In particular, Cohen sought to avoid the naive FUNCTIONALISM of some Marxists who believe that by merely pointing to the beneficial consequences of an event serves to explain it. Cohen's solution is to provide an alternative functional argument based on consequence laws. Although Cohen's revamped functional approach has been rejected by many of the analytical Marxists, the form of his argument established the tone and style for the school.

It is the American economist John Roemer (1981, 1982) who really brought analytical Marxism to a wider attention, following the publication of two pioneering monographs. Rejecting all vestiges of functionalism, Roemer argues that Marxists must provide explanations of events and actions at the micro-level using 'rational choice models: general equilibrium theory, game theory, and the arsenal of modelling techniques developed by neoclassical economics' (Roemer, 1986, p. 192).

In particular, the postulate of RATIONAL CHOICE, and the attendant position of METHODOLOGICAL INDIVIDUALISM, forms the foundation for much of the constructive analytical work that followed. This is best seen in Roemer's two theories of CLASS and exploitation, which in many ways lie at the core of analytical Marxism. The beginning point for both is a set of rational individuals who are endowed with a given share of society's economic resources, and who are intent on maximizing utility. From these two axioms Roemer endogenously derives the existence of exploitation and class.

In the first theory, rational individuals with given resource endowments choose among three labour-market options: working for oneself; hiring labour; or labouring for others. Roemer proves analytically that it is not rational to choose all three options simultaneously, although it can be rational to choose two of them. He thus derives five employment choices that are then taken as equivalent to class categories: pure capitalists who only hire labour; small capitalists who hire labour and also work for themselves; petite bourgeoisie who work only for themselves; a mixed proletariat who work for others and for themselves; and pure proletarians who only work for others. Using the terms *class-wealth correspondence principle* and *class-exploitation correspondence principle*, Roemer then demonstrates first, that there is a homology between wealth ownership and class status (greater wealth holdings imply greater class status) and, second, using a bastardized form of the labour theory of value, that there is a homology between class status and exploitation (capitalists both large and small are always exploiters, proletariat both mixed and pure are always exploited, and the petite bourgeoisie are neither).

Roemer's second theory begins with the same assumptions, but defines classes and exploitation using so-called withdrawal rules that are not specific to capitalism. For any mode of production, individuals rationally compare the actual distribution of that society's principal asset with the counterfactual one in which assets are distributed equally among all members of society. The principal asset varies historically. For example, in feudalism it is labour power, while in capitalism it is the means of production. Comparing the consequences of the actual distribution with the hypothetical one, Roemer argues that those who are worse off under the existing distribution are exploited, those who are better off are exploiters, and those whose material circumstances do not change are neither. Interpreting these results in terms of the traditional classes of capitalism, the first group are capitalists, the second workers, and the third the petite bourgeoisie.

Although Roemer's two schemes are different, there are strong commonalities. First, both make differences in resource ownership the basis of exploitation and class delineation. Second, both are used to understand different historical epochs, from feudalism to communism (Wright, 1985, ch. 2). Finally, and most controversially, both suggest that individuals choose their class positions. This is not a choice that individuals necessarily like to make, of course, but they do so because of the constraints that they are under (their society's share of assets), along with their desire to maximize.

Interestingly, analytical Marxism has been most criticized by those on the Left (Meiksins-Wood, 1989). Such criticisms include the following: that the preferences, and social contexts, of rational individuals are never explained, with the consequence that everything which is important to the investigation must be done *before* applying the rational choice model; that there is no

explanation of historical change among modes of production; that it rests on an economistic, market view of human nature, thereby aligning the movement intellectually with the resurgence of interest in right-wing thought; and, finally, that the METHODOLOGICAL INDIVIDUALISM of analytical Marxism is philosophically and politically bankrupt. The general response to these criticisms has been to argue that analytical Marxism is not a general theory explaining everything, but a specific one dealing with only a restricted range of questions.

There has been only limited use of the analytical Marxist framework by economic geographers. Sheppard and Barnes (1990) provide the most systematic treatment and, although sympathetic to the analytical approach, they argue that the incorporation of geography into either Roemer's work on class and exploitation, or Elster's on class formation, fundamentally disturbs the respective aspatial conclusions of each. In particular, Sheppard and Barnes (1990) show that negative exploitation can occur in a space-economy, which in turn vitiates both Roemer's class-exploitation and class-wealth principles. They also demonstrate that in a geographical economy Roemer's conclusions about technical choice and his dismissal of Marx's falling rate of profit thesis also cannot be sustained on analytical grounds. Finally, they criticize Elster's use of the rationality postulate and accompanying methodological individualism when he discusses class formation. For Elster collective action is a puzzle; it is not something in which rational individuals should engage, even though they do. Sheppard and Barnes (1990) argue that once such individuals are embedded in the geographical world of space and place, collective action is no longer a puzzle, but is the norm (see GAME THEORY).   TJB

References

Carling, A. 1986: Rational choice Marxism. *New Left Rev.* 160, pp. 24–62.

Cohen, G. A. 1978: *Karl Marx's theory of history: a defence.* Oxford: Oxford University Press.

Elster, J. 1985: *Making sense of Marx.* Cambridge: Cambridge University Press.

Meiksins-Wood, E. 1989: Rational choice Marxism: is the game worth the candle? *New Left Rev.* 177, pp. 41–88.

Roemer, J. 1981: *Analytical foundations of Marxian economic theory.* Cambridge: Cambridge University Press.

Roemer, J. 1982: *A general theory of exploitation and class.* Cambridge, MA: Harvard University Press.

Roemer, J., ed. 1986: *Analytical Marxism.* Cambridge: Cambridge University Press.

Sheppard, E. and Barnes, T. J. 1990: *The capitalist space economy: geographical analysis after Ricardo, Marx and Sraffa.* London: Unwin Hyman.

Wright, E. O. 1985: *Classes.* London: Verso.

Suggested Reading

Carling (1986).

Ruccio, D. F. 1988: The merchant of Venice or Marxism in the mathematical mode. *Rethinking Marxism* 1, pp. 36–68.

Sheppard and Barnes (1990).

anarchism A political philosophy that advocates the removal of the STATE and its replacement by voluntary groups of individuals who can sustain social order without any external authority. Such a social order may emphasize either individualism (and thus is a logical conclusion of liberalism, stressing the importance of individual liberty) or SOCIALISM (some versions of which reject private property as well as the state): Cook (1991) identifies five different forms of anarchism – individualism, collectivism, anarchism communism, anarch-syndicalism and pacifism. Among the early proponents of anarchist communism were Peter Kropotkin and Elisee Reclus, whose geographical writings were rediscovered by some of the advocates of RADICAL GEOGRAPHY. RJJ

Reference

Cook, I. 1990: Anarchistic alternatives: an introduction. In Cook, I. and Pepper, D., eds, *Anarchism and geography. Contemporary Issues in Geography and Education* 3(2), pp. 9–21.

Suggested Reading

Breitbart, M. 1981: Peter Kropotkin, the anarchist geographer. In Stoddart, D. R., ed., *Geography, ideology and social concern.* Oxford: Blackwell, pp. 134–53.

Cook and Pepper (1990).

Stoddart, D. R. 1975: Kropotkin, Reclus and 'relevant' geography. *Area* 7, pp. 180–90.

Annales school A school of French historians, distinctive in their interest in environmental and social topics, linked through the journal *Annales d'histoire économique et sociale,* which was founded in 1929 by Marc Bloch and Lucien Febvre (now *Annales Économies, Sociétés, Civilisations*). Together with Fernand Braudel and others, these authors advocated 'total history' as a synthesizing discipline underlying the human and social sciences in general, integrating long-run changes in ways of life and the short-term political events with which, they argued, historians were (wrongly) preoccupied. Numerous geographers have drawn on this tradition, both through explicit application of the long-/medium-/short-run framework of presentation and explanation, and through annalistes' discussions of relationships between social organization and spatial organization. PG

Suggested Reading

Baker, A. 1984: Reflections on the relations of historical geography and the Annales school of history. In Baker, A. and Gregory, D. eds, *Explorations in historical geography: interpretative essays.* Cambridge: Cambridge University Press, pp. 1–27.

Clark, S. 1985: The Annales historians. In Skinner, Q., ed., *The return of grand theory in the human sciences.* Cambridge: Cambridge University Press, pp. 177–98.

Lloyd, C. 1986: *Explanation in social history,* chapter 7. Oxford: Blackwell.

McClennan, G. 1981: Braudel and the Annales paradigm. In *Marxism and the methodologies of history.* London: Verso, pp. 129–51.

anomie A term introduced by the French nineteenth-century sociologist Emile Durkheim to denote a societal condition in which normative standards are absent. Individuals have no widely accepted behavioural guidelines in such contexts: they may be presented with two or more very contrasting and contradictory sets of norms, which create confusion and may stimulate problems of identity (hence the frequent confusion of anomie with ALIENATION, a state of individual estrangement which may not be related to an anomic society). Where anomie exists, according to the adherents to the CHICAGO SCHOOL, behaviours characteristic of social disorganization (such as crime, violence and suicide) are likely to be present, notably in INNER-CITY and SLUM areas. (See also ZONAL MODEL.)   RJJ

anthropogeography A school of human geography closely associated with the work of the German geographer Friedrich Ratzel (1844–1904). It was inaugurated by his *Anthropogeographie*. This was published in two volumes, in 1882 and 1891, and there were several differences in emphasis between them. To Hartshorne (1939), Ratzel organized his materials in the first volume 'largely in terms of the natural conditions of the earth, which he studied in their relation to human culture', thereby reworking the ideas of Karl Ritter, whereas in the second volume 'Ratzel himself largely reversed the process'; to Dickinson (1969), the first volume was essentially dynamic, 'an application of geography to history', whereas the second was static and treated 'the geographical distribution of man'. Both volumes have to be placed in the context of the contemporary debates within the German intellectual community over the place of the cultural sciences and their relation to the natural sciences (Smith, 1991) (see also DIFFUSION). For Ratzel, writing in the middle of what Bassin (1987a) describes as an 'imperialist frenzy', and indeed contributing to it, the cultural development of a STATE could not be separated from its spatial growth. His project was not an ENVIRONMENTAL DETERMINISM, as some later commentators have suggested, but it was distinguished by the attempt to conduct a nominally *scientific* study of the relations between society and NATURE through the elaboration of a system of concepts.

In many ways, Ratzel's *Politische Geographie*, published in 1897, represented the culmination of these ideals. There, Ratzel described the state as 'a living body which has extended itself over a part of the earth and has differentiated itself from other bodies which have similarly expanded'. The object of these extensions and expansions, Ratzel argued, was always 'the conquest of space', and it was this which became formalized in the concept of *LEBENSRAUM* ('living space'): 'the geographical area within which living organisms develop'. He was keenly aware of the dangers of organicism but, even so, insisted that: 'Just as the struggle for existence in the plant and animal world always centres about a matter of space, so the conflicts of nations are in great part only struggles for territory' (see GEOPOLITICS; TERRITORIALITY). Wanklyn (1961) treats *Lebensraum* as 'a fundamental geographical concept', therefore, and in her eyes Ratzel's writings were directed primarily towards 'thinking out the scope and content of biogeography'. There is certainly a distinguished tradition of biogeographical reflection within human geography, and in this sense there are important continuities between Ratzel's *Lebensraum*, Vidal de la Blache's *GENRE DE VIE* and, most recently, the concept of *rum* ('room') developed in Hägerstrand's TIME-GEOGRAPHY. If this is accepted, then Dickinson's (1969) view of Ratzel's original formulation, stripped of its distortions by the Third Reich, as 'one of the most original and fruitful of all concepts in modern geography' becomes peculiarly prescient. But such a purely 'biogeographical' or 'scientific' reading does scant justice to the context in which Ratzel was working and, in particular, ignores the fact that his vision of human geography had not only political implications: it also rested on – and was indeed made possible by – a series of political assumptions (Bassin, 1987a,b; Smith, 1991). (See also LAMARCK(IAN)ISM.)   DG

References

Bassin, M. 1987a: Imperialism and the nation–state in Friedrich Ratzel's political geography. *Progr. hum. Geogr.* 11, pp. 473–95.

Bassin, M. 1987b: Race *contra* space: the conflict between German Geopolitik and National Socialism. *Pol. Geogr. Q.* 6, pp. 115–34.

Dickinson, R. 1969: *The makers of modern geography*. London: Routledge and Kegan Paul/ New York: Praeger.

Hartshorne, R. 1939: *The nature of geography: a critical survey of current thought in the light of the past*. Lancaster, PA: Association of American Geographers.

Ratzel, F. 1897: *Politische Geographie*. Munich: Oldenbourg.

Smith, W. 1991: *Politics and the sciences of culture in Germany 1840–1920*. New York: Oxford University Press.

Wanklyn, H. 1961: *Friedrich Ratzel: biographical memoir and bibliography*. Cambridge: Cambridge University Press.

Suggested Reading

Bassin (1987a,b).

Dickinson (1969), pp. 64–76.

apartheid The policy of spatial separation of the races, as applied in South Africa after the National Party assumed political control in 1948, but now being dismantled. Under the Population Registration Act, all South Africans were classified as members of one of four race groups: Black (population almost 30 million in the early 1990s), White (5 million), Coloured (3.5 million) and Asian (1 million). RACE still provides the basis for separate political institutions, in both national and local government, until a new constitution is implemented. Racial discrimination has resulted in marked inequalities in levels of living, with Whites enjoying the highest standards overall, the Blacks experiencing the lowest and, between them, the Asians generally faring better than the Coloureds.

Apartheid, as originally implemented, operated at three spatial scales; personal, within residential space in towns and cities, and at the national level. Personal discrimination with respect to use of such public facilities as parks, theatres, transportation and lavatories was generally referred to as 'petty apartheid'. The extent of this form of discrimination had been reduced in recent years, before the abolition of the Separate Amenities Act removed its legal basis, although some conservative towns still use entrance fees and other devices to restrict Black access to certain facilities. Apartheid at the town or city level was implemented via the Group Areas Act, under which each portion of urban residential space was allocated for the exclusive occupation of a single race group. This ensured the perpetuation of almost complete residential SEGREGATION by race. However, integration was taking place in so-called 'grey areas' of the larger cities for some years before the announcement of the repeal of the Group Areas Act in 1991.

The most important aspect of apartheid was at the national level, where ten so-called 'homelands' (or 'Bantustans') were designated for the occupation of the major Black or African tribal groups. All Blacks were supposed to exercise their 'political rights' in their respective homelands, which were supposed ultimately to become independent states. Bophuthatswana, Ciskei, Transkei and Venda were granted 'independence', although this was not recognized by the United Nations or any government outside South Africa. The homelands are now likely to be re-incorporated into a new post-apartheid South African state, possibly within some version of FEDERALISM (see also TERRITORIALITY).

The South African government originally claimed that apartheid (sometimes known as 'separate development' or 'multi-nationalism') enables racial harmony and the rights of all groups to be protected in a heterogeneous, pluralistic society (see PLURAL SOCIETY; PLURALISM). The homelands were supposed to give Blacks their independence from White rule, and the same rights that the Whites enjoyed in their (White) residual republic. A more plausible explanation was that apartheid enabled the Whites to maintain their cultural identity, political power and exploitation of Black labour, by associating race with separation, externalizing the Black franchise and using the homelands as cheap labour reserves.

International economic sanctions undoubtedly played a part in the eventual abandonment of apartheid. However, the system was already breaking down from within, well before the government took the important step of releasing the African National Congress leader Nelson Mandela in February 1990 and legalizing the ANC and other opposition groups. Erosion of petty apartheid and residential segregation was accelerating, and the distinction between the homelands and White South Africa had always been artificial from an economic point of view. Half of the Black population lived in 'White South Africa', mainly in the cities where the jobs were, and large numbers were also drawn from the homelands as migrant workers or commuters (see MIGRANT LABOUR). By the early 1980s it was clear that restrictions known as 'influx control' could not prevent increasing numbers of Blacks settling in and around the metropolitan areas, especially the Witwatersrand (centred on Johannesburg), Cape Town and Durban. Millions now live in informal 'shack' settlements on the peri-urban fringe as well as in the older townships. Thus the legitimacy of the homelands as providing for the political rights of Blacks was increasingly called into question – and rising tension in the cities, expressed in violent unrest, made apartheid society increasingly difficult to control.

The Nationalist Party and the ANC are the principal protagonists in negotiations towards a new, non-racial constitution. Whatever the outcome of this process, the legacy of apartheid will take decades to eradicate. South Africa's towns and cities will remain highly segregated, as few Blacks can afford to move into White areas. It is more likely that Black residential space will become increasingly differentiated according to CLASS – a process which has been termed 'deracialized apartheid'. Whites, along with the better-off members of other race groups, may be able to protect some of their privileges on a neighbourhood basis; but the best that a growing proportion of the Black population can hope for is a place in one of the shack cities. The main uncertainties are how fast the economy can grow, to assist redistributive policies, and how much of the new political freedom will survive the control of unfulfilled material expectations.   DMS

Suggested Reading

Fair, T. J. D. 1982: *South Africa: spatial frameworks for development*. Cape Town: Juta, chs 5–7.

Lemon, A. 1987: *Apartheid in transition*. Aldershot: Gower.

Lemon, A., ed. 1991: *Homes apart: South Africa's divided cities*. London: Paul Chapman.

Pickles, J. and Weiner, D., eds 1991: *Rural and regional restructuring in South Africa*. Special issue of *Antipode*, 23(1).

Rogerson, C. M., ed. 1986: *South Africa: geography in a state of emergency*. Special issue of *Geo J.*, 12(2).

Rogerson, C. M., ed. 1988: *Urbanization in South Africa*. Special issue of *Urban Geogr.*, 9(6).

Simon, D. 1990: Crisis and change in South Africa: implications for the apartheid city. *Trans. Inst. Br. Geogr.* 14, pp. 198–206.

Smith, D. M., ed. 1982: *Living under apartheid: aspects of urbanization and social change in South Africa*. London: Allen & Unwin.

Smith, D. M. 1987: Conflict in South African cities. *Geogr.*, 72, pp. 153–8.

Smith, D. M. 1987: *Geography, inequality and society*. Cambridge: Cambridge University Press, ch. 6.

Smith, D. M. 1990: *Apartheid in South Africa*, third edition. Cambridge: Cambridge University Press. (*Update* series, Department of Geography, Queen Mary and Westfield College, University of London.)

Smith, D. M. 1991: South Africa's Shack Cities, *Geogr. Rev.* 4(5), pp. 25–9.

Smith, D. M., ed. 1992: *The apartheid city and beyond: urbanization and social change in contemporary South Africa*. London: Routledge.

Tomlinson, R. and Addleson, M., eds 1987: *Regional restructuring under apartheid: urban and regional policies in contemporary South Africa*. Johannesburg: Raven Press.

Tomlinson, R. 1990: *Urbanization in post-apartheid South Africa*. London: Unwin Hyman.

Wellings, P., ed. 1986: *South Africa: the development crisis*. Special issue of *Geoforum* 17(2).

applied geography The application of geographical knowledge and skills to the solution or resolution of problems within society. Until recent years, most applied geography in capitalist economies has been undertaken for the public sector, either by academics acting as consultants or by graduate geographers who are employed therein: many of them have worked in the field of URBAN AND REGIONAL PLANNING. More recently, geographers have been obtaining contracts and employment from private-sector firms in a wide variety of business types. In socialist countries, especially those of Eastern Europe and the former USSR, much of the work of academic geographers in the decades between 1950 and 1990 was directed by the STATE APPARATUS (of which they were a part) towards the solution of economic and environmental problems, and applied geography was volumetrically greater there than in most of the capitalist world.

As a subfield of the discipline, applied geography has lacked a coherent structure and has been characterized by a pragmatic approach – as suggested by Berry's (1973) categorization of approaches to planning problems. There is no central theoretical core or corpus of techniques; rather, the subfield has been characterized by *ad hoc* approaches to the problems posed, drawing on the perceived relevant skills and information. (Kenzer (1989) for example, writes that 'Regrettably the current spate of applied geography research (at least in North America) does not seem to have any philosophical or theoretical basis in being, other than its understood application to social needs' and, in a later 1992 piece, that 'the connection between applied and "pure" research was blurred by hazy, nebulous definitions and haughty, unrealistic expectations of what an autonomous, self-reliant applied geography could and could not achieve'.) Pacione (1990) attempted to develop such a structure, suggesting nine 'principles or guidelines' covering the main conceptual issues involved in the conduct of applied work, and Clark (1982) – stressing that academic applied geographers cannot be value-free in their work – offered four propositions to guide those who wished to be involved in policy analysis: academics should recognize their own values when tackling problems and formulating solutions; policy advocates should promote particular cases rather than seeking to be independent and objective adjudicators of competing formulations; policy scientists should be critical of the status quo; and sponsors of applied work should make the reports that they receive publicly available. (Kenzer (1992) also calls for applied geographers to be more 'openly self-critical'.)

The subfield's first major statement was L. D. Stamp's (1960) *Applied geography*, which presented the geographer's unique contribution as 'the holistic approach in which he sees the relationship between man and his environment, with its attendant problems, as a whole'. (Kenzer (1989, 1992) suggests that this holistic, synthesizing ability is being lost with the current expansion of applied geography and the narrow, technocratic specialisms that it is promoting.) That relationship, according to Stamp, is discerned 'by survey in the field, and the gathering of facts systematically and objectively', with the twin goals of survey and analysis 'achieved fully only when studied cartographically'. Such surveys and analyses were perceived as extremely relevant to many of the world's most pressing problems, such as population pressure on land, economic development, and improvement of living conditions. Stamp's own focus on the use and misuse of land in Great Britain – notably through the first Land Utilization Survey (Stamp, 1946) – led to his involvement in the development of town and country planning legislation after the Second World War.

Stamp presented the geographer as an information-gatherer and synthesizer, who could stand outside the political processes within which the formulation and pursuit of planning goals were set. Many trained geographers were employed in central and local government planning offices in the 1940s, 1950s and 1960s, where their skills were relevant to the focus on land-use survey and planning. Those skills were also called upon by national government agencies, notably in wartime when information about environments was needed as part of military intelligence. Many geographers were employed in the relevant agencies – and still are in the USA and elsewhere. In the UK, they played a major role in the preparation of the *Admiralty Handbooks*, which summarized knowledge about many areas. They were also involved in the interpretation of aerial photographs, out of which has grown the discipline's expertise in REMOTE SENSING, which is now called upon for a considerable amount of survey and mapping work.

From the 1960s onwards, developments in geographical approaches and techniques, notably those involved with the QUANTITATIVE REVOLUTION and, later, GEOGRAPHICAL INFORMATION SYSTEMS, enhanced the range of available applied contributions and led to employment of geographers for private- as well as public-sector work. Quantitative models were developed not only to describe but also to predict, as in the study of traffic flows. The GRAVITY

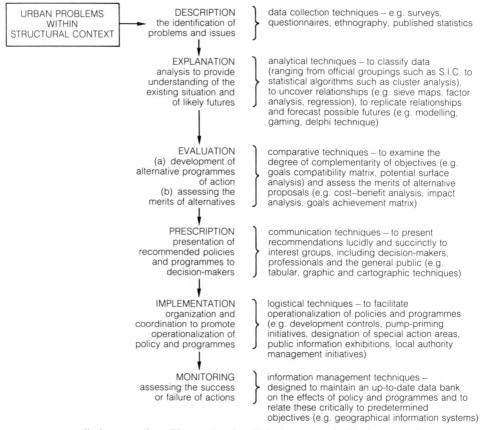

| URBAN PROBLEMS WITHIN STRUCTURAL CONTEXT | → | DESCRIPTION the identification of problems and issues | } | data collection techniques – e.g. surveys, questionnaires, ethnography, published statistics |

EXPLANATION analysis to provide understanding of the existing situation and of likely futures } analytical techniques – to classify data (ranging from official groupings such as S.I.C. to statistical algorithms such as cluster analysis), to uncover relationships (e.g. sieve maps, factor analysis, regression), to replicate relationships and forecast possible futures (e.g. modelling, gaming, delphi technique)

EVALUATION (a) development of alternative programmes of action (b) assessing the merits of alternatives } comparative techniques – to examine the degree of complementarity of objectives (e.g. goals compatibility matrix, potential surface analysis) and assess the merits of alternative proposals (e.g. cost–benefit analysis, impact analysis, goals achievement matrix)

PRESCRIPTION presentation of recommended policies and programmes to decision-makers } communication techniques – to present recommendations lucidly and succinctly to interest groups, including decision-makers, professionals and the general public (e.g. tabular, graphic and cartographic techniques)

IMPLEMENTATION organization and coordination to promote operationalization of policy and programmes } logistical techniques – to facilitate operationalization of policies and programmes (e.g. development controls, pump-priming initiatives, designation of special action areas, public information exhibitions, local authority management initiatives)

MONITORING assessing the success or failure of actions } information management techniques – designed to maintain an up-to-date data bank on the effects of policy and programmes and to relate these critically to predetermined objectives (e.g. geographical information systems)

applied geography *The practice of applied urban geography* (Pacione, 1990).

MODEL provided the basis for predicting likely flows between areas according to their land uses and distance apart (and was used, in a variety of forms, to predict the likely success of shopping centre developments, for example); more sophisticated procedures, such as the LOWRY MODEL and ENTROPY-MAXIMIZING MODELS, were later adapted to provide more comprehensive information (although see Batty, 1989, on the extent of their use). In this work, geographical analysis was closely linked to that of REGIONAL SCIENCE. The goal was to produce efficient patterns of land use which minimized movement costs (see LOCATION-ALLOCA-TION MODELS): intriguingly, such models were probably most widely used in the socialist states. Such work went beyond the information-gathering and synthesizing that

Stamp identified as the applied geographer's strengths: Pacione (1990) suggests a sequence of six tasks (see the figure) in the applied geographer's attack on urban problems, which involve policy formulation and monitoring as well as data collation and synthesis.

A second strand of work, developing out of Stamp's emphasis on land use, focused on society–environment interactions. Geographers in the USA were employed in the public agencies seeking to revive agriculture in the 1930s, for example (Kollmorgen, 1979), and the Australian Commonwealth Scientific and Industrial Research Organisation combined the work of physical and human geographers in its methods for evaluating land suitability for various uses. The developing field of HAZARD studies also led to geographers advising on a wide range of projects concerned with environmental use and rehabilitation (Burton et al., 1978): the journal *Applied Geography*, founded in 1981, concentrates on this type of work.

Despite the wide and increasing range of applied work in which geographers were involved, in the 1970s some senior academics were concerned that the discipline's expertise was insufficiently called-upon, especially within the public sector and relative to that of other social and environmental scientists. Thus the theme of 'geography and public policy' was taken up by both the Association of American Geographers (Ginsburg, 1972; White, 1972) and the Institute of British Geographers (Coppock, 1974); although others were concerned about the implications of this trend, not least because they felt that geographers were insufficiently prepared to perform the role being promoted for them (see Hare, 1974; Zelinsky, 1975): a further group felt that too great an emphasis on applied work could erode geography's traditional academic strengths, such as 'real world, field-oriented experience' (Rundstrom and Kenzer, 1989).

Throughout the 1980s there were increasing pressures on geographers to become more involved in applied work (although it was claimed at the onset of the decade that many already were; see Briggs, 1981). This reflects growing political requirements on universities and other higher education institutions to increase their contributions to tackling society's problems and to earn larger proportions of their incomes from such research and consultancy activity. It is also a consequence of recognition within the discipline of a responsibility to contribute to the resolution of an increasing range of perceived problems and of more students' requirements for a relevant training rather than a general education. Taylor (1985) has suggested that such pressures for greater concentration on 'applied' (as against 'pure') geography are typical of periods of major recession in the capitalist world-economy (see KONDRATIEFF CYCLES), but the current concentration may be enhanced because in the recessions of the 1980s (unlike that of the 1930s) there

was an emphasis – as part of the politics of the New Right – on reducing the role of the state and increasing the importance of market mechanisms in economic, and hence social, revival (Johnston, 1992a).

In the search for such 'marketable skills', some geographers have stressed the saleability of the technical advances characteristic of modern geography, notably those involved with GEOGRAPHICAL INFORMATION SYSTEMS and remote sensing. In societies in which information is a major source of power, the role of geographers not only as providers of information but also as people who 'add value' to such information has been stressed (e.g. Openshaw, 1989, 1991; Rhind, 1989). Spatially referenced information, and its manipulation in tackling a range of location-allocation problems, is presented as a key resource which geographers have to sell – alongside their understanding of places – thereby aiding their discipline's survival in an increasingly materialistic world of higher education: others have contested this claim, arguing that since information is power, geographers are allying themselves with the powerful groups within society (see Abler, 1992; Taylor and Johnston, 1994).

Applied geography as practised by geographers working outside academia is more apparent in North America than in the UK. There is much greater recognition of a graduate profession of geography in the former, and a willingness of practitioners to join and participate in the meetings of the main professional society, the Association of American Geographers, which has a very large and active Applied Geography Specialty Group.

Not all geographers have accepted this call for a particular form of applied geography, perceiving it as either or both of a narrow presentation of their discipline's expertise (especially the emphasis on technical skills – what Kenzer (1992) refers to as students 'being trained mainly to push buttons and learn software programs') and a value-laden approach to tackling societal problems. Some recognize three types of geography, each of which has its own applied programme (Johnston, 1992b): (1) that form of geography, such as

SPATIAL ANALYSIS, which adopts the tenets of POSITIVISM and seeks technical solutions to problems within an accepted political economy, as with the applications of GIS to location-allocation issues; (2) that activity – often termed HUMANISTIC GEOGRAPHY – which seeks to broaden individuals' understanding of themselves and others, thereby promoting greater tolerance and social peace; and (3) that branch of geography – often termed radical – the goal of which is to emancipate people by clarifying for them the nature of the society in which they live and thus enabling them to participate in its restructuring (see RADICAL GEOGRAPHY). Others accept the desirability of applied work but question the optimistic claims of some of its proponents, as illustrated in the discussion of Pacione's (1990) paper.

Much of the debate over applied geography has involved protagonists of the 'radical cause' in conflict with those promoting 'sociospatial engineering'. Thus, for example, Harvey (1974) posed the question 'What kind of geography for what kind of public policy?', and exposed the value judgements underpinning much applied geography, against which he set his 'people's geography' (Harvey, 1984): a later essay (1989) similarly exposed the implications of the private–public-sector partnerships being advanced as means of promoting economic revival. Stoddart (1987), on the other hand, has criticized much work for concentrating on relatively transient and trivial issues: he contends that members of the discipline should instead 'do some real geography' and focus on the large issue of people–environment relationships.   RJJ

References and Suggested Reading

Abler, R. F. 1992: Desiderata for geography: an institutional view from the United States. In Johnston, R. J. ed., *The challenge for geography: a changing world, a changing discipline*. Oxford: Blackwell.

Batty, M. 1989: Urban modelling and planning: reflections, retrodictions and predictions. In Macmillan, B. ed., *Remodelling geography*. Oxford: Basil Blackwell, pp. 147–69.

Berry, B. J. L. 1973: *The human consequences of urbanization*. New York: St Martin's Press/ London: Macmillan.

Briggs, D. J. 1981: The principles and practice of applied geography. *Appl. Geogr.* 1, pp. 1–8.

Burton, I., Kates, R. W. and White, G. F. 1978: *The environment as hazard*. Oxford: Oxford University Press.

Clark, G. L. 1982: Instrumental reason and policy analysis. In Herbert, D. T. and Johnston, R. J., eds, *Geography and the urban environment: progress in research and applications*, volume 5. Chichester: John Wiley, pp. 41–62.

Coppock, J. T. 1974: Geography and public policy: challenges and opportunities. *Trans. Inst. Br. Geogr.* 63, pp. 1–16.

Ginsburg, N. S. 1972: The mission of a scholarly society. *Prof. Geogr.* 24, pp. 1–6.

Hare, F. K. 1974: Geography and public policy: a Canadian view. *Trans. Inst. Br. Geogr.* 63, pp. 25–8.

Harvey, D. 1974: What kind of geography for what kind of public policy? *Trans. Inst. Br. Geogr.* 63, pp. 18–24.

Harvey, D. 1984: On the history and present condition of geography: an historical materialist manifesto. *Prof. Geogr.* 36, pp. 1–11.

Harvey, D. 1989: From managerialism to entrepreneurialism: the transformation of urban governance in late capitalism. *Geogr. Annlr* 71B, pp. 3–17.

Johnston, R. J. 1992a: The internal operations of the state. In Taylor, P. J., ed., *The political geography of the twentieth century*. London: Belhaven Press.

Johnston, R. J. 1992b: Face the challenge: make the change. In Johnston, R. J., ed., *The challenge for geography: a changing world; a changing discipline*. Oxford: Blackwell.

Kenzer, M. S. 1989: Applied geography: overview and introduction. In Kenzer, M. S., ed., *Applied geography: issues, questions, and concerns*. Dordrecht: Kluwer Academic, pp. 1–14.

Kenzer, M. S. 1992: Applied and academic geography and the remainder of the twentieth century. *Appl. Geogr.* 12, pp. 207–10.

Kollmorgen, W. 1979: Kollmorgen as bureaucrat. *Ann. Ass. Am. Geogr.* 69, pp. 77–89.

Openshaw, S. 1989: Computer modelling in human geography. In Macmillan, B., ed., *Remodelling geography*. Oxford: Blackwell, pp. 70–88.

Openshaw, S. 1991: A view on the GIS crisis in geography, or, using GIS to put Humpty Dumpty back together again. *Environ. Plann. A* 23, pp. 621–8.

Pacione, M. 1990: Conceptual issues in applied urban geography. *Tijdschr. econ. soc. Geogr.* 81, pp. 1–13.

Rhind, D. W. 1989: Computing, academic geography, and the world outside. In Macmillan, B., ed., *Remodelling geography*. Oxford: Blackwell, pp. 177–90.

Rundstrom, R. A. and Kenzer, M. S. 1989: The decline of fieldwork in human geography. *Prof. Geogr.* 41, pp. 294–303.

Stamp, L. D. 1946: *The land of Britain and how it is used*. London: Longman.

Stamp, L. D. 1960: *Applied geography*. London: Penguin.

Stoddart, D. R. 1987: To claim the high ground: geography for the end of the century. *Trans. Inst. Br. Geogr.* NS12, pp. 327–36.

Taylor, P. J. 1985: The value of a geographical perspective. In Johnston, R. J., ed., *The future of geography*. London: Methuen, pp. 92–110.

Taylor, P. J. and Johnston, R. J. 1994: GIS and geography. In Pickles, J., ed., *Geography, GIS and democracy*. New York: The Guilford Press.

White, G. F. 1972: Geography and public policy. *Prof. Geogr.* 24, pp. 101–4.

Zelinsky, W. 1975: The demigod's dilemma. *Ann. Ass. Am. Geogr.* 65, pp. 123–43.

areal differentiation The study of the areal variation of human and physical phenomena as they relate to other spatially proximate and causally linked phenomena. The classic statement of this view of geography as a field of inquiry is R. Hartshorne's *The nature of geography* (1939). Drawing from Hettner, Hartshorne's central claim about geography is its integrative or synthetic purpose. However, this does not entail the view, as many commentators on areal differentiation have asserted, that geography is on this definition solely concerned with the unique character of different areas of the Earth's surface. Rather, as argued by Agnew (1989), the logic of Hartshorne's discussion suggests that in order to recognize geographical difference in the covariation of phenomena one must necessarily examine geographical similarity and the causes of both. However, Hartshorne's repeated use of the term areal *differentiation* and his avowed indifference to 'phenomena themselves' deflected commentators away from the complexity of his presentation and towards an IDIOGRAPHIC interpretation of his work. The clash between Hartshorne and his critics over EXCEPTIONALISM and the impact of Kant on Hartshorne's work (see Smith, 1989) further simplified views to the extent that areal differentiation came to be seen as justifying a very particular definition of geography as CHOROLOGY, the expression of which was identified with traditional REGIONAL GEOGRAPHY, in which regions were regarded as mental constructs (on this confusion on the part of his critics, see Hartshorne, 1988). Thus, it could be claimed that 'areal differentiation dominated geography at the expense of areal integration' (Haggett, 1965). Defining geography as a SPATIAL SCIENCE thus involved moving the field in a totally antithetical direction from what was mistakenly seen as the *necessary* obsession of areal differentiation with areal particularity.

In the 1980s areal differentiation has been reinstated as a central perspective in human geography. Intellectual inspiration has come from three general directions, none of which either is directly connected to older positions in debates about areal differentiation or uses the same terminology as the others. The first is from the streams of thought referred to collectively as HUMANISTIC GEOGRAPHY. Their focus on the social construction of spaces (see SPATIALITY), PLACE as the context for human action, SENSE OF PLACE and the ICONOGRAPHY of landscape has generated an interest in the relationship between specific geographical 'settings' or LOCALES and social life or 'being in the world' in general, depending on the specific point of view (see, e.g., Tuan, 1977; Entrikin, 1990). The second focus of revival has been the analysis of UNEVEN DEVELOPMENT and the geography of LAYERS OF INVESTMENT associated with the concept of a changing spatial DIVISION OF LABOUR. Rejecting a model of an undifferentiated capitalism, a number of geographers have attempted to infuse into MARXIST GEOGRAPHY a concern for conjoining 'general processes' with 'particular circumstances' to explain spatial variation in economic activity and well-being (see Massey, 1984; Smith, 1990). The third influence has come from attempts in sociology and human geography to create CONTEXTUAL THEORY, in which the PLACE or REGION is viewed as geographically mediating the interpellation of HUMAN AGENCY and social structure and is thereby implicated directly in the production of geographical sameness and difference (e.g. Agnew, 1987). Various versions of STRUCTURATION THEORY and TIME-GEOGRAPHY have been especially influential in defining this direction (see Giddens, 1984).

The third direction could be seen as potentially integrating the other two, but this would be a superficial view. There are important philosophical differences between all three. For example, the first direction tends either to privilege or to emphasize the human subjective experience of place – more often than not that of the scholar engaged in writing about it – whereas the second and third view the division of space in terms of objective sociospatial processes with, for the third view, sense of place arising out of the conditions created by such processes. The second and third views part company over the first's insistence on separating general processes from local contingencies (Smith, 1987). This conflation of the general with the abstract (see ABSTRACTION) is denied by the philosophical REALISM that tends to underpin the third direction.

Persisting dilemmas have further limited the achievement of a new synthesis. One of these is the tension between analytical and narrative modes of thought and presentation (Sayer, 1989). Another is a general lack of attention to the multiscalar nature of the processes producing areal differentiation, with a given phenomenon (e.g. new jobs, or votes for a political party) showing a different scale of aggregation in different time periods because of a shifting balance of local and extra-local influences (see SCALE). This is a particular problem for so-called LOCALITY studies. The final and most challenging dilemma concerns the difficulty of neat BOUNDARY delimitation between places and regions when the TERRITORIALITY of social groups is dynamic and irreducible to a singular and temporally fixed set of spatial units.   JAA

References

Agnew, J. A. 1987: *Place and politics: the geographical mediation of state and society*. London: Allen and Unwin.

Agnew, J. A. 1989: Sameness and difference: Hartshorne's *The nature of geography* and geography as areal variation. In Entrikin, J. N. and Brunn, S. D., eds, *Reflections on Richard Hartshorne's The nature of geography*. Washington, DC: Association of American Geographers, pp. 121–39.

Entrikin, J. N. 1990: *The betweenness of place: towards a geography of modernity*. Baltimore, MD: Johns Hopkins University Press.

Giddens, A. 1984: *The constitution of society*. Cambridge: Polity Press.

Haggett, P. 1965: *Locational analysis in human geography*. London: Edward Arnold/New York: John Wiley.

Hartshorne, R. 1939: *The nature of geography: a critical survey of current thought in the light of the past*. Lancaster, PA: Association of American Geographers.

Hartshorne, R. 1988: Hettner's exceptionalism: fact or fiction? *Hist. Geogr. Newsletter* 6, pp. 1–4.

Massey, D. 1984: *Spatial divisions of labour: social structures and the geography of production*. London: Macmillan.

Sayer, R. A. 1989: The 'new' regional geography and problems of narrative. *Environ. Plann. D: Society and Space* 7, pp. 253–76.

Smith, N. 1987: Dangers of the empirical turn: some comments on the CURS initiative. *Antipode* 19, pp. 59–68.

Smith, N. 1989: Geography as museum. In Entrikin, J. N. and Brunn, S. D., eds, *Reflections on Richard Hartshorne's The nature of geography*. Washington, DC: Association of American Geographers, pp. 89–120.

Smith, N. 1990: *Uneven development: nature, capital, and the production of space*, second edition. Oxford: Blackwell.

Tuan, Y.-F. 1977: *Space and place: the perspective of experience*. London: Edward Arnold/Minneapolis: University of Minnesota Press.

Suggested Reading

Agnew (1987, 1989).

Entrikin, J. N. and Brunn, S. D., eds 1989: *Reflections on Richard Hartshorne's The nature of geography*. Washington, DC: Association of American Geographers.

Gregory, D. 1989: Areal differentiation and postmodern human geography. In Gregory, D. and Walford, R., eds, *New Horizons in Human Geography*. London: Macmillan, pp. 1–27.

Hartshorne (1939).

Massey (1984), chs 2–3.

areal unit problem   See MODIFIABLE AREAL UNIT.

Arrow's theorem A proposition concerning the possibility of deriving statements of social preferences from individual preferences. In NEOCLASSICAL ECONOMICS, individual preferences for goods and services are held to be capable of aggregation into a social-welfare function expressing social or community preferences (see also WELFARE GEOGRAPHY). Arrow (1951) showed how difficult the translation of individual preferences into social preferences would be in practice.

Arrow stated five axioms which he believed social-preference structures must satisfy to be minimally acceptable. Briefly, these are:

(a) that social preferences must be completely ordered by the relation 'is at least as well liked socially as' and must therefore satisfy the conditions of completeness, reflexivity and transitivity;

(b) that they must be responsive to individual preferences;

(c) that they must not be imposed independently of individual preferences;

(d) that they must not be dictatorial, i.e. totally reflecting the preference of a single individual;

(e) that the most preferred state in a set of alternatives must be independent of the existence of other alternatives.

These axioms reflect value judgements but are generally considered reasonable. Arrow's 'impossibility theorem' states that in general it is not possible to construct social preferences that satisfy all five axioms. The mathematical proof is complex and the issues raised have stimulated further work among mathematicians as well as economists. The significance of Arrow's theorem is that it called into question the validity of the concept of the social-welfare function as a set of social valuations of alternatives, e.g. collections of goods and services, that could be derived from individual preferences revealed in the marketplace or by some kind of voting procedure. DMS

Reference

Arrow, K. J. 1951: *Social choice and individual values.* New York: John Wiley.

Asiatic mode of production A

MODE OF PRODUCTION involving a form of 'communal appropriation' which Marx and Engels believed to be especially characteristic of Asiatic societies. They provided no consistent or systematic account of the Asiatic mode of production, however, which remains one of 'the most controversial and contested of all the possible modes of production outlined in the works of Marx and Engels' (Hindess and Hirst, 1975). In the most general terms it was usually described by three components which were supposedly *absent* from Asiatic societies. These were:

(a) private property (especially land, which was owned by the STATE);

(b) a bourgeoisie, whose role was replaced by a STATE APPARATUS which was able to appropriate a surplus from direct producers in the form of rents and taxes, by virtue of its centralized and often 'despotic' control over large-scale irrigation works on which communal subsistence depended (see HYDRAULIC SOCIETY);

(c) the CITY – direct producers lived in village communities which were 'self-sustaining' and 'compact wholes' with no developed social division of labour between them, and any cities which did exist were essentially 'parasitic' creatures of the state with no direct involvement in production.

The purpose of such an overwhelmingly negative series of definitions was to account for the genesis of CAPITALISM in Europe. If these *absences* could explain the 'unchangeability' of non-capitalist societies in the East then, so Marx and Engels believed, their *presence* would explain the dynamism of capitalist societies in the West.

The key to the supposed stasis of the Asiatic mode of production was the relation between the state and the local community:

Between the self-reproducing villages 'below' and the hypertrophied state 'above' dwelt no intermediate forces. The impact of the state on the mosaic of villages beneath it was purely external and tributary; its consolidation or destruction alike left rural society untouched (Anderson, 1974, p. 483).

Hence, as Marx himself wrote: 'The structure of the economic elements of society remains untouched by the storm clouds of the political sky'. Theoretically, however, a major problem is precisely the place this accords to the state, for it presupposes yet does not explain 'a state which already exists and the imposition of state rule on a hitherto stateless people' (Hindess and Hirst, 1975, p. 201). But in his later writings Marx shifted his emphasis from 'above' to 'below', from the state to the local COMMUNITY, and in doing so sought to extend the concept of the Asiatic mode of production beyond the confines of Asia (Anderson, 1974). Empirically, however, its application there is every bit as questionable as on its original terrain:

The image of Asia stagnating for millenia in an unfinished transition from classless to class society, from barbarism to civilisation, has not stood up to the findings of archaeology and history in the East and the New World (Godelier, 1978, p. 214).

Marx was undoubtedly right to emphasize the specificity of non-Western societies, and hence in some part to qualify the unilinear view of social evolution which some commentators have seen in his work, but his various constructions of the Asiatic mode of production were nevertheless so markedly Eurocentric that they have continued to attract major criticism (Giddens, 1981, p. 85) (see ETHNOCENTRISM).   DG

References

Anderson, P. 1974: *Lineages of the absolutist state.* London: New Left Books/Verso, pp. 462–549.

Giddens, A. 1981: *A contemporary critique of historical materialism,* volume 1, *Power, property and the state.* London: Macmillan, pp. 81–8.

Godelier, M. 1978: The concept of the 'Asiatic mode of production' and Marxist models of social evolution. In Seddon, D., ed., *Relations of production: Marxist approaches to economic anthropology.* London: Frank Cass, pp. 209–57.

Hindess, B. and Hirst, P. Q. 1975: *Pre-capitalist modes of production.* London: Routledge and Kegan Paul, ch. 4.

Suggested Reading

Anderson (1974).

Bailey, A. M. and Llobera, J. R. 1981: *Asiatic mode of production: science and politics.* London: Routledge and Kegan Paul.

Turner, B. S. 1978: *Marx and the end of Orientalism.* London: Allen and Unwin.

assimilation The process by which NATIONS or COMMUNITIES and the subnations or minorities within them intermix and become more similar: terms with loosely comparable meaning include acculturation, adjustment and INTEGRATION. The degree of assimilation is a vital influence on the level of residential SEGREGATION, and geographers have frequently studied the two processes as they relate to urban immigrants. Factors influencing the rate of assimilation include ETHNICITY, religion, economic status, attitudes, education and intermarriage. A distinction may be made between *behavioural assimilation*, implying a process whereby the members of a group acquire the memories, sentiments and attitudes of other groups and – by sharing their experience and history – are incorporated with them in a common cultural life, and *structural assimilation*, referring to the distribution of migrant ethnics through the groups and social systems of a society, including its system of occupational stratification. Differing political ideologies may underlie notions of assimilation. (See also MULTICULTURALISM.)   PEO

Suggested Reading

Boal, F. W. 1976: Ethnic residential segregation. In Herbert, D. T. and Johnston, R. J., eds, *Social areas in cities,* volume I, *Spatial processes and forms.* Chichester: John Wiley, ch. 2.

Gordon, M. M. 1964: *Assimilation in American life.* New York: Oxford University Press.

Petersen, W. 1975: *Population,* third edition. New York: Collier-Macmillan, ch. 4.

autocorrelation See SPATIAL AUTOCORRELATION.

B

balanced neighbourhood A planning concept intended to counter the process of SEGREGATION which produces NATURAL AREAS within urban residential mosaics (see also TERRITORIALITY). Instead of (ETHNIC, CLASS and perhaps other) social groups occupying separate residential districts they should be equally represented in all areas, with each NEIGHBOURHOOD thus comprising a balanced microcosm of the entire urban society. Such a mixture is supposed to bring social benefits and also to stabilize residential patterns, thereby preventing any process of INVASION AND SUCCESSION. Arguments against the concept contend that spatial proximity does not necessarily create a COMMUNITY and may instead generate conflict between unequals, which Sennett (1973) sees as a desirable first stage to inter-group accommodation. Others argue that balanced neighbourhoods are unlikely to survive in free markets for housing and property (see TIEBOUT MODEL).   RJJ

Reference

Sennett, R. 1973: *The uses of disorder*. London: Penguin.

Suggested Reading

Johnston, R. J. 1989: People and places in the behavioural environment. In Boal, F. W. and Livingstone, D. N., eds, *The behavioural environment*. London: Routledge, pp. 235–52.

Sarkissian, W. 1976: The idea of social mix in town planning, *Urban Stud.* 13, pp. 231–46.

barrio A Spanish term, widely used in Latin America for SQUATTER SETTLEMENTS.   RJJ

behaviour See PRISONER'S DILEMMA; SATISFICING BEHAVIOUR; SEARCH BEHAVIOUR.

behavioural environment The internal or perceptual environment in which the facts of the phenomenal world are organized into conceptual patterns and given meaning or values by individuals within particular cultural contexts. It forms the basis for environmental or locational DECISION-MAKING and is contrasted with the geographical or PHENOMENAL ENVIRONMENT (see the figure).

The term was developed within the German school of Gestalt psychology in the 1930s in reaction to atomistic, associationist theories of cognition (i.e. ones that posit that our complex mental representations are aggregations of sensations). Gestalt psychologists argued that perceptions are not simple aggregations of sensations; they are organized into wholes, the perception of each element determined by the context (see HOLISM).

William Kirk introduced the concept into geography in 1952 and expanded it in 1963 in an attempt to unify physical and human geography and mediate between the extremes of ENVIRONMENTAL DETERMINISM and POSSIBILISM. The concept is a remarkably elastic one. As Boal and Livingstone (1989) note, it is often unclear whether it is being used metaphorically or literally, in a REALIST or INSTRUMENTALIST way, and whether the processes that structure perceptions are supposed to be neurophysiological or sociocultural. In part because of this elasticity, Kirk's use of the concept is credited with spawning several different traditions: HUMANISTIC GEOGRAPHY, BEHAVIOURAL GEOGRAPHY,

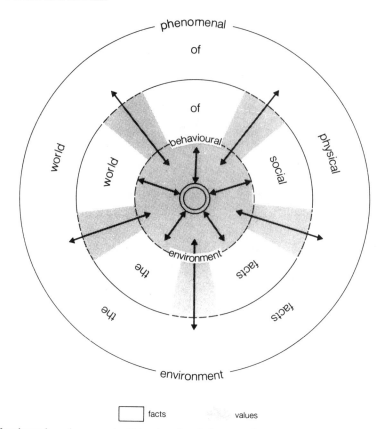

behavioural environment *Behavioural and phenomenal environments* (Gregory, 1978).

ENVIRONMENTAL PERCEPTION and the geography of HAZARDS. GP

References

Boal, F. and Livingstone, D. N. eds 1989: *The behavioural environment*. London: Routledge.

Gregory, D. 1978: *Ideology, science and human geography*. London: Hutchinson.

Kirk, W., 1952: Historical geography and the concept of the behavioural environment. *Indian Geographical Journal*, Silver Jubilee Volume, pp. 152–60.

Kirk, W. 1963: Problems of geography. *Geography* 48, pp. 357–71.

behavioural geography A psychological turn in human geography which emphasized the role of cognitive and decision-making variables as mediating the relationship between environment and spatial behaviour. The development of SPATIAL ANALYSIS was initially predicated

upon some simple and deterministic assumptions regarding human behaviour. People were posited to be both rational and optimizing in their actions: in geographical terms this meant that they were invariably concerned to minimize distance in their spatial behaviour. The simplicity of this fundamental postulate was steadily relaxed. First, in STOCHASTIC PROCESS work such as Hägerstrand's (1968) study of innovation DIFFUSION, the addition of a random variable in a SIMULATION model introduced some statistical variation to distance parameters. A second modification was the replacement of the random variable by a set of cognitive variables. This advance gave rise to the wide-ranging subfield of behavioural geography.

Research in behavioural geography converged from at least three empirical directions. In LOCATIONAL ANALYSIS the influential research of organization theorists such as Simon (1957) and Cyert and March (1963) introduced a more grounded emphasis on DECISION-MAKING to geographical studies. In an important paper, Wolpert (1964) showed that, for a sample of Swedish farmers, optimal farming practices were not attainable. He tested whether the farmers were indeed maximizing their utility functions, and were in possession of a complete stock of knowledge about available economic opportunities. Finding that neither of these conditions was met, he concluded that the farmers were not optimizers but, in Simon's term, *satisficers*. Not only did they lack complete knowledge and a perfect capacity for processing information, but there were other, and competing, values and aspirations which they held, as well as the force of habit which diverted them from new opportunities. A related study of industrial location (Pred, 1967) struck even closer to the core of conventional spatial analysis. Once again, the conclusion was that satisficing, the art (as well as the science) of making do, provided the most appropriate description of corporate decision-making, and thus of subsequent geographical patterns.

The extent to which behavioural geography departed from the paradigm of spatial analysis was contested. For some authors, locational theory was powerful enough to account for all but a 'residual domain' of spatial events, and 'this domain will presumably be colonized by a cognitive–behavioural location theory' (Harvey, 1969). But other authors saw the development of a cognitive–behavioural perspective in more substantial terms. In Olsson's (1969) oft-cited words, 'the earlier stress on the geometric outcome of the spatial game has lessened in favor of analyses of the rules which govern the moves of the actors who populate the gaming table'. Certainly, the decision-making rules of the actors were the major concern of a second influential body of research which examined the geography of natural HAZARDS. For in this domain, non-rational behaviour was palpable, as residents and businesses chose locations which placed them at risk from a natural hazard, including river or sea floods, avalanches and earthquakes. Why did such seemingly irrational locational

behaviour occur? In some instances, site selection was the product of incomplete information as, for example, revealed by a study of homeowners who had purchased property in seismically sensitive areas of California (Palm, 1981). In other instances, it seemed that geographical information was interpreted through the filter of distinctive personality dispositions. Here behavioural research was closest to psychology, and drew upon such personality measures as the thematic apperception test (T.A.T.), skilfully employed by Saarinen (1966) in his study of Great Plains wheat farmers operating in a region of marginal drought conditions.

The T.A.T. was one of a battery of paper and pencil tests used to assess attitudes, a practice that has been a distinctive methodological feature of behavioural geography. The third major field of research, ENVIRONMENTAL PERCEPTION, employed a range of attitudinal scales including REPERTORY GRIDS and the SEMANTIC DIFFERENTIAL to evaluate the meaning of places. The structured QUESTIONNAIRE was the fundamental research instrument. In his seminal study of MENTAL MAPS, for example, Gould asked college students to write down in rank order their residential preferences among different American states (Gould and White, 1974). More usually, geographers took their questionnaires out of the classroom and into the field as they probed the perceptions of such disparate phenomena as shopping centres, recreational sites or dangerous streets.

Behavioural research in human geography and related interdisciplinary fields has multiplied across a broad terrain of subject areas; a recent review has collected some 600 citations (Golledge and Timmermans, 1990; Timmermans and Golledge, 1990). But in certain respects despite its range, behavioural geography has become increasingly homogeneous, at least methodologically. Early contributions continued considerable methodological diversity, employing techniques that included such qualitative methods as PARTICIPANT OBSERVATION (Brookfield, 1969). In such a cognitive–behavioural approach, Mercer and Powell (1972) anticipated a contribution that would 'preserve and foster a "humanist" alternative to the popular mechanistic explanation'. That diversity has given way to a more squarely analytical methodology predicated upon a POSITIVIST philosophy of science (but see Couclelis and Golledge, 1983). As Harvey (1969) predicted, behavioural geography became 'an appendage' of the locational school and as such was irreversibly shaped by the QUANTITATIVE REVOLUTION, developing a preoccupation with MEASUREMENT, statistical analysis and a highly formalized methodology.

But does such a repertoire deal adequately with the realm of human consciousness and intersubjective realms (Ley, 1981; Lowenthal, 1987)? For, as Olsson (1974) has observed, in the realm of hopes and fears, two times two is not always equal to four. A second criticism has been directed against the intrusive nature of behavioural methodology, which either operates in a simplified quasi-laboratory format or else disrupts the flow of spontaneous action in the field and controls the nature of response in its use of a formalized research instrument. Such intrusion systematically removes the contexts which give meaning to events and actions. Perhaps the most serious severance of context is the manner in which questionnaires, administered to individuals, remove the social context in which decisions are made, and where actions originate.

As human geography shares something of a post-positivist scepticism of a highly formal scientific method, the criticisms of behavioural geography have assumed greater weight. To earlier criticisms another may be advanced: To what extent is research predicated upon a philosophy of observation able to discern realities which are not directly observable? Where do the contextual forces of ideology and social structure fit in a research programme concerned with the behaviour of individuals? (See also POSTSTRUCTURALISM; HUMAN AGENCY; HUMANISTIC GEOGRAPHY; SUBJECTIVITY.)   DL

References

Brookfield, H. 1969: On the environment as perceived. *Prog. Geog.* 1, pp. 51–80.

Couclelis, H. and Golledge, R. 1983: Analytic research, positivism and behavioral geography. *Ann. Ass. Am. Geogr.* 73, pp. 331–9.

Cyert, R. and March, J. 1963: *A behavioral theory of the firm.* Englewood Cliffs, NJ: Prentice-Hall.

Golledge, R. and Timmermans, H. 1990: Applications of behavioural research on spatial problems I: cognition. *Progr. hum. Geogr.* 14, pp. 57–99.

Gould, P. R. and White, R. 1974: *Mental maps.* London: Penguin.

Hägerstrand, T. 1968: *Innovation diffusion as a spatial process.* Chicago: University of Chicago Press.

Harvey, D. 1969: Conceptual and measurement problems in the cognitive-behavioral approach to location theory. In Cox, K. and Golledge, R., eds, *Behavioral problems in geography.* Evanston, IL: Northwestern Studies in Geography No. 17, pp. 35–67.

Ley, D. 1981: Behavioral geography and the philosophies of meaning. In Cox, K. and Golledge, R., eds, *Behavioral problems in geography revisited.* London: Methuen, pp. 209–30.

Lowenthal, D. 1987: Environmental perception: an odyssey of ideas. *Journal of Environmental Psychology* 7, 337–46.

Mercer, D. and Powell, J. 1972: *Phenomenology and related non-positivistic approaches in the social sciences.* Department of Geography, Monash University, Publications No. 1.

Olsson, G. 1969: Inference problems in locational analysis. In Cox, K. and Golledge, R., eds, *Behavioral problems in geography.* Evanston, IL: Northwestern Studies in Geography No. 17, pp. 14–34.

Olsson, G. 1974: The dialectics of spatial analysis. *Antipode* 6(3), pp. 50–62.

Palm, R. 1981: Public response to earthquake hazard information. *Ann. Ass. Am. Geogr.* 71, pp. 389–99.

Pred, A. 1967: *Behavior and location.* Lund Studies in Geography, Series B, No. 27.

Saarinen, T. 1966: *Perception of drought hazard on the Great Plains.* University of Chicago, Department of Geography, Research paper No. 106.

Simon, H. 1957: *Models of man.* New York: John Wiley.

Timmermans, H. and Golledge, R. 1990: Applications of behavioural research on spatial problems II: preference and choice. *Progr. hum. Geogr.* 14, pp. 311–54.

Wolpert, J. 1964: The decision process in spatial context. *Ann. Ass. Am. Geogr.* 54, pp. 537–58.

Suggested Reading

Cox and Golledge (1981).

Gold, J. 1980: *An introduction to behavioural geography*. Oxford: Oxford University Press.

Golledge, R. and Stimson, R. 1987: *Analytical behavioural geography*. London: Croom Helm.

Spencer, C. and Blades, M. 1986: Pattern and process: a review essay on the relationship between behavioural geography and environmental psychology. *Progr. hum. Geogr.* 10, pp. 230–48.

Walmsley, D. 1988: *Urban living: the individual in the city*. Harlow: Longman.

Berkeley School The collective term applied to the group of geographers influenced by Carl Sauer during his long years in the Department of Geography at the University of California, Berkeley. Most members of the School were graduate students of Sauer, and some became his colleagues at Berkeley: they included Homer Aschmann, Andrew Clark, William Denevan, Clarence Glacken, Leslie Hewes, Fred Kniffen, John Leighly, Marvin Mikesell, James Parsons, Fred Simoons, Dan Stanislawski and Philip Wagner.

The Berkeley School was not typical of such groups of scholars in other disciplines, in which the leader established a doctrinaire position which the disciples then followed uncritically. Rather, it was a series of individuals (Sauer taught at Berkeley from the 1920s until the 1970s) who shared Sauer's interests in LANDSCAPE creation as a representation of CULTURE, and who followed his emphasis on studies of the evolution of the CULTURAL LAND-SCAPE (cf. SEQUENT OCCUPANCE). Leighly and Parsons (1979) thus claimed that 'Sauer always disclaimed any intention of founding a school or of shaping students over a common last. He expected the individual to find his own object of curiosity': nevertheless, the distinctiveness of the group who followed his lead is clear.

That distinction reflects in part on Sauer's personal influence, and on the relative isolation of Berkeley geographers from developments elsewhere in the USA (which Sauer rejected) during the School's most formative years (Porter, 1978). Sauer himself was particularly influenced by the work of the anthropologist Kroeber and his definition of CULTURE (criticized by Duncan, 1980, as a form of reification). Thus Sauer's works on landscape development

were exercises in 'culture history', which involved appreciation of the 'natural environment', reconstruction of past landscapes, and processes of change through the spread of human agency (see DIFFUSION). This approach was defined in Sauer's (1925) classic early essay on 'The MORPHOLOGY of landscape' and crystallized in his Bowman memorial lectures on 'Agricultural origins and dispersals' (Sauer, 1952). The latter were characterized as 'a summary review of what man has done with the plants and animals at his disposal'.

Although Sauer and the Berkeley School were mainly concerned to elucidate past changes in the cultural landscape, especially in Latin America, with an emphasis on fieldwork as the main source of data, Sauer's own concerns extended to future landscape changes. The final paragraph of his Bowman lectures was as follows:

Our civilization still rests, and will continue to rest, on the discoveries made by peoples for the most part unknown to history. Historic man has added no plant or animal of major importance to the domesticated forms on which he depends. He has learned lately to explain a good part of the mechanisms of selection, but the arts thereof are immemorial and represent an achievement that merits our respect and attention. We remain a part of the organic world, and as we intervene more and more decisively to change the balance and nature of life, we have also more need to know, by retrospective study, the responsibilities and hazards of our present and our prospects as lords of creation.

This concern for the future landscape through appreciation of its past was also expressed in the major Wenner–Gren Symposium *Man's role in changing the face of the Earth* (Thomas, 1956), for which Sauer was a co-chair. In his introductory contribution, Sauer (1956) set out the theme of the symposium as 'an attempt to set forth the geographic effects, that is, the appropriation of habitat by habit, resulting from the spread of different cultures to all the *oikoumene* throughout all we know of human time', which summarizes well the overall approach of the Berkeley School.

The lack of any clear methodology – other than what Leighly and Parsons refer to as emphases on 'intellectual initiative, direct observation and a "good honest job of reporting"' – means that the School's output lacks many distinguishing characteristics. Most of it comprises major works of synthesis, often about an esoteric topic (as in Donkin's recent illustrations of its major themes: Donkin, 1989, 1991): they are major works of scholarship which enrich our understanding of the impacts of HUMAN AGENCY on the environment.

RJJ

References and Suggested Reading

Donkin, R. A. 1989: *The Muscovy duck*, Carina moschata domestica: *origins, dispersals, and associated aspects of the geography of domestication.* Rotterdam: A. A. Balkema.

Donkin, R. A. 1991: *Meleagrides: an historical and ethnogeographical study of the guinea fowl.* London: Ethnographica.

Duncan, J. S. 1980: The superorganic in American cultural geography. *Ann. Ass. Am. Geogr.* 70, pp. 181–98.

Leighly, J. and Parsons, J. J. 1979: Berkeley: drifting into geography in the twenties and the later Sauer years. *Ann. Ass. Am. Geogr.* 69, pp. 4–15.

Porter, P. W. 1978: Geography as human ecology. *Am. behav. Scient.* 22, pp. 15–40.

Sauer, C. O. 1925: *The morphology of landscape.* Berkeley, CA: University of California Publications in Geography, 2.

Sauer, C. O. 1952: *Agricultural origins and dispersals.* New York: American Geographical Society.

Sauer, C. O. 1956: The agency of man on Earth. In Thomas, W. L. Jr., ed., *Man's role in changing the face of the Earth.* Chicago: University of Chicago Press, pp. 49–69.

Thomas, W. L. Jr., ed., 1956: *Man's role in changing the face of the Earth.* Chicago: University of Chicago Press.

bid–rent curve A plot of the rent which people are prepared to pay against distance from some point, usually the city centre. Rent bids generally decrease with increasing distance from a city or its centre where land values are highest, so a bid–rent curve slopes down in a diagram with rent on the vertical axis and distance displayed horizontally. The curve is sometimes shown as convex to the origin of the graph, to reflect sharp decreases in rent with short distances from the city (centre), levelling off with increasing distance. Bid–rent curves are an important element in the ALONSO MODEL of urban land use and in the VON THÜNEN MODEL of agricultural land use.

DMS

bifurcation A change in the solution to a differential or difference equation at a critical value of a MODEL's parameter. Three types of change are common (see the figure): (a) there is a 'jump' in the relationship between X and T at the critical value of T (t_c), shown in the figure (a) as a discontinuous 'step function'; (b) there is a shift from a linear relationship at t_c to a periodic one; (c) there is shift at t_c from a linear to a chaotic relationship. (See also CHAOS and CATASTROPHE THEORY: the latter covers a special case of the general features of bifurcation.)

Bifurcations are common in models of SYSTEMS which involve interdependence

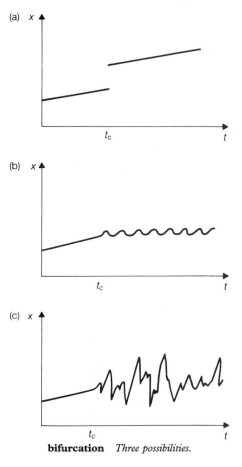

bifurcation *Three possibilities.*

among the variables, especially if the relationships among those variables are non-linear. Such systems are commonly studied in environmental science but are also typical of some aspects of human geography: 'jumps' may characterize the crossing of critical thresholds in the relationship between the percentage of the votes cast and the percentage of the seats won by a political party in first-past-the-post electoral systems, for example, whereas transitions to CHAOS may occur in the pattern of population change over time in a society the population of which has reached the CARRYING CAPACITY of the land occupied.   RJJ

Suggested Reading
Wilson, A. G. 1981: *Catastrophe theory and bifurcation: applications to urban and regional systems.* London: Croom Helm/Berkeley: University of California Press.

binomial distribution A theoretical frequency distribution used in statistical tests to indicate the likelihood of a particular characteristic being observed in a sample when the features of its parent population are known. For example, if half of the electorate of a town is female, then the probability of one female elector being sampled at random is 0.5, of two being sampled at random consecutively is 0.25 (0.5^2), of three being sampled consecutively is 0.125 (0.5^3), and so forth. With large samples, the binomial has the same form as a NORMAL DISTRIBUTION. It is used to test whether the characteristics of a sample are consistent with those of a known population, i.e. whether or not it is a true random sample.   RJJ

black economy See INFORMAL SECTOR.

blockbusting An American term for the process whereby the racial composition of a residential block changes from white to black, usually as a consequence of activity by real estate agents (cf. INVASION AND SUCCESSION). Agents or other speculators may trigger such a change by introducing a small number of black households to a block when vacancies arise, thereby putting pressure on the

remaining white households, many of which may not welcome the prospect of a 'mixed neighbourhood'. Some of them may be panicked into selling their homes relatively cheaply: the agents can then resell at higher prices to incoming blacks, thereby making large profits through stimulating rapid neighbourhood change on the basis of fear and prejudice.   RJJ

Suggested Reading
Ley, D. F. 1983: *A social geography of the city.* New York and London: Harper and Row.

boosterism See URBAN ENTREPRENEURIALISM.

Boserup thesis An argument put forward by Ester Boserup (1965) to explain historical change in agriculture. Her thesis was confined to subsistence farmers, who aim to provide themselves with food, are interested in maximizing their leisure time and thus choose farming systems that allow this (see SUBSISTENCE AGRICULTURE). They will thus only change their methods if population grows and they have to increase their food supply. Population growth is therefore the independent variable and compels an increase in food supplies, unlike in Malthus's system in which population increase is only possible after an increase in food supplies.

The increase in food supplies is obtained by the intensification of production, which is obtained in two ways. The first is the reduction of fallow (she excludes the possibility of the colonization of unoccupied land). As population density rises a series of stages occurs – forest fallow, bush fallow, short fallow, annual cropping and finally multiple cropping – in which the length of the fallow falls from 25 years to a negligible period. Second, as the fallow is reduced changes in farming methods are enforced to maintain or increase yields: the axe and digging stick are supplemented by the hoe and then replaced by the plough. In the early stages of forest fallow little or no weeding is done, no manure is used, and labour inputs are minimal. But with increasing density more manure is used, land is weeded more frequently, and in the final stages it is terraced and irrigated so that labour inputs increase. Thus, while output per hectare is increased, output per head is only maintained.

Boserup's thesis has attracted great attention from geographers, anthropologists and economists. Although devised to explain historical change, it has also been used to account for spatial differences in farming intensity in developing countries.

DBG

Reference

Boserup, E. 1965: *The conditions of agricultural change: the economics of agrarian change under population pressure.* London: Allen and Unwin.

Suggested Reading

Boserup (1965).

Boserup, E. 1981: *Population and technological change, a study of long-term trends.* Chicago: University of Chicago Press.

Grigg, D. B. 1979: Ester Boserup's theory of agrarian change: a critical review. *Progr. hum. Geogr.* 3, pp. 64–84.

boundary The dividing line between one spatial unit or group and another. Human spatial boundaries are defined by social activities and range from the precise to the fuzzy, depending upon the nature of the social activity in question. For example, political boundaries drawn to delimit the territory of a STATE mark the precise limits of the state's claim to SOVEREIGNTY. The boundaries of jurisdictions within a state serve to demarcate areas of legal responsibility for public-service delivery and revenue collection. Under FEDERALISM boundaries between the basic spatial units (provinces, cantons, states, etc.) are of special political importance. Social and cultural boundary-making are equally universal, and in certain circumstances the results show up vividly in the CULTURAL LANDSCAPE, as in, for example, contrasts in agricultural practices and building styles between English-settled and French-settled areas of Quebec. More often than not, however, social and cultural boundaries are dynamic and fluid, responding to shifts in social solidarity and mobilization. Often they are more akin to moving gradients. Moreover, linguistic, religious and economic boundaries are often cross-cutting and permeable rather than mutually reinforcing and impermeable (Weiss, 1962).

With increasing population MOBILITY, social and cultural boundaries have become especially complex and less susceptible to simple cartographic representation (Harley, 1989).

Human spatial boundaries are defined when, in the process of social interaction, groups form geographically and differentiate themselves from one another (Simmel, 1971). Socialization into group membership, therefore, is intrinsically spatial. A boundary between two social groups is the result of distinctive patterns of behaviour and systems of symbols that are formed geographically (Cohen, 1974). CONFLICT arises when boundaries are not well defined or there is contested TERRITORY. Although imprinted into consciousness in the process of learning, there is always an ambiguity about the meaning of symbols and the differences that they signify, so that the 'traditions' associated with a group are rarely static but constantly reinterpreted (Hobsbawm and Ranger, 1983). Ambiguity is especially evident when a social group, such as an ETHNIC GROUP, is deeply stratified by caste or CLASS or when large-scale social change challenges all existing boundaries.

The practice of TERRITORIALITY by groups is reinforced when social and economic differences between adjacent groups are perceived as relatively great. Boundaries then are not so much inclusionary as exclusionary in nature. Distancing and SEGREGATION between ethnic groups and classes become widespread. Physical barriers and legal devices are used to exclude those who threaten the 'security' and material interests of a group with sufficient power to exclude.

States and other forms of sociopolitical organization (such as hierarchical churches) exercise their power in part through their ability to engage in drawing and redrawing the boundaries inside and around their territory (Sack, 1986). Controlling and managing territory necessitates the demarcation of definite boundaries. These can be formal, as with the delegation of authority to local government units, or informal, as when national governments implement policies to favour their electorates or specific regional and ethnic groups within the national territory (MacLaughlin and Agnew, 1986).

The external boundaries of states have received the most attention from geographers, usually without much discussion of their genesis in social processes. The tendency has been either to tie them to physical features, as if the physical world was somehow responsible for their definition or, more realistically, to see them as the outcome of frontier settlement/development and inter-state conflict. Interest in the historical specificity of boundary-making by states is very recent. There is evidence that the rulers of the ancient empires, such as those of Rome and the early Chinese dynasties, did not define the edges of their territories in terms of fixed boundaries: 'Ancient IMPERIALISM saw control over peoples and towns as the essence of sovereignty . . . in antiquity territory was not a factor constituting the essence of the state at it is in our times' (Isaac, 1990, p. 417). In medieval Europe the hierarchical subordination of different strata (e.g. monarch, nobles and peasants) and the importance of local feudal links encouraged a plurality of social bonds without an exclusive identity based upon membership in the 'imagined community' (Anderson, 1983) of the NATION–STATE. Rigid spatial boundaries became important only when sovereignty of the state and CITIZENSHIP within its territory displaced that of the monarch in a rigid social order (Connolly, 1988). JAA

References

Anderson, B. 1983: *Imagined communities: reflections on the origins and spread of nationalism.* London: Verso.

Cohen, A. 1974: *Two-dimensional man: an essay on the anthropology of power and symbolism in complex society.* Berkeley, CA: University of California Press.

Connolly, W. 1988: *Political theory and modernity.* Oxford: Blackwell.

Harley, J. B. 1989: Historical geography and the cartographic illusion. *J. hist. Geogr.* 15, pp. 80–91.

Hobsbawm, E. and Ranger, T., eds, 1983: *The invention of tradition.* Cambridge: Cambridge University Press.

Isaac, B. 1990: *The limits of empire: the Roman army in the East.* Oxford: Oxford University Press.

MacLaughlin, J. G. and Agnew, J. A. 1986: Hegemony and the regional question: the political geography of regional policy in Northern Ireland, 1945–1972. *Ann. Ass. Am. Geogr.* 76, pp. 247–61.

Sack, R. D. 1986: *Human territoriality: its theory and history.* Cambridge: Cambridge University Press.

Simmel, G. 1971: *On individuality and social forms.* Chicago: University of Chicago Press.

Weiss, R. 1962: Cultural boundaries and ethnographic maps. In Wagner, P. and Mikesell, M., eds, *Readings in cultural geography.* Chicago: University of Chicago Press, pp. 62–74.

Suggested Reading

Agnew, J. A. 1989: Beyond reason: spatial and temporal sources of ethnic conflict. In Kriesberg, L. et al., eds, *Intractable conflicts and their transformation.* Syracuse, NY: Syracuse University Press, pp. 41–52.

Barth, F., ed., 1969: *Ethnic groups and boundaries.* Boston: Little, Brown.

Sack (1986).

Weiss (1962).

Brenner debate   One of the longest-running debates in the social sciences has concerned the causes and geography of the transition from FEUDALISM to CAPITALISM in medieval and early modern Europe (Hilton, 1975; Holton, 1985). In the mid-1970s the 'transition debate' entered a new phase stimulated by an American historian, Robert Brenner (1976, 1982). Brenner reworked an older argument (Dobb, 1946), that the structure of CLASS power and class relations (rather than demographic or commercial change) determined long-run patterns of European economic development, explaining the emergence of capitalism in England.

The editors of the journal *Past and Present*, in which Brenner's argument appeared, invited several responses, and a rejoinder from Brenner (all reprinted in Aston and Philpin, 1985). Subsequent debate spilled over into the literature of history, historical geography and social theory (Tribe, 1981; Heller, 1985).

Brenner rejected the notion that medieval European society underwent an ecological crisis from *c.*1300, produced by an underlying ecological dynamic (see POSTAN THESIS), reasserting the Marxian position that agrarian crises were socially precipitated. The legally dependent position of feudal tenants enabled lords to exact surplus above that produced by 'market' forces. Ever-greater surplus extraction from agricultural producers by feudal lords (to finance competition for political status), the Church and the Crown precipitated a crisis of reproduction in peasant agriculture, and threatened peasant subsistence. On this reading, 'the late-medieval crisis in seigneurial revenues was not a mere concomitant of a more general crisis in the economy: it was the very eye of the storm' (B. Harvey, in Campbell, 1991, p. 17).

However, class relations varied across Europe, causing demographic decline to have differing effects. Brenner claims that agrarian capitalism appeared in England because of the particular way in which English feudal society decayed during the later Middle Ages. Central to his argument are two geographical comparisons of social relations. The first comparison is between Western Europe (where lords lost their political control of feudal tenants) and Eastern Europe (where manorial lords strengthened their control over land and dependant peasantries). The second comparison is between France (where absolute peasant property rights became entrenched) and England (where peasants failed to establish absolute property rights, but achieved more flexible tenures). English tenants' initiatives rebounded on them when demographic expansion resumed after 1500: landlords evicted peasant producers and installed entrepreneurial tenants, thereby producing agrarian capitalism.

The main points of dispute between Brenner and his critics, on both the theoretical right and left, involved the extent to which he treated demographic and social causes of long-run change as mutually exclusive, rather than as interactive; and the extent to which he conflated exogenous and endogenous components of demographic and economic change (Hilton, 1978; Postan and Hatcher, 1978; Aston and Philpin, 1985). Within Marxist approaches, the most noteworthy skirmishing involved Wallerstein's world systems view of the emergent European world economy (Wallerstein, 1974, 1980; Brenner, 1977).

Brenner's rejoinder (1982) was more a clarified restatement than a sustained response to critics, and failed to problematize the relationship amongst the various components of 'agrarian capitalism' (Holton, 1985; Glennie, 1987). More recent work has also taken a more sophisticated view of power than Brenner's reduction of power to property relations (Mann, 1986; Biddick, 1990). Issues raised by the debate have been carried forward by theoretically informed intensive empirical studies (Searle, 1986; Glennie, 1988; Campbell, 1991). It is unfortunate that some medievalists and agrarian historians have more or less ignored this debate (e.g. Hallam, 1990). Analogous debates have been amongst the liveliest areas of contemporary agrarian geography, and of development studies, and comparative geographical work has much to offer in linking historical and contemporary work.

PG

References

Aston, T. H. and Philpin, C. E., eds, 1985: *The Brenner debate: agrarian class structure and economic development in preindustrial Europe.* Cambridge: Cambridge University Press.

Biddick, K. 1990: People and things: power in early English development. *Comp. Stud. Soc. Hist.* 32(1), pp. 3–23.

Brenner, R. 1976: Agrarian class structure and economic development in pre-industrial England. *Past and Present* 70, pp. 30–75.

Brenner, R. 1977: The origins of capitalist development: a critique of neo-Smithian Marxism. *New Left Rev.* 104, pp. 25–92.

Brenner, R. 1982: The agrarian roots of European capitalism. *Past and Present* 97, pp. 20–97.

Campbell, B. M. S., ed., 1991: *Before the Black Death: studies in the 'crisis' of the early fourteenth century.* Manchester: Manchester University Press.

Dobb, M. 1946: *Studies in the development of capitalism.* London: Routledge and Kegan Paul.

Glennie, P. D. 1987: The transition from feudalism to capitalism as a problem for historical geography. *J. hist. Geogr.* 13, pp. 296–302.

Glennie, P. D. 1988: In search of agrarian capitalism: manorial land markets and the acquisition of land in the Lea valley, c.1450–c.1560. *Continuity and Change* 3, pp. 11–40.

Hallam, H. E., ed., 1990: *The agrarian history of England and Wales* volume II, *1042–1348*. Cambridge: Cambridge University Press.

Heller, H. 1985: The transition debate in historical perspective. *Sci. Soc.* 49, pp. 208–13.

Hilton, R. H., ed., 1975: *The transition from feudalism to capitalism*. London: Verso.

Hilton, R. H. 1978: A crisis of feudalism. *Past and Present* 80, pp. 3–19.

Holton, R. J. 1985: *The transition from feudalism to capitalism*. London: Macmillan.

Mann, M. 1986: *The sources of social power.* Cambridge: Cambridge University Press.

Postan, M. and Hatcher, J. 1978: Population and class structure in feudal society. *Past and Present* 78, pp. 24–37.

Searle, C. 1986: Custom, class conflict and agrarian capitalism: the Cumbrian customary economy in the eighteenth century. *Past and Present* 110, pp. 106–30.

Tribe, K. 1981: The problem of transition and the question of origin. In *Genealogies of capitalism.* London: Routledge, ch. 1.

Wallerstein, I. 1974: *The modern world system I: capitalist agriculture and the origins of the European world-economy in the sixteenth century.* London: Academic Press.

Wallerstein, I. 1980: *The modern world system II: mercantilism and the consolidation of the European world-economy.* London: Academic Press.

Suggested Reading

Aston and Philpin (1985).

Campbell (1991).

Dyer, C. 1989: *Standards of living in the later Middle Ages: social change in England c.1200–1500.* Cambridge: Cambridge University Press.

Glennie (1987).

Holton (1985).

C

calibration   The procedure for fitting a theoretical model to an empirical data set. The GRAVITY MODEL, for example, specifies a relationship between a pattern of flows and certain other variables, the relative influence of which is weighted. The calibration procedure produces estimates of those weights in the particular empirical circumstances.   RJJ

capital   Commonly treated as synonymous with 'money', capital is more accurately understood as 'expanding social value'. Capital is a social relation rather than a thing, and it can take various material forms; it can be invested as MONEY, consumed as raw material, expended as wages for labour, operated as machinery and other means of production, or sold as commodities. Most succinctly, capital is 'value in motion' (Marx, 1987 edn, p. 149), insofar as it is social value that expands in the production process (see ACCUMULATION). Marx (1987 edn, ch. 4) describes the cyclical conversion from money into labour power, raw materials and commodities, and then back into money again, as the 'general formula of capital'. In all its forms, capital is the product of social labour performed in the production of commodities.

Historically, capital came to define the MODE OF PRODUCTION at the point when labour power itself became commodified as a form of capital. Thereafter the production of surplus value and the reproduction of capital was organized first and foremost as an economic result of market exchange rather than directly through social and political means. In the resulting capitalist society (see CAPITALISM), capital is owned and controlled by a specific social CLASS, the capitalist class, which profits from the expansion of capital and, by dint of its ownership of capital, forms a ruling class.

Different individual capitals (i.e. firms, individual capitalists, etc.) occupy different niches in the cyclical reproduction of capital (see CIRCUIT OF CAPITAL) and are associated with different factions of the capitalist class. Financial, industrial and rentier capital all represent specific interests within the capitalist class, and the role of the STATE is in part to mediate these intra-capitalist interests as well as to regulate class conflict between capital and labour.

Geographical research on capital has largely focused on the ways in which the social power and economic rationale of capital translate into systematic geographical patterns of DEVELOPMENT and UNDERDEVELOPMENT (see UNEVEN DEVELOPMENT), environmental degradation, and diverse experiences of local change (Harvey, 1982, 1989; Dunford and Perrins, 1983).   NS

References

Dunford, M. and Perrins, D. 1983: *The arena of capital.* London: Macmillan.

Harvey, D. 1982: *The limits to capital.* Oxford: Blackwell.

Harvey, D. 1989: *The urban experience.* Oxford: Blackwell.

Marx, K. 1987 edn: *Capital* volume I. New York: International Publishers, see esp. ch. IV.

capitalism   An *historically specific* form of economic and social organization in which:

(a) the direct producer is separated from ownership of the means of production and the product of the LABOUR PROCESS; and where

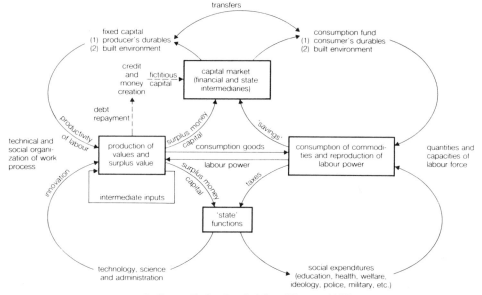

capitalism *Paths of capital flow* (Harvey, 1982).

(b) this separation is effected through the transformation of labour power into a COMMODITY to be bought and sold on a LABOUR MARKET regulated by price signals.

In NEOCLASSICAL ECONOMICS these exchanges are treated as identical to the price transactions which occur within and between all commodity markets, i.e. as an 'exchange of equivalents', so that the general structure of commodity exchange is sufficient to characterize the entire economy. Hence, in the course of the eighteenth and nineteenth centuries, the generalization of commodity exchange in Western Europe and North America ensured that 'the market mode of economic integration gradually bound society into one cohesive economic system' (Harvey, 1973) (see also MARKET EXCHANGE). Neoclassical economics is, of course, confined to the economy; its social and political counterpart is provided by Max Weber's description of 'the institutional foundations of the market' (Collins, 1980; see also Clarke, 1982).

Weber emphasized the importance of the legal and political framework established by the NATION-STATE, 'which afforded to capitalism its chance for development', and drew attention to the importance of

what he called *formal rationality*, i.e. the calculability of action, which can be oriented to any number of substantive ends, within the capitalist economy. In fact, rationality was the guiding thread of much of Weber's work. In his view, the generalization of formal rationality, its intrusion into all aspects of everyday life in the West, had as its climax the constitution of a generic *industrial society*, 'characterised by large-scale industrial production, the inexorable power of material goods, bureaucratic administration, and a pervasive "calculating attitude" ' (Bottomore, 1985). But where neoclassical economics can be read as a vindication, even a celebration, of formal rationality and the 'free market economy', Weber's writings are much more ambivalent:

In no sphere of human life, according to Weber, has rationalization unambiguously advanced human well-being. The rationalization of economic production, for example, has created the 'iron cage' of capitalism, a 'tremendous cosmos' that constrains individuals from without, determining their lives 'with irresistible force' (Brubaker, 1984).

Weber believed that there was a disjuncture between formal rationality and *substantive*

41

rationality: 'While capitalism is rational in the sense of enhancing the calculability of economic action, its rationality may well be problematic in terms of the [substantive] ends which it promotes or the [substantive] conditions of life which it imposes' (Bottomore, 1985). Weber's vision was thus profoundly pessimistic:

Consuming and replacing other forms of life, bourgeois rationalization processes tend to become an end in themselves. Under their monopolistic sway, contemporary capitalist societies knit themselves into a self-enslaving 'iron cage' of bondage. All spheres of daily life tend to become chronically dependent upon disciplined hierarchy, rational specialisation and the continuous deployment of impersonal systems of abstract–general rules. Bureaucratic domination is the fate of the present, whose future is likely to be more of the same. A 'polar night of icy darkness and hardness' is the spectre that haunts the modern world (Keane, 1984).

This sphere of the 'totally administered society' (see also SURVEILLANCE) confronts capitalism and socialism alike, so Weber argued, and it is the same spectre that post-Weberian CRITICAL THEORY has sought to lay. But its starting-point is Marx rather than Weber.

Marx recognized that capitalism is more than a system of generalized commodity exchange: it is also a system of generalized *commodity production*. It is this insight which acts as the lever for the characterization of capitalism provided by MARXIAN ECONOMICS and Marxian POLITICAL ECONOMY. In this perspective, capitalism is seen as an historically specific MODE OF PRODUCTION in which 'the reproduction of daily life depends upon the production of commodities produced through a system of circulation that has profit-seeking as its direct and socially accepted goal' (Harvey, 1985). Harvey has provided a summary account of the circuits of capital (see the figure). He emphasizes that such highly differentiated forms of circulation not only 'enable capitalism to shape its historical geography in accordance with the dictates of ACCUMULATION' but also 'increase immeasurably the possibilities for CRISIS formation.' Far from sustaining the general equilibrium posited by neoclassical economics, therefore, the dynamics of capital circulation generate a crisis-ridden historical geography of 'long waves' and spasmodic perturbations in time and of UNEVEN DEVELOPMENT in space (Harvey, 1982). One of the primary concerns of MARXIST GEOGRAPHY has been to analyse the SPACE-ECONOMY of capitalism and to disclose its 'inconstant geography', therefore, as a way of showing that the PRODUCTION OF SPACE is *integral* rather than incidental to the production of commodities (see Massey, 1984; Harvey, 1985; Storper and Walker, 1989) (see also LOCATION THEORY).

However, Marx argued that the circulation of capital is predicated on a CLASS relation – most starkly, between those who buy rights to the labour power of others in order to gain a profit ('capitalists') and those who sell rights to their own labour power in order to live ('workers') – and this entails not only chronic class struggle but, on occasion, overt *class conflict*. The relations between crisis and conflict are both complex and contingent: the one cannot be reduced to a simple and immediate expression of the other. For the paths and structures of capital circulation presuppose not only social relations between agents in the capitalist economy *but also social interactions between subjects in 'civil society'* (Urry, 1981) (see also HUMAN AGENCY). For this reason, there has been considerable interest in thinking through the multiple ways in which human beings are constituted *as* human subjects. This discussion has taken place inside Marxism (see STRUCTURAL MARXISM), outside Marxism (see POSTSTRUCTURALISM) and through a lively dialogue between the two (see POST-MARXISM). It is now generally accepted that the constitution of human subjects occurs not only through the inscriptions of CLASS that were the primary concern of classical Marxism, but also through the social construction and negotiation of the DIVISION OF LABOUR, of ETHNICITY, and of GENDER and sexuality (see also PATRIARCHY) (Wolch and Dear, 1988; Sayer and Walker, 1992).

Both CRISES and CONFLICTS may be (and usually are) mediated by the STATE in some way, and it is equally important not to reduce the state to the inner logic of capital, or so most writers would now accept.

Modern POLITICAL GEOGRAPHY has made considerable progress in clarifying the structure of the capitalist state and the STATE APPARATUS in terms of a 'society-centred' model which draws attention to their 'inherent qualities of autonomy and insulation from direct democratic control' (Clark and Dear, 1984); building in some part on this work and on critical legal studies there has also been extremely important work on the intersections between capitalism, law and space (Clark, 1989; Blomley, 1993). Crises and conflicts are also mediated through cultural politics, and the formation of a 'new' CULTURAL GEOGRAPHY has directed attention to the power of CULTURE, DISCOURSE and IDEOLOGY – and of their various 'maps of meaning' – to shape, regulate and legitimate the geographies of everyday life in modern capitalist societies (Harvey, 1989; Jackson, 1989) (see also POSTMODERNISM).

'Capitalism' is not the same everywhere and, as the previous paragraphs imply, there are considerable variations in its practices and structures over time and space. But it is also vitally important not to lose sight of the international span of capitalism and its intersections with MODERNITY. This raises a series of important questions about the *globalization* of capitalism and the dynamics of its world-economy (see WORLD-SYSTEMS ANALYSIS). These have been thrown into particularly sharp relief in contemporary debates over a putative transition to a regime of FLEXIBLE ACCUMULATION and its impact on both 'North' and 'South'; in discussions of the global debt crisis (Corbridge, 1992: see also DEPENDENCE; UNDERDEVELOPMENT); and in arguments over a market triumphalism that has emerged in the wake of the collapse of COMMUNISM in Eastern Europe and the former Soviet Union. But these debates bear directly on political, social and cultural questions, and the new sensitivity towards the global geography of capitalism also finds expression in the development of a critical GEOPOLITICS (Dalby, 1991), accentuated by the rhetoric of a 'New World Order' which is supposed to follow the demise of conflict between the two superpowers, and in a virtually unprecedented critical interest in the processes of 'othering' and of dispossession and exploitation which has accompanied (and, as a matter of fact, continues to accompany) capitalist expansion and transformation (see also POSTCOLONIALISM).   DG

References

Blomley, N. 1993: *Law, space and the geographies of power*. New York: Guilford Press.

Bottomore, T., 1985: *Theories of modern capitalism*. London: Allen and Unwin.

Brubaker, R. 1984: *The limits of rationality*. London: Allen and Unwin.

Clark, G. 1989: The geography of law. In Peet, R. and Thrift, N., eds, *New models in geography*. Volume 1. London: Unwin Hyman, pp. 310–37.

Clark, G. L. and Dear, M. J. 1984: *State apparatus: structures and language of legitimacy*. London: Allen and Unwin.

Clarke, S. 1982: *Marx, marginalism and modern sociology*. London: Macmillan.

Collins, R. 1980: Weber's last theory of capitalism: a systematization. *Am. Soc. R.*, 45, pp. 925–42.

Corbridge, S. 1992: *Debt and development*. Oxford: Blackwell.

Dalby, S. 1991: Critical geopolitics: discourse, difference, dissent. *Environ. Plann. D* 9, pp. 261–83.

Harvey, D. 1973: *Social justice and the city*. London: Edward Arnold.

Harvey, D. 1982: *The limits to capital*. Oxford: Blackwell.

Harvey, D. 1985: *The urbanization of capital*. Oxford: Blackwell.

Harvey, D. 1989: *The condition of postmodernity: an enquiry into the origins of cultural change*. Oxford: Blackwell.

Jackson, P. 1989: *Maps of meaning*. London: Unwin Hyman.

Keane, J. 1984: *Public life and late capitalism*. Cambridge: Cambridge University Press.

Massey, D. 1984: *Spatial divisions of labour*. London: Macmillan.

Sayer, A. and Walker, R. 1992: *The new social economy: reworking the division of labour*. Oxford: Blackwell.

Storper, M. and Walker, R. 1989: *The capitalist imperative: territory, technology and industrial growth*. Oxford: Blackwell.

Urry, J. 1981: *The anatomy of capitalist societies*. London: Macmillan.

Wolch, J. and Dear, M. 1988: *The power of geography*. London: Unwin Hyman.

Suggested Reading
Bottomore (1985).
Harvey (1985).

carrying capacity The maximum number of users that can be sustained by a given set of land resources. The concept originated in ecological studies in which the users were plants, and was later used to describe the number of livestock that could be sustained by different vegetation types. In agricultural geography it has been used to assess the maximum number of people that can be supported in a given area by a given farming system. Most attempts at measuring carrying capacity involve an assessment of the physical capacity of an area to produce crops and livestock with different levels of technology (Allan, 1965; Higgins, 1981). DBG

References
Allan, W. 1965: *The African husbandman.* Edinburgh: Oliver and Boyd.
Higgins, G. M. 1981: Africa's agricultural potential. *Ceres* 14, pp. 13–21.

cartogram (or transformation) A specific map PROJECTION transforming topographic space according to statistical factors (as in Kidron and Segal, 1984), so that the largest mapping units relate to greatest statistical values, e.g. census boundaries relative to population density. Topological relationship of units can be severely distorted, so research is aimed at:

(a) maintaining contiguity between units so that spatial proximity is not disrupted;

(b) maintaining correct shapes of units so that map readers can still easily recognize the topography; and

(c) reducing the complexity of construction since, as with any projection, considerable computational work is involved (this has presented COMPUTER-ASSISTED CARTOGRAPHY with a particularly difficult challenge, as yet not answered effectively).

Despite their intuitive appeal, cartograms still present a technical challenge to CARTOGRAPHY, and the best examples are still manually produced. Also, many people have difficulty in effectively perceiving space which is not represented as in a TOPOGRAPHIC MAP. MJB

Reference
Kidron, M. and Segal, R. 1984: *The new state of the world atlas.* London: Heinemann Educational.

Suggested Reading
Dougenik, J. A., Chrisman, N. R. and Niemeyer, D. R. 1985: An algorithm to construct continuous area cartograms. *Prof. Geogr.* 37(1), pp. 75–81.
Gatrell, A. C. 1991: Concepts of space and geographical data. In Maguire, D. J., Goodchild, M. F. and Rhind, D. W., eds, *Geographical information systems: principles and applications*, volume 1. London: Longman, pp. 119–34.
Upton, G. J. G. 1991: Displaying election results. *Pol. Geog. Q.* 10, pp. 200–20.

cartography A body of theoretical and practical knowledge that map-makers employ to construct maps as a distinct mode of visual representation (Harley, 1989). The study of cartography has in the past concentrated on the technical and professional practices of making maps. This has been set in the context of *progress*, whereby through time technology becomes more advanced (and therefore past technologies are inferior to present ones) and society more sophisticated (and therefore able to produce 'new' types of maps). Past cartographic practices would be studied in the context of current practices and technologies, and past cartographic products interpreted in the light of current assumptions of what constitutes a map (see Blakemore and Harley, 1981). Many texts on the history of cartography used to assess the positive role of maps in the exploration, discovery and opening up of new lands (see CARTOGRAPHY, HISTORY OF). In recent years such approaches have been challenged, in particular by the late Brian Harley (1989, 1990), who argued that many past cartographic practices were a function of colonial domination and exploitation, and were an act of forcible subjugation of the native populations. Such views are encouraging a reassessment of what cartography is: it can be a body of knowledge, as given in Harley's definition, or can it be a suite of techniques and practices. The latter is more in line with the International Cartographic Association, whose Working Group on Cartographic

Definitions, in 1991, defined cartography as 'The discipline dealing with the conception, production, dissemination and study of maps'.

Traditionalist views of cartography which prevailed up to the late 1950s are typified by Raisz (1962). He envisaged first that surveyors (see SURVEYING) would measure the land, that cartographers would then collect the measurements 'and render them on such a scale that the earth's wonderful patterns show at a glance', and that this pattern would be analysed by geographers, both examining the relation of society to that pattern as well as theorizing about its meaning. Such an interpretation saw cartography as heavily reliant on other specialists for data collection and on a further group for use of the finished product. Furthermore, the skills of cartography were primarily artistic (i.e. the manual skills of drafting) and aesthetic. The latter is typified by Raisz's belief that 'no rules can be given for generalisation' and that 'the rule of SYMBOLIZATION is that a symbol should be simple, yet distinctive, small and easy to draw. A good symbol can be recognized without a legend' (see MAP READING). These vague guidelines left considerable scope for personal interpretation, and therefore propagated a profusion of styles in designing the map image (see MAP IMAGE AND MAP), resulting in conflicting and confusing end-products.

In the late 1960s the artistic view declined, and has been replaced over the past 20 years by a more scientific and deterministic interpretation. A number of factors have influenced this: the emergence of computer usage; methodological changes in geography which embraced statistical and mathematical models (see QUANTITATIVE REVOLUTION); and changes in the educational system, which preferred science to art or social science. This development lasted until the late 1980s, when artistic and behavioural aspects of cartography resurfaced strongly in the context of new methodological critiques, and in trends within computer science such as artificial intelligence (see EXPERT SYSTEMS).

In the late 1960s and early 1970s, emphasis on the manual aspects of production was alleviated by the availability of stereotyped products (such as sheets of pre-prepared press-down symbols), and also by the growing influence of COMPUTER-ASSISTED CARTOGRAPHY and GEOGRAPHICAL INFORMATION SYSTEMS. There was also a general acceptance that cartography embraced all aspects of producing the map image. The production process encompassed the gathering of data (e.g. SURVEYING and REMOTE SENSING), the adjustment to a correct map base (see PROJECTION), and the reasoned and logical choice of the entities to be mapped, as well as the representation of those entities in symbol form (SYMBOLIZATION). This resulted in the eventual map image, which could be interpreted by the map reader. As with traditionalist approaches, the map was the focus of cartography, but the processes of creating the image no longer involved a direct transfer of surveyed reality to spatial summary. Cartographers saw cartography as a *communication system* that transmitted spatial messages, and subsequent discussions utilized the theme and terminology of communication.

One of the seminal papers was C. Board's 'Maps as models' (1967). Although specifically concerned with the map image and its role, he believed the overall cartographic purpose to be 'the human being's struggle to communicate to others something of the nature of the real world'. He foresaw that this involves communication, and that there are two overall stages in compiling the map image. The first involves concentrating the real world into a MODEL form, the map. The second is one whereby the model is tested against reality, and evaluated for errors or discrepancies so that it is possible to return to the first stage and improve the model; it is axiomatic that the cycle may begin again with a revised view of the real world. This complies with the feedback component of a communication system, and in cartography produced improvements in the quality of map images. Ultimately, the map image would match the reality it represents, in which case there would be no further need for work in cartography. In practice, the feedback element encompasses those attempts to evaluate and improve the processes of cartography, and two main approaches to achieving an optimal map image were proposed: the first was the iterative evaluation of the map by users; and the second was the scientific determination of formal ground rules for cartographers that obviated the need for iteratively testing each map with its own audience.

Robinson and Petchenik (1976) formalized the assimilation of communication theory in cartography. However, they stressed that direct integration of pure communication theory would not be very helpful; rather, it should be carefully adapted to suit the peculiar qualities of the map image. This approach modifies the basic communication model of source, encoder, transmitter, noise, receiver, decoder and destination. For them the source message is the real world, and the encoder and transmitter are encapsulated by the cartographer's conception of the world. The map as a physical artefact plays a somewhat more central role than does the message of communication theory. The receiver and decoder are the map reader, whose personal conception of reality leads to the resulting interpretation. Unlike the transmission noise of communication studies, consideration of error factors in cartography is important at every step. The optimal map image has a minimum of 'noise', which generally arises from confusion or misunderstanding of the use of projection, transformation (see CARTO-GRAM), CLASS INTERVALS for data, SYMBOLIZATION, generalization or design factors.

The 'noise' factor mostly results from the map reader's concept of a standardized language for map compilation differing from that of the cartographer. Morrison (1976) elaborated this point by viewing the process of cartographic communication as an interplay between the cognitive realms of the map maker and the map reader, with the map as the medium of communication (see also TEXT). A successful message involves no noise, and the message contained in the map image is totally understood. In reality it is unreasonable to expect no error factor, and thus the map image, being the vital link between the two cognitive realms, must be expertly encoded using the cartographic language of symbols, lines, lettering, colouring, etc. On one hand this involves the graphic skills of good drafting (sometimes called GRAPHICACY), but the drafting can only be as good as the cartographic signs that it portrays. To maximize the information transfer, Morrison stressed the need for an international standardization of cartographic signs and terminology. These aspects of cartographic communication are expounded at length in Taylor (1983) and Board (1984).

The task of standardization requires more than the use of a particular map symbol for a particular purpose. It has involved efforts to find out why map readers react differently to similar symbols, and why they react to certain symbols in a way that the cartographer does not foresee. This has conventionally been carried out using psychophysical experiments; for example, a sample of people would be tested on their perception of graduated symbol size, or on colour shading ranges. The problem with such tests, however, is in ensuring that the people being tested are truly representative of the general map-using public.

The critical area whereby information is fed back into the cartographic communication system was elaborated by others. Ratajski (1978), for example, proposed that it be called 'cartology', which he defines as 'an activity that consists of a scientific elaboration of theoretical principles and estimation, which leads to an important improvement of cartographical products and to the maximum functional optimization'. Whether this process is pursued exclusively by cartographers or in liaison with geographers is a matter for contention. Frulov (1978) stressed the Soviet view that cartography was still firmly integrated in geography, and supported Salichtchev's (1973) belief that 'contemporary scientific cartography should see its general purpose as the representation of spatial systems of varying complexity by their cartographic modelling'. Salichtchev (1978) further added that this modelling has ideological connotations because it should be based on the Marxist philosophical traditions of dialectical materialism. Since then, the breakdown of the communist system in Eastern Europe has led to a radical reappraisal of dogma-led approaches (see Blakemore, 1990). A new debate about the role of geography, cartography and technology is now focused on issues such as environment, with Berlyant (1991) being one of many former Soviet researchers who are exploring new roles in a rapidly changing political system.

The general situation is that cartographers and map users are not always under the same disciplinary umbrella, nor do they share a common conceptual framework: indeed, in 1992 the British Cartographic Society undertook a review of the changing profession of cartography, and what the Society's role should be. Geographers are not the only map users, and cartographers have to elicit and measure responses wherever possible and communicate them to a wider audience. After discussion and evaluation, new or adapted behavioural guidelines could be fed back into the formal structure known as the cartographic communication system.

In previous editions of this *Dictionary* the conclusion has been drawn that cartography is a discipline which involves the scientific refinement, elaboration and revision of a specialized communication system. However, a number of developments have challenged many of the research approaches that were dominant in the 1980s. Harley (1989) states that most people still accept traditional cartographers' definitions of what maps are supposed to be; this propagates what is professionally acceptable. He is surprised that there is no 'art' in most definitions of cartography, which are dominated more by 'science'. In a commentary on Harley's paper, Baldwin wrote that 'Harley's article threatens the whole credibility of an industry eager to assert its institutional stature, enhance the scientific and economic value of its product and expand a lucrative, national regional, and corporate patronage'. No more evident is this than in international scientific societies, and the International Cartographic Association's own 'corporate' definition can be contrasted with Harley's 'deconstructionist' approach. Harley argues that cartography

has developed along two sets of rules; the technical production rules (the 'skills' of cartography etc.) and the cultural production rules. The latter require attention to be given to politics, ethnicity, religion, social class and many others, and view cartography as part of an expanding information industry that ranges from private-sector profit to central-government policy-making, from the promotion and marketing of products to persuasion and propaganda. Two time-snaps (Olson, 1984; McMaster, 1991) illustrate the 'official' interpretation of US cartography as presented to the International Cartographic Association, as does Fairbairn (1991) for the UK, and Morrison (1991) evaluates the international organizational influences in cartography and GEOGRAPHICAL INFORMATION SYSTEMS.

Lastly, computer cartography and geographical information systems (GIS) have themselves contributed to a reappraisal of 'scientific' cartography. One reason why the artistic side of cartography declined was because the move to computerization required that cartographic practices be defined in terms of deterministic processes. Thus the process of generalization was relegated in computer packages merely to operations on the geometry of lines, and not to features in the whole map context. In the late 1980s the answer to this was perceived to lie in 'artificial intelligence' or 'expert systems', which would be 'trained' in the complex decision-making rules that cartographers use when creating maps. Because of such developments there is a growing realization that behavioural and artistic skills may still be a vital part of cartography. Furthermore, the provision, availability and cost of digital map data increasingly influence the way in which cartography can develop (see Muller, 1992).   MJB

References

Berlyant, A. M. 1991: Cartographic and remote sensing methods in ecological–geographical research. *Mapping Sciences and Remote Sensing* 28,(1), pp. 30–1.

Blakemore, M. J. 1990: Cartography. *Progr. hum. Geogr.* 14(1), pp. 101–11.

Blakemore, M. J. and Harley, J. B. 1981: Concepts in the history of cartography: a review and perspective. *Cartographica* 17(4).

Board, C. 1967: Maps as models. In Chorley, R. J. and Haggett, P., eds, *Models in geography.* London: Methuen, pp. 671–725.

Board, C., ed., 1984: New insights into cartographic communication. *Cartographica* 21(1), pp. 1–38.

Fairbairn, D., ed., 1991: British cartography 1987–1991: an overview. *Cartogr. J.* 28(1), pp. 1–107.

Frulov, Y. S. 1978: Theoretical aspects of the cartographic research method. *Soviet Geogr.* 19, pp. 151–60.

Harley, J. B. 1989: Deconstructing the map. *Cartographica* 26(2), pp. 1–20.

Harley, J. B. 1990: Cartography, ethics and social theory. *Cartographica* 27(2), pp. 1–23.

McMaster, R. B., ed, 1991: US National Report to ICA, 1991. History and development of academic cartography in the United States. *Cartogr. Geogr. Inform. Sys.* 18(3), pp. 1–216.

Morrison, J. L. 1976: The science of cartography and its essential process. *Int. Yearbook Cartogr.* 16, pp. 84–97.

Morrison, J. L. 1991: The organisational home for GIS in the scientific professional community. In Maguire, D. J., Goodchild, M. F. and Rhind, D. W., eds, *Geographical information systems: principles and applications,* volume 1. London: Longman, pp. 91–100.

Muller, J. C. ed., 1992: *Advances in cartography.* London: Elsevier Applied Science.

Olson, J. M. ed., 1984: *U.S. National Report to I.C.A.* Falls Church, VA: American Congress on Surveying and Mapping.

Raisz, E. J. 1962: *Principles of cartography.* New York: McGraw-Hill.

Ratajski, L. 1978: The main characteristics of cartographic communication as a part of theoretical cartography. *Int. Yearbook Cartogr.* 18, pp. 21–32.

Robinson, A. H. and Petchenik, B. B. 1976: *The nature of maps: essays towards understanding maps and mapping.* Chicago: University of Chicago Press.

Salichtchev, K. A. 1973: Some reflections on the subject and method of cartography after the Sixth International Cartographic Conference. *Can. Cartogr.* 10, pp. 106–11.

Salichtchev, K. A. 1978: Cartographic communication: its place in the theory of science. *Can. Cartogr.* 15, pp. 93–9.

Taylor, D. R. F., ed., 1983: *Graphic communication in contemporary cartography.* New York and Chichester: John Wiley.

Suggested Reading

Blakemore, M. J. 1992: Cartography, *Progr. hum. Geogr.* 16(1), pp. 75–87.

Morrison, J. L. 1977: Towards a functional definition of the science of cartography with an emphasis on map reading. In Kretschmer, I., ed., *Studies in theoretical cartography.* Vienna: Franz Deuticke, pp. 247–66.

Perkins, C. R. and Parry, R. B., eds, 1990: *Information sources in cartography.* London: Bowker–Sauer.

Robinson, A. H. 1979: Geography and cartography then and now. *Ann. Ass. Am. Geogr.* 69, pp. 97–102.

Robinson, A. H., Morrison, J. L. and Muehrcke, P. C. 1977: Cartography 1950–2000. *Trans. Inst. Br. Geogr.* n.s. 2, pp. 3–18.

cartography, history of The history of cartography is concerned with changes through time and in all human societies in the form, content, roles and values placed on graphical expressions of space and in the processes by means of which they were made. As such, it is part of and relates to the histories of ideas and technology and serves to help fashion the autonomy, scope and identity of modern cartography.

In recent decades, definitions of map have become increasingly catholic (see MAP IMAGE AND MAP). One of the most recent and probably the most catholic is that adopted for the University of Wisconsin-based History of Cartography Project: 'Maps are graphic representations that facilitate a spatial understanding of things, concepts, conditions, processes, or events in the human world' (Harley and Woodward, 1987). Likewise, the field of CARTOGRAPHY has been expanded from its traditional concern with and for the 'art, science and technology of making maps' to embrace 'their study as scientific documents and works of art' (British Cartographic Society, 1964). All production processes and fields of study have their histories, and in 1976 the International Cartographic Association recognized this by establishing a Commission for the History of Cartography. A comprehensive history of cartography must embrace the catholic definition of map, 'discuss the manifold technical processes that have contributed to the form and content of individual maps', and relate 'to the historically unique ability of map-using peoples to store, articulate, and communicate concepts and facts that have a spatial dimension' (Harley and Woodward, 1987). Consequently, the origins of cartography must be traced back to prehistory, its history must be seen in a multicultural perspective, and the study of that development will need to adopt several EPISTEMOLOGIES. Still in its infancy, once the history of cartography is more developed it should serve cartography in much the same way that the history of science now serves science by helping to 'fashion the autonomy, scope and scholarly identity of the modern subject' (Harley and Woodward, 1989). It should also provide for other fields new, better and more accessible map resources with improved descriptions and interpretations.

Like all thematic histories, the history of cartography needs to borrow or develop appropriate methodologies and apply a mix of epistemologies. For a long time description and classification were essentially the only methodologies. Recently, new ones have been applied to analyse the physical properties and geometrical characteristics of maps. Traditionally, epistemology was limited to tracing lineal developments through time. Recently, structuralist and humanist approaches have begun to place maps in new contexts and to expand understanding of both their overt and hidden roles within society (see HUMANISTIC GEOGRAPHY; STRUCTURALISM). Because these methodological and epistemological developments have been recent, they will be discussed after reviewing institutional developments and substantive work conducted in a traditional mould.

The history of cartography began to develop in its modern, more academic form in the early 1970s. Indicators include: the establishment by the International Cartographic Association in 1972 of a Working Group in the History of Cartography (precursor of the 1976 Commission); the endowment in that year of what was quickly to become the influential Hermon Dunlap Smith Center for the History of Cartography at the Newberry Library, Chicago; the publication in 1975 of the first *International directory of current research in the history of cartography and carto-bibliography*; and the preliminary planning in the same year for what was to become the History of Cartography Project, with its bold vision of a multivolume, multiauthored, comprehensive and authoritative global survey of maps and map making from prehistory up to and including the twentieth century (Harley and Woodward, 1982). The 1970s were also the decade in which the English-speaking (in particular, North American) world began to assume more importance in relation to the hitherto dominant continental European world. *Imago Mundi*, the only serial publication ever to have been concerned exclusively with the history of cartography, had been founded in 1935 and published successively in Berlin, London (1938–9 only), Stockholm, Leiden, The Hague and Amsterdam. In 1975 it returned to London and has been edited and published there ever since (Harley, 1986). It was also in the 1970s that the University of Chicago Press began to develop its influential list of books on the history of cartography; heralding the emergence of the Midwest as the heartland of North American scholarship in the field, and to some extent reflecting the establishment in 1966 at Newberry Library, Chicago, of the Kenneth Nebenzahl Jr. Lectures in the History of Cartography. Held every third year, many of the lecture series have been published by the University of Chicago Press. Of these, the first, *Maps: a historical survey of their study and collecting* (Skelton, 1972), is the datum against which later developments must be measured.

Because of their political, military, legal, commercial, scientific and educational importance, as well as their aesthetic properties and investment appeal, maps have long been collected. Many were not made to last and large sheets of paper are not robust. Furthermore, there has always been a period of vulnerability between the end of a map's practical usefulness and the realization that it has a significance beyond that of the purpose for which it was made. Of those maps that have survived, many remain in private hands: especially in the libraries, muniment rooms and estate offices of the royal and aristocratic families of Europe, and in the deed rooms of their legal advisers. Maps are increasingly passing into private hands. Collecting by individuals is on the increase, as reflected in the proliferation of map dealerships, the launch in 1977 of the successful quarterly, *The Map Collector*, the creation in the 1970s of several regional map societies, and the establishment in 1980 of the International Map Collectors' Society. The consequences of these developments for the history of cartography are debatable. Although rare items are sometimes discovered, the converse is equally common, and printed books and atlases are increasingly being broken up to satisfy the market for single maps of specific places and regions. Many sheet maps in public and other accessible collections remain essentially unknown, either because there is no catalogue or because they are included with associated items for cataloguing purposes. Because of their diverse sizes and proportions, maps in public institutions have usually been placed in special collections; horizontally drawered rather than vertically shelved. Regrettably, this has tended to separate sheet maps from the contexts in which they were made. Further segregation occurs because of the frequent institutional separation of printed and manuscript maps between library and archive collections. One welcome consequence of the placing of maps in special collections has been the emergence in recent decades of an increasingly professional body of map librarians. Conversely, museum curators remain for the most part unaware of the significance of map artefacts, and specialists in rock art have for the most part found it difficult to confirm supposedly cartographic content (Delano-Smith, 1987).

Printed maps that are not separated from the texts with which they were published are often difficult to find, although some progress has been made in providing bibliographical guides to the cartographic contents of major works. Printed catalogues to public map collections began to appear in the nineteenth century, and facsimile card catalogues of several major collections have been published in the third quarter of the twentieth century. Recently,

historians of cartography have been served by an ever-increasing number and diversity of published guides. A recent bibliography lists 333 pre–1985 items (Hodgkiss and Tatham, 1986). Since then the flow has accelerated with, for example, reference works to local maps and plans from medieval England, printed maps published before 1501, maps published in early periodicals and in early American books, maps in the Hudson's Bay Company and American Philosophical Society collections, maps of Africa and Ontario, American Civil War maps and the map resources of Washington, DC. Because of their near universality, two deserve special mention; guides to cartographers (Tooley, 1979, 1985) and to cartographic innovations (Wallis and Robinson, 1987). Reference works of this type are of a higher standard and a greater utility than ever before, reflecting demands arising from increasingly open access to public collections, a great willingness of custodial staff to publish, increases in institutional budgets, new techniques of compilation and book production, and an increasing use of maps. As far as the history of cartography is concerned, the last increase is a consequence of the greater mobility of researchers, more research funds, better focused research necessitating access to specific items, increasing opportunities to illustrate texts with quality facsimiles, and an increase in the number of researchers. Growing wear and tear on rare and unique items and the need to travel in order to consult them is to some extent being mitigated by increases in the number, quality and accessibility of facsimiles. Several recent examples combine superb scholarship with excellent reprography and high standards of book production. To date, however, it is rare to consult originals by means of electronic graphic communication systems, although maps from some collections are becoming available on disc. On-line searching for sheet maps is still unusual, but is becoming increasingly feasible for atlases.

Self-styled historians of cartography are still few; approximately 350 as of 1991, of which half lived in the European Community, a tenth in other European countries and a quarter in North America. Approximately half resided in the English-speaking world (Lowenthal, 1992). This residential imbalance continues to be reflected in the focus of most, and much of the best, research on the cartography of Europe and North America. However, there are some important exceptions. Several notable monographs have recently been published for Asia: early maps of India and China; Jainian cosmological maps; and a major survey of traditional Islamic and South Asian maps. Likewise, there has been an increased interest in the maps and mapping by past and present preliterate peoples. Stemming from earlier work on Mixtec place signs and maps, increasing attention is now being given to pre- and early post-contact maps of Meso America. Another recent development has been the interpretation and facsimile presentation of manuscript maps and atlases, examples of which include the English colonies in North America, Lake Champlain, Mughal India and maps associated with events such as the campaigns of Rochambeau's army during the American Revolutionary War and with the Lewis and Clark Expedition. There has also been an increase in interest in the less exotic but often very complex maps and map series of national surveys. Because these surveys were related so closely to political, social and technical developments, this interest is likely to increase. In the UK it is fostered by the Charles Close Society, and was stimulated by the work of Harley and others in the 1970s. Exhibitions of maps are not new, but in recent years they have been increasingly well researched, have often commemorated events, have been distinctive in their themes and have often been supported by catalogues that have made significant contributions to the field. For example, a map catalogue is the best single source of information on the early maps of New England. Regrettably, such catalogues are little known, rarely reviewed and often difficult to obtain via normal library services.

In recent years there has been an increase in the proportion of publications appearing as papers in periodicals, as distinct from the tradition of monographs. The range of periodicals is diverse and they are not adequately monitored. *Imago Mundi* contains an annual annotated bibliography, and the recent literature sections in *Cartographica*, *The Cartographic Journal* and *Cartography and Geographic Information Systems* each contain a history of cartography subsection. However, many of the listed papers fall short of what, in other fields, would be considered scholarly or original. Others are esoteric or parochial. The recent index to the topical interests of self-styled historians of cartography is revealing (Lowenthal, 1992). Atlases, map makers, surveyors, medieval cartography and military mapping are among the most frequent. Conversely, celestial mapping, commercial cartography, projections and thematic maps are among the least popular. The latter group is a serious omission because of the potential significance of these topics in relation to the history of pure and applied science; particularly thematic maps, interest in which does not appear to have been stimulated by the only serious book on the subject to date (Robinson, 1982). Methodology, theory and epistemology command similarly little interest. Although cartobibliography is the most frequent of all expressed interests, the following each have less than three adherents: cartochronology; cartographic representation; EPISTEMOLOGY; IDEOLOGY; MENTAL MAPS; MEASUREMENT; theoretical cartography; and the THEORY of the history of cartography. This paucity of interest does not suggest that the field is about to take what ought to be an important place in the history and philosophy of science, technology, the humanities and the graphic arts.

In 1974, Woodward proposed a framework within which to study the history of cartography (Woodward, 1974). Maps were presented as an end-product. The production process involved persons using techniques and appropriate tools at each of four stages; information gathering and processing, and document distribution and use. The proposal was in part responsible for stimulating serious research in topics such as materials dating, printing techniques and the map trade. The concept of the map as a document did not, however, place it in the context of the society in which it was produced, the use for which it was intended, or the roles that it eventually fulfilled (see TEXT). Nor were developments in style, geometry, symbolism and content placed in the contexts of wider developmental theories. Although internally comprehensive and dynamic, the framework was essentially a closed system. Within the next few years a few pseudo-structuralist attempts were made to relate maps to cognitive development (Wood, 1977; Harvey, 1980; Lewis, 1981). Another attempted to relate the development of mapping to biological evolution (Lewis, 1987). The next significant developments were the publication in 1980 of *Concepts in the history of cartography* (Blakemore and Harley, 1981) and in 1982 of the comments to which it gave rise (Gutsell, 1982). Of the comments, the most critical were by Wood, the self-appointed 'external' critic of epistemological developments – or inertia – in the history of cartography. *Concepts . . .* was 'ahistorical', refusing 'to deal with the history in the history of cartography' or to 'entertain the possibility that the history of cartography has a structure'. Blakemore and Harley denied that history 'might be developmental' and unrelentingly harassed the 'Darwinian position' without recognizing that 'hundreds of [other] evolutionary, historical and developmental models [were] waiting to be examined and deployed' (Wood, in Gutsell, 1982). The criticism did not stimulate more or better work in the structuralist–developmental tradition. Instead, it was in part responsible for stimulating Harley in particular to explore both more explicitly humanistic epistemologies and POST-STRUCTURALISM in order to interrogate the content and iconology of maps and to distinguish between their intended and actual roles within society (Harley, 1988, 1989, 1990a; see ICONOGRAPHY). Although rarely made explicit in interpretative works, their influence is becoming apparent (e.g. Konwitz, 1987; Harley, 1990b). However, they have essentially left unanswered Wood's final question: of the many things that 'need to be debated in the history of cartography, can't history be one of them?'. It will be less

than ironic if that history is eventually explored by developmental scientists in the contexts of cognition, knowledge, communication and behaviour, because the history of cartography has always been a field for and a beneficiary from 'outsiders' and, albeit less so, a laboratory for 'part-timers'. If so, it could mirror the revival and reorientation of much nineteenth-century natural history by the palaeosciences. Although considered desirable by some, it would be regrettable if it aborted the recent growth of interest in the roles of maps within societies and in the values placed on them by society. Achieving and maintaining a balance will be difficult. Infusing each with the insights of the other may be even more so. Not to do either would result in atrophy or, at best, information overload.

GML

References

Blakemore, M. J. and Harley, J. B. 1981: Concepts in the history of cartography: a review and perspective. *Cartographica* 17(4).

British Cartographic Society. 1964: Definition of cartography. *Cartogr. J.* 1, p. 17.

Delano-Smith, C. 1987: Cartography in the prehistoric period in the Old World: Europe, the Middle East, and North Africa. In Harley, J. B. and Woodward, D., eds, *The history of cartography*: volume 1, *Cartography in prehistoric, ancient, and medieval Europe and the Mediterranean*. Chicago: University of Chicago Press, pp. 54–101.

Gutsell, B. V., ed., 1982: Concepts in the history of cartography: some responses, with the authors' reply, especially to questions of definition. *Cartographica* 19(1), pp. 66–96.

Harley, J. B. 1986: *Imago Mundi*: the first fifty years and the next ten. *Cartographica* 23(3), pp. 1–15.

Harley, J. B. 1988: Maps, knowledge, and power. In Cosgrove, D. and Daniels, S., eds, *The iconography of landscape*. Cambridge: Cambridge University Press, pp. 277–312.

Harley, J. B. 1989: Deconstructing the map. *Cartographica* 26(2), pp. 1–20.

Harley, J. B. 1990a: Cartography, ethics and social theory. *Cartographica* 27(2), pp. 1–23.

Harley, J. B. 1990b: *Maps and the Columbian encounter: an interpretive guide to the travelling exhibition*. Milwaukee: The Golda Meir Library, University of Wisconsin.

Harley, J. B. and Woodward, D. 1982: The History of Cartography Project: a note on its organization and assumptions. *Technical Papers*, 43rd Annual Meeting, American Congress on Surveying and Mapping, March 1982, pp. 580–89.

Harley, J. B. and Woodward, D., eds, 1987: *The history of cartography*: volume 1, *Cartography in prehistoric, ancient, and medieval Europe and the Mediterranean*. Chicago: University of Chicago Press.

Harley, J. B. and Woodward, D. 1989: Why cartography needs its history. *Am. Cartogr.* 16(1), pp. 5–15.

Harvey, P. D. A. 1980: *The history of topographical maps: symbols, pictures and surveys*. London: Thames and Hudson.

Hodgkiss, A. G. and Tatham, A. F. 1986: *Keyguide to information sources in cartography*. London: Mansell.

Konwitz, J. 1987: *Cartography in France, 1660–1848: science, engineering, and statecraft*. Chicago: University of Chicago Press.

Lewis, G. M. 1981: Amerindian antecedents of American academic geography. In Blouet, B. W., ed., *The origins of academic geography in the United States*. Hamden, CT: Shoe String Press, pp. 19–35.

Lewis, G. M. 1987: The origins of cartography. In Harley, J. B. and Woodward, D., eds, *The history of cartography*: volume 1, *Cartography in prehistoric, ancient, and medieval Europe and the Mediterranean*. Chicago: University of Chicago Press, pp. 50–3.

Lowenthal, M. A. 1992: *Who's who in the history of cartography: an international directory of current research*. Tring, Herts, UK: Map Collector Publications.

Robinson, A. H. 1982: *Early thematic mapping in the history of cartography*. Chicago: University of Chicago Press.

Skelton, R. A. 1972: *Maps: a historical survey of their study and collecting*. Chicago: University of Chicago Press, for the Hermon Dunlap Smith Center for the History of Cartography, The Newberry Library.

Tooley, R. V., compiler, 1979: *Tooley's dictionary of mapmakers*. Tring, Herts, UK: Map Collector Publications.

Tooley, R. V., compiler, 1985: *Tooley's dictionary of mapmakers. Supplement*. New York: Liss.

Wallis, H. M. and Robinson, A. H., eds, 1987: *Cartographical innovations: an international handbook of mapping terms to 1900*. Tring, Herts, UK: Map Collector Publications, in association with the International Cartographic Association.

Wood, D. 1977: Now and then: comparisons of ordinary Americans' symbol conventions with those of past cartographers. *Prologue: J. Nat. Arch.* 9, 151–61.

Woodward, D. 1974: The study of the history of cartography: a suggested framework. *Am. Cartogr.* 1, pp. 101–15.

Suggested Reading

Harley, J. B. 1987: The map and the development of the history of cartography. In Harley, J. B. and Woodward, D., eds, *The history of cartography*: volume 1, *Cartography in prehistoric, ancient, and medieval Europe and the Mediterranean*. Chicago: University of Chicago Press, pp. 1–42.

Turnbull, D. 1989: *Maps are territories: science is an atlas*. Geelong, Victoria: Imagining Nature, Portfolio 5, Deakin University Press.

catastrophe theory A branch of mathematics, developed by Rene Thom (1975), concerned with discontinuous relationships (see also BIFURCATION). In a two-dimensional situation, as in figure 1, there is a portion of the relationship between the two variables (the end-points of which – A and B – are called the *fold-points*) where the value of a produces two separate values of b. Isnard and Zeeman (1976) illustrate this using the relationship between threat and military action. The graph shows that, in general, as the threat increases so does the probability of military action. However, between the two fold-points there are two values for the probability of a military action (i.e. at a_0 the probability may be either x_4 or x_6). Isnard and Zeeman identify two reactions to threat, that of the dove and of the hawk. There is an upper level of threat (B on the graph) beyond which public opinion will not accept the doveish option. Similarly, there is a lower level (A) below which it will not accept the hawkish reaction. Where the two overlap, we have what is termed a *hysteresis*, indicating that at certain threat levels the probable response is not readily predicted, and the shift from one relationship to the other can be understood in qualitative terms only.

In three-dimensional situations, in which the response variable is related to two stimuli (as in figure 2), a *fold curve* will develop (the area shown by M–G in figure 2) where the probability of the response is indeterminate. In the example shown, the stimuli are the degree of threat and the cost of countering it by military action; the

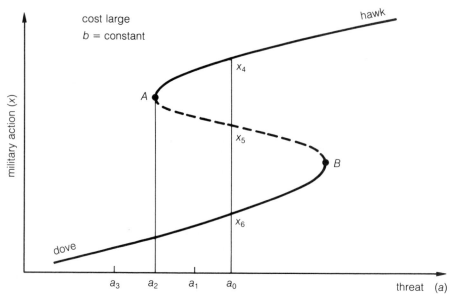

catastrophe theory   *1: A threat-action graph for high cost* (Isnard and Zeeman, 1976).

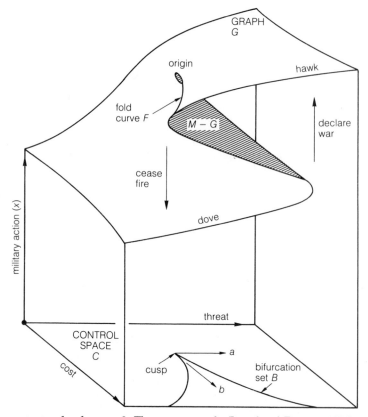

catastrophe theory   *2: The cusp catastrophe* (Isnard and Zeeman, 1976).

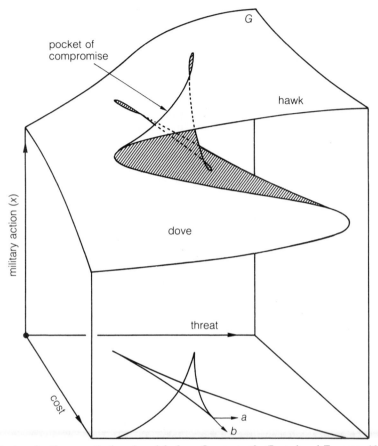

catastrophe theory   *3: A section of the butterfly catastrophe* (Isnard and Zeeman, 1976).

response variable is probability of military action, and within the *cusp* shown the probability of a military action takes on several values. There are several forms which the fold curve can take. Figure 3 shows a *butterfly catastrophe* which, according to Isnard and Zeeman, identifies a 'pocket of compromise' for those promoting the hawkish and doveish responses to a threat, at certain levels of threat and of cost of response.

The existence of catastrophes makes for difficulties in modelling SYSTEMS, and especially in predictive work, since the same conditions can produce different outcomes. Wilson (1981) has illustrated this using examples of the internal structure of cities.   RJJ

References and Suggested Reading

Isnard, C. A. and Zeeman, E. C. 1976: Some models from catastrophe theory in the social sciences. In Collins, L., ed., *The use of models in the social sciences*. London: Tavistock, pp. 44–99.

Thom, R. 1975: *Structural stability and morphogenesis*. Reading, MA: W. A. Benjamin.

Wilson, A. G. 1981: *Catastrophe theory and bifurcation: applications to urban and regional systems*. London: Croom Helm/Berkeley, CA: University of California Press.

categorical data analysis   A set of statistical procedures employed when one or more of the variables involved in an analysis is measured at a nominal scale only (see MEASUREMENT). Methods such as REGRESSION are not valid in the analysis of such data, because they violate several of the statistical assumptions underlying the general linear model. Categorical data analysis methods avoid those problems and provide robust procedures for estimating linear relationships with nominal data.

RJJ

Suggested Reading
Wrigley, N. 1985: *Categorical data analysis for geographers and environmental scientists*. London: Longman.

census The total process of collecting, compiling and publishing demographic, economic and social data pertaining to all persons in a defined territory at a specified time. The census thus provides the primary source of information about the population of a country. Given its government backing, its legal status, its coverage and the scale of the operation and resources devoted to it, it permits a far greater content and depth of analysis than can normally be produced by other methods.

Enumerations of population were carried out in ancient times, but the earliest modern censuses took place in Scandinavia and some Germanic and Italian states in the eighteenth century. The first census of Iceland, for example, was in 1703, and of Denmark in 1769. The first general census of the USA took place in 1790, although there had been earlier state censuses. In the UK and France the first censuses were held in 1801 and during the nineteenth century all European countries initiated periodic population censuses. During the present century, and especially since 1945, most countries of the world have begun to take censuses, although with widely varying frequency and reliability. Although critiques have been little developed by population geographers, census-taking may be seen as part of the wider monitoring by states of human activity (see, for example, SURVEILLANCE).

Two qualities in a census are particularly important: periodicity and universality, i.e. the need to hold regular censuses and to include every individual in a given area. The UK for example, has held regular censuses at ten-year intervals. SAMPLING is also used in many countries to establish certain categories of information within a full census, or to replace that census. There is also a general distinction in census method between a *de facto* approach, as in the UK, in which individuals are recorded at the place where they were found at the time of the census, and a *de jure* approach, as in the USA, where people are recorded according to their usual place of residence.

The types of data collected by censuses vary enormously from country to country. In an attempt to foster comparability, the United Nations has suggested that the census should include the following: total population; sex, age and marital status; place of birth, citizenship or nationality; first language, literacy and educational qualifications; economic status; urban or rural domicile; household or family structure; and fertility.

PEO

Suggested Reading
Benjamin, B. 1970: *The population census*. London: Heinemann.

Cox, P. R. 1976: *Demography*, fifth edition. Cambridge: Cambridge University Press.

Hakim, C. 1982: *Secondary analysis in social research: a guide to data sources and methods with examples*. London: Allen and Unwin, esp. Part One: The census, pp. 25–94.

Lawton, R., ed. 1978: *The census and social structure*. London: Frank Cass.

Petersen, W. 1975: *Population*, third edition. New York: Collier-Macmillan, ch. 2.

Rhind, D., ed., 1984: *A census-user's handbook*. London: Methuen.

census tract A small areal unit used in collecting and reporting CENSUS data. The first tracts were defined by the US Bureau of the Census for its 1920 enumeration, and were drawn so as to approximate NATURAL AREAS or NEIGHBOURHOODS wherever possible, thereby providing valuable data for analysing city district characteristics (see SOCIAL AREA ANALYSIS). Many census authorities report data for similar small areas (in the UK the term used is 'enumeration district'), but they are generally constructed on logistical grounds (ease of administration) rather than to meet analytical purposes.

RJJ

Suggested Reading
Openshaw, S., ed., 1992: *A census users' handbook*, second edition. London: Longman.

central business district (CBD)

The nucleus of an urban area, containing the main concentration of commercial land uses (shops, offices and warehouses). This concentration is associated – as both cause and effect – with both the most accessible point in the urban area and its peak land value (see ALONSO MODEL). The CBD contains the densest concentration of land uses and the tallest non-residential buildings within the urban area, and is spatially structured internally, with different uses and categories of use (e.g. clothing shops) concentrated in certain areas to benefit from the EXTERNAL ECONOMIES associated with AGGLOMERATION. (There may also be vertical segregation, with uses that can afford the highest rents on the ground floors of high-rise buildings.)

Most CBDs are in relative if not absolute decline, as their characteristic uses are increasingly decentralized to suburban and exurban locations, as with the growth of planned shopping centres and office parks close to major highway intersections. (See also CENTRIFUGAL AND CENTRIPETAL FORCES.)   RJJ

central place theory

A theoretical account of the size and distribution of settlements within an URBAN SYSTEM in which marketing is the predominant urban function. The theory assumes that both buyers (customers) and sellers (shopkeepers) make decisions which maximize their utilities: this is thus a NORMATIVE THEORY, providing a statement of what might appear in certain idealized circumstances.

The two main approaches to central place theory were both developed by German economic geographers, Walther Christaller (see CHRISTALLER MODEL) and August Losch. Christaller dealt only with retailing functions within settlements, and based his theory on two concepts: the *range* of a good (the maximum distance that a consumer will travel to purchase that good alone); and the *threshold* for a good (the minimum volume of business necessary for an establishment selling that good alone to be commercially viable). On the assumption of constant utilities for both consumers and shopkeepers, he then assumed that different goods would have different ranges and thresholds, which would determine both the number of establishments in an area with a given population and their distribution.

In presenting his theory, Christaller (1966) grouped the different types of retail establishment into seven orders, with similar thresholds and ranges within each. To derive the geography of the location of the different orders, he argued that shopkeepers would locate their establishments as close to their customers as possible, in order to minimize their travelling costs and so maximize both shop turnover and consumer satisfaction. Shops would thus be located centrally within the areas that they served (their HINTERLANDS).

If the distribution of population in an area is uniform, then meeting this centrality requirement will produce a hexagonal network of shop locations in central places. (Hexagons are the most efficient geometrical figures for the exhaustion of a territory without overlap.) Central places with the lowest order functions (having the smallest thresholds and ranges) have the densest network, those in the next order have a less dense hexagonal network, and so forth. According to Christaller's theory, all central places of a particular order will also contain all of the characteristic functions of the lower order centres (so that if first order central places are characterized by grocers' shops, second order places by butchers' shops, and third order places by hardware stores, then every third order central place will contain grocers' and butchers' shops as well as one or more hardware stores). This produces a hierarchy of central places, with seven levels according to the original theory (the details of which were much influenced by Christaller's empirical observations in southern Germany).

Christaller suggested three ways in which that hierarchical spatial structure would be organized, as shown in the figure. In the first (a in the figure) the structure minimizes the number of separate settlements serving an area by having each at the meeting point of three adjacent hexagons. This is his $k = 3$ (or *marketing principle*) model, so called because the number of

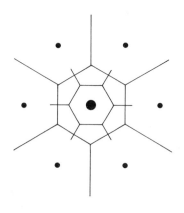
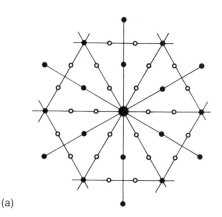

(a)

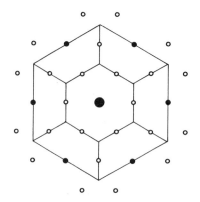
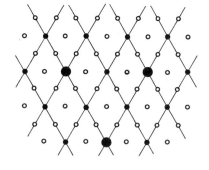

(b)

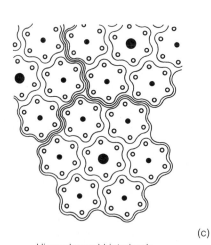
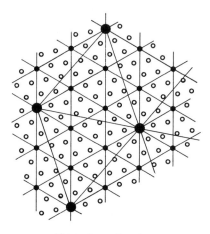

(c)

Hierarchy and hinterlands   Hierarchy and routes

central place theory   *The size and spacing of central places, plus their hinterlands (left) and routes (right), according to three variants of Christaller's model: (a) the market principle, which minimizes the number of centres: (b) the transport principle, which minimizes the road length: and (c) the administrative principle, in which hinterlands are nested hierarchically.*

settlements at each level of the hierarchy, below the second, is three times the number at the next highest. (Thus with one at the highest, seventh, order, the numbers are 1, 2, 6, 18, 54, 162 and 486.) The figure (a) illustrates this arrangement with a three-level hierarchy only.

In Christaller's $k = 4$ (or *transport principle*) model the criterion is to minimize the lengths of roads needed to join all adjacent pairs of central places. As shown in (b), this involves each settlement being placed centrally on each side of a hexagon, and each is on the boundary of two rather than three hinterlands. The number of settlements is thus greater than in the $k = 3$ model (in the ratio 1, 2, 8, 32, 128, 512 and 2048). Finally, he suggested a $k = 7$ (or *administrative principle*) model (c in the figure), in which each lower order hinterland nested exclusively within the hinterland of one higher order central place only, producing a sequence of 1, 6, 42, 294, 2058, 14 406 and 100 842 settlements.

Losch's (1954) model was less restrictive than Christaller's, because rather than bundle functions into orders he treated each as having a separate range, threshold and hexagonal hinterland. Wherever feasible, establishments in these functions were clustered in the same settlements, but in his system all central places with a function with a particular threshold need not contain examples of all functions with smaller thresholds. The result is a more complicated pattern of central places than in Christaller's simpler presentation – and one which can incorporate other urban functions (such as manufacturing). Whereas Christaller's theory predicted a stepped hierarchical form to the CITY-SIZE DISTRIBUTION (i.e. all places in an order had the same population), Losch's was consistent with a continuous distribution of population sizes.

These two theories were central to much of the early work undertaken during geography's QUANTITATIVE REVOLUTION in the 1960s. Christaller's theory, in particular, was used many times as the basis for searches for hierarchically structured, hexagonal arrangements of central places, both in rural areas and within cities (see also RETAILING, GEOGRAPHY OF), and

for distance-minimizing patterns of consumer shopping choice.   RJJ

References

Christaller, W. 1966: *Central places in southern Germany* (translated by C. W. Baskin). Englewood Cliffs, NJ: Prentice-Hall (original German edition, 1933).

Losch, A. 1954: *The economics of location.* New Haven, CT: Yale University Press/Oxford: Oxford University Press (original German edition, 1940).

Suggested Reading

Beavon, K. S. O. 1977: *Central place theory: a reinterpretation.* London: Longman.

Berry, B. J. L. 1967: *Geography of market centers and retail distribution.* Englewood Cliffs, NJ: Prentice-Hall.

Berry, B. J. L. and Parr, J. B. 1988: *Geography of market centers and retail distribution,* second edition. Englewood Cliffs, NJ: Prentice-Hall.

Preston, R. E. 1985: Christaller's neglected contribution to the study of the evolution of central places. *Progr. hum. Geogr.* 9, pp. 177–93.

central planning An omnipotent form of economic and social planning, associated with state centralized control and direction over the national economy and society. It is a type of planning associated particularly with state SOCIALISM, based on the Marxist supposition that central planning enables society to overcome both the anarchy of production and the CLASS conflict that is inherent in the capitalist mode of production. Under state socialism it is considered the only way of achieving rapid economic growth, an egalitarian income distribution and a strong defence against capitalist countries.

One of the major weaknesses of central planning has been the problem of calculating and implementing a plan for the efficient allocation of national resources in the absence of effective and realistic cost/profit criteria to guide investment decisions. Overcentralization of decision-making also tends to stultify local initiative and the ability of grassroots economic decision-makers to respond to changing circumstances.   GES

Suggested Reading

Ellman, M. 1979: *Socialist planning.* Cambridge: Cambridge University Press.

Smith, G. E. 1989: *Planned development in the socialist world*. Cambridge: Cambridge University Press.

centralization   See CONCENTRATION AND CENTRALIZATION.

centrifugal and centripetal forces

Terms borrowed from physics by Colby (1932) to describe the two counteracting forces producing patterns of land-use change within urban areas. Centrifugal forces push households and businesses away from the congested, polluted, high-density and expensive inner-city areas towards the suburbs and beyond (see also COUNTERURBANIZATION; DECENTRALIZATION; SPRAWL) whereas centripetal forces attract them towards the centre for the benefits of ACCESSIBILITY and AGGLOMERATION. The balance of these two forces at any period determines the evolution of the urban MORPHOLOGY. (For an alternative use of the term, see POLITICAL GEOGRAPHY.)   RJJ

Reference

Colby, C. C. 1932: Centripetal and centrifugal forces in urban geography. *Ann. Ass. Am. Geogr.* 23, pp. 1–20.

centrography   The study of descriptive

statistics for measuring the central tendency (such as the mean centre of a population distribution) and dispersion of point patterns across space. In the 1920s developments were undertaken by the Mendeleev Centrographic Laboratory in Leningrad. Their misuse of the techniques brought centrography into disrepute, until Bachi (1968) revived interest in the descriptive utility of such measures as standard distance, POPULATION POTENTIAL, mean centre and modal centre (see Smith, 1975).   MJB

References

Bachi, R. 1968: Statistical analysis of geographical series. In Berry, B. J. L. and Marble, D. F., eds, *Spatial analysis: a reader in statistical geography*. Englewood Cliffs, NJ: Prentice-Hall, pp. 101–9.

Smith, D. M. 1975: *Patterns in human geography: an introduction to numerical methods*. London: Penguin/New York: Crane Russak, pp. 188–200.

Suggested Reading

Kellerman, A. 1981: *Centrographic measures in geography*. Concepts and techniques in modern geography 32. Norwich: Geo Abstracts.

chain migration   The process whereby

migratory movements are sustained through kinship or other links. An initial migration stream of innovators who make the first moves from home may be followed by others, as information is passed back from destination to point of origin. For example, a village may be linked to a particular residential area of a city by this process. Thus, a primary group of migrants may be dominated by younger adults in search of better employment or a better standard of living, while the secondary group may be their dependents, children or parents, as well as neighbours and other members of the home community. The creation of distinct ETHNIC residential areas, e.g. by Italians or Chinese in North American cities, may be aided by this process. Chain migration is particularly evident in international movements over long distances, where information about opportunities for intending migrants is available mainly through the experiences of those who have already moved. (See also MIGRATION.)   PEO

Suggested Reading

Ogden, P. E. 1984: *Migration and geographical change*. Cambridge: Cambridge University Press.

White, P. E. and Woods, R. I., eds 1980: *The geographical impact of migration*. London: Longman/Seattle: University of Washington Press.

chaos   A mathematical term for relation-

ships between variables which show no order. The oscillations in the relationship contain no periodicity in either their frequency or their amplitude. Empirical and theoretical studies are producing an increasing volume of evidence of the existence of chaotic relationships, which makes forecasting and prediction of future SYSTEM states extremely difficult, if not impossible.   RJJ

Suggested Reading

Gleick, J. 1988: *Chaos: making a new science*. London: Cardinal Books.

chaotic conception An arbitrary abstraction from a whole. Almost all scientific analysis focuses on only some components of a SYSTEM. If they have some unity and autonomous existence, then their separation for study is a rational ABSTRACTION. However, if the selection either divides one or more wholes or amalgamates unrelated parts of separate wholes, then it is a chaotic conception, the study of which has little value. Sayer (1992) has argued that many human geographical studies deal with chaotic conception; for example, SERVICE industries, which cover a very wide range of dissimilar activities and about which few, if any, useful generalizations can be made.

RJJ

Reference

Sayer, A. 1992: *Method in social science: a realist approach*, second edition. London: Routledge.

chi-square A widely used NON-PARA-METRIC STATISTIC for the analysis of nominal data. SIGNIFICANCE TESTS employing chi-square are of two main types:

(1) Two empirical frequency distributions, such as the number of people in each of five separate ethnic categories in two city districts, are compared to see if they are probably drawn from the same population. (A significant difference between the two would suggest that they are not separate random samples from the same population, and so the two districts would almost certainly have populations with differing ethnic profiles.)

(2) An empirical frequency distribution is compared with another (which may be either theoretically or empirically derived) to identify the probability of the former being a random sample of the latter, as with the comparison of the age structure of one town in Wales with that of the total Welsh population. (A significant difference between the two would indicate that the town's age structure is not the same as that of the entire country, i.e. it is not a random sample of the country's population on that characteristic.)

RJJ

Suggested Reading

O'Brien, L. 1992: *Introducing quantitative geography: measurement, methods and generalised linear models*. London: Routledge.

Chicago School Members of the Department of Sociology at the University of Chicago, who activated a major research programme on the American city during the early twentieth century. Many academics over several generations have been associated with the school, but William Thomas (1863–1947), Robert Park (1864–1944), Ernest Burgess (1886–1966) and Louis Wirth (1897–1952) stand out, as their collective work established and sustained a new direction for American sociology (Bulmer, 1984). Drawing, paradoxically, on both PRAGMATISM and social DARWINISM, Chicago School sociologists combined painstaking ethnographic research with sweeping generalizations, steeped in physical metaphors and evolutionary logic, about urban society. The legacy of their work is complex and ambiguous, and contemporary authors range in their assessment of it from outright rejection, through a selective incorporation of certain insights and methodologies, to a celebration of the Chicago School as progenitor of humanistic social science.

Thomas introduced many issues that motivated subsequent research within the Chicago sociology department. *The Polish peasant in Europe and America*, published in 1918 (the year in which Thomas was dismissed over allegations of an extramarital affair; Deegan, 1988), is a key early text, in which Thomas and Znaniecki investigate both sides of a transatlantic flow of immigrants: conditions in rural Poland that led to emigration and the settlement of Poles in American cities. This four-volume work set the tone for scores of dense ethnographic studies undertaken by faculty and graduate students at the University of Chicago (see ETHNOGRAPHY). In each case researchers acquired new languages where appropriate, conducted social surveys, and engaged in PARTICIPANT OBSERVATION in an effort to chart the forces that bound communities together. Thomas and Znaniecki initiated perhaps the most enduring theme in Chicago School research: the dynamic between cultural retention among immigrants versus the pull to assimilate to American social mores. The residential clustering of Poles in American cities was seen as instrumental in allowing these immigrants to retain valued elements of their cultural heritage while, gradually but inevitably, assimilating to the society around them. The dual nature of 'ghettoized' neighbourhoods was further elaborated by Wirth (1928) in his seminal study of Chicago's Jewish community.

Park, who became the dominant intellectual figure in the department after the departure of Thomas, provided a formal theoretical backdrop for Chicago research by adapting principles of plant ecology to human society (Park, in Turner, 1967; see also McKenzie, in Hawley, 1968; Matthews, 1977). HUMAN ECOLOGY likens society to an organism, with each constituent part symbiotically related to all others in a web of relations that form around competitive and cooperative behaviour. On one level, which Park labelled 'biotic' (subsocial), human activities at all times are the product of an innate urge to compete in the struggle for survial, a struggle most clearly discernible in the economy, where individuals pursue their own ends. Competition over limited rewards sorts individuals based upon their given level of abilities. Those with similar abilities are 'naturally' channelled into groups that find appropriate occupational and residential niches in society, in much the same way that plant species proliferate in (and eventually dominate) places where environmental qualities favour their particular genetic composition. Within these ecological groups, or communities, individuals discover that it is in their interest to cooperate and regularize their relations with one another. Thus a 'moral order' emerges, reflecting the principle of cooperation which Park saw as a necessary complement to competition. Humans, in contrast to plant communities, temper the demands of the biotic level by developing a cultural superstructure in which rules are established to modify and control competition. Otherwise, Park believed, society would lack the basis to continue its existence, leading to a 'war of all against all'. Armed with these conceptualizations, Park's students set about defining 'natural' COMMUNITIES, such as immigrant groups, hobos, taxi dancers and street gangs, and documenting the moral orders shared by their members. These investigations are invariably rich in ethnographic detail, but the zeal of researchers to fit their data into the confines of ecological theory often seems forced.

Burgess was instrumental in transcribing the theory of human ecology to the urban arena, deriving a concentric model of the city based on the sorting behaviour of competition (Park, Burgess and McKenzie, 1925). In his model (see ZONAL MODEL), commercial and industrial activities capture the city centre (the CENTRAL BUSINESS DISTRICT [CBD]) because of their ability to generate profit and outbid other land uses for locations of highest spatial mobility. A Zone in Transition, where landlords allow their residential building stock to deteriorate in anticipation of the unearned profits they will reap as the CBD expands, surrounds the city centre. This district houses those least able to pay rent, typically recent immigrants and other racialized minorities. Beyond the Zone in Transition lies a belt of neighbourhoods housing the more settled working class, both American-born and immigrants who have achieved a modest level of social mobility. The middle class resides in manicured suburbs, or exurbs, on the periphery of the urbanized area, where they enjoy ample space and easy access to the countryside. Burgess set his model in motion by adding the concept of 'INVASION AND SUCCESSION', based on his assumptions that cities, as organisms, must grow, and that individuals are almost universally able to achieve upward social mobility. According to Burgess, as new commercial enterprises are established and new immigrants arrive, the CBD and Zone in Transition expand, pushing into the Zone of Workers' Homes. At the same time, new jobs are generated allowing working-class individuals to move up the occupational hierarchy and attain higher incomes, thereby opening new opportunities for immigrants to fill the jobs left behind. Working-class families direct their elevated incomes to the housing market and 'invade' middle-class suburbs, expanding their zone of the city outwards until they dominate the area that was once exclusive to middle-class residents. Invasion and succession therefore follows the cascading effect generated by the relentless growth of the CBD.

It is deeply ironic that the Burgess model continues to inform urban planning policy in most North American cities. Planners often reproduce the zonal pattern described above by fostering the development of homogeneous land uses in specified areas of the city. The city centre is therefore scheduled to house the commercial core of the urban economy, surrounded by progressively lower densities of residential land uses. However, Burgess believed that land uses sorted themselves into a concentric pattern at the biotic level through competition and 'natural' selection. Within the rubric of human ecology theory, planning would be seen as part of the cultural superstructure of society, where the negative effects of excessive competition are muted. Yet planners step in to reinforce (at times even force) a concentric pattern because processes that are supposed to develop 'naturally' do not; instead, the concentric pattern is 'naturalized' within a bureaucracy that operates at the cultural level.

Criticisms of human ecology have been numerous and comprehensive, although the Chicago School is not without its apologists. Early commentators focused on empirical inaccuracies of the Burgess model; of these Homer Hoyt's (1939) demonstration that urban land values vary more within concentric zones than between them is the most significant. Assessments published during the 1940–1965 period were part of a larger project to replace human ecology with STRUCTURAL FUNCTIONALISM as the basic paradigm for American sociology. Walter Firey (1947), for example, asserted that the distinction between the biotic and cultural levels of society is overdrawn within Chicago School research. Gideon Sjoberg (1960) focused his criticisms on the tendency for Park and

Burgess to universalize from the American experience, producing grand theories that result from time- and place-bound experiences. In particular, he argues that the Burgess model of urban land use only applies in the context of industrial capitalist societies (see SJOBERG MODEL). Recent authors have extended this criticism, arguing that the theories presented by the Chicago sociologists contain a substantial normative content – that they legitimate the competition characteristic of capitalism and the melting-pot ideology of American society (Harvey, 1973; Castells, 1977). Still others have shown that the Chicago sociologists were incorrect in portraying European immigrants and Afro-Americans as similar types of ethnic communities, and that they disregarded the depth of colour-based discrimination in American society (Philpott, 1978; Persons, 1987). Finally, feminist criticism has raised an equally serious charge. Deegan (1988) has documented the collaboration between members of the Chicago School and women social critics in the opening decades of the twentieth century. By the late 1910s, however, members of the Chicago Sociology Department sought to distance themselves from the pioneering social surveys and intellectual insights made by Jane Addams and other women residents of Hull House. In particular, Burgess and Park advocated a sharp distinction between social work (which they deemed an appropriate pursuit for women) and sociology (seen as an intellectual, rather than emotional, subject), and thereby trivialized the work of their former collaborators. Thus, in his introduction to her book, Park characterized Frances Donovan's (1929) study of saleswomen in Chicago as ' . . . impressionistic and descriptive rather than systematic and formal . . . ' and ' . . . more interested in the history than in the sociology of contemporary life . . . ', despite the fact that Donovan utilized the same ethnographic methodologies as male researchers.

Yet there are those who wish to salvage elements of Chicago School thought, and they too have presented cogent arguments. While it is true that Park and his colleagues portrayed Afro-Americans too simply (as one ethnic group among many), this fault was related to Park's critique of a biologically determined conception of race. Generally, Park emphasized the socially constructed aspects of race relations, stressing that ethnic groups (including blacks) would eventually be part of mainstream American society as they attained upward social mobility (Persons, 1987). Jackson has also argued that the grand theories produced by Chicago sociologists are overemphasized by critics, while the influences of PRAGMATISM in Chicago School research have been ignored. He further suggests that the participant observation studies characteristic of humanistic sociology and geography have their roots in the ethnography practised by students of Thomas, Park and Wirth (Jackson, 1984). Ultimately, the work of the Chicago School must be judged within its own context – early twentieth-century American thought; in that light it probably led to as many significant advances as strategic oversights.

DH

References

Bulmer, M. 1984: *The Chicago School of sociology: institutionalization, diversity and the role of sociological research.* Chicago: University of Chicago Press.

Castells, M. 1977: *The urban question: a Marxist approach.* London: Edward Arnold.

Deegan, M. J. 1988: *Jane Addams and the men of the Chicago School, 1892–1918.* New Brunswick, NJ: Transaction Books.

Donovan, F. R. 1929: *The saleslady.* Chicago: University of Chicago Press.

Firey, W. 1947: *Land use in central Boston.* Cambridge, MA: MIT Press.

Harvey, D. 1973: *Social justice and the city.* Baltimore: Johns Hopkins University Press.

Hawley, A. H. 1968: *Roderick D. McKenzie on human ecology.* Chicago: University of Chicago Press.

Hoyt, H. 1939: *The structure and growth of residential neighborhoods in American cities.* Washington, DC: Federal Housing Administration.

Jackson, P. 1984: Social disorganisation and moral order in the city. *Trans. Inst. Br. Geogr.* n.s. 9, pp. 168–180.

Matthews, F. H. 1977: *Quest for an American sociology: Robert E. Park and the Chicago School.* Montreal and London: McGill-Queen's University Press.

Park, R. E., Burgess, E. W. and McKenzie, R. D. 1925: *The city.* Chicago: University of Chicago Press.

Persons, S. 1987: *Ethnic studies at Chicago, 1905–45.* Urbana, IL: University of Illinois Press.

Philpott, T. L. 1978: *The slum and the ghetto: neighborhood deterioration and middle-class reform, Chicago, 1880–1930.* New York: Oxford University Press.

Sjoberg, G. 1960: *The pre-industrial city, past and present.* New York: The Free Press.

Thomas, W. I. and Znaniecki, F. 1918: *The Polish peasant in Europe and America,* volumes I and II. Chicago: University of Chicago Press. (Volumes III and IV were published two years later by Richard G. Badger, Boston.)

Turner, R. H., ed. 1967: *Robert E. Park: On social control and collective behaviour.* Chicago: University of Chicago Press.

Wirth, L. 1928: *The ghetto.* Chicago: University of Chicago Press.

Suggested Reading

Jackson, P. and Smith, S. 1984: *Exploring social geography.* London: Allen and Unwin.

Lal, B. B. 1990: *The romance of culture in an urban civilization: Robert E. Park on race and ethnic relations.* London: Routledge.

chorography See CHOROLOGY.

chorology (or chorography) The study of the AREAL DIFFERENTIATION of the Earth's surface. It represents the oldest tradition of Western geographical inquiry. It was first set forth by Hecataeus of Miletus in the sixth century BC, and codified most elegantly by Strabo in the 17 books of his *Geography* written sometime between 8 BC and AD 18. The geographer, he declared, is 'the person who attempts to describe the parts of the Earth' (in Greek, *chorographein*). The two key words were 'describe' and 'parts': in effect, Strabo was recommending what would now be called REGIONAL GEOGRAPHY as the core of geographical reflection. He was not interested in chorography for its own sake, but intended it to serve a higher purpose. 'If there is one science which is worthy to be practised by a "philosopher"', he argued, 'then it is geographical science'. For Strabo, geography described those worthwhile things from which one could learn about truth, nobility and virtue: it was 'a complement to political and ethical philosophy'. It was, in the original sense of the term, a *practical* activity. For this reason Strabo's geography was fundamentally concerned with human activities. It was directed towards social and political ends, and paid considerable attention to the interests of the military commander and the political ruler. Chorography was not supposed to provide a comprehensive gazetteer or a regional inventory. It was partial and purposive. 'I am neither required to enumerate all the many inhabited places nor to fix all the phenomena', Strabo insisted, and he said he began 'with Europe, because it is admirably adapted by nature for the development of excellence in men and governments' (van Paassen, 1957, pp. 1–32).

Strabo's conception of geography was challenged by Claudius Ptolemaeus, or Ptolemy, round about AD 150. In his view, the purpose of geography was to provide 'a view of the whole, analogous to the drawing of the whole head', and this meant that he separated geography from chorography which, so he said, 'has the purpose of describing the parts, as if one were to draw only an ear or an eye'. As this passage implies, for Ptolemy *graphein* did not mean describing but drawing and, specifically, mapping:

Ptolemy's 'geography' is geodesy and cartography and he preferred to leave out everything which had no direct connection with that aim: 'We shall expand our "guide" for so far as this is useful for the knowledge of the location of places and their setting upon the map, but we shall leave out of consideration all the many details about the peculiarities of the peoples' (van Paassen, 1957, p. 2).

The distance between Strabo and Ptolemy could not be plainer, and it is indelibly present in the constitution of a distinctively modern geography too. As late as the seventeenth century, Strabo and Ptolemy continued to provide the main models for European geography. The usual distinction was between a *special* geography, devoted to the description of particular regions (including a study of the human population), and a *general* geography, mathematically oriented and concerned with the globe as a whole. The premier illustration is provided by Bernhard Varenius, who published both studies in special geography and his famous *Geographia generalis* in which, for the first time, geography sought to engage with the ideas of Descartes, Bacon and Galileo (Bowen, 1981).

The modern case for geography as a 'chorographic science' was argued most forcefully by Hartshorne in *The nature of geography* (1939), and ever since the subsequent debate over EXCEPTIONALISM in geography – and despite the nuances and qualifications which Hartshorne had registered – chorology has often been used in polemical opposition to SPATIAL SCIENCE (cf. Sack, 1974). But the temper of the original version, with its acknowledgement of the importance of political power and philosophical reflection, is a forceful reminder of the continuing need to attend to the politics of geographical inquiry.   DG

References

Bowen, M. 1981: *Empiricism and geographical thought: from Francis Bacon to Alexander von Humboldt.* Cambridge: Cambridge University Press.

Hartshorne, R. 1939: *The nature of geography: a critical survey of current thought in the light of the past.* Lancaster, PA: Association of American Geographers.

Sack, R. 1974: Chorology and spatial analysis. *Ann. Ass. Am. Geogr.* 64, pp. 439–52.

van Paassen, C. 1957: *The classical tradition of geography.* Groningen: J. B. Walters.

Suggested Reading

van Paassen, 1957: pp. 1–32.

choropleth map A THEMATIC MAP displaying areally based data and tonal shadings proportional to density by areal units (see SYMBOLIZATION). The data types used in choropleth mapping are typically interval and ratio types (see MEASUREMENT). Chrisman (1991) differentiates between these and other categorical maps which use data types, such as soil classification. In choropleth mapping there are three main areas of concern. The first is that of SCALE, and the ECOLOGICAL FALLACY. The second is one of area groupings: most data types being mapped are aggregations of individual level data (e.g. population, industry, etc.) and the MODIFIABLE AREAL UNIT problem argues that there are many potential aggregations of data to a set number of aggregation units. Finally, there is the problem of effectively representing temporal processes by static maps (Monmonier, 1990).   MJB

References

Chrisman, N. R. 1991: The error component in spatial data. In Maguire, D. J., Goodchild, M. F. and Rhind, D. W., eds, *Geographical information systems: principles and applications*, volume 1. London: Longman, pp. 165–74.

Monmonier, M. S. 1990: Strategies for the visualisation of geographic time-series data. *Cartographica* 27(1), pp. 30–45.

Christaller model   A prediction of the spatial arrangement of urban places as service centres, combining nested hierarchies of settlements and market areas. (See CENTRAL PLACE THEORY.)   DMS

circuit of capital   The continuous transformation of CAPITAL into various forms: money, COMMODITIES, labour power, and means of production. Capital circulates into and out of the means of production and labour power in order to generate surplus value (see ACCUMULATION). As money, capital is advanced to purchase raw materials, the means of production (machinery, physical plant, etc.), and labour power which, when combined in production, results in a commodity that can then be exchanged back for money capital. Marx (1987 edn, ch. 4) summarized the circulation of capital as the 'expanded general formula of capital', which he denoted symbolically as follows:

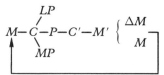

where M is the money capital advanced, C are the commodities purchased for productive consumption (LP = labour power, MP = means of production), P are the production processes, C' are the commodities produced for sale, M' is the money received in exchange for commodities C',

and ΔM is the increase over M (i.e. the surplus value).

Capital investment involves a circuit insofar as some of the M' redeemed after the first production period is reinvested in a second round of production. To the degree that the quantity of advanced capital increases with each circuit of capital, ACCUMULATION takes place.

In practice the circulation of capital is quite complex. In addition to direct investment in production, money capital may be: exchanged in a capital market; 'diverted' towards STATE functions of regulation and control; invested in the development of technology and science; or devoted to social expenditures such as education, health, welfare and the military. All of these activities help to reproduce capital in its expanded form. Although circulating in economic terms, capital may necessarily be 'fixed' in the built environment, for example, as factories, roads or fields; or it may be deployed in the 'consumption fund' to produce commodities for the reproduction of labour power, whether spatially fixed, as in houses, or not, as in cars (Harvey, 1982).

The circulation of capital presupposes the specific social relations of CAPITALISM i.e. labour and capital, or competitions between individual capitals. Economic CRISIS arises when the circulation of capital is halted or circumscribed. This can occur at any point in the circuit: money capital or labour power may be scarce or too expensive; existing means of production may be no longer competitive; final commodities may not sell in sufficient quantities or at a sufficient price (overproduction); or the rate of profit may have fallen too low to allow sufficient reinvestment. Where the circuit of capital is broken, this may lead to a 'switching crisis', in which capitalists switch investment from one circuit to another; for example, from industrial production to the built environment. To the extent that specific circuits of capital dominate certain regional economies, this can lead to regional crises. Crisis becomes global when insufficient profitable circuits exist for capital switching (Harvey, 1982).

The circuit of capital is central to understanding the geography of capitalism. Circuits of capital both produce the geographical structure of circulation and are at the same time constrained by it (Harvey, 1982; Smith, 1990; Lefebvre, 1991). NS

References

Harvey, D. 1982: *The limits to capital*. Oxford: Blackwell.

Lefebvre, H. 1991: *The production of space*. Oxford: Blackwell; transl. D. Nicholson-Smith.

Marx, K. 1987 edn: *Capital*, volume I. New York: International Publishers.

Smith, N. 1990: *Uneven development: nature capital and the production of space*, second edition. Oxford: Blackwell.

citizenship Refers to the terms of membership of a political unit (usually the NATION–STATE) which secure certain rights and privileges to those who fulfil particular obligations. Citizenship is a concept, rather than a theory, which formalizes the conditions for full participation in a community. In modern times, the idea owes most to the work of Marshall (1950), whose writings on the civil, social and political rights of citizenship laid the foundations of the European welfare states. In geography, there are at least two ways in which the concept can be useful (Smith, 1990).

First, the concept of citizenship can be used analytically, to expose differences in the *de jure* and *de facto* rights of different groups within and between nation–states. The assumption here is that recent changes in social entitlements are due not only to economic RESTRUCTURING and cultural transformation but also to political realignments. These realignments have renegotiated the boundaries between civil society and the STATE in ways which vary through time and over space. In charting these geographies of citizenship, analysts have: mapped variations in the patriarchal assumptions which underpin the social contracts of most developed societies (see PATRIARCHY); examined the racist and Eurocentric character of many countries' immigration and nationality laws (see ETHNOCENTRISM; RACISM); and specified some key inequalities between LOCALITIES and COMMUNITIES in the extent to which

residents' or members' social, economic and political entitlements can be mobilized.

Second, the concept of citizenship can be used normatively, as the basis for ideas about what a SOCIETY that is sensitive to individual rights as well as to social justice should look like. The quest for citizenship entitlements therefore provides a vision of, and a catalyst for, social transformation at a local, national, supranational and global scale. One project for POLITICAL GEOGRAPHY will be to explore the tensions between local and national states and between national and supranational units arising from the struggle to win both the political power required to define citizenship rights and the fiscal powers required to guarantee them.

This prescriptive content of the term is, nevertheless, at the heart of political debate. One argument, usually associated with the political Right, is that the condition of full participation in society is the protection of property rights and personal wealth. The opportunity to participate in the economy is seen as the gateway to and guarantor of all other rights and entitlements within a market democracy, on the grounds that free markets are the fairest means of exchanging and distributing resources. An opposing view argues that market inequalities deny some individuals their wider range of citizenship entitlements. The democratic Left favours state intervention to offset market inequalities, so ensuring that those without property rights or personal wealth have not only the opportunity but also the right – uncompromised by obligations – to participate in the full range of social affairs. SJS

References

Marshall, T. H. 1950: *Citizenship and social class*. Cambridge: Cambridge University Press.

Smith, S. J. 1990: Society, space and citizenship: human geography for the new times? *Trans. Inst. Br. Geogr.* n.s. 14, pp. 144–56.

city Originally a European urban settlement containing a cathedral and the seat of a bishop, the term is now generally applied to large urban places. The criteria for separately identifying cities from towns vary between countries: in some, population size is the determining factor; in others, the status of 'city' implies an administrative decision, and carries with it certain rights and privileges. RJJ

city-size distribution The FRE-QUENCY DISTRIBUTION of settlements of different sizes, often in different size categories. The observed distribution for an URBAN SYSTEM may be compared with a theoretical model, such as those provided by CENTRAL PLACE THEORY, the RANK-SIZE RULE and the law of the PRIMATE CITY. RJJ

Suggested Reading

Carroll, G. R. 1982: National city-size distributions: what do we know after 67 years of research? *Prog. hum. Geogr.* 6, pp. 1–43.

civil society That segment of the practices within a capitalist society which lie outside the sphere of production and the STATE. (Alternative terms are the *sphere of consumption* and the *sphere of reproduction*.) Relationships within civil society may involve divisions on a number of criteria, such as gender, RACE, ETHNICITY, RELIGION, and age.

The reproduction of society, individually and intergenerationally, biologically and culturally, is organized within civil society. According to Urry (1981), struggle over existence under CAPITALISM involves intersections with both the sphere of production, through the sphere of circulation (where money earned in the sphere of production is expended on reproduction), and the state (reproduction is regulated by the state, and is enhanced by it, through the provision of PUBLIC GOODS – see WELFARE STATE). These intersections define what Urry terms the 'sphere of struggle' (see the figure: see also SUPERSTRUCTURE). RJJ

Reference

Urry, J. 1981: *The anatomy of capitalist societies: the economy, civil society and the state.* London: Macmillan/Atlantic Highlands, NJ: Humanities Press.

Suggested Reading

Johnston, R. J. 1991: *A question of place: exploring the practice of human geography.* Oxford: Blackwell.

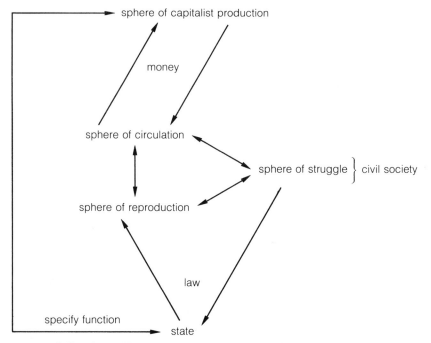

civil society *The basic structure of capitalist social formations* (Urry).

class A concept that describes systems of stratification derived from social relations of property and work. Given that it delineates major structural divisions and potential lines of societal conflict, class is central to most theoretical accounts of CAPITALISM, but there is a wide range of views as to the meaning of the concept. There is also debate as to whether classes exist in non-capitalist societies (see Giddens, 1987).

Geographers use a range of class definitions, drawn from different theoretical traditions (see the figure). In gradational approaches, classes are measured by attributes such as income, status and education, and tend to be descriptive rather than explanatory categories. With relational approaches, the social relations *between* classes are definitive, and gradations in income and status are taken as outcomes rather than defining characteristics of class position. David Harvey's book, *Social justice and the city* (1973), marked the transition from the use of gradational to relational

approaches to class in geography, in Harvey's case to Marxist CLASS theory.

There is a variety of relational approaches to class. A conception of class based on market relations is associated with Weberian theory. Max Weber used the term class to refer to 'objective' market interests that influence 'life-chances' (access to economic and cultural goods). He contrasted this to the concept of *status* groups, which are communities that are based on common 'styles of life' and perceptions of similarity. Although Weber restricts the notion of class to 'pure' economic relations, he presents a pluralistic model of them, distinguishing between: *property* classes that are based on command over forms of property that can be used to realize income in the market (see HOUSING CLASS); *acquisition* classes that are determined by marketable skills or services; and *social* classes that refer to clusters of class situations linked by common mobility chances (see Giddens, 1973, for a description and critique). Weber's definition of property classes has been used to argue that

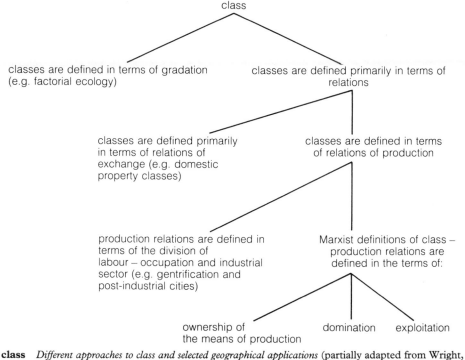

class *Different approaches to class and selected geographical applications* (partially adapted from Wright, 1979, and Sheppard and Barnes, 1990).

classes also emerge out of urban housing markets to form an important basis for CONFLICT in the city and within national politics (Saunders, 1984).

Other relational approaches ground class exclusively within the RELATIONS OF PRODUCTION but, once again, these relations are conceived in different ways. For some theorists, production relations are equivalent to occupation and industrial sector. This interpretation of class has been used by Ley (1980), for example, to explain the GENTRIFICATION of inner cities in terms of the expansion of professional occupations and the service sector. Marxist theorists conceive of the *division of labour* (the organization of work into, for example, occupations, industrial sectors and firms) as distinct from class (Walker, 1985) and usually define the latter in terms of ownership of the means of production, domination (control over labour) and exploitation (appropriation of surplus value). Sheppard and Barnes (1990) provide a critical discussion of the controversies within Marxism surrounding the centrality of each of these factors to the definition of class. At the most abstract level of theory, these criteria lead to the identification of two classes (capitalist and working), although considerable effort has been made over the past decade to revise Marxist class theory so as to theorize the middle classes in contemporary industrial societies (see Giddens, 1973; Wright, 1985).

Debates about and the use of class theory have shifted within geography over the past decade. Theoretical debate between Weberian and Marxist theorists – groups once considered irreconcilable – now assumes less importance. Weberians now tend to contain their use of the class concept to market relations within the production sphere, using different terminology to analyse distributive- and consumption-based exchange relations (Saunders, 1984). Similarly, Marxist theorists tend to use the concept more specifically, and admit the importance of other dimensions of power and social division (e.g. gender- and race-based forms of oppression). This creates the opportunity to explore the ways in which class and other relations and identities are intertwined. FEMINIST GEOGRAPHERS argue, for example, that gender relations are central to the restructuring of class relations. The increase in contingent forms of labour (e.g. part-time, temporary and other short-term contractual workers) is intrinsically linked to an increased female labour supply and gender relations within households.

A theoretical issue that continues to perplex many class theorists (both Marxist and Weberian) is how to move between abstractions about class *structure* to analyses of class *structure, consciousness* and *formation* in concrete societies. Walker (1985) reviews various attempts to resolve this difficulty and argues that the abstract definition of class must be 'recast' in each historical context. Most theorists, including Marxists, no longer expect a direct link between position in the class structure and class consciousness and action, and interpret the constitution of class identity as a highly contingent sociopolitical activity. (See Laclau and Mouffe (1985) for a critique of an essentialist Marxist reading of class that unproblematically roots individuals' identities in the class structure.) Attention is being given to the interrelations between different social identities; an early example is Willis's (1977) discussion of the links between masculinity and an affirmative manual, working-class culture.

Perhaps the most important recent development has been the vigorous insertion of SPACE and PLACE into class theory (Thrift and Williams, 1987). In the mid-1980s, Walker (1985) complained that geographical analyses of class suffered from 'the fallacy of sequential ordering' (i.e. class theory was applied to geographical problems, but the role of space in the constitution of classes was usually ignored). The linkages between space, place and class have since been expanded, and there is a vast literature, not only on the constitutive role of class in the production of space and places (see Pratt (1989) for a review at the urban scale and Corbridge (1989) for a review at the international scale), but also the place-specificity of class relations, and the role that space plays in class formation and the development of class consciousness and class practices. Sheppard and Barnes (1990, pp. 209–10) argue that the insertion of abstract Marxist theories of class *structure* into a spatial (as opposed to an aspatial) economy disrupts some of these theories' central conclusions. Focusing on class *politics*, Herod (1991) argues that spatial immobility leads some class actors to take up positions that are opposite to those that an aspatial class analysis would predict. Spatial proximity, residential SEGREGATION, and the specifics of the local history of a place play a role in class formation and the development of class consciousness. Architecture and landscape status markers are thought to be especially significant in the formation of an otherwise ambiguous middle-class identity (see Pratt, 1989, for a review of this literature).   GP

References

Corbridge, S. 1989: Marxism, post-Marxism, and geography of development. In Thrift, N. and Peet, R., eds, *New models in geography*, volume 1. London: Unwin Hyman, pp. 224–54.

Giddens, A. 1973: *The class structure of the advanced societies*. London: Hutchinson.

Giddens, A. 1987: *The nation–state and violence*. Berkeley, CA: University of California Press.

Harvey, D. 1973: *Social justice and the city*. London: Edward Arnold.

Herod, A. 1991: Local political practice in response to a manufacturing plant closure: how geography complicates class analysis. *Antipode*, 23(4), pp. 385–402.

Laclau, E. and Mouffe, C. 1985: *Hegemony and socialist strategy: towards a radical democratic politics*. London: Verso.

Ley, D. 1980: Liberal ideology and the post-industrial city. *Ann. Ass. Am. Geogr.* 70, pp. 238–58.

Pratt, G. 1989: Reproduction, class and the spatial structure of the city. In Thrift, N. and Peet, R., eds, *New models in geography*, volume 2. London: Unwin Hyman, pp. 84–108.

Saunders, P. 1984: Beyond housing classes: the sociological significance of private property rights in the means of consumption. *Int. J. urban and reg. Res.* 8, pp. 201–27.

Sheppard, E. and Barnes, T. 1990: *The capitalist space economy: geographical analysis after Ricardo, Marx and Sraffa*. London: Unwin Hyman.

Thrift, N. and Williams, P. 1987: *Class and space: the making of urban society*. London: Routledge and Kegan Paul.

Walker, R. 1985: Class, division of labour and employment in space. In Gregory, D. and Urry, J. eds, *Social relations and spatial structures*. New York: St. Martin's Press, pp. 164–89.

Willis, P. 1977: *Learning to labour*. Farnborough, Hants, UK: Saxon House.

Wright, E. O. 1979: *Class structure and income determination*. New York: Academic Press.

Wright, E. O. 1985: *Classes*. London: Verso.

Suggested Reading
Giddens (1973).

Thrift and Williams (1987).

Walker (1985).

class interval In CARTOGRAPHY, the statistical generalization of spatial data to a level suitable for inclusion in the map image (see MAP IMAGE AND MAP). It involves information loss, particularly so for class interval selection in CHOROPLETH MAPS. Various classification techniques are proposed: divide the data values into equal value ranges; examine statistical distributions for natural breaks; and use iteration to minimize within-class deviation (see CLASSIFICATION AND REGIONALIZATION). Computer-assisted methods were developed which obviate classification by using a continuous series of shading tones (see COMPUTER-ASSISTED CARTOGRAPHY), but these highlight the problems in user perception of classified data and the dilemma that the more sophisticated the classification, the less likely the general map-reading public is to understand the map (see FREQUENCY DISTRIBUTION). MJB

Suggested Reading
Evans, I. S. 1977: The selection of class intervals. *Trans. Inst. Br. Geogr.* n.s. 2, pp. 98–124.

Peterson, M. P. 1979: An evaluation of unclassed crossed-line choropleth mapping. *Am. Cartogr.* 6, pp. 21–37.

classification and regionalization Procedures for grouping individual observations into categories. Classification involves splitting a population into mutually exclusive categories, using predetermined criteria either deductively (using a previously determined set of classes) or inductively (finding the best set of classes for the particular data set). Some procedures take the entire population and divide it into classes, whereas others begin with each individual in a separate category and then group them into classes: in both cases, the outcome may be a hierarchy of classes (e.g. all people divided by gender; each gender group divided by ethnic origin; each ethnic group divided by age; etc.) With inductive classifications, the guideline is usually that each member of a class should be more like all of the other members of that class than it is like the members of any other class: the classes are thus internally homogeneous and externally heterogeneous.

Regionalization (see REGION) is a special case of the more general procedure of classification. The individuals comprising the population to be classified are areas and the resulting classes (regions) must form contiguous spatial units. Because of this additional criterion, regions defined for a population of areas may not be as internally homogeneous as a classification of the same areas without the contiguity constraint. RJJ

Suggested Reading

Johnston, R. J. 1976: *Classification in geography*. Concepts and techniques in modern geography 6. Norwich: Environmental Publications.

cleavage A division of a society into groups with similar political attitudes and partisan identifications. The classic study of Western European political systems identified four main cleavages (Lipset and Rokkan, 1967), two related to the growth of the NATION–STATE (subject versus dominant culture; church(es) versus state) and two related to the Industrial Revolution (primary versus secondary economy; workers versus employers). Other cleavages have been identified elsewhere; e.g. the sectional cleavage in the USA (see SECTION) and the POST-INDUSTRIAL in many 'advanced industrial' societies (Harrop and Miller, 1987). Cleavages are produced by political parties mobilizing the electors on the different sides of a social conflict, and are reflected in the geography of voting there (see ELECTORAL GEOGRAPHY). RJJ

References

Harrop, M. L. and Miller, W. L. 1987: *Electors and voters: a comparative perspective*. London: Macmillan.

Lipset, S. M. and Rokkan, S. E. 1967: Cleavage structures, party systems, and voter alignments: an introduction. In Lipset, S. M. and Rokkan, S. E., eds, *Party systems and voter alignments*. New York: The Free Press, pp. 1–64.

cohort A group of individuals who enter on some stage in the LIFE CYCLE simultaneously and are analysed as a unit throughout their lifetime. For example, 1000 babies all born in the same calendar year are a 'birth cohort', and 1000 couples all married for the first time in the same year are a 'marriage cohort'. Cohort, or LONGITUDINAL, DATA ANALYSIS is much used in demography; for example, in comparing FERTILITY behaviour in different generations. If cohorts are not the subject of study, but instead the experiences of particular periods of time are considered, the description *secular analysis* is sometimes employed. PEO

Suggested Reading

Cox, P. R. 1976: *Demography*, fifth edition. Cambridge: Cambridge University Press, ch. 3.

collective A form of farm organization associated with socialist countries in which the STATE retains ownership of land but leases it on a permanent basis to the members of the collective as an institutional unit. In theory each collective is self-governing, but in practice production quotas are invariably determined by the state as part of CENTRAL PLANNING. However, the collective is responsible for paying its employees and financing inputs (e.g. fertilizers or new machinery). Both former Soviet (*kolkhoz*) and Chinese (commune) forms of rural collectivism are being replaced by private forms of farm organization, in China since 1978 and in Eastern Europe and the successor states of the USSR since 1989. GES

Suggested Reading

Leeming, F. 1985: *Rural China today*. London: Longman.

Moskoff, W. 1990: *Perestroika and the countryside: agrarian reform in the Gorbachev era*. London: M. E. Sharpe.

Smith, G. E. 1989: Rural development. In Smith, G. E., *Planned development in the socialist world*. Cambridge: Cambridge University Press, pp. 82–97.

collective consumption

collective consumption A social process involving the consumption of services (see PUBLIC SERVICES) which are produced and managed on a collective basis and distributed on the basis of non-market choice (see Dunleavy, 1980, pp. 52–3; Pinch, 1985, pp. 12–14; Pinch, 1989, pp. 42–8). It is a concept associated especially with the French school of urban sociology, and in particular with the writings of Manuel Castells and Jean Lojkine (see Pickvance, 1976).

Collective consumption 'takes place not through the market but through the STATE APPARATUS' (Castells, 1977, p. 460). It involves the provision of the collective means of consumption of commodities, the production of which is not assured by capital, because of their 'lower than average profit rate', but which is, nevertheless, 'necessary to the reproduction of labour power and/or to the reproduction of social relations' (Castells, 1977, pp. 460, 461). The collective means of consumption 'refers today to the totality of medical, sports, educational, cultural and public transport facilities' (Lojkine, 1976, p. 121). A noticeable absentee from this list is public housing which, for Lojkine, is not collective, as housing is not consumed collectively. This criterion is not so significant for Castells, who is concerned mainly with STATE, i.e. collective, provision (cf. URBAN).

For Lojkine, the social expenses involved in the provision of collective means of consumption have the effect of lowering the rate of profit. Conversely, for Castells (1977, p. 461) the production of collective means of consumption 'plays a fundamental role in the struggle of capital against the tendency of the profit rate to fall', as unprofitable investments are taken over by the state, which thereby 'helps to raise proportionately the rate of profit attributed to social capital as a whole'. In fact, both effects may well occur simultaneously, the net effect on the rate of profit being an empirical matter affected by specific sets of circumstances. Both accounts are, in any case, highly functionalist (cf. FUNCTIONALISM), and imply acceptance of a theory in which the activities of the state are simply determined by the demands of capital.

The notion of collective consumption raises a range of issues that are crucial for urban analysis. It has given rise to a number of attempts to classify the expenditure of the state, especially at the local level. It has proved very difficult in practice to make theoretical categories of state expenditure (social investment, social consumption and social expenses) fit the concrete categories of state expenditure in precise terms (see FISCAL CRISIS). Nevertheless, the attempt to do so has produced some helpful insights into the role of the state and trends in its activities (e.g. Dunleavy, 1984; Saunders, 1980).

At a conceptual level the process of collective consumption has been used to define the city. For Castells (1976, p. 148) 'the "city" is a residential unit of labour power . . . defined as . . . a unit of collective consumption corresponding more or less to the daily organization of a section of labour power' which might be defined by patterns of commuting. Semantics aside, this view of the city certainly opens up a valuable perspective for urban research but, in divorcing production and consumption and in treating space as a mere container, such views also tend to separate in theory what is inseparable in practice and so to impose rationalist concepts upon the real world. This leads in turn to distinctions being made between, for example, 'urban political economy (analysis of the significance of space for capital accumulation), spatial sociology (analysis of the significance of spatial concentration for social relationships), and "urban" sociology (analysis of social provisions in the context of the relationship between the state, the private sector and the population of consumers)' (Saunders, 1981, p. 258).

Finally, the concept of collective consumption raises a range of political questions which, in Castells' formulation, are central to the urban question. As the state

73

assumes more and more responsibility for the provision of the means of collective consumption, rationality and fiscal crises affecting the provision become increasingly politicized and so involve sections of the population well beyond the working class alone (cf. CRISIS, CRITICAL THEORY). Crises in state provision therefore generate widely based urban struggles from which SOCIAL MOVEMENTS (e.g. Lowe, 1991) may arise to challenge capitalist social relations and/or the legitimacy of the current political order.

Two difficulties are immediately apparent in this account: the translation of contradiction and crisis into struggle; and the translation of struggle into an urban social movement. The individual consumption of services provided collectively may well undermine the development of a social consciousness of crisis, while divisions of collective interest in services provided both by the state and by private capital, e.g. housing, education, health care, will tend to fragment rather than to coalesce class interests. Such an argument lies behind the so-called DUAL THEORIES OF THE STATE (e.g. Saunders, 1981, 1984). Furthermore, the broadening of the field of potential conflict with the increasing importance of collective means of consumption also complicates the relationships between individuals, groups and political action. Formal political activity may well become increasingly significant and possibly destructive of more radical political challenges (e.g. Pickvance, 1976, 1977). Indeed, Castells (1983) shifts attention away from the structural generation of crisis and conflict, towards a concern for the diverse role of consciousness and social action in the transformation of the conditions of everyday life (Smith and Tardanico, 1987).

Although there are serious theoretical and practical problems associated with the notion of collective consumption, the problems lie in the way in which the concept has been used, not least by its originators, rather than in the concept itself, which remains both challenging and helpful, as its continued but modified use in urban political analysis testifies (see, e.g., Castells, 1983; Dunleavy, 1984; Pinch,

1985; Topalov, 1989). Nevertheless, the return to empiricism and the individual in urban research and the rise of the liberal state during the 1980s (Castells, 1988) poses questions not only for the concept itself but for the trajectory of urban development in an increasingly polarized society under conditions of intensified inter-urban competition.   RL

References and Suggested Reading

Castells, M. 1976: Theoretical propositions for an experimental study of urban social movements. In Pickvance, C. G., ed., *Urban sociology: critical essays*. London: Methuen, pp. 147–73.

Castells, M. 1977: *The urban question: a Marxist approach*. London: Edward Arnold, pp. 437–71 (originally published in 1972).

Castells, M. 1983: *The city and the grassroots: a cross-cultural theory of urban social movements*. London: Edward Arnold.

Castells, M. 1988: High technology and urban dynamics in the United States. In Dogan, M. and Kasarda, J., eds, *The metropolis era*, volume 1. *A world of giant cities*. Newbury park, CA: Sage, pp. 85–110.

Dunleavy, P. 1980: *Urban political analysis*. London: Macmillan.

Dunleavy, P. 1984: The limits to local government. In Boddy, M. and Fudge, C., eds, *Local socialism?* London: Macmillan, pp. 49–81.

Lojkine, J. 1976: Contribution to a Marxist theory of urbanization. In Pickvance, C. G., ed., *Urban sociology: critical essays*. London: Methuen, pp. 119–46.

Lowe, S. 1991: *Urban social movements: the city after Castells*. London: Macmillan.

Pickvance, C. G., ed. 1976: *Urban sociology: critical essays*. London: Methuen/New York: St. Martin's Press, pp. 1–32, 198–218.

Pickvance, C. G. 1977: Marxist approaches to the study of urban politics. *Int. J. urban and reg. Res.* 1, pp. 218–55.

Pinch, S. P. 1985: *Cities and services: the geography of collective consumption*. London: Routledge and Kegan Paul.

Pinch, S. P. 1989: Collective consumption. In Wolch, J. and Dear, M., eds., *The power of geography*. London: Unwin Hyman, pp. 41–60.

Saunders, P. 1980: *Urban politics*. London: Penguin, pp. 103–97.

Saunders, P. 1981: *Social theory and the urban question*. London: Hutchinson; New York: Holmes and Meier, ch. 8.

Saunders, P. 1984: Rethinking local politics. In Boddy, M. and Fudge, C., eds, *Local socialism?* London: Macmillan.

Smith, M. P. and Tardanico, R. 1987: Urban theory reconsidered: production, reproduction and collective action. In Smith, M. P. and Feagin, J. R., eds, *The capitalist city.* Oxford: Blackwell, ch. 4.

Topalov, C. 1989: A history of urban research: the French experience since 1965. *Int. J. urban and reg. Res.* 13, pp. 625–51.

collinearity A statistical problem in multiple REGRESSION analysis. If two or more of the independent variables are substantially intercorrelated, the resulting regression coefficients are biased and inefficient statements of the true relationships.   RJJ

colonialism The establishment and maintenance of rule, for an extended period of time, by a sovereign power over a subordinate and alien people that is separate from the ruling power. Colonialism has been associated with 'colonization' which involves the physical settlement of people (i.e. settlers) from the imperial centre to the colonial periphery (for example, the ancient Greek colonies, or British settlers in Kenya). Characteristic features of the colonial situation include political and legal domination over an alien society, relations of economic and political dependence and exploitation between imperial power and colony, and racial and cultural inequality (Fanon, 1966). Colonialism is a variant of IMPERIALISM, the latter understood as unequal territorial relationships among states based on subordination and domination, and typically associated with a distinct form of contemporary CAPITALISM, such as the emergence of monopolies and transnational enterprises. As a form of territorial expansion, colonialism is intimately related to uneven development within a developing global capitalist system and with new configurations of the international division of labour (see DEVELOPMENT; UNEVEN DEVELOPMENT; Barratt-Brown, 1974). In the modern period (since 1870), colonialism has emerged as a general description of the state of subjection of non-European societies as a result of specific forms of

European, American and Japanese imperial expansion, organization and rule (Fieldhouse, 1981). Colonialism and anti-colonialism have been fundamental forces in the making of the THIRD WORLD and in the shaping of the modern world system.

Modern colonialisms can be classified according to the timing and the manner in which alien territories were incorporated, usually through violent conquest and plunder, into a world system (see WORLD-SYSTEMS ANALYSIS). More precisely, variations in colonial experience arise from the specific combination of: (i) the form of capitalist political economy at specific moments in world time; (ii) different forms of colonial state and interests which they represented; and (iii) the diversity of pre-colonial societies upon which European domination was imposed. In the context of a geographical separation of colonizer and colonized, all colonialisms must confront the critical questions of how the colonies are to be administered, financed and made profitable. Colonial states were central to the establishment of conditions by which revenue could be raised (i.e. taxation and customs), labour regimes (based on various forms of free or servile labour) instituted to promote commodity production, and political alliances sealed to maintain the fiction of local participation and yet ensure imperial hegemony (see HEGEMONY; STATE).

The age of colonialism began in the fifteenth century with the European expansion in Africa, Asia and the New World. Led by Spain and Portugal, and secondarily other Western European powers, colonialism expanded by violent conquest and settlement after a period of extensive exploration. The most ambitious colonial project was established under Spanish auspices in the New World, involving complex forms of direct and indirect rule and administration, Spanish settlement through land and labour grants (the *encomienda* and the *repartimiento* systems), and new forms of economic exploitation associated with plantations and haciendas, and labour-intensive mining for bullion (Wallerstein, 1974). This first phase of colonialism is usually assumed to reflect the search for wealth in the form of gold, ivory and slaves, but the origins of European expansion also lie in the complex evolution of European mercantile competition, and in regional political developments associated with the crisis of European FEUDALISM (Wolf, 1982). Colonialism emerged in the context of both limited technological capability (the colonies were often geographically distant from the imperial centre and hence relatively autonomous) and at a specific moment in world time (late feudalism). While early colonialism is often seen as mercantile in nature, promoted by European states through merchant companies, its impact on production and international political economy generally was not simply confined to the promotion of exchange. For example, millions of slaves were forcibly taken from Africa to work on plantations in the Caribbean and the US South, while mining and ranching enterprises linked the New World into new circuits of international trade in mass commodities (Stavrianos, 1980).

The old colonial system erupted from the contradictions of European feudalism and lasted for three centuries. It was disrupted in the eighteenth century by the rapid advance of industrial capitalism in England, which ushered in a second phase of colonialism, much shorter in duration and rooted in an expansionary world capitalism (see IMPERIALISM). The century between 1820 and the First World War (1914–18) saw the growth of a modern colonial order backed by complete European hegemony over world trade, finance and shipping, and by new forms of political and military authority sustained by technology, applied science and information systems. Between 1870 and 1918, the colonial powers added an average of 240 000 square miles each year to their possessions; between 1875 and 1915 one-quarter of the globe's land surface was distributed or redistributed as colonies among half a dozen states (Hobsbawm, 1987). Britain, France and Germany increased their colonies by 4 million, 3.5 million, and 1 million square miles respectively; Belgium and Italy, and the USA and Japan, each increased their holdings by roughly 1 million and 100 000 square miles respectively. This phase of 'classical imperialism' was no longer cast in terms of *laissez faire* and mercantilism, but was rooted in a new phase of capitalist development and of inter-imperial rivalry.

Modern colonialism took a variety of forms. A useful taxonomy employs the coordinates of forms of commodity production, labour regime and political rule (Hicks, 1969). In the case of Africa there are three broad forms (Amin, 1974): settler colonies (e.g. Kenya or Mozambique) in which direct rule by a settler class was associated with plantation-based export commodity production (for example, cotton, tea and sugar); trade or trading post economies (e.g. Nigeria or Senegal) characterized by indirect rule (Britain's Dual Mandate) through local ruling classes who acted as colonial bureaucrats, and peasant-based production of export commodities such as palm oil and peanuts; and mine concessions (e.g. South Africa) in which transnational capital dominated the national economy, and migrant labour recruited, often by direct compulsion in the first instance, from 'native reserves' for work in the mines, overdetermined the shape of the local political economy (see MIGRANT LABOUR).

Efforts to explain the origins and timing, and the character and consequences, of modern colonialism have produced a vast literature. Colonialism has been seen as a benign force of economic modernization and social advancement (the so-called *mission civilatrice*) ensuring law and order, private property and contract, basic infrastructure and modern politico-legal institutions (Bauer, 1976; MODERNIZATION). It has also been posited within the Marxist theoretical tradition as an instrument of wholesale destruction, dependency and systematic exploitation, producing distorted economies, sociopsychological disorientation, and massive poverty and neocolonial dependency (Baran, 1957; Frank 1969; Rodney, 1972; see DEPENDENCE; MARXIST GEOGRAPHY; NEOCOLONIALISM). Some lines of neo-Marxist thinking have posited that colonial capitalism was 'progressive', acting as a powerful engine of social change (Warren, 1980); other, equally controversial, Marxist research has posited a distinctive colonial mode of production (Alavi, 1975). What is clear, however, is that the shift from informal spheres of influence to formal colonial rule in the nineteenth century is rooted in a new phase of capitalist transformation (sometimes called the 'second' industrial revolution) in which inter-capitalist rivalry and the growth of transnational forms of industrial and finance capital promoted a search for raw materials, new markets and new investment opportunities.

The colonial experience involved both resistance and adaptation to colonial rule. Western education and missionary activity, while introduced as a means of training lower order civil servants and as the civilizing arm of the colonial order, had contradictory consequences. The first generation of anti-colonial nationalist leaders were often products of the civil service and mission schools, who continued their education beyond the limits set by their colonial teachers. In the period after 1945, the rise of anti-colonial movements in the colonies and the economic crises within an ageing imperial system both contributed towards the rapid process of decolonization. The colonial system was found by the imperial powers to be expensive and increasingly ungovernable. Colonialism was politically and ideologically discredited by emergent nationalist movements, which were often actively supported by the Socialist bloc. Independence of colonial rule came quickly in the period after the Second World War although white settler colonies were especially resistant to any notion of indigenous rule. Independence was only achieved in such cases through organized insurrection (e.g. the Mau Mau in Kenya) or through a long guerilla war of liberation (e.g. Mozambique, Angola and Zimbabwe). There is a general sense throughout much of the THIRD WORLD that decolonization has not resulted in meaningful economic or political independence. The persistence of primary export production and of dependent political elites linked to former colonial powers suggests that colonialism has been transformed into 'perpetual neocolonialism' (Abdel-Fadil, 1989).   MW

References

Abdel-Fadil, M. 1989: Colonialism. In Eatwell, J., Milgate, M. and Newmans, P., eds, *Economic development*. Oxford: Blackwell, pp. 61–7.

Alavi, H. 1975: India and the colonial mode of production. In Miliband, R. and Saville, J., eds, *The socialist register*. London: Merlin, pp. 167–87.

Amin, S. 1974: *Unequal development*. New York: Monthly Review Press.

Baran, P. 1957: *The political economy of growth*. New York: Monthly Review Press.

Barratt-Brown, M. 1974: *The economics of imperialism*. London: Penguin.

Bauer, P. T. 1976: *Dissent on development*. Cambridge, MA: Harvard University Press.

Fanon, F. 1966: *The wretched of the Earth*. London: Penguin.

Fieldhouse, D. 1981: *Colonialism 1870–1945*. London: Weidenfeld and Nicolson.

Frank, A. G. 1969: *Development and underdevelopment in Latin America*. New York: Monthly Review Press.

Hicks, J. 1969: *A theory of economic history*. Oxford: Clarendon Press.

Hobsbawm, E. 1987: *Age of empire 1875–1914*. New York: Pantheon.

Rodney, W. 1972: *How Europe underdeveloped Africa*. London: Bogle.

Stavrianos, G. 1980: *Global rift*. New York: Free Press.

Wallerstein, I. 1974: *The modern world system*, volume 1. New York: Academic Press.

Warren, B. 1980: *Imperialism: pioneer of capitalism*. London: Verso.

Wolf, E. 1982: *Europe and the people without history*. Berkeley, CA: University of California Press.

Suggested Reading

Brewer, A. 1980: *Marxist theories of imperialism*. London: Routledge and Kegan Paul.

Etherington, N. 1984: *Theories of imperialism*. London: Croom Helm.

command economy An economy in which the means of production are owned and controlled by the STATE, and in which CENTRAL PLANNING of the structure and quantity of outputs prevails. The term is used to distinguish economies such as those previously found in Eastern Europe from CAPITALISM or a MIXED ECONOMY. The recent dismantling of command economies in Eastern Europe reflects their inability in actual practice to produce goods in the quantities that people had come to expect. While there are difficulties of coordination, the lack of incentives towards efficiency seems to have been a more serious problem. However, it must be recognized that change in Eastern Europe is an outcome of a crisis of political legitimacy and not simply of economic failure.   DMS

commercial geography One of the predecessors of ECONOMIC GEOGRAPHY, which was mainly concerned with amassing and presenting factual material about economic activity in the various parts of the world. Such compilations, of which the many editions of Chisholm's *Handbook of commercial geography* (1889) were the best known, were characteristic of an era in which geography was promoted as a major vehicle for informing colonial policies: Chisholm's book was in two main parts, the first giving details of the geography of production of various commodities, and the second providing a world regional catalogue of what was produced where. RJJ

Reference

Chisholm, G. G. 1889: *Handbook of commercial geography*. London: Longman.

Suggested Reading

Wise, M. J. 1975: A university teacher of geography. *Trans. Inst. Br. Geogr.* 66, pp. 1–16.

commodity Commodities are objects that are produced for the purpose of being exchanged; but this has not always been the case. For example, in many subsistence societies objects are produced simply so that people can carry out their everyday lives, without thought of exchange (see SUBSISTENCE AGRICULTURE). However, in a society driven by the production of commodities, entrepreneurs choose both the commodity and the method by which it is produced according to whether they expect that the commodity will sell at a high enough price to realize an adequate profit on the money that must be invested in its production. The mechanism of MARKET EXCHANGE is left to match up the hunt by commodity producers to realize a profit and the presumed needs of consumers.

Marx (1977, p. 163) stated that 'a commodity at first sight is an extremely obvious, trivial thing'. Thus, for some commentators, the market exchange of commodities defines what commodities are. But for other commentators, including Ricardo and Marx, this view does not go far enough. It *is* obvious and trivial. They want to look behind the mechanism of exchanging commodities at the value created in producing the commodity in order to understand fully what commodities are (Sheppard and Barnes, 1990). In particular, these commentators distinguish between a commodity's use value, exchange value and labour value. The *use value* is simply the usefulness of a product to an individual. The *exchange value* is defined as the number of units of another commodity for which a commodity is exchanged in the marketplace. Finally, the *labour value* is a general measure of the value created in the process of producing a commodity (see MARXIAN ECONOMICS).

Not all commodities are equal, however. Two types of commodity hold a special place in most economic theories. The first of these is labour itself: one of the abiding principles of capitalist societies is that people who work must themselves become commodities, exchanged in labour markets (see CAPITALISM). The second special commodity is MONEY, which has multiple functions – as a measure of value, a medium of exchange, a store of value and a means of payment. Money is also a good example of *commodity fetishism*, in which social relations appear as things. Thus, in the case of money, social relations with others are secured by the money form. Similarly, RENT transforms land into a commodity with a price on it, and 'makes it seem as though money comes from the soil' (Harvey, 1982).

What is certain is that the process of *commodification* has reached into every nook and cranny of modern life (see MODERNITY). Practically every human activity in Western countries either relies on or has certain commodities associated with it, from births through weddings to funerals, at work or in the home, in peace or in war. Increasingly, the process of commodification has also taken hold in non-Western societies, leading to notions of a global culture based, in part, on the ubiquity of certain commodities and commodity meaning (*Theory, Culture and Society*, 1990).

In some accounts of modern life, the commodity has travelled even deeper, burrowing into the human psyche. Thus the need to make commodities as attractive as possible, so that they will sell in large quantities (and make large profits), leads to the practice of *commodity aesthetics*. Commodities are fashioned that will, as near as possible, mirror consumers' desires. In turn, the potent combination of mass production and the mass media has led to attempts to *create* desire for commodities, through design, advertising and market research (see CONSUMPTION): no wonder that Richards (1991, p. 13) has argued that 'the commodity is the focal point and, increasingly, the arbiter of all representation in capitalist societies'.

Some commentators would go further again. They would have it that the images and signs used to create desire for commodities have become more important than the commodities themselves; people buy commodities because of the images and signs associated with them, rather than vice versa: 'The surface [of the commodity] has been detached and becomes its second skin, which as a rule is incomparably more perfect than the first; it becomes completely disembodied and drifts unencumbered like a multicoloured spirit into every household, preparing the way for the real distribution of the commodity' (Haug, 1986, p. 50). This description of the modern world, one in which the *simulation* of commodities has become its own reality (or 'hyper-reality'), in which the consumption of the images and signs of commodities has become more important than the consumption of commodities, reaches it zenith in the work of Baudrillard. In turn, Baudrillard's description of a world of simulation and hyper-reality has been a key component of work on POSTMODERNISM (Baudrillard, 1988; Gane, 1991a, b; Jameson, 1991).   NJT

References

Baudrillard, J. 1988: *Jean Baudrillard: selected writings*. Cambridge: Polity Press.

Gane, M. 1991a: *Baudrillard: critical and fatal theory*. London: Routledge.

Gane, M. 1991b: *Baudrillard's bestiary*. London: Routledge.

Harvey, D. 1982: *The limits to capital*. Oxford: Blackwell.

Haug, W. F. 1986: *Critique of commodity aesthetics: appearances, sexuality and advertising in capitalistic society*. Cambridge: Polity Press.

Jameson, F. 1991: *Postmodernism, or the cultural logic of late capitalism*. London: Verso.

Marx, K. 1977: *Capital*, volume 1. New York: Viking.

Richards, T. 1991: *The commodity culture of Victorian England*. London: Verso.

Sheppard, E. and Barnes, T. 1990: *The capitalist space economy: geographical analysis after Ricardo, Marx and Sraffa*. London: Unwin Hyman.

Theory, Culture and Society 1990: Special issue on global culture. *Theory, Culture and Society* 7(2–3).

Suggested Reading

Glennie, P., Thrift, N. J. and Whatmore, S. 1993: *Consumer culture*. London: Sage.

common market   One of the forms and stages of formal INTEGRATION between national economies. All restrictions on the movement of goods, labour, capital and enterprise should be removed within a common market which is, therefore, a product of negative integration. But a common market also involves positive integration in the creation of a common TRADE policy towards non-member states, often involving a common external TARIFF and the harmonization of other trading regulations over exports as well as imports. The most ambitious attempt to create a common market remains that of the European Community (EC), which set the Single European Market in place between its 12 member states at the end of December 1992. Other examples include the far less well-developed central American, east African, Andean and Caribbean common markets.

As a stage in the process of international economic integration, common markets involve the further development of more loosely integrated customs unions and FREE TRADE AREAS (for example, the North American Free Trade Area). It may lead on to the creation of closer forms of integration, such as economic and/or monetary union and full economic union, which involve substantial elements of positive as well as negative integration.

The logic behind the creation of a common market is the release of static (e.g. increased trade) and dynamic (e.g. ECONOMIES OF SCALE) gains from the geographical extension of the operation of nationally unencumbered markets. A consequence is the exposure of geographical diversity to more intense competition, and geographically UNEVEN DEVELOPMENT. RL

Suggested Reading

Knox, P. and Agnew, J. 1989: *The geography of the world economy.* London: Edward Arnold/New York: Routledge, Chapman and Hall, pp. 337–60.

Lee, R. 1990: Making Europe: towards a geography of European integration. In Chisholm, M. and Smith, D. M., eds, *Shared space – divided space.* London: Unwin Hyman, pp. 235–59.

Williams, A. M. 1991: *The European Community: contradictions of integration.* Oxford: Blackwell.

common pool resources RESOURCES (natural or otherwise) which are in common ownership because there is no alternative. The resource pool is so large that it is extremely difficult (although usually not entirely impossible) to exclude potential beneficiaries from exploiting them, which raises problems of RESOURCE MANAGEMENT so as to ensure that the pool is not depleted. (See also TRAGEDY OF THE COMMONS.) RJJ

Suggested Reading

Ostrom, E. 1990: *Governing the commons: illustrating the evolution of institutions for collective action.* New York: Cambridge University Press.

communism A body of ideas united by a common ideological tradition which, in modern form, can be traced back to the works of Karl Marx, and which takes as its point of reference the principle of communal ownership of all property. Marx identified two such classless societies (see CLASS): 'primitive communism', usually associated with tribal societies, in which basic economic resources (land and simple technology) were communally owned; and full communism, based on common ownership of the means of production, which could only come about in fully industrialized societies where goods were no longer scarce. According to Marx and his followers, such an end-stage society is preceded by a transitional period of SOCIALISM, characterized by the so-called 'dictatorship of the [industrial] proletariat'. With full communism, the STATE will 'wither away', while differences between town and country, between mental and physical labour, between nationality grouping, and between STATE and collective property will disappear, and social relations will be regulated by the principle 'from each according to his ability, to each according to his needs'. However, not all nineteenth-century Marxists agreed with the necessity of a socialist stage. For instance, the Russian anarchist (see ANARCHISM) and geographer, Peter Kropotkin, saw the driving forces of history in terms of *competition* and *cooperation,* and believed them to be analogous to laws of NATURE; he saw no need for any post-revolutionary state, regardless of its purpose or social composition, for he argued that, whatever the MODE OF PRODUCTION, the state would always be a primary source of exploitation. These views aside, today state socialist countries all derive their support and legitimation from the claim that they are implementing communist ideas (see FORM OF ECONOMIC INTEGRATION). GES

Suggested Reading

Breibart, M. 1981: Peter Kropotkin, the anarchist geographer. In Stoddart, D. R., ed., *Geography, ideology and social concern.* Oxford: Blackwell/New York: Barnes and Noble, pp. 134–53.

Evans, M. 1975: *Karl Marx.* London: Allen and Unwin/Bloomington: Indiana University Press.

Zinoviev, A. 1984: *The reality of communism.* London: Victor Gollancz.

community A SOCIAL NETWORK of interacting individuals, usually concentrated into a defined territory. The term has been very widely used and is applied in a wide range of (both academic and vernacular) contexts. It thus has a large number of separate (often implicit) definitions (Stacey, 1969) and as a consequence 'What community means has been disputed for even longer than the effects of place' (Bell and Newby, 1978): in the UK, for example, ETHNIC groups are often referred to as communities, irrespective of whether they occupy clearly identifiable TERRITORIES.

Bell and Newby follow Schmalenbach (1961) and define community as something more than the sense of belonging to an active social network – which they term 'communion'. Membership of a community involves 'a matter of custom and of shared modes of thought or expression, all of which have no other sanction than tradition': one belongs to a community, but may be conscious of that only when it is threatened. Thus a community does not involve emotional ties, which are characteristic of communion: a community may stimulate such experiences, providing the context within which they can develop, but all communities are not necessarily in communion.

Interest in communities in sociology and SOCIAL GEOGRAPHY can be linked to the work of the CHICAGO SCHOOL, and in particular its evaluation of the social and behavioural consequences of URBANIZATION (cf. URBANISM). Tönnies's original concept of *Gemeinschaft* identified communities as particular types of social network (i.e. community as a form of human association), and was not concerned with community as either a local social system or a finite, bounded physical location (i.e. a territorially defined social whole). Later workers brought the three together into an all-embracing definition, and thus stimulated the term's wide range of usages.

For the Chicago sociologists and their followers, the enhanced definition of community was consistent with their contrast of the (assumed) impersonality and social disorganization of urban life with the (also assumed) closely integrated social networks of rural areas, as expressed in their concept of a RURAL–URBAN CONTINUUM. Rural communities were presented not only as the norm against which urban societies could be compared (see URBAN VILLAGE) but also as the desirable condition: rural communities were integrated and stable and so not conducive to individual ALIENATION and social problems, whereas

urban societies were much more disorganized, and potentially characterized by ANOMIE and thus widespread social disorganization. This glorification of the rural was associated with anti-urban sentiments, as in the GARDEN CITY movement in late nineteenth- to early twentieth-century Britain (see Pepper, 1990): rural societies were good because their communities were in communion, whereas those in urban areas were not. Only later studies (such as Frankenberg, 1966) argued that whereas urban areas may lack certain positive characteristics relative to rural counterparts, they may also have their own positive features which are lacking from rural areas.

Community studies declined in popularity throughout the social sciences (except social anthropology) from the 1960s on. The introduction of the concept of LOCALITY in the 1980s suggested a returning interest in such local social systems to some observers, but Giddens (1984) nowhere equates LOCALE with community in his presentation of the former as central to STRUCTURATION THEORY. (See also CONTEXTUAL THEORY.) RJJ

References

Bell, C. and Newby, H. 1978: Community, communion, class and community action: the social sources of the new urban politics. In Herbert, D. T. and Johnston, R. J., eds, *Social areas in cities: processes, patterns and problems.* Chichester: John Wiley, pp. 283–302.

Frankenberg, R. 1966: *Communities in Britain: social life in town and country.* London: Penguin.

Giddens, A. 1984: *The constitution of society.* Cambridge: Polity Press.

Pepper, D. 1990: Geography and landscapes of anarchistic visions of Britain: the examples of Morris and Kropotkin. *Contemp. Issues Geogr. Ed.* 3(2), pp. 63–79.

Schmalenbach, H. 1961: The sociological category of communion. In Parsons, T. *et al.*, eds, *Theories of society* 1, pp. 331–47.

Stacey, M. 1969: The myth of community studies. *Br. J. Soc.* 20, pp. 134–47.

commuting The technical term for journeys to work. Because commuters are major generators of traffic flows within cities, models of commuting patterns (see LOWRY MODEL) have been developed to aid in transport planning and decisions on the location of new residential and employment areas. RJJ

compage All of the features of the physical, biotic and societal environments that are functionally associated with the human occupancy of the Earth. As a revival of an ancient term meaning 'a way of joining or connecting matter', it was introduced to geography by Derwent Whittlesey (1956) in an attempt to give greater precision to several aspects of REGIONAL GEOGRAPHY: it implies a highly diversified although unitary complex. MDB

Reference

Whittlesey, D. 1956: Southern Rhodesia: an African compage. *Ann. Ass. Am. Geogr.* 46, pp. 1–97.

comparative advantage The principle whereby individuals (or territories) produce those goods or services for which they have the greatest cost or efficiency advantage over others, or for which they have the least disadvantage. The outcome tends to be specialization. A gifted individual or resource-rich region may be able to produce everything more efficiently than others that are less well endowed, but as long as some comparative advantage exists specialization may benefit all. An example is that of the best lawyer in town who is also the best typist: it pays the lawyer to concentrate on the lucrative practice of the law and to hire a typist (who has a comparative advantage in typing relative to knowledge of the law). One region may be able to produce two goods more efficiently than another region, but it pays to concentrate on the good for which there is greatest comparative advantage and buy the other from the second region.

The notion of comparative advantage is important in understanding regional specialization, whereby all regions gain from the interchange of products even if they could satisfy their own needs. A condition for realizing the benefits of comparative advantage is free trade. At the international scale, market imperfections such as tariff barriers to free trade can impede specialization based on comparative advantage, protecting domestic production of goods which could not withstand open competition. The objective may be to ensure more 'balanced' economic development and to avoid problems associated with narrow product specialization. DMS

comparative cost analysis The practice of evaluating the COMPARATIVE ADVANTAGE of alternative locations with respect to the cost of production. Comparative cost analysis can serve both to judge the efficiency of existing locations and to assist with the choice of site for a new facility. The theoretical foundations are derived from VARIABLE COST ANALYSIS.

Comparative cost analysis is generally adopted when there are relatively few locations to evaluate and where the inputs involved are also few. Primary metal manufacturing lends itself to this approach. Alternative locations are identified, the cost of each of the inputs in each location is found, and these are aggregated into a figure for total cost. The COST STRUCTURE of the industry can provide initial guidance on which inputs are likely to be of greatest importance to total cost. Inputs that are insignificant in the general cost structure can be omitted with little effect on the final result, unless there is evidence that they may be unusually expensive in some of the locations to be considered. Inputs with constant cost in geographical space can be omitted, unless there is a subsequent analysis in which sales or revenue are considered to be sensitive to the total cost of production (see VARIABLE REVENUE ANALYSIS).

Comparative cost analysis is the most common practical means of making an informed choice among alternative locations. The major drawbacks are the difficulty of calculating total cost when more than a few inputs are involved, the problem of evaluating the effect of linkages and other EXTERNAL ECONOMIES, and failure to incorporate the demand factor. DMS

Suggested Reading

Smith, D. M. 1981: *Industrial location: an economic geographical analysis*, second edition. New York: John Wiley.

complementarity Complementarity between region A and region B implies that A produces (or has the potential to produce) goods or services of which B has a deficit (or potential deficit). The term was coined by Ullman (1956) to describe one of the bases of SPATIAL INTERACTION. He argued that complementarity may arise either from AREAL DIFFERENTIATION (in resource endowment, or in social, cultural and economic conditions) or as a result of ECONOMIES OF SCALE. In broader usage complementarity implies that regions produce (or could produce) quite different mixes of goods and services which are (or could be) exchanged between them: in this broad sense complementarity is related to the economic concepts of COMPARATIVE ADVANTAGE.   AMH

Reference

Ullman, E. L. 1956: The role of transportation and the bases for interactions. In Thomas, W. L., ed., *Man's role in changing the face of the Earth.* Chicago: University of Chicago Press, pp. 862–80.

components of change An accounting framework for studying the changing distribution of various components of a population, most commonly employment in various industries and/or occupations. Changes in the various areas of a larger spatial unit (such as regions of a country) over a defined time period are broken down into three components:

(1) *in situ* changes, reflecting the growth or decline of employment at industrial plants existing in the area at the start of the period;

(2) birth and death changes, resulting from the opening of new plants during the period and the closure of others; and

(3) migration changes, the outcome of some plants being moved to an area and others being moved from it.

The net change in an area (in its industrial employment in this example) is thus represented by the equation:

net change in employment = (employment in new plants opened during the period) - (employment in plants closed during the period) + (net change in employment in plants surviving through the period) + (employment in plants moved to the area from elsewhere) -

(employment in plants moved away from the area).

Studies of more than one area must subdivide the migration change component into plants which shed employment during the move, plants which increase their employment during the move, and plants which experience no change. (See also SHIFT-SHARE MODEL.)   RJJ

Suggested Reading

Mason, C. M. 1980: Industrial change in Greater Manchester 1966–1975: a components of change approach. *Urban Stud.* 17, pp. 173–84.

compositional theory An approach in which human activity is broken down into general categories based on principles of *similarity*, which are then recombined to constitute an explanation of (part of) social life. Kant described such an approach as the construction of a *logical* classification (see KANTIANISM), but in modern geography the term 'compositional theory' is derived from Hägerstrand (1974), who used it to accentuate the *theoretical* implications of such an approach. He particularly wanted to establish a difference between approaches of this kind, which he supposed to be characteristic of both mainstream natural and social sciences, and his own TIME-GEOGRAPHY, which he represented as a CONTEXTUAL THEORY.

Thrift (1983) has suggested that compositional approaches: (a) rely upon 'a formal–logical method based on the tool of abstraction'; and (b) correspond to the so-called 'immanent' explanations of natural science (Kennedy, 1979). Both claims are problematic. ABSTRACTION has a number of different meanings, but within the philosophy of REALISM it clearly entails the identification of INTERNAL RELATIONS which, unlike a compositional approach, are based on connection rather than similarity; and if immanent explanations are concerned with essentially *unchanging* properties and processes, then a number of theoretical foundations on which conventional human geography depends have provided more historically and geographically nuanced categories than Thrift implies. (See also CLASSIFICATION.)   DG

References

Hägerstrand, T. 1974: Tidgeografisk beskrivning – syfte och postulat. *Svensk Geogr. Arsbok* 50, pp. 86–94.

Kennedy, B. A. 1979: A naughty world. *Trans. Inst. Br. Geogr.* n.s. 4, pp. 550–8.

Thrift, N. J. 1983: On the determination of social action in space and time. *Environ. Plann. D, Society and Space* 1, pp. 23–58.

computer-assisted cartography

(or *digital mapping*) Cartographic applications that involve the use of the hardware and software components of digital computers. In the 1970s and early 1980s this distinguished between purely automated methods, which mainly speed up production, and those which assist in upgrading cartographic methods and practice. By the mid-1980s much of the latter were subsumed within GEOGRAPHICAL INFORMATION SYSTEMS (Maguire, 1991), while the former became more the domain of major mapping agencies whose goals included automated map production, and scale-free digital map databases.

Rhind (1977) discussed the benefits of 'computer-aided cartography', among which are four groups important to human geography:

(a) minimizing reliance on maps as data sources, since printed maps are often seriously out-of-date;

(b) allowing experimentation with graphical and statistical components of the map image, using the intermediary of a graphic display;

(c) enabling easy implementation of formal cartographic rules – computer-assisted methods obviate the requirement that cartographers be artistically skilled, since tools are automated and can comply with existing guidelines;

(d) by making the tools of cartography generally available, overcoming time and complexity problems of statistical processing, generalization and enhancement, it is now possible to create map images which would hitherto have been difficult.

At the time of Rhind's paper the cost of technology was a very substantial component of digital mapping. Computers were expensive and their power somewhat limited. Hardware is now a small component of overall applications costs (Dangermond, 1991). Similarly, software prices have also fallen – in the context of the functionality that they provide. The main area of attention in the late 1980s and early 1990s has been what Dangermond terms the 'data bottleneck', coupled with the high costs of staff for projects. The result of these developments is that research has moved away from system development (which is mainly undertaken in the commercial sector), to data provision, costs, accuracy and new software techniques of the 'blue skies' type. Examples include the following:

(a) The development of national digital map databases, mainly by national mapping agencies. Agencies need to meet the demands of dynamically changing societies by providing more frequently updated cartographic information at many scales. One goal here can be a 'scale-free' digital map database, although Sowton (1991) notes the extreme difficulty of meeting such a goal.

(b) Evaluating the accuracy, resolution, integration, costs and legal liability of cartographic information (Fisher, 1991).

(c) The generalization and representation of cartographic data (Buttenfield and McMaster, 1991).

(d) Different visualization methods, such as for those with visual difficulties (Nagel and Coulson, 1990), and also in areas such as 'virtual reality' (see SURFACE).   MJB

References

Buttenfield, B. P. and McMaster, R. B., eds 1991: *Map generalisation: making rules for knowledge representation.* London: Longman.

Dangermond, J. 1991: The commercial setting of GIS. In Maguire, D. J., Goodchild, M. F. and Rhind, D. W., eds, *Geographical information systems: principles and applications*, volume 1. London: Longman, pp. 65–75.

Fisher, P. F. 1991: Spatial data sources and data problems. In Maguire, D. J., Goodchild, M. F. and Rhind, D. W., eds, *Geographical information systems: principles and applications*, volume 1. London: Longman, pp. 175–89.

Maguire, D. J. 1991: An overview and definition of GIS. In Maguire, D. J., Goodchild, M. F. and Rhind, D. W., eds, *Geographical information systems: principles and applications*, volume 1. London: Longman, pp. 9–20.

Nagel, D. L. D. and Coulson, M. R. C. 1990: Tactual mobility maps: a comparative study. *Cartographica* 27(2), 47–63.

Rhind, D. W. 1977: Computer-aided cartography. *Trans. Inst. Br. Geogr.* n.s. 2, pp. 71–97.

Sowton, M. 1991: Development of GIS-related activities at the Ordnance Survey. In Maguire, D. J., Goodchild, M. F. and Rhind, D. W., eds, *Geographical information systems: principles and applications*, volume 2. London: Longman, pp. 23–38.

Suggested Reading

Cowen, D. J. 1988: GIS versus CAD versus DBMS: What are the differences? *Photogramm. Engng. Remote Sensing* 54(11), pp. 1551–4.

Tomlinson, R. F. 1988: The impact of the transition from analogue to digital cartographic representation. *Am. Cartogr.* 15(3), 249–62.

concentration and centralization

The tendency towards localization of economic activity in and around a relatively small number of urban centres. This condition is also referred to as polarization or AGGLOMERATION. It arises from the spatial concentration of the market, sources of information, bases for control and decision-making, inter-activity linkages and other EXTERNAL ECONOMIES. Concentration and centralization increase the disadvantages of peripheral locations and contribute to the economic and social deprivation commonly found with greater distance from the core (see CORE–PERIPHERY MODEL).

Spatial concentration and centralization are associated with the tendency for economic activity to be organized in units of increasing size and within a hierarchical organizational structure. The growing concentration of ownership of capitalist business activity was evident during the nineteenth century, decades before the contemporary emergence of the transnational or MULTINATIONAL CORPORATION. The large capitalist corporation of today may have productive capacity and sales outlets in many different nations, but ownership and control remain vested in the headquarters that are usually located within one of the major financial centres of Europe or North America. Concentration of capital in a non-spatial sense, i.e. in the hands of fewer larger owners, is an important feature of advanced capitalism, and a source of concentration of political, as well as economic, power that transcends that of NATION-STATES. The associated geographical concentration of certain kinds of economic activity facilitates the flow of capital between different uses and the pace of circulation and turnover on which profits depend.

The spatial organization of the ministries that controlled productive activity under Eastern European SOCIALISM bore some resemblance to that of the multi-plant firm under CAPITALISM. Production was dispersed, but control concentrated at the top of the hierarchy and hence spatially concentrated. Similar questions concerning local autonomy of action and the capacity for information feedback up the hierarchy arise under this type of state-bureaucratic organization as under capitalism. The crucial issue is the degree of local control of local affairs that is possible under either arrangement. The alternative would be some kind of locally dispersed system of production without central control, as proposed by adherents of ANARCHISM.

DMS

confirmatory data analysis

The use of statistical procedures, including SIGNIFICANCE TESTS, to evaluate HYPOTHESES. (See also EXPLORATORY DATA ANALYSIS.)
RJJ

conflict

A situation involving struggle among two or more protagonists. Within geography, studies of conflict are characteristic not only of POLITICAL GEOGRAPHY, but also of much of SOCIAL and ECONOMIC GEOGRAPHY. It is increasingly recognized that many of the patterns that geographers analyse are the outcome of conflicts, and that those outcomes themselves provide the context for further conflicts.

Much of the study of conflict focuses on the activities of the STATE. Those in control of the STATE APPARATUS operate what is known as the 'police power', which enables them to restrict individual freedoms in order to promote what they identify as the 'general good'. (In some arguments, this is a necessary state function, since individuals operating freely are unlikely to achieve what is in their own, let alone society's, best interests overall: see TRAGEDY OF THE COMMONS.) Urban land-use ZONING is a good example of the police power in operation, whereby individual freedom to use land for any purpose is constrained to those purposes considered best for the community as a whole.

The state also acts to defend its sovereign TERRITORY (see SOVEREIGNTY, TERRITORIALITY) against external aggressors and, in certain circumstances, to extend that territory, which may involve military activity: the study of GEOPOLITICS is central to the description and analysis of such conflicts.

Finally, the state is frequently called upon to arbitrate in conflicts and to identify and ensure a resolution. Such conflicts as are resolved – usually, although not always, through its quasi-independent judicial apparatus (see LAW, GEOGRAPHY OF) – involve either two or more parties which are claiming some breach of a law (such as a breach of contract) or the state itself claiming that individuals have violated a law or regulation.

Many of the conflicts considered by the state are over the use of land. With the growing realization that the Earth's environment is under very serious threat from human use and abuse (see SUSTAINABLE DEVELOPMENT), the exploitation of natural resources is becoming an increasing concern of states: the issues of CONSERVATION and PRESERVATION are central to many such conflicts at all spatial scales (see LAW OF THE SEA, for example). The use of land is also a source of conflicts among neighbours – for example, between the residents of a district who wish to protect its character and those who are promoting alterations to it – with the potential for EXTERNALITIES that will affect their own properties and levels of living (see Cox and Johnston, 1982).

Many empirical studies of conflicts and their outcomes have been undertaken by geographers, but a substantial number have focused on their appearance only and have failed to understand the context in which they have emerged. Increasingly, however, conflicts – especially those over the environment and land use – are being studied

within a theoretical structure provided by the understanding of CAPITALISM. It is argued that conflict is inherent to the MODE OF PRODUCTION: its fundamental conflict is between the two main economic CLASSES, the bourgeoisie and the proletariat, but within this there are many others involving fractions of the two classes, and even fractions of the same class. In most of such conflicts the issue is the manipulation of space and the use of NATURE to promote the accumulation of wealth, as shown in Massey's (1984) studies of the conflicts between employers and their labour forces in the restructuring of British industry, and Clark's (1988) analysis of the role of trades unions in the reorganization of the American space economy (see also Griffiths and Johnston, 1991).

At the international scale, the growing intersection of studies in political geography and international relations is providing a structure for analysing the geography of conflicts between countries. Taylor (1989), for example, has linked the changing geography of UNEVEN DEVELOPMENT to the rise and fall of particular nations as world powers, and has related the pattern of conflicts, and the geopolitical transitions that often follow from their resolution, to the KONDRATIEFF CYCLES that characterize the operation of the capitalist economy (see WORLD-SYSTEMS ANALYSIS).   RJJ

References

Clark, G. L. 1988: *Unions and communities under siege*. Cambridge: Cambridge University Press.

Cox, K. R. and Johnston, R. J., eds 1982: *Conflict, politics and the urban scene*. London: Longman.

Griffiths, M. J. and Johnston, R. J. 1991: What's in a place? An approach to the concept of place as illustrated by the British National Union of Mineworkers' strike, 1984–85. *Antipode* 23, pp. 185–213.

Massey, D. 1984: *Spatial divisions of labour: social structures and the geography of production*. London: Macmillan.

Taylor, P. J. 1989: *Political geography: world-economy, nation–state and community*, second edition. London: Longman.

congestion This arises where the existing use of some facility exceeds its CARRYING CAPACITY, often generating additional costs for individuals and the wider society. While most commonly discussed with respect to traffic problems, especially urban ones (see Hanson, 1986), congestion can also arise in other circumstances and at much lower population densities (for example, wilderness recreation). In the urban transport case congestion levels depend on traffic volumes, NETWORK characteristics, MODAL SPLIT and the public perception of acceptable levels of service. The costs of any given congestion incident can also vary from one individual to another. The consequences of congestion include frustration and costs of time delays borne by travellers, increased accident rates and environmental POLLUTION (noise and fumes), so creating an EXTERNALITY to the urban economy.   AGH

Reference

Hanson, S., ed. 1986: *The geography of urban transportation.* New York: Guilford Press.

connectivity The degree to which a NETWORK is internally connected. The term is often used in the restricted context of GRAPH THEORY, where it refers to the degree to which nodes are directly connected to each other.   AMH

conservation In some contexts, the efficient and non-wasteful use of NATURAL RESOURCES; in others, any form of environmental protection. The former meaning held sway throughout the 1950s in the United States. It distinguished conservationists (such as Gifford Pinchot) from preservationists (notably John Muir and later Aldo Leopold): the utilitarian concern of the former with RESOURCE MANAGEMENT, or in Samuel Hays' words 'the gospel of efficiency', clashed on a number of occasions with the inherent value which the latter ascribed to NATURE and WILDERNESS. Conservation and preservation are no longer sharply distinct, but the terms are still sometimes used to describe different emphases within ENVIRONMENTALISM (e.g. Passmore, 1974). In the UK, the term conservation has tended not to carry its narrower American connotations; 'nature conservation' represents concerns akin to those of the American preservationists and 'resource conservation' those of the

American conservationists. (In the UK, PRESERVATION denotes the saving of human rather than natural features of the landscape, or what is usually called 'historic preservation' in the US.) To these classic concerns, others such as POLLUTION and the conservation of biodiversity, have been added in recent decades.

The concerns of conservation reflect scepticism about the ability of market mechanisms to guide the use of resources or of the environment towards desirable ends. A narrow version of conservation adopts the utilitarian criteria of NEOCLASSICAL ECONOMICS, but identifies situations of market failure in which STATE intervention is required to achieve optimal ends. Economists have long recognized the endemic nature of market failure in such COMMON POOL RESOURCES as oil, groundwater and ocean fisheries, and the need for management to prevent rapid depletion. Market failures in these and other varieties form central concerns of environmental economics, as does the calculation of optimal rates of use of both renewable and non-renewable resources.

Resource use and conservation, however, increasingly appear to be the products as much of an array of political and social forces as of the forces of market allocation (Blaikie, 1985; Rees, 1985). Government programmes promoting, for example, soil conservation, nature and wildlife protection and energy efficiency, particularly in the developed world, represent a form of conservation concerned not only with the narrow goals of utilitarian efficiency but also with social goals (such as distribution) and with the needs of political interest groups. Many broad versions of conservation now reject the utilitarian criteria of maximizing the discounted present value of resources. Much recent discussion has pointed to the way in which the discounting of future values by the market weighs against sustainable resource use and encourages rapid exploitation, and has addressed the calculation of a lower social discount rate that better protects the interests of future generations. Notions of ecodevelopment or SUSTAINABLE DEVELOPMENT, although still imperfectly conceptualized, hold more promise than the narrowly economic approach for integrating the varied strands of conservation, particularly those of nature conservation or preservation, with the human use of the natural resource base. JEM

References

Blaikie, P. 1985: *The political economy of soil erosion in developing countries*. London: Longman.

Passmore, J. 1974: *Man's responsibility for nature*. London: Duckworth.

Rees, J. 1985: *Natural resources: allocation, economics and policy*. London: Methuen.

Suggested Reading

Emel, J. and Peet, R. 1989: Resource management and natural hazards. In Peet, R. and Thrift, N., eds, *New models in geography*, volume 1. London: Unwin Hyman.

Hays, S. P. 1959: *Conservation and the gospel of efficiency: the progressive conservation movement, 1890–1920*. Cambridge, MA: Harvard University Press.

Mitchell, B. 1989: *Geography and resource management*, second edition. London: Longman Scientific and Technical.

consociationalism A concept and practice of governance based on near unanimous consent among leaders drawn from major sectors of a polity (LANGUAGE, CLASS, REGION or RELIGION) in which the overriding objective is to ensure a politically stable and effective democracy. As a form of socioterritorial control, it is most closely associated with Belgium, Holland and Switzerland. To succeed, political elites must possess the ability to accommodate divergent interests, transcend the most salient cultural CLEAVAGES, be committed to STATE cohesion, and reflect support from each sector of their divergent COMMUNITIES. The recent politicization of ethnoterritorial and linguistic cleavages, however, has questioned the effectiveness of consociational solutions (see PLURALISM). GES

Suggested Reading

Duchacek, I. 1986: *The territorial dimension of politics. Within, Among, and Across Nations*. Boulder, CO: Westview Press.

Lijphart, A. 1977: *Democracy in plural societies*. New Haven: Yale University Press.

consumer services Services which are ordinarily supplied to individual consumers (cf. PRODUCER SERVICES). This definition encompasses a large array of different economic activities and until recently, precisely for this reason, the study of the geography of consumer services was effectively subsumed under a whole set of different headings, such as the geography of RETAILING, the geography of PUBLIC SERVICES, and the geography of TOURISM. However, the geography of consumer services is *now* more likely to be approached under one heading because of an increasing interest in the geography of the workings of private consumer markets, and especially so-called 'quasi-markets' in which public services are supplied on partially marketized lines. (See also COLLECTIVE CONSUMPTION; CONSUMPTION, GEOGRAPHY OF; MONEY, GEOGRAPHY OF; SERVICES, GEOGRAPHY OF.) NJT

Reference

Le Grand, J. and Estrin, S. 1989: *Market socialism*. Oxford: Clarendon Press.

consumption, geography of The study of the geography of consumption of commodities. Until very recently, the study of the geography of consumption had only a fitful history. The BERKELEY SCHOOL had shown an interest in certain issues to do with consumption, most notably food taboos and diets. The geographies of RECREATION and RETAILING sometimes showed tangential concern. But in the 1970s and early 1980s most interest in consumption was, in effect, focused on one commodity only – housing (see HOUSING CLASS, HOUSING STUDIES). In the mid-1980s, this narrow focus began to broaden out, especially through work on 'consumption sectors', but it was not until the late 1980s that consumption started to become an important point of attention in and for itself; for example, through work in social and cultural geography on the 'service class' (see CLASS) (Thrift, 1987). That consumption should have remained undiscovered for so long as an object of human geographical enquiry is certainly remarkable because of its ubiquity in everyday life, its massive economic importance and the large amount of effort that has gone into its understanding elsewhere in the social sciences (Miller, 1987; McCracken, 1990; Willis, 1990). It is all the more remarkable because the landscape of consumption is such an integral and obtrusive part of MODERNITY, whether in the form of the shopping mall, the theme park, the heritage centre or the humble main street (Knox, 1991; Shields, 1989).

Currently, the geography of consumption is chiefly fixed on social and cultural issues to do with the way in which COMMODITIES and their meanings have become intertwined. Four of these issues stand out. The first is an interest in the historical geography of consumption and its lessons for modern consumption (McKendrick, Brewer and Plumb, 1978; Glennie and Thrift, 1992). The second issue is the symbolic work that is done on commodities which invests them with rich and varied meanings by producers (through the design of commodities), by advertisers, by retailers and by consumers themselves. Special attention has been paid to how specific commodities feature in particular kinds of social activity, such as shopping, in the creation of certain kinds of social group identity (Jackson, 1991), and in the construction of certain kinds of PLACE (Sack, 1988). A third issue has been the extent to which a common global capitalist CULTURE has been created by the spread of commodities and commodity meanings around the world. In other words, does the spread of Madonna tapes, Coca-Cola cans and the like herald the end of local cultures? The consensus is that, instead, it is producing new forms of local culture, and new meanings of 'the local'. Finally, interest in a geography of consumption must be seen as part and parcel of the fascination with POSTMODERNISM. In the most apocalyptic of post-modern pronouncements the chief reason for existence is consuming, signs of the commodity have become more important than the commodity itself, and people have begun to lose their identity in the welter of consumption. In this conception, people function as if they were automata navigating through and navigated by programmed spaces of consumption.   NJT

References

Glennie, P. and Thrift, N. J. 1992: Modernity, urbanism and modern consumption. *Environ. Plann. D, Society and Space* 10, pp. 423–44.

Jackson, P. 1991: The cultural politics of masculinity: towards a social geography. *Trans. Inst. Br. Geogr.* 16, pp. 199–213.

Knox, P. 1991: The restless urban landscape: economic and social cultural change and the transformation of metropolitan Washington DC. *Ann. Ass. Am. Geogr.* 81, pp. 181–209.

McCracken, G. 1990: *Culture and consumption.* Bloomington: Indiana University Press.

McKendrick, N., Brewer, J. and Plumb, J. 1978: *The birth of consumer society.* London: Methuen.

Miller, D. 1987: *Mass consumption and material culture.* Oxford: Blackwell.

Sack, R. D. 1988: The consumer's world: place as context. *Ann. Ass. Am. Geogr.* 78, pp. 642–64.

Shields, R. 1989: Social spatialisation and the built environment: the West Edmonton Mall. *Environ. Plann. D, Society and Space.* 7, pp. 147–64.

Thrift, N. J. 1987: The geography of late twentieth-century class formation. In Thrift, N. J. and Williams, P., eds, *Class and Space: The Making of Urban Society.* London: Routledge and Kegan Paul, pp. 207–53.

Willis, P. 1990: *Common culture.* Milton Keynes: Open University Press.

contextual effect A concept used in ELECTORAL GEOGRAPHY to account for spatial variations in voting patterns.

Most studies of electoral behaviour present the voters as being mobilized to support particular parties (and their candidates) according to perceptions of their personal self-interest. The result is one or more electoral CLEAVAGES in each society, of which the most common are those based on economic CLASS. However, attempts to predict how people vote (both individually and in aggregate) based on those cleavages often fail (Miller, 1977; Johnston et al., 1988). This, it is suggested, is because people are also influenced in their voting decisions by others, of whom the most important are those they have most social contact with, such as their neighbours and workmates (cf. NEIGHBOURHOOD EFFECT). Thus their social contexts must also be analysed to appreciate how they interpret their social positions and how they translate those interpretations into votes for political parties.

Cox (1969) identified two processes that operate to produce contextual effects. According to the *acquaintance-circle process*, individuals are influenced by the weight of opinion in their contact networks, so that in any area in which a majority view prevails some of those who might – from knowledge of their individual characteristics – be expected to support the minority view are 'converted' by the dominant information flows to the majority view. (It is assumed that information spreads through a network, as does a rumour or a disease: see DIFFUSION.) Second, according to the *forced-field process* a local political culture is established in an area by the political parties; these mobilize opinions in a particular way – perhaps around local issues. In some places a singular local culture may develop which results in a voting pattern that deviates substantially from the national trend, as illustrated by Agnew's (1987) studies of nationalist voting in Scotland.

Many geographical studies have produced evidence of voting patterns that are consistent with the contextual effect hypothesis. The great majority of them use aggregate data only, however, and so face the problems of the ECOLOGICAL FALLACY. Recent developments in MULTILEVEL MODELLING have produced direct evidence of contextual effects (Jones et al., 1992).   RJJ

References

Agnew, J. A. 1987: *Place and politics: the geographical mediation of state and society.* Boston: Allen and Unwin.

Cox, K. R. 1969: The voting decision in a spatial context. In Board, C. et al., eds, *Progress in geography*, volume 1. London: Edward Arnold, pp. 81–117.

Johnston, R. J., Pattie, C. J. and Allsopp, J. G. 1988: *A nation dividing? The electoral map of Great Britain 1979–1987.* London: Longman.

Jones, K., Johnston, R. J. and Pattie, C. J. 1992: People, places and regions: exploring the use of multi-level modelling in the analysis of electoral data. *Brit. J. Polit. Sci.* 22, pp. 343–80.

Miller, W. L. 1977: *Electoral dyamics.* London: Macmillan.

contextual theory An approach which regards the *time–space settings* and *sequences* of human activity as essential to its constitution. Contextual explanations thus depend upon identifying relations of coexistence, connection or 'togetherness', rather than the relations of 'similarity' that characterize COMPOSITIONAL THEORY: 'In contrast to the compositional approach, and in many cases in reaction to it, the contextual approach is an attempt to recapture the flow of HUMAN AGENCY as a series of situated events in space and time' (Thrift, 1983).

The term derives from Hägerstrand, who speaks of it as an approach which 'encloses' a 'pocket' of the world 'as it is found, with its mixed assortment of beings', in contrast to more conventional approaches which remove different classes of beings 'from their habitats and place them in a classification system' (Hägsterstrand, 1984). In his view, the contextual approach is absolutely central to modern geography:

Being a geographer basically means to appreciate that when events are seen located together in a block of space–time they inevitably expose relations which cannot be traced any more, once we have bunched them into classes and drawn them out of their place in the block (Hägerstrand, 1974).

His own formulation of TIME-GEOGRAPHY thus focuses on what he calls *collateral processes* in *bounded regions*, i.e. on 'processes which cannot unfold freely . . . but have to accommodate themselves under the pressures and opportunities which follow from their common existence in terrestrial space and time' (Hägerstrand, 1976).

To think in terms of 'space as provider of room' (Swedish, *rum*), rather than 'space as made up of distances' (Hägerstrand, 1973), is characteristic of a long-established continental European tradition: compare Hägerstrand's *rum* with the conception of *Raum* in Ratzel's ANTHROPOGEOGRAPHY. Partly in consequence, it has something in common with 'closed space' doctrines such as Turner's FRONTIER THESIS, which drew upon organismic analogies. If this seems broadly naturalistic, however – and certainly Hägerstrand's own work has been criticized in precisely these terms – it nevertheless departs from physicalism in one vital particular. A number of commentators have drawn parallels between the contextual approach and so-called *configurational* explanations, the elements of which relate to unique conditions of time and space. Additionally, Kennedy (1979) claims that:

The configurational elements which must be taken into account in attempts to explain the past, present and future behaviour of the world in a geographical sense *are extremely difficult to handle in an explanatory framework which derives too narrowly from physics*, where such concerns are generally defined as irrelevant' (Kennedy, 1979, emphasis added).

Certainly, although Hägerstrand is clearly impressed by SOCIAL PHYSICS in other respects, he has himself accentuated how modern science ignores the ways in which 'phenomena are locally connected', a circumstance which, so he believes, 'leads to structural patterns and outcomes of processes which can seldom be derived from the laws of science as these are formulated today' (Hägerstrand, 1976).

Perhaps not surprisingly, therefore, contextuality has been accorded a central place in those social theories that are most sensitive to the difficulties of modelling the humanities and the social sciences directly on the natural sciences (see NATURALISM). Many of them have developed Hägerstrand's original notions, stripping away their outer layers of physicalism in order to expose an inner core of ideas about 'togetherness'. In STRUCTURATION THEORY, for example, contextuality does not denote uninteresting boundaries of social life but rather features that are inherently involved in its constitution. Accordingly, Giddens (1984) provides a set of concepts which represent contextuality as inherently involved in the connection of social integration and system integration: in the connection of face-to-face interaction with more extensive systems of mediated interaction. These thread out from the immediate, here-and-now setting of interaction and trace the progressive stretching of social relations over time and space (see TIME–SPACE DISTANCIATION). The link to Hägerstrand is more direct than a common

recognition of time–space routinization, For Hägerstrand (1984) also recognizes that:

Every action is situated in space and time and for its immediate outcome [is] dependent on what is present or absent as help or hindrance where the events take place. The secondary consequences in their turn are dependent on a new set of presences and absences, and so it goes further and further out from the initial action (Hägerstrand, 1984).

Pred (1983, 1984) builds on both time-geography and structuration theory to provide a 'theory of place as historically contingent process that emphasizes institutional and individual practices as well as the structural features with which those practices are interwoven'. This is supposed to lay the foundations for a reconstituted REGIONAL GEOGRAPHY in which human activity quite literally takes place, and in which 'place' itself becomes a process. Similarly, Thrift (1983) conceives of human activity in a region as a continuous discourse 'rooted in a staggered series of shared material situations that constantly arise out of one another in a dialectically linked distribution of opportunity and constraint, presence and absence'. For Thrift too, therefore, the REGION is a pivotal concept, because it is the 'actively passive' meeting place of social structure and human agency, substantive enough to be the generator and conductor of structure, but still intimate enough to ensure that the 'creature-like aspects of human beings are not lost'. It is precisely those intimate, corporeal, existential dimensions which Simonsen (1991) thinks are marginalized in Giddens's account (and in those writings which derive directly from it). Simonsen presents an ambitious codification of the contextuality of social life in which the *situated life story* occupies the central place (see the figure):

In the heart of the mediation between individual and collectivity stands individuals' biographies or life stories in time and space. It is here that human practice and consciousness are connected with the temporal–spatial context . . . through the notions of generation and locality. It is here that the concrete production of individuals takes place, and it is here that the complex texture of

Time/Space	Longue durée	Dasein	Durée of daily life
institutional spatial practice	sociospatial development (historical geography)	life strategies in spatial context	geographical conditioning of daily routines
place	local history, culture and tradition	biography in time and space – identity	spatially based 'natural attitudes'
individual spatial practice	historical conditioning of spatial practices	relation between life strategies and spatial practices	daily time–space routines (time-geography)

contextual theory *Temporality, spatiality and social life* (Simonsen, 1991).

daily temporal–spatial routines is organised (Simonsen, 1991).

Schatzki (1991) goes some way beyond these authors by suggesting that, for the most part, they fail to distinguish sufficiently clearly between *objective space* – the domain of Hägerstrand's (objectivist) time-geography – and *social space*. He conceives of social space as the opening and occupation of sites for human existence, and claims that it is within social space that webs of interconnection are inscribed to constitute 'social reality' (see EXISTENTIALISM, ONTOLOGY). Schatzki's proposals intersect with Soja's discussion of SPATIALITY. He defines his terms somewhat differently to those of the preceding discussion, contrasting a physically based *contextual space* (which corresponds to Schatzki's 'objective space') with a socially based *created space* ('social space'). In his view, 'the organization, use and meaning of space is a product of social translation, transformation and experience'; the social construction of space thus occurs 'within the physical frame of ubiquitous, contextual space' but is nevertheless clearly distinguishable from it. The vocabulary of human geography has been so permeated by the analysis of the latter, 'objective' and in his terms 'contextual' space, that 'the term "spatial" typically evokes the image of something physical and external to the social context and to social action, a part of the environment, a context *for* society – its container – rather than a structure created *by* society' (Soja, 1980; see also Soja, 1989). This is an important reminder that contextual approaches in the more general sense defined above must be concerned with space as both context and creation: as both 'condition' and 'consequence' of human activity. DG

References

Giddens, A. 1984: *The constitution of society.* Cambridge: Polity Press.

Hägerstrand, T. 1973: The domain of human geography. In Chorley, R. J., ed., *Directions in human geography.* London: Methuen.

Hägerstrand, T. 1974: Commentary. In Buttimer, A., *Values in geography.* Association of American Geographers, Commission on College Geography, Resource paper 24, pp. 50–4.

Hägerstrand, T. 1976: Geography and the study of interaction between nature and society. *Geoforum* 7, pp. 329–34.

Hägerstrand, T. 1984: Presences and absences: a look at conceptual choices and bodily necessities. *Reg. Stud.* 18, pp. 373–80.

Kennedy, B. A. 1979: A naughty world. *Trans. Inst. Br. Geogr.* n.s. 4, pp. 550–8.

Pred, A. 1983: Structuration and place: on the becoming of a sense of place and structure of feeling. *J. T. S. Behav.* 13, pp. 45–68.

Pred, A. 1984: Place as historically contingent process: structuration and the time-geography of becoming places. *Ann. Ass. Am. Geogr.* 74, pp. 279–97.

Schatzki, T. 1991: Spatial ontology and explanation. *Ann. Ass. Am. Geogr.* 81, pp. 650–70.

Simonsen, K. 1991: Towards an understanding of the contextuality of social life. *Environ. Plann. D: Society and Space* 9, pp. 417–32.

Soja, E. 1980: The socio-spatial dialectic. *Ann. Ass. Am. Geogr.* 70, pp. 207–25.

Soja, E. 1989: *Postmodern geographies: the reassertion of space in critical social theory.* London: Verso.

Thrift, N. 1983: On the determination of social action in space and time. *Environ. Plann. D: Society and Space* 1, pp. 23–57.

Suggested Reading

Hägerstrand (1984).

Schatzki (1991).

Simonsen (1991).

Thrift (1983).

contiguous zone An area of the high seas, beyond the TERRITORIAL SEAS, and extending up to 24 nautical miles from the baseline delimiting the internal waters of a state. The zone was first defined in the 1958 UN Convention on the Territorial Sea and the Contiguous Zone as extending up to 12 nautical miles from the baseline, but this was replaced by the present definition under the 1982 UN Convention on the Law of the Sea, although the Convention has still not formally come into force. At the time, there was some debate as to whether it was still necessary actually to define a contiguous zone. It was eventually decided to retain it, because it can play an important role in domestic law enforcement, even against foreign vessels, although it has little standing in international law.   MB

continental shelf The area of submerged continental rock forming the continental margin lying closest to the shore. It terminates abruptly at varying depths and distances out to sea, but is everywhere relatively clearly defined physically. The political significance of the continental shelf has increased rapidly during the second half of the twentieth-century, as the exploitation of underwater resources, in addition to fisheries, has become a realistic prospect. The earliest claim was made by Argentina in 1944, when it asserted rights over offshore mineral resources. A year later President Truman issued Proclamation 2667, claiming USA SOVEREIGNTY over the sea bed and the subsoil of the continental shelf, although not over the waters above. Other states were quick to follow suit, but in the absence of any clear definition of the continental shelf much confusion ensued. In 1958 the UN Convention on the Continental Shelf gave states the right to exploit the mineral resources of their coastal waters to a depth of 200 m or beyond if exploitation was technically feasible. In the furtherance of such exploitation, STATES were permitted to build (or agree to the construction of) permanent structures, such as oil wells, as long as they were not accorded the status of islands with territorial waters of their own, and provided that they did not pose an undue hazard for shipping. The Convention also gave states rights to sedentary species of living things on the sea bed, such as shellfish and crustacea, but not fish. Once it comes into force, the 1982 UN Convention on the Law of the Sea will radically revise this definition. In legal terms, the continental shelf will extend for 200 nautical miles from the coastal baseline of a state, and in a few instances further, up to 350 nautical miles. Within this area states will have exclusive rights to explore and exploit the natural resources.   MB

Suggested Reading

Glassner, M. I. 1990: *Neptune's domain.* Boston: Unwin Hyman.

conurbation A term coined by Patrick Geddes to describe a built-up area created by the coalescence of once-separate urban settlements, initially through RIBBON DEVELOPMENT along the main inter-urban routes. With greater urban SPRAWL the term has now largely been replaced by concepts such as DAILY URBAN SYSTEM, MEGALOPOLIS, METROPOLITAN AREA and METROPOLITAN LABOUR AREA.   RJJ

convergence, regional The tendency for regional incomes or levels of living within a nation to become more equal over time. That this should be the case is a prediction derived from NEO-CLASSICAL ECONOMICS, which portrays labour, capital and other FACTORS OF PRODUCTION moving from one region to another, seeking the best possible returns (wages and profits), until there is nothing to gain from further movement because returns are the same in all regions. Thus a competitive free-market economy under CAPITALISM should tend towards regional equality, subject to constraints on the spatial mobility of factors of production.

Evidence to support this prediction can be found for individual nations. For example, regional incomes in the USA show steady convergence from the latter part of the nineteenth century up to the 1970s. However, individual regions can have their own trajectory, reflecting their own historical experience of greater or lesser movement towards the national average income, which complicates a simple picture of regular convergence. In addition, the convergence thesis depends on the geographical scale adopted: the trend towards reduced inequality at a broad regional scale can be contradicted more locally, e.g. between core and periphery and within the city.

Regional convergence is not confined to capitalist economies. Indeed, this trend may be more marked under a socialist system which has the equalization of regional living standards as an explicit objective. For example, a strong convergence tendency could be observed among the former republics of the Soviet Union, although this may have been reversed during the so-called 'era of stagnation' which preceded *perestroika*.

There is also evidence of recent reversals of convergence in the capitalist world, including the USA. For example, the best-off region of the UK (the South East) had 120.6 per cent of national average Gross Domestic Product per capita in 1989 compared with 116.2 in 1979, while the worst-off (Northern Ireland) had only 76.4 per cent in 1989 compared with 78.3 per cent ten years before. Interregional inequality had clearly increased. The fact that this occurred during a decade of government dedicated to the free market suggests limits to the extent of regional convergence towards perfect equality under capitalism, in practice if not in theory. Indeed, the earlier decades of more positive regional planning may have taken the country further in the direction of equality than would have been the case under less restrained market forces. This suggests that, after a certain level in the convergence process has been reached, state intervention in the form of regional development policy is a necessary if not sufficient condition for further convergence. DMS

Suggested Reading
Smith, D. M. 1987: *Geography, inequality and society*. Cambridge: Cambridge University Press.
Williamson, J. G. 1966: Regional inequality and the process of national development: a description of the patterns. *Ec. Dev. cult. Ch.*, 13, pp. 3–45.

cooperative An organization of farmers for their mutual benefit in production or marketing, or both. Farmers group together to form a larger buying unit for their farm inputs, or to create a larger marketing unit. The aims are to enable farmers to gain the financial advantages of bulk trading while maintaining the independence of their farms. Marketing cooperatives are an alternative to government-controlled marketing boards, although state aid may be available to set up such cooperatives. Some cooperatives own processing plants; for example, for wine making and bottling and for egg packing. Others also purchase machinery for use or hire by individual farmers. PEW/DBG

Suggested Reading
Anschel, K. R., Brannon, R. H. and Smith, E. D., eds 1969: *Agricultural cooperatives and markets in developing countries*. New York: Praeger.

core area A loose term frequently used to refer to some central area within a STATE that acts as the mainspring for its subsequent economic growth. Many states, particularly in Europe, have grown in this way. Some would also argue that the continued vitality of a state depends on whether the core functions efficiently as a central focus. Others disagree, pointing to the many instances, particularly in Africa and South America, in which states have been established without reference to a core area and the territory has subsequently been coherently organized through the creation of a socio-economic infrastructure. (See also BOUNDARY; FRONTIER.) MB

core–periphery model A model of the spatial organization of human activity based upon the unequal distribution of POWER in economy, society and polity. The core dominates (although it in turn may be dominated from outside), while the periphery is dependent. This DEPENDENCE is structured through the relations of exchange (see MODE OF PRODUCTION) between the core and the periphery. Although it uses similar terms to those adopted in WORLD-SYSTEMS ANALYSIS, and accepts that geographically UNEVEN DEVELOPMENT is a long-term process, the core–periphery model tends to accept spatial equilibrium as a policy goal and so does not recognize the structurally uneven development of the DIVISION OF LABOUR in the capitalist world-economy.

Unequal exchange (see TRADE), the concentration of economic power, technical progress and productive activity at the core, and the emanation of productive innovations from the core, help to maintain the flow of surplus value (see MARXIAN ECONOMICS) from the core to the periphery. For example, increases in productivity in the core may, with an effective labour movement, be translated into higher wages. At the same time a more plentiful supply of unorganized labour in the periphery may serve to sustain a downward pressure on wages. If wage levels are reflected in the relative prices of the products exchanged between the core and the periphery, the consequence of higher wages in the core will either be to generate a balance-of-payments crisis in the periphery or to enforce increased exports from the periphery to finance the increased cost of imports. In either case autonomous development in the periphery is made more difficult and

may, indeed, be subverted. Such unequal relations may also be maintained by the implementation of economic and commercial policies that favour the core at the expense of the periphery (see COLONIALISM, NEOCOLONIALISM) and may be reinforced by migration and capital flows from the periphery to the core.

Core–periphery relations were seen by Friedmann (1966), with whom the core–periphery model is most closely associated, as the second in a four-stage sequence of the development of the space economy. The stages outlined by Friedmann are: (a) preindustrial society with localized economies; (b) core–periphery; (c) dispersion of economic activity and, to a lesser extent, control into certain parts of the periphery; and (d) the emergence of spatial INTEGRATION in which the various and now more or less fully developed spatial parts of the economy relate in a more truly interdependent manner (see INTERDEPENDENCE).

Although it implies interregional conflict rather than equilibrium, and so emphasizes the uneven nature of economic DEVELOPMENT, the core–periphery model has several deficiencies stemming, in the main, from its reliance upon exchange relations (see Brenner, 1977) and the abstract nature of power in the model (see also UNEVEN DEVELOPMENT). Critics argue that it is false to assume that the social concentration of power necessarily leads to spatial concentration, and that the redistribution of power is somehow associated with development and the emergence of an integrated SPACE-ECONOMY. Many insist that the spatial arrangement and transformation of a capitalist economy at a particular moment in time reflects, above all, the current requirements of accumulation and the historical legacy of a landscape created by previous rounds of accumulation and LAYERS OF INVESTMENT. Storper and Walker (1989, p. 183), for example, argue that 'the main shape of territorial development in capitalist societies' is a product of the 'spatial expansion, integration, and division of growing industries and industrial ensembles'. They stress that it is the geography of production rather than exchange that acts as the dynamic of geographically uneven development.

It may be argued that economic power stems less from its location than the locus of control over the means of production, and that it derives its specific historical characteristics from the nature of this control. Thus, although the spatial redistribution of productive activity and the decentralization of decision-making over the productive process may generate what appears to be a more highly integrated form of spatial organization, it does not necessarily shift power over the means of production to a more democratic base. Nor does it imply that the spatial location of control over the means of production has been decentralized. In fact, the concentration of control is more likely to be intensified rather than reduced, as the economy becomes more highly integrated in spatial terms and its geographical development evolves in accordance with a development plan.

The second and third stages of Friedmann's model and the policies of regional development with which they may be associated (see GROWTH POLE) would certainly lead to a less unequal exchange between core and periphery. But they ought, more correctly, to be seen as a means whereby surplus may be extracted from the economy as a whole rather than as a means of diffusing development. A more genuine redistribution of development would, necessarily, involve a fundamental transformation of the relations of control over the means of production.   RL

References and Suggested Reading

Agnew, J. 1987: *The United States in the world-economy: a regional geography*. Cambridge: Cambridge University Press, pp. 89–127.

Brenner, R. 1977: The origins of capitalist development: a critique of neo-Smithian Marxism. *New Left Rev.* 104, pp. 25–92.

Dicken, P. E. and Lloyd, P. 1990: *Location in space: theoretical perspectives in economic geography*, third edition. New York: Harper and Row, pp. 239–46.

Friedmann, J. 1966: *Regional development policy: a case study of Venezuela*. Cambridge, MA: MIT Press.

Keeble, D. E. 1989: Core–periphery disparities, recession and new regional dynamisms in the European Community. *Geogr.* 74, pp. 1–11.

Perloff, H. S., Dunn, E. S., Lampard, E. E. and Muth, R. F. 1960: *Regions, resources and economic growth*. Lincoln, NE: University of Nebraska Press/Baltimore, MD: Johns Hopkins University Press.

Storper, M. and Walker, R. 1989: *The capitalist imperative*. Oxford: Blackwell.

corporatism   A mode of operation for the capitalist STATE in which major interest groups – notably those representing capital on the one hand and labour on the other – share power with the elected representative government. In the latter, power is competed for through the electoral process, as in PLURALISM: under corporatism, governments share that power with unelected representatives of functional interest groups. Corporatism is especially strong in some Western European countries (notably Austria and Germany), where employers' groups and trades unions are routinely consulted on major issues of economic policy: it is much weaker in the UK and the USA.   RJJ

Suggested Reading

Cawson, A. 1986: *Corporatism and political theory*. Oxford: Blackwell.

Johnston, R. J. 1992: The internal operations of the state. In Taylor, P. J., ed., *The political geography of the twentieth century*. London: Belhaven Press, pp. 115-70.

correlation   The degree of association between two or more variables, mainly used in the statistical analysis of interval and ratio data. A correlation coefficient measures the goodness-of-fit of a REGRESSION line to a scatter of points: its value ranges from +1.0 through 0.0 to -1.0. A value of +1.0 indicates that all of the points lie on the regression line, as does one of -1.0: the latter indicates a negative slope to the relationship (i.e. as the values of one variable increase, those of the other decrease). Usually represented by r, the square of this coefficient (r^2) is interpreted as the proportion of the variation in the independent variable that can be accounted for by the variation in the independent variable. For multiple regression equations,

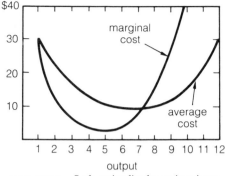

cost curve *Scale optimality for an imaginary plant under imperfect competition, as derived from the cost and revenue curves.*

the multiple correlation coefficient is represented as *R*.   RJJ

Suggested Reading
Johnston, R. J. 1978: *Multivariate statistical analysis in geography*. London: Longman.

cost curve A plot of the relationship between the cost of production and the volume of output. An *average cost curve* typically slopes downwards to the right at low levels of output, to rise again with diseconomies of scale after a minimum average unit cost has been reached. The *marginal cost curve* plots the cost of each additional (i.e. marginal) unit of production (see the figure). The *total cost curve* (not shown) plots the total cost of a given volume of output, i.e. the average cost multipled by the quantity produced.   DMS

cost structure The division of the total cost of production into its constituent parts, or the costs of individual inputs. For example, the cost structure of the iron and steel industry would indicate absolute (or relative) amounts of expenditure on iron ore, coking coal, limestone, labour, capital equipment and so on. The cost structure thus reveals whether a particular activity is material intensive, capital intensive, labour intensive, etc., with respect to expenditure on inputs. This information can provide an initial clue to the inputs that are likely to have the greatest bearing on the location of the activity in question.   DMS

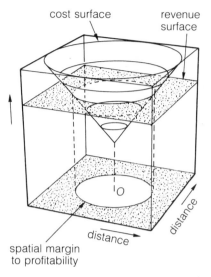

cost surface *The cost surface, revenue surface and spatial margin to profitability* (Smith, 1981).

cost surface Spatial variations in the cost of production, depicted as a three-dimensional surface, with distance along the two horizontal axes and cost in pecuniary units on the vertical axis (see the figure). When related to a REVENUE SURFACE, a SPATIAL MARGIN to profitability can be identified, defining the area in which revenue exceeds cost and some profit can be made. In practice as well as in theory, cost surfaces are typically portrayed by contour lines, such as ISODAPANES. The surface may represent spatial variations in the cost of single inputs, such as labour, land or individual materials. It may also represent total operating costs at a given scale, although this is more difficult to identify empirically. (See also VARIABLE COST ANALYSIS.)   DMS

Reference
Smith, D. M. 1981: *Industrial location: an economic geographical analysis*, second edition. New York: John Wiley, p. 112.

cost–benefit analysis An analytical procedure for the comprehensive, often pre-construction, economic evaluation of major public investment projects, embracing their full positive and negative societal consequences over the range of investment options. As such, cost–benefit analysis covers a wider range of considerations than does the profit-and-loss accounting of private-sector investment decision-making. Originally applied to public river and harbour projects in the USA, its contemporary uses extend to issues such as urban air quality, dam and irrigation schemes, refuse recycling, transport deregulation, roadway maintenance, coastal protection against sea-level rise induced by global warming, disposal of hazardous waste, choices among electricity generation systems, and job creation by regional policy (see also Walshe and Daffern, 1990).

Cost–benefit analysis involves three stages. First, costs and benefits associated with public projects have to be identified, including intangible EXTERNALITIES such as noise and POLLUTION. Second, these must be quantified, including their discounting to a common base date, since the various costs and benefits are often experienced over very different time periods. Finally, the resulting cost–benefit ratios are incorporated into the decision-making, or project-evaluation, stage, alongside political and other judgemental inputs.

Economists differ as to the appropriate ways to apply these general principles, and over the validity of the exercise as a whole. Some argue that cost–benefit analysis attempts to measure the immeasurable. Certainly, it raises several implementation problems. Defining all costs and benefits is one such: it is difficult to be comprehensive without double-counting. Not all variables have an easily determined market value, and some estimates may be little more than guesses. The discount value, whether taken as prevailing market interest rates or some arbitrary, government-determined figure, can be crucial to the outcome, and endangers undervaluing the welfare of future generations. Finally, distributional issues are important – a $1 million benefit to poor residents from one freeway route should outweigh a $1 million gain to rich citizens from an alternative one.   AGH

References

Walshe, G. and Daffern, P. 1990: *Managing cost-benefit analysis*. London: Macmillan.

Suggested Reading

Schofield, J. 1987: *Cost–benefit analysis in urban and regional planning*. London: Allen and Unwin.

counterfactual explanation An extension of the comparative method which seeks to check 'hypothetical reconstructions' of what might have happened in the past 'against the record of what actually took place' (Prince, 1971). While there is nothing especially novel about counterfactuals as such – indeed, Cohen (1953) argued that 'the significance of historical fact [is] revealed by asking what might have happened if things had been different', which would make the construction of counterfactuals intrinsic to historical method – they nevertheless played a particularly prominent part in the so-called 'New Economic History' (or *econometric* history), in which their supposed success encouraged calls for their formal deployment in HISTORICAL GEOGRAPHY. The emphasis on a *formal* methodology is important, because what is distinctive about counterfactual explanation in econometric history is its connection with formal MODEL-building: its commitment 'to the efficacy of theory in specifying useful counterfactuals and to quantitative methods in implementing them' in such a way that they indicate 'the latent tendencies of the SYSTEM being studied' (Fishlow and Fogel, 1971); these two authors have in fact provided classic demonstrations of the method (Fishlow, 1965; Fogel, 1964). While counterfactuals restore an essential contingency to historical eventuation and explanation, their viability clearly depends on the specification of an adequate theoretical system and on the use of sufficiently powerful techniques of SIMULATION or SPACE–TIME FORECASTING. But even then, their interpretation is riddled with difficulties, since historical events and processes are contextual: this means that 'we cannot [readily] decide what we must *subtract* from the real past' along with the event or process under investigation, and so we cannot easily decide whether the counterfactual construction is legitimate (Gould, 1969). These difficulties have proved so formidable that many historical geographers seem to have implicitly endorsed M. M. Postan's claim (see Gould, 1969) that 'the might-have-beens of history are not a profitable subject for discussion.'   DG

References

Cohen, M. R. 1953: *Reason and nature: essay on the meaning of scientific method*, second edition. Glencoe, IL: Free Press.

Fishlow, A. 1965: *American railroads and the transformation of the antebellum economy*. Cambridge, MA: Harvard University Press/Oxford: Oxford University Press.

Fishlow, A. and Fogel, R. 1971: Quantitative economic history: an interim evaluation. *J. econ. Hist.* 21, pp. 15–42.

Fogel, R. 1964: *Railroads and American economic growth: essays in econometric history*. Baltimore: Johns Hopkins University Press.

Gould, J. D. 1969: Hypothetical history. *Econ. Hist. R.* 22, pp. 195–207.

Prince, H. C. 1971: Real, imagined and abstract worlds of the past. *Prog. Geog.* 3, pp. 1–86.

Suggested Reading

Gould (1969).

counterurbanization

A process of population deconcentration away from the large URBAN settlements. The process was first identified in the USA in the 1970s, where population statistics indicated that the METROPOLITAN AREAS, especially the largest and oldest, were losing population by net migration to non-metropolitan areas. The number of places experiencing such decline increased in the following years as people and jobs moved: (a) beyond the SUBURBS to the smaller settlements of the METROPOLITAN LABOUR AREAS; and (b) to the smaller, rapidly growing metropolitan centres of the sunbelt (see SUNBELT/SNOWBELT). Evidence from the 1980s suggested that counterurbanization was widespread in the advanced industrial countries, although there is some evidence that large cities are beginning to grow again in some countries, suggesting that counterurbanization was but a brief episode.

Attempted explanations for the decline of large cities and the growth of the smaller towns focus on the latter's attractions and the disadvantages of the former for both employers and householders. Smaller towns offer cheaper, more extensive tracts of land, and more pliant labour forces who lack strong traditions of militant trade unionism, and these advantages more than counter the greater costs of movement of goods, which in any case are reducing with the trend to higher value, less bulky goods and better road transport. For householders, the smaller places are more attractive than the congested and polluted cities, even for commuters who are prepared to trade longer, more expensive journeys for the more pleasant environments. And with an ageing population with a greater percentage of retired, healthy and relatively affluent people, the smaller towns (and even the more remote rural areas) offer a better quality of life, usually at lower cost, than the large cities.   RJJ

Suggested Reading

Berry, B. J. L., ed., 1976: *Urbanization and counterurbanization*. Beverly Hills, CA: Sage Publications.

Champion, A. G. 1991: *Counterurbanization*. London: Edward Arnold.

crime, geography of

A subdiscipline which elucidates the relevance of SPACE to the study of criminal offenders, the incidence of crime and the characteristics of victims. An explicit geography of crime was discussed by Cohen (1941), although its modern practitioners did not publish widely until the early 1970s. The spatial tradition, however, was established in the nineteenth century by Europe's 'cartographic criminologists', and close relationships between urban structure and the distribution of crime and criminals were documented by Chicago's ecologists in the early 1920s (see CHICAGO SCHOOL; HUMAN ECOLOGY).

Recent large-scale (urban and regional) studies in the geography of crime involve: (a) the mapping and distribution of crime patterns (areal analyses); and (b) comparisons of the distribution of crime and offender rates with spatial variations amongst socio-economic or environmental indicators (ecological analyses). High rates of offender residence have been found in INNER-CITY areas and (in the UK) on some public-sector housing estates (apparently related to the operation of the housing allocation system). Enduring relationships have emerged between high crime and offender rates and substandard housing, poverty, high population mobility, social heterogeneity and (more controversially) economic inequality. These findings underpin a revival of interest in the links between crime and COMMUNITY (Reiss and Tonry, 1986).

At a more detailed level, four facets of offender behaviour have received attention:

(a) Offenders' 'journeys-to-crime', which vary according to: (i) offenders' socio-economic and demographic characteristics; (ii) the type of crime committed; and (iii) the size of pay-off expected in different target areas.

(b) Criminals' images of the city (see MENTAL MAP), which indicate what crime targets fall within the ACTION SPACE and ACTIVITY SPACE of offenders from different environments.

(c) Economic analyses of criminal behaviour, which conceptualize property crimes as the outcome of rational DECISION-MAKING processes, enabling analysts to predict the distribution of some offences.

(d) Subcultural delinquency, which has been analysed as a manifestation of relationships between residential proximity, joint offending, shared delinquent values and attachment to PLACE.

The traditional emphasis on offenders has been displaced in recent years by analyses of the environments in which crime occurs. High crime rates have been implicated in the process of urban decline and in the direction of neighbourhood change. Crime can halt the impulse for URBAN RENEWAL by encouraging a spiral of disinvestment and a wave of outmigration (Taub, Taylor and Dunham, 1984). Studies are also exploring whether high property crime rates characterize economically heterogeneous areas and/or residential 'border zones' (where offenders find a greater degree of anonymity than in neighbourhood interiors).

Recent research on the defensibility of space (examining the availability of opportunities for crime to potential offenders) has developed Newman's (1972) idea that a sense of TERRITORIALITY sufficient to enhance informal, communal, crime-

prevention strategies can be encouraged by modifications to the built environment. Geographers have now become enmeshed in debate on the relative merits of 'architectural determinism' versus 'social engineering' for 'defending' neighbourhood space (Coleman, 1985; Smith, 1987a).

Recently, the geography of crime has focused more explicitly on victims (e.g. Smith, 1984), following the introduction of national and local crime surveys in the USA and Western Europe. Such surveys have democratized the definition of crime by recognizing the authenticity of victims' experiences (whether or not these are known to the police). The risks of victimization have been explained in terms of two broad geographical themes: lifestyle and activity patterns (the most active segments of the population are the most vulnerable); and residential location (urban – especially INNER-CITY – residents face greater risks than their rural counterparts).

Fear of crime also varies geographically, peaking in the inner cities. Moreover, fear is rapidly gaining credence as a social problem in its own right, as an emotion triggered not only by the experience of victimization, but also by a range of other 'environmental incivilities' (Smith, 1987b). Fear of crime is particularly widespread among women, both within and outside the home. Attempts to document, explain and control this have become an important area of FEMINIST GEOGRAPHY, since fear of sexual harassment, rape and domestic violence restricts women's use of space and curtails their social and employment opportunities (Pain, 1992).

Most research within the geography of crime has embraced the empirical–analytical tradition (see EMPIRICISM), often seeking findings that are relevant to policy. The historical–hermeneutic tradition is also represented (see HERMENEUTICS), e.g. in Ley's (1974) account of the meaning of delinquency in Philadelphia's inner city. The proponents of CRITICAL THEORY are less concerned with the meaning or measurement of crime than with a critique of the construction of the laws which define it. In geography, this perspective has furthered the tradition of Leftist idealism:

inter-class crime represents a rejection of laws protecting the distribution of wealth, and it involves the transfer of property over space from areas of surplus to areas of want (Peet, 1976). Critical reformism, an alternative radical perspective, is concerned with the legitimacy and effects of the law, and with flaws in legal administration that allow the law to discriminate against the powerless (cf. Lowman, 1982; see LAW, GEOGRAPHY OF).

The geography of crime ranges widely in its subject matter, methodologies and philosophical bases. A unifying theme is the analyst's concern to relate crime closely to the social and spatial contexts in which it arises: demonstrably, crime reflects the organization of the built environment, the spatial structure of social relations, and the distribution of power and wealth.   SJS

References

Cohen, J. 1941: The geography of crime. *Ann. Am. Acad. Pol. Soc. Sci.* 217, pp. 29–37.

Coleman, A. 1985: *Utopia on trial.* London: Hilary Shipman.

Ley, D. 1974: *The black inner city as frontier outpost.* Washington, DC: Association of American Geographers.

Lowman, J. 1982: Crime, criminal justice policy and the urban environment. In Herbert, D. T. and Johnston, R. J., eds, *Geography and the urban environment: progress in research and applications,* volume V. Chichester: John Wiley, pp. 307–41.

Newman, O. 1972: *Defensible space.* New York: Macmillan.

Pain, R. 1992: Space, sexual violence and social control: integrating geographical and feminist analyses of women's fear of crime. *Progr. hum. Geogr.* 15, pp. 415–31.

Peet, J. R. 1976: Further comments on the geography of crime. *Prof. Geogr.* 28, pp. 96–100.

Reiss, A. J. and Tonry, M. 1986: *Communities and crime.* Chicago: University of Chicago Press.

Smith, S. J. 1984: Crime and the structure of social relations. *Trans. Inst. Br. Geogr.* n.s. 9, pp. 427–42.

Smith, S. J. 1987a: Design against crime? Beyond the rhetoric of residential crime prevention. *Journal of Property Management* 5, pp. 146–50.

Smith, S. J. 1987b: Fear of crime: beyond a geography of deviance. *Progr. hum. Geogr.* 11, pp. 1–23.

Taub, R. P., Taylor, D. G. and Dunham, J. D. 1984: *Paths of neighbourhood change.* Chicago: University of Chicago Press.

Suggested Reading

Davidson, R. N. 1981: *Crime and environment.* London: Croom Helm.

Evans, D. J. and Herbert, D. T. 1989: *The geography of crime.* London: Routledge.

Herbert, D. 1982: *The geography of urban crime.* London: Longman.

Smith, S. J. 1986: *Crime, space and society.* Cambridge: Cambridge University Press.

crisis An interruption in the reproduction of economic, cultural, social and/or political life.

The most systematic theories of crisis and crisis formation are provided by HISTORICAL MATERIALISM, in which accounts of social change are underwritten by the operation of opposing principles of societal organization ('contradictions') (see DIALECTIC). A number of Marxist historians have spoken of a crisis of FEUDALISM in these terms (although in different ways), but most discussion in geography has centred on crisis in CAPITALISM conceived as a MODE OF PRODUCTION: indeed, in conventional MARXIAN ECONOMICS a crisis is an objective interruption in the accumulation of capital. However, there is no single (let alone simple) theory of crisis in Marx's writings, and in *The limits to capital* (1982) Harvey goes some way beyond Marx to distinguish the following:

(a) A 'first-cut' theory of crisis. Here, so Harvey claims, Marx seeks to disclose the 'underlying rationale' for the instability of capitalist *production*. This is usually exemplified by the falling rate of profit, and in particular by the tendency for capitalism to produce both a surplus of capital ('overaccumulation') and a surplus of labour power (unemployment and underemployment, a strategic moment in 'devaluation').

(b) A 'second-cut' theory of crisis which focuses on *temporal displacement*: on the ways in which these surpluses of capital and labour power can be absorbed through new forms of *circulation* and, in particular, through financial and monetary arrangements which are themselves structurally implicated in financial and monetary crises.

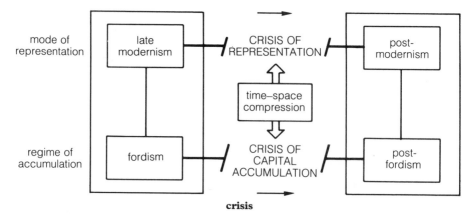

crisis

This second cut enables Harvey to differentiate

between periodic crashes . . . and long-run problems . . . [which] are strongly affected by the increasing socialization of capital itself, first via the agency of the credit system and ultimately through socially necessary interventions on the part of the state (Harvey, 1982).

The introduction of the STATE into the analysis is of considerable importance since, Harvey emphasizes, once we drop the assumption of a closed system and consider international aspects to crisis formation, then it becomes clear that

The struggle to export inflation, unemployment, idle productive capacity, excess commodities, etc., becomes the pivot of national policy. The costs of crises are spread differentially according to the financial, economic, political and military power of rival states (Harvey, 1982).

(c) This leads directly to a 'third-cut' theory of crisis which focuses not only on 'temporal dynamics' but also on the possibility of a *spatial fix*: in other words, on the historical geography of capitalism and, in particular, on the ways in which surpluses of capital and labour power might be inscribed in the built environment and, still more important, 'be disposed of and remunerated by entering into external relations with other regions'. This is one of Harvey's central insights; Marx's formulations, in his view, are 'powerful with respect to time but weak with respect to space' and Marx's political vision is thus

'undermined by his failure to build a systematic and distinctively geographical and spatial dimension into his thought' (Harvey, 1985a; see also MARXIST GEOGRAPHY). Harvey is therefore concerned, first, to integrate the geography of UNEVEN DEVELOPMENT into crisis theory (Harvey, 1982, 1985b) and, second, to incorporate the state into crisis theory through an analysis of the GEOPOLITICS of capitalism (Harvey, 1985a; see also REGIONAL ALLIANCE).

Throughout these discussions capitalism is held to be both *crisis-ridden* and *crisis-dependent*. In so far as this means that crisis is a mechanism of autoregulation, however, there is undoubtedly a danger of a covert FUNCTIONALISM in some of these formulations. To blunt the force of these objections, O'Connor (1981; see also 1984) insists that crises are not limited to system integration but also threaten *social integration*. Such a claim evidently owes something to Habermas's CRITICAL THEORY, which treats not only economic crises but also (and more particularly) 'rationality crises' and 'legitimation crises' (Habermas, 1976). But O'Connor argues that Habermas does not break sufficiently with classical Marxism. In his view, crises 'originate in the emancipatory practices of human beings': 'the essence of crisis is not social disintegration but social struggle'. In fact, although Habermas has used a model of crisis formation and resolution to account for the evolution of modern societies, he now argues that contemporary social struggles are provoked not only (or even primarily) by spasmodic economic or political crises but also by the *colonization* of the LIFEWORLD by economic and political–administrative systems (see CRITICAL THEORY). In any event, it seems clear that these various struggles have their own geographies, the contours of which cannot be read directly from a map of economic crisis. It is equally clear that social struggles are not always automatically translated into political or even parapolitical forms because, as Morgan (1983) accentuates, 'formidable integrative mechanisms . . . [can] prevail within the most radical restructuring process . . . .[to produce] what might be called a subdued social crisis'. And, as Morgan shows, one of the most powerful ways in which such struggles can be contained is through their fragmentation and localization (see also Massey, 1984).

All of these concerns have been mobilized in recent discussions of the so-called crisis of FORDISM and its (supposed) resolution through the installation of a regime of FLEXIBLE ACCUMULATION. Shifts and tremors within 'the inconstant geography of capitalist production' remain immensely important foci of debate (Storper and Walker, 1989; see also Webber, 1991), and the ramifications of the international debt crisis have received increasing attention (Corbridge, 1992), but there has also been a definite movement beyond exclusively economic geographies of crisis formation. Indeed, Harvey (1989) has himself sought to explore the political and cultural implications of the contemporary crisis of capital accumulation by connecting it to a *crisis of representation* brought about by TIME–SPACE COMPRESSION (see the figure), although many of his critics object to the reductionism of his account. Whatever one makes of these particular claims, however, they thread out into a wider discussion of MODERNITY and its constant 'creative destruction' of a world in which, as Marx put it, 'all that is solid melts into air' (see Berman, 1982; Gregory, 1989). Marx's own concerns were the economic and political crises of nineteenth-century capitalism, of course, but the multiple crises which are inscribed within the trembling foundations of the late twentieth-century world have such vitally important *cultural* and *ecological* dimensions (Emel, 1991; Jackson, 1991) that their critical analysis poses considerable challenges to historical materialism inside and outside geography. (See also POSTCOLONIALISM; POSTMODERNISM; POST-MARXISM.) DG

References

Berman, M. 1982: *All that is solid melts into air: the experience of modernity*. London: Verso.

Corbridge, S. 1992: *Debt and development*. Oxford: Blackwell.

Emel, J. 1991: Ecological crisis and provocative pragmatism. *Environ. Plann. D: Society and Space* 9, pp. 384–90.

Gregory, D. 1989: The crisis of modernity? Human geography and critical social theory. In Peet, R. and Thrift, N., eds, *New models in geography*, volume 2. London: Unwin Hyman, pp. 348–85.

Habermas, J. 1976: *Legitimation crisis*. London: Heinemann.

Harvey, D. 1982: *The limits to capital*. Oxford: Blackwell.

Harvey, D. 1985a: The geopolitics of capitalism. In Gregory, D. and Urry, J., eds, *Social relations and spatial structures*. London: Macmillan, pp. 128–63.

Harvey, D. 1985b: *The urbanization of capital*. Oxford: Blackwell.

Harvey, D. 1989: *The condition of postmodernity: an enquiry into the origins of cultural change*. Oxford: Blackwell.

Jackson, P. 1991: The crisis of representation and the politics of position. *Environ. Plann. D: Society and Space* 9, pp. 131–4.

Massey, D. 1984: *Spatial divisions of labour: social structures and the geography of production*. London: Macmillan.

Morgan, K. 1983: The crises of labour and locality in Britain. *Int. J. urban and reg. Res.* 7, pp. 175–201.

O'Connor, J. 1981: The meaning of crisis. *Int. J. urban and reg. Res.* 5, pp. 301–25.

O'Connor, J. 1984: *Accumulation crisis*. Oxford: Blackwell.

Storper, M. and Walker, R. 1989: *The capitalist imperative: territory, technology and industrial growth*. Oxford: Blackwell.

Webber, M. 1991: The contemporary transition. *Environ. Plann. D: Society and Space* 9, pp. 165–82.

Suggested Reading
Gregory (1989).
Harvey (1985a).
Johnston, R. J. and Taylor, P. J. eds 1989: *A world in crisis? Geographical perspectives*, second edition. Oxford: Blackwell.

critical rationalism   A philosophy of science developed by Karl Popper, originally as a critical response to the LOGICAL POSITIVISM of the VIENNA CIRCLE. (Neurath, a member of the Circle, nicknamed Popper 'the Official Opposition'; see Popper, 1976). Popper's philosophy is wide-ranging, and detailed discussions have been provided by Burke (1983) and O'Hear (1980), but two connected components have been of special significance for human geography.

a) *The principle of falsification*   In *The logic of scientific discovery* (1934; translated into English in 1959) Popper challenged the 'principle of verification' which was at the heart of logical positivism by suggesting that 'not the *verifiability* but the *falsifiability* of a [theoretical] system' should be taken as a 'criterion of demarcation' between the empirical sciences on the one hand and mathematics, logic and metaphysics on the other. This was not the same as a criterion of meaning, Popper emphasized, and 'falsifiability separates two kinds of perfectly meaningful statements': a view which made him still further at odds with the Vienna Circle, for whom metaphysics was indeed meaningless. Within human geography, Wilson's (1972) programme for a 'theoretical geography' was explicitly based on Popper's procedures, i.e.:

The essence of the scientific method is the construction of theories and the continual testing of these by comparing them with observation. The essence of such testing is an attempt to disprove a theory – to marshall observations which contradict the predictions of the theory. In this sense, theories are never proved to be generally true. The ones in which we believe represent the best approximations to truth at any one time . . . We expect, then, that theories will be subject to constant development and refinement: sometimes a falsified theory can be patched up; sometimes, radically different theory is needed (Wilson, 1972, p. 32).

As the last sentence implies, Popper's principle is often *methodologically* intractable, whatever its *logical* attractions. Even though Popper himself recognized this and attempted to stipulate a number of safeguards against *ad hoc* tinkering, Sayer (1992), from the perspective of REALISM, dismisses the principle of FALSIFICATION as 'virtually impossible to put into practice' (cf. Marshall, 1982). It is certainly the case that the principle has rarely been used in human geography but, as Wilson (1972) noted, this was as much a result of the inductivist bias of the QUANTITATIVE REVOLUTION as any considered rejection of critical rationalism. (This never prevented some quantitative geographers from using Popper to object to Marxism because, as Popper (1945) himself objected, it either *cannot be* falsified, or *has been* falsified and hence loses any claim to be a 'science'.)

(b) *The progress of science*   Popper used the iterative sequence described by Wilson to argue, further, that 'the growth of knowledge' depends upon a method of 'rational criticism'. He usually represented it like this:

$$P_1 \rightarrow TS \rightarrow EE \rightarrow P_2$$

Thus, we are supposed to start from a problem (P_1), then formulate a trial solution (TS) 'which we then subject to the severest possible test [that is, falsification] in a process of error elimination' (EE), which in turn leads to the creative formulation of a new problem (P_2). Hence, in Popper's view, the progress of science depends upon a creative response to error – upon what he called *Conjectures and refutations* (1963). Many commentators, and Popper too, have contrasted this normative model with Kuhn's account of the changing structure of scientific knowledge (see PARADIGM). So, for example, Bird (1975) correctly recognized that 'the implications for geography to be drawn from Popper's works are quite different from those to be drawn from the writings of Thomas Kuhn'. And Marshall (1982), although he mistakenly assumes Kuhn to stand 'in the mainstream of the logical positivist tradition' by virtue of the very tactic which Popper (1976) rejects (namely judging books 'by their covers or editors'), urged geographers 'to look elsewhere if

[they] are concerned to understand the logic of the process by which knowledge advances' (i.e. Popper) rather than 'the sociology of academic life' (i.e. Kuhn). Kuhn's whole object was indeed to confront what Barnes (1985) terms 'the myth of rationalism' on which Popper's project is founded. Barnes provides a number of general reasons why rationalism might properly be called a 'myth'; but perhaps the most telling specific objection comes from Sayer (1992, p. 230): 'What do we learn when a deductive theory is legitimately falsified? . . . Only that we must try a different deductive theory . . . *only* that *something* is wrong and not *what* is wrong'. The essential weakness, Sayer contends, is that Popper's strategy 'ignores the content of theory' and so cannot distinguish causal explanation from instrumentalist 'deviation' (see INSTRUMENTALISM; REALISM).

But Chouinard, Fincher and Webber (1984) have used I. Lakatos's critique and reformulation of Popper's proposals to argue that it is possible to conduct *scientific research programmes* in human geography in ways which are none the less conformable with REALISM. Lakatos (1978) believes that Popper is too ready to reject theories and argues for a more cautious, 'conservative' strategy: in his view, scientific progress ought to depend on the careful evaluation of what he calls *problemshifts*. A series of scientific theories is to be counted as *theoretically progressive* 'if each new theory has some excess empirical content over its predecessor, that is, if it predicts some novel, hitherto unexpected fact', and as *empirically progressive* if some of this excess empirical content is also corroborated, that is, if each new theory leads us to the actual discovery of some new fact'. Unless a problemshift satisfies both of these conditions it will be *degenerating* rather than progressive and ought not to replace the existing formulation (Lakatos, 1979). In much the same way, Chouinard, Fincher and Webber (1984, p. 375) argue that

It does not make sense, when dealing with an open system and therefore with a reality without invariant cause and effect relationships, to reject one's core propositions about causal mechanisms and processes only because of apparently disconfirming empirical evidence. Instead, the

criteria for accepting or rejecting a particular research tradition in human geography must be programmatic, that is, they must evaluate the coherence and creativity of a particular approach in terms of expansion in the conceptual and empirical scope of explanation.

Be that as it may, Lakatos's proposals are not immune to objection (Barnes, 1982) and it is by no means clear that, even in this revised form, 'the critical rationalist viewpoint can provide a new and welcome coherence' in human geography (Marshall, 1982; cf. Bird, 1989).   DG

References

Barnes, 1982: *T. S. Kuhn and social science*. London: Macmillan.

Barnes, B. 1985: Thomas Kuhn. In Skinner, Q., ed., *The return of grand theory to the human sciences*. Cambridge: Cambridge University Press, pp. 83–100.

Bird, J. H. 1975: Methodological implications for geography from the philosophy of K. R. Popper. *Scott. geogr. Mag.* 91, pp. 153–63.

Bird, J. H. 1989: *The changing worlds of geography*. Oxford: Clarendon Press.

Burke, T. 1983: *The philosophy of Popper*. Manchester: Manchester University Press.

Chouinard, V., Fincher, R. and Webber, W. 1984: Empirical research in scientific human geography. *Progr. hum. Geogr.* 8, pp. 346–80.

Lakatos, I. 1978: *The methodology of scientific research programmes*. Cambridge: Cambridge University Press.

Lakatos, I. 1979: Falsification and the methodology of scientific research programmes. In Lakatos, I. and Musgrave, A., eds, *Criticism and the growth of knowledge*. Cambridge: Cambridge University Press, pp. 91–196.

Marshall, J. 1982: Geography and critical rationalism. In Wood, J. D., ed., *Rethinking geographical inquiry*. Downsview, Ontario: Department of Geography, Atkinson College, York University, pp. 73–171.

O'Hear, A. 1980: *Karl Popper*. London: Routledge and Kegan Paul.

Popper, K. 1945: *The open society and its enemies*. London: Routledge and Kegan Paul.

Popper, K. 1959: *The logic of scientific discovery*. London: Hutchinson/New York: Basic Books.

Popper, K. 1963: *Conjectures and refutations: the gorwth of scientific knowledge*. London: Routledge and Kegan Paul.

Popper, K. 1976: Reason or revolution? In Frisby, D., ed., *The positivist dispute in German sociology*. London: Heinemann/New York: Harper and Row, pp. 288–300.

Sayer, A. 1992: *Method in social science: a realist approach*. London: Routledge.

Wilson, A. G. 1972: Theoretical geography: some speculations. *Trans. Inst. Br. Geogr.* 57, pp. 31–44.

Suggested Reading

Bird (1975).

Chouinard et al. (1984).

Sayer (1992), ch. 8.

critical theory A tradition of social and political thought, the central concern of which is the historicity of social action: in particular, the connections between HUMAN AGENCY and social structure which exist under CAPITALISM and which can be recognized and restructured through a process of critical reflection. Critical theory owed its inspiration to classical Marxism, but it was also a vital presence within the critical reformulations and extensions of HISTORICAL MATERIALISM associated with so-called 'Western Marxism': that is to say, it sought to move away from the priorities of political economy in order to address, in full and equal measure, the concerns of philosophy, aesthetics and culture (cf. Merquior, 1986).

It is usual to distinguish between two main schools (although there are connections and continuities between them): (i) the original FRANKFURT SCHOOL; and (ii) the later work of Jürgen Habermas, the focus of attention here, which includes and is variously described as a 'reconstruction of historical materialism' and a 'theory of communicative action' (see Held, 1980). There are three main planks to Habermas's platform.

(a) In his early writings Habermas argued that critical theory had to reflect on the conditions that made it possible: more specifically, he claimed that a critique of EPISTEMOLOGY is only possible as a social theory. To that end, he developed a concept of cognitive (or 'knowledge-constitutive') interests. In his view, any society necessarily entails both (i) social labour, which is organized through a system of *instrumental action*, and (b) social interaction, which is organized through a system of *communicative action*. The first of these involves the realization of a *technical interest*, so Habermas claimed, because any labour process has to have some means of achieving control over its materials and components (including human beings considered as objects); the second involves the realization of a *practical interest*, because any communication process requires some means of ensuring that the participants understand one another. These two interests, which are supposed to be deep-seated or 'quasi-transcendental' structural rules, thus constitute two different but dependent forms of knowledge by specifying their domains of study and the criteria for making valid statements about them: the

	COGNITIVE INTEREST	FORM OF KNOWLEDGE	DOMAIN	CRITERION OF VALIDITY	MODE OF SOCIAL ORGANIZATION
SOCIAL LABOUR ↓ forces of production	TECHNICAL	empirical–analytic	'object world'	successful explanations	instrumental action
relations of production SOCIAL INTERACTION	PRACTICAL	historical–hermeneutic	'subject world'	successful interpretations	communicative action

quasi-transcendental – – – – –▶ methodological – – – – – – ▶ sociological

critical theory *1: Cognitive interests.*

Type of society	Organization principle ——→	Characteristic form of crisis
PRIMITIVE	kinship relations	ecological–demographic crisis
TRADITIONAL	class domination through the state	political crisis
EARLY CAPITALISM	class domination through capital–labour relation	economic crisis
LATE CAPITALISM	class domination through state mediation of (corporate) capital–labour relation	sociocultural crisis

critical theory 2: *Society, organization principle and crisis in Habermas*

empirical–analytical sciences, which deal with a world of objects and make predictions about their interactions; and the *historical–hermeneutic sciences*, which deal with a world of subjects and provide interpretations of their interactions (Habermas, 1972). These twin trajectories are summarized in figure 1. At the time, Habermas suggested that a *critical science* would be directed towards the realization of a third, *emancipatory* interest which would necessarily involve the considered conjunction of both forms of knowledge – neither of them was self-sufficient. This scheme has been used in human geography to advance the critique of POSITIVISM and, in particular, to argue for the development of a *critical human geography* that would be committed neither to the 'objectivist' analysis of spatial systems and SPATIAL STRUCTURES nor to the 'subjectivist' construction of PLACE, but would use and rework both traditions together (Gregory, 1978; see also REALISM).

(b) Habermas subsequently proposed that a critical social theory is possible only as a theory of social evolution, and his reconstruction of historical materialism depends on the 'argumentation sketch' summarized in figure 2 (Habermas, 1975, 1979). There, different forms of society are supposed to be characterized by different 'organizational principles', each of which is vulnerable to a distinctive form of CRISIS. Habermas's central claim is that a crisis is both 'objective' and 'subjective', both caused and 'experienced', so that a crisis is *caused* by an interruption in the prevailing mode of system integration but will only be realized (in the fullest sense of the term) if it is consciously *experienced*; in other words, if human subjects 'feel their social identity threatened'. Habermas's argument is that the resolution of successive crises depends on an evolutionary learning process which takes place in two dimensions: technically useful knowledge and moral–practical consciousness. It is that 'learning process' which Habermas sees inscribed within the Enlightenment project of MODERNITY and which has prompted a number of critics to charge him with ETHNOCENTRISM. Habermas's major concern, however, is with the distortion of the project of modernity by the development of capitalism – through the intrusion of domination into labour (ALIENATION) and interaction ('systematically distorted communication') – in such a way that the possibilities of informed democratic debate within a genuinely public sphere have been foreshortened: issues are increasingly constructed as purely technical matters which may be decided without the involvement of a moral–practical consciousness (Habermas, 1989; see also Gregory, 1980). Here too Habermas is vulnerable to criticism, and feminist scholars in particular have objected to his failure to recognize the significance of gender as an axis of discrimination and domination; it is also necessary to offer an historically and geographically more nuanced account than Habermas was able to provide at the time (see Fraser, 1987; Calhoun, 1992). But Habermas's commitment to the project

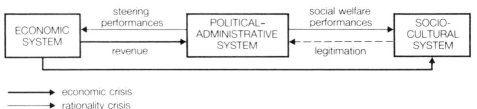

critical theory   *3: Crises in late capitalism.*

of modernity is unwavering and has generated sharp criticism of POSTMODERNISM and POSTSTRUCTURALISM (see Habermas, 1981, 1987b; Bernstein, 1985).

(c) In the early 1970s Habermas focused on the involvement of the STATE in mediating and managing the various crises of so-called *late capitalism,* and he paid particular attention to its propensity for sociocultural crisis or *legitimation crisis* (figure 3; see also Habermas, 1975; McCarthy, 1978). This model was widely if informally used in POLITICAL GEOGRAPHY. Although Harvey and Scott (1989) have implied that it was subsequently overtaken by events – notably by what they saw as the shift from FORDISM to FLEXIBLE ACCUMULATION – Habermas has since revised his account in the direction of a *theory of communicative action.* In the late twentieth-century world, he now argues, the instrumental and strategic rationalities of social systems (the domains of technically useful knowledge) have been over-extended: the economic system and the politico-administrative system have encroached on the LIFE-WORLD through processes of monetization and bureaucratization (figure 4). At the limit, Habermas suggests, this amounts to a *colonization of the lifeworld,* which occurs as soon as those processes reach 'beyond their mediating roles and penetrate those spheres of the lifeworld which are responsible for cultural transmission, socialization and the formation of personal identity'. When the scope of communicative action is confined in this way, Habermas concludes, people are made to feel less like persons and more like things. New conflicts may arise at the seam between system and lifeworld, around 'the grammar of forms of life', where they are articulated by new SOCIAL MOVEMENTS which overlie the traditional politics of economic, social and military security, and revolve around the symbolic reproduction of the lifeworld itself (Habermas, 1984, 1987a; see also Ingram, 1987; White, 1988).

These are important and provocative suggestions, and as such they have been subject to considerable critical scrutiny (see Honneth and Joas, 1991). Oddly, however, neither Habermas nor his critics have paid

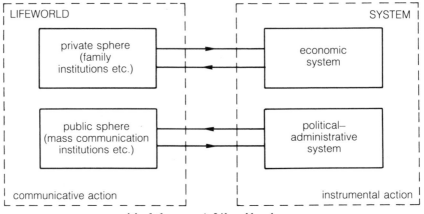

critical theory   *4: Lifeworld and system.*

much attention to the different spatialities involved: although the theory of communicative action is plainly deeply embedded in the dilemmas of postwar Germany, it is none the less a GRAND THEORY (Giddens, 1985) which pays no attention to the significance of webs of difference and connection over space. But it is possible to bring Habermas's project into dialogue with human geography, in particular with concepts of SPACE and PLACE (Gregory, 1989), to chart the territoriality of social struggles (Miller, 1992), and to explore some of the parallels and contrasts between Habermas's advance of the system into the lifeworld and Lefebvre's account of the superimposition of *abstract space* over *concrete space* (Lefebvre, 1992; Gregory, 1993). It may even be possible to turn the ethnocentrism of Habermas's project against itself, and to examine the imposition of colonial systems and spatialities on the lifeworlds of native peoples (Harris, 1991).   DG

References

Bernstein, R. J., ed. 1985: *Habermas and modernity*. Cambridge: Polity Press.

Calhoun, C. 1992: *Habermas and the public sphere*. Cambridge, MA: MIT Press.

Fraser, N. 1987: What's critical about critical theory? Habermas and gender. In Benhabib, S. and Cornell, D., eds, *Feminism as critique: essays on the politics of gender in late-capitalist societies*. Cambridge: Polity Press, pp. 31–56.

Giddens, A. 1985: Jürgen Habermas. In Skinner, Q., ed., *The return of grand theory in the human sciences*. Cambridge: Cambridge University Press, pp. 121–39.

Gregory, D. 1978: *Ideology, science and human geography*. London: Hutchinson.

Gregory, D. 1980: The ideology of control: systems theory and geography. *Tijdschr. econ. soc. Geogr.* 71, pp. 327–42.

Gregory, D. 1989: The crisis of modernity? Human geography and critical social theory. In Peet, R. and Thrift, N., eds, *New models in geography*, volume 2. London: Unwin Hyman, pp. 348–85.

Gregory, D. 1993: *Geographical imaginations*. Oxford: Blackwell.

Habermas, J. 1972: *Knowledge and human interests*. London: Heinemann.

Habermas, J. 1975: *Legitimation crisis*. London: Heinemann.

Habermas, J. 1979: *Communication and the evolution of society*. London: Heinemann.

Habermas, J. 1981: Modernity versus postmodernity. *New German Critique* 22, pp. 3–14.

Habermas, J. 1984: *The theory of communicative action*, volume 1: *Reason and the rationalization of society*. London: Heinemann.

Habermas, J. 1987a: *The theory of communicative action*, volume 2: *The critique of functionalist reason*. Cambridge: Polity Press.

Habermas, J. 1987b: *The philosophical discourse of modernity*. Cambridge: Polity Press.

Habermas, J. 1989: *The structural transformation of the public sphere*. Cambridge, MA: MIT Press.

Harris, C. 1991: Power, modernity and historical geography. *Ann. Ass. Am. Geogr.* 81, pp. 671–83.

Harvey, D. and Scott, A. 1989: The practice of human geography. In Macmillan, B. ed., *Remodelling geography*. Oxford: Blackwell, pp. 217–29.

Held, D. 1980: *Introduction to critical theory: Horkheimer to Habermas*. London: Hutchinson.

Honneth, A. and Joas, H. 1991: *Communicative action: essays on Jürgen Habermas's The theory of communicative action*. Cambridge, MA: MIT Press.

Ingram, D. 1987: *Habermas and the dialectic of reason*. New Haven: Yale University Press.

Lefebvre, H. 1992: *The production of space* (translated by D. Nicholson-Smith). Oxford: Blackwell.

McCarthy, T. 1978: *The critical theory of Jürgen Habermas*. London: Hutchinson.

Merquior, J. 1986: *Western Marxism*. London: Paladin.

Miller, B. 1992: Collective action and rational choice: place, community and the limits to individual self-interest. *Econ. Geogr.* 68, pp. 22–42.

White, S. 1988: *The recent work of Jürgen Habermas: power, justice and modernity*. Cambridge: Cambridge University Press.

Suggested Reading

Giddens (1985).

Gregory (1989).

Holub, R. 1991: *Jürgen Habermas: critic in the public sphere*. London: Routledge.

Ingram, D. 1990: *Critical theory and philosophy*. New York: Paragon House, chs 1 and 7.

cross-section A description of a SOCIETY and (particularly) its LANDSCAPE at a specific moment in time: in effect, a horizontal 'slice'. The use of cross-sections as a working methodology in HISTORICAL

GEOGRAPHY was popularized by H. C. Darby's classic *Historical geography of England before A.D. 1800* (1936), which used 'a sequence of cross-sections taken at successive periods' to represent 'reconstructions of past geographies', a device which owed much to Macaulay's famous description of the landscape of England in 1685 in his *The history of England* (1849). At the time, Darby recalled, 'the method of cross-sections [was] hailed as being essentially geographical as opposed to historical', but drawing boundaries around subjects was soon forgotten since, as Darby himself recognized, 'the moment we ask "Why does this landscape look like it does?" that moment we are committed to something more than mere description or a mere cross-section' (see Darby, in Finberg, 1962). Hence, in his later compilation, *A new historical geography of England* (1973), Darby employed an intercalation of cross-section and vertical theme to try to capture stabilities and transformations and to combine description and explanation (see also SEQUENT OCCUPANCE). But the move from 'description' to 'explanation' is not so readily accomplished by a trajectory between 'cross-section' and 'vertical theme', and the implied identifications are misleading. First, the advance of FUNCTIONALISM in geography through the formal protocols of SYSTEMS ANALYSIS represented a recognizable revival of Darby's traditional methodology and could claim to provide a theoretical rationale for what had originally been a largely pragmatic procedure, *but in explanatory rather than descriptive terms*. Second, questions of temporal phrasing are considerably more complicated than the early discussions seemed to suggest, and the recognition of hierarchies of process domains (or 'temporal levels') within SOCIAL FORMATIONS make the cutting of cross-sections more than the simple empirical manoeuvre it was once made out to be (see, e.g., Thrift, 1977) DG

References

Darby, H. C., ed. 1936: *Historical geography of England before A.D. 1800*. Cambridge: Cambridge University Press.

Darby, H. C., ed. 1973: *A new historical geography of England*. Cambridge: Cambridge University Press.

Finberg, H. P. R., ed. 1962: *Approaches to history: a symposium*. London: Routledge and Kegan Paul/Toronto: University of Toronto Press.

Macaulay, T. B. 1849: *The history of England from the accession of James II*, volume 1. London: Longman, Green and Co.

Thrift, N. 1977: Time and theory in human geography. *Prog. hum. Geogr.* 1, pp. 65–101.

cultivation See SHIFTING CULTIVATION.

cultural capital Coined by the French sociologist Pierre Bourdieu, the term refers to social status acquired through the ability to make cultural distinctions. Cultural (or symbolic) capital represents 'a transformed or disguised form of physical or "economic" capital' (Bourdieu and Passeron, 1977, p. 183). Related to Bourdieu's broader interest in 'cultural competence' (the cognitive process that enables us to understand the cultural codes through which meanings are communicated), 'cultural capital' originated in the context of educational research and was later extended to the whole range of social distinctions through which 'tastes' (e.g. in music and the arts) function as markers of CLASS.   PAJ

Reference

Bourdieu, P. and Passeron, J.-C. 1977: *Reproduction in education, society and culture*. London: Sage.

Suggested Reading

Bourdieu, P. 1984: *Distinction: a social critique of the judgement of taste*. London: Routledge and Kegan Paul.

cultural ecology An approach to the study of the relations between a cultural group (a mode of life associated with specific material and symbolic practices) and its natural environment. It is most closely associated with the work of Julian Steward (1955) and with the study of THIRD WORLD peasantries, pastoralists, hunter–gatherers and tribal peoples (see SUBSISTENCE). Cultural ecology proposes that similar configurations of environment and technology tend to be functionally and causally related to similar social organizations. Cultural ecology was therefore the study of the adaptive processes by which human societies and CULTURES adjust through subsistence patterns to the specific parameters of their local habitat (see ECOLOGY and ENVIRONMENTAL PERCEPTION). Steward emphasized that adaptive processes could be explored through a 'cultural core' of human activities; social evolution was not a series of stages through which all societies passed but a multilinear process of differing patterns of environmental adaptation. Cultural ecology can be seen as a subset of HUMAN ECOLOGY, an approach which attempts to link culture as a material and symbolic realm and Darwinist evolutionary theory.

Since Steward's time, cultural ecology has developed in two directions. First, it can be seen as a variant of Marx's materialism in which 'techno-environmental determinism' becomes the motor of history. The second interpretation refines the concept of ecology by introducing notions drawn from ECOSYSTEMS analysis and GENERAL SYSTEMS THEORY. Cultural practices are related to wider movements of energy, matter and information, and fulfil homeostatic or regulatory functions to ensure environmental sustainability (see FEEDBACK). In this latter view, cultural ecology is strongly influenced by cybernetics and ecological theory, such that human populations are seen conceptually as the same as any other animal population struggling for survival amidst the complex webs of ecosystemic relations. Many geographers and anthropologists attempted to develop this theory of adaptation in which culture (for example, pig-killing rituals in highland New Guinea, or cosmological beliefs in the Kalahari) functions as a self-regulating adaptive mechanism with respect to local environmental systems (CARRYING CAPACITY). Cultural ecology has been heavily criticized for its functionalism and teleology, its heavily reliance on organic analogies, and its incapacity to take account of politico-economic processes of surplus extraction and appropriation. (See also BERKELEY SCHOOL.) MW

Reference

Steward, J. 1955: *The theory of culture change.* Urbana: University of Illinois Press.

cultural geography Traditionally a subfield of HUMAN GEOGRAPHY that focused upon the patterns and interactions of human CULTURE, both material and non-material, in relation to the natural environment. Today the term 'cultural geography' covers a diverse range of studies with only tenuous links to a common tradition. Theories of CULTURE are important in differentiating between the various approaches to cultural geography.

The major tradition of cultural geography in the twentieth century has been American, and courses in cultural geography, common in the USA and Canada, have until recently been relatively rare in European geographical teaching outside Germany. American cultural geography has long been dominated by the writings and teachings of Carl O. Sauer (1952, 1966) and his students of the BERKELEY SCHOOL. Sauer was interested in the range of human interventions in transforming the natural world across defined regions of the Earth's surface: plant and animal domestication; the DIFFUSION of domesticates; fire ecology and hydrological engineering; modes of cultivation; and human conduct of all kinds that bears upon human occupancy and geographical diversity apparent in landscapes. Sauer approached the human use of the Earth ecologically, and although deeply critical of the school of ENVIRONMENTAL DETERMINISM that was current in American geography in the early part of the century, he was himself influenced by ecological concepts of culture traceable to the same German intellectual sources, notably Friedrich Ratzel's biologically based ANTHROPOGEOGRAPHY. Sauer's understanding of culture was strongly influenced by the American student of native cultures, the anthropologist A. L. Kroeber. From German geography he adopted the concept of *Landschaft* which he translated as LANDSCAPE, outlining the method of cultural geography in his 1925 paper 'The morphology of landscape'. In his work on the American South West and Spanish America, Sauer modified his early distinction between natural and cultural landscapes, and he introduced into cultural geography a focus on plant and animal domestication, diffusion of innovations and a strong commitment to rural, folk societies that were understood historically.

Sauer's concern in later life that the human use of the Earth was becoming increasingly destructive anticipates contemporary worries about environmental degradation. This concern found expression, and Sauerian cultural geography its apotheosis, in the conceptually vast and hugely influential *Man's role in changing the face of the Earth* (Thomas, 1956), which emerged from a conference of which Sauer was the guiding spirit. Its essays and discussions demonstrate the breadth of his conception of cultural geography and his global commitment, as well as his resistance to many aspects of modern, urbanized life. The continued significance of this ecological approach to cultural geography is evidenced by a recent re-examination of the issues considered in *Man's role . . .* (Turner, 1990) and by its strength in the research and teaching activities of American geography departments, particularly in the West and South.

Sauer's concept of CULTURE has been attacked by modern cultural geographers who are keen to ground the idea of culture in social relations of production and reproduction (Cosgrove, 1983). The centrality given to questions of culture within critical social science and the humanities in the years since Sauer's death has led some to proclaim a 'new' cultural geography (Jackson, 1989) that is more closely aligned to social theory than to biology and history. In fact, the texts of the late 1960s in the series 'Foundations of cultural geography' (Wagner, various dates), which address issues such as culture and communication, the symbolism of house forms and the cultural diversity of the USA, both reflect the Berkeley agenda and anticipate many of the concerns of the 'new' cultural geography (Duncan, 1990), while Clarence Glacken's masterpiece *Traces on the Rhodean shore* (1967), which examines European intellectual history with respect to questions of environmental relations, may be regarded as foundational for renewed scholarly interest in the historiography of environmental attitudes (Livingstone, 1988).

Despite such continuities, it is possible to draw distinctions between the Berkeley project and some new directions in cultural geography (Cosgrove and Jackson, 1987). The relative decline of the former during the period of the QUANTITATIVE REVOLUTION, with its promotion of SPACE rather than environment as the central geographical concept, has yielded to a *rapprochement* of cultural and SOCIAL GEO-GRAPHY in recent years. The influence of linguistic theory within human geography has led to greater attention to culture as a process of self- and social signification, wherein *meaning* is unstable and contested because it is always constituted through the shared discourses of specific human groups. The new cultural geography has responded to the MULTICULTURALISM of contemporary urban societies in Europe and North America and to the claims of POSTMODERNISM to give a voice to the 'other'; that is, to the discourses of those traditionally excluded from consideration in Western social science and the humanities. In this perspective, recent writers have insisted on the cultural integrity of formerly colonized peoples, and of women, the materially dispossessed and other minorities within a dominantly white, male and bourgeois culture. The traditional view of CULTURE as constituted by a uniform and normative set of beliefs, attitudes and material artefacts has been criticized as the ideology of a dominant group seeking hegemonic power over what it regards as 'other' to itself. The concept of culture traditionally used by cultural geographers has thus been displaced by a theory of *cultural politics*, in which different cultural discourses engage each other in a constant struggle for POWER. The new perspective places emphasis on issues of representation, and cultural geography today is faced with a problem – common to all social science – of a *crisis of representation*, because any claim to represent the 'other' is potentially a denial of the integrity of that 'other' and its own separate language.

One aspect of this concern with the politics of representation is the interest among some cultural geographers with national identity. Recognition of the fact that environmental, territorial and other geographical myths have been and remain significant in constructing alternative nationalist ideologies has renewed the links between cultural and POLITICAL GEOGRAPHY. Research on the role of landscape in the construction of 'Englishness' (Cox, 1988), or of landscape icons such as Niagara Falls in defining American national identity (McGreevey, 1988), recast in new ways cultural geography's traditional interest in landscape and environmental relations. Radical changes in the world order during the late 1980s, notably the collapse of the Soviet imperial system in Eurasia, and the rise of religious fundamentalism, have given these questions a renewed urgency and contemporary relevance.

The centrality now afforded to questions of culture within geography has thus led both to a powerful revival of cultural geography and to the loss of a single theory, method and set of questions within a defined subfield. In this, cultural geography reflects the collapse of foundationalism and metatheory generally within human geography. However, the continued strength of cultural ecology in the USA (Turner, 1989), the renewed interest in historical and contemporary environmental attitudes and conduct, the growing desire to find ways to represent multiple voices within geography, and the powerful restatement of national identities across the world all suggest that cultural geography will remain a diverse but vital part of the discipline. (See also CULTURE; CULTURAL LANDSCAPE; POSTMODERNISM.)   DEC

References

Cosgrove, D. 1983: Towards a radical cultural geography: problems of theory. *Antipode*, 15(1), pp. 1–11.

Cosgrove, D. and Jackson, P. 1987: New directions in cultural geography. *Area*, 19, pp. 95–101.

Cox, G. 1988: 'Reading nature': reflections on ideological persistence and the politics of the countryside. *Landscape Res.* 13, pp. 24–34.

Duncan, J. 1990: *The city as text: the politics of landscape interpretation in the Kandyan kingdom.* Cambridge: Cambridge University Press.

Glacken, C. 1967: *Traces on the Rhodean shore: nature and culture in Western thought from ancient times to the end of the eighteenth century.* Berkeley, CA: University of California Press.

Jackson, P. 1989: *Maps of meaning: an introduction to cultural geography.* London: Unwin Hyman.

Livingstone, D. N. 1988: Science, magic and religion: a contextual reassessment of geography in the sixteenth and seventeenth centuries. *Hist. Sci.* 26, pp. 269–94.

McGreevey, P. 1988: The end of America: the beginning of Canada. *Can. Geogr.* 32, pp. 307–18.

Sauer, C. O. 1925: The morphology of landscape. Reprinted in Leighly, J. ed., 1963: *Land and life: selections from the writings of Carl Ortwin Sauer.* Berkeley, CA: University of California Press, pp. 315–50.

Sauer, C. O. 1952: *Agricultural origins and dispersals.* Bowman Memorial Lecture Series 2, New York: American Geographical Society.

Sauer, C. O. 1966: *The early Spanish Main.* Berkeley, CA: University of California Press.

Thomas, W. L. 1956: *Man's role in changing the face of the Earth.* Chicago: University of Chicago Press.

Turner, B. L. II 1989: The specialist–synthesist approach and the revival of geography. *Ann. Ass. Am. Geogr.* 79, pp. 269–79.

Turner, B. L. II et al., eds 1990: *The Earth as transformed by human action: global and regional changes in the biosphere over the past 300 years.* Cambridge: Cambridge University Press.

Wagner, P. ed., various dates: Foundations in cultural geography series. Englewood Cliffs, NJ: Prentice-Hall.

Suggested Reading

Cosgrove, D. and Daniels, S., eds 1988: *The inconography of landscape: essays on the symbolic representation, design and use of past environments.* Cambridge: Cambridge University Press.

Glacken (1967).

Jackson (1989).

Leighly (1963).

Short, J. R. 1991: *Imagined country: culture, society, environment.* London: Routledge.

cultural hearth   The area of origin of a cultural group involved in the creation of a particular CULTURAL LANDSCAPE. The concept is associated with Sauer and the Berkeley School (cf. CULTURAL GEOGRAPHY): it represents the core area in a process of DIFFUSION whereby new cultural practices (especially, given Sauer's interests, agricultural practices) spread through

HUMAN AGENCY to create cultural regions (see Sauer, 1969).

Sauer (1952) argued that cultural hearths emerged through the combination of especially favourable circumstances, reflecting the available natural resources, including climate and vegetation. Such hearths were few, he claimed:

Now and then, in a few and, I may repeat, physically favored areas some such center has burst forth into a great period of significant invention, from which ideas spread, and in part changed as they spread afield. These centers of major and sustained innovation were always few. In the history of man, unless I misread it greatly, diffusion of ideas from a few hearths has been the rule; independent, parallel invention the exception.   RJJ

References

Sauer, C. O. 1952: *Agricultural origins and dispersals*. New York: American Geographical Society.

Sauer, C. O. 1969: *Seeds, spades, hearths and herds: the domestication of animals and foodstuffs*. Cambridge, MA: MIT Press.

cultural landscape   Traditionally, the principal object of study in CULTURAL GEOGRAPHY; the classic definition is Carl Sauer's:

The cultural landscape is fashioned from a natural landscape by a culture group. Culture is the agent, the natural area is the medium, the cultural landscape is the result. Under the influence of a given culture, itself changing through time, the landscape undergoes development, passing through phases, and probably reaching ultimately the end of its cycle of development. With the introduction of a different – that is, alien – culture, a rejuvenation of the cultural landscape sets in, or a new landscape is superimposed on remnants of an older one (Sauer, 1925; see the figure).

Drawing a clear parallel with W. M. Davis' ideas of cyclical evolution over time in physical landscapes, Sauer sought to stress the agency of CULTURE as a force in shaping the visible features of delimited regions on the Earth's surface. In his conception, which came to dominate the work of the BERKELEY SCHOOL of geography, Sauer was concerned to counter the influence of ENVIRONMENTAL DETERMINISM while recognizing the significance of the physical environment as the medium with and through which human cultures act (see CULTURE AREA). Thus elements of the physical environment such as watercourses, plants and animals are included in the cultural landscape in so far as they evoke human responses and adaptations, or have been altered by human activity; for example, hydrological management and plant domestication (Voeks, 1990). It is clear in Sauer's model that he regarded visible forms as the principal features for study in the cultural landscape, and that his

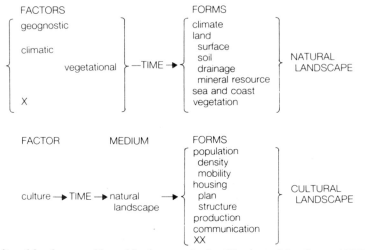

cultural landscape   *Natural landscape and cultural landscape (after Sauer, 1925).*

approach to it was highly empirical.

Numerous studies of particular cultural LANDSCAPES, especially in the American Southwest, were influenced by Sauer's ideas. The model was perhaps more successful in such a stark physical environment over which a succession of distinct cultural groups have recently had influence (Meinig, 1973; Norwood and Monk, 1987) than in more deeply modified regions such as Western Europe (Jordan, 1973). More recent work has paid greater attention to non-material aspects of culture, examining the role of beliefs, attitudes and expectations in shaping cultural transformations of physical enviroments (Doughty, 1983, 1987).

Attempts to distance cultural geography from Sauer's influence have yielded different and more fluid conceptions of landscape in cultural geography. Daniels and Cosgrove (1988, p. 1) claim that 'a landscape is a cultural image, a pictorial way of representing, structuring or symbolising surroundings. This is not to say that landscapes are immaterial. They may be represented in a variety of materials and on many surfaces – in paint on canvas, in writing on paper, in earth, stone, water and vegetation on the ground'. Here the emphasis remains on the visual character of landscapes, but is not restricted to their visible features: all forms of landscape are regarded as cultural signifiers, the interpretation of which reveals cultural attitudes and processes (see CULTURE; ICONOGRAPHY).

Less attention is now paid in cultural landscape studies to the direct relations between human societies and the physical environment. Empirically, it is recognized that the 'natural landscape' that Sauer regarded as the *tabula rasa* upon which culture inscribed itself cannot be established with any certainty over most regions of the world. Theoretically, the recognition that the meanings of NATURE itself vary between cultures means that it offers no single, stable object for study in cultural geography (see CULTURE). Thus all landscapes may be regarded as cultural, even in their 'natural' state. Although landscape thus remains a significant concept within cultural geography, in terms of usage, the phrase *cultural landscape* usually still implies the traditional Sauerian concept.   DEC

References and Suggested Reading

Daniels, S. and Cosgrove, D. 1988: Iconography and landscape. In Cosgrove, D. and Daniels, S., eds, *The iconography of landscape: essays on the symbolic representation, design and use of past environments*. Cambridge: Cambridge University Press, pp. 1–10.

Doughty, R. W. 1983: *Wildlife and man in Texas: environmental change and conservation*. College Station: Texas A&M Press.

Doughty, R. W. 1987: *At home in Texas: early views of the land*. College Station: Texas A&M Press.

Jordan, T. 1973: *The European cultural area*. New York: Harper and Row.

Meinig, D. W. 1973: *Southwest: three peoples in geographic change*. Oxford: Oxford University Press.

Norwood, V. and Monk, J. 1987: *The desert is no lady: southwestern landscapes in women's writing and art*. New Haven: Yale University Press.

Sauer, C. O. 1925: The morphology of landscape. Reprinted in Leighly, J., ed., 1974: *Land and life: selections from the writings of Carl Ortwin Sauer*. Berkeley, CA: University of California Press, pp. 315–50.

Voeks, R. 1990: Sacred leaves of Brazilian candomble. *Geogr. Rev.* 80, pp. 118–31.

cultural politics Deriving from the field of cultural studies, 'cultural politics' signifies the domain in which meanings are constructed, negotiated and resisted. The term demands a plural definition of CULTURE as 'whole ways of life', ranked hierarchically in relations of dominance and subordination and ranging from abstract 'maps of meaning' to the objectification of those meanings in concrete social practices and spatial forms (Hall and Henderson, 1977, p. 10). The concept of 'cultural politics' draws attention to the unequal distribution of power that inheres within cultural conceptions of RACE, GENDER and sexuality, extending to personal identities as well as social relations.   PAJ

Reference

Hall, S. and Henderson, J., eds 1977: *Resistance through rituals*. London: Hutchinson/Centre for Contemporary Cultural Studies.

Suggested Reading

Hall and Henderson (1977).

Hall, S. et al., eds 1980: *Culture, media, language.* London: Hutchinson/Centre for Contemporary Cultural Studies.

Hooks, B. 1990: *Yearning: race, gender, and cultural politics.* Toronto: Between the Lines.

Jackson, P. 1989: *Maps of meaning.* London: Unwin Hyman.

culture One of the most complex yet important concepts in the social sciences, most writers now agree that culture is best approached historically. Williams (1976) has pointed out how over the course of the modern period the meaning of culture has changed from reference to skilled human activity (as in agriculture, viticulture, etc.) to refer to the whole set of activities through which a human group encompasses and transforms nature, including 'human nature' (Yoruba culture, bourgeois culture) and the refined individual spirit (as in being a person of culture), and finally to the collection of intellectual and artistic practices deemed to indicate and be produced by such spirits (the culture that impelled Goering to reach for his revolver). Consistently throughout this history of changing meanings in Western thought, culture has been theoretically counterposed to NATURE. Following Williams' lead, attention has recently been focused on recovering the ways in which the changing meanings of culture have reflected and promoted sectional interpretations of individual and collective human nature.

In CULTURAL GEOGRAPHY attention was originally focused on *material culture*, as opposed to the social heritage of collective mental and spiritual products and forms of human conduct (but see Tuan, 1974, 1984). In this, geographers followed definitions developed in cultural anthropology. Explicit theorizing of culture was rare among geographers of both the BERKELEY SCHOOL and the Aberystwyth School, whose students concentrated on relations between apparently static folk cultures and their physical environment. Geography's persistent economism rendered culture a weak and epiphenomenal concept in explaining human occupance, although Carl Sauer, the most influential geographical writer on culture until the 1970s, himself recognized that the economy is culturally encompassed (Sauer, 1941).

In both anthropology and geography the past two decades have seen a renewed interest in the theorizing of culture (Geertz, 1973; Clifford and Marcus, 1986) and greater concentration on contemporary cultures. Culture is now seen as an active force in social reproduction, the negotiated process and product of the discourses through which humans signify their experiences to themselves and others. The linguistic turn in SOCIAL THEORY has led to the concept of culture as a TEXT which the outsider is obliged to interpret ethnographically through processes of representation which are themselves textual (Duncan and Duncan, 1988). The realization that all human activity is culturally encompassed and thus open to variable interpretations according to different perspectives has been a feature of POST-MODERNISM, and accounts in part for postmodern geography's rejection of univocal explanation and its celebration of difference.

The cause and consequence of the renewed attention paid to cultural theory has been the development of CULTURAL POLITICS (Bonnett, 1989; Jackson, 1989). Challenges to what are seen as ideologically dominant cultural discourses (CAPITALISM; PATRIARCHY; RACISM) are identified in the cultural codes and signification systems of *other*, subaltern groups in Western societies: ethnic and religious minorities, feminists, gays and lesbians. Such conscious promotion of cultural identity, often involving the invention of traditions, can be subverted by the capacity of dominant cultures to incorporate and neutralize cultural signifiers. Thus styles of American black music and speech, or graffiti art, are rapidly introduced into mainstream culture and their subversive political potential reduced. The main agency for this transmission is the mass media, which have become a subject of considerable attention within cultural geography (Zonin, 1990).

Attention to cultural politics within SOCIAL GEOGRAPHY focuses upon increasingly multicultural metropolitan regions. In both ECONOMIC GEOGRAPHY and geographical studies of DEVELOPMENT, emphasis has also turned towards cultural questions. In the former this derives from recognition of the significance of leisure and consumerism in POST-INDUSTRIAL societies and their post-Fordist production systems which concentrate on product differentiation adjusted to rapidly changing fashion seen as a form of cultural self-signification (Harvey, 1989; Cooke, 1990) (see also FLEXIBLE ACCUMULATION; POST-FORDISM). In the latter it results from the recognition that the grass-roots reception of development ideas is significantly affected by local cultural assumptions and attitudes.

The traditional distinction between culture and NATURE that found expression within geographical studies of culture and environment has been challenged by both 'green' and feminist philosophies, which seek to collapse the separate spheres of humanity and the natural world, emphasizing environmental unity, species rights and 'ecological reason' (Diamond and Orestein, 1990; see ENVIRONMENTALISM). Although as yet underdeveloped within geography (Cosgrove, 1990; Kay, 1989), such challenges to the meaning of culture will undoubtedly have an impact there during the 1990s. (See also CULTURAL LANDSCAPE; ICONOGRAPHY.)   DEC

References and Suggested Reading

Bonnett, A. 1989: Situationism, geography and poststructuralism. *Environ. Plann. D: Society and Space* 7, pp. 131–46.

Clifford, J. and Marcus, G., eds 1986: *Writing culture: the politics and poetics of ethnography.* Berkeley, CA: University of California Press.

Cooke, P. 1990: *Back to the future: modernity, postmodernity and locality.* London: Unwin Hyman.

Cosgrove, D. 1990: Environmental thought and action: pre-modern and post-modern. *Trans. Inst. Br. Geogr.* n.s. 15, pp. 344–58.

Diamond, I. and Orenstein, F. 1990: *Reweaving the world: the emergence of ecofeminism.* San Francisco: Sierra Club.

Duncan, J. and Duncan, N. 1988: (Re)reading the landscape. *Environ. Plann. D: Society and Space* 6, pp. 117-26.

Geertz, C. 1973: *The interpretation of cultures.* New York: Basic Books.

Harvey, D. 1989: *The condition of modernity: an enquiry into the origins of cultural change.* Oxford: Blackwell.

Jackson, P. 1989: *Maps of meaning: an introduction to cultural geography.* London: Unwin Hyman.

Kay, J. 1989: Human dominion over nature in the Hebrew Bible. *Ann. Ass. Am. Geogr.* 79, pp. 214–32.

Sauer, C. O. 1941: Foreword to historical geography. Reprinted in Leighly, J., ed., 1974: *Land and life: selections from the writing of Carl Ortwin Sauer.* Berkeley, CA: University of California Press, pp. 351–79.

Tuan, Y.-F. 1974: *Topophilia: a study of environmental attitudes, perceptions and values.* Englewood Cliffs, NJ: Prentice-Hall.

Tuan, Y.-F. 1984: *Dominance and affection: the making of pets.* New Haven: Yale University Press.

Williams, R. 1976: *Keywords: a vocabulary of culture and society.* London: Fontana/New York: Oxford University Press.

Zonin, L. 1990: *Place images in media: portrayal, experience, meaning.* Savage, MD: Rowman & Littlefield.

culture area   A concept derived from CULTURAL ECOLOGY, referring to the geographical REGION over which a degree of homogeneity in cultural traits may be identified (see also CULTURE). The concept owes its origins to Ratzel's notion of a *Kulturprovinz*, and to the concern among German geographers in the first part of the twentieth century to delimit the true boundaries of the German *Reich* using cultural indicators. Germanic influences on inter-war American anthropological and geographical studies of native American cultures (Benedict, 1935) introduced the concept into Anglophone geography. Students using the culture area concept frequently subclassified such areas into three contiguous zones: (a) the *core*, the area over which the culture in question has exclusive or quasi-exclusive influence; (b) the *domain*, over which its identifying traits are dominant but not exclusive; and (c) the *realm*, over which such traits may be found but are subdominant to those of other cultures. A classic example of such a study is Meinig's (1965) identification of a Mormon culture area centred on the Great Basin of Utah. The organismic dimension given to the original concept by Ratzel's biologically based ideas of environmental relations, and of expansion and conflict between culture areas struggling for survival, is absent from such morphological studies (Jordan, 1973). Today, interpretations of culture areas often concentrate on urban subcultures, or lifestyles dominating sections of cities, as Jackson's (1989) of the gay community in San Francisco.   DEC

References

Benedict, R. 1935: *Patterns of culture*. London: Routledge and Kegan Paul.

Jackson, P. 1989: *Maps of meaning: an introduction to cultural Geography*. London: Unwin Hyman.

Jordan, T. 1973: *The European culture area*. New York: Harper and Row.

Meinig, D. 1965: The Mormon culture region: strategies and patterns of the American West. *Ann. Ass. Am. Geogr.* 55, pp. 191–220.

cycle of poverty   Self-perpetuating poverty and deprivation transmitted inter-generationally (see the figure). Whereas some of the causes of this process lie in a child's home background, others reflect spatial variations in life chances, as with the quality of local schools, the quantity and quality of local jobs available, health and crime problems in the NEIGHBOUR-HOOD, and so forth. Thus the cycle of poverty is particularly associated with the INNER CITY in many urban areas, and is the reason for it being the focus of many policies of POSITIVE DISCRIMINATION there. The operation of cycles of poverty can be found in a wide variety of contexts, however, both rural and suburban, wherever disadvantaged members of society are concentrated in areas in which the local situation harms their life chances (cf. UNDERCLASS). In some presentations, drawing on the work of Oscar Lewis (e.g. 1966, 1969), the victims of the cycle are interpreted as contributing to their own situation – a 'blaming the victim' argument that is strongly condemned in critiques.

RJJ

References

Johnston, R. J. 1984: *City and society: an outline for urban geography*. London: Penguin.

Lewis, O. 1966: *La vida*. London: Secker and Warburg.

Lewis, O. 1969: The possessions of the poor. *Scient. Am.* 221, pp. 114–24.

Suggested Reading

Rutter, M. and Madge, N. 1976: *Cycles of disadvantage*. London: Heinemann.

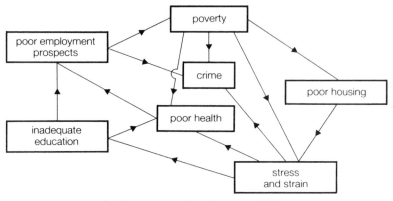

cycle of poverty   (after Johnston, 1984).

D

daily urban system The area surrounding an urban centre with which there is a substantial amount of daily COMMUTING traffic. (See METROPOLITAN LABOUR AREA.)   RJJ

Darwinism While it certainly can be said that Darwinism refers to the version of evolutionary theory originating with Charles Darwin (1809–1882), it is actually extraordinarily difficult to provide more precise definition. The reasons are manifold. For one thing, Darwin's theory of evolution (which involved also commitments to common organic descent, gradualism and the multiplication of species) encompassed a range of mechanisms for effecting organic transformation; as well as natural selection, Darwin also spoke of sexual selection, family selection, correlative variation, use inheritance and directed variation (Mayr, 1985; Provine 1985). Besides this, there is much to be said for the view that Darwinism is itself a historical entity that has evolved over time (Hull, 1985). What it was to be a Darwinian was different for different people at different times and in different places – and all of these forms of Darwinism bear different relationships to Darwin's own theories. Indeed, on some readings, Darwin himself would not qualify as a Darwinian! (see La Vergata, 1985). Evidently, Darwinism is a group or system of ideas more related by family resemblance than by genetic identity.

For all that, in the *Origin of species* (1859) Darwin did specify one major mechanism – natural selection – by which the transmutation of species could be effected. (A similar theory was simultaneously put forward by Alfred Russel Wallace (1823–1913).) Here Darwin showed how the multitude of living things in our world, so finely adapted to their environments, could have come into being without any recourse to a divine master-plan, in a plain, causal, naturalistic way (Desmond and Moore, 1991). Given the self-evident facts of heredity and variation among organisms, and the MAL-THUSIAN parameters of population increase, Darwin argued that a struggle for existence must take place; it followed that those who survived were better adapted to their environments than competitors (Young, 1969). This was essentially a theory of reproductive success in which relatively superior adaptations increase while relatively inferior ones are steadily eliminated. As Gould (1980, p. 11) summarizes Darwin's insight:

(a) Organisms vary, and these variations are inherited (at least in part) by their offspring.
(b) Organisms produce more offspring than can possibly survive.
(c) On average, offspring that vary most strongly in directions favored by the environment will survive and propagate. Favorable variations will therefore accumulate in populations by natural selection.

The implications of Darwin's theory of natural selection were far-reaching. It was, for example, a non-progressivist account of organic change. It assumed that variations in animals were random (or at least obeyed laws as yet unknown) and therefore that there was no inevitable movement of evolutionary history towards some ultimate goal. In this way the older teleological conception of NATURE was profoundly challenged (see TELEOLOGY). Additionally, Darwin had come to the realization that the

119

real units of organic history were populations, not types or species. The change from one species to another was simply the by-product of the process of a population becoming increasingly adapted to its particular environment. Here, then, was an account of population change that accounted in naturalistic terms for differential reproductive success among organic groups.

The network of Darwinian commitments, of course, had repercussions beyond biology and biogeography. Disciplines from anthropology to zoology registered at least some of the currents of the Darwinian vision. In addition, Darwinism had a considerable cultural impact, although interpreting the significance of this 'revolution' has proved to be an infernally stubborn problem (Bowler, 1988). Some have seen its significance as the triumph of science over religion, the substitution of natural law for natural theology, or the shift from a creationist to an epistemology of POSITIVISM. Others, such as R. M. Young, stress the ideological continuity between religion and science, regarding both as the socially sanctioned IDEOLOGIES (see discussions in Gillespie, 1979; Moore 1982; Young, 1985; Brooke, 1991).

Given the ambiguities over the term 'Darwinism' and the fact that it cannot be reduced *just* to an acceptance of the natural selection mechanism, it is understandable that the percolation of Darwinian themes into geography did not take place in any systematic way. Notions such as change through time, interrelationships between organism and environment, organic analogies, and selection and struggle, certainly became commonplace in the geographical literature (Stoddart, 1966, 1981). But these, as often as not, were derived from the LAMARCKIAN version of evolution which emphasized that organisms could consciously adapt themselves to their surrounding and pass on acquired characteristics to offspring. Still, whatever the sources, aspects of the evolutionary PARADIGM found expression in almost every subdisciplinary specialism of geography. Davis's cycle of erosion expressed his interpretation of LANDSCAPE evolution;

Clements's plant geography displayed his fascination with organic modes of thought; Ratzel's ANTHROPOGEOGRAPHY disclosed his organismic conception of the STATE and provided a human geographical articulation of Moritz Wagner's Lamarckian-based MIGRATION theory; Whittlesey's scheme of SEQUENT OCCUPANCE and Fleure's geographical anthropology were also evidently imbued with evolutionary thinking. Besides these individuals, a variety of key issues within the geographical tradition drew heavily on evolutionary *motifs*. Statements of ENVIRONMENTAL DETERMINISM by figures such as Semple, Huntington and Taylor were invariably couched in evolutionary categories (Livingstone, 1987); debates about acclimatization were similarly connected up to questions about heredity and adaptation (Livingstone, 1992a); and early theoretical statements about REGIONAL GEOGRAPHY, such as those of Herbertson and Geddes, were supported by appeals to the need for elucidating evolutionary mechanisms in specific contexts (Livingstone, 1992b).

DNL

References

Bowler, P. 1988: *The non-Darwinian revolution: reinterpreting a historical myth*. Baltimore, MD: John Hopkins University Press.

Brooke, J. H. 1991: *Science and religion*. Cambridge: Cambridge University Press.

Desmond, A. and Moore, J. 1991: *Darwin*. London: Michael Joseph.

Gillespie, N. C. 1979: *Charles Darwin and the problem of creation*. Chicago: University of Chicago Press.

Gould, S. J. 1980: *Ever since Darwin: reflections in natural history*. London: Penguin.

Hull, D. L. 1985: Darwinism as a historical entity: a historiographical proposal. In Kohn, D. ed., *The Darwinian heritage*. Princeton, NJ: Princeton University Press, pp. 773–812.

La Vergata, A. 1985. Images of Darwin. A historiographic overview. In Kohn, D. ed., *The Darwinian heritage*. Princeton NJ: Princeton University Press, pp. 901–75.

Livingstone, D. N. 1987: Human acclimatization: perspectives on a contested field of inquiry in science, medicine and geography. *Hist. Sci.* 25, pp. 359–94.

Livingstone, D. N. 1992a. 'Never shall ye make the crab walk straight': an inquiry into the scientific sources of racial geography. In Driver, F. and Rose, G., eds, *Nature and science: essays in the history of geographical knowledge*. Historical Geography Research Series, No. 28. Norwich: Geobooks, pp. 37–48.

Livingstone, D. N. 1992b: *The geographical tradition: episodes in the history of a contested enterprise*. Oxford: Blackwell.

Mayr, E. 1985: Darwin's five theories of evolution. In Kohn, D. ed., *The Darwinian heritage*. Princeton, NJ: Princeton University Press, pp. 755–72.

Moore, J. R. 1982: 1859 and all that: remaking the story of evolution-and-religion. In Chapman, R. and Duval, C. T., eds, *Charles Darwin: a centennial commemorative*. Wellington, NZ: Nova Pacifica, pp. 167–94.

Provine, W. P. 1985: Adaptation and mechanisms of evolution after Darwin: a study in persistent controversies. In Kohn, D., ed., *The Darwinian heritage*. Princeton, NJ: Princeton University Press, pp. 825–66.

Stoddart, D. R. 1966: Darwin's impact on geography. *Ann. Ass. Am. Geogr.* 56, pp. 683–98.

Stoddart, D. R. 1981: Darwin's influence on the development of geography in the United States, 1859–1914. In Blouet, B. W., ed., *The origins of academic geography in the United States*. Hamden, CN: Archon Books, pp. 265–78.

Young, R. M. 1969: Malthus and the evolutionists: the common context of biological and social theory. *Past and Present* 43, pp. 109–45.

Young, R. M. 1985: *Darwin's metaphor: nature's place in Victorian culture*. Cambridge: Cambridge University Press.

Suggested Reading

Bowler, P. J. 1984: *Evolution: the history of an idea*. Berkeley, CA: University of California Press.

Kohn, D., ed. 1985: *The Darwinian heritage*. Princeton, NJ: Princeton University Press.

Oldroyd, D. R. 1980: *Darwinian impacts: an introduction to the Darwinian revolution*. Milton Keynes, UK: Open University Press Atlantic Highlands, NJ: Humanities Press.

Ruse, M. 1979: *The Darwinian revolution: science red in tooth and claw*. Chicago: University of Chicago Press.

data analysis See CATEGORICAL DATA ANALYSIS; CONFIRMATORY DATA ANALYSIS; EXPLORATORY DATA ANALYSIS; LONGITUDINAL DATA ANALYSIS; SECONDARY DATA ANALYSIS.

databases Collections of information records in digital form. A database will probably contain more than one type of record, with information on the linkages or relationships between different types, since the term 'file' implies a simpler collection of only one type of record. To qualify as a database, there is often some degree of 'transparency', a term implying that access to the records does not require detailed knowledge of how they are stored. Transparency is provided by a Database Management System (DBMS), which contains the necessary information on formats and coding schemes, and handles requests expressed by the user in convenient terms. Many DBMS have adopted the standardized query language SQL (Structured Query Language) which allows the user to formulate queries in a simple English-like syntax. Some widely known DBMS include Oracle, INGRES, INFO, DBase and SIR. The database approach is being used increasingly to handle, distribute and access the large collections of social and economic data maintained by national census and other agencies.   MG

decentralization A process of spatial change produced by centrifugal forces (see CENTRIFUGAL AND CENTRIPETAL FORCES). Within urban areas, demands for space and the desire to escape the congestion, pollution and high land values of the CENTRAL BUSINESS DISTRICT are increasingly encouraging businesses (both commercial and industrial) to move their premises to the SUBURBS and beyond, where custom-built, accessible industrial estates, office parks and shopping complexes are increasingly common. At a larger scale, the negative EXTERNALITIES of vast cities encourage movement to smaller settlements (a process also known as deconcentration – see also COUNTER-URBANIZATION).   RJJ

decision-making The process whereby alternative courses of action are evaluated and a decision taken. The decision-making perspective attracted great interest after it was introduced to geography during the 1960s as part of the behavioural movement (see BEHAVIOURAL GEOGRAPHY). It broadened the more traditional perspectives, making them more realistic with respect to actual human practice. Industrial location theory provides an illustration.

The crux of the decision-making perspective is the recognition that real-world location decisions are seldom if ever optimal in the sense of maximizing profits or minimizing RESOURCES used. Similarly, consumer behaviour hardly ever accords with the rational calculus of utilities assumed in conventional economic formulations. The all-knowing and perfectly able rational actor (see RATIONAL CHOICE THEORY) of NEOCLASSICAL ECONOMICS bears only slight resemblance to actual human beings.

Suboptimal location decision-making may be incorporated into conventional location theory by the use of SPATIAL MARGINS to profitability, within which some profit is possible anywhere, and the business is free to locate away from the optimal (profit-maximizing) location at some pecuniary cost. However, this tells us nothing about how the actual choice of location is arrived at within the economically determined constraints.

A step further was taken by Allen Pred (1967, 1969) in his concept of the *behavioural matrix*. According to this, decision-makers have a position in a matrix, with the information available on one axis and the ability to use it on the other: the more information and the greater the ability, the higher the probability of a 'good' location within the spatial margin, i.e. near the optimal location on cost/ revenue grounds. Decision-makers with very limited ability and information are more likely to locate beyond the margins and fail, but a good location could still be chosen by chance.

Pred was greatly influenced by H. A. Simon's (1957) concept of SATISFICING BEHAVIOUR, as an alternative to the unrealistic optimizing capacity attributed to economic decision-makers who are viewed by Simon as considering only a limited number of alternatives, and

choosing one that is broadly satisfactory rather than optimal. The introduction of a more realistic perspective on location decision-making corresponded with a similar move in the study of business behaviour in general, within a broad context of industrial organization.

The decision-making perspective in location analysis followed two routes – theoretical and empirical. The search for a theoretical framework for studies of location behaviour under conditions of RISK and UNCERTAINTY led geographers and regional scientists into fields such as GAME THEORY and organization theory. However, the light shed on actual decision-making was very limited.

An empirical approach promised more, in a field where the emphasis is so much on individual practice. There was a tradition of SURVEY ANALYSIS in industrial location studies well before the behavioural movements penetrated the subject. Such research often revealed the importance of 'purely personal' factors. Later empirical research preferred to take sets of firms and examine the actual process of decision-making. Some perceived problem (such as undercapacity) sets in motion a sequence of decisions beginning with whether to expand *in situ*, to set up a branch or to acquire an existing plant; the sequence continues with the process of searching for a site, the evaluation of alternatives, the final decision and the feedback of the learning experience into some subsequent decision of a similar nature. This empirical approach held out the prospect of generalizations that relate the process of location decision-making to the nature of the organization concerned.

After more than two decades of behavioural studies of industrial location decision-making, the findings seem rather limited. The behavioural decision-making approach promised more than it was able to deliver. A critique was mounted by Doreen Massey (1979), who pointed to objections on epistemological grounds (see EPISTEMOLOGY) to the practice of adopting ideal type constructs (whether 'satisficing' or otherwise) and of making a distinction between behaviour that accords with the ideal type and that which must be attributed to other factors. Massey argued that the focus on individual decision-making distracts attention from the structural features of the economy to which firms react, and that what firms actually do with respect to the setting up or closure of plants is best understood in this broader context of POLITICAL ECONOMY.

Other aspects of human geography in which the decision-making perspective assumed importance include the response to environmental hazards (e.g. Kates, 1962), residential choice (e.g. Brown and Moore, 1970), shopping behaviour (e.g. Rushton, 1969; see also DISCRETE CHOICE MODELLING) and the decision to migrate (e.g. Wolpert, 1965). Again, neoclassical economics was originally influential, the concept of PLACE UTILITY being an obvious geographical extension of the theory of consumer behaviour. While qualities of place as people evaluate them do influence decisions including locational choice or movement, there are many other considerations of a fortuitous and seemingly irrational nature. Indeed, geographers can easily exaggerate the spatial element in decision-making.

Contemporary research involving QUALITATIVE METHODS is seeking a more sensitive understanding of how people assign meaning to various aspects of life and how decisions follow from this. For example, the decision to seek health care, involving the coverage of distance, is influenced by culturally specific conceptions of the meaning of illness, personal and shared experience of being ill, assessment of the benefit likely to be derived from the doctor's advice based on past contacts, the felt need for treatment or reassurance, and so on. Such work helps to set the spatial aspects of decision-making and -taking in a broader context, getting away from crude notions of human behaviour as some stimulus–response mechanism and allowing greater scope for the way in which meaning is interpreted and translated into action.   DMS

References

Brown, L. A. and Moore, E. G. 1970: The intra-urban migration process: a perspective. *Geogr. Annlr.* 52B, pp. 1–13.

Kates, R. W. 1962: *Hazard and choice perception in flood plain management.* Chicago: University of Chicago, Department of Geography, Research Paper 78.

Massey, D. B. 1979: A critical evaluation of industrial location theory. In Hamilton, F. E. I. and Linge, G. J. R., eds, *Spatial analysis, industry and the industrial environment,* volume I. *Industrial systems.* New York: John Wiley, pp. 57–72.

Pred, A. 1967, 1969: *Behavior and location: foundations for a geographic and dynamic location theory,* Parts 1 and 2. Lund studies in geography, series B, 27 and 28. Lund: C. W. K. Gleerup.

Rushton, G. 1969: Analysis of spatial behavior by revealed space preference. *Ann. Ass. Am. Geogr.* 59, pp. 391–400.

Simon, H. A. 1957: *Models of man: social and rational.* New York: John Wiley.

Wolpert, J. 1965: Behavioral aspects of the decision to migrate. *Pap. Proc. reg. Sci. Assoc.,* 15, pp. 159–72.

Suggested Reading

Chapman, K. and Walker, D. 1991: *Industrial location: principles and policies,* second edition. Oxford: Blackwell.

Lever, W., ed. 1987: *Industrial change in the United Kingdom.* London: Longman.

Smith, D. M. 1981: *Industrial location: an economic geographical analysis,* second edition. New York: John Wiley, ch. 5.

Wolpert, J. 1964. The decision process in a spatial context. *Ann. Ass. Am. Geogr.* 54, pp. 337–58.

deconstruction   See POSTSTRUC-TURALISM.

deindustrialization   A sustained decline in industrial (especially manufacturing) activity (cf. INDUSTRIALIZATION). It may involve the absolute and/or relative decline of industrial output, employment and means of production. Such changes are quite normal in the course of economic development. However, when they are linked to the declining competitiveness of industrial production to meet extra-regional, domestic and international demand within reasonable levels of employment and a sustainable balance of payments, deindustrialization represents a process of UNDERDEVELOPMENT. The causes of deindustrialization are complex.

In the contemporary global economy, they lie in a combination of local circumstance and locational adjustment to global conditions. In a capitalist economy, the rate of profit and its determinants must lie at the centre of any explanation.   RL

Suggested Reading

Bluestone, B. and Harrison, B. 1982: *The deindustrialization of America.* New York: Basic Books.

Martin, R. and Rowthorn, B. eds, 1986: *The geography of deindustrialization.* London: Macmillan.

demand curve A plot of the volume of demand for a product in relation to its price, with demand on the horizontal axis and price on the vertical axis (see the figure). A demand curve typically slopes downwards to the right, reflecting the tendency of people to consume less of a product as its price increases. The slope of the demand curve at any point reflects the *elasticity of demand,* or the sensitivity of the level of demand to changes in price. A vertical demand curve indicates perfectly elastic demand, with all output sold irrespective of price; while a horizontal demand curve indicates the other extreme, with only one price at which the commodity can be sold. When multiplied by price, the plot of demand becomes a

revenue curve. In conventional economic theory, the market price is determined by the intersection of the demand curve with the SUPPLY CURVE. (See also EQUILIBRIUM.)   DMS

Reference

Smith, D. M. 1977: *Human geography: a welfare approach.* London: Edward Arnold/New York: St. Martins Press, ch. 3.

demographic transition A general model describing the evolution of levels of FERTILITY and MORTALITY over time. It has been devised with particular reference to the experience of developed countries which have passed through the processes of INDUSTRIALIZATION and URBANIZATION, and it has attracted considerable criticism as a general model. The model suggests four highly stylized phases in the process (see the figure). In the first, or high stationary, phase both birth and death rates are high. Deaths, due to FAMINES, diseases or wars, are the most important influence on population growth, which tends to be at a low level. In the second, or early expanding, phase the population begins to grow, as a result of a stable birth rate and a rapidly declining death rate. The latter falls as a result of improved nutrition, sanitation and medicine. The third, or late expanding, phase is characterized by a

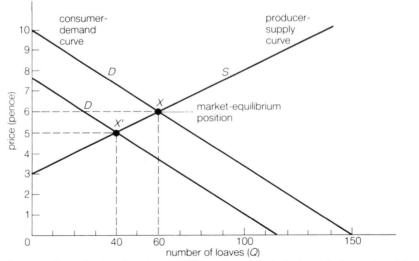

demand curve *Determination of market equilibrium output and price for bread by intersection of demand and supply curves (Smith, 1977).*

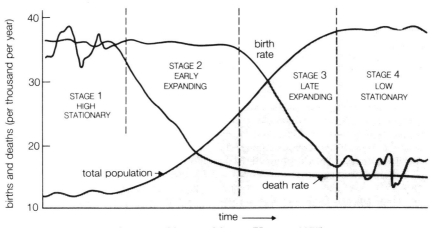

demographic transition   (Haggett, 1975).

slowing in the growth rate as the death rate stabilized at a low level and the birth rate declines. This decline is associated with the growth of an urban/industrial society. In the fourth, or low stationary, phase birth and death rates have stabilized at a low level, population growth is very slow, and the birth rate is more likely to fluctuate than the death rate.

There is much variety in the way in which demographic transition applies to individual countries. Most countries of Europe, North America and the rest of the developed world not have very low rates of fertility and mortality, with low levels of population growth. By contrast, many countries of the THIRD WORLD are experiencing high rates of growth, as the decline in mortality has not been matched by a decline in fertility. Great care must be taken in applying the model of demographic transition to individual countries. For example, recent research has shown that the first stage of the model is rather over-simplified for the currently developed world; that post-1945 fluctuations in the birth rates of the developed world are more complex than the model implies; and that it is far from certain that the currently underdeveloped world will follow the form of transition depicted in the figure.   PEO

Reference

Haggett, P. 1975: *Geography: a modern synthesis*. New York: Harper and Row.

Suggested Reading
Chesnais, J.-C. 1986: *La transition démographique: étapes, formes, implications économiques*. Paris: Presses Universitaires de France.

Coale, A. J. and Watkins, S. C., eds 1986: *The decline of fertility in Europe*. Princeton, NJ: Princeton University Press.

Davis, K., Bernstam, M. S. and Ricardo-Campbell, R., eds 1986: *Below replacement fertility in industrial societies: causes, consequences, policies*. (Supplement to *Population and Development Review*, volume 12). New York: The Population Council.

Watkins, S. C. 1991: *From provinces into nations: demographic integration in western Europe 1870–1960*. Princeton, NJ: Princeton University Press.

Woods, R. and Rees, P. 1986: *Population structures and models: developments in spatial demography*. London: Allen and Unwin.

density gradient   The rate of falling-off of land-use intensity (or population density etc.) with distance from a central point, as in the DISTANCE DECAY relationship identified in the ALONSO and VON THÜNEN MODELS of land-use distributions.

One density gradient that has received considerable attention from geographers is the intra-urban distribution of population. Clark (1951) noted that population density declines exponentially with distance from the CENTRAL BUSINESS DISTRICT, and further empirical studies have replicated his findings: in general they show that the younger the city, the shallower the gradient.   RJJ

Reference

Clark, C. 1951: Urban population densities. *J. R. Statist. Soc.*, Ser. *A* 114, pp. 110–16.

dependence A dependent relationship between two or more societies. Dependence implies that the ability of a society to survive and to reproduce itself derives, in large measure, from its links with other dominant, imperialist societies. Without such links (manifest, for example, in flows of value, technology, AID, political influence and control) a dependent society may be unable to sustain the conditions for its own continued existence.

Before relations of dependence can develop it is necessary for the means of communication between societies to exist. It follows that dependence cannot be an original condition and must, therefore, relate to the development of such means of communication. For Keith Griffin (1969) the origins of dependence are to be found in the expansion of European influence. He stresses the symbiotic relationship between the development of dependence and the development of UN-DERDEVELOPMENT:

Nearly all of the people in today's underdeveloped areas were members of viable societies which could satisfy the economic needs of the community. Yet these societies were shattered when they came into contact with an expanding Europe. Europe did not 'discover' the underdeveloped countries, on the contrary it created them. In many cases, in fact, the societies with which Europe came into contact were sophisticated, cultured and wealthy.

According to this view, relations of dependence are produced by the disintegration of viable societies resulting from their contact with a powerful external social influence. It is hardly surprising that Griffin concludes from his analysis that 'the essence of development is institutional reform'.

The nature of dependence goes much deeper than this. Andre Gunder Frank (1969) has argued that dependence is closely related to the process of ACCUMULATION in capitalist societies (see CAPITALISM). Capitalism involves the production of surplus value by the application of labour power to the productive task,

and the extraction and concentration of surplus value by capital (see MARXIAN ECONOMICS). The geography of this process involves, according to Frank, a flow of surplus value from local, peripheral producers, dependent upon external sources of capital, to regional, national and world metropolitan centres of accumulation. As a result the course of economic and social change in the peripheral satellite is directed, constrained and governed by its dependence upon the dynamic (or motive force) of the metropolis (see NEW INTERNATIONAL DIVISION OF LABOUR). Nevertheless, the maintenance by capital of ownership and control over the means of production in capitalist societies ensures their dominance in structuring the relations of dependence in social and cultural terms, albeit in a contradictory manner.

However, such a view of the world is restrictive in a number of ways. Not only are developed societies more dependent upon a resource- and capital-intensive technology than are underdeveloped societies, but they are also dependent upon the labour, resources and markets of the latter for their own continued development. Furthermore, the internal transformation of dependent societies, resulting from their relations of dependence, is tending to lead them, too, to greater dependence on resources and capital. Under such circumstances it becomes difficult to distinguish who is dependent upon whom (Brookfield, 1975).

The more determinist versions of dependency thereby imply that change can come only from without, so that the only possibility of development lies in isolation from the world-economy, and that the distinction between metropolis and satellites is permanent and structurally determined, with little room for contextual variation or local action. Thus the distinction is permanent (Foster-Carter, 1985). Yet the dramatic growth of the newly industrializing countries suggests that it is the combination of internal and external factors that conditions industrial growth.

Dependence is as much a social as a material relationship, and genuine INTERDEPENDENCE will necessarily involve the creation and realization of non-exploitative relations of production. Thus although dependent economies may develop through the structural transformation of their economies (e.g. by import substitution or export-led growth), their degree of dependency will remain a function of the social relations of production underpinning such structural transformation. And this comment points to the major limitation of dependency as an explanation of underdevelopment – its reliance solely upon relations of exchange rather than upon the duality of exchange and production (Brenner, 1977). (See also DEVELOPMENT; DUAL ECONOMY; SUBALTERN STUDIES; WORLD-SYSTEMS ANALYSIS.) RL

References and Suggested Reading

Brenner, R. 1977: The origins of capitalist development: a critique of neo-Smithian Marxism. *New Left Rev.* 104, pp. 25–92.

Brookfield, H. 1975: *Interdependent development.* London: Methuen/Pittsburgh, PA: University of Pittsburgh Press.

Corbridge, S. 1986: *Capitalist world development.* London: Macmillan.

Foster-Carter, A. 1985: *The sociology of development.* Ormskirk, UK: Causeway.

Frank, A. G. 1969: *Capitalism and underdevelopment in Latin America.* New York: Monthly Review Press/London: Penguin.

Gilbert, A. 1985: *An unequal world: the links between rich and poor nations.* London: Macmillan.

Griffin, K. 1969: *Underdevelopment in Spanish America.* London: Allen & Unwin/Cambridge, MA: MIT Press.

Peet, R. 1991: *Global capitalism.* London: Routledge, ch. 4.

dependency ratio The number of children (aged 0–14) and elderly people (aged 65 or over) in a population as a ratio of the number of adults (aged 15–64). The dependency ratio is a useful comparative indication of the number that the active or potentially active (i.e. employed) population has to support. The definitions by age group are to an extent arbitrary and may be varied to take account of, for example, changes in retirement or school-leaving age. The general definition of adults as aged 15–64 tends to overstate the actual size of the active population in a typical Western society. PEO

deregulation The reduction or elimination of STATE control of economic activity. This may involve opening up a publicly provided activity, such as rail or bus services, to private enterprise. It can also take the form of less or no regulation of private-sector activity, perhaps to encourage competition. The usual objective of deregulation is to encourage efficiency by removing what may be obstacles to free enterprise and competition. Deregulation was a popular feature of the free-market oriented regimes that dominated British and United States politics during the 1980s. Some efficiency benefits have been claimed, against which have to be set poorer working conditions that can arise when state regulation is relaxed and competition becomes intense. DMS

desertification The process whereby an area of land becomes a desert. This normally involves the impoverishment of an ECOSYSTEM, through either climatic change or human impact (or a combination of the two), so that the land develops the characteristics of a desert area. Desertification thus involves long-term change in an area's floral and faunal characteristics, its soil productivity, and its biological potential; it is not the short-term fall in an area's productivity and CARRYING CAPACITY which results from a period of drought – although a drought may catalyse the human impacts which result in long-term desertification.

The relative importance of the two main causes is the focus of much debate, because of the apparent advance of deserts in recent years, especially on the margins of the Sahara: Dregne (1983) and Mabbutt (1984), for example, estimated that some 33–37 per cent of the world's land suffering at least moderate desertification is in Africa (between 7500 and 10 000 km^2). Increased pressure on the land is brought about by greater demands resulting from both population pressure and the penetration of traditional farming systems by capitalist imperatives (Blaikie, 1985; Watts, 1983). Overgrazing, overcropping, poor management of irrigation systems, and deforestation can all accelerate natural processes which lead to deterioration in the soil resource, especially where rainfall totals are falling, as appears to have been the case recently in the Sahel region.

Desertification may be reversible, if it has not proceeded too far. Many fear, however, that even if the technical ability to counter its spread (which is usually both sporadic and locally confined) were available, the political will to achieve the needed changes in land management practices is generally absent (Johnston, 1989). RJJ

References

Blaikie, P. M. 1985: *The political economy of soil erosion*. London: Longman.

Dregne, J. 1983: *Desertification of arid lands*. Chur, Switzerland: Harwood Academic Publishers.

Johnston, R. J. 1989: *Environmental problems: nature, economy and the state*. London: Belhaven Press.

Mabbutt, J. A. 1984: A new global assessment of the status and trends of desertification. *Environ. Conserv.* 11, pp. 100–13.

Watts, M. 1983: *Silent violence*. Berkeley, CA: University of California Press.

Suggested Reading

Grainger, A. 1990: *The threatening desert: controlling desertification*. London: Earthscan.

determinism See ENVIRONMENTAL DETERMINISM.

development A process of becoming and a potential state of being. The achievement of a state of development would enable people in societies to make their own histories and geographies under conditions of their own choosing. The process of development is the means by which such conditions of human existence might be achieved. The suggestion here is that development would necessarily involve people in a productive, crisis-free and non-exploitative set of relations with NATURE in the production of their material lives and in the struggle to remove oppression and exploitation from the relations between themselves.

By these standards, no society in history has ever achieved a state of development, and it may be argued that no society has ever engaged in a process of development.

SUSTAINABLE DEVELOPMENT (Redclift, 1987) has not yet materialized. And yet development is widely used to describe the state of particular societies and the processes of change experienced by them. What, then, does development mean in this common usage?

Part of the difficulty in providing an answer is that common usage frequently reflects an unconscious acceptance of a particular point of view, which is then generalized as if it were universal (see ETHNOCENTRISM). Thus the term is commonly used to refer to an amalgam of characteristics (related to economic growth, welfare and MODERNIZATION) that are ascribable to particular societies. Four interconnected sets of phenomena appear most often:

- levels of, changes in and the technology of material production and consumption
- technological change
- associated social, cultural and political changes, and
- the distribution of the costs and benefits of production and consumption

The *World development report*, produced annually by the World Bank, contains a compilation of world development indicators (see also Hoogvelt, 1982, ch. 1) for countries grouped together in the following categories: industrial market economies; eastern European countries; high-income oil exporters; low-income developing countries; and middle-income developing countries. This provides statistical details of production, consumption and investment, demand, industrialization, energy consumption and supply, trade, capital flows, population growth, fertility, the labour force, urbanization, life expectancy, health, education and income distribution for nation–states throughout the world. The Human Development Index (HDI), constructed by the United Nations as a counterweight to monetary measures of development, combines life expectancy, literacy and GNP per capita figures in a weighted average.

The state of development may be defined by such variables and, by bringing them into quantitative or qualitative relationship with each other, the process of development may be modelled. They may also be used to calibrate a scale of development against which comparisons of the level and changes in the level of development within each nation–state may be made. Thus Williamson and Milner (1991, p. 283) define economic development as

the process by which a traditional society employing primitive techniques and therefore capable of sustaining only a modest level of per capita income is transformed into a modern, high-technology, high-income economy. The process involves the replacement of labour-intensive subsistence production by techniques that use capital, skilled labour and scientific knowledge to produce the wide variety of different products consumed in an affluent society.

Between 1950 and 1989 real incomes per head in Asia went up by 3.6 per cent per year. By contrast, growth in Latin America was only 1.2 per cent per year and, in sub-Saharan Africa, 0.8 per cent per year. According to the World Bank such discrepancies are caused largely by variations in national economic policy in, for example, the foreign exchange markets. However, such analyses and the conclusions which flow from them must make the assumption that national economies are, in fact, rational abstractions (rather than CHAOTIC CONCEPTIONS) in the context of global development (Murray, 1971; Corbridge, 1986; Dicken, 1992).

There are several objections that may be raised against the conventional meaning given to development and the use to which such a restricted understanding may be put. First, it restricts itself to surface appearances and defines development in terms of a number of apparently characteristic outputs without either specifying the way in which such outputs are produced or clarifying the social relationships between them – although for those with eyes to see (e.g. Dicken, 1992, ch. 13) it makes clear the heterogeneity of development. Thus countries with low levels of development as measured by the HDI relative to their GNP ranking include those in which the rights of women are circumscribed, while a number of communist countries such as Vietnam

and Cuba perform well. The USA has the worst HDI of the industrialized countries.

An alternative approach to an understanding of the meaning of development would be to begin by recognizing that it is a historically and socially specific process. Its meaning may be perceived only in the context of particular social relations. The development of CAPITALISM has dominated world history from the seventeenth century, if not before. The social relations of capitalism have facilitated great progress in terms of material production and the generation and recirculation of a surplus. The basis of this development lies in increases in productivity but, as Brenner (1977) argues, such a tendency rests in turn upon the social relations of capitalism. Thus the maintenance of such progress rests upon contradictions endemic to capitalism between people and between people and NATURE (e.g. Watts, 1983) and upon the relationships established between capitalist and non-capitalist SOCIAL FORMATIONS (see Corbridge, 1986). It is because of such characteristics that the spread of capitalism – its development – has been accompanied by DEPENDENCE and UNDERDEVELOPMENT in those societies articulated with it. This contradiction is critical not merely because of its implications for social justice (see WELFARE GEOGRAPHY) but because it poses a threat to survival. Opposition to such a threat involves people in a creative struggle – development – vitally necessary and not restricted to its economic dimensions (Slater, 1989) if social existence is to be maintained.

A second difficulty with the conventional meaning given to development is that it is interpreted in a non-dialectical (see DIALECTIC) and ahistorical manner. An *a priori* definition of development is made from a very narrow base and is then imposed upon the diversity of the situations and conditions of change of human existence. Thus the particular ways in which specific social formations respond to, restrict, transform and are themselves transformed by an inseparable combination of external and internal processes of change are ignored. Development is an historical and essentially geographical process not only because of its own variable and particular characteristics, but also because it is a product of conscious human labour operating in specific sets of social, material and natural conditions. It is not a process that can be defined in universal terms: rather, it is a contradictory, often perverse, course of change. It may involve evolutionary change within specific sets of social relations of production, or the revolutionary transformation of the social relations and means of production. Thus O'Riordan (1989, p. 94), for example, argues that

the self-perpetuating imperatives of international capitalism, international aid, national militarism and counter-insurgency, and cultural conflict . . . renders impossible any realistic hope of achieving sustainable [environmental] utilization in much of the Third World.

The success of a struggle to develop is by no means assured. Social revolution is not achieved overnight. The type of social change implied by a transformation of the relations of production may take decades, if not centuries, to achieve. Furthermore, the progress of evolutionary change cannot be laid down in a blueprint. It is itself a contradictory process in which local conjunctural circumstances are of critical importance.

In short, the widespread and conventional attempts to define the state of development in one-dimensional and universal terms and to build similarly restrictive models of change is at odds with the geographical and historical circumstances and social processes of change by which development may be achieved. For Hettne (1990, p. 2)

[T]here can be no fixed and final definition of development, only suggestions of what development should imply in particular contexts.

Development is historical, diverse, complex and contradictory; it is the central feature of the human condition. To reduce it to a number of asocial characteristics and their interaction is to trivialize the experience of real societies and the struggle of their peoples to make a living. (See also WORLD-SYSTEMS ANALYSIS.)   RL

References and Suggested Reading

Allen, T. and Thomas, A., eds 1992: *Development in the 1990s*. Oxford: Oxford University Press.

Brenner, R. 1977: The origins of capitalist development: a critique of neo-Smithian Marxism. *New Left Rev.* 104, pp. 25–92.

Brookfield, H. 1975: *Interdependent development*. London: Methuen/Pittsburgh. PA: University of Pittsburgh Press.

Corbridge, S. 1986: *Capitalist world development*. London: Macmillan.

Dicken, P. 1992: *Global shift: the internationalization of economic activity*, second edition. London: Paul Chapman.

Harrison, P. 1981: *Inside the Third World: an anatomy of poverty*, second edition. London: Penguin.

Hettne, B. 1990: *Development theory and the three worlds*. London: Longman.

Hoogvelt, J. M. M. 1982: *The Third World in global development*. London: Macmillan.

Keeble, D. E. 1967: Models of economic development. In Chorley, R. J. and Haggett, P. eds, *Models in geography*. London: Methuen, ch. 8.

Murray, R. 1971: The internationalization of capital and the nation state. *New Left Rev.* 67, pp. 84–109.

O'Riordan, T. 1989: The challenge for environmentalism. In Peet, R. and Thrift, N., eds, *New models in geography*, volume 1. London: Unwin Hyman, pp. 77–102.

Peet, R. 1991: *Global capitalism*. London: Routledge.

Redclift, M. 1987: *Sustainable development: exploring the contradictions*. London: Routledge.

Slater, D. 1989: Peripheral capitalism and the regional problematic. In Peet, R. and Thrift, N., eds, *New models in geography*, volume 2. London: Unwin Hyman, pp. 267–94.

Watts, M. 1983: *Silent violence: food, famine and peasantry in northern Nigeria*. Berkeley, CA: University of California Press.

Williamson, J. and Milner, C. 1991: *The world economy: a textbook in international economics*. Hemel Hempstead: Harvester Wheatsheaf/New York: Simon and Schuster.

World Bank annual: *World development report*. New York: Oxford University Press.

developmentalism   A form of analysis of social change that treats each country separately in an evolutionary manner. Two assumptions are made: first, countries are deemed to be autonomous in terms of social change; and, second, all countries follow the same stages of change. This was a very common way of thinking about economic DEVELOPMENT in the optimistic period following the Second World War. The most famous of such models was undoubtably Rostow's (1960) 'STAGES OF ECONOMIC GROWTH'. There were many examples in geography, of which the most widely cited was Taaffe, Morrill and Gould's (1963) model of stages of transport growth.

These models have been widely criticized for their ETHNOCENTRISM and their neglect of the international context within which modern social change occurs. In particular, WORLD-SYSTEMS ANALYSIS has been constructed to counter both liberal and Marxist versions of the error of developmentalism (Taylor, 1989, 1992).

PJT

References

Rostow, W. W. 1960: *The stages of economic growth*. Cambridge: Cambridge University Press.

Taaffe, E. J., Morrill, R. L. and Gould, P. R. 1963: Transport expansion in underdeveloped countries: a comparative analysis. *Geogrl. Rev.* 53, pp. 503–29.

Taylor, P. J. 1989: The error of developmentalism in human geography. In Gregory, D. and Walford, R. eds, *Horizons in human geography*. London: Macmillan, pp. 303-19.

Taylor, P. J. 1992: Understanding global inequalities: a world-systems approach. *Geogr.* 77, pp. 1–11.

devolution The process of devolving political power from central to more local levels of government. This can frequently involve the creation of regional assemblies with limited law-making and tax-raising powers. Devolution has been an issue of growing importance in Europe in recent years, as linguistic and cultural minorities have begun to assert their independence more strongly, notably within the framework of the European Community (see NATIONALISM). In Spain the government has devolved considerable regional autonomy to the Basques, the Catalans and the Andalusians since the re-establishment of democracy in 1976. In the UK the possibility of regional assemblies for Scotland and Wales was not supported by referenda in 1979, but the issue is once again firmly on the political agenda.   MB

Suggested Reading
Nairn, T. 1977: *The break-up of Britain*. London: NLB.

dialect See LANGUAGE AND DIALECT, GEOGRAPHY OF.

dialectic The perpetual resolution of binary oppositions: a metaphysics most closely associated in European philosophy and social thought with G. W. F. Hegel (1770–1813) and K. Marx (1818–1883). In human geography, a simple example would be the following, essentially Hegelian, reading of Lösch's LOCATION THEORY. There:

a perfectly homogeneous landscape with identical customers, working inside the framework of perfect competition, would necessarily develop, from its inner rules of change, into a heterogeneous landscape with both rich, active sectors and poor, depressed regions. The homogeneous regional system negates itself and generates dialectically its contradiction as regional inequalities appear (Marchand, 1978).

But the dialectic is usually deployed outside this framework of NEOCLASSICAL ECONOMICS, and in fact it is a characteristic of the Löschian system that once the heterogeneous landscape has emerged it is 'frozen' in equilibrium rather than convulsed through transformation. As such, it is really an example of a *categorical* rather than a fully dialectical paradigm, i.e. one in which change is simply the kaleidoscopic recombination of the same and ever-present, fixed and precise categories and elements (Gregory, 1978). The most developed dialectical paradigms in geography are derived from Marx's HISTORICAL MATERIALISM, and have been deployed to elucidate the inner workings of CAPITALISM as a MODE OF PRODUCTION, but even within MARXIST GEOGRAPHY the politico-intellectual implications of dialectical thought have rarely been systematically discussed.

The most sustained philosophical reflections on dialectics in human geography have come from different sources. In a series of writings, Olsson has argued that our conventional modes of analysing thought, action and SPATIALITY typically fail to recognize the essential interpenetration of form and process, subject and object: within a categorical paradigm, he claims, our propositions reveal more about the language we are talking *in*, whereas 'statements in dialectics will say more about the worlds we are talking *about*'. To be sure, 'words' and 'worlds' are connected, and for this reason Olsson insists on the importance of attending to what he once called 'the dialectics of spatial analysis' (Olsson, 1974, 1980, 1991). But this interest in language and its system of differences has impelled some writers to follow the so-called 'linguistic turn' in the humanities and social sciences much further, and those who have been persuaded by the claims of *deconstruction* have set dialectics aside: for deconstruction challenges the metaphysics of binary opposition on which dialectics depends, and refuses to conceive of difference as contradiction (Doel, 1992).   DG

References

Doel, M. A. 1992: In stalling deconstruction: striking out the postmodern. *Environ. Plann. D: Society and Space* 10, pp. 163–79.

Gregory, D. 1978: *Ideology, science and human geography*. London: Hutchinson.

Marchand, B. 1978: A dialectic approach in geography. *Geogr. Anal.* 10, pp. 105–19.

Olsson, G. 1974: The dialectics of spatial analysis. *Antipode* 6 (3), pp. 50–62.

Olsson, G. 1980: *Birds in egg/eggs in bird*. London: Pion.

Olsson, G. 1991: *Lines of power, limits of language*. Minneapolis: University of Minnesota Press.

Suggested Reading

Doel (1992).

Marchand (1978).

Olsson (1991), pp. 66–77.

diaspora Literally the scattering of a population, the word was originally applied to the dispersal of the Jews following the Roman conquest of Palestine and the destruction of Jerusalem in AD 70. It is now applied more generally to other (non-voluntary) population dispersals, such as the Black diaspora that resulted from the slave trade.   PAJ

Suggested Reading

Keller, W. 1971: *Diaspora: the post-Biblical history of the Jews* (transl. R. Winston and C. Winston). London: Pitman.

diffusion The spread of a phenomenon over space and through time. There is a long and distinguished tradition of diffusion studies in CULTURAL GEOGRAPHY. According to Sauer (1941), it was Ratzel who 'founded the study of the diffusion of cultural traits, presented in the nearly forgotten second volume of his *Anthropogeographie*' (see ANTHROPOGEOGRAPHY). In Sauer's view, diffusion – 'the filling of the spaces of the earth' – was a 'general problem of social science': 'A new crop, craft or technique is introduced to a CULTURE AREA. Does it spread, or diffuse vigorously or does its acceptance meet resistance?'. The *specific* contribution of geography, so Sauer argued, was to reconstruct diffusion pathways and to evaluate the influence of (physical) barriers (see Sauer, 1952; more generally, Wagner and Mikesell, 1962). Both of these tasks were pursued energetically by various members of the BERKELEY SCHOOL, but they reappeared in a starkly different guise in Hägerstrand's much more formal study of INNOVATION diffusion. In fact, Hägerstrand's original Swedish monograph was introduced to Anglo-American geography in a short note by Leighly (1954), himself an associate of Sauer. 'No one who essays in the future to interpret the distribution of culture elements in the process of diffusion can afford to ignore Hägerstrand's methods and conclusions', Leighly declared, and he drew particular attention to Hägerstrand's emphasis on the importance of 'chance' (see STOCHASTIC PROCESS). Even so, it was some 14 years before an English translation of Hägerstrand's *Innovation diffusion as a spatial process* appeared (1968), although in the interim his basic ideas had already become better known (see Duncan, 1974).

The theoretical structure behind Hägerstrand's MODEL is summarized in the figure. An interaction matrix suggests the

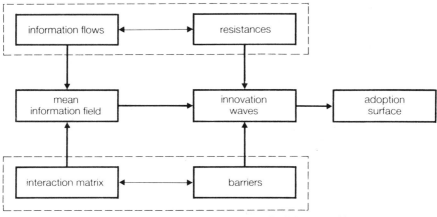

diffusion *The structure of Hägerstrand's diffusion model.*

contours of a generalized or MEAN INFOR-MATION FIELD, which structures the way in which information circulates through a regional system; these flows are modulated by both physical barriers and individual resistances which together check the transformation of information into innovation and so shape successive diffusion waves which break onto the adoption surface (Gregory, 1985; see also Haggett et al., 1977). Most discussion has been about the operationalization of the model – about Hägerstrand's use of Monte Carlo SIMU-LATION methods, the comparison of 'observed' and 'predicted' patterns of adoption, and the detection of a NEIGH-BOURHOOD EFFECT – rather than about its theoretical basis (but see below). Within the modelling tradition initiated by Häger-strand, the most important developments have included:

(a) a formalization of the mathematical relations between the structure of the mean information field and the form and velocity of diffusion waves, indicating the connections between different DISTANCE-DECAY curves and the classic neighbourhood effect (although it is, of course, scarcely surprising that a distance-bound mean information field should generate a broadly contagious pattern of adoptions);

(b) a demonstration that the Hägerstrand model is only a special instance of the simple epidemic model, and the subsequent derivation of more complex *epidemic models* – particularly through the remarkable contributions of Haggett, Cliff and Ord (see Haggett et al., 1977, ch. 7) – whose replication of a range of supposedly 'spatial processes' (see PROCESS) has confirmed;

(c) the recognition of *hierarchical* diffusion, typically through central place systems (see CENTRAL PLACE THEORY) and frequently operating alongside the distance-bound, *contagious* processes of the classical model (see Hudson, 1969; Pedersen, 1970);

(d) the incorporation of rejection and removal processes and the modelling of competitive diffusions (see Webber, 1972).

These changes have entailed a move away from simulation techniques towards the use of more analytical methods, which Agnew (1979) sees as a shift from EMPIRICISM and INSTRUMENTALISM towards REALISM. But to some critics outside the abstract domains of LOCATION THEORY or MEDICAL GEOGRAPHY (where these advances have been immensely important: see Cliff et al., 1981) the move towards a post-positivist formulation remains strategically incomplete. Blaikie (1978) even spoke of a 'crisis' in diffusion research, which he attributed to a reluctance to reverse out from a 'spacious cul-de-sac' – by which he meant a preoccupation with spatial form and space–time sequence – and Gregory (1985) attributed the 'stasis' of diffusion theory to an unwillingness to engage with social theory and social history in ways which clarified both the *conditions* and the *consequences* of diffusion processes. In the most general terms, this critique notes that the spatial circulation of information is the strategic element in most applications of the Hägerstrand model and its derivatives to human geography. Although the flow of information through different 'propagation structures' and contact networks has been exposed in more detail (e.g. Blaikie, 1973, 1975; Brown, 1975), most critics claim that the primacy accorded to the pattern of these pathways obscures two other, more fundamental, elements (cf. the critique of BEHAVIOURAL GEOGRAPHY):

(a) The Hägerstrand model 'is concerned with the locational attributes and communication habits of potential adopters' and 'does not explicate the process by which potential adopters are identified' (Yapa and Mayfield, 1978). The alternative is a model of *biased innovation* which takes as primary the ways in which 'social access to the means of production' can be closed off through the CLASS structure of the MODE OF PRODUCTION. In this perspective, 'non-diffusion is not to be equated with the passive state of lack of adoption due to low levels of awareness [or] apathy .... It is an active state arising out of the structural arrangements of the economic [base of] society' (Yapa, 1977; see also Blaikie, 1978 and Gregory, 1985). Claims of this sort carry with them a demand for diffusion theory to be located within a more general political economy, although it is clearly not necessary to endorse the economic reductionism of classical Marxism implicit in Yapa's commentary. At the very least, the significance of ETHNICITY and GENDER needs to be admitted alongside that of class (see Blaikie, 1975).

(b) The Hägerstrand model postulates 'a uniform cognitive region' and does not explicate the selective social processes through which information flows are differentially constituted as socially meaningful. Hence Blaut (1977) has called for the forging of closer links with the older tradition of cultural diffusion, which is capable of treating diffusion in what Blaut takes to be 'its broadest, most adequate sense' by locating diffusion theory within a more general cultural geography. Such a manoeuvre is not the return to Sauer which

it seems to be, however, for it is clear from Blaut's other writings that here too the model is to be Marx (see Blaut, 1980). Whatever one thinks of this – and there is certainly a vibrant cultural perspective within HISTORICAL MATERIALISM – no model of biased innovation can equate 'resistance' with ignorance or insufficient information. Access to information, like any other means of production, is indeed socially structured, but resistance equally (and, one might say, usually) connotes a process of sustained struggle: considered and collective action on the part of people whose evaluation of the available information may be strikingly different to that of the 'potential adopters' (see Gregory, 1985).

Hägerstrand has himself conceded the force of some of these objections; rather than explore the claims of contemporary Marxism, however, he has returned to some of those themes which exercised him before he constructed his diffusion model, and he has developed them beyond the confines of its spatial formalism into TIME-GEOGRAPHY.

Many of the continuing tensions within diffusion studies are exemplified by the recent interest in the diffusion of AIDS. Mapping and modelling the spread of the disease has been the major focus of geographical inquiry (see, e.g. Shannon and Pyle, 1989; Casetti and Fan, 1991; Shannon, Pyle and Bashshur, 1991; Smallman-Raynor, Cliff and Haggett, 1992). Where this work has referred to the Hägerstrand model at all, it has usually been to its capacity to *describe* patterns of spread: their spatial *analysis* has involved epidemiological modelling. An interest in the cultural, social and political geography of AIDS diffusion has been much slower to develop – and even then it has often been subordinated to the objectivist logics of spatial science (see, e.g., Wallace and Fullilove, 1991) – but there have been many relevant studies outside the discipline (Crimp, 1988; Patton, 1990; Shilts, 1987).

DG

References

Agnew, J. A. 1979: Instrumentalism, realism and research on diffusion of innovation. *Prof. Geogr.* 31, pp. 364–70.

Blaikie, P. 1973: The spatial structure of information networks and innovative behaviour in the Ziz valley, S. Morocco. *Geogr. Annlr. B* 55, pp. 83–105.

Blaikie, P. 1975: *Family planning in India: a socio-geographical approach.* London: Edward Arnold/ New York: Holmes and Meier.

Blaikie, P. 1978: The theory of the spatial diffusion of innovations: a spacious cul-de-sac. *Prog. hum. Geogr.* 2, pp. 268–95.

Blaut, J. 1977: Two views of diffusion. *Ann. Ass. Am. Geogr.* 67, pp. 343–9.

Blaut, J. 1980: A radical critique of cultural geography. *Antipode* 12, pp. 25–9

Brown, L. A. 1975: The market and infrastructure context of adoption: a spatial perspective on the diffusion of innovation. *Econ. Geogr.* 51, pp. 185–216.

Casetti, E. and Fan, C. 1991: The spatial spread of the AIDS epidemic in Ohio: empirical analyses using the expansion method. *Environ. Plann. A* 23, pp. 1589–608.

Cliff, A. D., Haggett, P., Ord, J. K. and Versey, G. R. 1981: *Spatial diffusion: an historical geography of epidemics in an island community.* Cambridge: Cambridge University Press.

Crimp, D., ed., 1988: *AIDS: cultural analysis, cultural criticism.* Cambridge, MA: MIT Press.

Duncan, S. S. 1974: The isolation of scientific discovery: indifference and resistance to a new idea. *Sci. Stud.* 4, pp. 109–34.

Gregory, D. 1985: Suspended animation: the stasis of diffusion theory. In Gregory, D. and Urry, J., eds, *Social relations and spatial structures.* London: Macmillan, pp. 296–336.

Hägerstrand, T. 1968: *Innovation diffusion as a spatial process* (translated by A. Pred). Chicago: University of Chicago Press.

Haggett, P., Cliff, A. D. and Frey, A. E. 1977: *Locational analysis in human geography,* second edition. London: Edward Arnold/New York: John Wiley.

Hudson, J. C. 1969: Diffusion in a central place system. *Geogr. Anal.* 1, pp. 45–58.

Leighly, J. 1954: Innovation and area. *Geogrl. Rev.* 44, pp. 439–41.

Patton, C. 1990: *Inventing AIDS.* London: Routledge.

Pedersen, P. O. 1970: Innovation diffusion within and between national urban systems. *Geogr. Anal.* 2, pp. 203–54.

Sauer, C. 1941: Foreword to historical geography. *Ann. Ass. Am. Geogr.* 31, pp. 1–24.

Sauer, C. 1952: *Agricultural origins and dispersals.* New York: American Geographical Society.

Shannon, G. W. and Pyle, G. F. 1989: The origin and diffusion of AIDS: a view from medical geography. *Ann. Ass. Am. Geogr.* 79, pp. 1–24.

Shannon, G. W., Pyle, G. F. and Bashshur, R. L. 1991: *The geography of AIDS: origins and course of an epidemic.* New York: Guilford Press.

Shilts, R. 1987: *And the band played on: politics, people and the AIDS epidemic.* New York: Penguin.

Smallman-Raynor, M., Cliff, A. D. and Haggett, P. 1992: *London international atlas of AIDS.* Oxford: Blackwell.

Wagner, P. L. and Mikesell, M. W., eds 1962: *Readings in cultural geography.* Chicago: University of Chicago Press.

Wallace, R. and Fullilove, M. 1991: AIDS deaths in the Bronx 1983–1988: spatiotemporal analysis from a sociogeographic perspective. *Environ. Plann. A* 23, pp. 1701–23.

Webber, M. J. 1972: *The impact of uncertainty on location.* Cambridge, MA: MIT Press.

Yapa, L. S. 1977: The green revolution: a diffusion model. *Ann. Ass. Am. Geogr.* 67, pp. 350–9.

Yapa, L. S. and Mayfield, R. C. 1978: Non-adoption of innovations. *Econ. Geogr.* 54, pp. 145–56.

Suggested Reading

Blaikie (1978).

Cliff et al. (1981).

Gregory (1985).

Wagner and Mikesell (1962), part 3.

digitizing The translation of an analogue line into discrete digital co-ordinates. The resulting co-ordinate strings are suitable for COMPUTER-ASSISTED CARTOGRAPHY. In the past the process was mostly effected using digitizing tables and was time-consuming and prone to error. More common now are semi-automatic line followers and automatic raster scanners. Human and machine imprecision require map bases to be carefully prepared before digitizing starts. Considerable post-processing is often required before information is 'clean' enough for cartographic use. MJB

Suggested Reading

Fisher, P. F. 1991: Spatial data sources and data problems. In Maguire, D. J., Goodchild, M. F. and Rhind, D. W., eds, *Geographical information* systems: principles and applications, Volume 1. London: Longman, pp. 175–89.

Jackson, M. J. and Woodsford, P. A. 1991: GIS data capture hardware and software. In Maguire, D. J., Goodchild, M. F. and Rhind, D. W., eds, Geographical information systems: principles and applications, Volume 1. London: Longman, pp. 239–49.

disaggregate travel demand modelling An approach to modelling travel behaviour (especially choice of mode and choice of destination) which identifies the individual (person or household) as the appropriate unit for modelling travel behaviour. That identification gave rise to the use of DISCRETE CHOICE MODELLING (to represent the choice process), attitudinal and cognitive modelling (to represent the role of respondents' subjective perceptions, judgements and evaluations) and activity modelling (which stresses the complex of household and individual activities which underlie the demand for travel). In general, the approach requires complex strategies for the collection and analysis of information.   AMH

Suggested Reading
Pipkin, J. S. 1986: Disaggregate travel models. In Hanson, S., ed., The geography of urban transportation. New York: Guilford Press, pp. 179–206.

discourse The ensemble of social practices through which the world is made meaningful and intelligible to oneself and to others: 'frameworks that embrace particular combinations of narratives, concepts, ideologies and signifying practices, each relevant to a particular realm of social action' (Barnes and Duncan, 1992). There are many different definitions of discourse, but what is important about this (admittedly loose) version is as follows:

(a) *The embeddedness of discourse.* Discourses are not free-floating, independent constructions, but are materially implicated in the conduct of day-to-day life where they have substantial, constitutive effects. This view has been particularly helpful in clarifying the historical constitution of human geography: for example, the social foundations of urban and regional discourse (Scott, 1982) or the complicity of

human geography in COLONIALISM and IMPERIALISM (Driver, 1992).

(b) *The naturalizing function of discourse.* Discourses shape the contours of the TAKEN-FOR-GRANTED WORLD: they 'naturalize' and often implicitly universalize a particular view of the world and position subjects within it. This has been particularly helpful in examining IDEOLOGY as unexamined discourse (Gregory, 1978) and, more recently, in exploring the different ways in which human subjects are constituted in time and space (Laclau and Mouffe, 1985; cf. HUMANISTIC GEOGRAPHY).

(c) *The situated character of discourse.* Discourses always provide partial, situated knowledges: as such they are characterized by particular constellations of POWER and knowledge and are always open to contestation and negotiation. This has been particularly helpful in elucidating the part played by RHETORIC in legitimizing social and intellectual practice; for example, the connections between poetics and politics (Crush, 1991), and most of all in disclosing the ETHNOCENTRISM and PHALLOCENTRISM of much mainstream geography. Since discourses are never self-sufficient, one of the principal strategies of *deconstruction* is to show how supposedly closed and totalizing discourses are always vulnerable to disruption, displacement and interruption (cf. POSTSTRUCTURALISM).

These three characterizations are interconnected. For the most part they are influenced by poststructuralism in general and the work of Michel Foucault and Jacques Derrida in particular. In Foucauldian terms, one might say that they enable us to understand 'how *what* is said fits into a network that has its own history and conditions of existence' (Barrett, 1992; see also Hall, 1992): one might also add that it has its own geography and that a central concern of critical human geography is to elucidate the connections between power, knowledge and SPATIALITY (Driver, 1985; Philo, 1992).   DG

References

Barnes, T. and Duncan, J., eds 1992: *Writing worlds: discourse, text and metaphor in the representation of landscape.* London: Routledge.

Barrett, M. 1992: *The politics of truth: from Marx to Foucault.* Stanford, CA: Stanford University Press.

Crush, J. 1991: The discourse of progressive human geography. *Progr. hum. Geogr.* 15, pp. 395–414.

Driver, F. 1985: Power, space and the body: a critical assessment of Foucault's *Discipline and punish. Environ. Plann. D: Society and Space* 3, pp. 425–46.

Driver, F. 1992: Geography's empire: histories of geographical knowledge. *Environ. Plann. D: Society and Space* 10, pp. 23–40.

Gregory, D. 1978: *Ideology, science and human geography.* London: Hutchinson.

Hall, S. 1992: The West and the rest: discourse and power. In Hall, S. and Gieben, B., eds, *Formations of modernity.* Cambridge: Polity Press, pp. 275–332.

Laclau, E. and Mouffe, C. 1985: *Hegemony and socialist strategy: towards a radical democratic politics.* London: Verso.

Philo, C. 1992: Foucault's geography. *Environ. Plann. D: Society and Space* 10, pp. 137–61.

Scott, A. 1982: The meaning and social origins of discourse on the spatial foundations of society. In Gould, P. and Olsson, G., eds, *A search for common ground.* London: Pion, pp. 141–56.

Suggested Reading
Barrett (1992), ch. 6.

discrete choice modelling
A cluster of statistical methods designed to model the way in which individuals choose between discrete alternatives; for example, the choice of a house, the mode of travel for a trip, or the destination for a holiday. The first key argument is that any alternative (house, travel mode or holiday destination) has a total utility to the user which is itself a combination of the weighted utilities of each of its attributes (e.g. a house has a price, garden, garage, architectural style and number of rooms) to the individual user. The second argument is that the probability of choosing the ith alternative is given by the equation:

$$P = v_i \Big/ \sum_j v_j,$$

where v_i is the utility associated with the ith alternative. This equation is the basis for the multinomial LOGIT model, which has proved to be an extremely powerful tool in modelling travel behaviour, including an extension to handle multilayered choices, but it is very demanding in terms of data and computation. It also poses some very important questions: first, the summation over j alternatives requires that the set of alternatives be known; secondly, the use of the utilities (v_i) raises a question as to how they are related to the quantities of the various attributes; thirdly, it may be that these quantities and their utilities are in part determined by the subjective attitudes, beliefs and preferences of the individuals.

AMH

Suggested Reading
Hensher, D. A. 1981: *Applied discrete choice modelling.* London: Croom Helm.
Pipkin, J. S. 1986: Disaggregate travel models. In Hanson, S., ed., *The geography of urban transportation.* New York: Guilford Press, pp. 179–206.

discrimination
See APARTHEID; POSITIVE DISCRIMINATION; RACISM.

disorganized capitalism
A term coined by Lash and Urry (1987) to describe a new form of CAPITALISM that came into existence in the 1960s and 1970s as a result of the demise of organized capitalism.

Organized capitalism, a term that dates back to Hilferding but has been developed more recently by Kocka (1974), refers to a mature form of capitalism that began to evolve out of so-called 'liberal capitalism' in the final decades of the nineteenth century and became dominant in many Western countries in the early and middle parts of the twentieth century. It was characterized by the growth of large bureaucratic organizations in the economy, the STATE and civil society, by the growth of a middle class employed in these organizations, by a form of partnership (or 'corporatist agreement') between companies, states and workers, and by modernist cultural orms. In contrast, *disorganized capitalism* is a process of disorganization and RESTRUCTURING typified by large, global corporations striving to become less bureaucratized and by nation–states which find it increasingly difficult to make economic interventions, by the growth of a 'service class' of managers and professionals (see CLASS), by the breakdown of corporatist agreements (cf. CORPORATISM), and by postmodern cultural forms.

Put baldly, the distinction between organized and disorganized capitalism might seem to be simply a way of synthesizing distinctions that are often made: between FORDISM and POST-FORDISM in the case of the economy, between industrial and POST-INDUSTRIAL SOCIETY, and in the sphere of culture between MODERNISM and POSTMODERNISM. To some extent, this is true. But the idea of disorganized capitalism has more bite than this. In particular, it can be distinguished from these formulations by three important emphases. First, it is particularly attentive to the importance of geography; changing spatial forms are clearly implicated in the shift from organized to disorganized capitalism. Second, it stresses that disorganized capitalism is a process that moves hesitantly rather than triumphantly. Third, it is methodologically catholic; Lash and Urry are not willing to declare a fixed allegiance to any 'ism' but instead offer a list of diagnostic elements which cannot be reduced to any single, central generating mechanism.

Since the original book, the authors have developed their thesis in a number of different ways, especially through work on culture and the cultural industries (Lash, 1990), tourism (Urry, 1991) and travel (Lash and Urry, 1992). NJT

References

Kocka, J. 1974: *Organiserter Kapitalismus. Göttingen: Vandenhock and Ruprecht.*

Lash, S. 1990: *Sociology of postmodernism.* London: Routledge.

Lash, S. and Urry, J. 1987: *The end of organised capitalism.* Cambridge: Polity Press.

Lash, S. and Urry, J. 1992: *Economics of signs and space: after organised capitalism.* Cambridge: Polity Press.

Urry, J. 1991: *The tourist gaze.* London: Sage.

distance decay The attenuation of a pattern or process with distance. Distance was one of the 'fundamental spatial concepts' identified by Nystuen (in Berry and Marble, 1968) and the importance of distance decay (sometimes called a distance *lapse rate*) was enshrined in Tobler's famous 'first law of geography: everything is related to everything else, but near things

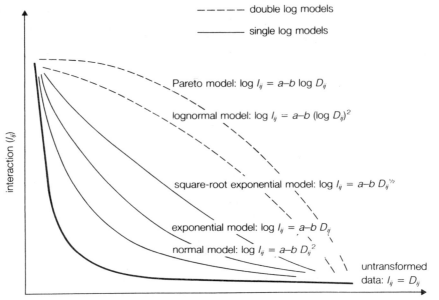

distance decay   *Distance decay curves and transformations* (Taylor, 1971).

are more related than distant things' (Tobler, 1970). The empirical significance of this had of course been recognized in the early formulations of SOCIAL PHYSICS, but only achieved wider formal significance within geography with the emergence of the search for general theorems of spatial organization. Underlying many of the classical models of SPATIAL STRUCTURE, for example, the CENTRAL PLACE models of Christaller and Lösch and the DIFFUSION models of Hägerstrand, are assumptions about SPATIAL INTERACTION which, in the typical GRAVITY MODEL form, postulate a definite inverse 'distance effect', which is capable of a series of mathematical expressions (see the figure). These various transformations have such a powerful effect on the lapse rate that Olsson (1980) argued that the identification of a distance decay 'may reveal as much about the language I am talking *in* as it does about the phenomena I am talking *about*'. But in any event the lapse rate is evidently not independent of the geometry of the system within which interaction takes place, and in some locational models this is partially recognized through a parallel discussion of the accessibility of points arrayed on a movement surface (or network) around some hypothetical centre; for example, the VON THÜNEN MODEL of agricultural land use or the density gradients of conventional urban land-use models. Because of these logical connections Bunge (1962) represented interaction and geometry as 'the inseparable duals of geographic theory'; but the matter clearly does not end there, because such interdependence poses formidable interpretative difficulties (e.g., see Cliff et al., 1975, 1976; Curry, 1972). Hence, while distance-decay curves can be identified empirically it is by no means clear how far their form depends on the model structures used to replicate them; nor to what extent their parameters can be given substantive meaning.   DG

References

Berry, B. J. L. and Marble, D. F., eds 1968: *Spatial analysis: a reader in statistical geography.* Englewood Cliffs, NJ: Prentice-Hall.

Bunge, W. 1962: *Theoretical geography.* Lund: C. W. K. Gleerup.

Cliff, A., Martin, R. L. and Ord, J. K. 1975 and 1976: Map pattern and friction of distance parameters. *Reg. Stud.* 9, pp. 285–8 and 10, pp. 341–2.

Curry, L. 1972: A spatial analysis of gravity flows. *Reg. Stud.* 6, pp. 131–47.

Olsson, G. 1980: *Birds in eggs/eggs in bird.* London: Pion/New York: Methuen.

Taylor, P. J. 1971: Distance transformation and distance decay functions. *Geogr. Anal.* 3, pp. 221–38.

Tobler, W. 1970: A computer movie. *Econ. Geogr.*, 46, pp. 234–40.

Suggested Reading

Olsson (1980), ch. 13.

Sheppard, E. S. 1984: The distance decay gravity model debate. In Gaile, G. L. and Willmott, C. J. eds, *Spatial statistics and models.* Dordrecht: D. Reidel, pp. 367–88.

districting algorithm A procedure, usually programmed for a computer, for defining the boundaries of electoral constituencies. Such algorithms became popular in the USA after the Supreme Court outlawed MALAPPORTIONMENT in the 1960s; they are used to produce constituencies which conform to the equal-population requirement.   RJJ

Suggested Reading

Johnston, R. J. and Rossiter, D. J. 1983: Constituency building, political representation and electoral bias in urban England. In Herbert, D. T. and Johnston, R. J., eds, *Geography and the urban environment: progress in research and applications,* Volume 5. Chichester: John Wiley, pp. 113–56.

division of labour An aspect of the RELATIONS OF PRODUCTION of society which involves the separation of tasks within the LABOUR PROCESS and their allocation to different groups of workers. Two forms are commonly identified:

(a) *Social division of labour* – the division of workers between product sectors (e.g. 'car workers' or 'textile workers').

(b) *Technical division of labour* – the division of the production process into tasks, and the specialization of workers in one or a small number of these (e.g. managers, supervisors and assembly workers).

To these we may add the following:

(c) *Gender division of labour* – in which specific jobs are assigned to men or women: in Western societies nurses tend to be women, and coalminers men. This extends beyond paid employment, so that unwaged domestic labour is largely performed by women (see GENDER AND GEOGRAPHY; PATRIARCHY).

(d) *Cultural division of labour* – according to the theory of internal colonialism (see NATIONALISM), regional minorities bear the same relationship to the majority as a colony does to the metropolitan power under COLONIALISM. The periphery supplies the core with raw materials and labour, forming a division of labour between the minority and majority cultures (see CORE–PERIPHERY MODEL).

(e) *International division of labour* – characteristically, less-developed countries produce raw materials and developed countries produce manufactured goods. More recently, a NEW INTERNATIONAL DIVISION OF LABOUR has involved the development by MULTINATIONAL CORPORATIONS of production facilities in less-developed countries, although normally at the routine and low-skill end of the production process. This is a special case of:

(f) *Spatial division of labour* – a concept proposed by Massey (1984), which involves the concentration of particular sectors and/or production tasks in specific geographical areas. JP

Reference

Massey, D. 1984: *Spatial divisions of labour*, London: Macmillan.

domino theory A GEOPOLITICS theory adopted by the American government in the 1950s to justify its policies of military and political involvement in other countries. The theory contended that if one country fell into the Soviet Union's sphere of influence its neighbours could well follow, setting up a ripple effect similar to that of a toppling line of dominoes. Its main use was to justify American involvement in Southeast Asia, being propounded by President Eisenhower in 1953. It continues to influence American foreign policy, including attitudes towards governments in Central America, it being pointed out in

the late 1980s that Nicaragua is closer to Texas than is Washington, DC.

RJJ

Suggested Reading

O'Sullivan, P. 1982: Antidomino. *Pol. Geogr. Q.* 1, pp. 57–64.

dry farming A farming technique for crop cultivation without irrigation in areas of low and variable rainfall. Fallowing, reserving two seasons' rainfall for one crop, is the most common, with mulching and frequent weeding. Low-rainfall areas are subject to erosion, and thus soil conservation methods are essential. Dry farming areas can have only a narrow range of crops and low yields. Traditional dry farming is found in the Near East, North Africa, the Sahel and north-west India. These methods allowed the extension of crop cultivation into the semi-arid areas of North America and Australia in the nineteenth century, and into the Virgin Lands of the USSR in the 1950s. DBG

Suggested Reading

Andreae, B. 1981: *Farming development and space: a world agricultural geography*. New York: De Gruyter, pp. 174–87.

Swindale, L. D. and Virmani, S. M. 1981: Climatic variability and crop yields in the semi-arid tropics. In Bach, W., Pankrath, J. and Schneider, S. H., eds, *Food–climate interactions*. London: D. Reidel, pp. 139–66.

dual economy An economy that appears to consist of two separate parts, each having a distinctive history and dynamic.

Early this century, J. H. Boeke (see Boeke, 1953; Furnivall, 1939) argued that Indonesian society was divided into two separate CULTURES – a Western and an Eastern. These cultures were considered to be structurally and behaviourally so different that Western principles of social analysis were quite inappropriate for an understanding of Eastern culture or, indeed, for an understanding of Eastern culture or, indeed, for an understanding of the dual whole. Insofar as Western culture is highly organized along lines which facilitate the fulfilment of material objectives by rational means of production

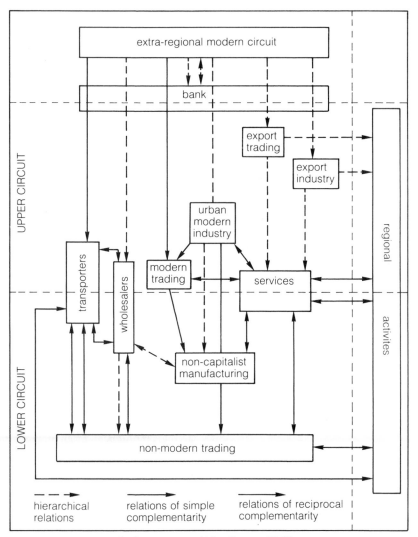

dual economy   (After Santos, 1979).

(production for gain) and Eastern culture is loosely organized, fatalistic, passive and concerned with production for use, the central problem of DEVELOPMENT in dual economies (the context in which they have, in the main, been analysed) is the relationship between the two cultures.

Such an emphasis upon development generates an economistic and universal view of the world, and so legitimates dualist thinking by imposing a particular and singular Western view of the world on all 'others' (see ETHNOCENTRISM). It thereby encourages the simplistic division of the world in dualist terms (see Said (1985) for a critique of such a manoeuvre). Any SOCIAL FORMATION is made up of a variety of MODES OF PRODUCTION. There may be two or more, and sensitive social dissection would reveal the variety of social discontinuities.

Two particularly influential accounts of the world-economy (Braudel, 1985; Wallerstein, 1979; see WORLD-SYSTEMS ANALYSIS) each identify three, rather different, underlying structures. But to

141

look for two is to find two – to generalize in such a way that the resulting classification is binary in form. In developed industrial economies, for example, distinctions are sometimes drawn between the small number of very large firms which dominate economies and the large number of small firms, the conditions of existence of which are set by the former group.

Nevertheless, Brookfield (1975) asserts that 'it is a matter of simple observation that the economies of a great many developing countries are organized in two parts . . . the point must be emphasized that a phenomenon called "dualism" exists . . .'. The question is whether 'simple observation' is an adequate basis for such an assertion. On the basis of evidence on the complexity, recency and incompleteness of class structures in the underdeveloped world (Roxborough, 1979), the answer must be that it is not.

An alternative but associated conception of dualism – elucidated most explicitly in the writings of Santos (1979; see Chatterjee, 1989 for a critical evaluation) – is that of the emergence of two circuits of production and exchange. Santos (1979, p. 19) refers to these circuits as the 'upper circuit' and the 'lower circuit' (see the figure):

In simple terms, the upper circuit consists of banking, export trade and industry, modern urban industry, trade and services, and wholesaling and trucking. The lower circuit is essentially made up of non-capitalist-intensive forms of manufacturing, non-modern services generally provided at the 'retail' level and non-modern and small-scale trade.

The circuits correspond to what Geertz (1963, p. 34) speaks of as the 'firm-centred economy' and the 'bazaar economy': the distinction between them is based primarily upon the non-modern/modern cleavage. Thus, whereas the upper circuit is characterized by modern capital-intensive industry, extensive trade and complex commercial flows, the lower circuit involves labour-intensive manufacturing, local services and limited trade. Access by the individual to the products of the upper circuit is restricted by income; the distribution of which is increasingly polarized as

the landless and jobless live alongside those productively involved in, and highly remunerated for, their participation in the upper circuit. Yet the poor and dispossessed must somehow create the conditions of their own existence: they do so through their participation in a lower circuit (see INFORMAL SECTOR).

Simple and reciprocal forms of complementarity (inputs and outputs) form the material relationships between the circuits but, insofar as the upper circuit is based upon capitalist production and exchange, the two circuits may be constantly intertwined through the activities of merchants and moneylenders, who facilitate a flow of capital in both directions. However, in terms of material linkages, the relationship between the circuits is asymmetric: the lower circuit serves as a market for the upper, but the former finds its markets amongst households and producers elsewhere in the informal sector (Lubell, 1991).

A view of the circuits based upon the informal sector and the differentiation both of capital as self-expanding value and of its sources of expansion begins to undermine a simple dualism embodied in the dual circuit. This dualism is based on the notion that the hegemony of the upper circuit is reproduced by an inherent process of quantitative expansion (see CAPITALISM) and provides not only the context to which the lower circuit must constantly adapt but the very reason for its existence.

The notion of dualism serves a significant ideological purpose (see IDEOLOGY). On the one hand, and stemming from the work of Lewis (1954), economists have tried to build theories of development based upon the assumed existence of dualism. Such theories, operating under various assumptions such as the abundance of unemployed labour power in the traditional sector, try to uncover the implications of economic growth and structural change for both parts of the economy, for their interrelationship and for economy-wide change. As a result the dominant sector may be imposed upon the subdominant, and the latter may well disintegrate and be transformed into the image of its dominant partner (see DEPENDENCE).

Leaving aside the question of whether or not dualism is an adequate description of the economy in question, problems arise over the nature of the two parts. The solution is to set up ideal types which more or less correspond to observed characteristics (see ABSTRACTION). But such problems are intensified when such relatively unreal ideal types are brought into interrelationship with each other. Without a detailed social specification of the two parts – which would, in any case, serve to break down a simplistic dualism – it is difficult to build an operational model.

On the other hand, the sustenance of the ideology of dualism may serve the interests of those who promote MODERNIZATION (or, more correctly, those who promote the development of a particular MODE OF PRODUCTION) on the grounds that everything associated with change is identified with progress and everything associated with the *status quo* is identified with stagnation. Furthermore, dualism implies that UNDERDEVELOPMENT is the consequence of resistance to change. It suggests that underdevelopment is caused by development-restrictive conditions within the underdeveloped society (such as may be manifest in a backward-sloping supply curve of labour) rather than through its relationships with the world outside. For Santos (1979) the objective of development is to open up the upper circuit to participation by those in the lower, in order to increase their skills and productivity. This is classical dualist thinking and, despite assertions to the contrary, implies a 'dichotomized or fragmented urban economy'.

Dualism is a powerful idea. It has given rise to a substantial body of development theory and practice and insofar as it emphasizes the UNEVEN nature of DEVELOPMENT and the barriers to its progress, it is useful. The major problem is that it imposes a simplistic, misleading and teleological predefinition of the world into two parts (development-facilitative and development-restrictive), rather than emphasizing either the causal links between them or offering a critique of the universalism implied. These two parts are defined by external criteria derived from the process of development under advocacy. In this way dualism acts as a kind of intellectual as well as practical imperialism, serving to deny the complete structure and vitality of incorporated societies.   RL

References and Suggested Reading

Boeke, J. H. 1953: *Economics and economic policy of dual societies, as exemplified by Indonesia.* Haarlem: H. D. Tjeenk Willink and Zoon/New York: Institute of Pacific Relations. (Reprinted 1976, New York: AMS Press.)

Braudel, F. 1985: *Civilization and capitalism 15th–18th Century* Volume I, *The perspective of the world.* London: Fontana.

Brookfield, H. 1975: *Interdependent development.* London: Methuen/Pittsburgh, PA: University of Pittsburgh Press, ch. 3.

Chatterjee, L. 1989: Third World cities. In Peet, R. and Thrift, N., eds, *New models in geography,* Volume 2. London: Unwin Hyman, pp. 127–46.

Furnivall, J. S. 1939: *Netherlands India: a study of plural economy.* Cambridge: Cambridge University Press. (1944 edition reprinted 1977. New York: AMS Press.)

Geertz, C. 1963: *Peddlars and princes.* Chicago: Chicago University Press.

Lewis, W. A. 1954: Economic development with unlimited supplies of labour. *Manchester Sch. Econ. Soc. Stud.* 22, pp. 139–91.

Lubell, H. 1991: *The informal sector in the 1980s and 1990s.* OECD Development Centre Studies. Paris: OECD.

Roxborough, I. 1979: *Theories of underdevelopment.* London: Macmillan/Atlantic Highlands, NJ: Humanities Press, chs 6 and 7.

Said, E. W. 1985: *Orientalism.* London: Penguin (originally published in 1978).

Santos, M. 1979: *The shared space.* London: Methuen.

Wallerstein, I. 1979: *The capitalist world economy.* Cambridge: Cambridge University Press/ Paris: Editions de la Maison des Sciences de l'Homme.

dual theory of the state A theory developed by Peter Saunders (1986) which separates analytically the STATE's roles in promoting production (and thus wealth creation) in a capitalist society and in ensuring satisfactory levels of consumption for its resident population. Saunders argued that these two functions involve two separate, though overlapping, arenas of CONFLICT – what he termed the 'politics of production' and the 'politics of consumption'. The actors in these two political arenas are mobilized in different ways. In the politics of production, the conflicts are largely CLASS–based (involving, for example, employers' organizations on the one hand and trades unions on the other, in conflict with each other and with the state: cf. CORPORATISM); in the politics of consumption the interested parties are sectoral groups (such as those reliant on different sources for housing, transport, health services, education and so forth) which may not be mobilized across a class CLEAVAGE.

The main geographical component of Saunders' theory is the claim that whereas the politics of production are largely organized at the national or regional level, the politics of consumption are played out at the local scale (see LOCAL STATE). Major contentious issues, conflicts over which might threaten the rate of capital accumulation, are focused on the national state, where the interests of capitalists can best be safeguarded. Other issues, which are local rather than national in their impact and carry less threat to the capitalist imperative, remain at the local level: most of these are concerned with consumption issues, with conflict over relative access to PUBLIC GOODS rather than over shares of the national wealth, and these can be relatively safely left to the more pluralist political ethos of local governments (see PLURAL-ISM), while production issues are handled in the national government, which is more influenced by corporatism.

On a simple reading, this theory suggests a clear distinction between central and local governments in their respective roles within the STATE APPARATUS. Saunders stresses that the relative allocation of functions varies over time and between places, but contends that in Great Britain at least it is atypical for class politics to dominate at the local level.   RJJ

Reference

Saunders, P. 1986: *Social theory and the urban question,* second edition. London: Hutchinson.

Suggested Reading

Dunleavy, P. 1980: *Urban political analysis.* London: Macmillan.

E

ecological fallacy The problem of inferring characteristics of individuals from aggregate data referring to a population. Since such data are frequently used in geographical work, referring to the populations of defined areas, the problem is frequently a serious one for geographical analyses.

The problem was initially highlighted by Robinson (1950). Using data from the 1930 US CENSUS, he obtained a high CORRELATION coefficient of 0.773 for the REGRESSION of the percentage of each state's population who were illiterate on the percentage who were black. From this it could be inferred that blacks were much more likely to be illiterate than were non-blacks. However, using data on individuals from the same source, he found a correlation of only 0.203: there was a higher level of illiteracy among blacks than non-blacks, but much less than the state-level analysis suggested. The lesson was clear: just because blacks were concentrated in the states with the highest levels of illiteracy did not necessarily imply a much higher level of illiteracy among blacks.

Robinson's identification of the possibility of implying spurious correlations from analyses of aggregate data has been advanced by others. Alker (1969) identified five other fallacies:

(1) the *individualistic fallacy*, which involves the assumption that the whole is no more than the sum of its parts (see HOLISM; REGIONALISM) – many societies are more than mere aggregations of their individual members;

(2) the *cross-level fallacy*, which assumes that a relationship observed in one aggregation of a population (i.e. one set of spatial units) applies to all others, and is thus a universal feature of that population – research on the MODIFIABLE AREAL UNIT problem has demonstrated that this is invalid;

(3) the *universal fallacy*, which assumes that the pattern observed in a sample – often not randomly selected according to the principles of SAMPLING – holds for its population;

(4) the *selective fallacy*, in which data from carefully chosen cases are used to 'prove' a point; and

(5) the *cross-sectional fallacy*, the assumption that what is observed at one point in time (i.e. for a sample of one observation only) applies to other times.

Recognition of these fallacies and the pitfalls that they create for aggregate data analysis calls for careful interpretation of the results of studies based on ecological data. An observed relationship may be consistent with a HYPOTHESIS, but a causal relationship should never be assumed: as Robinson's example showed, very wrong conclusions can be drawn from aggregate data analyses.   RJJ

References

Alker, H. R. 1969: A typology of ecological fallacies. In M. Dogan and S. Rokkan, eds, *Quantitative ecological analysis in the social sciences*. Cambridge, MA: The MIT Press, pp. 69–86.

Robinson, W. S. 1950: Ecological correlations and the behavior of individuals. *Am. Soc. Rev.* 15, pp. 351–7.

Suggested Reading

Duncan, O. D., Cuzzort, R. P. and Duncan, B. 1961: *Statistical geography*. Glencoe, IL: The Free Press.

ecology The study of interrelations between organisms and their biotic and abiotic environments. The term 'ecology' entered the English language in the late nineteenth century as 'oecology', a translation of the word *Oecologia*, coined in 1866 by the German biologist Ernst Haeckel. Many early uses of the word itself – Haeckel's included – bore little resemblance in practice to what the word now signifies. Some historians have sought to reconstruct a history of ecological ideas pre-dating the coining of the term. Worster (1985), for example, traces one such current of thought, the 'arcadian', back to the English natural historian Gilbert White of Selborne. Bramwell (1989) examines sources of nineteenth- and twentieth-century ecological thinking, ranging from British and German fascism to the anarchist Kropotkin. Glacken (1967) traces a lineage as far back as Greek TELEOLOGY.

The word clearly has two meanings, one denoting the environmental science and the other a normative or ethical position that is protective of and reverent towards ecological processes and communities. As a central discipline in biology, ecology is concerned primarily with the distribution and abundance of organisms, populations (individuals of the same species), and communities of populations. COMMUNITY ecology, the subdiscipline of scientific ecology most familiar to laypersons, deals with the composition or structure of communities and with the movement of matter and energy through them (see ECOSYSTEM). Community ecology was pioneered at the turn of the century by Cowles and Clements, who studied the development and dynamics of plant communities and were themselves influenced by geographers such as Humboldt, De Candolle, Engler, Gray and Kerner. Population dynamics developed from the theoretical approaches of Lotka and Volterra in the 1920s, and from the later field studies of Lack. Darwin's theory of evolution, along with the genetic theories of Mendel and S. Wright (in 1931), influenced the growth of 'population genetics', the study of evolution and adaptation. Two limnologists, Birge and Juday, developed the idea of primary production in the 1940s. From their studies came the trophic-dynamic concept of ecology introduced by

Lindeman in 1942. In the 1950s Hutchinson and H. T. and E. P. Odum pioneered work on energy flow and energy budgets, which was complemented by Ovington, Rodin and Bazilevic's work on the cycling of nutrients (see Smith, 1974).

Several ecological concepts have been borrowed by geographers, economists and anthropologists (see HUMAN ECOLOGY). Cultural ecologists and hazards geographers have used the concept of adaptation rather uncritically to describe human adjustments to environmental change (see ENVIRONMENTAL HAZARD). Energy accounting, the concepts of multiple equilibria and surprise (in which system collapse occurs for no predictable or known reason), and other ecological ideas such as CARRYING CAPACITY, have informed resource and hazards geography (and economics) with varying degrees of success. URBAN ECOLOGY and landscape ecology are two relatively new multidisciplinary areas of study of interest to geographers. Urban ecology challenges the dualism of 'natural' and 'built' environments, although it emphasizes biogeophysical over social structures and processes. Landscape ecology considers the development and maintenance of spatial heterogeneity and exchanges across heterogeneous landscapes. Dispensing with notions of homogeneity and equilibrium, landscape ecology principles appear promising for RESOURCE MANAGEMENT. Yet the focus upon spatial patterns (including SCALE) suggests a need for collaboration between geographers and biologists in order to avoid another round of atheoretical spatial modelling.

The word ecology has also come to be associated with the belief that drastic change within an ECOSYSTEM is wrong or ill-advised. Normative ecological thinking thus advocates the preservation of species, habitats and ecological processes. In popular usage, 'ecology' is often equated with ENVIRONMENTALISM or the ENVIRONMENTAL MOVEMENT. As Bramwell (1989) illustrates, normative ecologies do not fit into any one ideological category: they run the gamut from Left to Right, from anthropocentric to ecocentric, from anarchist to authoritarian, from romantic to technocratic, and so on. Geographers have an important contribution to make to debates within and between scientific and normative ecology. JEm

References

Bramwell, A. 1989: *Ecology in the 20th century: a history*. New Haven, CN: Yale University Press.

Glacken, C. 1967: *Traces on the Rhodian shore*. Berkeley, CA: University of California Press.

Smith, R. L. 1974: *Ecology and field biology*. New York: Harper and Row.

Worster, D. 1985: *Nature's economy: a history of ecological ideas*. Cambridge: Cambridge University Press.

Suggested Reading

Crosby, A. W. 1986: *Ecological imperialism: the biological expansion of Europe, 900–1900*. Cambridge: Cambridge University Press.

Gorz, A. 1980: *Ecology as politics*. Boston, MA: South End Press/London: Pluto Press.

Martinez-Alier, J. 1987: *Ecological economics: energy, environment and society*. Oxford: Blackwell.

economic base theory A theory that explains urban and regional growth in terms of a division of employment into *basic* and *non-basic* sectors. The basic sector (*B*) comprises those industries that meet external or export demand, and the location and growth of this sector is seen as a function of national and international forces. The non-basic sector (*S*) is locally oriented employment, servicing the total local population (*P*). The total population is a function of the total employment (*E*), and the economic base relationships are:

$$E = S + B, \qquad P = \alpha E, \qquad S = \beta P.$$

The coefficients α and β can be obtained by REGRESSION using observations for a sample of cities or for one city or region over time. Growth (or decline) in local population and employment is controlled by changes in the basic sector, and the impacts (MULTIPLIERS) of such changes can be calculated from the economic base equations:

$$E = (1 - \alpha\beta)^{-1}B,$$
$$P = \alpha(1 - \alpha\beta)^{-1}B,$$
$$S = \alpha\beta(1 - \alpha\beta)^{-1}B.$$

A unit increase in *B* generates $\alpha/(1 - \alpha\beta)$ units of additional local population.

Economic base theory is very simplistic in its assumptions, but because its data demands are simple it has been widely employed in regional economic analysis. It is used, for example, in ACTIVITY ALLOCATION MODELS and LOWRY MODELS. Correct identification of the basic sector is crucial, and LOCATION QUOTIENTS are frequently used for this purpose. Either industries with high indices of specialization are defined as basic industries, or the quotient is used to define a proportion of employment in an industry as basic; so that, for example, one-third of employment in an industry with a quotient of 1.5 is designated as basic employment. A more sophisticated approach is to use INPUT–OUTPUT analysis to trace actual interindustrial linkages, but this is very data-demanding and expensive.

The major limitations of economic base theory spring from its aggregative nature: the difficulties of sector definition; the dubious assumption that the aggregate multipliers will remain constant; and an inability to trace the impact of particular basic sector shifts, such as a rise in oil exports, on specific sectors of the local economy. LWH

Suggested Reading

Glickman, N. J. 1977: *Econometric analysis of regional systems: explorations in model building and policy analysis*. New York and London: Academic Press, pp. 15–27.

economic geography A geography of people's struggle to make a living. As such it should concern itself with the sustainable and humane production, use and reproduction of the social, natural and material conditions of human existence. Such a perspective is easily lost in the analysis of the complex technicalities and apparently impersonal processes of change in the contemporary economic world. And yet, as Peter Dicken (1992, chapter 13) reminds us, even in the powerful realm of global production and MULTINATIONAL CORPORATIONS, economies are for people, and the concern for 'making a living in the global economy' is always and should always be present in any economic geography which insists upon the subordination of the merely economic for the richly human.

Making a living is a process profoundly structured by geography:

(a) *It is becoming more and more unevenly developed* (see UNEVEN DEVELOPMENT). By 1990, the richest 20 per cent of the world's population by country had incomes 60 times greater than the poorest 20 per cent, whereas in 1960 the equivalent ratio was only 30. But the reality is even worse, because if the distribution of income *within* countries is taken into account, the richest 20 per cent have incomes over 150 times greater than the poorest 20 per cent. (United Nations Development Programme, 1992). Under such circumstances and the even more grossly unequal underlying productive mechanisms which generate such distributive inequality, any concept of the world-economy which assumes uniformity in global process and form – and is, therefore, not geographical in structure – is simply inadequate (hence the relevance and popularity of WORLD-SYSTEMS ANALYSIS in geography); and any economic geography which is not aimed at the explanation and removal of such obscene inequalities is self-indulgent.

(b) *The social bases of economic activity* (Brenner, 1977; Lee, 1989) *are themselves geographically structured*: 'the historical geography of capitalism has been nothing short of remarkable' (Harvey, 1982, p. 373).

(c) *The reproduction of social life rests upon the struggle to establish modes of DEVELOPMENT capable of gentle and subtle responses to what are, ultimately, internal relations with NATURE;* in other words, it rests upon the ability of human societies to devise workable models of SUSTAINABLE DEVELOPMENT a term that should recognize that the production of nature (Smith, 1984) extends to gender and race relations as well as to environmental relations (Redclift, 1987).

(d) *The production and reproduction of the social and material conditions of human existence are subject to the logics of geography,* which shape their territorial dynamics and so precondition them (see, for example, Massey, 1984; Storper and Walker, 1989).

(e) *The resultant geography of production and reproduction and of the DIVISION OF LABOUR* (Sayer and Walker, 1992) *forms the material basis of international relations and, at the same time, sets the local context for urban and regional development and the social conflict/acquiescence/support which underpins such development.* Scott and Storper (1986, p. 311) conclude that 'the question of the geographical anatomy of industrial capitalism is likely to become rapidly of major significance throughout the social sciences at large'.

An inclusive economic geography would include the study of:

- the cultural and environmental origins of economic activity, articulated through socially constructed gender and kinship relations, and struggle to establish a particular set of social relations of production and their geographical extent
- the conceptualization of nature
- the forms of calculation and measurement of value
- the processes and forms of production and consumption generated by such relations and value systems
- the division of labour
- the conditions of development within a particular set of social relations
- the forms of STATE and politics which support and legitimize particular social relations and processes of production and consumption
- the construction of cultural and ideological forms which shape the basis of discourse within a particular value system
- the structuring of relationships within and between different sets of social relations
- the conditions of transformation from one set of social relations of production to another

In fact, however, economic geography remains fragmented and asocial. Emphasis has traditionally been placed upon the production and use of the environmental and technological conditions of existence. It is argued by Paterson (1976) that economic geography is concerned with the human usefulness of Earth features, the amount of support they can offer, and with the measures which people may take to bring them into use. Such an emphasis is critical if 'spaceship Earth' is to maintain its systems of life support. But an understanding of the present economic use of known natural resources (see, e.g., Manners, 1971) is becoming less significant than the imaginative but realistic analysis of their use (e.g. Rees, 1990) in conditions which recognize the ecological limits to growth and the imperatives of sustainable development which yet remains shaped and constrained by the dynamics and logic of capitalism. Thus any significant modification of the social production of nature will necessarily involve a transformation of social relations – the relations between people themselves (Emel and Peet, 1989; Johnston, 1989; O'Riordan, 1989).

The social construction of nature is complex and dynamic (Sayer, 1979). Through production people change the nature around them. They thereby quite consciously change the material and mental conditions of their own existence and, in the process, modify their own nature as they bring a new relationship within nature into being. In contrast to other social animals, human beings 'do not just live in society, they *produce society in order to live*' (Godelier, 1986, p. 1; italics in original). Despite this dialectical process of the production of nature, which may be established only within definite social relations of production (Lee, 1989), geographers tend to insist on the relations *between* people and nature in an asocial methodology which has relied upon environmental – and, more recently, economic – determinism (Peet, 1991). In this they acquiesce in the practice of orthodox (neoclassical) economics which simply ignores the significance of social relations.

And yet as early as 1935, in a study of *The pastoral industries of New Zealand*, R. O. Buchanan pointed out that 'geographical conditions . . . are dependent on the precise nature of the economic conditions'. He went on to suggest that such a relationship 'will be recognized as merely specifying one type of instance of the generally accepted view that geographical values are not absolute, but are relative to the cultural stage [see CULTURAL GEOGRAPHY;

CULTURE] achieved by the human actors'. Such a view may be 'generally accepted' outside economic geography, but it is rarely incorporated within the subdiscipline. Nevertheless, it carries with it the implication that understanding will be distorted unless environmental and cultural relations are interpreted in a dialectical manner.

The appropriation of nature necessitates the development of the productive forces. These are the material and intellectual means which are combined together in the LABOUR PROCESS through which nature is transformed and socialized into use values (which are simply items of use to people). Despite its central significance for material production, the labour process (and certainly its social parameters) has not, with a few notable exceptions (e.g. Franklin, 1969; Dunford and Perrons, 1983), been considered of central importance in economic geography. The same might also be said of the economic geographical interest in the division of labour (Sayer and Walker, 1992). Rather, the emphasis has been placed upon the geographically distinctive characteristics of the commodities produced and, to a lesser extent, upon the productive capacities of particular places.

Thus the early development of economic geography was largely atheoretical and characterized by a not altogether innocent EMPIRICISM concerned to amass factual detail about production in different parts of the world. As G. G. Chisholm shows in his *Handbook of commercial geography* – first published in 1889 and remaining in print for almost a century – such factual compilations were not entirely without economic substance. Furthermore, the availability of systematically compiled data was strategically important for colonial powers, especially during the nineteenth century. The colonists were able to use geography and geographers to provide information to aid the expansion of colonial investment, commerce, trade and settlement and the control of vital strategic resources (see COLONIALISM). Even if the subdiscipline of economic geography was economically naive, the economic and political use to which it was put was highly sophisticated.

Such an emphasis upon COMMODITIES and the geographical conditions and material means of their production led to a fragmentation of economic geography: the subdiscipline is conventionally subdivided by economic sector – AGRICULTURAL GEOGRAPHY, INDUSTRIAL GEOGRAPHY, TRANSPORT GEOGRAPHY and the geographies of SERVICES and TRADE. Progress in such subdivisions has been marked by a move from description to analysis and from ENVIRONMENTAL to economic DETERMINISM. This transformation was achieved initially by the gradual incorporation of NEOCLASSICAL ECONOMICS into economic geography (Hodder and Lee, 1974). Some of the relationships between geography and (neoclassical) economics have been explored by Michael Chisholm (1966). They become clear from the many detailed studies of particular economic activities and of location in space (Dicken and Lloyd, 1990) in which the definitional categories used and the causal mechanisms analysed are derived directly from neoclassical economic theory.

Such academic developments reflect the world in which they take place. The emergence of neoclassical economics was closely associated with the rise of CAPITALISM, as it presents an ideologically non-threatening image of the world (Galbraith, 1974) which sidesteps the issue of CLASS conflict in class-based systems of wealth generation. Neoclassical economics bases its analysis both upon an asocial and apparently universal set of markets rather than a historically specific type of SOCIETY, and upon a concern for the allocation of resources to alternative uses rather than the processes and conflicts – both economic and social – of the generation of wealth.

It is hardly surprising, then, that neoclassical theory provides the conceptual channel for the mainstream of LOCATION THEORY (see, for example, Michael Chisholm's classic application – well ahead of its time – of Von Thünen's agricultural location theory in his *Rural settlement and land use*, first published in 1962: see VON THÜNEN MODEL), and REGIONAL SCIENCE (see also CENTRAL PLACE THEORY; TRADE; URBAN SYSTEM),

which themselves employ universal geometric concepts and physical processes to analyse the space economy, and for much APPLIED economic GEOGRAPHY. However, the mechanical and non-human assumptions concerning rational economic action made by neoclassical theory generated a reaction in the form of behavioural and humanistic perspectives (see BEHAVIOURAL GEOGRAPHY; HUMANISTIC GEOGRAPHY; RATIONAL CHOICE THEORY: for an application of the latter to economic geography, see Wallace, 1978). These accept a wider range of stimuli to and constraints upon individual action than can be admitted by neoclassical theory but do not incorporate a fully developed view of the relationships between individuals and the societies and nature in which they find their conditions of existence.

The increasing consciousness of international and domestic contradictions stemming from the operation of the economy (especially those associated with UNEVEN DEVELOPMENT, DEVELOPMENT and UNDERDEVELOPMENT) has led economic geography to develop a concern for some of the outcomes of economic processes. The emergence of WELFARE GEOGRAPHY represents one geographical response to this concern. However, the methodology underpinning welfare geography implies an acceptance of the conventional image of the ahistoric market economy, and so prevents a thorough understanding and critique of the historically specific and socially reproductive characteristics of the economy. The STATE is interpreted as an autonomous means of redistribution rather than as an implicated means of social reproduction.

A definite set of social relations of production is a vital prerequisite for material production. By establishing the bases and purposes of communication and thereby establishing the criteria by which the production and circulation of the surplus may be valued, social relations define the nature and purpose of production and reproduction (Lee, 1989). The appearance of David Harvey's *Social justice and the city* in 1973 – nearly 40 years after R. O. Buchanan's comments on the definitive relations between culture and economy – brought such basic issues, and an EPISTEMOLOGY with which they could be handled, to the attention of geographers. The later chapters of Harvey's book represent a first attempt to interpret the structure and functioning of economies as cultural, social and historic entities, while his *The limits to capital* (1982) presents a review of and remarkable response to criticisms of Marxist economic theory (see MARXIAN ECONOMICS; MARXIST GEOGRAPHY). It is not surprising, then to read (in, for example, Sheppard and Barnes, 1990) that recent attempts to continue to provide a theoretical outline of this much more sophisticated view of the interconnections between economics and geography – a view which accepts that economies are social constructs (Lee, 1989) and goes beyond Marxist theory – acknowledge the continuing, primary influence of David Harvey (see ANALYTICAL MARXISM, GEOGRAPHY AND).

The recognition of the social bases of economic geography has led to a rewriting of economic geography with a number of distinctive features:

(a) *An explicit concern for the significance of social relations of production for understanding in economic geography.* Social relations both provide the means and define the purpose and meaning of economic communication between people. Such a concern is manifest in interpretations of the bases of economic development under capitalism (Brenner, 1977) and in the construction of the world economy (see, e.g. WORLD-SYSTEMS ANALYSIS), in studies of particular SOCIAL FORMATIONS (e.g. Allen and Massey, 1988; Dunford, 1988; Storper and Scott, 1989); and in the recognition (e.g. Martin, 1988) of the significance of regimes of accumulation (see REGULATION SCHOOL) and socio-institutional structures of accumulation which provide the essential conditions of existence for ACCUMULATION and development in the form of a stable and conformable social and political environment in which the role of the state is critical (e.g. Hudson, 1989). In this view, the widespread economic crises of the 1920s and 1930s and of the 1970s, 1980s and 1990s – whether or not they are associated with KONDRATIEFF CYCLES – are not simply quantitative interruptions to

economic growth but may be interpreted as transitions from one phase of socio-economic development to another (Harvey, 1989; see FORDISM; POST-FORDISM).

(b) *A recognition that although social relations of production are central to understanding in economic geography, they may hide more than they reveal.* If their provenance is seen merely in the social struggle over control of production and of the means of production, an oppressively economic domination of society and of its investigation results. The massive but frequently contested – or worse, ignored – contribution of FEMINIST GEOGRAPHY (see, e.g. Bowlby et al. 1989) and of the geography of RACE and, more pertinently, of RACISM has not been merely to reveal gender blindness by adding women to the economic landscape (e.g. Duncan, 1991) or to recognize discrimination and even oppression but, far more fundamentally, to challenge the very social bases on which the economy, society and the individual are constituted and develop (e.g. Jackson, 1989; McDowell, 1991). The division of labour combines with CLASS, gender, race and racism in a complex interaction of multiple structures (Sayer and Walker, 1992).

(c) *An appreciation of the crucial socio-cultural role of money in capitalist economies* (Harvey, 1982, 1989: see MONEY, GEOGRAPHY OF). Money is not only a means of communication but a store, an arbiter and a ready, if thoroughly deficient, means of measuring value. More neutral but highly influential in sustaining and shaping communication is the *information economy* – a manifestation of high technology developed in response to the needs for the high-speed transactions around an increasingly global economy (e.g. Castells, 1989: see INFORMATION CITY; WORLD CITY).

(d) *A reintegration of economic geography expressed directly and clearly by the CIRCUIT OF CAPITAL* through which, for example, the geography of production may be re-evaluated (e.g. Morgan and Sayer, 1988). One consequence of such reintegration is that finance capital has, at last, received attention from economic geographers (e.g. Thrift, 1987) not only as a determinant of productive activity (Ingham, 1984) and urban economic development (King 1990;

Sassen, 1991) but, along with the geography of PRODUCER SERVICES (Daniels, 1991), as a phenomenon in its own right (e.g., Thrift, 1987 on commercial capital).

(e) *A rediscovery of the global economy* (Gordon, 1988; see WORLD-SYSTEMS ANALYSIS for another interpretation; see also Johnston, 1984; Knox and Agnew, 1989; Thrift, 1989; Wallace, 1990) *and of its significance for regions within it* (e.g. Agnew, 1987; Dixon, 1991; Richardson, 1992). The world economy is hardly new, but the contemporary internationalization of production (Dicken, 1992) intensifies both the level of global integration long established in the forms of flows of TRADE, capital and labour and, along with the speed of interaction around the global circuit of capital, the degree of competition in the world economy.

(f) *A recognition of the significance of the combined impact of high technology and what Piore and Sabel (1984) call 'the second industrial divide'.* In the context of an increasingly competitive world economy, attention has been given to the creation of 'new industrial spaces' (Scott, 1988) – often based upon high technology and flexible production (Storper and Scott, 1989). This new geography of production combines in complex fashion (Hudson, 1989) with earlier spaces of industrial production, spatial DIVISIONS OF LABOUR (Massey, 1984) and the contemporary globalization of production.

(g) *A reassessment of the nature of DEVELOPMENT and UNDERDEVELOPMENT.* Emphasis within economic geography has traditionally been placed upon the natural and human-made material conditions of growth and the asocial human constraints upon it (see Keeble, 1967). But with the emergence of a methodology which insists that the social relations of production are central to social understanding, the causal connections between the processes of development and underdevelopment are being exposed and analysed (Slater, 1973, 1977; Brookfield, 1975).

The shift to a more inclusive concept of economic geography is related in part to the realization that development for anyone is increasingly dependent upon development for all. No matter how dynamic and influential, the capitalist world-economy is merely 'an order among other orders' (Braudel, 1985, p. 45) – both social and natural – and so generates local contradictions and continues to threaten the stability of the world system as a whole. In such a context, Keith Buchanan's (1970) assertion that the contribution of this world-economy 'to alleviating the lot of the damned of the earth is derisory' should remain as the first item to be addressed on the agenda of economic geography.   RL

References and Suggested Reading

Agnew, J. A. 1987: *The United States in the world-economy: a regional geography*. Cambridge: Cambridge University Press.

Allen, J. and Massey, D. 1988: *The economy in question*. Newbury Park, CA: Sage.

Bowlby, S., Lewis, J., McDowell, L. and Foord, J. 1989: The geography of gender. In Peet, R. and Thrift, N. eds, *New models in geography*, vol. 2. London: Unwin Hyman; pp. 157–75.

Braudel, F. 1985: *Civilization and capitalism 15th–18th century*, vol. III, *The perspective of the world*. London: Fontana.

Brenner, R. 1977: The origins of capitalist development: a critique of neo-Smithian Marxism. *New Left Rev.* 104, pp. 25–92.

Brookfield, H. 1975: *Interdependent development*. London: Methuen/Pittsburgh, PA: University of Pittsburgh Press.

Buchanan, K. M. 1970: *The transformation of the Chinese earth*. London: Bell/New York:Praeger.

Buchanan, R. O. 1935: *The pastoral industries of New Zealand: a study in economic geography*. Institute of British Geographers publications 2. London: George Philip.

Castells, M. 1989: *The informational city*. Oxford: Blackwell.

Chisholm, G. G. 1975: *Chisholm's handbook of commercial geography*, nineteenth edition. London: Longman (first published 1889).

Chisholm, M. 1962: *Rural settlement and land use*. London: Hutchinson.

Chisholm, M. 1966: *Geography and economics*. London: Bell/Boulder, CO: Westview Press.

Daniels, P. 1991: A world of services? *Geoforum* 22, pp. 359–76.

Dicken, P. 1992: *Global shift: the internationalization of economic activity*, second edition. London: Paul Chapman.

Dicken, P. E. and Lloyd, P. 1990: *Location in space: theoretical perspectives in economic geography*, third edition. New York: Harper and Row.

Dixon, C. 1991: *South-east Asia in the world-economy*. Cambridge: Cambridge University Press.

Duncan, S. 1991: The geography of gender divisions of labour in Britain *Trans. Inst. Br. Geogr.* n.s. 16, pp. 420–39.

Dunford, M. 1988: *Capital, the state and regional development*. London: Pion.

Dunford, M. and Perrons, D. 1983: *The arena of capital*. London: Macmillan/New York: St. Martin's Press.

Emel, J. and Peet, R. 1989: Resource management and natural hazards. In Peet, R. and Thrift, N., eds, *New models in geography*, vol. 1. London: Unwin Hyman, pp. 49–76.

Franklin, S. H. 1969: *The European peasantry: the final phase*. London: Methuen.

Galbraith, J. K. 1974: *Economics and the public purpose*. London: André Deutsch/Boston: Houghton Mifflin.

Godelier, M. 1986: *The mental and the material*. London: Verso.

Gordon, D. 1988: The global economy: new edifice or crumbling foundations? *New Left Rev.* 168, 24–64.

Harvey, D. 1973: *Social justice and the city*. London: Edward Arnold/Baltimore, MD: Johns Hopkins University Press.

Harvey, D. 1982: *The limits to capital*. Oxford: Blackwell/Chicago: Chicago University Press.

Harvey, D. 1989: *The condition of postmodernity*. Oxford: Blackwell.

Healey, M. J. and Ilbery, B. W. 1990: *Location and change: perspectives on economic geography*. Oxford: Oxford University Press.

Hodder, B. W. and Lee, R. 1974: *Economic geography*. London: Methuen/New York: St. Martin's Press.

Hudson, R. 1988: Uneven development in capitalist societies: changing spatial divisions of labour, forms of spatial organization of production and service provision and their impacts on localities. *Trans. Inst. Br. Geogr.* n.s. 13, pp. 484–96.

Hudson, R. 1989: *Wrecking a region*. London: Pion.

Ingham, G. 1984: *Capitalism divided? The city and industry in British social development*. London: Macmillan.

Jackson, P. 1989: Geography, race and racism. In Peet, R. and Thrift, N., eds, *New models in geography*, vol. 2. London: Unwin Hyman, pp. 176–95.

Johnston, R. J. 1984: The world is our oyster. *Trans. Inst. Br. Geogr.* n.s. 9, pp. 443–59.

Johnston, R. J. 1989: *Environmental problems*. London: Belhaven Press.

Keeble, D. E. 1967: Models of economic development. In Chorley, R. J. and Haggett, P., eds, *Models in geography*. London: Methuen, pp. 243–302.

King, A. D. 1990: *Global cities: post-imperialism and the internationalization of London*. London: Routledge.

Knox, P. L. and Agnew, J. A. 1989: *The geography of the world-economy*. New York: Edward Arnold.

Lee, R. 1989: Social relations and the geography of material life. In Gregory, D. and Walford, R., eds, *Horizons in human geography*. London: Macmillan/New York: St. Martin's Press, pp. 152–69.

Manners, G. 1971: *The changing world market for iron ore 1950–1980: an economic geography*. Baltimore, MD: Johns Hopkins University Press.

Martin, R. 1988: Industrial capitalism in transition: the contemporary reorganization of the British space-economy. In Massey, D. and Allen, J., eds, *Uneven re-development: cities and regions in transition*. London: Hodder and Stoughton, p. 10.

Massey, D. 1978: Regionalism: some current issues. *Capital and Class* Autumn, pp. 106–25.

Massey, D. 1984: *Spatial divisions of labour*. London: Macmillan.

McDowell, L. 1991: Life without father and Ford: the new gender order of post-Fordism. *Trans. Inst. Br. Geogr.* n.s. 16, pp. 400–19.

Morgan, K. and Sayer, A. 1988: *Microcircuits of capital: 'sunrise' industry and uneven development*. Oxford: Polity Press.

O'Riordan, T. 1989: The challenge for environmentalism. In Peet, R. and Thrift, N., eds, *New models in geography*, vol. 1. London: Unwin Hyman, pp. 77–102.

Paterson, J. H. 1976: *Land, work and resources: an introduction to economic geography*, second edition. London: Edward Arnold/New York: Crane Russak.

Peet, R. 1991: *Global capitalism: theories of societal development*. London: Routledge.

Piore, M. and Sabel, C. 1984: *The second industrial divide*. New York: Basic Books.

Redclift, M. 1987: The production of nature and the reproduction of the species. *Antipode* 19, pp. 222–30.

Rees, J. 1990: *Natural resources: allocation, economics and policy*. London: Routledge.

Richardson, B. C. 1992: *The Caribbean in the wider world, 1492–1992: a regional geography*. Cambridge: Cambridge University Press.

Sassen, S. 1991: *The global city*. Princeton, NJ: Princeton University Press.

Sayer, A. 1979: Epistemology and conceptions of people and nature in geography. *Geoforum* 10, pp. 19–43.

Sayer, A. and Walker, R. 1992: *The social economy: reworking the division of labour*. Oxford: Blackwell.

Scott, A. J. 1988: Flexible production systems and regional development: the rise of new industrial spaces in north America and western Europe. *Int. J. urban and reg. Res.* 12, pp. 171–86.

Scott, A. J. and Storper, M., eds, 1986: *Production, work, territory: The geographical anatomy of industrial capitalism*. London: Allen and Unwin.

Sheppard, E. and Barnes, T. J. 1990: *The capitalist space economy: geographical analysis after Ricardo, Marx and Sraffa*. London: Unwin Hyman.

Slater, D. 1973, 1977: Geography and underdevelopment, parts I and II. *Antipode* 5(3), pp. 21–32; *ibid*. 9 (3), pp. 1–31.

Smith, N. 1984: *Uneven development*. Oxford: Blackwell.

Storper, M. and Scott, A. J. 1989: The geographical foundations and social regulation of flexible production complexes. In Wolch, J. and Dear, M., eds, *The power of geography: how territory shapes social life*. London: Unwin Hyman, pp. 21–40.

Storper, M. and Walker, R. 1989: *The capitalist imperative*. Oxford: Basil Blackwell.

Thrift, N. 1987: The fixers. The urban geography of international commercial capital. In Henderson, J. and Castells, M., eds, *Global restructuring and territorial development*. Newbury Park, CA: Sage; pp. 203–33.

Thrift, N. 1989: The geography of international economic disorder. In Johnston, R. J. and Taylor, P. J. eds, *A world in crisis?* Oxford: Blackwell, pp. 16–78.

United Nations Development Programme 1992: *Human Development Report*. Oxford: Oxford University Press.

Wallace, I. 1978: Towards a humanized conception of economic geography. In Ley, D. and Samuels, M. S., eds, *Humanistic geography: prospects and problems*. Chicago: Maaroufa Press; pp. 91–108.

Wallace, I. 1990: *The global economic system*. London: Unwin Hyman.

'economic man' See RATIONAL CHOICE THEORY.

economies of scale The cost advantages gained by large-scale production, as the average cost of production falls with increasing output. Total production costs increase less than proportionately with output, up to a point at which diseconomies of scale (cost disadvantages) set in.

Economies of scale generally arise from conditions that are internal to the operation of the plant in question. Some important internal sources of scale economies are as follows: (a) *indivisibilities*, where the plant is built to a certain capacity below which the average cost of production will be higher than at full capacity, and the plant cannot be divided up into smaller units working with the same efficiency as the larger one; (b) *specialization* and division of labour associated with expansion of scale, which can increase efficiency and hence lower costs; and (c) *overhead processes* such as the design of a product, which must be undertaken and paid for irrespective of scale so that the larger the output the lower the overhead cost per unit. Certain EXTERNAL ECONOMIES may also be associated with expansion of scale of output; for example, if the growth of an entire industry reduces costs in each individual firm.

The existence of economies of scale encourages the expansion of productive capacity up to the point at which diseconomies eventually pull the cost of the additional (marginal) unit above the price that it will fetch. In some modern industries it may be that this point is reached only at a very high volume of output; thus the average cost continues to fall with rising output, well beyond the level at which diseconomies might be expected to arise. However, in other activities a trend towards more flexible and differentiated production may lead to diseconomies at relatively small scales of output. (See also ECONOMIES OF SCOPE.)   DMS

economies of scope The cost advantages that may arise when performing two or more activities together within a single firm rather than performing them separately. When economies of scope exist, firms have an incentive to internalize (that is, perform in-house) the production of goods or services that otherwise would be acquired through transactions with external suppliers (see TRANSACTIONAL ANALYSIS). Economies of scope may arise where the outputs in question share inputs to their production (e.g. by using excess capacity in power generation or indivisible machinery), are related to one another through INPUT-OUTPUT relations (one good being an input to the production of the other good), draw upon common technical or manual skills for their production, or can be most efficiently produced at roughly the same scale of output. This concept, when combined with the idea of ECONOMIES OF SCALE, provides an understanding of the forces that determine firm size and the nature of inter-firm relations in localized clusters of producers (Scott, 1988). (See PRODUCTION COMPLEX.)   MSG

Reference

Scott, A. J. 1988: *New industrial spaces*, London: Pion.

ecosystem   The North American ecologist E. P. Odum (1969) defined an ecosystem thus: 'Any unit that includes all of the organisms in a given area interacting with the physical environment so that a flow of energy leads to . . . exchange of materials between living and non-living parts of the system . . . is an ecosystem'. This amplifies the earlier definition given by A. G. Tansley who coined the term in 1935, and thus confirms the concept of the ecosystem in an aggregative hierarchy. Individuals aggregate into populations, populations come together in communities, and a COMMUNITY plus its physical environment comprises an ecosystem. In many ways, the concept is independent of SCALE, for the definition is as valid for a drop of water with a few micro-organisms in it as for the whole of planet Earth. But in usual practice the term is used for units below the scale of the major world units, the biomes.

Although an ecosystem may be characterized in terms of synoptic terms, i.e. by inventory of its components, both biotic and physical, the essential features of the term are: (a) that it implies a functional and dynamic relation between the components, going beyond a frozen mosaic of species distribution: and (b) that it is holistic,

implying that the whole possesses emergent qualities which are not predictable from our knowledge of the constituent parts (see HOLISM). The study of functional relationships in ecosystems has usually concentrated on phenomena which can be accurately measured and which are common to both biotic and abiotic parts of the system: energy, water and mineral nutrients are frequent examples. ENERGY flow through the various trophic levels of a system and its dissipation into heat can be used to see how the system has in its evolution partitioned the energy and how efficiently it is passed on from level to level. (However, doubt has recently been cast on the notion of trophic levels as realistic structural elements of ecosystems: the concepts that they lead to are often rather simplistic.) Likewise, studies of nutrients have often revealed mechanisms for keeping the nutrients 'tight' within the ecosystem: under natural conditions relatively little of the nutrient capital of the system is lost in runoff or animal migration.

The temporal dimensions of the system are also amenable to study, e.g. population numbers through time are often followed. For most species each ecosystem has a carrying capacity, i.e. an optimum level for a particular population, which may be a simple number or subject to fluctuations of various kinds. Again, the changes in species composition and physiognomy of an ecosystem through time may be studied, as in the succession from bare ground left by a glacier through various types of vegetation to a stable, self-reproducing forest. When succession has apparently terminated at an ecosystem type which sustains itself and gives way, under natural conditions, to no other, then this is said to be a mature or climax ecosystem.

The applied side of the concept is evident in the idea of PRODUCTIVITY, which is the rate of organic matter production per unit area per unit time by an ecosystem, and which can be used to compare natural ecosystems with those affected by human activity and, indeed, with totally human-made ecosystems. The concept of stability is important in the human/biophysical interface because it relates to the resilience of an ecosystem to perturbation. If there is a particular act of environmental manipulation, will an ecosystem recover its former state (given the cessation of the impact) or will it, for example, change stochastically?

That a perturbation may be human-induced has led to the introduction of ecosystem-type thinking and practice into geography. It ties in with ideas of geography as HUMAN ECOLOGY and URBAN ECOLOGY, links geographic work to wider bodies of thought such as GENERAL SYSTEMS THEORY and SYSTEMS ANALYSIS, and to operational systems such as ENVIRONMENTAL IMPACT ASSESSMENT. So geographers among others have studied ecosystems with a large human-induced and directed component such as agriculture (the term 'agroecosystem' is sometimes used), pastoralism, fisheries, and even cities, where studies of inputs and outputs of energy and matter have been quantified. One difficulty of such work can be the reductionist tendency in quantifying such flows, losing the cultural forces which can equal in importance those of nature or technology. IGS

References

Odum, E. P. 1969: The strategy of ecosystem development. *Sci.* 164, pp. 262–70.

Tansley, A. G. 1935: The use and abuse of vegetational concepts and terms. *Ecol.* 16, pp. 284–307.

Suggested Reading

Boyden, S., Miller, S., Newcombe, K. and O'Neill, B. 1981: *The ecology of a city and its people: the case of Hong Kong.* Canberra: ANU Press.

Douglas, I. 1983: *The urban environment.* London: Edward Arnold.

Gregory, K. J. 1985: *The nature of physical geography.* London: Edward Arnold.

Odum, E. P. 1989: *Ecology and our endangered life-support systems.* Sunderland, MA: Sinauer.

Polunin, N. ed., 1986: *Ecosystem theory and application.* Chichester: John Wiley.

Roberts, N. S. 1981: *The holocene.* Oxford: Blackwell.

Simmons, I. G. 1981: *Changing the face of the Earth.* Oxford: Blackwell.

Stoddart, D. R. 1965: Geography and the ecological approach. The ecosystem as a geographic principle and method. *Geography* 50, pp. 242–51.

education See GEOGRAPHICAL SOCIETIES.

education, geography of The study of spatial variations in the provision, uptake and outputs of educational facilities and resources.

The provision of educational resources involves both the fixed facilities and the wherewithal to make use of them. Thus the location of play-centres, schools and colleges is important not only to the structuring of educational provision but also, because such facilities fall within the class of PUBLIC GOODS, to the structured inequality in provision which characterizes many societies (as in the CONFLICT over proposed school closures: Bondi, 1987). Linked to this is the pattern of expenditure on education, which varies at many scales and can be used progressively in a programme of POSITIVE DISCRIMINATION (Pattie, 1986).

The uptake of facilities reflects a range of factors which also operate at a variety of scales, from the individual and the home through the NEIGHBOURHOOD to the authority responsible for provision and even the region and nation. The same is true of the outputs of the educational system, and many studies have shown that students' aspirations and performance reflect their parents' aspirations for them, the nature of their home environment, the characteristics of their peers in class and school (and thus the characteristics of the school catchment area), and the quality of the school and its teaching – including the resources available (Bradford, 1991). Thus the concept of the NEIGHBOURHOOD EFFECT has been central to much analysis of the geography of educational outcomes, for which specialist statistical procedures have been adopted (see MULTILEVEL MODELLING). RJJ

References

Bondi, L. 1987: School closures and local politics. *Polit. Geogr. Q.* 6, pp. 203–24.

Bradford, M. J. 1991: School performance indicators, the local residential environment, and parental choice. *Environ. Plann. A* 23, pp. 319–33.

Pattie, C. J. 1986: Positive discrimination in the provision of primary education in Sheffield. *Environ. Plann. A* 18, pp. 1249–58.

Suggested Reading
Bondi, L. and Matthews, M. H., eds, 1988: *Education and society: studies in the politics, sociology and geography of education.* London: Routledge.

efficiency A measure of the work achieved relative to the energy expended. This physical concept has been appropriated for analyses of capitalist economies, by relating the volume of output (as in manufacturing industry) to input, usually measured in monetary terms; the concept is thus similar to PRODUCTIVITY. Both major modes of analysis of CAPITALISM (cf. MARXIAN ECONOMICS; NEOCLASSICAL ECONOMICS) argue that increased efficiency (greater financial returns from production relative to the costs of inputs) is central to the MODE OF PRODUCTION's dynamic.

The concept is now widely applied to all productive and non-productive activities within a capitalist economy, as a means of evaluating performance and providing targets for its improvement. (In the early 1990s, for example, the British government required universities to increase the efficiency of their teaching operations by 2.5 per cent per annum: i.e. the same volume of students had to be taught, to the same – or better – standards, with only 97.5 per cent of the financial resources – in real terms – made available in the previous year.)

The concept of efficiency has been adapted by adherents of the LOCATIONAL ANALYSIS school of human geography, who have emphasized the importance of *spatial efficiency* in the development of LOCATION THEORY: Smith (1977) defines spatial efficiency in the context of industrial location theory as 'equal marginal costs in all production locations', for example, but the concept is more generally associated with the minimization of TRANSPORT COSTS as the major geographical contribution to efficient sociospatial organization (cf. LINEAR PROGRAMMING).

Analysts have argued that using the concepts of both efficiency and EQUITY may introduce conflicts into the planning of spatial organization, as in the distribution of PUBLIC SERVICES (see LOCATION-ALLOCATION MODELS; PUBLIC ADMINISTRATION, GEOGRAPHY OF). An efficient spatial distribution of fire stations, for example, may minimize total costs within certain constraints, but may be inequitable because it provides a much better service to some parts of a territory relative to others.

RJJ

Reference
Smith, D. M. 1977: *Human geography: a welfare approach.* London: Edward Arnold.

electoral geography The study of the geographical aspects of the organization, conduct and results of elections. Pioneering studies (including those by French geographers following the lead of André Siegfried; e.g. Siegfried, 1913) were published early in the twentieth century, but most of the small literature dates from the 1960s on, and few identify themselves specifically as electoral geographers. Many studies are empirical investigations of voting patterns, with a relatively weak theoretical base, and Taylor (1989) has criticized them for their lack of integration into the expanding field of POLITICAL GEOGRAPHY.

Many aspects of elections are inherently spatial in their form, and five separate aspects of the subfield can be identified:

(1) the *spatial organization of elections*, especially the definition of constituencies (see DISTRICTING ALGORITHM);

(2) *spatial variations in voting patterns*, plus the relationships between these and other characteristics of the population (see CLEAVAGE);

(3) the *influence of local factors on political attitudes* and voting decisions (see CONTEXTUAL EFFECT; FRIENDS-AND-NEIGHBOURS EFFECT);

(4) *spatial patterns of representation* which result from the translation of votes into seats in a representative body; and

(5) the *spatial variations in POWER and policy implementation* which reflect the patterns of representation (see PORK BARREL).

The study of the second and third of these in particular was advanced by the adoption of quantitative methods for analysis of spatial data in the 1960s. Voting returns offer a great deal of data which can be analysed spatially, and these can be combined with areal data from CENSUSES to investigate the relationships between population characteristics and partisan choices. Greater sophistication in the analysis of such data has been achieved in the 1980s (in the context of awareness of both the ECOLOGICAL FALLACY and the MODIFIABLE AREAL UNIT problem), including the integration of survey (obtained from QUESTIONNAIRES) and aggregate data (Johnston, Pattie and Allsopp, 1988: see ENTROPY-MAXIMIZING MODELS; MULTI-LEVEL MODELLING). Most of the work is concerned to identify the relative importance of various cleavages and their variation among places.

In most countries the translation of votes into seats involves the use of spatially delimited constituencies. Manipulation of their boundaries can generate electoral bias (favouring one party or interest group over another) away from the 'norm' of proportional representation (a party's percentage of the seats allocated should be consistent with its percentage of the votes cast). This bias may be the result of deliberate attempts, through MALAPPORTIONMENT and GERRYMANDER strategies, or it may, as Gudgin and Taylor (1979) demonstrated, be the unintended consequence of the disinterested application of neutrally conceived rules for constituency construction.

The outcome of an election gives power to individuals and groups within the STATE APPARATUS, who may use it to promote their own interests, including their own re-election, through the selective allocation of PUBLIC GOODS (Johnston, 1980). RJJ

References

Gudgin, G. and Taylor, P. J. 1979: *Seats, votes and the spatial organization of elections*. London: Pion.

Johnston, R. J. 1980: *The geography of federal spending in the United States*. Chichester: John Wiley.

Johnston, R. J., Pattie, C. J. and Allsopp, J. G. 1988: *A nation dividing? The electoral map of Great Britain 1979–1987*. London: Longman.

Siegfried, A. 1913: *Tableau politique de la France de l'Ouest*. Paris: A. Colin.

Taylor, P. J. 1989: *Political geography: world-economy, nation–state and community*, second edition. London: Longman.

Suggested Reading

Johnston, R. J. 1979: *Political, electoral and spatial systems*. Oxford: Clarendon Press.

Reynolds, D. R. and Knight, D. B. 1989: Political geography. In Gaile, G. L. and Willmott, C. J., eds, *Geography in America*. Columbus, OH: Merrill, pp. 582–618.

Taylor, P. J. and Johnston, R. J. 1979: *Geography of elections*. London: Penguin.

empiricism A philosophy of science which accords a special privilege to empirical observations over theoretical statements. Specifically, it assumes that observational statements are the only ones which make direct reference to phenomena in the real world (*ontological privilege* – see ONTOLOGY) and that they can be declared true or false without reference to the truth or falsity of theoretical statements (*epistemological privilege* – see EPISTEMOLOGY). Empiricism is a fundamental assumption of POSITIVISM and is challenged by most modern philosophies of science, which establish connections between theoretical and observation languages in terms which allow for varying degrees of theoretical (co-)determination (see REALISM); it is also out of sympathy with those versions of POSTMODERNISM which insist on the importance of partial perspectives and multiple voices and with critiques derived from POSTSTRUCTURALISM which seek to establish the social construction of different regimes of truth.

It is important, therefore, to distinguish between (a) an *empiricist* inquiry, which assumes that its facts somehow 'speak for themselves' and represses the concepts and technologies that make its observations possible; and (b) an empirical inquiry, which is a substantive study that does not necessarily make any assumptions of ontological and epistemological privilege. DG

enclave A small piece of territory lying within a STATE but which does not fall under its jurisdiction. A number are in Europe and are evidence of the continent's confused political history. The microstates of San Marino and the Vatican City in Italy and Andorra in Spain are classical examples. Elsewhere, the city territories of Ceuta and Melilla on the northern coast of Africa are Spanish enclaves in Morocco. It is not uncommon for areas in which a minority from one state is actually isolated within the territory of a neighbouring state to be referred to as enclaves. A good example is the region known as Ngorno Kharabach on the isthmus between Turkey and Russia. It is overwhelmingly populated by Armenians, but rather than being part of Armenia it is actually located entirely within the neighbouring republic of Azerbaydzhan. MB

enclosure Land demarcation using boundaries, usually associated with the restriction of rights of ownership or use on that land, and the processes through which these physical and tenurial restrictions are achieved. However, the physical separation of land parcels and the restriction of use-rights need not change in parallel. Much discussion has involved the consequences of enclosure for economic development: for example, during conversion of co-operative FIELD SYSTEMS to individualistic landownership and control, often accompanied by changes in LAND TENURE, in the emergence of agrarian CAPITALISM. PG

energy The capacity of a physical system for doing work. According to Einstein's theory of relativity, matter is a key energy form: the conversion or annihilation of mass releases of energy in, for example, nuclear reactions and solar radiation. Other forms of energy arise through the motion of mass (kinetic energy), the configuration of masses (gravity and electromagnetic fields), and the existence of forces between elementary particles. Energy is one of the most important concepts in physics and the ability of human beings to harness, release, convert and deploy these fundamental forms of energy to do productive work and yield desired goods and services has been the basis for the evolution of human societies over time.

All life on Earth is dependent on solar energy which sustains the biogeochemical cycles of the global ecosphere. At the beginning of their history, human beings had to satisfy their energy needs (for food, heat and movement) by using their own muscle power and gathering or hunting naturally available plants, animals and wood. It is estimated that primitive hunting–gathering communities used a mere 5000 kilocalories of energy per person per day, compared with over 230 000 consumed by each modern American. Each stage in the evolution of human society – the development of farming, domestication of animals, harnessing of wind and water power – increased the average per capita energy use, but it was the INDUSTRIAL REVOLUTION and the exploitation of fossil fuels which marked the transformation of societies into the energy-intensive economies of today.

Since the eighteenth century the industrializing countries have come to rely on non-renewable energy sources, and at present 80 per cent of the world's commercial energy is derived from oil, coal and gas. In the early STAGES OF economic GROWTH, energy consumption grows rapidly and is closely correlated with increases in GROSS NATIONAL PRODUCT. For more mature economies, trends in energy efficiency and the development of high technology and tertiary industries have broken the link between GNP and energy consumption. Japan's GNP, for example, grew by 46 per cent between 1973 and 1985 with virtually no increase in energy use. This means that the greatest rates of growth in energy consumption are occurring in the industrializing countries of the THIRD WORLD, although the advanced nations still consume the bulk of world commercial energy (20 per cent of the world's population consumes over 70 per cent of commercial energy).

Since the fossil fuels are stock RESOURCES, consumed by use, current consumption patterns are unsustainable, and it is recognized that energy conservation and the development of renewable energy sources will be needed to sustain economic growth. The quantity of ultimately recoverable fossil fuels remains a matter of conjecture, but few analysts today accept the popular view of the 1970s that scarcity was imminent (see LIMITS TO GROWTH). The notion that the 1973 Oil Crisis marked the transition from abundant, low-cost energy to an era of scarcity and increasing real energy prices lost credibility as surpluses of coal and oil forced fuel prices down from the mid-1980s. Today concerns over scarcity have been overtaken by the question of whether human beings can afford to meet the environmental costs of continued fossil fuel consumption (see GLOBAL WARMING and SUSTAINABLE DEVELOPMENT).

It is now widely accepted that CO_2 emissions from the burning of fossil fuels must be curbed, but there is little agreement over how this can be done and who will bear the costs. The industrialized countries are talking about stabilizing their emissions at 1990 levels by the years 2000–2005, and some are prepared to actually reduce their CO_2 output by 20–30 per cent. However, Third World nations question the equity of having to stabilize their own CO_2 outputs, which would perpetuate existing inequalities in energy use.   JAR

Suggested Reading

Aitchison, J. and Heal, D. 1990: Which fuel? Diversity in world energy consumption. *Geography Rev.* 3(5), pp. 18–21.

Allen, J. 1992: *Energy: resources for a changing world.* Cambridge: Cambridge University Press.

Krause, F., Bach, W. and Koomey, J. 1990: *Energy policy in the greenhouse.* London: Earthscan Publications.

Millar, G. T. 1990: *Living in the environment,* sixth edition. Belmont, CA: Wadsworth.

Odell, P. R. 1989: *Oil and world power.* London: Penguin.

enterprise zone   An area within which special policies apply to encourage economic DEVELOPMENT through private investment. Enterprise zone (EZs) provide tax concessions and reduced planning restrictions for companies establishing plants. They represent a neoliberal approach to the development of declining areas by promoting market solutions to economic problems. Duncan and Goodwin (1988) argue that in the UK, 'economically the effects of EZs seem minor and mostly redistributive, and they have mainly shifted existing jobs around as some firms have relocated to take advantage of EZ subsidies'. They suggest that the real impact has involved concentration of power in the central state and loss of control by the LOCAL STATE over development strategies. Similar areas of deregulation have been established in a number of countries in different forms (e.g. 'freeports'): examples include Singapore and, more recently, the People's Republic of China.   JP

Reference

Duncan, S. and Goodwin, M. 1988: *The local state and uneven development.* Cambridge: Polity Press.

entropy   A measure of the amount of UNCERTAINTY in a probability distribution or a SYSTEM subject to constraints. The term originated in thermodynamics, but has been used in a wide variety of contexts, notably in INFORMATION THEORY and as the basis for the ENTROPY-MAXIMIZING MODELS of SPATIAL INTERACTION.

The concepts of macrostate and microstate are central to entropy analysis (note that some writers use the term mesostate where macrostate is employed here). Consider the distribution of 100 people into ten regions: individual B to region 6, individual K to region 4, and so on. A *microstate* is an aggregate frequency distribution of people across regions. Several different microstates may correspond to or give rise to the same *macrostate*: different individuals go to different regions, but the frequency distributions are the same. Entropy measures the relationship between a macrostate and the possible microstates that correspond to it. At one extreme, one macrostate (all 100 people in one region) has only one associated microstate, whereas the macrostate with ten people in each region corresponds to a large number of different microstates. The number of microstates corresponding to a macrostate is denoted here by W, and finding this entropy measure is a combinatorial calculation, given by:

$$W = N! \Big/ \prod_i n_i!$$

the factorial of the total number of individuals N, divided by the product of the factorials for each n_i (the number in each region).

An alternative entropy measure, used in information theory, is the statistic:

$$H = -\sum_i p_i \log 1/p_i$$

where p_i is the probability (or proportion) in a given region. H is perfectly related to $\log W$. The entropy statistics W and H measure the uncertainty of a macrostate distribution with regard to its microstates. Minimum entropy ($H = 0$) occurs for one p_i equal to unity and the rest to zero: there is complete certainty because there is only one microstate. H is at a maximum when all the p_i are equal (maximum uncertainty; all microstates are equally likely). W and H can be used to assess either the expected entropy of distributions and allocations, or the actual entropy of empirical patterns.

In geography, the information theory approach has used H to assess and compare entropy levels for settlement patterns and for trends in population distributions. The entropy-maximizing approach uses entropy as the basis for finding the most likely macrostate of a system subject to specific constraints.   LWH

Suggested Reading

Thomas, R. W. and Huggett, R. J. 1980: *Modelling in geography: a mathematical approach.* New York: Harper and Row, pp. 153–66 and 197–200.

Wilson, A. G. and Bennett, R. J. eds 1986: *Mathematical methods in human geography and planning.* Chichester: Wiley.

entropy-maximizing models   Statistical models for identifying the 'most likely' spatial allocation pattern in a system subject to constraints. The approach was introduced into geographical modelling by A. G. Wilson in 1967 as the basis for a more rigorous interpretation of the GRAVITY MODEL, and has been extensively used since for SPATIAL INTERACTION modelling in urban regions and for modelling interregional flows of traffic and commodities. It

is based on the concept of entropy, a measure of the UNCERTAINTY or 'likelihood' in a probability distribution.

A journey-to-work model illustrates the method. For a city divided into k zones, we wish to calculate the best estimate of interzonal commuting flows T_{ij} without detailed information on each individual movement. Assume that there are N total commuters. Any specific trip distribution pattern T_{ij}, known as a 'macrostate' (see ENTROPY), can arise from many different sets of individual commuting movements or 'microstates'. Entropy measures the number of different microstates that can give rise to a particular macrostate:

$$W(\{T_{ij}\}) = N! \Big/ \sum_i^k \sum_j^k T_{ij}!.$$

In the absence of detailed microstate data, we assume that each microstate is equally probable, and the macrostate $\{T_{ij}\}$ with the maximum entropy value is the most probable or most likely overall pattern.

Additional information is also normally available, notably the total number of commuters originating from each zone O_i, the total number of jobs available in each zone, D_j, and estimates of the average or total travel expenditure for the city, C (usually based on survey data). The entropy-maximizing method then consists of maximizing $W(\{T_{ij}\})$ subject to the constraints

$$\sum_j T_{ij} = O_i, \quad \sum_i T_{ij} = D_j, \quad \sum_i \sum_j T_{ij} c_{ij} = C,$$

where c_{ij} is the travel cost from zone i to zone j. This maximization is a non-linear optimization problem, and must be solved by iterative search methods, systematically trying out different sets of values until the maximum is found.

Entropy-maximizing models not only fit empirical trip-distributions well, but also facilitate easy calculation of the effects of new housing or jobs (altering the Q_i and D_j terms), and so have been widely used in more general urban models (see LOWRY MODEL). Wilson and his colleagues at Leeds have extended the model in many ways, making it dynamic, linking it to industrial and urban LOCATION THEORY, and including several types of disaggregation. Other applications include the prediction of 'flows' or changes in voting behaviour.

The entropy-maximizing trip distribution, based on fixed total cost, can be related to the optimizing minimum-cost distribution generated by the TRANSPORTATION PROBLEM.   LWH

Reference

Wilson, A. G. 1967: A statistical theory of spatial distribution models. *Transport. Res.* 1, pp. 253–69.

Suggested Reading

Wilson, A. G. 1974: *Urban and regional models in geography and planning.* Chichester: John Wiley.

Wilson, A. G. and Bennett, R. J., eds 1986: *Mathematical methods in human geography and planning.* Chichester: John Wiley.

environment   See BEHAVIOURAL ENVIRONMENT; ENVIRONMENTAL DETERMINISM; NATURE; PHENOMENAL ENVIRONMENT.

environmental audit   An inventory of the 'pollutants' (see POLLUTION) generated by a firm or corporation that are regulated by the state. An audit usually involves tracking quantities of inputs, outputs and geographical disposal.   JEm

environmental determinism   The doctrine that human activities are controlled by the environment (Lewthwaite, 1966). Since ancient times a belief in the moulding power of the physical environment on human culture and constitution has attracted many advocates (Glacken, 1967). Hippocrates, for instance, linked the characteristics of people in particular places to the influence of environmental factors such as humidity, altitude and terrain; while Aristotle believed that the world's climatic zones (frigid, temperate and torrid) determined global habitability. The widespread publicizing of such environmental doctrines during the Enlightenment owed much to the writings of Montesquieu, and in particular to his volume on *The spirit of the laws* (1748). To be sure, many others had flirted with

the idea, notably Jean Bodin and John Arbuthnot. But Montesquieu's project, of locating legislative regulation within the framework of the entire social and environmental conditions of which they were a part, was exceptionally influential. Thereby contextualizing law and custom, and drawing from a burgeoning travel literature, Montesquieu disclosed how climatic conditions governed both the degeneration and persistence of cultural traits. Because everything from human physiology to social practices, from religious principles to moral judgements, was geographically conditioned, he presented the case for cultural relativism (Shklar, 1987).

Notwithstanding the critiques of figures such as Herder, ENVIRONMENTALISM flourished in the pre-Darwinian period among those such as Henry Buckle who sought for a historicist history that subjected human activities to natural law (Bowler, 1989), among regional sociologists such as Le Play (see LE PLAY SOCIETY) who causally connected up *travail* and *famille* with *lieu* (Brooke, 1970), and among ethnologists who accounted for racial differentiation in climatic terms (Stocking, 1987). In the aftermath of the 'Darwinian Revolution' the naturalistic construal of human CULTURE in the categories of natural law received further encouragement (see also DARWINISM, SOCIAL DARWINISM, LAMARCKIANISM and HUMAN ECOLOGY). It clearly surfaced, for example, among those writers working at the interface of geography, history and anthropology, who continued to read the human story through racial lenses (cf. RACE, RACISM). The role of the environment in shaping racial 'achievement' was thus emphasized in the writings of figures such as A. R. Wallace, Sir John Lubbock and A. H. Keane (Stepan, 1982).

These currents of thought were clearly registered within the geographical tradition. After all, Friedrich Ratzel and Oscar Peschel in Germany acquired distinguished reputations in anthropology as well as geography. Yet, for all that, there is much to be said for the view that evolution's reinforcement of environmental determinism sprang less from classical Darwinism than from the Neo-Lamarckian version (Campbell and Livingstone, 1983; see LAMARCKIANISM). Ratzel's *Anthropogeographie*, with its cardinal notion of *LEBENSRAUM* and his organismic conception of the STATE, owed much to the MIGRATION theories of the Lamarckian Moritz Wagner; and while the environmental determinist element in his early work has perhaps been overestimated, the evolutionary *Weltanschauung* of figures such as Wagner and Haeckel did much to legitimate any such tendencies in Ratzel's project (Livingstone, 1992; see also ANTHROPOGEOGRAPHY).

The Ratzelian programme, in its more sternly environmental determinist guise, found its American voice largely through the writings of Ellen C. Semple. Her *American history and its geographic conditions* (1903) and *Influences of geographic environment* (1911), while not so crude as some commentators have implied, nevertheless did much to establish environmentalism as American geography's *Leitmotif* in the early decades of the twentieth century. And with the reinforcement of earlier works from writers such as Shaler and Brigham, its scientific stature seemed secured (Livingstone, 1987). Such was also the conviction of Ellsworth Huntington, whose voluminous writings on climate and civilization displayed his predilection for racial typecasting and environmentalist explanations. Yet here again we find another victim of the historical stereotype, for even while he advocated human history on the grand environmental scale, Huntington constantly reiterated the importance of genetic constitution and thus threw his weight behind various eugenic enterprises (Spate, 1968).

Elsewhere similar conceptual manoeuvres were discernible. Griffith Taylor, for example, advocated what he called 'stop and go' determinism in an attempt to modulate the shrillest tones of inexorable necessitarianism. And in Britain Halford Mackinder, who at one point insisted that the only rational basis for human geography was as a causal science built upon physical foundations, nevertheless left space for humanity's wresting the initiative from nature through the exercise of what he came to call the Going Concern (Ó Tuathail, 1992).

Given this sense of equivocation, it is evident that the distinctions between environmental determinism, POSSIBILISM and probabilism turn out to be far from clear cut. To the contrary, figures widely regarded as paradigm cases actually displayed greater ambivalence and conceptual nuance than is usually acknowledged. Vidal de la Blache, for instance, was convinced that *genres de vie* were themselves reflective of NATURE even as they transformed it, and it would therefore be mistaken to consider his as an altogether radical voluntarism. Never psychologistic, Vidal always conceived of human geography as a *natural*, not a *social* science (Buttimer, 1971; Livingstone, 1992). Similarly, the anthropologist Franz Boas's polemical crusade against an unsophisticated environmentalism (a campaign that influenced Carl Sauer's repudiation) must not be taken to imply an entire dismissal of the conditioning power of environment, as is clearly evident in his celebrated study of the environmental modification of the immigrant headform (Stocking, 1965; Speth, 1978). In the light of such revelations it seems that the labels 'determinism' and 'possibilism' were retained with a degree of polemical typecasting compatible with the suspicion that other interests were at stake in the controversies.

Considerable debate on the subject also characterized Soviet geography (Matley, 1966). With the official endorsement of Lysenko's Lamarckism, and the stimulus of Plekhanov's evolutionized Marxism that causally connected the forces and relations of production to natural environment (Gregory, 1986), environmental determinism mobilized considerable support among Soviet geographers, notwithstanding the early critiques of Karl Wittfogel (Matley, 1966). During the second quarter of the century, many more came to query environmental determinism in the wake of Stalin's repudiation. Yet despite such spurnings, V. Anuchin felt justified in reasserting the salience of at least a neodeterminism because he was convinced that classical Marxism was implicated in the attempt to trace causal links between the material and the social (see also MARXIST GEOGRAPHY).

Any acceptable account of the intellectual mainsprings of environmental determinism will have to recognize its plural origins and purposes. Among these are the ways in which it was connected up to the philosophy of scientific explanation, how it articulated the ideological interests of its academic advocates, and the role that it played in bids to control disciplinary identity (Livingstone, 1992; Martin, 1951; Montefiore and Williams, 1955; Peet, 1985). DNL

References and Suggested Reading

Bowler, P. J. 1989: *The invention of progress: the Victorians and the past.* Oxford: Blackwell.

Brooke, M. Z. 1970 *Le Play: engineer and social scientist. The life and work of Frederic Le Play.* London: Longman.

Buttimer, A. 1971: *Society and milieu in the French geographic tradition.* Chicago: Rand McNally.

Campbell, J. A. and Livingstone, D. N. 1983: Neo-Lamarckism and the development of geography in the United States and Great Britain. *Trans. Inst. Br. Geogr.* n. s. 8, pp. 267–94.

Glacken, C. J. 1967: *Traces on the Rhodian shore: nature and culture in western thought from ancient times to the end of the eighteenth century.* Berkeley, CA: University of California Press.

Gregory, D. 1986: Environmental determinism. In Johnston, R. J., Gregory, D. and Smith, D. M., eds, *The dictionary of human geography,* second edition. Oxford: Blackwell, pp. 131–3.

Lewthwaite, G. 1966: Environmentalism and determinism: a search for clarification. *Ann. Ass. Am. Geogr.* 56, pp. 1–23.

Livingstone, D. N. 1987: *Nathaniel Southgate Shaler and the culture of American science.* London: University of Alabama Press.

Livingstone, D. N. 1992: *The geographical tradition: episodes in the history of a contested enterprise.* Oxford: Blackwell.

Martin, A. F. 1951: The necessity for determinism. *Trans. Inst. Br. Geogr.* 17, pp. 1–12.

Matley, I. M. 1966: The marxist approach to the geographical environment. *Ann. Ass. Am. Geogr.* 56, pp. 97–111.

Montefiore, A. and Williams, W. 1955: Determinism and possibilism. *Geogr. Stud.* 2, pp. 1–11.

Ó Tuathail, G. 1992: Putting Mackinder in his place: material transformations and myth. *Pol. Geogr. Q.* 11, pp. 100–18.

Peet, R. 1985: The social origins of environmental determinism. *Ann. Ass. Am. Geogr.* 75, pp. 309–33.

Semple, E. C. 1903: *American history and its geographic conditions.* Boston: Houghton Mifflin.

Semple, E. C. 1911: *Influences of geographic environment.* New York: H. Hold.

Shklar, J. N. 1987: *Montesquieu.* Oxford: Oxford University Press.

Spate, O. H. K. 1968: Ellsworth Huntington. In Sills, D. L., ed., *International encyclopedia of the social sciences,* Vol. 7. New York: Macmillan & Free Press, pp. 26–7.

Speth, W. 1978: The anthropogeographic theory of Franz Boas. *Anthropos* 73, pp. 1–31.

Stepan, N. 1982: *The idea of race in science: Great Britain 1800–1960.* London: Macmillan.

Stocking, G. W. Jr., 1965: From physics to ethnology: Franz Boas' Arctic expedition as problem in the historiography of the behavioral sciences. *J. Hist. behav. Sci.* 1, pp. 211–18.

Stocking, G. W. Jr., 1987: *Victorian anthropology.* New York: Free Press.

environmental hazard Generally refers to short- or long-term geophysical events that pose economic and physical threats to people. The category usually includes earthquakes, volcanic activity, drought, flooding, lightning, current shifts, high winds, waterlogging, plant or animal invasions, and other natural phenomena that may interfere with socio-economic processes or health and well-being.

The leading school of natural or environmental hazards research in geography developed out of White's (1945) work on human adjustment to floods. Drawing upon his experience in river basin planning, White analysed the range of alternatives in human adjustments to flood hazards. He found that planners emphasized 'technological fixes' (dams, for example) and left the possibilities for behavioural change with respect to floods largely unexplored. White's research showed that despite heavy spending on technological measures, the losses due to floods increased steadily throughout the United States. For White, this problem stemmed from an increasing separation between knowledge and practice. On the one hand, sophisticated economic and technical analyses designed theoretically efficient combinations of resource use. But such guides for optimal adjustment did little to explain present adjustments and, more importantly, seemed unable to offer effective means for better human behaviour with respect to floods.

Sceptical about the approaches of water economists, White elaborated an alternative model to analyse resource use decisions: a 'practical range of choice', determined by sociocultural restraints and lack of awareness, sets the limits within which individuals can decide upon specific adjustments. Emphasis on individual DECISION-MAKING units prompted an association with psychology as the source for methodological inspiration. Cognitive aspects of the human relationship with the environment were explored in order to show how managers confronted risk and uncertainty.

The dominant view in hazards research was criticized from both critical theory and more explicitly Marxist perspectives, most extensively by Watts (1983a, 1985). The critique begins with themes explored by Hewitt (1983): knowledge is shaped by the preoccupations brought to it; the world is interpreted within an historically conditioned imagination; theories and concepts cannot be taken for granted. In analysing disasters such as FAMINES, Watts finds that 'both hazards research and human ecology have suffered from neurotic obsession with individual rationality, a profound ahistoricism and not least a neglect of political economic structure' (1983b, p. 14). As a result of these critiques and alternative theorizations, environmental hazards are now viewed as a 'complex web of interactions among peoples, environments, and technologies, characterized by multiple causes and consequences' (Mitchell, 1990, p. 131).   JEm

References

Hewitt, K. 1983: The idea of calamity in a technocratic age. In Hewitt, K., ed., *Interpretations of calamity*. Boston: Allen and Unwin, pp. 3–31.

Mitchell, J. K. 1990: Human dimensions of environmental hazards: complexity, disparity, and the search for guidance. In Kirby, A., ed., *Nothing to fear*. Tucson: University of Arizona Press, pp. 131–78.

Watts, M. 1983a: On the poverty of theory: natural hazards research in context. In Hewitt, K., ed., *Interpretations of calamity*. Boston: Allen and Unwin, pp. 23–62.

Watts, M. 1983b: *Silent violence: food, famine and peasantry in Northern Nigeria*. Berkeley, CA: University of California Press.

Watts, M. 1985: Social theory and environmental degradation. In Gradus, Y., ed., *Desert development: man and technology in sparselands*. Dordrecht: D. Reidel, pp. 14–32.

White, G. 1945: *Human adjustment to floods*. Research paper no. 29. Chicago: University of Chicago, Department of Geography.

Suggested Reading

Emel, J. and Peet, R. 1989: Resource management and natural hazards. In Peet, R. and Thrift, N., eds, *New models in geography*, volume 1. London: Unwin Hyman, pp. 49–76.

Hewitt (1983).

Kirby, A. 1990: *Nothing to fear*. Tucson: University of Arizona Press.

Palm, R. 1990: *Natural hazards: an integrative framework for research and planning*. Baltimore, MD: The Johns Hopkins University Press.

environmental impact assessment In a narrow sense, a report required under the US National Environmental Policy Act of 1969, assessing the impact of any federal project having a potentially significant effect on the environment. More broadly, assessments or environmental impact statements of this sort are now required by many countries and subnational level governments. Some reports merely catalogue the assorted environmental consequences of the project in question, leaving their evaluation to the political decision-making process; others attempt a quantitative comparison of the environmental costs and benefits, typically using some form of cost–benefit analysis and employing a variety of means to compute monetary values for non-market benefits. (See also ENVIRONMENTAL AUDIT.)   JEm

environmental movement The organized political expression of ENVIRONMENTALISM. The birth of the modern environmental movement is usually traced back to the 1960s, with the coming together in North America and Western Europe of a range of concerns (such as wilderness protection, resource depletion and pollution of various kinds). The environmental movement in the United States has its roots in the turn-of-the-century CONSERVATION and preservation movements. It has largely taken the form of pressure and advocacy groups working within the established political framework. American public support for environmental causes has shown remarkable persistence despite the supposed conflict between environmental protection and economic growth. In Western Europe, although environmental concerns have won some support within the established political framework, separate Green parties have also emerged. The Greens have coupled their environmentalist goals with a broader and more radical social agenda than is found in the mainstream of the American movement. They scored some notable electoral successes during the 1980s, winning parliamentary representation in West Germany and seats from several countries in the European parliament (cf. SOCIAL MOVEMENTS).

Environmental degradation and dissatisfaction have engendered environmental movements outside North America and Western Europe as well. Movements in Hungary, the Commonwealth of Independent States, Poland, India and Nepal have protested against dam building, industrial pollution and forestry practices, for example; the Chipko Movement in India is perhaps the most well known of these grassroots movements.   JEm

Suggested Reading

Bandyopadhyay, J. 1993: Sustainability and survival in the mountain context: reflections on the environmental movements in Garhwal Himalaya. *AMBIO.*

Lowenthal, D. 1990: Awareness of human impacts: changing attitudes and emphases. In Turner, B. L. II et al., eds, *The earth as transformed by human action.* Cambridge: Cambridge University Press, pp. 121–35.

Redclift, M. 1989: Turning nightmares into dreams: the green movement in Eastern Europe. *The Ecologist* 19(5), pp. 177–83.

environmental perception   'Decision-makers operating in an environment base their decisions on the environment as they perceive it, not as it is. The action

resulting from decision, on the other hand, is played out in a real environment' (Brookfield, 1969). The study of environmental perception in geography focuses on the ways in which the actors' understanding of their surroundings conditions their behaviour within their surroundings. The ordinary-language use of the term notwithstanding, 'environmental perception' does not exclude such elements as values, ideas and cognition.

Perception studies in geography stem from several traditions. Work in psychology and decision sciences modifying NEO-CLASSICAL ECONOMIC models through such notions as 'bounded rationality' and 'SATISFICING BEHAVIOUR' had a strong influence on geographical studies of ENVIRONMENTAL HAZARDS in the 1960s and 1970s. Apparently, irrational behaviour such as the occupance of hazardous floodplains was understood as the response of the occupants to their perceived opportunities and constraints. Another stream of research developed independently in work on historical geography and the history of geographical thought; R. H. Brown, John K. Wright, David Lowenthal and others emphasized the variety of perceptions of the human environment (see GEOSOPHY) and the significance of geographical ideas in accounting for past behaviour. Urban and economic geographers developed BEHAVIOURAL and perceptual studies, with strong ties to psychology, addressing topics such as urban travel behaviour, neighbourhood design and MIGRATION as related to images and MENTAL MAPS of place preferences. A fourth stream of environmental perception research by geographers involves the study of indigenous environmental knowledge or folk science as a theme in CULTURAL ECOLOGY.

Some criticism of perception research has been methodological in nature, focusing on the difficulties in eliciting accurate representations of a subject's perceptions and in linking perceptions with behaviour. More damaging has been the claim that real constraints on choice and behaviour are played down and the voluntary choices of individuals over-emphasized in this approach, which has been accused of locating the source of apparently irrational behaviour in the imperfectly rational psyche of the individual actor rather than in the wider system of power relations. Such has particularly been an objection lodged against the perception focus in the study of ENVIRONMENTAL HAZARDS. Approached differently, however, the issues raised in the study of environmental perception are important in clarifying the degree to which actors understand the environments in which they operate, an understanding that is usually profound but never complete, and that forms part of the circumstances under which they make and remake their geographies.   JEm

Reference

Brookfield, H. C. 1969: On the environment as perceived. *Prog. Geog.* 1, pp. 51–80.

Suggested Reading

Aitken, S. C., Cutter, S. L., Foote, K. E. and Sell, J. L. 1989: Environmental perception and behavioral geography. In *Geography in America*, Gaile, G. L. and Wilmott, C. J., eds. Columbus, OH: Merrill, pp. 218–38.

environmentalism[1] A wide range of ideas and practices evincing a concern for nature–society or human–environment relations. Much existing literature considers the increasing salience of environmentalism to be a product of new social cleavages developing in POST-INDUSTRIAL, post-material or post-scarcity society (Habermas, 1976, 1987; Touraine, 1981). But ecological or environmental philosophies and causes are not new: they have been subjects of discourse since antiquity and, in some ways, have changed little. According to Glacken (1967), three modes of characterizing nature–society or human–environment relations have persisted over the history of Western thought. These are humanity (society) in harmony with nature, humanity as determined by nature, and humanity as modifier of nature. The last of these is the dominant element of contemporary environmentalism, but elements of all three tend to mingle in particular perspectives.

The prescription of living in harmony with nature goes back at least as far as the traditions of the eighteenth century (Worster, 1977; Pepper, 1984; Kates, Turner

and Clark, 1990). 'Deep ecology' is a major twentieth-century movement in Europe and North America, espousing the principle of living in harmony with the biotic community. Borrowing widely from Buddhist, Native American and other transcendental world views, the movement has sought an alternative to material progress. It has been roundly criticized as lacking the ethics, cosmology and eschatology necessary to replace the dominant scientific–empiricist world view (see, for example, Skolimowski, 1988). The hard Left has tended to write it off as trivial, politically naive and doomed to failure (Elkins, 1990). Yet it is clear that the values of 'Deep Ecology' have taken root in numerous ways, from 'New Age' personal health agenda to militant activists using force to preserve wilderness areas or release laboratory animals.

Espousing a less transcendental and more materialist (albeit ambiguous) view of nature–society relations are the 'Greens', who represent a shift from individual lifestyles and citizen action groups to institutionalized forms of action such as lobbying and the establishment of political parties. Within this form of environmentalism or 'ecologism', the focus is on questions of political theory and practice. The Green Party in Germany, established in 1979, is a convincing expression of this new force. Several national green parties have campaigned on a common European manifesto during the last two elections for the European Parliament (McGrew, 1990).

Geographers have a long but limited (in terms of numbers of researchers) history of involvement with questions of appropriate balance in nature–society relations. The HUMAN ECOLOGY 'school', the roots of which can be traced to Harlan Barrows at the University of Chicago, includes a number of scholars (notably Gilbert White) who are deeply committed to applied work and policy formulation. In critical CULTURAL ECOLOGY (or 'political ecology' as it is sometimes called), new approaches have been tried to correct what is widely regarded as the major problem in human ecological theory of nature–society relations; the small amount of attention paid to the role of economic, social and political structures in explaining human experience with nature. JEm

References

Elkins, S. 1990: The politics of mystical ecology. *Telos* 82, pp. 52–70.

Glacken, C. J. 1967: *Traces on the Rhodian shore: nature and culture in western thought from ancient times to the end of the eighteenth century.* Berkeley, CA: University of California Press.

Habermas, J. 1976: *Legitimation crisis.* London: Heinemann.

Habermas, J. 1987: *The theory of communicative action,* volume 2. Cambridge: Polity Press.

Kates, R., Turner, B. L. and Clark, W. C. 1990: The great transformation. In Turner, B. L. et al., eds, *The earth as transformed by human action: global and regional changes in the biosphere over the past 300 years.* Cambridge: Cambridge University Press, pp. 1–17.

McGrew, A. 1990: The political dynamics of the new environmentalism. *Industrial Crisis Quarterly* 4, pp. 291–305.

Pepper, D. 1984: *The social roots of modern environmentalism.* London: Croom Helm.

Skolimowski, H. 1988: Eco-philosophy and deep ecology. *The Ecologist* 18(4/5), pp. 124–7.

Touraine, A. 1981: *The voice and the eye: an analysis of social movements.* Cambridge: Cambridge University Press.

Worster, D. 1977: *Nature's economy: a history of ecological ideas.* Cambridge: Cambridge University Press.

Suggested Reading

Dobson, A. 1990: *Green political thought.* London: Unwin Hyman.

O'Riordan, T. 1981: *Environmentalism,* second edition. London: Pion.

Pepper (1984).

environmentalism[2] In some of the social sciences (such as psychology), an approach that explains human behaviour as the product of its social surroundings, usually in contrast to others that emphasize heredity (cf. CONTEXTUAL EFFECT).
JEm

environmentalism[3] A synonym for ENVIRONMENTAL DETERMINISM. JEm

epistemology 'The study of knowledge and the justification of belief' (Dancy, 1985). According to Hindess (1977), an epistemology is a THEORY which seeks to determine the correspondences between a *realm of knowledge,* e.g. concepts and propositions, and a *realm of objects,* e.g. experiences and things. It is, so Hindess claims, inherently circular: 'for however it may conceive the distinction between knowledge and the world, its theory of knowledge logically presupposes a knowledge of the conditions in which knowledge takes place'. Against this, however, Thompson (1984) argues that epistemology may be not so much a defence of a particular version of 'knowledge as representation' but rather 'an attempt to elucidate what is presupposed by *claims to know*'. Such claims, Thompson continues, are embedded in structures of language and social action – an insight which is central to Habermas's CRITICAL THEORY – and their elucidation 'is vital for social theory in general and for the analysis of IDEOLOGY in particular'. In modern human geography, 'epistemology' has been used in both a general sense – to examine 'all geographical knowledge, scientific and other: how it is acquired, transmitted, altered and integrated into conceptual systems; and how the horizon of geography varies among individuals and groups' (Lowenthal, 1961; cf. GEOSOPHY); and – in a more particular sense – to interrogate the 'claims to know' made by POSITIVISM and other non-positivistic philosophies (Gregory, 1978). Until recently, the dominant epistemologies in human geography were *foundational.* In other words, they made systematic claims about the conditions which made knowledge possible, and they used those claims to adjudicate, decisively and unambiguously, between 'legitimate' and 'illegitimate' knowledges: see, for example, CRITICAL RATIONALISM, PHENOMENOLOGY, (LOGICAL) POSITIVISM and REALISM. Foundationalism was always challenged by PRAGMATISM, but the more recent critique of GRAND THEORY has ushered in a new series of *non-foundationalist* epistemologies: see, for example, POSTMODERNISM and POSTSTRUCTURALISM. These changes, which human geography shares with the other humanities and social sciences, have prompted: (a) a reappraisal of the privileges which have traditionally been accorded to 'Philosophy with a capital P' (Baynes, Bohman and McCarthy, 1987); (b) a new interest in the politics of 'local knowledges' and their associated regimes of truth (Rouse, 1987; Barrett, 1991); and (c) an awareness of the positions from which subjects can (and cannot) speak (Spivak, 1988; Pratt, 1992). Intersecting with these developments is an important feminist critique which regards the dominant epistemologies as thoroughly *masculinist* – as treating knowledge as mastery by a sovereign (masculine) subject – and which seeks to oppose them through the construction of distinctively feminist epistemologies (Lloyd, 1984; Harding, 1986; Haraway, 1991: see PHALLO-CENTRISM). DG

References

Barrett, M. 1991: *The politics of truth: from Marx to Foucault.* Cambridge: Polity Press/Stanford, CA: Stanford University Press.

Baynes, K., Bohman, J. and McCarthy, T., eds, 1987: *After philosophy: end or transformation?* Cambridge, MA: MIT Press.

Dancy, J. 1985: *Introduction to contemporary epistemology.* Oxford: Blackwell.

Gregory, D. 1978: *Ideology, science and human geography.* London: Hutchinson.

Haraway, D. 1991: Situated knowledges: the science question in feminism and the privilege of partial perspective. In her *Simians, cyborgs and women: the reinvention of nature.* London: Routledge, pp. 183–201.

Harding, S. 1986: *The science question in feminism.* Ithaca, NY: Cornell University Press.

Hindess, B. 1977: *Philosophy and methodology in the social sciences.* Brighton: Harvester Press.

Lloyd, G. 1984: *The man of reason: 'male' and 'female' in Western philosophy.* London: Methuen.

Lowenthal, D. 1961: Geography, experience and imagination: towards a geographical epistemology. *Ann. Ass. Am. Geogr.* 51, pp. 241–60.

Pratt, G. 1992: Spatial metaphors and speaking positions. *Environ. Plann. D: Society and Space* 10, pp. 241–4.

Rouse, J. 1987: *Knowledge and power: toward a political philosophy of science.* Ithaca, NY: Cornell University Press.

Spivak, G. C. 1988: Can the subaltern speak? In Nelson, C. and Grossberg, L., eds, *Marxism and the interpretation of culture.* London: Macmillan, pp. 271–313.

Thompson, J. B. 1984: *Studies in the theory of ideology.* Cambridge: Polity Press.

Suggested Reading

Barrett (1991).
Dancy (1985).
Haraway (1991).

equality The same, in an arithmetic sense. Individual incomes are equal if the people concerned receive the same number of pounds, dollars or whatever in the same period of time. Equality in a geographical context is a more difficult concept, because it is dependent on the nature and level of territorial aggregation adopted. For example, a set of regions may have the same income per capita and thus exhibit equality, while differences (inequality) may exist between per capita income at a subregional or local level. Furthermore, equality among population aggregates at any spatial scale can obscure inequality among individuals and groups, such as racial minorities. (See also INEQUALITY, SPATIAL.) DMS

equilibrium A state in which the forces making for change are in balance. This concept is central to NEOCLASSICAL ECONOMICS, where a free market working perfectly is supposed to tend towards a state of equilibrium in which the balance of opposing forces will maintain the status quo. Thus, once a state of equilibrium has been achieved, any change will set in motion other changes which will eventually restore equilibrium. If the forces of supply and demand for all goods and services and all FACTORS OF PRODUCTION are balanced in such a way that all supply is consumed and all demand is met, and no participant(s) in the economy can derive any further income or satisfaction from doing anything other than what is presently done, this would constitute a state of equilibrium, which would be maintained until a change took place. Such a change might be internal to the economy under consideration, such as a price rise associated with resource depletion, or it could be external, such as a change in demand in an overseas market.

Suppose that, in a perfectly competitive economy in equilibrium, the extraction of coal becomes more difficult or resources are depleted, and that the coal owners put up the price of coal so as to meet the rising cost of mining. As the consumption of coal is to some extent sensitive to its price, demand for coal is reduced. The mine owners may then find that they have unsold coal and they may reduce its price a little to get rid of it. Eventually the balance of forces of supply and demand will be regained by these market adjustments, at a point at which the prevailing price just clears the coal supplied. Equilibrium will have been restored. This process may, of course, involve bringing back into balance other elements of the economy disturbed by change in the coal market; for example, if there is less coal produced than before under the new state of equilibrium this may effect employment in mining, coal delivery and so on, while if the new market price is higher some customers may substitute other sources of fuel for coal.

In reality, even an economy with perfectly free markets working perfectly will be in a process of perpetual adjustment to change. Equilibrium is an ideal state, never achieved in practice but helpful as a concept in the understanding of a market-regulated economy. A distinction is sometimes made between 'general equilibrium analysis' which relates to the entire economy and 'partial equilibrium analysis' which considers the effect of change on a single market or limited set of related activities.

'Spatial equilibrium' refers to the state of balance identified above, but in a spatially disaggregated economy. Change in such a system can be spatially selective: the rise in the price of coal may be confined to a specific region and restoration of equilibrium may involve change and its repercussions working their way from place to place as well as from one market to another. The spatial version of neoclassical economics suggests the equalization of income as a feature of spatial equilibrium, since regional disparities in wages should encourage labour to move to regions where wages are highest and/or capital to move to regions where wages are lowest until equality is achieved and no advantage is to be obtained from further movement (see CONVERGENCE, REGIONAL). Just as imperfection in market mechanisms can frustrate the achievement of equilibrium in general,

so, in geographical space, obstacles to the free mobility of labour, capital and so on impede adjustment to wage and price differentials.

The concept of spatial equilibrium has been partly responsible for some misconceptions in regional development theory and planning practice. The terms equilibrium and balance have desirable connotations, and the idea of a self-regulating space economy tending towards equalization of incomes encourages a view that market mechanisms are capable of promoting more even development if planners somehow harness them to a public purpose. However, the tendency of market economies under capitalism in reality is more one of CONCENTRATION AND CENTRALIZATION, characterized by UNEVEN DEVELOPMENT and inequality of living standards, especially in the less-developed world. DMS

Suggested Reading
Gore, C. 1984: *Regions in question: space, development theory and regional policy*. London: Methuen.

equity Fairness or justice, usually applied to the distribution of income and other aspects of human life chances. Equity may be manifest in EQUALITY, but the two are not necessarily synonymous. An unequal distribution may be fair or just. For example, it is widely accepted that payment by results or at different rates for different levels of skill and responsibility is fair in most societies, socialist as well as capitalist. That social services should be distributed according to need is commonly held to be just; different levels of need can therefore justify unequal treatment. In a geographical context, equity in distribution among areas is achieved when any differences or departures from equality are proportional to differences in accepted entitlement such as need. DMS

estimate See FORECAST.

ethics, geography and The content of moral philosophy, concerned with the judgement of ends and means as good or bad, desirable or undesirable. Ethics contain both a *descriptive* dimension, an assessment of what is, and a *normative* dimension, an evaluation of what should be. Ethical standards ultimately find their basis in cosmology, a set of fundamental control beliefs. Ethics point to the pervasive role of VALUES, choice and responsibility in the actions of individuals and collectivities.

In the pursuit of value-free research, positivist philosophies of science have dismissed or repressed the role of human SUBJECTIVITY and intersubjectivity. Such a view is no longer tenable, less because it is undesirable than because it is unattainable. Moreover, the pursuit of value-free science is itself the pursuit of a set of values, the Enlightenment values of rationality and pragmatism, that readily translate into the needs of a rational–bureaucratic society, but may do little to enhance creativity, individuality or other, less tangible, objectives (Buttimer, 1974).

Ethics enter into geographical research at many levels. In professional practice ethical integrity is presumed in the transmission of research, avoiding such errors as plagiarism or self-plagiarism. Equally, a clear balance should be followed between career advancement or other personal objectives and the pursuit of scholarly goals. As Curry (1991) has noted, academic goals are also compromised from other directions, and not least from the profit orientation of publishers. In addition, ethical standards are required, and frequently prescribed, in the conduct of research, to protect the interests of people whose attitudes or actions are subsequently reported in publications. Safeguards concerning confidentiality, privacy, and even the health and safety of subjects included in research are routinely included in protocols defining acceptable research practices. These guidelines have expanded to include also the dignity of subjects, and their freedom to terminate the research process at any point.

Recently, the range of ethical concerns has broadened further to include the representation of people who are more distant in time or space. The historical geographer has immense power to remake the identity of historical actors who have no capacity to answer back. The cultural geographer is similarly empowered to represent the cultural other in terms of his or her own making. This crisis of representation has received considerable attention in ETHNOGRAPHY (Clifford, 1986), for ethnographic description is inevitably framed by the positioning of the author (see POSTMODERNISM). Writing is not just a transparent statement of facts, but also an ethical and political presentation. If the scholar is indeed condemned to meaning, if published facts are a condensation of personal and social values, then the sociology of knowledge is all pervasive: 'there is no discipline, no structure of knowledge, no institution or epistemology that can or has ever stood free of the various socio-cultural, historical and political formations that give epochs their peculiar individuality' (Said, 1989). Confronted with a task of this magnitude the author must become acutely self-critical to locate biases of both inclusion and exclusion (see also FEMINIST GEOGRAPHY; POSTCOLONIALISM).

However, another strategy is to adopt a specific value-position, and press selected values as a normative prescription of what should be. Such an argument in favour of advocacy and social relevance was advanced by human geographers in critical debates around 1970 (Mitchell and Draper, 1982). Normative values clearly influence deeply both HUMANISTIC and MARXIST viewpoints in human geography. Buttimer (1974), for example, has advanced an ethic of human dignity and empowerment, and Harvey (1973) an ethic of social justice.

In an increasingly plural society there is mounting concern to establish a workable ethical structure, for with the erosion of previous standards predicated upon religious revelation or rational protocols, 'the language of morality is in the . . . state of grave disorder' (MacIntyre, 1984, p. 2). If the realm of ethics begins in the murmurings of cosmology it ends in the disputations of politics and law. The political and legal discourse of rights would also seem to include the right to receive ethical treatment from others. Such an insight throws fresh light on some conventional geographical problems, including locational decision-making (Clark, 1990; cf. LAW, GEOGRAPHY OF). DL

References

Buttimer, A. 1974: *Values in geography*. Washington, DC: Association of American Geographers, Resource Paper No. 24.

Clark, G. 1990: Unethical secrets, lies and legal retaliation in the context of corporate restructuring in the United States. *Trans. Inst. Br. Geogr.* 15, pp. 403–20.

Clifford, J. 1986: Partial truths. In Clifford, J. and Marcus, G., eds, *Writing culture: the poetics and politics of ethnography*. Berkeley, CA: University of California Press, pp. 1–26.

Curry, M. 1991: On the possibility of ethics in geography. *Progr. hum. Geog.* 15, pp. 125–48.

Harvey, D. 1973: *Social justice and the city*. London: Edward Arnold.

MacIntyre, A. 1984: *After virtue*. Notre Dame: University of Notre Dame Press.

Mitchell, B. and Draper, D. 1982: *Relevance and ethics in geography*. London: Longman.

Said, E. 1989: Representing the colonized: anthropology's interlocutors. *Critical Inquiry* 15, pp. 205–25.

Suggested Reading

Buttimer (1974).

Mitchell and Draper (1982).

ethnicity The etymology of this term dates back to ancient Greece, where the word *ethnos* was used to refer to a distinct 'people'. In contemporary usage, ethnicity is seen as both a way in which individuals define their personal identity and a type of social stratification that emerges when people form groups based on their real or perceived common origins. Members of *ethnic groups* believe that their specific ancestry and CULTURE mark them as different from others. As such, ethnic group formation always entails both inclusionary and exclusionary behaviour, and ethnicity is a classic form of the distinction people make between 'us' and 'them'. However, ethnicity is not uniformly important to all people: the degree of ethnic attachment varies strongly between and within societies. Typically, the most cohesive ethnic groups form when an area is invaded by an external power or when people migrate to new countries. In both cases people affiliate because the survival of their culture, religious practices, and access to employment opportunities are threatened as they become minorities. Generally, ethnic solidarity grows as the degree of discrimination against minority groups increases. Conversely, those in the majority population tend to play down their own origins and culture, assuming that they are 'normal' while others are 'different', or 'ethnic'. For example, few middle-class, white Americans identify with their European origins, even though these origins may have been decisive in privileging their ancestors in labour and housing markets.

Given the variability of ethnic attachments, sociologists have long debated the ultimate causes of ethnic consciousness. Sociobiologists believe that ethnicity is a primordial human value that is, at bottom, the legacy of a deep-seated drive to ensure access to food and shelter. In this highly controversial perspective, ethnic solidarity is seen as an extension of the biologically driven feelings that link individuals to their nuclear family and kin. These researchers find it difficult to explain why some people place no value on their ethnic origin and culture while others choose to express their ethnicity even when it is disadvantageous to do so. Until recently, Marxists have played down the importance of ethnicity by arguing that it is a displaced form of CLASS consciousness (Bonacich, 1972). In its crudest form, this argument implies a rigid instrumentalism wherein the STATE, viewed as a straightforward extension of the ruling class, enacts colonial and immigration policies designed to create differences within the working class in order to fragment its solidarity. More sophisticated Marxist treatments of ethnicity have emerged in light of growing ethnic and nationalist movements of the late twentieth century; even these, however, tend to portray ethnicity as a regressive force deflecting people from their 'real' material interests. A third important interpretation of ethnicity emphasizes a multifaceted social causation, in which ethnic identities and affiliations are seen to emerge for specific reasons in specific contexts. For example, early twentieth-century immigrants from the southern Italian peninsula to North America brought the parochial loyalties of their village origins; once in

North America, these local affiliations were united into a broader consciousness of being 'Italian'. This emergent ethnicity was the product of a host of factors, including similar religious expressions, common languages, geopolitical events, occupational segmentation, residential segregation and the way in which these immigrants were perceived and categorized as Italians by others around them (Yancey et al., 1976). While researchers following this system of thought are best able to account for the variety of ethnic expression and conflict, their insistence on the need to contextualize renders the construction of a systematic theory of ethnicity virtually impossible. In fact, the very factors that some identify as crucial to the emergence of ethnic consciousness are interpreted by others as sources of dissension. There is no consensus, therefore, on the origins and nature of ethnic affiliation.

Yet another ambiguity is added when researchers use the terms ethnicity and *race* interchangeably. Although the same circumstances may lead to both racialization and the formation of ethnic groups, the two terms should not be confused. While it is possible to identify distinct ethnic groups, the definition of separate 'races' is far more contentious. Even though there are obvious phenotypic differences between people, there is only one human race. Throughout history, however, people have been *racialized* by others for particular reasons. Most commentators agree that racialization is necessarily a negative process, where one group (usually in a more powerful position) chooses to define another as morally and/or genetically inferior in order to dominate and oppress it: racialization is always an *imposed* category. Phenotypical differences, such as skin colour or facial structure, are then interpreted as evidence that the two groups are indeed separate 'types' of people and are used strategically to demark the boundaries between groups. Once defined, such boundaries are virtually impossible to cross. Racialized minorities become ethnic groups when they achieve social solidarity on the basis of their distinct culture and social background. Racialization therefore facilitates the development of ethnic consciousness, which may be harnessed by minorities in their struggle against discrimination (e.g. the Black Power movement of the 1960s in the US, or the contemporary Palestinian Intefadah), but does not *necessarily* lead to ethnic group formation. While external forces are important in the generation of ethnic consciousness, the most basic difference between race and ethnicity is that ethnic affiliation arises from *inside* a group: ethnicity is a process of self-definition.

Over time, ethnic solidarity may be perpetuated or may dissipate. The processes governing the dynamic between assimilation and cultural retention are exceedingly complex, but researchers generally agree that the nature of the social boundaries between ethnic groups is critical. Boundaries are maintained when individuals maximize their interactions with those in their ethnic group while minimizing their interactions with others. This occurs when separate social, political and educational institutions are established within different groups. In many cases ethnic boundaries become entrenched in space, such as in the formation of ethnic neighbourhoods in cities.

Geographers have shown a long-standing interest in documenting the causes and consequences of urban ethnic segregation. Much of this work stems from the conceptualization of human ecology articulated by Robert Park and other members of the CHICAGO SCHOOL in the early twentieth century. During the 1960s attention focused on plotting ethnic 'GHETTOS', devising ways to measure the degree of ethnic segregation (see INDICES OF SEGREGATION), and formulating public policy to integrate ethnic and racialized groups across the city. By the end of the decade, a concern for ethnic residential patterns entered the mainstream of urban theory as increasingly sophisticated models of urban land use were devised. This type of work came under intense criticism in the 1970s and 1980s, particularly because of its reliance on census data. Ethnicity is defined in most censuses by respondents' national or 'racial' origin, and is therefore a poor indicator of ethnic affiliation (e.g. all those of Polish extraction are considered to be alike, whether or not they identify with their cultural heritage). Furthermore, such classification of people perpetuates the idea that there are distinct races, and the census itself may be implicated in the racialization of minorities. Given these criticisms, data-intensive studies of ethnicity have been increasingly abandoned within human geography. Research energy has instead begun to focus more squarely on the racialization process, especially as it impinges on people's access to housing and the labour market. The regulatory practices of government are highlighted in this work because immigration, housing, employment equity and other policies directly affect the way in which individuals experience discrimination and ethnic or racial difference. While this research has led to important insights, it tends to ignore social processes that operate within groups; that is, discrimination and racialization are emphasized without a corresponding interest in the agency of individuals to create ethnic consciousness and use this to struggle against domination (Leitner, 1992).

Human geographers have also begun to examine the intersections between ethnicity/race and other forms of personal identity and stratification, notably CLASS and GENDER. Here emphasis is placed on the ways in which each dimension of identity affects all others; for example, masculinity and feminity may well be defined and lived differently in different ethnic groups. This type of investigation is both conceptually difficult, since researchers must study many facets of experience and social structure simultaneously, and controversial, since it destabilizes traditional definitions of class and gender.   DH

References

Bonacich, E. 1972: A theory of ethnic antagonism: the split labor market. *Am. Soc. R.* 37, pp. 547–59.

Leitner, H. 1992: Urban geography: responding to new challenges. *Prog. hum. Geogr.* 16, pp. 105–18.

Yancey, W. L., Ericksen, E. P., and Juliani, R. N. 1976: Emergent ethnicity: a review and reformulation. *Am. Soc. R.* 41, pp. 391–402.

Suggested Reading

Anderson, K. J. 1991: *Vancouver's Chinatown: racial discourse in Canada, 1875–1980*. Montreal and Kingston: McGill–Queen's University Press.

Banton, M. 1983: *Racial and ethnic competition*. Cambridge: Cambridge University Press.

McColl, C. 1990: *Class, ethnicity, and social inequality*. Montreal and Kingston: McGill–Queen's University Press.

Peach, C., Robinson, V. and Smith, S. J., eds 1981: *Ethnic segregation in cities*. London: Croom Helm.

Rex, J. and Mason, D. eds 1986: *Theories of race and ethnic relations*. Cambridge: Cambridge University Press.

Smith, S. J. 1989: *The politics of 'race' and residence; citizenship, segregation and white supremacy in Britain*. Cambridge: Polity Press.

ethnocentrism   A form of prejudice or stereotyping that assumes the superiority of one's own CULTURE or ETHNIC GROUP; a milder version of RACISM or xenophobia, which assumes that one's own way of doing things is the normal or 'natural' way and that other ways are inherently inferior. Whereas prejudice may be directed against specific groups, ethnocentrism is directed against everyone who is perceived to belong to a different ethnic group. McGee (1991) has criticized geography for its own form of ethnocentrism, arguing that the discipline has defined Asia in Eurocentric terms. (See also ORIENTALISM, POSTCOLONIALISM.)
                                                      PAJ

Reference

McGee, T. G. 1991: Eurocentrism in geography: the case of Asian urbanization. *Can. Geogr.* 35, pp 332–44.

ethnography   Based on first-hand observation in the field, ethnography employs PARTICIPANT OBSERVATION and other QUALITATIVE METHODS to convey the inner life and texture of a particular social group or neighbourhood. An intensive, contextual and holistic approach, ethnography aims for depth rather than coverage. Originally focusing on 'primitive' societies in distant settings, ethnographers now face a crisis of representation (Marcus and Fisher, 1986) concerning their authority to provide accurate accounts of societies other than their own. Various alternatives to the conventional monograph or documentary film are being explored (e.g. Clifford and Marcus, 1986), including experiments with textual strategy and representational style (Atkinson, 1990).   PAJ

References

Atkinson, P. 1990: *The ethnographic imagination: textual constructions of reality*. London: Routledge.

Clifford, J. and Marcus, G. E., eds 1986: *Writing culture: the poetics and politics of ethnography*. Berkeley, CA: University of California Press.

Marcus, G. E. and Fisher, M. M. J. 1986: *Anthropology as cultural critique: an experimental moment in the human sciences*. Chicago: University of Chicago Press.

Suggested Reading

Clifford and Marcus (1986).

Hammersley, M. 1992: *What's wrong with ethnography? methodological explorations*. London: Routledge.

Hammersley, M. and Atkinson, P. 1983: *Ethnography: principles in practice*. London: Tavistock.

Jackson, P. 1985: Urban ethnography, *Progr. hum. Geogr.* 9, pp. 157–76.

ethnomethodology Procedures to discover the general and universal methods by which people make sense of, and give order to, the world. It concentrates on how the *appearance* of order and the *impression* of shared rules are maintained by, for example, employing PARTICIPANT OBSERVATION, examining the use and construction of official records (see TEXT), and disrupting everyday situations to expose background assumptions. Deriving from Schutz's phenomenological sociology (see PHENOMENOLOGY), ethnomethodology's strength lies in its critique of conventional social science, particularly the latter's neglect of the contextual determination of meaning, which is utterly dependent on unique situations which provide the indexical expressions used to make sense of the world. Ethnomethodology thus concentrates on the unique, the descriptive and the IDIOGRAPHIC. It does not see the point or possibility of generalization.   JE

Suggested Reading

Bauman, Z. 1973: On the philosophical status of ethnomethodology. *Soc. Rev.* 21, pp. 5–23.

Garfinkel, H. 1967: *Studies in ethnomethodology*. Englewood Cliffs, NJ: Prentice-Hall (republished 1984, Cambridge: Polity Press).

exceptionalism The belief that geography and history are methodologically distinct from other fields of inquiry because they are peculiarly concerned with the study of the unique and the particular. The idea is closely associated with KANTIANISM, but in geography the term is usually identified with Schaefer's (1953) posthumous challenge to what he regarded as the IDIOGRAPHIC orthodoxy enshrined in Hartshorne's *The nature of geography* (1939). Schaefer rejected exceptionalism to argue for a NOMOTHETIC geography which would furnish 'morphological laws' about spatial patterns. Hartshorne's views were in fact more nuanced than Schaefer maintained, and he never accepted any clear division between the idiographic and the nomothetic because they were both 'present in all branches of science'. But he did insist that any general concepts used in geography should be directed towards the analysis of specific REGIONS, and that its essential task was the study of AREAL DIFFERENTIATION rather than (as Schaefer preferred) the elucidation of the laws of location that were supposed to underpin these regional configurations.   DG

References

Hartshorne, R. 1939: *The nature of geography: a critical survey of current thought in the light of the past*. Lancaster, PA: Association of American Geographers.

Schaefer, F. K. 1953: Exceptionalism in geography: a methodological examination. *Ann. Ass. Am. Geogr.* 43, pp. 226–49.

Suggested Reading

Johnston, R. J. 1991: *Geography and geographers: Anglo-American human geography since 1945*, fourth edition. London: Edward Arnold/New York: Halsted, pp. 51–8.

exclave A small part of a STATE, separated from the main territorial unit and surrounded by the land of a neighbour, such as the area of Spain around Llivia on the French side of the Pyrenees. There are several variations on this basic form. *Pene-exclaves* are part of the state which, although not physically separate, can only be reached conveniently via another country. *Quasi-exclaves* are areas that for all practical purposes have ceased to be treated as exclaves. *Virtual exclaves* are the reverse, areas that enjoy the status of an exclave without the legal entitlement. Finally, *temporary exclaves* result from inconclusive territorial arrangements being made after an armistice. (See also ENCLAVE.)   MB

Suggested Reading
Robinson, G. W. S. 1959: Exclaves: *Ann. Ass. Am. Geogr.* 49, pp. 283–95.

existentialism A philosophy the central concern of which is with the human subject's existential 'being' in the world (which Heidegger called *Dasein*). Existentialism posits that all persons are typically estranged from their intrinsic creativity and live instead in worlds of objects which exist for them only as externalized 'things' – a passive attitude which Tuan (1971, 1972) called ENVIRONMENTALISM – and that any attempt to realize a truly human condition through an active 'openness' to the world necessarily involves a freely entered struggle against estrangement. Following in some part the ideas of Buber, Heidegger and Sartre, Samuels (1978) has argued that this struggle entails an *essentially spatial* ONTOLOGY: that it is 'a history of human efforts to overcome or eliminate detachment, which is to say, to eliminate distance' through the creation of meaningful, so to speak 'authored' places (see PLACE). Many of the early existentialist explorations in human geography were concerned not so much with the elaboration of a spatial ontology, however, as with a more general assault on those 'technical' conceptions of the subject, usually closely associated with POSITIVISM, which reduced it to a so-called 'scientism'. 'For the existentially aware geographers', Buttimer (1974) suggested, the human being:

is more than a cultural, 'rational' or dynamically-charged decision maker out there to be observed, analysed and modelled: he [or she] is a 'subject' of lived experience, past, present and future. An existentially aware geographer is thus less interested in establishing intellectual control over [people] through pre-conceived analytical models than . . . in encountering people and situations in an open, intersubjective manner.

(See also Gibson (1978) for the Weberian alternative.)

As Buttimer's remarks indicate, existentialism involves a critique of both rationalism and IDEALISM, which certainly extends to Weber's interpretative sociology – because it (quite literally) regards *existence* as primary. And while it has important connections with both PHENOMENOLOGY and HISTORICAL MATERIALISM, especially through some of the contributions of Sartre (see Poster, 1975), it can be distinguished from both by its fundamental concern with what Buttimer describes as 'the quality and meaning of human life in the everyday world'. Hence, Buttimer invokes Heidegger's distinction between *Herrschaftswissen* ('knowledge of meaning and overlordship') and *Bildungswissen* ('knowledge of meaning and creativity') to support her plea for a 'more concerned, caring approach to knowledge and action' which can resist and ultimately transcend the rationalist impulse for technical control, and the estrangement which this entails, and thereby provide for a truly human existence (Buttimer, 1979a,b) (cf. CRITICAL THEORY). Not surprisingly, these sorts of criticisms have been applied *a fortiori* to the *relations* between human geography and planning (e.g. see Cullen and Knox, 1982), but they are clearly intended to have a much more general purchase.

Indeed, Relph (1981) widened the existentialist critique within the subject far beyond the sphere of spatial science to confront what he calls the 'ontological triviality' of HUMANISTIC GEOGRAPHY (p. 155). In his view, too, Heidegger's writings are an indispensable source for a genuinely human geography; but whereas 'Heidegger's philosophy was a form of contemplation', the 'environmental humility' which Relph is concerned to foster must embrace not only 'an openness to Being' – 'allowing things to disclose themselves as they are', 'letting ourselves be claimed by Being' – but also 'a manifest guardianship for the individuality of places and landscapes' (pp. 187–91). Similar ideas were pursued by Samuels (1979, 1981) in his search for 'an existential geography' directed towards the elucidation of what he termed 'the biography of landscape'. They have been developed most rigorously by Pickles (1985), who has drawn upon Heidegger to identify the significance of the 'existential analytic' for the human sciences in general and human geography in particular. He seeks to clarify the fundamental importance of what, following Heidegger, he terms a 'regional ontology' of human SPATIALITY for both enterprises.

Present in virtually all of these discussions is the idea of 'openness to Being', and in a remarkable essay Gould (1981) worked with *Daseinanalysis* to recover the root-meaning of the word 'theory' (*theoria*) in a way which connects up to the foregoing. He suggests that *theoria* connotes both openness and 'the reverent paying heed to phenomena'. If we see conventional 'theory-building' from this perspective, then Gould believes that 'our deep and legitimate concern for a scientific geography' may have gone astray:

In attempting to map the description of human phenomena onto the forms of science generated by those who assault the inanimate or non-conscious physical and biological worlds with their questions, we have objectified, cut off, 'templated' the very beings-in-the-world that should be of our deepest concern in any geography where the adjective 'human' is genuinely deserved. There seems to be little 'reverent paying heed' in the everyday research and questioning of the human sciences today, and the old meanings of *theoria* seldom seem to shine through the methodical, and often mechanistic, processes of inquiry in these realms.

Gould objects to 'con-*templation*', therefore, because it involves partition and enclosure – the construction of a *template* – and prefers instead to explore descriptive languages more appropriate to (open to) human spatiality: in particular languages in which we do not project 'the multidimensional character that seems to characterize the complexity of contemporary life onto the traditional space of the geographic map.'

Much of this discussion has evidently been preoccupied with broadly methodological questions – with mobilizing a philosophical literature to displace the assumptions of SPATIAL SCIENCE – but there has recently been a considerable revival of interest in the historical grounding and substantive implications of Heidegger's work across the humanities and the social sciences as a whole. This has followed four interconnected paths, all of which bear directly on work in contemporary human geography:

(a) the politics of Heidegger's philosophy and, in particular, the complex connections between his intellectual work and his involvement in National Socialism (see Wolin, 1990) – this examination connects with parallel attempts to establish the contextuality of geographical inquiry;

(b) Heidegger's critique of MODERNITY, and in particular of its technocratic consciousness (Zimmerman, 1990) and its 'enframing' of what Mitchell (1989) calls the world-as-exhibition – these examinations intersect with attempts to explore human geographies of modernity, to think through society's involvement in and responsibility towards NATURE, and to consider the concept of LANDSCAPE as a 'way of seeing';

(c) the filiations between Heidegger's ethical concerns and those of POSTMODERNISM (White, 1991) – this examination feeds in to contemporary interests in the geographies of postmodernism and 'post-modernity' and, in particular, to processes of 'Othering';

(d) the construction of a spatial ontology (Schatzki, 1991) – this effort contributes directly to attempts to clarify the importance of space and spatiality in the constitution of social life.   DG

References

Buttimer, A. 1974: *Values in geography*. Washington, DC: Association of American Geographers, Commission on College Geography, resource paper 24.

Buttimer, A. 1979a: Erewhon or nowhere land. In Gale, S. and Olsson, G., eds, *Philosophy in geography*. Dordrecht and Boston: D. Reidel, pp. 9–37.

Buttimer, A. 1979b: Reason, rationality and human creativity. *Geogr. Annlr.* 61B, pp. 43–9.

Cullen, J. and Knox, P. 1982: The city, the self and urban society. *Trans. Inst. Br. Geogr.* 7, pp. 276–91.

Gibson, E. 1978: Understanding the subjective meaning of places. In Ley, D. and Samuels, M. S., eds, *Humanistic geography: prospects and problems*. London: Croom Helm, pp. 138–54.

Gould, P. 1981: Letting the data speak for themselves. *Ann. Ass. Am. Geogr.* 71, pp. 166–76.

Mitchell, T. 1989: The world as exhibition. *Comp. Stud. Soc. Hist.* 31, pp. 217–36.

Pickles, J. 1985: *Phenomenology, science and geography: spatiality and the human sciences.* Cambridge: Cambridge University Press.

Poster, M. 1975: *Existential Marxism: from Sartre to Althusser.* Princeton, NJ: Princeton University Press.

Relph, E. 1981: *Rational landscapes and humanistic geography.* London: Croom Helm/Totowa, NJ: Barnes & Noble.

Samuels, M. 1978: Existentialism and human geography. In Ley, D. and Samuels, M. S., eds, *Humanistic geography: prospects and problems.* London: Croom Helm, pp. 22–40.

Samuels, M. 1979: The biography of landscape: cause and culpability. In Meinig, D., ed., *The interpretation of ordinary landscapes.* Oxford: Oxford University Press, pp. 51–88.

Samuels, M. 1981: An existential geography. In Harvey, M. E. and Holly, B. P., eds, *Themes in geographic thought.* London: Croom Helm, pp. 115–32.

Schatzki, T. 1991: Spatial ontology and explanation. *Ann. Ass. Am. Geogr.* 81, pp. 650–70.

Tuan, Y.-F. 1971: Geography, phenomenology and the study of human nature. *Can. Geogr.* 15, pp. 181–92.

Tuan, Y.-F. 1972: Structuralism, existentialism and environmental perception. *Environ. Behav.* 4, pp. 319–42.

White, S. 1991: *Political theory and postmodernism.* Cambridge: Cambridge University Press.

Wolin, R. 1990: *The politics of Being: the political thought of Martin Heidegger.* New York: Columbia University Press.

Zimmerman, M. 1990: *Heidegger's confrontation with modernity: technology, politics and art.* Bloomington, IN: Indiana University Press.

Suggested Reading

Samuels (1978, 1981).

Schatzki (1991).

White (1991).

Zimmerman (1990).

exit, voice and loyalty A theory of consumer influence on the quality of PUBLIC GOODS: it was developed by Hirschman (1970), who contends that in a monopoly situation the quality of such goods is likely to be lower than when consumers have a range of potential suppliers. In the latter situation, consumers can react to an inefficient/ineffective service by taking one of the following options: (1) *exit*, which involves transferring their custom to an alternative supplier; (2) *voice*, complaining about the quality of provision and threatening exit if it is not improved; and (3) *loyalty*, remaining with the current supplier without either voicing complaints or threatening exit. The higher the exit costs (i.e. of switching suppliers) the lower the likely impact of voice, because the supplier can assume loyalty. If exit is impossible, because of a monopoly, then loyalty is virtually guaranteed and voice will have little impact.

Several consequences have been deduced from this argument, and some were put into effect by New Right governments during the 1980s. One is that to obtain efficient and effective service-delivery public-sector monopolies should be dismantled, either by their PRIVATIZATION in a way that will create competitive situations or by the creation of a quasi-market system within the sector (as with the British National Health Service from 1990 on: see also TIEBOUT MODEL). Another is that although individual voice may be ineffective, collective protest may not, since powerful pressure groups may be able to mobilize effective collective voice and/or exit: against this, it is argued that those with least political POWER to organize are least likely to have effective exit options open to them (e.g. transferring their consumption of such items as education and health care from the public to the private sector). RJJ

Reference

Hirschman, A. O. 1970: *Exit, voice and loyalty.* Cambridge, MA: Harvard University Press.

Suggested Reading

Johnston, R. J. 1992: The internal operations of the state. In P. J. Taylor, ed., *The political geography of the twentieth century.* London: Belhaven Press, pp. 115–70.

Laver, M. 1981: *The politics of private desires.* London: Penguin Books.

expert systems Software packages that attempt to mimic the behaviour of an expert in a given field. The notion that a computer could emulate an expert is attractive, since it implies that such expert systems could be used to standardize many DECISION-MAKING processes, reduce errors and improve the performance of regulatory agencies. An expert system consists of a rule base, containing a digital representation of the known decision rules, and a processor to evaluate the rules in a given instance and reach an appropriate decision. The builder of an expert system will commonly make use of a set of generic tools known as a 'shell', which takes care of the storage of the rule base, and the processing functions. Expert systems have often been coupled with GEOGRAPHICAL INFORMATION SYSTEMS (GIS), which provide many of the inputs and may also display and manage the outputs, in supporting decision-making in forestry, RESOURCE MANAGEMENT, hydrology, and URBAN AND REGIONAL PLANNING. The success of expert system approaches depends on the degree to which all relevant rules can be expressed in the highly constrained forms required of a rule base, and on the credibility of an expert system's output to its users. Rules are often imprecise or 'fuzzy', and expert systems based on fuzzy reasoning have become popular in many geographical applications. Finally, an expert system can provide a useful formal structure for studying decision-making processes. MG

Suggested Reading

Giddens, A. 1991: *Consequences of modernity.* Cambridge: Polity Press.

Kim, T. J., Wiggins, L. L. and Wright, J. R., eds 1990: *Expert systems: applications to urban planning.* New York: Springer-Verlag.

exploration While it is generally taken to refer to the growth of knowledge of the globe that resulted from various voyages of discovery and scientific expeditions, the label 'exploration' disconcerts. Its controverted character arises from the clash over the appropriate vocabulary in which to speak of this essentially contested concept. The very terms *discovery* and *exploration*, according to revisionists, should be replaced by *invasion, conquest* or *occupation*, for the simple reason that these unmask the pretended innocence and moral neutrality

that the standard scientific-sounding idioms convey.

Whatever the allocation of moral accountability, there can be no doubting the significance of 'exploration' on the scientific enterprise in general and the discourse and discipline of geography in particular. Traditional chroniclers of these exploits have thus tended towards a progressivist interpretation of scientific knowledge, cartographic history and global awareness (Baker, 1931). The vast maritime expeditions of Chêng Ho in the early decades of the fifteenth century (1405–1433), for example, have been commended for their contributions to Chinese marine CARTOGRAPHY and descriptive geography; although, in contrast to later voyages, the purpose of the mission was neither the garnering of 'scientific' information nor commercial conquest (Needham, 1959; Chang, 1971). In similar vein, the writings of the Muslim traveller Ibn Battuta during the late Middle Ages are typically interpreted as an encyclopaedic conspectus of Islamic life and culture in different climatic regimes (Boorstin, 1983; James, 1972).

It is, however, with the European voyages of Reconnaissance during the fifteenth and sixteenth centuries that putative connections between scientific 'progress' and geographical 'exploration' are even more closely associated. Parry (1981, p. 3), for example, argues that, save for the arts of war and military engineering, geographical exploration was 'almost the only field' in which 'scientific discovery and everyday technique became closely associated before the middle of the seventeenth century'. Similarly, Hale (1967) suggests that the first scientific laboratory was the world itself, and O'Sullivan (1984, p. 3) that 'the voyages of discovery were in a way large scale experiments, proving or disproving the Renaissance concepts inherited from the ancient world'. In such scenarios the names of Bartholomew Dias, Vasco da Gama, Christopher Columbus, Fernand Magellan, and, perhaps most of all, 'Prince Henry the Navigator' assume hagiographic status. For these reasons, the Portuguese and Spanish voyages have been interpreted as precursors to the Scientific Revolution (Hooykaas, 1979).

Francis Bacon later reflected in his *Novum Organum* of 1620 (§ lxxxiv) that the opening up of the geographical world through the voyages of discovery foreshadowed the expansion of the 'boundaries of the intellectual globe' beyond the confines of 'the narrow discoveries of the ancients'. Support for this interpretation has come from those who attach crucial significance to the Portuguese encouragement of navigational science and mathematical practice through the work of the Jewish map- and instrument-maker Mestre Jacome. This Jewish tradition of Mallorcan cartography, instrumentation and nautical science was perpetuated by Abraham Zacuto and Joseph Vizinho, while Francesco Faleiro, Garcia da Orta and Pedro Nunes did much to further medicinal botany, cartography and natural history during the first half of the sixteenth century (Goodman, 1991). Accordingly, such accomplishments have recently been canvassed to substantiate the claim that this Jewish style of science practised in sixteenth-century Portugal provided the template for the Scientific Revolution in England and the 'catalyst inducing the emergence of modern science in Western Europe' (Banes, 1988, p. 58).

Nevertheless, even partisan commentators concede that the scientific advances of the 'Age of Discovery' were by-products of the commercial, evangelistic and colonial motives that undergirded these expeditionary enterprises. Ostensibly more scientific were the Pacific exploits of Enlightenment figures such as Louis Antoine de Bougainville, James Cook, Joseph Banks, the Forsters, Jean François de la Pérouse and George Vancouver (Beaglehole, 1966). And yet with them too political factors loomed as large as scientific ones: prevoyage briefings on settlement possibility, resource inventory and the staking of colonial claims all revealed the strategic significance of everything from cartographic survey to geodesic experiment and ethnographic illustration (Frost, 1988). Still, the scientific achievements were not insubstantial: Cook, for instance, carried with him landscape painters, natural history draughtsmen and professional astronomers, surgeons and naturalists, and successfully completed an accurate recording of the transit of Venus (Goetzmann, 1986). Indeed, the Pacific became something of a laboratory for the testing of scientific methodologies and artistic representational styles (Smith, 1960). Precisely the same was true of later explorations in South America and Central Africa. Alexander von Humboldt and Aimé Bonpland, for example, used their South American findings to break the bonds of the static taxonomic system of Linnaeus, and ultimately to create a distinctive mode of scientific investigation – what Cannon labelled 'Humboldtian science' – in which 'the accurate, measured study of widespread but interconnected real phenomena' were interrogated 'in order to find a definite law and a dynamic cause' (Cannon, 1978, p. 105). Again, Roderick Murchison, who has been dubbed England's scientist of empire, virtually orchestrated the British colonial assault on Central Africa through his oversight of the Royal Geographical Society, and used a variety of explorers to test his own geological theories there. In the expansive personage of Murchison, geography's complicity in the colonial project found expression (Stafford, 1989).

There is not space here to delineate, even in outline, the scientific contributions of a host of other exploratory ventures: the Napoleonic survey of Egypt, Baudin's deadly mission to 'New Holland', the succession of Russian voyages into the Pacific by Krusentern, Kotzebue and Lütke, the Royal Geographical Society's efforts to reduce the Australian outback to cartographic enclosure, Lewis and Clark's western territorial expedition orchestrated by Thomas Jefferson, Darwin's *Beagle* circumnavigation, the United States Exploring Expedition under Charles Wilkes, the voyage of T. H. Huxley on *The Rattlesnake*, A. R. Wallace's sojourn in Borneo, and the oceanographic survey of *The Challenger*, to name but a very few. Their role in the evolution of geographical knowledge has been so engrained in the discipline's collective memory that various expeditionary ventures continue to receive the sponsorship of institutions such as the Royal Geographical Society and the National Geographic Society, and to provide a language in which to speak of geographical excursions into other threatening environments, such as urban ethnic 'no-go' areas (Horvath, 1971).

However, as already hinted, to interpret the significance of these SURVEILLANCE exploits solely in terms of cognitive 'progress' is highly questionable. Moreover, merely to state that the growth of these scientific knowledges was situated within the framework of IMPERIALISM is to pay scant attention to a whole suite of issues to do with the construction of Western identity, the representations of 'exoticism', the inscription of 'otherness', the reciprocal constitution of scientific discourse and colonial praxis (see COLONIALISM), and the deconstruction of cartographic ICONOGRAPHY.

It was indeed as a consequence of the European Age of Exploration/Reconnaissance/Conquest that the idea of the 'West' and 'Western-ness' received its baptism (see ORIENTALISM). Europe's sense of distinctiveness from the other worlds that the navigators encountered was embedded in a discourse about identity that represented 'the West' and 'the Rest' – to use Stuart Hall's (1992) words – in the categories of superiority–inferiority, power–impotence, enlightenment–ignorance and civilization–barbarism. Seen in these terms, Europe's rendezvous with the New World in the fifteenth and sixteenth centuries was as much a moral event as a commercial or intellectual one, and induced what Pagden (1986) calls a sense of 'metaphysical unease' because it confounded standard conceptions of human nature.

The construction of this 'discourse of the West', of course, depended crucially on the idioms in which the new worlds were represented. The categories, vocabularies, assumptions and instruments which the explorers brought to the encounter were, understandably, thoroughly European, and so the worlds of 'the other' were interrogated, classified and assimilated according to European norms. Moreover, that the language of the engagement was invariably gendered facilitated the representation of new landscapes in the exotic categories of a potent sexual imagery intended to indicate mastery and submissiveness.

If the foundations of Western discourse were laid during the fifteenth and sixteenth centuries, they were reinforced during the following centuries when Eurocentric modes of representation actually constituted regional identities. One such construction was what Edward Said has termed 'ORIENTALISM' – a discursive formation through which, he writes, 'European culture was able to manage – and even produce – the Orient politically, sociologically, militarily, ideologically, scientifically and imaginatively during the post-Enlightenment period' (Said, 1978, p. 3). And if the construction of Orientalism was crucially dependent on the scientific, historical and literary crafts of Western exploration, its evocation also owed much to the supposedly realist works of visual art later produced by painters such as Jean-Léon Gérôme (Nochlin, 1991).

The procedures facilitating the marginalization of the Oriental realm (and – at the same time – its constitutive role in European self-definition) were also perpetuated in other places and in other terms. The variety of representational devices that Cook and his coterie of naturalists and draughtsmen deployed – whether Banks' abstract taxonomics or Parkinson's evocation of anthropological variety – succeeded in encapsulating the Pacific world within the confines of European EPISTEMOLOGIES. Moreover, their penchant for designating names – the naming of places, peoples and individuals – at once invented, brought into cultural circulation and domesticated the very entities that were the subjects of their enquiries (Carter, 1987). That Cook's team was engaged in what Salmond (1991, p. 15) terms 'mirror-image ETHNOGRAPHY' is beyond dispute. But just because their modes of categorization were suffused with the expectations of eighteenth-century society – from descriptions of social status (governors and kings make their appearance) to the evaluation of character (courage, honour and virtue figure prominently) – should not be permitted to gainsay the remarkable accuracy of their accounts of physical phenomena. Their New Zealand portrayals, for example, 'check well against the surviving evidence of the places and objects which they described', Salmond writes (p. 294). So much is that so that Cook's vivid depictions of the 'regional variability of tribal life' (Salmond, p. 431) exposes the ahistorical idealization of pre-European 'traditional Maori society' which in fact only began to be systematically constructed a century later.

Space does not permit further elucidation of these motifs in other regions. Suffice it to note that in the African context, according to the Comaroffs (1991, p. 313), European colonization 'was often less a directly coercive conquest than a persuasive attempt to colonize consciousness, to remake people by redefining the taken-for-granted surfaces of their everyday worlds'. Yet here too the temptation towards 'monolithizing' the encounter must be resisted: the moral significance of African environments became a source of endless debate about the effects of a tropical climate on white constitution and the connections between black racial character, biological make-up, and physical geography (Livingstone, 1991). In South America it was Humboldt's 'interweaving of visual and emotive language' that contributed so powerfully towards what Pratt (1992) calls the 'ideological reinvention' of 'América' – a reimagining so vivid and so vital that Humboldt's writings provided founding visions for *both* the older elites of northern Europe *and* the newer independent elites of Spanish America.

If these machinations, however tangled their genealogies, satisfied a European sense of superiority through constituting the peripheral regions of the globe in its own terms, those self-same arenas were soon to become pivotal laboratories for scrutiny into human prehistory. In this way the threat that resided in 'alien' human natures could be rendered benign if those RACES turned out to be the persistent remnants of earlier phases in the story of human evolution. Just as earlier Scottish and French Enlightenment thinkers, such as Smith, Ferguson and Buffon, regularly crafted their image of the bestial or noble savage into evolutionary schemes depicting a transition from barbarism to civilization, so early twentiety-century students of human archaeology used 'the peoples defined as living at the uttermost ends of the imperial world as examples of living prehistory' (Gamble, 1992, p. 713). Thereby their identity remained engulfed within the imperatives of Western scientific scrutiny. They also remained subordinated in the cartographic representations that invariably accompanied the exploratory process. Whether in their use as military tools, in their advocacy of colonial promotion, in their marginal decorations, in their systems of hierarchical classification, or in their imposition of a regulative geometry that bore little reference to indigenous peoples, maps became the conductors of imperial POWER and Western IDEOLOGY (Harley, 1988: see CARTOGRAPHY, HISTORY OF).

The history of 'exploration', then, turns out to be far from antiquarian chronology. Rather, it focuses centrally on the identity of people, the wielding of power, and the construction of knowledge; and it is precisely because these are entangled in such complex and intricate ways that their elucidation is of crucial importance to the future course of human history.   DNL

References

Baker, J. N. L. 1931: *A history of geographical discovery and exploration.* London: Harrap.

Banes, D. 1988: The Portuguese voyages of discovery and the emergence of modern science. *J. Wash. Acad. Sci.* 28, pp. 47–58.

Beaglehole, J. C. 1966: *The exploration of the Pacific*, third edition. Stanford, CA: Stanford University Press.

Boorstin, D. 1983: *The discoverers: a history of man's search to know his world and himself.* New York: Random House.

Cannon, S. F. 1978: *Science in culture: the early Victorian period.* New York: Dawson and Science History Publications.

Carter, P. 1987: *The road to Botany Bay: an essay in spatial history.* London: Faber.

Chang, K.-S. 1971: The Ming maritime enterprise and China's knowledge of Africa prior to the Age of Great Discoverers. *Terrae Incognitae* 3, pp. 33–4.

Comaroff, J. and J. 1991: *Of revelation and revolution: Christianity, colonialism, and consciousness in South Africa*, volume 1. Chicago: University of Chicago Press.

Frost, A. 1988: Science for political purposes: European explorations of the Pacific Ocean, 1764–1806. In MacLeod, R. and Rehbock, P. E., eds, *Nature in its greatest extent: Western science in the Pacific*. Honolulu: University of Hawaii Press, pp. 27–44.

Gamble, C. 1992: Archaeology, history and the uttermost ends of the Earth – Tasmania, Tierra del Fuego and the Cape. *Antiquity* 66, pp. 712–20.

Goetzmann, W. H. 1986: *New lands, new men: America and the second Great Age of Discovery*. New York: Viking.

Goodman, D. 1991: Iberian science: navigation, empire and counter-reformation. In Goodman, D. and Russell, C. A., eds, *The rise of scientific Europe, 1500–1800*. Sevenoaks, Kent: Hodder & Stoughton, pp. 117–44.

Hale, J. R. 1967: A world elsewhere. In Hay, D. ed., *The age of renaissance*. London: Thames and Hudson.

Hall, S. 1992: The West and the Rest: discourse and power. In Hall, S. and Gieben, B., eds, *Formations of modernity*. Oxford: Polity Press in association with the Open University.

Harley, J. B. 1988: Maps, knowledge, and power. In Cosgrove, D. and Daniels, S., eds, *The iconography of landscape: essays in the representation, design and use of past environments*. Cambridge: Cambridge University Press, pp. 277–312.

Hooykaas, R. 1979: *Humanism and the voyages of discovery in 16th century Portuguese science and letters*. Amsterdam: North Holland.

Horvath, R. 1971: The 'Detroit Geographical Expedition and Institute' experience, *Antipode* 3, pp. 73–85.

James, P. E. 1972: *All possible worlds: a history of geographical ideas*. Indianapolis: Bobbs-Merrill.

Livingstone, D. N. 1991: The moral discourse of climate: historical considerations on race, place and virtue, *J. Hist. Geogr.* 17, pp. 413–34.

Needham, J. 1959: *Science and civilization in China*, volume 3. Cambridge: Cambridge University Press.

Nochlin, L. 1991: The imaginary Orient. In *The politics of vision*. London: Thames and Hudson, ch. 3.

O'Sullivan, D. 1984: *The age of discovery 1400–1550*. London: Longman.

Pagden, A. 1986: The impact of the New World on the Old: the history of an idea. *Renaissance and Modern Studies* 30, pp. 1–11.

Parry, J. H. 1981: *The age of reconnaissance: discovery, exploration and settlement 1450 to 1650*. Berkeley, CA: University of California Press.

Pratt, M. L. 1992: *Imperial eyes: travel writing and transculturation*. London: Routledge.

Salmond, A. 1991: *Two worlds: first meetings between Maori and Europeans 1642–1772*. Auckland, NZ: Viking.

Said, E. W. 1978: *Orientalism: Western conceptions of the Orient*. London: Routledge & Kegan Paul.

Smith, B. 1960: *European vision and the South Pacific, 1768–1850: a study in the history of art and ideas*. Oxford: Oxford University Press.

Stafford, R. A. 1989: *Scientist of empire: Sir Roderick Murchison, scientific exploration and Victorian imperialism*. Cambridge: Cambridge University Press.

Suggested Reading

Brosse, J. 1983: *Great voyages of discovery: circumnavigators and scientists, 1764–1843* (translated by S. Hochman). New York: Facts on File Publications.

Penrose, B. 1967: *Travel and discovery in the Renaissance 1420–1620*. Cambridge, MA: Harvard University Press.

Van Orman, R. A. 1984: *The explorers: nineteenth century expeditions in Africa and the American West*. Albuquerque: University of New Mexico Press.

Viola, H. J. and Margolis, C. eds, 1985: *Magnificent voyagers: the U.S. exploring expedition, 1838–1842*. Washington, DC: Smithsonian Institution Press.

exploratory data analysis Statistical procedures for describing the major features of a data set, from which HYPOTHESES for further testing may be generated. Whereas many statistical analyses follow the rules of scientific INFERENCE in the evaluation of hypotheses (see CONFIRMATORY DATA ANALYSIS), exploratory data analysis makes few initial assumptions about the expected findings.

Exploratory analyses are of particular value in geographical work for two reasons. First, much geographical investigation has only a weak theoretical base and the empirical expectations are thus relatively imprecise: exploratory data analysis is more sympathetic to such situations, because it lacks the constraints of formal hypothesis-testing. Secondly, few of the data sets employed by geographers are specifically collected for those purposes in properly controlled experimental conditions, so that the investigator has an incomplete appreciation of their structure. Exploratory data analysis, with its emphasis on graphical display, allows researchers to penetrate their data sets, appreciate their peculiarities, and draw conclusions which are constrained neither by prior expectations nor by the limitations of inferential techniques. RJJ

Suggested Reading
Sibley, D. 1990: *Spatial applications of exploratory data analysis.* Concepts and techniques in modern geography 49. Norwich: Environmental Publications.
Wrigley, N. 1983: Quantitative methods: on data and diagnostics. *Prog. hum. Geogr.* 7, pp. 567–77.

export platform A location for industrial activity, the primary purpose of which is to produce for export. The term is usually applied to a location where cheap labour is available and industrial activity is not closely linked with other elements of the local economy. Export platforms are typically found in underdeveloped countries, where labour costs are kept down by low living standards and sometimes also by governments which condone poor working conditions and discourage unionization. Such locations may be attractive to MULTI-NATIONAL CORPORATIONS seeking to disperse production from places such as Western Europe where labour is more expensive. Because of the external orientation of the activities involved, export platforms often contribute little to the development of the host nation, by way of local multiplier effects, but they do provide some employment and the opportunity to tax any profits not transferred to the country from which the investment originated. DMS

extensive agriculture Farming carried on with a low number of inputs per hectare. It occurs under a number of circumstances. Farming near markets is generally characterized by high inputs (see VON THÜNEN MODEL), but with increasing distance from the market income is maximized with lower inputs, and large-scale grain products replace horticulture and dairying. Population density may influence intensity. In areas of low population density land is abundant, labour is scarce and farmers use few yield-increasing inputs and attempt to maximize output per head.

In high-density areas where land is scarce but labour cheap, inputs are used to maximize yields and labour productivity is low. DBG

Suggested Reading
Chisholm, M. 1979: *Rural settlement and land use: an essay in location,* third edition. London: Hutchison/Atlantic Highlands, NJ: Humanities Press.
Hayami, Y. and Ruttan, V. W. 1985: *Agricultural development an international perspective,* second edition. Baltimore, MD: Johns Hopkins University Press.

extensive research Research that is directed towards discovering common properties and *empirical regularities* and that aims to offer *generalizations* about them. The term is derived from the philosopher Rom Harré, and in geography would apply to much of the work conducted under the signs of EMPIRICISM and POSITIVISM with spatial science and BEHAVIOURAL GEOGRAPHY. Sayer (1992) suggests that extensive research typically relies on QUANTITATIVE METHODS – including descriptive and inferential statistics and numerical analysis – and on large-scale questionnaires and formal interviews. The term has been widely used in discussions of REALISM as a more appropriate philosophy for human geography, where it is contrasted with strategies of INTENSIVE RESEARCH. 'Extensive studies are weaker for the purpose of explanation not so much because they are a 'broad-brush' method lacking in sensitivity to detail', Sayer (1992) argues, 'but because the relations they discover are formal, concerning similarity, dissimilarity, correlation and the like, rather than causal, structural and substantial'. DG

Reference and Suggested Reading
Sayer, A. 1992: *Method in social science a realist approach,* second edition. London: Routledge, pp. 241–51.

external economies Cost advantages obtained from sources external to the individual industrial organization. These comprise reductions in operating costs, associated with such considerations as the local availability of a skilled labour force, workers familiar with the industry in question, a technical college providing appropriate training, research facilities and the existence of ancillary industries providing materials, components, machinery or specialized services. External economies typically develop in a localized concentration of a particular activity. If not available externally, such facilities have to be provided internally, i.e. by the individual organization, which increases costs and requires a certain level of scale and resources. Thus external economies are especially important to small firms.   DMS

externalities The (usually unintended) effects of one person's actions on another, over which the latter has no control. Externalities may be either positive (bringing benefits to the recipients) or negative (creating costs for them). Good examples are provided by a neighbourhood environment: well-kept gardens in an area can generate positive externalities (pleasant contexts for domestic life), whereas noisy factories there can create costs for people in the locality. Each type of externality may have an influence on property values in the neighbourhood.

Most externalities are local in their impact only, with a DISTANCE DECAY effect in their extent and intensity. (There is usually a DENSITY GRADIENT in the spread of a negative externality such as noise, for example: the further you are from its source, the less it affects you.) For this reason, and because externalities have impacts on both people's quality of life and the value of their properties, there is CONFLICT over the location of land uses which generate externalities. People compete – through the pricing system in the property market, for example – to be near sources of positive externalities (as shown in studies of the geography of house values in many cities) and they become involved in political action (often of a collective kind) to exclude negative externality generators from their neighbourhoods. Because of unequal power in housing markets, the more affluent are usually better able to succeed in the elimination of negative externalities from their home areas, and thus to protect their property values.   RJJ

Suggested Reading

Cox, K. R. 1973: *Conflict, power and politics in the city: a geographic view*. New York: McGraw-Hill.

Saunders, P. 1979: *Urban politics: a sociological interpretation*. London: Penguin.

Smith, D. M. 1977: *Human geography: a welfare approach*. London: Edward Arnold.

F

factor analysis A statistical procedure for transforming an (observations by variables) data matrix so that the variables in the new matrix are uncorrelated. Unlike PRINCIPAL COMPONENTS ANALYSIS, which has a similar goal, factor analysis does not identify as many new variables (termed factors) as there are in the original matrix because it ignores that portion of the variance in each of the original variables that is unique to it, i.e. is uncorrelated with any other variable.

The first stage in a factor analysis involves using one of the available methods of identifying and eliminating the unique variance. The technique then follows the same general sequence of procedures as in principal components analysis, with the successive extraction of factors which maximize the common variance accounted for. The results – the eigenvalues and the matrices of factor loadings and factor scores – are interpreted in the same way as the comparable matrices of component loadings and scores.

Factor analysis concentrates on identifying the commonalities in the interrelationships among variables. It can be used either inductively (as in EXPLORATORY DATA ANALYSIS), to separate groups of variables with common relative distributions across the observations, or deductively, to test HYPOTHESES regarding the existence of such groups. Few geographical applications have rigorously followed the second route, because the available theory gives only very general expectations concerning the loadings.

To facilitate the inductive search for groups of related variables (as in applications which fall under the general term FACTORIAL ECOLOGY), the factor loading matrix may be rotated mathematically to maximize the relationship of each of the original variables to just one factor. Of the many rotation procedures available in computer statistical packages, most fall into one of two types: (1) orthogonal rotations (of which the most popular is Varimax), which maintain the uncorrelated nature of the factors; and (2) oblique rotations, which allow correlations among the factors.   RJJ

Suggested Reading

Johnston, R. J. 1978: *Multivariate statistical analysis in geography: a primer on the general linear model*. London: Longman.

factorial ecology The application of either FACTOR ANALYSIS or PRINCIPAL COMPONENTS ANALYSIS to matrices of socio-economic, demographic and housing data for small intra-urban districts (see CENSUS TRACT) to test the hypothesis that the pattern of residential differentiation (see SEGREGATION) can be accounted for by a small number of general constructs. SOCIAL AREA ANALYSIS provides the framework within which factorial ecology was developed: it is generally applied inductively, thereby allowing the constructs to emerge from the data rather than testing for the existence of hypothesized relationships (other than in a qualitative sense of expecting certain broad patterns). Factorial ecology is thus a relatively sophisticated technology for describing the main elements of urban social structure in space, dependent for its outputs on the nature of the data input – almost invariably obtained from censuses.   RJJ

Suggested Reading
Davies, W. K. D. 1984: *Factorial ecology*. Aldershot: Gower.

Timms, D. W. G. 1969: *The urban mosaic*. Cambridge: Cambridge University Press.

factors of production
The ingredients necessary to the production process, i.e. those things that must be assembled at one place before production can begin. The three broad headings conventionally adopted are land, labour and capital. Sometimes the fourth factor of 'enterprise' is added, to recognize the contribution of the 'entrepreneur' or risk-taker and the legitimacy of a special return to this particular participant in the productive process. However, in the current complexity of economic organization it is hard to distinguish enterprise from general management functions, so this factor is more appropriately subsumed under labour. The combination of factors of production reflects the state of technology applied in the activity in question, e.g. whether it is capital-intensive or labour-intensive.

Land is necessary for any productive activity, whether it is agriculture, mining, manufacturing or services. Land may be a direct source of raw material, as is the case with mining. It may be required for the cultivation of a crop or to support the physical plant of a manufacturing activity. Modern industry requires increasing quantities of land, as factory sites and for associated uses such as storage, roadways and parking.

Labour requirements vary with the nature of the activity in question. Some need numerous unskilled workers while others require more skilled operatives, technicians, office personnel, etc. The availability of particular types of labour can have an important bearing on the location of economic activity. Despite the growing capital intensity of modern industry, cheap labour with a record of stability is still an attraction. That the value of production can ultimately be traced to the factor of labour is central to the LABOUR THEORY OF VALUE.

CAPITAL includes all things deliberately created by humans for the purpose of production. This includes the physical plant, buildings and machinery, i.e. fixed capital. It also includes the circulating capital in the form of stocks of raw materials, components, semi-finished goods, etc. Private ownership of capital and land is the major distinguishing feature of the capitalist mode of production, which carries with it important implications for the distribution of income and wealth.

The conventional categories of land, labour and capital (and enterprise) can serve an ideological role in legitimizing the differential rewards of the various contributors to production under capitalism. The concept of PRODUCTIVE FORCES is preferred in socialist economics. In any event, for practical purposes these broad categories tend to be subdivided into the individual inputs actually required in particular productive activities. (See MARXIAN ECONOMICS, NEOCLASSICAL ECONOMICS.)   DMS

Suggested Reading
Smith, D. M. 1981: *Industrial location: an economic geographical analysis*, second edition. New York: John Wiley.

falsification
The distinguishing principle of an empirical science, according to the philosophy of CRITICAL RATIONALISM. The progression of such a science involves the articulation of a THEORY which is evaluated empirically by creation of a critical test designed to refute it.   RJJ

family reconstitution
A technique of nominal linkage in demographic analysis. Family reconstitution creates accurate FERTILITY and MORTALITY rates from data about vital events (births, marriages and deaths): such data are sometimes available in cases in which the absence of a CENSUS inhibits the calculation of demographic measures. The researcher assembles all information relating to one marriage on a family reconstitution form: date of marriage, birth and death dates of spouses and of children, and socio-economic information (e.g. occupation). A range of measures may then be calculated, including age-at-marriage, proportion of adult males and females ever married, age-at-death, and childbirth patterns among women.

187

Two major, and linked, areas of complexity involve identifying the population covered by registers, and the interpretation of demographic measures obtained. The former problem is approached through 'observation rules'. These are conventions for deciding whether particular individuals are 'in observation' in a parish register at any given time, and are necessitated by the open nature of communities affected by high levels of local MIGRATION. For example, following a baptism it is necessary to know whether an infant continues to be resident, if that infant is to be used in calculating infant mortality rates. This is inferred according to the subsequent appearance in the register of other events relating to the same family. The significance of precise rules for establishing an individual's 'presence in observation' was first set out by Fleury and Henry (1956); see also Henry (1967). Henry's rules were adapted for English registers, available from 1538, by Wrigley (1966).

Obviously, measures which require data relating to an individual over many years use fewer data than those which require presence in observation for only a short period. Thus infant mortality rates are typically based upon 80 per cent or more of legitimate births, whereas age-at-marriage calculations rarely involve more than half of marriage partners, and age-specific fertility rates are typically based upon 15–20 per cent of legitimate births. Some debate surrounds the representativeness of the immobile population that remains in observation within a single parish, especially for topics requiring long observation periods of individual families (Schofield, 1972; Souden, 1984).

The main application of family reconstitution has been for pre-census Europe and colonial North America, and based on church registers of baptisms, marriages and burials (note that the first and last of these may not equate exactly with births and deaths). The procedures are very time-consuming, but some progress in computerizing them has been made at the ESRC Cambridge Group for the History of Population and Social Structure. By 1992, family reconstitutions for the whole parish register period had been completed for 25 English parishes, with reconstitutions for shorter time periods for numerous others.

These studies have indicated the predominance of natural fertility in preindustrial European and American populations, with only very limited family limitation before the late nineteenth century. They also enable the beginnings of analysis of long-run geographical variations in nuptiality, FERTILITY and MORTALITY, and comparisons with nineteenth-century CENSUS data (Wrigley and Schofield, 1983; Wilson, 1984; Woods and Wilson, 1991). Substantial geographical variations in marriage patterns and timing, and in infant mortality, are apparent.   PG

References

Fleury, M. and Henry, L. 1956: *Nouveau manuel de depouillement et d'exploitation de l'etat civil ancien.* Paris: Institut National d'Etudes Demographiques.

Henry, L. 1967: *Manuel de demographie historique.* Geneva: Libraire Droz.

Schofield, R. S. 1972: Representativeness and family reconstitution. *Annls dem. Hist.,* pp. 121–5.

Souden, D. 1984: Movers and stayers in family reconstitution populations. *Local Pop. Stud.* 33, pp. 11–27.

Wilson, C. 1984: Natural fertility in preindustrial England. *Pop. Stud.* 38, pp. 225–40.

Woods, R. and Wilson, C. 1991: Fertility in England: a long-term perspective. *Pop. Stud.* 45, pp. 399–415.

Wrigley, E. A. 1966: Family reconstitution. In Wrigley, E. A., ed., *An introduction to English historical demography.* London: Weidenfeld and Nicholson. pp. 96–159.

Wrigley, E. A. and Schofield, R. S. 1983: English population history from family reconstitutions: summary results 1600–1799. *Pop. Stud.* 37, pp. 157–84.

Suggested Reading

Knodel, J. 1988: *Demographic behaviour in the past: a study of fourteen German village populations in the eighteenth and nineteenth centuries.* Cambridge: Cambridge University Press.

Wrigley (1966).

Wrigley and Schofield (1983).

family types Families are units of kinsfolk within which decisions of everyday life are made; they are defined with respect to blood and marital relationships.

In almost all human societies, families form significant units of social recognition and social interaction, but the composition of 'the family' varies widely. Different family types vary in the number and proximity of kin involved in prevailing definitions of 'family' (Wall et al., 1983; Plakans, 1984).

An important distinction separates simple 'nuclear' families (those consisting of one or more parents with their children) from various 'extended' family types (where a nuclear family unit may be extended upwards or downwards to include three generations, or laterally to include the families of more than one sibling). Besides natural (i.e. biological) kinship, family types vary in respect of the senses in and degree to which family members are created by affinity (through marriage or illegitimate carnal unions); by legal kinship (adoption); or by spiritual kinship (through godparenthood).

Debates on family types overlap with debates on household composition, but these debates are not equivalent, because family and household unit need not be synonymous (in part depending on INHERITANCE SYSTEMS), and because household composition may vary through the family life-cycle (Flandrin, 1979).

The family also has an important symbolic role in cultural and political systems. Some claim that 'the family is best understood as a moral system' (Casey, 1989), although the household remains central to most conceptions of the family. The emotional/cultural significance of family ideals may not be directly related to prevailing patterns of family or household behaviour (Anderson, 1980). Some claim that variations in family structure and kinship structure condition geographical variations in social ideology and belief (Todd, 1985).   PG

References

Anderson, M. 1980: *Approaches to the history of the Western family*. London: Macmillan.

Casey, J. 1989: *The history of the family*. Oxford: Blackwell.

Flandrin, J.-L. 1979: *Families in former times: kinship, household and sexuality*. Cambridge: Cambridge University Press.

Plakans, A. 1984: *Kinship in the past: an anthropology of European family life 1500–1900*. Oxford: Blackwell.

Todd, E. 1985: *The explanation of ideology: family structures and social systems*. Oxford: Blackwell.

Wall, R. et al., eds 1983: *Family forms in historic Europe* Cambridge: Cambridge University Press.

Suggested Reading

Plakans (1984).

Wall et al (1983).

famine A relatively sudden event involving mass mortalities from starvation within a short period. Famine is typically distinguished from chronic hunger, understood as endemic nutritional deprivation on a persistent basis (as opposed to seasonal hunger, for example). Definitions of famine are fraught with danger because: (i) cultural, as opposed to biological, definitions of starvation vary around diverse, locally defined norms; and (ii) deaths from starvation are frequently impossible to distinguish from those of disease. However, the dynamics and characteristics of mass starvation have similar structural properties; typically, such famines involve sharp price increases for staple foodstuffs, decapitalization of household assets, gathering of wild foods, borrowing and begging, and out-migration (Watts, 1983).

Hunger, and famine in particular, is intolerable in the modern world because it is unnecessary and unwarranted (Sen and Dreze 1989). According to the Hunger Program at Brown University, famine casualities have been moving downward since 1945, but in the late 1980s states with a combined population of 200 millions failed to prevent famine within their national borders.

Famine causation has often been linked to natural disasters, population growth and war, producing a reduction in food supply. But some major famines (for example, Bengal in 1943) were not preceded by a significant decline in food production or absolute availability, and in some cases have been associated with food export. Recent analyses have focused on access to and control over food resources. Sen (1981) argues that what we eat depends on what food we are able to acquire. Famine therefore is a function of the failure of socially specific entitlements through which individuals command bundles of commodities. Entitlements vary in relation to property rights, asset distribution, CLASS and GENDER. Famine is therefore a social phenomenon rooted in the institutional and political economic arrangements which determine the access to food by different clases and strata. Mass poverty and mass starvation are obviously linked via entitlements. Mass poverty results from long-term changes in entitlements associated with social production and distribution mechanisms; famines arise from short-term changes in these same mechanisms. Famine and endemic deprivation correspond to two forms of public action to eradicate them: famine policy requires entitlement protection ensuring that they do not impact upon vulnerable groups (i.e. landless labourers, women). Chronic hunger demands entitlement promotion to expand the command that people have over basic necessities (Sen and Dreze, 1989). Since 1945 India has implemented a successful anti-famine policy, and yet has conspicuously failed to eradicate endemic deprivation; conversely, China has overcome the hunger problem, but failed to prevent massive famine in the 1950s. Africa has witnessed a catastrophic growth in the incidence of both mass starvation and chronic hunger.   MW

References

Sen, A. 1981: *Poverty and famines.* Oxford: Clarendon Press.

Sen, A. and Dreze, J. 1989: *Hunger and public action.* Oxford: Clarendon Press.

Watts, M. 1983: *Silent violence: food, famine and peasantry in northern Nigeria.* Berkeley, CA: University of California Press.

farm fragmentation The scattering of the fields of a farm, so that it is not composed of a single unit of land, and so that the fields are intermixed with those of other farms. Fragmentation can be the result of the fossilization of old open-field systems, of equal-inheritance practices, of piecemeal land reclamation, or of the commercial amalgamation of non-contiguous farm holdings. Chisholm (1979, ch. 3) has demonstrated the inefficiency of fragmentation. Plot consolidation into

farms or contiguous fields (often known by the French term *remembrement*) is usually sponsored or directed by governments: an historic form of such consolidation was ENCLOSURE. Fragmentation often involves settlement nucleation, while farm consolidation involves settlement dispersal, so that the farmstead is at the centre of its land (see SETTLEMENT CONTINUITY).

PEW/DBG

Reference

Chisholm, M. 1979: *Rural settlement and land use: an essay in location,* third edition. London: Hutchinson/Atlantic Highlands, NJ: Humanities Press.

Suggested Reading

Clout, H. D. 1984: *A rural policy for the EEC?* London: Methuen, pp. 102–17.

King, R. and Burton, S. 1982: Land fragmentation: notes on fundamental rural spatial problems. *Progr. hum. Geogr.* 6, pp. 475–94.

Smith, E. G. 1975: Fragmented farms in the United States. *Ann. Ass. Am. Geogr.* 65, pp. 58–70.

farming See DRY FARMING; MIXED FARMING; PART-TIME FARMING.

farming, type of The classification of farms or agricultural census areas on the basis of measurable attributes. The classes or types may also be mapped to give type of farming areas. An early deductive and qualitative classification of the world's agriculture into 13 classes or types, such as shifting, cultivation and nomadic herding, was based upon five attributes (Whittlesey, 1936); Weaver (1954) classified parts of the United States according to crop combinations. More recently farms and agricultural census areas have been assigned to types by determining the *dominant enterprise*; that is, the most important product or combination of related products. Importance has been measured either by the proportion of total work time devoted to that product or by the proportion of total net returns earned (Napolitan and Brown, 1962; Ministry of Agriculture, Fisheries and Food, 1963–1976, 1969; Church et al., 1968). A more complex approach has been to take a number of measurable attributes for each unit under consideration and use some statistical method to determine the grouping into types by similarity (Anderson, 1975: see CLASSIFICATION AND REGIONALIZATION). The most notable of such investigations is that by Jerzy Kostrowicki and colleagues in the International Geographical Union Commission for Agricultural Typology, who have attempted to produce a typography for the whole world (Kostrowicki, 1980, 1982). They have used 27 variables to produce six types of the first order, 30 of the second order and over 100 of the third order. The methodology has been applied to a number of countries, and a map of Europe has been produced (Asztalos et al., 1966; Kostrowicki and Szczesmy, 1972; Troughton, 1982.) DBG

References

Anderson, K. E. 1975: An agricultural classification of England and Wales. *Tijdschri. econ. soc. Geogr.* 66, pp. 148–58.

Asztalos, I., Enyedi, G., Sarfalvi, B. and Laslo, S. 1966: *Geographical types of Hungarian agriculture.* Budapest: Akadémiai.

Church, B. M., Boyd, D. A., Evans, J. A. and Sadler, J. I. 1968: A type of farming map based on agricultural census data. *Outlook on Agriculture,* 5, pp. 191–6.

Kostrowicki, J. 1980: A hierarchy of world types of agriculture. *Geogr. Pol.* 43, pp. 125–48.

Kostrowicki, J. 1982: The types of agriculture map of Europe. *Geogr. Pol.* 48, pp. 79–91.

Kostrowicki, J. and Szczesmy, R. 1972: *Polish agriculture: characteristics, types and regions* (in Hungarian). Budapest: Akadémiai.

Napolitan, L. and Brown, C. J. 1962: A type of farming classification of agricultural holdings in England and Wales according to enterprise patterns, *J. agric. Econ.* 15, pp. 595–617.

Ministry of Agriculture 1963–1976: *Farm classification in England and Wales.* London: ADAS.

Ministry of Agriculture, Fisheries and Food 1969: *Type of farming maps of England and Wales.* London: MAFF.

Troughton, M. J. 1982: *Canadian agriculture.* Budapest, Akadémiai Kiado.

Weaver, J. C. 1954: Crop combination regions in the Middle West. *Geogr. Rev.* 44, pp. 175–200.

Whittlesey, D. 1936: Major agricultural regions of the earth. *Ann. Ass. Am. Geogr* 26, pp. 199–240.

federalism A form of government in which central and regional authorities divide powers and functions, with the aim of maintaining a high degree of autonomy in the regional units. Federal systems are usually designed to prevent one level from dictating to the other as, at one extreme, with unitary government and, at another, with confederation. A written constitution serves to entrench this aim. Some matters such as foreign policy, defence and international trade are usually reserved for the central government, with all others, in theory, left in the hands of the regional units. This geographical division of functions is also often planned as a device to prevent the concentration of public POWER, especially when combined, as in the US case, with a divided central government (executive, legislature and judiciary). This can lead to charges of a system-wide lack of 'decisional focus' and the usurping of public power by the best organized private interests (Ollman and Birnbaum, 1990).

In practice federations vary widely. Some, such as the USSR under its 1936 Constitution, have been fictive rather than real. Most of those established in former colonies have foundered (e.g. the Central African Federation and the West Indian Federation). Interdependence rather than true separation of functions marks many others. Most have become more centralized over time as citizens have called upon central governments to establish equal rights (as in the US Civil Rights movement of the 1960s) or to engage in national redistributive policies (as in the US 'New Deal' of the 1930s). But certain others, particularly those with geographically concentrated ethnic groups (see ETHNICITY), have become more decentralized (e.g. Canada) or have broken up (e.g. Yugoslavia.) In the US since 1978 the regional units (the states) in general have become more assertive with respect to services, revenue collection and economic development. This trend was reinforced by the election in the 1980s of presidents who were ideologically committed to limiting the role of the central government and deregulating the national economy. Many of the states have since joined the central government in FISCAL CRISIS. JAA

Reference

Ollman, B. and Birnbaum, J. eds 1990: *The United States Constitution: 200 years of antifederalist, abolitionist, feminist, muckraking, progressive, and especially socialist criticism.* New York: New York University Press.

feedback The reciprocal effect in a SYSTEM, whereby a change in one variable (*A*) influences change in others (*B* and *C*, perhaps), which in turn influence change in *A*. The influences may be either negative or positive.

With negative feedback the system's EQUILIBRIUM is maintained, as in ECO-SYSTEMS: an increase in species *A*'s abundance, for example, may generate an increase in the number of predators (*B*) which feed on it; as a consequence, the availability of *A* is reduced, the number of *B* predators that can be sustained falls, and the system returns to its former state. Such a system is said to be *morphostatic*, and in a condition of dynamic equilibrium.

With positive feedback an increase in *A* stimulates an increase in *B*, which in turn stimulates a further increase in *A*, as in the MULTIPLIER process central to INPUT–OUTPUT analysis and in the process of CHAIN MIGRATION. Such a system is termed *morphogenetic*.

The example in the figure shows a system which has both morphogenetic and morphostatic feedback loops. The left-hand loop (P–G–B–D) is morphostatic: population growth induces disease, which subsequently limits population growth. The right-hand loop (P–M–C–P) is morphogenetic: a growing city is modernized, attracts more immigrants, and so grows even further. The two loops are also linked via variable *S*: as MODERNIZATION proceeds so there is greater control over disease and the negative checks are reduced – thereby presumably making the morphogenetic loop dominant and advancing the rate of population growth.   RJJ

Reference

Langton, J. 1972: Potentialities and problems of adopting a systems approach to the study of change in human geography. In C. Board et al., eds, *Progress in geography*, volume 4. London: Edward Arnold, pp. 125–79.

feminist geographies Perspectives that draw on feminist politics and theories to explore how GENDER relations AND GEOGRAPHIES are mutually structured and transformed. The tradition dates from the mid-1970s, drawing inspiration from the women's movements of the 1960s. Although there are distinctive strands, some common concerns cut across all feminist geographies.

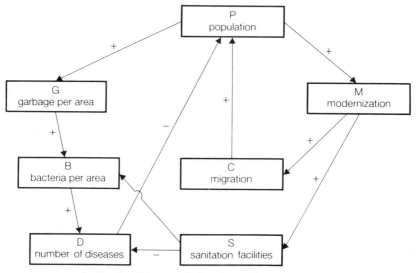

feedback *Urban population change* (Langton, 1972).

(a) First, they have developed as critical discourses, critical not only of women's oppression in society, but also of the various ways that this is reproduced in geographical theory. Reflecting their different theoretical and substantive starting points, each refutes a different aspect of geographical theory. This has built towards a comprehensive critique of geographical traditions: for example, POLITICAL GEOGRAPHY (Kofman and Peake, 1990); HISTORICAL GEOGRAPHY (Kay, 1990); SOCIAL AREA ANALYSIS and FACTORIAL ECOLOGY (Pratt and Hanson, 1988); GENTRIFICATION studies inspired by Weberian and MARXIST theory (Rose, 1984); and POSTMODERN geographies (Deutsche, 1991; Massey, 1991).

(b) Second, sexism within geographical institutions (in the teaching of geography, the staffing of academic departments, and through the publication process) has been a constant concern (Zelinsky, Monk and Hanson, 1982; McDowell, 1988).

(c) Third, most feminist geographers share a commitment to situating knowledge, to the view that interpretations are context-bound and partial, rather than detached and universal. This feeds into the discussion and use of QUALITATIVE METHODS. McDowell (1988) provides an excellent overview of the ways in which feminism structures the empirical research process, from shaping research questions to writing about and disseminating research findings.

(d) Fourth, feminist geographies trace the interconnections between all aspects of daily life, across the subdisciplinary boundaries of ECONOMIC, SOCIAL and, more recently, CULTURAL GEOGRAPHY.

Despite these common themes, there is a great deal of variation among feminist geographers. Bowlby et al. (1989) sketch a useful history of feminist geographies, in which they identify two breaks, one in the late 1970s and the other towards the end of the 1980s (see figure). The first break identified within feminist geography seems less decisive in the US, where the influence of the geography of women approach has been stronger.

The first task of feminist geographers was to make women visible, by developing a geography of women. Two points were made: women's experiences and perceptions often differ from those of men; and women have restricted access to a range of opportunities, from paid employment to services. This is largely an empirical tradition, loosely influenced by liberal feminism and WELFARE GEOGRAPHY. It has tended to focus on individuals, documenting how women's roles as caregivers and 'housewives', in conjunction with the existing urban SPATIAL STRUCTURE, housing design and policy, and patterns of accessibility to transport and other services such as childcare, conspire to constrain women's access to paid employment and other urban resources.

This geography of women approach has been criticized because gender inequality is typically explained in terms of the concept of gender roles, especially women's roles as housewives and mothers, in conjunction with some notion of spatial constraint. Foord and Gregson (1986) argue that the concept of gender roles narrows the focus to women (as opposed to male power and the relations between women and men), emerges out of a static social theory, and presents women as victims (as passive recipients of roles). Furthermore, although the geography of women shows how spatial constraint and separation enters into the construction of women's position, it provides a fairly narrow reading of space, conceived almost exclusively as distance (e.g. the journey to work, the separation of SUBURBS from paid employment). Little consideration has been given to variations in gender relations across places. However, there has been a very useful, pragmatic planning component to this literature which suggests ways in which to restructure the city so as to reduce gender inequalities (Wekerle, 1984). Frustrations with attempts to implement some of these reforms have led to critical reconsiderations of the limits of liberal feminism and towards a fuller institutional analysis (Wekerle, 1984), confirming Eisenstein's (1981) point that the practical and theoretical limits of liberalism are frequently discovered by liberal feminists themselves.

Socialist feminist geographers have reworked Marxian categories and theory to

PHASE ONE: THE GEOGRAPHY OF WOMEN (mid- to late 1970s)

topical focus:	theoretical influences:	geographical focus:
description of the effects of gender inequality	welfare geography, liberal feminism	constraints of distance and spatial separation

PHASE TWO: SOCIALIST-FEMINIST GEOGRAPHY (early to late 1980s)

topical focus:	theoretical influences:	geographical focus:
explanation of gender inequality, and relation between capitalism and patriarchy	Marxism, socialist feminism	spatial separation, place, localities

PHASE THREE: POSTCOLONIAL FEMINIST GEOGRAPHIES (late 1980s to present)

topical focus:	theoretical influences:	geographical focus:
the construction of gendered identities, differences among women, gender and nature, gender and nationalism	cultural, poststructural, postcolonial, psychoanalytical theories; writings of women of colour, lesbian women, gay men, women from 'developing' countries	microgeographies of the body, distance, separation, place, imaginative and symbolic spaces, colonialism, environment

feminist geographies

explain the interdependence of geography, gender relations and economic development under CAPITALISM (see MARXIST GEOGRAPHY). One of the key theoretical debates within socialist feminist geography has revolved around the question of how best to articulate gender and CLASS analyses. At its most abstract, the question has been addressed in terms of PATRIARCHY and capitalism, and the relative autonomy of the two systems (Foord and Gregson, 1986; McDowell, 1986).

Socialist feminist geographers have worked mostly at the urban and regional scales. At the urban scale, the social and spatial separation of suburban homes from paid employment is seen as crucial to the day-to-day and generational reproduction of workers and the development and continuation of 'traditional' gender relations in capitalist societies (MacKenzie and Rose, 1983: see SUBURB). Efforts have been made to read these processes in non-functionalist terms and as strategies to manage the effects of a capitalist economy. For example, MacKenzie and Rose argue that the isolation of women as housewives in suburban locations emerged from the combined influence of working-class household strategies, governmental policy and male power within families and trade unions. Attempts to break away from strictly economistic and functionalist explanations have led some socialist feminists to explore links to HUMANISTIC GEOGRAPHY and STRUCTURATION THEORY (MacKenzie, 1989).

Socialist feminist geographers have been increasingly attentive to the ways in which gender relations differ from place to place and not only reflect but partially determine local economic changes. At the urban scale,

Nelson (1986) argues that employers of clerical workers in the US are now moving to suburban locations to gain access to middle-class, suburban 'housewives' who are willing to work for relatively low wages on a part-time basis. Broadly similar arguments, about the importance of local gender relations and the attractions of cheaper, female labour for industrial and geographical restructuring, have been made at the regional scale (Massey, 1984), in studies that have been influenced by the LOCALITIES tradition.

Since the late 1980s, feminist geographers have moved away from an exclusive focus on gender and class systems and the modernist debates typical of socialist feminists. This new phase can be identified as postcolonial feminist geography (see POSTCOLONIALISM). It has three characteristics. First, the category of gender is contested and expanded beyond the man/woman duality. Feminist geographers are increasingly attentive to the differences in the construction of gender relations across races, ethnicities, religions, sexual orientations and nationalities, and to exploitative relations among women who are positioned in varying ways along these multiple axes of difference (McDowell, 1991). Secondly, postcolonial feminist geographers are drawing on a broader range of social, and particularly cultural, theory, including psychoanalysis and POSTSTRUCTURALISM, in order to develop a fuller understanding of how gender relations and identities are shaped and assumed (see SEXUALITY AND GEOGRAPHY; SUBJECTIVITY, HUMAN). As one consequence, theoretical differences among feminist geographers are much more obvious than in the past. Third, there has been a more explicit shift away from objectivist epistemologies through the espousal of situated knowledge claims (see EPISTEMOLOGY). A key area of discussion concerns the distinction between relativism and *situated knowledge* (Haraway, 1991), and ways in which to reconcile partial perspectives with commitments to political action and social change.

New areas, some of which entail different conceptions of geography and space, are receiving attention. A body of writing is developing around gender and cultural REPRESENTATION, which extends the focus to imaginative and symbolic spaces. Norwood and Monk (1987) explore the landscape perceptions of women writers and the gendering of the American Southwest landscape in textual representations. Pollock (1988) reads the visual spaces created by female and male modernist painters through the lens of gender and class: not only did male and female modernist painters develop different spatial orders in their paintings, but male painters battled over their sexuality through the representation of female bodies. There is a vast literature in film studies, as yet untapped by feminist geographers, on distance, space, filmic representations and the problematic of women as spectators (Doane, 1987). Bondi (1991) draws on Lacan to explore the ways in which gender identities are embedded in and reproduced through language. Some feminist geographers have scrutinized geographers' own representations: Domosh (1991) examines the exclusionary narratives constructed by historians of geography and Deutsche (1991) and Massey (1991) are critical of disembodied and sexist representations of postmodern geographies (cf. POSTMODERNISM. Although little has yet been published, feminist geographers are also expanding their consideration of geography to include environmental concerns – this area is likely to receive much more attention in coming years.   GP

References

Bondi, L. 1991: In whose words? On gender identities and speaking positions. Paper presented at the AAG Annual Conference, Miami, April.

Bowlby, S., Lewis, J., McDowell, L. and Foord, J., 1989: The geography of gender. In Peet, R. and Thrift, N. eds, *New models in geography*, volume 2. London: Unwin Hyman, pp. 157–75.

Deutsche, R. 1991: Boys town. *Environ. Plann. D: Society and Space* 9, pp. 5–30.

Doane, M. A. 1987: *The desire to desire.* Bloomington: Indiana University Press.

Domosh, M. 1991: Towards a feminist historiography of geography. *Trans. Inst. Br. Geogr*, n.s. 16, pp. 95–104.

Eisenstein, Z. 1981: *The radical future of liberal feminism.* New York: Longman.

Foord, J. and Gregson, N. 1986: Patriarchy: towards a reconceptualisation. *Antipode* 18(2), pp. 186–211.

Haraway, D. 1991: Situated knowledges: the science question in feminism and the privilege of partial perspective. In her *Simians, cyborgs, and women: the reinvention of nature*. New York: Routledge, pp. 183–201.

Kay, J., 1990: The future of historical geography in the United States. *Ann. Ass. Am. Geogr.* 80, pp. 618–21.

Kofman, E. and Peake, L., 1990: Into the 1990's: a gendered agenda for political geography: *Pol. Geogr. Q.* 9, pp. 313–36.

MacKenzie, S. 1989: Restructuring the relations of work and life: women as environmental actors, feminism as geographic analysis. In Kobayashi, A. and MacKenzie, S., eds, *Remaking human geography*. Boston: Unwin Hyman, pp. 40–61.

MacKenzie, S. and Rose, D. 1983: Industrial change, the domestic economy and home life. In Anderson, J. et al., eds, *Redundant spaces in cities and regions*. New York: Academic Press.

McDowell, L. 1986: Beyond patriarchy: a class-based explanation of women's subordination. *Antipode* 18(3), pp. 311–21.

McDowell, L. 1988: Coming in from the dark: qualitative feminist research in geography. In Eyles, J. and Smith, D. M. eds, *Research in Human Geography*. Oxford: Basil Blackwell, pp. 155–73.

McDowell, L., 1991: The baby and the bath water: diversity, deconstruction and feminist theory in geography. *Geoforum* 22, pp. 123–33.

Massey, D. 1984: *Spatial divisions of labor*. New York: Methuen.

Massey, D. 1991: Flexible sexism. *Environ. Plann. D: Society and Space* 9, pp. 31–57.

Nelson, K. 1986: Female labor supply characteristics and the suburbanization of low-wage office work. In Scott, A. and Storper, M. eds, *Production, work, territory: the geographical anatomy of industrial capitalism*. London: Allen and Unwin.

Norwood, V. and Monk, J. eds 1987: *The desert is no lady: southwestern landscapes in women's writing and art*. New Haven: Yale University Press.

Pollock, G. 1988: *Vision and difference*. London: Routledge.

Pratt, G. and Hanson, S. 1988: Gender, class and space. *Environ. Plann. D: Society and Space* 6, pp. 15–35.

Rose, D. 1984: Rethinking gentrification: beyond the uneven development of marxist urban theory. *Environ. Plann. D: Society and Space* 1, pp. 47–74.

Wekerle, G. 1984: A woman's place is in the city. *Antipode* 16(3), pp. 11–19.

Zelinsky, W., Monk, J. and Hanson, S. 1982: Women and geography: a review and prospectus. *Progr. hum. Geogr.* 6, pp. 317–66.

fertility The number of live births produced by a woman. Fertility is generally distinguished from *fecundity*, a biological term used to express the ability of a female to conceive. Fertility, MORTALITY and MIGRATION are the three fundamental influences on population size in any area. Although they have recognized the importance of spatial variations in fertility, geographers have made relatively few contributions to research in this field. Demographers, on the other hand, have developed sophisticated measures of fertility and have made considerable progress towards establishing and explaining fertility trends in both developed and developing countries. Fertility behaviour is still imperfectly understood, however, and projections are problematic.

Measures of fertility range from the very simple to the very complex. A general distinction may be drawn between *period fertility* and *cohort fertility*. The former is the most straightforward and relates to the study of births occurring to all females in their reproductive period, i.e. to groups of females of given ages at a certain point in time or over a relatively short period. The latter is used to trace the reproductive history of a group of females who were born or married at the same time, so illuminating the ways in which families are built up through time, plus changes in completed family size and the spacing of births. The cohort approach requires long series of accurate vital statistics and so is most commonly applied to the populations of developed countries in the twentieth century (see COHORT).

The most simple and widely used fertility measure is the *crude birth rate*, which expresses the number of live births in a given period as a ratio of the average total population alive during that period in parts per 1000. Crude birth rates vary from about 10 to 55 per 1000, the latter being an estimate of the biological maximum. The crude birth rate has the advantage of being easy to calculate and is one element in the basic demographic equation of birth, death and migration for any areas, but it may be an extremely misleading measure of underlying fertility patterns, because of variations in age structure in the base population. Other more sophisticated measures have therefore been devised. The simplest is the *general fertility rate*, or the number of births per 1000 women in the fecund ages (defined variously as 15–49 or 15–44). The *marital fertility rate*, on the other hand, expresses the number of legitimate live births per 1000 married women. These rates are thus useful in relating births to the actual section of the population responsible for them. A further refinement is the *age-specific fertility rate*, defined as the number of births to a specified age-group per 1000 women in those ages, usually taken in five-year periods. This allows more detailed analysis and comparisons of fertility experiences. The *total fertility rate* tells us how many children on average each 1000 women have while passing through their fecund years. In the developed world, a rate of 2.1 children per women is necessary to ensure replacement of generations (see REPLACEMENT RATES). Replacement may also be measured by the *gross reproduction rate*, the average number of daughters produced by a woman during her reproductive lifetime, and the *net reproduction rate*, where mortality is taken into account. A net reproduction rate greater than 1.0 ensures replacement of one generation by the next. Of the cohort fertility measures, completed family size is the most useful, expressing the average number of children ever born to women currently aged 45 or over.

Factors affecting fertility levels have given rise to much discussion. The general ideas of the DEMOGRAPHIC TRANSITION have been only partially acceptable, given recent fertility behaviour in both developed and developing nations. Explanations have been sought in relation both to the long-term decline of fertility over the past two centuries in much of the developed world and to cross-cultural variations in contemporary fertility patterns. Fertility is linked to other aspects of demographic behaviour, to mortality and particularly to marriage

patterns, for age at marriage and overall NUPTIALITY are important. Explanations of fertility decline in Europe, which began in France in the later eighteenth century, have been sought in the broad pattern of URBANIZATION, INDUSTRIALIZATION and MODERNIZATION, which changed attitudes to birth control, marriage and family formation and were associated with, for example, higher levels of education and changes in religious attitudes. Interestingly, other links, for example with issues raised in FEMINIST GEOGRAPHY, have been slow to develop; although for a Marxist critique, see Seccombe (1983).

Considerable geographical variations in fertility exist within states today, and these too have been related to a very broad series of factors, including social and occupational status, rural or urban residence, education, religion and the changing role of women in society. Great care must be taken in analysing fertility trends in the THIRD WORLD. Because of less complete sources, it is difficult to estimate accurately even recent trends, and there is no guarantee that relationships postulated for developed countries hold true either to explain the past or to predict future trends. Certainly fertility levels, and their geographical variations, represent one of the most important fields for research in population studies.   PEO

Reference
Seccombe, W. 1983: Marxism and demography, *New Left Rev.* 137, pp. 22–47.

Suggested Reading
Andorka, R. 1978: *Determinants of fertility in advanced societies.* London: Methuen/ New York: Free Press.

Jones, H. R. 1990: *Population geography*, second edition. London: Paul Chapman.

Lutz, W., ed. 1990: *Future demographic trends in Europe and North America.* London: Academic Press, part 2.

Tilly, C., ed. 1978: *Historical studies of changing fertility.* Princeton, NJ: Princeton University Press.

Woods, R. I. 1979: *Population analysis in geography.* London: Longman.

feudalism A term used in the analysis of pre-capitalist societies, especially in

Europe, with senses ranging from a broad type of social formation (originating within Marxist analyses, but variously defined therein) to a narrower definition based on legal terminology formulated by nineteenth-century legal historians (Postan, 1983). Indeed, the range of contexts to which the label is applied enrages some, who advocate its abandonment (Brown, 1974). The earlier formulations focused on the 'fief' (see below) and whether notional military obligations were realized, but this focus has largely passed out of use. So too have identifications of feudalism with subsistence society as opposed to capitalist production for profit through market exchange (e.g. Wallerstein, 1974).

The broadening of definitions reflects twentieth-century interest in comparative history, and has been much stimulated by analyses relating the emergence of agrarian CAPITALISM to the decline of feudalism (Kula, 1976; Martin, 1983; Dodgshon, 1987). Were the decline of feudalism and the rise of agrarian capitalism (Hilton, 1976; Holton, 1985; Glennie, 1987) two separate phenomena, or two facets of a single process?

In its most general sense, feudalism possesses, in common with other pre-capitalist social formations, two component social groups. One group comprises direct producers (peasants, broadly speaking) who maintain direct (i.e. non-market) access to the means of production (land, tools, seedcorn and livestock), even though they may not legally own them (especially land). Direct producers are subject to politico-legal domination by a second group, of social superiors who form a status hierarchy headed by a monarch. The monarch ultimately owns all land, but landownership is effectively decentralized through Crown land grants to feudal lords, in return for military and political support. Thus social RELATIONS OF PRODUCTION are not defined primarily through markets (as under CAPITALISM). And the means by which direct producers' surplus is extracted by social superiors differ from social formations such as slavery.

The key social relationships in feudalism were vassalage and serfdom. *Vassalage* was an intra-elite relationship by which a subordinate vassal held landed property, the 'fief' (Latin *feodum, feudum,* hence feudalism), from a lord, ultimately the Crown, in return for military service required by the Crown. The Crown's vassals were tenants-in-chief, who in turn sub-infeudated their estates to raise their own military service. Thus a hierarchy of tenants came to 'own' estates of various sizes, composed of territorial jurisdictions called manors.

Serfdom was the legal subjection of peasant tenants to lords through lords' manorial jurisdictions, of which unfree tenants were legally held to be part. Dependent peasant tenants held land from their lord in return for varying combinations of money rents and services in kind, especially labour services on the lord's own land, the demesne. The legal dependence of tenants enabled feudal lords both to extract higher than market rents from their tenants and to impose a range of other dues. These feudal dues included heriot (a tenant's best animal, payable on inheritance); and licences to marry, to migrate, to mill or to brew ale. Tenants were fined at a manorial court if these activities were carried out without appropriate licence, and courts also exercised a degree of moral regulation (Bonfield, 1985).

The level of rents and dues, it is held, were set more by lords' income requirements than by market forces, although lords gained from the latter, as population growth made land scarce relative to labour. Seigneurial income requirements progressively increased as lords competed for political status through conspicuous consumption. Moreover, since feudal lords could raise income from intensified surplus-extraction, they were comparatively indifferent to innovations to raise agricultural productivity, which explains why feudalism was characterized by relatively stagnant technology (see BRENNER DEBATE). Implied here is a strong view about the explanatory value of the geography of manorialism (estate size and fragmentation, seigneurial character), and of lord–tenant struggle, in accounting for geographical diversity in population density, agricultural systems and productivity, and standards of living (Hilton, 1973;

Dyer, 1989; Hallam, 1989; Campbell, 1990). This is currently an active research area, also stimulated by the Brenner debate (Aston and Philpin, 1985; Campbell, 1991).

As lordly surplus extraction intensified, and medieval European populations grew (for reasons as yet imperfectly understood), feudal society exhibited certain CRISIS tendencies, because the surplus removal process failed to generate any significant feedback into the productive capacity of agriculture through investment. A crisis of social reproduction was inevitable since (Hilton, 1985, p. 244):

In the first place, production for the market and the stimulus of competition only affected a very narrow sector of the economy. Secondly, agricultural and industrial production were based on the household unit and the profits of small peasant and small artisan enterprise were taken by landowners and usurers. Thirdly, the social structure and the habits of the landed nobility did not permit accumulation for investment for the extension of production.

However, vigorous discussions continue on the relative importance of excessive surplus-extraction and of medieval agriculture's ecological frailties (emphasized by the POSTAN THESIS) in medieval agrarian contraction.

The quoted passage from Hilton also leads into other important research areas in HISTORICAL GEOGRAPHY. One is the extent of commercialization within medieval agrarian economies, and its geographical impact (Campbell and Power, 1992). It is now recognized that towns and trade were an integral part of the feudal economy, not an exogenous factor automatically solvent of feudal social relations (Langton and Hoppe, 1983; Hilton, 1985).

There has been a general move to more sophisticated theorizations, which broaden analysis of feudal society beyond property relations. Greater attention has been paid to accumulation and differentiation within the class of primary producers (Poos, 1991). Important developments in social technologies changed the geographical structuring of feudal society. Over time, status came to be increasingly embodied in property, rather than in interpersonal relations. Notable geographical compon-

ents stemmed from this shift, including new legal, fiscal and administrative technologies to control time and space (Clanchy, 1979; Bean, 1989; Biddick, 1990). Finally, certain social continuities across the feudalism–capitalism transition, especially in the functioning of geo-demographic and cultural systems, have begun to receive serious attention (Poos, 1991).   PG

References

Aston, T. H. and Philpin, C. E., eds 1985: *The Brenner debate: agrarian class structure and economic development in pre-industrial Europe*. Cambridge: Cambridge University Press.

Bean, J. M. W. 1989: *From lord to patron: lordship in late-medieval England*. Manchester: Manchester University Press.

Biddick, K. 1990: People and things: power in early English development. *Comp. Stud. Soc. Hist.* 32, pp. 3–23.

Bonfield, L., 1985: The nature of customary law in the manor courts of medieval England. *Comp. Stud. Soc. Hist.* 31, pp. 514–34.

Brown, E. A. R. 1974: The tyranny of a construct: feudalism and historians of medieval Europe. *Am. Hist. Rev.* 37, pp. 1063–88.

Campbell, B. M. S. 1990: People and land in the middle ages, 1066–1500. In Butlin, R. and Dodgshon, R., eds, *An historical geography of England and Wales*, second edition. London: Academic Press, pp. 69–122.

Campbell, B. M. S. 1991: Land, labour, livestock, and productivity trends in English seignorial agriculture 1208–1450. In Campbell, B. M. S. and Overton, M., eds, *Land, labour and livestock: historical studies in European agricultural productivity*. Manchester: Manchester University Press, pp. 144–82.

Campbell, B. M. S. and Power, J. 1992: Cluster analysis and the classification of medieval demesne-farming systems. *Trans. Inst. Br. Geogr.*, n.s. 17, pp. 227–45.

Clanchy, M. T. 1979: *From memory to written record: England 1066–1307*. London: Edward Arnold.

Dodgshon, R. A. 1987: *The European past: social evolution and spatial order*. London: Macmillan.

Dyer, C. 1989: *Standards of living in the later middle ages: social change in England c. 1200–1520*. Cambridge: Cambridge University Press.

Glennie, P. D. 1987: The transition from feudalism to capitalism as a problem for historical geography. *J. hist. Geogr.* 13, pp. 296–302.

Hallam, H. E., ed. 1989: *The agrarian history of England and Wales*, volume II, 1042–1350. Cambridge: Cambridge University Press.

Hilton, R. H. 1973: *Bond men made free: medieval peasant movements and the English rising of 1381*. London: Temple Smith.

Hilton, R. H., ed. 1976: *The transition from feudalism to capitalism*. London: Verso.

Hilton, R. H. 1985: *Class conflict and the crisis of feudalism: essays in medieval social history*. London: Hambledon Press.

Holton, R. J. 1985: *The transition from feudalism to capitalism*. London: Macmillan.

Kula, W. 1976: *An economic theory of the feudal system*. London: New Left Books.

Langton, J. and Hoppe, G. 1983: *Town and country in the development of early modern western Europe*. Cheltenham: HGRG Historical Geography Research Series.

Martin, J. E. 1983: *Feudalism to capitalism: peasant and landlord in English agrarian development*. London: Macmillan.

Poos, L. 1991: *A rural society after the Black Death: late-medieval Essex*. Cambridge: Cambridge University Press.

Postan, M. 1983: Feudalism and its decline: a semantic exercise. In Aston, T. H. et al., eds, *Social relations and ideas: essays in honour of R. H. Hilton*. Cambridge: Cambridge University Press, pp. 73–87.

Wallerstein, I. 1974: *The modern world system I: capitalist agriculture and the origins of the European world-economy in the sixteenth century*. London: Academic Press.

Suggested Reading

Bloch, M. 1961: *Feudal society*. London: Routledge.

Dodgshon (1987).

Dyer (1989).

Hilton (1985).

Martin (1983).

field system The fields and other agricultural lands of a community considered as a functioning whole. Field systems vary in several ways, including the character of LAND TENURE, the sets of rules through which agricultural activities were coordinated, and the physical disposition of land holdings. Particular importance attaches to the scope of individual control and of social coordination, in land ownership, use rights and in agricultural decision-making. Many traditional societies have been dominated by complex co-operative systems of rights over both arable land (especially in 'open field' systems, in which the holdings of individuals were scattered) and pasture, and have been much altered by ENCLOSURE which redefined field systems in more individualistic terms.

The rise of POLITICAL ECONOMY approaches within human geography has helped to focus attention on field systems as spatial expressions of social POWER relations. For historical and contemporary geographers, important debates surround at least five questions: first, about the origins of different types of field systems, and their connection with familial, social and territorial forms; second, about their development trajectories, and the extent to which they were flexible and able to evolve, or inflexible and resistant to non-revolutionary change; third, about how field systems functioned as channels of social control over agricultural production; fourth, about the relationship between different types of field system and processes and rates of agricultural change; and fifth, about connections between field systems and rural standards of living and poverty.   PG

fieldwork A traditional means of data collection within geography, based on the assumption that reality is present in appearance (see EMPIRICISM), and can therefore be directly apprehended through observation (see REALISM). In quantitative human geography (see QUANTITATIVE METHODS) this view is epitomized in the implementation of sample QUESTIONNAIRE surveys of people's attributes, attitudes, actions, aspirations and motivations. Such surveys may be conducted in person or by post, and depend for success on a relatively high response rate from a random sample of households (see SAMPLING). This quantitative approach regards social data as analogous to the raw material of much of natural science: something which is discrete and stable and exists independently of the analyst, and which therefore yields findings which could be replicated and verified by others. Such fieldwork is part of the practical project of empirical-analytical science, and is generally used to establish cause and effect relationships in order to predict and control the future.

However, there is an alternative view of fieldwork, associated with the advent of HUMANISTIC GEOGRAPHY and with the rediscovery of meaning. This philosophy requires an approach more akin to the CASE STUDY methods of anthropology than to the statistical generalizations of positivistic social science. Within this tradition, fieldwork is preocupied with the project of understanding and communication rather than with the goal of prediction and intervention. The generalizations arising from this approach are not, therefore, of a statistical nature, and the validity of the approach does not hinge on the randomness or typicality of the cases selected for study. Such research often takes the form of PARTICIPANT OBSERVATION, written up in the form of ethnographic description (see ETHNOGRAPHY), although it may also include in-depth individual or group INTERVIEWING. These QUALITATIVE METHODS all locate social scientists within, rather than apart from, the social world, and acknowledge that 'reality' is constructed – not uncovered – through the research process. SJS

filtering A process of NEIGHBOURHOOD change whereby housing passes from one social group to another. Most filtering involves relatively old housing in an area moving down the social scale: as the former inhabitants move out to better-quality dwellings, their previous homes become relatively cheaper and so accessible to lower-income groups. Thus the full filtering process involves the highest-income groups moving to new homes, thereby initiating a rippling process whereby all homes, and thus (to the extent that they are homogeneous) all NEIGHBOURHOODS, are moved down the income scale: this should release the lowest-quality homes at the end of the process for demolition, if the rate of new building for the rich at least equals the total demand for new homes in the system. If new homes are constructed on the urban periphery, then the filtering process ripples inwards towards the city centre, with every income group moving out one neighbourhood (as proposed in the original SECTORAL MODEL).

Filtering is a continuous process, with at any time some neighbourhoods being mixed in their composition until the shift from one occupant group to another is complete. It may be 'interrupted' by the construction of new housing for middle-income groups, who release neighbourhoods somewhere in the centre of the idealized sequence, or by the construction of public housing for lower-income groups: it may be initiated by pressure for more housing among the lower-income groups at the centre of the city, as in the INVASION AND SUCCESSION process associated with the ZONAL MODEL.

One widely remarked deviation from the general process of filtering, which associates newer housing with higher-income groups, is GENTRIFICATION, whereby higher income groups reoccupy and regenerate older housing in attractive INNER-CITY districts.

According to some writers, the operation of filtering mechanisms ensures that the housing needs of all, including the poor and otherwise disadvantaged, are met through market structures. The existence of HOMELESSNESS in many cities and of poor-quality housing for the less affluent in most (see SLUM) leads critics to argue that filtering rarely succeeds in providing adequate housing for all: hence the need for government subsidies and various forms of 'social housing' (see HOUSING STUDIES). RJJ

Suggested Reading
Gray, F. and Boddy, M. 1979: The origins and use of theory in urban geography: household mobility in filtering theory. *Geoforum* 10, pp. 117–27.

Johnston, R. J. 1971: *Urban residential patterns.* London: Bell.

fiscal crisis The tendency for a government's expenditure to increase more rapidly than its income from taxation and other sources. Any budget deficit could thus be labelled a fiscal crisis; O'Connor's (1973) classic study argues that a fiscal crisis of the state is a logical consequence of the evolution of monopoly CAPITALISM.

According to O'Connor – following Habermas, Offe and other theorists – the STATE (see also STATE APPARATUS) has two main functions within a capitalist economy: to promote successful accumulation strategies for private capitals, and to ensure their legitimation. The former involves it in providing social capital, such as the physical infrastructure within which enterprises operate and the trained labour force which they require. For the latter function, it promotes social harmony through social expenses on items such as welfare services and the maintenance of law and order. O'Connor argues that with monopoly capitalism an increasing proportion of investment costs must be met by the state, while at the same time legitimation of the problems created by monopolies also demands greater expenditure. Thus the state must spend more, relative to GNP. To do so, it must tax more heavily, which, by discouraging investment and enterprise, can counter its pro-accumulation policies. Increasing demands on the state – from both capital (for social capital) and labour (for social expenses) – outpace its ability to meet them, stimulating a fiscal crisis. To counter it, social expenses may be cut (especially on the welfare state), while more is spent on using the ideological and repressive components of the STATE APPARATUS to protect accumulation (for an extension of these arguments, see Held, 1987).

In several countries the greatest pressure involved in a fiscal crisis is felt at the LOCAL STATE level, which is allocated particular responsibility for welfare service provision (see DUAL THEORY OF THE STATE: see also Newton, 1980). This has been very apparent in the 1980s – in the UK and in New Zealand, for example (Johnston, 1992) – as governments seek to tackle the crisis by 'rolling back the frontiers of the state' and promoting PRIVATIZATION and DEREGULATION. (See CRISIS.)   RJJ

References and Suggested Reading

Held, D. 1987: *Models of democracy*. Cambridge: Polity Press.

Johnston, R. J. 1992: The internal operations of the state. In P. J. Taylor, ed., *The political geography of the twentieth century*. London: Belhaven Press, pp. 115–70.

Newton, K. 1980: *Balancing the books*. Beverly Hills, CA: Sage.

O'Connor, J. 1973: *The fiscal crisis of the state*. New York: St Martin's Press.

fiscal migration A MIGRATION undertaken for fiscal advantage, usually to reduce the level of taxation paid. Such migration occurs at all spatial scales. Within an urban area with fragmented local government, for example, according to the TIEBOUT MODEL land users should move to that administration which optimizes their 'tax/service package'. Internationally, different STATES offer similar variations in packages the potentials of which are especially realized by the affluent who are seeking tax havens and by MULTINATIONAL CORPORATIONS. Within countries, the reduction of tax burdens in some areas to stimulate investment can similarly attract firms that wish to reduce their tax bills and for which the costs of the move are far outweighed by the financial advantages gained. (See also ENTERPRISE ZONE.)   RJJ

flexible accumulation A collection of industrial technologies, labour practices, inter-firm relations and consumption patterns characterized by the pursuit of greater flexibility. Borrowing from the REGULATION SCHOOL of political economy, Harvey (1988) identifies this idea with a new REGIME OF ACCUMULATION:' "Flexible accumulation", as I shall call it, is marked by a direct confrontation with the rigidities of FORDISM. It rests on a startling flexibility with respect to labor processes, labor markets, products, and patterns of consumption. It is characterized by the emergence of entirely new sectors of production, new ways of providing financial services, new markets, and, above all, greatly intensified rates of commercial, technological, and organizational innovation'. Adopted in response to the increasing rigidities of the classical Fordist era (particularly rigid rules for the deployment and remuneration of labour, rigid, dedicated machinery, and the rigid organizational structures of large industrial corporations), these practices are seen by Harvey and others as constituting a set of responses to the productivity slowdown, increasing competition from Third World industrialization, and the saturation and fragmentation of home markets that characterized North American and European economies beginning in the late 1960s and early 1970s. Scott (1988) adds that this emergent regime is also 'focused . . . on the search for *external* ECONOMIES OF SCALE in the organization of the industrial apparatus'. The desire to circumvent labour market rigidities and to exploit EXTERNAL ECONOMIES has, according to Scott, produced major shifts in the geography of capitalist production, consisting of 'the twofold tendency (a) to a definite spatial *reagglomeration* of production in selected areas, combined with (b) active evasion of labor pools dominated now or in the recent past by Fordist industry'. However, while this would imply that flexible accumulation is associated primarily with 'new industrial spaces . . . comprehended as *transactions-intensive agglomerations of human labor and social activity*' (Scott, 1988), it is also true that some firms in older industrial regions (notably within the automotive industry) are adopting more flexible methods in an attempt to respond to intensified competition pressures. (See also ECONOMIES OF SCOPE; INDUSTRIAL GEOGRAPHY; JUST-IN-TIME PRODUCTION; LOCATION THEORY; POST-FORDISM; PRODUCTION COMPLEX; TRANSACTIONAL ANALYSIS.)   MSG

References

Harvey, D. 1988: The geographical and geopolitical consequences of the transition from Fordist to flexible accumulation. In Sternlieb, G. and Hughes, J. W., eds, *America's new market geography*. New Brunswick, NJ: Rutgers Center for Urban Policy Research, pp. 101–34.

Scott, A. J. 1988: *New industrial spaces*. London: Pion.

footloose industry   An industry which can locate virtually anywhere because it has no strong MATERIAL ORIENTATION or MARKET ORIENTATION in its locational requirements and very wide SPATIAL MARGINS; transport usually involves only a small proportion of its total cost structure.   RJJ

forces of production   See PRODUCTIVE FORCES.

Fordism   A set of industrial and broader societal practices associated with the workplace innovations pioneered by Henry Ford in Detroit, Michigan in the second decade of the twentieth century. In its original usage, Gramsci (1971) wrote of 'Americanism and Fordism' in his description of Ford's strategy to reorganize shopfloor production while at the same time forging a new relationship with his workers. Automobile production was being revolutionized through the use of the mass-production assembly lines and application of the principles of TAYLORISM to organize workers' tasks (with higher productivity and internal ECONOMIES OF SCALE producing a cheaper final product). At the same time, Ford hoped that by paying his workers a high wage commensurate with their enhanced PRODUCTIVITY, and by shortening the working day to eight hours, he could create an efficient workforce with a stable family life and incomes large enough to acquire the very products they themselves were producing.

More recently, members of the REGULATION SCHOOL of political economy have used 'Fordism' to describe a broader system of social relations transcending the practices of any single firm. Here, the Fordist REGIME OF ACCUMULATION refers to a period stretching roughly from the end of the Second World War to the mid-1970s. The era was, in this view, characterized by the widespread mass production of standardized goods using inflexible, dedicated machinery, exploitation of internal scale economies, a Taylorist fragmentation and deskilling of work, and relatively narrow and rigidly defined job descriptions. The key to this regime's sustained success was a unique and unprecedented social compromise struck between workers and owners, manifested in a set of institutions governing wage determination, collective bargaining and social welfare functions. Collectively, these institutions served to link annual wage increases to the productivity increases being realized from mass-production techniques. Their net result was to distribute sufficient income to workers to support consumption of industrial products on a mass scale. Geographers have associated this historical period with the rise of major regional concentrations of mass-production industries in the more developed countries (e.g. automobile manufacturing in the American Midwest, the British West Midlands and northwestern Italy). The later stages of this period have also seen the spatial fragmentation of manufacturing functions, with routinized assembly of standardized products occurring increasingly in branch plants in peripheral regions of industrialized countries, or in Third World production sites. (See also FLEXIBLE ACCUMULATION; NEW INTERNATIONAL DIVISION OF LABOUR; POST-FORDISM.)

MSG

Reference

Gramsci, A. 1971: *Selections from the prison notebooks*. New York: International.

Suggested Reading

Harvey, D. 1989: *The condition of postmodernity*. Oxford: Blackwell.

forecast The creation of an estimated value for an observation unit, usually through the application of a REGRESSION model. Of the two types of estimate, a *forecast* is less certain – because it involves extrapolation from the known to the unknown – than a *prediction*: a forecast is an estimated value for an observation unit not involved in the CALIBRATION of the regression equation, whereas prediction is an estimated value for one of the observations used in the calibration. RJJ

forecasting See SPACE–TIME FORECASTING MODELS.

form of economic integration A concept proposed by Karl Polanyi to describe the means by which an economy 'acquires unity and stability, that is the interdependence and recurrence of its parts' (cf. SYSTEM). Polanyi distinguished three main forms of economic integration: RECIPROCITY, REDISTRIBUTION and MARKET EXCHANGE. 'Since they occur side by side on different levels and in different sectors of the economy', Polanyi argued, 'it may often be possible to select one of them as dominant so that they could be employed for a classification of economies as a whole'. Dominance was to be identified by the degree to which any one of them 'comprises land and labour in a society' (Polanyi in Dalton, 1971, pp. 148–56). Polanyi's purpose was thus to treat the economy as an *instituted process*: 'instituted' because coherent structures were imposed on economies through historically specific institutions and 'process' because these various structures were reproduced through transactions across space and over time.

This approach came to be the cornerstone of what Polanyi called *substantivist anthropology*, whose focus on the historical specificity of different forms of economic integration was in sharp contrast to 'formalist' approaches, the generalizations of which assumed price-fixing markets to be the universal economic mechanism (cf. NEOCLASSICAL ECONOMICS). 'The error was in equating the human economy in

after Karl Polanyi

form of economic integration *1: Schemes of form of economic integration* (after Wheatley, 1973).

mode of production	social system
reciprocal-lineage ⟶	MINI-SYSTEM
redistributive-tributary ⟶	WORLD-EMPIRE
capitalist ⟶	WORLD-ECONOMY

form of economic integration 2: *Modes of production and social systems.*

general with its market form', Polanyi wrote, and in assuming that every DIVISION OF LABOUR implied the existence of market exchange. Such a formalism, so he believed, ignored 'the shifting place occupied by the economy in society' and made it impossible to understand the various ways in which precapitalist economies were 'embedded' in distinctive social relations (Polanyi in Pearson, 1977, pp. 6 and 104).

Polanyi's ideas have attracted considerable (and sometimes critical) attention within both anthropology and history (see Humphreys, 1969; North, 1977). Within geography, they were used by Wheatley in his seminal investigation of URBAN ORIGINS, which focused on the shift from reciprocity to redistribution (Wheatley, 1971). Wheatley later developed a series of connections between Polanyi's economic schema and what he regarded as the comparable social schema contained within Parsons's version of STRUCTURAL FUNCTIONALISM (Wheatley, 1973) (see figure 1). Wheatley's original arguments were extended in different directions by Harvey in his parallel examinations of URBANISM. Although his primary concern was market exchange within contemporary capitalism, he regarded all three concepts of 'reciprocity, redistribution and market exchange [as] simple and effective tools for dissecting the relationship between societies and the urban forms manifest within them'. Indeed, these concepts were treated as both superior to Marx's concept of a MODE OF PRODUCTION, which at the time Harvey thought 'too broad and all-embracing' for his purpose, and yet essentially compatible with Marx's views. They offered 'the conceptual means to characterise a social and economic formation' and provided 'consistent threads to trace the transformation from one mode of production to another' (Harvey, 1973, pp. 206–15). But there are important differences between Marx and Polanyi, and

Polanyi was consistently critical of 'the economistic fallacy' which he considered to be common to both formalist anthropology and HISTORICAL MATERIALISM (Block and Somers, 1984). In his later writings, certainly, Harvey paid little attention to Polanyi and concentrated on Marx (e.g. Harvey, 1982). Even so, the emergence of WORLD-SYSTEMS ANALYSIS has once again brought Polanyi's ideas to the attention of a *Marxisant* audience. In particular, Wallerstein's (1978, 1984) identification of three distinctive 'social systems' depends upon 'the existence within [each of them] of a division of labour, such that the various sectors or areas with [each one] are dependent upon economic exchange for the smooth and continuous provisioning of the needs of the area'. Wallerstein calls these divisions of labour and systems of exchange 'modes of production' but, as figure 2 shows, they are in fact formally equivalent to Polanyi's forms of economic integration and betray a similar emphasis on functionalist constructions (Aronowitz, 1981).   DG

References

Aronowitz, S. 1981: A metatheoretical critique of Immanuel Wallerstein's *The modern world system. Theory and Society* 9, pp. 503–20.

Block, F. and Somers, M. 1984: Beyond the economistic fallacy: the holistic social science of Karl Polanyi. In Skocpol, T., ed., *Vision and method in historical sociology*. Cambridge: Cambridge University Press, pp. 47–84.

Dalton, G., ed. 1968, 1971: *Primitive, archaic and modern economies: essays of Karl Polanyi*. Boston: Beacon Press.

Harvey, D. 1973: *Social justice and the city*. London: Edward Arnold/Baltimore, MD: Johns Hopkins University Press.

Harvey, D. 1982: *The limits to capital*. Oxford: Blackwell/Chicago: Chicago University Press.

Humphreys, S. C. 1969: History, economics and anthropology: the work of Karl Polanyi. *Hist. Theor.* 8, pp. 165–212.

North, D. C. 1977: Markets and other allocation systems in history: the challenge of Karl Polanyi. *J. Eur. econ. Hist.* 6, pp. 703–16.

Pearson, H., ed. 1977: *The livelihood of man: essays of Karl Polanyi.* New York: Academic Press.

Wallerstein, I. 1978: *The capitalist world-economy.* Cambridge: Cambridge University Press.

Wallerstein, I. 1984: *The politics of the world-economy.* Cambridge: Cambridge University Press.

Wheatley, P. 1971: *The pivot of the four quarters.* Edinburgh: Edinburgh University Press/Chicago: Aldine.

Wheatley, P. 1973: Satyantra in Suvarnadvipa: from reciprocity to redistribution in ancient South-East Asia. In Sabloff, J. A. and Lamberg-Karlovsky, C., eds, *Ancient civilization and trade.* Albuquerque: University of New Mexico Press, ch. 6.

Suggested Reading
Dalton (1968).

Humphreys (1969).

North (1977).

fragmentation   See FARM FRAGMENTATION.

Frankfurt School   A group of radical scholars associated with the Institute of Social Research founded in Frankfurt, Germany in 1923. Their writings established CRITICAL THEORY as a central moment in the wider currents of 'Western Marxism' as it emerged in the wake of the Bolshevik Revolution. The label is misleading, however, since the 'Frankfurt School' was only referred to as such after the parent Institute had been closed by the Nazis in 1933 and its members forced to flee the country. Their exile lasted until 1950, but this was arguably the most intellectually productive period for the group as a whole. It was then that their critique of POSITIVISM was developed most forcefully and conjoined to a critique of domination which stressed the relations between theory and practice and between material and mental CULTURE. Even then, however, the contributions of the most prominent members of the group – M. Horkheimer, T. Adorno, W. Benjamin, H. Marcuse, L. Lowenthal and F. Pollock – were sufficiently distinctive to require a carefully differentiated

analysis rather than the casual attribution of a collective project.

Some critics have regarded their work as being preoccupied with abstract philosophy and aesthetic theory, to such a degree as to represent a radical departure from the concrete historical and economic emphases of orthodox Marxism: Connerton (1980) speaks of an 'enveloping orgy of abstractions' and Bottomore (1984) of the 'extremely limited' range of their interests. Others, by contrast, regard 'the way connections [were] established between apparently disparate fields of inquiry' as one of the features confirming the Frankfurt School as a 'major source for contemporary social and political thought' (Held, 1980). Certainly, its revivification and extension by Habermas, Offe and Schmidt in the 1960s and 1970s had a major impact on all the social sciences, and in geography informed both general discussions, e.g. the RELEVANCE of teaching and resarch, and specific analyses, e.g. of social movements and of the capitalist STATE.   DG

References
Bottomore, T. 1984: *The Frankfurt School.* London: Tavistock.

Connerton, P. 1980: *The tragedy of enlightenment: an essay on the Frankfurt School.* Cambridge: Cambridge University Press.

Held, D. 1980: *Introduction to critical theory: Horkheimer to Habermas.* London: Hutchinson.

Suggested Reading
Bottomore (1984).

Jay, M. 1973: *The dialectical imagination: a history of the Frankfurt School and the Institute of Social Research 1923–50.* London: Heinemann.

free port   A port designed as a FREE TRADE AREA, so that exports are exempt from customs duties and subject to minimal customs regulations. Hong Kong is one important contemporary example. From 1945 to 1954, Trieste in the northern Adriatic Sea was a free port under joint British and American supervision, prior to its incorporation into Italy.   MB

free trade area   A group of STATES that have agreed to remove all artificial barriers to trade between themselves, such as import and export duties, export guarantees and quota restrictions, while at the same time maintaining their own separate policies on trade with other countries. This can cause problems and rules of origin have to be agreed, so that imports from countries outside the free trade area do not flood into all the countries in the group through the member with the lowest duty levels. The European Free Trade Association (EFTA), founded in 1959, has been one of the most successful free trade areas in recent years, although there have been other experiments in Latin America and the Caribbean (cf. COMMON MARKET). MB

Suggested Reading

Blacksell, M. 1981: *Post-war Europe: a political geography*, second edition. London: Hutchinson.
Dell, S. 1963: *Trade blocs and common markets*. London: Constable.

freight rates The money charged for the movement of goods by land, sea or air. Such charges often discriminate between commodities (on the basis of handling characteristics or value); they often taper with distance (the charge per tonne kilometre falls as distance increases – see DISTANCE DECAY) and may have a stepped form (it is easier for an operator to quote for distance bands than to have separate charges for every destination or distance). The setting of freight rates may be subject to competitive pressures but is often determined under conditions of monopoly or collusive oligopoly. AMH

frequency distribution A tabulation of the number of occurrences of the values of a variable into classes, which may be arbitrarily defined.

An empirical frequency distribution is usually displayed ordinally, as in:

Number of shops per settlement	Number of settlements
0	20
1–2	15
3–4	4
5–6	3
7–8	1

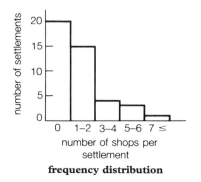

frequency distribution

This information can be displayed graphically as a *histogram* (see the figure).

A theoretical frequency distribution (such as the NORMAL DISTRIBUTION and the Poisson distribution) is a tabulation of the expected number of occurrences in each class according to an algebraic formulation (usually known as the 'generating function'). Most theoretical distributions are smooth because they are based on infinitely large populations. RJJ

friction of distance The frictional or inhibiting effect of distance on human interactions in all forms (including MIGRATION, tourist flows, movement of goods and transmission of information – see DIFFUSION). It is usually seen as a combined effect of the time and cost of overcoming distance and is directly related to TRANSFERABILITY. The friction of distance is geographically variable (being lowest in regions with well-developed transport and communciation systems) and is generally believed to have declined with technological improvements in transport and communications. Its measurement will depend on the context, but the exponential terms in GRAVITY MODELS are often interpreted as being indicative of the friction of distance. Empirically, its effects are evident in patterns of DISTANCE DECAY. (See also TIME-SPACE CONVERGENCE; TIME–SPACE DISTANCIATION.) AMH

friends-and-neighbours effect A particular CONTEXTUAL EFFECT identified in ELECTORAL GEOGRAPHY whereby voters favour local candidates (even if this means abandoning their traditional party preferences), either because they have personal knowledge of the candidate or in the belief that his/her election should promote local interests. RJJ

fringe belt A region of mixed land uses at the edge of a built-up area, the heterogeneity of which reflects the concentration of activities propelled there by centrifugal forces (see CENTRIFUGAL AND CENTRIPETAL FORCES). The study of fringe belts is central to Conzen's methodology of town-plan analysis, which focuses on TOWNSCAPE morphology. (See also RURAL–URBAN FRINGE.) RJJ

Suggested Reading
Whitehand, J. W. R. 1967: Fringe belts: a neglected aspect of urban geography. *Trans. Inst. Br. Geogr.* 41, pp. 223–33.

frontier A zone of varying width that refers either to the political division between two countries or to the division between the settled and uninhabited parts of a country. Prior to the twentieth century frontiers were a common feature of the political landscape, but most have now disappeared under the global tide of human settlement and economic development, to be replaced by BOUNDARIES, which are lines. In the nineteenth century land on the frontier was generally regarded as a necessary 'safety valve' for accommodating the populations of fast-growing states, such as the United States (see FRONTIER THESIS). Although this view is now somewhat discredited the Canadian Northlands and Alaska are still referred to as the last great frontier in North America, and similar descriptions are applied to Russian Siberia and the Australian outback. In reality, however, the opportunity for access to such areas is a luxury open to few states in the modern world, when boundaries on land and sea are now so tightly drawn. MB

Suggested Reading
Prescott, J. V. R. 1987: *Political frontiers and boundaries.* London: Unwin Hyman.

frontier thesis Frederick Jackson Turner's claim that the 'existence of an area of free land, its continuous recession, and the advance of American settlement

westward, explain American development' (Turner, 1894). For Turner, the frontier was 'the line of most rapid and effective Americanization': as it moved westward, so the successive 'primitive' engagements between the colonist and the wilderness entailed 'a steady movement away from the influence of Europe', which could be traced through a series of settlement 'waves' which corresponded to identifiable evolutionary 'stages':

Stand at Cumberland Gap and watch the procession of civilization, marching single file – the buffalo following the trail to the salt springs, the Indian, the fur trader and hunter, the cattle raiser, the pioneer farmer – and the frontier has passed by. Stand at South Pass in the Rockies a century later and see the same procession with wider intervals between.

Through these continuous movements, the frontier was supposed to have provided a 'safety valve' for the relief of poverty outside the west and, in so doing, to have encouraged a determined individualism which 'promoted democracy'. Thus, with the closing of the frontier ended 'the first period of American history', a claim which in part prompted Malin to describe the thesis as a 'closed-space doctrine' (cf. Mackinder's HEARTLAND thesis). But whatever its contemporary political resonances – and these were clearly important – Turner's thesis was also intellectually formative: Ratzel regarded it as an important *organic* theory and it was in fact exactly this conjunction of biology and geography, treating the 'struggle for space' as a requirement of the 'social organism', which was largely responsible for Malin's description (Kearns, 1984; see also ANTHROPOGEOGRAPHY; LAMARCKIAN-ISM).

With the emergence of a more clearly defined spatial perspective in geography, Meinig (1960) could still say that Turner's thesis contained four embryonic concepts (AREAL DIFFERENTIATION, connectivity, cultural succession and SPATIAL INTERACTION) which were 'undoubtedly the most influential of their type ever to come from American scholarship'; and 20 years on Block (1980) hailed it as 'the classic

American essay in speculative historical geography'.

The thesis was also subject to weighty criticism, however, most notably from Sauer who dismissed it as both 'easy and wrong' and reversed its conjectures at virtually every point: succeeding frontiers were 'a series of secondary culture hearths' so that 'there was no single type of frontier, neither was there a uniform series of stages'; insofar as there had been any convergence in frontier development, this was due more to 'a growing common political consciousness radiating from the older sections of the country' (see also CULTURAL HEARTH) (reprinted in Leighly, 1963). These criticisms have been extended by more recent studies which point to the *economic barriers* to frontier settlement, the *discontinuous movement* of the frontier, and the significance of *reverse flows* and MIGRATION streams. But as Gulley (1959) and Mikesell (1960) noted, few modern studies of the frontier can ignore Turner's seminal contribution.   DG

References

Block, R. 1980: Frederick Jackson Turner and American geography. *Ann. Ass. Am. Geogr.* 70, pp. 31–42.

Gulley, J. L. M. 1959: The Turner thesis. *Tijdschr. econ. soc. Geogr.* 50, pp. 65–72 and 81–91.

Kearns, G. P. 1984: Closed space and political practice: Frederick Jackson Turner and Halford Mackinder. *Environ. Plann. D*: Society and Space 2, pp. 23–34.

Leighly, J. ed. 1963: *Land and life: a selection from the writings of Carl Ortwin Sauer.* Berkeley, CA: University of California Press.

Meinig, D. W. 1960: Commentary on W. P. Webb, 'Geographical–historical concepts in American history'. *Ann. Ass. Am. Geogr.* 50, pp. 95–6.

Mikesell, M. W. 1960: Comparative studies in frontier history. *Ann. Ass. Am. Geogr.* 50, pp. 62–74.

Turner, F. J. 1894: *The significance of the frontier in American history.* Annual report of the American Historical Association for 1893, Washington, DC: US Government Printing Office.

functional classification of cities

Categorizations of towns and cities according to their economic functions, usually as indicated by their occupational and industrial structures. Most classifications are inductive, employing methods such as PRINCIPAL COMPONENTS ANALYSIS.   RJJ

functionalism A perspective from which the world is seen as a set of differentiated and interdependent systems, the collective actions and interactions of which are 'instances of repeatable and predictable regularities in which form and function can be assumed to be related' (Bennett and Chorley, 1978), and which explains these form–function relations in terms of their role in maintaining the continuity or integrity of the system(s). Modern functionalism is usually traced back to advances in evolutionary biology in the nineteenth century (see DARWINISM; LAMARCK(IAN)ISM), but in geography 'organismic' analogies of the Earth, its REGIONS and its STATES pre-dated Darwinian evolutionary theory. Although Darwin provided for the formal articulation of functionalism in many social sciences (as well as the natural sciences), his impact on human geography was, in these terms, less decisive (see Stoddart, 1986): the discipline 'rarely claimed for itself a philosophy of functionalism in the way that anthropology and sociology [did]' and while 'much of the empirical work in geography could be construed as functionalist in form' its precepts 'tended to remain implicit rather than overt in geographical thinking' (Harvey, 1969).

Before the end of the Second World War, the most explicit discussions of functionalism were to be found in Ratzel's ANTHROPOGEOGRAPHY and in some of the writings of the French school of human geography (particularly in the notions of 'terrestrial unity' proposed by Vidal de la Blache and Brunhes) (see POSSIBILISM): but this was scarcely surprising, since Vidal was influenced by the programmatic sociology of Durkheim, who was 'without doubt the most important single influence upon the development of functionalism in the present century' (Giddens, 1977; see also Berdoulay, 1978). Sauer's CULTURAL GEOGRAPHY was strongly functionalist in tone, and this was especially evident in his conception of LANDSCAPE as 'a reality as a whole that is not expressed by a consideration of the constituent parts separately' and which has 'form, structure and function and hence position in a system, and [which] is subject to development, change and completion', and also in his conception of CULTURE itself, which was heavily indebted to Kroeber's functionalist anthropology and which was largely responsible for the incorporation of what Duncan (1980) called the 'superorganic' into American cultural geography.

Until the 1970s, however, most of postwar human geography showed little interest in (and even a distrust of) social theory and social science, and preferred instead to draw upon models provided by the physical sciences. These provided two points of entry for functionalism. The indirect route was through the advance of NEOCLASSICAL ECONOMICS into ECONOMIC GEOGRAPHY: the so-called 'marginal revolution' of Jevons, Walras and others, with its central concern with the maintenance of an equilibrium between interdependent markets, depended in large measure on a deliberate analogy with statistical mechanics. The more direct route was through SYSTEMS ANALYSIS, the principles and procedures of which emerged from control engineering and thermodynamics, and which often displayed a similar concern with the maintenance of (dynamic) equilibrium (see Bennett and Chorley, 1978). Because of this double history, functionalism in postwar human geography advanced with scant acknowledgement of parallel developments in social theory. Even in SOCIAL GEOGRAPHY there were few excursions into the STRUCTURAL FUNCTIONALISM proposed by Parsons and others despite the affinities between some of its formulations and those of the various systems approaches being canvassed within the discipline.

In the 1970s, as human geography moved closer to the social sciences, functionalism advanced on a broader front. Particularly important was the rapid incorporation of ideas from HISTORICAL MATERIALISM, sometimes under the sign of STRUCTURAL MARXISM but more usually as a somewhat diffuse STRUCTURALISM, by means of which CAPITALISM was conceived as a crisis-ridden but self-regulating MODE OF PRODUCTION. The language of many of these discussions was not burdened with the baggage of traditional functionalism: the watchword was now usually capitalism as a *totality*. In the 1980s, however, many of these assumptions were called into question. The critique of functionalism was reinvigorated through a series of major debates over the relations between functionalism and Marxism (see Cohen, 1982; Elster, 1982). The most frequent objections to functionalism were at once *logical*, e.g. the unintended or unanticipated consequences of a form of social conduct cannot be used to explain its existence in the first place, and *substantive*, e.g. functionalism characteristically assumes a purpose ('needs' or 'goals') without a purposive agent. Indeed, it was the concern with HUMAN AGENCY that united most of these critical commentaries. Some of them insisted on the importance of methodological individualism and refused purely 'structural' explanations (e.g. Duncan and Ley, 1982; Elster, 1982: see HUMANISTIC GEOGRAPHY), others argued for a bounded conception of human agency within a more inclusive STRUCTURATION THEORY (which was advertised as a 'non-functionalist manifesto': Giddens, 1981). The language of totality was not immune to critique. In the course of the 1980s the rise of POSTMODERNISM, with its suspicion of GRAND THEORY and its totalizing claims to knowledge, threatened to hammer another nail in the coffin of functionalism; and as the 1980s became the 1990s so the assault on the hypothesized coherence of *both* human subjects *and* social systems has been raised to a new level of intensity by POSTSTRUCTURALISM

However, there are many who would prise those nails out again. In social theory there has undoubtedly been a revival of interest in functionalism, particularly in the work of Luhmann (1981). Within historical materialism Habermas has always opposed Luhmann's ideas, and his own theory of communicative action revolves around 'a critique of functionalist reason': and yet the presence of Parsons in his work is still considerable (Habermas, 1987; see also

Joas, 1991; McCarthy, 1991: and see CRITICAL THEORY). In geography, too, there are several thinkers who insist that it is possible – and indeed necessary – to retain a concept of totality without lapsing into functionalism (see Harvey and Scott, 1989). DG

References

Bennett, R. J. and Chorley, R. J. 1978: *Environmental systems: philosophy, analysis, control*. London: Methuen.

Berdoulay, V. 1978: The Vidal–Durkheim debate. In Ley D., and Samuels, M., eds, *Humanistic geography: prospects and problems*. London: Croom Helm, pp. 77–90.

Cohen, G. A. 1982: Functional explanation, consequence explanation and Marxism. *Inquiry* 25, pp. 27–56.

Duncan, J. S. 1980: The superorganic in American cultural geography. *Ann. Ass. Am. Geogr.* 70, pp. 181–98.

Duncan, J. S. and Ley, D. 1982: Structural Marxism and human geography: a critical assessment. *Ann. Ass. Am. Geogr.* 72, pp. 30–59.

Elster, J. 1982: Marxism, functionalism and game theory: the case for methodological individualism. *Theory and Society* 11, pp. 453–82.

Giddens, A. 1977: *Studies in social and political theory*. London: Hutchinson.

Giddens, A. 1981: *A contemporary critique of historical materialism*, volume 1: *Power, property and the state*. London: Macmillan.

Habermas, J. 1987: *The theory of communicative action*, volume 2: *A critique of functionalist reason*. Cambridge: Polity Press.

Harvey, D. 1969: *Explanation in geography*. London: Edward Arnold.

Harvey, D. and Scott, A. 1989: The practice of human geography. In B. Macmillan, ed., *Remodelling geography*. Oxford: Blackwell, pp. 217–29.

Joas, H. 1991: The unhappy marriage of hermeneutics and functionalism. In Honneth, A. and Joas, H., eds, *Communicative action*. Cambridge: Polity Press, pp. 97–118.

Luhmann, N. 1981: *The differentiation of society*. New York: Columbia University Press.

McCarthy, T. 1991: Complexity and democracy: or the seducements of systems theory. In Honneth, A. and Joas, H., eds, *Communciative action*. Cambridge: Polity Press, pp. 119–39.

Stoddart, D. R. 1986: *On geography and its history*. Oxford: Blackwell.

Suggested Reading

Elster (1982).

Giddens (1977), ch. 2.

Harvey (1969), ch. 22.

G

game theory A theory of interactive decision-making according to which individuals ('players') must select strategies for action while remaining ignorant of other players' choices, but with knowledge of the costs and benefits ('pay-offs') of all the resulting potential outcomes. Game theory arose at the turn of the century, but was solidified as a subdiscipline in the mid-1940s with the publication of von Neumann's and Morgenstern's (1944) *The theory of games and economic behavior*. Because game theory represents a set of general theorems about behaviour, it has been subsequently utilized in a swath of disciplines – political science, sociology, philosophy, economics, human geography and even biology – generating an enormous literature.

The simplest case is the strictly competitive two-person, zero-sum game. Here there is no potential for cooperation, because whatever one person gains the other must lose. In geography the classic example is of the HOTELLING MODEL, usually presented as two ice-cream vendors on an elongated beach who must decide where to locate given a uniform distribution of sunbathers. Given the propensity of customers always to buy from the closest vendor, both ice-cream sellers will end up in the middle of the beach, back-to-back. It is a zero sum game because if one vendor should move even slightly off centre towards one end, s/he will immediately lose some business while the other vendor will correspondingly gain. Under such conditions, the best strategy is one of MAXIMIN; that is, acting in such a way which guarantees at least a minimum pay-off regardless of the actions of the other player. In the Hotelling case, the maximin solution is always to stand in the middle of the beach, because a minimum market of at least half the total customers is always guaranteed irrespective of the actions of the other ice-cream seller. When both vendors adopt a maximin strategy, equilibrium obtains.

More complicated games have been devised that involve non-zero sum pay-offs, i.e. through interaction all players can potentially gain. Here the bargaining model of Nash (1950) has proved immensely useful, demonstrating that non-cooperative strategies can be the basis of non-zero-sum games. Other assumptions modified include increasing the number of players, allowing for incomplete information, running a sequence of games ('supergames') rather than assuming that each one is a single play, and postulating SATISFICING BEHAVIOUR instead of RATIONAL CHOICE. This latter modification has proven particularly difficult to undertake, reinforcing the point that game theory sits squarely within the tradition of rational choice theory, and its concomitant approach of METHODOLOGICAL INDIVIDUALISM.

Some of the more interesting recent work in game theory revolves around the possibility of cooperation. The problem is that usually it is not rational for rational individuals to cooperate in a game or, more generally, to engage in any form of collective action. At issue is the so-called free-rider problem. High individual costs are often associated with collective action if others do not cooperate (for example, being shot if you are only one of a few revolutionaries to mount a rebellion), but large collective gains obtain if they do (for example, political freedom for all). Given this structure of pay-offs (exemplified by the PRISONER'S DILEMMA), it is individually rational not to engage in collective action, but instead to free-ride on the actions of others (Olson, 1965). By so doing, any losses, such as being shot, are minimized, while any gains, such as greater liberty, can still be obtained provided that others act collectively. Of course, if everyone free-rides then there is no collective action, and as a consequence collective suboptimality eventuates from individual rational choice (cf. TRAGEDY OF THE COMMONS).

The free-rider argument has proven powerful. Many political theorists, beginning with Hobbes, have used it to justify the necessity of the STATE – if everyone free-rides important public goods such as domestic security would never be provided (Taylor, 1987). This said, *voluntary* cooperation and collective action clearly do occur: workers go on strike, students defend democracy, and residents defend their neighbourhoods against pimps and pushers (cf. TURF POLITICS). In each case, individuals act in a way to benefit collective interests, rather than their narrowly defined self-interest. But why does this happen? Four reasons have been proposed. First, the pay-off structure may not reflect all of the incentives impinging on collective action – for example, feelings of guilt or injustice with respect to others; second, the very interactions into which individuals enter can endogenously alter preferences in favour of collective action – for example, being swept up in revolutionary fervour; third, individuals may irrationally believe that if they engage in collective action then others will too; and, finally – and the one most discussed – that there may be more than a single play to the game, in which case players are able to devise certain meta-strategies that favour cooperation (the most successful of which is tit-for-tat; Axelrod, 1984). In each case, because of some form of interdependence among individuals the norm of free-riding is replaced by one of collective action.

Very little geographical work exists on cooperative game playing. However, Sheppard and Barnes (1990) attempt to ground geographically the four justifications for collective action given above. They argue that the interdependencies among individuals necessary for cooperative behaviour most readily occur in PLACE. This is further justified by Olson's (1965) original work which suggested that free-rider effects are most likely to break down within small groups of people, such as found within specific locales. Thus, this is yet another case in which the introduction of the geographical dimension fundamentally disturbs the conclusions of an aspatial analysis.   TJB

References

Axelrod, R. 1984: *The evolution of cooperation.* New York: Basic Books.

Nash, J. F. 1950: The bargaining problem. *Econometrica* 18, pp. 155–62.

Olson, M. 1965: *The logic of collective action: public goods and the logic of groups.* Cambridge, MA: Harvard University Press.

Sheppard, E. S. and Barnes, T. J. 1990: *The capitalist space economy: geographical analysis after Ricardo, Marx and Sraffa.* London: Unwin Hyman.

Taylor, M. 1987: *The possibility of cooperation.* Cambridge: Cambridge University Press.

von Neumann, J. and Morgenstern, O. 1944: *The theory of games and economic behavior.* Princeton, NJ: Princeton University Press.

Suggested Reading

Axelrod (1984).
Sheppard and Barnes (1990), ch. 10.
Taylor (1987).

garden city A planned and relatively self-contained settlement, developed to a plan stressing spaciousness, environmental quality and 'greenness'. It represents the first successful modern attempt to exploit these principles for whole settlements, the success of which is attributed to the theoretical ideas and practical promotion of a City of London stenographer, Ebenezer Howard (1850–1928). His vision, as outlined in his *Garden cities of tomorrow* (1902, first published in 1898 under a different title), saw them as combining the social, economic and cultural benefits of big-city living with the advantages to the individual of a more healthy rural environment. Each city would accommodate some 32 000 people on a 6000 acre site, planned according to a concentric land-use pattern in which residential and commercial land were segregated. Openness was injected through wide boulevards, low-density development and public parks within, with farmland and GREEN BELT beyond. On a city reaching its capacity, additional growth was directed to further garden cities, so creating a system of planned centres around their parent metropolis, the whole being interconnected by efficient rail and road links.

In 1899 Howard founded the Garden City Association which, four years later, bought a 3918 acre site in Hertfordshire on which Barry Parker and Raymond Unwin designed the world's first garden city, Letchworth, only one-third of which became built upon, the rest remaining variously as open space. A second followed at Welwyn, also in Hertfordshire, in 1920.

The garden city movement showed how DECENTRALIZATION could contribute to the planned improvement of congested urban centres, a theme taken up in Britain's postwar NEW TOWN and URBAN RENEWAL programmes, while the Garden City Association led to the founding of the Town and Country Planning Association in 1918, still a potent pressure group in British urban and regional planning.

These ideas have also been adopted internationally, and although settlements called 'garden cities' outside Britain show variations from the Howard model, high-quality residential environments, low densities and greenness are still central themes. Both in Britain and elsewhere, too, similar ideas have been adopted on a smaller scale in the intra-urban development of garden villages and garden suburbs. While the debt that these owe to Howard's ideas is a point of debate, it is clear that Howard in his turn was influenced by the utopian ideas of Victorian urban thinkers and philanthropic industrialists.   AGH

Suggested Reading
Beevers, R. 1988: *The garden city utopia: a critical biography of Ebenezer Howard.* Basingstoke: Macmillan.

Gastarbeiter A German term for foreign (guest) workers, now widely applied to migrant labourers who are temporarily resident in European cities.   RJJ

gatekeepers See URBAN MANAGERS AND GATEKEEPERS.

gateway city A settlement linking two areas, and usually located at a favourable physical situation which allows it to command entrance to and exit from its HINTERLAND. As control centres, such settlements often develop into locally dominant PRIMATE CITIES. (See also MERCANTILIST MODEL.)   RJJ

gender and geography The study of the various ways in which genders and geographies are mutually constituted. Haraway (1991) provides a thorough discussion of the history and meaning of the term 'gender' within feminist theory. The term has a broadly similar history within geography, with a movement away from theories of gender roles to gender relations and towards a fuller exploration of how gender relations are constructed in all spheres of life (see FEMINIST GEOGRAPHIES).

'Gender' is usually contrasted with 'sex' in an effort to remove women from NATURE and place them within CULTURE as constructed and self-constituting social subjects. The treatment of gender within geography is slightly unusual in this regard, as it has not been 'quarantined from the infections of biological sex' (Haraway, 1991, p. 134) to the same extent as in other disciplines. In an effort to theorize PATRIARCHY, Foord and Gregson (1986) attempt to identify the necessary relations that constitute gender relations. Following the analytical procedures of REALISM, they reason that two genders, male and female, are the basic characteristics of gender relations. In order to theorize the necessary relations between these basic characteristics, they ask: 'Under what conditions do men and women require each other's existence?', to which they answer, for biological reproduction and the practice of heterosexuality. Foord and Gregson's analysis was quickly criticized, because it made it difficult to theorize how capitalism structures gender relations (McDowell,

214

1986) and for its biologism, especially in terms of its portrayal of heterosexuality as biologically or psychologically fixed (Knopp and Lauria, 1987). The influence of POSTSTRUCTURALISM extends the latter criticism, calling attention to the function of gender as a regulatory concept that fixes identity around SEXUALITY and gender difference (see also SUBJECTIVITY).

Feminist geographers have also evinced some scepticism concerning the extent to which the use of the concept of gender within geography has effectively severed the link between women and nature, insofar as women are often portrayed as the naturally gendered sex. Bondi (1991, p. 8), for example, is critical of Pred's (1990) reliance on the feminine to explore the gendering of space and language because it 'perpetuates the familiar process whereby masculine terms of reference remain free from the mark of sexual difference'. She invites male geographers to explore their own gendering through an examination of masculinity and geography.   GP

References

Bondi, L. 1991: In whose words? On gender identities and speaking positions. Paper presented at the AAG Annual Conference, Miami, April.

Foord, J. and Gregson, N. 1986: Patriarchy: towards a reconceptualisation. *Antipode* 18, pp. 186–211.

Haraway, D. 1991: 'Gender' for a Marxist dictionary: the sexual politics of a word. In her *Simians, cyborgs, and women: the reinvention of nature*. New York: Routledge, pp. 127–48.

Knopp, L. and Lauria, M. 1987: Gender relations as a particular form of social relations. *Antipode* 19, pp. 48–53.

McDowell, L. 1986: Beyond patriarchy: a class-based explanation of women's subordination. *Antipode* 18, pp. 311–21.

Pred, A. 1990: In other wor(l)ds: fragmented and integrated observations on gendered languages, gendered spaces and local transformation. *Antipode* 22, pp. 33–52.

general linear model The collective term for the body of statistical procedures (such as ANALYSIS OF VARIANCE, FACTOR ANALYSIS, PRINCIPAL COMPONENTS ANALYSIS and REGRESSION) based on the analysis of covariation among variables. Many statistical packages for computer applications of these procedures are available, including GLIM (General LInear Model).

Application of the general linear model to a data set assumes a number of characteristics of the variables being analysed and the interrelationships among them. The most important of these are that: (1) the relationship between any pair of variables should be linear; (2) the residuals from the estimated value of the dependent variable for each value of an independent variable in a regression should have a mean of zero; (3) the same residuals should be normally distributed and with equal variances (i.e. they should be *homoscedastic*, not *heteroscedastic*); (4) values on each independent variable should not be autocorrelated (i.e. the value at one observation should not determine the value of an adjacent observation – see SPATIAL AUTOCORRELATION); and (5) all variables should be measured without error. In addition, in multiple regression there should be no COLLINEARITY among the independent variables (i.e. they should be uncorrelated). If some of these requirements are not met, it may be possible to manipulate the data in order that they are (see, for example, TRANSFORMATION OF VARIABLES): if they cannot, then strict application of general linear model methods is not possible.   RJJ

Suggested Reading

Johnston, R. J. 1978: *Multivariate statistical analysis in geography: a primer on the general linear model*. London: Longman.

O'Brien, L. 1992: *Introducing quantitative geography: measurement, methods and generalised linear models*. London: Routledge.

general systems theory An attempt to develop general statements about the common properties of superficially different SYSTEMS, usually identified with the work of von Bertalanffy (1968). This was introduced to geographers during the 1960s as a structure which could draw together various strands of work undertaken during the discipline's QUANTITATIVE REVOLUTION: it was dismissed by Chisholm (1967) as an 'irrelevant distraction'.

The search for isomorphisms among different systems focused on three main principles:

(a) *allometry* – the growth rate of a subsystem is proportional to that of the system as a whole (Ray et al., 1974);
(b) *hierarchical structuring* – as in CENTRAL PLACE THEORY (for isomorphisms, see Woldenberg and Berry, 1967); and
(c) ENTROPY (see Wilson, 1970).

Chorley (1962) suggested that appreciation of the commonality of these principles across systems studied in both human and physical geography would advance the integration of those two fields – a task promoted in Bennett and Chorley's (1978) *Environmental systems*, the subtitle of which – *philosophy, analysis and control* – mimics von Bertalanffy's.

Little was achieved by the small number who sought to apply general systems theory principles within human geography, however (although the early work on MACROGEO-GRAPHY was a partial exception), and most members of the discipline have now moved away from such searches for universals.   RJJ

References

Bennett, R. J. and Chorley, R. J. 1978: *Environmental systems: philosophy, analysis and control*. London: Methuen/Princeton, NJ: Princeton University Press.

Chisholm, M. 1967: General systems theory and geography. *Trans. Inst. Br. Geogr.* 42, pp. 45–52.

Chorley, R. J. 1962: *Geomorphology and general systems theory*. Geological Survey Professional Paper 500-B. Washington, DC: US Government Printing Office.

Ray, D. M., Villeneuve, P. Y. and Roberge, R. A. 1974: Functional prerequisites, spatial diffusion and allometric growth. *Econ. Geogr.* 50, pp. 341–51.

von Bertalanffy, L. 1968: *General systems theory: foundation, development, applications*. New York: G. Braziller/London: Allen Lane.

Wilson, A. G. 1970: *Entropy in urban and regional modelling*. London: Pion.

Woldenberg, M. J. and Berry, B. J. L. 1967: Rivers and central places: analogous systems? *J. reg. Sci.* 7, pp. 129–40.

genre de vie A form of livelihood functionally characteristic of a human group; for example, transhumants and peasant agriculturalists (see PEASANT; TRANSHUMANCE). Collective organization for the purposes of producing and reproducing social and economic life within a particular geographical setting (*milieu*) is regarded as the foundation for an integrated set of environmental, cultural and spiritual practices.

Along with *milieu* and *circulation*, *genre de vie* was a pivotal concept in Vidalian geography (Vidal de la Blache, 1911: see POSSIBILISM), and in the early twentieth century it informed the writing of French regional monographs which sought to identify localized CULTURAL LANDSCAPES to which the interaction of the three concepts gave rise. Recognition of parallels between Vidal's *genre de vie* and the concept of 'mode of life' developed in Marx's discussion of the MODE OF PRODUCTION (the foundation of social consciousness) has been significant in recent CULTURAL GEOGRAPHY, as has recognition of the concept's nostalgic and folkloric aspects, which signal geography's connections with European nationalist discourses at the turn of the century (see NATIONALISM).   DEC

Reference

Vidal de la Blache, P. 1911: Les genres de vie dans la géographie humaine. *Annls Géogr.* 20, pp. 193–212.

Suggested Reading

Buttimer, A. 1971: *Society and milieu in the French géographic tradition*. Chicago: Rand McNally.

gentrification A process of NEIGH-BOURHOOD regeneration by relatively affluent incomers, who displace lower-income groups and invest substantially in improvements to homes the quality of which has deteriorated (cf. FILTERING). Such neighbourhoods are usually accessible to the city centre and comprise substantial older dwellings – as in parts of Islington in London and Society Hill in Philadelphia.

The process of gentrification is often similar to that of INVASION AND SUCCESSION. A few gentrifiers obtain properties in a relatively run-down condition within a small area and improve them, thereby increasing the attractiveness of the area to others who would prefer such a location, so that eventually the entire area (often only a few streets) changes its socio-economic status, and property values are substantially enhanced. Real estate agents and property developers may participate in the process, as they seek to enhance the exchange value of an area and to reap substantial profits from promoting UNEVEN DEVELOPMENT at the intra-urban scale.

Most early gentrifications involved individual decision-making within the operations of the property market, but in recent years it has been promoted by governments (both central and local) seeking to rehabilitate INNER-CITY areas – as in the work of the London and Merseyside Dockland Development Corporations in the 1980s. Their attempts to attract affluent residents to such areas – many of them relatively young, childless households – involve either or both of the construction of new high-density, expensive flats and houses and the conversion of former non-residential buildings (such as waterfront warehouses) into luxury apartment blocks.

Early work on gentrification was largely descriptive, illustrating processes of neighbourhood change which contradicted those of the traditional models of urban residential patterns (see ALONSO MODEL; ZONAL MODEL). They also showed how, in some cases, the ousting of the lower-income residents from an area and their replacement by 'yuppies' was achieved with questionable tactics used by landlords and estate agents wishing to generate large profits from property sales; in addition, they showed how in some places government grants intended to assist the improvement of low-quality inner-city residential areas were used to subsidize the costs of improvement and thus the large financial gains made by the more affluent classes (Hamnett and Williams, 1980).

As gentrification became more common, attention focused on the general conditioning factors which stimulated its development across a large number of places (Ley, 1986). In addition, the process was analysed in the context of theoretical developments in the understanding of the making and remaking of urban residential differentiation, as part of the operation of the CIRCUITS OF CAPITAL being invested in the built environment and in creating UNEVEN DEVELOPMENT (Smith and Williams, 1986). RJJ

References
Hamnett, C. and Williams, P. R. 1980: Social change in London: a study of gentrification. *Urban Affairs Quarterly* 15, pp. 469–87.
Ley, D. F. 1986: Alternative explanations for inner-city gentrification: a Canadian assessment. *Ann. Ass. Am. Geogr.* 76, pp. 521–35.
Smith, N. and Williams, P. R., eds 1986: *Gentrification of the city.* Boston: Allen and Unwin.

geographical imagination A sensitivity towards the significance of PLACE, SPACE and LANDSCAPE in the constitution and conduct of social life. Probably the most influential use of the term, on which this particular definition is based, was that of Harvey (1973), who claimed that a geographical imagination

enables . . . individual[s] to recognize the role of space and place in [their] own biograph[ies], to relate to the spaces [they] see around [them], and to recognize how transactions between individuals and between organizations are affected by the space that separates them . . . to judge the relevance of events in other places . . . to fashion and use space creatively, and to appreciate the meaning of the spatial forms created by others.

Harvey used the term both to contrast the 'geographical imagination' with and to connect it to what Mills (1959) had called the 'sociological imagination' which he said 'enables us to grasp history and biography and the relations between the two in society'. Neither Harvey nor Mills confined the terms to their own disciplines: they both said that they were talking about 'habits of mind' or, more formally, *discourses* which transcended particular disciplines. 'It has been a fundamental concern of mine for several years now', Harvey wrote, 'to heal the breach in our thought between what appears to be two distinctive and indeed irreconcilable modes of analysis', and he presented his seminal *Social justice and the city* as (in part) a 'quest to bridge the gap between sociological and geographical imaginations'.

This seemed particularly important in the wake of a SPATIAL SCIENCE that, in its most extreme forms, had removed people and societies from human geography and concentrated instead on the mathematical and statistical analysis of spatial patterns and structures. It was urgently necessary to *humanize* human geography, and ideas and concepts were drawn in from the humanities and the social sciences: in particular, from political economy, social theory and cultural studies (see CULTURAL GEOGRAPHY; HUMANISTIC GEOGRAPHY; MARXIST GEOGRAPHY). En route, however, it became clear that the reverse movement was equally (and ecumenically) important, because most of these were COMPOSITIONAL THEORIES which took no account of place, space and landscape. Some ten years after *Social justice*, therefore, Harvey had this to say:

'The insertion of space, place, locale and milieu into any social theory has a numbing effect upon that theory's central propositions . . . Marx, Marshall, Weber and Durkheim all have this in common: they prioritize time over space and, where they treat the latter at all, tend to view it unproblematically as the site or context for historical action. Whenever social theorists of whatever stripe actively interrogate the meaning of geographical categories, they are forced either to make so many ad hoc adjustments to their theory that it splinters into incoherence, or else to abandon their theory in favour of some language derived from pure geometry. The insertion of spatial concepts into social theory has not yet been successfully accomplished. Yet social theory that ignores the materialities of actual geographical configurations, relations and processes lacks validity (Harvey, 1984).

Since then, there has been considerable progress in sensitizing social theory and social thought more generally to these concerns: there has been an immensely productive dialogue between Marxist geography and urban and regional political economy; many commentators have hailed POSTMODERNISM as being emblematic of a distinctively geographical (or at any rate 'spatial') imagination (Soja, 1989); and the recent interest in POSTCOLONIALISM and POSTSTRUCTURALISM has contributed in still more radical ways to the critique of abstract and universal models of 'the human subject' and 'society' (cf. CONTEXTUAL THEORY; GRAND THEORY) and

helped to bring about a clearer understanding of the significance of *situated knowledges*. At the same time, a series of changes in the organization and experience of social space (what is sometimes called 'the culture of space') have been registered not only in the academy (Harvey, 1990), but also in the media and through an explosion of interest in travel-writing and 'travelling theory' which has also had a major impact on social thought and cultural criticism (Gregory, 1993).

But there are, of course, other geographical imaginations: 'other' in the sense that there are geographies outside the Western academy (including indigenous geographies in other areas of the world and informal geographies inscribed in the TAKEN-FOR-GRANTED WORLD); and 'other' in the sense that there are (human) geographies which focus much more directly on CULTURAL ECOLOGY and the 'culture of nature' which, while they are connected to place, space and landscape, are by no means reducible to those concerns (Turner, 1991; Wilson, 1992).

DG

References

Gregory, D. 1993: *Geographical imaginations*. Oxford: Blackwell.

Harvey, D. 1973: *Social justice and the city*. London: Edward Arnold.

Harvey, D. 1984: On the history and present condition of geography: an historical materialist manifesto. *Prof. Geogr.* 36, pp. 1–11.

Harvey, D. 1990: Between space and time: reflections on the geographical imagination. *Ann. Ass. Am. Geogr.*, 80, pp. 418–34.

Mills, C. W. 1959: *The sociological imagination*. Oxford: Oxford University Press.

Soja, E. 1989: *Postmodern geographies: the reassertion of space in critical social theory*. London: Verso.

Turner, B. L., ed. 1991: *The Earth as transformed by human action*. Cambridge: Cambridge University Press.

Wilson, A. 1992: *The culture of nature: North American landscapes from Disney to the Exxon Valdez*. Oxford: Blackwell.

Suggested Reading

Gregory (1993).

Harvey (1990).

Turner (1991).

geographical information systems (GIS) Integrated computer tools for the handling, processing and analysing of geographical data. The software of a GIS is normally self-contained, and most often runs on a personal computer or workstation, although mainframes are common in many larger applications. Conservative estimates put the size of the GIS software industry's total business in 1991 at between US$ 1 and US$ 2 billion. In addition to software and processing hardware, a GIS normally includes specialized peripherals for input (digitizing) and output (printing or plotting) of mapped data. The cost of a modest GIS package and associated hardware and peripherals would be about US$ 15 000.

Although the first mention of GIS occurred in the literature in the mid-1960s, massive growth began only in 1980, with the introduction of superminicomputers by manufacturers such as Digital Equipment Corporation and Prime Computer. Growth in the software industry followed, led by Intergraph Corporation and the Environment Systems Research Institute (ESRI). The technology of GIS found practical applications in RESOURCE MANAGEMENT, particularly forestry, local government, utility companies and market research. More specifically, its uses include the automated measurement and analysis of geographically distributed resources, and the management of distributed facilities. Scientific applications also developed in the 1980s, as GIS was applied to the wide range of sciences and social sciences that deal with geographically distributed data and find value in a spatial perspective (see APPLIED GEOGRAPHY). These include epidemiology, archaeology, geology, ecology, geophysics, oceanography, REGIONAL SCIENCE and, of course, geography. The methods and concepts of GIS overlap strongly with the concerns of many more established disciplines, including CARTOGRAPHY (particularly COMPUTER-ASSISTED CARTOGRAPHY), REMOTE SENSING, photogrammetry, geodesy and SURVEYING.

Two major traditions have developed in GIS for representing geographical distributions. The *raster* approach divides the study area into an array of rectangular cells, and describes the content of each cell; while the *vector* approach describes a geographical distribution as a collection of discrete objects (points, lines or areas), and describes the location of each. In essence, the raster approach 'tells what is at every place' and the vector approach 'tells where everything is'. In addition, a GIS database contains information on the attributes of each cell or object, and on various kinds of relationships between objects. Broadly, the continuous view of space embedded in the raster approach is most commonly associated with environmental and physical science applications of GIS, while the view of space as a collection of discrete objects that is implicit in the vector approach has found more applications in the social and policy sciences, in the mapping industry, and in the management of geographically distributed facilities. Most currently available GIS software products can be identified with one approach, although most provide limited capabilities for handling the other.

The ability to couple the input and output functions of a GIS with its more exploratory functions of browsing and simple statistical analysis, and with more sophisticated CONFIRMATORY DATA ANALYSIS techniques, has led to many GIS applications in human geography and related disciplines. GIS has been used to implement models of regional economies, transportation systems and urban growth; to develop hypotheses from complex catalogues of spatially distributed artefacts; to develop understanding from patterns of social deprivation and disease; to analyse voting behaviour; and to understand the sacred meaning that many cultures give to space. In short, GIS has become a powerful tool for automating the geographer's processes of analysis and synthesis.

Currently, GIS remains firmly bound to its cartographic roots: maps continue to be the primary means of input and output. It provides tools for recording and processing the positions of features in space (as in SPATIAL SCIENCE), but has yet to develop much sophistication in its handling of time dependence (see TIME-GEOGRAPHY) or interaction. In this sense GIS preserves a

219

container-like view of SPACE, and cannot yet deal effectively with the temporal changes and interactions that drive or result from many social processes. However, current basic research efforts are likely to yield significant advances in these areas in the next few years. Moreover, the growth of GIS has led to renewed interest in many of the more fundamental issues of geography and cartography: the accuracy of abstracted views of geographical distributions; the effects of scale and resolution; languages for describing spatial relations; methods for exploring the spatial perspective; the role of geographical information in empowerment and domination; and the importance of geographical information to the decision-making process.   MG

Suggested Reading

Burrough, P. A. 1986: *Principles of geographical information systems for land resources assessment.* Oxford: Clarendon Press.

Chrisman, N. R., Cowen, D. J., Fisher, P. F., Goodchild, M. F. and Mark, D. M. 1989: Geographic information systems. In Gaile, G. L. and Willmott, C. J., eds, *Geography in America.* Columbus, OH: Merrill, pp. 776–96.

Maguire, D. J., Goodchild, M. F. and Rhind, D. W., eds 1991: *Geographical information systems: principles and applications* (2 volumes). London: Longman.

Marble, D. F. 1990: The potential methodological impact of geographic information systems on the social sciences. In Allen, K. M. S., Green, S. W. and Zubrow, E. B. W., eds, *Interpreting space: GIS and archaeology.* London: Taylor and Francis, pp. 9–21.

geographical societies Voluntary bodies established to promote the discipline of geography. Some of the early societies, both national (e.g. the Royal Geographical Society of London and the American Geographical Society of New York) and regional (e.g. the Manchester Geographical Society), were major forces in the nineteenth-century development of geography and its establishment as a school and university discipline. They continue to play major roles in promoting geography, both as an academic discipline and as a subject of wider general interest.

Alongside these general societies, the late nineteenth and early twentieth centuries saw the establishment of a number of professional societies for geographers, such as the Geographical Association (for teachers, mainly at school level) and the Institute of British Geographers (mainly for researchers and for teachers in higher education) in the UK; the National Council for Geographical Education and the Association of American Geographers fulfil the comparable roles in the USA. These societies, through conferences, seminars, specialist meetings and publications, participate in the promotion and dissemination of material about research advances and promote the discipline both politically and professionally.   RJJ

Suggested Reading

Freeman, T. W. 1980: The Royal Geographical Society. In Brown, E. H., ed., *Geography – yesterday and tomorrow.* Oxford: Oxford University Press, pp. 1–99.

James, P. E. and Martin, G. J. 1978: *The Association of American Geographers: the first seventy-five years 1904–1979.* Washington, DC: Association of American Geographers.

Steel, R. W. 1984: *The Institute of British Geographers: the first fifty years.* London: Institute of British Geographers.

geography Geography can be formally defined as the study of the Earth's surface as the space within which the human population lives (Haggett, 1990), or simply as the study of the Earth as the home of people (Tuan, 1991). The word is derived from the Greek *geo*, the Earth, and *graphein*, to write.

Perhaps the best known formal definition of the field was provided by the American geographer, Richard Hartshorne, in his *Perspective on the nature of geography* (1959): 'geography is concerned to provide accurate, orderly, and rational description and interpretation of the variable character of the Earth surface'. The last two terms in this definition need some elaboration. By 'variable character' geographers mean the spatial variation that can occur between the character of the Earth's surface at one location and another. This variation may occur at all map SCALES from the globe itself, say between continent and continent, down to a very local level, say between one district and another within an urban area. By 'Earth surface' is meant that rather thin shell, only about one-thousandth of the planet's circumference thick, that forms the habitat or environment within which the human population is able to survive.

As defined above, geography occupies a puzzling position within the traditional organizations of knowledge. It is neither a purely natural science nor a purely social science. Its intellectual origins as a distinctive field of study pre-date such a separation, going back to classical Greece; people were viewed then as an integral part of NATURE. In that period a geography of any area would be written so as to include descriptions of both the animate and inanimate things found there (See CHOROLOGY.). Although individual scholars or small clusters of scholars wrote geographical descriptions of various parts of the world over the ensuing centuries, and although GEOGRAPHICAL SOCIETIES flourished from the early nineteenth century onward, geography established itself as a university discipline rather late. (Separate departments of geography had emerged in German-speaking countries by the 1870s but not generally until the present century in the case of Great Britain and the USA: Taylor, 1985.) By then, the division of academic studies within universities into the natural sciences on the one hand and the humanities and social sciences on the other had already become crystallized in formal faculty organization. In practice, therefore, geography had to be fitted, albeit somewhat awkwardly, into an already established scholarly order. Sometimes it found itself part of a natural-sciences faculty, sometimes in an arts or social sciences faculty, sometimes divided between the two. In consequence there have been rather powerful external forces (as well as an internal logic) which have tended to split geography into two parts: a geography of the natural world, termed 'physical geography', and a geography of the human-created world, termed 'HUMAN GEOGRAPHY'. This pressure has sometimes been sufficiently strong, as in some Scandinavian and all Dutch universities, to lead to the establishment of separate departments of physical geography and human geography with rather tenuous cross-links.

While the short-term advantages of this separation were apparent in terms of the integration of one part of geography with its neighbouring science, e.g. geomorphology with geology, most geographers have viewed such moves with concern. They argue that the distinction between natural phenomena and those made by humans is unhelpful, since it obscures some of the essential characteristics of geographical study and therefore undermines its long-term rationale as a university discipline.

What, then, are these essential geographical characteristics, and why were they considered so important? At least three can be readily identified.

(a) The first characteristic is an emphasis on *location*. Geography is concerned with the locational or spatial variation in both physical and human phenomena at the Earth's surface. It tries to establish locations accurately, to represent them effectively and economically (see CARTOGRAPHY), and to disentangle the factors that lead to particular spatial patterns (see, for example, LOCATION THEORY). In human geography it may also propose alternative spatial patterns which are more equitable (see WELFARE GEOGRAPHY) or more efficient (see ECONOMIC GEOGRAPHY). It is significant that many of the techniques developed within geography for the study of such spatial variation are general in character, and not specific to phenomena studied in either physical or human geography.

(b) A second characteristic is geography's ecological emphasis on *society–land relations* (see ECOLOGY). Here the stress is on the interrelations of phenomena, the links between aspects of the natural environment of a particular area, and the human population occupying or modifying it. In this type of analysis, geographers shift their emphasis from the study of spatial variations between areas (these may be thought of as horizontal bonds) to the study of ecological links within a bounded geographical area (vertical bonds). It is worth noting that the bonds may be two-way (i.e. the impact of people on land, as well as land on people) and that the bounded area may be anything from the globe itself to a very small locality.

(c) A third characteristic of geography is *regional analysis*, in which the spatial and ecological approaches described under (a) and (b) are fused. Appropriate spatial segments of the Earth's surface, termed REGIONS, are identified, their internal (intraregional) morphology and ecological linkages traced, and their external (extraregional) relations established (see REGIONAL GEOGRAPHY).

For some geographers the process of region building, sometimes termed the AREAL DIFFERENTIATION of the Earth's surface, represented the core area of the field; for others, the most significant advances were seen to come from more systematic studies, often in association with a neighbouring discipline. The relative importance of regional and systematic approaches to geography forms a second area of methodological debate: for although the subject matter of geography is logically indivisible, the study of the Earth's surface must be divided into compartments in order to be manageable. There are two traditional ways of doing this: either we can consider each part of the Earth's surface in turn, region by region, or we can consider a significant theme or element and trace it systematically over the whole of the Earth's surface. The first approach is termed regional geography; the second, systematic geography.

Studies in REGIONAL GEOGRAPHY are characteristically broad-based and include consideration not only of the environment but also of the population of an area: its demographic characteristics, its occupational structure (e.g. primary, secondary, tertiary and quaternary groupings), and its social and political behaviour (e.g. MIGRATIONS and voting patterns). Emphasis is placed on the spatial dimension of each component, and on such local associations of environment and population characteristics in particular areas as give rise to distinctive subregions within the overall area being considered. Where the evidence is available, emphasis is placed on the stability or instability of regional structures over time, to underscore whether those being described are static or undergoing modification. It is characteristic of such regional studies in geography that they try to integrate a number of phenomena within a single area, and have a combinatorially complex array of links between the phenomena. SYSTEMS ANALYSIS provides one way of attempting to reduce this complexity to a simpler architectural form, in which it may be more easily comprehended and on which models can be constructed.

Systematic studies in geography take one or a few aspects of the human environment or the human population and study their varying performance over a predefined geographical space. Such studies are usually labelled with reference either to the phenomenon concerned or to the subfield of the natural or social science with which it may be identified. Thus a spatial study of voting behaviour may be termed ELECTORAL GEOGRAPHY (under the first label) or POLITICAL GEOGRAPHY (under the second). This second type of labelling causes dilemmas in library classification, commonly leading to books on geography being shelved in different sections of a library with their systematic discipline rather than gathered together into a single geography section.

Three types of overlap between geography and a systematic field commonly occur. We illustrate them here by the overlap of geography with a neighbouring medical field, epidemiology. In the first type, cartographic or locational methods may be used as a mapping or allocational process to study the distribution of disease over the Earth's surface. In the second, geographers may use diseases as causal factors in a broader geographical study. Thus, a geographical study of settlement in the humid tropics may need to take into account the distribution of malaria. In the third, epidemiologists may use geographical phenomena as one of the causal factors in an epidemiological study; the distribution of disease reservoirs may be critically related to the size and density of human settlements. In short-hand terms we might caricature the three approaches as 'the geography of disease distribution', 'the disease behind geography' and 'the geography behind disease'. We have only to substitute in the above short-hand account another field from the natural or social sciences or the humanities, e.g. hydrology or demography in place of epidemiology, to appreciate the range and variety of literature which may arise in this area. Such literature forms a continuum, with the geographical concern (e.g. regional detail) and language (e.g. cartographic analysis) decreasing as one moves away from the geographical core area towards that of another discipline.

Today, geography represents a well-established tradition of research and scholarship within the corpus of academic disciplines. It is one in which the legacy of past ideas remains strongly embedded but current thinking is still being worked out. In some respects it resembles a city with districts of different ages and vitalities. There are some long-established districts dating back to a century ago and sometimes in need of repair; and these are areas which were once fashionable but are so no longer, while others are being rehabilitated. Other districts have expanded recently and rapidly; some are well built, others rather gimcrack. If we use the city metaphor, then geography has extended beyond its medieval walls to form a sprawling CONURBATION with other subjects. Its dictionary definition must then represent a partial view of an evolving field at a particular historical stage in its evolution. PH

References

Haggett, P. 1990: *The geographer's art*. Oxford: Blackwell.

Hartshorne, R. 1959: *Perspective on the nature of geography*. Chicago: Rand McNally/London: John Murray.

Taylor, P. J. 1985: The value of a geographical perspective. In Johnston, R. J., ed., *The future of geography*. London: Methuen, pp. 92–108.

Tuan, Y.-F. 1991: A view of geography. *Geogrl. Rev.* 81, pp. 99–107.

Suggested Reading

Cloke, P., Philo, C. and Sadler, D. 1991: *Approaching human geography*. London: Paul Chapman.

Haggett, P. 1983: *Geography: a modern synthesis*, third revised edition. New York: Harper and Row.

James, P. E. and Martin, G. J. 1981: *All possible worlds: a history of geographical ideas*, second edition. New York: John Wiley.

Johnston, R. J. 1991: *A question of place*. Oxford: Blackwell.

Johnston, R. J. 1991: *Geography and geographers: Anglo-American human geography since 1945*, fourth edition. London: Edward Arnold/New York: Halstead.

Stoddart, D. R. 1986: *On geography: and its history*. Oxford: Blackwell.

geography, history of Because the term 'geography' means, and has meant, different things to different people in different times and places, there is no agreed-upon consensus on what constitutes the project of writing the history of this enterprise. Moreover, while the story of geography as an independent scholarly *discipline* is inescapably bound up with the history of the professionalization of academic knowledge since around the middle of the nineteenth century, it is clear that the history of geography as a DISCOURSE not only operates without such constraints but also reaches beyond the historical and institutional confines of the modern-day discipline. Of course, geography as discourse and discipline are interrelated in intimate ways – one might even say that the purpose of a discipline is precisely to 'discipline' discourse. Nevertheless, there is frequently a considerable difference in both substance and style between those writing the history of these respective geographies.

So far as the modern *discipline* of geography is concerned, those chronicling the course of historical change have conducted their investigations in a variety of ways. Some have concentrated on the subject's institutional expression, and accordingly have produced histories of such bodies as the Royal Geographical Society (Freeman, 1980b), the American Geographical Society (Wright, 1952), the Institute of British Geographers (Steel, 1984) and the Association of American Geographers (James and Martin, 1978) (see GEOGRAPHICAL SOCIETIES). Others have organized their material around national traditions or schools, such as the French School (Buttimer, 1971; Berdoulay, 1981), the German tradition (Schultz, 1980) and the British School (Freeman, 1980a,c). Still others have considered the biographies of key professional geographers: Halford Mackinder (Parker, 1982; Blouet, 1987), Isaiah Bowman (Martin, 1980), Ellsworth

Huntington (Martin, 1973) and W. M. Davis (Chorley et al., 1973) have all been the subject of full-length biographies; while shorter biographical sketches of a wider range of figures have appeared in the series *Geographers: biobibliographical studies*. Biographical treatments are also available of figures who loom large in the story of the subject's pre-professional past, such as Humboldt (Beck, 1958–61; Botting, 1973), Ritter (Beck, 1979), Reclus (Dunbar, 1978), Marsh (Lowenthal, 1958) and Shaler (Livingstone, 1987). And in addition to one or two standard autobiographies (Taylor, 1958), newer experiments in this genre have been promoted using both written (Buttimer, 1983; Billinge et al., 1984) and audiovisual means of retrieval.

Inevitably those works dealing with geographical *discourses* come in a variety of guises. Crucial here is the definition of what passes as 'geographical' by the historian in question. Numerous candidates have been offered. Dealing with the pre-professional period, for example, Glacken's (1967) monumental *Traces on the Rhodian shore* explored the contact zone between nature and CULTURE, acknowledging that he had thereby to transcend the conventional limits of the modern discipline. J. K. Wright's (1965) *Geographical lore of the time of the Crusades* focused more on earth description with its cartographic and cosmographical correlates, and similarly commented that his project covered 'a wider field than most definitions of geography' (p. 2). By contrast, Beazley's (1897–1906) *The dawn of modern geography* emphasized the history of medieval travel and exploration, whereas for Eva Taylor (1930) mathematical practice, surveying and navigation assumed greater importance in her investigations into the character of *Tudor geography*. More recently, Bowen's (1981) compendious survey of geographical thought from Bacon to Humboldt constitutes a sophisticated historical apologia for an ecological, anti-positivistic vision of geography through a revivification of the Humboldtian project. By contrast, in a survey of 'Theoretical geography', Wilson (1972) presented his own alternative history of geography as SPATIAL SCIENCE in which the names of

mathematically inclined economists and sociologists loomed large. Alongside these treatments of geographical discourse by geographers is a range of related works by historians of science dealing with allied subjects such as biogeography (Browne, 1983), meteorology (Frisinger, 1977), geology (Laudan, 1987), geomorphology (Davies, n.d.; Tinkler, 1985), and environmental science (Bowler, 1992), and by historians of CARTOGRAPHY, of which the first volumes of the projected series spearheaded by Harley and Woodward (1987) promise to be the most comprehensive investigation to date (cf. CARTOGRAPHY, HISTORY OF).

These relatively specialist studies are supplemented by a number of what Aay (1981) calls 'textbook chronicles', synthetic treatments designed for student consumption that provide an overview of the field (Dickinson, 1969; James, 1972; Holt-Jensen, 1988). It is now plain, however, that these surveys all too frequently lapsed into apologetics for some particular viewpoint – geography as regional interrogation, the study of occupied space, or some such. Moreover, their strategy was typically: *presentist*, namely using history to adjudicate present-day controversies; *internalist*, in the sense that they paid scant attention to the broader social and intellectual contexts within which geographical knowledges were produced; and *cumulative*, portraying history in terms of progress towards some perceived contemporary orthodoxy. It is precisely these assumptions, however, that a greater sensitivity to currents of historiographical thinking has questioned. Accordingly, there have recently been a number of appeals for contextual readings of the tradition (Livingstone, 1979; Stoddart, 1981), and a range of strategies have therefore been deployed in the endeavour to achieve this aim.

Some have turned to Kuhn's paradigmatic perspective – with varying degrees of integrity towards Kuhn's original formulations – and have sought to characterize the history of geography in terms of an overlapping succession of PARADIGMS enshrined in a number of key texts: Vidal's 'possibilism', Huntington's 'determinism', Sauer's 'landscape morphology',

Hartshorne's 'areal differentiation' and Schaefer's 'exceptionalism' are typical candidates for paradigm status (Harvey and Holly, 1981; Mair, 1986). In such scenarios, however, a good deal of historical typecasting and editorial management has had to be engaged in. Others have begun to take more seriously the work of the sociologists of scientific knowledge and have examined, for instance, the role of 'invisible colleges' and 'socio-scientific networks' (Lochhead, 1981), and the relationships between cognitive claims and institutional arrangements (Capel, 1981). At the same time the Marxist historical materialist perspective has been marshalled as a means of elucidating the way in which geographical knowledge and practices have been used to legitimate the social conditions that produced that knowledge in the first place (Harvey, 1984). Still others have seen in the philosophical literature on the cognitive power of metaphor a key to unlocking aspects of geography's history (Buttimer, 1982; Barnes and Duncan, 1992), through delineating the different uses of, say, mechanistic, organic, structural and textual metaphors. The insights of Foucault on the intimate connections between SPACE, SURVEILLANCE, POWER and knowledge, and of Said on the Western construction of 'non-Western' realms (see ORIENTALISM) have also begun to be mobilized and to open up new vistas to the history of geography by unmasking the pretended neutrality of spatial discourse in a variety of arenas both within and beyond the academy (Driver, 1985; Philo, 1992).

Cumulatively, such calls for re-reading geography's history have begun to contribute towards a growing variety of revisionist accounts of particular episodes, among which mention might be made of the links between magic, mysticism and geography at various times (Livingstone, 1988; Matless, 1991), the intimate connections between geography, empire and racial theory (Driver, 1992; Livingstone, 1991), the complicity of German geography in the Nazi programme (Sandner, 1988, Rössler, 1989), the relations between landscape representation and artistic convention (Cosgrove and Daniels, 1988) and calls for a feminist reading of the tradition (Domosh, 1991). Embedded within at least of some of these accounts is a conviction that 'geography' is a negotiated entity, and that a central task of its historians is to ascertain how and why certain practices and procedures come to be accounted authoritative, and hence normative, at certain moments in time, and in certain spatial settings.

It is plain, then, that the 'history of geography' comprises a variety of enterprises that have been engaged in various ways. Nevertheless, a broad shift can be detected from the 'encyclopaedism' of earlier works (which operated in a cumulative-chronological fashion) towards a more recent 'genealogical' perspective (which aims to disclose the tangled connections between power and knowledge). The subversive character of the latter has been embraced with differing degrees of enthusiasm: some now insist that the very idea of history is a Western 'myth' (Young, 1990) while others, either unenamoured of an altogether radical relativism or suspicious that the genealogist is implicated in an impossible self-referential dilemma, suggest that there is more value in thinking of discourses as 'contested traditions' – socially embodied and temporally extended conversations that act as stabilizing constraints on the elucidation of meaning (MacIntyre, 1990). Insofar as 'encyclopaedia', 'genealogy' and 'tradition' as modes of historical interrogation reflect differing attitudes towards what has come to be called the Enlightenment project, the history of geography has a significant role to play in debates within the discipline over the relations between knowledge, power, representation and social constitution. Moreover, the recent reassertion of the significance of PLACE and space in historical investigations of human knowing suggests that 'the history of geography' as an undertaking could benefit (ironically perhaps) by taking 'geography' more seriously; namely, by reconceptualizing the enterprise as 'the historical geography of geography'.   DNL

References

Aay, H. 1981: Textbook chronicles: disciplinary history and the growth of geographic knowledge.

In Blouet, B. W., ed., *The origins of academic geography in the United States*. Hamden, CN: Archon Books, pp. 291–301.

Barnes, T. J. and Duncan, J. S. 1992: *Writing worlds: discourse, text and metaphor in the representation of landscape*. London: Routledge.

Beazley, C. R. 1897–1906: *The dawn of modern geography*, three volumes. Oxford: Clarendon Press.

Beck, H. 1979: *Carl Ritter, Genius der Geographie: Zu Seinem Leben und Werk*. Berlin: Dietrich Reimer Verlag.

Beck, N. 1958–61: *Alexander von Humboldt*, two volumes. Wiesbaden: Ranz Steiner Verlag.

Berdoulay, V. 1981: *La formation de l'école française de géographie (1870–1914)*. Paris: Bibliothèque Nationale.

Billinge, M., Gregory D. and Martin, R., eds 1984: *Recollections of a revolution: geography as spatial science*. London: Macmillan.

Blouet, B. W. 1987: *Halford Mackinder: a biography*. College Station, Texas; Texas A & M University Press.

Botting, D., 1973: *Humboldt and the cosmos*. London: Sphere.

Bowen, M. 1981: *Empiricism and geographical thought: from Francis Bacon to Alexander von Humboldt*. Cambridge: Cambridge University Press.

Bowler, P. J. 1992: *The Fontana history of the environmental sciences*. London: Fontana.

Browne, J. 1983: *The secular ark: studies in the history of biogeography*. New Haven: Yale University Press.

Buttimer, A. 1971: *Society and milieu in the French geographic tradition*. Chicago: Rand McNally.

Buttimer, A. 1982: Musing on Helicon: root metaphors and geography. *Geogr. Annlr*, Series B, 64, pp. 89–96.

Buttimer, A., ed. 1983: *The practice of geography*. London: Longman.

Capel, H. 1981: Institutionalization of geography and strategies of change. In Stoddart, D. R., ed., *Geography, ideology and social concern*. Oxford: Blackwell, pp. 37–69.

Chorley, R. J., Beckinsale, R. P. and Dunn, A. J. 1973: *The history of the study of landforms or the development of geomorphology*, volume 2: *The life and work of William Morris Davis*. London: Methuen.

Cosgrove, D. and Daniels, S., eds 1988: *The iconography of landscape: essays on the symbolic representation, design and use of past environments*. Cambridge: Cambridge University Press.

Davies, G. L. n.d.: *The Earth in decay: a history of British geomorphology 1578 to 1878*. London: MacDonald.

Dickinson, R. E. 1969: *The makers of modern geography*. London: Routledge & Kegan Paul.

Domosh, M. 1991: Towards a feminist historiography of geography. *Trans. Inst. Br. Geogr.*, n.s., 16, pp. 95–104.

Driver, F. 1985: Power, space, and the body: a critical assessment of Foucault's *Discipline and punish*. *Environ. Plann. D: Society and Space* 3, pp. 425–46.

Driver, F. 1992: Geography's empire: histories of geographical knowledge. *Environ. Plann. D: Society and Space* 10, pp. 23–40.

Dunbar, G. S. 1978: *Elisée Reclus: historian of nature*. Hamden, CN: Archon Books.

Freeman, T. W. 1980a: *A history of modern British geography*. London: Longman.

Freeman, T. W. 1980b: The Royal Geographical Society and the development of geography. In Brown, E. H., ed., *Geography – yesterday and tomorrow*. Oxford: Oxford University Press, pp. 1–99.

Freeman, T. W. 1980c: The British school of geography. *Organon* 14, pp. 205–16.

Frisinger, H. 1977: *The history of meteorology to 1800*. New York: Science History Publications.

Glacken, C. 1967: *Traces on the Rhodian shore: nature and culture in western thought to the end of the eighteenth century*. Berkeley, CA: University of California Press.

Harley, J. B. and Woodward, D., eds 1987: *History of cartography*, volume 1: *Cartography in prehistoric, ancient, and medieval Europe and the Mediterranean*. Chicago: University of Chicago Press.

Harvey, D. 1984: On the history and present condition of Geography: an historical materialist manifesto. *Prof. Geogr.* 36, pp. 1–10.

Harvey, M. E. and Holly, B. P. 1981: Paradigm, philosophy and geographic thought. In Harvey, M. E. and Holly, B. P., eds, *Themes in geographic thought*. London: Croom Helm, pp. 11–37.

Holt-Jensen, A. 1988: *Geography: history and concepts*, second edition. London: Paul Chapman.

James, P. E. 1972: *All possible worlds: a history of geographical ideas*. Indianapolis: Bobbs-Merrill.

James, P. E. and Martin, G. J. 1978: *The Association of American Geographers: the first seventy-five years, 1904–1979*. Washington, DC: Association of American Geographers.

Laudan, R. 1987: *From mineralogy to geology: the foundations of a science, 1650–1830*. Chicago: University of Chicago Press.

Livingstone, D. N. 1979: Some methodological problems in the history of geographical thought. *Tijdschr. econ. soc. Geogr.* 70, pp. 226–31.

Livingstone, D. N. 1987: *Nathaniel Southgate Shaler and the culture of American science.* Tuscaloosa, AL: University of Alabama Press.

Livingstone, D. N. 1988: Science, magic and religion: a contextual reassesssment of geography in the sixteenth and seventeenth centuries, *Hist. Sci.* 26, pp. 269–94.

Livingstone, D. N. 1991: The moral discourse of climate: historical considerations on race, place and virtue. *J. hist. Geogr.* 17, pp. 413–34.

Lochhead, E. 1981: Scotland as the cradle of modern academic geography in Britain. *Scott. geogr. Mag.* 97, pp. 98–109.

Lowenthal, D. 1958: *George Perkins Marsh: versatile Vermonter.* New York: Columbia University Press.

MacIntyre, A. 1990: *Three rival versions of moral enquiry: encyclopaedia, genealogy, and tradition.* Notre Dame, IN: University of Notre Dame Press.

Mair, A. 1986: Thomas Kuhn and understanding geography. *Progr. hum. Geogr.* 10, pp. 345–69.

Martin, G. J. 1973: *Ellsworth Huntington: his life and thought.* Hamden, CN: Archon Books.

Martin G. J. 1980: *The life and thought of Isaiah Bowman.* Hamden, CN: Archon Books.

Matless, D. 1991: Nature, the modern and the mystic: tales from early twentieth-century geography. *Trans. Inst. Br. Geogr.* n.s. 16, pp. 272—86.

Parker, W. H. 1982: *Mackinder: geography as an aid to statecraft.* Oxford: Clarendon Press.

Philo, C. 1992: Foucault's geography. *Environ. Plann. D: Society and Space* 10, pp. 137–61.

Rössler, M. 1989: Applied geography and area research in Nazi society: central place theory and planning, 1933 to 1945. *Environ. Plann. D: Society and Space* 7, pp. 419–31.

Sandner, G. 1988: Recent advances in the history of German geography 1918–1945: a progress report for the Federal Republic of Germany. *Geogr. Z.* 76, pp. 120–33.

Schultz, H.-D. 1980: *Die Deutschsprachige Geographie von 1800 bis 1970: ein Beitrag zur Geschichte ihrer Methodologie.* Berlin: Geographische Institut der Freien Universität.

Steel, R. 1984: *The Institute of British Geographers: the first fifty years.* London: Institute of British Geographers.

Stoddart, D. R., ed. 1981: *Geography, ideology and social concern.* Oxford: Blackwell.

Taylor, E. G. R. 1930: *Tudor geography.* London: Methuen.

Taylor, T. G. 1958: *Journeyman Taylor*, ed. A. A. MacGregor. London: Robert Gale.

Tinkler, K. J. 1985: *A short history of geomorphology.* Totowa, NJ: Barnes & Noble.

Wilson, A. G. 1972: Theoretical geography. *Trans. Inst. Br. Geogr.* 57, pp. 31–44.

Wright, J. K. 1952: *Geography in the making: the American Geographical Society, 1851–1951.* New York: American Geographical Society.

Wright, J. K. 1965: *The geographical lore of the time of the Crusades. A study in the history of medieval science and tradition in Western Europe.* New York: Dover. First published in 1925.

Young, R. 1990: *White mythologies: writing history and the West.* London: Routledge.

Suggested Reading

Johnston, R. J. 1991: *Geography and geographers: Anglo-American human geography since 1945,* fourth edition. London: Edward Arnold.

Livingstone, D. N. 1992: *The geographical tradition: episodes in the history of a contested enterprise.* Oxford: Blackwell.

Stoddart, D. R. 1986: *On geography and its history.* Oxford: Blackwell.

geopiety A term initially coined by J. K. Wright (1966) to denote the sense of thoughtful piety aroused by human awareness of the natural world and geographical space, and thus closely connected to TOPOPHILIA. In a localized context this may yield a specific sense of human TERRITORIALITY in which a people (or NATION) develop an almost mystical, organic bond of attachment to their homeland, giving rise to powerful nationalist sentiments (*Blut und Boden*). More generally, geopiety can refer to sentiments of human attachment to elemental spaces (telluric, aquatic, etc.). The rise of deep ECOLOGY in the late twentieth century has extended this meaning of geopiety to a quasi-religious belief in a universal, autochthonous bond between human life and a holistic, living Earth, and the moral duty of reverential environmental conduct that this entails. DEC

Reference

Wright, J. K. 1966: *Human nature in geography: fourteen papers 1925–1965.* Cambridge, MA: Harvard University Press/Oxford: Oxford University Press.

Suggested Reading

Kohak, E. 1984: *The embers and the stars: a philosophical enquiry into the moral sense of nature.* Chicago: Chicago University Press.

Tuan, Y.–F. 1976: Geopiety: a theme in man's attachment to nature and to place. In Lowenthal, D. and Bowden, M. J., eds, *Geography of the mind: essays in historical geosophy in honor of John Kirkland Wright.* New York: Oxford University Press, pp. 11–39.

geopolitical transition The replacement of one geopolitical world order by another. Some students of WORLD-SYSTEMS theory suggest that a single world power is dominant during each KONDRATIEFF CYCLE, and that the declining years of each (its B phase) involve a contest (in some cases including a 'hegemonic war') for world political leadership during the next. Thus the onset of the Cold War in the late 1940s is interpreted as one such transition (Taylor, 1990), and the collapse of the socialist states in the late 1980s – leading to the initiation of a so-called 'new world order' – as the next. (See also GEOPOLITICS.)   RJJ

Reference

Taylor, P. J. 1990: *Britain and the Cold War: 1945 as geopolitical transition.* London: Belhaven Press.

geopolitics A long-established area of geographical enquiry which considers SPACE to be important in understanding the constitution of international relations. Its contemporary usage should not be confused with GEOPOLITIK, however, which is a crude form of ENVIRONMENTAL DETERMINISM popularized in foreign-policy circles to legitimize STATE action. In the search for an explanation of the global geopolitical order, three main approaches can be singled out.

(a) *Traditional geopolitics* has its roots in the early-twentieth-century works of the British geographer, Halford Mackinder who, in an age of British expansion and overseas interests, drew attention to the geostrategic advantages of land power over sea power. For Mackinder, the pivotal position of the HEARTLAND within the Eurasian land mass meant that whoever occupied the heartland could exert a dominating influence over world politics. By interpreting European history as a record of struggle to achieve and prevent control over the heartland, Mackinder was arguing that location and the physical environment were important determinants of the global power structure. Like many other geopolitical theoreticians, Mackinder's conception of the geopolitical order was prescriptive and ethnocentric, and subject to rapid obsolescence, although it remains one of the most widely read and influential of geographical expositions. It was this heartland thesis, along with Ratzel's organic theory of the state, which was to have a formative influence on *Geopolitik*. The organic theory held that all components of the state 'grow' together into one body which has a 'life' of its own. As a German geographer, Friedrich Ratzel was clearly influenced by the specifically Hegelian concept of the state as a community based on a transcendental spiritual union in which and through which all nationals are bound spiritually into an organic 'oneness'. The biological analogy of state with NATURE was taken further by Otto Maull and Rudolph Kjellen, and later used in interwar Germany to provide spurious intellectual justifications for national paranoia, territorial claims and geopolitical objectives (see *LEBENSRAUM*). This exploitation of political geographical ideas to serve political purposes ensured that *Geopolitik* and geopolitics both became war casualties, for anything that even notionally resembled the latter became politically sensitive. By the 1970s, however geopolitics was again undergoing a renaissance amongst US foreign policy analysts focusing on the Cold War. Here containment and DOMINO THEORY were utilized in conjunction with Mackinder's heartland and Spykman's rimland theory to justify the continuing necessity for Western geomilitary alliances and interventions in order to prevent COMMUNISM'S spatial expansion from the (Soviet) heartland.

(b) The *power-relations* perspective focuses on the hierarchical character of states within the global order by examining a polity's ability to influence or change the behaviour of other states in a desired direction. Drawing in particular upon the realist school of international relations, power relations between states have been conceived in terms of global geopolitical equilibrium, by formulating postwar international relations as a model of bipolarity in the late 1940s and early 1950s, loose bipolarity in the late 1950s and 1960s, and the multipolar world of the 1970s, 1980s and 1990s. With the end of the Cold War, however, the geopolitical world order has moved away from one characterized in this approach by an hierarchical, integrated but flexible structure of states, linked in one way or another with the two major geopolitical power blocks of the United States and Soviet Union (Cohen, 1991), to a post-Cold-War era in which the geopolitical influence of both the United States and the former Soviet Union in structuring the world order is in decline, a thesis compatible with Kennedy's (1988) compelling modern geopolitical history in which he argues that Great Powers that overextend themselves geopolitically but are unable to innovate and reform at home, become victims of their own 'imperial overstretch' (see GEOPOLITICAL TRANSITION; KONDRATIEFF CYCLES; WORLD-SYSTEMS ANALYSIS).

(c) The *political economy* approach is based on the underlying assumption that geopolitics cannot be understood fully without considering the dynamics of the global economy. By interpreting the state and its external relations as the political organization of the world economy, world-systems analysis moves away from the state-centrism of realist-based accounts. Thus Wallerstein (1984) considers the links between the processes of capital accumulation, resource competition and foreign policy as part of a singular and interdependent global system in which CAPITALISM determines the character and hierarchical configuration of states (see WORLD-SYSTEMS ANALYSIS). Thus for world-systems theorists, the more peripheral location of the former USSR in the world economy helps us to understand why it was unable to compete effectively with the United States during the later stages of the Cold War. By taking economic forces as, in the last instance, the basis for determining relations between states, there is a tendency to relegate the importance of political and sociocultural processes at the state level, when in fact both politics and cultural processes can and do play an important and independent part in determining the nature of geopolitics. Such concerns have led Agnew and Corbridge (1989) to advocate a more dynamic and nuanced approach to geopolitics, which moves away from the hypostatization of the world simply into economically differentiated core and periphery states. Their call for a new geopolitics based on a *geopolitical economy* perspective focuses on the importance of both economic and political processes shaping post–1945 world orders, in which neither process is simply reducible to the other and in which non-state actors (such as multinational companies and the International Monetary Fund) play a key role. GES

References

Agnew, J. and Corbridge, S. 1989: The new geopolitics: the dynamics of global disorder. In Johnston, R. J. and Taylor, P. J., eds, *A world in crisis? Geographical perspectives.* Oxford: Blackwell, pp. 266–88.

Cohen, S. B. 1991: Global geopolitical change in the post-Cold War era. *Ann. Ass. Am. Geogr.* 81, pp. 551–80.

Kennedy, P. 1988: *The rise and fall of the Great Powers: economic change and military conflict from 1500 to 2000.* London: Unwin Hyman.

Wallerstein, I. 1984: *The politics of the world economy.* Cambridge: Cambridge University Press.

Suggested Reading

Ashley, R. 1987: The geopolitics of political space: toward a critical social theory of international politics. *Alternatives* 12, pp. 403–34.

Dalby, S. 1991: Critical geopolitics: discourse, difference and dissent. *Environ. Plann. D: Society and Space* 9, pp. 261–83.

Linklater, A. 1990: *Beyond realism and Marxism: critical theory and international relations.* London: Macmillan.

O'Loughlin, J. and Wusten, H. van der 1994: *The political geography of international relations.* London: Frances Pinter.

Parker, G. 1985: *Western geopolitical thought in the twentieth century.* London: Croom Helm.

Smith, G. E. 1992: Ends, geopolitics and transitions. In Johnston, R. J., ed., *The challenge for geography: a changing world, changing discipline.* Oxford: Blackwell, pp. 76–99.

Taylor, P. 1990: *Britain and the Cold War: 1945 as a geopolitical transition*. London: Frances Pinter.

Geopolitik A school of political geography developed in interwar Germany, associated with the geographer, Karl Haushofer, and with the journal *Zeitschrift für Geopolitik* (1922–44). The term *Geopolitik*, however, originated with the Swedish political scientist, Rudolph Kjellen, whose ideas, along with Ratzel's organic theory of the STATE and Mackinder's HEARTLAND concept, provided a basis and spurious rationale to justify German expansionism. The state was portrayed as an organism which needed to expand territorially (*LEBENSRAUM*) in order to fulfil its destiny. However, important differences did exist between *Geopolitik* and national socialism, a fact which has not always been appreciated by geographers. Whereas *Geopolitik* was influenced by the significance of natural laws in its understanding of social and political life, national socialism saw societies as determined by biological inheritance. Nonetheless, the relationship which undoubtedly existed between *Geopolitik* and 1930s German foreign policy meant that it is only recently that geography, and in particular German geography, has begun to investigate its unhappy past. GES

Suggested Reading

Bassin, M. 1987: Race contra space: the conflict between German *Geopolitik* and national socialism. *Pol. Geogr. Q.* 6, pp. 115–34.

Parker, G. 1985: *The development of Western geopolitical thought in the twentieth century*. London: Croom Helm.

Smith, W. 1980: Friedrich Ratzel and the origins of *Lebensraum. German Studies Review* 3, pp. 51–68.

geosophy The study of colloquial knowledge from all or any points of view (a neologism coined by J. K. Wright).

Geosophy is geography's equivalent of historiography, and thus the study of 'geographical ideas both true and false held by all manner of people accounting for human desires, motives and prejudice'. Wright's (1947) plea for the study of such 'geographies of the mind' anticipated the entry into geography of Foucauldian notions of power-knowledge and recognition of the significance of the geographical imagination in the invention of tradition. Much contemporary research may be counted as geosophical in its critique of scientific geographical foundationalism and its extension of studies into geography's history beyond formally systematized disciplinary knowledge. DEC

Reference

Wright, J. K. 1947: 'Terrae incognitae': the place of the imagination in geography. *Ann. Ass. Am. Geogr.* 37, pp. 1–15.

Suggested Reading

Allen, J. L., ed. 1992: The invention of American tradition. Special issue of *J. hist. Geogr.* 18.

geostrategic regions Large-scale international regions comprising groups of states sharing a common political or economic philosophy. The best-known attempt at devising such a system of world regions is by S. B. Cohen who, in the context of the Cold War, proposed a fundamental twofold division of the globe.

The *Trade-dependent Maritime World* comprised Western Europe, the Americas, and most of Africa and Australasia, and was held together by a complex network of maritime trading links. The *Eurasian Continental World* was a land-based grouping, with IDEOLOGY rather than TRADE as the prime cohesive force. Cohen's model was an attempt to provide a more sophisticated and detailed successor to the HEARTLAND theory that was so popular in the early twentieth century, but it too has now been overtaken by events. The collapse and fragmentation of the Soviet Union in the course of 1990 and 1991 into a number of independent republics, all committed to introducing market economies, renders Cohen's monolithic twofold global division meaningless. He has begun to sketch out a new order, but in the present uncertain political climate his ideas are, at best, provisional. MB

Suggested Reading

Cohen, S. B. 1973: *Geography and politics in a world divided*, second edition. New York: Oxford University Press.

Cohen, S. B. 1982: A new map of global geopolitical equilibrium. *Pol. Geogr. Q.* 1, pp. 223–41.

Cohen, S. B. 1992: Policy prescriptions for the post-Cold War world. *Prof. Geogr.* 44, pp. 13–15.

gerrymandering The deliberate drawing of the boundaries of electoral constituencies to produce an advantage for an interested party. The term was coined by the enemies of Republican Governor Elbridge Gerry of Massachusetts, who redrew a district's boundaries to his party's advantage in 1812: that district was shaped like a salamander, hence the neologism and the widespread (though false) belief that gerrymandering necessarily involves odd-shaped district boundaries. Although the widespread practice of gerrymandering has long been appreciated in the USA, it has only recently been tackled by the willingness of the Supreme Court to interpret it as a constitutional violation (Grofman, 1990).

RJJ

Reference

Grofman, B., ed. 1990: *Political gerrymandering and the courts*. New York: Agathon Press.

ghetto An urban residential district which is almost exclusively the preserve of one ETHNIC or cultural group. The term originally referred to the legally separate quarter reserved for Jewish residents in medieval European cities, but its application has been broadened in the present century.

The original ghettos were areas in which a group was required to live by its host society (although in his classic work, Wirth (1928) argued that ghettos existed because Jews chose to live together long before they were legally required to): after the removal of such legal barriers to freedom of choice of residence (APARTHEID in late twentieth-century South Africa providing the last major example of such restrictions) it was applied more generally to areas in which certain groups were concentrated. Through a combination of prejudice and discrimination in housing and labour markets which substantially restricts the ability to exercise freedom of choice, plus in many cases their wish to live together in order to defend their culture and provide relative security from hostile other groups, including the host society, certain groups have come to occupy separate residential areas which are often termed ghettos.

As a descriptive term, therefore, ghetto now confuses voluntary and involuntary SEGREGATION within cities: Boal (1976) suggested that the term 'ghetto' should be reserved for the latter, where ethnic concentration results from discrimination, and that 'enclave' should be used for ethnic separation which largely reflects a group's choice – but this has not been widely followed. The term is frequently used, especially in the vernacular, as synonymous with a SLUM, but not all ghettos have been the homes of low-income households living in relatively deprived conditions: 'gilded ghettos' for the affluent members of an ethnic group have been identified in many cities, such as Chicago.

RJJ

References

Boal, F. W. 1976: Ethnic residential segregation. In Herbert, D. T. and Johnston, R. J., eds, *Social areas in cities*, volume 1: *Spatial processes and form*. Chichester: John Wiley, pp. 41–79.

Wirth, L. 1928: *The ghetto*. Chicago: Chicago University Press.

Suggested Reading

Ward, D. 1982: The ethnic ghetto in the United States: past and present. *Trans. Inst. Br. Geogr.* n.s. 7, pp. 257–75.

global futures Broadly defined, the study of global futures has a rich past, exemplified in such venerable traditions of thought as the idea of progress and countervailing notions of cyclical change and of the decay and deterioration of the world. The utopian (also the dystopian) genre has long served as a device to explore the future, as much as a means of criticizing or clarifying the present as for its own sake. Most such works are best understood as commentaries on their own time, and are misjudged when judged simplistically on the basis of the correspondence of their imagined future to what has actually happened. Much the same can be said of a quite different set of exercises in exploring global futures – those to which a narrower definition of the term would confine itself – that of mathematical MODELLING such as the Club of Rome report on *The limits to growth* (Meadows et al., 1972) and its numerous progeny. Many modellers themselves take pains to emphasize that their goal is not to predict or FORECAST as such but to clarify and elucidate the consequences of certain starting assumptions. Indeed, works such as *The limits to growth*, have sought to become examples of the 'Cassandra effect' or of the 'self-refuting prophecy' – statements about the future that do not come true precisely because their statement has caused behaviour to be altered. It is apparent, however, that the choice of assumptions that a modeller makes reflect some beliefs about the key driving forces of global change, and do to some degree construct futures regarded by the author as more plausible or likely than others. Moreover, when published, the results are often interpreted by a wider audience as forecasts, and even as scientific certainties.

A substantial literature has grown up in the ground pioneered by the Club of Rome report – issues of human–environment relationships and global environmental change. The approach of *The limits to growth*, that of extrapolating current trends in resource demand and pollution to a point of collapse, was immediately criticized by economists and others (e.g. Cole et al., 1973) for ignoring the processes of technological innovation and substitution induced by scarcity through price signals. A neo-Malthusian point of view, associated with, among others, Paul Ehrlich, Earl Cook and Herman Daly, continues to emphasize absolute physical limits and the need to limit economic and demographic growth to avoid future environmental catastrophe. The opposing 'cornucopian' position (e.g. Simon, 1981; Simon and Kahn, 1984) argues that population is less a drain on resources than itself, 'the ultimate resource' of labour and ingenuity, and that innovation constantly redefines physical limits. Others have sought to steer a different course that emphasizes the issues of distribution and conflict elided in both of these positions, and adopts the notion of SUSTAINABLE DEVELOPMENT expounded

by the World Commission on Environment and Development (1987) as a guide to global policy and planning. Global social and economic change – itself an integral part of models dealing with environment and resources – has its own vast modelling literature.

Surprises that may be essentially unpredictable have in the past tended to frustrate global-future study as a predictive enterprise, and those not sympathetic to that enterprise argue its essential futility. The emphasis in contemporary social theory on the contingency of outcomes of social action and the asymmetry of explanation and prediction points to a similar judgement. Yet the paradox of studying futures – global or otherwise – is that all rational action depends on some such forecast, in that ends can only be sought by taking means expected to produce them, even though accurate prediction has long been and remains an intractably elusive goal.

JEm

References

Cole, H. S. D., Freeman, C., Jahoda, M. and Pavitt, K. L. R., eds 1973: *Thinking about the future: a critique of The limits to growth.* London: Chatto and Windus.

Meadows, D. H., Meadows, D. L., Randers, J. and Behrens, W. W. 1972: *The limits to growth.* New York: Universal Books.

Simon, J. L. 1981: *The ultimate resource.* Princeton, NJ: Princeton University Press.

Simon, J. L. and Kahn, H., eds 1984: *The resourceful Earth.* Oxford: Blackwell.

World Commission on Environment and Development. 1987. *Our common future.* Oxford: Oxford University Press.

global warming (and greenhouse effect)

Increased global temperatures caused by human activities that enhance the atmospheric greenhouse effect. Various trace components of the atmosphere (including carbon dioxide, methane and nitrous oxide) reabsorb and retain certain wavelengths of heat radiated from the Earth's surface. Human activities – burning of fossil fuels and land-cover change (especially deforestation) – have increased the tropospheric concentrations of all of these compounds, while adding a new class of greenhouse gases, the chlorofluorocarbons (CFCs). Monitoring of carbon dioxide levels conducted since 1957 has shown a steady yearly increase; concentrations now exceed the preindustrial level by some 25 per cent. Whether and to what degree human-induced global warming has already occurred are quite controversial, and the physical and social consequences of warming remain shrouded in great uncertainty. The climatic models used to forecast patterns of regional and local change offer as yet only broad generalizations: that warming is expected to be greatest in the high latitudes, for example; and that particularly severe impacts may be expected along coastlines through sea-level rise; although high-latitude warming might even increase polar ice accumulation and lead to sea-level decline. Paradoxically, the uncertainties of impact have in some ways stimulated broad-based initiatives to slow the accumulation of greenhouse gases in a way that a more clear-cut pattern of gainers and losers would not have done. However, international agreement has been hampered by the reluctance of some countries to slow economic growth in face of an uncertain threat, and by disputes about the relative shares of responsibility for emissions and their consequences.   JEm

Grand Theory   A term devised by the sociologist C. Wright Mills (1959) to attack what he took to be the obsessive concern of postwar social science with empty conceptual elaboration ('the associating and dissociating of concepts') at high levels of ABSTRACTION. In his view, 'Grand Theory' was more or less severed from the irredeemably concrete concerns of everyday social life and largely indifferent to its immense variety in time and space. His main target was Talcott Parsons, the architect of STRUCTURAL FUNCTIONALISM, against whom he insisted that 'there is no "grand theory"', no one universal scheme in terms of which we can understand the unity of social structure, no one answer to the tired old problem of social order'. Since Mills wrote, and despite his spirited objections, a number of other candidates for 'grand theory' have emerged (see, for example,

CRITICAL THEORY; STRUCTURAL MARXISM; STRUCTURALISM; STRUCTURATION THEORY): in such numbers, indeed, that Skinner (1985) writes of 'the *return* of Grand Theory'. This has not gone unremarked by the critics, and in human geography Ley (1989) has complained of a *fixation* upon THEORY, of the privilege currently accorded to the 'theorization of theories', second-order abstractions 'doubly removed from the empirical world', the proliferation of which is producing what he sees as a disturbing fragmentation of intellectual inquiry. Set against this, however, and from the perspective of a broadly MARXIST GEOGRAPHY, Harvey and Scott (1989) agonize over what they see as a *withdrawal* from 'the theoretical imperative' and, in consequence, the dissolution of intellectual inquiry into a host of empirical particulars and fragments. But the pervasive fragmentation that dismays all of these writers (in different ways) is itself often a product of theoretical work outside the traditional confines of (and in large measure working against) 'grand theory': see, for example, POSTMODERNISM, POSTSTRUCTURALISM and PRAGMATISM.
                                    DG

References

Harvey, D. and Scott, A. 1989: The practice of human geography: theory and empirical specificity in the transition from Fordism to flexible accumulation. In Macmillan, B., ed., *Remodelling geography*. Oxford: Blackwell, pp. 217–29.

Ley, D. 1989: Fragmentation, coherence and limits to theory in human geography. In Kobayashi, A. and Mackenzie, S., eds, *Remaking human geography*. London: Unwin Hyman, pp. 227–44.

Mills, C. W. 1959: *The sociological imagination*. New York: Oxford University Press.

Skinner, Q., ed. 1985: *The return of grand theory in the human sciences*. Cambridge: Cambridge University Press.

Suggested Reading

Harvey and Scott (1989).
Ley (1989).
Skinner (1985), ch. 1.

graph theory   A branch of mathematics that investigates the properties of the topological diagrams known as graphs, which can be drawn to represent many

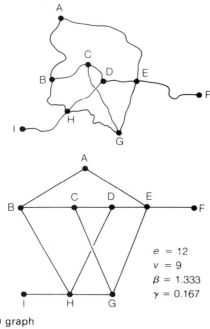

$$e = 12$$
$$v = 9$$
$$\beta = 1.333$$
$$\gamma = 0.167$$

(a) graph

	A	B	C	D	E	F	G	H	I
A	–	1	0	0	1	0	0	0	0
B	1	–	1	0	0	0	0	1	0
C	0	1	–	1	0	0	1	0	0
D	0	0	1	–	1	0	0	1	0
E	1	0	0	1	–	1	1	0	0
F	0	0	0	0	1	–	0	0	0
G	0	0	1	0	1	0	–	1	0
H	0	1	0	1	0	0	1	–	1
I	0	0	0	0	0	0	0	1	–

(b) binary connectivity matrix

graph theory *The interpretation of a railway network as a graph (a) and as a binary connectivity matrix (b).*

different types of geographical NETWORK, especially transport networks. These diagrams represent the terminals and junctions of a network (as nodes or vertices) and the routes or links between them (called edges). The graph as a whole may be either *directed* (i.e. the existence of a direct link from A to B does not imply a link in the opposite direction) or *undirected*. Most road networks yield undirected graphs, but an urban area with one-way streets would be represented

by a directed graph (*digraph*). Most geographical applications use *binary* graphs in which only the presence or absence of a link is recorded, but *valued* graphs are also used.

Another important distinction is between *planar* graphs, which can be topologically represented in a single plane without edges intersecting except at vertices, and *nonplanar* graphs, where such a representation is impossible (airline networks are typically non-planar). Finally, there is a distinction between *unitary* graphs (where every vertex is connected, however indirectly, with every other vertex) and *divided* graphs (where several disconnected subgraphs exist).

Graph theory was first emphasized in TRANSPORT GEOGRAPHY by W. L. Garrison, D. F. Marble and their associates. The simplest graph theory measures (see the figure) are based upon the number of vertices (*v*), the number of edges (*e*) and the number of subgraphs (*p*):

$$\beta = e/v$$

and

$$\gamma = e/[3(v - 2)] \qquad \text{for planar graphs}$$

or

$$\gamma = e/[v(v - 1)] \qquad \text{for non-planar graphs.}$$

The β index not only describes the mean number of edges per node, but values less than one indicate a tree-like network with no circuits. The γ index compares the actual number of edges present with the maximum number possible (for given *v*), so that the closer it approaches unity the more the network approaches maximal CONNECTIVITY. In addition, use is made of other combinations of *e*, *v* and *p*, and of the *diameter* of the network (the greatest number of edges on the shortest path, in edge terms, between pairs of vertices). Early studies demonstrated that these measures could be correlated with independent variables (e.g. terrain, shape of a region or level of economic development).

The simple graph can also be used to characterize individual vertices. The *degree* of a vertex is the number of edges serving that vertex (and, by implication, the number of other vertices with which it has a direct connection). The *centrality* or *associated number* of a vertex is the number of edges in the shortest path to the most remote of all the other vertices.

Graphs can also be represented and manipulated in the form of binary connectivity matrices (C) in which each row and each column represents a vertex and the cell entry 1 or 0 represents the presence or absence of a link (see the figure). This matrix is suited to analysis by matrix algebra and is most often used to examine the ACCESSIBILITY of individual vertices within the network. The row and column totals represent the degree of each vertex, but more importantly the matrix can be used to construct a power series:

$$C^1 \ C^2 \ C^3 \ C^4 \ \ldots \ C^n$$

The cell values in the ijth cell of the nth power of C give the number of ways in which it is possible to move from i to j by traversing exactly n edges or links. So cells of the summed series:

$$C^1 + C^2 + C^3 + C^4 + \ldots + C^n$$

will give the number of direct and indirect routes between places, up to and including routes which are n edges in length. Other authors have favoured summing the series

$$S^1C^1 + S^2C^2 + S^3C^3 + S^4C^4 + \ldots + S^nC^n$$

because if the value of the scalar S is set at less than one the more indirect links are discounted by the powering procedure. There are also questions as to which power should be chosen to terminate the series; some argue that n should equal the diameter of the network, but other values can be chosen.

The adoption of these methods in transport geography (in the early waves of the QUANTITATIVE REVOLUTION) led to a recognition that the problems involved are shared by other areas of human geography (e.g. studies of social contacts within a community), and physical geography (e.g. interconnecting distributaries within a river delta). However, they have proved to be of limited usefulness, for two reasons: first, there is substantial loss of information in representing links which vary greatly in length, quality etc. by a single binary value; second, the expansion of computer capacity and programming methods now makes it possible to represent and analyse a network in much greater detail. (See also SPATIAL STRUCTURE.)   AMH

Suggested Reading

Hoggett, P. and Chorley, R. J. 1969: *Network models in geography*. London: Edward Arnold.

Taaffe, E. J. and Gauthier, H. L. 1973: *Geography of transportation*. Englewood Cliffs, NJ: Prentice-Hall.

Tinkler, K. J. 1977: *An introduction to graph theoretical methods in geography*. Concepts and techniques in modern geography 14. Norwich: Geo Books.

Wilson, R. J. 1979: *Introduction to graph theory*. New York: Academic Press.

graphicacy The visual–spatial component of human intelligence, complementing literacy, numeracy and articulacy. The term was coined by Balchin (1972) to cover 'the communication of spatial information that cannot be conveyed adequately by verbal or numerical means'. It focuses on the map rather than photographs and works of art, therefore, and promotion of this skill is presented as a major goal of geographical education. (See CARTOGRAPHY.)   RJJ

Reference

Balchin, W. G. V. 1972: Graphicacy. *Geogr.* 57, pp. 185–95.

gravity model A mathematical model which has been used to account for a wide range of flow patterns in human geography (MIGRATION, telephone traffic, passenger movements, commodity flow, etc.).

The original model, proposed by exponents of SOCIAL PHYSICS, was based on a crude analogy with Newton's gravitational equation:

$$G_{ij} = g \ M_iM_j/d_{ij}{}^2$$

This can be interpreted as follows: the gravitational force (G_{ij}) between two masses (M_i and M_j) is proportional to a gravitational constant (g) and to the product of their masses (M_iM_j), and inversely proportional to the square of the distance between them ($d_{ij}{}^2$).

The analogy with migration, for example, was given as:

$$F_{ij} = g \, P_i P_j / d_{ij}{}^2,$$

where the migrant flow (F_{ij}) from i to j was seen as being proportional to the product of the populations of the two places. In such a model the constant g was empirically determined by simple arithmetic methods. At a later stage the model was fitted by regression methods in logarithmic form:

$$\log(F_{ij}/P_i P_j) = \log g + b \log d_{ij},$$

in which case both g and the exponent for distance (b) were empirically determined by CALIBRATION. Planning applications soon revealed that these forms gave poor fits to real data sets, so *ad hoc* adjustments were made to the form of the model. Some focused upon the relationship with distance, fitting, for example, the exponential model (see DISTANCE DECAY):

$$F_{ij} = gP_i P_j e^{-bd_{ij}}$$

(where e is the root of Napierian logarithms). Other adjustments were made to the P_i and/or P_j terms to ensure that the total flow predicted by the model, either from an origin, or to a destination, or both, equalled the actual flow. Where only one of these was attempted the model was termed either *origin constrained* or *destination constrained*; where both were attempted the model was termed *doubly constrained* and took the form:

$$F_{ij} = A_i P_i B_j P_j e^{-bd_{ij}}$$

where the new symbols A_i and B_j were calibrating constants which had to be empirically determined by an iterative procedure. But such forms were a long way from the original analogy with physics and a stronger rationale was required. There have been several attempts to provide this on the basis of likelihood maximizing, utility maximizing and ENTROPY-MAXIMIZING; the last, due to Wilson (1974), has been widely accepted. His method also demonstrated close links between gravity models on one hand and models based on INTERVENING OPPORTUNITY and the TRANSPORTATION PROBLEM.

Despite its problems the gravity model is widely used in transport planning: the great variety of forms means that an approximate fit to data can nearly always be achieved, although a number of questions have been raised about a number of technical aspects. Those who believe that its theoretical content is weak fear that it may prove to be a bad predictive tool and advocate other methods (e.g. with a stronger behavioural basis – see DISAGGREGATE TRAVEL DEMAND MODELLING): others note that using gravity models to plan will in any case lead to a perpetuation of the status quo or even to a more unequal distribution of welfare (Sayer, 1971). (See also DISTANCE DECAY; FRICTION OF DISTANCE.)   AMH

References

Sayer, A. 1971: Gravity models and spatial autocorrelation, or atrophy in urban and regional modelling. *Area* 9, pp. 183–89.

Wilson, A. G. 1974: *Urban and regional models in geography and planning.* Chichester: John Wiley.

Suggested Reading

Fotheringham, A. S. 1991: Migration and spatial structure: the development of the competing destination model. In Stillwell, J. C. and Compton, P., eds, *Migration models.* London: Belhaven, pp. 57–72.

Senior, M. L. 1979: From gravity modelling to entropy maximising: a pedagogic guide. *Prog. hum. Geogr.* 3, pp. 179–211.

Taylor, P. J. 1975: *Distance decay models in spatial interactions.* Concepts and techniques in modern geography 2. *Norwich: Geo Books.*

Tocalis, T. R. 1978: Changing theoretical foundations for the gravity concept of human interaction. In Berry B. J. L., ed., *The nature of change in geographic ideas.* DeKalb, IL: Northern Illinois University Press, pp. 66–124.

green belt   An area of open, low-density land use surrounding existing major cities and CONURBATIONS where further extension, including the possible merging of urban areas, is strictly controlled. Green belts represent the largest element in the land-use planning of metropolitan England since the Second World War, and feature prominently in some URBAN

AND REGIONAL PLANNING strategies, especially in South-east England. Although the term is sometimes now also applied overseas, its origins, implementation and significance are predominantly English.

The first such formal proposal appeared in Ebenezer Howard's GARDEN CITY scheme, where the green belt provided for agriculture and recreation and acted as a buffer against excessive urban growth and coalescence. A variety of green belts were advocated around London from the 1890s onwards (Elson, 1986), but land-acquisition costs to local authorities proved prohibitive until the 1947 Town and Country Planning Act. This allowed green belt designations to be proposed under county Development Plans and, subsequently, Structure Plans, a trend encouraged by a central government circular of 1955 extolling their virtues. Although many proposals have not been formally approved by central government, and others only after an extended delay, approved green belts still cover some 11 per cent of England, with the acreage doubling between 1979 and 1988.

The 1980s saw a renewal of interest and controversy. For some, green belts are to restrain urban growth, while others emphasize the provision of recreation and amenity space, or safeguarding agriculture and mineral workings in urban England. (Indeed, the majority of green belt land is in private ownership.) For their opponents (especially in the housing lobby) green belts are negative devices, preventing development by 'NIMBY'-minded residents and planning authorities, thereby raising the cost of development of the national economy by insulating such land from 'normal' development pressures and processes. Government resolve on the green belts was also perceived as weakening in the 1980s, despite two further (controversial) circulars in 1983 and 1984.   AGH

Reference

Elson, M. 1986: *Green belts*. London: Heinemann.

Further Reading

Munton, R. J. C. 1983: *London's green belt: containment in practice*. London: Allen and Unwin.

green revolution A term formerly used about land reform in Eastern Europe in the 1920s and 1930s, but since the 1960s used to describe the adoption of a package of agricultural practices in developing countries, particularly in Asia. New High Yielding Varieties (HYV) of wheat were bred in Mexico in the 1950s and of rice in the Philippines in the early 1960s, and distributed to farmers in the mid-1960s. Yields were much higher than those obtained with indigenous varieties, but required optimum growing conditions. They were most successfully grown when chemical fertilizers were used, and there was liberal use of irrigation. The early HYVs lacked the immunity to disease that local varieties possessed. They are dwarf varieties, highly responsive to fertilizer, and not sensitive to day length, and so can be grown widely: they mature more rapidly than traditional varieties, thus allowing double cropping. Where double cropping is practised the package requires extra labour, and as the inputs are divisible they can be adopted as easily on small as on large farms, although in the 1960s and 1970s they were adopted more rapidly on the larger farms, and the rate of adoption was most rapid in areas where irrigation already existed. The HYV package has been widely adopted in Asia – including China, where new varieties were independently bred – and have had least impact in tropical Africa, where wheat and rice are little grown and irrigation is uncommon.

Although the adoption of the new HYVs has undoubtedly led to marked increases in output since the 1960s, there have been many criticisms of their impact upon the social structure of the communities in which they have been adopted: there is a large and often controversial literature on the subject (Karim, 1986).   DBG

Reference

Karim, M. B. 1986: *The green revolution, an international bibliography*. New York: Greenwood Press.

Suggested Reading

Bayliss-Smith, T. and Wanmali, S., eds 1984: *Understanding green revolutions: agrarian change and development planning in South Asia*. Cambridge: Cambridge University Press.

Dalrymple, D. 1979: The adoption of high yielding grain varieties in developing nations. *Ag. Hist.* 53, pp. 704–26.

Farmer, B. H., ed. 1977: *Green Revolution? Technology and change in rice-growing areas of Tamil Nadu and Sri Lanka.* London: Macmillan/ Boulder, CO: Westview Press.

Lipton, M. with Richard Longhurst 1989: *New seeds and poor people.* London: Unwin Hyman.

Rigg, J. 1989: The green revolution. *Geogr.* 74, pp. 144–50.

greenhouse effect See GLOBAL WARMING.

gross domestic product (GDP) A monetary measure of the value at market prices of goods and services produced within a (national) economy over a given period of time, normally a year or a quarter. The value of intermediate products – most notably raw materials – is excluded and incorporated in the market price of goods for final consumption or investment. No allowance is made for expenditure on the replacement of capital assets, and the use of market prices incorporates the value of indirect taxes and subsidies. The subtraction of indirect taxes and the addition of subsidies produces GDP at factor cost. GDP may be valued at current prices or in real terms.

GDP provides a better guide to domestic production than GROSS NATIONAL PRODUCT (GNP), and tends to be favoured as a measure of performance by industrial economies because it excludes net income from abroad. In most countries (e.g. the USA, the UK and Japan), this adjustment makes little difference. But in countries such as Kuwait, with large overseas investments, GNP is about 35 per cent greater than GDP, whereas in the Republic of Ireland and Brazil, for example, GNP is about 14 per cent less than GDP.

Like GNP, GDP is seriously deficient as a measure of economic activity, omitting whole areas of work undertaken in the non-monetary part of the economy (see, e.g. Waring, 1989) and perversely counting as wealth creation that which destroys the natural foundations of all productive activity (see, e.g., Anderson, 1991).   RL

References

Anderson, V. 1991: *Alternative economic indicators.* London: Routledge.

Waring, M. 1989: *If women counted: a new feminist economics.* London: Macmillan.

gross national product (GNP) GROSS DOMESTIC PRODUCT (GDP) plus net income from abroad (i.e. GNP equals GDP plus profits, dividends and income earned overseas minus such overseas payments to other countries). GNP at factor cost is the market value of GNP net of indirect taxes and subsidies. Although many industrial economies favour GDP as a measure of domestic economic performance, Germany and Japan currently use GNP. International comparisons of GNP avoiding exchange rate fluctuations may be facilitated by the use of purchasing power parities (a measure of the quantity of goods that nominal GNP will buy in each country) in converting currencies to a common base.

Like GDP, GNP is seriously deficient as a measure of economic activity, omitting whole areas of work undertaken in the non-monetary part of the economy (see, e.g. Waring, 1989) and perversely counting as wealth creation that which destroys the natural foundations of all productive activity (see, e.g., Anderson, 1991).   RL

References

Anderson, V. 1991: *Alternative economic indicators.* London: Routledge.

Waring, M. 1989: *If women counted: a new feminist economics.* London: Macmillan.

growth See DEVELOPMENT; LIMITS TO GROWTH; ZERO POPULATION GROWTH.

growth pole A dynamic and highly integrated set of industries organized around a propulsive leading sector or industry (*industrie motrice*). A growth pole is capable of rapid growth and of generating growth through spillover and multiplier effects in the rest of the economy.

This idea, associated with François Perroux (1955), was translated into spatial terms by Boudeville (1966). On the bases of EXTERNAL ECONOMIES and economies of AGGLOMERATION, Boudeville argued that the set of industries forming the growth pole (or *pôle de croissance*) might be clustered spatially and linked to an existing urban area. He also pointed to the regionally differentiated growth that such a spatial strategy might generate. The precise meaning of the term 'growth pole' has been made difficult to pin down, however, because it is frequently used in a far looser fashion to denote any (planned) spatial clustering of economic activity.

The apparent simplicity of the notion, its suggestion of dynamism and its ability to wed problems of sectoral growth and planning with those of intra- and inter-regional growth and physical planning led to its ready acceptance and widespread use in URBAN, REGIONAL and national PLANNING. However, there are several difficulties associated with both the idea and practice of growth poles. These difficulties fall into three broad groups. First, there are the technical problems. These include: (a) the interdependent decisions to be made on an appropriate location, threshold size and sectoral composition of a growth pole within an urban or regional network of firms; (b) the distinction between spontaneous and planned poles with the need, in the latter case at least, for integrated social and physical planning; (c) the nature of the intersectoral and interregional transmission of growth; (d) the facilitative relationship between state-provided services and INFRASTRUCTURE and the success of the growth pole; (e) the relationships between the pole and the existing, unevenly developed, city distributions; and (f) the need for monitoring and management to avoid diseconomies. Second, the appropriate time span over which to judge success or failure – say, 15–25 years – may be too long in political terms, as elected governments will wish positive results of policy to be clear over the length of the electoral cycle (which

is usually less than four years). Third, the success of a growth pole must depend upon the extent to which it conforms to the productive and reproductive demands of the society in which it is located. The process of production both helps to create and necessarily takes place in an existing landscape. As production itself changes, it makes fresh demands upon the landscape, demands which may not be met within its existing dimensions. As a result the landscape must be changed. A growth pole is a planned insertion into this constantly changing landscape. It must, therefore, combine with what is already there in both physical and functional terms as well as provide an appropriate location for the extension or reorganization of production. In short, growth poles – like any other planned spatial strategy for production – can never be autonomous of the underlying productive dynamic. As a result they may also generate problems relating to UNEVEN DEVELOPMENT. Growth poles provide a particularly clear and direct example of the implication of the STATE in the structure and dynamic of the wider society of which it is an inseparable part.   RL

References

Boudeville, J. R. 1966: *Problems of regional economic planning*. Edinburgh: Edinburgh University Press.

Perroux, F. 1955: Note sur la notion de pôle de croissance. *Économie Appliquée* 7, pp. 307–20.

Suggested Reading

Buttler, F. A. 1975: *Growth pole theory and economic development*. Farnborough: Saxon House/Lexington, MA: Lexington Press.

Dicken, P. and Lloyd, P. E. 1990: *Location in space: theoretical perspectives in economic geography*. New York: Harper and Row, ch. 6.

Healey, M. J. and Ilbery, B. W. 1990: *Location and change: perspectives on economic geography*. Oxford: Oxford University Press, ch. 15.

H

habitus A system of internalized dispositions that mediates between social structures and practical activity. The concept derives from the work of Bourdieu (1971, 1990) and has both a vertical and a horizontal dimension. 'Vertically', Bourdieu offers the concept as a means of overcoming the dichotomy between STRUCTURALISM and the philosophy of the subject. In French, *'disposition'* means both 'the result of an organizing action' and 'a predisposition', and the recursive movement between *result* and *predisposition* within the flow of practical activity, spiralling through the reproduction of objective structures, has something in common with Giddens's STRUCTURATION THEORY. Indeed, in much the same way Bourdieu insists that the habitus is reducible neither to the imperative of structures nor to the intentionality of agents, and offers his theory of practice as a way of transcending the opposition between them (Brubaker, 1985). But it is not difficult to see why some of his critics disagree. Honneth (1986) claims that the habitus must depend on a reductionist model, because it is in some substantial degree the lateral extension of social structures that shapes and underwrites the horizontal span of the habitus as 'the locus of practical realization of the "articulation" of fields'. Bourdieu argues that the coherence of different social practices is the result of 'the coherence which the generative principles constituting that habitus owe to the social structures of which they are a product and which they tend to reproduce.' By extension, therefore, and 'horizontally', Bourdieu intends the habitus to harmonize and homologize social practices from one sphere of social life to another. Hence:

One of the fundamental effects of the orchestration of habitus is the production of a common-sense world endowed with the objectivity secured by consensus on the meaning . . . of practices and the world . . . The homogeneity of habitus is what – within the limits of the group of agents possessing the schemes (of production and interpretation) implied in their production – cause practices and works to be immediately intelligible and foreseeable and hence taken-for-granted.

The concept of the habitus is thus a way of elucidating the coherence of social life: its systematicity is always partial and precarious – always an achievement, something to be negotiated through social practice rather than imposed through a trans-situational logic – but it is none the less real. In human geography, the concept has been deployed in two ways: as part of the general discussion of HUMAN AGENCY (Thrift, 1983) and, more specifically, as part of a discusssion of the dislocating effects of TIME–SPACE COMPRESSION on the habitus (Harvey, 1989).   DG

References

Bourdieu, P. 1971: *Outline of the theory of practice.* Cambridge: Cambridge University Press.

Bourdieu, P. 1990: *The logic of practice.* Stanford, CA: Stanford University Press.

Brubaker, R. 1985: Rethinking classical theory: the sociological vision of Pierre Bourdieu. *Theory and Society* 14, pp. 747–75.

Harvey, D. 1989: *The condition of postmodernity: an enquiry into the origins of cultural change.* Oxford: Blackwell.

Honneth, A. 1986: The fragmented world of symbolic forms: reflections on Pierre Bourdieu's sociology of culture. *Theory, Culture and Society* 3, pp. 55–66.

Thrift, N. 1983: On the determination of social action in space and time. *Environ. Plann. D: Society and Space* 1, pp. 23–57.

Suggested Reading
Harker, R., Mahar, C. and Wilkes, C. 1990: *An introduction to the work of Pierre Bourdieu: the practice of theory.* London: Macmillan.

hazard, human-made Human-made hazards are products, processes and other conditions that potentially threaten individuals and/or their reproduction (in all senses). These hazards are somewhat distinguishable from ENVIRONMENTAL HAZARDS by the level of human involvement in causation: for example, a volcanic eruption would be considered an environmental or natural hazard, whereas radioactive wastes would be considered a human-made hazard. Yet although the event of the eruption and the event or process of waste production may be thus distinguished, their human consequences which transform them from events into hazards are not so readily separated into human and non-human categories. A natural event becomes a hazard only because social processes have left some people exposed to its effects. Moreover, with the growing recognition of the human impact on the environment, some (although not all) environmental hazard events have been seen as possessing a human component (e.g. floods, exacerbated by deforestation, or drought by GLOBAL WARMING). Thus, the dualism between 'natural' and 'human-made' hazards has collapsed in recent years.

Much discussion of human-made hazards has centred upon technological risk (cf. RISK). Technological risks are considered to be 'side-effects' or contingencies of technological systems or processes. Researchers have developed taxonomies of risk that identify characteristics of production (e.g. incidental versus purposive causation) or of consequence (e.g. pervasive or isolated in time and space, or catastrophic and transgenerational: see Hohenemser et al., 1983). This sort of hazards or risk profiling has contributed to understanding about social perception and acceptance of risks, and to the development of priorities for managing or reducing risk.

Geographers have contributed immeasurably to expanding the notion of risk in society. Physical scientists tend to express risks as conditional probabilities for experiencing harm, and frequently seek to use these probabilities as bases for prescribing social response. In contrast, the public judges on more complex scales (Hohenemser et al., 1982), and some progress has been made in integrating social, cultural and psychological paradigms of risk or hazards perception and assessment (Kasperson et al., 1988). Personal histories and psychological dispositions, the media, experts, institutions, local history – these and many other factors coincide to shape outlooks, judgments and fears when it comes to specific hazards (Johnson and Covello, 1987; Sood et al., 1987).   JEm

References
Hohenemser, C., Kasperson, R. E. and Kates, R. W. 1982: Causal structure: a framework for policy formulation. In Hohenemser, C. and Kasperson, J., eds, *Risk in the technological society*, AAAS Selected Symposium 65. Boulder, CO: Westview Press, pp. 109–40.

Hohenemser, C., Kates, R. W. and Slovic, P. 1983: The nature of technological hazard. *Science* 220, pp. 378–84.

Johnson, B. B. and Covello, V. T., eds 1987: *The social construction of risk.* Dordrecht: D. Reidel.

Kasperson, R. et al. 1988: The social amplification of risk. *Risk Analysis* 8(2), pp. 194–200.

Sood, R., Stockdale, S. G. and Rogers, E. M. 1987: How the news media operate in natural disasters. *J. Commun.* 37(3), pp. 27–41.

Suggested Reading
Kasperson, R. E. and Pijawka, K. D. 1985: Societal response to hazards and major hazard events: comparing natural and technological hazards. *Publ. Admin. Rev.*, Special Issue.

Johnson and Covello (1987).

Zeigler, D. J., Johnson, J. H. and Brunn, S. D. 1983: *Technological hazards.* Washington, DC: Association of American Geographers.

health and health care, geography of The application of geographical perspectives and methods to the study of the health of populations, the health of individuals and human activities that relate to health.

These are topics which have growing importance in the field of MEDICAL GEOGRAPHY. There is an increasing emphasis in this field on *health* in a broad sense, rather than the traditional perspective of medical geography which focused on specific medically *diagnosed diseases*. The interpretation of health now being adopted often reflects the definition proposed by the World Health Organisation, which suggests that health is complete mental and physical well-being, rather than just the absence of disease.

Health care can be interpreted quite broadly to include a range of care intended to promote good health, prevent illness and treat people who have become ill. Health care is often viewed as comprising both *primary health care* services (provided in community-based clinics and surgeries or in people's homes) and *secondary and tertiary services* (which are usually hospital-based). Most studies of health care focus on professional health care services organized or provided by the STATE (in the *public sector*) or by the *independent sector* (commercial health care organizations or non-profit-making agencies). However, health care might also be taken to include both 'informal' care, provided by non-professional carers such as relatives, neighbours and friends, and self-help.

Health is still often studied by medical geographers in terms of indicators of morbidity and mortality (see MEDICAL GEOGRAPHY), and there is an important area of medical geography which seeks to analyse the spatial distribution of diseases and their association with factors in the social and physical environment. However, geographers have also become more concerned with the theoretical and methodological questions of definition and measurement of health. Illness, as perceived by lay people as well as by doctors, and more positive aspects of health, such as well-being and healthy growth, are among the dimensions of health investigated. This approach has often involved the use of social SURVEY methods which seek to measure and compare self-reported health and illness in the population of particular areas and, more recently, more ETHNOGRAPHIC techniques (also employed by sociologists and anthropologists) have also been used by medical geographers to improve our understanding of how the social and physical environments interact with personal perceptions and beliefs to influence the experience of health for particular individuals. These studies have often focused on less privileged members of society, and have revealed how the constraints of material and social deprivation interact with access to health care and individual lifestyles and beliefs about health to influence people's experience of health and illness. Theories of social inequality and social position, including theories of poverty, GENDER relations and RACE relations, are therefore relevant to the geographical study of health.

The focus on health care in medical geography is also a rather recent development. Studies of health care services which are organized or provided by the state also form part of the geography of PUBLIC SERVICES. Studies of health care provision in the independent sector have shown that these have a geography which is different from that of public health services.

Early studies in the geography of health care tended to concentrate on physical access for patients to services which treat diseases – in hospitals, clinics and doctors' surgeries. More recent studies have examined preventative services (e.g. uptake of immunization and health screening services) and have looked at a wider range of factors likely to influence access to and use of these services. These factors include time constraints and access to transportation, as well as the effects of distance, people's knowledge and/or perception of the service, and the impact of economic, social and cultural barriers to obtaining care (including the effects of poverty, social position, gender role and RACISM).

Part of the objective of studies of the geography of health care is to investigate how well the spatial variation in health care provision matches spatial differences in a population's need for services. The definition of population need for health services presents numerous theoretical and methodological challenges. The analysis of geographical patterns of health care provision is also complex, and may involve analysis of the quality of services (whether they are appropriate and acceptable to the populations of particular areas) as well as the quantity of provision (numbers of facilities and personnel provided for those needing to use them in particular geographical areas).

The geography of health services may be compared at the international as well as the intranational scale. Health care varies between different countries, and also between areas within the same country, in ways which reflect numerous factors including demography, health status, variations in social and economic conditions, and political ideologies concerning health care objectives and the appropriate roles of the WELFARE STATE and the independent sector in health care. These analyses address important issues of EQUALITY, EQUITY and EFFICIENCY in the spatial distribution of need and resources for health care which are informed by theories of social and TERRITORIAL JUSTICE and the economy of welfare which are also important to the geography of public services.

SC

Suggested Reading

Eyles, J. and Donovan, J. 1990: *The social effects of health policy.* Brookfield, Ill.: Avebury.

Eyles, J. and Woods, K. 1983: *The social geography of medicine and health.* London: Croom Helm.

Jones, K. and Moon, G. 1987: *Health, disease and society: an introduction to medical geography.* London: Routledge and Kegan Paul.

Joseph, A. and Phillips, D. 1984: *Accessibility and utilization: geographical perspectives on health delivery.* New York: Harper and Row.

Phillips, D. R. 1990: *Health and health care in the Third World.* London: Longman.

heartland A geopolitical concept first coined by the British geographer Sir Halford Mackinder in 1904, and later used in cold war discourse to denote an area of Eurasia roughly synonymous with the boundaries of the Russian Empire/USSR. Mackinder suggested that the Columbian era of sea power, which had given Europe its pivotal role for the past four centuries, was coming to a close and was being eclipsed by the ascendancy of land-based powers and in particular with a new 'geopolitical pivot of history', namely the

'heart-land' of 'Euro-Asia' (Mackinder, 1904, pp. 430–1). For Mackinder, whoever could gain control of this world island would be in an almost unstoppable position to dominate the entire globe. The key to control of the heartland, Mackinder later argued, lay in Eastern Europe, reflecting a powerful strand of pre- and post-Versailles geopolitical thinking concerning the need to separate the two land powers of Russia and Germany through the creation of a series of 'buffer states'. Despite the ENVIRONMENTAL DETERMINISM inherent in much of Mackinder's geopolitical writings, the simplicity of the heartland concept was to play an influential part in Western geopolitical thinking concerning the image of an expansionist USSR. (See also GEOPOLITICS.)

GES

References and Suggested Reading

Hauner, M. 1990: *What is Asia to us? Russia's Asian heartland yesterday and today.* London: Unwin Hyman.

Mackinder, H. J. 1904: The geographical pivot of history. *Geogrl. J.* 23, pp. 421–37.

Mackinder, H. J. 1919: *Democratic ideals and reality: a study in the politics of reconstruction.* London: Constable.

hegemony, cultural The capacity of a dominant group to exercise control, not through visible rule or the deployment of force, but rather through the willing acquiescence of citizens to accept subordinate status by their affirmation of cultural, social and political practices and institutions which are fundamentally unequal. Current use of the term is derived from the prison writings of Antonio Gramsci (1971), incarcerated by the Italian Fascist state between 1928 and 1935. Like other critical intellectuals of the era (most notably the Frankfurt School) who lived through the rise of totalitarian government in democratic nations, Gramsci reflected on the problem of social order, on how citizens might willingly lend their assent to forms of government that curtailed their freedoms and denied other democratic ideals.

Hegemony incorporates more than the IDEOLOGY of a dominant elite, the VALUES and beliefs which it disseminates. It also includes the sedimentation of these values and interests in everyday practices and institutional arrangements. It is, therefore, 'a lived system of meanings and values – constitutive and constituting – which as they are experienced as practices appear as reciprocally confirming' (Williams, 1977, p. 110). Buried in everyday life, hegemonic processes become taken for granted and 'natural'. As a result, popular culture plays a significant theoretical and political role in the achievement of hegemony – or, indeed, resistance to it.

The concept has proven valuable in cultural studies, and a new CULTURAL GEOGRAPHY is examining the reproduction of domination by elite groups. In an interpretation of North American Chinatowns, Anderson (1988, 1991) has noted how the use of RACE as a dominant colonial discourse impregnated the routine practices of the STATE and reproduced the marginal status of 'the oriental'. 'Chinatown' as a category, rather than as a place, was not innocent in the fabrication of this cultural fiction. In a different context, Duncan (1990) has detailed the critical role of a ritualized landscape and its supportive meanings to sustain royal power in pre-colonial Kandy, Sri Lanka. Resistance to the centralized and often tyrannical rule of the king by an oppositional elite proceeded by de-naturalizing his building projects. This deconstruction of the king's landscapes was simultaneously a challenge to the king's power and right to rule.

These examples introduce two additional developments of the concept of hegemony. Although presented by Gramsci primarily in the context of HISTORICAL MATERIALISM and its characteristic focus on CLASS relations, hegemony is applicable to the interpretation of other sources of domination, such as RACISM and PATRIARCHY. Second, the penetration of dominant values into the 'whole social process' does not mean that its terms are not negotiated, or indeed resisted. There has sometimes been a tendency to treat hegemonic forces as systemic and total, as a static and paralysing presence, with their effects assumed rather than demonstrated. Such a theorization negates Gramsci's view of cultural hegemony as 'a moving equilibrium', dynamic, evolving, yet oscillating around a consensual form. One of the contributions of the Birmingham Centre for Contemporary Cultural Studies has been to document the 'rituals or resistance' of a number of working-class, youth subcultures to mainstream norms (Hall and Jefferson, 1976). In these instances, resistance has often been symbolic; that is, the subculture has assumed a style of dress or ornament (a safety pin, for example) intended to be subversive to the pervasive and accepted forms of the dominant culture. The rapid onset and departure of many of these subcultures underscores the constantly changing and renegotiated nature of cultural forms. Gramsci noted that such fluidity may also exist within the elite itself, a point well-illustrated in the Kandyan Kingdom.   DL

References

Anderson, K. 1988: Cultural hegemony and the race definition process in Chinatown, Vancouver. *Environ. Plann. D: Society and Space* 6, pp. 127–49.

Anderson, K. 1991: *Vancouver's Chinatown: racial discourse in Canada, 1875–1980.* Montreal and Kingston: McGill–Queens Press.

Duncan, J. 1990: *The city as text: the politics of landscape interpretation in the Kandyan Kingdom.* Cambridge: Cambridge University Press.

Gramsci, A. 1971: *Selections from the prison notebooks.* London: Lawrence and Wishart.

Hall, S. and Jefferson, T., eds 1976: *Resistance through rituals: youth subcultures in post-war Britain.* London: Hutchinson/Centre for Contemporary Cultural Studies.

Williams, R. 1977: Hegemony. In *Marxism and literature.* Oxford: Oxford University Press, pp. 108–14.

Suggested Reading

Anderson (1988).

Lears, T. J. 1985: The concept of cultural hegemony: problems and possibilities. *Am. hist. Rev.* 90, pp. 567–93.

Williams (1977).

hermeneutics   The study of interpretation and meaning. Originating with the exegesis of biblical texts, hermeneutical theological scholars used philological methods to clarify the meaning of God's word, as well as to adjudicate among the competing interpretations of it. With the work of F. Schleiermacher (1768–1834), by the end of the eighteenth century hermeneutics had broadened to include the interpretation of historical texts more generally. By suggesting that the interpretation of a text required scrutinizing the very intentions of its author, advocates of hermeneutics were implicitly challenging the relevance for the human sciences of the emerging scientific method.

Wilhelm Dilthey's (1833–1911) late-nineteenth-century writings both generalized hermeneutics and made its critique of natural science explicit. He argued that the human sciences (*Geisteswissenschaften*), because of their subject matter, required a special methodology – hermeneutics – which was very different from the empirical methodology of the natural sciences (*Naturwissenschaften*). In both cases, though, 'objective' knowledge was obtainable. Specifically, Dilthey argued that meaning is found in all kinds of activities and objects: in written texts, certainly, but also in the non-textual; for example, in tools, in landscapes and in individual lives. However, the methodology of natural science would deny such meanings. It would examine each of these things by means of an abstract universal vocabulary: physical properties, geometrical relations and physiological processes. But in so doing the very object of study of the human sciences is abandoned, for meanings are precisely what the human sciences need to understand. How is that meaning to be explicated? The hermeneutical model of interpreting a text provides the key. When we try to understand a piece of writing we bring to it a whole set of presuppositions. By tacking back and forth both between our presuppositions and the text itself, as well as between individual parts of the text and its whole, we eventually gain meaning and understanding. Known as the 'hermeneutical circle', this same procedure can be used to clarify meanings within the sphere of the non-textual. More generally, this approach to interpretation is a creative, progressive and open-ended process in which there is no final truth. Dilthey makes clear, though, that this lack of finality does not imply that interpretation is then a result of personal whim and fancy – that it is purely

subjective. Rather, our interpretations are always made against a set of socially agreed-upon canons and texts, which are themselves publicly accessible in the case of disputations (Rouse, 1987).

In the twentieth century Gadamer (1975) has been the most important proponent of the hermeneutical approach. Arguing that Dilthey was not radical enough, Gadamer rejects the very notion of a general method for arriving at objectivity (Bernstein, 1983). Instead, to use Rorty's (1979) vocabulary, Gadamer is primarily interested in human 'edification', which means being ever open to new evidence and ideas, even though they may be incommensurate with our existing ones. Such openness to challenging the old by the new, the known by the unknown, is only another way of restating the importance of the hermeneutical circle (Bernstein, 1983). In addition, it also highlights hermeneutics' critical edge. Implied by hermeneutics' openness is a critique of the closed nature of GRAND THEORY and other forms of foundationalism. Here we can also see an elective affinity between hermeneutics and POSTMODERNISM, for both are engaged in an anti-foundationalist enterprise. More broadly, the use of a hermeneutical approach has become widespread across a wide range of disciplines during the past two decades, and is found in anthropology (Geertz, 1983), the history and philosophy of science (Feyerabend, 1975) and economics (Mirowski, 1989). The result has been a major challenge to the approach of natural science and, in particular, to the notion that there are fixed methods for revealing the truth.

In geography hermeneutics was originally introduced to contest EMPIRICISM and POSITIVISM as manifest in SPATIAL SCIENCE. Buttimer's (1974) 'dialogical approach', which involved bringing together inside and outside views, was an important early contribution, as was Tuan's (1974) reflexive approach to 'topophilia' ('to know the world is to know oneself'). These early forays were codified in the late 1970s under two different rubrics, HUMANISTIC GEOGRAPHY and CRITICAL THEORY. Humanistic geography made human meaning and intentionality

245

the very core of its concern, while critical theory, as proposed by Gregory (1978), attempted to link the hermeneutical approach to a critique of, in particular, traditional historical and regional geography. This critical impulse has been more generally formalized by Harrison and Livingstone (1980) under their presuppositional approach. Over the past decade the explicit working out of the hermeneutical approach has become less important. None the less, the spirit of hermeneutical inquiry, that is the recognition of the importance of interpretation, open-mindedness, and a critical, reflexive sensibility, is as great as it has ever been (Barnes and Curry, 1983).

TJB

References

Barnes, T. J. and Curry, M. R. 1983: Towards a contextualist approach in human geography. *Trans. Inst. Br. Geogr.* n.s. 8, pp. 467–82.

Bernstein, R. J. 1983: *Beyond objectivism and relativism: science, hermeneutics and praxis.* Philadelphia: University of Pennsylvania Press.

Buttimer, A. 1974: *Values in geography.* Washington, DC: Association of American Geographers, Commission on College Geography, resource paper 24.

Feyerabend, P. 1975: *Against method.* London: Verso.

Gadamer, H.-G. 1975: *Truth and method.* New York: Seabury Press.

Geertz, C. 1983: *Local knowledge: further essays in interpretive anthropology.* New York: Basic Books.

Gregory, D. 1978: *Ideology, science and human geography.* London: Hutchinson.

Harrison, R. T. and Livingstone, D. N. 1980: Philosophy and problems in human geography: a presuppositional approach. *Area* 12, pp. 25–31.

Mirowski, P. 1989: *More heat than light. Economics as social physics: physics as nature's economics.* Cambridge: Cambridge University Press.

Rorty, R. 1979: *Philosophy and the mirror of nature.* Princeton, NJ: Princeton University Press.

Rouse, J. 1987: *Knowledge and power: toward a political philosophy of science.* Ithaca, NY: Cornell University Press.

Tuan, Y.-F. 1974: *Topophilia: a study of environmental perception, attitudes and values.* Englewood Cliffs, NJ: Prentice-Hall.

Suggested Reading

Bernstein (1983).

Gregory (1978).

hinterland The tributary area of a port, from which it collects material to be exported and through which it distributes imports; its complementary area – connected to the port by ship – is termed the *foreland*. In more general usage, the term now refers to the spatial extent of the sphere of influence of any settlement (or of an establishment within a settlement): it is the area for which the settlement is the trading nexus (as in the hexagonal hinterlands of CENTRAL PLACE THEORY). RJJ

historical geography The human geography of the past. Historical geography was being taught as soon as geography became institutionalized as a university discipline in the late nineteenth century. In this early period topics in historical geography included geographies of the Holy Land, the history of discovery and exploration, and the histories of changing state boundaries. Generally speaking, historical geography was fragmented then and did not constitute a distinct subdiscipline within geography.

The origins of modern historical geography date from the 1920s and 1930s when, according to Darby, 'came the rise of historical geography as a *self-conscious* discipline' (Darby, 1983). Darby edited a major text on English historical geography, published in 1936, although E. H. Carrier's *Historical geography of England and Wales,* which covered changing geographies from the prehistoric period to the present day, had appeared in 1925.

In tracing the fortunes of historical geography as the geography of the past we can distinguish between the work of those who consider themselves part of this 'self-conscious' discipline (or subdiscipline), whose prime concern lies with the study of the past, and other geographers who also make reference to the past although their prime concern lies with the present. The subdiscipline of historical geography has produced an overwhelming number of introspective reviews, summaries and methodological articles, so there is no shortage of information on its achievements (e.g. Darby, 1953, 1983; Clark, 1954; Harris, 1971, 1991; Baker, 1972; Baker and Billinge, 1982; Baker and

Gregory, 1984; Norton, 1984; Dennis, 1985; Pacione, 1987; Kearns, 1988; Earle et al. 1989; Meinig, 1989). Both the fortunes of historical geography as a subdiscipline and the attitudes of other geographers towards the role of the past in their own studies can be divided conveniently into three periods.

From the 1930s to the 1960s historical geography was seen as central to the subject of geography as a whole: according to Darby (1953) 'the foundations of geographical study lie in geomorphology and historical geography'. Thus most REGIONAL GEOGRAPHY included a strong historical component as a prelude to the discussion of contemporary issues. Specifically historical regional geographies were produced by historical geographers, particularly in North America (e.g. Clark, 1959), where geographers from the BERKELEY SCHOOL were also involved in reconstructing CULTURAL LANDSCAPES (Williams, 1983). Although British historical geographers expressed an interest in landscape development (e.g. Darby, 1951), as did economic historians (e.g. Hoskins, 1955; Beresford, 1957), the more common approach was to re-create geographies of the past as historical 'cross-sections', often as cartographic reconstructions based on individual historical sources. The most famous of these is Darby's series of volumes on Domesday England (1952–77; see also Lawton and Butlin, 1989) although many other sources were given a similar treatment (see the collection in Baker et al., 1970). These geographies have been criticized for their 'source bound empiricism', almost as though they were adhering to Gilbert's dictum of 1932: 'Historical geography should confine itself to a *descriptive* geographical account of a region at some past period and should *not* endeavour to make the explanation of historical events its main objective'.

The central role of historical geography within geography was challenged by the QUANTITATIVE REVOLUTION. During the 1960s and early 1970s the subdiscipline of historical geography became marginalized as historical approaches were eschewed by other geographers. The descriptive EMPIRICISM of most historical geographers

was out of step with the attempts to 'explain' the world through general theories of spatial organization. Moreover, many historical geographers found the statistical methods of the quantitative revolution alien to their ways of working with historical sources, which were often not amenable to such treatment. For other geographers the past was no longer seen as central to the understanding of the present, as perspectives new to geography such as FUNCTIONALISM campaigned against historical forms of explanation.

Some historical geographers carried on much as before, although their historical geographies were no longer limited to mere description (e.g. Baker and Butlin, 1973; Fox and Butlin, 1979; Langton, 1979). Others rather cautiously began to incorporate new quantitative techniques into their work (e.g. Overton, 1977). At the same time, given their isolation from the rest of geography, it is not surprising that historical geographers heeded Baker's call (1972) and began to look outside their discipline for inspiration – towards economic and social history, and historical anthropology.

The demise of the quantitative revolution as the intellectual dynamic within geography characterizes the third phase in this account of historical geography. In fact, the criticisms from historical geographers were among the most important in contributing to that demise. The attack came on two fronts. First, from the perspective of HISTORICAL MATERIALISM, which obviously brought history to the forefront in understanding the present and, second, from the HUMANISTIC perspective of IDEALISM, which brought human beings back into geography. Perhaps even more important, it was an historical geographer who made geographers confront the notion of examined and unexamined discourse (Gregory, 1978), bringing the wider world of philosophy to their attention, and encouraging them to confront their own philosophical positions.

The subdiscipline of historical geography remains, as it always has been, a relatively small community of scholars. New work in established traditions continues (e.g. Dennis, 1984; Meinig, 1986; Mitchell and Groves 1987; Langton, 1988; Powell,

1988; Ward, 1989; Dodgshon and Butlin, 1990), there are some new departures – e.g. the historical geography of LANGUAGE (Withers, 1984) and of madness (Philo, 1989) – and some former themes are being re-examined (e.g. Driver, 1991).

Meinig (1989) has recently commented that the subdiscipline of historical geography is a 'dangerously weak field' because the number of its practitioners is small. But outside the narrow confines of the 'self-conscious' subdiscipline human geography is increasingly giving a more central role to an historical perspective, the incorporation of which is evident in many areas of geography, although several conceptions of the 'historical' are employed.

Substantive examples of this broader historical approach include studies based on the perspective of POLITICAL ECONOMY, whether they be in ECONOMIC GEOGRAPHY (e.g. Martin, 1988), in POLITICAL GEO-GRAPHY (e.g. WORLD-SYSTEMS ANALY-SIS), in LOCALITY studies, or in THIRD-WORLD studies from the viewpoint of DEPENDENCY theory.

Closer links are also being forged between the subdisciplines of historical geography and CULTURAL GEOGRAPHY, although the two are already closely connected, especially in North America. A major attack on the POSITIVISM of the quantitative revolution and re-affirmation of historical geography came from historical geographers writing from a HUMANISTIC perspective (e.g. Harris, 1971, 1978; Guelke, 1982; see also Daniels, 1985). In Britain studies in the ICONOGRAPHY of landscape are bringing work by historical geographers (e.g. Cosgrove, 1984; Cosgrove and Daniels, 1988) to the heart of a revitalized cultural geography.

However, perhaps the most significant contribution of historical geography to the discipline as a whole is in the construction of an explicit social theory within geography (Harris, 1991). This process is already under way (e.g. Gregory, 1982; Pred, 1990) and its outcome might well be the emergence of time–space structures at the centre of social theory. For the first time in its history, the discipline of geography, with an essential contribution from historical

geography, is taking a lead in theory building for the social sciences as a whole.

Just as an historical perspective is gaining ground in geography so too is a geographical perspective gaining ground in history once again: 'During the last decade or so the long and debilitating separation of geography from history, and more broadly, the social sciences, has begun to be overcome' (Genovese and Hochberg, 1989). In a sense this is a resurgence of the notion of the 'geography behind history' (Darby, 1953). Historians and geographers are also converging in the study of regions (e.g. Langton, 1984; Gregory, 1988): ironically (in Britain at least) a growing concern for regional differences by historians in the 1960s coincided with their abandonment by geographers.   MO

References and Further Reading

Baker, A. R. H., ed. 1972: *Progress in historical geography.* Newton Abbot: David and Charles/New York: Wiley Interscience.

Baker, A. R. H. and Billinge, M. D., eds 1982: *Period and place: research methods in historical geography.* Cambridge: Cambridge University Press.

Baker, A. R. H. and Butlin, R. A., eds 1973: *Studies of field systems in the British Isles.* Cambridge: Cambridge University Press.

Baker, A. R. H. and Gregory, D., eds 1984: *Explorations in historical geography: some interpretive essays.* Cambridge: Cambridge University Press.

Baker, A. R. H., Hamshere, J. and Langton, J., eds 1970: *Geographical interpretations of historical sources.* Newton Abbot; David and Charles/New York: Barnes and Noble.

Beresford, M. 1957: *History on the ground: six studies in maps and landscapes.* London: Methuen.

Carrier, E. H. 1925: *Historical geography of England and Wales.* London: Allen and Unwin.

Clark, A. H. 1954: Historical geography. In James, P. E. and Jones, C. F., eds, *American geography: inventory and prospect.* Syracuse, NY: Syracuse University Press, pp. 70–105.

Clark, A. H. 1959: *Three centuries and the island: a historical geography of settlement and agriculture in Prince Edward Island, Canada.* Toronto: University of Toronto Press.

Cosgrove, D. 1984: *Social formation and symbolic landscape.* London: Croom Helm.

Cosgrove, D. and Daniels, S., eds 1988: *The iconography of landscape: essays on symbolic representation, design and use of past environments.* Cambridge: Cambridge University Press.

Daniels, S. 1985: Arguments for a humanistic geography. In Johnston, R. J., ed., *The future of geography.* London: Methuen, pp. 143–58.

Darby, H. C., ed. 1936: *An historical geography of England before AD 1800.* Cambridge: Cambridge University Press.

Darby, H. C. 1951: The changing English landscape. *Geogrl. J.* 67, pp. 377–98.

Darby, H. C. 1952–77: *The Domesday geography of England,* seven volumes. Cambridge: Cambridge University Press.

Darby, H. C. 1953: On the relations of geography and history. *Trans. Inst. Br. Geogr.* 19, pp. 1–11.

Darby, H. C. 1983: Historical geography in Britain, 1920–1980: continuity and change. *Trans. Inst. Br. Geogr.* n.s. 8, pp. 421–8.

Dennis, R. J. 1984: *English industrial cities in the nineteenth century: a social geography.* Cambridge: Cambridge University Press.

Dennis, R. J. 1985: Historical geography: landscape with figures. *Prog. hum. Geogr.* 9, pp. 575–84.

Dodgshon, R. A. 1987: *The European past: social evolution and the spatial order.* London: Macmillan.

Dodghson, R. A. and Butlin, R. A., eds 1990: *An historical geography of England and Wales,* second edition. London: Academic Press.

Driver, F. 1991: Henry Morton Stanley and his critics: geography, exploration and empire. *Past and Present,* 133, pp. 134–66.

Earle, C. et al. 1989: Historical geography. In Gaile, G. L. and Willmot, C. J., eds, *Geography in America.* Columbus, OH: Merrill, pp. 156–91.

Fox, H. S. A. and Butlin, R. A., eds 1979: *Change in the countryside: essays on rural England 1500–1900.* I. B. G. Special Publication 10.

Genovese, E. D. and Hochberg, L., eds 1989: *Geographic perspectives in history.* Oxford: Blackwell.

Gilbert, E. W. 1932: What is historical geography? *Scott. geogr. Mag.* 48, pp. 129–36.

Gregory, D. 1978: *Ideology, science and human geography.* London: Hutchinson/New York: St. Martin's Press.

Gregory, D. 1982: *Regional transformation and industrial revolution.* London: Macmillan.

Gregory, D. 1988: The production of regions in England's industrial revolution. *J. hist. Geogr.* 14, pp. 50–8.

Guelke, L. 1982: *Historical understanding in geography: an idealist approach.* Cambridge: Cambridge University Press.

Harris, R. C. 1971: Theory and synthesis in historical geography. *Can. Geogr.* 15, pp. 157–72.

Harris, R. C. 1978: The historical mind and the practice of geography. In Ley, D. and Samuels, M. S., eds, *Humanistic geography: prospects and problems.* London: Croom Helm, pp. 123–37.

Harris, R. C. 1991: Power, modernity, and historical geography. *Ann. Ass. Am. Geogr.* 81, pp. 67–83.

Hoskins, W. G. 1955: *The making of the English landscape.* London: Hodder and Stoughton.

Jakle, J. A. 1971: Time, space and the geographic past: a prospectus for historical geography. *Am. hist. Rev.* 76, pp. 1084–103.

Kearns, G. 1988: Historical geography. *Progr. hum. Geogr.* 12, pp. 103–10.

Langton, J. 1979: *Geographical change and industrial revolution.* Cambridge: Cambridge University Press.

Langton, J. 1984: The industrial revolution and the regional geography of England. *Trans. Inst. Br. Geogr.* n.s. 9, pp. 145–67.

Langton, J. 1988: The two traditions of geography, historical geography and the study of landscape. *Geogr. Annlr.* 70B, pp. 17–26.

Lawton, R. and Butlin, R. A. 1989: Clifford Darby: an appreciation. *J. hist. Geogr.* 15, pp. 14–19.

Martin, R. 1988: The political economy of Britain's north–south divide. *Trans. Inst. Br. Geogr.* n.s. 13, pp. 389–418.

Meinig, D. W. 1986: *The shaping of America: a geographical perspective on 500 years of history,* volume 1: *Atlantic America, 1492–1800.* New Haven, CN: Yale University Press.

Meinig, D. W. 1989: The historical geography imperative. *Ann. Ass. Am. Geogr.* 79, pp. 79–87.

Mitchell, R. D. and Groves, P. A., eds 1987: *North America: the historical geography of a changing continent.* Totowa, NJ: Rowman and Littlefield.

Norton, W. 1984: *Historical analysis in geography.* London: Longman.

Overton, M. 1977: Computer analysis of an inconsistent data source: the case of probate inventories. *J. hist. Geogr.* 3, pp. 317–26.

Pacione, M. 1987: *Historical geography: progress and prospect.* London: Croom Helm.

Philo, C. 1989: 'Enough to drive one mad': the organisation of space in nineteenth-century lunatic asylums. In Wolch, J. and Dear, M., eds, *The power of geography: how territory shapes social life.* London: Unwin Hyman, pp. 258–90.

Powell, J. M. 1988: *An historical geography of modern Australia: the restive fringe.* Cambridge: Cambridge University Press.

Pred, A. 1990: *Making histories and constructing human geographies: the local transformation of practice, power relations, and consciousness.* Boulder, CO: Westview Press.

Ward, D. 1989: *Poverty, ethnicity, and the American city, 1840–1925: changing conceptions of the slum and the ghetto.* Cambridge: Cambridge University Press.

Williams, M. 1983: 'The apple of my eye': Carl Sauer and historical geography. *J. hist. Geogr.* 9, pp. 1–28.

Withers, C. W. J. 1984: *Gaelic in Scotland 1698–1981: the geographical history of a language.* Edinburgh: John Donald.

historical materialism An analytical method that emphasizes the material basis of society, and looks to the historical development of social relations to comprehend societal change. Opposed to IDEALISM, historical materialism is generally associated with Marxism, and the term itself was coined by Engels. Historical-materialist analysis assumes the importance of ideas and argues that 'life is not determined by consciousness, but consciousness by life'. As social beings, men and women develop 'their material production and their material intercourse', and thereby alter 'their history and the products of their thinking' (Marx and Engels, 1970, p. 47). In geographical research, historical materialism rose to prominence in the 1970s; it attempts to explain patterns and processes of spatial and environmental change as the result of the specific social relations of capitalism or other MODES OF PRODUCTION (see MARXIST GEOGRAPHY). NS

Reference

Marx, K. and Engels, F. 1970: *The German ideology* (transl. C. J. Arthur). New York: International.

Suggested Reading

Harvey, D. 1984: On the present condition of geography; an historical materialist manifesto. *Prof. Geogr.* 36, pp. 11–18.

Marx, K. 1967: *Capital,* volume I. New York: International.

Marx, K. 1971: Preface. *A contribution to the critique of political economy.* London: Lawrence and Wishart.

holism A belief that the whole organism is greater than simply the sum of its parts. In biology, this implies that there are characteristics of organisms which are not a function of their individual components, which produces laws of the whole (as studied in systematic biology: see COMPOSITIONAL THEORY) as well as laws of the parts (as in molecular biology). In geography, some approaches to the study of REGIONS have adopted an holistic, organismic analogy (see also ECOSYSTEM) and the concept of *LEBENSRAUM,* central to the 1930s German School of *GEOPOLITIK,* was similarly based on such an analogy. RJJ

Suggested Reading

Stoddart, D. R. 1967: Organism and ecosystem as geographic models. In Chorley, R. J. and Haggett, P., eds, *Models in geography.* London: Methuen, pp. 511–48.

homelessness Most operational definitions characterize homelessness as the absence of a place where one can sleep and receive mail. But researchers also emphasize the loss of support networks and the progressive social disaffiliation that are typical of the descent into homelessness (see ALIENATION; ANOMIE). People who become homeless in industrialized societies usually pass through an extended sequence of deteriorating circumstances, often involving (for example) a move to a cheaper rental accommodation, doubling up with friends or family, and temporary housing in a hotel or shelter, before being cast out onto the street.

Definitional problems make it difficult to achieve accurate counts of the homeless population. Historically, the homeless in industrialized societies have tended to be middle-aged men, often alcoholic, who have elected voluntarily to dissociate themselves from the rest of society. Today, however, this group has been joined on the streets by the deinstitutionalized mentally disabled, women and children (the former often victims of domestic violence), troubled youth, and (in the USA) war veterans, among others.

The factors causing the enormous increase in the numbers of 'new' homeless in industrialized societies vary according to national and regional specificities. But most

Western industrialized nations have, during the past decade, experienced the following: (a) a massive economic RESTRUCTURING, associated with DEINDUSTRIALIZATION and the rise of POST-FORDISM, that has caused recession and unemployment; (b) a restructuring of the welfare state that has reduced levels of, and eligibility for, public assistance – at a time when demand for such assistance has sky-rocketed; and (c) a collapse of government-supported afford-able housing programmes (such as public housing). These broad trends have created a class of 'proto-homeless', i.e. economic-ally and residentially marginalized indivi-duals only a pay cheque or two away from destitution.

In the absence of effective programmes to aid the homeless, many individuals have gathered in the inner-city ZONE OF DE-PENDENCE, where human services are concentrated (also see SKID ROW). There, the homeless are able to rebuild street-based social networks that substitute for previous home-based networks.   MJD

Suggested Reading

Dear, M. and Wolch, J. 1987: *Landscapes of despair*. Princeton, NJ: Princeton University Press.

Rowe, S. and Wolch J. 1990: Social networks in time and space: homeless women in skid row, Los Angeles. *Ann. Ass. Am. Geogr.* 80(2), pp. 184–204.

Wolch, J. and Dear, M. 1993: *Inside outside: homelessness in Los Angeles*. San Francisco: Jossey Bass.

Hotelling model An analysis of the location strategy of two firms competing for market territory. Hotelling was one of the first economists to address the question of the spatial arrangement of competing firms, and his analysis has provided a starting point for a number of illustrative extensions. Hotelling (1929) postulated the highly simplified situation of two producers competing to supply identical goods to consumers evenly spread along a linear market. The usual textbook exam-ple (though not in Hotelling's original presentation) is of two ice-cream sellers competing to supply people evenly distrib-uted on a beach. Under circumstances such as these, Hotelling deduced the seemingly

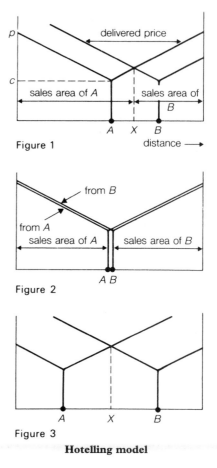

Figure 1

Figure 2

Figure 3

Hotelling model

unlikely conclusion that the two sellers would end up standing back-to-back in the centre of the beach, each supply-ing one half of the market (see GAME THEORY). This was then extended into a generalization concerning industrial AGGLOMERATION under certain demand conditions. Hotelling's model is thus an illustration of the useful practice of deduc-tive generalization in spatial economic analysis.

Hotelling's argument and some of its implications with respect to competition between two firms (duopolists) in space may be illustrated diagrammatically (see figures 1–3). Two producers are competing to serve the linear market (a beach) represented by the horizontal axis. Produc-tion costs (c) are the same in all locations and the product is sold at a price p that reflects the transport cost to the consumer

251

(in the case of ice-cream this is the effort of customers walking to the seller's location). In figure 1, firm A locates in the centre of the market; B locates some distance to the right. The respective sales areas split at X, where the delivered prices from the two suppliers are the same (see MARKET AREA ANALYSIS). But under the conditions of infinitely inelastic demand when every consumer will buy one unit of the product in one unit of time irrespective of price (or effort of acquisition), firm B loses nothing by moving to the left, as in figure 2, and taking part of A's sales area, even though this raises the delivered price to customers on the right: hence the conclusion that B will join A at the centre of the market, where neither firm can gain further sales by relocating. This conclusion holds irrespective of the initial location of the producers, as long as conditions of infinitely inelastic demand exist. The introduction of sensitivity of demand level to price will discourage sales to distant customers, and producers seeking to maximize sales will move apart to the so-called 'quartile' positions, as in figure 3. Thus the general deduction is that elasticity of demand will stimulate industrial dispersal.

Hotelling's model has been applied in other competitive situations, as in PUBLIC CHOICE THEORY.   DMS

Reference

Hotelling, H. 1929: Stability in competition. *Econ. J.* 39, pp. 40–57.

Suggested Reading

Smith, D. M. 1981: *Industrial location: an economic geographical analysis*, second edition. New York: John Wiley, pp. 91–7.

housing class A group of people characterized by their access to a particular housing type, usually defined by tenure. The term was coined by a British sociologist John Rex (1968, 1971) who identified three access routes to housing: possession of capital and credit, thereby allowing entry to the owner–occupier market; possession of a tenancy in a public (social) housing sector; and possession of a tenancy in a private housing rental sector. With these, he identified seven housing classes: (1) outright owners; (2) mortgagees; (3) tenants in purpose-built public housing; (4) tenants in publicly acquired SLUM properties awaiting demolition; (5) tenants of whole properties belonging to private owners; (6) house-owners who must sublet parts of their properties in order to afford the repayments; and (7) lodgers who occupy one or more rooms in a dwelling shared with other households.

Rex developed the concept and the classification as part of an attempt to understand the operation of the British housing market and the position of immigrant groups within it (Rex and Moore, 1967). He showed that access to housing was not a function of socio-economic status alone, because of the discrimination operated by the URBAN MANAGERS AND GATEKEEPERS who control access to the various tenure types; such as financial institutions which may discriminate in the allocation of mortgages, and managers who discriminate in creating and operating the rules for allocating public housing.

The concept was adopted by students of urban residential patterns in the late 1970s as providing a better appreciation of how SEGREGATION was produced than the models based on the free operation of a property market (cf. ALONSO MODEL). However, it has been criticized as being no more than an inductive generalization from a particular case (a point which Rex himself accepted: Rex and Tomlinson, 1979), for its assumption of common value systems regarding the desirability of certain types of housing and housing tenure, and for its confusion of CONSUMPTION sectors within a society with people's CLASS position (Saunders, 1986). Nevertheless, its clarification of the role of constraints as well as choices within urban housing markets (along with the comparable work of Pahl, 1975) made a major contribution to the sophistication of analysis and understanding in this aspect of URBAN GEOGRAPHY and HOUSING STUDIES.   RJJ

References

Pahl, R. E. 1975: *Whose city?* London: Penguin.

Rex, J. 1968: The sociology of a zone in transition. In Pahl, R. E. ed., *Readings in urban sociology*. Oxford: Pergamon Press, pp. 211–31.

Rex, J. 1971: The concept of housing class and the sociology of race relations. *Race* 12, pp. 293–301.

Rex, J. and Moore, R. 1967: *Race, community and conflict.* Oxford: Oxford University Press.

Rex, J. and Tomlinson, S. A. 1979: *Colonial immigrants in a British city.* London: Routledge and Kegan Paul.

Saunders, P. 1986: *Social theory and the urban question,* second edition. London: Hutchinson.

housing studies   Housing is a form of shelter, a refuge, a welfare service, an investment and a gateway to jobs, services and social support. In most societies, housing is available both according to need (in areas where housing provision is an element of social policy) and according to ability to pay (where housing policy is more directly geared to market principles). Housing studies therefore investigate the patterning of both a basic human right and a COMMODITY or capital asset.

Whether as state-subsidized shelter or as a saleable commodity, housing is a spatially uneven resource of variable cost and quality. Its variety stems partly from the process of housing production, which itself reflects the changing fortunes of the dwelling construction industry (Ball, 1978). This unevenness is also a consequence of differences in the extent of maintenance, repair and rehabilitation effected by either private individuals or corporate owners. There is, then, a geography of housing production which is one element of the PRODUCTION OF SPACE more generally.

Because qualitative differences in housing character and condition (use value), as well as quantitative price differences (exchange value), vary over space, the geography of housing consumption has a bearing on the study of social inequality (see also INEQUALITY, SPATIAL). This geography of CONSUMPTION can be explored in several ways.

First, housing outcomes may be viewed simply as a spatial reflection of social differentiation. Access to housing is fundamentally mediated by income and wealth. This is most obvious when examining access to the private sector, which depends on a regular income at a given level to sustain mortgage repayments or market rents in different residential areas. But even in the public sector, where income is supposed to be less important than housing need in mediating access to shelter, economic factors are an important determinant of residential SEGREGATION (Clapham and Kintrea, 1987).

Access to housing is also mediated by other qualities in a way which cannot wholly be explained by financial considerations. Direct and indirect discrimination, effected by individuals, institutionalized within housing allocation systems and inherent in the wider organization of society, underpin the gender, 'race' and health inequalities currently embedded in the organization of residential space.

Watson (1988), for instance, shows how the operation of the housing system in Britain and Australia reflects and reinforces the patriarchal character of such societies by marginalizing those 'non-family' households which do not reproduce the traditional family form. Henderson and Karn (1987) show how, in the allocation of public housing, 'racial' stereotypes become associated with scales of distinction and disrepute which are translated into offers of better tenancies (for 'white' applicants) and worse homes (for their 'black' counterparts). Smith (1990) argues that neither the public nor the private sector of the housing system provides adequate accommodation for people with health problems. Despite their position among the 'deserving' poor, many sick people may be forced into some of the poorest and least healthy homes and, at worst, find themselves disproportionately vulnerable to homelessness (Shanks and Smith, 1992).

From this *first* perspective on housing consumption, *where* people live – whether in the public or the private sector, or in the most or least affluent neighbourhood – is largely a function of who they are. Groups high in the income or status hierarchy tend to benefit most (in terms of the quality and quantity of their living space as well as in the potential to secure returns on housing investment) from prevailing patterns of housing provision. Moreover, in many countries those who are better off reap most benefits from the system of housing subsidies and tax exemptions.

From a *second* perspective, housing attainment can be viewed not as an outcome giving spatial expression to social attributes but rather as a resource which itself, in part, determines what characteristics (associated with wealth, status and service availability) residents can acquire. The attainment of owner-occupation is the best example.

Owner-occupation is the dominant, politically favoured and most widely aspired after tenure sector in Britain, Australia and North America. For homeowners in these nations, dwelling locations – in national, regional and urban space – may be a significant determinant of house price appreciation and of dwelling saleability. Thus where people live affects the exchange value of their home. Over a period of time, this determines owners' ability to make capital gains from their housing investment. The potential to increase personal wealth and social standing through home ownership is therefore geographically uneven.

As a consequence of the differing ability of homes in different locations to hold their price, gain value and store equity, owner-occupation is becoming increasingly differentiated and spatially polarized into low- and high-value sectors. Low-income home ownership often denotes a risky investment of limited capital into properties which require high expenditure on maintenance and repair; higher-income groups can make a better investment into appreciating homes which provide a store of equity and a source of cheap housing services in old age.

For all households – owners and renters alike – housing outcomes also have a bearing on access to jobs, services and social support, as well as to a range of risks and opportunities which are themselves unevenly spread over space. For instance, poor-quality housing is often a health hazard (Smith, 1989), a crime risk (Smith, 1986) and a financial liability when the costs of upkeep and insurance are considered (Karn et al., 1985). Residential location affects access to health services (see HEALTH AND HEALTH CARE, GEOGRAPHY OF), police services (Lea and Young, 1984), reasonably priced shopping facilities, and educational and recreational facilities (Tunley et al., 1979; Hallsworth et al., 1986).

Where people live is not, then, simply a passive product of who they are; it is also a factor affecting what they can do and who they can become. Housing attainment is therefore implicated in the structuring of society and in the processes of SOCIAL REPRODUCTION. This occurs through the practice of social segregation which reinforces spatial inequalities within tenure sectors; it is implicit in the consumption sector cleavages identified by Saunders (1986) between those able to secure housing in the marketplace and those reliant on state provisioning; and it is exemplified in the gulf between those with any kind of permanent home and the growing number of homeless people in virtually all societies in the developed and developing worlds (cf. HOMELESSNESS).

Because housing outcomes not only reflect but also shape social difference and inequality, a third perspective on the geography of housing can be gained from a consideration of housing policy (see also PUBLIC POLICY). Housing interventions affect both the production and consumption of residential space, and they are a key factor determining (either deliberately or inadvertently) the extent to which housing attainment passively reflects or actively moulds the social structure.

Housing policy can be viewed in at least three perspectives (Clapham et al., 1990):

(a) Housing interventions may be conceived of as a tool of macro-economic policy. Investment in housing can be used to pump-prime both national and local economies, and to stimulate the construction industry and the finance markets. This may be achieved *either* directly by state subsidies to dwelling production and to the consumption of public housing; *or* it may be achieved indirectly through tax exemptions (which effectively allow the state to subsidize the market), or through the manipulation of interest rates. The trend over most of Europe, North America and Australasia in recent years has been towards the latter practice, completing a cycle of commodification, decommodification and recommodification which is discussed by Dickens et al. (1985) (see COMMODITY).

(b) Housing policy may be used as an instrument of urban change and as the motor of NEIGHBOURHOOD revitalization. In much of Western Europe, for example, area-based housing policies have been a popular alternative to the cycle of SLUM clearance and redevelopment which once displaced and fragmented INNER-CITY communities. *In situ* revitalization policies were designed to facilitate the gradual upgrading and renewal of older urban areas without disturbing the existing social fabric. In some areas, however, the (generally low) level of grant assistance was sufficient to stimulate the socio-economic changes associated with GENTRIFICATION, while in others it was inadequate to halt a spiral of disinvestment and selective out-migration (by young people and white households). Some housing factors affecting the direction of neighbourhood change in urban areas are discussed by Taub et al. (1984).

(c) Housing policy plays a part in promoting public welfare and may therefore be seen as an element of social policy. This is the area of housing consumption in which the STATE has a central role, and can therefore use housing provision to meet health needs, facilitate community care, offset income inequalities and so on. However, most developed societies are now engaged in a process of welfare restructuring, so that SOCIAL WELL-BEING is becoming one of the most neglected aims of housing provision.

The changing social role of housing is exemplified in Britain, where over a million public dwellings were sold into private ownership during the 1980s. These sales were spatially and socially uneven: better-quality homes in suburban locations were bought by better-off tenants, leaving a residual sector housing the benefit-dependent poor and other marginalized groups (Forrest and Murie, 1988). Public housing became the welfare arm of the housing system at the moment it was least suited to perform this role – when it had become restricted in its geography and had undergone a decline in overall quality.

To summarize, housing studies contribute to many areas of human geography: there is a link between labour markets and the housing system which has a bearing on the pattern of economic restructuring; housing often forms the leading edge of welfare restructuring and so affects the geography of disadvantage; and as well as providing shelter, housing functions as a home – it has a meaning and a symbolism which insert it firmly into the CULTURAL LANDSCAPE. In short, even a few examples indicate that studies of housing policy, production and consumption comprise an important interface between geography and the social sciences.   SJS

References

Ball, M. 1978: British housing policy and the housebuilding industry. *Capital and Class* 4, pp. 78–99.

Clapham, D., Kemp, P. and Smith, S. J. 1990: *Housing and social policy*: London: Macmillan.

Clapham, D. and Kintrea, K. 1987: Rationing choice and constraint: the allocation of public housing in Glasgow. *J. soc. Policy* 15, pp. 51–67.

Dickens, P., Duncan, S., Goodwin, M. and Gray, F. 1985: *Housing, states and localities*. London: Methuen.

Forrest, R. and Murie, A. 1988: *Selling the welfare state: the privatisation of public housing*. London: Routledge and Kegan Paul.

Hallsworth, A. G., Wood, A. and Lewington, T. 1986: Welfare and retail accessibility. *Area* 18, pp. 291–8.

Henderson, J. and Karn, V. 1987: *Race, class and state housing*. Aldershot: Gower.

Karn, V., Kemeny, J. and Williams, P. 1985: *Home ownership in the inner city: salvation or despair*. Aldershot: Gower.

Lea, J. and Young, J. 1984: *What is to be done about law and order?* London: Penguin.

Saunders, P. 1986: *Social theory and the urban question*, second edition. London: Hutchinson.

Shanks, N. and Smith, S. J. 1992: British public policy and the health of homeless people. *Policy and Politics* 20, pp. 35–46.

Smith, S. J. 1986: *Crime, space and society*. Cambridge: Cambridge University Press.

Smith, S. J. 1989: Housing and health: a review and research agenda. Discussion Paper 27, Centre for Housing Research, University of Glasgow.

Smith, S. J. 1990: Health status and the housing system. *Soc. Sci. Med.* 31, pp. 753–62.

Taub, R. P., Taylor, D. G. and Dunham, J. D. 1984: *Paths of neighborhood change*. Chicago: University of Chicago Press.

Tunley, P., Travers, T. and Pratt, J. 1979: *Depriving the deprived*. London: Kogan Page.

Watson, S. 1988: *Accommodating inequality: gender and housing*. Sydney: Allen and Unwin.

Suggested Reading

Ball, M., Harloe, M. and Martens, M. 1988: *Housing and social change in Europe and the USA*. London: Routledge.

Forrest and Murie (1988).

Karn, V. and Wolman, H. 1992: *Comparing housing systems: housing performance and housing policy in the United States and Britain*. Oxford: Clarendon Press.

Morris, J. and Winn, M. 1990: *Housing and social inequality*. London: Hilary Shipman.

human agency The capabilities of human beings. Human agency is a central concern of HUMANISTIC GEOGRAPHY in particular and of 'humanism' in the social sciences more generally (see Gregory, 1981). Concepts of human agency have occasioned several major disagreements, including disputes over the following:

(a) The relations between *agents* and *human agents*. For Cutler et al. (1977), for example, 'an agent is an entity capable of occupying the position of a locus of decision in a social relation' and recognized as such by other potential agents and by law or custom. They explicitly reject the view that 'to be an agent is to be a subject [and] to act in terms of the functioning of a will and a consciousness endowed with a faculty of "experience"' and they insist that 'there can be no basis for maintaining that agents must be conceptualised as human subjects'. Indeed, 'there may be agents other than human individuals', e.g. companies, corporations and states. But Giddens (1979) dismisses these views as:

wholly unenlightening; they do not address the philosophical problem of agency at all. It is perfectly true that a corporation can be an agent in law. But laws have to be interpreted and applied; it takes human agents to do that, as well as to frame them in the first place. . . . [N]o approach which *ignores* the will and consciousness of human subjects is likely to be of much use in social theory.

(b) The relations between *intentions* and *actions*. For Giddens (1984), for example, although 'it has frequently been supposed that human agency can be defined only in terms of intentions', agency refers 'not to the intentions people have in doing things but to their capability of doing those things in the first place'. Such capabilities, he contends, are logically tied to POWER: 'an agent ceases to be such if he or she loses the capability to "make a difference", that is, to exercise some sort of power' (but see Thompson, 1984). Giddens acknowledges that these practical interventions 'cannot be examined apart from a broader theory of the acting self' and hence elaborates what he calls a *stratification model* of action (see the figure). Not all action is purposive, therefore, in the sense of being directed by definite intentions, but it is purposeful in the sense of being 'reflexively monitored' by actors. Even so, Philo (1984) claims that

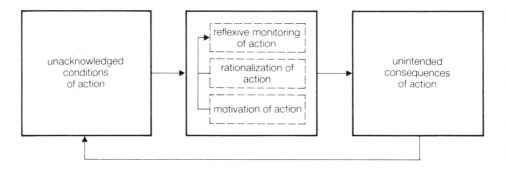

human agency *Stratification model of action* (after Giddens, 1984).

Giddens often collapses agency into action and thereby obscures the integrity of 'thought-and-action' explored by Olsson (1980): thus, 'what is obscured in [Giddens's] presentation is the claimed status of agency beyond the poles of intentional activity and reactive behavior' (Dallmayr, 1982).

(c) The relations between *agency* and *structure*. In both STRUCTURAL FUNCTIONALISM and STRUCTURAL MARXISM for example, Thompson (1978) complains that 'systems and sub-systems, elements and structures, are drilled up and down the pages pretending to be people': human agency is evicted from history other than 'as the "supports" or vectors of ulterior structural determinations' (see also Duncan and Ley, 1982). Against this, however, Anderson (1980) has noted that 'agency' is such 'a dominant in [Thompson's] vocabulary' that he continually trembles on the edges of a voluntarism. Anderson regards 'area of self-determination' as a much more precise term than agency; and even if this has been widening in the past 150 years, Anderson argues, 'it is still very much less than its opposite'. What is at stake here is not simply the deeply sedimented dualism between 'agency' and 'structure' which STRUCTURATION THEORY seeks to transcend, but the development of an *historical*, as opposed to a purely axiomatic, approach which would trace the changing 'curve' of human agency over time and space (see also Thrift, 1983).

All of these disputes intersect with debates about the constitution of human subjects (cf. Hirst and Woolley, 1982). Across the whole field of the humanities and the social sciences there has been considerable interest in the displacement or 'decentering' of the autonomous subject of traditional humanism, a figure who also occupied a central place in HUMANISTIC GEOGRAPHY. This critique has been driven by POSTSTRUCTURALISM and psychoanalytical theory and revolves around the possibility of identifying multiple and competing subject-positions, so that subjectivities are constituted at the intersection of different discourses (see Smith, 1987). These ideas have far-reaching consequences. In FEMINIST GEOGRAPHY they have helped to clarify the ways in which human agency and human subjects have been tacitly gendered in mainstream ('malestream') social theory and inquiry. Those discourses are also usually profoundly ETHNOCENTRIC, and POSTCOLONIALISM has played a vital part in contesting the privileges typically accorded to 'the European subject' and to the collective power of European agency in such narratives: concepts of *hybridity* and *subalternity* have been particularly important to this counterproject. Finally, the incorporation of more complex constructions of human agency and identity within POST-MARXISM has disrupted the classical Marxian thesis of ALIENATION and identified the salience of social struggles that are not sutured around a CLASS subject. But the most profound impact of these ideas has been in the braiding of these three streams: in seeking to situate human agency at the intersection of these different discourses (see, for example, Spivak, 1988; Watts, 1991). DG

References

Anderson, P. 1980: *Arguments within English Marxism*. London: Verso.

Cutler, A., Hindess, B., Hirst, P. and Hussain, A. 1977: *Marx's Capital and capitalism today*. London: Routledge and Kegan Paul.

Dallmayr, F. 1982: The theory of structuration: a critique. In Giddens, A., *Profiles and critiques in social theory*. London: Macmillan, pp. 18–25.

Duncan, J. and Ley, D. 1982: Structural Marxism and human geography: a critical assessment. *Ann. Ass. Am. Geogr.* 72, pp. 30–59.

Giddens, A. 1979: *Central problems in social theory: action, structure and contradiction in social analysis*. London: Macmillan.

Giddens, A. 1984: *The constitution of society*. Cambridge: Polity Press.

Gregory, D. 1981: Human agency and human geography. *Trans. Inst. Br. Geogr.* n.s. 5, pp. 1–16.

Hirst, P. and Woolley, J. 1982: *Social relations and human attributes*. London: Tavistock/New York: Methuen.

Olsson, G. 1980: *Birds in egg/eggs in bird*. London: Pion/New York: Methuen.

Philo, C. 1984: Reflections on Gunnar Olsson's contribution to the discourse of contemporary human geography. *Environ. Plann. D.: Society and Space* 2, pp. 217–40.

Smith, P. 1987: *Discerning the subject*. Minneapolis: University of Minnesota Press.

Spivak, G. C. 1988: *In other worlds: essays in cultural politics*. London: Routledge.

Thompson, E. P. 1978: *The poverty of theory and other essays*. London: Merlin.

Thompson, J. B. 1984: The theory of structuration: an assessment of the contribution of Anthony Giddens. In Thompson, J. B., *Studies in the theory of ideology*. Cambridge: Polity Press.

Thrift, N. 1983: On the determination of social action in space and time. *Environ. Plann. D: Society and Space* 1, pp. 23–57.

Watts, M. 1991: Mapping meaning, denoting difference, imagining identity: dialectical images and postmodern geographies. *Geogr. Annlr.* 73B, pp. 7–16.

Suggested Reading

Anderson (1980), ch. 2.

Hirst and Woolley (1982).

Smith (1987).

Watts (1991).

human ecology The extension of concepts drawn from ECOLOGY to the social realm: if ecology deals with the relationships of organisms with their environments, human ecology studies the relationships of human beings with their environments, both physical and social. The term has had a chequered history and a wide range of meanings. As developed in the early decades of the twentieth century by sociologists of the CHICAGO SCHOOL – Robert Park, Ernest Burgess, and others – human ecology represented an interactive perspective on social life as a scientifically respectable replacement for various forms of ENVIRONMENTAL DETERMINISM. In their work, the ecological theme represented more a borrowing of then-current concepts and analogies from ecology (such as COMMUNITY, competition, disturbance, climax equilibrium, and INVASION AND SUCCESSION) than it did a concern with the natural environment. Its kinship with human geography lay much more in its focus on the spatial dimension of society, best represented in the Burgess–Park concentric ring model of urban structure (see ZONAL MODEL), than in a sustained interest in nature–society relationships. Later systematizers of sociological human ecology, such as Hawley (1950, 1986), have tended to play down the spatial focus of the Chicago School (even as geographers

in the 1960s rediscovered it) in favour of an emphasis on the demographic and institutional dimensions of society (Saunders 1981), although at the same time they have shown a strengthened interest in human interaction with the physical environment. Sociological human ecology has also moved away from those aspects of the Chicago School – embodied more in its ETHNOGRAPHIC research monographs than in its theoretical pronouncements – that some have cited as exemplary models for humanistic social geography (Ley, 1977; Jackson and Smith, 1984).

When the University of Chicago geographer Harlan H. Barrows (1923) defined geography as 'the science of human ecology', he gave the term a quite different sense than did his sociological colleagues. For Barrows, geography was best conceived as addressing 'the relationships existing between natural environments and the distribution and activities of man', with a focus on human 'adjustment'; to those environments (p. 3). For Park, geography was an idiographic discipline analogous to history; human ecology dealt with the same issues but with the goal of generalization (Entrikin, 1980). Barrows's definition (which excluded physical geography as such from the discipline) would have given geography the NOMOTHETIC character that Park would have denied it (Entrikin, 1980). This aspect, as well as its environmental focus in a period newly wary of its heritage of environmental determinism, may have been responsible for its failure to take hold. The term 'human ecology' is none the less frequently used in contemporary nature–society geographies (e.g., Kates, 1971; Butzer, 1982) that continue Barrows's focus on human adjustment to the natural environment, emphasizing the interactive and adaptive character of the human–nature interaction and its mediation by social institutions. The focus of the interdisciplinary journal *Human Ecology* closely resembles this approach, which is largely that of the influential subfield of geography and anthropology better known as CULTURAL ECOLOGY (cf. URBAN ECOLOGY).

JEm

References

Barrows, H. H. 1923: Geography as human ecology. *Ann. Ass. Am. Geogr.* 13, pp. 1–14.

Butzer, K. W. 1982: *Archaeology as human ecology.* Cambridge: Cambridge University Press.

Entrikin, J. N. 1980: Robert Park's human ecology and human geography. *Ann. Ass. Am. Geogr.* 70, pp. 43–58.

Hawley, A. H. 1950: *Human ecology: a theory of community structure.* New York: Ronald Press.

Hawley, A. H. 1986: *Human ecology: a theoretical essay.* Chicago: University of Chicago Press.

Jackson, P. and Smith, S. 1984: *Exploring social geography.* London: Allen and Unwin.

Kates, R. W. 1971: Natural hazard in human ecological perspective: hypotheses and models. *Econ. Geogr.* 47, pp. 438–51.

Ley, D. 1977: Social geography and the taken-for-granted world. *Trans. Inst. Br. Geogr.* n.s. 2, pp. 498–512.

Saunders, P. 1981: *Social theory and the urban question.* New York: Holmes & Meier.

human geography That part of the discipline of GEOGRAPHY concerned with the spatial differentiation and organization of human activity and with human use of the physical environment.

The separation of human from physical geography as a major division of the discipline is relatively recent. It has its roots in both German (cf. ANTHROPO-GEOGRAPHY) and French writings in the late eighteenth and early nineteenth centuries, but most works in English continued to cover both human and physical topics, with an emphasis on the society–environment interrelationship and its regional variations. Thus the main texts in the first half of the present century – Hartshorne's (1939) *The nature of geography* in North America and Wooldridge and East's (1951) *The spirit and purpose of geography* in the UK – covered the entire corpus of the discipline. Nevertheless, during the 1918–1939 interwar period specialization in either human or, especially, physical geography by individual workers became more common. Freeman (1980) suggests a fourfold division of interests at that time – physical, historical, regional and human: his review groups the last two together, and concentrates on REGIONAL GEOGRAPHY, LAND-USE SURVEY and the study of settlement types, especially villages. He quotes Fawcett (1934):

We are as yet in the early stages of investigation of the many problems of human geography, and have not reached well-established generalisations. The study is in the stage of collecting facts, and framing and establishing hypotheses, most of which can only mark stages in its development.

Thus it was not until after the Second World War that human geography came to equal physical geography in its standing within the discipline in the UK, as regional geography was further denigrated and the subdisciplines of URBAN, SOCIAL, POLITICAL and INDUSTRIAL GEOGRAPHY began to attract considerable attention (Johnston and Gregory, 1984).

Many of the stimuli for this new work in the UK came from other countries, both European and North American; with the latter in some cases acting as an intermediary, as with the 1960s appreciation there of the work of the Swedish geographer Torsten Hägerstrand on MIGRATION and DIFFUSION (Duncan, 1974) and the 'discovery' of the German developments of CENTRAL PLACE THEORY by geographers at the University of Washington, Seattle (Johnston, 1991a). Urban geography, for example, was influenced by German work, introduced – along with much American material – to the UK by Dickinson (1947) and by Conzen (1960). In North America, there were also continental European stimuli (as illustrated in Garrison's (1959) review of books on LOCATIONAL ANALYSIS) but in addition much local innovation (Johnston, 1991a).

During the 1960s and 1970s, many human geographers, especially those trained since the war, enthusiastically adopted the QUANTITATIVE REVOLUTION then being advanced, and they promoted the subdiscipline as LOCATIONAL ANALYSIS or SPATIAL SCIENCE. The main texts of the period (Haggett, 1965; Morrill, 1970; Abler et al., 1971) did not subdivide the subdiscipline further: nor did the two pathbreaking books of essays (Chorley and Haggett, 1965, 1967) – although separate topical chapters were included and the latter, under the heading 'Models of socio-economic systems', had chapter titles covering demographic models, socio-logical models, economic development models, models of urban geography and settlement location, models of industrial location, and models of agricultural activity, which together presaged the growth of some of the later specialisms (population, social, urban, economic, industrial and agricultural) but not others (political and cultural).

British, although not North American, geographers continued with attempts to sustain the links between human and physical geography through shared interests in models and (quantitative) methods – as illustrated by the two books edited by Chorley and Haggett and by Haggett's (1972) major student text, although the last contained less physical than human geography material. (Physical geography was relatively weak in North America at that time, as indicated by its total absence from the retrospective essays published in a special issue of the *Annals* in 1979 to mark the Association of American Geographers' seventy-fifth anniversary.) By this time, however, physical and human geographers were very largely going their separate ways and although, for political and pedagogical reasons, they remained together in higher education institutions (with some claims that the discipline as a whole integrated material from the natural and social sciences and the humanities: Johnston, 1983), the nature of their work became ever more divorced (Johnston, 1986, 1989).

Within human geography, the 1970s and 1980s saw two main trends – internal specialization and philosophical pluralism. Internal specialization was in part a consequence of the discipline's rapid growth (Stoddart, 1967), with scholars seeking to establish their own niches, and in part it reflected the wide range of links developed by geographers with the literature, if not the practitioners, of most of the other social sciences. (The flow of influence was very asymmetrical: geographers quoted other social scientists much more than other social scientists quoted geographers.) Specialist subgroups were established within the main professional societies to cater for these particular

interests, and to a considerable extent they operate as separate organizations, with their members owing greater allegiance to the part than to the whole: each runs its own sections at major conferences, many organize their own conferences too, and some publish their own journals and book series. (For analyses of these groups, see Good-child and Janelle, 1988; Johnston, 1990, 1991b). At the same time, other specialized journals – both subdisciplinary and inter-disciplinary – were launched by commercial publishers to realize the potential of new niche markets, and so the literature of the discipline has become increasingly segmented and specialized (see Johnston, 1991b).

Of the many specializations within the discipline, initially URBAN GEOGRAPHY and ECONOMIC GEOGRAPHY were the growth areas, with a shared interest in locational analysis and the development of quantitative methods. Other subfields grew later, with a growing emphasis on SOCIAL GEO-GRAPHY, on a revived and revised POLI-TICAL GEOGRAPHY, on a restructured CULTURAL GEOGRAPHY, and on a range of issues to do with society–nature relationships, such as RESOURCE MANAGEMENT. Despite the popularity of the PARADIGM model of disciplinary change, especially in the 1970s, these shifts in substantive emphasis – and in philosophical orientation too – did not involve the wholesale replacement of one type of work by another. Instead, more were added and those already present retained vitality, occasionally being rejuvenated – as with the continued sophistication of quantitative work by a relatively small group of workers in the late 1970s and early 1980s, and then the rapid growth of interest in GEOGRAPHI-CAL INFORMATION SYSTEMS in the late 1980s.

Philosophical pluralism also reflected geographers' increasing involvement with the literature of other social science disciplines, which provided bases for critiques of current geographical practice (notably Harvey, 1973; Gregory, 1978) and attempts to restructure the discipline (e.g. Smith's, 1977, volume with its focus on relevance, inequality and social justice). Thus, for example, critiques of locational analysis and spatial science were launched in the 1970s from two directions: one, drawing on history and the humanities more generally, attacked positivist approaches for their derogation of the individual human and the attitudes, values and feelings (as in SENSE OF PLACE) which could not be appreciated through the search for quantitatively stated laws; the other criticized the same work for its implicit acceptance of the political status quo and its inability to match its quantitative descriptions with meaningful understanding. These two strands of work – often known as HUMANISTIC GEOGRAPHY and RADICAL GEOGRAPHY, respectively – meant that geographical scholarship in the 1980s was marked by three very different approaches to the discipline, or to parts of it (humanistic geography was particularly associated with cultural and with HISTORICAL GEOGRAPHY, for example, and radical geography with urban and economic studies).

Through the past two decades these three strands of work have been complexly interwoven within the fabric of geographical activity as individual scholars seek to come to terms with them, and occasionally suggest how they might be integrated to a greater or lesser extent. At the same time, geographers continue to explore other literatures – and to open their own up to other disciplines in ways rarely seen previously: this continues to bring new stimuli to the discipline – empirical, methodological and philosophical. Thus developments such as POSTMODERNISM have attracted considerable attention, with some (e.g. Soja, 1989) embracing it wholeheartedly and suggesting that it offers a basis for reconstructing geographical practice (around the main themes of economic, political and social geography, according to Dear, 1988), whereas others see it, and many other '-isms' (Harvey, 1990), as adding little to what is already known (Harvey, 1989). Others promote greater attention to APPLIED GEOGRAPHY, however, and see the debates within the discipline as both intellectually and politically damaging.

The late 1980s saw the publication of a substantial number of books which reflected two or more decades of internal specialization and philosophical pluralism. Some sought to review the richness of the discipline, in all-embracing compendia, of which the best example is Gaile and Willmott's (1989) 840 pages on *Geography in America*; whereas others, such as Gregory and Walford (1989), were more selective in the topics selected for review. Peet and Thrift (1989) produced a two-volume work which brought together major reviews of work done in the radical geography mould; Gregory and Urry (1985) and Wolch and Dear (1990) edited volumes which promoted a new perspective on the study of spatial structures of society; Macmillan's (1989) volume was largely prepared, despite some dissenting voices from within, as a defence of the quantitative-dominated approach, as was Haggett's (1990) personal view of 30 years in the discipline; and others, such as Kobayashi and Mackenzie (1989) sought accommodations – in their case between the humanistic and the radical view – promoting the restructured cultural geography (Jackson, 1989).

Throughout much of this period geography as an academic discipline has, like most others – and certainly most social sciences – been pressed to prove its value in an increasingly materialist society (see Taylor, 1985). Within the discipline some have embraced this call wholeheartedly, calling for more applied work, whereas others have been more critical, arguing that geography has much to offer those who want to understand the world better before they seek to change it (as the essays in Johnston, 1992, illustrate).

In 1978 a senior American geographer edited a special issue of a general social science journal to which he gave the title 'Human geography coming of age' (Zelinsky, 1978). In retrospect, I am sure he would see that as a premature conclusion. In the quarter-century since, human geography has certainly not displayed the characteristics of maturity and staidness which might be associated with a coming-of-age. Instead, it has continued to demonstrate the vitality and vibrancy of youth. To some this is unfortunate; to others, it is the basis of their excitement in the discipline. Certainly much has changed, and will continue to change. A comparison of Chorley and Haggett's (1967) volume with Peet and Thrift's (1989) volume will illustrate just how much change, as will one for the longer span provided by James and Jones's (1954) mid-century compilation on American geography and Gaile and Willmott's (1989) later work. Human geography is changing fast, with the rapidly changing world of which it is part and which its researchers are seeking to understand. The nature of that change is illustrated by the two themes identified here. The next decades will undoubtedly stimulate major change too. In 1973, Chorley invited several authors to consider *Directions in geography*: their essays bear little resemblance to those produced by another group 12 years later in *The future of geography* (Johnston, 1985); and a further collection only seven years later again once more illustrates how rapidly the discipline is changing (Johnston, 1992) – as indeed does comparison of the three editions (1981, 1986, 1993) of the present work.

Human geography is one of the smaller social sciences, but it is also one of the liveliest. Its subject matter – the spatial organization of their societies and the relationships between people and their environments – offers innumerable opportunities for research in a great variety of styles, opportunities to which geographers are responding vigorously.   RJJ

References

Abler, R. F., Adams, J. S. and Gould, P. R. 1971: *Spatial organization: the geographer's view of the world.* Englewood Cliffs, NJ: Prentice-Hall.

Chorley, R. J., ed. 1973: *Directions in geography.* London: Methuen.

Chorley, R. J. and Haggett, P., eds 1965: *Frontiers in geographical teaching.* London: Methuen.

Chorley, R. J. and Haggett, P., eds 1967: *Models in geography.* London: Methuen.

Conzen, M. R. G. 1960: Alnwick, Northumberland: a study in town-plan analysis. *Trans. Inst. Br. Geogr.* 27.

Dear, M. J. 1988: The postmodern challenge: reconstructing human geography. *Trans. Inst. Br. Geogr.* n.s. 13, pp. 262–74.

Dickinson, R. E. 1947: *City, region and regionalism.* London: Routledge and Kegan Paul.

Duncan, S. S. 1974: The isolation of scientific discovery: indifference and resistance to a new idea. *Science Studies* 4, pp. 109–34.

Fawcett, C. B. 1934: *Geogr. J.* 84, p. 427.

Freeman, T. W. 1980: *A history of modern British geography.* London: Longman.

Gaile, G. L. and Wilmott, C. J., eds 1989: *Geography in America.* Columbus, OH: Merrill.

Garrison, W. L. 1959: Spatial structure of the economy I. *Ann. Ass. Am. Geogr.* 49, pp. 232–9.

Goodchild, M. F. and Janelle, D. G. 1988: Specialization in the structure and organization of geography. *Ann. Ass. Am. Geogr.* 78, pp. 11–28.

Gregory, D. 1978: *Ideology, science and human geography.* London: Hutchinson.

Gregory, D. and Urry, J., eds 1985: *Social relations and spatial structures.* London: Macmillan.

Gregory, D. and Walford, R., eds 1989: *Horizons in human geography.* London: Macmillan.

Haggett, P. 1965: *Locational analysis in human geography.* London: Edward Arnold.

Haggett, P. 1972: *Geography: a modern synthesis.* New York: Harper and Row.

Haggett, P. 1990: *The geographer's art.* Oxford: Blackwell.

Hartshorne, R. 1939: *The nature of geography.* Lancaster, PA: Association of American Geographers.

Harvey, D. 1973: *Social justice and the city.* London: Edward Arnold.

Harvey, D. 1989: *The condition of postmodernity.* Oxford: Blackwell.

Harvey, D. 1990: Between space and time: reflections on the geographical imagination. *Ann. Ass. Am. Geogr.* 80, pp. 418–34.

Jackson, P. 1989: *Maps of meaning.* London: Unwin Hyman.

James, P. E. and Jones, C. F., eds 1954: *American geography: inventory and prospect.* Syracuse, NY: Syracuse University Press.

Johnston, R. J. 1983: Resource analysis, resource management and the integration of human and physical geography. *Progr. phys. Geogr.* 7, pp. 127–46.

Johnston, R. J., ed. 1985: *The future of geography.* London: Methuen.

Johnston, R. J. 1986: *On human geography.* Oxford: Blackwell.

Johnston, R. J. 1989: *Environmental problems: nature, society and the state.* London: Belhaven Press.

Johnston, R. J. 1990: The Institute, study groups, and a discipline without a core? *Area* 22, pp. 407–14.

Johnston, R. J. 1991a: *Geography and geographers: Anglo-American human geography since 1945* (fourth edition). London: Edward Arnold/New York: Routledge.

Johnston, R. J. 1991b: *A question of place: exploring the practice of human geography.* Oxford: Blackwell.

Johnston, R. J., ed. 1992: *The challenge for geography: a changing world, a changing discipline.* Oxford: Blackwell.

Johnston, R. J. and Gregory, S. 1984: The United Kingdom. In Johnston, R. J. and Claval, P., eds, *Geography since the Second World War: an international survey.* London: Croom Helm/Totowa, NJ: Barnes and Noble, pp. 107–31.

Kobayashi, A. and Mackenzie, S., eds 1989: *Remaking human geography.* London: Unwin Hyman.

Macmillan, B., ed. 1989: *Remodelling geography.* Oxford: Blackwell.

Morrill, R. L. 1970: *The spatial organization of society.* Belmont, CA: Wadsworth.

Peet, R. and Thrift, N. J., eds 1989: *New models in geography.* London: Unwin Hyman (two volumes).

Smith, D. M. 1977: *Human geography: a welfare approach.* London: Edward Arnold.

Soja, E. W. 1989: *Postmodern geographies.* London: Verso.

Stoddart, D. R. 1967: Growth and structure of geography. *Trans. Inst. Br. Geogr.* 41, pp. 1–19.

Taylor, P. J. 1985: The value of a geographical perspective. In Johnston, R. J., ed., *The future of geography.* London: Methuen, pp. 92–110.

Wolch, J. and Dear, M. J., eds 1990: *The power of geography: how territory shapes social life.* Boston: Unwin Hyman.

Wooldridge, S. W. and East, W. G. 1951: *The spirit and purpose of geography.* London: Hutchinson.

Zelinsky, W., ed. 1978: Human geography coming of age. *Am. behav. Scient.* 22, pp. 1–167.

humanistic geography An approach to human geography distinguished by the central and active role that it gives to human awareness and HUMAN AGENCY, human consciousness and human creativity (cf. Soper, 1986). Humanistic geography is at once an attempt at 'understanding meaning, value and [the] human significance of life events' (Buttimer, 1979) and 'an expansive view of what the human person is and can do' (Tuan, 1976).

Although humanism in the modern discipline is often traced back to the French school of human geography, Vidal de la Blache's writings bear many of the hallmarks of FUNCTIONALISM and of what Duncan (1980) called the 'super-organic' which most humanistic geographers would repudiate: although Vidal was himself trained in both history and geography, and much of his work displayed an aesthetic sensibility usually identified with the humanities, he advertised human geography as a *natural* science. There are affinities between the prewar French school of human geography and the postwar Anglophone school of humanistic geography, but these need careful nuancing and sensitive reconstruction (Andrews, 1984). Whatever the strength of the French connection, it has been claimed that humanistic geography (especially those versions which draw upon SYMBOLIC INTERACTIONISM) is also descended from the neo-Kantianism and pragmatism of Park and the CHICAGO SCHOOL of sociology (see KANTIANISM; PRAGMATISM): 'Park's practical concerns clearly have immense contemporary relevance, offering the basis of a much-needed methodological armoury capable of sustaining the variety of humanistic philosophies currently pervading social geography' (Jackson and Smith, 1984) (for a parallel claim that Vidal's position was also neo-Kantian, see Berdoulay, 1978).

However much one might profitably invest these twin legacies, and the others that might be discovered – the gentle ANARCHISM of Kropotkin and Reclus, for example, or the sensibilities of Fleure and Herbertson – it is clear that the formalization and advance of humanism in Anglophone geography in the 1970s owed much to a deep dissatisfaction with the mechanistic models of SPATIAL SCIENCE that had been developed during the QUANTITATIVE REVOLUTION. For this reason, its early steps were made alongside BEHAVIOURAL GEOGRAPHY (Gold and Goodey, 1984); but the two soon parted company as humanistic geography came to insist upon the essential subjectivity of both the investigator and the investigated in ways which departed (often dramatically) from the formal strictures of behaviouralism.

Indeed, humanistic geography shared in the more general critique of POSITIVISM's claim to objectivity (in which behavioural geography was itself implicated) and so came to be represented as 'a form of criticism' through which 'geographers can be made more self-aware and cognizant of many of the hidden assumptions and implications of their methods and research', rather than as a coherent and robust 'methodology for the "postbehavioural revolution" in geography' (Entrikin, 1976).

However, humanism was intended to be more than just a critical philosophy. Insofar as it was also a rejection of the 'geometric determinism' in which men and women were made to respond autonomically to the dictates of universal spatial structures and abstract spatial logics, it was at the same time a claim for a human geography with the human being at its very centre, 'a "people's geography", about real people and *for* the people in the sense of contributing to the enlargement of human being for all' (Smith, 1977), i.e. one concerned with the social construction of PLACE, SPACE and LANDSCAPE rather than the spatial confinement of people and societies (see also MARXIST GEOGRAPHY; WELFARE GEOGRAPHY).

During the next ten years humanistic geography moved far from the position plotted by Entrikin. It advanced from its early attack on positivism to make an assault on STRUCTURALISM and STRUCTURAL MARXISM (Duncan and Ley, 1982); at the same time it moved beyond a simple IDEALISM that would have limited enquiry to a recovery of the intentions that lay behind actions, to develop a more incisive methodology for empirical investigation that allowed for a bounded conception of human agency. Two basic streams of work can be distinguished.

(a) The first of these was characterized by 'a self-conscious drive to connect with that special body of knowledge, reflection and substance about human experience and human expression, about what it means to be a human being on this earth': namely the *humanities* (Meinig, 1983). Its methods were essentially those of HERMENEUTICS and historiography, literary criticism and

art history (see, for example, Tuan, 1976; Cosgrove, 1979; Meinig, 1979; Pocock, 1981). Its interest in the recovery of the meanings and actions embedded in different places and in the ICONOGRAPHY of LANDSCAPE was often associated with HISTORICAL GEOGRAPHY (Harris, 1978; Daniels, 1985). It displayed a deep concern with particularity and specificity, rather than with general theories of spatial organization, but this did not preclude the sensitive and imaginative use of theoretical constructs often (and increasingly) derived from cultural theory and historical materialism (see, for example, Thrift, 1983; Cosgrove, 1984). Many of these developments contributed directly to the revival of CULTURAL GEOGRAPHY.

(b) The second stream was more self-consciously theoretical from the very start. One of its central concerns was to clarify the 'theoretical attitude' itself (Christensen, 1982), and it drew on a range of ideas and insights derived from the (philosophies of the) *human and social sciences*, including EXISTENTIALISM and PHENOMENOLOGY. Its concrete enquiries were often informed by ETHNOMETHODOLOGY and SYMBOLIC INTERACTIONISM; its methods were typically those of ETHNOGRAPHY; and in seeking to make its studies speak to wider concerns it used 'logical' rather than statistical inference and paid increasing attention to questions of reflexivity (Smith, 1984; Jackson, 1985; Pile 1991). Its contemporary interests in the social construction of spaces, in the incursions of rationalized landscapes into the geographies of the LIFEWORLD and of the TAKEN-FOR-GRANTED WORLD, and in the geographies of social action and interaction, meant that it was closely associated with SOCIAL GEOGRAPHY (see, for example, Ley, 1978; Relph, 1981; Western, 1981). But this stream also fed into studies in the historical geography of social struggle that were influenced by a humanist tradition within historical materialism and which intersected with a STRUCTURATION THEORY that was in large measure inspired by Marx's writings (Gregory, 1981).

Towards the close of the 1980s these two streams braided in intricate ways. The theoretical sensibilities of many of those working in the humanities were accorded far greater prominence in human geography, for example, and this coincided with the explosion of interest in cultural theory and cultural studies and the formation of a new cultural geography (see Barnes and Duncan, 1992; Grossberg et al., 1992); for those conducting a dialogue between social theory and human geography, the interest in GRAND THEORY slackened and the claims of multiple and competing local knowledges were increasingly recognized and negotiated (Ley, 1989). Both of these developments involved a constructive but none the less critical engagement with historical materialism (see Kobayashi and Mackenzie, 1989). These various interconnections have made it increasingly difficult to identify a distinctively humanistic geography in the 1990s (cf. Buttimer, 1990). If anything, perhaps one should speak of the emergence of a post-humanistic geography: there is certainly no shortage of 'posts'. Many of those who had been most closely associated with the development of humanistic geography have since been drawn to POSTMODERNISM, POSTCOLONIALISM and even POSTSTRUCTURALISM: all of which, in various ways, have made problematic the conception of human agency and the human subject that was originally focal to humanistic geography. It is now widely accepted that the autonomous, neutered and sovereign human subject at its core was a fiction, implicated in an IDEOLOGY of humanism which suppressed the multiple ways in which subjects were constructed in order to promote a white, masculine, bourgeois subject as the norm, from which others were to be seen as departures or deviants (Gregory, 1993). What is more, Cosgrove has shown how, in its Renaissance origins at least, humanism was implicated in the very geometricization of knowledge which, in its modern geographical form, it sought to contest (Cosgrove, 1989). And humanism has also been indicted through an ecological critique which favours an *ecocentric* (rather than anthropocentric) perspective on the world and the place of human beings within it.   DG

References

Andrews, H. 1984: The Durkheimians and human geography: some contextual problems in the sociology of knowledge. *Trans. Inst. Br. Geogr.* n.s. 9, pp. 315–36.

Barnes, T. and Duncan, J., eds 1992: *Writing worlds: discourse, text and metaphor in the representation of landscape.* London: Routledge.

Berdoulay, V. 1978: The Vidal–Durkheim debate. In Ley, D. and Samuels, M., eds., *Humanistic geography: prospects and problems.* London: Croom Helm, pp. 77–90.

Buttimer, A. 1979: Reason, rationality and human creativity. *Geogr. Annlr.* 61B, pp. 43–9.

Buttimer, A. 1990: Geography, humanism and global concern. *Ann. Ass. Am. Geogr.* 80, pp. 1–33.

Christensen, K. 1982: Geography as a human science: a philosophical critique of the positivist-humanist split. In Gould, P. and Olsson, G., eds, *A search for common ground.* London: Pion, pp. 37–57.

Cosgrove, D. 1979: John Ruskin and the geographical imagination. *Geogrl. Rev.* 69, pp. 43–62.

Cosgrove, D. 1984: *Social formation and symbolic landscape.* London: Croom Helm.

Cosgrove, D. 1989: Historical considerations on humanism, historical materialism and geography. In Kobayashi, A. and Mackenzie, S., eds, *Remaking human geography.* London: Unwin Hyman, pp. 189–205.

Daniels, S. 1985: Arguments for a humanistic geography. In Johnston, R. J., ed., *The future of geography.* London: Methuen, pp. 143–58.

Duncan, J. 1980: The superorganic in American cultural geography. *Ann. Ass. Am. Geogr.* 70, pp. 181–98.

Duncan, J. and Ley, D. 1982: Structural Marxism and human geography. *Ann. Ass. Am. Geogr.* 72, pp. 30–59.

Entrikin, J. N. 1976: Contemporary humanism in geography. *Ann. Ass. Am. Geogr.* 66, pp. 615–32.

Gold, J. R. and Goodey, B. 1984: Behavioral and perceptual geography: criticisms and responses. *Progr. hum. Geogr.* 8, pp. 544–50.

Gregory, D. 1981: Human agency and human geography. *Trans. Inst. Br. Geogr.* n.s. 6, pp. 1–16.

Gregory, D. 1993: *Geographical imaginations.* Oxford: Blackwell.

Grossberg, L., Nelson, C. and Treichler, P., eds 1992: *Cultural studies.* London: Routledge.

Harris, R. C. 1978: The historical mind and the practice of geography. In Ley, D. and Samuels, M., eds, *Humanistic geography: prospects and problems.* London: Croom Helm, pp. 123–37.

Jackson, P. 1985: Urban ethnography. *Progr. hum. Geogr.* 9, pp. 157–76.

Jackson, P. and Smith, S. J. 1984: *Exploring social geography*. London: Allen and Unwin.

Kobayashi, A. and Mackenzie, S., eds 1989: *Remaking human geography*. London: Unwin Hyman.

Ley, D. 1978: Social geography and social action. In Ley, D. and Samuels, M., eds, *Humanistic geography: prospects and problems*. London: Croom Helm, pp. 41–57.

Ley, D. 1989: Fragmentation, coherence and the limits to theory in human geography. In Kobayashi, A. and Mackenzie, S., eds, *Remaking human geography*. London: Unwin Hyman, pp. 223–44.

Meinig, D. ed., 1979: *The interpretation of ordinary landscapes*. New York: Oxford University Press.

Meinig, D. 1983: Geography as an art. *Trans. Inst. Br. Geogr.* n.s. 8, pp. 314–28.

Pile, S. 1991: Practising interpretative geography. *Trans. Inst. Br. Geogr.* n.s. 16, pp. 458–69.

Pocock, D., ed. 1981: *Humanistic geography and literature: essays on the experience of place*. London: Croom Helm.

Relph, E. 1981: *Rational landscapes and humanistic geography*. London: Croom Helm.

Smith, D. M. 1977: *Human geography: a welfare approach*. London: Edward Arnold.

Smith, S. 1984: Practising humanistic geography. *Ann. Ass. Am. Geogr.* 74, pp. 353–74.

Soper, K. 1986: *Humanism and anti-humanism*. London: Hutchinson.

Thrift, N. 1983: Literature, the production of culture and the politics of place. *Antipode* 15(1), pp. 12–24.

Tuan, Y.-F. 1976: Humanistic geography. *Ann. Ass. Am. Geogr.* 66, pp. 266–76.

Western J. 1981: *Outcast Cape Town*. London: Allen and Unwin.

Suggested Reading

Cloke, P., Philo, C. and Sadler, D. 1991: *Approaching human geography: an introduction to contemporary theoretical debates*. London: Paul Chapman/New York: Guilford Press, ch. 3.

Kobayashi and Mackenzie (1989).

Ley, D. and Samuels, M., eds 1978: *Humanistic geography: prospects and problems*. London: Croom Helm.

Smith (1984).

human subjectivity See SUBJECTIVITY, HUMAN.

hydraulic society An agrarian society based on large-scale hydraulic constructions, typically irrigation systems. According to Wittfogel (1957, p. 27):

> The effective management of these works involves an organizational web which covers either the whole, or at least the dynamic core, of the country's population. In consequence, those who control this network are uniquely prepared to wield supreme political power.

The result, Wittfogel contended, was that the STATE 'occupied an unrivaled position of operational leadership and organizational control'. It mobilized *corvée* labour (forced labour raised on a temporary but recurrent, because seasonal, basis) and enforced such an inordinately powerful control over its subject population that it was, in effect, 'a state stronger than society'. It depended on a monopoly of the means of violence, on legitimation through a theocracy which identified the state with the divine order, and on a STATE APPARATUS which took the form of a *hydraulic bureaucracy*. Wittfogel took the latter term from Max Weber, but whereas Weber regarded localizing tendencies as pervasive in all precapitalist bureaucracies, Wittfogel insisted on the contrary: on the overwhelming centralization of what he called 'Oriental despotism' (see Hindess and Hirst, 1975, pp. 217–18; cf. ASIATIC MODE OF PRODUCTION). Even so, many of the 'hydraulic societies' which have been investigated seem, in this respect at least, much closer to the Weber model (see, e.g., Leach, 1959; Eberhard, 1970) and although Wittfogel's thesis has been used to account for URBAN ORIGINS precisely because it is supposed to provide a rationale for centralization and concentration, Wheatley (1971, pp. 256–98) has provided a forceful summary of its 'structural inadequacies' in such a context.

Modern discussions of such agrarian societies offer much more detailed reconstructions of their ecological regimes (see, e.g., Butzer, 1976) and much more incisive examinations of their power structures (e.g. Mann, 1986).   DG

References

Butzer, K. 1976: *Early civilization in Egypt: a study in cultural ecology*. Chicago: Chicago University Press.

Eberhard, W. 1970: *Conquerors and rulers: social forces in medieval China.* Leiden: Brill.

Hindess, B. and Hirst, P. Q. 1975: *Pre-capitalist modes of production.* London: Routledge and Kegan Paul.

Leach, E. R. 1959: Hydraulic society in Ceylon. *Past and Present* 15, pp. 2–25.

Mann, M. 1986: *The sources of social power,* volume 1, *A history of power in agrarian societies.* Cambridge: Cambridge University Press.

Wheatley, P. 1971: *The pivot of the four quarters.* Edinburgh: Edinburgh University Press/Chicago: Aldine.

Wittfogel, K. 1957: *Oriental despotism.* New Haven: Yale University Press.

Suggested Reading

Mann (1986).

Wheatley (1971), pp. 289–98.

Wittfogel, K. 1956: The hydraulic civilizations. In Thomas, W. L., ed., *Man's role in changing the face of the earth.* Chicago: Chicago University Press, pp. 152–64.

hyperspace A dominant and often disorienting SPATIALITY of POSTMODERNISM and 'postmodernity'. The term derives from Frederic Jameson's (1991) celebrated reading of the 'experience of space' in the Bonaventure Hotel in Los Angeles as a figure for a postmodern space which, so he said, transcends 'the capacities of the individual human body to locate itself, to organize its immediate surroundings perceptually, and cognitively to map its position in a mappable external world'. Jameson's characterization of hyperspace has something in common with the observations of two other influential critics and theorists. Castells (1983) writes of a late-twentieth-century 'space of flows', 'a space of variable geometry, formed by locations hierarchically ordered in a continuously changing network of flows', in which the meaning of places for the people who live in them dissolves and disappears: 'Life is transformed into abstraction, cities into shadows'. And Lefebvre (1992) describes the history of the modern PRODUCTION OF SPACE as a process of abstraction in which space has been progressively decorporealized (see Gregory, 1993, chapter 6).

Jameson (1988; see also 1991) has called for a new *cognitive mapping* to chart post-

modern hyperspace, and in human geography its constitution has been explored through a conjunction between political economy and cultural theory which has paid particular attention to the globalization of MODERNITY and the TIME–SPACE COMPRESSION of late-twentieth-century CAPITALISM (Harvey, 1989; Swyngedouw, 1989) and to various experimental ways of representing the postmodern city (cf. Soja, 1989, chapter 9; Gregory, 1993, chapter 4).

DG

References

Castells, M. 1983: *The city and the grassroots.* Berkeley, CA: University of California Press.

Gregory, D. 1993: *Geographical imaginations.* Oxford: Blackwell.

Harvey, D. 1989: *The condition of postmodernity: an enquiry into the origins of cultural change.* Oxford: Blackwell.

Jameson, F. 1988: Cognitive mapping. In Nelson, C. and Grossberg, L., eds, *Marxism and the interpretation of culture.* Urbana, IL: University of Illinois Press, pp. 347–60.

Jameson, F. 1991: *Postmodernism or, the cultural logic of late capitalism.* Durham, NC: Duke University Press.

Lefebvre, H. 1992: *The production of space.* Oxford: Blackwell.

Soja, E. 1989: *Postmodern geographies: the reassertion of space in critical social theory.* London: Verso.

Swyngedouw, E. 1989: The heart of the place: the resurrection of locality in an age of hyperspace. *Geogr. Annlr.* 71B, pp. 31–42.

Suggested Reading

Jameson (1988).

Jameson (1991), ch. 1.

hypothesis A provisional statement which guides empirical work in several scientific EPISTEMOLOGIES.

Within POSITIVISM, a hypothesis is an empirical statement not yet accepted as true: the purpose of the positivist methodology is to test its veracity, thereby establishing the statement's truth through empirical investigation. The hypothesis, derived from a body of THEORY, should be general in its application and not refer to a specific place or event only. Hypotheses are therefore the means of structuring empirical research programmes within this philosophy, which was strongly promoted

267

during geography's QUANTITATIVE REVO-
LUTION.

In CRITICAL RATIONALISM hypotheses
are designed not to be validated but to
be refuted – or falsified: science advances,
it is argued, not by accumulating evidence
of verified hypotheses (because any
verification can only be provisional)
but by discarding false hypotheses. In
PRAGMATISM, too, they are provisional
statements which guide action until a
superior hypothesis is derived. Similarly,
in aspects of REALISM hypotheses are
used in the cumulative process of
knowledge acquisition, but not with
the goal of producing statements of
universal generality, which characterizes
positivism.   RJJ

Suggested Reading

Harvey, D. 1969: *Explanation in geography.*
London: Edward Arnold.

Newman, J. L. 1973: The use of the term
'hypothesis' in geography. *Ann. Ass. Am. Geogr.*
62, pp. 22–7.

Sayer, A. 1992: *Method in social science: a realist
approach.* London: Routledge.

hysteresis A switch in the relationship
between two variables from one smooth
curve to another. (See also BIFURCATION;
CATASTROPHE THEORY.)   RJJ

I

iconography The description and interpretation of visual images in order to disclose their symbolic meanings. Conventionally applied to religious icons and painted images, 'iconography' was initially introduced into geography by Jean Gottmann (1952) alongside 'movement' as one of two counterposing forces moving the political geography of NATIONS: the latter acting to integrate territories, and the former to separate them through local allegiances. Iconography has more recently been promoted as a method of cartographic and LANDSCAPE interpretation in CULTURAL GEOGRAPHY. Landscapes, both on the ground and represented on various surfaces, are thus regarded as deposits of cultural meanings (Woodward, 1987; Cosgrove and Daniels, 1988). The iconographic method seeks to explore these meanings through describing the form and composition of landscapes, interpreting their symbolic content and re-immersing landscapes in their social and historical contexts. Successful iconographic interpretation allows us to see human landscapes as both shaped by and themselves shaping broader social and cultural processes, and thus having ideological significance. Geographical iconography today accepts that landscape meanings are unstable, contested and highly political. Recognition of the role of landscape images, such as the English village, or dams and hydroelectric schemes in the American West, in shaping national identity bids to re-introduce iconography as a valuable approach in POLITICAL GEOGRAPHY. DEC

References

Cosgrove, D. and Daniels, S., eds 1988: *The iconography of landscape: essays on the symbolic representation, design and use of past environments.* Cambridge: Cambridge University Press.

Gottmann, J. 1952: *La politique des états et leur géographie.* Paris: Armand Colin.

Woodward, D., ed. 1987: *Art and cartography: six historical essays.* Chicago: University of Chicago Press.

ideal type A theoretical construction proposed by the sociologist Max Weber as a means of understanding the complexity and variety of social action (see ABSTRACTION). It provides a generalization, either through the use of a case study or by creating a hypothetical norm, against which comparisons can be made and understanding of particular events obtained: the use of ideal types often suggests dichotomies, as in the RURAL–URBAN CONTINUUM. Ideal types are often used ideologically, as in the concept of a 'free market', which most critiques of CAPITALISM suggest cannot exist.

According to some versions of PHENOMENOLOGY, ideal types are constructs that individuals use in the creation of their TAKEN-FOR-GRANTED WORLDS – they are means of simplifying reality in order to come to terms with it, as suggested in the work of Sennett (1973) on stereotypes. RJJ

Reference

Sennett, R. 1973: *The uses of disorder.* London: Penguin.

Suggested Reading

Jackson, P. and Smith, S. J. 1984: *Exploring social geography.* London: Allen and Unwin.

idealism A philosophy which *either* regards reality as residing in or constituted by the mind ('metaphysical idealism') *or* limits human understanding to perceptions of external objects ('epistemological idealism') (cf. the *materialism* of MARXIST GEOGRAPHY): in human geography, however, it has also come to connote a particular perspective which seeks 'to understand the development of the earth's cultural landscapes by uncovering the thought that lies behind them' (Guelke, 1974; see also Guelke, 1982). It is this emphasis on the mind, 'on rethinking the thoughts of geographical agents', which Guelke claims entitles him to represent his programme as an idealist one (cf. Lowther, 1959). On this reading, 'the human geographer does not need theories of his [or her] own because he [or she] is concerned with the theories expressed in the actions of the individual being investigated'; and indeed, 'any attempt to describe human behavior in theoretical terms seems doomed' to Guelke because the geographer 'must take full account of the special nature of human theoretical behavior' (Guelke, 1974, 1976). It is perhaps not surprising that, when confronted with formulations such as this, Chappell (1976) should complain that Guelke's insistence that 'human geographers cannot achieve sound general theory for the very reason that human thought is theoretical in character' left him 'groping for a logical handle'. According to Chappell, such a peculiar suppression of the theoretical attitude is not idealist at all, but IDIOGRAPHIC; while to Harrison and Livingstone (1979) it is simply a version of EMPIRICISM rather than the telling critique of POSITIVISM which Guelke intends it to be (see Guelke, 1971). But in fact a 'logical handle' can be constructed which distances Guelke's project from both of these critical readings (if not from other objections). This has two elements:

(a) *Interpretative sociology.* Guelke takes the 'special nature of human theoretical behavior' to be its rationality and its intentionality, so that a proper understanding of social life depends on the method of *Verstehen*, i.e. the imaginative 'immersion' of the observer in the 'experiential context' of the subject (Hufferd, 1980); but because empirical validation of the reasons behind actions cannot be achieved within this realm of subjective meaning, Guelke's idealist geography has to proceed via the construction of 'ideal models' which 'map out rational courses of action' and so allow entry into a realm of objective action where verification can take place (Guelke, 1974). This is formally equivalent to Max Weber's attempt to conjoin *Verstehen* to empirically verifiable explanation (*Erklären*) through the use of 'IDEAL TYPES' which project intentions on the actions (see Outhwaite, 1975).

(b) *Constitutive PHENOMENOLOGY.* The connections between intentions and actions depend on a criterion of adequacy, which Alfred Schutz formulated as follows: 'each term in a scientific model of human action must be constructed in such a way that a human act performed within the lifeworld by an individual actor would be understandable for the actor himself as well as for his fellow-men in terms of common-sense interpretation of everyday life' (Schutz, 1962). This raises all sorts of difficulties (see the discussion in Gregory, 1978), but it is this need for congruence between the actor's explanation and the audience's explanation which makes general theorems about such specific theoretical constructions and codifications inadmissible for Guelke.

However, rather than draw upon these two sources and examine them in detail, Guelke has predicated his programme on Collingwood's *The idea of history* (1946), and in particular on Collingwood's 'crucial' contention that 'all history is the history of thought' (see Guelke, 1982). But to many commentators this is both less developed and more restrictive than Guelke requires: Collingwood's conception of mind excluded 'immediate experience and unconscious acts' (Watts and Watts, 1978) and failed to explore the different ways in which Weber, for example, conceived of 'rational' action. Indeed, when Guelke claims that an idealist interpretation involves sorting out the intentions of actors 'in such a way that their actions can be seen as rational responses to their situations as they saw them' he glosses over *who* is to regard them as rational and on *what* basis: these are vital questions in any comparative or historical work – which is one of Guelke's major concerns (see Guelke, 1982). Furthermore, as Curry (1982) has argued, Guelke's search for reasons involves an essentialism – thoughts are supposed to be 'behind' actions – whereas not all actions entail consciously entertained reasons. Without a more rigorous account of his principles and procedures and without a convincing demonstration of their practical consequences it is hard to see how Guelke's programme can register a genuine advance over pre-existing interpretative traditions in human geography and social theory (see Giddens, 1976; Gregory, 1978) (see also HUMANIST GEOGRAPHY; QUALITATIVE METHODS).

Despite these criticisms, Guelke has not modified his views (see Guelke, 1989), but few geographers have taken up his ideas. Instead, there has been a growing interest in examining, in distinctly *non*-idealist ways, the model of rational choice and rational behaviour which lies at the heart of his project. This critical examination has taken place without direct reference to Guelke's version of idealism, but it has broken the tie between 'rational choices' and 'rational consequences' on which his method depends (Barnes and Sheppard, 1992) and provided a more comprehensive account of different forms of rationality than he allows (Miller, 1992).   DG

References

Barnes, T. and Sheppard, E. 1992: Is there a place for the rational actor? A geographical critique of the rational choice paradigm. *Econ. Geogr.* 68, pp. 1–21.

Chappell, J. E. Jr 1976: Comment in reply. *Ann. Ass. Am. Geogr.* 66, pp. 169–73.

Collingwood, R. G. 1946: *The idea of history*. Oxford: Oxford University Press.

Curry, M. 1982: The idealist dispute in Anglo-American geography. *Can. Geogr.* 27, pp. 35–50 (see also responses, pp. 51–9).

Giddens, A. 1976: *New rules of sociological method*. London: Hutchinson/New York: Basic Books.

Gregory, D. 1978: *Ideology, science and human geography*. London: Hutchinson/New York: St. Martin's Press.

Guelke, L. 1971: Problems of scientific explanation in geography. *Can. Geogr.* 15, pp. 38–53.

Guelke, L. 1974: An idealist alternative in human geography. *Ann. Ass. Am. Geogr.* 64, pp. 193–202.

Guelke, L. 1976: The philosophy of idealism. *Ann. Ass. Am. Geogr.* 66, pp. 168–9.

Guelke, L. 1982: *Historical understanding in geography: an idealist approach*. Cambridge: Cambridge University Press.

Guelke, L. 1989: Intellectual coherence and the foundations of geography. *Prof. Geogr.* 41, pp. 123–30.

Harrison, R. and Livingstone, D. N. 1979: There and back again – towards a critique of idealist human geography. *Area* 11, pp. 75–9 (and discussion, pp. 80–2).

Hufferd, J. 1980: Idealism and the participant's world. *Prof. Geogr.* 32, pp. 1–5.

Lowther, G. R. 1959: Idealist history and historical geography. *Can. Geogr.* 14, pp. 31–6.

Miller, B. 1992: Collective action and rational choice: place, community and the limits to individual self-interest. *Econ. Geogr.* 68, pp. 22–42.

Outhwaite, W. 1975: *Understanding social life: the method called 'Verstehen'*. London: Allen & Unwin/New York: Holmes and Meier.

Schutz, A. 1962: *Collected Papers*, volume 1. The Hague: Martinus Nijhoff.

Watts, S. J. and Watts, S. J. 1978: The idealist alternative in geography and history. *Prof. Geogr.* 30. pp. 123–7.

Suggested Reading

Curry (1982).

Guelke (1974).

Harrison and Livingstone (1979).

ideology The term *idéologie* was originally used by Enlightenment philosopher Destutt de Tracy in 1796 to describe (and to recommend) a new, rigorous 'science of ideas' which, 'by overcoming religious and metaphysical prejudices, may serve as a new basis for public education'. It was, thus, profoundly 'positive' (cf. POSITIVISM), and only assumed a negative and indeed pejorative meaning in the course of the nineteenth century – and in this Marx was instrumental, for 'with Marx, the concept of ideology came of age' (Larrain, 1979).

Since then, however, the concept has taken on a number of different meanings, so that it is impossible to provide a single definition (within HISTORICAL MATERIALISM alone, see Eagleton, 1991). In the most general terms, most writers use 'ideology' in one of two conventional senses, each of which bears the marks of its eighteenth- and nineteenth-century origins. Thompson (1981) distinguishes them thus:

(a) 'the lattice of ideas which permeate the social order, constituting the collective consciousness of an epoch', i.e. a *generalized* system of ideas; and

(b) 'a consciousness which is in some way "false" [and] which fails to grasp the real conditions of human existence', i.e. a *distorted* system of ideas.

In Thompson's view, neither is satisfactory. He objects to the first 'because it is too *wide*: by anchoring ideology in the very nature of consciousness, it conceals the specificity of the ideological phenomenon and renders the latter unsurpassable'. He objects to the second 'because it is too *narrow*: by defining ideology in opposition to science, it precludes the possibility that science itself may be ideological'. (cf. Harvey, 1974: 'The use of a scientific method is of necessity founded in ideology, and . . . any claim to be ideology-free is of necessity an ideological claim'.)

Thompson (1981, 1984) prefers to treat ideology as 'a system of signification which facilitates the pursuit of particular interests' and sustains specific 'relations of domination'. This formulation draws on both Habermas's CRITICAL THEORY and Giddens's STRUCTURATION THEORY. So, for example, Giddens (1979, emphasis below added) argues that 'to analyse the ideological aspects of symbolic orders' is to examine '*how structures of signification are mobilised to legitimate the sectional interests of hegemonic groups*' (see HEGEMONY) within specific '*structures of domination*' (cf. Gregory, 1980). But Thompson, like Habermas, emphasizes the signal importance of *language*. 'It is only in recent years', he notes, that the theory of ideology 'has been enriched and elaborated through a reflection on languages...':

For increasingly it has been realized that ideas do not drift through the social world like clouds in a summer sky, occasionally divulging their contents with a clap of thunder and a flash of light. Rather, ideas circulate in the social world as utterances, as expressions, as words which are

spoken or inscribed. Hence to study ideology is, in some part and in some way, to study language in the social world. It is to study the ways in which language is used in everyday social life, from the most mundane encounter between friends and family members to the most privileged forms of political debate (Thompson, 1984).

The 'linguistic turn' in social theory is multifaceted, but within human geography it has been echoed by Gregory's (1978) critique of ideology as 'unexamined discourse', by Olsson's (1980, 1991) investigations of the connective imperative between language and 'thought-and-action', and by a series of inquiries informed by PRAGMATISM. What these explorations indicate – and this is vital – is that ideology is *not* merely 'illusion':

Once we recognize that ideology operates through language and that language is a medium of social action, we must also acknowledge that ideology is partially constitutive of what, in our societies, 'is real'. Ideology is not a pale image of the social world but is part of that world, a creative and constitutive element of our social lives (Thompson, 1984).

This much would now probably be acknowledged by most geographers, although their interest in ideology extends beyond spoken and written forms of communication to the constellations of power inscribed in visual images (see ICONOGRAPHY; LANDSCAPE). These ideas thread out into the more general analysis of DISCOURSE: even Eagleton (1991) concedes that 'ideology is a matter of "discourse" rather than of language'. It represents, so he says, 'the points where power impacts upon certain utterances ["knowledges"] and inscribes itself tacitly within them'. The most sustained examinations of discourse in these terms have been conducted under the sign of POST-STRUCTURALISM, where particular interest attaches to the identification of *regimes of truth* and the conjunctions between power and knowledge (see Barrett, 1991). What this implies, in turn, is that investigations are needed not only of *the ideology of geography* – and the critical literature which bears on this terrain is now extensive, including critiques of ETHNOCENTRISM, ORIENTALISM and PHALLOCENTRISM and the correspondingly 'white' and masculinist ideologies of geography – but also of *the geography of ideology*. There is more or less general agreement on the need to avoid those versions of 'hegemony' and of the 'dominant ideology thesis' which over-emphasize the degree of coherence, integration and stability of societies (Abercrombie et al., 1980), and of the importance of recovering the multiple ideologies which inform and are invigorated by diverse social struggles (Eyles, 1981). Such a project will require a much more inclusive account of geographies of knowing and unknowing (Thrift, 1985) and of the geographies of discourse and the mediatization of modern culture (Thompson, 1990). It will include analyses of the relations between power, knowledge and SPATIALITY (Gregory, 1993) and of the inscription of those often unacknowledged and taken-for-granted constellations of power and knowledge in maps (Harley, 1988, 1992) and landscapes (Cosgrove, 1984, Baker and Biger, 1992).   DG

References

Abercrombie, N., Hill, T. and Turner, B. S. 1980: *The dominant ideology thesis*. London: Allen and Unwin.

Baker, A. R. H. and Biger, G. 1992: *Ideology and landscape in historical perspective*. Cambridge: Cambridge University Press.

Barrett, M. 1991: *The politics of truth: from Marx to Foucault*. Stanford, CA: Stanford University Press.

Cosgrove, D. 1984: *Social formation and symbolic landscape*. London: Croom Helm.

Eagleton, T. 1991: *Ideology: an introduction*. London: Verso.

Eyles, J. 1981: Ideology, contradiction and struggle: an exploratory discussion. *Antipode* 13(2), pp. 39–46.

Giddens, A. 1979: *Central problems in social theory*. London: Macmillan.

Gregory, D. 1978: *Ideology, science and human geography*. London: Hutchinson.

Gregory, D. 1980: The ideology of control: systems theory and geography. *Tijdschr. econ. soc. Geogr.* 71, pp. 327–42.

Gregory, D. 1993: *Geographical imaginations*. Oxford: Blackwell.

Harley, J. B. 1988: Maps, knowledge and power. In Cosgrove, D. and Daniels, S., eds, *The iconography of landscape*. Cambridge: Cambridge University Press, pp. 277–312.

Harley, J. B. 1992: Deconstructing the map. In Barnes, T. and Duncan, J., eds, *Writing worlds: discourse, text and metaphor in the representation of landscape*. London: Routledge, pp. 231–47.

Harvey, D. 1974: Population, resources and the ideology of science. *Econ. Geogr.* 50, pp. 256–77.

Larrain, J. 1979: *The concept of ideology*. London: Hutchinson.

Olsson, G. 1980: *Birds in egg/eggs in bird*. London: Pion.

Olsson, G. 1991: *Lines of power/limits of language*. Minneapolis: University of Minnesota Press.

Thompson, J. B. 1981: *Critical hermeneutics*. Cambridge: Cambridge University Press.

Thompson, J. B. 1984: *Studies in the theory of ideology*. Cambridge: Polity Press.

Thompson, J. B. 1990: *Ideology and modern culture*. Cambridge: Polity Press.

Thrift, N. 1985: Flies and germs: a geography of knowledge. In Gregory, D. and Urry, J., eds, *Social relations and spatial structures*. London: Macmillan, pp. 366–403.

Suggested Reading

Barrett (1991).

Harley (1992).

Thompson (1990), chs 1 and 2.

idiographic Concerned with the unique and the particular (cf. NOMOTHETIC). The appellation originated at the end of the nineteenth century when W. Windelband and N. Rickert made a famous distinction between the nomothetic and idiographic sciences which, they claimed, entitled history to be regarded as radically different from other forms of intellectual inquiry (see KANTIANISM). Their arguments have been challenged by other historians and philosophers of science, but made a forceful entry into geography through the Hartshorne–Schaefer debate over EXCEPTIONALISM, when traditional REGIONAL GEOGRAPHY was represented as essentially idiographic and incapable of contributing towards effective generalization. These claims were subsequently revived during the QUANTITATIVE REVOLUTION: both Bunge (1962) and Haggett (1965) argued that 'one can do little with the unique except contemplate its uniqueness', and although Chorley and Haggett's influential *Models in geography* (1967) did 'not propose to alter the basic Hartshorne definition of geography's prime task', attempts there and elsewhere to establish a model-based PARADIGM nevertheless marked the re-emergence of a nomothetic geography 'after the lapse into ideography' (Burton, 1963). Some geographers would (then and now) reverse this charge, in the belief that a preoccupation with abstract models constituted the real lapse: certainly, the emergence of IDEALISM within geography has been accompanied by equally polemical claims that the human geographer 'does not need theories of his [or her] own' (Guelke, 1974). Whatever one thinks of Guelke's specific proposals, a number of traditions which would otherwise contest his philosophy would nevertheless agree that 'the avoidance of the unique is not a requirement of science' (Guelke, 1977). From the perspective of historical materialism, for example, Massey (1984) contends that:

Variety should not be seen as a deviation from the expected; nor should uniqueness be seen as a problem. 'General processes' *never* work themselves out in pure form. There are always specific circumstances, a particular history, a particular place or location. What is at issue . . . is the articulation of the general with the local (the particular) to produce qualitatively different outcomes in different localities.

It is exactly this issue which is at the very centre of the revival of interest in AREAL DIFFERENTIATION and the reconstruction of a theoretically informed REGIONAL GEOGRAPHY. Thus, Johnston (1985) argues that:

[R]egional geography must focus on the *unique* characteristics of the place being studied, but must not express them as if they were *singular* [emphasis added]. This means that regions must not be studied solely as separate entities. They are part of a much larger whole. . . . We need a regional geography that finds a middle course between on the one hand the generalising approaches, which allow for no real freedom of individual action, and on the other the singular approaches, which argue that all is freedom of action.

(Cf. CONTEXTUAL THEORY; STRUCTURATION THEORY.)

All of these formulations are simplifications, of course: it is not so much a matter of connecting 'the' general to 'the' particular as one of recognizing the *hierarchy of concepts* which are involved (see REALISM). But they all register a significant advance over the combative opposition of the nomothetic and the idiographic.   DG

References

Bunge, W. 1962: *Theoretical geography*. Lund, Sweden: C. W. K. Gleerup.

Burton, I. 1963: The quantitative revolution and theoretical geography. *Can. Geogr.* 7, pp. 151–62.

Chorley, R. J. and Haggett, P., eds 1967: *Models in geography*. London: Methuen

Guelke, L. 1974: An idealist alternative in human geography. *Ann. Ass. Am. Geogr.* 64, pp. 193–202.

Guelke, L. 1977: The role of laws in human geography. *Prog. hum. Geogr.* 1, pp. 376–86.

Haggett, P. 1965: *Locational analysis in human geography*. London: Edward Arnold/New York: John Wiley.

Johnston, R. J. 1985: The world is our oyster. In King, R., ed., *Geographical futures*. Sheffield: Geographical Association, pp. 112–28.

Massey, D. 1984: Introduction. In Massey, D. and Allen, J., eds, *Geography matters! A reader*. Cambridge: Cambridge University Press, pp. 1–11.

Suggested Reading

Harvey, D. 1969: *Explanation in geography*. London: Edward Arnold/New York: St. Martin's Press, pp. 49–54.

Johnston (1985).

imperialism An unequal territorial relationship, usually between STATES, based on domination and subordination. Such a relationship does not necessarily imply COLONIALISM, for imperialist control over a subordinate territory's economic and political activities can exist without military intervention and the establishment of a colonial regime.

There is a number of economic theories of imperialism, the most influential being that put forward by the English liberal economist, J. A. Hobson, in 1902, which was later elaborated upon by the Russian Marxist, V. I. Lenin. In his 1915 thesis, Lenin argued that both the causes of the

First World War and the continuation of CAPITALISM were linked to the following five main features of imperialism:

(a) in the epoch of imperialism, production and capital are concentrated to such a degree that they give rise to monopolies, which play the decisive part in the economic life of capitalist states;

(b) monopoly banking CAPITAL merges with monopoly industrial capital, forming finance capital, the financial oligarchy;

(c) the export of capital, as distinct from the export of goods, acquires particular importance;

(d) the process of monopolization brings about the formation of international monopolies which divide the world among themselves economically;

(e) the territorial division of the world between a handful of the largest capitalist states is completed.

(For Lenin, this heralded in the last stage of CAPITALISM, for competing imperialisms would lead to war, which in turn would bring revolution and capitalism's eventual destruction.)

The nature of imperialism has changed dramatically since 1915, however. The post-1945 decolonization of the Third World has resulted in the establishment of a large number of sovereign states, the vast majority of which remain economically dependent on the developed world (see SOVEREIGNTY). Recent decades have also seen the meteoric rise of the MULTINATIONAL CORPORATION, the global reach of which is not just characterized by worldwide acquisition of financial assets and exercise over financial control, but also by a production process which follows the spatial logic of capitalism, which in turn has contributed to an international spatial DIVISION OF LABOUR (see also NEW INTERNATIONAL DIVISION OF LABOUR). For Mandel (1975), there are three possible models for the corresponding internationalization of capital:

(a) *super-imperialism* – the dominance of a single, advanced capitalist state, which corresponds to control over an increasing share of internationalized capital by a single national class of capitalists;

(b) *ultra-imperialism* – the emergence of a supranational imperialist 'world state' which corresponds to a multinational capital;

(c) *inter-imperialist competition* – between the major Western blocs (USA, Western Europe, Japan), which corresponds to multinational capital on a continental scale, but not on a fully international basis.

Contemporary imperialism should not be considered as purely economic, however, for the expansion of the area of the operation of capital is more often than not associated with an expansion of political influence of the state with which that capital is associated, and it often has vitally important cultural dimensions.   GES

Reference

Mandel, E. 1975: *Late capitalism*. London: Verso.

Suggested Reading

Blaut, J. M. 1975: Imperialism: the Marxist theory and its evolution. *Antipode*, 7(1), pp. 1–19.

Brown, M. B. 1974: *The economics of imperialism*. London: Penguin.

Elson, D. 1984: Imperialism. In McLennan, G., Held, D. and Hall, S., eds, *The idea of the modern state*. Milton Keynes: Open University Press, pp. 154–82.

Lenin, V. I. 1915: *Imperialism, the highest form of capitalism*. Moscow: Foreign Languages Publishing House.

indices of segregation Measures of the degree of residential separation of subgroups within a wider population. The development of meaningful indices of SEGREGATION has been fundamental to the study of social stratification and residential differentiation in urban areas. A simple graphical method of showing segregation is the *Lorenz curve*. In the figure are shown curves for several ethnic groups in Melbourne in 1961. The x axis shows the cumulative percentage of each ethnic group, and the y axis the cumulative percentage of the remaining groups over the sub-areas of the city. A diagonal line indicates no segregation, i.e. the percentages within each sub-area are absolutely consistent with the percentages of the city population as a whole. Normally, the segregation line is a curve the distance of which from the diagonal indicates the degree of segregation. The Lorenz curve

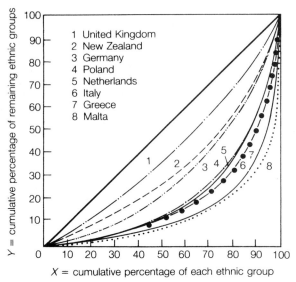

Y = cumulative percentage of remaining ethnic groups

1 United Kingdom
2 New Zealand
3 Germany
4 Poland
5 Netherlands
6 Italy
7 Greece
8 Malta

X = cumulative percentage of each ethnic group

indices of segregation   *Concentration curves of the residential distribution of ethnic groups in 611 census areas of Melbourne* (Lancaster Jones, 1967).

is widely used in other contexts as a general measure of inequalities in distributions.

Most studies of segregation have used one of two simple indices to summarize differences between two spatial distributions. The indices vary from 0 to 100 and indicate the percentage redistribution necessary before two groups are similarly distributed over a set of districts. First, the *index of residential dissimilarity* indicates the percentage difference between the distributions of two component groups of population:

$$I_d = \frac{1}{2} \sum_{i=1}^{k} |x_i - y_i|,$$

where x_i represents the percentage of the x population in the ith areal sub-unit, y_i the percentage of the y population in the ith sub-unit, and the summation is given over all of the k sub-units making up the given territory, such as a city. Second, the *index of residential segregation* indicates the percentage difference between one group's distribution and that of the rest of the population:

$$I_s = I_d / [1 - (\Sigma x_{ai} / \Sigma x_{ni})],$$

where I_d is the index of dissimilarity between the subgroup and the total population (including the subgroup), Σx_{ai} represents the total number of the subgroup in the city and Σx_{ni} represents the total population of the city. For example, for Chicago in 1950 the index of dissimilarity for professional groups compared to labourers was 54 per cent; the index of segregation for professional groups was 30 per cent and for labourers 35 per cent.

A further simple measure is the LOCATION QUOTIENT, which shows the relative concentration of a population within any one sub-area. Variations on these basic measures, and the problems associated with scale, the size of subgroups and the nature of areal units have been much discussed. (See also GHETTO; RACE; RACISM; URBAN GEOGRAPHY.)   PEO

Reference

Lancaster Jones, F. 1967: Ethnic concentration and assimilation: an Australian case study. *Social Forces* 45, pp. 412–23.

Suggested Reading

Jones, E. and Eyles, J. 1977: *An introduction to social geography.* Oxford: Oxford University Press.

Peach, C., ed. 1975: *Urban social segregation.* London: Longman.

Peach, C., Robinson, V. and Smith, S., eds 1981: *Ethnic segregation in cities.* London: Croom Helm/ Athens, GA: University of Georgia Press.

indifference curves A plot of combinations of quantities of two things, such that an individual is indifferent as to which combination to choose (see the figure). Indifference curves are part of the analytical geometry of NEOCLASSICAL ECONOMICS. In their usual form they show combinations of two commodities, which provide consumers with the same level of satisfaction of utility. As consumers move along the curve, they are trading off one commodity for the other; if behaving rationally, they would choose the combination which costs least. In the ALONSO MODEL of urban land use, people have indifference curves with respect to combinations of a fixed amount of money spent on commuting and on housing, which assist the analysis of residential choice. In welfare economics, communities are assumed to have indifference curves reflecting the aggregation of individual preferences, which are used in the analysis of collective consumption.

DMS

industrial geography The study of the spatial arrangement of industrial activity. Industrial geography is a subfield of ECONOMIC GEOGRAPHY and deals with manufacturing or secondary activity. It is distinguished by the fact that the study of industrial location has brought geography and economics closer together than any other branch of geographical inquiry.

Until the quantitative and model-building movement gathered strength in the latter part of the 1950s, the study of industrial geography was largely confined to the verbal description of the distribution of individual manufacturing activities. Explanation tended to emphasize the historical evolution of the patterns and to place undue emphasis on the role of physical–environmental factors, such as the availability of raw materials and natural sources of power. There was little attempt to generalize from the case studies; there was no explicit theoretical framework, and hardly any economic analysis.

In the latter part of the 1950s statistical methods began to be used on the measurement of industrial location patterns. Then, as human geography became more interested in theory and models, industrial geography was able to benefit from existing work in economics. The birth of modern industrial location theory dates back to 1909, when the German economist

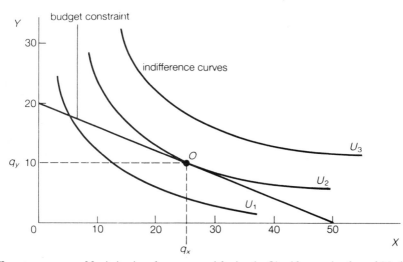

indifference curves *Maximization of consumer satisfaction (at O) with ten units of y and 25 of x, where the highest indifference curve just touches the budget constraint representing what the customer has to spend.*

Alfred Weber published his *Uber den Standort der Industrien* (translated into English in 1929 as *Alfred Weber's theory of the location of industries*; see WEBER MODEL). This book provided the foundations for VARIABLE COST ANALYSIS, which T. Palander and E. M. Hoover had significantly extended by the end of the 1930s (see Palander, 1935; Hoover, 1948). Parallel to this was the development of theory on LOCATIONAL INTERDEPENDENCE, which formed the basis for VARIABLE REVENUE ANALYSIS. This approach grew out of the recognition that firms can derive SPATIAL MONOPOLY advantages from location, contrary to the assumptions of the model of perfect competition in economic theory.

Throughout most of the 1960s the variable cost approach dominated theory in industrial geography. Developments on the revenue side, mainly in MARKET AREA ANALYSIS, found their most obvious expression in the context of CENTRAL PLACE THEORY. The fusion of the variable cost and variable revenue approaches has proved to be very difficult in theory. The most influential attempts at synthesis in the tradition of spatial economic analysis were those of Lösch (1954), Greenhut (1956) and Isard (1956). Important contributions by geographers during this phase of development of industrial location analysis were few, a major exception being E. M. Rawstron's concept of SPATIAL MARGINS to profitability.

Geographical contributions became more prominent towards the end of the 1960s, when traditional or 'neoclassical' LOCATION THEORY came under assault during the ascendancy of the behavioural school (see BEHAVIOURAL GEOGRAPHY). The shift from abstract models based on assumptions of optimizing objectives and capacity on behalf of decision-makers towards observation of actual location practice accorded with the traditionally more empirical predilections of the geographer. The case study thus reasserted itself. The practical application of location theory in the tradition of spatial economic analysis had always proved difficult, by virtue of the data demands of variable cost and variable revenue models. The empirical identification of locational decision-making was easier to undertake.

The 1970s saw two distinct but interconnected themes emerging in the more behaviourally oriented industrial geography. The first focused on the location DECISION-MAKING process, frequently using SURVEY methods to elicit from individuals the considerations relevant to locational choice and how final selection was made. The second theme has stressed the role of INDUSTRIAL ORGANIZATION in the location decision, and in the spatial organization of industrial activity in general. The perspective has gradually broadened, from preoccupation with the location of single-plant firms, through the complexities of giant multiplant and multiproduct firms, to concern with entire spatial industrial systems.

More recent developments have reflected the application of MARXIAN ECONOMICS to industrial location problems, in place of the NEOCLASSICAL ECONOMICS on which traditional location theory was based. The RESTRUCTURING of industrial activity in a spatial context has attracted increasing attention, within the broader context of change in the capitalist economy. As FLEXIBLE ACCUMULATION has come to characterize this kind of economy, the small firm nas re-emerged as a focus of interest. Increasing attention is also being given to networks of information exchange, which may be replacing traditional concerns such as input costs as factors influencing the location of some industries.

Despite these and other contemporary developments, neoclassical location theory in the space–economics tradition still has its adherents. Considerations such as cost minimization and spatial control of markets remain important to firms in a competitive capitalist economy, and the traditional models still have some utility as both predictive and prescriptive devices.

Since the introduction of location theory into industrial geography there has always been an interest in problems of planning industrial development. In the advanced capitalist world the focus has been primarily on problems of economic decline in older industrial regions and on plans to encourage the dispersal of manufacturing firms from prosperous metropolitan centres into the periphery. More recently, attention has shifted to the decline of industry in the INNER CITY. In the underdeveloped world the problem is how to stimulate industrial development, in circumstances that may include limitations of resources, capital and skills, in the general context of dependency on the advanced capitalist world.

As with other specialized subfields of economic (and human) geography, industrial geography finds its independent existence increasingly at variance with the tendency towards integration of subject matter, which was originally stimulated by the quantitative and model-building movements, was further encouraged by the emergence of regional economics and REGIONAL SCIENCE, and is an important feature of the political-economy perspective that seeks an holistic view of society. DMS

References

Greenhut, M. L. 1956: *Plant location in theory and in practice: the economics of space*. Chapel Hill, NC: University of North Carolina Press.

Hoover, E. M. 1948: *The location of economic activity*. New York: McGraw-Hill.

Isard, W. 1956: *Location and space economy: a general theory relating to industrial location, market areas, land use, trade and urban structure*. Cambridge, MA: MIT Press/London: Chapman and Hall.

Losch, A. 1954: *The economics of location*, translated by W. H. Woglom. New Haven: Yale University Press/Oxford: Oxford University Press. (First German edition 1940.)

Palander, T. 1935: *Beitrage zur Standorts-theorie*. Uppsala, Sweden: Almqvist and Wiksell.

Weber, A. 1929: *Alfred Weber's theory of the location of industries*, translated by C. J. Friedrich. Chicago: University of Chicago Press. (Reprinted 1971, New York: Russell and Russell; first German edition 1909.)

Suggested Reading

Carr, M. 1983: A contribution to the review and critique of behavioural industrial location theory. *Prog. hum. Geogr.* 7, pp. 386–402.

Chapman, K. and Walker, D. 1991: *Industrial location: principles and policies*, second edition. Oxford: Blackwell.

Hayter, R. and Watts, H. D. 1983: The geography of enterprise: a reappraisal. *Prog. hum. Geogr.* 7, pp. 157–81.

Massey, D. 1984: *Spatial divisions of labour: social structures and the geography of reproduction*. London: Macmillan.

O hUallachain, B. 1989: Industrial geography. *Prog. hum. Geogr.*, 13, pp. 251–8.

O hUallachain, B. 1991: Industrial geography. *Prog. hum. Geogr.*, 15, pp. 73–80.

Scott, A. J. 1988: *New industrial spaces*. London: Pion.

Scott, A. and Storper, M. 1986: *Production, work, territory: the geographical anatomy of industrial capitalism*. Boston: Allen and Unwin.

Sheppard, E. and Barnes, T. J. 1990: *The capitalist space economy: analysis after Ricardo, Marx and Sraffa*. London: Unwin Hyman.

Smith, D. M. 1981: *Industrial location: an economic geographical analysis*, second edition. New York: John Wiley.

Smith, D. M. 1987: Neoclassical location theory. In Lever, W., ed., *Industrial change in the United Kingdom*. London: Longman, pp. 23–37.

Storper, M. and Walker, R. A. 1989: *The capitalist imperative: territory, technology and industrial growth*. Oxford: Blackwell.

Walker, R. A. and Storper, M. 1981: Capital and industrial location. *Prog. hum. Geogr.* 5, pp. 473–509.

industrial inertia The tendency for industry, once established, to remain in its existing location rather than to move with changing economic circumstances. Industrial inertia arises because many industries will, in the course of time, build up local advantages, such as skilled labour and ancillary activities, as EXTERNAL ECONOMIES. These can be lost if a firm moves away from an area that may have a traditional concentration on the activity in question. Industrial inertia also arises from more general economies associated with AGGLOMERATION and from the relative immobility of fixed capital in the form of plant and machinery. DMS

industrial location policy The manner in which the STATE seeks to influence the location of industrial activity, generally justified by the pursuit of welfare objectives. Industrial location policy under CAPITALISM is usually directed towards the economic regeneration of declining industrial districts, such as parts of northern England and certain inner-city areas (see INNER CITY). In the underdeveloped world industrial location policy may be directed towards the initiation of economic development, or MODERNIZATION.

Industrial location policy normally comprises goals, instruments and strategy. The goals represent the policy objectives, such as the creation of new jobs or raising local income. The instruments are the specific measures adopted to induce industry to become established in the areas in question. These can comprise grants towards the cost of plant and machinery, favourable rates for writing off capital investment, a financial premium for each job created, and tax concessions. The instruments can also take the form of state-provided industrial premises, industrial estates laid out with the necessary utilities, and general investment in local or regional INFRASTRUCTURE. The strategy is the way in which the various measures adopted are related to one another.

An important element in any industrial location policy is the spatial strategy. Financial inducements to new industry may be dispersed or concentrated in geographical space. In the latter case, some kind of GROWTH-POLE policy is often adopted, with certain places selected for special consideration by virtue of their apparent growth potential. A further step in the direction of concentration is the creation of a planned industrial complex (see TERRITORIAL PRODUCTION COMPLEX). Another kind of spatial strategy, favoured by governments committed to the encouragement of market forces, involves local relaxation of constraints on development, for example in an ENTERPRISE ZONE or FREE TRADE AREA.

Under capitalism, the extent to which industrial location policy can succeed is constrained by the profit-seeking objectives of private-sector industry. The inducements that the STATE is able to offer may be insufficient to offset the disadvantages of a relatively high-cost location. Under SOCIALISM, industrial location policy is an integral part of national economic and social planning. But there are limits to the freedom of the state to locate industry in pursuit of welfare objectives, for dispersal to high-cost locations can impair overall efficiency – as some Eastern European countries have discovered.   DMS

industrial location theory A branch of LOCATION THEORY concerned with manufacturing and providing a theoretical basis for INDUSTRIAL GEOGRAPHY. Classical industrial location theory was concerned with VARIABLE COST ANALYSIS, built on the foundations of Alfred Weber, to which was added VARIABLE REVENUE ANALYSIS to accommodate the effects of demand and the market. More recent developments have been concerned with the roles of INDUSTRIAL ORGANIZATION and DECISION-MAKING, and with the interpretation of industrial location and change within the broader structure of regional, national and international economic processes (see LAYERS OF INVESTMENT).   DMS

industrial organization The structure within which the functions of control and DECISION-MAKING are exercised in the process of industrial production. The impact of industrial organization on the location of economic activity was neglected in the early development of LOCATION THEORY, but subsequently became a matter of major concern. This was partly because of shifts in theoretical perspective and partly because of significant changes in industrial organization itself.

In the early days of modern industrial development the typical unit of production was organized very simply, with a single owner–operator often exercising complete control. The theory of the firm in economics tended to perpetuate the figure of the individual entrepreneur making all the major production decisions with a single-minded dedication to profit maximization. The growing complexity of industrial organization with increasing scale of operation proceeded somewhat ahead of the recognition of this change, both in economics and in location theory. However, a more realistic view subsequently emerged, stimulated by the adoption in location analysis of some concepts from organization theory (which seeks to explain the general behaviour of organizations). The single unit of production run by the individual owner–operator was replaced by the multiplant, multilocational firm in which the control functions are much more dispersed (see MULTINATIONAL CORPORATION).

The expansion of industrial production in geographical space had an important bearing on this growing organizational complexity. The simple distinction between parent plant or head office on the one hand and branch or sales outlet on the other requires some division of responsibility. As industrial production became steadily more extensive in scale and in the spatial scope of its operations, an hierarchical structure of control grew up parallel to an hierarchical structure of spatial organization. The major control functions are exercised in major cities or centres of finance, secondary control and coordinating functions will be more dispersed in smaller towns and cities, while production and its day-to-day control will be most dispersed. Such a structure is typical of the modern transnational corporation. It has important implications for the economic DEVELOPMENT of those peripheral territories (generally the THIRD WORLD) that perform the lower-order functions in the organizational hierarchy controlled from elsewhere (generally the advanced capitalist world).

The adoption of more flexible forms of manufacturing, involving less assembly-line mass production and more emphasis on various kinds of subcontracting, has added to organizational complexity in recent years (see FLEXIBLE ACCUMULATION).   DMS

Suggested Reading
Chapman, K. and Walker, D. 1991: *Industrial location: principles and policies*, second edition. Oxford: Blackwell.
Lever, W., ed. 1987: *Industrial change in the United Kingdom*. London: Longman.
Smith, D. M. 1981: *Industrial location: an economic geographical analysis*, second edition. New York: John Wiley, ch. 5.

industrial revolution A transformation of the forces of production, centring on (but not confined to) the circuit of industrial capital (see CAPITALISM). The term is most usually applied to the series of changes within the British economy

between *c.*1750 and *c.*1850, but it has also been used in a number of other contexts. Some writers claim to have identified an 'industrial revolution' in Europe in the sixteenth and seventeenth centuries, based on technical change and the growth of large-scale capitalist organizations (Nef, 1934–5; see Musson, 1978); others speak of a 'Second Industrial Revolution' at the close of the nineteenth and beginning of the twentieth centuries, in which industrial hegemony passed from Britain, 'the first industrial nation', to Germany and the USA, based on the growth of steel, engineering and electricity and a new 'scientific' organization of the labour process (TAYLORISM: see Landes, 1969); yet others speak of a further industrial revolution in the late twentieth century, based on the emergence of high-technology, so-called sunrise industries with a new global geography of production (see FLEXIBLE ACCUMULATION; NEW INTERNATIONAL DIVISION OF LABOUR).

However, virtually all of these variant usages take as their point of reference the classical Industrial Revolution in Britain. Most writers attribute the term to Blanqui in 1837: 'Just as the French revolution witnessed great social experiences of earth-shaking proportions, England began to undergo the same process on the terrain of industry' (see Tribe, 1981). As the comparison implied, the process was as much social and political as it was economic, but it was far from being as 'revolutionary' as Blanqui and most subsequent commentators assumed. The epic image of the Industrial Revolution as 'Prometheus Unbound' (Landes, 1969) – in Greek mythology Prometheus stole fire from the gods for the benefit of humankind – has been sharply qualified in recent years: it now seems likely that industrial growth started earlier in the eighteenth century (see PROTOINDUSTRIALIZATION), that the industrial sector was then much larger (and its growth more diffuse), and that its expansion later in the eighteenth century was correspondingly less dramatic than conventional accounts allowed (Crafts, 1985).

This is not to say that industrialization was a smooth and uninterrupted process, however, and investment in industrial production was often jagged and punctuated by national and regional crises of capital accumulation and circulation (see CRISIS: Gregory, 1984); industrialization was also uneven over space, and indeed one of the most striking features of the new industrial SPACE-ECONOMY was its heterogeneity (see Langton and Morris, 1986). Over 40 years ago, Dobb (1946) argued that 'the unevenness of development as between different industries' was 'one of the leading features of the period', and later studies have confirmed his views. Marx, whose critique of POLITICAL ECONOMY in *Capital* was centred around an analysis of the Industrial Revolution in Britain, was undoubtedly right to draw attention to the significance of the transformation of the LABOUR PROCESS and in particular in the transition from *manufacture* to *machinofacture* in the emergence of industrial capitalism (see Dunford and Perrons, 1983); and several geographers have outlined the contributions made by 'heavy industries' such as textiles, coal and iron to the transformation of the manufacturing sector (e.g. Warren, 1976). Their growth was connected to important and sometimes dramatic changes – in the resource base of industrialization, and these often excited the imaginations and aroused the fears of those who had to live through them (Wrigley, 1988; Gregory, 1990). But in so far as capitalism is characterized by a process of UNEVEN DEVELOPMENT it is scarcely surprising that, as Samuel (1977) put it:

If one looks at the economy as a whole rather than at its most novel and striking features, a less orderly canvas might be drawn – one bearing more resemblance to a Bruegel or even a Hieronymus Bosch than to the geometrical regularities of a modern abstract. The industrial landscape would be seen to be full of diggings and pits as well as tall factory chimneys. Smithies would sprout in the shadows of the furnaces, sweatshops in those of the looms. Agricultural labourers might take up the foreground, armed with sickle or scythe, while behind them troops of women and children would be bent double over the ripening crops in the field . . . In the middle distance there might be navvies digging sewers and paviours laying flags. On the building sites there would be a bustle of man-powered activity,

with house-painters on ladders and slaters nailing roofs. Carters would be loading and unloading horses, market-women carrying baskets of produce on their heads; dockers balancing weights. The factories would be hot and steamy, with men stripped to the singlet and juvenile runners in bare feet. At the lead works women would be carrying pots of poisonous metal on their heads, in the bleachers, shed they would be stitching yards of chlorined cloth, at a shoddy mill sorting rags. Instead of calling [the] picture 'machinery' the artist might prefer to label it 'toil'.

This is indeed to speak of a LANDSCAPE rather than a space-economy, and to conjure up a series of changes in cultural forms and sensibilities that have only recently attracted attention in human geography (see Daniels, 1992). Those sensibilities were, of course, more than aesthetic and they entered into the construction of a vigorous geography of popular CULTURE through which many of the new work-disciplines, their divisions of CLASS and GENDER, and the framing assumptions of the new 'political economy' were sharply contested (see Thompson, 1968; Pinchbeck, 1969). But these have attracted comparatively little attention in geography; where they have been considered the focus has usually been on contours of class struggle (Gregory, 1984) rather than geographies of GENDER and PATRIARCHY (but see McDowell and Massey, 1984). For the most part, however, discussion has centred on the economic integuments of the REGIONAL GEOGRAPHY of the Industrial Revolution.

Indeed, Berg (1985) attributes the 'persistence of traditional forms of organization and labour-intensive techniques' so vividly present in Samuels's vignettes to what she calls 'the different micro-economies of the various sectors and industries' and to 'the *regional and cyclical* pattern of industrialization' (emphasis added). A number of studies have reconstructed the geographies of regional production systems during the Industrial Revolution (e.g. Langton, 1979; Gregory, 1982; Hudson, 1989), but it has also been argued that the Industrial Revolution *accentuated* the regional specialization of production. The most sustained discussion of the question has been provided by Langton (1984,

1988), who attributed 'the essentially regional structure of the emerging manufacturing economy of the time' to its dependence on canal transportation. Far from forming a coherent system, the canals were disjointed and disarticulated, and long-distance flows along them were interrupted by transfers between one carrier and another. The vast majority of shipments were therefore over short distances, to and from the major ports, and in consequence the canal-based economies 'became more specialised, more differentiated from each other and more internally unified' (Langton, 1984; see also Turnbull, 1987). This growing fragmentation between regions was more than economic; in Langton's view it was repeated in the dissolution of REGIONAL ALLIANCES, in the disunity of social protests and in the dismemberment of trades unions once they reached out from their regional bases. Regional economies found expression in coherent regional cultures. It was not until the coming of the railways, Langton concluded, that 'long-term processes of integration were set in motion'. It was then that 'London again began to exert the sway over national commerce that it had lost to the canal-based regional capitals' (see also Calhoun, 1987).

Against these views, or as a supplement to them, Freeman (1984) argued that Langton 'over-stated the case for economic regionalism during the earlier phases of industrialization and under-stated it for the later ones'. The importance of the canal system is undeniable, Freeman concedes, but much of it was not operational until 1800 and both coastwise shipping and land carriage over the turnpike system ensured that spheres of trade were much less circumscribed than Langton allowed (see Pawson, 1977; Freeman, 1980; Freeman and Aldcroft, 1983). Furthermore, Freeman dismissed 'the view which casts railways as a uniform cohesive agency' as 'a convenient, if widely current fiction'. On the contrary, the railway network was divided 'between a multiplicity of independent companies, sometimes serving highly discrete geographical areas and much of the time operating freight pricing policies which discriminated in favour of

the part of the country they served'. The result, Freeman (1984) concluded, was 'to describe for the railways much the same role that Langton conceives for the inland waterway system': that is to say, much rail traffic was also short-haul, 'between consuming or producing areas and major ports', and although this system of flows was evidently part of the internationalization of the Victorian economy it neither required nor resulted in the systematic integration of the space-economy.

However, this exchange revolved around the production and circulation of commodities, and later contributions have focused on *non-commodity* forms. Analyses of the mobility of skilled labour (Southall, 1988, 1991a,b) of the circulation of capital (Black, 1989) and the dissemination of public and private information (Gregory, 1987) have revealed an even more complex picture in which regional differentiation and integration are two sides of the same coin, and in which London acted as a vital commercial and financial pivot between Britain and the world-economy. But it is also important not to lose sight of London's national political and cultural functions (Gregory, 1988). Although there has been considerable interest in municipal government, however, and in the social geographies of industrial towns and cities (Dennis, 1984), historical geographers have paid little attention to the formal domains of national politics – to ELECTORAL GEOGRAPHIES, the geographies of the STATE APPARATUS and its institutions – or to the more subterranean modes of regulating and 'disciplining' the new industrial society: but there are encouraging signs that this is beginning to change (see Driver, 1988, 1993; Ogborn, 1992). In any event, there remain many other geographies of industrialization to be reconstructed and interrogated, and to feed in to debates within the wider discipline. DG

References

Berg, M. 1985: *The age of manufacturers: industry, innovation and work in Britain 1700–1820.* London: Fontana.

Black, I. 1989: Geography, political economy and the circulation of finance capital in early industrial England. *J. hist. Geogr.* 15, pp. 366–84.

Calhoun, C. 1987: Class, place and industrial revolution. In Thrift, N. and Williams, P., eds, *Class and space: the making of urban society*. London: Unwin Hyman, pp. 51–72.

Crafts, N. 1985: *British economic growth during the Industrial Revolution*. Oxford: Clarendon Press.

Daniels, S. 1992: The implications of industry: Turner and Leeds. In Barnes, T. and Duncan, J., eds, *Writing worlds: discourse, text and metaphor in the representation of landscape*. London: Routledge, pp. 38–49.

Dennis, R. 1984: *English industrial cities of the nineteenth century: a social geography*. Cambridge: Cambridge University Press.

Dobb, M. 1946: *Studies in the development of capitalism*. London: Routledge.

Driver, F. 1988: Moral geographies: social science and the urban environment in mid-nineteenth century England. *Trans. Inst. Brit. Geogr.* n.s. 13, pp. 275–87.

Driver, F. 1993: *An historical geography of the Poor Law in England*. Cambridge: Cambridge University Press.

Dunford, M. and Perrons, D. 1983: *The arena of capital*. London: Macmillan.

Freeman, M. 1980: Road transport in the English industrial revolution: an interim reassessment. *J. hist. Geogr.* 6, pp. 17–28.

Freeman, M. 1984: The industrial revolution and the regional geography of England: a comment. *Trans. Inst. Br. Geogr.* n.s. 9, pp. 502–12.

Freeman, M. and Aldcroft, D., eds 1983: *Transport in the industrial revolution*. Manchester: Manchester University Press.

Gregory, D. 1982: *Regional transformation and industrial revolution: a geography of the Yorkshire woollen industry*. London: Macmillan.

Gregory, D. 1984: Contours of crisis? Sketches for a geography of class struggle in the early industrial revolution in England. In Baker, A. R. H. and Gregory, D., eds, *Explorations in historical geography: interpretative essays*. Cambridge: Cambridge University Press, pp. 68–117.

Gregory, D. 1987: The friction of distance? Information circulation and the mails in early nineteenth-century England. *J. hist. Geogr.* 13, pp. 130–54.

Gregory, D. 1988: The production of regions in England's Industrial Revolution', *J. hist. Geogr.* 14, pp. 50–8.

Gregory, D. 1990: 'A new and differing face in many places': Three geographies of industrialization. In Dodgshon, R. A. and Butlin, R. A., eds, *An historical geography of England and Wales*, second edition. London: Academic Press, pp. 351–99.

Hudson, P., ed., 1989: *Regions and industries: a perspective on the industrial revolution in Britain*. Cambridge: Cambridge University Press.

Landes, D. 1969: *The unbound Prometheus: technological change and industrial development in Western Europe from 1750 to the present*. Cambridge: Cambridge University Press.

Langton, J. 1979: *Geographical change and industrial revolution: coal mining in south west Lancashire 1590–1799*. Cambridge: Cambridge University Press.

Langton, J. 1984: The Industrial Revolution and the regional geography of England. *Trans. Inst. Br. Geogr.* n.s. 9, pp. 145–67.

Langton, J. 1988: The production of regions in England's Industrial Revolution: a reponse. *J. hist. Geogr.* 14, pp. 170–4.

Langton, J. and Morris, R. J., eds 1986: *Atlas of industrializing Britain* London: Methuen.

McDowell, L. and Massey, D. 1984: A woman's place? In Massey, D. and Allen J., eds, *Geography matters! A reader*. Cambridge: Cambridge University Press, pp. 128–47.

Musson, E. 1978: *The growth of British industry*. London: Batsford.

Nef, J. 1934–5: The progress of technology and the growth of large-scale industry in Britain, 1540–1640. *Econ. Hist. R.* 5, pp. 3–24.

Ogborn, M. 1992: Love-state-ego: 'centres' and 'margins' in nineteenth-century Britain. *Environ. Plann. D: Society and Space* 10, pp. 287–305.

Pawson, E. 1977: *Transport and economy: the turnpike roads of eighteenth-century Britain*. London: Academic Press.

Pinchbeck, I. 1969: *Women workers and the industrial revolution 1750–1850*. London: Virago.

Samuel, R. 1977: Workshop of the world: steam power and hand technology in mid-Victorian Britain. *Hist. Workshop J.* 3, pp. 6–72.

Southall, H. 1988: Towards a geography of early unionization: the spatial organization and distribution of early British trade unions. *Trans. Inst. Br. Geogr.* n.s. 13, pp. 466–83.

Southall, H. 1991a: The tramping artisan revisited: labour mobility and economic distress in early Victorian England. *Econ. Hist. R.* 44, pp. 272–96.

Southall, H. 1991b: Mobility, the artisan community and popular politics in early nineteenth-century England. In Kearns, G. and Withers, C., eds, *Urbanising Britain: essays on class and community in the nineteenth century*. Cambridge: Cambridge University Press, pp. 103–30.

Thompson, E. P. 1968: *The making of the English working class*. London: Penguin.

Tribe, K. 1981: *Genealogies of capitalism*. London: Macmillan.

Turnbull, G. 1987: Canals, coal and regional growth during the industrial revolution. *Econ. Hist. R.* 40, pp. 537–60.

Warren, K. 1976: *The geography of British heavy industry since 1800.* Oxford: Oxford University Press.

Wrigley, E. A. 1988: *Continuity, chance and change: the character of the Industrial Revolution in England.* Cambridge: Cambridge University Press.

Suggested Reading

Gregory (1990).

Langton (1984).

Langton and Morris (1986).

Samuel (1977).

industrialization The process whereby industrial activity comes to play a dominant role in the economy of a nation or region. Industrialization may take place spontaneously or as a result of some process of development planning. Manufacturing (literally, making by hand) has always been a necessary human activity, ever since the first fashioning of a plough or spear from the branch of a tree. The advantages of DIVISION OF LABOUR eventually created specialist producers of particular types of commodities.

Industrialization as a spontaneous activity refers to the augmentation or replacement of small-scale production for either personal use or a limited local market by a type of activity characterized by a much larger scale of productive unit and by mechanization. Such a change can be stimulated by the growth of the market to such an extent that the pre-existing system of manufacturing cannot maintain an adequate supply; but other necessary conditions exist, such as the accumulation of capital in quantities required for investment in large plants and the development of a technology appropriate to the task.

The process of industrialization under CAPITALISM involves important changes in the social relations of production. In the early stages of the development of manufacturing industry, apprentices may be bound to masters in a manner that constrains their mobility and their freedom to sell their labour as they choose. As large-scale industry grows, it is important to have a supply of labour capable of responding to market forces, and this contributes to the breakdown of the existing system of organization.

Industrialization is often considered to be the panacea for the problems of poverty in the underdeveloped world. The process is constrained not only by the shortage of capital but also by the predominance of the role of primary producers assigned to underdeveloped countries in the international division of labour. Industrialization depends to a large extent on the infusion of capital, technology and business organization from outside, and carries the risk of DEPENDENCY. The advent of modern industry may destroy existing manufacturing activity and exacerbate inequality by reinforcing a distinction between those employed in the traditional sector and those in the modern. Planned industrialization forms an important element in the development strategy of most Third World countries. An indigenous process of industrialization under socialist central planning may avoid many of the problems associated with externally induced industrialization, but at the price of limiting access to outside capital and know-how.

Industrialization is no longer regarded as universally beneficial. In addition to some of the negative side-effects observed in the underdeveloped world, there are the ecological implications of indiscriminate resource exploitation and unrestrained POLLUTION of land, sea and air. The continued 'advance' of industrialization also requires sources of energy, the availability and safety of which are no longer assured. (See also PROTOINDUSTRIALIZATION.)   DMS

inequality, spatial The unequal distribution of some particular kinds of attribute among spatially defined population aggregates. Whereas spatial *differentiation* refers to the uneven incidence of any condition, inequality refers to those over which moral questions of right or wrong can arise. In general, it is recognized that some differences among individuals do not raise moral questions (for example, their height or free choice of leisure activities), whereas references to their wealth or educational qualifications could be described as inequality. Thus regional variations in topography or the type of goods produced would be differentiation, while regional variations in income or health would be inequality.

The geographical expression of inequality is an important element in WELFARE GEOGRAPHY, but preoccupation with spatial patterns can obscure inequality by individuals or groups such as RACE and CLASS, and risks losing sight of the structural basis of inequality. Spatial inequality cannot automatically be judged wrong and might be approved of, especially among the 'New Right'. The crucial and extremely difficult question of SOCIAL JUSTICE concerns the circumstances in which inequality can be justified in some moral sense. In a world with such extreme inequalities as are evident today, the onus may well be on those advocating inequality to justify their position, or at least to explain the morality behind the actual degree of inequality manifest in real life. (See also UNEVEN DEVELOPMENT.)   DMS

Suggested Reading

Bennett, R. J. 1989: Whither models and geography in a post-welfarist world? In Macmillan, B., ed., *Remodelling geography*. Oxford: Blackwell, pp. 273–90.

Smith, D. M. 1987: *Geography, inequality and society*. Cambridge: Cambridge University Press.

inference Drawing a conclusion from incomplete evidence. The body of procedures known as inferential statistics has been developed to assess the degree of certainty with which a statement about a population can be made when data are only available from a SAMPLING of that population. The degree of certainty is expressed in probabilistic terms; for example, one can be 95 per cent certain that what has been observed in the sample will hold for the population because under the theory of sampling that conclusion would be drawn from similar analyses of at least 95 out of every 100 samples (see CONFIRMATORY DATA ANALYSIS).   RJJ

informal sector That part of an economy beyond official recognition and record which performs productive, useful

and necessary labour without formal systems of control and remuneration. It is sometimes referred to as the *black economy*.

For Braudel (1985, pp. 23–4), the informal sector is one of the 'several economies' evolving within the world economy. It is a

shadowy zone, often hard to see for lack of adequate historical documents, lying underneath the market economy: this is . . . basic activity which went on everywhere and the volume of which is truly fantastic. This rich zone, like a layer covering the earth, I have called . . . *material life* or *material civilization*. These are obviously ambiguous expressions. But . . . a proper term will one day be found to describe this infraeconomy, the informal other half of economic activity, the world of self-sufficiency and barter of goods within a very small radius.

The very nature of the informal sector and its differentiation, associated particularly with prevailing forms of technology and levels of INDUSTRIALIZATION in different regions of the world, makes a precise and uncontested definition almost impossible. Lubell (1991, p. 11) is forced into a minimalist position:

After years of controversy . . . two characteristics have emerged as operational criteria for identifying informal sector enterprises: small size . . . and the extent to which an enterprise avoids official regulations and taxes.

Mingione (1991) notes that informal activities may be ranged along various continua: formal–informal, legal–not provided for by law–illegal, monetary–non-monetary, and public–private. The informal sector is also characterized by a range of scales of activity, from individual, part-time activity (e.g. taxi driving, do-it-yourself) to small-scale commercial service (e.g. window cleaning, prostitution) and takes place throughout the world economy (Pahl, 1984; Portes et al., 1989).

This diversity points to the wide variety of activities such as handicrafts, shoe repair, machinery repair, street marketing and the bazaar economy, domestic labour, painting and decorating, car washing, dog-walking and casual labour which make up the informal economy. Within THIRD WORLD cities petty trading is the predominant form of informal activity (Lubell, 1991). The wide range of activities is also suggestive of close links between the formal and the informal economy. In fact, Lubell (1991) reports that backward LINKAGES to formal-sector suppliers are relatively strong, whereas forward linkages are limited to households and other informal-sector producers (see DUAL ECONOMY).

The low productivity and high labour intensity of most informal activities makes them attractive as a means of absorbing unemployment. Survey evidence (e.g. Lubell, 1991: Gilbert and Gugler, 1982) suggests that between 40 and 70 per cent of the labour force in Third World cities may work in the informal sector. Clearly, the informal economy contributes substantially to the absorptive capacity of cities (see, e.g., Rogerson, 1992).

Bartering enables some participants to make a living outside the formal market economy, but the informal sector may be regarded with suspicion verging on outright opposition by official agencies/states. One reason is that states lose tax revenues as informal transactions take place outside the tax collection system. One estimate suggests that in 1985 the black economy in the UK amounted to over 14 per cent of GDP, with households spending up to £40 per week within it.

However, despite the fact that its growth generates powerful social and political consequences – for example, it is highly gendered (Waring, 1989) and unequal (according to Lubell (1991), remuneration is often well below official minimum wage levels, although the heads of informal enterprises generally receive incomes above such levels) – the ideological significance of the informal sector for the state is ambiguous (see, e.g., Khosa, 1992). One reason for this is that the informal sector not only offers employment but, in so doing, also contributes to a form of social control. But such 'control' is not without conflict, which may reach violent – even murderous – proportions in cities throughout the world.

The informal conomy poses profound questions about the legitimacy and developmental effectiveness of the formal economy. Nevertheless, one strategy of DEVELOPMENT (see, e.g., Santos, 1979; Dickenson et al., 1983) is to organize the informal economy and integrate it more fully into the formal. More positively, the continuing dynamism of the informal sector points to the demonstrable possibility of the construction of social relations of production and consumption 'beyond the market paradigm' (Mingione, 1991).   RL

References and Suggested Reading

Braudel, F. 1985: *Civilization and capitalism 15th–18th Century*, volume I, *The structures of everyday life*. London: Fontana.

Dickenson, J. P., Clark C. and Thomas-Hope, E. 1983: *A geography of the Third World*. London: Methuen.

Gilbert, A. and Gugler, J. 1982: *Cities, poverty and development: urbanisation in the Third World*. Oxford: Oxford University Press.

Khosa, M. M. 1992: Changing state policy and the black taxi industry in Soweto. In Smith, D. M., ed., *The apartheid city and beyond: urbanization and social change in South Africa*. London: Routledge, pp. 182–92.

Lubell, H. 1991: *The informal sector in the 1980s and 1990s*. OECD Development Centre Studies. Paris: OECD.

Mingione, E. 1991: *Fragmented societies: a sociology of life beyond the market paradigm*. Oxford: Blackwell.

Pahl, R. 1984: *Divisions of labour*. Oxford: Blackwell.

Portes, A., Castells, M. and Benton, L. A., eds 1989: *The informal economy: studies in advanced and less developed countries*. Baltimore, MD: Johns Hopkins University Press.

Rogerson, C. M. 1992: The absorptive capacity of the informal sector in the South African city. In Smith, D. M., ed., *The apartheid city and beyond: urbanization and social change in South Africa*. London: Routledge, pp. 161–71.

Santos, M. 1979: *The shared space*. London: Methuen.

Waring, M. 1989: *If women counted: a new feminist economics*. London: Macmillan.

information city   A city which acts as a focus for information flows, via high-technology media, and has a large proportion of its labour force employed in those service industries which are based on the manipulation of information – such as banking, insurance and legal services (see

SERVICES, GEOGRAPHY OF). Such cities are major centres of economic decision-making, at a variety of spatial scales. (See also WORLD CITY.) RJJ

Suggested Reading

Castells, M. 1989: *The informational city: information technology, economic restructuring and the urban–regional process.* Oxford: Blackwell.

information theory A mathematical approach in communication science which attempts to measure the information or degree of organization in a SYSTEM. The theory and its associated methods have been used to describe settlement and population distributions in geographical space. Its mathematical formulation exhibits a close relationship with the mathematics of ENTROPY in statistical thermodynamics, and ENTROPY-MAXIMIZING MODELS in geography and planning.

The basic equation is due to Shannon:

$$H = \sum_{i=1}^{N} x \, \log \frac{1}{x_i} = \sum_{i=1}^{N} -x_i \, \log \, x_i,$$

where $\sum_{i=1}^{N} x_i$ and H is the information statistic.

The individual x_is might therefore be probabilities of the N possible outcomes of a stochastic experiment, proportions of a population in N census tracts, proportions of a land area in N counties, etc. It can be shown, both by example and by algebraic proof, that H approaches zero as one of the x_i approaches unity (statistically, as one outcome becomes a near certainty). On the other hand, if all of the x_is are approximately equal (at $1/N$) then H approaches a maximum given by $\log N$. In information studies these results are used to define an index R:

$$R = 1 - H/H_{max}$$

which is variously termed a measure of redundancy (Shannon) and order (von Foerster). Ambiguities in interpretation arise in geography because a highly concentrated spatial pattern ($H = 0$, $R = 1$) and a uniform spatial pattern ($H = H_{max}$, $R = 0$) both suggest order, albeit of quite different kinds.

Marchand (1972) points out that in CARTOGRAPHY a CHOROPLETH MAP conveys most information if each of the class intervals has approximately the same proportion of the mapping units, i.e. H is maximized. He also shows that the maximum possible information on such a map is controlled by the number of mapping units and classes utilized – however much raw data may have been used in the compilation. A similar approach uses the H statistic to distinguish within group and between group information as an aid to CLASSIFICATION. AMH

References and Suggested Reading

Marchand, B. 1972: Information theory and geography. *Geogr. Anal.* 4, pp. 234–57.

Shannon, C. E. and Weaver, W. 1949: *The mathematical theory of communication.* Champaign, IL: University of Illinois Press.

Thomas, R. W. 1981: *Information statistics in geography.* Concepts and techniques in modern geography 31. Norwich: Geo Books.

infrastructure[1] The underlying structure of services and amenities (social overhead capital, SOC) needed to facilitate directly productive activity (DPA). Examples include public services, transport, telecommunications, public utilities, public environmental installations, human capital investment installations and social and community facilities.

Infrastructure tends to be immobile, labour-intensive, indivisible, open of access and to have economy-wide effects. There is considerable argument (Hirschman, 1958; Hodder and Lee, 1974) over the extent to which infrastructural investment is a sufficient (or even a necessary) precondition for economic development; whether it should be provided *before* DEVELOPMENT in the form of excess capacity or whether scarce resources should be devoted primarily to DPA, so allowing bottlenecks to build up as a result of the underprovision of SOC; and whether it should be publicly or privately owned. RL

References

Hirschman, A. O. 1958: *The strategy of economic development.* New Haven: Yale University Press.

Hodder, B. W. and Lee, R. 1974: *Economic geography.* London: Methuen, pp. 148–55.

infrastructure[2] (see also SUPER-STRUCTURE) Within classical Marxism, a concept that emphasizes the significance of material practice and the structures of the production of material life in giving rise to political and legal systems and in shaping ideas. As such, it contrasts with the Hegelian conception of history in which the 'idea' is seen as the guiding force.

The general argument, that social action proceeds from social reality, not from abstract categories, intellectual constructs or self-originating and unproblematic ideas, is summarized by Marx:

It is not the consciousness of men that determines their being, but their social being that determines their consciousness (Marx, 1968).

But Carver (1982, p. 34) suggests that this is not a deterministic view because in German the word for 'determines' is not the same word as for 'causes'. More accurate meanings would be given by ' "defines', 'delimits', 'structures' or even 'decides" '.

Furthermore, Marx's much quoted relational account (first published in 1859) of infrastructure, base or foundation (*Grundlage*) and superstructure (*Uberbau*) may suffer in nuance from its translation into English but fails to suggest either that the superstructure is determined by the infrastructure or that consciousness is determined by the superstructure. What it does suggest is that consciousness is not formed directly out of material practice but is a far more complex consequence of the relationships between material, political and legal practices:

In the social production of their life, men enter into definite relations that are indispensable and independent of their will, relations of production which correspond to a definite stage of development of their material productive forces. The sum total of these relations of production constitutes the economic structure of society, the real foundation, on which rises a legal and political superstructure and to which correspond definite forms of social consciousness (Marx, 1968, p. 181).

This passage has been the object of much debate, focusing particularly upon the apparently implied dichotomy between base or infrastructure ('the real foundation') and superstructure, and the determination of the latter by the former. Few would now accept this simple dualism, and the passage does not justify such a simplistic interpretation. Furthermore, it is important to realize that Marx refers to this statement as the 'guiding thread' of his studies; it is not a law-full or even law-like statement. Rather, it is a general HYPOTHESIS, a guide (Carver, 1982). Nevertheless, the essentially DIALECTICAL concern for the *relationships* between human labour and ideas in Marxist thought is often interpreted as a *distinction* between infrastructure and superstructure.

The analytical problem is to provide a more satisfactory theorization of the interconnections and indivisibilities between what are otherwise seen as separate and, therefore, conceptually inadequate spheres of social life (see also HISTORICAL MATERIALISM; STRUCTURATION THEORY). Carver (1982, pp. 34-5) makes the following suggestion:

For a given state of social being (social production of material life within particular relations using material productive forces from which rises a legal and political superstructure) some forms of consciousness (ideas, belief, opinions) are likely to be widely held, commonplace, encouraged etc., and others are likely to be absent, eccentrically held by only a few, discouraged, dismissed, made illegal etc . . . We do not have the particular elements of our social being that we have because God intended that we should, nor do we have them because man has been consciously or unconsciously striving to realise an idea, such as truth or freedom . . . On the contrary, our social being is as it is because of what men have actually accomplished in the economic sphere of material needs and desires.

RL

References and Suggested Reading

Carver, T. 1982: *Marx's social theory.* Oxford: Oxford University Press.

Godelier, M. 1978: Infrastructures, societies and history. *New Left Rev.* 112, pp. 84-96.

Marx, K. 1968: Preface to *A critique of political economy.* In Marx, K. and Engels, F., *Selected works.* London: Lawrence and Wishart (first published 1859).

inheritance system Rules, either customary or legal, that govern transmission of property (particularly real estate) between generations. Inheritance rules may define the number and gender of heir(s) to whom property should pass, the ways in which property shall be divided between multiple heirs, and the degree to which heirs' claims through inheritance are binding on property holders regardless of their own will.

Geographers have paid particular attention to the effects of different inheritance systems, especially impartible (single-heir) versus partible (multi-heir) systems: on the physical layout of landholdings; on structures of landholding (see FARM FRAGMENTATION); on the operation of FIELD SYSTEMS; on the ability of local agrarian societies to absorb population growth; and on levels of geographical mobility (generally higher in impartible systems).

Analysts have also sought to explore the relative importance of inheritance systems in channelling property transmission, compared with other means of transfer (by gift, via grants from landlords or, most importantly, through land markets). The power of market or other mechanisms to offset or override property transfers through inheritance has often been emphasized as a central component of MODERNIZATION, as in debates on the transition from FEUDALISM to CAPITALISM (see BRENNER DEBATE). PG

Suggested Reading

Goody, J., Thirsk, J. and Thompson, E. P. 1976: *Family and inheritance: rural society in western Europe 1200–1800.* Cambridge: Cambridge University Press.

Smith, R. M. ed. 1984: *Land, kinship and lifecycle.* Cambridge: Cambridge University Press.

inner city An ill-defined area close to the CENTRAL BUSINESS DISTRICT, usually associated with dilapidation, poor housing and economic and social deprivation (see CYCLE OF POVERTY; SLUM). In the ZONAL MODEL which was developed by Chicago sociologists in the 1920s (see CHICAGO SCHOOL), and which informed much writing about urban residential patterns for the next half-century, the inner city was characterized as:

(a) the reception area for new migrants to the city, from which they were launched on their search for economic and social improvement and associated moves into the SUBURBS; and

(b) as a zone in transition, the other residents of which are either transients or members of the lowest status, geographically and socially immobile, economic groups.

More recently, the term 'inner city' has been associated, not least in political rhetoric (as in the British Prime Minister's reference immediately after her 1987 general election victory to the work that needed to be done in 'those inner cities': Robson, 1988), with portions of urban areas suffering substantial economic and social difficulties and requiring programmes of regeneration and revitalization. A range of policies was introduced – such as Model Cities in the US and the Urban Programme in the UK – which targeted public money on environmental improvement and job attraction to such areas, while academic analysis (see Hall, 1981) was pointing out that the inner-city problem could not be appreciated apart from an understanding of the wider forces of UNEVEN DEVELOPMENT which were currently stimulating COUNTERURBANIZATION, DECENTRALIZATION and other processes of spatial change that were not favouring congested, run-down, expensive inner-city areas (many of which may also have suffered problems of political leadership: Bennett, 1989). RJJ

References

Bennett, R. J. 1989: Resources and finances for the city. In Herbert, D. T. and Smith, D. M., eds, *Social problems and the city: new perspectives.* Oxford: Oxford University Press, pp. 100–125.

Hall, P. G., ed., 1981: *The inner city in context.* London: Heinemann.

Robson, B. T. 1988: *Those inner cities.* Oxford: Clarendon Press.

innovation The introduction of a new phenomenon – or the new phenomenon itself. Geographical attention to innovations has focused particularly on: (a) their spatial origins, and the question of whether they are more likely to emerge in certain areas than others; and (b) the spread of innovations from their original sites (cf. CULTURAL HEARTH) through DIFFUSION.

RJJ

input–output An analytical framework developed by the economist Wassily Leontief to describe and model the inter-industry linkages within the economy, and to use this information to examine economic and policy impacts. The basic building block is the recognition that the production (or outputs) of one sector become the inputs for other sectors. Thus the machine-tools sector uses inputs of energy, steel, metals and other components (all in turn outputs of other sectors) to produce outputs to other industries, such as car or aircraft producers.

Information on inter-industry inputs and outputs is collected by survey or from administrative records, and recorded in an input–output table. The rows and columns represent the different industries or sectors, and the entries or coefficients measure the exchanges between them. Leontief's innovation was to see that this table could be manipulated as a matrix, and used mathematically. If the final demands of consumers are specified, the input–output matrix can be analysed as a set of simultaneous equations to trace out all the backward linkages involved in producing for those final demands, calculating what each sector must produce. By changing the final demands, we can assess the impacts of different policies and economic changes. The model (in its basic form anyway) is a comparative equilibrium model: it measures the medium- or long-term adjustments, but does not track the short-term path.

Very detailed input–output models have been constructed for most advanced economies, and the method has been extended to regional and multiregional analyses: examining linkages within a region (e.g. the Philadelphia region) and their dependence on the national economy, and explicitly tracing exchanges between sectors in different regions, using information on commodity flows and transport charges. Full multiregional models have been built for countries such as Japan and the Netherlands, and (with some simplifying adjustments) for the 51 states of the USA. One application of this USA model has been to examine the sectoral and regional impacts of alternative tax policies: tax changes shift the final consumer demands, and the multiregional input–output model computes the effects on industrial production across the regions. Such detailed models are very demanding of data, and so are difficult and expensive to construct. A limitation is that one then has to assume that coefficients remain stable (or project technical changes by some method).

Recent attention has focused on using the framework to trace the energy use and other activities such as environmental POLLUTION associated with production. Pollution generation can be included as an output, and the costs of pollution abatement or control can be included as an input. Dutch economists have included this in a multiregional framework, so that pollution emissions (to air, river or sea) diffuse into neighbouring regions.   LWH

Suggested Reading
Miller, R. E. and Blair, P. D. 1985: *Input–output analysis: foundations and extensions*. Englewood Cliffs, NJ: Prentice-Hall.

instrumentalism A philosophy of science which directs attention towards (and is in turn legitimated by) the establishment of technical control over the environment; because it is this end-result which matters, the truth or falsity of the theoretical statements which are called upon is never at issue (cf. POSITIVISM) and so they become literally *instruments*, 'computational devices for the generation of successful predictions about observables', which are to be judged solely in terms of their practical utility (Keat and Urry, 1975). Instrumentalism was extremely important during geography's QUANTITATIVE REVOLUTION as a means of qualifying the status of the 'LAWS' of a projected SPATIAL SCIENCE while retaining the commitment to some form of scientific explanation: thus Harvey (1969) argued that the identification of laws in geography is 'partly a matter of our own willingness to regard geographical phenomena *as if* they were subject to universal laws, *even when they are patently* *not so governed*' (emphasis added). The ability of geography to provide NOMO-THETIC statements in these more restricted terms was translated into empirical studies which were concerned more with the 'goodness of fit' between one spatial pattern and another than with the explication of the processes which produced them (e.g. the surrogates employed in SIMULATION and in SPACE–TIME FORE-CASTING). Many of these models were clearly capable of generating direct inputs to the formulation of public policy, since they enabled a ready comparison of a range of policy options and their associated outcomes without the need to specify the mechanisms which linked them; but the conception of RELEVANCE which they entailed was evidently a starkly pragmatic one and it was soon vigorously contested by the emergence of other philosophies of science, such as REALISM (Sayer, 1992).

DG

References

Harvey, D. 1969: *Explanation in geography.* London: Edward Arnold/New York: St. Martin's Press.

Keat, R. and Urry, J. 1975: *Social theory as science.* London: Routledge and Kegan Paul.

Sayer, R. A. 1992: *Method in social science: a realist approach.* London: Routledge.

Suggested Reading

Gregory, D. 1978: *Ideology, science and human geography.* London: Hutchinson/New York: St. Martin's Press, pp. 40–2.

integration The creation and maintenance of intense and diverse patterns of interaction and control within and between social groups, political units, economic activities, economies and modes of production. The objectives of integration are commonly disputed and range from the creation of a unity (e.g. economic and political union – exemplified, for example, by the reunification of Germany in 1990; a takeover of one firm by another; ASSIM-ILATION), to diversity within some form of unity (e.g. the EC as a community of nations; a COMMON MARKET; FEDERAL-ISM; MULTICULTURALISM; a joint venture) and links between independent units

(e.g. a FREE TRADE AREA; a common-wealth; subcontracting).

The achievement of unity must involve both *positive integration,* in which new structures and institutions (e.g. a common currency) are created to replace the extant, more divisive structures and institutions; and *negative integration,* the removal of pre-existing barriers and impediments to integration (e.g. TARIFF barriers). Anything less than the achievement of unity may involve either positive or negative integration or a combination of the two.

Within the sphere of production (see, e.g. Storper and Walker, 1989, ch. 3), integration (or disintegration) may be: *vertical,* a process which refers to the extent to which successive stages in production and distribution are placed under the control of a single firm, shaped by internal ECONOMIES OF SCOPE; or *horizontal,* the extent to which firms producing related products (competitive, complementary or by-products) operate under central control. The disintegration of production is often interpreted as a manifestation of the emergence of flexibility in production (see ECONOMIC GEO-GRAPHY).

Integration may be formal or informal:

Informal integration consists of those patterns of interaction which develop without the impetus of deliberate political decisions, following the dynamics of markets, technology, communications networks and social change. *Formal integration* consists of those changes in the framework of rules and regulations which encourage – or inhibit, or redirect – informal flows. *Informal integration* is a continuous process, a flow; it creeps unawares out of the myriad transactions of private individuals pursuing private interests. Formal integration is discontinuous: it proceeds decision by decision, bargain by bargain, treaty by treaty (Wallace, 1990, p. 9).

Helpful as this distinction is, it fails to acknowledge that social relations underpin the tendency towards integration and the possibilities of achieving it; it conceives of integration in universal terms. The emergence of CAPITALISM as a dominant set of social relations implies both geographical and quantitative expansion (Smith, 1984, ch. 3; Lee, 1989: see ECONOMIC GEOGRA-PHY; WORLD-SYSTEMS ANALYSIS). Integration is, therefore, a tendency accelerated and intensified by capitalism. Thus in the attempt to understand integration within Europe, Lee (1976, p. 12) wished to escape from the narrow view of institutional (formal) approaches to integration:

Both the supposed dichotomy between economic and political integration and the atomistic concept of the self-determining state are inadequate starting points for the analysis of integration. The international economy is not a simple aggregation of national economies but a total system in which nations are subordinate, but not necessarily subdominant, structures and economic integration is, in fact, a fundamental concept determined by the mode of production.

He went on to outline a historical geography of European integration in terms somewhat less reminiscent of STRUC-TURALISM but which, nevertheless, explored the process of STRUCTURATION between economic, political and social processes in the context of the dynamic geography of the CIRCUIT OF CAPITAL (Lee, 1990).

Although the expansionary nature of capitalist world economy continuously poses the question of integration, it is important to remember that other forces may resist it. During the sixteenth century 'Islam and Christendom faced each other along the north–south divide between the Levant and the western Mediterranean, a line running from the shores of the Adriatic to Sicily and then on to the coast of present-day Tunisia' and although 'merchant vessels sailed across it every day' (Braudel, 1985, p. 22), the cultural and social divisions remain highly influential. The integrative world economy is, as Braudel (1985, p. 45) points out, simply 'an order among other orders', and the struggle between integration and distinction remains a powerful determinant of economic, political and social relations. RL

References and Suggested Reading

Braudel, F. 1985: *Civilization and capitalism 15th–18th Century*, volume III, *The perspective of the world*. London: Fontana.

Lee, R. 1976: Integration, spatial structure and the capitalist mode of production in the EEC. In Lee, R. and Ogden, P. E., eds, *Economy and society in the EEC*. Farnborough, Hants, UK: Saxon House, pp. 11–37.

Lee, R. 1989: Social relations and the geography of material life. In Gregory, D. and Walford, R., eds, *Horizons in human geography*. London: Macmillan/New York: St. Martin's Press, pp. 152–69.

Lee, R. 1990: Making Europe: towards a geography of European integration. In Chisholm, M. and Smith, D. M., eds, *Shared space divided space*. London: Unwin Hyman, pp. 235–59.

Smith, N. 1984: *Uneven development*. Oxford: Blackwell. (Second edition 1985.)

Storper, M. and Walker, R. 1989: *The capitalist imperative*. Oxford: Blackwell.

Wallace, W. 1990: Introduction: the dynamics of European integration. In Wallace, W. ed., *The dynamics of European integration*. London: Frances Pinter, pp. 1–24.

intensive agriculture Farmers may use a large number of inputs per hectare or few inputs per hectare: this is the intensity of farming. A large number of inputs – high intensity – gives high gross and net returns per hectare, whereas few inputs per hectare – low intensity – give low returns. The terms 'intensive agriculture' and EXTENSIVE AGRICULTURE are thus relative and can be applied to a farm or a farming system. Intensity is measured by the cost per hectare of all inputs, but farming systems are often distinguished in relation to only labour inputs (viz. labour-intensive agriculture) or only variable capital inputs (fertilizers etc.) viz. capital intensive agriculture. (See also VON THÜNEN MODEL.) DBG

Suggested Reading
Chisholm, M. 1979: *Rural settlement and land use: an essay in location*, third edition. London: Hutchinson/Atlantic Highlands, NJ: Humanities Press.

intensive research Research strategies which are concerned to reconstruct the causal chains that connect social structures, social practices and individual agents in particular contexts. Sayer (1992) claims that intensive research typically

	Intensive	Extensive
research question	How does a process work in a particular case or small number of cases? What produces a certain change? What did the agents actually do?	What are the regularities common patterns, distinguishing features of a population? How widely are certain characteristics or processes distributed or represented?
relations	substantial relations of connection	formal relations of similarity
type of groups studied	causal groups	taxonomic groups
type of account produced	causal explanation of the production of certain objects or events, although not necessarily representative ones	descriptive 'representative' generalizations, lacking in explanatory penetration
typical methods	study of individual agents in their causal contexts, interactive interviews, ethnography – qualitative analysis	large-scale survey of population or representative sample, formal questionnaires, standardized interviews – statistical analysis
limitations	actual concrete patterns and contingent relations are unlikely to be 'representative', 'average' or generalizable – necessary relations discovered will exist wherever their relata are present, e.g. causal powers of objects are generalizable to other contexts as they are necessary features of these objects	although representative of a whole population, they are unlikely to be generalizable to other populations at different times and places – problem of ecological fallacy in making inferences about individuals – limited explanatory power
appropriate tests	corroboration	replication

intensive research *Sayer's summary of intensive and extensive research* (Sayer, 1992, p. 243).

involves QUALITATIVE METHODS, including ETHNOGRAPHY, and argues that these strategies are particularly appropriate for research conducted under the sign of REALISM. This does not mean that they are 'subjective' or parochial; Sayer makes a detailed comparison with EXTENSIVE RESEARCH (see the figure) and emphasizes that intensive studies can be every bit as 'objective' as extensive studies and that they may well produce 'abstract knowledge [that is] more generally applicable.' DG

Reference and Suggested Reading

Sayer, A. 1992: *Method in social science: a realist approach*. London: Routledge, pp. 241–51.

interaction See SPATIAL INTERACTION.

interdependence Relations of mutual dependence. Human societies are highly influential participants in wider ECOSYSTEMS – so influential in fact that some go beyond the interdependence of society and NATURE to recognize nature as a social product (Smith, 1984). Interdependence is applied in a particularly direct way to the understanding of DEVELOPMENT. Here interest lies in the making and extent of interdependence and in the challenge that it poses to monocausal, unilinear explanations of the human condition (Brookfield, 1975).

The contemporary world economy is often presented as a single interdependent whole with overtones of STRUCTURAL FUNCTIONALISM, and emphasis is placed on the systemic mechanics rather than the politics of development. The danger of such a conception is that the conflicts and contradictions stemming from the social bases of interdependence are overlooked in the assumption of an ecological unity of purpose (see WORLD-SYSTEMS ANALYSIS). The emergence of a world economy is the result of the development of social relations capable of conducting human activity at a global scale: the social relations of CAPITALISM provides such a basis. They are both further developed by and cause developments in the generalization of the market and the structure and geography of TRADE, flows of capital and labour, and the scale and organization of production. In short, the social relations of production are the language through which interdependence may be realized (see ECONOMIC GEOGRAPHY).

In precapitalist societies, interdependence was both highly localized and restricted in scope (see WORLD-SYSTEMS ANALYSIS), although in some cases international trade helped to supply the demand for luxury consumption from an elite. In the contemporary capitalist world economy, interdependence is worldwide. And, in recent years, capitalist social relations have experienced further geographical expansion with the collapse of state socialism in Eastern Europe and the former USSR. The ensuing social vacuum was quickly, but hardly effectively, filled by the agencies of capitalism, the agility of which was encouraged by limited, restricted and conditional flows of AID from West to East.

The political implications of interdependence are clear: human survival is itself reliant upon relations of mutual dependence operating at a world scale. Metropolitan economies are as much if not more dependent upon the societies of the so-called periphery as the latter are upon the former (see DEPENDENCE). In fact, the apparently peripheral societies may, in so far as their social relations of production are characterized by RECIPROCITY rather than by exploitation and their productive use of nature is co-operative rather than exploitative, have a greater capacity for self-sufficiency and independence. But in economies and societies organized at a world scale, development may proceed only with the acceptance of mutual interdependence. This was the underlying message of the Brandt Reports (Brandt Commission, 1980, 1983). Their argument was that it was in the interests of the developed 'north' to aid the underdeveloped 'south', on the grounds that both would benefit from increased levels of economic activity and interaction.

However, this is to pose the issue of interdependent development only in terms of IDEALISM rather than of the relations between materialism and idealism (see HISTORICAL MATERIALISM). All societies need to be able to produce or appropriate a surplus to ensure their material and social reproduction. The expansion of capitalism, and the struggle for strategic domination within the capitalist and non-capitalist world and between these spheres of influence, is a product of this material imperative. The struggle for dominance involves the incorporation and subjugation of formerly independent SOCIAL FORMATIONS. The existence of such a struggle, unproductive as it is, is itself a major cause of UNDERDEVELOPMENT. Furthermore, struggle for domination generates a reaction in the form of a countervailing struggle for freedom from domination. Thus, while ecological interdependence remains, the question is whether it can withstand the ravages – both social and material – of exploitative modes of production which generate economic, political and ideological conflict throughout the world. It is, perhaps, rather more realistic to speak of an international balance of power based upon the economic geography of productive capacity and output.   RL

References and Suggested Reading

Brandt Commission, The 1980: *North–south: a programme for survival.* London: Pan.

Brandt Commission, The 1983: *Common crisis: north–south cooperation for world recovery.* London: Pan/Cambridge, MA: MIT Press.

Brookfield, H. 1975: *Interdependent development.* London: Methuen/Pittsburgh, PA: University of Pittsburgh Press.

Smith, N. 1984: *Uneven development.* Oxford: Blackwell.

internal relations Necessary relations between objects or practices; formally, 'a relation R_{AB} may be defined as *internal* if and only if A would not be what it *essentially* is unless B is related to it in the way that it is' (Bhaskar, 1979). The relation between landlord and tenant, for example, is an internal relation, and in this case presupposes the other, so that the relation is

symmetrical. The relation between the STATE and local-authority housing is also an internal relation; in this example, however, the latter presupposes the former but the former does *not* presuppose the latter, so that the relation is *asymmetrical.* These distinctions are important for the process of rational ABSTRACTION which is the main-spring of the philosophy of REALISM, where they guard against so-called 'CHAOTIC CONCEPTIONS' which 'combine the unrelated' and 'divide the indivisible' (Sayer, 1982).

Sets of internal relations may be termed *structures*: an example is shown in the figure (Sayer, 1984). Within geography, this terminology was first used by Harvey (1973). Drawing upon Ollman's (1971) exegesis of Marx's writings and upon Piaget's operational or genetic STRUCTURALISM, Harvey proposed that: 'A structure must be defined . . . as a system of internal relations which is in the process of being structured through the operation of its own transformation rules'. Such a definition enabled Harvey to pose fundamental questions of ONTOLOGY, to do with our most basic understanding of the nature of URBANISM, of CAPITALISM and of MODES OF PRODUCTION in general. Thus: 'Should we regard urbanism as a structure which can be derived from the economic base of society (or from superstructural

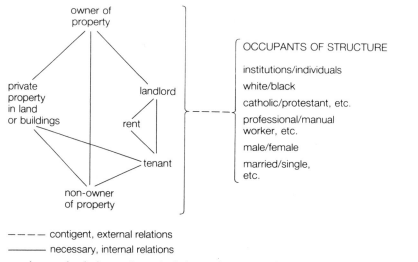

---- contigent, external relations
———— necessary, internal relations

internal relations *Internal relations and structure* (after Sayer, 1984).

elements) by way of a transformation? Or should we regard urbanism as a separate structure in interaction with other structures?' His answer was, in fact, to favour the second: 'Urbanism possesses a separate structure – it can be conceived as a separate entity – with a dynamic of its own. But this dynamic is moderated through interaction and contradiction with other structures'. Insofar as he clearly sought to distinguish one structure from another – 'structures may be regarded as separate and differentiable entities when no transformation exists whereby one may be derived from another' – then it is less than fair to say that Harvey somehow *universalizes* internal relations 'at the expense of external [or contingent] relations' (Sayer, 1982). In Sayer's view, to do so is to 'nullify' the power of the concept of internal relations: 'if everything is internally related to everything else, then the concept does not help us say anything *particular* about *specific* structures' (emphases added). This may well be so, but such a charge cannot be levelled at Harvey.

It may have more force, however, when brought to bear on Olsson's (1980) investigations of 'thought-and-action'. Like Harvey, Olsson commends Ollman's 'relational' interpretation of Marx, but he seemingly comes closer to the 'universalization' of internal relations which Sayer condemns. To Olsson, thought, language and action are internally related:

Within that philosophy of internal relations, thought is conceived as both being and knowledge of being . . . . It follows that internal relations are ontological in its parts. The implication is that truth is a single, all-embracing entity in which each component has its particular place. No component can be separated from any of the others.

'It is a central tenet of this attitude', Olsson continues (and one which is broadly Hegelian), that 'the world and our ideas are so entangled in each other that they cannot be separated'. Hence, he claims, we need to see that 'social relations between people [are] like logical relations between propositions' and 'logical relations between propositions [are] like social relations between people': and all such relations are internal relations. It is for this reason, of course, that Olsson undertakes the so-called 'linguistic turn' (cf. IDEOLOGY) and embarks upon a series of linguistic experiments which take him into the realms of surrealism: 'we enter a new world by acquiring a new language'. But this very centrality of language, whatever else one might think about such a claim, offers some sort of defence against Sayer's objection. For, presumably, Olsson would insist that Sayer's critique of the universalization of internal relations only 'makes sense' from inside the framework of one particular 'language-game' – and Olsson is playing a very different one.   DG

References

Bhaskar, R. 1979: *The possibility of naturalism: a philosophical critique of the contemporary human sciences.* Brighton: Harvester/Atlantic Highlands, NJ: Humanities Press.

Harvey, D. 1973: *Social justice and the city.* London: Edward Arnold/Baltimore, MD: Johns Hopkins University Press.

Ollman, B. 1971: *Alienation: Marx's conception of man in capitalist society.* Cambridge: Cambridge University Press.

Olsson, G. 1980: *Birds in egg/eggs in bird.* London: Pion/New York: Methuen.

Sayer, A. 1982: Explanation in economic geography: abstraction versus generalization. *Progr. hum. Geogr.* 6, pp. 68–88.

Sayer, A. 1984: *Method in social science: a realist approach.* London: Hutchinson (second edition, 1992, London: Routledge).

Suggested Reading

Harvey (1973), pp. 286–314.
Olsson (1980).
Sayer (1982).

intervening opportunities A concept developed by the American sociologist S. A. Stouffer (1940) to explain the pattern of human MIGRATION, but since then applied in studies of commodity flow, passenger trips, traffic movements, etc. The concept states that the number of movements from an origin to a destination is proportional to the number of opportunities at that destination and inversely proportional to the number of intervening opportunities between the origin and the destination. Stouffer also argued that distance itself has no deterrent effect, and that any observed decline in the volume of movement with distance (see DISTANCE DECAY) is due to an increase in the number of intervening opportunities. AMH

Suggested Reading
Clark, C. and Peters, G. H. 1965: The intervening opportunities method of traffic analysis. *Traffic Quarterly* 19, pp. 101–19.
Stouffer, S. A. 1940: Intervening opportunities: a theory relating mobility to distance. *Am. Soc. Rev.* 5, pp. 845–67.

interviewing One of human geography's most widely used FIELDWORK methods. As a key means of data collection in household surveys, face-to-face interviewing forms a cornerstone of the extensive cross-sectional, cohort and panel surveys that underpin large-scale quantitative social science (see QUANTITATIVE METHODS). Structured QUESTIONNAIRE data are often collected by professional interviewers employed by commercial market research firms who provide varying amounts of project-specific training. The quality of the data thus varies enormously from interviewer to interviewer, from study to study (depending on the complexity and sensitivity of the questionnaire and on the character of the target sample), from survey company to survey company (depending on the nature and extent of quality control in the field), from place to place and from time to time.

There are also technical problems related to SAMPLING procedures, response rates, and debates over the nature, use and calculation of inferential statistics, especially for the cluster sampling which forms the basis of so many large-scale surveys (see INFERENCE). Perhaps more crucially, there are important ethical questions related to the storage and analysis of individual computerized records, especially when these are tagged to spatial co-ordinates.

The advantage of the structured questionnaire is that it provides comparability between regions and through history among some key demographic and socio-economic characteristics of large populations. Pieced together, the various national surveys that currently exist already offer a fairly comprehensive map of the social world – at least for the developed countries. The disadvantage of this approach is that it masks individual variety, attributes a consistency and stability to attitudes and opinions that is rarely found in everyday life, and limits the kinds of responses that the interviewees can make. The questions reflect the purposes and presuppositions of the analyst, which respondents have little scope to challenge or augment.

Interview data can, however, also be collected from groups and individuals in less structured settings (see QUALITATIVE METHODS). This approach sacrifices comprehensiveness for intensity, and is less preoccupied with mapping society than with exploring the relationships between society and space. Individual and group interviews have thus been used in geography to explore the relationships between people and their environments providing, among other things, a commentary on the value, utility and safety of ACTIVITY SPACE.

In-depth individual interviews allow researchers to study subjective meanings and motives alongside the more objectifiable attributes and aspirations that can be tapped by structured questionnaires. They are a means of explaining and understanding the kinds of relationships which can only be described by more extensive quantitative approaches. They also allow the research subjects more scope to speak for themselves than do structured questionnaires. Group interviews take this commitment to the authenticity of everyday life and experience a step further, allowing participants not only to speak for themselves but also to begin to negotiate their own shared views. This can be seen as a contribution to the democratization of the research process: it allows ordinary people to generalize about their lives and futures, rather than relying on the analyst to derive aggregate statements from a set of individual observations. SJS

Suggested Reading
Burgess, J., Limb, M. and Harrison, C. M. 1988: Exploring environmental values through the medium of small groups, part one: theory and practice. *Environ. Plann. A* 20, pp. 309–26.
Eyles, J. ed. 1988: *Research in human geography*. Oxford: Blackwell.

invasion and succession A term adopted from ECOLOGY to describe a process of NEIGHBOURHOOD change whereby one social group succeeds another in a residential area. The term is particularly associated with the ZONAL MODEL developed by the CHICAGO SCHOOL of sociologists in the 1920s, which suggested that change was initiated by pressure on INNER-CITY housing, usually by migrant groups of low socio-economic status. They moved into adjacent residential areas, forcing the current occupants to move out into the next zone, thus stimulating a rippling process of change outwards from the city centre which ended with the highest-status groups on the edge of the built-up areas moving to newly built suburban homes further out (cf. FILTERING). The process of invasion and succession, frequently associated with the movement of an ethnic minority group (see ETHNICITY) into an area (cf. BLOCK-BUSTING), thus involves changing the characteristics of many of the city's NATURAL AREAS: in its idealized form it suggests periods of equilibrium in the urban residential pattern punctuated by, probably brief, periods of wholesale change, but in most cities the processes are continuous, although substantially accelerated in some districts at particular times. RJJ

Suggested Reading
Know, P. L. 1987: *Urban social geography: an introduction*, second edition. London: Longman.
Ley, D. F. 1983: *A social geography of the city*. New York: Harper and Row.

investment See LAYERS OF INVESTMENT.

irredentism The assertion by the government of a country that a minority living across the border in a neighbouring country belongs to it historically and culturally, and the mounting of a propaganda campaign, or even a declaration of war, to effect that claim.

Currently, some of the most serious irredentist conflicts are being fuelled by the break-up of Yugoslavia. There are large Serbian ENCLAVES in the newly formed state of Croatia, formerly one of the northern Yugoslav republics, and a fierce civil war was initiated in 1991 to try and incorporate them into Greater Serbia, a Serbian nationalist aspiration dating back to the nineteenth century. MB

isarithms See ISOLINES.

isodapane A line joining points of equal additional transportation cost, drawn about the point of minimum transport cost. The concept originated in the work of Alfred Weber (see LOCATIONAL TRIANGLE; VARIABLE COST ANALYSIS). The term isodapane is sometimes used (incorrectly) to describe any equal-trans-port-cost or equal-cost line. A map of isodapanes is a form of COST SURFACE. Weber's isodapane concept is the origin of various forms of cartographic analysis adopted in industrial location theory. DMS

isolines Lines on a map connecting points of equal data value. Known also as isopleths or isarithms, they are two-dimensional representations of three-dimensional reality (the x, y location plus a z data value). Major problems with their use include: (a) the isoline value interval – some important features may be generalized out by poor choices; and (b) generating lines, which involves interpolation from sample points.

'Local fitting' methods involve regular control points, their value determined according to adjacent values, and placing isolines onto gradients between control points. In most present-day computer systems the process of generating isolines involves TINs (Triangulated Irregular Networks) and Digital Terrain Modelling. MJB

Suggested Reading
Raper, J. F. and Kelk, B. 1991: Three-dimensional GIS. In Maguire, D. J., Goodchild, M. F. and Rhind, D. W., eds, *Geographical information systems: principles and applications*, volume 1. London: Longman, pp. 299–317.
Robinson, A. H., Sale, R., Morrison, J. and Muerhcke, P. C. 1985: *Elements of cartography*, fifth edition. New York: John Wiley.

isopleths see ISOLINES.

J

just-in-time production A system of manufacturing in which inputs are supplied and outputs delivered very soon after demand for a finished good has been registered. Perfected by Japanese automobile producers, and now emulated by North American and European assemblers, this set of practices has spread to other industrial sectors. As one objective is to reduce the quantity of producers' capital tied up in inventories of parts and finished products, producers no longer keep large buffer stocks of parts on hand. This has the consequent effect of forcing lower defect rates in parts supplied, and hence improved overall quality. Because suppliers are able to meet buyers' varying requirements (in both number and type) at short notice, the system allows manufacturers to respond more flexibly to changing market demands. The adoption of such practices may exert an agglomerative force, bringing buyers and suppliers closer together to facilitate rapid delivery at short notice. (See also POST-FORDISM; PRODUCTION COMPLEX.)

MSG

justice See SOCIAL JUSTICE; TERRITORIAL JUSTICE.

justice, geography and The empirical and theoretical study of the justice or fairness of the geographical apportionment of social benefits. Such a definition derives from the concerns of distributional justice; that is, the allocation of some gain. There are other forms of justice, retributive for example, but these have not been discussed by geographers. Within the confines of distributional justice various theories have been proposed, such as utilitarianism, naturalism and intuitivism, and those based upon the idea of a social contract (see Walzer, 1983). Despite their differences, all such theories assume, first, that justice only becomes an issue when there is a conflict of interests and, second, that there exists a general set of principles for resolving such disputes. It is the nature of those principles that then defines the meaning of justice within a given theory.

David Harvey, in *Social justice and the city* (1973, chs 2 and 3), was the first geographer to examine the issue of justice explicitly. He was concerned: to delineate the variegated forms in which social benefits are manifest (from private income to public goods); to demonstrate that such benefits varied according to location; to define a geographical theory of justice (based upon need, contribution to the common good, and merit); and to show the means by which the just spatial distribution could be realized (see PUBLIC FINANCE, GEOGRAPHY OF). Curiously, though, by the end of that book, the theories of justice that he had discussed were passed over in favour of a Marxism which seemed to offer no clear-cut theory of justice at all. Although David Smith (1977) later also took up the idea of social justice in his programmatic WELFARE GEOGRAPHY, Harvey's ambiguity set the tone for subsequent discussion. Justice seemed important to geographers (seen in the debate on RELEVANCE), but somehow traditional theories were not the right vocabulary.

More recently, geographers interested in FEMINISM and POSTCOLONIALISM have also raised issues of justice, but in doing so they have revealed perhaps that source of ambiguity first seen in Harvey's work. For them, principles of justice are not something that can be definitively defined, but are forever shifting in response to changing configurations of POWER in society. In this sense, traditional definitions of justice are as much part of the problem as they are part of the solution, in determining a just geography. (See also ETHICS.) TJB

References

Harvey, D. 1973: *Social justice and the city.* London: Edward Arnold.

Smith, D. M. 1977: *Human geography: a welfare approach.* London: Edward Arnold.

Walzer, M. 1983: *Spheres of justice: a defense of pluralism and equality.* New York: Basic Books.

Suggested Reading

Harvey (1973).

Walzer (1983).

K

Kantianism A philosophy devoloped by Immanuel Kant (1724–1804). The Kantian tradition has been incorporated within contemporary human geography in three main (increasingly interconnected) ways.

(a) Kant's conception of the nature of geography and of its location within the sciences as a whole has provided the basis for a series of major disagreements (see May, 1970). Kant considered that knowledge could be classified in two ways: either *logically* or *physically*. 'The logical classification collects all individual items in separate classes according to similarities of morphological features; it could be called something like an "archive" and will lead, if pursued, to a "natural system"' (Büttner and Hoheisel, 1980). In a 'natural system', Kant noted, 'I place each thing in its class, even though they are to be found in different, widely separated places' (cited in Hartshorne, 1939). The physical classification, in contrast, collects individual items which 'belong to the same time or the same space'. In this connection, Kant asserted:

History differs from geography only in the consideration of time and [space]. The former is a report of phenomena that follow one another (*Nacheinander*) and has reference to time. The latter is a report of phenomena beside each other (*Nebeneinander*) in space. History is a narrative, geography a description.

Geography and history fill up the entire circumference of our perceptions: geography that of space, history that of time (cited in Hartshorne, 1939).

Although Kant's views on geography were broadly similar to those of von Humboldt and Hettner, they appear to have had 'no *direct* influence' other than 'as a form of confirmation' (Hartshorne, 1958; but cf. Büttner and Hoheisel, 1980). Indeed, they were not explicitly endorsed in any major programmatic statement of the scope of geography (in English) until Hartshorne's account of *The nature of geography* (1939), which accepted that geography's basic task was essentially Kantian:

Geography and history are alike in that they are integrating sciences concerned with studying the world. There is, therefore, a universal and mutual relation between them, even though their bases of integration are in a sense opposite – geography in terms of earth spaces, history in terms of periods of time (Hartshorne, 1939).

Others were more sceptical. Blaut (1961) concluded that, for Kant:

Knowledge about the spatial location of objects is quite distinct from knowledge about their true nature and the natural laws governing them. The latter sorts of knowledge are eternal and universal, are truly scientific . . . [whereas] spatial and temporal co-ordinates are separate and rather secondary attributes of objects, and spatial and temporal arrangement of objects is not a matter for science.

Like Schaefer (1953), therefore, Blaut represented Kant as the originator of an EXCEPTIONALISM which was inimical to the 'explanations' and 'generalisations' (rather than mere 'descriptions') required if geography were to be reconstituted as a SPATIAL SCIENCE. More recently, however, Kant's basic distinction has been revitalized by Hägerstrand; although his TIME-GEOGRAPHY is self-evidently predicated on a repudiation of divisions between 'history' and 'geography', 'time' and 'space', the contrast which he draws between COMPOSITIONAL THEORY and CONTEXTUAL THEORY clearly corresponds (in its essentials) to that between 'logical' and 'physical' classification (cf. Parkes and Taylor, 1975).

(b) Most of the foregoing formulations depend on Kant's early lectures on (physical) geography, but other commentators have drawn attention to Kant's *Critique of pure reason* (1781) and its emphasis on 'the structuring activity of the thinking subject':

Space is not something objective and real, nor is it a substance or an accident, or a relation, but it is *subjective* and *ideal* and proceeds from the nature of mind by an *unchanging law*, as a schema for coordinating with each other absolutely all things externally sensed (Kant, cited in Richards, 1974; emphasis added).

This stress upon 'the epistemic structuring of the world by the human actor [is] the essence of the Kantian heritage', so it is claimed, and 'constitutes the common theme which has, in practice, been distilled from the variety of humanistic philosophies to which geographers of a subjectivist orientation have turned in their endeavour to transcend the dichotomy inherent in subject–object relations' (Livingstone and Harrison, 1981) (see BEHAVIOURAL GEOGRAPHY; HUMANISTIC GEOGRAPHY).

Many of these endeavours might more properly be described as 'neo-Kantian'. *Neo-Kantianism* emerged in Germany in the closing decades of the nineteenth century. Whereas Kant had held the *a priori* to be 'externally fixed and eternally immutable' – the 'unchanging law' in Richards's quotation above – the neo-Kantians rejected the vision of a unitary scientific method which this allowed. They substituted a distinction between:

(i) the cultural and historical sciences (the *Geisteswissenschaften*), which dealt with an intelligible world of 'non-sensuous objects of experience' which had to be understood (*verstehen*), and which were thus concerned with the IDIOGRAPHIC – this was the focus of the 'Baden school', which included Windelband and Rickert; and

(ii) the natural sciences (the *Naturwissenschaften*), which dealt with the 'sensible world of science' which could be explained (*erklären*), and which were thus concerned with the NOMOTHETIC – this was the focus of the 'Marburg school', which included Cassirer.

Within human geography, neo-Kantianism has been attributed to (*inter alia*) the POSSIBILISM of the French school of human geography (Berdoulay, 1976), to the programme of the CHICAGO SCHOOL of sociology (Park completed a doctoral dissertation under Windelband: see Entrikin, 1980), and to modern humanistic geography more generally (see Jackson and Smith, 1984). In a still more fundamental sense, Entrikin (1981) has proposed that Hartshorne's views of the nature of geography (above) incorporated a number of patently neo-Kantian arguments, and that Cassirer's writings might provide a means of reinvigorating (and even bringing together) geography's heterogeneous perspectives upon SPACE (see Entrikin, 1977).

(iii) until very recently, most geographers limited their interest in Kant to his lectures on physical geography and his first critique, largely – one suspects – because of their interest in (or objections to) the scientificity of geography. But several writers have started to reflect on Kant's second and third critiques. This new-found interest has been expressed in a widespread (if often tacit) acceptance of an essentially Kantian distinction between three forms of knowledge or reason. Following Habermas, for example, many writers associate the Enlightenment project that is inscribed within the so-called project of MODERNITY with the formation of three autonomous spheres:

science	truth and knowledge cognitive–instrumental rationality
morality	norms and justice moral–practical rationality
art	authenticity and beauty aesthetic–expressive rationality

The task of Habermas's version of CRITICAL THEORY is, in part, to bring these three spheres back into balance with one another: to guard against the inflation of 'science' (and the detachment of its 'expert culture' from public scrutiny) which, so he claims, was characteristic of CAPITALISM in the early and middle twentieth century; and, more recently, against the inflation of the aesthetic that he sees within late-twentieth-century POSTMODERNISM (Ingram, 1987). Certainly, Kantian aesthetics have played an extremely important part in discussions of postmodern sensibilities, and particular attention has been paid to the 'aestheticization of politics' which can be found in versions of both MODERNISM and postmodernism (Harvey, 1989; Eagleton, 1990). DG

References

Berdoulay, V. 1976: French possibilism as a form of neo-Kantian philosophy. *Proc. Ass. Am. Geogr.* 8, pp. 176–9.

Blaut, J. 1961: Space and process. *Prof. Geogr.* 13, pp. 1–7.

Büttner, M. and Hoheisel, K. 1980: Immanuel Kant. *Geographers: Biobibliographical Studies* 4, pp. 55–67.

Eagleton, T. 1990: *The ideology of the aesthetic.* Oxford: Blackwell.

Entrikin, J. N. 1977: Geography's spatial perspective and the philosophy of Ernst Cassirer. *Can. Geogr.* 21, pp. 209–22.

Entrikin, J. N. 1980: Robert Park's human ecology and human geography. *Ann. Ass. Am. Geogr.* 70, pp. 43–58.

Entrikin, J. N. 1981: Philosophical issues in the scientific study of regions. In Herbert, D. T. and Johnston, R. J., eds, *Geography and the urban environment. Progress in research and applications,* volume 4. Chichester: John Wiley, pp. 1–27.

Hartshorne, R. 1939: *The nature of geography: a critical survey of current thought in the light of the past.* Lancaster, PA: Association of American Geographers.

Hartshorne, R. 1958: The concept of geography as a science of space, from Kant and Humboldt to Hettner. *Ann. Ass. Am. Geogr.,* 48, pp. 97–108.

Harvey, D. 1989: *The condition of postmodernity: an enquiry into the origins of cultural change.* Oxford: Blackwell.

Ingram, D. 1987: *Habermas and the dialectic of reason.* New Haven: Yale University Press.

Jackson, P. and Smith, S. J. 1984: *Exploring social geography.* London: Allen and Unwin.

Livingstone, D. N. and Harrison, D. T. 1981: Immanuel Kant, subjectivism and human geography: a preliminary investigation. *Trans. Inst. Br. Geogr.* n.s. 6, pp. 359–74.

May, J. A. 1970: *Kant's conception of geography and its relation to recent geographical thought.* Toronto: University of Toronto, Department of Geography, Research Publication 4.

Parkes, D. and Taylor, P. J. 1975: A Kantian view of the city: a factorial ecology experiment in space and time. *Environ. Plann. A* 7, pp. 671–88.

Richards, P. 1974: Kant's geography and mental maps. *Trans. Inst. Br. Geogr.* 61, pp. 1–16.

Schaefer, F. K. 1953: Exceptionalism in geography: a methodological examination. *Ann. Ass. Am. Geogr.* 43, pp. 226–49.

Suggested Reading

Büttner and Hoheisel (1980).
Entrikin (1981).
Livingstone and Harrison (1981).
May (1970).

kibbutz An Israeli agricultural commune (plural: kibbutzim). The kibbutz movement began in the early twentieth century and was one of the principal means whereby Jews recolonized Palestine. Early proponents of the movement combined elements of Zionism (the belief that Jewish people must exercise self-determination by creating a Jewish-majority nation–state in Palestine) and European socialism. Kibbutzim were established in rural areas both to introduce Jewish settlers to agriculture and to gain territorial control. The new settlements were organized as COLLECTIVES and were autonomous from the surrounding (often hostile) Palestinian-Arab agricultural economy. Many kibbutzim were armed and protected by stockades and watchtowers. While kibbutzim were joined in three separate federations, decisions on each kibbutz were collectively reached, meals were eaten in common, and children were normally housed and raised in communal facilities. After 1948, the military role of kibbutzim waned and was replaced by a stronger emphasis on industrialization and export-oriented agriculture. Standards of living rose as more land was acquired, and a state-controlled water distribution system was implemented. In recent years this standard has been difficult to maintain, and kibbutzim face mounting annual deficits. Collectivist ideologies are also challenged as more individuals seek work and education off the kibbutz; moreover, recent statistics indicate that 50 per cent of kibbutz-born children do not settle on kibbutzim. Still, the movement survives and continues to attract approximately 3 per cent of the Israeli population, thereby maintaining a vital national symbol of idealism and collective self-determination.   DH

Suggested Reading

Mittelberg, D. 1988: *Strangers in paradise: the Israeli kibbutz experience.* New Brunswick, NJ: Transaction Books.

Rayman, P. 1981: *The kibbutz community and nation building.* Princeton, NJ: Princeton University Press.

Kondratieff cycles *Long waves* of economic development with a wavelength of about 40–60 years. Shorter oscillations in the level of business activity may be superimposed upon such long waves, but Kondratieff cycles imply fundamental qualitative transformations of economic systems rather than mere quantitative fluctuations. The figure illustrates both the sequence of Kondratieffs since the late eighteenth century (each wave is composed of a growth (A) and a stagnation (B) phase), and the range of economic, social and political changes which are thought to accompany them.

Kondratieff waves are named after the Soviet economist N. D. Kondratieff (see, for example, Kondratieff, 1935) who worked during the 1920s on long-term fluctuations in economic activity. Empirical evidence for the existence of long waves is strongly disputed (e.g. Maddison, 1982, 1991) but the interest lies in the HYPOTHESES about and insights into the dynamics of capitalist development that have been generated by long-wave theorizing (Freeman et al., 1982) and in the two-way relationships between UNEVEN DEVELOPMENT and the generation and geographical implications of long waves (Marshall, 1987; Allen and Massey, 1988; Hall and Preston, 1988; Berry, 1991; Kleinknecht et al., 1992).

Ernest Mandel (1980) strongly supports the existence of long waves. He argues that the four waves identified to the present represent segments of the overall history of CAPITALISM that have definite distinguishing characteristics: (a) 1789–1848, the industrial and bourgeois revolutions and Napoleonic wars, and the constitution of a world market for industrial goods; (b) 1848–93, free competition; (c) 1893–1940, IMPERIALISM, the rise of finance CAPITAL and the consequent interimperialist wars; and (d) 1940–present, late capitalism. For Mandel there are serious technical and economic difficulties facing a capitalist path out of the current decline, which began in the late 1960s after the long postwar boom and, as a result of such difficulties, some even more severe social and political problems.

Maddison (1982) accepts that 'major changes in growth momentum have occurred since 1820'. He argues that these changes have given rise to 'phases of growth', but suggests that their explanation is not to be found in 'systematic long waves, but in specific disturbances of an *ad hoc* character'. Each of Maddison's phases (1870–1914, the liberal phase; 1920–38, the beggar-your-neighbour phase; 1950–73, the golden age; 1973–present, the phase of blurred objectives) is characterized by quantitative and qualitative characteristics, and the latest phase coincides in its onset with the contemporary crisis described by long-wave theorists.

A common theme in the analysis of the causes of long waves is the generation and implications of technological change. Schumpeter (1939) and Mensch (1979) point to a bunching of INNOVATIONS. This bunching, Schumpeter suggests, is stimulated by the leadership of pioneering entrepreneurs searching for ways of resuscitating rates of profit during a recession. The innovations create expansionary and transformative systemic effects but, eventually, they too are subject to falling rates of profit. Long waves are, therefore, distinguished by particular types of technological revolution. Thus the first four Kondratieff waves were associated respectively with major innovations in: steam power, cotton and iron; railways and iron and steel;

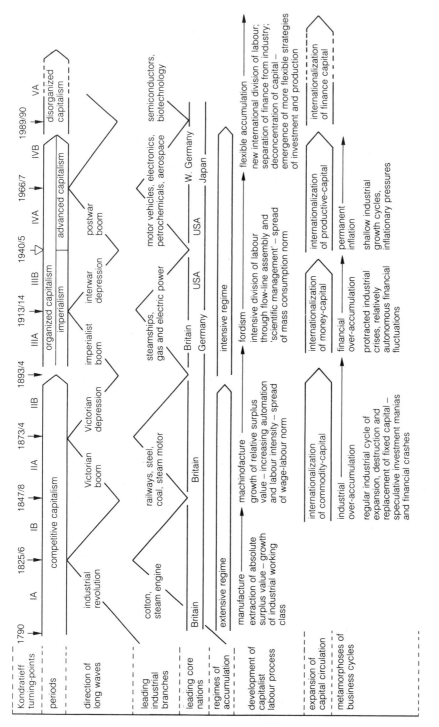

Kondratieff cycles *A schematic representation of the major features associated with long-wave economic cycles (Knox and Agnew, 1989: adapted from Marshall, 1987).*

electricity, chemicals and automobiles; and electronics, synthetics and petrochemicals. Speculation continues as to the basis of the fifth Kondratieff, with likely contenders being information technology, and tele-communications, and biotechnology. Free-man et al. (1982) point rather to the effects of the DIFFUSION of innovations in stimu-lating change and, like Gordon et al. (1982, 1983), suggest that long waves reflect the social and institutional circumstances (what Gordon et al. (1983) call 'the social structure of accumulation': (see ECON-OMIC GEOGRAPHY) in which technical change is stimulated and diffused as well as the particular characteristics of the technology itself. Certainly, long waves are thought to be associated with the transformation of other features of capital-ist society (Knox and Agnew, 1989) such as regimes of accumulation (see ECONOMIC GEOGRAPHY). This approach to the UN-EVEN DEVELOPMENT of capitalism is similar to, but broader in scope than, that propounded by Dunford and Perrons (1983), who point to critical transforma-tions in the LABOUR PROCESS as an explanation of long waves.

Insofar as Kondratieffs are generated by systemic technical change, successive cycles imply quite different geographical conditions of existence for production and, in addition, the associated social, political and regulatory changes themselves present new geographical constraints and possibi-lities. The geographical implications of Kondratieffs or, rather, the complex of changes that they represent, are profound and may be associated with the rise and fall of regions and places of production (see, e.g., Hall, 1985; Massey, 1988). Broadly, there are two schools of thought on the implications of Kondratieff cycles for geographically uneven development. Peter Hall (1985) adopts a technological–deter-minist position, and argues that places are differentially endowed with respect to the development and growth of new technol-ogy, that uneven development will and should result and that such differences should be intensified in policies for eco-nomic growth. By contrast, others (e.g. Freeman et al., 1982; Marshall, 1987; Massey, 1988) argue that technical change

is facilitative and that places may be adapted to such change. Marshall points out that new or high technology rarely represents a sudden or complete break with the past, and that 'low' technology may be modified by high technology via process innovations.

Little attention has been paid to the possibilities of geography being implicated in the generation of technical change (see Allen and Massey, 1988), despite the suggestion that peripheral regions are inherently less hidebound by fixed invest-ment and are, therefore, more open to innovation (see, e.g., Dodgshon, 1987). However, insofar as geography represents an integral part of the conditions of existence of productive activity, it seems likely that the geography of the generation of long waves is not reducible merely to local conditions of innovation, but to contradictions and potentials in the geo-graphical structure of economic develop-ment at particular places and points of time, to which technical change and innovation may represent a positive re-sponse.

It is important to remember, however, that the application of long-wave theory to geographical change remains highly econ-omistic. Avoidance of the catastrophic future predicted by Mandel in emerging from the fourth Kondratieff would depend upon political and social struggle and leadership rather than on a resigned acceptance of the inevitability of economic-ally determined and potentially damaging social, cultural and political change.   RL

References and Suggested Reading

Allen, J. and Massey, D., eds 1988: *The economy in question*. Newbury Park, CA: Sage.

Berry, B. J. L. 1991: *Long-wave rhythms in economic development and political behavior*. Balti-more, MD: The Johns Hopkins University Press.

Dodgshon, R. A. 1987: *The European past: social evolution and spatial order*. London: Macmillan/ New York: St. Martin's Press.

Dunford, M. and Perrons, D. 1983: *The arena of capital*. London: Macmillan/New York: St. Martin's Press, ch. 9.

Freeman, C., Clark, J. and Soete, L. 1982: *Unemployment and technical innovation: a study of long waves and economic development*. London: Francis Pinter/Westport, CN: Greenwood Press.

Gordon, D. M., Edwards, R. and Reich, M. 1982: *Segmented work, divided workers*. Cambridge: Cambridge University Press, ch. 2.

Gordon, D. M., Weisskopf, T. E. and Bowles, S. 1983: Long swings and the non-reproductive cycle. American Economic Association, *Papers and Proceedings* 73 (2), pp. 152–7.

Hall, P. 1985: The geography of the Fifth Kondratieff. In Hall, P. and Markusen, A., eds, *Silicon landscapes*. Winchester, MA: Allen and Unwin, ch. 1.

Hall, P. and Preston, P. 1988: *The carrier wave: new information technology and the geography of innovation 1846–2003*. London: Unwin Hyman.

Kleinknecht, A., Mandel, E. and Wallerstein I. 1992: *New findings in long wave research*. London: Macmillan.

Knox, P. and Agnew, J. 1989: *The geography of the world-economy*. London: Edward Arnold.

Kondratieff, N. D. 1935: The long waves in economic life. *Rev. Econ. St.* 17, pp. 105–15.

Maddison, A. 1982: *Phases of capitalist development*. Oxford: Oxford University Press, ch. 4.

Maddison, A. 1991: *Dynamic forces in capitalist development*. Oxford: Oxford University Press.

Mandel, E. 1980: *Long waves of capitalist development: the Marxist interpretation*. Cambridge: Cambridge University Press.

Marshall, M. 1987: *Long waves of regional development*. London: Macmillan/New York: St. Martin's Press.

Massey, D. 1988: What's happening to UK manufacturing? In Allen, J. and Massey, D., eds, *The economy in question*. Newbury Park, CA: Sage, ch. 2.

Mensch, G. 1979: *Stalemate in technology: innovations overcome the depression*. New York: Ballinger.

Schumpeter, J. A. 1939: *Business cycles: a theoretical, historical and statistical analysis of the capitalist process*. New York: McGraw-Hill.

L

labour See DIVISION OF LABOUR; FAC-
TORS OF PRODUCTION; *GASTARBEITER*;
LABOUR MARKET; METROPOLITAN
LABOUR AREA: MIGRANT LABOUR; NEW
INTERNATIONAL DIVISION OF LABOUR;
SEGMENTED LABOUR MARKET.

labour market A mechanism whereby
labour power is exchanged for the material
conditions of its reproduction. From the
perspective of MARXIAN ECONOMICS this
involves, in capitalist societies, the transformation of labour power into variable
CAPITAL. The NEOCLASSICAL ECONOMICS
theory of labour markets reduces *Homo
sapiens* to *Homo economicus*; the market is
assumed to be continuous and to work
smoothly towards EQUILIBRIUM on the
basis of the marginal productivity of labour.

However, labour power is a special
commodity in that it is produced by and
is the property of sentient human beings
(see LABOUR PROCESS). In this sense it is
inalienable, while work is a ubiquitous
feature of human life. Thus Storper and
Walker (1989, p. 156) point out that the
'most fundamental difference between
labour and true commodities is that there
is no guarantee that you get what you pay
for'. Thus, although it is possible to speak,
for example, of singular national, international or even global labour markets in
terms of the forms of legislation which
govern them and/or the migration of labour
(always limited in relation to total labour
supply) within them, all labour markets are
in a sense local, shaped by the daily
journey-to-work and intensified by the
processes and experience of reproduction
within particular localities. The practical
implementation of legislation and the social
character of labour markets will have a

geography shaped by the experience of
production.

The complex mosaic of bounded labour
markets (see Cooke, 1983) is formed by
geographically uneven LAYERS OF IN-
VESTMENT and creates opportunities for
capital to relocate and to change and
diversify the LABOUR PROCESS. But it also
represents a differentiation of resistance on
the part of labour. An important point here
is that the dynamics of the capital–labour
relation are two-sided and imply a perpetual process of change in production; there
is not necessarily a pre-given and rationalist
spatial structure which induces certain
responses by capital or labour. Rather,
geography is an integral part of a continuing struggle which serves to differentiate
labour markets. On the one hand, capital
must exert control but, on the other, labour
must perform actively in production. Both
the geography and the politics of this
relationship are, therefore, crucial and the
bases of neoclassical analyses profoundly
unsatisfactory.

Labour markets are also characterized by
internal discontinuities, such as those
induced by gender, race, age or skill (see
SEGMENTED LABOUR MARKET). However,
such differences may be created as much by
the participants in the market as by any
inherent differences that may, *a priori*, be
assumed to exist. Thus skill, for example, is
a social construct created by the intersection of sectorally diverse production dynamics, technology, the nature and extent
of the market and division of labour, the job
specification, social evaluation and the
active participation of labour in shaping
the nature of work. Although such diverse
influences are resolved in the market, the
processes involved in their resolution are

not reducible to marginal analysis. The debate on deskilling or reskilling is complex and indeterminate: these processes are neither one-sided (labour or capital) nor explained monocausally (by technology, for example). Nor can the context of such dynamics be restricted to the space within the factory gate or office door. The social character of localities is shaped in part by the character of local production but, by the same token, reproduction shapes the possibilities for productive change.

The essential politics of negotiating performance and control between labour and capital in establishing the employment relation (Burawoy, 1985) is reflected in the segmentation of labour markets. Storper and Walker (1989, p. 171) suggest that segmentation is an unintended consequence of the indeterminate politics of 'the conflict between labour and capital within socially- and technically-defined strategic conditions'. Until the mid-1970s, the labour markets of the USA and Western Europe were characterized by an 'independent primary segment' in which rewards, security and autonomy were high; a 'subordinate primary' sector with reasonably high rewards and stable employment but lower levels of autonomy and higher risks of lay-offs; and a 'secondary' labour market characterized by high levels of social control, no autonomy, physical discomfort and low rewards. This segmentation was reproduced and regulated by institutions (including trades unions) within the labour market. Since the mid-1970s, however, transitions within contemporary economies have served to restructure the subordinate secondary and, to a much lesser extent, the independent primary segments. Fordist production, which was enabled by the development of the former segment, is in decline (in relative if not absolute terms) and productivity increases are essential for maintaining competitiveness. By contrast, subcontracting and outwork, with conditions typical of the secondary labour market segment, are on the increase.

If the head of a pin is an inappropriate locale for understanding the economy, it is doubly inappropriate in the analysis of the labour market. Human beings are place-bound not only in terms of limited mobility in relation to capital – which can, therefore, use locational adjustment in the politics of negotiation with labour – but in terms of their own identity and reproduction. But the very place-boundedness of labour presents mobile capital with a problem, in that the employment relation must be re-established in a new location with its own geographically distinctive labour. The labour market is, therefore, always a product of present political consciousness and possibilities and past experience and the continuing presence of historical economic geographies.   RL

References and Suggested Reading
Burawoy, M. 1985: *The politics of production.* London: Verso.

Cooke, P. 1983: *Theories of planning and spatial development.* London: Hutchinson, ch. 9.

Storper, M. and Walker, R. 1989: *The capitalist imperative.* Oxford: Blackwell, ch. 6.

labour process   '. . . a process by which man, through his own actions, mediates, regulates and controls the metabolism between himself and nature' (Marx, 1976). The *sexism* in this definition reflects the widespread tendency to assume (correctly in some places at some times, but not inherently so) both that participation in the labour process is restricted to wage labour and that males dominate the waged labour force.

The universal characteristics of the labour process include work itself, the object upon which work is undertaken, and the instruments of labour. But human labour is characterized above all by thought and symbolism (Godelier, 1986). Despite the fact that it is this aspect of the labour process that has been most profoundly modified in capitalist production.

Marx distinguishes between the formal subsumption of labour by CAPITAL, in which labour is subordinated by capital simply by the compulsion for people to sell their labour power in order to survive, and the real subsumption of labour by capital in which capital reorganizes the labour process itself. In the former circumstance, capital has to accept labour as it finds it, and so remains dependent upon its workers' bargainable skills and crafts. Under these conditions, the best that can be achieved is the production of absolute surplus value, involving an extension of the working day (see MARXIAN ECONOMICS). With the capitalist transformation of the labour process, the attempt is made formally to subsume labour to capital. But the special nature of labour power as a commodity turns this process into an indeterminate political rather than purely economic or technical dynamic (compare Storper and Walker, 1989 with Dunford and Perrons, 1983; see LABOUR MARKET).

Beginning with the capitalist organization of co-operation between craft workers, capital may secure an ever more rigorous hold over the labour process through the DIVISION OF LABOUR and manufacture, the introduction of machinery, the growth of large-scale industry and the emergence of the factory system (see INDUSTRIAL REVOLUTION). With these developments comes the ability to modify the labour process in order to increase PRODUCTIVITY and so to produce relative surplus value (see MARXIAN ECONOMICS). Associated with these changes comes a monumental physical and geographical revolution in production and the re-evaluation of skill (see LABOUR MARKET).

Scientific management, developed from the practices of Henry Ford and the principles of F. W. Taylor (see FORDISM), takes this process further by the pre-planning and complete specification of every aspect of the labour process. Scientific management further separates the mental and the manual aspects of work and intensifies the demand for management, engineering and design specialists, increases the specialization of skilled and semi-skilled labour, and increases the demand for that labour to operate but not control machines. This separation has facilitated the NEW INTERNATIONAL DIVISION OF LABOUR, as capital has been able to separate its productive operations into a hierarchy of activities, with global management at the top of the hierarchy and production at the bottom (see Massey, 1984).

These changes may be summarized (see, e.g., Dunford and Perrons, 1983) as four phases of development of the labour process:

(a) *manufacture* – independent workers gathered together into workshops, rudimentary division of labour;

(b) *machinofacture* – mechanization, the application of inanimate power and the division of labour extending human labour power and individual production;

(c) *scientific management and Fordism* – scientific division of work into specialized tasks and the introduction of the moving assembly line;

(d) *neo-Fordism* – further fragmentation of tasks and increasing automation, and mechanization of thought through computer-aided design and production.

Despite this apparent progression of change, the crisis of Fordism is due in large measure to the limitations of its labour process. It is inflexible, capital-intensive, producer-orientated and, notwithstanding its rhetoric of labour control, susceptible to disruption by labour – a contradiction which provided the theme for Charlie Chaplin's 1936 film, *Modern Times*.

Microelectronic technology now allows the complete reintegration of material and information handling (formerly integrated by labour) at the corporate level and so completes the subordination of labour by capital. The crisis of Fordism is thought to be leading not only to the restructuring of the workplace (Meegan, 1988) but also of the workforce and labour process too (Harvey, 1989). Functional and numerical flexibility are seen as critical responses to the increasingly intense levels of global competition in an uncertain environment, although the evidence for such changes is far from fully convincing (Allen, 1988).

As always with the labour process, the future is uncertain and far from determined in a simple fashion. It seems likely that specialization, standardization and routinization will continue – with all the implications that such processes may have for the segmentation of labour – and, at the same time, an increasing flexibility of the production process and of the organization of production will develop further. The combined effect of these processes will increase the geographical and sectoral diversity of the labour process.

Labour is far from being a passive element in the development of the labour process: Marx's own account of the course of the Industrial Revolution stresses that point. The development of capitalist production has followed certain tendencies to which labour has responded in a variety of ways, many of which have, paradoxically, tended to stabilize and ensure the reproduction of capitalist production (Urry, 1981). Changes in the forces of production do not automatically bring forth appropriate changes in the relations of production, and the labour force remains influential in the effectiveness of production technology.

Neither is geography passive: on the contrary, geography matters. Geography is an active element which shapes the labour process by presenting a diverse range of conditions for production by conditioning production strategies and, through the influence of local social structures and cultures, by influencing the detailed operation of particular processes of production.

RL

References and Suggested Reading

Allen, J. 1988: Fragmented firms, disorganized labour? In Allen, J. and Massey, D., eds, *The economy in question*. Newbury Park, CA: Sage, ch. 5.

Braverman, H. 1974: *Labour and monopoly capital: the degradation of work in the twentieth century*. New York: Monthly Review Press.

Dunford, M. and Perrons, D. 1983: *The arena of capital*. London: Macmillan/New York: St. Martin's Press, part III.

Godelier, M. 1986: *The mental and the material*. London: Verso.

Harvey, D. 1982: *The limits to capital*. Oxford: Blackwell/Chicago: University of Chicago Press, ch. 4.

Harvey, D. 1989: *The condition of postmodernity*. Oxford: Blackwell, ch. 9.

Marx, K. 1976: *Capital*, volume 1. London: Penguin, ch. 7 (first published 1867).

Massey, D. 1984: *Spatial divisions of labour*. London: Macmillan.

Meegan, D. 1988: A crisis of mass production? In Allen, J. and Massey, D., eds, *The economy in question*. Newbury Park, CA: Sage, ch. 4.

Storper, M. and Walker, R. 1989: *The capitalist imperative*. Oxford: Blackwell, ch. 6.

Urry, J. 1981: *The anatomy of capitalist societies*. London: Macmillan/Atlantic Highlands, NJ: Humanities Press, ch. 7.

labour theory of value A central argument of MARXIAN ECONOMICS is that the value of goods reflects the amount of labour time involved in their production under average conditions. Surplus value is obtained under CAPITALISM because the wages paid for labour are less than the value added by its application. CLASS conflict within capitalist societies focuses on this expropriation of surplus value through the exploitation of labour by capital (see CONFLICT). In NEOCLASSICAL ECONOMICS, surplus value is interpreted as the reward paid for enterprising investment of capital in situations of RISK and UNCERTAINTY. RJJ

Suggested Reading

Harvey, D. 1982: *The limits of capital*. Oxford: Blackwell.

Lamarck(ian)ism A non-Darwinian theory of evolutionary change originating with the French naturalist Jean Baptiste de Lamarck. As a doctrine of organic progression, Lamarckism in the pre-Darwinian period differed substantially from its post-Darwinian *neo-Lamarckian* successor. Lamarck himself did *not* conceive of evolution as a system of common descent, but rather of 'separate lines progressing in parallel along the same hierarchy' (Bowler, 1989, p. 85). The dynamic behind this organic progress was the active power of nature impelling life along predetermined sequences. What facilitated this *tendance de la nature* was the conjoint processes of environmental stimulus and the efforts of organisms to adapt to modified conditions through changed habits and the use and disuse of organs (Burkhardt, 1977).

In the post-Darwinian period it was the Lamarckian insistence on the inheritance of acquired characteristics that provided an alternative mechanism to that of classical Darwinism (Bowler, 1983). In the decades around 1900, when Darwinism itself was in eclipse as a consequence of a series of criticisms within the scientific community, Larmackian mechanisms achieved considerable support. These neo-Lamarckians perpetuated certain elements in Lamarck's system and married them to the principle of natural selection as a secondary mechanism in a distinctively non-Darwinian way.

Particularly in the United States, but also in Britain, this alternative evolutionary theory attracted widespread support (Pfeifer, 1965): Cope and Hyatt spearheaded the movement among palaeontologists; LeConte and King added their geological approval; and Argyll and Romanes in anthropology and psychology also helped to swell the tide. Soon a loose coalition of dissident evolutionary theory was available for those with a passion for socializing evolution. Of those conventionally labelled Social Darwinians – not least Spencer himself – many drew more inspiration from neo-Lamarckian dogma than from classical DARWINISM (see also SOCIAL DARWINISM). Thus in neo-Lamarckian evolution many found grounds for looking to environment as the driving force behind social processes; others, more taken with the evolutionary significance that Lamarckism attributed to mind and will, took a more idealist turn. Either way, Lamarckism could be mobilized to justify the politics of interventionism (Jones, 1980). The ramifications of engaging social Lamarckism were many and diverse (Stocking, 1962). Lester Frank Ward, for example, found there the justification for educating his children with the right values, for he believed that they would then become part of the race's inherited repertoire. Similarly, the geologist Joseph Le Conte could only find firm scientific grounds for education in the principles of neo-Lamarckian inheritance (Russett, 1976).

Given these particular conceptual alignments it is not surprising that a number of geographers would find the neo-Lamarckian construal of evolution to their liking, not least because the environment played such a key directive role in the scenario (Campbell and Livingstone, 1983; Livingstone, 1992). In the United States numerous advocates of ENVIRONMENTAL DETERMINISM, such as Shaler, Davis, Semple, Brigham and Huntingdon, betray the infiltration of neo-Lamarckism.

Similarly, the recapitulationist strains in Turner's FRONTIER THESIS drew inspiration from Lamarckian environmentalism (Coleman, 1966). In Britain similar convictions are discernible among those who were drawn to Lamarckism's emphasis on the directive evolutionary significance of consciousness. Geddes, for instance, used it to advocate various urban planning and educational reforms; Kropotkin, critical of the cut-throat ethics of a capitalist competitive struggle, found in Lamarckism the grounds for a more benign social order – an anarchistic humanism – built upon mutual aid; and Herbertson and Fleure both mobilized the idea in their considerations of REGIONAL GEOGRAPHY.

In more general terms, neo-Lamarckism facilitated geography's transition from a natural theology framework to that of evolutionary naturalism, largely due to the ease with which it could be given a teleological reading (Livingstone, 1984). And this, together with its widespread influence on numerous key individuals, demonstrates how profound its impact on the modern geographical tradition has been.   DNL

References

Bowler, P. J. 1983: *The eclipse of Darwinism: anti-Darwinian evolution theories in the decades around 1900*. Baltimore, MD: Johns Hopkins University Press.

Bowler, P. J. 1989: *Evolution. The history of an idea*, second edition. Berkeley, CA: University of California Press.

Burkhardt, R. W. 1977: *The spirit of system: Lamarck and evolutionary biology*. Cambridge, MA: Harvard University Press.

Campbell, J. A. and Livingstone, D. N. 1983: Neo-Lamarckism and the development of geography in the United States and Great Britain. *Trans. Inst. Br. Geogr.* n.s. 8, pp. 267–94.

Coleman, W. 1966: Science and symbol in the Turner frontier hypothesis. *Am. hist. Rev.* 72, pp. 22–49.

Jones, G. 1980: *Social Darwinism and English thought: the interaction between biological and social theory*. Brighton: Harvester Press.

Livingstone, D. N. 1984: Natural theology and neo-Lamarckism: the changing context of nineteenth century geography in the United States and Great Britain. *Ann. Ass. Am. Geogr.* 74, pp. 9–28.

Livingstone, D. N. 1992: *The geographical tradition: episodes in the history of a contested enterprise.* Oxford: Blackwell.

Pfeifer, E. J. 1965: The genesis of American neo-Lamarckism. *Isis* 56, pp. 156–67.

Russett, C. E. 1976: *Darwin in America: the intellectual response 1865–1912.* San Francisco: W. H. Freeman.

Stocking, G. W. Jr 1962: Lamarckianism in American social science: 1890–1915. *J. hist. Ideas* 23, pp. 239–56.

land reform   See LAND TENURE; FARM FRAGMENTATION.

land tenure   The system of ownership of land and of title to its use, generally in agriculture. Land ownership is usually relatively straightforward, but rights to land use are complex and varied. Types of land tenure may be classified according to their legal basis; the relative rights of landowner and land user; the conditions and forms of payment from the latter to the former, if any; and the security of tenants (defined either in terms of duration or of predictability). Many forms of tenure involve very complex combinations of use-rights.

The following are important types of land tenure:

(a) *Owner-occupation.* This can involve large-scale modern farms, where the owners utilize wage labour alongside their own; family farms; and PEASANT systems. In the last case, land ownership and use may be vested in a family group rather than a single individual. The continuity of owner-occupation is affected by INHERITANCE SYSTEMS, whereby partible inheritance may lead to FARM FRAGMENTATION, a problem that occurs less often under tenancy systems.

(b) *Tenancy.* This is the most complex type of land tenure, embracing a very wide variety of conditions. Tenancy involves the tenant repaying the landowner in some way for being granted the right to use land. Most frequently this payment is in one of three forms: (i) labour supply for work on land retained by the owners for their personal or institutional use, as in certain forms of FEUDALISM; (ii) cash payment; or (iii) some form of SHARECROPPING. Often, the landowner's return on leasing the land

is made up of a blend of these three elements.

(c) *Use-right.* This is characteristic of SHIFTING CULTIVATION, whereby the question of long-run land ownership is of no significance, and where an individual or communal group establishes a right to the land by using it. Many more intensive agricultural systems include elements of use-right over common land, especially for the grazing of animals.

(d) *Institutional with wage labour.* Under this form of tenure, land is owned by an institution, such as a private company, and agricultural production is the result of a contract employment system. The PLANTATION is the most common example of land held by this form of tenure.

(e) *Collectivist.* This form of tenure is also complex. Land is owned by some collectivist interest, such as the state or whole village (e.g. the *ujamaa* village of Tanzania; see also KIBBUTZ), and individuals participate in a communal farming programme; they have shares in the produce or in the revenue from sales.

Land tenure systems, especially considered dynamically, are more complex than this simple classification allows, for five main reasons. First, individual tenures may not fall neatly into just one category. For example, a large landowner may farm some of the land and lease out the remainder. The largest estates held under this system, *latifundia* or *hacienda* estates, often involve the existence of very small tenant holdings, with the part of the estate kept for the landlord's own use being worked by day labourers. Likewise, the state farms that dominated agriculture in socialist countries at certain periods of the twentieth century can be thought of as an intermediate stage between the 'collectivist' and 'institutional with wage labour' systems of tenure: the land is state-owned (i.e. collectivist) but the farm workers are wage earners rather than participants in the produce of the farms (see also COLLECTIVE).

Second, many tenure systems are combinations of various tenure types. Third, the relative frequency of different tenure types may not be the most important facet of a tenurial system. For example, Newby (1986) discusses how the legacy of previously dominant property relations can continue to have greater local effects on social and economic change than their contemporary significance might imply. Fourth, it may be important to distinguish between the formal–legal components of tenurial relationships and the customary components. The latter are the informally accepted 'normal' practices, but may be poorly protected in law at times of stress.

Fifth, agricultural property rights have become divided in new and more complex ways, as in Western agriculture during the 1980s, necessitating more sophisticated geographical analyses. In particular, the diverging interests of various fractions of capital, and the growing indirect involvement of banking capital in land ownership, via the accumulation of land as collateral for loans, have produced new and complex interrelations between ownership, occupation and use-rights over agricultural property (Whatmore et al., 1990).

Issues of land tenure feature prominently in debates about both historical and contemporary agrarian change. Compared with earlier debates, however, current work examines land tenure less as a topic in itself than as a component of rural power relations in general (e.g. Cloke, 1989). Key historical debates concern the relationships between land tenure and broader social trends (Tawney, 1912; Snell, 1985; Allen, 1992); between land tenure and agricultural productivity (Campbell and Overton, 1991); and between land tenures and the appearance of the agricultural landscape.

Active debates on actual or proposed land reform in many LDCs mostly concern the break-up of very large estates, often focused on export crops, in favour of the redistribution of land to owner–occupiers or secure tenants concentrating on labour-intensive crops, especially food for domestic consumption. Although such changes involve state planning, not only of tenure but also of agricultural institutions and infrastructure, there are widely differing views as to the appropriate balance of state and market forces in new tenurial arrangements (Ghose 1983; Smith, 1989; Christodolou, 1990; Harvey, 1990; Platteau, 1991). PG

References

Allen, R. C. 1992: *Enclosure and the yeoman.* Oxford: Clarendon Press.

Campbell, B. M. S. and Overton, M., eds 1991: *Land, labour and livestock: historical studies in European agricultural productivity.* Manchester: Manchester University Press.

Christodolou, D. 1990: *The unpromised land: agrarian reform and conflict worldwide.* London: Zed Books.

Cloke, P. 1989: Rural geography and political economy. In Peet, R. and Thrift, N., eds, *New models in geography* volume 1: *the political-economy perspective.* London: Unwin Hyman, pp. 164–97.

Ghose, A. K., ed. 1983: *Agrarian reform in contemporary developing countries.* London: Croom Helm.

Harvey, N. 1990: *The new agrarian movement in Mexico, 1979–1990.* London: Institute of Latin American Studies.

Newby, E., 1986: Locality and rurality: the restructuring of rural social relations. *Reg. Stud.* 20, pp. 209–26.

Platteau, J.-P. 1991: *Formalization and privatization of land-rights in sub-Saharan Africa: a critique of current orthodoxies and structural adjustment programmes.* London: Suntory–Toyota International Centre, London School of Economics.

Smith, G. A. 1989: *Livelihood and resistance: peasants and the politics of land in Peru.* Berkeley, CA: University of California Press.

Snell, K. D. M. 1985: *Annals of the labouring poor: social change and agrarian England 1660–1900.* Cambridge: Cambridge University Press.

Tawney, R. H. 1912: *The agrarian problem in the sixteenth century.* London: Allen and Unwin.

Whatmore, S., Munton, R. and Marsden, T. 1990: The rural restructuring process: emerging divisions of agricultural property rights. *Reg. Stud.* 24, pp. 235–45.

Suggested Reading
Whatmore et al. (1990).

land-use survey The investigation and cartographic representation of land use. Large-scale land-use surveys were initiated in Britain by L. Dudley Stamp in the 1930s, and detailed studies have now been conducted in many countries – increasingly using the technologies of RE-MOTE SENSING and GEOGRAPHICAL INFORMATION SYSTEMS for the data collection, collation and display. Land-use surveys are largely descriptive exercises: their use was long advanced by geographers as the initial stage in the development of a land-use plan, for both urban and rural areas (see APPLIED GEOGRAPHY).   RJJ

Suggested Reading
Rhind, D. and Hudson, R. 1980: *Land use.* London: Methuen.

landscape A polysemic term referring to the appearance of an area, the assemblage of objects used to produce that appearance, and the area itself. According to Mikesell (1968), during the Middle Ages in England the term referred to the land controlled by a lord or inhabited by a particular group of people. By the early seventeenth century, however, under the influence of the Dutch *landschap* painters, the term 'landscape' came to refer to the appearance of an area, more particularly to the representation of scenery. By the late nineteenth century, as Mikesell points out, the basis for the contemporary definition of landscape took shape as 'a portion of land or TERRITORY which the eye can comprehend in a single view, including all the objects so seen, especially in its pictorial aspect'.

The term 'landscape' was introduced into American geography in 1925 by Sauer with the publication of his 'The morphology of landscape' (see Leighly, 1963). This influential article drew on the concept of LANDSCHAFT developed by German geographers, most prominently Passarge and Schluter. Sauer put forward the concept of landscape as an alternative to the currently popular form of geographical explanation known as ENVIRONMENTAL DETERMINISM. While the latter sought to specify the causal influences of the environment on humans, the landscape approach sought to describe the interrelations between humans and the environment, with primary attention given to the human impact on the environment. Sauer played down the subjective aspects of the concept of landscape and stressed that landscape was an objective area to be studied scientifically through observation. Although he paid lip service to the subjective in the latter part of 'Morphology', it is clear that he envisaged the study of landscape in geography as a scientific endeavour. Under this view the landscape was defined as 'an area made up of a distinct association of forms, both physical and cultural'. Sauer's position was that geographers should proceed genetically and trace the development of a natural landscape into a CULTURAL LANDSCAPE. The difficulty with this methodology, as Sauer himself soon realized, was that it was seldom possible to reconstruct the appearance of the natural landscape, because the human impact on the face of the Earth had been pervasive for many millennia. In effect, all landscapes had become cultural landscapes. Thus the study of landscapes by Sauer and his students (who constituted the so-called BERKELEY SCHOOL) became the study of culture history.

Beginning in the 1950s, two scholars outside this Berkeley tradition became influential. The first was the English historian W. G. Hoskins, who conducted detailed studies of landscape history and whose *The making of the English landscape* (1955) remains a classic in the genre. The second was J. B. Jackson, who founded *Landscape Magazine* in 1951 and went on to write numerous books of essays on the meaning of the American landscape (1984). To a very large extent, the intellectual context for landscape studies from the 1960s on was set by the troika of Sauer and his students, Hoskins and Jackson. David Lowenthal's influential studies, both alone (1985) and with Hugh Prince (1964), enriched the tradition by demonstrating the impact of national taste and social class on landscape creation. The single most significant work to emerge during this period was a volume entitled *The interpretation of ordinary landscapes*, edited by Donald Meinig (1979). This explicitly recognized the influence of Sauer, Hoskins and Jackson, and contained contributions from such well known cultural geographers as J. B. Jackson, Peirce Lewis, David Lowenthal, Donald Meinig, Marwyn Samuels, David Sopher and Yi-Fu Tuan. While this volume did not for the most part break new ground, it elegantly summarized the work of this period. A geographer who was not included in this collection, but whose work fits within this genre and who has been one of the most prolific and insightful interpreters of the American landscape, is

Wilbur Zelinsky (1973). This tradition of landscape analysis focusing upon Sauerian themes of artifactual analysis and culture history continues to flourish.

During the 1980s and early 1990s some new directions in landscape interpretation have been charted. Although this newer work maintains important connections with the older landscape tradition, it diverges in explicitly applying social and cultural theory to landscape interpretation, and showing greater concern for both the sociocultural and political processes that shape landscapes, as well as the role that landscapes play in these processes. A number of different theoretical stances have been adopted. Samuels (1979) and Kobayashi (1989) both explore EXISTEN-TIALISM as a basis for landscape interpretation. Cosgrove (1984) has redefined landscape as a 'way of seeing' rather than as an image or an object. He argued that this way of seeing is ideological, representing the way in which a particular class has represented itself and its property. Both Cosgrove (1984) and Daniels (1989) draw upon Marxian cultural critics such as Raymond Williams and John Berger to inform their writings, and together (Cosgrove and Daniels, 1988) apply the notion of ICONOGRAPHY drawn from art history to landscape interpretation. Ley (1987) has employed postmodern architectural theory and theories of postindustrialism, while James and Nancy Duncan (Duncan and Duncan, 1988; Duncan, 1990) have applied poststructural notions of TEXT and intertextuality drawn from literary theory to the landscape, thereby incorporating landscape interpretation into the debate surrounding POSTMODERNISM. The thrust of this new landscape work over the past decade has been not only to theorize the concept of landscape but to show how it forms an important part of social, cultural and political systems. JD

References

Cosgrove, D. 1984: *Social formation and symbolic landscape*. London: Croom Helm.

Cosgrove, D. and Daniels, S. 1988: *The iconography of landscape*. Cambridge: Cambridge University Press.

Daniels, S. 1989: Marxism, culture, and the duplicity of landscape. In Peet, R. and Thrift, N.,

eds, *New models in geography*, volume 2. London: Unwin Hyman, pp. 196–220.

Duncan, J. 1990: *The city as text: ,he politics of landscape interpretation in the Kandyan kingdom*. Cambridge: Cambridge University Press.

Duncan, J. and Duncan, N. 1988: (Re)reading the landscape. *Environ. Plann. D: Society and Space* 6, pp. 117–26.

Hoskins, W. G. 1955: *The making of the English landscape*. London: Hodder and Stoughton.

Jackson, J. B. 1984: *Discovering the vernacular landscape*. New Haven: Yale University Press.

Kobayashi, A. 1989: A critique of dialectical landscape. In Kobayashi, A. and Mackenzie, S., eds, *Remaking human geography*. London: Unwin Hyman, pp. 164–85.

Leighly, J., ed. 1963: *Land and life: selections from the writings of Carl Ortwin Sauer*. Berkeley, CA: University of California Press, pp. 315–50.

Ley, D. 1987: Styles of the times: liberal and neo-conservative landscapes in inner Vancouver, 1968–86. *J. hist. Geogr.* 13, pp. 40–56.

Lowenthal, D. 1985: *The past is a foreign country*. Cambridge: Cambridge University Press.

Lowenthal, D. and Prince, H. 1964: English landscape tastes. *Geogrl. Rev.* 54, pp. 309–46.

Meinig, D. W. 1979: *The interpretation of ordinary landscapes*. New York: Oxford University Press.

Mikesell, M. 1968: Landscape. In Sills, D. L., ed., *International encyclopedia of the social sciences*, volume 8. New York: Crowell, Collier and Macmillan, pp. 575–80.

Samuels, M. 1979: The biography of landscape: cause and culpability. In Meinig, D., ed., *The interpretation of ordinary landscapes*. New York: Oxford University Press.

Zelinsky, W. 1973: *The cultural geography of the United States*. Englewood Cliffs, NJ: Prentice-Hall.

Suggested Reading

Cosgrove (1984).

Cosgrove and Daniels (1988).

Duncan (1990).

Duncan and Duncan (1988).

Leighly (1963).

Meinig (1979).

Mikesell (1968).

Landschaft Literally and most generally LANDSCAPE, but the German term is more particularly associated with the continental European school of *Landschaftsgeographie*, a tradition which can be traced back to the end of the nineteenth century when

German geographers started to define the subject as 'landscape science'. Viewed in these terms, geography was fundamentally concerned with the form of the landscapes of particular REGIONS, and a number of schemes were proposed to classify landscapes and their elements and to provide for formal procedures of analysis (for a review, see Hartshorne, 1939). Several of these distinguished the *natural landscape* from the *cultural landscape*, and in so doing recognized the importance of HUMAN AGENCY. Many others, however, were circumscribed by a commitment to a genetic MORPHOLOGY, which progressively distanced them from human geography altogether:

Increasingly the trend was to classify on the basis of process, and to trace these forms back to more and more remote forms . . . The final step was that some of these specialists lost sight completely of actual land forms and devoted themselves to the construction of theoretical forms deducted from individual physical processes. The defeat of geographic ends was therefore almost complete and such geomorphology became part of general earth science (Leighly, 1963).

This was not strictly true of British geography, which maintained a strong interest in geomorphology as the 'physical basis' of the subject. Even in the USA, where Sauer's BERKELEY SCHOOL did much to restore the cultural concerns of Passarge's *Landschaftskünde*, an interest in the physical features of the landscape was retained: 'American geography cannot dissociate itself from the great fields of physical geography' (Leighly, 1963). But in practice the connections were closer in Britain, where a 'landscape school' of HISTORICAL GEOGRAPHY was excavated alongside geomorphology as twin 'foundations' for the rest of the subject (Darby, 1953). Yet here, too, enquiry was frequently restricted to the morphology of past landscapes treated as assemblies of artefacts: where processes were reconstructed at all, they were often described as VERTICAL THEMES inscribed directly in the landscape – 'clearing the wood', 'draining the marsh', etc.

It is precisely these morphological restrictions that have been challenged by the development of other enquiries which have (a) sought to explain landscape change in terms of social processes and practices, and (b) subjected the cultural construction of the concept of landscape as a 'way of seeing' to searching investigation, often drawing upon aesthetics, art history and cultural studies (Cosgrove, 1985; Daniels, 1992) and feminist theory (Rose, 1992). (See also ICONOGRAPHY.)   DG

References

Cosgrove, D. 1985: *Social formation and symbolic landscape.* London: Croom Helm.

Daniels, S. 1992: *Fields of vision.* Cambridge: Polity Press.

Darby, H. C. 1953: On the relations of geography and history. *Trans. Inst. Br. Geogr.* 19, pp. 1–11.

Hartshorne, R. 1939: *The nature of geography: a critical survey of current thought in the light of the past.* Lancaster, PA: Association of American Geographers.

Leighly, J., ed. 1963: *Land and life: a selection from the writings of Carl Ortwin Sauer.* Berkeley, CA: University of California Press, ch. 16.

Rose, G. 1992: Geography as a science of observation: the landscape, the gaze and masculinity. In Driver, F. and Rose, G., eds, *Nature and science; essays in the history of geographical knowledge.* Institute of British Geographers, Historical Geography Research Series, No. 28, pp. 8–18.

Suggested Reading

Hartshorne (1939), ch. 5.

Leighly (1963).

language   A set of terms, and rules for their combination (a *grammar*), with which concepts are transmitted interpersonally, in both written and oral forms. The importance of language in the understanding of geography has been increasingly stressed in recent years (cf. DISCOURSE; HERMENEUTICS; TEXT).   DG

Suggested Reading

Barnes, T. and Duncan, J., eds 1991: *Writing worlds: discourse, text and metaphor in the representation of landscape.* London: Routledge.

Pred, A. 1991: *Lost words and lost worlds: modernity and the language of everyday life in late nineteenth century Sweden.* Cambridge: Cambridge University Press.

language and dialect, geography of

The study of the distribution and social usage of language. It is possible to distinguish four broad phases in the geographical study of language:

(1) Initial interest is evident in several nineteenth-century projects to map European languages by ethnic group as part of the development of ANTHROPOGEOGRAPHY (Berghaus, 1848–52).

(2) The mapping of language areas or language groups, past or present, either as expressions of CULTURE or culture contact or as part of POLITICAL GEOGRAPHY, has been a principal part of the geography of language, especially in Britain and North America. In Canada, maps have been produced of native language groups from the sixteenth to the eighteenth centuries, of areas dominated by English, French, German and Gaelic in the late 1700s, and of French- and English-speaking areas in 1871. In the United States, language mapping has concentrated on English and German. There is a strong tradition of language mapping in the British Isles (Price, 1984; Zelinsky and Williams, 1988). This cartographic concern with language change over space and time has centred upon 'the geographic area of certain languages' (Delgado de Carvalho, 1962; see also CARTOGRAPHY).

(3) 'Dialect geography' or 'linguistic geography' considers local differentiations within speech areas, and the changing geography of particular linguistic forms (Trudgill, 1984). Trudgill (1975) noted that 'Traditionally, linguistic geography has been geographical only in the sense that it has been concerned with the spatial distribution of linguistic phenomena'. This is a well-developed field of enquiry in the United States and has close links with the study of PLACE-NAMES (Conklin and Lowrie, 1983; Carver, 1987). In Britain, the development of dialect geography has focused around internal variations in the geography of English speaking (Wakelin, 1981; Kirk et al., 1985; Langton, 1986). Attention to the geography of the Celtic languages, in part linguistic in orientation, has centred on the decline of language areas in relation to agencies of political and cultural transformation (Withers, 1984; Hindley, 1990).

(4) More recent concerns have examined the relationships between language, social practice and meaning. This work represents a significant departure from more traditional concern and is closely linked to developments in CULTURAL GEOGRAPHY (see also STRUCTURATION THEORY). For Jackson (1989), 'Language is a structure of signification that is reproduced in social practice. Like other practices, however, it does not exist outside social relations of power. . . . There is, in other words, a *politics of language*' (see also CULTURAL POLITICS). If, in part, the politics of language is an issue in POLITICAL GEOGRAPHY and NATIONALISM (Zelinsky and Williams, 1988; Williams, 1991), it also offers particular richness at local scales. Pred's examination of conflicts of meaning articulated in different language usage in nineteenth-century Stockholm (Pred, 1990a) and in other studies (Pred, 1989, 1990b), has emphasized the need for study of the locally spoken word (see also LOCALE; LOCALITY; SENSE OF PLACE). Jackson (1989) has suggested that '. . . a revitalised cultural geography must go beyond the mapping of languages and the geography of dialect, towards the study of language itself as the medium through which intersubjective meaning is communicated.

Interests in language in these ways have converged with those on DISCOURSE and on the very nature of the social sciences (see also ONTOLOGY; POSTSTRUCTURALISM). Curry (1991) has claimed that 'The use of language in post-modern works appears to express a radically new view of the nature of the social sciences and of the place of the social scientist in society'. Billinge (1983) provides a cautionary discussion on language and the articulation of (postmodern) geographical complexity. For Pred (1989), writing of the connections between language and geography as a whole, 'A vast terrain of enquiry lies open': for Jackson, 'Geographical "discovery" is an inherently linguistic process'.   CWJW

References

Berghaus, H. 1848–52: *Physikalischer Atlas.* Gotha: Peterman.

Billinge, M. D. 1983: The Mandarin dialect: an essay on style in contemporary geographical writing. *Trans. Inst. Br. Geogr.* n.s. 8, pp. 400–20.

Carver, C. M. 1987: *American regional dialects: a word geography.* Ann Arbor: University of Michigan Press.

Conklin, N. F. and Lowrie, M. A. 1983: *A host of tongues: language communities in the United States.* New York: Free Press.

Curry, M. R. 1991: Postmodernism, language and the strains of modernism. *Ann. Ass. Am. Geogr.* 81, pp. 210–28.

Delgado de Carvalho, C. M. 1962: The geography of languages. In Wagner, P. L. and Mikesell, M. W., eds, *Readings in cultural geography.* Chicago; University of Chicago Press, pp. 75–93.

Harrison, R. T. and Livingstone, D. N. 1982: Understanding in geography: structuring the subjective. In Herbert, D. T. and Johnston, R. J., eds, *Geography and the urban environment,* volume 5. Chichester: John Wiley, pp. 1–39.

Hindley, R. 1990: *The death of the Irish language: an obituary.* London: Routledge.

Jackson, P. 1989: *Maps of meaning: an introduction to cultural geography.* London: Unwin Hyman.

Kirk, J., Sanderson, S. and Widdowson, J. 1985: *Studies in linguistic geography.* London: Croom Helm.

Langton, J. 1986: Languages and dialects. In Langton, J. and Morris, R. J., eds, *Atlas of industrializing Britain.* London: Methuen.

Pred, A. 1989: Survey 14: the locally spoken word and local struggles. *Environ. Plann. D: Society and Space,* 7, pp. 211–33.

Pred, A. 1990a: *Lost words and lost worlds: modernity and the language of everyday life in late-nineteenth century Stockholm.* Cambridge: Cambridge University Press.

Pred, A. 1990b: In other wor(l)ds: fragmented and integrated observations on gendered languages, gendered spaces and local transformation. *Antipode,* 22, pp. 33–52.

Price, G. 1984: *The languages of Britain.* London: Edward Arnold.

Trudgill, P. 1975: Linguistic geography and geographical linguistics. *Prog. Geog.* 7, pp. 227–52.

Trudgill, P. 1984: *On dialect: social and geographical perspectives.* Oxford: Blackwell/New York: New York University Press.

Wakelin, M. 1981: *English dialects.* London: Athlone Press.

Williams, C. H., ed. 1991: *Linguistic minorities: society and territory.* Clevedon and Philadelphia: Multilingual Matters.

Withers, C. W. J. 1984: *Gaelic in Scotland 1698–1981: the geographical history of a language.* Edinburgh: John Donald/Atlantic Highlands, NJ: Humanities Press.

Zelinsky, W. and Williams, C. H. 1988: The mapping of language in North America and the British Isles. *Progr. hum. Geogr.* 12, pp. 337–68.

Suggested Reading

Jackson (1989), ch. 7.

Pred (1990a).

Zelinsky and Williams (1988).

law An integral component of a scientific THEORY, the nature of which can vary according to the EPISTEMOLOGY.

In POSITIVISM, a law is a statement which is universally true, independent of time and place. It thus represents a constant conjunction – of the form 'if X, then Y': given certain antecedent conditions, a particular consequence will follow (perhaps at some specified level of probability). Laws differ from factual statements, which refer to specific events (times and/or places) only, through their generality: they are produced by the empirical testing of HYPOTHESES and are linked together in coherent theories.

A law in REALISM is a statement of a causal connection: it indicates a necessity in a particular situation but implies neither universality nor regularity. In positivism, laws are frequently produced through the identification of regularities which can be equated with causation (perhaps because the theory posits such a relationship): the implication is that future events can be predicted as further occurrences of the universal regularity – 'if X again, then Y will follow again'. In realism, on the other hand, causation is identified by an analysis of the circumstances of the event(s) being considered: there is no implication that the conditions will be repeated, so the validity of the law does not imply that it occurs repeatedly. (Thus laws identified in positivist science are special cases of those of realist science, since positivism implicitly assumes that the same conditions do recur, with the same result: see Chouinard et al., 1984). However, many realists argue that the observation of repeated examples of the same conditions is very rare in social science.

There has been much debate within the social sciences concerning the relevance of the positivist conception of a law. According to realists, it is possible to conceive of laws which are particular to a finite domain – as with the Marxian law of the falling – rate of profit (see MARXIAN ECONOMICS) which applies only to capitalist societies. The domain for any law must be precisely specified, however; i.e. it must be a rational ABSTRACTION and not a CHAOTIC CONCEPTION.

Where such laws are identified, they are frequently descriptive statements only, presenting empirical regularities but no insights into the mechanisms that produce them. Thus realists prefer to focus on uncovering causal connection laws rather than describing unaccounted-for regularities.   RJJ

Reference

Chouinard, V., Fincher, R. and Webber, M. 1984: Empirical research in scientific human geography. *Progr. hum. Geogr.* 8, pp. 347–80.

Suggested Reading

Golledge, R. G. and Amedeo, D. W. 1968: On laws in geography. *Ann. Ass. Am. Geogr.* 58, pp. 560–74.

Harvey, D. 1969: *Explanation in geography.* London: Edward Arnold.

Sayer, A. 1992: *Method in social science: a realist approach*, second edition. London: Routledge.

law, geography of It is difficult to provide a neat definition of the geography of law. This is due to the diverse approaches to both geography and law – and their interrelation – that have been adopted at different times, and to the somewhat indistinct analytical focus of recent scholarship. Any working definition would have to encompass such concerns as the analysis of the spatial variability of law, the link between the LOCALITY and legal interpretation, the effects of legal DECISION-MAKING on spatial configurations, and the spatial representations contained within legal discourse, amongst others.

Recent years have seen a heightened interest in the exploration of the law–geography link. Such an interest should not be seen as unprecedented, given a lengthy engagement with legal–geographical questions. Previous research can be broadly divided according to emphasis. An older body of writing, concerned with mapping the regional diversity of law, tends towards an account of the geographical environment as a vital structuring agent of law. Another, more recent, literature, inverts the relation, and explores the manner in which law affects space. More recently, a 'critical' perspective on law and space has sought to transcend the unilinear causality of both schools by an exploration of the complex interrelations of the legal, the spatial and the social.

Although an interest in the REGIONAL GEOGRAPHY of law can be traced as far back as the sixteenth-century writings of Jean Bodin, or the eighteenth-century treatise of Montesquieu, perhaps the first academic treatment was given by John Wigmore who, alerted to the geographical diversity of legal systems by a detailed study of Japanese law, produced a three-volume geographical survey of the world's legal systems (Wigmore, 1928, 1929). Exploring the relation between law and geography in broad, descriptive terms, he suggested that 'the influence of geography has operated in two ways – immediately, through natural features, and mediately, through race and race traits' (Wigmore, 1929, p. 115). Along with Albert Kocourek, Wigmore co-edited a three-volume set on legal evolution, one volume of which included papers by sociologists and geographers. These vary to the extent that 'race' and the natural environment are assumed to determine spatial variations in law. The geographer Ellen Semple, for example, describes the evolution of the 'land-bond' (defined, broadly, in terms of property relations) that she sees as characteristic of diverse human societies. Evoking naturalistic analogies, she refers to the 'fibres of the land which become woven into the whole fabric of the nation's life. These are the geographic elements constituting the soil in which empires are rooted; they arise in the sap of the nation' (Semple, 1918, p. 223).

Although the ENVIRONMENTAL DETER-MINISM of these accounts might seem somewhat dated, one recent legal exploration of geography and law notes that 'geography is fate . . . not only for a country but also its culture and law' (Grossfeld, 1984, pp. 1512–13).

In an influential paper, Derwent Whittlesey (1935) inverted the law–environment relation by attending to the 'impress of effective central authority upon the landscape'. Although noting that environmental forces may be important, the thrust of his account is clear: 'phenomena engendered by political forces should have a recognized place as elements in the geographic structure of every region' (Whittlesey, 1935, p. 97). Importantly, several laws resulting in 'landscape modification' are identified, including tariffs, property and resource law. As Clark (1989a) notes, a similar 'spatial impact' emphasis best characterizes many recent geographical analyses of law. These accounts, in tracking the effect that a given law or ruling has on a SPATIAL STRUCTURE, such as a housing market, are generally applied, pragmatic and non-theoretical, sharing common ground with the orthodox policy-analysis literature. Typical of this literature, for example, is Briggs's (1980) assessment of the impact of federal public transit assistance on travel behaviour in US cities.

Although both regional and impact analyses offer some useful insights, they have been criticized on a number of grounds (Blomley, 1989b; Clark, 1989a). Most important, perhaps, is the assertion that both perspectives, although with different emphases, assume an analytical separation of law, space and society. The impact analysis literature tends to regard law as acting upon a passive spatial structure, on the assumption that there are two realms – one legal, the other spatial. Similarly, there is a tendency within the regional literature to root law in certain immutable and often naturalized forces. Again, an implicit divide is made between social life and certain non-conditional and asocial legal principles. This is problematic on several counts. For example, the location of law either in an asocial

and aspatial realm, as implied by the impact literature, presents a picture of law as in a higher, 'closed' sphere, beyond the world of local struggle and politics. Not only can this be questioned on certain theoretical grounds (where, for example, is this uniquely legal realm?), but also in political terms. Similarly, the submergence of law beneath the suffocating effects of the geographical environment implies legal immutability and naturalness.

Both impact and regional analyses make implicit assumptions of the determinacy of legal meaning. An extensive poststructuralist literature has emerged to question this claim, arguing that legal meaning is deeply ambiguous, and that legal interpretation must be understood as situated, occurring with reference to certain implicit assumptions concerning social and political life (Hutchinson, 1988; Clark, 1989b: see CONTEXTUAL THEORY; POSTSTRUCTURALISM). The categories and vocabulary of liberalism are often assumed to be important in this regard. Finally, the legal-geographical orthodoxy has been challenged in terms of its account of the effects of law itself. Law, it is noted, is often understood exclusively as a restrictive and instrumental code. However, such a reading underplays the other dimensions of law, including its power to define or constitute the terms of social life, or to empower certain groups. On this account, law is not simply an external imperative, but is in important senses *constitutive* of social and political life (Griffiths, 1979).

It is in response to these sorts of assertions that we can understand the rise of what might be termed a *critical legal geography* over the past decade. Influenced by debates within geographical, social and legal theory, this perspective has a very different reading of law, space and their mutual relation, with a scepticism of existing legal structures and the social relations that they embody. The distinguishing feature of this perspective is its refusal to accept either law or space as pre-political, or as the unproblematic outcome of external forces. Both are regarded as deeply social and political. Law is seen both as a site at which competing values and meanings are fought over, and also as the means by which certain meanings become fixed and naturalized. Similarly, space is regarded as both socially produced and as socially constitutive, with attention being directed to the 'politics' of space (see SPATIALITY). The relation between law, space and society is redefined and extended in important ways, opening up many new areas to critical geographical enquiry. To date, certain areas have received some study, including the following:

(a) The analysis of the manner in which legal interpretation produces space (see PRODUCTION OF SPACE). This departs from 'impact analyses' by virtue of its attention to such matters as the complexities of interpretation and the local context of legal interpretation. The role of the legal apparatus – especially the judiciary – is given prominence, it being noted that court decisions have profound (and often problematic) effects within local settings in both material and discursive terms, given the manner in which legal categories and discourse can come to frame local debates (see STATE APPARATUS). Examples include Clark's (1991) discussion of legal decision-making in redistricting disputes in Los Angeles, and the work of both Johnston (1984) and Clark (1985) on the role of the US judiciary in local disputes relating to housing, labour and planning.

(b) The study of the situated nature of legal interpretation, it being noted that legal practice is often bound up in the LOCALE in which it occurs. For example, a study of the enforcement of retail regulatory law in England (Blomley, 1989a) reveals a surprising degree of local knowledge amongst enforcement authorities, with interpretation being structured according to local political imperatives and a historically acquired local 'common sense' based on a delicate set of local negotiations between LOCAL STATE and local retail capital. Such local knowledge is fragile, however, and subject to review by other legal agencies, including higher courts (cf. Lake and Johns, 1990). The study of such local legal cultures has a related political implication. If it is accepted that interpretation – including legal interpretation – is necessarily structured by the diverse spatial and temporal settings of social life, then

formal legal interpretation, with its claims concerning the autonomy of the individual legal subject and the balance between universal and particularized legal knowledge, implies an untenuous rejection of the situated contextuality of law. Diverse and contingent legal understandings are presented as 'Law'; a form of higher truth, removed from the vagaries and political conflicts of 'real life'. Wesley Pue (1990), in a trenchant critique of the relation between legal discourse and the multiple geographies of social life, argues that law is in this sense 'anti-geographical', to the extent that legal relations are frequently understood within law as existing in a purely conceptual space divorced from the heterogeneity and contextuality of local legal understandings. It follows that an assertion of the spatiality of legal knowledge constitutes, at least implicitly, a powerful critique of certain widely held legal beliefs and concepts of legal 'closure' (Clark, 1989a; Blomley, 1992).

(c) The study of the geographical claims and representations contained within legal discourse, it being noted that in much the way that law relies on claims concerning history and time, so it both defines and draws upon a complex range of geographies and spatial understandings. While struggling to make sense of the complexity and ambiguity of social life, legal agents – whether judges, legal theorists, administrative officers or ordinary people – represent and evaluate space in various ways. These juridical representations touch all aspects of legal life, including property, contractual relations, crime and intergovernmental law. The construction of such spaces can be seen, for example, when legal actors designate boundaries between 'public' and 'private' spaces (see PRIVATE AND PUBLIC SPHERES); make decisions concerning the local autonomy of governmental units; consider questions of personal mobility or spatial equality; and explore CITIZENSHIP or SOVEREIGNTY (Engel, 1990; Blomley, 1992).

(d) The politics of the law–space relation. Recent scholarship has maintained that both law and space – in their strategic use and representation – are deeply political. Rather than being simply 'pre-political' and 'natural', they are both constituted by, and constitutive of, political struggles. A study of their conjunction, then, is revealing. Santos (1987) notes, for example, that the spatial SCALE at which law is analysed – local, national and supranational – is not 'innocent', but has profound implications for social life. Other writers have similarly explored the 'geo-politics' of law in terms of: local working-class opposition and the delivery of legal services (Chouinard, 1989); a critique of legal closure (Kobayashi, 1990); with reference to worker safety (Blomley, 1990); and the regulation of US labour unions (Clark, 1990).

However useful these insights may be, recent scholarship on law and geography is still in an undeveloped state. Several issues need to be addressed. First, a deeper engagement with legal theory is needed. As noted by Bakan and Blomley (1992), intriguing parallels exist between critical writings in both law and geography. To date, however, little exchange has occurred between the two fields. Second, many potential areas of geographical enquiry remain unexplored. These include a detailed account of local legal cultures and a consideration of the importance of space within legal discourse. Third, attention needs to be given to the 'geographies of liberalism', including the legal representation of citizenship, property or public and private spaces. Fourth, the connections to other branches of the discipline need to be clarified, such as the geography of crime and policing, and political geography in general (cf. Fyfe, 1991: see also CRIME, GEOGRAPHY OF; LAW OF THE SEA; POLICING, GEOGRAPHY OF; POLITICAL GEOGRAPHY). Finally, the 'critical' aspects of this enquiry need to be explicated. It might be suggested that they are considerable, given an implicit attention to legal critique and the politics of law (Blomley, 1993). (See also CRITICAL THEORY.)   NB

References

Bakan, J. C. and Blomley, N. K. 1992: Spatial boundaries, legal categories and the judicial mapping of the worker. *Environ. Plann. A* 24, pp. 629–44.

Blomley, N. K. 1989a: Interpretive practices, the state and the locale. In Wolch, J. and Dear, M.,

eds, *The power of geography*. Boston: Unwin Hyman, pp. 175–96.

Blomley, N. K. 1989b: Text and context: rethinking the law–geography nexus. *Progr. hum. Geogr.* 13, pp. 512–34.

Blomley, N. K. 1990: Federalism, law and the regulation of worker safety. *Econ. Geogr.* 66, pp. 22–46.

Blomley, N. K. 1992: The business of mobility. *Can. Geogr.* 26.

Blomley, N. K. 1993: *Law, space and power: the geographies of liberalism.* New York: Guilford Press.

Briggs, R. 1980: The impact of federal local public transportation assistance upon travel behavior. *Prof. Geogr.* 36, pp. 316–25.

Chouinard, V. 1989: Transformations in the capitalist state: the development of legal aid clinics in Canada. *Trans. Inst. Br. Geogr.* n.s. 14, pp. 329–49.

Clark, G. L. 1985: *Judges and the cities: interpreting local autonomy.* Chicago: University of Chicago Press.

Clark, G. L. 1989a: The geography of law. In Peet, R. and Thrift, N., eds, *New models in geography* volume 1. London: Unwin Hyman, pp. 310–37.

Clark, G. L. 1989b: Law and the interpretive turn in the social sciences. *Urban Geogr.* 10, pp. 209–28.

Clark, G. L. 1990: The virtues of location: do property rights 'trump' workers' rights to self organization? *Environ. Plann. D: Society and Space* 8, pp. 53–72.

Clark, W. A. V. 1991: Geography in court: expertise in adversarial settings. *Trans. Inst. Br. Geogr.* n.s. 16, pp. 5–20.

Engel, D. M. 1990: Litigation across space and time: courts, conflict, and social change. *Law and Society Review*, 24, pp. 333–44.

Fyfe, N. R. 1991: The police, space and society: the geography of policing. *Progr. hum. Geogr.* 15, pp. 249–67.

Griffiths, J. 1979: Is law important? *New York University Law Review* 54, pp. 339–74.

Grossfeld, B. 1984: Geography and law. *Michigan Law Review* 82, pp. 1510–19.

Hutchinson, A. 1988: *Dwelling on the threshold: critical essays on modern legal thought.* Toronto: Carswell.

Johnston, R. J. 1984: *Residential segregation, the state and constitutional conflict in American urban areas.* London: Academic Press.

Kobayashi, A. 1990: Racism and the law in Canada: a geographical perspective. *Urban Geogr.* 11, pp. 447–73.

Lake, R. W. and Johns, R. A. 1990: Legitimation conflicts: the politics of hazardous waste siting law. *Urban Geogr.* 11(5), pp. 488–508.

Pue, W. W. 1990: Wrestling with law: (geographical) specificity vs. (legal) abstraction. *Urban Geogr.* 11, pp. 566–85.

Santos, B. 1987: Law: a map of misreading: toward a postmodern conception of law. *J. Law Soc.* 14, pp. 279–302.

Semple, E. C. 1918: The influences of geographic environment on law, state and society. In Kocourek, A. and Wigmore, J. H. eds, *Formative influences of legal development*. Boston: Little, Brown, pp. 215–33.

Whittlesey, D. 1935: The impress of central authority upon the landscape. *Ann. Ass. Am. Geogr.* 25, pp. 85–97.

Wigmore, J. H. 1928: *A panorama of the world's legal systems* (three volumes). St Paul, MN: West Publishing Company.

Wigmore, J. H. 1929: A map of the world's law. *Geogr. Rev.* 19, pp. 114–20.

Suggested Reading

Blacksell, M. C., Economides, K. and Watkins, C. 1991: *Justice outside the city: access to legal services in rural areas*. London: Longman.

Blacksell, M., Watkins, C., and Economides, K. 1986: Human geography and law: a case of separate development in social science. *Progr. hum. Geogr.* 10, pp. 371–96.

Blomley, N. K. and Clark, G. L. 1990: Law, theory and geography. *Urban Geogr.* 11, pp. 433–46.

Emel, J. 1990: Resource instrumentalism, privatization and commodification. *Urban Geogr.* 11, pp. 527–47.

Frug, G. 1980: The city as a legal concept. *Harvard Law Review* 93, pp. 1059–154.

Harries, K. D. and Brunn, S. D. 1978: *The geography of laws and justice: spatial perspectives on the criminal justice system*. New York: Praeger.

Hunt, A. 1990: The Big Fear: law confronts postmodernism. *McGill Law Journal* 35, pp. 507–40.

law of the sea Prior to 1958 most of the law of the sea derived from customary law, but subsequently three United Nations Conferences on the Law of the Sea have resulted in a series of conventions which have had some success in bringing the oceans within a single body of international law. The most recent is UNCLOS III, agreed on 17 December 1982 at Montego Bay, Jamaica, and signed by the majority of maritime states. Although it has still not formally come into force, its provisions are now being implemented by most countries.

The convention defines seven maritime jurisdictional zones (see the figure):

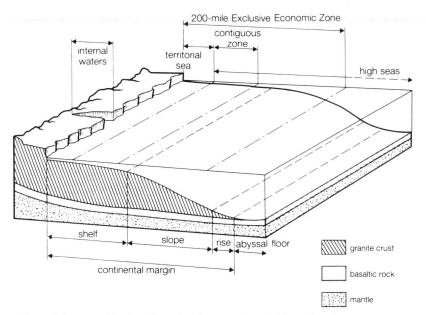

law of the sea *The three-dimensional nature of sea divisions* (after Couper, 1978).

(a) *Internal waters:* all waters landward of the baseline from which the territorial sea is measured, such as rivers, lakes, bays, ports and any waters landward of the low-tide line.

(b) *The* TERRITORIAL SEA: STATES exercise total SOVEREIGNTY over these waters, except for rights of innocent passage. They extend out to sea for 12 nautical miles from the baseline, unless this impinges on the territorial seas of a neighbouring state, when a compromise has to be agreed.

(c) *The* CONTIGUOUS ZONE: an area 12 nautical miles beyond the limit of the territorial sea, within which states are free to apply customs and other national regulations.

(d) *The* CONTINENTAL SHELF: an area extending 200 nautical miles from the baseline, within which states may claim virtually exclusive rights to the seabed resources.

(e) *Fishing:* most states now claim and exercise exclusive fishing rights up to 200 nautical miles out to sea from their coasts.

(f) *Exclusive economic zone:* synonymous with the redefined continental shelf described in (d) above.

(g) *The high seas:* these include all waters other than those defined in (a)–(f) above, and there is complete freedom of movement within them. However, proposals are still under negotiation for the exploitation of seabed resources to be subject to UN control – a controversial proposal for many states.

Finally, all habitable islands are subject to the same regulations as coastal states, but it is not permissible to claim an Exclusive Economic Zone around small, uninhabitable rocks.   MB

Reference

Couper, A. 1978: *Geography and law of the sea.* London: Macmillan.

Suggested Reading

Couper, A. 1983: *The Times atlas of the ocean.* London: Times Books/New York: Van Nostrand Reinhold.

Glassner, M. I. 1990: *Neptune's domain.* London: Unwin Hyman.

layers of investment The successive cycles of economic DEVELOPMENT of particular PLACES or REGIONS. The concept was first developed by Doreen Massey (1978) as a way of characterizing the changing SPATIAL STRUCTURE of the economy.

According to Massey (1984) 'the structure of local economies can be seen as a product of the combination of "layers", of the successive imposition over the years of new rounds of investment, new forms of activity'. With each successive round of investment, the local economy acquires a particular place in a wider spatial DIVISION OF LABOUR: 'if a local economy can be analysed as the historical product of the combination of layers of activity, those layers also represent in turn the succession of roles the local economy has played within wider national and international spatial structures'. Gregory (1989) has represented this process as a game of cards, in which regions are dealt different cards as a result of the operation of successive rounds of investment to make up a complete, and unique, 'hand' (see the figure).

However, Massey does not see this sort of analysis as an exercise in structural determinism. Rather, the existing character of the area interacts with the new 'layer' in a process of 'mutual determination':

the internal necessity of a spatial structure does not get 'acted out' in the real world in pure form. What takes place is the interrelation of the new spatial structure with the accumulated results of the old. The 'combination' of layers, in other words, really does mean combination, with each side of the process affecting the other (Massey, 1984, p. 121).

In seeking to relate the operation of processes of capital ACCUMULATION to the evident AREAL DIFFERENTIATION of the SPACE-ECONOMY, this approach to INDUSTRIAL GEOGRAPHY was an explicit challenge to conventional LOCATION THEORY. Regional change is seen as part and parcel of wider processes of economic restructuring, but also the character of each region and LOCALITY is seen as stamping its own imprint on those processes.

layers of investment *Phases of capital accumulation – translated into a game of cards* (Gregory, 1989).

Massey exemplifies her arguments by discussing the impact of new branch-plant investment on the coalfield areas of Britain. The decline of coal, steel and heavy engineering began to break down the existing social structures in these areas. The new factories provided new jobs in areas of high unemployment, but their branch-plant status made the security of employment questionable. Of particular significance was the recruitment of women to work in the factories, often for relatively low wages. The largely male-dominated character of the labour movement in these areas ensured that the new female workforces had little experience of trade union militancy. These sorts of changes often involved quite deliberate spatial strategies within as well as between regions on the part of firms – as Morgan and Sayer (1985) have shown. (See also SUBURB.)

The causes of new phases of investment have been the subject of some debate. For Harvey (1985) they are a response to successive crises (see CRISIS) in the process of capital accumulation: a product of the 'spatial fix' through which the built-up contradictions of the previous phase of capitalist development are temporarily resolved. Marshall (1987) suggests that they are the result of KONDRATIEFF CYCLES, with each long wave producing a new pattern of UNEVEN DEVELOPMENT.

Massey's concept has acted as a stimulus both to a wide range of empirical work in INDUSTRIAL GEOGRAPHY and beyond and to considerable debate about the appropriate ways of conceptualizing regional and urban change. (See Environment and Planning A (1989) for examples.) JP

References

Environment and Planning A 1989: Spatial Divisions of Labour in practice. Environ. Plann. A 21, pp. 655–700.

Gregory, D. 1989: Areal differentiation and post-modern human geography. In Gregory, D. and Walford, R., eds, Horizons in human geography. London: Macmillan, pp. 67–96.

Harvey, D. 1985: The geopolitics of capitalism. In Gregory, D. and Urry, J., eds, Social relations and spatial structures. London: Macmillan, pp. 128–63.

Marshall, M. 1987: Long waves of regional development. London: Macmillan.

Massey, D. 1978: Regionalism: some current issues. Capital and Class 6, pp. 106–25.

Massey, D. 1984: Spatial divisions of labour. London: Macmillan.

Morgan, K. and Sayer, A. 1985: A 'modern' industry in a mature region: the remaking of management–labour relations. Int. J. urban and reg. Res. 9, pp. 383–403.

Suggested Reading

Environmental Planning A (1989).

Gregory, D. (1989), pp. 75–6.

Massey (1984).

Massey, D. 1988: Uneven development: social change and spatial divisions of labour. In Massey, D. and Allen, J., eds, Uneven redevelopment: cities and regions in transition. London: Hodder and Stoughton, pp. 250–76.

Warde, A. 1985: Spatial change, politics and the division of labour. In Gregory, D. and Urry, J., eds, Social relations and spatial structures. London: Macmillan, pp. 190–212.

le Play Society A society founded in England in 1930 to promote FIELDWORK and regional survey in sociology and geography. It was named after a nineteenth-century engineer, Frederic le Play, who published accounts of the places that he visited (e.g. Les ouvriers européens, 1855) and who developed a schema (with strong overtones of ENVIRONMENTAL DETERMINISM) of place–work–family to encapsulate the major features of local societies: his ideas were taken up and promoted by Sir Patrick Geddes. The Society was disbanded in 1960, having organized 71 major field surveys and published eight major monographs during its existence. RJJ

Suggested Reading

Beaver, S. H. 1962: The le Play Society and fieldwork. Geogr. 40, pp. 225–40.

Herbertson, D. 1950: The life of Frederic le Play. Ledbury, UK: le Play House Press.

lead–lag models Statistical models for identifying timing differences ('leads' and 'lags') in the transmission of fluctuations through urban and regional systems. These models have been widely used for studies of REGIONAL CYCLES of economic activity and for studies of the spatial DIFFUSION of epidemics such as influenza or measles. Three types of timing differences can be studied: (a) leads/lags between different variables within a region; (b) lead/lags between regions or cities; (c) lead/lags between a regional series and the national aggregate series. The models require detailed time-series data for the variables and regions, e.g. unemployment data by month or quarter for Canadian cities.

The lead–lag structure can be identified using lagged CORRELATION (sometimes called cross-correlation). To find the lead–lag between employment cycles in two regions X and Y, the time series for region X is first correlated with that for region Y to give the usual correlation coefficient r. This is then repeated, but with the Y series lagged by one period, i.e. X_t is related to Y_{t-1} for $t = 2,3,\ldots,T$ to give r_{-1}. This is done for several lags, generating r_{-2}, r_{-3}, etc., and then for Y_t related to X lagged by several periods to give r_{+1}, r_{+2}, r_{+3}, etc. The set of cross-correlations r_{+k} to r_{-k}, is then examined to find the highest correlation, so identifying the lead–lag. It is sometimes appropriate then to use such a lead–lag in a lagged REGRESSION model, e.g. when examining local fluctuations to national economic cycles. Here Y_t might be local unemployment, and X_t the national unemployment series. If k is the best-fit lag, the regression has the form:

$$Y_t = bX_{t-k} + e_t$$

and b measures the cyclical sensitivity of the local economy. It is increasingly recognized, however, that such responses are gradual or distributed, and that accurate modelling requires the incorporation of several lags in the form of a 'distributed lag model'. SPECTRAL ANALYSIS is also used to examine lead–lags between regions for different types of cycles.

A drawback of lead–lag models is that, like most statistical models, they assume that the relationship is constant across the whole time period under study, e.g. over 12 years and four economic cycles. But each cycle may have very different origins and causes, generating different patterns of leads and lags: downturns may have different timings across space to those of the subsequent upturns, and so it is important to also examine changing relationships, either graphically or by time-varying parameter models.   LWH

Suggested Reading
Cliff, A. D., Haggett, P. and Ord, J. K. 1985: *Spatial aspects of influenza epidemics*. London: Pion.

Lebensraum Literally 'living space' or 'the geographical area within which living organisms develop'. In his book on POLITICAL GEOGRAPHY, Ratzel equated a nation with a living organism, and argued that a country's search for territorial expansion was similar to a growing organism's search for space (see HOLISM): CONFLICT between nations was thus seen as a contest for TERRITORY within which to expand, with the fittest surviving. The concept was appropriated by the German school of *GEOPOLITIK* in the 1920s and 1930s and used to justify the Nazi programme of territorial expansion. (See also ANTHROPOGEOGRAPHY.)   RJJ

Suggested Reading
Dickinson, R. E. 1943: *The German Lebensraum*. London: Penguin.

Parker, G. 1985: *The development of Western geopolitical thought in the twentieth century*. London: Croom Helm.

leisure, geography of The activity patterns of people during their non-working hours, studied over space and time. Leisure is a general term embracing all free time from work and other obligations; much of this time is occupied by RECREATION, which can include anything from active participation in SPORT to watching television or social drinking. There has recently been a marked increase in the amount of leisure time available to most people living in advanced industrial societies, producing important changes in patterns of social and economic activity.

The increase in the amount of leisure time enjoyed by the majority of the population results from a combination of factors. The early twentieth century saw a marked shortening of the working week in most industrial countries. The present average in the UK is 44 hours, which leaves a considerable amount of time free for things other than routine activities. More important in the past two decades has been the reorganization of work time, rather than any absolute reduction in hours of employment. Almost everyone in the UK who has a job can now expect at least three weeks' holiday on full pay each year and a five-day week, thus providing regular blocks of time free for new activities. In many countries the general ageing of the population has led to a growing number of retired, but still active, people who are eager to find activities to fill their new-found leisure time. At the other end of the demographic spectrum, the progressive raising of the school leaving age and the growing participation in higher education have delayed entry into the workforce for many more young people. For most people, increased leisure time has been accompanied by greater affluence in real terms, thus removing many of the financial barriers to participation in recreational pursuits. Technology has also played a part: developments in transportation, especially widespread car ownership and cheap air travel, have dramatically improved levels of personal mobility; while innovations such as washing machines in the home have removed much of the drudgery from household chores, leaving people free to do other things.

The increase in leisure time and the new activities that it has engendered have stimulated whole new areas of economic activity. In both the developed and the developing worlds, TOURISM is now a major element in the foreign currency earnings of many countries; while in industrialized societies expenditure on leisure activities accounts for a substantial proportion of overall domestic economic activity (Kirby, 1985). In the UK, for example, expenditure on leisure goods and leisure services accounts for over 13 per cent of total household expenditure (Central Statistical Office, 1991).

Geographical studies of leisure have tended to be subsumed into more specific research on topics such as RECREATION, SPORT and TOURISM, although there are some notable exceptions, looking at the changes in leisure lifestyles (Glyptis, 1981) and the impact of these changes on patterns of land use, particularly in rural areas (Patmore, 1983).   MB

References

Central Statistical Office 1991: *Family spending: A report on the 1990 Family Expenditure Survey.* London: HMSO.

Glyptis, S. 1981: Leisure life-styles. *Reg. Stud.* 15, pp. 311–26.

Kirby, A. M. 1985: Leisure as commodity. *Progr. hum. Geogr.* 9, pp. 64–84.

Patmore, J. A. 1983: *Recreation and resources. Leisure patterns and leisure places.* Oxford: Blackwell.

Suggested Reading

Owens, P. L. 1984: Rural leisure and recreation research: a retrospective evaluation. *Progr. hum. Geogr.* 8, pp. 157–88.

Patmore (1983).

Wearing, B. and Wearing, S. 1988: All in a day's leisure: gender and the concept of leisure. *Leisure Studies* 7, pp. 111-23.

life-cycle The process of growth, adulthood and old age which human beings experience, each stage being associated with various forms of social, economic and political behaviour. The idea of stage in the life-cycle has been much used in FACTORIAL ECOLOGIES of urban areas. Crucial stages in the life-cycle include first marriage, a pre-child stage, birth and rearing of children, a post-child stage, and finally family dissolution with the death of one spouse. These stages affect mobility, income, demand for housing and recreational activities, among other things. The life-cycle is reflected in the AGE AND SEX STRUCTURE of particular areas.   PEO

Suggested Reading

Bongaarts, J., Burch, T. K. and Wachter, K. W. 1987: *Family demography: methods and their application.* Oxford: Clarendon Press.

life expectancy The average number of years to be lived, generally derived from the LIFE TABLE calculations, either from birth or from a particular age (usually denoted as e_x where x is age). *Life expectancy at birth*, e_0, is frequently used as a summary measure of MORTALITY for the whole population. Life expectancy at birth is usually less than after the first year because of infant mortality, but thereafter the decline is generally steady. Life expectancy has improved dramatically in most countries over the past few decades: in the USA, e_0 for the population as a whole was around 75 years in 1989; and in Europe e_0 for males was in the lower seventies, for females well into the seventies or early eighties; for example, in Sweden, 80.6 years for females and 74.8 years for males in 1989.   PEO

Suggested Reading
Woods, R. I. 1979: *Population analysis in geography.* London: Longman, ch. 3.

life table A table showing what the probability is of surviving from any age to any subsequent age, according to the age-specific death rates prevailing at a particular time and place. It may be assumed for the purposes of calculation that 100 000 babies are all born on the same day, and the experience of this COHORT is followed until its last surviving member dies: the summary is the life table. Life tables were first compiled for actuarial purposes in order to calculate for each age group the possibility of dying, the number of deaths, the number of survivors, and the average LIFE EXPECTANCY of the latter, as a basis for life assurance premiums. They may also be used as structural models for studying population growth (see STABLE POPULATION) and projections (see POPULATION PROJECTION) and as a summary of mortality experiences in different countries or regions.   PEO

Suggested Reading
Pressat, R. 1972: *Demographic analysis.* London: Edward Arnold/Chicago: Aldine, ch. 6.
Woods, R. I. 1979: *Population analysis in geography.* London: Longman, ch. 3.

lifeworld 'The culturally defined spatio-temporal setting or horizon of everyday life' (Buttimer, 1976); in other words, the totality of a person's direct involvement with the PLACES and environments experienced in ordinary life.

The term originates in German PHENOMENOLOGY as *Lebenswelt*, which signifies a relationship of *intentionality* between a conscious and imaginative human subject and the external world as it is naively given to our attention. It is in the lifeworld that meaning is given to external phenomena

through our intuitive experiences and relationships with them. Phenomenological philosophies give attention to the apparently trivial phenomena of the lifeworld – my bodily existence, my being in this place, my home – which are taken as presuppositions in positive science (see POSITIVISM) but left largely unexamined in its analyses. Close attention to such phenomena, freed as far as possible from *a priori* assumptions, as they are constituted in consciousness, gives access to truths about them and about ourselves. Thus the lifeworld is fundamental to much HUMANISTIC GEOGRAPHY concerned to understand places and environments without analytical separation of subject and object. From this perspective, places, environments and COMMUNITIES become 'regions of care'.

In geography the concept of lifeworld has directed attention to the significance of everyday life and the personal, meaningful geographies developed and practised within it (see TAKEN-FOR-GRANTED WORLD). The concept implicitly criticizes more distant, analytical and manipulative approaches to spatial behaviour and organization. Thus, from the person-centred perspective of the lifeworld, place becomes more important than SPACE, and geographical investigation is required to honour the experiences, imagination and attachments of intentional human subjects.   DEC

Reference
Buttimer, A. 1976: Grasping the dynamism of the lifeworld. *Ann. Ass. Am. Geogr.* 66, pp. 277-92.

Suggested Reading
Eyles, J. 1985: *Senses of place.* Warrington, UK: Silverbrook Press.
Seamon, D. 1979: *A geography of the lifeworld: movement, rest and encounter.* London: Croom Helm/New York: St. Martin's Press.

limits to growth A phrase that gained currency as the title of a report issued in 1972 by the Club of Rome on global resource and POLLUTION trends (Meadows et al., 1972). The classic work in the broader history of thought on limits to growth remains Thomas Robert Malthus's *Essay on the principle of population,* first published in 1798, which depicted food supply as a fundamental check to demographic and economic growth; the modern neo-Malthusianism represented by the Club of Rome report has extended the argument to other NATURAL RESOURCES and to the Earth's capacity to absorb POLLUTION. *The limits to growth* reported the results of computer modelling of the world system carried out by the authors and by Jay Forrester (1971) of MIT. Extrapolating the interactions of global trends into the future, they asserted the likelihood of an overshoot of the Earth's resource capacity and a consequent collapse of population and economy. They argued from their findings for immediate attempts to achieve a global-scale equilibrium between human demands and environmental resources, focusing on the stabilization of population and of per capita consumption levels.

The limits to growth was widely discussed upon publication. Telling criticisms were quickly made, both of its methods and of its disregard for processes such as innovation and substitution as responses to resource scarcity (e.g., Cole et al., 1973; see GLOBAL FUTURES). From a different angle, the notions of physically defined limits to growth and of overpopulation were criticized as ideological constructs that diverted attention from questions of CLASS and distribution (Harvey, 1974). The limits to growth concept has retained its currency in some circles (e.g., Daly, 1977; Ehrlich and Holdren, 1988). That eventual physical limits to population and economic expansion do exist is hardly contested, but the limits to growth concept in its original form has not appeared to most researchers to be the most promising framework within which to investigate environmental problems. That the concept has been widely influential outside academia is, in any case, questionable, and Buttel et al. (1990) claim that '[t]he only lasting residue of the limits to growth notion in contemporary politics is its localization in the form of NIMBY movements and local growth control politics that are often motivated as much by the preservation of life-styles and property values as by environmental or health concerns'.   JEm

References

Buttel, F. H., Hawkins, A. P. and Power, A. G. 1990: From limits to growth to global change: constraints and contradictions in the evolution of environmental science and ideology. *Global Environmental Change* 1, pp. 57–66.

Cole, H. S. D., Freeman, C., Jahoda, M. and Pavitt, K. eds 1973: *Thinking about the future: a critique of* The limits to growth. London: Chatto and Windus.

Daly, H. 1977: *Steady-state economics: the economics of biophysical equilibrium and moral growth*. San Francisco, CA: W. H. Freeman.

Ehrlich, P. R. and Holdren, J. P., eds 1988: *The Cassandra conference*. College Station, TX: Texas A&M University Press.

Forrester, J. W. 1971: *World dynamics*. Cambridge, MA: Wright-Allen.

Harvey, D. 1974: Population, resources, and the ideology of science. *Econ. Geogr.* 50, 256–71.

Meadows, D. H., Meadows, D. L., Randers, J. and Behrens, W. W. III 1972: *The limits to growth*. New York: Universe Books.

linear programming   A mathematical tool for seeking optimal solutions to allocation problems. It was devised to identify optimal configurations for whole SYSTEMS in terms of an objective function (i.e. a quantity to be maximized or minimized), subject to constraints. The methods of solution, except in the simplest cases, are iterative: in other words, they converge upon an optimal solution by a series of adjustments to an initial feasible solution.

The first step in any linear programming study is the statement of the *objective function*. In economic studies this is usually stated in monetary terms – maximization of revenues or minimization of costs – but the same approach may be used to optimize other quantities; for example, the minimum aggregate distance travelled by pupils to secondary schools, the minimum average distance of fire stations from potential sites of fires, or the maximum food output from a farming enterprise.

The second step is to establish the *constraints* upon the system. These may be equalities, such as that the number of pupils in each school district shall equal the number of school places, or inequalities, such as that the number of school pupils shall be less than or equal to the

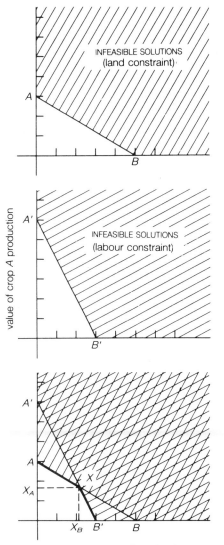

value of crop *B* production

linear programming *The graphical solution to a simple linear programming problem, showing the effect of constraints, the convex set of feasible solutions lying within the convex hull AXB' and the optimal solution at X.*

number of places. A requirement of the method is that the production functions shall be linear; for example, that the aggregate travel for school pupils is an additive linear function of distances travelled and numbers of pupils.

The simplest linear programming problems may be solved graphically. Consider,

for example, a farmer who wishes to maximize the cash output from two crops (the objective function) subject to the two constraints of the land and labour available. The various possible combinations of the two crops can be plotted in graph form (see the figure). In the upper graph, the proportions of land allocated to the two crops range from monoculture (crop *A*) through various mixes to monoculture (crop *B*). The constraint on land available means that any solution above and to the right of the line in the diagram is not feasible, whereas any solution to the left and below the line uses less than all the available land. The middle graph shows the possible proportional allocations of labour in the same way: once again, infeasible solutions are identified, as also are those which fail to use all the labour available. The superimposition of the two graphs (bottom) reveals that some solutions are infeasible because of labour constraints, some because of land constraints and some for both reasons (double shading). It can be shown that the maximum feasible cash yield will be achieved by producing the combination X (X_A of crop *A* and X_B of crop *B*). The line AXB' is known as the 'convex hull' and the unshaded area lying below it is known as the 'convex set'. Because there are two constraints the hull has only two sides (AX and XB'), and because the example involves only two crops the hull can be plotted in two-dimensional space. More complex problems will have more sides to the hull, which will then lie in multidimensional space. For this reason most problems in linear programming cannot be solved graphically, and use the more general simplex algorithm or attempt to recast the problem as a TRANSPORTATION PROBLEM.

The solution to the farmer's problem illustrates the concept of *shadow prices*. Once the solution has been identified the farmer might (for reasons other than optimization) reduce production of crop *A*, but there will be an OPPORTUNITY COST in so doing. Most linear programming solutions identify the opportunity costs of sub-optimal behaviour – a concept which is closely related to the idea of economic RENT being an opportunity cost. Finally, it may be noted that all linear programming problems have an alternative formulation: in cases in which the main (primal) problem is to maximize, there will be a *dual problem* to minimize a mathematical expression (which may or may not have a physical interpretation). The dual has two features of importance: first, many problems which are difficult to solve in their primal form prove more tractable in dual form; and, second, in some cases the dual problem has a geographically interesting interpretation (for example, the least transport cost solution to a VON THÜNEN agricultural location problem is also that which maximizes location rent).

Although originally designed for use in management problems, linear programming has proved capable of application to a wide range of problems (if the linearity condition can be met), including the planning of agriculture, transport, industrial plant and warehouse location, the delimitation of school districts and the location of medical facilities: it has been used in such contexts by applied geographers. Other geographers have used the technique either as a quasi-explanatory model or as a normative model to test the efficiency of geographical patterns. They have seldom found close matches: it seems that the constraints and objective functions used by decision-makers are too complex to be adequately modelled in this way.

Shortcomings of the approach have stimulated the development of other forms of programming (non-linear programming, recursive programming etc.), but these have not, as yet, been widely applied in geography. AMH

Suggested Reading

Abler, R., Adams, J. S. and Gould, P. R. 1971: *Spatial organization: the geographer's view of the world*. Englewood Cliffs, NJ: Prentice-Hall.

Killen, J. E. 1979: *Linear programming: the simplex method with geographical applications*. Concepts and techniques in modern geography 24. Norwich: Geo Books.

Vajda, S. 1960: *An introduction to linear programming and the theory of games*. London: Methuen/New York: John Wiley.

linkages The contacts and flows of information and/or materials between two or more individuals. The term is most widely used in INDUSTRIAL GEOGRAPHY, to indicate the interdependence among firms and its effects on location choice (see AGGLOMERATION). For any one firm, linkages can be divided into: (1) backward – providing goods and services for the firm's production activities; (2) forward – links with customers for its products; and (3) sideways – interactions with other firms involved in the same processes. (See also LOCATIONAL INTERDEPENDENCE.) RJJ

local state The set of institutions charged with the maintenance and protection of social relations at the sub-national level. This set includes local government, local judiciary, licensing authorities and the machinery of local politics, as well as *quangos* and other local administrative agencies (representative of, for instance, central government). The term is most commonly invoked with reference to metropolitan-level governance, although it can also refer to state/provincial, county or regional scales.

The local state is part of the STATE APPARATUS: its existence is predicated on the need for CRISIS avoidance at the local level. The local state is a vital component in the control of spatially extensive and socially heterogeneous territories. No matter what the nature of the state organization (democratic, totalitarian, etc.), surveillance and social integration of the populace is facilitated by a decentralized structure of state organs. The local state also has an important political function, in that it legitimates central state actions through such means as party organizations or electoral politics. Local elections are buttressed by an IDEOLOGY of participation or democracy which often insists on the right to local self-determination (cf. TIEBOUT MODEL).

Conservative and liberal analysts, who simply view the business of government as the provision of PUBLIC GOODS and services, tend to be primarily concerned with EFFICIENCY and control of local state operations. Other social theorists have concentrated on the reasons for the existence of a separate local state. For them, the fundamental theoretical question is the authority relationship between central and local states: To what extent is the local state autonomous from the central state? The local state is alternatively viewed as the 'Achilles heel' of the state, and as the 'creature' of the central state. In the former case, it is perceived as the weak and vulnerable gap in the central state's armour, because well-organized local SOCIAL MOVEMENTS may be able to capture the local state and, hence, practise a potentially threatening local autonomy. In the latter case, the local state is regarded as simply the puppet of the central agencies.

The question of local autonomy has fundamental political significance, since many pressure groups have attempted to 'capture' the local state. The resolution of the question of the autonomy of the local state is most likely to be achieved only at the empirical level. The degree of autonomy is a function of the extent of local powers of initiative, and local immunity from interference by other tiers of the state apparatus. By examining the power and role of significant human agents, such as URBAN MANAGERS AND GATEKEEPERS, it would be possible to determine the value of attempting to capture the local state. (For other views of local urban politics, see COLLECTIVE CONSUMPTION and DUAL THEORY OF THE STATE.)

In the fragmented politics characteristic of POSTMODERN society, the potential for political power at the local level is critically important in the fate of non-class-based social movements, such as those involving women, gays and minorities. (See also STATE; STATE APPARATUS.)   MJD

Suggested Reading

Castells, M. 1983: *The city and the grassroots.* Berkeley, CA: University of California Press.

Clark, G. L. and Dear, M. J. 1984: *State apparatus.* Boston: Allen and Unwin.

Wolch, J. R. 1990: *The shadow state.* New York: The Foundation Center.

locale A setting or context for social interaction. The term was proposed by Anthony Giddens in his development of STRUCTURATION THEORY. Giddens's notion of structuration suggests how the flow of HUMAN AGENCY 'binds' time and SPACE. The social interactions involved in

this are integrative. *Social* integration involves individual actors who are 'co-present' in time and space, while *system* integration involves relations between actors, groups and collectivities outside conditions of 'co-presence'. In both cases interactions are situated in time and space, and this setting furnishes the resources on which the actors draw in their interaction. It is this context which Giddens labels 'locale'. In an early (1979) formulation he defines it thus:

'Locale' is in some respects a preferable term to that of 'place', more commonly employed in social geography: for it carries something of the connotation of space used as a *setting* for interaction. A setting is not just a spatial parameter, and physical environment, in which interaction 'occurs': it is these elements mobilised as part of the interaction. Features of the setting of interaction, including its spatial and physical aspects . . . are routinely drawn upon by social actors in the sustaining of communication.

On a number of occasions Giddens refers to locales as the characteristic physical settings associated with different types of collectivities: 'virtually all collectivities have a *locale* of operation, spatially distinct from that associated with others' (1979, pp. 206–7) and 'all collectivities have defined *locales* of operation: physical settings associated with the "typical interactions" composing those collectivities as social systems' (1981, p. 39). Thus the typical locale of the school is the classroom; that of the prison, the cell block; that of the bureaucracy, the office; that of the army, the barracks (1987, pp. 153–62).

Moreover, Giddens distinguishes between *organizations* and *social movements* and claims that 'unlike organizations, SOCIAL MOVEMENTS do not characteristically operate within fixed locales' (1984, p. 204). Elsewhere, however, he makes it clear that he means the concept of locale to have 'very general applicability' and that it applies in principle to all social interaction (1981, p. 40). The reason for stressing the typical locales of certain types of institutions (barracks, schools etc.) is that *in some cases* locales can take on a fixed physical form, but this form does not completely specify the nature of a locale, and indeed

335

Type of society	Dominant locale organization	Power-container
Tribal societies	band groups or villages	villages (?)
Class-divided societies	symbiosis of city and countryside	cities
Class societies	'the created environment'	nation–states

locale *Dominant locales and time–space distanciation* (Giddens, 1981).

some locales may not have a physical form in that sense at all:

Locales provide for a good deal of the 'fixity' underlying institutions, although there is no clear sense in which they 'determine' such 'fixity'. It is *usually* possible to designate locales in terms of their physical properties, either as features of the material world or, more commonly, as combinations of those features and human artefacts. But *it is an error to suppose that locales can be described in those terms alone* . . . A house is grasped as such only if the observer recognizes that it is a 'dwelling' with a range of other properties specified by the modes of its utilization in human activity (1984, p. 118, emphases added).

However, the idea that 'locale' is applicable to all social interaction introduces a further ambiguity. On the one hand, Giddens (1984, p. 71) implies that interactions situated in locales necessarily involve the 'co-presence' of the actors: on the other, he stresses that 'locales may range from a room in a house, a street corner, the shop floor of a factory, towns and cities, to the territorially demarcated areas occupied by nation states' (1984, p. 118), or to put it, as Nigel Thrift (1983) does more concisely, 'a locale does not have to be local'. The apparent contradiction here is partially resolved by Giddens' (1984, p. 68) comments on media of communication:

Although the 'full conditions of co-presence' exist only in unmediated contact between those who are physically present, mediated contacts that permit some of the intimacies of co-presence are made possible in the modern era by electronic communications, most notably the telephone.

However, elsewhere Giddens (1987, p. 137) insists that 'co-presence' must involve literal 'face-to-face' interaction:

Interaction in contexts of co-presence obviously has characteristics not found in 'mediated' interaction – via the telephone, recordings, the mail and so on.

Although there is a confusion here, it seems fairly clear that Giddens regards a 'locale' as something which can have (potentially considerable) spatial and temporal extension. The interactions for which locales form the setting can therefore in principle be subject to TIME–SPACE DISTANCIATION. This allows for the existence within locales of REGIONS which provide for the 'zoning' of social practices in time and space.

According to Giddens (1981) some locales dominate in particular types of society and form their principal 'power containers' (see the figure).

A number of writers have discussed the relationship between locale and the apparently related concept of LOCALITY. Cooke (1989) sees them as competing alternatives such that acceptance of one would imply the rejection of the other. Favouring the concept of locality, Cooke claims that the idea of locale should be rejected because 'it reproduces the passive connotations of community in the way it refers to setting and context for action rather than as a constituting element in action' (Cooke, 1989, p. 10). Giddens' insistence on the constitutive nature of context suggests that this is a misreading, but, as Duncan (1989) points out, locale and locality in any case refer to different things. This is recognized by Massey (1991), who briefly hints that localities could be conceptualized as 'the intersection of sets of locales', while her insistence that localities should be seen as socially constructed applies equally to locales. (See.also CONTEXTUAL THEORY; HABITUS; PLACE; SPATIALITY; TIME-GEO-GRAPHY.) JP

References

Cooke, P. 1989: *Localities: the changing face of urban Britain*. London: Unwin Hyman.

Duncan, S. 1989: What is locality? In Peet, R. and Thrift, N., eds, *New models in geography*, volume 2. London: Unwin Hyman, pp. 221–52.

Giddens, A. 1979: *Central problems in social theory*. London: Macmillan.

Giddens, A. 1981: *A contemporary critique of historical materialism*, volume 1, *Power, property and the state*. London: Macmillan.

Giddens, A. 1984: *The constitution of society*. Cambridge: Polity Press.

Giddens, A. 1987: *Social theory and modern sociology*. Cambridge: Polity Press.

Massey, D. 1991: The political place of locality studies. *Environ. Plann. A* 23, pp. 267–81.

Thrift, N. 1983: On the determination of social action in space and time. *Environ. Plann. D: Society and Space* 1, pp. 23–57.

Suggested Reading

Giddens (1984), especially ch. 3.

Giddens (1987), ch. 6.

Thrift (1983).

locality In lay terms, a PLACE or REGION of sub-national spatial SCALE. Despite, or perhaps because of, considerable debate about the concept, there is no consensus concerning its technical meaning within HUMAN GEOGRAPHY. The origins of the debate lie in attempts in the 1980s to explain the RESTRUCTURING of economies and their SPATIAL STRUCTURES. At a time of significant transformations in the human geography of the UK, Urry (1981) and Massey (1984) argued that an understanding of spatial variations in social, political and economic change was particularly important (see also Massey, 1991).

The UK Government's Economic and Social Research Council (ESRC) translated this concern into substantive research programmes: the 'Changing Urban and Regional System' initiative (CURS), the 'Social Change and Economic Life' initiative (SCEL), and the 'Economic Restructuring, Social Change and the Locality' programme. At the centre of each was a series of studies of the impact of restructuring on particular places or regions. A key concern of these 'locality studies' was to collect detailed empirical evidence to assist the identification of the nature, causes and consequences of spatial differentiation in processes of change.

As well as substantive results (Dickens, 1988; Cooke, 1989a; Bagguley et al., 1990), this research effort raised a series of methodological and theoretical issues which became bound up with wider debates:

(a) *The delimitation of localities for research.* Despite extensive deliberations on the nature of localities, many studies have in practice used (statistically defined) local LABOUR MARKET areas. By contrast, Massey (1991) argues that 'localities are not simply spatial areas you can easily draw a line around' but should be 'defined in terms of the sets of social relations or processes in question'. Savage et al. (1987) claim to have adopted this sort of approach in defining the localities for the Economic Restructuring, Social Change and the Locality programme.

(b) *The relationship between locality research and critical realism.* Many writers have explicitly or implicitly linked locality research to the EPISTEMOLOGY of REALISM (e.g. Urry, 1987; Duncan, 1989). From this perspective: (i) localities are the concrete outcome of the contingent combination in particular places of a number of causal PROCESSES; (ii) localities may become causally powerful social objects in their own right, with effects on wider processes (e.g. by influencing STATE policy or the locational decisions of firms); and (iii) locality *studies* are exercises in INTENSIVE RESEARCH which seek to unravel these processes and hence to identify through ABSTRACTION the necessary relations which define social structures (Sayer, 1984). Sayer himself, however, has objected to the ways in which some protagonists in the debate have mistakenly conflated the distinctions of realist philosophy (Sayer, 1991).

(c) *The theoretical status of the concept of locality.* According to Cooke (1989b, p. 12) 'locality is a concept attaching to a process characteristic of MODERNITY, namely the extension, following political struggle, of civil, political and social rights of citizenship to individuals'. Since there are considerable differences between apparently

337

similarly constituted localities, Cooke argues that this link with CITIZENSHIP forms a basis for local 'pro-activity', with localities 'actively involved in their own transformation' (Cooke, 1989c, p. 296).

Despite the stress on citizenship, this formulation leaves unclear the relationship between HUMAN AGENCY and the pro-activity of localities. Cooke asserts that 'localities are not simply places or even communities: they are the sum of social energy and agency resulting from the clustering of diverse individuals, groups and social interests in space' (Cooke, 1989c, p. 296). However, the heterogeneous character of this clustering casts doubt on the possibility of grounding pro-activity in a notion of universal citizenship, and in practice Cooke reduces pro-activity to the policies of the LOCAL STATE.

Duncan, Savage and their co-workers regard the idea that localities are pro-active, causally powerful objects as a worrying return to SPATIAL FETISHISM. They argue that while social processes vary spatially, and are sometimes constituted at the local scale, unique 'locality effects' (such as local political cultures) are extremely unusual (Savage et al., 1987, p. 32). This scepticism leads them to abandon the concept in favour of an existing vocabulary of spatial variation: 'most of the time, instead of writing about "locality" researchers should more simply talk about "case study areas", "towns", "labour market areas", or just "areas", "places" and "spatial variations"' (Duncan and Savage, 1989, p. 192).

Cox and Mair (1991) retain the concept of locality, and like Cooke they argue that localities can have an impact on wider processes. Where they differ is in teasing out in detail the mechanisms through which this operates.

Although they have involved much dissent, these debates have largely been conducted among those engaged in locality studies or otherwise connected with the ESRC programmes. In addition, several writers who have not been directly involved in the empirical research projects have criticized this form of research from a variety of perspectives.

Smith (1987) expressed doubts about the wisdom of detailed empirical studies.

According to him they run the risk of EMPIRICISM because their stress on the unique character of localities makes it difficult to produce generalizations and to draw out theoretical conclusions. While his reminder about the role of theory may have been timely, Smith's apparent equation of theory with generalization might itself be read as an empiricist position, and would not necessarily be accepted either by the locality researchers or within the tradition of MARXIST GEOGRAPHY from which Smith was writing.

Through an empirical (but not empiricist) study of Poplar in the 1920s, Rose (1989) argues that the theoretical contributions of locality studies have been compromised by their stress on the sphere of waged labour. The radical politics of 1920s Poplar, she suggests, were largely constituted outside the workplace in the home and the community. Jackson (1991) develops this line of argument through his 'cultural critique of locality studies'. He suggests that, notwithstanding frequent references to local cultures and regional traditions, most studies have failed adequately to theorize cultural relations.

Those who seek to retain the idea of locality might argue that these criticisms do not undermine it in principle, but are addressed to the use made of it in practice. With the ending of the formal research programmes it remains to be seen how far the concept will continue to be used and further developed by other researchers.   JP

References

Bagguley, P., Mark-Lawson, J., Shapiro, D., Urry, J., Walby, S. and Warde, A. 1990: *Restructuring: place, class and gender*. London: Sage.

Cooke, P., ed. 1989a: *Localities: the changing face of urban Britain*. London: Unwin Hyman.

Cooke, P. 1989b: Locality, economic restructuring and world development. In Cooke, P., ed., *Localities: the changing face of urban Britain*. London: Unwin Hyman, pp. 1–44.

Cooke, P. 1989c: The local question – revival or survival? In Cooke, P., ed., *Localities: the changing face of urban Britain*. London: Unwin Hyman, pp. 296–306.

Cox, K. and Mair, A. 1991: From localised social structures to localities as agents. *Environ. Plann. A* 23, pp. 197–213.

Dickens, P. 1988: *One nation? Social change and the politics of locality.* London: Pluto Press.

Duncan, S. 1989: What is locality? In Peet, R. and Thrift, N., eds, *New models in geography,* volume 2. London: Unwin Hyman, pp. 221–52.

Duncan, S. and Savage, M. 1989: Space, scale and locality. *Antipode,* 21, pp. 179–206.

Jackson, P. 1991: Mapping meanings: a cultural critique of locality studies. *Environ. Plann. A* 23, pp. 215–28.

Massey, D. 1984: *Spatial divisions of labour.* London: Macmillan.

Massey, D. 1991: The political place of locality studies. *Environ. Plann. A* 23, pp. 267–81.

Rose, G. 1989: Locality studies and waged labour: an historical critique. *Trans. Inst. Br. Geogr.* n.s. 14, pp. 317–28.

Savage, M., Barlow, J., Duncan, S. and Saunders, P. 1987: 'Locality research': the Sussex programme on Economic Restructuring, Social Change and the Locality. *Q. J. soc. Aff.* 4, pp. 27–51.

Sayer, A. 1984: *Method in social science: a realist approach.* London: Hutchinson.

Sayer, A. 1991: Behind the locality debate: deconstructing geography's dualisms. *Environ. Plann. A* 23, pp. 283–308.

Smith, N. 1987: Dangers of the empirical turn: some comments on the CURS initiative. *Antipode* 19, pp. 59–66.

Urry, J. 1981: Localities, regions and social class. *Int. J. urban and reg. Res.,* 5, 455–74.

Urry, J. 1987: Society, space and locality. *Environ. Plann. D: Society and Space,* 5, pp. 435–44.

Suggested Reading
Cooke (1989).

Duncan (1989).

Environmental Planning A 1991: Special issue on new perspectives on the locality debate. *Environ. Plann. A* 23(2).

location quotient A coefficient comparing some quality of an area with a specified norm. The quality may be the percentage of a country's employment in the manufacture of silicon chips in area i (S_i) and the norm the percentage of the country's total employment there (T_i). The location quotient for area i (LQ_i) is obtained as:

$$LQ_i = S_i/T_i.$$

If LQ_i is greater than 1.0, employment in silicon-chip manufacturing is concentrated in area i, relative to the percentage of all manufacturing there: if LQ_i is less than 1.0, silicon-chip manufacturing is relatively under-represented there.   MJB

Suggested Reading
Smith, D. M. 1975: *Patterns in human geography: an introduction to numerical methods.* London: Penguin/New York: Crane Russak, pp. 161–71.

location theory A body of theories which seek to account for the location of economic activities. An interest in the POLITICAL ECONOMY of location can be traced back to the seventeenth and eighteenth centuries, when several writers attempted to explicate patterns of agricultural land use (see Scott, 1976), and these efforts can now be seen to have culminated in the classical VON THÜNEN MODEL (1826). But the parallel rise of Ricardian political economy, and in particular its establishment of the 'machinery question' as the primary spur to economic growth, effectively displaced these traditional concerns; the relegation of agriculture underwrote the simultaneous suppression of SPACE. Its residual, essentially derivative status was confirmed later in the nineteenth century by A. Marshall's *Principles of economics* (1890; see Marshall, 1952), which judged time to be 'more fundamental' than space. And ever since, according to W. Isard (1956), 'the architects of our finest [economic–]theoretical structures have 'intensified [his] prejudice'. But the cardinal exception to this, as Isard noted, was the German school of location theory, whose contribution – for all their differences – reclaimed and reinvigorated the constructs of an earlier generation and did much to prefigure the general theories of the SPACE-ECONOMY which were Isard's own objective: especially important here were the formulations of Alfred Weber (1909), Walter Christaller (1933) and August Lösch (1944) (for historical summaries, see Isard, 1956, chapter 2; Smith, 1981, chapter 8: see also REGIONAL SCIENCE).

In geography the significance of the German school was recognized by R. Hartshorne, whose *The nature of geography*

(1939) was based on an exegesis of a primarily German intellectual tradition. While he believed that 'the determination of principles governing location of units of production . . . requires more training in economics than in geography', he nevertheless accepted it as an identifiably 'geographical problem'. But his evident hesitation turned out to be shared by most of his contemporaries, and with some notable exceptions – particularly W. Smith (1949) and E. M. Rawstron (1958) – Anglo-American ECONOMIC GEOGRAPHY remained resolutely empirical and ignored these theoretical excursions. As a reviewer of Friedrich's translation of Weber's industrial location theory had predicted, 'the great majority of geographers' found it 'too theoretical'. Location theory was not formally admitted into the developing corpus of HUMAN GEOGRAPHY until the early 1960s, mainly through the efforts of W. L. Garrison and the Washington school in the USA and, on the other side of the Atlantic, through P. Haggett's *Locational analysis in human geography* (1965). Haggett drew attention to the 'fundamental role of locational concepts within human geography' and called for a reaffirmation of its 'geometric tradition'; but clearly, as Hartshorne had realized, location theory could not depend on geometry alone, on the articulation of purely spatial concepts, and during this formative period it drew much of its theoretical strength from NEOCLASSICAL ECONOMICS. In particular, attempts were made to use general equilibrium theory to provide a theory of industrial location capable of integrating VARIABLE COST ANALYSIS and VARIABLE REVENUE ANALYSIS (see Smith, 1981), while UTILITY THEORY was used to reconstruct SPATIAL PREFERENCE structures within the framework of CENTRAL PLACE THEORY (see Rushton, 1969). Yet location theory encountered formidable problems in translating these formulations into the spatial domain, because 'the working assumptions and abstractions that the neoclassicist uses as a starting point for his analysis could never be justified in a world which recognizes the existence of space as well as time' (Richardson, 1973). These special

misgivings were reinforced by a growing awareness of the more general critique of neoclassical economics, and together these objections forced a series of responses from location theory. Three main developments can be distinguished, although it must be remembered that there are connections between and differences within them.

(a) A long-standing concern with the spatial behaviour of rational *economic man* (*sic*; see METHODOLOGICAL INDIVIDUALISM) was replaced as the emergence of BEHAVIOURAL GEOGRAPHY allowed for the incorporation of more realistic behavioural assumptions into location theory; in other words, for the construction of what H. Stafford (1972) called 'the geography of manufactur*ers*' rather than 'the geography of manufactur*ing*'. Typical of these various studies, in roughly chronological order, were investigations of SATISFICING BEHAVIOUR, the formalization of A. Pred's BEHAVIOURAL MATRIX, and whole series of models of corporate DECISION-MAKING. Although D. Harvey (1969) had been sceptical about the possibility of a viable 'cognitive–behavioural location theory', and had been particularly scathing about the analytical rigour of 'satisficing' concepts, sufficient advances had been registered by the early 1970s for several textbooks and research collections to be published (e.g. Eliot Hurst, 1974; Toyne, 1974). Renewed criticisms of behaviouralism did not stop the search for a location theory informed by an 'interpretive' social science and in the second edition of *Locational analysis in human geography* (1977), P. Haggett, A. D. Cliff and A. Frey recorded their optimism about 'major developments in human microgeography' (including ENVIRONMENTAL PERCEPTION, PHENOMENOLOGY and TIME-GEOGRAPHY) which promised to 'enrich' the 'somewhat formal areas of aggregate MODEL-building' with which mainstream location theory continued to be preoccupied. This continuity can, in part, be attributed to the persistence of the problems Harvey had previously identified, and certainly both of his alternative avenues – the development of NORMATIVE THEORY (e.g. Chisholm, 1971) and the incorporation of

STOCHASTIC PROCESSES (e.g. Webber, 1972) – have been vigorously pursued.

(b) The single-plant, single-product firm was displaced as the primary object of industrial location theory, and earlier work on industrial AGGLOMERATION and LOCATIONAL INTERDEPENDENCE was extended as the structural context of corporate behaviour gradually became more clearly defined. This was achieved in part through the refinement of the decision-making models referred to above – indeed, Martin (1981) still claims that 'behavioural theory remains predominant in new work in industrial geography' – but more particularly through what has come to be called the *'geography of enterprise'* approach. This is distinguished by its concern with 'the interrelationships between firm organization, development and spatial behaviour, in the context of [economic–] environmental change'. Apart from its empirical importance, its proponents also believe that it has 'prospective significance as a *theoretical* framework which might replace Weberian and neoclassical theory' (Keeble, 1979; see also special issue of *Regional Studies*, 1978; McDermott and Taylor, 1982; Hayter and Watts, 1983).

(c) The ahistorical nature of location theory was challenged through a more considered recognition of the historical specificity of the space-economy of CAPITALISM. This had in fact been treated by Weber in summary form (see Gregory, 1981) and it is also latent within both of the previous approaches, but what is distinctive about its explicit acknowledgement is the conjoint denial of any autonomy for location theory: 'spatial development can only be seen as part of the overall development of capitalism' (Massey, 1977: see also Scott, 1980; Harvey, 1982; Cooke, 1983a). (The restriction to capitalism is deliberate: there have been very few theoretical accounts of location under precapitalist or non-capitalist modes of production.) Most of these discussions depend upon MARXIAN ECONOMICS and POLITICAL ECONOMY, and most of them have taken place within INDUSTRIAL GEOGRAPHY rather than AGRICULTURAL GEOGRAPHY (but see Scott (1979) for a

translation of the VON THÜNEN MODEL into NEO-RICARDIAN ECONOMICS). Indeed, Taylor (1984) considers that 'it has been the Marxist approach which has done most to stimulate theoretical thinking in industrial geography'. To speak of 'the' Marxist approach is somewhat misleading, however, since HISTORICAL MATERIALISM includes a number of different perspectives: and by no means all of them are as severely economistic as Harvey's (1982) account of *The limits to capital* implies. Even so, Harvey's exegesis of classical Marxism – most of all his treatment of money, credit and finance capital – and his development of a so-called 'third-cut' theory of capitalist crisis capable of addressing many of the traditional concerns of location theory provide an essential benchmark. Some of the most imaginative contributions (which, although they can be situated within a recognizably Marxist tradition, are nevertheless far from fideistic: as Harvey admits, Marx's original formulations are 'powerful with respect to time but weak with respect to space') have been, very broadly, theorizations of UNEVEN DEVELOPMENT and of the changing spatial DIVISION OF LABOUR (for general accounts see Clark, 1980; Browett, 1984). Of particular interest here are theorizations of the differential geographies of different LAYERS OF INVESTMENT (see, e.g., Massey, 1978), of strategies of industrial RESTRUCTURING which transform the LABOUR PROCESS and impact on geographies of both CLASS and GENDER (see, e.g., Walker and Storper, 1981; Storper and Walker, 1983; Massey, 1984), and of the segmentation and differentiation of the LABOUR MARKET and its implications for theories of spatial development (see, e.g., Cooke, 1983b). This stream of studies is much wider and deeper than a cursory list can indicate, but its focus on the dynamics of capitalism and on the structuration of both economic *and* social relations over time and space encompasses three fundamental features:

(i) the *historical particularity* of different phases of capitalist development – hence the attention paid to 'long waves' (see KONDRATIEFF CYCLES) and to the differentiation of 'sub-modes of production' (see, e.g., Gibson and Horvath, 1983);

341

(ii) the *global context* of different phases of capitalist development – hence the attention paid to the NEW INTERNATIONAL DIVISION OF LABOUR, to MULTINATIONAL CORPORATIONS and to theories of the 'geographical transfer of value' and of unequal exchange (see, e.g., Foot and Webber, 1983; Bradbury, 1985: see also WORLD-SYSTEMS ANALYSIS);

(iii) the *structural interdependencies* between commodity production, social reproduction and the URBANIZATION of the space-economy (see, e.g., Cooke, 1983a; Harvey, 1985: see also COLLECTIVE CONSUMPTION).

In the most general terms, then, it is clear that since the early 1970s the highly schematic representations of the geometry of the space-economy have yielded to much more substantive specifications of the processes (see PROCESS) which produce and reproduce constellations of economic activities in time and space. In effect, an insistence on the importance of careful specification and conceptualization (see ABSTRACTION) evident in the first-generation location theory has provided a basis for constructive critiques of the theoretical approaches underlying the non-Marxian tradition (Sayer, 1982; Clark et al., 1986; Storper and Walker, 1989). Furthermore, as a sign of maturation of the newer work in this field, a healthy self-critical literature has recently emerged, beginning with Sayer (1985). As but one example, the NEW INTERNATIONAL DIVISION OF LABOUR thesis has recently been criticized for its excessive determinism and inability to account for the notable reconcentration of particular economic activities in the Western industrialized countries (see Sayer, 1986; Schoenberger, 1988). Similarly, the continuing relevance of the concept of spatial DIVISION OF LABOUR has also been the subject of spirited debate (e.g. see the exchange between Gertler, 1988, and Schoenberger, 1989).

Further signs of this maturation are evident in the new questions now being posed in this 'post-Weberian' literature, and have served to broaden the scope of location theory away from its traditional narrow concern with explaining the location of economic activities. First, the increasing locational influence ascribed to local social relations in the workplace and community (evident in the literature on RESTRUCTURING and spatial DIVISION OF LABOUR), has spawned considerable interest in the processes which produce local geographies of labour and community in the first place (see various contributions in the collections edited by Gregory and Urry, 1985, and Scott and Storper, 1986; see also Clark, 1989). This emphasis is also present in Scott and Storper (1987), Scott (1988), and Storper and Walker (1989), who note the coincidence of dynamic new local growth phenomena with particular, characteristic politics of PLACE.

A second broad question receiving much recent attention concerns how economic geography, with its sensitivity to locational variation, might contribute to a reconstruction of the other social sciences which followed Marshall's advice in privileging time over space. In doing this, geographers have, with strange irony, returned to Isard's original mission. However, while their motives may be similar, their approaches are rather different. Three distinct thrusts have recently emerged.

(a) Within the tradition of analytical political economy, economic geographers have addressed the more mathematically inclined body of work associated with economists such as Marx, Ricardo, Sraffa, Kalecki and Pasinetti (see Barnes, 1990 and accompanying papers; see also Sheppard and Barnes, 1990). Their intent and effect has been to mount a serious challenge to the logical deductions arising from this (as well as more traditional neoclassical) theory when the spatial dimension of the economy is explicitly introduced. In showing how the determinate conclusions of Marxian economics – e.g. that profit rates will tend to fall over time – are thrown into doubt when space is admitted into the analysis, this work has been of key importance in illustrating the contribution of geographical theory to the wider body of economic analysis.

(b) Still within a political–economic tradition, but employing a non-mathematical discourse, other economic geographers have rejected the logical separation between the 'growth question' and the 'location question' implicit in earlier location theory, and have instead sought to demonstrate how the basic theory of economic growth itself can only be properly constructed when it is explicitly couched in spatial terms (Storper and Walker, 1989). In this work, the history of economic change is viewed as the 'inconstant geography of capitalism' and, by invoking the central analytical concept of 'geographical industrialization', Storper and Walker demonstrate how the series of major upheavals in this history have each found their origins in the specific physical, economic and social configurations of individual places. Furthermore, the willing acceptance of an *a priori* spatial variation in factors of production that is evident within the Weberian tradition of location theory is explicitly rejected here. Thus, the notion of local industrial growth arising 'in passive response to endowment-based local comparative advantages' (see COMPARATIVE ADVANTAGE) is instead conceived of as 'an active shaping of local factor supplies by industry itself' (Gertler, 1991).

(c) Geographers have also made a major contribution to the relatively new body of theory emerging from the REGULATION SCHOOL of French political economy. While economists such as Boyer (1990) have openly professed an interest in 'how economic and social dynamics vary over space and time', their analysis has not penetrated below the spatial scale of the nation–state. Thus, Harvey (1988, 1989), Scott (1988), and Storper and Walker (1989) have argued that the transformation from a Fordist (see FORDISM) to a post-Fordist (see POST-FORDISM) REGIME OF ACCUMULATION has been founded upon the shifting geographical configuration of production systems, labour markets and communities. Indeed, the central concept of FLEXIBLE ACCUMULATION itself, now in wide usage within the social sciences, was originally coined by Harvey (1988) and Scott (1988). Geographical work in this area has been concerned to show how apparently national and international changes in markets, competition and state regulations have influenced the nature and geography of industrial organization. However, perhaps more fundamentally, a

second objective has been to demonstrate how the spatial construction of production systems (and, to a lesser extent, consumption patterns) have made feasible the responses to these macroeconomic challenges and, in the process, contributed to the creation of the next macrogeography of economic activity. Interestingly, some of this work (see Scott, 1988) has been based explicitly on the time-honoured tradition of importing aspatial economic theory for extension and application within economic geography. Perhaps as a further measure of the discipline's maturation, this bid to replace the more traditional construct of TRANSPORT COSTS with the newer concept of transaction costs (see TRANSACTIONAL ANALYSIS) has not met with unanimous approval (Lovering, 1990). Nevertheless, the vitality of this and related debates seems to indicate that location theory is still high on the agenda of human geography, although its form may have changed and its ambit broadened substantially in recent years.

DG/MSG

References

Barnes, T. J. 1990: Analytical political economy: a geographical introduction. *Environ. Plann A*, 22, pp. 993–1006.

Boyer, R. 1990: *The regulation school: a critical introduction*. New York: Columbia University Press.

Bradbury, J. H. 1985: Regional and industrial restructuring processes in the new international division of labour. *Progr. hum. Geogr.* 9, pp. 38–63.

Browett, J. 1984: On the necessity and inevitability of uneven spatial development under capitalism. *Int. J. urban and reg. Res.* 8, pp. 155–76.

Chisholm, M. 1971: In search of a basis for location theory: micro-economics or welfare economics. *Prog. Geog.* 3, pp. 111–33.

Clark, G. 1980: Capitalism and regional inequality. *Ann. Ass. Am. Geogr.* 70, pp. 226–37.

Clark, G. L. 1989: *Unions and communities under siege*. Cambridge: Cambridge University Press.

Clark, G. L., Gertler, M. S. and Whiteman, J. E. M. 1986: *Regional dynamics: studies in adjustment theory*. Boston: Allen and Unwin.

Cooke, P. 1983a: *Theories of planning and spatial development*. London: Hutchinson.

Cooke, P. 1983b: Labour market discontinuity and spatial development. *Progr. hum. Geogr.* 7, pp. 543–65.

Eliot Hurst, M. E. 1974: *A geography of economic behavior: an introduction.* North Scituate, MA: Duxbury Press/London: Prentice-Hall.

Foot, S. and Webber, M. 1983: Unequal exchange and uneven development. *Environ. Plann. D: Society and Space* 1, pp. 281–304.

Gertler, M. S. 1988: The limits to flexibility: comments on the post-Fordist vision of production and its geography. *Trans. Inst. Br. Geogr.* n.s. 13, pp. 419–32.

Gertler, M. S. 1991: Review: Storper and Walker's *The capitalist imperative. Econ. Geogr.* 67, pp. 361–64.

Gibson, K. and Horvath, R. 1983: Aspects of a theory of transition within the capitalist mode of production. *Environ. Plann. D: Society and Space* 1, pp. 121–38.

Gregory, D. 1981: Alfred Weber and location theory. In Stoddart, D. R., ed., *Geography, ideology and social concern.* Oxford: Blackwell/New York: Barnes and Noble.

Gregory, D. and Urry, J. eds, 1985: *Social relations and spatial structures.* London: Macmillan.

Haggett, P. 1965: *Locational analysis in human geography.* London: Edward Arnold/New York: St. Martin's Press.

Haggett, P., Cliff, A. D. and Frey, A. E. 1977: *Locational analysis in human geography,* second edition. London: Edward Arnold/New York: John Wiley.

Hartshorne, R. 1939: *The nature of geography: a critical survey of current thought in the light of the past.* Lancaster, PA: Association of American Geographers.

Harvey, D. 1969: Conceptual and measurement problems in the cognitive–behavioural approach to location theory. (Reprinted in Cox, K. and Golledge, R. G., eds, *Behavioral problems in geography revisited,* 1981 edition. London: Methuen, pp. 18–42.)

Harvey, D. 1982: *The limits to capital.* Oxford: Blackwell/Chicago: Chicago University Press.

Harvey, D. 1985: *The urbanization of capital.* Oxford: Blackwell.

Harvey, D. 1988: The geographical and geopolitical consequences of the transition from Fordist to flexible accumulation. In Sternlieb, G. and Hughes, J. W., eds, *America's new market geography.* New Brunswick, NJ: Rutgers Center for Urban Policy Research, pp. 101–34.

Harvey, D. 1989: *The condition of postmodernity.* Oxford: Blackwell.

Hayter, R. and Watts, H. D. 1983: The geography of enterprise: a reappraisal. *Progr. hum. Geogr.* 7, pp. 157–81.

Isard, W. 1956: *Location and space economy.* Cambridge, MA: MIT Press/London; Chapman and Hall.

Keeble, D. E. 1979: Industrial geography. *Progr. hum. Geogr.* 3, pp. 425–33.

Lovering, J. 1990: Fordism's unknown successor: a comment on Scott's theory of flexible accumulation and the re-emergence of regional economies. *Int. J. urban and reg. Res.* 14, pp. 159–74.

McDermott, P. and Taylor, M. 1982: *Industrial organization and location.* Cambridge: Cambridge University Press.

Marshall, A. 1952: *Principles of economics,* eighth edition. London and New York: Macmillan. (First edition 1890.)

Martin, J. E. 1981: Location theory and spatial analysis. *Progr. hum. Geogr.* 5, pp. 258–62.

Massey, D. 1977: Towards a critique of industrial location theory. In Peet, R., ed., *Radical geography: alternative viewpoints on contemporary social issues.* London: Methuen/Chicago: Maaroufa, pp. 181–96.

Massey, D. 1978: Regionalism: some current issues. *Capital and Class* 6, pp. 106–25.

Massey, D. 1984: *Spatial divisions of labour: social structures and the geography of production.* London: Macmillan.

Rawstron, E. M. 1958: Three principles of industrial location. *Trans. Inst. Br. Geogr.* 25, pp. 135–42.

Regional Studies 1978: Organisation and industrial location in Britain. *Reg. Stud.* 9, Part 2.

Richardson, H. W. 1973: *Regional growth theory.* London: Macmillan/New York: John Wiley.

Rushton, G. 1969: Analysis of spatial behavior by revealed space preference. *Ann. Ass. Am. Geogr.* 59, pp. 391–400.

Sayer, R. A. 1982: Explanation in economic geography. *Progr. hum. Geogr.* 6, pp. 68–88.

Sayer, R. A. 1985: Industry and space: a sympathetic critique of radical research. *Environ. Plann. D: Society and Space* 3, pp. 3–30.

Sayer, R. A. 1986: Industrial location on a world scale: the case of the semiconductor industry. In Scott, A. J. and Storper, M., eds, *Production, work, territory.* Boston: Allen and Unwin, pp. 107–23.

Schoenberger, E. 1988: Multinational corporations and the new international division of labor: a critical appraisal. *Int. reg. Sci. Rev.* 11, pp. 105–19.

Schoenberger, E. 1989: Thinking about flexibility: a response to Gertler. *Trans. Inst. Br. Geogr.* n.s. 14, pp. 109–12.

Scott, A. J. 1976: Land and land rent: an interpretative review of the French literature. *Prog. Geog.* 9, pp. 101–45.

Scott, A. J. 1979: Commodity production and the dynamics of land-use differentiation. *Urban Stud.* 16, pp. 95–104.

Scott, A. J. 1980: *The urban land nexus and the state.* London: Pion.

Scott, A. J. 1988: *New industrial spaces.* London: Pion.

Scott, A. J. and Storper, M., eds, 1986: *Production, work, territory.* Boston: Allen and Unwin.

Scott, A. J. and Storper, M. 1987: High technology industry and regional development: a theoretical critique and reconstruction. *Int. Soc. Sci. J.* 112, pp. 215–32.

Sheppard, E. and Barnes, T. J. 1990: *The capitalist space economy: analysis after Ricardo, Marx and Sraffa.* London: Unwin Hyman.

Smith, D. M. 1981: *Industrial location: an economic geographical analysis,* second edition. New York: John Wiley.

Smith, W. 1949: *An economic geography of Great Britain.* London: Methuen.

Stafford, H. 1972: The geography of manufacturers. *Prog. Geog.* 4, pp. 181–215.

Storper, M. and Walker, R. 1983: The theory of labour and the theory of location. *Int. J. urban and reg. Res.* 7, pp. 1–41.

Storper, M. and Walker, R. A. 1989: *The capitalist imperative; territory, technology, and industrial growth.* Oxford: Blackwell.

Taylor, M. 1984: Industrial geography. *Progr. hum. Geogr.* 8, pp. 263–74.

Toyne, P. 1974: *Organisation, location and behaviour: decision making in economic geography.* London: Macmillan/New York: Halsted.

Walker, R. and Storper, M. 1981: Capital and industrial location. *Progr. hum. Geogr.* 5, pp. 473–509.

Webber, M. J. 1972: *The impact of uncertainty on location.* Cambridge, MA: MIT Press.

Suggested Reading

Bradbury (1985).

Cooke (1983a), chs. 6–10.

Harvey (1982), chs. 11–13.

Smith (1981).

Storper and Walker (1989), chs 1–4.

location–allocation models Models used to determine the optimal location of central facilities (hospitals, offices, warehouses, etc.) in order to minimize movement and other costs. A public-sector example is the location of two new hospitals in a city: the objectives would be to minimize the aggregate travel cost to patients and to arrive at an optimal assignment of patients to the hospitals. A private-sector example is the location of warehouse facilities between factories and markets in order to minimize total distribution costs.

Unlike TRANSPORTATION PROBLEM models, in which all of the locations are fixed and the optimal assignment can be determined by LINEAR PROGRAMMING, in location-allocation models the siting of the central facilities and the assignment of least-cost flows must be determined simultaneously. The choice of location (whether or not to build a hospital at any given location) is a discrete or integer variable, and linear programming only deals with continuous variables. This makes the solution of these models more difficult, and many applications use heuristic or trial-and-error procedures that search for, but cannot be guaranteed to find, the true optimum. The degree of difficulty is a function of the number of unknowns: a two-hospital problem with fixed hospital capacities is much easier than a five-hospital problem with variable hospital sizes.

Two important classes of location-allocation models are distinguished: location on a continuous surface or plane, and location on a NETWORK. The continuous surface form has been widely used in theoretical analysis, and is related to the WEBER MODEL, but its limitations are increasingly recognized. Straight-line distance is often a poor proxy for real travel costs, which occur on a route network, and potential locations are usually restricted. Recent work has increasingly used the network form, where potential locations are defined as nodes and are linked to sources (and destinations in the warehousing case) by a route network. Mixed integer-continuous techniques are now available to find a true optimum for such problems. LWH

Suggested Reading

Killen, J. E. 1983: *Mathematical programming for geographers and planners*. London: Croom Helm.

locational analysis An approach to HUMAN GEOGRAPHY which focuses on the spatial arrangement of phenomena: its usual methodology is that of SPATIAL SCIENCE. The philosophy of POSITIVISM underpins the approach, which concentrates on the identification of THEORIES of spatial arrangements and so is closely linked to the discipline's QUANTITATIVE REVOLUTION.

Work within the locational analysis framework was taken up by several groups of geographers in the US in the 1950s, although it has much deeper roots in the work of pioneers who were later adopted by geographers (Johnston, 1991). Bunge (1966), for example, wrote a thesis on *Theoretical geography* based on the premises that 'nearness [is] a candidate for the central problem in geography' and that geography is 'the science of locations'. Others, such as McCarty, were strongly influenced by developments in the field of economics, to which they introduced the spatial variable (as in McCarty and Lindberg, 1966): these links led to the close interrelationships between geographers and regional scientists in the 1960s and 1970s, and are illustrated by attempts to build economic geography theories of spatial arrangements (as in Smith, 1981).

It was an English geographer who, in the classic way, codified the PARADIGM in a textbook – *Locational analysis in human geography* (first published in 1965). In this book, which rapidly attained the status of a classic within the field, Haggett established the pedigree of locational analysis by linking its *geometrical* focus to the work of early Greek cartographers. Bunge (1966), too, had argued that 'of the three classic areas of mathematics, geometry would appear to be the most promising for geography' (which discipline he defined as the 'discovery of predictive patterns'), and Harvey (1969) similarly presented a strong case for using geometry as the language for the study of spatial form (but see Sack, 1972, on the issue of whether geometry is a language for explaining as well as describing form).

Haggett's appeal to the relatively neglected geometrical tradition within geography emphasized an approach 'placed squarely on asking questions about the order, locational order, shown by the phenomena studied traditionally as human geography'. Such a focus needed: (1) to adopt a SYSTEMS approach which concentrates on the patterns and linkages within a whole assemblage; (2) to employ MODELS (a theme also advanced in Chorley and Haggett, 1965) as the stimuli for understanding; and (3) to use quantitative procedures to make precise statements (generalizations) about locational order (see also MACROGEOGRAPHY). Thus his book, and its successor (Haggett et al., 1977), comprised two halves: the first dealt with the models and the second with the methods.

Haggett's major innovation in this work was his framework for classifying the models of locational order. (Interestingly, his schema is paralleled by one developed contemporaneously by Cole and King, 1968.) In the first presentation this contained five components: the sixth (diffusion) was added in the second edition. Each component was given a separate chapter, and they were ordered in what he saw as a logical sequence (see the figure). The first (a) was concerned with interactions, or flows across space; the second (b) analysed the networks along which those flows moved; and the third (c) considered the major nodes, or organizational centres, on those networks. In the fourth (d) the hierarchical structure of the nodal system (see CENTRAL PLACE THEORY; URBAN SYSTEMS) was decomposed, whereas in the fifth (e) the organization of the space between the nodes – the surfaces – was the focus. The final component (f) looked at DIFFUSION down the hierarchy, along the networks and across the surfaces. Haggett decomposed the systems, therefore, but – despite his discussion of regions – did not recombine them into wholes, as promoted in the then fashionable REGIONAL SCIENCE.

With regard to methods, there was a major shift of emphasis between the two editions of Haggett's book. In the first, he

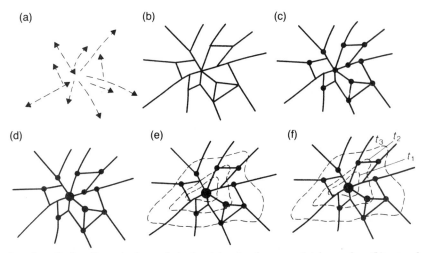

(a) (b) (c)

(d) (e) (f)
t_3 t_2 t_1

locational analysis *Stages in the analysis of nodal regional systems: (a) interaction: (b) networks: (c) nodes: (d) hierarchies: (e) surface: (f) diffusion* (Haggett et al., 1977).

accepted the then-conventional view that the methods associated with the GENERAL LINEAR MODEL could be adopted for SPATIAL ANALYSIS without difficulty; but a decade later, influenced by his empirical analyses of diffusion and the work of his colleague Andrew Cliff on SPATIAL AUTOCORRELATION, he argued that such application were 'more difficult than might at first appear' so that, for example, conventional REGRESSION procedures were omitted.

From this pioneering conspectus, Haggett set out to explore the component parts of his framework in more detail. The first output was a book on network analysis, combining human and physical geography (Haggett and Chorley, 1969), but most of his work has focused on aspects of diffusion (Cliff et al., 1975, 1981), especially in the context of MEDICAL GEOGRAPHY.

Haggett's major role was thus as a synthesizer and stimulant, and he promoted both the search for locational order as a major goal of contemporary geography and its adopted positivist philosophy, although he wrote very little himself on the latter. Others followed his lead, providing their own perspectives on the study of what became known to some as SPATIAL STRUCTURES (Johnston, 1973). Morrill (1970), for example, was also strongly influenced by the geometrical tradition adopted by Bunge and Haggett, and

focused his text *The spatial organization of society* on what he termed the 'nearness principle': people, he argued, seek to maximize spatial interaction at minimum cost and so bring related activities into proximity – the result is that 'human society is surprisingly alike from place to place . . . [because of] the predictable, organized pattern of locations and inter-relations'. Whereas Morrill focused entirely on substantive illustration of his principle (which he later revised somewhat, thereby playing down the geometrical component: see Morrill and Dormitzer, 1979), Abler et al. (1971) spent the first third of *Spatial organization* discussing the nature of science and the methods to be used in locational analysis.

Critiques of locational analysis developed during the 1970s. Initially, they focused on the validity of NORMATIVE THEORY in geographical studies, on the grounds that this did not reflect the reality of DECISION-MAKING and so was of little value in predicting locational arrangements; the outcome was BEHAVIOURAL GEOGRAPHY, with its more inductive approach (see EMPIRICISM). Nevertheless, this also assumed that generalizations about spatial behaviour and patterns are feasible, a position countered in a further critique – generally termed that of HUMANISTIC GEOGRAPHY – which argued that locational analysis studies imply an absence

347

of individual human free will and suggest little more than a programmed automaton responding in set ways to defined stimuli (van der Laan and Piersma, 1982). Later still, those attracted to one or both of Marxism (see STRUCTURALISM) and REALISM argued against the search for generalization in a dynamic society comprising individuals with the capacity to remember, learn and promote change. As a consequence, while the study of spatial patterns, the use of relevant quantitative methods and the implied search for laws of spatial organization remain part of human geography, their dominance of the discipline was restricted to the 1960s and early 1970s.

Some historians of human geography are concerned to determine whether the development of locational analysis in the 1960s reflected the influence of persuasive leaders such as Haggett, whether it came about because of greater awareness of the existence of relevant models and methods in other disciplines, as Pooler (1977) suggests, or whether it was just a general realization that the traditional form of regional analysis was increasingly less suited to study of the contemporary world. Cox (1976) argued that until the nineteenth century societies were predominantly local in their orientation and the main influence on their livelihood was the local physical environment – hence traditional regional geography and its society-land focus. But the twentieth-century integration of societies into a global world-economy (see WORLD-SYSTEMS ANALYSIS) means that spatial interdependence has become much more important and 'locally experienced environmental dependencies lost their rationale: men [sic] relate less and less to the land on which they stand and more and more to socially-created geographical patterns over a much wider area': recognition of this by geographers led to locational analysis ousting regional analysis as the discipline's dominant paradigm.

Whatever the reason for its origin, there is little doubt that locational analysis substantially changed the nature of human geography from the mid-1960s on, although there is some doubt that it ever

dominated the discipline (Mikesell, 1984). It presented geography as a positivist social science, concerned to develop precise, quantitatively stated generalizations about patterns of spatial organization, thereby enriching and being enriched by LOCATION THEORY, and to offer models and procedures which could be used in physical planning. By 1978, therefore, Haggett could write that:

the spatial economy is more carefully defined than before, we know a little more about its organization, the way it responds to shocks, and the way some regional sections are tied into others. There now exist theoretical bridges, albeit incomplete and shaky, which span from pure, spaceless economics through to a more spatially disaggregated reality.

Twelve years later, he continued to promote the search for 'scientific generalizations' (Haggett, 1990), while accepting that in the search for spatial order 'the answer largely depends on what we are prepared to look for and what we accept as order': for only a minority of geographers now can we claim that order is the focus of their quest.

RJJ

References

Abler, R. F., Adams, J. S. and Gould, P. R. 1971: *Spatial organization: the geographer's view of the world.* Englewood Cliffs, NJ: Prentice-Hall.

Bunge, W. 1966: *Theoretical geography.* Lund: C. W. K. Gleerup.

Chorley, R. J. and Haggett, P., eds 1965: *Frontiers in geographical thinking.* London: Methuen.

Chorley, R. J. and Haggett, P., eds 1967: *Models in geography.* London: Methuen.

Cliff, A. D., Haggett, P., Bassett, K., Ord, J. K. and Davies, R. 1975: *Elements of spatial structure: a quantitative approach.* Cambridge: Cambridge University Press.

Cliff, A. D., Haggett, P., Bassett, K., Ord, J. K. and Davies, R. 1981: *Spatial diffusion.* Cambridge: Cambridge University Press.

Cole, J. P. and King, C. A. M. 1968: *Quantitative geography.* London: John Wiley.

Cox, K. R. 1976: American geography: social science emergent. *Soc. Sci. Q.* 57, pp. 182–207.

Haggett, P. 1965: *Locational analysis in human geography.* London: Edward Arnold.

Haggett, P. 1978: The spatial economy. *Am. behav. Scient.* 22, pp. 151–67.

Haggett, P. 1990: *The geographer's art*. Oxford: Blackwell.

Haggett, P. and Chorley, R. J. 1969: *Network analysis in geography*. London: Edward Arnold.

Haggett, P., Cliff, A. D. and Frey, A. E. 1977: *Locational analysis in human geography*, second edition. London: Edward Arnold.

Harvey, D. 1969: *Explanation in geography*. London: Edward Arnold.

Johnston, R. J. 1973: *Spatial structures: introducing the study of spatial systems in human geography*. London: Methuen.

Johnston, R. J. 1991: *Geography and geographers: Anglo-American human geography since 1945*, fourth edition. London: Edward Arnold.

McCarty, H. H. and Lindberg, J. B. 1966: *A preface to economic geography*. Englewood Cliffs, NJ: Prentice-Hall.

Mikesell, M. W. 1984: North America. In Johnston, R. J. and Claval, P., eds, *Geography since the Second World War: an international survey*. London: Croom Helm, pp. 185–213.

Morrill, R. L. 1970: *The spatial organization of society*. Belmont, CA: Wadsworth.

Morrill, R. L. and Dormitzer, J. 1979: *The spatial order: an introduction to modern geography*. North Scituate, NJ: Duxbury.

Pooler, J. A. 1977: The origins of the spatial tradition in geography: an interpretation. *Ontario Geography* 11, pp. 56–83.

Sack, R. D. 1972: Geography, geometry and explanation. *Ann. Ass. Am. Geogr.* 62, pp. 61–78.

Smith, D. M. 1981: *Industrial location: an economic geographical analysis*, second edition. New York: John Wiley.

van der Laan, L. and Piersma, A. 1982: The image of man: paradigmatic cornerstone in human geography. *Ann. Ass. Am. Geogr.* 72, pp. 411–26.

locational interdependence The dependence of locational choice on the location chosen by others. In reality, there are very few situations in which locational choice can legitimately be regarded as totally independent of the location of other participants in the activity in question, or in related activities. For example, the location of any factory will be dependent to some extent on the location of suppliers or consumers. But locational interdependence generally refers to situations in which the choice of location depends on that of competitors. The analysis of locational interdependence thus concerns the strategies adopted in seeking control of sales areas that bestow some degree of SPATIAL MONOPOLY, in circumstances in which the location of competitors is a relevant consideration.

The locational interdependence approach in INDUSTRIAL LOCATION THEORY is closely associated with the theory of imperfect competition, in which it is recognized that geographical space necessarily introduces imperfections in market competition. (See also HOTELLING MODEL; MARKET AREA ANALYSIS; VARIABLE REVENUE ANALYSIS.)   DMS

locational triangle A simple graphic model devised by Alfred Weber for the analysis of industrial location. Weber's classic work on LOCATION THEORY was published in 1909 as *Über den standort der Industrien*, and issued in English translation 20 years later. It has probably had more influence on INDUSTRIAL LOCATION THEORY than any other single contribution. Weber's graphic analysis had its origin in the work of Wilhelm Launhardt, an earlier German economist.

Weber's attempt to derive 'pure' rules of location involved a number of simplifying assumptions. There were materials, markets and cheap-labour locations at fixed points, and movement was possible in any direction at the same cost per unit of distance. From this idealized world Weber abstracted sources of two materials (M_1 and M_2) and a single market point (C) and posed the question of where would be the least-cost location (P) for production within this triangle (see the figure). Given the weight of commodities to be shipped from M_1 to M_2 and to C, and given the transport costs per unit of distance, the problem may be solved by a physical analogue model, known as Varignon's frame, using weights and pulleys. There is also a number of computer algorithms designed to identify as closely as possible this point of minimum transport cost or minimum 'aggregate travel'.

From information on the cost of the two materials and of delivering the products to the market it is possible to calculate total transport cost at alternative locations. This enables contours of equal additional transportation cost (ISODAPANES) to be

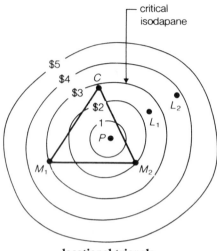

locational triangle

interpolated. Weber used these isodapanes to demonstrate the circumstances in which the optimal location could be diverted from the least-transport-cost location (P) by economies of AGGLOMERATION or by a cheap labour location. The cheap labour case is illustrated in the figure. Cheap labour at L, could provide a cost saving of $3 (per unit of output). According to Weber, this would provide lower overall production costs at L_1, being within the 'critical isodapane', i.e. the isodapane with a value equivalent to the saving on labour cost ($3), as shown in the figure. This cheap labour source would therefore become the optimal location. A second cheap labour source L_2 is beyond the critical isodapane and would not divert the factory from P.   DMS

References

Launhardt, W. 1885: *Mathematische Begründung der Volkswirtschaftslehre*, Leipzig: W. Englemann.

Weber, A. 1929: *Alfred Weber's theory of the location of industries*, translated by C. J. Friedrich. Chicago: University of Chicago Press. (Reprinted 1971, New York: Russell and Russell; first German edition 1909.)

Suggested Reading

Smith, D. M., 1981: *Industrial location: an economic geographical analysis*, second edition. New York: John Wiley, pp. 69–75.

log-linear modelling   Procedures for analysing data measured at the nominal level of MEASUREMENT only. The goal, as in REGRESSION, is to fit an equation which predicts the values in a contingency table (i.e. the entries in each cell) in terms of the values of independent variables (which may themselves also be measured at the nominal level only). The terms in the model, presented in logarithmic form, are the deviations for the relevant cell (defined by the values of the independent variables) from a control value, usually the grand mean for the entire sample.   RJJ

Suggested Reading

O'Brien, L. G. 1990: *The statistical analysis of contingency table designs*. Concepts and techniques in modern geography 51. Norwich: Environmental Publications.

O'Brien, L. G. 1992: *Introducing quantitative geography: measurement, methods and generalised linear models*. London: Routledge.

logical positivism   A particular development of the philosophy of POSITIVISM which was formulated by the VIENNA CIRCLE in the 1920s and 1930s and which in its modern form is usually associated with the writings of Ayer, Hempel and Nagel (among others). Unlike earlier versions of positivism, logical positivism recognized two (and only two) kinds of statement as scientifically meaningful: (a) *empirical* (or 'synthetic') statements, the truth of which had to be established by verification; and (b) *analytical* statements of logic and mathematics, which were judged to be true by definition. Much of the specific critique of logical positivism, as opposed to the more general critique of positivism, has concentrated on the problems posed by this central 'principle of verification' and on the physicalism which it was often supposed to entail. Indeed, Popper (1976) insisted that 'everybody knows nowadays that logical positivism is dead' and declared 'I must admit responsibility'. He believed that his formulation of CRITICAL RATIONALISM in the 1930s, and especially its contrary 'principle of falsification', had decisively discredited the claims of logical positivism. Certainly Suppe (1977), from a rather more catholic perspective, reckoned that 'virtually all of the positivistic program for philosophy of science has been repudiated by contemporary philosophy of science' and that today 'its influence is that of a movement historically important in shaping the landscape of a much-changed contemporary philosophy of science'. Even so, according to Guelke (1978), 'from Hartshorne to Harvey geographical writing on philosophy and methodology has to a greater or lesser degree shown the influence of logical positivist ideas'. Its most sharply focused application came during the QUANTITATIVE REVOLUTION:

In the 1950s and 1960s, many geographers in emphasising the importance of laws, theories and prediction in empirical research *implicitly* adopted a logical positivist view of science and scientific explanation. The connection between geography and logical positivism was made *explicit* by Harvey [in his *Explanation in geography* (1969)] who presented a thorough logical positivist analysis of geographical explanation (Guelke, 1978, p. 46).

Whether or not it is fair to use Harvey's text as an index of human geography as a whole, it is certainly clear that today, as the critique of logical positivism has become more widely known, fewer geographers now cheerfully accept the label and most resist the suggestion that logical positivism represents 'the' scientific method.   DG

References

Guelke, L. 1978: Geography and logical positivism. In Herbert, D. T. and Johnston, R. J., eds, *Geography and the urban environment*, volume 1. Chichester: John Wiley, pp. 35–61.

Harvey, D. 1969: *Explanation in geography*. London: Edward Arnold/New York: St. Martin's Press.

Popper, K. 1976: *Unended quest: an intellectual autobiography*. London: Fontana.

Suppe, F., ed. 1977: *The structure of scientific theories*, second edition. Urbana, IL: University of Illinois Press.

Suggested Reading
Guelke (1978).

logit   A transformation of a variable, usually to meet the criteria for statistical analyses within the GENERAL LINEAR MODEL. Logit transformations are usually performed on binary data (i.e. the variable can only take the values of 0 and 1) to avoid estimating equations which might produce 'nonsense' answers outside that range.   RJJ

Suggested Reading
O'Brien, L. G. 1992: *Introducing quantitative geography: measurement, methods and generalised linear models*. London: Routledge.

longitudinal data analysis   The study of repeated measurements of one or more variables on the same observation units over a period of time. Such study allows consideration of change over time without potentially committing a cross-level fallacy (see ECOLOGICAL FALLACY) which might be done by inferring change processes from cross-sectional studies of different samples over time.   RJJ

Lowry model   A MODEL of the generation and spatial allocation of urban activities and land uses, developed by I. S. Lowry in 1964 for the Pittsburgh urban region. The urban activities are total population, basic (manufacturing and primary) employment and service employment, and the corresponding land uses are residential, industrial and service.

The Lowry model uses ECONOMIC BASE THEORY to generate the overall activity levels: basic employment is exogenous, and from it the service employment and total population are predicted. The activities are then allocated to the zones of the urban region, using the concept of POPULATION POTENTIAL. Population is allocated to zones in proportion to the population potential of each zone, and service employment in proportion to the market or employment potential of the zone. The Lowry model also includes constraints on land use in the zones, notably maximum densities of housing (population) and minimum sizes for clusters of services. Lowry allowed three different levels of service clusters: neighbourhood, district and metropolitan. The allocation procedure is iterative, with the activities being reallocated until land-use constraints are met, and also until the final population distribution corresponds with the distribution used to compute potentials.

The model is a comparative static one: given an initial pattern and then an injection (or loss) of basic employment, the model calculates the new equilibrium pattern. The Lowry model was characteristic of the first generation of urban and subregional planning models; in later models the economic base mechanism was both refined and disaggregated, and the crude allocation by population potential was replaced by GRAVITY and ENTROPY-MAXIMIZING MODELS. (See also ACTIVITY ALLOCATION MODELS.) LWH

Suggested Reading

Weber, M. J. 1984: *Explanation, prediction and planning: the Lowry model.* London: Pion.

M

macrogeography The use of techniques of CENTROGRAPHY to identify empirical regularities in spatial distributions and hence to derive abstract generalizations about space-occupying systems. From its original base in SOCIAL PHYSICS, and owing much to the pioneering work of John Q. Stewart, macrogeography moved out to become identified more explicitly with GENERAL SYSTEMS THEORY. But from the outset Stewart and his collaborators had insisted that the hallmark of macrogeography was abstraction rather than SCALE.

The size of the area portrayed by a map does not indicate whether the approach was microscopic or what we shall call 'macroscopic'. The mere assembling of more and more areas, even with an increase in detail, does not mean a shift in point of view from microscopic to macroscopic. A heightening of the level of abstraction is the significant thing, an insistence on the functional consistency and organic unity of the whole, a recognition that no part of a true system can be understood without reference to the whole (Stewart and Warntz, 1958).

Thus the core of macrogeography was the concept of POPULATION POTENTIAL. The cartographic surfaces which could be produced from these calculations expressed a belief in the importance of elemental spatial concepts to an explanation of systems in both natural and social domains, so that although some of the basic ideas were derived from thermodynamics no analogies were intended; as Warntz argued, 'the similarity in structure of patterns derived from no *a priori* determination. Rather, this result was obtained because both kinds of abstractions are logically related to each other' (Warntz, 1973). On this basis macrogeography was seen to prefigure 'a dimensional social science', and both Stewart and Warntz believed that 'much of the lag in the development of social science stems from the impatient attempts to understand . . . more difficult problems [what they called 'the loftier human characteristics'] before time and space regularities are understood' – a claim which has resurfaced (at least in part) in TIME-GEOGRAPHY. In the event, however, the success of macrogeography was more limited, although the American Geographical Society's Macrogeography Project made a number of seminal contributions to SPATIAL ANALYSIS (e.g. Neft, 1966) and Warntz's substantive work on so-called *income fronts* proved highly suggestive (see Warntz, 1965). DG

References

Neft, D. 1966: *Statistical analysis for areal distributions*. Philadelphia: Regional Science Research Institute.

Stewart, J. Q. and Warntz, W. 1958: Macrogeography and social science. *Geogrl. Rev.* 48, pp. 167–84.

Warntz, W. 1965: *Macrogeography and income fronts*. Philadelphia: Regional Science Research Institute.

Warntz, W. 1973: New geography as general spatial systems theory – old social physics writ large? In Chorley, R. J., ed., *Directions in geography*. London: Methuen.

Suggested Reading

Warntz (1973).

Warntz, W. 1984: Trajectories and coordinates. In Billinge, M., Gregory, D. and Martin, R. L., eds, *Recollections of a revolution: geography as spatial science*. London: Macmillan/New York: St. Martin's Press, pp. 134–50.

malapportionment An electoral abuse in which a party promotes its own interests by defining constituencies of differing (population or electorate) sizes. The most successful method involves creating small constituencies for your own party to win and much larger ones for opposition party victories. As a strategy, malapportionment is only potentially successful if the parties' supporters are spatially separated to some extent. Malapportionment was ruled as unconstitutional and subsequently outlawed as a practice in the US in the 1960s, and British legislation requires the definition of constituencies the electorates of which are 'as equal as is practicable'. RJJ

Suggested Reading

Taylor, P. J. and Johnston, R. J. 1979: *Geography of elections*. London: Penguin.

Malthusian model The economist Thomas Robert Malthus (1766–1834) published *An essay on the principle of population* in 1798, and it is to his ideas that subsequent thinking on the economic approach to demography may be traced. While he modified his own position, and subsequent developments of Malthusian theory are complex, his general view was that population tends to increase faster than the means of subsistence, thus absorbing all economic gains, unless controlled by what he termed 'preventative' and 'positive' checks. He maintained that population, if unchecked, tended to increase at a geometric rate (i.e., 1, 2, 4, 8, 16 ...) while subsistence increased at an arithmetic rate (1, 2, 3, 4, 5, ...) and 'in two centuries the population would be to the means of subsistence as 256 to 9; in three centuries as 4096 to 13, and in two thousand years the difference would be almost incalculable'. His 'positive and preventative checks' which occur in human populations to prevent excessive growth relate to practices affecting MORTALITY and FERTILITY respectively. So his 'positive' checks included wars, disease, poverty and, especially, lack of food; while his 'preventative' checks included principally 'moral restraint', or the postponement of marriage, and 'vice', in which he included adultery, birth control and

abortion. He saw the tension between population and RESOURCES as a major cause of the misery for much of humanity. Malthus was not, however, in favour of contraceptive methods, since their use did not generate the same drive to work hard as would a postponement of marriage. He stressed the negative correlation between station in life and number of children and, in order to induce in the lower classes the self-control and social responsibility he saw in the middle classes, Malthus asserted that the poor should be better paid and educated.

Malthus's views have been challenged in a great variety of ways. He certainly established the thesis that population was growing quickly and that people are biological as well as social beings, depending on sexual drive and food. Yet he has been criticized, for example, for confusing moralist and scientific approaches and for being a very poor prophet of events. Marx was one of the most powerful critics of Malthus, asserting that poverty is the result of the unjust social institutions of CAPITALISM rather than of population growth. No country of Europe or North America, except possibly Ireland, conformed to the Malthusian prediction. During the nineteenth century economic growth far outdistanced population growth, resulting in rising standards of living; and, despite this, birth rates declined first in France and Sweden and then more generally. It has also been argued that Malthus's reactionary views impeded the development of demography as a science. PEO

Suggested Reading

Coleman, D. and Schofield, R., eds 1986: *The state of population theory: forward from Malthus*. Oxford: Blackwell.

Dupâquier, J., Fauve-Chamoux, A. and Grebenik, E., eds 1983: *Malthus past and present*. London: Academic Press.

James, P. 1979: *Population Malthus: his life and times*. London: Routledge and Kegan Paul.

Malthus, T. R. 1970 edn: *An essay on the principle of population and a summary view of the principle of population*, ed. A. Flew, London: Pelican.

Petersen, W. 1979: *Malthus*. London: Heinemann/Cambridge, MA: Harvard University Press.

map image and map The map image is a structured cartographic representation of selected spatial information. The image becomes a map when represented physically (e.g. classical topographic map, or braille), virtually (e.g. on a computer screen) or linguistically (e.g. verbal or written spatial instructions) (see CARTO-GRAPHY).

The encoded real-world conception of a cartographer (or others such as a national mapping agency) is transmitted to a map reader through the map image, itself the result of processes such as generalization, SYMBOLIZATION etc. Whether or not the map image has been constructed according to formal guidelines of scientific cartography (Openshaw (1989) for example, uses simulation techniques to produce a highly significant map that is not produced to any formal guidelines), it has somehow to be represented so that a map reader may interpret it.

Historically (see CARTOGRAPHY, HIS-TORY OF), transfer and storage have been the constraining factors on the size and detail of a physical map image: Babylonian and Mesopotamian maps of the fifth and thirtieth centuries BC were simple and small because the clay tablet used would crack if made too large, and their surfaces were given only to crude linework. Early maps produced on printing presses had a maximum size placed on them by the woodblock, which was prone to warping if made too large. Furthermore, updating such maps proved difficult, and so the map images not only exhibited quite poor linework but often were badly out of date. Additionally, some media have a very short life span during which the image can be retained. Aboriginal maps drawn on sand or birch bark are impermanent for this reason. Indeed, the shortest life span for a map image must be the instance in which people draw maps in the air when giving guidance to others.

Early map images were constrained by available technology. By contrast, contemporary cartography has abundant means at its disposal, but despite the new technological opportunities most physical maps produced assume that the map reader has perfect colour perception and excellent eyesight (see O'Brien and McFetridge, 1991). Maps for those with physical or other disabilities tend to be relegated to special projects rather than being a part of core cartography. MJB

References

O'Brien, L. G. and McFetridge, M. 1991: Mapping geographic space for the disabled. In Rybaczuk, K. and Blakemore, M. eds, *Mapping the nations: Proceedings of the ICA 15th Conference*, volume 1. London: ICA 1991 Ltd, pp. 149–56.

Openshaw, S. 1989: Automating the search for cancer clusters. *Prof. Statist.* 8(9), pp. 7–8.

Suggested Reading

Mark, D. M. 1987: On giving and receiving directions: cartographic and cognitive issues. In Chrisman, N. R., ed., *Proceedings of Auto Carto 8.* Falls Church, VA: ACSM/ASPRS, pp. 562–71.

Monmonier, M. S. 1982: *Technological transitions in cartography.* Madison, WI: University of Wisconsin Press.

Robinson, A. H. and Petchenik, B. B. 1976: *The nature of maps: essays towards understanding maps and mapping.* Chicago: University of Chicago Press, pp. 1–22.

Vasilev, I., Freundschuh, S., Mark, D. M., Theisen, G. D. and MacAvoy, J. 1990: What is a map? *Cartogr. J.* 27, pp. 119–23.

White, M. 1991: Car navigation systems. In Maguire, D. J., Goodchild, M. F. and Rhind, D. W., eds, *Geographical information systems: principles and applications*, volume 2. London: Longman, pp. 115–25.

map reading The perceptual and physical processes of interpreting and analysing map images (see MAP IMAGE AND MAP). Determining and evaluating such processes play an important part in improving cartographic communication: they include the psycho-physical movements of the eye when observing detail and short- and long-term memory which differentiate between initial cursory scanning and subsequent detailed examination, and extend to the wider consideration of visualization. Buttenfield and Mackaness (1991) examine the ways in which reading, analysis and interpretation are interrelated with the ways in which people organize and extract information from maps. MJB

Reference

Buttenfield, B. P. and Mackaness, W. A. 1991: Visualization. In Maguire, D. J., Goodchild,

M. F. and Rhind, D. W., eds, *Geographical information systems: principles and applications*, volume 1. London: Longman, pp. 428–43.

Suggested Reading
Moellering, H. M., ed. 1991: Analytical cartography. *Cartogr. geogr. Inform. Sys.* 18(1), 78pp.

market See CENTRAL PLACE THEORY; COMMON MARKET; MARKET EXCHANGE; PERIODIC MARKET SYSTEMS.

market area analysis The examination of the conditions under which the market area of the firm is determined. This type of analysis is important both to industrial location and to the provision of services. For an industrial organization, control over a sales territory is of some relevance to locational choice and plant viability. Some further aspects of market area analysis in industrial location are discussed under HOTELLING MODEL and VARIABLE REVENUE ANALYSIS.

The derivation of a market area for the single plant is explained in the figure. A plant is located at A, in the (one-dimensional) space represented by the horizontal axis. The cost of producing one unit or a

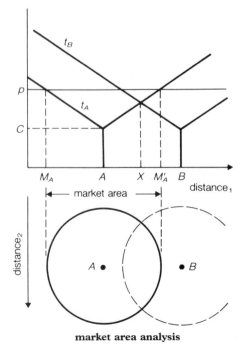

market area analysis

given volume of output is represented by C. The commodity is sold to the customers, ranging along the distance axis, at a price that includes production cost and transport costs (represented by t_A). A price p is the most that the consumers are prepared to pay for the commodity, a condition assumed to be constant in space. Under these simple conditions, the market area for the firm located at A will be bounded by the points M_A and M'_A, where delivered price is just equal to the maximum that the consumer is prepared to pay. Introducing the second distance dimension and rotating the edge of the market line about A would generate a circular market area.

Relaxing the assumption of a single firm in isolation and introducing a second plant at B, the figure illustrates the effect of LOCATIONAL INTERDEPENDENCE on market competition. Firm B is able to offer the commodity at a lower delivered price (t_B) than A in the section of A's market area extending from M_A to X. On the assumption that consumers purchase from the cheapest source of supply, this area would now be transferred to the market area of firm B. As other firms enter the industry, space should gradually be filled up and market areas whittled down to the minimum size consistent with profitable operation by a process of competition, as elaborated in the CENTRAL PLACE THEORY associated with Walter Christaller and August Lösch.

In reality, market areas will be more complex in both form and derivation than in this simple model, because of the actual nature of consumer preferences, behaviour, pricing policies and competitive practice.

DMS

Suggested Reading
Smith, D. M. 1981: *Industrial location: an economic geographical analysis*, second edition. New York: John Wiley, chs 4 and 9.

market exchange A system of exchange organized through price-fixing markets. Market exchange was one of three FORMS OF ECONOMIC INTEGRATION identified by Karl Polanyi. When he used it to characterize an entire economy (rather than segments within an economy) Polanyi spoke of a *market economy* thus: 'an economic system controlled, regulated and directed by markets alone; order in the production and distribution of goods is entrusted to this self-regulating mechanism . . . [and] ensured by prices alone' (Polanyi, 1957). Three features of market exchange are especially important.

(a) Market exchange depends upon a characteristic SPATIAL STRUCTURE involving the transmission of price signals and the interdependence of markets in time and space. 'Price-making markets are integrative only if they are linked up in a system that tends to spread the effects of prices to markets other than those directly affected' (Polanyi, in Dalton, 1968). Much of mainstream LOCATION THEORY assumed, and on occasion addressed, these matters but attention was usually focused on the pattern of markets – for example, as in Christaller's CENTRAL PLACE THEORY – with comparatively little regard to the diffusion of price signals. Notable empirical exceptions include Lösch's (1954, pp. 496–504) suggestive descriptions of 'spatial differences in the movement of commodity prices' and Pred's (1973) reconstruction of the circulation of information (including prices current) through systems of American cities between 1790 and 1840. Most of the theoretical formulations depended upon NEOCLASSICAL ECONOMICS, however, which assumes: (i) the universality of market exchange; and (ii) its tendency toward equilibrium. Polanyi contested both of these assumptions: see (b) and (c) respectively.

(b) Market exchange is historically specific. Before the INDUSTRIAL REVOLUTION in England, Polanyi argued, 'the economic system was submerged in general social relations; markets were merely an accessory feature of an institutional setting controlled and regulated . . . by social authority'. In preindustrial societies, therefore, 'the self-regulating market was unknown': and it was precisely because he believed that the emergence of 'the idea of self-regulation was a complete reversal of the trend of development' that Polanyi entitled his celebrated account of the INDUSTRIAL REVOLUTION *The great transformation* (1957). Within geography, the historical specificity of market exchange has

been accentuated most sharply by those approaches which have drawn upon MARXIAN ECONOMICS to recognize 'integration through price-fixing markets [as] characteristic of the capitalist mode of production' (Harvey, 1973: see CAPITALISM). Even so, Harvey described the Industrial Revolution in terms which were as close to Polanyi as they were to Marx:

The slow build-up of the Industrial Revolution in Britain . . . represented a gradual penetration of market exchange into production (as distinct from trade and commerce) through the penetration of land and labour. As the industrial revolution gained momentum, more and more sectors of activity became integrated through market exchange, and distribution and service activities were also drawn in. The circulation of surplus value in its capitalist form finally broke free from the restraining influence of the rank society and then, through its domination of all the key sectors of society became the medium through which the market mode of economic integration gradually bound society into one cohesive economic system (Harvey, 1973, p. 243).

This slippage between Marx and Polanyi is problematic – Polanyi was not a Marxist and there are important differences between his formulations and those of HISTORICAL MATERIALISM – but Harvey was not alone in seeking to connect them. More recently, Wallerstein's discussions of the formation of the capitalist world-economy and what he calls 'historical capitalism' rely on similar connections and accord a peculiar primacy to systems of (unequal) exchange (see Brenner, 1977; Skocpol, 1977). This is not to argue for an intellectual fideism, of course: Marx's formulations have no necessary privilege over Polanyi's and, indeed, one commentator has claimed that Wallerstein's schema is deficient because it pays *too little* attention to Polanyi's work (Dodgshon, 1977). But the rise of this WORLD-SYSTEMS ANALYSIS has confirmed the continuing significance of Polanyi's writings and has underscored the historical specificity of market exchange.

(c) Market exchange entails relations of CONFLICT. According to Polanyi, 'exchange at fluctuating prices aims at a gain that can be attained only by an attitude involving a distinctive antagonistic relationship between the partners . . . [which] is ineradicable' (Polanyi, in Dalton, 1968). In his first formulations Harvey (1973) thus identified market exchange with *stratified* societies, but he soon acknowledged that this begged the central question. Giddens (1981) had emphasized that for both Marx and Weber '*the market is intrinsically a structure of power*' (emphasis added) and that for any account seeking to build on either of these foundations 'the problem . . . is not the recognition of the diversity of the relationships and conflicts created by the capitalist market as such, but that of making the *theoretical* transition from such relationships and conflicts to identification of classes as structured forms'. In a later essay Harvey (1974) drew upon Giddens's writings to provide a thumbnail sketch of the connections between class structure and residential differentiation; and although this derived 'primarily from a reading of Marx', it also gave a special prominence to differential 'market capacities' in a way which plainly owed just as much to Weber (see CLASS). The past 15 years have seen a number of developments from this baseline (see, e.g., Cox, 1978) and particular interest continues to be attached to studies of the relations between housing markets and LABOUR MARKETS (see, e.g., Harvey, 1978; Thorns, 1982; Hamnett, 1984; Saunders, 1984). More recently still, the collapse of communism in Eastern Europe and the dissolution of the Soviet Union has ushered in a new period of so-called 'market triumphalism', but many of the former command economies have experienced considerable problems in making the transition to a market economy, which seems to confirm the conflicts and asymmetries which Polanyi believed to be inherent within market exchange.   DG

References

Brenner, R. 1977: The origins of capitalist development: a critique of neo-Smithian Marxism. *New Left Rev.* 104, pp. 25–92.

Cox, K. R., ed. 1978: *Urbanization and conflict in market societies.* London: Methuen.

Dalton, G., ed. 1968: *Primitive, archaic and modern economies: essays of Karl Polanyi.* Boston: Beacon Press.

Dodgshon, R. A. 1977: Review symposium; *The modern world system* by Immanuel Wallerstein. A spatial perspective. *Peasant Studies* 6, pp. 8–19.

Giddens, A. 1981: *The class structure of the advanced societies,* second edition. London: Hutchinson.

Hamnett, C. 1984: The postwar restructuring of the British housing and labour markets. *Environ. Plann. A* 12, pp. 147–61.

Harvey, D. 1973: *Social justice and the city.* London: Edward Arnold/Baltimore, MD: Johns Hopkins University Press.

Harvey, D. 1974: Class structure in a capitalist society and the theory of residential differentiation. In Peel, R., Chisholm, M. and Haggett, P., eds, *Processes in physical and human geography: Bristol essays.* London: Heinemann, pp. 354–69.

Harvey, D. 1978: Labor, capital and class struggle around the built environment in advanced capitalist societies. In Cox, K. R., ed., *Urbanization and conflict in market societies.* London: Methuen/Chicago; Maaroufa Press, pp. 9–37.

Lösch, A. 1954: *The economics of location.* New Haven: Yale University Press.

Polanyi, K. 1957: *The great transformation: the political and economic origins of our time.* Boston: Beacon Press.

Pred, A. 1973: *Urban growth and the circulation of information: the United States system of cities 1790–1840.* Cambridge, MA: Harvard University Press.

Saunders, P. 1984: Beyond housing classes. *Int. J. urban and reg. Res.* 8, pp. 202–25.

Skocpol, T. 1977: Wallerstein's world capitalist system: a theoretical and historical critique. *Am. J. Soc.* 82, pp. 1075–90.

Thorns, D. C. 1982: Industrial restructuring and changes in the labour and property markets in Britain. *Environ. Plann. A* 14, pp. 745–63.

Suggested Reading

Cox (1978).

Harvey (1973), pp. 210–15, 241–5, 261–84.

Polanyi (1957).

market orientation The tendency of an economic activity to locate in proximity to its market. This will be the case where the cost of shipping the product to the consumer accounts for a relatively high proportion of total cost, or where the effort involved in consumers getting to the source of supply, along with the attraction of the good or service, is such that only short distances will be travelled. Historically, the operation of market orientation has changed with the distribution of population and the nature of the productive process. Formerly, market orientation applied mainly at the local level, with small-scale producers supplying a small local market, while today the pull of the market is rather a factor in the AGGLOMERATION of economic activity in major metropolitan areas. (Cf. MATERIAL ORIENTATION.) DMS

market potential model A device for estimating the likely volume of sales attainable from alternative plant locations. It is an application of the general concept of POPULATION POTENTIAL, which also forms the basis of the GRAVITY MODEL. It rests on some very specific assumptions as to the prevailing demand situation; that the level of sales at any market will be proportional to some initial local magnitude there, and that this will decrease with increasing distance from the source of supply. There is thus the implicit assumption of a downward-sloping DEMAND CURVE and an f.o.b. price (whereby the cost of transportation is met by the consumer; see PRICING POLICIES).

The market potential or estimated volume of sales (M) attainable from any plant location i is given by:

$$M_i = \sum_{j=1}^{n} Q_j / T_{ij},$$

where Q is some initial measure of magnitude of the size of the local market at j, and T is some measure of the transfer cost from i to j, or the rise in delivered price with increasing distance from the plant. The magnitude of Q is usually measured by the size of the local population or by per capita income or retail sales, in the absence of a more accurate basis for the estimation of size of market for the commodity in question. T may be measured by the prevailing TRANSPORT COSTS, but this is more usually taken simply as linear distance between production points and markets.

When M is calculated for a set of possible plant locations, the one with the largest market potential can be identified. Market potential at alternative locations can be used to interpolate a market potential

surface. If revenue is expected to be proportional to volume of sales, and if this is actually identified by the market potential formulation, then a market potential surface can act as a REVENUE SURFACE.

The practical application of the concept of market potential is severely limited by the stringency of the assumptions on which its prediction of likely sales is based. These rarely exist in reality. The market potential concept has been used rather indiscriminately in economic geography, often in circumstances in which it is not appropriate to the empirical situation. (See also POPULATION POTENTIAL.) DMS

Suggested Reading
Smith, D. M. 1981: *Industrial location: an economic geographical analysis*, second edition. New York: John Wiley, pp. 275–8.

Markov process (or **Markov chain**) A type of STOCHASTIC PROCESS: if the probability of being in a state (or states) at time t is wholly dependent upon the state(s) at some preceding time(s) it is said to be a Markov process. Where only the immediately preceding time and state is considered it is said to be a first order Markov process, but higher order processes (i.e. dependence on earlier states) can be modelled. The process is frequently represented by a transition probability matrix in which the rows and columns represent states and the cells represent the probabilities of movement between states. For example, land-use changes between the categories 'residential', 'commercial' and 'industrial' could be modelled by the matrix:

		State at time $t+1$:		
		Res.	Comm.	Ind.
State	Res.	0.90	0.06	0.04
at time	Comm.	0.02	0.85	0.13
t	Ind.	0.00	0.10	0.90

The matrix is interpreted as follows: between time t and time $t+1$, 90 per cent of the residential land remains in the same use, 6 per cent is transferred to commercial use, and 4 per cent becomes industrial. The second and third rows are similarly interpreted: note that each of the rows sums to unity (no land is lost or gained in the conversion process). The repeated operation of such a matrix results in a stable distribution between the states, which is independent (in general) of the initial distribution. The Markov model has been used to study the growth of firms (movement between size categories) and the migration of firms and households (movement between geographical locations). AMH

Suggested Reading

Collins, L., Drewett, R. and Ferguson, R. 1974: Markov models in geography. *Statistician* 23, pp. 179–210.

Marxian economics
A body of theory that seeks to provide an explanation of how an economy functions, derived from the POLITICAL ECONOMY of Karl Marx (1818–83) and from its elaborations and extensions by Friedrich Engels (1820–95). The alternative body of theory is NEOCLASSICAL ECONOMICS, which forms the basis of the analysis usually accepted in the West, or the capitalist world.

The 1960s and 1970s saw a resurgence of interest in Marxian economics. What Marxists describe as 'bourgeois economics' appeared to be increasingly inadequate as a basis for understanding how a capitalist economy actually functions, as evident from the failure of Western governments and their economic advisers to manage economic crises (see CRISIS). Marxian economics provides an alternative and (for Marxists) more persuasive interpretation of how CAPITALISM operates.

Marxian economics does not form a prominent component in conventional textbooks and courses in economics in the capitalist world. Marx himself has been described by Paul Samuelson as 'a minor post-Ricardian', although Samuelson gives Marxian economics a few pages in his popular textbook, *Economics* (Samuelson and Nordhaus, 1989). This comparative neglect of Marxian economics, along with wilful misrepresentations, has led to considerable misunderstanding of what Marx was actually trying to do when he addressed himself to economic matters. Contrary to popular belief, Marxism is not merely a guide to revolutionary practice, although Marx did make some predictions concerning the demise of capitalism. Similarly,

Marxian analysis does not offer a blueprint for the operation of a centrally planned socialist economy, as the former Soviet Union discovered to its cost. The purpose of Marxian analysis is to provide a general historical perspective on economic affairs, focused particularly on laying bare the operation of the capitalist system.

Marxian economics and neoclassical theory share common roots in the so-called classical economics of the late eighteenth and early nineteenth centuries. The strongest link between Marx and the classical tradition is provided by the LABOUR THEORY OF VALUE associated with the economist David Ricardo, and assigned a central place in Marxian theory. It is in the treatment of value that the fundamental difference between Marxian economics and the alternative perspective is to be found. In the classical labour theory of value, the prices of all goods are seen as derived from the current labour input and from the labour input embodied in the materials of production. In neoclassical economics the role of value theory is similarly to explain relative prices, but with the explicit recognition that capital and land as well as labour make a contribution and are entitled to a return. For Marx, value theory was the key to understanding the nature of capitalist society as an historically specific form of economic organization. Whereas the neoclassical analysis sees value (reflected in prices and income distribution) arising from some almost mechanical processes of market determination, Marxian economics uses the concept of value to expose the social (CLASS) relations seen to be at the root of the inequality manifest under capitalism.

Marxian analysis is thus more of a general theory of society than an approach to economics. Indeed, to separate out from the rest of Marx's work those notions that might be labelled 'economic' is contrary to the very spirit of Marxism, with its emphasis on the holistic perspective of POLITICAL ECONOMY. What follows is thus inevitably a highly selective summary of the basics of Marxian analysis as applied to economic processes. [Those seeking additional insight may refer to the

Suggested Reading listed at the end of this entry, as well as to *Capital* and other writings of Marx himself.]

The general perspective of Marxism is sometimes referred to as HISTORICAL MATERIALISM. The emphasis is on identifying those relationships that are of fundamental importance in determining a social system's overall direction of movement and change, as unfolded in history. The economic base or MODE OF PRODUCTION is seen as the key to understanding the complex web of interconnections involving the institutions, patterns of behaviour, beliefs and so on that make up a society. The mode of production consists of the PRODUCTIVE FORCES or capacity to produce (these are labour, resources and instruments of labour) and the RELATIONS OF PRODUCTION whereby people participate in the productive process. The social relations involve class cleavages, as for example between landlords and peasants or capitalists and workers. The base or *substructure* of the mode of production is connected with the SUPERSTRUCTURE of religion, ethics, laws, mores and institutions via reciprocal cause and effect relationships, but the effect of economic base on superstructure is held to be dominant.

Historically, four successive modes of production are recognized before the advent of SOCIALISM: primitive COMMUNISM, slave (see SLAVERY), FEUDALISM and CAPITALISM. As the forces of production develop to increase productive capacity, CONFLICT or tension arises within the prevailing relations of production which threaten their self-perpetuating tendencies. For example, as long as feudal social relations remained it was impossible to take full advantage of the increased production capacities generated by technological advances that took place prior to the INDUSTRIAL REVOLUTION. The ties of apprentice to master and peasant to landlord prevented the redeployment of labour required for rapid economic growth. The resolution of this type of contradiction is the motive force for change, which can lead to the replacement of one mode of production by another – as in the transition from feudalism to capitalism, during which labour was gradually freed from its old obligations. Capitalist social relations, with the distinctions between labour on the one hand and capital on the other, facilitated the full development of the productive forces in an era of major technological change. This made possible rapid increases in production, and a rise in general living standards that would have been frustrated under feudalism. But capitalism brought its own contradictions, as Marx was able to demonstrate. Crucial to the resolution of contradictions between the forces of production and the social relations of production is the class struggle, under which the CLASS controlling the means of production (i.e. the slave owners, feudal landlords or capitalists) is opposed to the mass of the working people (the 'proletariat'). In Marx's analysis, the proletariat would eventually be driven to overthrow the capitalist ruling class, to create socialism and ultimately the classless communist society (cf. COMMUNISM).

The rise of capitalism not only changed the status of labour but also began to divest it of the means of production (in the form of tools and the land), over which many feudal craftsmen and small farms had direct control. To sustain itself, this 'freed' labour had to offer its services to those who owned the new means of production – the capitalists. Whereas conventional economics views the sale of labour, like that of other commodities, as part of a system of exchange relationships, Marxian analysis uses the theory of value to reveal the exploitive social relationships of capitalism: the class relations hidden beneath commodity transactions.

This process may be explained by reference to some basic categories and relationships in Marxian economics. It is necessary first to distinguish two concepts of value: *exchange value*, or the value at which a commodity can be exchanged for other commodities; and *use value* or the usefulness of commodities to their possessor. All economic systems produce things with use value to satisfy human needs; capitalism is distinguished by its emphasis on production for exchange and profit. Marx directed his analysis towards the determination of the exchange value of commodities. According to the labour theory of value, the basis of the exchange of commodities (i.e. their prices) should be the amount of labour time required to produce them under the conditions normally obtaining; the labour thus required is termed *socially necessary* labour. This theory applies to labour itself just as to other commodities: the exchange value of *labour power* (i.e. the commodity that workers sell) is determined by the socially necessary labour required for subsistence, or the cost of production (and reproduction) of labour itself. The exchange value of labour is thus (theoretically) decided independently of the specific job that the labourer might do. Once sold to capital, labour power may be employed to produce something that can be sold at a price greater than the cost of labour reflected in its price in the form of wages paid. Thus the use value of labour to the capitalist exceeds its exchange value. The difference is *surplus value*, which accrues to the capitalist and forms the basis for profit. It is ownership of the means of production that enables the capitalist to engage in *exploitation*, whereby part of the value of the product of labour is appropriated by the capitalist. Value and class relations are thus inextricable elements of the social practice of production under capitalism.

Labour enters into the production process in two forms. One is the direct living labour expended, which is *variable capital* (*v*) in Marxian terminology. The other is the past or 'dead' labour embodied in the means of production (materials and machinery), known as *constant capital* (*c*). If surplus value is *s*, then the total value of a commodity (*y*) is given by:

$$y = c + v + s.$$

The ratio of variable capital to surplus value defines the rate of *surplus value* (*r*), or rate of exploitation, as follows:

$$r = s/v;$$

that is, the higher the surplus value (or difference between exchange value and use value of labour) in relation to exchange value (or wages paid), the higher the rate of exploitation. The *rate of profit* (*p*) is:

$$p = s/(c + v),$$

which reveals the importance of surplus value itself to the capitalist seeking profits. A final relationship that occupies an important place in Marxian economics is the *organic composition of capital* (*q*):

$$q = c/(c + v)$$

which, in conventional terminology, is the capital intensity of production.

Money plays a crucial part in the creation of surplus value, and this is explained by some further simple relationships that can be expressed symbolically. The capitalist advances a sum of money (*M*) for the commodities of materials, machines and labour power (*C*), and sells the final product for more money (*M'*). This may be represented by the simple cycle of *M–C–M'*. The commodities *C* may be subdivided into labour power (*L*) for which wages are paid and means of production (*MP*) purchased or rented from other capitalists, the total expenditure (*M*) being defined as productive material (*P*). The production process now creates new commodities (*C'*) which can be sold for more money than the initial outlay. The source of the difference between *M* and *M'* can only be the surplus value created by labour. The additional money or profits accruing to the capitalist can then be advanced again for a second round of production (see the figure). At the end of each round labour has 'reproduced' itself; capital has accumulated wealth. The distinction arises from the inequality of power in capitalist class relations, manifest in the buying and selling of labour power – hence Marx's stress on value as a social relationship rather than as something merely associated with exchange relations. The Marxist critique of conventional (neoclassical) economics is that exploitive class relations are hidden beneath the technicalities of market pricing, resource allocation, production functions and so on, with the formal abstraction of mathematics obscuring social reality.

This framework for analysing the capitalist system helps to reveal certain imperatives for any economy. The process of material production carries with it certain necessary consumption, required to maintain the productive forces in the form of the producers themselves (met via wages) and

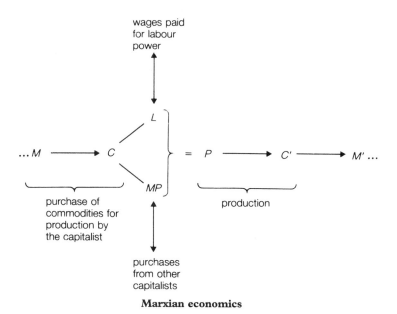

Marxian economics

the means of production (met via funds set aside for depreciation). However, discretion exists over the disposition of the remaining surplus, accruing as private profits under capitalism. This surplus could be returned to labour in the form of higher wages to support higher living standards. It could all be spent on luxury consumption, e.g. by an extravagant capitalist and landowning elite. Alternatively, it could be invested in new means of production or measures to enhance labour's capacity to produce, so as to develop the productive forces. The proportion that is reinvested (i.e. how much of M' in the figure goes into the next round of production) governs the rate of economic growth. Marx's analysis of *expanded reproduction*, whereby society's productive capacity is increased by reinvestment, anticipated by almost a century the INPUT–OUTPUT growth model that is so influential in conventional economics today. This particular contribution was adopted in economic planning under socialism, although the full technical development of input–output analysis was achieved in the USA.

An important tenet of Marxian economics is that capitalism will eventually be destroyed by its own internal contradictions. The extraction of surplus value from labour is the starting point of the process of capital accumulation, whereby wealth piles up in growing quantities in the hands of the capitalist class while the working class remains living at a bare subsistence level. Some use must be found for the surplus capital, there being limits to the capacity of the capitalist class for the self-indulgence of luxury consumption. The capital can be recycled into new production, but the masses must have the purchasing power to consume what is produced; it is only when commodities are sold that the capitalist can realize surplus value in its money form. There is thus a basic contradiction under capitalism between the pressure to increase surplus value by keeping wages low and the need for people to purchase commodities from their wages so that surplus value can be realized. Capital can be used to produce more machines to replace living labour, but this contributes to unemployment and immiserization of the proletariat. The inherently competitive nature of capitalism squeezes profits, which creates further pressure to reduce labour costs or substitute machines for labour. As the most successful firms grow and the weak go to the wall, capital becomes steadily more concentrated, until major monopolies confront the impoverished working class. The exploited masses are finally driven to the revolutionary overthrow of capitalism.

While the contradictions identified by Marx are certainly important features of the dynamics of capitalism, the final revolutionary outcome in an advanced industrial society has thus far failed to materialize. Among the more obvious reasons for this has been the growing power of organized labour to bargain with capital for increases in real wages, which capital has been able to concede to some extent by virtue of the great success of the capitalist system in expanding the capacity to produce. It may also be the case that affluence, at least in the advanced capitalist world, has helped to diffuse working-class consciousness – a trend assisted by use of the mass media to stimulate materialistic values and reinforce the prevailing IDEOLOGY of capitalism.

Contemporary Marxism is more concerned with dissecting the actual operation of capitalism in its modern form than with the veracity or otherwise of Marx's prediction of revolutionary change. Of special geographical interest is the general theory of UNEVEN DEVELOPMENT that traces its origins to the works of Lenin and Rosa Luxemburg on IMPERIALISM. Whereas neoclassical economics suggests the convergence of territorial income levels via self-adjusting markets for factors of production, Marxian analysis points to the tendency towards spatial concentration of economic activity under capitalism, and to a perpetuation and even exacerbation of spatial inequality. The spatial expansion of capitalism in the search for new investment opportunities, materials and markets has tied up much of the world into a web of interdependencies. Each nation or region plays a role in this international (or regional) division of labour, determined not by national interest or local need but by the capital accumulation process itself. The beneficiaries are the affluent of the advanced nations of North America and Western Europe, together with the elites in the rest of the capitalist world. The losers are the masses of the Third World poor, together with the less affluent inhabitants of the richer nations. The MULTINATIONAL CORPORATIONS are viewed as major instruments in this process, operating beyond the control of national governments but themselves subject to the imperatives by which the capitalist system operates. Local manifestations of uneven development, such as depressed regions and declining inner-city areas, can be related to the broader structural features of the national and international economy via Marxian economic analysis.

While the basics of Marxian economics are timeless, there have been some extensions and revisions in recent years. These include highly technical aspects of the 'transformation problem' of calculating under the labour theory of value. Of more interest to geographers has been the exploration of the KONDRATIEFF CYCLES, which are supposed to represent rather regular fluctuations of a capitalist economy over time, and are influential in the study of UNEVEN DEVELOPMENT, including WORLD-SYSTEMS ANALYSIS. The changing nature of the capitalist economy is reflected in attention given to the so-called REGULATION SCHOOL and to the concept of the REGIME OF ACCUMULATION which remains relatively stable over a period of time, as well as to the notion of FLEXIBLE ACCUMULATION which is supposed to capture important aspects of contemporary capitalism.

The political-economy perspective derived from Marx and his modern interpreters offers the geographer the nearest thing yet devised to a plausible general theory in which historically and locationally specific events can be related to one another in a broader context. The danger with Marxian analysis is the tendency of some of its adherents to adopt an unduly dogmatic interpretation, in the face of a changing world that requires flexibility on the part of any body of knowledge claiming to facilitate the understanding of human affairs as they actually unfold. Despite ideological opposition to Marxian analysis, and the rise of 'New Right' thinking in the 1980s, this approach is likely to maintain its interest and relevance to geography. (See also MARXIST GEOGRAPHY; NEO-RICARDIAN ECONOMICS.)   DMS

Reference

Samuelson, P. A. and Nordhaus, W. D. 1989: *Economics: an introductory analysis*, 13th edition. New York: McGraw-Hill.

Suggested Reading

Bottomore, T. ed. 1991: *A dictionary of Marxist thought*, second edition. Oxford: Blackwell.

Cohen, G. A. 1986: Forces and relations of production. In Roemer, J. ed., *Analytical Marxism*. Cambridge: Cambridge University Press.

Desai, M. 1974: *Marxian economic theory*. Oxford: Blackwell/Totowa, NJ: Rowman & Littlefield.

Fine, B. 1989: *Marx's Capital*, third edition. London: Macmillan.

Harvey, D. 1982: *The limits to capital*. Oxford: Blackwell.

Kay, G. 1975: *Development and underdevelopment: a Marxist analysis*. London: Macmillan/New York: St. Martin's Press (published as *Development, underdevelopment and the law of value: a Marxist analysis*).

Mandel, E. 1968: *Marxist economic theory*, two volumes, transl. B. Pearce. London: Merlin/New York: Monthly Review Press.

Mandel, E. 1978: *Late capitalism*, transl. J. de Bres, revised edition. London: Verso/New York: Schocken.

Marx, K. 1976 edn: *Capital*, volume 1. London: Penguin/New York: International.

Sheppard, E. and Barnes, T. J. 1990: *The capitalist space economy: analysis after Ricardo, Marx and Sraffa*. London: Unwin Hyman.

Marxist geography The study of geographical questions using the analytical insights, concepts and theoretical framework of Marxism (see HISTORICAL MATERIALISM). Although not inherently limited to one kind of society, Marxist geography has tended to focus on the various geographies of capitalist society.

Compared with most other social sciences, pre-1960s geography had experienced very limited radical critique (but see Galois, 1976), and postwar Soviet geography was more technocratic than radical. In the English-speaking world, Marxist geography emerged in the early 1970s in response to two sets of events: the critique of 'establishment geography' (Eliot Hurst, 1973), and the political uprisings of the late 1960s. REGIONAL GEOGRAPHY dominated the postwar period until the so-called QUANTITATIVE REVOLUTION brought a new POSITIVIST paradigm in geography, emphasizing SPATIAL ANALYSIS. Marxist geography emerged as a critique of this newly dominant paradigm, seeking to place geography questions in their broader social and political context.

Marxists argued that positivist spatial analysis was flawed in three basic ways. First, insofar as existing geographical realities were treated uncritically as spatial rather than social patterns, ruling social ideologies were reaffirmed; geographers might map urban SEGREGATION according to CLASS and RACE, for example, but never interrogate the political and economic processes that led to such unequal geographies. Second, despite its avowed scientific objectivity, spatial analysis was devoted to providing 'socially useful' results that amounted to a 'spatial technology' for capital; LOCATIONAL ANALYSIS sought to identify the most efficient locations for factories, supermarkets and social services, for example, accepting traditional class-based economic definitions of 'efficient location' (Massey, 1973). Third, universal spatial laws of the sort sought by positivist spatial analysis are a misnomer, and very different spatial arrangements obtain in different societies (Gregory, 1978; Smith, 1979a).

This critique of positivist spatial analysis as both IDEOLOGY and technology for capital emerged in the late 1960s, when the civil rights, anti-war and feminist movements provoked a fundamental challenge to the political establishment (see RADICAL GEOGRAPHY). The emergence of a radical and eventually Marxist geography was as much a response to these events as a critique of academic geography. Amidst the social and political turmoil of the time, the geometrical abstractions of spatial analysis seemed irrelevant for understanding the origins of CRISIS, the geographies of inequality implicated in these uprisings, and the political questions of social justice that they provoked.

If the emergence of a radical alternative to establishment geography can be dated to 1969, when a group of graduate students and faculty at Clark University published the first volume of *Antipode: A Radical Journal of Geography*, its consummation came in 1973 with the publication of David Harvey's highly influential *Social justice and the city*. First, this book traced an anguished personal and logical journey from a constellation of unsatisfying liberal assumptions towards a systematic Marxist analysis. Second, it demonstrated the ways in which spatial form and urban geographies are integral to an exploitative social and economic system. Ghetto formation, for example, is the result of a housing market that discriminates on the basis of class and race and yet is also a convenient urban form through which the costs of social reproduction are minimized. In this light, supposed scientific objectivity seems both unrealistic and politically motivated to endorse rather than criticize the exploitation and oppression inherent to capitalism. This in turn called for revolutionary theory, Harvey argued, theory that not only helps comprehend current geographies but embodies the practical intent to change those geographies and the societies that gave rise to them (Harvey, 1984; Harvey and Smith, 1984).

The substantive contributions of Marxist geography are more difficult to encapsulate. While adopting a broad purview, Marxist geographical research and writing can be treated under three (albeit overlapping) headings: political economy, theories of space, and questions of nature and environment.

Political economic analyses explain the geography of capitalism as the outcome primarily of political and economic relationships and processes in the wider society. Documentation of spatial inequality and community advocacy (see Bunge, 1971) was superseded by critique and theory (Peet, 1977a; Harvey, 1982). The urban geographies of capitalism can thereby be understood as resulting from the inherent contradiction between CLASS struggle and ACCUMULATION (Harvey, 1978, 1985). URBANIZATION is both the most rational geographical means (for capital) of centralizing productive capital, and at the same time an encouragement to oppositional struggle insofar as it congregates large numbers of people with similar experiences of exploitation and oppression in a single place. Capitalist urbanization

represents a further contradiction: on the one hand it brings about an extraordinary economic and geographical fixation of capital in the built environment – as factories, offices and infrastructure – as a condition of economic expansion. Yet at the same time, the changing conditions of production, circulation and realization of capital demand that capital investments be infinitely fluid. Given the long-term fixity of capital investment in the built environment, it is not surprising that economic crises have a particularly sharp effect on urban areas.

Other researchers have rewritten the story of surburbanization less as a heroic fable of the middle-class consumer, and more as a distinct geographical form of urban development that expresses the social geography of class inequality and the economic geography of class-based consumption. Suburbanization (see SUBURB) was actively planned and publicly subsidized, and represented a putative solution to the crisis of accumulation in the 1920s and 1930s (Walker, 1977, 1978; Chekoway, 1980). At the urban core, GENTRIFICATION can be seen as an economic as well as social question, resulting as much from geographical patterns of investment and disinvestment in the urban space economy as from consumer choice (Smith, 1979b), and as part of a larger pattern of urban RESTRUCTURING and UNEVEN DEVELOPMENT at the urban scale (Smith, 1982; Beauregard, 1984). There is also an intricate connection between class and other social relationships. Socialist feminists have shown the importance of gender relations in the making of contemporary urban form (McDowell, 1983; Mackenzie, 1989; Pratt, 1989). The requirements of social reproduction, the patterns of women's labour, and class-differentiated ideologies of a woman's proper place have all shaped capitalist urbanization (McKenzie and Rose, 1983; Marston, 1988). Suburbanization was premised on the gender relations of postwar expansion (Seguin, 1989), while gentrification results in part from changing social and economic roles of women, changing definitions of the family, and the restructuring of the Fordist regime of accumulation (Markusen, 1980; Rose, 1984; Bondi, 1991).

Regional geographies have been transformed by similar processes, by DEINDUSTRIALIZATION, and by changes in the organization of labour and capital (Massey, 1984; Schoenberger, 1986) and technology (Saxinien, 1984). These shifts are integrally connected with economic and social crises and bring new geographies of industrial and non-industrial growth, new ensembles of production (Scott, 1989).

At the global scale, greatest attention has been paid to the geography of UNDERDEVELOPMENT. Since before postcolonialism came into vogue, Blaut consistently questioned Western versions of the origins of capitalism and capitalist ideologies of NATIONALISM (Blaut, 1976, 1987). How has colonial and imperial expansion led to specific geographical patterns and structures in underdeveloped societies (cf. COLONIALISM; NATIONALISM)? The answer comes in a number of forms. In environmental terms, underdevelopment has led to a highly destructive social ecology characterized by chronic FAMINE (Franke and Chasin, 1980; Watts, 1983) and the systematic disruption of the means of social reproduction (Katz, 1991). In social and economic terms, underdevelopment leads to a de-centred and imbalanced regional structure that emphasizes communications with the colonial capital and Europe rather than between neighbouring regions (Slater, 1975; Moulaert and Wilson, 1983): thus the fastest way from Mali to neighbouring Niger is via Paris. Today the focus has shifted from understanding the ways in which imperial societies imposed specific geographies towards a more engrained understanding of the way in which specific societies responded differently and turned imperial domination in very different directions (see POSTCOLONIALISM).

The temporal rhythms of capital investment, accumulation and crisis are matched by a geographical logic of economic expansion and decline. Capital seeks a *spatial fix* for economic crises (Harvey, 1982), whether by disinvesting heavily in one place or investing heavily in another. In Marx's (1973 edn, p. 524) renowned phrase, the accumulation of capital relies upon a highly dynamic 'annihilation of space by time'. This implies the simultaneous development of the forces of communication and the cyclical creation of newly built environments for production, consumption and reproduction. But it also implies an equally fervid destruction of capital invested in the built environment, thereby creating new opportunities for expansion. This is the process that Schumpeter (1942), following Marx, later called 'creative destruction'. More broadly, the geography of capitalism is a perpetual maelstrom of construction and destruction that is captured in the general theory of UNEVEN DEVELOPMENT (Smith, 1990; Peet, 1991).

There are, of course, widespread debates in all of this (for a broad review, see Peet and Thrift, 1989): How possible is 'revolutionary theory' and what does it look like? Is wage labour the key to the historical geography of capitalism, or is it commerce? Is uneven development systemic to global capitalism, and to what extent should the unevenness of development be seen as a product also of underdeveloped economies? Are LOCALITIES the appropriate scale at which to examine the processes and results of restructuring?

Marxist geographical research has also focused on a second theme, *theories of* SPACE. The critique of positivism and of abstract spatial analysis called into question the conceptions of space employed in geographical research. Geographical discourse has been dominated by the familiar concept of abstract space – space as a field or container, primordially empty until filled with objects and events. The Marxist critique objected that this was only one of various possible concepts of space, and that when twinned with dubious assumptions of scientific objectivity it encouraged geographers to see abstract spatial forms and processes separate from the concrete social processes that created them. Social processes were elided as spatial forms and spatial processes, in an ideological move that Marxist geographers identified as SPATIAL FETISHISM (Anderson, 1973). There were many debates over the question of space and how to retheorize it. Peet

(1977b) argued that geographers needed to develop a 'spatial dialectics', and a debate emerged concerning the appropriateness of dividing the DIALECTIC in this way (Smith, 1979a; Eliot Hurst, 1980; Peet, 1981). Soja (1980) proposed the compromise of a 'socio-spatial dialectic'.

For a reconstruction of space, Marxist geography looked to physics and beyond – to relative conceptions of space, to the connection of space and time (Thrift, 1983) and to the PRODUCTION OF SPACE. Space was seen in relation to material events and processes (social as well as natural), no longer prior to NATURE: material objects do not so much fill up space; rather, their placement *produces* space. Absolute space is not entirely vanquished, but it is rendered relational; for example, privately owned land represents socially constructed absolute space (Harvey, 1973; Smith, 1990).

Henri Lefebvre has suggested that it is more appropriate to think in terms of the production of space (1991 edn). We do not know why capitalism has survived since Marx's time, he says, but we do know how: by producing space (Lefebvre, 1976, p. 21). Lefebvre argues that a contemporary science of society was necessarily a science of space. In opposition to the homogeneity of abstract space continually imposed by capitalism, he identifies a differential space constructed through opposition to capitalism, class struggle, and the actions of emerging SOCIAL MOVEMENTS. The production of differential space is the object of revolutionary theory and practice.

A third focus of Marxist research in the past two decades involves *theories of nature and society–nature relations*. It is a common misconception that Marx had little to say about nature and the ENVIRONMENT, but his critique of capitalist society was built on an explicit vision of the relationship between society and nature. Rather than assuming that nature and society represent separate realms, Marxist theory posits the fundamental interconnectedness of society and nature, achieved practically in the performance of social labour. Labour converts naturally occurring material into social commodities, and in transforming the form of nature it simultaneously

changes its own (human) nature (Marx, 1987 edn, p. 177). Capitalist society produces wealth 'only by sapping the original sources of all wealth – the soil and the labourer' (1987 edn, p. 507).

This has led to the suggestion that geographers ought to develop a 'geographical materialism' comparable to Marx's HISTORICAL MATERIALISM (Wittfogel, 1987; Peet, 1987). Others have suggested a more socially centred vision of nature (Schmidt, 1971; Burgess, 1978). But it is also possible to derive from Marx the argument that human societies, and especially capitalism, are involved in the 'production of nature' (Redclift, 1987; Smith, 1990). It may sound quixotic to talk about the production of nature since, after all, nature is precisely that which we are used to thinking of as the antithesis of human society and social construction. Yet the strangeness of the idea may belie a persistent bifurcated ideology of nature: nature is deemed either external to human society or else as universal, including quite literally everything in the world. To the extent that the form of the Earth has been entirely altered by productive human activity, however, and no part of the world remains unaffected, the production of nature is a reality. This does not imply that somehow natural laws of gravity or chemical interaction cease to operate, nor that nature is thereby controlled. Control and production are two quite separate issues. It does suggest forcefully that the natural world can no longer be separated conceptually or ontologically from the social world, and that an environmental politics is a quintessentially social politics. This has two results. First, it disqualifies the romantic appeal – from deep ecologist to conservationist – to a pre-existing, Edenic nature unaffected by social production and social change, to which we ought to return; or the appeal to biological essentialism that gives authority to much ecofeminism. Second, it disqualifies the technocratic appeal to 'society–nature interactions' insofar as this perspective also assumes the initial separation of society and nature. As Cosgrove (1984, p. 180) has put it, it 'is not the relationship between human beings and the land that governs their social organization, but ultimately their relations with each other in the course of production'. 'The production of nature' suggests the political question: How do we as a society want to produce nature, and how will these decisions be made?

Notwithstanding that nature and environment have become a subsidiary concern for Marxist geographers (FitzSimmons, 1989), *vis-à-vis* space, numerous writers have addressed concrete as well as theoretical environmental issues. Considerable effort has been aimed at reinterpreting the conventional wisdom on environmental HAZARDS. Where traditional hazard specialists draw a distinction between natural and technological hazards, Marxists have stressed that this distinction perpetuates the ideology of a nature separate from society and encourages a belief in natural hazards as inevitability. 'Natural' hazard is in fact a misnomer, since all hazards (as opposed to natural events) are by definition social (O'Keefe et al., 1976). With a clear correlation between income and social class on the one side and vulnerability to hazard on the other, a disproportionate number of deaths due to so-called natural disasters are in the underdeveloped world. By the same token, any given environment has vastly different meanings for different people: a hazard for one population may be a recreational resource for another.

This research has focused on reinterpreting supposedly natural events such as the Sahel famine of 1968–74 and the wider African famine of the 1980s and 1990s as quintessentially social events traceable to the broad structure and specific operation of capitalist social relations (Franke and Chasin, 1980; Watts, 1983). Likewise, the Irish starvation of the 1840s, traditionally blamed on potato blight, resulted from the dependence – enforced by British imperialism – of Irish peasants on the potato: as peasants starved, English landlords continued to export large quantities of Irish beef to the English market (Regan, 1980, p. 11). The production of food in general involves an extraordinary appropriation of nature along class lines (Goodman and Redclift, 1991), and the class politics of rainforest destruction are now evident (Hecht and Cockburn, 1990). In the consumption

sphere, too, access to nature is privatized (Heiman, 1988; Emel and Roberts, 1989), and the disruption of local patterns of social ecology due to capitalist expansion fundamentally disrupts established processes and traditions of SOCIAL REPRODUCTION (Katz, 1991).

A central ideological plank of traditional environmental geography holds that the population and RESOURCES of a place are intricately dependent on each other, and that 'OVERPOPULATION' should be defined in relation to available resources. There is an implicit retention here of MALTHUSIAN assumptions about the separateness and fixity of nature *vis-à-vis* population (Harvey, 1974). Given economic trade, global financial flows, and very unequal patterns of political power, it is fallacious to assume that a place's resources have a determining effect on population growth or even development. Resource availability and resource scarcity are themselves social constructions.

* * *

The first phase of Marxist research in geography, lasting until the early 1980s, was concerned above all else to demonstrate the ways in which capitalism as a coherent social system was responsible for the configuration of specific LANDSCAPES – the urban geography of capitalism, its regional patterns, environmental depredation and underdevelopment at the global scale. The primary intent was to import Marxist ideas and a Marxist framework into geography as a means of analysing questions of traditional geographical concern. This involved a prolonged rediscovery of Marx and Marxist ideas and their application to geography, but it was only half the battle; Marxists were no more convinced about geography than most geographers were about Marxism. And yet by the early 1980s, Marxism had come to hold an unprecedented influence within geography, compared to the other social sciences. In part this was a result of uneven intellectual development: in the 1960s geography embodied virtually no social theory beyond positivism, at a time when social theory was dearly needed. Geographers compensated for this lacuna with such an embrace of Marxism that within 15–20 years a disproportionate number of the most influential geographers were Marxists (Bodman, 1992).

The next phase of Marxist geography began in the early 1980s and was marked by several shifts. First, the focus was no longer so much on unearthing Marx and Marxism but on using them critically. This involved a significant broadening of Marxist geography and an involvement with other social theories that were being imported into geography, especially the work of Weber. But, second, it involved an expansion and simultaneous reversal of the project. It was no longer simply a matter of convincing geographers that Marxism had something to offer – which had already been achieved – but rather of taking the case to Marxism that a geographical, and especially a spatial, perspective was vital for Marxism and SOCIAL THEORY more broadly. This ambitious 'spatialization of social theory' (Soja, 1989) gathered steam precisely as Marxism itself was subject to increasingly critical analysis by geographers. The second phase of Marxist research also heralded an attempt to rewrite cultural geography in a radical vein (Cosgrove, 1983) and the reconsideration of 'landscape' as a central geographical concept (Cosgrove, 1984; Olwig, 1984; Cosgrove and Daniels, 1987; Daniels, 1989).

The broadening of Marxist geography in the 1980s was the product of internal maturity as well as of increasing challenges from outside, as geographers became more versed in social theory and the political climate lurched decisively to the right. These challenges came from several directions. The humanist critique (Duncan and Ley, 1982), which galvanized widespread discomfiture with Marxism, portrayed it as a form of structuralism whereby structures, not people, embodied social purposefulness. This approach was complemented by Giddens (1979, 1981), whose STRUCTURATIONIST theory took apart the Marxist DIALECTIC, explicitly separating 'structure' and 'human agency' in order to investigate their connectedness. A related challenge came from REALISM, the proponents of which argued that Marxism overestimated

the range of 'necessary' (i.e. structurally determined) relationships in contemporary capitalism, and that contingent relationships accounted for much contemporary geography (Sayer, 1984): the geography of capitalism, they argued, accounts for only a small proportion of current geographical forms and processes.

A more total challenge has been mounted by POSTMODERNISM. Postmodernist writers have argued that an entire modern epoch of Western thought is over. The product of the Enlightenment, 'Modern' thought has emphasized rationality over irrationality, science over subjectivity, the global over the local, and the total and the universal over the partial and the fragmented. Marxism and POSITIVISM, communism and capitalism – all are either discarded as modernist or variously reinterpreted to capture the fragmentation and differentiation of social experience. Social critique is increasingly seen as a cultural rather than political and economic project. If more extreme versions of postmodernism involve a complete dismissal of Marxism, along with all other forms of Enlightenment and Modern thought (Dear, 1988), and seek a wholesale displacement of social theory by cultural analysis (Deutsche, 1991), it is also possible to see postmodernism as a deeply sympathetic critique. It fundamentally questions the existence of a 'universal subject' – a generalized 'we' usually defined from the perspective of ruling-class white men; it rejects the ambition of a total critique based on some essential set of causes or relationships; and it opens up Marxism and other social theory to additional kinds of social difference and uncertainty (Graham, 1990). Postmodernism has especially resonated within geography insofar as it embodies what might be called a 'spatial turn', in which space more than time is now on the social theory agenda (Soja, 1989). Postmodernism can also be seen less as an alternative to modernism than as a reconnection between basic themes of fixity and fluidity of social experience that were increasingly separated in the twentieth century. This is the power of Harvey's (1989) *The condition of postmodernity*, which attempts an engagement between political, economic and cultural analysis (see also Jameson, 1984).

The feminist engagement with Marxism has a longer history. FEMINIST GEOGRAPHY first emerged in the early 1970s in close connection with radical and Marxist analyses, exploring issues of social reproduction, community and women's work, and connecting broader feminist debates with geographical questions, mostly at the urban scale. By the late 1980s, feminism took a much more critical approach to Marxism, in part out of frustration that a newly influential Marxism only marginally considered questions of gender. Debate flared around Harvey's (1989) *The condition of postmodernity* (see Deutsche, 1991; Massey, 1991; Harvey, 1992). A middle ground is already evident among some feminists who have sought to integrate questions of class and gender: (Pratt, 1989; Mackenzie, 1989; Bondi 1991). Linda McDowell (1991) especially warns that the baby of Marxist insights and class analysis not be thrown out with the bathwater of a male-centred vision. In this respect, postmodernism has been very fruitful. It has opened up a wider space for the engagement of feminism and Marxism than would otherwise have been available (Bondi, 1990).

If the challenges to Marxist geography in the 1990s are in part the inevitable result of Marxism's success in academic geography amidst a wider gathering conservatism, they also embody genuine shortcomings to which Marxist geography must respond. Ironically, while the defeat of official Communist Parties in the Soviet Union and Eastern Europe has caused the capitalist class throughout the West to rejoice, it also frees Marxist ideas from a particularly oppressive social system which, however much the reality diverged from Marx's own vision of democratic workers' control, nonetheless governed in the name of socialism. In that respect the agenda is open for a re-thought, integrative Marxism, committed still to political action as well as ideas. It will be achieved only through debate about new and old political directions for the Left (Walker, 1989; Folke and Sayer, 1990; McDowell, 1992).   NS

References

Anderson, J. 1973: Ideology in geography: an introduction. *Antipode* 5, pp. 1–6.

Beauregard, R. 1984: Structure, agency and urban redevelopment. In Smith, M., ed., *Capital, class and urban structure*. Beverly Hills, CA: Sage, pp. 51–72.

Blaut, J. 1976: Where was capitalism born? *Antipode* 8(2), pp. 1–11.

Blaut, J. 1987: *The national question: decolonising the theory of nationalism*. London: Zed Books.

Bodman, A. 1992: Holes in the fabric: more on the master weavers in human geography. *Trans. Inst. Br. Geogr.* n.s. 17, pp. 21–37.

Bondi, L. 1990: Feminism, postmodernism, and geography: space for women? *Antipode* 22, pp. 156–67.

Bondi, L. 1991: Gender divisions and gentrification: a critique. *Trans. Inst. Br. Geogr.* n.s. 16, pp. 190–8.

Bunge, W. 1971: *Fitzgerald: the geography of a revolution*. Cambridge, MA: Schlenkman.

Burgess, R. 1978: The concept of nature in geography and Marxism. *Antipode* 10, pp. 1–11.

Chekoway, B. 1980: Large builders, Federal housing programs, and postwar suburbanization. *Int. J. urban and reg. Res.* 4, pp. 21–44.

Cosgrove, D. 1983: Towards a radical cultural geography: problems of theory. *Antipode* 15, pp. 1–11.

Cosgrove, D. 1984: *Social formation and symbolic landscape*. London: Croom Helm.

Cosgrove, D. and Daniels, S., eds 1987: *The iconography of landscape*. Cambridge: Cambridge University Press.

Daniels, S. 1989: Marxism, culture and the duplicity of landscape. In Peet, R. and Thrift, N., eds, *New models in geography*, volume 2. London: Unwin Hyman, pp. 196–220.

Dear, M. 1988: The postmodern challenge: reconstructing human geography. *Trans. Inst. Br. Geogr.* n.s. 13, pp. 262–74.

Deutsch, R. 1991: Boys town. *Environ. Plann. D: Society and Space* 9, pp. 5–30.

Duncan, J. and Ley, D. 1982: Structural Marxism and human geography: a critical assessment. *Ann. Ass. Am. Geogr.* 72, pp. 30–59.

Eliot Hurst, M. 1973: Establishment geography: how to be irrelevant in three easy lessons. *Antipode* 5(2), pp. 40–59.

Eliot Hurst, M. 1980: Geography, social science and society: towards a de-definition. *Aust. geogr. Stud.* 18, pp. 3–21.

Emel, J. and Roberts, R. 1989: Ideologies of property: property rights in Texas and New Mexico groundwater resources. *Econ. Geogr.* 65.

FitzSimmons, M. 1989: The matter of nature. *Antipode* 21, pp. 106–20.

Folke, S. and Sayer, A. 1990: What's left to do? Two views from Europe. *Antipode* 23, pp. 240–8.

Franke, L. and Chasin, B. 1980: *Seeds of famine.* Totowa, NJ: Rowan and Littlefield.

Galois, B. 1976: Ideology and the idea of nature: the case of Peter Kropotkin. *Antipode* 8, pp. 1–16.

Giddens, A. 1979: *Central problems in social theory.* London: Macmillan.

Giddens, A. 1981: *A contemporary critique of historical materialism.* London: Macmillan.

Goodman, D. and Redclift, M. 1991: *Refashioning nature: food ecology and culture.* London: Routledge.

Graham, J. 1990: Theory and essentialism in Marxist geography. *Antipode* 22, pp. 53–66.

Gregory, D. 1978: *Ideology, science and human geography.* London: Hutchinson.

Harvey, D. 1973: *Social justice and the city.* London: Edward Arnold.

Harvey, D. 1974: Population, resources and the ideology of science. *Econ. Geogr.* 50, pp. 256–77.

Harvey, D. 1978: The urban process under capitalism: a framework for analysis. *Int. J. urban and reg. Res.* 2, pp. 101–30.

Harvey, D. 1982: *The limits to capital.* Chicago: University of Chicago Press.

Harvey, D. 1984: On the history and present condition of geography. *Prof. Geogr.* 36, pp. 1–11.

Harvey, D. 1985: *The urbanization of capital.* Oxford: Blackwell.

Harvey, D. 1989: *The condition of postmodernity.* Oxford: Blackwell.

Harvey, D. 1992: Postmodern morality plays. *Antipode* 25, pp. 300–26.

Harvey, D. and Smith, N. 1984: From capitals to Capital. In Ollman, B. and Vernoff, E., eds, *The left academy: Marxist scholarship on American campuses,* volume 2. New York: Praeger, pp. 99–121.

Hecht, S. and Cockburn, A. 1990: *The fate of the forest: developers, destroyers and defenders of the Amazon.* London: Penguin.

Heiman, M. 1988: *The quiet evolution.* New York: Praeger.

Jameson, F. 1984: Postmodernism, or the cultural logic of late capitalism. *New Left Rev.* 146, pp. 53–92.

Katz, C. 1991: Sow what you know: the struggle for social reproduction in rural Sudan. *Ann. Ass. Am. Geogr.* 81, pp. 488–514.

Lefebvre, H. 1976: *The survival of capital.* London: Allison and Busby.

Lefebvre, H. 1991 edn: *The production of space.* Oxford: Blackwell.

McDowell, L. 1983: Toward an understanding of the gender division of urban space. *Environ. Plann. D: Society and Space* 1, pp. 59–72.

McDowell, L. 1991: The baby and the bathwater: deconstruction and feminist theory in geography. *Geoforum* 22.

McDowell, L. 1992: Multiple voices: speaking from inside and outside the project. *Antipode* 24, pp. 56–72.

Mackenzie, S. 1989: Women in the city. In Peet, R. and Thrift, N. eds, *New models in geography,* volume 2. London: Unwin Hyman, pp. 109–26.

Mackenzie, S. and Rose, D. 1983: Industrial change, the domestic economy and home life. In Anderson, J., Duncan, S., and Hudson, R., eds, *Redundant spaces in cities and regions: studies in industrial decline and social change.* London: Academic Press.

Markusen, A. 1980: City spatial structure, women's household work, and national policy. *Signs* 5, pp. 23–44.

Marston, S. A. 1988: Neighborhood and politics: Irish ethnicity in 19th century Lowell, Massachusetts. *Ann. Ass. Am. Geogr.* 78, pp. 414–32.

Marx, K. 1973 edn: *Grundrisse.* London: Penguin.

Marx, K. 1987 edn: *Capital.* New York: International.

Massey, D. 1973: Towards a critique of industrial location theory. *Antipode* 5, pp. 33–9.

Massey, D. 1984: *Spatial divisions of labour: social structures and the geography of production.* London: Methuen.

Massey, D. 1991: Flexible sexism. *Environ. Plann. D: Society and Space* 9, pp. 31–57.

Moulaert, F. and Wilson, P., eds 1983: *Regional analysis and the international division of labor.* The Hague: Kluwer Nijhoff.

O'Keefe, P., Westgate, B. and Wisner, B. 1976: Taking the naturalness out of natural disasters. *Nature* 260, 15 April.

Olwig, K. 1984: *Nature's ideological landscape.* London: Allen and Unwin.

Peet, R. 1977a: The development of radical geography in the United States. *Progr. hum. Geogr.* 1, pp. 64–87.

Peet, R. 1977b: *Radical geography: alternative viewpoints on contemporary social issues.* Chicago: Maaroufa.

Peet, R. 1981: Spatial dialectics and Marxist geography. *Progr. hum. Geogr.* 5, pp. 105–10.

Peet, R. 1987: The geographical ideas of Karl Wittfogel. *Antipode* 17, pp. 35–50.

Peet, R. 1991: *Global capitalism: theories of social development*. London: Routledge.

Peet, R. and Thrift, N., eds 1989: *New models in geography*, two volumes. London: Unwin Hyman.

Pratt, G. 1989: Reproduction, class, and the spatial structure of the city. In Peet, R. and Thrift, N., eds, *New models in geography*, volume 2. London: Unwin Hyman, pp. 84–108.

Redclift, M. 1987: The production of nature. *Antipode* 19, pp. 222-30.

Regan, C. 1980: Economic development in Ireland: the historical dimension. *Antipode* 11, pp. 1–14.

Rose, D. 1984: Rethinking gentrification: beyond the uneven development of Marxist urban theory. *Environ. Plann. D: Society and Space* 2, pp. 47–74.

Saxinien, A. 1984: The urban contradictions of Silicon Valley: regional growth and restructuring in the semiconductor industry. In Tabb, W. and Sawers, L, eds, *Sunbelt/Snowbelt*. Oxford: Oxford University Press.

Sayer, A. 1984: *Method and social science*. London: Hutchinson.

Schmidt, A. 1971: *The concept of nature in Marx*. London: New Left Books.

Schoenberger, E. 1986: Competition, competitive strategy, and industrial change: the case of electronic components. *Econ. Geogr.* 62, pp. 321-33.

Schumpeter, J. 1942: *Capitalism, socialism and democracy*. New York: Harper and Row.

Scott, A. 1989: *New ensembles of production*. London: Pion.

Seguin, A. 1989: Madame Ford et l'espace: lecture feministe de la suburbanisation. *Recherches feministes* 2, pp. 51–68.

Slater, D. 1975: The poverty of modern geographical inquiry. *Pacific Viewpoint* 16, pp. 159–76.

Smith, N. 1979a: Geography, science and post-positivist modes of explanation. *Progr. hum. Geogr.* 3, pp. 356–83.

Smith, N. 1979b: Toward a theory of gentrification: a back to the city movement by capital not people. *J. Am. Plann. Assoc.* 45, pp. 538–48.

Smith, N. 1982: Gentrification and uneven development. *Econ. Geogr.* 58, pp. 139–55.

Smith, N. 1990: *Uneven development: nature, capital and the production of space*, second edition. Oxford: Blackwell.

Soja, E. 1980: The socio-spatial dialectic. *Ann. Ass. Am. Geogr.* 70, pp. 207–25.

Soja, E. 1989: *Postmodern geographies*. London: Verso.

Thrift, N. 1983: On the determination of social action in space and time. *Environ. Plann. D: Society and Space* 1, pp. 23–57.

Walker, R. 1977: The suburban solution. Ph.D. dissertation, Johns Hopkins University.

Walker, R. 1978: The transformation of urban structure in the nineteenth century and the beginnings of suburbanization. In Cox, K., ed., *Urbanization and conflict in market societies*. Chicago: Maaroufa, pp. 165–211.

Walker, R. 1989: What's left to do? *Antipode* 21, pp. 133–65.

Watts, M. 1983: *Silent violence*. Berkeley, CA: University of California Press.

Wittfogel, K. 1987: Geopolitics, geographical materialism and Marxism. *Antipode* 17(1), pp. 21–34.

Suggested Reading

Harvey (1982, 1989).

Harvey and Smith (1984).

Peet (1977b).

Soja (1989).

material orientation The tendency of an economic activity to locate close to sources of materials. This is likely to be the case where the cost of the material(s) in question forms a large share of total cost and/or where material costs are subject to substantial spatial variations. Historically, the importance of material orientation in industrial location has declined, with a reduction in the proportion of all industry using bulky materials and with the reduction in transfer costs associated with advances in transportation technology. Industries that remain predominantly material-oriented are largely confined to primary metal manufacturing and the processing of agricultural products. (Cf. MARKET ORIENTATION.)   DMS

maximin criterion The rational decision-making strategy in RISK situations, according to GAME THEORY. From a range of choices, the decision-maker selects that which maximizes the minimum return. Thus a farmer, for example, would select either the single crop or the combination of crops which produces the best return under the worst possible anticipated climatic and/or market conditions.   RJJ

Suggested Reading
Gould, P. R., 1963: Man against his environment: a game theoretic framework. *Ann. Ass. Am. Geogr.* 53, pp. 290–7.

mean information field (m.i.f.)

The representation of a DISTANCE DECAY pattern in a SIMULATION model, used especially in analyses of the DIFFUSION of an innovation and of MIGRATION. The m.i.f. is usually presented as a 5×5 matrix in which the central square represents the origin (e.g. of a migration) and the value in each of the other cells represent the probability of it being the destination. The m.i.f. values may be defined arbitrarily, on the basis of *a priori* theory, or from empirical analyses.   RJJ

Suggested Reading
Hägerstrand, T. 1967: *Innovation diffusion as a spatial process*, transl. A. Pred. Englewood Cliffs, NJ: Prentice-Hall.

measurement   A classification of data types in statistical analysis. Four levels of measurement are generally recognized:

(1) *nominal*, in which each individual (member of a population or sample) is allocated to one only of two or more exclusive categories;

(2) *ordinal*, in which either the individuals or the categories to which they are allocated are rank-ordered in some way;

(3) *interval*, which involves a quantitative assessment between two individuals along a predetermined scale (such as °C); and

(4) *ratio*, which allows relative quantitative assessment of differences along a scale. Thus, for example, nominal measurement would allocate three million people to Birmingham and nine million to London; ordinal measurement of the same data would say that London is larger than Birmingham; interval measurement would provide the information that London has six million more people than Birmingham; and ratio measurement would indicate that London is three times the size of Birmingham.   RJJ

medical geography   The application of geographical perspectives and methods to the study of health, disease and health care. The study of geographical aspects of health-related problems has a long history, but has tended in the past to be viewed as part of disciplines such as epidemiology, medicine, demography etc. Meade et al. (1988) suggest that medical geography was first recognized as a geographical discipline in 1952, when the Commission on Medical Geography (Ecology) of Health and Disease first reported to the International Geographical Union. Medical geography is now well established in many countries and incorporates two broad areas of study. The first, which has the longer tradition, concerns the spatial ECOLOGY of disease and geographical aspects of the health of populations. The second, which has developed more recently, emphasizes the geographical organization of health care (see also HEALTH AND HEALTH CARE, GEOGRAPHY OF). Medical geography retains associations with other disciplines outside geography concerned with health-related problems, reflecting the complexity of these problems and the need to examine them from a multidisciplinary perspective.

Health is often measured and compared in terms of indicators of ill-health such as illness (*morbidity*) and death (*mortality*). Some of the earliest studies in medical geography studied morbidity and mortality by examining their distribution in space, often by mapping them and comparing their occurrence in different geographical areas. The objective of these studies is usually to search for environmental factors with a spatial pattern associated with that of the disease, which may help to explain the *aetiology* ('natural history') of the disease. An often-cited early example of this approach is the map of cases of cholera in part of the Soho district of London, produced by Dr John Snow in the 1850s, when the cause of the disease was not understood. Those dying from the disease were found to be from households which were close to a particular pump, which they used for their domestic water supplies. This led Snow to suspect infected water in the pump as the source of infection, and when the pump was shut off the number of new cases of the disease rapidly declined (Snow, 1855).

This area of medical geography (reviewed by Learmonth, 1988, and Meade et al., 1988) is closely related to studies in epidemiology, and has been developed using more advanced methods to analyse the spatial distribution of both physical and mental illnesses and to test spatial COR-RELATIONS between diseases and associated environmental factors. There are many such studies, covering such diverse problems as the relationship between nuclear power stations and childhood leukaemia (Openshaw et al., 1988), the spatial patterning of mental illness (Giggs, 1983) and, in tropical areas, the association between schistosomiases in humans and their use of water sources supporting snails which carry the disease-causing agent (reviewed in Learmonth, 1988, ch. 11).

Some studies have examined the spread of diseases through human populations in time and space. These have focused, for example, on cholera in nineteenth-century America (Pyle, 1969), on epidemics of diseases such as measles in island communities (Cliff and Haggett, 1984), on influenza epidemics (Pyle and Patterson, 1983) and on AIDS (Smallman-Raynor and Cliff, 1990). Many diseases are associated with a complex of environmental factors (air, water and soil POLLUTION, noxious flora and fauna and climatic effects, as well as various aspects of the domestic and social environment), so that it is not yet possible to provide complete explanations of the relationships between environment and health. However, the spatial analysis of diseases often provides a useful starting point for research on these relationships.

Studies by geographers of variations in the health of the population across different geographical areas have made an important contribution to the discussion of social inequalities in health and welfare. Research in many parts of the world has shown that, at various spatial scales, population health is often associated not only with differences in the physical environment, but also with varying social factors such as housing and living conditions, lifestyle and access to health services (Jones and Moon, 1987; Meade et al., 1988; Phillips, 1990). Although it is important to avoid extending these ecological relationships too rigidly to the level of individuals, many studies have shown that in areas in which material and social deprivation is relatively high, morbidity and mortality in the population are also greater than in areas in which the population is more privileged. This means that there is an important social, economic and political dimension to spatial differences in population health, and that theories concerning socio-economic inequalities in different societies are relevant to explanation of health inequalities (cf. CONTEX-TUAL EFFECT). The strong links between health and living conditions and socio-economic position have proved very persistent, even in more advanced contemporary societies with highly developed medical systems. This has led to continuing concern with issues of public health, and debate over the effectiveness of modern medicine as a means of improving the health of the population by preventing illness and promoting good health, rather than treating illness.

There are also a number of geographical perspectives which have been usefully applied to the study of *health-care services* (see HEALTH AND HEALTH CARE, GEOGRA-PHY OF). Since population health varies from place to place, population need for health services also varies spatially. Medical geography is therefore concerned with the geographical relationship between health-care needs and service provision. The definition and measurement of health, health-care need and health-care provision of different populations presents a number of theoretical and practical problems (discussed, for example, by Eyles and Woods, 1983, and Jones and Moon, 1987). The analysis is often focused on the degree of EQUALITY and EQUITY apparent in the spatial distribution of need and resources for health care (see, e.g., Shannon and Dever, 1974; Powell, 1990). This approach has an important application to health-service planning in countries in which indicators of population health-care needs, such as population size, demographic structure, mortality levels and socio-economic deprivation, are used to plan the allocation of funds to regions for state health-care provision (Pacione, 1986; Haynes, 1987; Jones and Moon, 1987). At the international scale, the question of distribution of health-care resources between more and less developed countries is also an important issue (Phillips, 1990). This field of medical geography draws upon concepts of need and of territorial social justice, which are also employed in studies of the geography of PUBLIC SERVICES.

Another application of geography to health-care planning concerns the location and accessibility of specific health-care facilities such as hospitals or clinics (including the effects of DISTANCE DECAY in the use of health care associated with distance to be travelled to health facilities). These questions are of greatest importance in less developed countries, where health-care facilities are often sparsely distributed and distance presents a major obstacle to access (Phillips, 1990). However, models of health-care utilization (often adopted by geographers from medical sociology) show that there is a whole complex of social and economic factors which affect the ways in which people use health care, in addition to questions of spatial accessibility of services. Much of the research carried out in urban areas of advanced countries, where distances travelled to health-care facilities are typically relatively short, has produced equivocal results concerning distance decay effects on health service use. Nevertheless, for those with limited spatial mobility (e.g. elderly people and mothers with children) and in some types of region (e.g. in very remote rural areas and in countries which have a very limited and sparsely distributed system of health-care facilities) spatial ACCESSIBILITY may have an important impact on use of health care and its outcome for the patient (Haynes, 1987). This is also true for services such as accident and emergency units which are usually centralized in hospitals and must be accessed quickly when the need arises. LOCATION-ALLOCATION MODELLING has been used in a number of studies to investigate the 'efficient' siting of medical facilities to minimize as far as possible the aggregate distance to be travelled by patients needing to use them (see, e.g. Taket, 1989). In practice, locational benefits in terms of reduction of travel costs

usually have to be weighed against other factors affecting the location of facilities (such as the availability of sites, etc.; Joseph and Phillips, 1984).

Until recently, medical geography has been dominated by research methods which study aggregate populations using statistical techniques. However, more recently some medical geographers have been using more 'qualitative' and individualistic methods to study the more complex social factors which influence people's experience of health, illness and health care. Often, these studies are carried out in particular geographical settings and involve specific social groups (for example, poor people and ethnic minorities in INNER-CITY areas: see, e.g., Dear et al., 1980; Cornwell, 1984; Donovan, 1986; Eyles and Donovan, 1990). This area of medical geography has stronger links with medical sociology and anthropology than with epidemiology or medicine, and it draws upon a range of theories, including those concerned with health-related behaviour, RACE relations and GENDER relationships.

Because of the importance of health to human well-being and productivity, and because of the large amounts of resources which many nations devote to health care, medical geography has much potential for application to important contemporary issues, both in developed and developing countries. It has seen a considerable expansion over recent decades, and it brings geographers into close collaboration with researchers from other disciplines.   SC

References

Cliff, A. and Haggett, P. 1984: Island epidemics. *Scient. Am.* 250(5), pp. 110–17.

Cornwell, J. 1984: *Hard earned lives: accounts of health and illness from East London.* London: Tavistock.

Dear, M., Taylor, S. and Hall, G. 1980: Attitudes toward the mentally ill and reactions to mental health facilities. *Soc. Sci. Med.* 14D, pp. 281–90.

Donovan, J. 1986: *We don't buy sickness, it just comes: health, illness and health care in the lives of black people in London.* Aldershot, UK: Gower.

Eyles, J. and Donovan, J. 1990: *The social effects of health policy.* Aldershot, UK: Avebury.

Eyles, J. and Woods, K. 1983: *The social geography of medicine and health.* London: Croom Helm.

Giggs, J. 1983: Schizophrenia and ecological structure in Nottingham. In McGlashan, N. and Blunden, J., eds, *Geographical aspects of health.* London: Academic Press, pp. 197–222.

Haynes, R. 1987: *The geography of health services in Britain.* London: Croom Helm.

Jones, K. and Moon, G. 1987: *Health, disease and society: an introduction to medical geography.* London: Routledge and Kegan Paul.

Joseph, A. and Phillips, D. 1984: *Accessibility and utilization: geographical perspectives on health delivery.* New York: Harper and Row.

Learmonth, A. 1988: *Disease ecology.* Oxford: Blackwell.

Meade, M., Florin, J. and Gesler, W. 1988: *Medical geography.* New York: Guilford.

Openshaw, S., Charlton, M., Craft, A. and Birch, J. 1988: Investigation of leukaemia clusters by use of a geographical analysis machine. *The Lancet,* 6 February, pp. 272–3.

Pacione, M., ed. 1986: *Medical geography: progress and prospect.* London: Croom Helm.

Phillips, D. R. 1990: *Health and health care in the Third World.* London: Longman.

Powell, M. 1990: Need and provision in the National Health Service: an inverse care law? *Policy and Politics* 18, pp. 31–7.

Pyle, G. F. 1969: The diffusion of cholera in the United States in the nineteenth century. *Geogr. Anal.* 1, pp. 59–75.

Pyle, G. F. and Patterson, K. D. 1983: Influenza diffusion in European history: patterns and paradigms. *Ecology of Diseases* 2, pp. 173–84.

Shannon, G. and Dever, G. 1974: *Health care delivery: spatial perspectives.* New York: McGraw-Hill.

Smallman-Raynor, M. and Cliff, A. 1990: Acquired Immune Deficiency Syndrome (AIDS): literature, geographical origins and global patterns. *Progr. hum. Geogr.* 14, pp. 157–213.

Snow, J. 1855: *On the mode of communication of cholera.* Cambridge, MA: Harvard University Press. (See also: Meade, M., Florin, J. and Gesler, W. 1988: *Medical geography.* New York: Guilford, pp. 19–20.)

Taket, A. 1989: Equity and access: exploring the effects of hospital location on the population served – a case study in strategic planning. *J. Op. Res. Soc.* 40, pp. 1001–10.

megalopolis A Greek word (combining the terms for 'great' and 'city') adapted by Jean Gottmann (1964) to describe the urban complex of the northeastern seaboard of the US. (Cf. CONURBATION.) RJJ

Reference

Gottmann, J. 1964: *Megalopolis: the urbanized northeastern seaboard of the United States.* Cambridge, MA: The MIT Press.

mental map A term referring to the psychological representation of space as shown by simple paper and pencil tests. A psychological turn in human geography in the late 1960s directed attention to the central role of perception as a mediation between the environment and human action. To specify a key role for cognition was also to relax the determinism of LOCATIONAL ANALYSIS with its assumption of fully rational spatial behaviour. Research led to a proliferation of terms describing mental configurations of space. Lynch (1960) asked residents in several American cities to provide him with an image of their city; Downs and Stea (1973) referred to *cognitive maps* which, following Tolman's (1948) early work with rats, are particularly concerned with way-finding behaviour; and other terms included spatial cognition, spatial schemata and awareness space. All of these concepts implied knowledge of the configuration and structure of space: some of them also included an evaluation of that structure, a concern with the meaning of space (Ley, 1983).

The most influential research was Peter Gould's innovative experiments exploring the content of what he called mental maps (Gould, 1965; Gould and White, 1974). In the initial experiments, undergraduates in several American universities were asked to rank order the states in which they would like to live following graduation. The results invariably showed a national preference surface onto which was superimposed a preference for the home region. The research was extended to Europe and Africa, and included a study of the developmental sequence of place learning by children, as well as the effects of 'MODERNIZATION' upon mental maps (Gould and White, 1974). It was implied that the mental maps were not only preference surfaces but also predictors of consequent spatial behaviour. Later research found significant correlations between the mental maps of students in several regions and the patterning of migration flows (Lloyd, 1976).

More qualitative assessments of the meaning of space have been a primary objective of HUMANISTIC GEOGRAPHY. Tuan's (1974) seminal volume on topophilia (the love of place) was the first of many studies informed by EXISTENTIALISM, PHENOMENOLOGY and SYMBOLIC INTER-ACTIONISM, and which demarcated the variable meeting of subject and object, and of place and identity. However, the meanings of PLACE are not necessarily either supportive or innocent. Association with settings which are, for example, stigmatized or stressful may engender spoiled identities. The image of places may also be deliberately manipulated in order to achieve a desired end. Such a manipulation of meanings has been a constant feature of urban and regional 'boosterism', with its objective of stimulating investment by representing an attractive image of a locality. (See also BEHAVIOURAL GEOGRAPHY; ENVIRONMENTAL PERCEPTION; URBAN ENTREPRENEURIALISM.) DL

References

Downs, R. and Stea, D., eds 1973: *Image and environment: cognitive mapping and spatial behaviour*. Chicago: Aldine.

Gould, P. 1965: On mental maps. Discussion Paper No. 9, Michigan Inter-University Community of Mathematical Geographers, Ann Arbor.

Gould, P. and White, R. 1974: *Mental maps*. London: Penguin.

Ley, D. 1983: *A social geography of the city*. New York: Harper and Row.

Lloyd, R. 1976: Cognition, preference and behaviour in space. *Econ. Geogr.* 52, pp. 241–53.

Lynch, K. 1960: *The image of the city*. Cambridge, MA: The MIT Press.

Tolman, E. C. 1948: Cognitive maps in rats and men. *Psychol. Rev.* 55, pp. 189–208.

Tuan, Y.-F. 1974: *Topophilia*. Englewood Cliffs, NJ: Prentice-Hall.

Suggested Reading

Gould and White (1974).

mercantilist model An approach to the study of URBAN SYSTEMS devised by

Vance (1970) to counter the dominance of CENTRAL PLACE THEORY. The key urban function in the model is wholesaling, and the system's development is founded on the articulation of long-distance trade, especially through GATEWAY and PRIMATE CITIES. RJJ

Reference

Vance, J. E. Jr. 1970: *The merchant's world: the geography of wholesaling*. Englewood Cliffs, NJ: Prentice-Hall.

merit good A particular type of pure PUBLIC GOOD, usually defined as the national minimum standard for its provision. Public policy is written to ensure that the entire population of the relevant territory obtains at least that standard level of provision of the good in question (such as the purity of a water supply) – and thereby implies that others (those in control of the STATE APPARATUS) are able to determine what it is best for people to consume, in opposition to the widely lauded concept of consumer sovereignty. Any provision above the merit good standard involves the creation of impurely distributed public goods. RJJ

methodological individualism The view that explanations of society are reducible to the properties (e.g. beliefs) and relations (e.g. employer–employee) of the *individuals* that compose it. Because for the methodological individualist all macro-level social entities are decomposable into more basic micro-level ones, it follows that 'there are no societies, [but] only individuals who interact with one another' (Elster, 1989, p. 248). The usual justification for methodological individualism is that by beginning with the desires, intentions and reasons of individuals the specific causes of aggregate social action are illuminated. But despite the seemingly greater explanatory detail offered by methodological individualism, it typically presumes that individuals are governed by the universal of RATIONAL CHOICE. Because of this association with the rationality postulate, methodological individualism is found most readily in NEOCLASSICAL ECONOMICS (and its spatial counterpart REGIONAL

SCIENCE), and more recently in ANALYTICAL MARXISM. TJB

Reference
Elster, J. 1989: *The cement of society*. Cambridge: Cambridge University Press.

Suggested Reading
Levine, A., Sober, E. and Wright, E. O. 1987: Marxism and methodological individualism. *New Left Rev.* 162, pp. 67–84.

Przeworski, A. 1985: Marxism and rational choice. *Pol. Soc.* 14, pp. 379–409.

metropolitan area A general term, originating in the US, to describe a very large urban settlement. Metropolitan districts were first defined in the 1910 American CENSUS to group together large cities (administrative districts) with their contiguous SUBURBS into single data-reporting units. The term was changed to 'Standard Metropolitan Area' in 1950 and to 'Standard Metropolitan Statistical Area' (SMSA) in 1960, when 219 were defined. The criteria for defining SMSAs are population size, population density and occupational structures: the basic building blocks are US counties. Within SMSAs the US Bureau of the Census also defines 'Urbanized Areas', comprising the built-up portions only. Many countries now have defined metropolitan areas, on widely varying criteria. RJJ

metropolitan labour area (MLA)
The commuting HINTERLAND of a METROPOLITAN AREA, a term coined by Brian Berry, who also invented 'daily urban system' to indicate the interdependence of the area's parts. Berry's maps for the 1960 census showed that nearly all US counties 'exported' at least five per cent of their workers to an SMSA and were thus part of at least one MLA. The concept is now widely adopted for reporting CENSUS data (the British term is 'Local Labour Market Area' – LLMA). RJJ

Suggested Reading
Berry, B. J. L., Goheen, P. G. and Goldstein, H. 1969: *Metropolitan area definition: a reevaluation of concept and statistical practice*. Washington, DC: US Bureau of the Census.

Coombes, M. G., Dixon, J. S., Goddard, J. B., Openshaw, S. and Taylor, P. J. 1979: Daily urban systems in Britain: from theory to practice. *Environ. Plann. A* 11, pp. 565–74.

microsimulation A statistical procedure for estimating the characteristics of individuals from knowledge of the aggregate characteristics of the population of which they are part. For example, a CENSUS may indicate the number of public housing units in a small area, the number of single-parent heads of household there, and the number of households living below the poverty level. With microsimulation, estimates are made of the number in the area having all of those characteristics, i.e. the number of single-parent head of households living below the poverty level in a public housing unit. (See also ENTROPY-MAXIMIZING MODELS.) RJJ

Suggested Reading
Longley, P. A., Clarke, M. and Williams, H. C. W. L. 1991: Housing careers, asset accumulation and subsidies to owner–occupiers – a microsimulation. *Housing Studies* 6, pp. 57–69.

migrant labour Workers who migrate in order to find employment. MIGRATION may be temporary or permanent and over long or short distances, often involving movement across international frontiers. In the contemporary world there are many examples of economies that have come to rely to a significant extent upon migrant labour.

Two aspects are crucial to understanding the distinction between migrant labour and other types of migration. First, for the individual the principal motivation is economic, the search for a better wage and more secure employment. While much migrant labour involves the temporary movement, often of young individuals, more mature streams may lead to permanent settlement of migrants and their families. Thus, migrant labour often becomes a permanent part of the labour force at the point of destination, sometimes indistinguishable from the population at large or, particularly with culturally distinct international migrations, forming distinct ethnic groups (see ETHNICITY). Second, migrant labour may be seen in a wider economic structural context, e.g. in the development of CAPITALISM. Thus, since capitalist development is uneven in both time and space, MOBILITY of the labouring population in, for example, nineteenth-century Great Britain was essential for the continuing development of INDUSTRIAL-IZATION. Similarly, in north-west Europe after the Second World War, migrant labour became an essential part of economic growth and of urban and industrial CONCENTRATION AND CENTRALIZATION. Thus, countries such as the UK, France and West Germany came to rely increasingly upon labour from southern Europe and from the THIRD WORLD: the UK from the West Indies and South Asia; France from Italy, Spain, Portugal and North Africa; and West Germany from Greece and Turkey (see *GASTARBEITER*). Equally, in the USA comparable migration flows came from Mexico and the Caribbean. Labour migrants are found in many other parts of the world and in varying circumstances; for example, seasonal or periodic migrants in West Africa find employment in both agriculture and industry. Migrant labour was an important feature of the South African economy under APART-HEID. Workers were drawn into 'White' South Africa from the Black 'Homelands' on year-long contracts. One advantage of this system is that, as elsewhere, the receiving territory is relieved of some of the cost of production and reproduction of the labour which it uses, as such costs are borne in the territory of origin where families remain.   PEO

Suggested Reading

Cohen, R. 1987: *The new helots: migrants in the international division of labour.* Aldershot, UK: Gower.

Miles, R. 1982: *Racism and migrant labour.* London: Routledge and Kegan Paul.

migration   Permanent or semi-permanent change of residence of an individual or group of people. Geographers have devoted much more attention to the study of migration than to other branches of population study. The collection of data on migration requires a boundary of some sort to have been crossed and a certain length of time to have been spent over that boundary in a new area of residence.

Migration, together with FERTILITY and MORTALITY, is a fundamental element determining population growth and structure in an area. *Gross migration* includes all flows, and *net migration* the balance of moves into and out of an area. MOBILITY is a rather more general term than migration, covering all kinds of territorial movements of whatever distance, duration or degree of permanence. A distinction is sometimes drawn between migration and *circulation*, a term given to short-term, repetitive or cyclical movements. Reviewing the whole process of mobility in history, Zelinsky (1971) has developed the idea of the 'mobility transition', related to the general model of the DEMOGRAPHIC TRANSITION, in which he hypothesizes a relationship between different types of movement and general processes of URBANIZATION, INDUSTRIALIZATION and MODERNIZATION in space and time.

SCALE provides an essential criterion for classification, and so migration may be international or inter-regional, or inter-urban, rural–urban or intra-urban. Other criteria include time (temporary/permanent), distance (long/short), decision-making (voluntary/forced), numbers involved (individual/mass), social organization of migrants (family/clan/individuals), political organization (sponsored/free), causes (economic/social) and aims (conservative/innovative). Different aspects of migration flows are also distinguished: stepwise migration generally implies movement through a series of places, such as from a village up the urban hierarchy; the related idea of CHAIN MIGRATION links flows to established kinship ties between, for example, rural areas and the city.

Migration has been enormously influential in determining cultural and social change at all scales. Research has concentrated on both empirical and theoretical aspects of the economic and social causes and consequences of migration: its selectivity by age, sex, marital status, education, occupation and stage in the life-cycle; spatial patterns of flow and distance, including migration models; and behavioural aspects of the decision to migrate.

However, there is no comprehensive theory of migration, although attempts have been made to integrate migration into economic and social theory, spatial analysis and behavioural theory. In the late nineteenth century, E. G. Ravenstein formulated what he called 'laws of migration', on which much subsequent work has been based (see Grigg, 1977). These were as follows:

(a) the majority of migrants go only a short distance;

(b) migration proceeds step by step;

(c) migrants going long distances generally go by preference to one of the great centres of commerce or industry;

(d) each migration current produces a compensating counter-current;

(e) the natives of towns are less migratory than those of rural areas;

(f) females are more migratory than males within their country of birth, but males more frequently venture beyond;

(g) most migrants are adults – families rarely migrate out of their country of birth;

(h) large towns grow more by migration than by natural increase;

(i) migration increases in volume as industries and commerce develop and transport improves;

(j) the major direction of migration is from the agricultural areas to the centres of industry and commerce; and

(k) the major causes of migration are economic.

These 'laws' have been modified by subsequent research rather than fundamentally disproved.

Geographers have paid particular attention to the relationship between migration and DISTANCE DECAY. Most studies show migration to be inversely related to distance and Hägerstrand and others have used REGRESSION techniques to describe this relationship, the basis of the idea of the MEAN INFORMATION FIELD. In his basic formulation of the GRAVITY MODEL, Zipf (1949) revealed the relationship between population size, distance and migration. S. A. Stouffer (1940) refined this further by showing that migration was determined by opportunities at origin and destination and by INTERVENING OPPORTUNITIES between the two. Others provided more elaborate multivariate models, relating distance to a variety of other factors.   PEO

References

Grigg, D. B. 1977: E. G. Ravenstein and the 'laws of migration'. *J. hist. Geogr.* 3, pp. 41–54.

Stouffer, S. A. 1940: Intervening opportunities: a theory relating mobility and distance. *Am. Soc. R.* 5, pp. 845–67.

Zelinsky, W. 1971: The hypothesis of the mobility transition. *Geogrl. Rev.* 61, pp. 219–49.

Zipf, G. K. 1949: *Human behavior and the principle of least effort.* New York: Hafner.

Suggested Reading

Champion, A. and Fielding, A. eds 1992: *Migration processes and patterns,* volume 1, *Research progress and prospects.* London: Belhaven.

Cohen, R. 1987: *The new helots: migrants in the international division of labour.* Aldershot, UK: Gower.

Kosinski, L. A. and Prothero, R. M., eds 1975: *People on the move: studies on internal migration.* London: Methuen/New York: Barnes and Noble.

Lewis, G. J. 1982: *Human migration.* London: Croom Helm/New York: St. Martin's Press.

Lutz, W., ed. 1990: *Future demographic trends in Europe and North America.* London: Academic Press, Part 3.

McNeill, W. H. and Adams, R. J. 1978: *Human migration: patterns and policies.* Bloomington, IN: Indiana University Press.

Ogden, P. E. 1984: *Migration and geographical change.* Cambridge: Cambridge University Press.

Stillwell, J. and Congdon, P. 1991: *Migration models: macro and micro approaches.* London: Belhaven.

White, P. E. and Woods, R. I., eds 1980: *The geographical impact of migration.* London: Longman.

mixed economy A term sometimes applied to an economy which combines private and state-owned productive activities. As all capitalist economies have some STATE activities and all countries with a centrally planned COMMAND ECONOMY some private activity, mixed economy is not a helpful term. In fact, it is misleading if taken to describe some intermediate between a fully capitalist and a socialist economic system, because the predominant MODE OF PRODUCTION usually remains capitalist.   DMS

mixed farming An agricultural system in which crops and livestock are produced on the same farm; livestock provide manure for crops and some crops feed the livestock. A range of products can be sold off the farm, making it less vulnerable to price fluctuations, and production variety reduces seasonal unemployment. Mixed farming evolved in Western Europe and simplified forms were found in North America, but it has been largely replaced by more specialized livestock and crop production since 1950. It is unusual in Latin America and Africa, but still occurs in a less integrated form in Asia.   DBG

Suggested Reading

Grigg, D. B. 1974: *The agriculture systems of the world: an evolutionary approach.* Cambridge: Cambridge University Press, ch. 9.

Grigg, D. B. 1989: *English agriculture: a historical perspective.* Oxford: Blackwell, ch. 14.

mobility A general term which includes all types of territorial movements, including MIGRATION. Strictly, a distinction is necessary between this spatial or geographical mobility and 'social mobility', a term used to cover changes in socio-economic status. Not all forms of spatial mobility may be regarded as migration. The latter usually implies a permanent or semi-permanent change of residence and therefore excludes, for example, commuters, holiday-makers and students moving termly between family home and college. These forms of mobility are often designated as *circulation*, which covers a 'great variety of movements, usually short-term, repetitive or cyclical in character, but all having in common the lack of any declared intention of a permanent or long-lasting change in residence' (Zelinsky, 1971).   PEO

Reference

Zelinsky, W. 1971: The hypothesis of the mobility transition. *Geogrl. Rev.* 61, pp. 219–49.

Suggested Reading

Jones, H. R. 1990: *Population geography,* second edition. London: Paul Chapman.

Ogden, P. E. 1984: *Migration and geographical change.* Cambridge: Cambridge University Press, ch. 1.

modal split The division of transport flows (passengers or freight) between competing transport modes. The proportion carried by a particular mode varies between countries and between regions within countries, and there is also evidence that particular types of flow 'favour' particular modes: for example, long-distance movements of very low value goods tend to be by water or rail transport, very long distance movements of passengers are increasingly dominated by air transport, but short-distance movement of people in the advanced economies are increasingly dominated by the motor car.

Geographical studies of the determinants of modal split are important not only because modal split is an aspect of AREAL DIFFERENTIATION, but also because modal split is an important policy variable in attempts to reduce traffic congestion and the environmental consequences of the motor vehicle. Initial attempts to represent modal split for aggregate data used the diversion curve technique, but since the mid-1970s attempts to model modal split increasingly use the methods of DISAGGRE-GATE TRAVEL DEMAND and DISCRETE CHOICE MODELLING, which incorporate properties of alternative modes (price, speed, comfort and safety) and characteristics of the decision-maker in the calculus.   AMH

Suggested Reading

Bruton, M. J. 1985: *Introduction to transportation planning,* third edition. London: Hutchinson, ch. 7.

McKinnon, A. C. 1989: *Physical distribution systems.* London: Routledge, ch. 6.

mode of development A term devised by Castells (1983) to refer to 'the particular form in which labour, matter and energy are combined in work to obtain the product'. Castells distinguished between the *industrial mode of development,* in which PRODUCTIVITY derives from a quantitative increase in labour, matter and/or energy, and the *informational mode of development,* in which productivity derives from 'knowledge and results from the organizational methods of combining the three elements of production'. Castells cross-cuts these two modes of development with two MODES OF PRODUCTION to obtain the 'grid of modernity' shown in the figure (see Gregory, 1989).

Mode of production		
	Capitalism	State socialism
Mode of development — Industrial	profit maximization: increasing the appropriation of surplus value economic growth: increasing output	power maximization: increasing the military capacity of the political apparatus economic growth: increasing output
Mode of development — Informational	profit maximization: increasing the appropriation of surplus value technological development: accumulation of knowledge	power maximization: increasing the military capacity of the political apparatus technological development: accumulation of knowledge

mode of development *Modes of production and modes of development* (Gregory, 1989: after Castells).

References

Castells, M. 1983: *The city and the grassroots.* Berkeley, CA: University of California Press.

Gregory, D. 1989: The crisis of modernity? Human geography and critical social theory. In Peet, R. and Thrift, N. eds, *New models in geography*, volume 2. London: Unwin Hyman, pp. 348–85.

Suggested Reading

Castells (1983), pp. 306–17.

mode of distribution A term sometimes used to refer to the way in which societies organize their distributive activities. This term does not have the centrality of MODE OF PRODUCTION in Marxism, being more of a loose descriptive category. Under CAPITALISM, the prevailing mode of distribution is by markets, whereas under SOCIALISM the state prescribes and organizes the distribution of most services and controls the overall supply of most goods – the distribution of which will depend on state-determined income differentials. The extent to which the former socialist societies of Eastern Europe developed a highly bureaucratized administrative system of distribution which accorded privilege to state functionaries tempted some observers to see this as a distinctive mode of distribution. DMS

mode of production The structured social relationships through which human societies organize productive activity, the extraction of surplus value and the reproduction of social life. 'Mode of production' is a periodizing concept, suggesting the historical development of human societies through a series of such modes.

Although Marx was much more circumspect, orthodox Marxist theory, originating with Engels, identified several different modes of production which are seen, in the broadest terms, to succeed each other; primitive communism, SLAVERY, FEUDALISM, CAPITALISM, SOCIALISM and COMMUNISM. In each of these, different social relationships structure the way in which a society's productive and reproductive activity are organized. The definition of modes of production revolves around who performs the social labour and who reaps the benefit. Under primitive communal societies any means of production (land, tools, etc.) were held in common; these societies had subsistence economies, were egalitarian, and experienced no permanent internal class differences. Typified by hunter–gatherers, these societies had only the most elementary DIVISION OF LABOUR (often along age and gender lines). In the slave mode of production, the labourer is owned *as* a means of production (property), and can therefore be bought and sold, and the benefits of labour accrue entirely to the owner (Marx, 1964). Under feudalism, the labourers are peasants who, while not themselves owned as slaves, remain legally tied to the land as agricultural serfs and servants; a landlord retains rights to peasants' labour integral with ownership of the land. Peasants own some of the means of production (especially elementary tools) and live on a portion of what they produce, the remainder being retained by the landlord. With the advent of capitalism, the wage labourer is 'freed' from both the land and the means of production and is obliged to sell his/her labour power for a wage. The working class performs the society's work while the capitalist class, by dint of its ownership of CAPITAL, performs no work.

Socialism was envisaged by Marx as transitional. It represents a mode of production in which the capitalist class has been defeated and class distinctions are being broken down through civil as well as state action. Communism is the mode of production in which egalitarian social relationships have been achieved, class differences have been eroded, and the state has withered away in favour of direct popular control of economy, politics and society.

Although modes of production are identified primarily by their distinctive social relationships, there is a clear connection between RELATIONS OF PRODUCTION and forces of production. Each mode of production is identified with a specific range and type of technologies which develop along with the division of labour. Furthermore, each mode of production implies a specific set of social and cultural relationships, and a specific kind of STATE. Whereas feudalism incorporated a legal system that identified different levels of privilege (enforced by the Court) and was buttressed by an ideology of knowing one's 'rightful place' in an established hierarchical order, the legal structure and social ideologies of capitalist societies emphasize freedom, democracy and equality, despite the obvious inequality in economic relations between classes which defines capitalism.

A mode of production therefore incorporates not just social relations of production but also a complex of political, economic and cultural relations and institutions. Cohesion between these different elements in a mode of production is vital. Marx argued that under capitalism there developed a systematic disjuncture between the rapidly expanding forces of production and the increasingly antiquated social (class) relations of production such that the creation of greater social wealth depended on the continued impoverishment of a large part of humanity. As this situation becomes increasingly untenable, it brings not only social malaise but also political organization, the threat of revolution and the potential to abandon capitalism in favour of a new mode of production.

There are extensive theoretical and empirical debates concerning 'modes of production'. First, while the notion of transnational, historical social structures, common to different times and places, makes considerable sense, human history should not be seen as following a tight evolutionary progression of modes of production. Second, this schema of modes of production was constructed largely on the basis of European history and may not apply more widely. Additional modes of production have been identified: Marx, for example, spoke of an 'Asiatic mode of production' (see Wittfogel, 1957; Peet, 1985).

For geographers, each mode of production can be seen as creating its own distinctive geography, and indeed changing geographies as the mode of production itself develops. Under capitalism, the inequality between capital and labour becomes inscribed in the landscape as the distinction between developed and underdeveloped areas at different scales from the global to the local. UNEVEN DEVELOPMENT is therefore a systematic more than a haphazard aspect of capitalist geographical change. In the twentieth century the geographical unevenness of development has played a central role in defining the fate and directions of capitalist expansion. Likewise, changes in the composition of capitalism have led to a continually transforming geography (Dunford and Perrons, 1983); David Gordon (1984), for example, has shown how the transformation of the US economy from a mercantile to industrial and then to corporate capitalism has involved a parallel transformation in US city structure and spatial form.   NS

References

Dunford, M. and Perrons, D. 1983: *The arena of capital*. London: Macmillan.

Gordon, D. 1984: Capitalist development and the history of American crisis. In Tabb, W. and Sawers, L., eds, *Marxism and the metropolis*, second edition. New York: Oxford University Press, pp. 21–53.

Marx, K. 1964 edn: *Pre-capitalist economic formations*. London: Lawrence and Wishart.

Peet, R., ed. 1985: The geographical ideas of Karl Wittfogel. *Antipode* 17(1), pp. 35–50.

Wittfogel, K. 1957: *Oriental despotism*. New Haven: Yale University Press.

Suggested Reading

Marx (1964).

Hilton, R. et al. 1976: *The transition from feudalism to capitalism*. London: New Left Books.

model   An idealized and structured representation of the real (cf. ABSTRACTION). Model-building has a long history in many sciences, but its formal incorporation into geography is of comparatively recent origin and is most closely associated with postwar attempts to establish geography as a SPATIAL SCIENCE. Indeed, *scientificity* was central to the benchmark collection of essays edited by Chorley and Haggett as *Models in geography* (1967). They argued that model-building depends on 'analogue theory', which treats models as 'selective approximations which, by the elimination of incidental detail [or 'noise'], allow some fundamental, relevant or interesting aspects of the real world to appear in some generalized form'. The accent on *generalization* was vital: these procedures were often formalized in statistical and (less often) mathematical terms and played a vital role in the search for general theories of spatial organization that could underwrite the seemingly endless heterogeneity and differentiation of human landscapes. Ten years later, Haggett, Cliff and Frey (1977) spoke of 'essential links' between model-building and the QUANTITATIVE REVOLUTION, and many of the first-generation models were attempts to represent the abstract geometry of an idealized landscape through various transformations of DISTANCE DECAY functions. Since the itinerary from abstraction through generalization to disclosure was supposed to provide for further extensions and explorations, model-building was seen as a necessary moment in the 'puzzle-solving' activity required for the foundation of a new scientific PARADIGM. It was no accident, therefore, that Chorley and Haggett's advocacy of a model-based paradigm for geographical inquiry should have been phrased in resolutely Kuhnian terms.

Since Chorley and Haggett wrote, however, the claims and concepts which provided the architecture for their pioneer collection of essays have been re-evaluated on three main levels:

(a) The models themselves have been subject to a (limited) reformulation. In the second edition of *Locational analysis* the authors admitted that 'the present stock of models may be unprepossessing', and a comparison with the first edition (1965) shows that the intervening years had seen remarkably few attempts to construct new locational models, although some of the old ones had been reworked: for example, Hägerstrand's DIFFUSION model was shown to be a special case of a more general epidemiological model, the classical GRAVITY MODEL was shown to be an instance of a more general class of ENTROPY-MAXIMIZING MODELS, and the VON THÜNEN MODEL was recast as the dual of the TRANSPORTATION PROBLEM in LINEAR PROGRAMMING. This limited advance was, in part, because the autonomy of LOCATION THEORY had been compromised and more inclusive models of the SPACE-ECONOMY had been constructed outside the domain of spatial science. Those who continued to work within the conventional modelling framework were more concerned with developing statistical and mathematical models which could break open complicated data sets than with seeking to establish in any direct way the theorems of a general spatial science.

(b) Partly as a consequence, the original claim for analytical model-building as the object of geographical inquiry was displaced, and efforts were directed towards methods as *means* rather than as ends in themselves. This effort was originally entangled with the critique of (LOGICAL) POSITIVISM, but the use of analytical methods has since been resituated within a wider intellectual landscape which is much more sensitive to the limitations of such methods: so, for example, Sheppard and Barnes (1990) 'recognize that many aspects of society and economy are not subject to analytical treatment, and even those aspects that are may well be more sensitively treated by non-analytical methods'. The same authors direct modelling towards the identification of substantive processes and causal mechanisms rather than mathematical processes and idealized landscapes:

> Distances are not some physical constraint to which all realizations of a process are subject in identical ways, as in the laws of physics, because spatial structures are socially constructed and far more complex than the isotropic and stationary spaces that are generally relied on in [locational] analysis (Sheppard and Barnes, 1990).

(c) Those reformulations have had some impact on conventional modelling, and a conference held to mark the twentieth anniversary of the original *Models in geography* included both revisionists who sought to rethink and resituate the modelling enterprise and dissidents who were sceptical of its ability to address important practical questions: 'Those who have stuck with modelling since those heady days have largely been able to do so', Harvey suggested, 'by restricting the nature of the questions they ask'. Modelling was a quintessential expression of MODERNISM, Cosgrove argued, and was quite incapable of responding to the contemporary (political and moral) challenges of POSTMODERNISM. But the conference also included a large number of unrepentant spatial scientists who had no time for such concerns, and who reaffirmed their faith in the central importance of modelling as a way of making an accommodation with the new right (Bennett) or meeting the demands of the commercial marketplace (Openshaw) (Macmillan, 1989). Their priorities and profiles have been boosted by the rapid expansion of GEOGRAPHICAL INFORMATION SYSTEMS. DG

References

Chorley, R. J. and Haggett, P., eds, 1967: *Models in geography*. London: Methuen.

Haggett, P., Cliff, A. and Frey, A. 1977: *Locational analysis in human geography*, second edition. London: Edward Arnold.

Macmillan, B., ed. 1989: *Remodelling geography*. Oxford: Blackwell.

Sheppard, E. and Barnes, T. 1990: *The capitalist space-economy*. London: Unwin Hyman.

Suggested Reading

Harvey, D. 1969: *Explanation in geography*. London: Edward Arnold, chs 10 and 11.

Macmillan (1989).

modernism A mode of representation most closely identified with twentieth-century movements in the arts that challenged the conventions of realism and romanticism. Some commentators dismiss 'modernism' as the emptiest of labels, and certainly the diversity of modernisms needs emphasis, but Lunn (1985) identifies four major preoccupations of aesthetic modernism in the early twentieth century:

(a) *Aesthetic self-consciousness.* 'Modern artists, writers and composers often draw attention to the media or materials with which they are working', Lunn argues, and in doing so establish the status of their work as a 'fiction' in the literal sense of 'something made': they thus seek to escape from the idea of art as a direct reflection of the world.

(b) *Simultaneity and juxtaposition.* Modernism often disrupts, weakens or dissolves temporal structure in favour of an ordering based on simultaneity: different perspectives are often juxtaposed within the same frame.

(c) *Paradox, ambiguity and uncertainty.* Modernism often explores what Lunn calls 'the paradoxical many-sidedness of the world': instead of an omniscient narrator, for example, modernist writers may deploy multiple, limited and partial vantage-points from which to view events.

(d) *The demise of the centred subject.* Modernism often exposes and disrupts the fiction of the sovereign individual or the 'integrated subject'.

These shifts did not emerge in a vacuum, and many commentators treat modernism – and in particular the avant-garde

(Bürger, 1984) – as both a critique of and a response to a major CRISIS within early twentieth-century MODERNITY. Its European co-ordinates include the restructuring of CAPITALISM, especially the Agricultural Depression at the end of the nineteenth century and the technical changes brought about by the 'Second INDUSTRIAL REVOLUTION'; the aggressive advance of COLONIALISM and IMPERIALISM; and the turbulence of the First World War and the Russian Revolution (Anderson, 1984; Hobsbawm, 1987; Eksteins, 1989). Even in such an abbreviated form, this cultural mapping has two implications of direct relevance to human geography. First, these episodes brought with them significant changes in conceptions of time and space in the West (Kern, 1983) which also had dramatic repercussions far beyond Europe and North America (Rabinow, 1989; Wright, 1991) and which were directly implicated in a process of 'othering' (see, e.g., Torgovnick, 1990). Secondly, modernism was connected to philosophical reflection and the formation of the social sciences, including the critical inquiries of the FRANKFURT SCHOOL, as well as to experimentation in the arts (see, e.g., Berman, 1989; Pippin, 1991).

Lunn's characterizations make most sense when applied to modern art and literature – in discussions of movements such as surrealism and cubism – and have less purchase on modern architecture, which has its own chronologies and concerns (Frampton, 1985; Holston, 1989). These assumed a wider significance in the 1950s and 1960s when a 'high modernism' emerged as a dominant cultural thematic, distinguished by what Bürger (1984) describes as a 'pathos of purity'. 'In the same way as architecture divested itself of ornamental elements', he argues, so 'painting freed itself from the primacy of the representational, and the *nouveau roman* liberated itself from the categories of traditional fiction (plot and character)'. And in much the same way, and at much the same time, one could see SPATIAL SCIENCE divesting human geography of its interest in difference and differentiation, which became so many 'residuals' and so much 'noise', in order

to reveal the purity of universal geometric form (often, like architecture, cast in terms of a FUNCTIONALISM). It would not be difficult to present other modern movements in social thought in the same way: for example, STRUCTURALISM.

From such a perspective, POSTMODERNISM becomes a critique of high modernism. But equally important are its echoes and filiations with the early twentieth-century avant-garde: connections which, as Lunn (1985) shows, were particularly important for the development of Western Marxism. Not for nothing does Berman (1983, 1992) urge the importance of reclaiming that earlier modernism. In fact, he suggests that it has its roots even earlier, in the nineteenth-century writings of Baudelaire and Marx, both of whom (in different ways) sought to come to terms with a world in which 'all that is solid melts into air'. Those most interested in elucidating such connections have often been concerned to establish the ways in which both modernism and POSTMODERNISM bear on (and yield particular insights into) the production of space and spatiality. There is, of course, a geography of modernism – it is, above all, 'an art of cities' (Bradbury, 1976; Timms and Kelley, 1985) – but the exploration of these matters has by no means been confined to CULTURAL GEOGRAPHY and extends to political economy (Harvey, 1989). Far from eclipsing modernism, therefore, the rise of postmodernism has provoked an unprecedented interest (in human geography) in the early twentieth-century avant-garde (see, e.g., Gregory, 1991; Bonnett, 1992).   DG

References

Anderson, P. 1984: Modernity and revolution. *New Left Rev.* 144, pp. 96–113.

Berman, M. 1983: *All that is solid melts into air: the experience of modernity.* London: Verso.

Berman, R. 1989: *Modern culture and critical theory: art, politics and the legacy of the Frankfurt School.* Madison, WI: University of Wisconsin Press.

Berman, M. 1992: Why modernism still matters. In Lash, S. and Friedman, J., eds, *Modernity and identity.* Oxford: Blackwell, pp. 33–58.

Bonnett, A. 1992: Art, ideology and everyday space: subversive tendencies from dada to postmodernism. *Environ. Plann. D: Society and Space* 10, pp. 69–86.

Bradbury, M. 1976: The cities of modernism. In Bradbury, M. and McFarlane, J., eds, *Modernism 1890–1930*. London: Penguin, pp. 96–104.

Bürger, P. 1984: *Theory of the avant-garde*. Minneapolis: University of Minnesota Press.

Eksteins, M. 1989: *The rites of spring: the Great War and the birth of the modern age*. Toronto: Lester and Orpen Dennys.

Frampton, K. 1985: *Modern architecture: a critical history*. London: Thames and Hudson.

Gregory, D. 1991: Interventions in the historical geography of modernity: social theory, spatiality and the politics of representation. *Geogr. Annlr.* 73B, pp. 17–44.

Harvey, D. 1989: *The condition of postmodernity: an enquiry into the origins of cultural change*. Oxford: Blackwell.

Hobsbawm, E. 1987: *The age of empire, 1875–1914*. London: Cardinal.

Holston, J. 1989: *The modernist city*. Chicago: University of Chicago Press.

Kern, S. 1983: *The culture of time and space, 1880–1918*. Cambridge, MA: Harvard University Press.

Lunn, E. 1985: *Marxism and modernism*. London: Verso.

Pippin, R. 1991: *Modernism as a philosophical problem*. Oxford: Blackwell.

Rabinow, P. 1989: *French modern: norms and forms of the social environmental*. Cambridge, MA: MIT Press.

Timms, E. and Kelley, D., eds 1985: *Unreal city: urban experience in modern European literature and art*. Manchester: Manchester University Press.

Torgovnick, M. 1990: *Gone primitive: savage intellects, modern lives*. Chicago: University of Chicago Press.

Wright, G. 1991: *The politics of design in French colonial urbanism*. Chicago: University of Chicago Press.

Suggested Reading

Anderson (1984).

Harvey (1989), chs 2 and 16.

Lunn (1985), ch. 2.

modernity A particular constellation of POWER, knowledge and social practices which first emerged in Europe in the sixteenth and seventeenth centuries, and the forms and structures of which changed over time and extended themselves over space until, by the middle of the twentieth century, they constituted the dominant social order on the planet. In the West the term 'modern' had long been used to distinguish a new social order from previous social orders. In post-Roman Europe, for example, the Latin *modernus* was used from the late fifth century to distinguish the Christian present from the pagan past, and for centuries the term was used to dramatize a renewed relationship to the ancient world. But the first recorded English-language use of 'modernity' as a noun was not until 1627, and many intellectual historians place the origins of modernity as a world-view, a horizon of meaning and expectation, in the seventeenth century (for a critical review, see Toulmin, 1990). Most writers continued to speak of 'our age' when describing their own present, but in the course of the eighteenth century many of them started to talk instead of *nova aetas* (the 'new age'). Towards the end of that century the idea of being modern came to be associated not only with novelty but, more particularly, with looking forward rather than backward: with the so-called 'Enlightenment project' of reason, rationality and progress towards truth, beauty and the just life. The Enlightenment project had its critics and its successors, of course, and the experience of two world wars left deep marks on what Habermas (1981) identified more generally as 'the project of modernity' (see, for example, Horkheimer and Adorno, 1974; Eksteins, 1989). But common to virtually all of these post-Enlightenment discussions of modernity is an emphasis on novelty, change and 'progress'. In the middle of the nineteenth century, to take what turned out to be a particularly fruitful example, Marx saw an essential connection between modernity and the revolutionary dynamics of CAPITALISM. With Engels, he described a turbulent world in which:

All fixed, fast-frozen relations, with their train of ancient and venerable prejudices, are swept away, all new-formed ones become antiquated before they can ossify. All that is solid melts into air . . . (see Berman, 1982, for an extended discussion).

This imagery was by no means confined to Marx and Engels, and it raised two fundamental, closely connected questions.

On the one side was the problem of *representation–authorization*. In a world of such volatility how was it possible to convey – to capture on the canvas or on the page – what Baudelaire, in his essay on 'The Painter of Modern Life' (which was also composed in the middle of the nineteenth century), now saw as fully one half of any properly modern artistic endeavour, namely 'the ephemeral, the fugitive, the contingent'? This was the question that haunted MODERNISM through the nineteenth and into the twentieth centuries, but it also had implications far beyond the creative arts. For these changes in time were embedded in changes in the PRODUCTION OF SPACE. Although it is perhaps possible to identify the emergence of a 'modern world system' centred on Europe as early as the sixteenth century – and, by implication, to conceive of modernity as a system of politico-economic structures and transactions organized around MARKET EXCHANGE (Wallerstein, 1974; see also WORLD-SYSTEMS ANALYSIS) – it seems clear that processes of globalization and TIME–SPACE COMPRESSION had intensified to such a degree in the course of the nineteenth and twentieth centuries, most acutely in Western metropolitan and colonial cities, that many commentators declared a profound crisis of representation not only in the arts but in the humanities and social sciences as well (Frisby, 1985; Harvey, 1989). What Jay (1992) saw as the dominant 'scopic regime of modernity' – namely 'Cartesian perspectivalism' – was called into question, new separations were installed between PLACE and SPACE (Entrikin, 1991), and constructions of *abstract space* multiplied endlessly (Lefebvre, 1992). These compound dilemmas eventually issued in what Clifford (1988) calls 'the predicament of culture', of 'ethnographic modernity' itself. As he put it elsewhere,

One cannot [now] occupy, unambiguously, a bounded cultural world from which to journey out and analyse other cultures. Human ways of life increasingly influence, dominate, parody, translate and subvert one another (Clifford, 1988, p. 22).

To some writers, this predicament has necessitated a renewed period of experimentation with modes of representation and a move supposedly 'beyond' modernism: hence, in part, the interest in POSTMODERNISM. But these cultural configurations also raise serious ethical and political problems. If all knowledge is 'situated knowledge', then by what right – and in whose voice – can one claim to speak about (or on behalf of) other people in other situations? This is the pivot around which much of the postcolonial critique in the humanities revolves, and it draws attention to the ETHNOCENTRISM of modernism and, indeed, that of many versions of postmodernism too (see POSTCOLONIALISM).

On the other side, and moving with these developments, there is the question of *analysis prescription*. To many commentators, modernity was an unqualified human good which promised to banish ignorance, misery and despotism: to free human beings from myth and superstition, disease and hunger, oppression and arbitrary rule. In the middle years of the twentieth century these assumptions culminated in models of MODERNIZATION, the DEVELOPMENT programmes of which sought to remake the so-called 'traditional' world in the image of the West. There have, of course, been spectacular advances in science and technology, politics and production, but this view has its own blindspots. The triumph of modernity was not accomplished without various attendant violences; not only did it involve warfare, plunder and exploitation, but it also carried within it an instrumental attitude to NATURE, it institutionalized new forms of PHALLOCENTRISM, and it was deeply implicated in COLONIALISM, IMPERIALISM and ORIENTALISM. These are by no means confined to the past but continue to intrude in the present (see, e.g., Taussig, 1992). To other commentators, therefore, modernity has always had its dark side, and many of them argued (in different ways) that European modernity installed new grids of POWER and SURVEILLANCE which, in Max Weber's well-known image, confined human agency, consciousness and creativity within an 'iron cage' of bureaucracy and regulation.

(a)   The Institutionalized politics of modernity (Giddens, 1990)

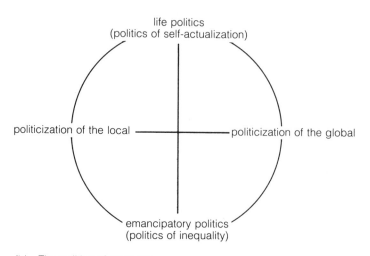

(b)   The politics of modernity

modernity

A recognition of this Janus-face has prompted the construction of complex architectures of modernity. These do not simply identify modernity with capitalism, although that connection remains of vital importance, and their multidimensional models typically draw not only on Marx but also on Weber and other more recent thinkers (see Sayer, 1991). Thus, for example, Habermas (1987a) has suggested that the rationalization processes characteristic of modernity have over-extended themselves to such a degree that one now confronts a multifaceted *colonization* of the LIFEWORLD by the modern SYSTEM (see CRITICAL THEORY), while Giddens (1990) has identified four major institutional dimensions of modernity and proposed an equivalent nexus of political strategies which emphasizes the interlacing of the local and the global and of life-politics and emancipatory politics (see the figure). Many of these analyses draw attention to the staccato dynamics of modernity – to its various shocks, disorientations and CRISES – and, indeed, Beck (1992) likens the experience of modernity to 'living on the volcano of civilization' and identifies modernity with the inauguration of what he calls the 'risk society'. Again, these are not narrowly analytical questions but situate themselves within an ethical–political horizon. Habermas treats modernity as 'the epoch that lives for the future, that opens itself up to the novelty of the future' precisely because it cannot appeal to myth or tradition for legitimation:

Modernity can and will no longer borrow the criteria by which it takes its orientation from the models supplied by another epoch; *it has to create its normativity out of itself*. Modernity sees itself cast back upon itself without any possibility of escape (Habermas, 1987b, p. 7).

Giddens (1990, pp. 38–9) similarly regards what he calls *reflexivity* – the constant examination and modification of social practices – as focal to the configuration of modernity. His is not the Foucauldian reading of the human sciences – the emergence of a specifically modern intellectual grid which focuses on the body, the human subject and the population – although, plainly, the emergence of these specialized discourses has had an immense bearing on the conduct of social life (Rabinow, 1989); Giddens is also interested in the ways in which these processes of monitoring and modification contribute to the volatility of the modern world: 'New knowledge (concepts, theories, findings) does not simply render the social world more transparent, but alters its nature, spinning it off in novel directions' (p. 153). This has reached such a pitch, Giddens argues, that the world is presently in a condition of *radicalized modernity*.

And yet, while Habermas makes the metaphor of 'colonization' central to his thesis and Giddens accentuates the importance of the local and the global, there is no doubt that many of these studies remain ethnocentric, centred more or less unproblematically on an imaginary geography of 'the West'. This also applies to many of those other commentators who insist that the modern epoch has come to an end, and 'history' with it, and who prefer to speak instead of a condition of POSTMODERNITY. But there are signs that new (historical) geographies of modernity are emerging, more attentive to the complex articulations between different social orders in time and space (Harris, 1991; Pred and Watts, 1992). And it seems clear that these studies will have to attend to the situatedness of their own theories and to the complicity of their constructions in the worlds that they seek to represent and analyse (Young, 1990).   DG

References

Beck, U. 1992: *Risk society: towards a new modernity*. London: Sage.

Berman, M. 1982: *All that is solid melts into air: the experience of modernity*. New York: Simon and Schuster/London: Verso (1983).

Clifford, J. 1988: *The predicament of culture: twentieth-century ethnography, literature and art*. Cambridge, MA: Harvard University Press.

Eksteins, M. 1989: *Rites of spring: the Great War and the birth of the modern age*. Toronto: Lester and Orpen Dennys.

Entrikin, J. N. 1991: *The betweenness of place: towards a geography of modernity*. London: Macmillan.

Frisby, D. 1985: *Fragments of modernity*. Cambridge: Polity Press.

Giddens, A. 1990: *The consequences of modernity*. Stanford, CA: Stanford University Press/Cambridge: Polity Press.

Habermas, J. 1981: Modernity versus postmodernity. *New German Critique* 22, pp. 3–14.

Habermas, J. 1987a: *The theory of communicative action*, volume 2, *The critique of functionalist reason*. Cambridge: Polity Press.

Habermas, J. 1987b: *The philosophical discourse of modernity*. Cambridge: Polity Press.

Harris, R. C. 1991: Power, modernity and historical geography. *Ann. Ass. Am. Geogr.* 81, pp. 671–83.

Harvey, D. 1989: *The condition of postmodernity: an enquiry into the origins of cultural change*. Oxford: Blackwell.

Horkheimer, M. and Adorno, T. W. 1974: *Dialectic of enlightenment*. New York: Seabury.

Jay, M. 1992: Scopic regimes of modernity. In Lash, S. and Friedman, J., eds, *Modernity and identity*. Oxford: Blackwell, pp. 178–93.

Lefebvre, H. 1992: *The production of space*. Oxford: Blackwell.

Pred, A. and Watts, M. J. 1992: *Reworking modernity: capitalisms and symbolic discontent*. New Brunswick, NJ: Rutgers University Press.

Rabinow, P. 1989: *French modern: norms and forms of the social environment.* Cambridge: MA: The MIT Press.

Sayer, D. 1991: *Capitalism and modernity: an excursus on Marx and Weber.* London: Routledge.

Taussig, M. 1992: *The nervous system.* London: Routledge.

Toulmin, S. 1990: *Cosmopolis: the hidden agenda of modernity.* New York: The Free Press.

Wallerstein, I. 1974: *The modern world system: capitalist agriculture and the origins of the European world-economy in the sixteenth century.* London: Academic Press.

Young, R. 1990: *White mythologies: Writing History and the West.* London: Routledge.

Suggested Reading

Harris (1991).

Harvey (1989), ch. 2.

Pred and Watts (1992), ch. 2.

modernization A process of social change resulting from the DIFFUSION and adoption of the characteristics of expansive and apparently more advanced societies through societies which are apparently less advanced. Modernization involves social mobilization, the growth of a more effective and centralized apparatus of political and social control, the acceptance of scientifically rational norms and the transformation of social relations (see MODE OF PRODUCTION) and aesthetic forms. The five linear stages of economic growth proposed by Rostow (1960, 1978) provide the conceptual spectacles – or rather blinkers (Hobsbawm, 1979; Taylor, 1989) – within which such a view of DEVELOPMENT may be seen.

However, such an IDEOLOGY merely abstracts from the deeper and wider tendency towards modernization and a postmodern world (Harvey, 1989) associated with the 'remarkable . . . historical geography of capitalism' (Harvey, 1982, p. 373) and its dramatic transformation of values, societies and landscapes across the globe (See POSTMODERNISM).

The translation of modernization into a geography of development was closely associated with the 'new' geography of spatial organization and LOCATIONAL ANALYSIS of the mid- to late-1960s (e.g. Soja, 1968; Gould, 1970; Riddell, 1970; Soja and Tobin, 1972: see SPATIAL SCIENCE). It conceived of modernization as the creation and spread of a network of urban GROWTH POLES orientated to external markets and through which innovations, and therefore development, would diffuse throughout a nationally based central place hierarchy (see CENTRAL PLACE THEORY). Modernization is seen as a recursive process as the social and environmental changes which it induces redefine the framework within which it continues to take place.

Like all models of change based upon the STAGES OF GROWTH, modernization emphasizes the temporally uneven nature and complexity of social change. However, the notion also implies a unilinear and teleological process of change (see TELEOLOGY). Modernization is an apparently unproblematic process of asocial adoption throughout a universal society. The outcome is known in advance: modernization is defined in Eurocentric terms (Hettne, 1990), and the process and direction of change are, therefore, predetermined. Notions of empowerment and disempowerment (see UNDERDEVELOPMENT) and the contested establishment of particular forms of social and environmental relations are ignored. The modernizing society is, apparently, infinitely pliable and may be pulled and stretched to conform with the requirements of modernization. The implication of modernization is that its subject societies have no history, culture or developed set of social or environmental relations. This is an example of a profoundly culturally racist view of the world (see Blaut, 1992).

Furthermore, modernization is often conceived as an autonomous process of change rather than as the product of the integration of pre-existing societies and their subsequent disintegration and restructuring in line with the tenets of modernization. One consequence of such a view and of its influence upon policy and the legitimation of economic and social action is the generation of underdevelopment. For example, industrialization is still often seen as the path to modernity but, as Knox and Agnew (1989, p. 301) point out, this view is based on three 'ideas of mythic proportions': the apparently limited multiplier effects of agriculture, the notion that agriculturalists are inherently conservative, and the belief that only industry is productive in terms of its potential for PRODUCTIVITY increases and increasing marginal returns through ECONOMIES OF SCALE. The value of locally based, often environmentally sensitive systems of production are thus replaced and their practitioners displaced by a process of change which leads to unsustainable social, environmental and geographical disruption and polarization (see SUSTAINABLE DEVELOPMENT).

In short, modernization is more than an abstraction, a 'comfortable myth' (Brookfield, 1975, p. 76), which denies the concrete and complex processes of change and struggle in real social formations. It is an environmentally and socially destructive IDEOLOGY (Watts, 1983; Blaikie, 1985; Blaikie and Brookfield, 1987) which still retains a power to shape trajectories of economic development within which sustainability is problematic (Adams, 1990). And it is still more than that: as a global set of social relations providing the predominant conditions of existence in the struggle to make a living, CAPITALISM provides the immensely powerful social and material commonality in which postmodern struggles and conflicts are played out.   RL

References

Adams, W. 1990: *Green development: environment and sustainability in the third world.* London: Routledge.

Blaikie, P. M. 1985: *The political economy of soil erosion in developing countries.* London: Longman.

Blaikie, P. and Brookfield, H., eds 1987: *Land degradation and society.* London: Methuen.

Blaut, J. 1992: Fourteen ninety-two. *Pol. Geogr. Q.* 11, pp. 355–85.

Brookfield, H. 1975: *Interdependent development.* London: Methuen/Pittsburgh, PA: University of Pittsburgh Press.

Gould, P. 1970: Tanzania 1920–63: the spatial impress of the modernisation process. *World Pol.* 22(2), pp. 149–70.

Harvey, D. 1982: *The limits to capital.* Oxford: Blackwell.

Harvey, D. 1989: *The condition of postmodernity.* Oxford: Blackwell, ch. 5, pp. 99–112.

Hettne, B. 1990: *Development theory and the three worlds.* London: Longman.

Hobsbawm, E. J. 1979: The development of the world economy. *Camb. J. Econ.* 3, pp. 305–18.

Knox, P. L. and Agnew, J. A. 1989: *The geography of the world economy.* London: Edward Arnold.

Riddell, J. B. 1970: *The spatial dynamics of modernisation in Sierra Leone: structure, diffusion and response.* Evanston, IL: Northwestern University Press.

Rostow, W. W. 1960: *The stages of economic growth: a non-Communist manifesto.* Cambridge: Cambridge University Press.

Rostow, W. W. 1978: *The world economy: history and prospect.* London: Macmillan.

Soja, E. W. 1968: *The geography of modernization in Africa.* Syracuse, NY: Syracuse University Press.

Soja, E. W. and Tobin, R. J. 1972: The geography of modernisation: paths, patterns and processes of spatial change in developing countries. In Brunner, R. and Brewer, G., eds, *A political approach to the study of political development and change.* Beverly Hills, CA: Sage.

Taylor, P. J. 1989: The error of developmentalism in human geography. In Gregory, D. and Walford, R., eds, *Horizons in human geography.* London: Macmillan, ch. 5.1, pp. 303–19.

Watts, M. 1983: Hazards and crisis: a political economy of drought and famine in northern Nigeria. *Antipode* 15, pp. 24–34.

Suggested Reading

Brookfield (1975), pp. 76–84, 110–16.

Corbridge, S. 1986: *Capitalist world development.* London: Macmillan, ch. 1, pp. 3–17.

Hobsbawm (1979).

Taylor, J. G. 1979: *From modernisation to modes of production: a critique of the sociologies of development and underdevelopment.* London: Macmillan/Atlantic Highlands, NJ: Humanities Press.

Taylor (1989).

Watts (1983).

modifiable areal unit problem

A particular form of ECOLOGICAL FALLACY associated with the aggregation of data into areal units for geographical analysis.

Most geographical data refer to points in space – such as an individual dwelling or workplace – but in CENSUSES and many other sources these data are aggregated into spatial units (such as CENSUS TRACTS) in order to retain anonymity for the people there. Those spatial units are then the 'individuals' used in geographical analysis, and INFERENCES are often drawn about the people within the units: Robinson's classic exposé of the ecological fallacy, for example, showed that a high correlation between two variables at one spatial aggregation (in his case, between percentage black and percentage illiterate at the state scale in the US) is taken to imply a similar correlation at the individual level (that blacks are more likely to be illiterate).

Openshaw (1977, 1984) extended Robinson's work by showing that when data are aggregated spatially the ecological fallacy should be decomposed into two effects. The first is a *scale effect*: the larger the unit of aggregation, the larger on average is the CORRELATION between two variables. The second is an *aggregation effect*. There is a very large number of different ways in which, for example, the 500 000 or so residents of the city of Sheffield could be grouped into 29 wards, each comprising a contiguous block of territory and containing about 18 500 residents. Openshaw has shown that if you construct a large number of the possible aggregations for such a situation, you can obtain a FREQUENCY DISTRIBUTION for the correlation between two variables across those aggregation units which, although it may be leptokurtic and have most of its values around the distribution mean, could cover the full range of possible values from -1.00 to $+1.00$ (hence the title of Openshaw and Taylor, 1979).

As with the other ecological fallacies, Openshaw's arguments regarding scale and aggregation effects in the modifiable areal unit problem caution against inferring individual relationships from one aggregation only. (Taylor and Johnston (1979), for example, report on regressions between the percentage voting for Richard Nixon in the 1960 US Presidential election and the percentage of an area's residents classified as 'rural non-farm': they obtained a correlation of $r = +0.44$ using the US Bureau of the Censuses nine-region division, and $r = -0.22$ for the four-region division.) To the extent that the spatial division used is arbitrary and unrelated to the nature of the phenomena being analysed, therefore, Openshaw's findings indicate a clear need for care in data analysis and interpretation – and the possibility that researchers wanting to produce a particular result could do so by evaluating the many possible optional aggregations open to them! (See also MULTILEVEL MODELLING.)

The development of computer programs with which to assess the extent of the modifiable areal unit problem (i.e. by generating the frequency distribution for the correlation under consideration) has also allowed advances in the evaluation of procedures for aggregating smaller areal units into larger ones. In the UK, for example, Parliamentary constituencies are constructed by grouping contiguous electoral wards, Johnston and Rossiter (1982) have shown that in many parts of England the relative success of the two main political parties can be substantially influenced by the particular aggregation selected by the neutral Parliamentary Boundary Commission.   RJJ

References

Johnston, R. J. and Rossiter, D. J. 1982: Constituency building, political representation and electoral bias in urban England. In Herbert, D. T. and Johnston, R. J., eds, *Geography and the urban environment: progress in research and applications*, volume 5. Chichester: John Wiley, pp. 113–55.

Openshaw, S. 1977: A geographical study of scale and aggregation problems in region-building, partitioning and spatial modelling. *Trans. Inst. Br. Geogr.* n.s. 2, pp. 459–72.

Openshaw, S. 1984: *The modifiable areal unit problem*. Concepts and techniques in modern geography 38. Norwich: Geo Books.

Openshaw, S. and Taylor, P. J. 1979: A million or so correlation coefficients: three experiments on the modifiable areal unit problem. In Bennett, R. J., Thrift, N. J. and Wrigley, N., eds, *Statistical applications in the spatial sciences*. London: Pion.

Taylor, P. J. and Johnston, R. J. 1979: *The geography of elections*. London: Penguin.

Suggested Reading

Duncan, O. D., Cuzzort, R. P. and Duncan, B. 1961: *Statistical geography*. Glencoe, IL: The Free Press.

money, geography of The study of the geography of money and financial institutions. The importance of money in the modern world hardly needs stating, but human geographers only became interested in money as a geography in the 1980s. There were four main stimulants to this belated discovery. The first was the publication of Harvey's *The limits to capital* in 1982, with its chapters on money, credit and finance. The second was that the 1980s was a decade of dynamic expansion of financial instruments, financial institutions, financial services and financial workforces worldwide. The third was that the 1980s was also a decade overshadowed by periodic crises of insolvency and debt, which bouts of government financial DEREGU-LATION and reregulation seemingly did little to overcome (see CRISIS). Finally, the geography of money and financial institutions had become ever more obvious; money formed a spatial grid of social POWER which overlaid the globe.

Money and credit have to be produced and distributed, and this production and distribution chiefly takes place through a few 'WORLD CITIES' such as London, New York and Tokyo, urban centres where financial institutions and intermediaries gather. Geographical research has concentrated on these cities (see, e.g., Thrift, 1987, 1990; King, 1990; Pryke, 1991; Sassen, 1991; Budd and Whimster, 1992; Thrift and Leyshon, 1993) but this research has increasingly expanded to take in smaller urban centres which may have fewer financial service workers *in toto* but may also have similar relative proportions of these workers (Leyshon et al., 1989). The production and distribution of money and credit clearly demands some degree of state regulation. A second important focus of geographical research on money has therefore concentrated on the relations between NATION–STATES and financial systems that are forged by regulatory systems. This has become a focus of the utmost importance, encompassing the geographical effects of: the creation of new international systems of monetary regulation, such as the European Monetary System (Leyshon and Thrift, 1992); the changing borders between different kinds of financial activity (such as those inspired by the Glass–Steagall Act in the US); and the proper running of all kinds of mutual funds, such as building societies in Britain and thrifts in the US.

The process of the production and distribution of money and credit creates a geography of debt, and this has been a third focus of geographical endeavour. It is a geography that encompasses the 'silent violence' dealt out to many poor people by the Third World debt crises (Watts, 1983; Thrift and Leyshon, 1988; Corbridge, 1992), the deficits run by the US federal government (Corbridge and Agnew, 1991) and all manner of private debt crises that resulted from the invention of new fiscal instruments in the 1980s (Clark, 1989).

Financial systems do not exist in an isolated state, cut off from the rest of society. They are intertwined in many different ways with the productive economy, and some of these ways go by the label of 'finance capital'. Most especially, they are connected with the production of the built environment. Increasingly, commercial and residential property markets dance to the tunes of financial systems (Warf, 1993).

The link between money and CON-SUMPTION was first made explicit by Veblen, while the links between space, time, money and social identity were first forged in any detail by Marx and Simmel. Geographers have subsequently drawn on these authors to provide accounts of the social and cultural consequences of the production and distribution of money and credit (Harvey, 1985; Watts, 1993). In so doing, they have demonstrated yet again that money reaches into every nook and cranny of modern life (see MODERNITY).

NJT

References

Budd, L. and Whimster, S., eds 1992: *Global finance and urban living*. London: Routledge.

Clark, G. L. 1989: The arbitrage economy of the 1990s. *Environ. Plann. A*, 21, pp. 997–1000.

Corbridge, S. 1992: *Debt and development*. Oxford: Blackwell.

Corbridge, S. and Agnew, J. 1991: The US trade and budget deficits in global perspective: an essay in geopolitical economy. *Environ. Plann. D: Society and Space* 9, pp. 91–116.

Harvey, D. 1982: *The limits to capital*. Oxford: Blackwell.

Harvey, D. 1985: Money, time, space and the city. In *The urbanisation of consciousness*. Oxford: Blackwell.

King, A. D. 1990: *Global cities*. London: Routledge.

Leyshon, A. and Thrift, N. J. 1992: Liberalisation and consolidation: the Single European Market and the remaking of European financial capital. *Environ. Plann. A* 24, pp. 49–81.

Leyshon, A., Thrift, N. J. and Tommey, C. 1989: The rise of the provincial financial centre. *Progr. Plann.* 31, pp. 151–229.

Pryke, M. 1991: An international city going global: spatial change in the City of London. *Environ. Plann. D: Society and Space*, 9, pp. 197–222.

Sassen, S. 1991: *The global city*. Princeton, NJ: Princeton University Press.

Thrift, N. J. 1987: The fixers: the urban geography of international commercial capital. In Henderson, J. and Castells, M. eds, *Global restructuring and territorial development*. London: Sage, pp. 203–33.

Thrift, N. J. 1990: Doing global regional geography: the City of London, the South East of England and the new international financial system. In Johnston, R. J., Hauer, J. and Hoekveld, G., eds, *Regional geography*. London: Routledge, pp. 180–207.

Thrift, N. J. and Leyshon, A. 1988: The gambling propensity: banks, developing country debt expo issues and the new international financial system. *Geoforum* 19, pp. 55–70.

Thrift, N. J. and Leyshon, A. 1993: *Making money*. London: Routledge.

Warf, B. 1993: Vicious circle: financial markets and commercial real estate in the US. In Corbridge, S., Martin, R. L. and Thrift, N. J. eds, *The space of money*. Oxford: Blackwell.

Watts, M. 1983: *Silent violence*. Berkeley, CA: University of California Press.

Watts, M. 1993: The devil's excrement: oil money and the spectacle of black gold. In Corbridge, S., Martin, R. L. and Thrift, N. J., eds, *The space of money*. Oxford: Blackwell.

Suggested Reading

Corbridge, S., Martin, R. L. and Thrift, N. J., eds 1993: *The space of money*. Oxford: Blackwell.

Sassen (1991).

Thrift and Leyshon (1993).

morphogenesis Evolutionary or revolutionary change in form. There have been two main areas of application in human geography:

(a) The transformation of a LANDSCAPE. Sauer established such a concern as focal to HISTORICAL GEOGRAPHY in his essay on 'The morphology of landscape' (1925), when he emphasized that 'we cannot form an idea of landscape except in terms of its time relations as well as of its space relations'. This approach has been especially prominent in American and European studies of the rural landscape (see, e.g., Helmfrid, 1961) but there are also classical counterparts for the urban landscape (in particular, Conzen, 1960) which have provided impetus for modern and more theoretically informed studies of changing urban morphologies (Whitehand, 1987; Vance, 1990). (See also MORPHOLOGY; SEQUENT OCCUPANCE; VERTICAL THEME.)

(b) The transformation of a SYSTEM. Biology has been an especially important source of inspiration for many morphogenetic studies within this tradition, providing both informal, typically 'organic' analogies of the Earth, its REGIONS and STATES (see Stoddart, 1967), and much more formal methods and models, most of which usually acknowledge a debt to D'Arcy Thompson's celebrated *On growth and form*, first published in 1917 (see Tobler, 1963). Thus, Bunge's *Theoretical geography* (1962) hailed Thompson's work as 'most suggestive' and Haggett's *Locational analysis in human geography* (1965) found 'common ground' in its focus on 'movement and geometry'. In many ways, CATASTROPHE THEORY represents a radical development of this tradition.

The connections between (a) and (b) were explored in an early essay by Harvey (1967), which was much more concerned with the elucidation of the PROCESSES which sustained morphogenesis rather than with the changing forms themselves. Many subsequent attempts at SYSTEMS ANALYSIS reflected Maruyama's (1963) distinction between a 'first cybernetics' which studies *morphostasis* – ' "deviation counteracting" mutual causal processes', i.e. negative FEEDBACK – and a 'second cybernetics' which studied *morphogenesis* – ' "deviation amplifying" mutual causal processes', i.e. positive feedback. The distinction between positive and negative feedback is more complicated than this implies, however, and involves no necessary correspondence with instability and stability (see, e.g., Bennett and Chorley, 1978, pp. 41–3). DG

References

Bennett, R.J. and Chorley, R. J. 1978: *Environmental systems: philosophy, analysis and control*. London: Methuen.

Bunge, W. 1962: *Theoretical geography*. Lund: C. W. K. Gleerup.

Conzen, M. 1960: Alnwick: Northumberland: a study in town plan analysis. *Trans. Inst. Br. Geogr.* 27.

D'Arcy Thompson, W. 1942: *On growth and form*. Cambridge: Cambridge University Press.

Haggett, P. 1965: *Locational analysis in human geography*. London: Edward Arnold.

Harvey, D. 1967: Models of the evolution of spatial patterns in human geography. In Chorley, R. J. and Haggett, P., eds, *Models in geography*. London: Methuen, pp. 549–608.

Helmfrid, S. 1961: Morphogenesis of the agrarian landscape. *Geogr. Annlr.* 43, pp. 1–328.

Maruyama, M. 1963: The second cybernetics: deviation-amplifying mutual causal processes. *Am. Scient.* 51, pp. 164–79.

Sauer, C. 1925: The morphology of landscape. In Leighly, J., ed., *Land and life: a selection from the writings of Carl Ortwin Sauer*. Berkeley, CA: University of California Press. (Reproduced 1963.)

Stoddart, D. R. 1967: Organism and ecosystem as geographical models. In Chorley, R. J. and Haggett, P., eds, *Models in geography*. London: Methuen, pp. 511–48.

Tobler, W. 1963: D'Arcy Thompson and the analysis of growth and form. *Pap. Mich. Acad. Sci.* 48, pp. 385–90.

Vance, J. 1990: *The continuing city: urban morphology and Western civilization*. Baltimore, MD: Johns Hopkins University Press.

Whitehand, J. 1987: *The changing face of cities: a study of development cycles and urban form*. Oxford: Blackwell.

Suggested Reading

Harvey (1967).
Helmfrid (1961).

morphology Strictly, the science of form, but often used as a synonym for form itself. (Thus, for example, 'geomorphology' is used both to refer to 'the science of landform study' and as a synonym for 'landform'.)

Within the social sciences, morphology has sometimes been used as an alternative term for 'structure', as in Halbwachs' (1960) *Morphologie sociale*, which is concerned with society's demographic and socio-economic structure. Halbwachs drew on Durkheim's classic writings, which also influenced French geography through Vidal de la Blache. Durkheim identified geographers' proper role as the study of social morphology, which comprises 'the mass of individuals who comprise the society, the manner in which they are disposed upon the earth, and the nature and configuration of objects of all sorts which affect collective relations'.

In human geography, the term's classic use is Sauer's (1925) statement on *The morphology of landscape*. He argued that morphological method is a particular form of synthesis, an inductive procedure for identifying the major structural (form) elements in the landscape and arranging them in a developmental sequence (see MORPHOGENESIS). He emphasized the CULTURAL LANDSCAPE, and that study of its creation involved: (a) general geography, or the study of the form-elements themselves (what today is called systematic geography); (b) regional geography, or comparative morphology; and (c) HISTORICAL GEOGRAPHY, which studies the development sequence, as in SEQUENT OCCUPANCE. (Sauer also identified COMMERCIAL GEOGRAPHY, which deals with the forms of production and means of distribution in an area, but he made little reference to this in his later work.)

The study of elements of the TOWNSCAPE is frequently referred to as the study of urban morphology (see FRINGE BELT). RJJ

References

Halbwachs, M. 1960: *Morphologie sociale*, transl. O. D. Duncan and H. W. Pfautz, Glencoe, IL: The Free Press.

Sauer, C. O. 1925: *The morphology of landscape*. Berkeley, CA: University of California Publications in Geography 2, pp. 19–54.

Suggested Reading

Leighly, J., ed. 1963: *Land and life: a selection from the writings of Carl Ortwin Sauer.* Berkeley, CA: University of California Press.

morphometry The measurement of shape. In geography, morphometric techniques have been widely used to provide quantitative depictions of spatial form. Much of the early work took place in geomorphology and depended on the elementary analysis of topographic maps, but the advent of the QUANTITATIVE REVOLUTION saw an increasing sophistication in the derivation of morphological indices and the decomposition of isarithmic surfaces (e.g. Chorley, 1972). This brought with it the realization that these methods could be extended into the domain of human geography too: that 'much of morphometric analysis (conventionally restricted to topographic studies) may be applicable to the topography of all isarithmic surfaces' (Haggett et al., 1977; see also TREND SURFACE ANALYSIS). Morphometry has been of special importance to studies in spatial archaeology and HISTORICAL GEOGRAPHY which continue to be concerned with 'assemblies of artefacts' (Langton, 1972), where the most elaborate application has undoubtedly been the system of *metrological analysis* developed by Hanneberg for the retrogressive study (see RETROGRESSIVE APPROACH) of village tofts and field units.   DG

References

Chorley, R. J., ed. 1972: *Spatial analysis in geomorphology.* London: Methuen/New York: Harper and Row.

Haggett, P., Cliff, A. D. and Frey, A. E. 1977: *Locational analysis in human geography,* second edition. London: Edward Arnold/New York: John Wiley.

Langton, J. 1972: Potentialities and problems of adopting a systems approach to the study of change in human geography. *Progr. Geog.* 4, pp. 125–79.

Suggested Reading

Haggett et al. (1977).

mortality Together with FERTILITY and MIGRATION, death is an essential determinant of population structure and growth. Geographers have been interested in the role of mortality in population change; in the influences of environment on mortality (see HEALTH AND HEALTH CARE); in the ways in which particular diseases are diffused; and in the relationship with economic and social conditions.

The measurement of mortality may be achieved in a number of ways. The simplest is the *crude death rate,* the number of deaths in a specific period per 1000 of the population. Like the crude birth rate (see FERTILITY), this simple measure is severely distorted by age-structure variations which are obviously fundamental to determining overall mortality. *Age-specific mortality rates* express the number of deaths of persons of a certain age per 1000 of the population in that age group. In order to produce single-number indicators of mortality, *standardized mortality rates* may be calculated which take into account variations in age structure and make comparisons between regions or countries possible. Mortality rates may also be related to causes, which can be most informative about the incidence of disease in different age groups and different areas. LIFE TABLES and the measures derived from them, such as LIFE EXPECTANCY, provide the most detailed and sophisticated measures of mortality and are widely used in population models.

One most important group of measures relates to infant mortality, often given special attention because of its sensitivity to social and environmental conditions. The most frequently used *infant mortality rate* is the number of deaths of infants under one year old per 1000 live births in a given year. More precise measures include *neonatal mortality,* defined as those deaths occurring during the first four weeks of life, and *post neonatal mortality,* those occurring within the remainder of the first year. There is also an important distinction in the causes of infant mortality between endogenous and exogenous mortality. The former refers to deaths from congenital malformations or delivery complications and the latter to deaths from infections or poor care. Improvements in modern medicine and health services have brought the most dramatic decline in infant mortality, and general reductions in infant mortality are usually the first stage in overall mortality decline. In some underdeveloped countries, and in past centuries in the presently developed world, infant mortality might account for 30 per cent or more of all deaths. In most developed states, this figure is now very low (see the figure).

The decline in general mortality levels in the developed world has been fairly constant throughout the nineteenth and twentieth centuries, with the result that fertility is generally more important than mortality in determining short-term fluctuations in population. In the developing world, however, mortality has often been reduced dramatically over a few years, producing very rapid population growth. Mortality decline is an essential element in the DEMOGRAPHIC TRANSITION model. Ascribing causes to mortality decline is not as simple as it may seem. Many of the worst diseases have certainly disappeared or been greatly reduced, and FAMINE and subsistence crises are now less influential as the world's social and economic environment has improved. Causes of death have changed dramatically: plague, smallpox, cholera and tuberculosis are not the killers they once were, and in developed countries mortality is now associated more with cancer, heart disease and road accidents.

The major argument about causes of the general decline in mortality centres around the conflict between the role of medicine and the general improvements in standards of living. Improvements in public health provision, techniques of diagnosis and surgery, inoculation and the development of drugs were undoubtedly influential, but probably more so in recent decades in the THIRD WORLD than in nineteenth- and early twentieth-century Europe. For it has been shown that general increases in living standards – improvements in the quantity and quality of food, better sanitation, hygiene and housing conditions – were just as important as changes in medical care. Research has also concentrated on the varying susceptibility of sections of the population to disease and death: differential mortality rates may be calculated to show the influence of racial or ethnic background, education, income and social

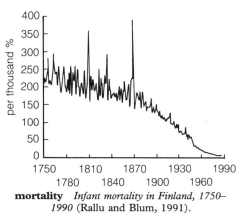

mortality *Infant mortality in Finland, 1750– 1990* (Rallu and Blum, 1991).

or occupational status, sex and rural or urban evidence. (See also MEDICAL GEO-GRAPHY.)   PEO

Reference

Rallu, J.-L. and Blum, A., eds 1991: *European population. 1. Country analysis.* London: John Libbey, p. 153.

Suggested Reading

Howe, G. M. 1976: *Man, environment and disease in Britain: a medical geography of Britain through the ages.* London: Penguin/New York: Barnes and Noble.

Jones, H. R. 1990: *Population geography*, second edition. London: Paul Chapman.

Lutz, W. ed. 1990: *Future demographic trends in Europe and North America.* London: Academic Press, Part 1.

McKeown, T. 1976: *The modern rise of population.* London: Edward Arnold/New York: Academic Press.

Schofield, R. S., Reher, D. R. and Bideau, A., eds 1991: *The decline of mortality in Europe.* Oxford: Clarendon Press.

Woods, R. I. 1979: *Population analysis in geography.* London: Longman.

multiculturalism A policy that endorses the right of different cultural or ethnic groups (see ETHNICITY) to remain distinct rather than assimilating to a dominant society's cultural 'mainstream'. Often restricted to education and the arts, some such policies are more wide-ranging. A weakness of much multicultural rhetoric is its apparent application only to minority cultures rather than to whole societies. Multiculturalism can also be criticized as a celebration of cultural diversity (looking backwards to each group's ethnic heritage) rather than making a positive commitment to equal rights (irrespective of ethnocultural background). (See also ASSIMILATION; PLURAL SOCIETY; PLURALISM.) PAJ

Suggested Reading
Kobayashi, A. 1993: Multiculturalism: representing a Canadian institution. In Duncan, J. S. and Ley, D., eds, *Place culture representation*. London: Routledge.

multidimensional scaling (MDS) A method for simplifying and replicating a matrix, showing the distances between a set of points (n) and – as far as possible – retaining the relative ordering of those distances. MDS locates the points in a smaller number of dimensions than n, and so reduces a multidimensional representation to more comprehensible proportions. It can also be used to transform MAPS, basing them, for example, on the time-distance between places rather than the distance as the crow flies. RJJ

Suggested Reading
Gatrell, A. C. 1983: *Distance and space: a geographical perspective*. Oxford: Clarendon Press.
Haggett, P. 1990: *The geographer's art*. Oxford: Blackwell.

multilevel modelling A method of statistical analysis developed by educational researchers for examining the nature of a relationship at several spatial SCALES. In educational work, for example, children's examination performance within a town may be related to: (1) their personal and home characteristics (level 1); (2) the class in which they are taught (level 2); and (3) the school which they attend (level 3). It is argued that the school and classroom contexts are important influences on performance, in addition to individual ability (Goldstein, 1987).

The multilevel modelling strategy has many potential applications in geography, reflecting the contention that there are NEIGHBOURHOOD and CONTEXTUAL EFFECTS operating on individuals. The strategy is much superior to conventional ecological analyses using CORRELATION and REGRESSION methods to investigate the conjoint influences of individual and areal characteristics. (See also ECOLOGICAL FALLACY; MODIFIABLE AREAL UNIT PROBLEM.) RJJ

Reference
Goldstein, H. 1987: *Multilevel models in educational and social research*. London: Charles Griffin.

Suggested Reading
Jones, K. 1991: *Multi-level models for geographical research*. Concepts and techniques in modern geography 54. Norwich: Environmental Publications.
Jones, K., Johnston, R. J. and Pattie, C. J. 1992: People, places and regions: an exploration of the use of multi-level modelling in the analysis of electoral data. *Brit. J. Polit. Sci.* 22, pp. 343–80.

multinational corporation (MNC) A large business organization operating in a number of national economies: a transnational corporation (TNC) operates in at least two countries. No longer integrated (see INTEGRATION) merely by flows of merchant CAPITAL and TRADE or by finance capital and indirect (portfolio) investment, or even by the internationalization of industrial capital (see ECONOMIC GEOGRAPHY), the world economy is increasingly tied together by the corporate organization of large enterprises which operate at a worldwide scale.

The growth of MNCs has now gone beyond their mere spatial expansion (including their origins and the ever-increasing diversity of the geography of their investments); instead, it is characterized by the intensification of corporate control over the global operating environment. Between one-fifth and one-quarter of total world production in market economies is undertaken by TNCs, and Dicken (1992, p. 47) argues that the 'TNC is the single most important force creating global shifts in economic activity'. Electronic communications and management systems allow the centralization of information and decision-making and the decentralization of operations (see INFORMATION CITY), while the freeing of national controls over the international movement of finance capital and the establishment of international money markets and financial systems combine to increase the international mobility of capital.

This combination of centralization, de-centralization and global structure facilitates locational flexibility and the reduction of RISK, as corporate strategy is able to respond quickly with the use of what are, in corporate terms, ephemeral branch plants and national subsidiaries, to changes in the world economy, without destabilizing the organization as a whole. But however ephemeral such investments may be for the corporation, for the host nation they often represent a significant part of the national economy, over which local interests may have little or no control.

MNCs are now multinational in their origin as well as their destination: many American corporations are now outstripped in size by Japanese and even by Western European MNCs and, although generally small in size, MNCs are now emerging from the leading newly industrializing countries. As a result, there is an increase in the interpenetration of capital around the world which serves to break down the possibilities for integrated and locally controlled indigenous development in particular economies. Furthermore, given the enormous size of the largest MNCs, which rival medium-sized national economies and many underdeveloped economies (although only 4 or 5 per cent of the total number of MNCs are truly global) and their profit-making interest in national currency differentials articulated through the multinational network of banking corporations, they are capable of both the stimulation and destabilization of national economies. MNCs dominate world TRADE, with over 50 per cent of the total trade of Japan and the USA accounted for by intra-firm trade. MNCs are also able to indulge in the largely invisible practice of *transfer pricing*, an accounting practice which enables the allocation of costs and the pricing of goods moving within the corporation to be made in the most profitable fashion, regardless of the accuracy of the costs, the prices or their allocation.

The balance sheet of advantages and disadvantages of MNCs is far from clear; for the CIRCUIT OF CAPITAL as a whole (its overall efficiency and responsiveness to change and the potential for change), for the various forms of CAPITAL around the circuit, or for the places caught up in the influence of MNCs. Judged from the perspective of DEVELOPMENT, their influence is malignant insofar as at the same time that they connect economies into the global circuit of capital and so increase supply lines and markets, by imposing a particular understanding and measure of value and progress they displace control over the making of history and geography from people struggling to make their living and define their own identities.   RL

Reference and Suggested Reading
Dicken, P. 1992: *Global shift: the internationalization of productive activity*. London: Paul Chapman.

multiple nuclei model A model of intra-urban land-use distributions developed by Harris and Ullman (1945), which combines the features of the earlier ZONAL and SECTORAL models. They argued that the residential districts of most urban areas are organized around several nodes and not just the one CENTRAL BUSINESS DISTRICT (see the figure on page 402).   RJJ

References
Harris, C. D. and Ullman, E. L. 1945: The nature of cities. *Ann. Am. Acad. Pol. Soc. Sci.* 242, pp. 7–17.
Harris, C. D. and Ullman, E. L. 1959: The nature of cities. In Mayer, H. M. and Kohn, C. F., eds, *Readings in urban geography*. Chicago: Chicago University Press/Cambridge: Cambridge University Press, pp. 277–860.

multipliers It is widely observed that a new basic primary or secondary economic activity, such as the development of a mine or the construction of a steel plant, triggers off additional economic activities nearby, especially in the local tertiary sector which provides services to the new industry or to its employees and their households: this is termed a multiplier effect, and the multiplier is an attempt to measure the magnitude of such impacts. This magnitude has great potential importance, for high multipliers would indicate to planners the places and the activities where investment would create, directly and indirectly, the greatest

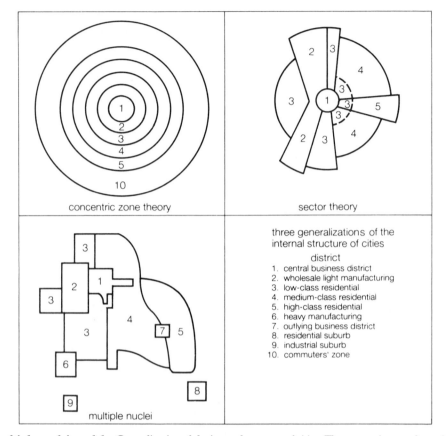

multiple nuclei model *Generalization of the internal structure of cities. The concentric-zone theory is a generalization for all cities. The arrangement of the sectors in the sector theory varies from city to city. The diagram for multiple nuclei represents one possible pattern among innumerable variations* (Harris and Ullman, 1959).

amount of new economic activity (see GROWTH POLE).

The exact method for estimating the multipliers depends upon the theoretical base of the researcher and the data available. The simplest multiplier calculations are derived from ECONOMIC BASE THEORY, but in other cases multipliers are derived from INPUT–OUTPUT analysis. There are two fundamental distinctions in all these studies. The first is between *employment multipliers* (where the focus is on the number of jobs created) and *income multipliers* (where the extra economic activity is measured in value terms). The second is between *aggregate* and *incremental multipliers*. The aggregate multiplier is the

ratio between the total regional economic activity (Y) and its economic base (X):

$$K = Y/X$$

The incremental multiplier is the ratio between a change in X (ΔX) and the consequent change in Y (ΔY). The former is easier to measure: the latter is more correct theoretically, but extremely difficult to measure except in the simplest cases.

The value of multiplier studies has been called into question on a number of grounds. First, it can be shown that multipliers are unstable over time, and that incremental multipliers differ according to whether the change in base activity (ΔX) is an increase or decrease. Second, it is often stressed that multiplier studies, like

ECONOMIC BASE THEORY, essentially deal with short-run effects. Third, it is clear that the value of the multiplier is very sensitive to the size and shape of the study region. Very small regions tend to have very low multipliers because effects leak across boundaries; much larger units have much larger multipliers simply because they are larger and more of the service activities are provided internally. A US study suggested that multipliers will be around 1.5 to 2.0 for smaller cities, greater than 2.0 for cities such as Cincinnati and Denver, and over 3.0 for New York City.   AMH

Suggested Reading

Pred, A. R. 1977: *City systems in advanced economies.* London: Hutchinson/New York: John Wiley.

Smith, D. M. 1981: *Industrial location: an economic geographical analysis,* second edition. New York: John Wiley.

N

nation A COMMUNITY of people whose members are bound together by a sense of solidarity rooted in an historic attachment to TERRITORY and a common CULTURE, and by a consciousness of being different from other nations. The term is frequently but misleadingly used interchangeably with STATE or NATION–STATE on the assumption that every state is a nation and vice versa, although nationalist writings generally hold that they are destined for each other because neither is complete without the other (see NATIONALISM). Anderson (1990) considers the nation to be above all else an 'imagined community' for four reasons: (a) despite the limited bounds of an individual's activities, the nation is associated with *a larger sense of communion* to that of his or her local environment; (b) it is imagined as *limited* in geographical reach by finite, if elastic, boundaries beyond which lie other nations; (c) it is imagined as *sovereign* and thus the ideal is freedom in a sovereign state (see SOVEREIGNTY; and (d) it is imagined as *community* based on a territorial relationship which subsumes other community CLEAVAGES.   GES

Reference

Anderson, B. 1990: *Imagined communities*. London: Verso.

Suggested Reading

Gellner, E. 1983: *Nations and nationalism*. Oxford: Blackwell/Ithaca, NY: Cornell University Press.

Knight, D. 1982: Identity and territory: geographical perspectives on nationalism and regionalism. *Ann. Ass. Am. Geogr.* 72, pp. 514–31.

Smith, A. 1991: *National identity*. London: Penguin.

nation–state A complex array of modern institutions involved in governance over a spatially bounded territory which enjoys monopolistic control over the means of violence.

There are two central components to nation–state formation. First, the process of *state-building* is bound up with the territorialization of state power, a set of centralizing processes which, to paraphrase Mann, can be defined as the capacity of the state to penetrate CIVIL SOCIETY, and to implement logistically political decisions throughout its territory. Such infrastructural powers would include the collection and storage of information (what Giddens, 1985, calls the SURVEILLANCE aspect of state power), imposition of an administrative–territorial order, the regulation of movements of ideas, goods and people across national boundaries, and the growth of a centralized bureaucracy to coordinate and carry out increasingly complex functions within its territorial realm. Second, there is *nation-building*, which, in classic nation–states was facilitated by state-building and the development of industrial capitalism. Nation-state building involves, in particular, the utilization of the NATION by state elites in which a sense of territorial identity and of belonging to a national culture is important, aided by the spread of a common vernacular and national educational system (see IDEOLOGY). Nation-building is therefore also bound up with creating citizens. In one sense, the nation–state is an IDEAL TYPE, for there are few cases in which state boundaries are coextensive with a national community to which all citizens possess an identical culture. It is particularly problematic when the territorial boundaries of the state exceed national identific boundaries.

In this sense, historically, the nation–state has often been a conquest state.

However, processes of globalization, both in the form of the internationalization of capital and the growth of global and regionalized forms of inter-state organization, challenge the ability of the nation–state effectively to practice its claim to a sovereign monopoly over its bounded space and to protect its citizens from external incursion. (See TERRITORIALITY.)   GES

Reference

Giddens, A. 1985: *The nation–state and violence.* Oxford: Polity Press.

Suggested Reading

Cooke, P. 1989: Nation, space, modernity. In Peet, R. and Thrift, N., eds, *New models in geography.* London: Unwin Hyman, pp. 267–91.

Giddens (1985).

Hall, J., ed. 1986: *States in history.* Oxford: Blackwell.

Mann, M. 1984: The autonomous power of the state: its origins, mechanisms and results. *Archives européennes de sociologie* 25, pp. 185–213.

Smith, G. 1994: Political theory and political geography. In Gregory, D., Martin, R. and Smith, G., eds, *Human geography: society, space and the social sciences.* London: Macmillan.

national parks Areas placed under national government protection for their natural significance. The International Union for the Conservation of Nature defines national parks as areas of protection and restricted human access containing 'ECOSYSTEMS not materially altered by human exploitation and occupation', of 'special scientific, educational and recreational interest', or 'containing a natural landscape of great beauty'. The definition, on a broad reading, may also incorporate national forests, game preserves, and nature reserves that are not classified as national parks in a strict sense. Many federal systems (e.g. the US, Canada and Germany) also have state or provincial park systems that are functionally indistinguishable from national parks.

The scenic preserves created at Yosemite (1864) and Yellowstone (1872) in the United States are generally regarded as the first national parks. Numerous countries created similar parks before the First World War. After long agitation, a British system began with the National Parks and Access to the Countryside Act of 1949. The early emphasis on scenic preservation has increasingly broadened to include rare and endangered ecosystems, and the largely recreational functions of developed-world national parks have of necessity expanded to embrace concepts of sustainable use by resident or neighbouring populations in Third World settings. The World Resources Institute (1990) estimates the global extent of 'protected natural areas' of all types to be 530 million hectares, or about 4 per cent of the world's land surface.   JEm

References

World Resources Institute 1990: *World Resources, 1990–1991: a guide to the global environment.* New York: Oxford University Press.

Suggested Reading

Allin, W., ed. 1990: *International handbook of national parks and nature reserves.* New York: Greenwood Press.

nationalism 1. A feeling of belonging to the NATION. 2. A corresponding political IDEOLOGY which holds that the territorial and national unit should be allowed to coexist in an autonomously congruent relationship. Nationalism is chameleon-like, for it can accommodate itself to such diverse socio-territorial backgrounds and contrasting environments as authoritarian collectivism (e.g. fascism and right-wing movements) and democratic movements struggling against domination by another nation, state or empire. Consequently, it is not necessarily 'emancipatory', although its central claim rests on securing social justice (Buchanan, 1991). Nationalism draws upon the doctrine of SELF-DETERMINATION, in which the nation considers itself to have a natural right to determine its own affairs.

As Gellner (1983) has argued, nationalism is a phenomenon connected not so much with INDUSTRIALIZATION or MODERNIZATION, but rather with its uneven DIFFUSION. Originating in Western Europe with the consolidation of 'NATION-STATES', it later brought about the reorganization of the nineteenth- and twentieth-century maps of Europe, and has been the prime force in the political awakening of the THIRD WORLD. However, nationalism does take on a variety of forms, differing in their relationships to the nation and to those objective conditions which determine its opportunity to achieve or maintain the aim of territorial autonomy. On the one hand, there is a *state nationalism*, which reinforces or even exalts the idea of the nation–state. On behalf of the nation's myths and *iconographies*, state actions can be legitimized in both the domestic and the international arena by appealing to 'national unity' and 'national interests' (see ICONOGRAPHY). On the other hand, there is a variety of minority or *substate nationalisms*. These include irredentist (borderland people striving for secession and unity with co-nationals in a neighbouring state; see IRREDENTISM), anti-colonial (in which nationalist demands are based primarily, although not exclusively, on an ethnically heterogeneous people's common response to, and rejection of, colonial rule) and ethnic causes (where shared experience, CULTURE and often language legitimize demands for territorial autonomy or outright separtism). The last category is associated particularly with the European experience.

Until recently, conventional academic wisdom held that ethnic nationalism was destined to dissolve in the acid bath of modernity as a consequence of both the successful regional penetration of the centralized and uniform state and the homogenizing forces associated with mass society. However, far from being a spent force, the persistence of ethnic-based territorial units and their politicization throughout ethnically plural industrialized societies has in a number of instances threatened the stability of many well-established states and, in the case of socialist federations, their very existence (see PLURALISM). The reasons offered for ethnic nationalism have tended to follow one of three lines of explanation:

(a) The first emphasizes the importance of ethnocultural markers – based on language, religion, ethnic background, kinship patterns, etc. – as providing the automatic reference point for ethnoterritorial communities seeking security, survival and regeneration under conditions of socio-economic and political pressure to conform to a state-wide, territorializing process (e.g. Mayo, 1974). But this line of reasoning is too ready to assume that, for the peripheral region, cultural differences provide the most compelling basis upon which such politicization might occur, although there is no doubt that threats to COMMUNITY and the increased impersonalization of growing centralized and bureaucratic states can fuel the engines for political action.

(b) The second approach, which has found much sympathy in Marxist writings, sees the politicization of ethnoterritories as a reaction to historically formed peripheral predicaments, in which the spatial logic of CAPITALISM generates discontinuous and disruptive patterns or waves, conferring advantages on some regions (see UNEVEN DEVELOPMENT), while relegating minority ethnoterritorial communities to a marginal and subordinate status. Hechter (1975), for instance, sees minority nations as being conditioned by the historical development of a culturally backward and economically exploited internal colony, while the state 'core' ethnoterritory, by accumulating capital from and inhibiting its flow into these regions, develops a more advanced and diversified economic base. Such CORE–PERIPHERY differences become institutionalized into a coextensive cultural DIVISION OF LABOUR, forming a basis for political mobilization along ethnoterritorial lines. Besides underestimating the emotional and cultural appeal of nationalism and its capacity to serve human needs better than instrumental groups and satisfactions, such a view does not account for the revival of nationalism in Europe since the 1960s: nor does it explain why ethnic nationalism can propel both relatively prosperous (e.g. Spanish, Basques, Croats, Latvians and Scots) and relatively poor (e.g. Québecois, Bretons, Welsh and Kirgiz) peoples alike into political action.

(c) The third perspective focuses on the spearheading role played by the ethnic intelligentsia in the 'discovery' and politicization of the nation. Their changing expectations in a state which may no longer be able to meet their material and status aspirations thrust them to the forefront of the manufacture, organization and mass mobilization of nationalism. On this basis, time- and place-specific mechanisms and events (e.g. the potential for regional development, a flagging core economy or increased remoteness from government) not only help us to understand why the ethnic intelligentsia are usually at the forefront but also highlight the key role that they play in popularizing the nationalist cause throughout their constituencyGES

References

Buchanan, A. 1991: *Succession*. Boulder, CO: Westview Press.

Gellner, E. 1983: *Nations and nationalism*. Oxford: Blackwell.

Hechter, M. 1975. *Internal colonialism: the Celtic fringe in British national development 1536–1966*. London: Routledge and Kegan Paul.

Mayo, P. 1974: *The roots of identity: three national movements in contemporary European politics*. London: Allen Lane.

Suggested Reading

Agnew, J. 1987: *Place and politics: the geographical mediation of state and society*. London: Allen and Unwin.

Anderson, B. 1990: *Imagined communities: reflections on the origins and spread of nationalism*. London: Verso.

Blaut, J. 1987: *The national question*. London: Zed Books.

Forsyth, M., ed. 1989: *Federalism and nationalism*. Leicester: Leicester University Press.

Hobsbawm, E. 1990: *Nations and nationalism since 1780: programme, myth, reality*. Cambridge: Cambridge University Press.

Johnston, R. J., Knight, D. B. and Kofman, E., eds 1988: *Nationalism, self-determination and political geography*. London: Croom Helm.

Mikesell, M. W. and Murphy, A. B. 1991: A framework for comparative study of minority-group aspirations. *Ann. Ass. Am. Geogr.* 81, pp. 581–604.

Smith, A. 1986: *The ethnic origins of nations*. Oxford: Blackwell.

Smith, A. 1991: *National identity*. London: Penguin.

Smith, G. 1985: Nationalism, regionalism and the state. *Environ. Plann. C: Government and Policy* 3, pp. 3–74.

Smith, G., ed. 1990: *The nationalities question in the Soviet Union*. London: Longman.

Williams, C. and Kofman, E., eds 1989: *Community conflict, partition and nationalism*. London: Routledge.

natural area A residential district within an urban area characterized by its physical individuality and, especially, the cultural and other characteristics of its inhabitants. The concept was introduced by the sociologists of the 1920s CHICAGO SCHOOL, who saw a natural area as the outcome of an unplanned process of sorting of similar people through the operations of the housing market, although some adherents to the HUMAN ECOLOGY perspective saw them as statistical constructs rather than the homogeneous outcomes of ecological sorting processes suggested by some proponents. (See also SEGREGATION.) RJJ

Suggested Reading

Hatt, P. K. 1946: The concept of natural area. *Am. Soc. R.* 11, pp. 423–7.

Zorbaugh, H. W. 1926: The natural areas of the city. *Publ. Am. Sociol. Soc.* 20, pp. 188–97.

natural resources Properties of the physical environment that are considered useful for satisfying human wants. These properties exist independently of humankind, and in physically finite quantity; at the same time, their value, scarcity and usefulness are socially defined: 'Resources are not; they become' (Zimmerman, 1951). (See also RESOURCE.) JEm

Reference

Zimmerman, E. 1951: *World resources and industries*, revised edition. New York: Harper and Row.

naturalism 'The thesis that there is (or can be) an essential unity of method between the natural and the social sciences' (Bhaskar, 1979). Put like that, one might expect naturalism to have played an important part in the history of geography, in making possible a conversation between physical geography and human geography. Certainly, those geographers who have worked with philosophies of science such as CRITICAL RATIONALISM, (LOGICAL)

POSITIVISM and REALISM have accepted a (sometimes modified) version of naturalism. But the situation is more complicated than this implies, for two reasons which work in different directions. On the one side are those human geographers who are suspicious of social science, not least because of the shadows which naturalism casts over them, and who think of themselves as working within the *humanities*. Their central concern is with questions of intention, interpretation and VALUES as these emerge within a world which is intrinsically meaningful to the beings who inhabit it, and this situation (so they suppose) has no direct counterpart in the natural sciences (see HUMANISTIC GEOGRAPHY). On the other side, however, are those who would challenge that last sentence: in their view, *all* 'sciences' involve questions of intention, interpretation and values; their findings are the product of negotiations and practices which are carried out in specific field or laboratory settings, and the dissemination and generalization of their 'local knowledges' involves issues of HERMENEUTICS, power and RHETORIC (Rouse, 1987; Woolgar, 1988).   DG

References

Bhaskar, R. 1979: *The possibility of naturalism: a philosophical critique of the contemporary human sciences*. Brighton: Harvester.

Rouse, J. 1987: *Knowledge and power: toward a political philosophy of science*. Ithaca, NY: Cornell University Press.

Woolgar, S. 1988: *Science: the very idea*. London: Tavistock.

Suggested Reading

Bhaskar (1979).
Woolgar (1988).

nature 1. The essence of something (as in Richard Hartshorne's *The nature of geography*, 1939). 2. Areas unaffected or unaltered by human action. 3. The physical world in general, as the totality of its phenomena or processes or as a topic of study. These three principal meanings in modern geography prompted Williams (1976) to suggest that nature is 'perhaps the most complex word in the language'. In any of these senses, 'nature' can also be used normatively as a standard of value; what is most 'natural' is judged to be best, a standard that has not lacked critics since at least the time of John Stuart Mill (1873).

The second sense – areas unaffected by human action – is akin to the notion of WILDERNESS: McKibben (1989) has written in this vein of *The end of nature*. With the onset of GLOBAL WARMING, he argues, 'nature' (defined as 'the separate and wild province, the world apart from man to which he has adapted') no longer exists 'now that we have changed the most basic forces around us'. Long-term and pervasive human impacts have been so widespread, however, that (like wilderness), nature in this sense is often more an imaginative construct than an historical or physical reality.

The third sense is the most significant, and also the broadest in the questions it raises regarding the human relation to nature. A long-standing debate centres on the extent to which the approaches of the natural sciences (however defined) are appropriate to the study of social life (see NATURALISM). From a different viewpoint, the question asked in 1864 by George Perkins Marsh, 'whether man is of nature or above her' – and repeated in 1973 by Richard Chorley, 'To what extent is it proper to regard Man as a part of Nature or as standing apart from it?' – is of central importance for the study of human–environment relationships. Glacken (1967), in a history of Western thought before the nineteenth century, identified three views of the relationship: humankind in harmony with nature; dominated by nature (see ENVIRONMENTAL DETERMINISM); and dominating nature. The rise of ENVIRONMENTALISM has focused particular attention on the last of these issues. Leiss (1972), in a study of the idea of the human domination of nature, added a key historical dimension in showing that the concept has at different times been used in the interests of social domination or of social liberation – as have the other two views identified by Glacken. Historically specific social relations are often legitimated and made to seem inevitable by being 'naturalized' (see Smith, 1992), yet 'nature' has also been used as a standpoint from which to criticize existing social forms (as at the time of the French Revolution).

In Marxism and Marxist geography, nature has been regarded as a social construction given significance principally through its transformation by human labour in the process of production creating use-values (Schmidt, 1971; Sayer, 1979; Smith, 1984). Human relations with nature are determined by social relations and thus are historically specific. Failure to recognize this point, it is argued, vitiates the insights of Malthusianism or of environmental determinism and the more recent ones of LIMITS TO GROWTH. Critics of the Marxist view of nature as diverse as Heidegger and the FRANKFURT SCHOOL have found it reductionistic in its narrow focus on nature as a resource for production. Recent writings on the concept of nature have emphasized its standing as a negotiated construct and a complex web of often contested meanings.   JEm

References

Chorley, R. 1973: Geography as human ecology. In Chorley, R. J., ed., *Directions in geography.* London: Methuen/New York: Barnes and Noble, pp. 155–69.

Glacken, C. 1967: *Traces on the Rhodian shore: nature and culture in western thought to the end of the eighteenth century.* Berkeley, CA: University of California Press.

Hartshorne, R. 1939: *The nature of geography: a critical survey of current thought in the light of the past.* Lancaster, PA: Association of American Geographers.

Leiss, W. 1972: *The domination of nature.* New York: George Braziller.

Marsh, G. P. 1864: *Man and nature.* New York: Scribner.

McKibben, B. 1989: *The end of nature.* New York: Random House.

Mill, J. S. 1873: Nature. In *Three essays on religion*, pp. 3–65. New York: Henry Holt.

Sayer, A. 1979: Epistemology and conceptions of people and nature in geography. *Geoforum* 10, pp. 19–44.

Schmidt, A. 1971: *The concept of nature in Marx.* London: New Left Books.

Smith, N. 1984: *Uneven development: nature, capital and the production of space.* Oxford: Blackwell.

Smith, S. J. 1992: Social landscapes: continuity and change. In Johnston, R. J., ed., *The challenge for geography.* Oxford: Blackwell.

Williams, R. 1976: *Keywords: a vocabulary of society and nature.* London: Fontana.

nearest neighbour analysis   A method for comparing the distribution of points in an area with a theoretical norm based on their random distribution within the same area. The theoretical distribution gives an expected average distance between all pairs of nearest neighbour points, which is compared to the observed distribution for the mapped pattern. The test statistic R_n is derived by dividing the observed by the expected average distance, and ranges through 0.0 (indicating that the observed distribution is more clustered than expected from a random allocation of the points in that space), through 1.0 (a random distribution), to 2.149 (a more uniform distribution than expected): the scale of values is not linear, however (i.e. a value of 0.4 does not imply a distribution twice as clustered as shown by a value of 0.8), which creates interpretive difficulties. The size of R_n for any set of points is also influenced by the size of the area analysed: what is clustered at one SCALE may be uniform at another. (See also QUADRAT.)
                                                         RJJ

Suggested Reading

Aplin, G. J. 1983: *Order-neighbour analysis.* Concepts and techniques in modern geography 36. Norwich: Geo Books.

neighbourhood   A district within an urban area. Although the term was coined to describe a district within which there was a COMMUNITY of individuals, it is frequently applied in general usage for any small residential district, irrespective of the degree of social integration of the residents. A neighbourhood *sensu stricto* is a defined area within which there is an identifiable subculture to which the majority of its residents conform (cf. NEIGHBOURHOOD EFFECT). Many now doubt the existence of such spatially specific social units, given the general level of population mobility in cities and the myriad opportunities for social, economic and political interaction outside one's immediate residential milieu: they are certainly not easy to identify empirically. (See also BALANCED NEIGHBOURHOOD.)
                                                         RJJ

Suggested Reading
Keller, S. 1968: *The urban neighbourhood: a sociological perspective.* New York: Random House.
Ley, D. 1983: *A social geography of the city.* New York: Harper and Row.

neighbourhood effect A process of local influence, whereby the characteristics of people's local social milieux are believed to influence the ways in which they think and act. Neighbours present individuals with MODELS of attitudes and behavioural patterns, which (1) may conform to their own, and thus reinforce their self-identity, but alternatively (2) may contradict them and thus influence some, although not necessarily all, to modify their own attitudes and behaviour in order to be consistent with those of their local peer groups (cf. CONTEXTUAL EFFECT).

The neighbourhood effect has been used to account for certain geographical patterns – of attitudes towards educational achievement, for example, and of voting – which indicate greater spatial concentration of a certain attitude than anticipated from knowledge of the characteristics of an area's residents alone. The inference drawn from the ecological relationships identified, but rarely tested (thus potentially committing an ECOLOGICAL FALLACY), is that people initially predisposed to a minority view within an area will be influenced by the majority opinion there: since this influence comes about through interpersonal interaction it is sometimes termed 'conversion through conversation'.

Belief in the operation of a neighbourhood effect stimulated proposals for BALANCED NEIGHBOURHOODS in the planning of urban residential areas, in a form of social engineering.   RJJ

neighbourhood unit A relatively self-contained residential area. Most identified neighbourhood units are in planned residential developments, either of new suburban districts to existing towns and cities or in NEW TOWNS and comparable settlements.

The concept of the neighbourhood unit, first used in Chicago in 1916 and formally enunciated by Clarence Perry in 1929, was introduced to suggest the importance of SCALE in planning residential districts. It was intended that each new district should be of a sufficient size that it would be socially self-contained for most regular activities – such as daily and weekly shopping, the provision of primary schools and health-care facilities, and so on – and thus would develop as an integrated COMMUNITY (cf. BALANCED NEIGHBOURHOOD). British GARDEN CITIES were planned to have such units containing about 5000 persons each, and the pattern of roads and public transport was arranged to maximize the perceived gains of such separation, with the unit populations living within walking distance (segregated from motorized traffic as far as possible) of all unit facilities.

The validity of the assumption that people wished to live in such bounded communities and would constrain their activities and spatial movements largely within them has led to criticisms of the concept, but much urban planning continues to promote such a cellular division of residential space.   RJJ

Suggested Reading
Hall, P. G. 1988: *Cities of tomorrow: an intellectual history of urban planning and design in the twentieth century.* Oxford: Blackwell.

neoclassical economics Economics has been defined as the study of people earning a living, or more specifically as the study of the allocation of scarce means among alternative ends. In other words, economics is concerned with how human needs and wants are satisfied in a world of limited resources, where not everyone can have as much as he or she wants of everything. Neoclassical economics forms the basis of the view of how economic activity functions, as conventionally adopted in capitalist society. It represents the refinement and extension of ideas from the formative or classical phase of economics as an academic discipline. The classical period of economics is usually defined by the publication of Adam Smith's *Wealth of nations* in 1776 and John Stuart Mill's *Principles of political economy* in 1848. It was dominated by the work of David Ricardo (see NEO-RICARDIAN ECONOMICS), who developed a theory of relative prices based on costs of production, in which labour cost played the dominant role. The LABOUR THEORY OF VALUE was taken up by Karl Marx, to become a central feature of MARXIAN ECONOMICS. The classical economists placed great emphasis on the ability of *laissez-faire* to resolve conflicting self-interest in a manner that would benefit the community as a whole, via the 'invisible hand' of market competition recognized by Adam Smith. It was the liberalism of the classical economists rather than the labour theory of value that characterized the neoclassical perspective. A view of human affairs that stressed individualism, *laissez-faire* and reverence for market mechanisms (see MARKET EXCHANGE) was more in accordance with the prevailing ethics of CAPITALISM than one which attributed all value produced to the expenditure of labour.

The classical conception of an economy was one composed of many small enterprises, none of which could exercise a significant influence on market prices or on the total quantity of goods sold. The actions of any firm were dictated by consumer tastes as expressed in the marketplace, and by the competition of innumerable other small firms seeking consumer expenditure. The utilitarianism of Jeremy Bentham provided a concept whereby consumer satisfaction could be represented. As this framework became formalized in mathematics, the new school of neoclassical economists emerged from the tradition of classical liberalism.

The rise of neoclassical economics is closely associated with three well-known texts published in the early 1870s. These were William Stanley Jevon's *The theory of political economy* (see Jevons, 1970), Karl Menger's *Grundsatze der Volkswirtschaftslehre* and Leon Walras's *Elements d'economie politique*. Although there were differences between their analyses, the basic approach and content of these works was similar. The framework set down is still highly influential in economics and ECONOMIC GEOGRAPHY today.

Neoclassical theory portrays an economy comprising a large number of small producers and consumers without the power to influence the operation of the market significantly. Firms purchase or hire FACTORS OF PRODUCTION (land, labour and capital) which they utilize in the production process in such a way as to maximize their profits. The prices of factors and of finished goods sold are taken as given, and beyond the control of the firm. The decisions facing the firm are the productive process to be adopted (combination of factors) and the volume of output (or scale); plant location is disregarded. Households sell the factors of production that they possess: their land and capital if they have some, otherwise just their labour. They accept the given market price, and use the resulting income to purchase goods and services in quantities selected so as to maximize individual satisfaction or *utility*. The entire system is regulated by the interaction of supply and demand in the marketplace, which serves both to allocate resources and to distribute income through the determination of prices for goods and factors of production.

This is essentially how conventional economics textbooks see the operation of a capitalist free-enterprise system. For example, Paul Samuelson's *Economics* (see Samuelson and Nordhaus, 1989) portrays the competitive price system solving the basic economic problem of what to produce, how and for whom, in a manner summarized in the figure. Two groups of participants in the economy are recognized – 'the public' and 'business'. The markets for goods and for factors of production set the prices at which things are exchanged. The public offer their labour, land and capital goods for sale to business, and the interaction of supply and demand in the factor markets determines the prices paid as wages, rent and interest, i.e. it determines the distribution of income. The public takes its income onto the markets for consumer goods, expressing its preferences in the form of what Samuelson refers to as 'dollar votes'. (The implicit analogy with the electoral process evokes the principles of democracy in support of free-market mechanisms: see PLURALISM.) Consumer demand interacts

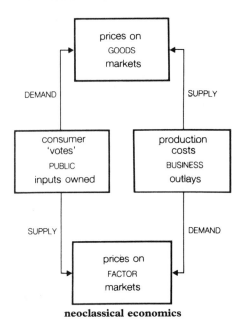

neoclassical economics

with the costs at which business is able to supply goods, to determine their prices.

All the elements of the economy represented in the figure are related to one another, so that a change in one will have repercussions for others. Thus a change in the willingness of capital owners or labour to offer their services will affect prices on the factor markets, which will affect the cost of production, the price of goods, and the willingness of the public to consume them. Markets are supposed to adjust automatically to these changes, tending towards the restoration of a state of EQUILIBRIUM at a price that brings supply and demand into balance. It is this self-regulating property that gives free-market mechanisms much of their attraction as means of allocating factors among alternative uses, and of distributing returns among the various participants in the productive process.

The consumption and production sides of the economy are themselves the subject of elaborate and sophisticated theory, formalized by the use of algebra and simple geometrical models. The concept of UTILITY is crucial to the theory of consumer behaviour. Consumers are held to possess a *utility function* incorporating their tastes and preferences. They alone know what suits them best: this is the principle of 'consumer sovereignty'. Consumers allocate their expenditure among alternative 'bundles of goods' so as to maximize utility, subject to the 'budget constraint' represented by income and to the prevailing set of prices. For a long time utility was assumed to be measurable, at least on an ordinal scale, but even this was found unnecessary as the level of abstraction from reality became such that consumer behaviour could be analysed without any empirical frame of reference. Economists of the neoclassical school went to great lengths to minimize the ethical content of their theories, which meant avoiding any reference to the actual specification of the utility function. The objective was to identify the general necessary and sufficient conditions for the maximization of utility, irrespective of the actual goods involved and the actual magnitude of the utility to be derived from their consumption in specific combinations. Consumers maximize utility when the utility derived from the last (or marginal) unit consumed, expressed as a ratio over the price of that commodity, is an equal proportion for all commodities. In other words, marginal utility per unit of expenditure should be the same for all goods or services consumed; otherwise, there is additional utility still to be gained by the reallocation of expenditure from things offering low marginal utility to things offering more (cf. UTILITY THEORY).

This analysis is then extended into the COLLECTIVE CONSUMPTION of an entire community. Individual utility functions are aggregated into a *social welfare function* expressing community preferences for various goods and services. The resources and technology available create certain production possibilities (the community equivalent of the budget constraint), which place limits on what can actually be made available for consumption. Community welfare is maximized through the maximization of the individual utility functions. This simple exposition of welfare theory in neoclassical economics (welfare economics) has been the subject of much development and debate, including some geographical extensions (see

PARETO OPTIMALITY; WELFARE GEO-GRAPHY).

The neoclassical analysis of the operation of the firm on the business side of the figure is analogous to that of consumer behaviour. To maximize profits, the firm operates at the highest level of EFFICIENCY in its use of resources and hence produces at the lowest possible cost. It purchases factors of production up to the point at which contribution to production of the last (marginal) unit of each factor, expressed as a ratio over the price of the factor, is an equal proportion for all factors. Thus the last unit of expenditure on each factor should yield the same increase in production; otherwise, additional output could be achieved by reallocating outlays among factors or inputs (just as in the consumer's attempt to maximize utility). When production and consumption are brought together, resources are allocated among alternative goods and services in such a way that no reallocation is possible without diminishing the total value of production of the entire economy and the overall utility or welfare derived from it. Income is distributed according to the prevailing marginalist principles, each factor being paid according to its marginal productivity.

Although neoclassical economics traditionally ignores geographical space, attempts have been made to overcome this obvious defect through regional economics (see REGIONAL SCIENCE). For the most part, this is a repetition of the conventional neoclassical formulations. For example, a strict interpretation of the notion of factors of production being allocated according to marginalist principles requires labour to move to places of shortage from places of surplus, and for capital to do the same, until no further addition to output can be achieved by spatial reallocation. This leads to a prediction that market forces will tend to equalize factor returns, and hence incomes, in geographical space. The Swedish economist Bertil Ohlin published a book, *Interregional and international trade*, in 1933, which showed how specialization and trade would lead to regional equality, given certain assumptions, which he acknowledged would not necessarily be fulfilled in reality. The truth is that imperfect mobility of factors prevents the instantaneous adjustment that the market is supposed to achieve. The fact that the FRICTION OF DISTANCE is an important impediment to factor mobility makes the neoclassical perspective especially inappropriate as a general theory of how the SPACE-ECONOMY actually functions. However, the rise of regional economics had some benefit for both geography and conventional economics, with the recognition that space is neither non-existent nor neutral in economic processes.

Regional growth theory in the neoclassical tradition has had an important influence on spatial economic planning. Albert Hirschman, in *The strategy of economic development* (1958), argued that the selective development of particular sectors of the economy is the most effective way of promoting the interregional transmission of growth. This was similar to François Perroux's argument (1950) for the stimulation of propulsive industry as a GROWTH POLE, a concept which was translated geographically into that of the growth point or location selected for investment. Selective spatial development strategies depend on how effectively growth is transmitted from one place to another, or what Hirschman termed the 'trickle down' effect.

Brian Berry (1970) and others have elaborated a view of 'growth impulses' spreading down the urban hierarchy, rather like the DIFFUSION of innovation. The tendency towards equalization may be frustrated by 'polarization' effects arising from efficiency advantages maintained where growth was initiated. Gunnar Myrdal's (1957) concept of circular and cumulative causation suggests that the 'spread' effects would be counteracted by 'backwash' effects, thus perpetuating uneven development or regional inequality. Particularly important is the process of CONCENTRATION AND CENTRALIZATION, which implies continuing growth in the core region or a metropolis at the expense of the periphery, as EXTERNAL ECONOMIES are built up and capital generated in the periphery is transferred back as returns to investors in the core (cf. CORE-PERIPHERY MODEL).

Neoclassical economic theory has some obvious attractions. It provides an elegant general theory, in the sense that all aspects of economic activity can be brought together in a set of statements that define the necessary and sufficient conditions for social welfare to be maximized. The assocation of all this with a market-regulated, free-enterprise system provides what can appear to be objective scientific support for the capitalist system. What is produced, how and for whom, can be conveyed as something ultimately depending on the 'democratic' sanction of the people as they spend their money votes in the marketplace. Thus, however perverse the structure of consumption may appear to be, and however unequal the distribution of rewards, these can be traced logically to the free expression of popular preference and to the response of business under the discipline of the marketplace. Government intervention will merely impede the operation of processes which, if left to themselves, will adjust to change and resolve all conflict in the general interest.

Neoclassical theory is obviously at variance with reality in some important respects. Some of the defects have been addressed in subsequent modifications. For example, it is recognized that buyers and sellers may be large enough to affect prices, so that competition is not perfect. In fact, there is a tendency in the competitive process for inefficient firms to be eliminated to the extent that monopoly, or something close to it, can develop. This in its turn distorts or constrains the very competition on which efficient production is supposed to depend. Thus anti-monopoly laws usually form part of the attempt by the STATE to regulate a capitalist economy.

In addition to the monopolistic tendencies conventionally considered, SPATIAL MONOPOLY is a source of market imperfection. Another refinement includes the introduction of the category of PUBLIC GOODS which do not lend themselves to supply under market conditions, and for which society usually accepts collective responsibility even under capitalism, e.g. defence, certain social services and aspects of INFRASTRUCTURE. Social costs and EXTERNALITIES (unpriced benefits and burdens) are also seen as major distortions of the free-market model.

More fundamental defects of neoclassical theory have also been recognized. The existing pattern of factor ownership and income distribution is taken as given and its legitimacy is unquestioned. Social institutions characteristic of CAPITALISM, such as the private ownership of land and capital, are portrayed as the natural order of things. The analysis of consumer behaviour is highly individualistic, emphasizing freedom of choice at the expense of examining the origins of personal preference and of the budget constraint. For all their formal elegance (or because of it) the analytical devices of neoclassical theory are confined to technical matters and ignore social relationships, such as those among *classes* under capitalism.

Much of the criticism of neoclassical theory has come from within mainstream economics itself. It was J. de V. Graaff's *Theoretical welfare economics* (1957) that originally laid bare the long and restrictive list of assumptions necessary for a competitive, free-market capitalist economy to realize the optimally efficient and welfare-maximizing outcomes with which it is credited. J. K. Galbraith (1975) was responsible for a sustained critique on the grounds of the changed nature of business organization and control, while E. J. Mishan (1969) pointed to problems in welfare economics arising from such considerations as the negative externalities of economic growth.

Different lines of critique have been followed by radical and Marxist economists. The ideological content of neoclassical theory has been exposed by M. Dobb (1973) and others, who see the perpetuation of the self-regulating, free-market model with its welfare-maximizing properties, in the face of such evident logical flaws and discordance with reality, as attributable in part to its role in supporting the capitalist system. As seen from the Marxist perspective, the focus on purely technical relationships diverts attention from the exploitive nature of capitalism. Furthermore, capitalism is inherently cyclical (see KONDRATIEFF CYCLES), leading to considerable fluctuations in prosperity over time and with great hardship generated by periods of 'downturn'. The repeated crises of recession/depression, inflation, industrial unrest, business scandals, etc., do little to improve confidence either in the capitalist system as a benign, self-regulating mechanism or in the control capacity of those professional economists who claim to understand it (and whose training tends to be in the neoclassical tradition).

The critique of neoclassical theory can be overdone, however. As a theory of how capitalism (or indeed any economic system) actually operates, it is clearly defective. But the analytical devices used to demonstrate optimality in resource allocation in pursuit of efficiency and even the maximization of social welfare do have some practical applicability if adopted with sensitivity to their limitations. Central planning of the kind at one time followed in Eastern Europe and the former Soviet Union used some neoclassical devices in the pursuit of allocational optimality, although the actual operation of these societies frustrated its achievement.

The 1980s saw a resurgence of interest in 'free-market' processes. This came first in the West, in Reagan's United States and Thatcher's Britain, for example, and then in Eastern Europe with the collapse of socialism and central planning. While market mechanisms do have the capacity to improve economic efficiency in certain circumstances, their adoption in both West and East is often a matter of political ideology and faith rather than an outcome of careful understanding. In the enthusiasm of free-market fanatics to implement their favoured panacea, the very specific conditions required for markets to work in reality as they are supposed to in theory are all too frequently overlooked.   DMS

References

Berry, B. J. L. 1970: City size and economic development. In Jacobson, L. and Prakash, V., eds, *Urbanization and national development*. Beverly Hills, CA: Sage, pp. 111–56.

Dobb, M. 1973: *Theories of value and distribution since Adam Smith: ideology and economic theory*. Cambridge: Cambridge University Press.

Galbraith, J. K. 1975: *Economics and the public purpose*. London: Penguin/New York: New American Library.

Graaff, J. de V. 1957: *Theoretical welfare economics*. Cambridge: Cambridge University Press.

Hirschman, A. O. 1958: *the strategy of economic development*. New Haven: Yale University Press.

Jevons, W. S. 1970: *The theory of political economy*. London: Penguin.

Mishan, E. J. 1969: *The cost of economic growth*. London: Penguin/New York: Praeger.

Myrdal, G. 1957: *Economic theory and underdeveloped regions*. London: Duckworth.

Ohlin, B. 1933: *Interregional and international trade*. Cambridge, MA: Harvard University Press.

Perroux, F. 1950: Economic space, theory and applications. *Q. J. Econ.* 64, pp. 89–104.

Samuelson, P. A. and Nordhaus, W. D. 1989: *Economics: an introductory analysis*, 13th edition. New York: McGraw-Hill.

Suggested Reading

Dobb (1973).

Galbraith (1975).

Hunt, E. K. and Sherman, H. J. 1978: *Economics: an introduction to traditional and radical views*, third edition. New York: Harper and Row.

Mishan (1969).

Samuelson and Nordhaus (1989).

Smith, D. M. 1977: *Human geography: a welfare approach*. London: Edward Arnold/New York: St. Martin's Press.

neocolonialism   A means of economic and political control articulated through the powerful STATES of developed economies (notably the USA, the former USSR, Japan and, collectively, the member states of the EC) over the economies and societies of the underdeveloped world (see DEVELOPMENT; UNDERDEVELOPMENT). The dominated states are apparently independent – there is no formal or direct rule (see COLONIALISM) and they exhibit all the outward trappings of independence. But in reality their economic and political systems are controlled from outside (see DEPENDENCE).

This control may be exerted in a variety of ways. The presence of foreign industrial and finance capital (Radice, 1975) has an effect not merely upon the external economic relations of the neocolonial societies but, in addition, serves to restructure their CLASS relations and exerts foreign domination by the maintenance of a *comprador* bourgeoisie (see NEW INTERNATIONAL DIVISION OF LABOUR). Participation in special commercial relations, such as those linking France with its West African dependencies and those within the Sterling Area, helps not only to tie underdeveloped to developed economies by means of trade and investment but also to enforce an internal economic discipline upon the policies of the underdeveloped economies. The Lomé Conventions negotiated between the EC and 60 or so African, Caribbean and Pacific states develop the techniques of neocolonialism by means of aid, trade and investment agreements (Kirkpatrick, 1979). At an even more extensive multilateral scale, the International Monetary Fund enforces a form of capitalist discipline upon the states of those underdeveloped societies which turn to it for help. Political control may also be manipulated more directly and carried out covertly by agencies such as the US Central Intelligence Agency (Agee, 1975).

The objective of neocolonialism is to keep the dominated societies secure within the wider sphere of influence. With the growth of INTERDEPENDENCE in the world economy – based upon the internationalization of production and access to raw materials – the attempt to maintain this security will be intensified. As a result, neocolonialism, with its associated unproductive and high costs of maintenance and with the inherent potential for conflict carried with it, is likely to grow and extend. It will thereby contribute directly as well as indirectly to the continued development of underdevelopment.   RL

References

Agee, P. 1975: *Inside the company: C.I.A. diary.* London: Penguin/New York: Bantam

Kirkpatrick, C. 1979: The renegotiation of the Lomé Convention. *National Westminster Bank Quarterly Review* May, pp. 23–33.

Radice, H., ed. 1975: *International firms and modern imperialism.* London: Penguin.

Suggested Reading
Buchanan, K. M. 1972: *The geography of empire.* Nottingham: Spokesman Books.

Crow, B., Thomas, A., Jenkins, R. and Kimble, J. 1983: *Third World atlas.* Milton Keynes: Open University Press; see especially section III.

Frobel, F., Heinrichs, J. and Kreye, O. 1980: *The new international division of labour.* Cambridge: Cambridge University Press/Paris: Éditions de la Maison des Sciences de l'Homme.

Warren, B. 1981: *Imperialism: pioneer of capitalism.* London: Verso.

neo-Ricardian economics   A school of economics associated with the University of Cambridge that provides criticisms of, and an alternative to, both NEOCLASSICAL and MARXIST ECONOMICS by drawing upon the ideas of the nineteenth-century English economist David Ricardo (1772–1823). Although the historical antecedents of neo-Ricardianism include the Russian economist V. Dmitriev and the Prussian statistician L. von Bortkewicz (both writing at the turn of the century), it was Piero Sraffa (1898–1983) in his book *Production of commodities by means of commodities* (1960) that effectively established the school.

The model of the economy that Sraffa presents has two components (see the figure):

(a) The technical conditions of production are represented by a series of input–output linear production equations implying that demand conditions do not affect relative prices. Following the classical economic tradition, production is conceived as a circular and interdependent process, in which the output in one production period is used as an input for

neo-Ricardian economics

the next production period. Peculiar to Sraffa's analysis is that there are no underlying constants that determine value. Although Ricardo, and later Marx, adopted a similar view of production, both grounded their analysis in some form of the LABOUR THEORY OF VALUE. In contrast, for Sraffa the price of a good in one sector is determined by the prices of goods produced in all other sectors in a previous production period, and in turn those prices were determined by the prices of goods in the production period before that, and so on. At no point are prices derived from some bedrock entity such as labour values.

(b) When outputs exceed inputs a 'surplus' exists, which then forms the basis for the social conditions of distribution, for it is from this surplus that each CLASS draws its respective share of national income. In common with other proponents of the circular view of production, Sraffa demonstrates that to obtain a determinant system of prices at least one of the income shares must be given from outside the system of production. This is important because it means that, unlike neoclassical economics, neo-Ricardianism necessarily makes reference to relations external to the purely economic. The effect is to redraw the boundaries of economics as conceived by orthodoxy to include the wider array of social, political and cultural institutions that bear on income distribution. Furthermore, because the surplus is finite, the relationship among social classes is necessarily adversarial. One class's gain is another class's loss.

It is significant that the subtitle of Sraffa's book is *Prelude to a critique of economic theory*. Although Sraffa does not present that critique himself, his model has provided the wherewithal for others to launch penetrating appraisals of both neoclassical and Marxist theories. These critiques were first taken up in the *capital controversy*, in which the neoclassical marginal productivity theory was attacked, and then later in the *value controversy*, in which the Marxist labour theory of value was criticized.

The *capital controversy* raged during the 1960s. Although initiated by Joan Robinson's query about the meaning of capital in the neoclassical aggregate production function, it was not until Sraffa's demonstration of 'capital reswitching' and 'capital reversing' that a decisive assault on neoclassicism was made. According to neoclassical theory the income accruing to any factor of production is equal to its marginal product – the output of the last unit of the factor hired. Because it is assumed that marginal productivity falls as a greater amount of a factor is used, there is a negative relationship between the rate of profit (the marginal product of capital) and the amount of capital employed (the capital intensity of a production technique). In this way profits act as an index of capital's scarcity. When capital is abundant, profit rates are low, and therefore capitalists in a competitive economy will use capital-intensive techniques of production because they employ relatively large amounts of cheap capital, and vice versa when capital is scarce. Sraffa's findings of capital reswitching and reversing undermine this neoclassical 'parable'. Reswitching suggests that while a capital-intensive technique may be the most profitable when profits are low (conforming to the neoclassical prediction), that very same technique can also be the most profitable one at very high profits, even though less-capital-intensive techniques are most profitable in between. In contrast, capital reversing occurs when the value of capital, a measure of its abundance, rises when a switch is made to a more profitable technique rather than falling as the neoclassical analysis suggests. In both cases, capital reswitching and reversing demonstrate logical flaws in the neoclassical analysis of the marginal productivity of capital. In so doing they open the way to a new interpretation of the meaning of profit, one that eschews a justification based on the scarcity of capital.

The *value controversy* began in the mid-1970s. Associated in particular with Ian Steedman (1977), the debate on Marx's labour theory of value has centred around the 'transformation problem'; that is, finding a correct procedure to convert labour values into prices. Steedman argues that for a number of reasons Marx's original solution to the problem was incorrect. This failing is not simply due to a mathematical error on Marx's part, however, but is a result of employing labour values in the first place. Following Sraffa, Steedman shows that prices can be determined independently of labour values. Steedman's critique is not meant as a sweeping dismissal of the whole of Marxist economics, however; rather, the neo-Ricardians believe that a coherent and logically consistent theory of capitalism can only be elaborated once such metaphysical entities as labour values are expunged.

Neo-Ricardianism, in its turn, has been criticized by neoclassical and Marxist economists. The complaints include: that neo-Ricardianism is empty formalism; that it contains no theory of history or change; that it draws upon the discredited class categories of Weber; that it provides no discussion of the labour process; that it emphasizes market over production relationships; and that it is a theory based upon commodity fetishism. In response, the supporters of neo-Ricardianism argue that such criticisms miss the point of Sraffa's work. Sraffa is not concerned with constructing a grand theory to explain everything, but is rather offering a CONTEXTUAL approach (Barnes, 1989); one concerned only with a few precisely defined issues within political economy, saying nothing about broader questions that are only resolvable within the context at hand.

Economic geographers have made some use of neo-Ricardian economics. The work begins with Scott's (1976) pioneering paper linking Sraffa's model of production with von Thünen's models of agricultural rent (cf. VON THÜNEN MODEL). More recently, other topics within economic geography examined from a neo-Ricardian perspective include: agricultural land use (Huriot, 1981), intra-urban location (Webber, 1984), interregional trade (Barnes, 1985), spatial reswitching (Pavlik, 1990), urban growth dynamics (Sheppard, 1983) and urban fixed capital (Sheppard and Barnes, 1990, ch. 7). To date there has been no direct empirical application of Sraffa's work in economic geography. Rather, most proponents have sought to integrate spatial relations into the neo-Ricardian model in order to undermine, in particular, a number of the propositions found in the neoclassical-inspired REGIONAL SCIENCE movement. Curiously, in making that integration, it also has been established that the introduction of geography into Sraffa's work can produce indeterminancy in his otherwise determinant aspatial conclusions (for example, with respect to technical change and trade; Sheppard and Barnes, 1986). In fact, the only means to resolve that indeterminancy is through engaging in contextual studies, which, in the end, may be Sraffa's main point.   TJB

References

Barnes, T. J. 1985: Theories of interregional trade and theories of value. *Environ. Plann. A* 17, pp. 729–46.

Barnes, T. J. 1989: Space, place and theories of economic value: contextualism and essentialism in economic geography. *Trans. Inst. Br. Geogr.* n.s. 14, pp. 299–316.

Huriot, J. M. 1981: Rente forcière et modèle de production. *Environ. Plann. A* 13, pp. 1125–49.

Pavlik, C. 1990: Technical switching: a spatial case. *Environ. Plann. A* 22, pp. 1025–34.

Scott, A. J. 1976: Land use and commodity production. *Reg. Sci. Urban Econ.* 6, pp. 147–60.

Sheppard, E. 1983: Pasinetti, Marx, and urban accumulation dynamics. In Griffith, D. and Lea, A. C., eds, *Evolving geographical structures*. The Hague: Martinus Nijhoff, pp. 293–322.

Sheppard, E. and Barnes, T. J. 1986: Instabilities in the geography of capitalist production: collective versus individual profit maximization. *Ann. Ass. Am. Geogr.* 76, pp. 493–507.

Sheppard, E. and Barnes, T. J. 1990: *The capitalist space economy: geographical analysis after Ricardo, Marx and Sraffa*. London: Unwin Hyman.

Sraffa, P. 1960: *Production of commodities by means of commodities*. Cambridge: Cambridge University Press.

Steedman, I. 1977: *Marx after Sraffa*. London: New Left Books.

Webber, M. J. 1984: *Explanation, prediction and planning: the Lowry model*. London: Pion.

Suggested Reading

Harcourt, G. C. 1982: The Sraffian contribution: an evaluation. In Bradley, I. and Howard, M., eds *Classical and Marxian political economy*. London: Macmillan, pp. 255–75.

Rowthorn, R. 1974: Neo-classicism, neo-Ricardianism and Marxism. *New Left Rev.* 86, pp. 63–87.

Wolff, R. P. 1982: Piero Sraffa and the rehabilitation of classical political economy. *Soc. Res.* 49, pp. 209–38.

network In human geography, a term mainly used to refer to a transport network either of permanent facilities (road, rail or canal) or of scheduled services (bus, train or air). It has also been extended to cover many types of line patterns including political and administrative boundaries, social contacts and telephone calls.

In most cases it is possible to identify two main categories of elements in a network: the *nodes* or vertices (junctions and terminals) and the *links* or edges which connect them (routes and scheduled services). In transport studies the nodes are usually the main terminals and junctions, but there is some dispute as to whether (or under what conditions) locations which have important traffic-generating functions (but which are neither junctions nor terminals) should be treated as nodes. Some authors prefer the term 'access points', but this still confuses the issue because some important junctions are neither traffic generators nor points of access to the network.

Intuitively, it is possible to identify several characteristics of network form, including *density*, *connectedness* and *orientation*. Some of these may be measured using GRAPH THEORY, but they may also be measured in other ways. Network *density* (length of network per unit area) is important because it bears a mathematical and empirical statistical relationship to the maximum distance and the average distance of points in an area from the nearest route or access point, thus having implications for ACCESSIBILITY.

The concept of *connectedness* (CONNECTIVITY has a more restricted use) identifies whether movements can be made between locations on the network and how directly such movement may be made. In measuring the latter property, use is made of the ratio between route distance and geodetic distance (this ratio is variously called the route factor, index of circuitry, etc.); high ratios suggest a poorly connected network, but may also reflect the indirect route adopted by individual links (a phenomenon commonly observed in regions of rugged terrain). Empirical evidence suggests that there are contrasts between rail networks (route factor ratios around 1.8) and road networks (1.3–1.4).

The route factor may also reveal the existence of *orientation*; in other words, a network which favours movements in specific directions, such as east–west routes, or movements to and from a capital city.

In addition to descriptive studies, transport geographers have attempted to account for the existence and location of individual network elements (ports, airports, canals, railway lines and roads) and for the pattern of whole networks. Although a relationship can be demonstrated between network form and other geographical variables (terrain, population density, economic development, etc.) it is generally recognized that a full explanation must include reference to the changing historical context (economic, political and social) of the decision-makers. (See also SOCIAL NETWORK.)   AMH

Suggested Reading
Chorley, R. J. and Haggett, P. 1974: *Network analysis in geography*, second edition. London: Edward Arnold/New York: St. Martin's Press.

new international division of labour (NIDL)

An emergent form of the worldwide DIVISION OF LABOUR associated with the internationalization of production and the spread of INDUSTRIALIZATION, especially in a number of rapidly growing newly industrializing countries (NICs).

The term has been used most explicitly by Fröbel et al. (1980) in their account of the DEINDUSTRIALIZATION of the old industrial countries. It is associated with the outflow of investment as CAPITAL operating on a global scale, and taking advantage of transportation and communications technology and the fragmentation and locational separability of the productive process, attempts to tap the global reserve army of labour and to seek out cheap production sites in order better to face competitive pressures. An alternative interpretation suggests that MNCs are pushed out of highly industrialized economies by the falling rate of profit, and yet another that the NIDL reflects rational geographical developments within the CIRCUIT OF CAPITAL as a whole. The implication here is that the NIDL is one strategic response to the continuous imperative of accumulation in CAPITALISM. MULTINA-TIONAL CORPORATIONS (MNCs) – the major agents of the NIDL – reorganize the geography of their productive structure and so stimulate the growth of industrial production in the NICs and elsewhere. However, the resultant industrialization process within the host economies is limited in its effects:

Only rarely do developing countries end up with the establishment of reasonably complex industrial branches . . . And even in the very few developing countires where such centres of partial industrialization have been established there are no signs that they are being supplemented by a wider industrial complex which would enable them to free themselves from their dependency on the already industrialized countries for imports of capital and other goods, and for the maintenance of their industrial installations . . . Instead, industrial production is confined to a few highly specialized manufacturing processes . . . in world market factories . . . with no connection to the local economy except for their utilization of extremely cheap labour and occasionally some local inputs (Fröbel et al., 1980, p. 6).

A central feature of such accounts is the stress upon the role of multinational capital (Schoenberger, 1988) in shaping the world economy, especially in the expansion/relocation of production: 'One form of this relocation . . . is the closing down of certain types of manufacturing operations . . . in the industrial nations and the subsequent installation of these parts of the production process in foreign subsidiaries of the same company' (Fröbel et al., 1980). The NIDL is, in this view, the result of the multinational RESTRUCTURING of production. Only incidentally would the interests of MNCs coincide with the build-up of an integrated and complex industrial structure in a developing country. The countries remain passive and *dependent* (see DEPENDENCY).

Less critical than this dependency view of the NIDL is that presented by the *diffusionist* theorists (see, e.g., Chisholm, 1982; Corbridge, 1986). Here most emphasis is placed upon the leading forces within the industrializing economies to mobilize available resources and to develop distinctive patterns of COMPARATIVE ADVANTAGE in

exploiting the opportunities for development presented by the international environment. The primacy of multinational capital is replaced in this account by the primacy of NATION–STATES assisted by an assumed and unspecified, but apparently beneficent, transfer of developmental resources from the core nations to those of the periphery (see CORE–PERIPHERY MODEL).

While it is right to move away from determinist accounts of the emergence of the NIDL and to point out that NATIONS need not necessarily be passive, it is also necessary to situate the process in the overarching context of the structure and dynamics of the world economy (see WORLD-SYSTEMS ANALYSIS for one interpretation) and to enquire into the national politics and potential for national resistance to the dominant forces of international development. It is in this context that Chisholm's entirely appropriate insistence upon the significance of geographical variations from place to place in the working out of the development process should be, but is not, most apparent.

The central importance of international CAPITAL in shaping the NIDL is clearly apparent in the recognition that only a very small number of developing countries have developed a significant level of industrialization (Dicken, 1992), and in the suggestion that investment may switch back to the old industrial economies as computer-aided production increases the capital intensity of the LABOUR PROCESS. Under such circumstances, the requirements of production change and the global locational strategies of multinational corporations, which, in any case, are not motivated merely by the search for cheap labour but by the appropriate combination of circumstances for profitable reproduction, will also change. The new international division of labour could, thereby, soon become old.   RL

References and Suggested Reading

Chisholm, M. 1982: *Modern world development*. London: Hutchinson/Totowa, NJ: Barnes and Noble.

Corbridge, S. 1986: *Capitalist world development*. London: Macmillan, ch. 4.

Dicken, P. 1992: *Global shift: the internationalization of economic activity*, second edition. London: Paul Chapman, ch. 5.

Fröbel, F., Heinrichs, J. and Kreye, O. 1980: *The new international division of labour*. Cambridge: Cambridge University Press.

Schoenberger, E. 1988: Multinational corporations and the new international division of labour: a critical appraisal. *Int. reg. Sci. Rev.* 11, pp. 105–19.

new town A free-standing, self-contained and socially balanced urban centre, primarily planned to receive overspill population and employment from nearby CONURBATIONS. In one sense any planned settlement or virgin soil is a 'new town'; including, for example, the *bastides* of medieval Europe, company towns built by enlightened industrialists for their workers, settlements of colonial powers in overseas empires, and 'artificial' capital cities in established independent states. But as more commonly used, the phrase owes its genesis to Britain's post Second World War solution to excessive metropolitan area growth, itself a natural successor of Howard's GARDEN CITY concept (indeed, Welwyn Garden City became one of the first London New Towns). Some New Towns are also intended to serve as instruments of REGIONAL POLICY.

Abercrombie's influential 1944 Greater London Plan advocated ten New Town reception areas for London overspill beyond a GREEN BELT, and the New Towns Act two years later established the necessary administrative and financial structures, including their management by non-elected development corporations. In total, 14 New Towns were designated in the UK in a frenzy of activity from 1947 to 1950, and a further 17 since. Whether based on substantial existing settlements (for example, Basildon and Peterborough) or built largely from scratch, the general principles of economic self-containment (including minimal non-local COMMUTING), social balance, landscaping and recreation provision, and high-quality transport provision have been followed.

British New Towns have also undergone detailed changes over time. Their planned eventual size has risen from the 25 000–80 000 range for the first postwar tranche to upwards of a quarter of a million for their successors, such as Milton Keynes and Central Lancashire, designed in 1967–8. The amount of private development incorporated has also risen, and the NEIGHBOURHOOD UNIT principles in the early schemes have been abandoned. Instead, Milton Keynes embraces a number of pre-existing communities, whereas those designated in 1955–67 (for example, Runcorn and Cumbernauld) emphasized centralized facilities and efficient transport networks from suburbs to town centres, and generally favoured higher-density development.

Although not without their critics in Britain on other grounds (see, e.g., Aldridge, 1979) an earlier accusation that New Towns contributed to INNER-CITY decline is now discounted. In the 1980s many early development corporations ceased and their settlements adopted conventional local government structures. Government policy, by now opposed to further state-sponsored New Towns, turned to encouraging (often controversial) 'new town' initiatives by private consortia in South-East England.

The concept has been widely admired and copied worldwide: Osborn and Whittick (1977) list parallel developments in 67 countries, including over 140 New Towns in the USA, where details of practice vary from the British experience and, indeed, the oldest pre-dates it (for example, Radburn, designed in 1928). Private development is more to the fore (for example, Reston, Virginia); free-standing locations are less commonplace (such as the 'town within a town' at Cedar-Riverside to revitalize downtown Minneapolis/St. Paul); and the social balance is not sacrosanct (Soul City, North Carolina, is designed to house poor blacks).   AGH

References

Aldridge, M. 1979: *The British New Towns – a programme without a policy*. London: Routledge and Kegan Paul.

Osborn, F. J. and Whittick, A. 1977: *New Towns*, third edition. London: Leonard Hill/Boston: Routledge and Kegan Paul.

NIMBY The acronym for 'Not-in-my-Back-Yard', an attitude towards locational issues typical of individuals who resist the siting of a source of negative EXTERN-ALITIES next to their homes and campaign for its location elsewhere. (See also CON-FLICT.)   RJJ

nomadism A high degree of spatial mobility or wandering as a basis for a particular way of life (Salzman, 1980). Nomadism implies no or very limited reliance upon sedentary cultivation. In general, nomadism is presumed to be synonymous with the movements of herds (animal husbandry) and livestock rearing (Johnson, 1969) especially in the semi-arid tropics and in montane regions. But hunter–gatherers (for example, the San peoples of the Kalahari desert) who typically have no domesticated livestock are also defined by their 'nomadic style'. In both of these cases nomadism is distinguished from the very limited seasonal movements of animals associated with sedentary agriculture (see TRANSHU-MANCE). Nomadism is often classified in terms of the degree of spatial mobility. So-called full or true nomads have no permanent dwellings and practice no agriculture, although they do participate in exchange relations to acquire grain (e.g. the Wodaabe of the West African Sahel). Semi-nomads practice wet-season agriculture but are usually mobile during the dry season (e.g. the Masai of East Africa) as they search for pasture and water with their herds (see PASTORALISM).   MW

References

Johnson, D. 1969: *The nature of nomadism: a comparative study of pastoral migrations in Southeast Asia and Northern Africa.* Chicago: University of Chicago, Department of Geography Research Paper no. 118.
Salzman, P. 1980: Is nomadism a useful concept? *Nomadic Peoples* 6, pp. 1–7.

nomothetic Concerned with the universal and the general. The term derived from neo-Kantian EPISTEMOLOGY, and most notably from an 1894 address by the philosopher Windelband, who used it to signify one of two possible goals of concept formation:

The theoretical interests associated with nomothetic concept formation highlight those common qualities of objects of experience that lead to the formulation of general laws of nature. The process is one of continual ABSTRACTION, in which the special qualities of an object are filtered out and the object is seen as a general type that exists with certain relations to other general types (Entrikin, 1991).

Windelband contrasted this with IDIO-GRAPHIC concept formation which is concerned to achieve a complete understanding of the *individual* case (see also KANTIANISM).

The term gained currency in geography after the middle of the twentieth century, in the wake of the Hartshorne–Schaefer exchange over EXCEPTIONALISM, when the proponents of SPATIAL SCIENCE claimed that geography should be directed towards the formulation (rather than simply the application) of scientific theories and LAWS. Guelke (1977) saw that mid-century debate as being 'of crucial importance in changing the direction of research . . . away from any consideration of the unique' and towards the search for general laws of spatial organisation (see Golledge and Amedeo, 1968). Much of that search, itself part of the formalization of POSITIVISM within geography, took place within the existing framework of LOCATION THEORY; but its rapid extension into the very centre of the discipline and its displacement of more traditional objectives soon produced a host of claims that geography should be concerned with intrinsically spatial theory if it was to be a distinctive science. Harvey's *Explanation in geography* (1969) thus concluded that 'by our theories you shall know us'. The status of many of these laws and theories was often qualified (see INSTRUMENTALISM), and their autonomy was challenged by those who thought that 'the spatial position's aim of prying apart a subject matter from the systematic sciences by arguing for spatial questions and spatial laws does not seem viable' (Sack, 1974a,b). Even so, these efforts were a vitally important input to the development of SPACE–TIME FORE-CASTING and also a formative influence on the growth of a greater theoretical awareness within the subject. Today that awareness rarely hinges on the idiographic–nomothetic distinction: on the one side, the interest in the philosophy of REALISM and in the formulation of CONTEXTUAL THEORY, and on the other side, the critique of the totalizing claims of GRAND THEORY and the interest in situated knowledges, has produced a much more nuanced understanding of both the powers and the limits of 'theory'.   DG

References

Entrikin, J. N. 1991: *The betweenness of place: towards a geography of modernity*. London: Macmillan.

Golledge, R. G. and Amedeo, D. 1968: On laws in geography. *Ann. Ass. Am. Geogr.* 58, pp. 760–74.

Guelke, L. 1977: The role of laws in human geography. *Progr. hum. Geogr.* 1, pp. 376–86.

Harvey, D. 1969: *Explanation in geography*. London: Edward Arnold.

Sack, R. 1974a: Chorology and spatial analysis. *Ann. Ass. Am Geogr.* 64, pp. 439–52.

Sack, R. 1974b: The spatial separatist theme in geography. *Econ. Geogr.* 50, pp. 1–19.

Suggested Reading

Entrikin (1991), pp. 93–8.

Guelke (1977).

non-parametric statistics A family of statistical procedures used in the analysis of data at either the nominal or ordinal level of MEASUREMENT. They are contrasted with parametric statistics, which are used with interval and ratio level data and which make certain assumptions about the FREQUENCY DISTRIBUTIONS of those data: non-parametric statistics are sometimes referred to as distribution-free statistics. By far the most popular of these statistical tests is CHI-SQUARE.   RJJ

normal distribution A theoretical FREQUENCY DISTRIBUTION the identifying characteristic of which is its bell-shaped symmetry around the three measures of its central tendency – mean, median and mode (see the figure). As with all theoretical distributions, it has a smooth shape based on a histogram for an infinitely large population of values. Using the two major measures of its form (its mean and standard deviation – S.D.) it is possible to identify the exact location of an individual value

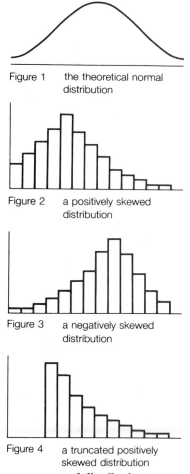

Figure 1   the theoretical normal distribution

Figure 2   a positively skewed distribution

Figure 3   a negatively skewed distribution

Figure 4   a truncated positively skewed distribution

normal distribution

within it, i.e. how far that value is from the mean in S.D. units.

Many of the test statistics used in CONFIRMATORY DATA ANALYSIS have normal distributions, which allow precise statements of the probability of an observed value being obtained from a random allocation procedure (e.g. what is the probability of obtaining a CORRELATION coefficient, r, of 0.67 with a random allocation of the values across that number of observations). Thus the normal distribution is central to much statistical analysis.

Deviations from the normal distribution involve *skewness* (in which the mean and the median do not share the same value) and *kurtosis*. A positively skewed distribution has a longer right-hand than left-hand tail, for example, with the reverse for a negatively skewed distribution: a truncated distribution lacks one of the tails (see the figure). A special case of a truncated, positively skewed distribution is the Poisson, in which the mean is equal to the standard deviation: this can be generated by random processes in which the probability of an event is small, and is used by geographers in QUADRAT ANALYSIS.

Regarding *kurtosis*, a platykurtic distribution is 'flatter' than the normal (i.e. has a relatively large S.D.) and a leptokurtic distribution is more 'peaked' (i.e. has a relatively small S.D.).   RJJ

Suggested Reading

Gardiner, V. and Gardiner, G. 1978: *Analysis of frequency distributions.* Concepts and techniques in modern geography 19. Norwich: Geo Books.

normative theory A theory which 'concerns what *ought* to be'. Unlike 'positive theory', which 'concerns what *is, was,* or *will be*', normative theory cannot be adjusted by 'an appeal to the facts' but depends instead on the disclosure of competing VALUE systems (Lipsey, 1966). This distinction was of some importance to ECONOMIC GEOGRAPHY, where Chisholm drew on Lipsey's NEOCLASSICAL ECONOMICS and the philosophy of POSITIVISM which underwrote it to argue that the 'greatest casualty' of geography's QUANTITATIVE REVOLUTION was the mistaken belief that 'positive theory would lead to normative insights' (Chisholm, 1978). Hence 'to criticize normative theory because it fails to yield positive results is to tilt at windmills' (Chisholm, 1975). On this reading it was illegitimate to attempt an empirical validation of most of classical LOCATION THEORY since its constructions were for the most part explicitly normative: 'The question of the best location is far more dignified than the determination of the actual one' (Lösch, 1954). In his own *Geography and economics* (1966) Chisholm used neoclassical concepts to sketch the outlines of a 'positive' economic geography, and subsequently turned to welfare economics to suggest a new 'normative' basis for location theory (Chisholm, 1971; see also WELFARE GEOGRAPHY).

However, Smith (1977) argued that the distinction had been irredeemably blurred during geography's RELEVANCE revolution: the critique of positivism had demolished claims for a 'value-free geography' and it was no longer tenable to assume that an 'appeal to the facts' was as straightforward as these views supposed. One might think that normative questions would have loomed large in post-positivist human geography, but most attention has been directed towards what Benhabib (1985) calls more generally an *explanatory–diagnostic moment* – particularly to the critique of modern CAPITALISM – and there has been considerably less attention paid to an *anticipatory–utopian moment*: to detailed discussions of what ought to be and, indeed, could be (cf. CRITICAL THEORY). Even so, Smith's central point remains as sharp as ever, because *both* moments are underwritten by implicit normative claims.

DG

References

Benhabib, S. 1985: *Critique, norm and utopia: a study of the foundations of critical theory.* New York: Columbia University Press.

Chisholm, M. 1966: *Geography and economics.* London: Bell.

Chisholm, M. 1971: In search of a basis for location theory: micro-economics or welfare economics. *Prog. Geogr.* 3, pp. 111–34.

Chisholm, M. 1975: *Human geography: evolution or revolution?* London: Penguin.

Chisholm, M. 1978: Theory construction in geography. *S. Afr. Geogr. J.* 6, pp. 113–22.

Lipsey, R. G. 1966: *An introduction to positive economics.* London: Weidenfeld and Nicolson.

Lösch, A. 1954: *The economics of location.* New Haven: Yale University Press.

Smith, D. M. 1977: *Human geography: a welfare approach.* London: Edward Arnold.

North–South A dichotomous term used in macropolitical economy to identify one of the most pervasive biopolar divisions in the current global system. 'North' is a rather loose, portmanteau term for the wealthy advanced industrial countries, both socialist and capitalist. In this sense it is roughly synonymous with the term 'First World' which is employed widely in political economic analyses (see CORE-PERIPHERY DEVELOPMENT MODEL). The

'South' corresponds to those poor, largely non-industrial and ex-colonial states that are seen to constitute a Third World (mostly in Africa, Asia and Latin America), a term which arose in the postwar period, emerging from the Non-Aligned Movement (see THIRD WORLD). The language of First and Third Worlds, or North and South, is often conspicuously absent among the major multilateral and national development agencies (for example, the World Bank or the International Monetary Fund) who stratify nations according to income (low, middle and so on). The average per capita income of the South is currently about 50 times less than that of the industrialized North.

North–South is the title of an influential book which became popularly known in the 1980s as the Brandt Report (Brandt, 1980). It meant to signal divisions between rich and poor nations, in contradistinction to the East–West divide of the Cold War. The events of the late 1980s, including the collapse of many state socialisms, have in any case made the East–West divide increasingly less relevant. The Brandt Report sought to address the growing economic, political and military polarities at the beginning of a decade during which the material circumstances of the Third World were to deteriorate seriously. The North–South dialogue was part of ongoing political debates within the United Nations during the 1970s and elsewhere over the need for a 'New International Economic Order'. The single greatest difficulty with the North–South concept is the question of economic and political coherence. While it might be argued that the collapse of many state socialisms has produced a more homogeneous capitalist core associated with capitalist regional trade blocs, the South is extremely diverse, and becoming more so. On the one hand, the newly industrializing states (the NICs) such as Taiwan and South Korea are no longer primary commodity producers, and on the other the South has rarely had a unified political position, even within the Non-Aligned Movement. The appearance of a Fourth World of extreme poverty (the so-called famine belt), particularly in Africa, suggests a growing economic polarization *within* the South coeval with a deepening polarization *between* North and South. MW

References

Brandt, W. 1980: *North–South: a programme for survival*. London: Pan.

nuptiality The extent to which a population marries. Marriage is extremely important in most societies in determining demographic behaviour, particularly FERTILITY. The simplest nuptiality rate expresses the number of marriages celebrated (or the total number of persons marrying) in a given year as a ratio of the average number of persons alive in that year, expressed in parts per 1000. Consideration must also be given to two fundamental aspects of the marriage pattern: the intensity of nuptiality, expressed as the proportion of the population that is single at any one time and in certain age groups; and the precocity of marriage, expressed as age at first marriage for both sexes.   PEO

Suggested Reading

Pressat, R. 1972: *Demographic analysis*. London: Edward Arnold/Chicago: Aldine, ch. 7.

O

occupance   See SEQUENT OCCUPANCE.

ontology   THEORIES – sometimes called 'meta-theories' – which seek to answer 'the question of what the world must be like for [knowledge] to be possible' (Bhaskar, 1978; cf. EPISTEMOLOGY). Bhaskar contends that 'every account of science presupposes an ontology' and distinguishes three broad ontological traditions within the philosophy of science:

(a) Classical EMPIRICISM, in which 'the ultimate objects of knowledge are atomistic events'. From this perspective, Bhaskar claims, 'knowledge and the world may be viewed as surfaces whose points are in isomorphic correspondence': there is a direct, one-to-one relation between them (see also POSITIVISM).

(b) Transcendental IDEALISM, in which the ultimate objects of knowledge are artificial constructs – models and idealizations – imposed upon the world. From this perspective, 'knowledge is seen as a structure rather than a surface', but a structure which is constituted by the thinking subject (see also KANTIANISM).

(c) Transcendental REALISM, which regards the ultimate objects of knowledge as 'the structures and mechanisms that generate phenomena' and which are *intransitive* in the sense that 'such objects exist and act independently of their identification'.

Bhaskar himself endorses (c) and claims that a concept of ontological depth – of 'the multi-tiered stratification of reality' – is indispensable for the natural, the social

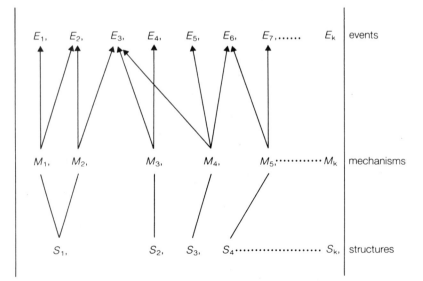

ontology   *1: A realist ontology: structures, mechanism and events* (after Sayer, 1984).

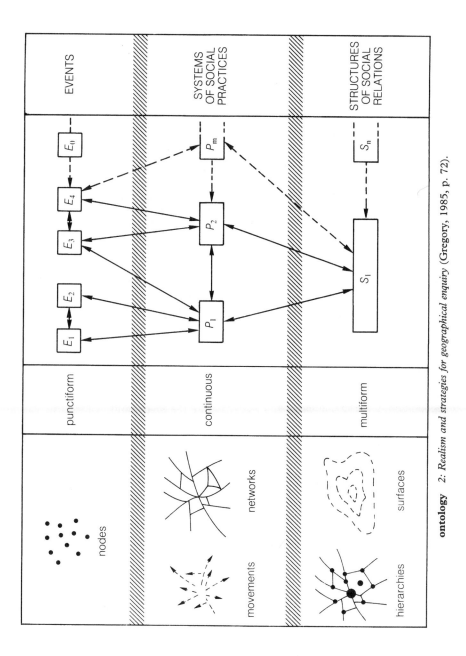

ontology 2: *Realism and strategies for geographical enquiry* (Gregory, 1985, p. 72).

and the human sciences (Bhaskar, 1979). An example is given in figure 1: analysis conducted under the sign of realism is thus directed towards the elucidation of *structures* which possess particular 'causal powers'; these powers are realized, under specific conditions, through *mechanisms* that result in a pattern of empirical *events*. This is a highly general skeleton, however, and Keat and Urry (1981) emphasize that a realist *philosophy* of social science does not automatically usher in a specific *theory* of social life: one is not provided with 'a ready-made social ontology and a set of substantive theoretical propositions about the social world'. One possible mapping of this model is shown in figure 2 (Gregory, 1985). It is important to understand that, from this perspective, 'it is not the character of science that imposes a determinate pattern or order upon the world; but the order of the world that, under certain determinate conditions, makes possible the cluster of activities that we call "science" ' (Bhaskar, 1978; see also Bhaskar, 1986).

Although Bhaskar means to explore the possibility of NATURALISM within the human and social sciences, and in this sense moves in a radically different direction to Husserl and his followers, a recognition of the fundamental and *foundational* role of ontology is also the starting-point for PHENOMENOLOGY. Within human geography, Pickles (1985) has drawn upon Husserl's writings to indicate the importance of *regional ontologies* for the 'grounding' of empirical enquiry. These 'regions' are not those of REGIONAL GEOGRAPHY: the object of the exercise is to identify, through philosophical reflection, spaces ('regions') in which particular knowledges are made possible. Pickles particularly wants to challenge research programmes which 'impose constructions on phenomena, without the careful and necessary prior clarification, through descriptive phenomenology, of the domain of the phenomena under consideration'. In the case of human geography, so he claims, geographers have 'unreflectively adopted an ontology of physical nature as the fundamental and underlying logic of geographical DISCOURSE and inquiry'. In his

view, this physical ontology has been dervied from a KANTIANISM which stands in the closest of associations to Newtonian conceptions of SPACE, and so takes 'human SPATIALITY to be the same as, or a modification (or distortion) of, the spatiality appropriate to the physical world'. Pickles accepts that 'if spatial organization and interaction, conceived geometrically, are fundamental, and if the ontology of material nature and Newtonian space on which they are predicated is unquestioned, then modelling such spaces is an exercise in SOCIAL PHYSICS' (see also MACROGEOGRAPHY). But if this implication is rejected, Pickles continues, then 'it becomes necessary to rethink not merely methodology *but also ontology*: to fashion a place-centred ontology of *human* spatiality for a geographical *human* science' (cf. PRODUCTION OF SPACE).

It is precisely this task that has been taken up by Pickles's colleague Schatzki (1991) in his account of 'spatial ontology'. He draws on Heidegger to distinguish between *objective space* which is composed by or contains 'objects' (including human beings), and *social space*, which he conceives as the opening and occupation of sites for human existence: of *places* which are the preconditions for particular human activities to (literally) *take place*. This is a profoundly ontological claim, for Schatzki is arguing that 'human existence *ipso facto* constitutes a space', that 'human agency is always embedded within a space which it shapes and is shaped by', and it is within this *social* space (not the objective space of TIME-GEOGRAPHY) that overlapping and hierarchical webs of interconnection are inscribed to constitute 'social reality' (see also EXISTENTIALISM).

Other writers are equally critical of spatial science and make similar claims about the importance of *social* space and spatiality, but by no means all of them would accept the need for making foundational claims of the sort advanced above: both PRAGMATISM and POSTMODERNISM have encouraged a certain scepticism towards *foundationalism* and the aspirations of GRAND THEORY. DG

References

Bhaskar, R. 1978: *A realist theory of science.* Brighton: Harvester.

Bhaskar, R. 1979: *The possibility of naturalism: a philosophical critique of the contemporary human sciences.* Brighton, UK: Harvester.

Bhaskar, R. 1986: *Scientific realism and human emancipation.* London: Verso.

Gregory, D. 1985: People, places and practices: the future of human geography. In King, R., ed., *Geographical futures.* Sheffield: Geographical Association.

Keat, R. and Urry, J. 1981: *Social theory as science,* second edition. London: Routledge.

Pickles, J. 1985: *Phenomenology, science and geography: spatiality and the human sciences.* Cambridge: Cambridge University Press.

Sayer, A. 1984: *Method in social science: a realist approach.* London: Hutchinson.

Schatzki, T. 1991: Spatial ontology and explanation. *Ann. Ass. Am. Geogr.* 81, pp. 650–70.

Suggested Reading

Bhaskar (1979).

Pickles (1985).

Schatzki (1991).

opportunity cost Used in NEOCLASS-ICAL ECONOMICS to express costs in terms of opportunities foregone (whether or not money was paid out to cover these costs). For example, if rural land is kept as open moorland there will be a cost to society and to the landowner in terms of the net value of agricultural products not produced. The concept is used by geographers to explain the allocation of productive resources (land, labour and capital) among alternative productive activities. It plays an important part in theories of RENT and COMPARATIVE ADVANTAGE, and in LINEAR PROGRAMMING.   AMH

optimization models Models, often adopted from mathematics and operational research, which seek to define the optimal solution to a problem situation. They often relate to NORMATIVE THEORIES of SPATIAL STRUCTURE.

Common to all these models is a quantity (or, but less often, quantities) to be maximized or minimized. This quantity is often termed the *objective function*: for example, the objective might be to max-imize food production in an agricultural system or to minimize the total transport costs in an industrial location problem. In addition, most optimization problems have constraints – parameters within which the solution must lie if it is to be either acceptable or feasible: for example, agri-cultural production may be maximized subject to certain constraints on labour supply and fertilizer inputs, while an industrial location problem may have constraints on raw material inputs and the capacity of transport links. It is also important to differentiate between a sys-tem optimum and the optimum for individual actors within the system, be-cause there is no certainty that the aggregate of optimal solutions for indivi-duals will produce a global optimum.

Some optimization models assume that the operating environment is predictable, but an important group of methods based on GAME THEORY assumes that some elements in the system are themselves uncertain. In such cases the objective function may need to be specially defined: for example, a farming system might be optimized to allocate land to maximize the minimum output even if the most un-favourable weather conditions should occur.

The methods of modelling and solving optimization problems are extremely var-ied; a few problems are capable of direct mathematical or graphical solution but many can only be solved by iteration – a stepwise search which converges upon the optimal solution (see LINEAR PROGRAM-MING).

The scope of such models is very wide, including industrial location, agricultural location (see VON THÜNEN MODEL), retail location, transport network development, transport flows (see TRANSPORTATION PROBLEM), political geography (see DIS-TRICTING ALGORITHM) and regional de-velopment. The use made may be of three types: explanatory, normative-critical or prescriptive. In a few cases it can be argued that the model adequately repre-sents the causal processes and can therefore be used as an explanatory device. More generally, optimization models may be used to demonstrate the inadequacies of existing solutions. Finally, in applied and planning studies the optimization model may be used to prescribe solutions to location problems – if the model is truly capable of representing the objectives and constraints present in the situation. AMH

optimum city size A city size below which the benefits of further growth outweigh the costs, but above which costs exceed benefits. Some analysts believe that URBANIZATION has seen the optimum city size exceeded in many cases but – as in many other cases in which society's best interests and those of its members individually are not met by unregulated market operations (see TRAGEDY OF THE COMMONS) – no mechanism exists to restrain growth beyond the desirable level. (Thus, for example, an additional 10 000 people in a city of 1 million may lead to a 10 per cent increase in traffic congestion, but the individuals concerned share the additional costs with those already there – which amounts to only 0.01 per cent each.) Some argue that planning policies are needed to identify the optimum and ensure that it is not breached, but against this view, those supporting the free-market approach argue that when the optimum is reached then urbanization will halt – hence the COUNTERURBANIZATION currently being experienced in several parts of the world and, perhaps, the reduced concern about the issue in the past decade. RJJ

Suggested Reading

Richardson, H. W. 1973: *The economics of urban size*. Farnborough, UK: Saxon House/Lexington, MA: Lexington Books.

optimum population The number of people that, in relation to given economic, military or social goals, produces the maximum return. The idea of population optima has long been discussed, especially in relation to OVERPOPULATION and the general notions of the MALTHUSIAN MODEL. Very difficult to define with any precision, it has most often been seen in economic terms of total production or real income per head, its definition and usefulness being hotly disputed by each generation of economists. (See also OPTIMUM CITY SIZE.) PEO

Suggested Reading

Sauvy, A. 1969: *General theory of population*, transl. C. Campos. London: Weidenfeld and Nicolson/New York: Basic books, ch. 4.

organized capitalism See DISORGANIZED CAPITALISM.

Orientalism A Western construction of the East, imposed from outside and connoting a mythical 'Orient', Orientalism is the inverse of all things European. Its boundaries have constantly shifted, sometimes restricted to the Arab and Islamic worlds, while at other times including everything east of Suez. Orientalism incorporates what Edward Said (1978) calls an 'imaginative geography': a set of contradictory ideas and attitudes about the East which combine an admiration for Arab and Islamic cultures as the source of European languages and civilization with a set of derogatory stereotypes about 'Orientals'. Orientalism works ideologically through a series of oppositions (between 'us' and 'them', the familiar and the exotic, the near and the far): East assumes West; the Orient assumes the Occident. The two geographical entities support and reflect each other (Said, 1978, p. 5). Despite his insistence that Orientalism is a European invention, Said acknowledges that the relationship between East and West is not a purely imaginative one but is based on very real material foundations in the history of IMPERIALISM. Said also shows how the discipline of geography has contributed to the creation of 'the Orient', a cultural, political and historical entity the destiny of which was under European control. Said's work has attracted a substantial amount of criticism for failing to provide an alternative to the phenomenon that he analyses, for ignoring the highly gendered nature of Orientalism, and for perpetuating his own form of 'totalizing', essentialist and ahistorical thinking (Young, 1990). The concept has also been criticized for exaggerating the degree of coherence and consistency in Western attitudes towards the East, a weakness which Said's comparison between British and French attitudes only partly overcomes. Geographers have begun to respond to Said's work (see, e.g.,

Driver, 1992) and to apply his ideas in specific empirical studies (see, e.g., Anderson, 1991). (See also ETHNOCENTRISM; POSTCOLONIALISM.)   PAJ

References

Anderson, K. 1991: *Vancouver's Chinatown: racial discourse in Canada, 1875–1980.* Montreal and Kingston: McGill–Queen's University Press.

Driver, F. 1992: Geography's empire: histories of geographical knowledge. *Envir. Plann. D: Society and Space* 10, pp. 23–40.

Said, E. W. 1978: *Orientalism.* London: Routledge.

Young, R. 1990: Disorienting Orientalism. In *White mythologies: writing history and the West.* London: Routledge, pp. 119–40.

Suggested Reading

Said (1978).

Said, E. W. 1986: Orientalism reconsidered. In Barker, F. et al., eds, *Literature, politics and theory.* London: Methuen, pp. 210–29.

Young, R. (1990).

overpopulation An excess of population in an area in relation to resources or to other broader economic or social goals. Since Malthus first propounded his ideas on population, economists and demographers have tried to refine the concepts of overpopulation, underpopulation and OPTIMUM POPULATION, often with little success. Overpopulation may exist at rural, regional or national levels, and today is most frequently seen in underdeveloped rural areas where the outstripping of RESOURCES by population growth may be evident in undernourishment or underemployment. Some Marxists deny the possibility of overpopulation in a socialist society, attaching more importance to the distribution of resources in a population than to the rate of population growth itself (Harvey, 1974). (See also CARRYING CAPACITY; MALTHUSIAN MODEL.)   PEO

Reference

Harvey, D. 1974: Population, resources and the ideology of science. *Econ. Geogr.* 50, pp. 256–77.

Suggested Reading

Sauvy, A. 1969: *General theory of population,* transl. C. Campos. London: Weidenfeld and Nicolson/New York: Basic Books, ch. 23.

overurbanization A concept used in comparisons of URBANIZATION rates and levels in the contemporary THIRD WORLD with those in the First World (the 'advanced industrial countries') at similar levels of DEVELOPMENT. In the 1950s and 1960s it was argued that many Third World cities had too many residents relative to their industrial base, which led to policy proposals (and in a few cases their – usually unsuccessful – implementation) for the return of recent inmigrants, especially the residents of SQUATTER SETTLEMENTS, to the countryside. Later analyses claimed that nineteenth-century European urbanization, which was based on labour-intensive factory industries, could not legitimately be compared with the current Third World situation, in which outmigration from the countryside is needed to promote an efficient agricultural sector, with the cities absorbing new residents not into capital-intensive manufacturing industries but rather into labour-intensive service industries. What is crucial to some of those analyses is not the size of the city but whether it is either parasitic on its HINTERLAND or stimulates growth there (Hoselitz, 1955).   RJJ

Reference

Hoselitz, B. F. 1955: Generative and parasitic cities. *Econ. Develop. Cult. Change* 3, pp. 270–8.

Suggested Reading

Sovani, N. V. 1964: The analysis of overurbanization. *Econ. Develop. Cult. Change* 12, pp. 113–22.

P

paradigm The working assumptions, procedures and findings routinely accepted by a group of scholars, which together define a stable pattern of scientific activity; this in turn defines the community which shares in it (cf. PROBLEMATIC). The term comes from Kuhn (1962, 1970), who argued that 'normal science' proceeds uninterrupted through the cumulative sedimentation of theoretical systems and empirical materials, until it begins to be disrupted by a cluster of 'anomalies' which cannot be explained away or subsumed within the existing framework; the pressure is temporarily accommodated by what Kuhn called 'extraordinary research' which, if successful, eventually produces a 'revolution', i.e. a 'paradigm shift', which inaugurates the emergence of a new disciplinary matrix.

Criticisms of the concept have been registered at two levels. First, and most generally, Kuhn's original formulation is questionable; even though he modified his views between the first and second editions, his usages remained unclear (e.g. Mastermann, in Lakatos and Musgrave, 1970, recorded 21 different meanings of 'paradigm' in his work) and yet at the same time overbold, e.g. the consensus within any one science is seldom complete and stable, and the negotiation of systems of concepts is not an autonomous activity carried out entirely within the confines of a particular discipline or discourse (see Mulkay, 1979). Indeed, Karl Popper – whose *The logic of scientific discovery* (1959) has been a formative influence on many philosophers and historians of science, including Kuhn – thought that 'one ought to be sorry for' Kuhn's 'normal' scientist because, as a matter of empirical record, any scientist worthy of the name is necessarily engaged in 'extraordinary research': in short, normal science is not so normal. His objections to the theory of paradigms as 'the myth of the framework' (see also CRITICAL RATIONALISM) were extended and refined by Imre Lakatos (in Lakatos and Musgrave, 1970), who claimed that science in fact advances (and, prescriptively, that it *ought* to advance) through progressive 'problemshifts'. A series of propositions is judged as 'theoretically progressive' if 'each new theory has some excess empirical content over its predecessors, i.e. if it predicts some novel, hitherto unexpected fact', and as 'empirically progressive' if 'some of this empirical content is also corroborated', i.e. if each new theory leads us to the discovery of some new fact (see also Chouinard et al., 1984; Wheeler, 1982). Against these various objections, however, Kuhn has himself acknowledged that he 'made unnecessary difficulties for many readers'. In writing *The structure of scientific revolutions*, he recalled:

[P]aradigms took on a life of their own, largely displacing the previous talk of consensus. Having begun simply as exemplary problem solutions, they expanded their empire to include, first, the classic books in which these accepted examples initially appeared and, finally, the entire global set of commitments shared by members of a particular scientific community. The more global use of the term is the only one most readers of the book have recognized, and the inevitable result has been confusion: many of the things said there about paradigms apply only to the original sense of the term. Though both senses seem to me important, they do need to be distinguished, and the word 'paradigm' is appropriate only to the first (Kuhn, 1977, pp. xix–xx).

Hence, the 'more fundamental' (localized) sense of paradigm is what Kuhn now refers to as an *exemplar*; the other (global) sense of paradigm is what Kuhn now calls a *disciplinary matrix*. He attaches considerable importance to the empirical identification of scientific communities and to the scrutiny of the disciplinary matrix in which their members share because this is '*central to the cognitive operation of the group*' (emphasis added): in other words, Kuhn's model is *descriptive, not prescriptive*. It is this central point which most of Kuhn's critics have missed (see Barnes, 1982).

Second, and more specifically, the application of the concept of a paradigm (in either sense) to geography is open to objection. Kuhn himself restricted his account to the natural sciences – indeed, one of the reasons he formulated the notion of 'paradigms' in the first place was his perception of deep-rooted disagreements about basic premises that seemed to him to characterize social science but not natural science: except in certain phases of transformation – so it is hardly surprising that attempts to apply Kuhn to the history of human geography should be so unsuccessful (Johnston, 1991). Most of the early applications of Kuhn, however, were prescriptive rather than descriptive. Chorley and Haggett, for example, (in their *Models in geography*, 1967) drew on Kuhn to argue that the QUANTITATIVE REVOLUTION represented the establishment of a 'model-based paradigm' for geography, but their usage was at best polemical (Stoddart, 1981; but cf. Stoddart, 1967). Certainly, they did not identify any 'anomalies' in the Kuhnian sense within the framework of traditional REGIONAL GEOGRAPHY, and in so far as they sought to overthrow the regional 'paradigm' and replace it with a ('revolutionary') model-based spatial science, then their use of Kuhn was patently as prescriptive as most of Kuhn's critics. What is more, Kuhn's whole conception of science was irredeemably *non*-positivist (cf. Marshall, 1982) and there is something perverse in using his writings to legitimize the rise of a largely *positivist* geography (see POSITIVISM) (Billinge et al., 1984). Kuhn's project has much more in common with HERMENEUTICS

(Bernstein, 1983), and more recent investigations of the history of human geography which have focused on *communication* between members of particular 'communities' (e.g. Gatrell, 1984) and on the wider and intrinsically societal *contexts* in which this takes place (e.g. Barnes and Curry, 1983) come much closer to reclaiming the spirit of that hermeneutic tradition.   DG

References

Barnes, B. 1982: *T. S. Kuhn and social science.* London: Macmillan.

Barnes, T. and Curry, M. 1983: Towards a contextualist approach to geographical knowledge. *Trans. Inst. Br. Geogr.*, n.s. 8, pp. 467–82.

Bernstein, R. J. 1983: *Beyond objectivism and relativism: science, hermeneutics and praxis.* Oxford: Blackwell/Philadelphia: Pennsylvania University Press.

Billinge, M., Gregory, D. and Martin, R. L. 1984: Reconstructions. In Billinge, M., Gregory, D. and Martin, R. L., eds, *Recollections of a revolution: geography as spatial science.* London: Macmillan/New York: St. Martin's Press, pp. 1–24.

Chorley, R. J. and Haggett, P., eds 1967: *Models in geography.* London: Methuen.

Chouinard, V., Fincher, R. and Webber, M. 1984: Empirical research in scientific human geography. *Progr. hum. Geogr.* 8, pp. 347–80.

Gatrell, A. 1984: The geometry of a research speciality: spatial diffusion modelling. *Ann. Ass. Am. Geogr.* 74, pp. 437–53.

Johnston, R. J. 1991: *Geography and geographers: Anglo-American human geography since 1945*, fourth edition. London: Edward Arnold/New York: John Wiley.

Kuhn, T. S. 1962 and 1970: *The structure of scientific revolutions*, first and second editions. Chicago: University of Chicago Press.

Kuhn, T. S. 1977: *The essential tension: selected studies in scientific tradition and change.* Chicago: University of Chicago Press.

Lakatos, I. and Musgrave, A., eds 1970: *Criticism and the growth of knowledge.* Cambridge: Cambridge University Press.

Marshall, J. D. 1982: Geography and critical rationalism. In Wood, J. D., ed., *Rethinking geographical inquiry.* Downsview, Ontario: Department of Geography, Atkinson College, York University, pp. 75–171.

Mulkay, M. 1979: *Science and the sociology of knowledge.* London: Allen and Unwin.

Popper, K. 1959: *The logic of scientific discovery.* New York: Basic Books.

Stoddart, D. R. 1967: Organism and ecosystem as geographical models. In Chorley, R. J. and Haggett, P., eds, *Models in geography*. London: Methuen, pp. 511–48.

Stoddart, D. R. 1981: The paradigm concept and the history of geography. In Stoddart, D. R., ed., *Geography, ideology and social concern*. Oxford: Blackwell, pp. 70–80.

Wheeler, P. B. 1982: Revolutions, research programmes and human geography. *Area* 14, pp. 1–6.

Suggested Reading

Bernstein (1983), part 2.

Johnston (1991), chs 1 and 7.

Kuhn (1977), ch. 12.

Mair, A. 1986: Thomas Kuhn and understanding geography. *Progr. hum. Geogr.* 10, 345–70.

Pareto optimality A situation in which it is impossible to make some people better off without making others worse off. This criterion of 'economic efficiency' was devised by the economist and sociologist V. F. D. Pareto, and is an important element in NEOCLASSICAL ECONOMICS. The Pareto criterion may be applied to efficiency of RESOURCE allocation, optimality being achieved when it is impossible to reallocate resources to produce an outcome that would increase the satisfaction of some people without reducing the satisfaction of others. A more direct application to distributional issues would be to recognize as Pareto optimal a distribution of income that cannot be changed in favour of one individual or group without taking some income from another individual or group.

The attainment of Pareto optimality is illustrated in the figure. Resources are available to generate a certain amount of income, which may be distributed among A and B – these could be individuals, groups of people or even the inhabitants of two different territories. The line AB indicates the possible distributions of the maximum total income available, ranging from all going to A and none to B (at point A) and all to B (at B). Point X is a position of Pareto optimality, where any redistribution in the direction of either A or B (along the line) will make the other party worse off. In fact, any starting position on the line is Pareto optimal. It would be impossible to increase A's share from X to Z (thus leaving B in the same position) because this conflicts with the resource constraint. However, point Y inside the triangle ABO is suboptimal by the Pareto criterion because available resources are not fully utilized and it is possible to incease A's income to X, for example, without taking anything away from B. Such a move would be a 'Pareto improvement'.

The Pareto criterion figures prominently in traditional welfare economics, where it is argued that acceptance of Pareto optimality as a rule for allocative efficiency or distributive equity involves minimal ethical content. However, adoption of the Pareto criterion carries some important implications that tend to strengthen the status quo. Once society has reached the limit of production possibilities, i.e. there is no more growth, the poor cannot be made better off without conflicting with the Pareto criterion, for any such move would be at the expense of others (the rich). Thus however badly off the poor may be, they can be made better off only if more income (or whatever) is produced. In practice, the application of the Pareto criterion in a no-growth economy would prevent redistribution in the direction of the poor, no matter how unequal the existing distribution. DMS

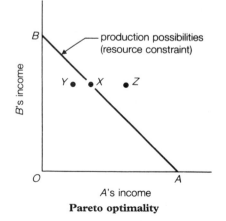

Pareto optimality

participant observation Defined by Florence Kluckhohn as 'conscious and systematic sharing, in so far as circumstances permit, in the life-activities and, on occasion, in the interests and affects of a group of persons' (1940, p. 331), participant observation originated in anthropological research on 'primitive' societies and has since been employed in sociological and geographical studies of urban NEIGHBOURHOODS. One of the principal methods for conducting ETHNOGRAPHY, participant observation is based on first-hand fieldwork over an extended period of time. Debate focuses on the extent to which participant observation can be regarded simply as a *technique* that can be applied like any other, on the extent to which it is *complementary* to more quantitative approaches, and on the *ethical and moral issues* raised by covert observation. PAJ

Reference
Kluckhohn, F. R. 1940: The participant-observer technique in small communities. *Am. J. Soc.* 46, 331–43.

Suggested Reading
Burgess, R. G. 1982: *In the field*. London: Allen and Unwin.

Jackson, P. 1983: Principles and problems of participant observation. *Geogr. Annlr.* 65B, pp. 39–46.

Spradley, J. P. 1980: *Participant observation*. New York: Holt, Rinehart and Winston.

Whyte, W. F. 1955: *Street corner society*, second edition. Chicago: University of Chicago Press.

part-time farming A situation in which farmers also have some other regular occupation. Part-time farms are of a multiplicity of types, but two major groups may be identified: (a) those of a worker-peasantry, where an industrial occupation is added alongside smallholding agriculture (common in much of Central and Eastern Europe) and in which part-time farming is a transition stage out of full-time farming; and (b) hobby farming, where farming is added to an existing non-farming (usually urban) occupation. Hobby farming may sometimes be used as an entry into full-time agriculture. The falling real incomes of farmers in the past 15 years have led to an increase in the number of part-time farmers in Western Europe and North America. PEW/DBG

Suggested Reading
Gasson, R. 1988: *The economics of part-time farming*. London: Longman.

Geojournal 1982:6. Theme issue on part-time farming.

pastoralism The breeding and rearing of certain domesticated herbivorous animals and ruminants as a primary means to satisfy food, clothing and shelter. Pastoral production involves an interaction between land, water and mineral resources, livestock and labour. Livestock as a capital good serves as a technology to transform otherwise unpalatable cellulose into consumable products. Pastoralism embraces both commercial livestock rearing (e.g. commercial stockrearing on the Argentinian pampas) and 'traditional' pastoral NOMADISM, which combines livestock husbandry and spatial mobility for the largely subsistence production of animal products. Pastoral nomadism is internally differentiated with respect to its dependence on agricultural production, forms of pasture ecology, and the animals herded. A common pastoral taxonomy distinguishes between flat and mountainous land, large and small animals, and the relationship to agriculture (i.e. pure pastoralists versus semi-pastoralists). Like PEASANTS, pastoralists exhibit significant differences in terms of household structure, property rights, sexual divisions of labour, patterns of consumption and exchange and labour processes (Galanty and Johnson, 1990). However, pastoralism is a distinctive form of ecological and cultural adaptation to specific sorts of ECOSYSTEMS (see CULTURAL ECOLOGY) in which humans and animals live in a symbiotic community typified by a fierce independence and self-determination. MW

Reference
Galanty, J. and Johnson, D. 1990: *The world of pastoralism: herding systems in comparative perspective*. New York: Guilford.

patriarchy A society in which gender relations are characterized by the domination of men over women and of masculinity over femininity. Patriarchy is a key concept and a central object of study for FEMINIST GEOGRAPHY. The relations of domination involved consist of systematic differences in POWER between genders. While there is no consensus about the source of these differences, three broad interpretations may be identified: (a) *biological or essentialist approaches*, which stress the control of women's bodies, sexuality and reproduction by men (see SEXUALITY AND GEOGRAPHY); (b) *economic approaches*, which derive patriarchal relations from the RELATIONS OF PRODUCTION in society; and (c) *cultural and political approaches*, which emphasize the role of masculinity as an IDEOLOGY and the significance of masculine values and meanings in controlling DISCOURSE. In addition, some writers combine more than one approach.

Walby (1990) identifies six sites of patriarchal relations: paid employment, household production, the STATE, male violence, sexuality, and cultural institutions. Each has a particular geography, and patriarchy is thus also geographically differentiated. Studies of GENDER AND GEOGRAPHY have focused on the causes and consequences of these patterns. Within ECONOMIC GEOGRAPHY there has been a concern with different traditions of female involvement in waged labour in different areas. POLITICAL GEOGRAPHY's focus on the state has included analyses of the changing role of welfare and family policy, while in SOCIAL GEOGRAPHY and CULTURAL GEOGRAPHY male violence, sexuality and masculinity are important research topics. It has also been pointed out that the institutions of GEOGRAPHY are themselves patriarchal, reinforcing the maxim that 'the personal is political'.   JP

Reference

Walby, S. 1990: *Theorizing patriarchy*. Oxford: Blackwell.

peasant A term in common use in English from the fifteenth century referring to individuals working on the land and residing in the countryside. By the nineteenth century 'peasant' was employed as a term of abuse (for example, Marx on the idiocy of rural life), and in the recent past it has been imbued with heroic and revolutionary connotations (Maoism, for example). In modern usage peasants are family farming households which function as relatively corporate units of production, consumption and reproduction (Chayanov, 1966). The particular social structural forms of the domestic unit (nuclear families, multigenerational extended families, and intra-household sexual divisions of labour and property systems), the social relations between households within peasant communities, and the ecological relations of production (the peasant ecotype) are, however, extremely heterogeneous (Wolf, 1966). Peasants are distinguished by direct access to their means of production in land, by the predominant use of family labour and by a high degree of self-sufficiency (see SUBSISTENCE AGRICULTURE). None the less, all peasants are by definition characterized by a partial engagement with markets (which tend to function with a high degree of imperfection) and are subordinate actors in larger political economies in which they fulfil obligations to holders of political and economic power. Peasants as forms of household enterprise rooted primarily in production on the land have a distinctive LABOUR PROCESS (the unity of the domestic unit and the productive group) and a unique *combination of labour and property* through partial market involvement. Peasants stand between those social groups who have lost all or most of their productive assets (proletarians or semi-proletarians) on the other hand, and farming households which are fully involved in the market (so-called petty or simple commodity producers) on the other. Seen in this way peasants have existed under a variety of economic, political and cultural circumstances (FEUDALISM, CAPITALISM and state SOCIALISM) spanning vast periods of history, and care 'part societies'. Peasant societies are often seen as transitional – they 'stand midway between the primitive tribe and industrial society' (Wolf, 1966, p. vii) – and yet are marginal or outsiders, 'subordinate to a group of controlling outsiders' (Wolf 1966, p. 13) who appropriate surpluses in a variety of forms (RENT, interest and unequal exchange).

In many THIRD WORLD societies in which peasants constitute an important and occasionally dominant stratum, a central question pertains to the fate of the peasantry in relation to growing state and market involvment (the so-called 'agrarian question'). Peasants are invariably the victims of MODERNITY. The question of growing commercialization and mechanization of peasant production and of the growth of off-farm income (MIGRATION, craft production and local wage labour), is reflected in the long-standing concern with *internal differentiation* among peasantries and hence their long-term survival (and also the debates over peasant persistence, de-peasantization and captured peasants). It is probably safe to say that the period 1950–75 witnessed an epochal shift in which the peasantry became for the first time a global minority.

The terms 'peasant' and 'peasantry' have often been employed loosely to describe a broad range of rural producers as generic types characterized by certain social, cultural or economic traits: the backward or anti-economic peasant, the rational and moral peasant, or the uncaptured peasant. However, these and other terms, such as traditional, subsistence or smallholder, detract from the important analytical task of situating peasants as specific social producers in concrete, historically specific political economies with their own dynamics and laws of motion.   MW

References

Chayanov, A. V. 1966: *The theory of peasant economy*, ed. D. Thorner, B. Kerblay and R. E. F. Smith and trans. R. E. F. Smith. Homewood, IL: American Economic Association. (First Russian edition 1912.)

Wolf, E. 1966: *Peasants*. Englewood Cliffs, NJ: Prentice-Hall.

perception   See ENVIRONMENTAL PERCEPTION.

periodic market systems   The provision of retail and other service functions in a settlement on a particular day or days of the week only. These may be all of the functions in the place, or they may complement a permanent set available throughout the week, as in British market towns.

Research into these systems was stimulated by analogies with CENTRAL PLACE THEORY: with relatively low *ranges* and high *thresholds*, a system of traders moving around a set cycle of markets could overcome the lack of sufficient trade to support a permanent establishment at any one.

Movement of the traders to be near their customers on set occasions is more efficient than the customers travelling long distances to permanent markets much less frequently. Detailed research has identified considerable variability in the ways in which traders work within such systems, however, and to some extent invalidates the analogy: each system must be analysed as a particular local cultural phenomenon. (See also MARKET EXCHANGE.)   RJJ

Suggested Reading

Bromley, R. F. 1980: Trader mobility in systems of periodic and daily markets. In Herbert, D. T. and Johnston, R. J., eds, *Geography and the urban environment: progress in research and applications*, volume 3. Chichester: John Wiley, pp. 133–74.

phallocentrism   A placing of man at the centre; a masculine way of representing and approaching the world which some theorists root in male genitalia and a masculine libidinal economy. It is characterized by a unified, self-controlled and distanced drive towards a singular truth or goal (i.e. a notion of progress). Cixous (1980) argues that it is intertwined with *logocentrism* (the fixing of meaning in concepts) such that meaning is fixed in a set of hierarchized and sexualized binary oppositions (hence the term *phallogocentrism*). Culture–nature is a central organizing dichotomy within phallogocentric thought, with CULTURE conceived as masculine and active, and NATURE as feminine and passive. Many critiques of phallocentrism have roots in psychoanalysis. They have led French feminists such as Cixous and male philosophers such as Lacan and Derrida to explore feminine (more open and multiple) ways of writing and reading, an exploration that Jardine (1985) terms *gynesis* and evaluates with some suspicion.

Geography intersects with phallocentrism in a number of ways. Jardine (1985) attributes the critiques of phallocentrism (e.g. the disbelief in origins, master narratives, humanism and progress) that have been developed throughout the twentieth century to the end of European imperial domination, as well as to the growing influence of feminist voices (see FEMINIST GEOGRAPHY). She interprets *gynesis*, the 'solution' to phallocentrism proposed by male philosophers, as a working out of male paranoia: men began to desire to be women as a way to avoid becoming the object of female desire. (The frequent feminization of non-European countries is especially interesting in the context of this interpretation.) Critiques of phallogocentrism also intersect with conceptions of NATURE insofar as they are tied to attempts to displace 'man' from the controlling centre and to refigure nature in active, equal terms. To the extent that humanism and phallocentrism are intertwined, the critiques of the latter extend to HUMANISTIC GEOGRAPHY. (See also SEXUALITY AND GEOGRAPHY.) GP

References

Cixous, H. 1980: Sorties. In Marks, E. and de Courtivron, I., eds, *New French feminisms*. Amherst, MA: The University of Massachusetts Press, pp. 90–8.

Jardine, A. 1985: *Gynesis: configurations of women and modernity*. Ithaca, NY: Cornell University Press.

phenomenal environment

The physical and cultural environment that lies outside individuals' perceptions. The term is attributed to William Kirk and has meaning in relation to the concept of BEHAVIOURAL ENVIRONMENT. Facts from the phenomenal environment constitute a part of the behavioural environment only after they are filtered through social and cultural values.

By including the manifestations of human activity, and not just the physical and biotic environment, the concept was intended to counteract a static conception of the natural environment. It has been less widely used than its twin concept (that of behavioural environment); Campbell (1989) speculates that this may reflect the fact that it tends to naturalize human activity. For example, human populations are assigned to the phenomenal environment, and Kirk claimed that 'areal variation in the physical constitution of mankind is no less a fact of nature than the ecological complexity of equatorial rain forest' (1963, pp. 364–5). Others (e.g., Relph, 1989) reject the idea of the phenomenal

environment because it is based in a realist dualism (i.e. real versus perceived worlds). GP

References

Campbell, J. A. 1989: The concept of 'the behavioural environment', and its origins, reconsidered. In Boal, F. and Livingstone, D. N., eds, *The behavioural environment*. London: Routledge, pp. 33–76.

Kirk, W. 1963: Problems of geography. *Geography* 48, pp. 357–71.

Relph, E. 1989: A curiously unbalanced condition of the powers of the mind: realism and the ecology of environmental experience. In Boal, F. and Livingstone, D. N., eds, *The behavioural environment*. London: Routledge, pp. 277–88.

phenomenology

A philosophy which is founded on the importance of reflecting on the ways in which the world is made available for intellectual inquiry: this means that it pays particular attention to the active, creative function of language and DISCOURSE in making the world intelligible. One of phenomenology's main concerns is 'to disclose the world as it shows itself before scientific inquiry, as that which is *pre-given* and *presupposed* by the sciences' (Pickles, 1985; emphases added). As such, phenomenology provides a powerful critique of POSITIVISM, which disavows any such reflection as meaningless metaphysics and, by virtue of its commitment to EMPIRICISM, assumes that there is no need to say anything at all about the preconceptions on which its various objectifications necessarily depend. Against this, phenomenology claims that 'observation' and 'objectification' are never the simple exercises which conventional forms of science assume them to be (cf. ABSTRACTION). Indeed, it rejects any assumption of the separation of subject ('the observer') and object ('the observed'), and insists instead that 'we exist primordially not as subjects manipulating objects in the external, "real", physical world, but as beings in, alongside and toward the world' (Pickles, 1985) (cf. EXISTENTIALISM). This contradicts our commonsense views, of course, which Edmund Husserl, the father of modern phenomenology, called the *natural attitude*, i.e. a set of views in which the possibility of cognition is simply taken for granted. For Husserl, the task of a truly rigorous and radical philosophy was to interrogate the natural attitude in order to show 'from what perspective things in the world are taken by the sciences and how the objects of each science are constituted' (Pickles, 1985). Husserl argued that this intrinsically critical examination could be achieved through an act of pure philosophical reflection, called the *epoché* or the 'phenomenological reduction' (see Johnson, 1983). This method – and, *contra* Billinge (1977) and others, phenomenology is indeed a method – involves:

(a) suspending one's taken-for-granted presuppositions;

(b) reflecting 'not upon the objects of our perception but on the way in which they are originally given . . . [on] the way in which we grasp the corresponding experiences' (Pickles, 1985) – Husserl called these experiences *phenomena*; and

(c) disclosing the very essence (*eidé*) of the phenomena.

These procedures may be connected to and contrasted with those of HERMENEUTICS and STRUCTURALISM (Gregory, 1978). Seen in this way, phenomenology becomes an *eidetic science* – not only a critique of positivism (Entrikin, 1976) but also an *alternative* to it. Its purpose is to establish, through the disclosure of 'essences', what Husserl called *regional ontologies* (see ONTOLOGY), i.e. it has to 'ground' the thematic frameworks of the various empirical sciences by revealing the really essential nature of the objects and concepts which constitute their empirical domains (cf. PRAGMATISM):

The purpose of a regional ontology is to describe the domain of entities appropriate to that science. This purpose is achieved through an ontological description of the a priori theoretical framework posited by a science when it engages in empirical work. Such a description lays out precisely the origin, the meaning and the functions of the concepts, principles and methods of a particular framework which has been assumed before that science can establish facts, develop hypotheses, or build theory (Christensen, 1982).

This makes it necessary to distinguish between:

(a) *descriptive phenomenology*, which deals with the 'essential structures' underlying and governing the facts of the various empirical sciences – with 'the a priori framework of meaning adopted by a particular empirical science'; and

(b) *transcendental phenomenology*, which deals with the 'essential structures' of INTENTIONALITY itself – with 'that realm which gives rise to the possibility of scientific reflection in the first place' (Pickles, 1985).

But in human geography the distinctions between (a) and (b) have usually been erased. Readings of Husserl have most frequently been closed around his transcendental phenomenology and, much more seriously, misrepresented to underwrite a patently 'subjectivist' critique of SPATIAL SCIENCE. To reinstate descriptive phenomenology is *not* to arrive at subjective constructions of 'the world naively given':

We do not arrive at 'phenomenological description' of everyday activities such as going to the mailbox [cf. Seamon, 1979]. Descriptive phenomenology provides us with formal and abstract universal structures through methodically conscious performance of the eidetic reduction (Pickles, 1985).

As an empirical science then, clearly, human geography is susceptible to interrogation by descriptive phenomenology: to the clarification of what Relph (1970) called 'the phenomenological basis of geography' through a systematic reflection on 'the elements and notions which characterize the nature of an entity within its empirical domain'. It is through procedures of this sort, in fact, that Pickles (1985) sought 'to retrieve two basic concepts of geographic concern – place and space – for a viable and vital regional ontology of the geographical, on the grounds of which geographical inquiry as a human science of the world can be explicitly founded' (see SPATIALITY).

But what about those 'everyday activities' (above)? Christensen (1982) contends that:

The *descriptive* component of given human science cannot guarantee that the theoretical framework of meaning employed by the empirical component is adequate and relevant to the lived world. This can be guaranteed only by an *interpretative* component to science which accounts critically for the meanings held by the agents in their lived world [emphases added].

Indeed, Husserl himself once complained that the scientist 'does not make it clear to himself that the constant foundation of his admittedly subjective thinking activity is the environing world of life. This latter is constantly presupposed as the basic working area, in which alone his questions and his methodology make sense'. And again: 'The sciences build upon the life-world as taken-for-granted in that they make use of whatever in it happens to be necessary for their particular ends. But to use the life-world in this way is not to know it scientifically in its own manner of being' (Husserl, 1954). According to Pickles (1985), however, the task of phenomenology is to clarify the *universal* and *general* structure of the LIFEWORLD – what he calls the *'universal a priori of the lifeworld'* – and *not*, 'contrary to the claims of much "geographical phenomenology", [to] be a capturing of the everyday lifeworld as it is lived'. Others disagree with this (to them, limited) objective and insist upon the importance of the 'interpretative component' identified by Christensen (1982). She associates the interpretative, above all, with the writings of Alfred Schutz, whose ideas 'align more comfortably with the tradition of Heidegger than with the tradition of Husserl' (see also Hirst, 1977), but which are also indebted to Weber's interpretative sociology (see Gorman, 1977). This requires us to distinguish:

(c) *constitutive phenomenology*, which deals with the structures of social meaning – with frames of reference and systems of typification – which constitute the 'multiple realities' embedded in the lifeworld.

It is only in this context that it makes sense to speak of 'a plurality of worlds' (Relph, 1970; see also Tuan, 1971). It was certainly not Husserl's intention to licence 'a multiplicity of different frames of reference; on the contrary, he made it perfectly clear that the purpose of the *epoché* was to ensure that the world could be "identically reconstituted in each individual through a similar reflective procedure" ' (Gregory, 1978; cf. Mercer and Powell, 1972). In so far as Husserl's

supposed 'preoccupation with the individual' has been contrasted with the 'fundamentally social' focus of Schutz (Jackson, 1981), then constitutive phenomenology has informed – Pickles (1985) would perhaps say '*mis*informed' – several studies in HUMANISTIC GEOGRAPHY. 'Rather than stressing experiences', Relph (1981) observes, such 'phenomenological studies can emphasise the phenomena of the geographical life-world'. This is not how Husserl understood 'experiences' and 'phenomena' (see above), and when Relph cites as examples his own *Place and placelessness* (1976) and Tuan's *Space and place* (1977) it should be noted that neither of these texts draws upon Husserl at all. Other studies have moved still further beyond 'the letter of the phenomenological law' to explore the dynamism of the LIFEWORLD (Buttimer, 1976) and the constitution of the TAKEN-FOR-GRANTED WORLD in ways which intersect directly with STRUCTURATION THEORY and SYMBOLIC INTERACTIONISM (Ley, 1977; Warf, 1986). (See also IDEALISM.)   DG

References

Billinge, M. 1977: In search of negativism: phenomenology and historical geography. *J. hist. Geogr.* 3, pp. 55–68.

Buttimer, A. 1976: Grasping the dynamism of the life-world. *Ann. Ass. Am. Geogr.* 66, pp. 277–92.

Christensen, K. 1982: Geography as a human science: a philosophic critique of the positivist–humanist split. In Gould, P. and Olsson, G., eds, *A search for common ground.* London: Pion, pp. 37–57.

Entrikin, J. N. 1976: Contemporary humanism in geography. *Ann. Ass. Am. Geogr.* 66, pp. 615–32.

Gorman, R. A. 1977: *The dual vision: Alfred Schutz and the myth of phenomenological social science.* London: Routledge and Kegan Paul.

Gregory, D. 1978: The discourse of the past: phenomenology, structuralism and historical geography. *J. hist. Geogr.* 4, pp. 161–73.

Hirst, P. 1977: *Philosophy and methodology in the social sciences.* Brighton: Harvester.

Husserl, E. 1954: *The crisis of European sciences and transcendental phenomenology.* Evanston, IL: Northwestern University Press.

Jackson, P. 1981: Phenomenology and social geography. *Area* 13, pp. 299–305.

Johnson, L. 1983: Bracketing lifeworlds: Husserlian phenomenology as geographical method. *Aust. geogr. Stud.* 21, pp. 102–8.

Ley, D. 1977: Social geography and the taken-for-granted world. *Trans. Inst. Br. Geogr.* n.s. 2, pp. 498–512.

Mercer, D. and Powell, J. M. 1972: *Phenomenology and related non-positivistic viewpoints in the social sciences.* Melbourne: Monash University publications in geography 1.

Pickles, J. 1985: *Phenomenology, science and geography: spatiality and the human sciences.* Cambridge: Cambridge University Press.

Relph, E. 1970: An inquiry into the relations between phenomenology and geography. *Can. Geogr.* 14, pp. 193–201.

Relph, E. 1976: *Place and placelessness.* London: Pion.

Relph, E. 1981: Phenomenology. In Harvey, M. E. and Holly, B. P., eds, *Themes in geographic thought.* London: Croom Helm/New York: St. Martin's Press.

Seamon, D. 1979: *A geography of the life-world.* London: Croom Helm/New York: St. Martin's Press.

Tuan, Y.-F. 1971: Geography, phenomenology and the study of human nature. *Can. Geogr.* 15, pp. 181–92.

Tuan, Y.-F. 1977: *Space and place.* London: Edward Arnold/Minneapolis: University of Minnesota Press.

Warf, B. 1986: Ideology, everyday life and principatory phenomenology. *Antipode* 18, pp. 268–83.

Suggested Reading
Christensen (1982).
Pickles (1985).

Phillips curve The relationship between the percentage change in money wages and the level of unemployment. In 1958 the economist A. W. H. Phillips set out empirical evidence of a significant relationship between these two variables, such that the lower the unemployment, the higher the rate of change of wages. As the rate of increase in wages influences the rate of inflation, the Phillips curve suggests that the lower the level of unemployment, the higher the rate of inflation. This implies that the aims of low unemployment and a low rate of inflation may be inconsistent. The change in Britain from low unemployment and high inflation in the 1970s to high unemployment and a reduced rate of inflation in the 1980s represents a shift along the Phillips curve arising from changing govenment policy. DMS

Reference

Phillips, A. W. H. 1958: The relation between unemployment and rate of change in money wage rate in the UK, 1861–1957. *Economica* 25, pp. 283–99.

Pirenne thesis With the publication of *Medieval cities* in 1925, Belgian historian Henri Pirenne (1862–1935) advanced a theory of medieval URBANIZATION that has only recently been superseded. According to Pirenne, the Arabian conquest of North Africa, Sicily and Spain in the eighth century finally closed the Mediterranean to trade between Europe and the Middle East. In the absence of systematic international trade, Europe fragmented into parochial REGIONS with largely self-sufficient economies. As a result cities became both unnecessary and unsupported, and were abandoned for some 200 years until east–west commerce was revived through Venice and Scandinavia. The reurbanization of Europe in the tenth century was led by merchants creating trade-based suburbs on the peripheries of ecclesiastical or military centres. Relations characteristic of FEUDALISM did not apply in these suburbs, which became progenitors of 'free labour' and a mercantile legal system.

Recent evidence drawn from archaeology, lexicology, topography and numismatics has shown that Pirenne underestimated the level of international trade during the Carolingian period, as well as the connections between agricultural and urban economies. The reurbanization of Europe is now interpreted as the result of internal population growth and an increased agricultural surplus which, together, underpinned a revival of both local and international trade. New interpretations of medieval urbanization seek to reveal the interdependence between city and countryside, and no longer see these as separately functioning economic and social systems. DH

Reference

Pirenne, H. 1925: *Medieval cities: their origins and the revival of trade*. Princeton, NJ: Princeton University Press.

Suggested Reading

Hodges, R. and Whitehouse, D. 1983: *Mohammed, Charlemagne and the origins of Europe: archaeology and the Pirenne thesis*. London: Duckworth.

Pirenne (1925).

place A portion of geographical SPACE occupied by a person or thing. Agnew (1987) identifies three major elements of place: 'LOCALE, the settings in which social relations are constituted (these can be informal or institutional); location, the geographical area encompassing the settings for social interaction as defined by social and economic processes operating at a wider scale; and SENSE OF PLACE, the local "structure of feeling" '.

Place, and in particular sense of place, was one of the key concepts used by HUMANISTIC GEOGRAPHY in the 1970s to distinguish its approach from that of positivist geographers. In particular, it was associated with the phenomenological approaches of Relph (1976) and Tuan (1977). Such a philosophical approach to place has been continued in the 1980s in the work of Seamon and Mugerauer (1985) and Black et al. (1989).

During the 1980s interest in the concept of place grew outside humanistic geography. Economic geographers such as Massey (see Massey and Allen, 1984) sought to theorize place as manifesting specificity within the context of general processes. Historical geographers such as Pred (1984), drawing upon Giddens, saw places as part of a STRUCTURATION process, both constituted by social practices and in turn constituting those practices. Agnew (1987) and Johnston (1991) have argued for place as one of the cornerstones of POLITICAL GEOGRAPHY. Entrikin (1991) has tried to mediate between notions of place by arguing that '[t]o seek to understand place in a manner that captures its sense of totality and contextuality is to occupy a position that is between the objective pole of scientific theorizing and the subjective pole of empathetic understanding'.   JD

References

Agnew, J. A. 1987: *Place and politics: the geographical mediation of state and society*. Boston: Allen and Unwin.

Black, D. W., Kunze, D., Pickles, J. 1989: *Commonplaces: essays on the nature of place*. New York: University Press of America.

Entrikin, J. N. 1991: *The betweenness of place: towards a geography of modernity*. Baltimore, MD: Johns Hopkins University Press.

Johnston, R. J. 1991: *A question of place: exploring the practice of geography*. Oxford: Blackwell.

Massey, D. and Allen, J., eds 1984: *Geography matters! A reader*. Cambridge: Cambridge University Press.

Pred, A. 1984: Place as historically contingent process: structuration and the time geography of becoming places. *Ann. Ass. Am. Geogr.* 74, pp. 279–97.

Relph, E. 1976: *Place and placelessness*. London: Pion.

Seamon, D. and Mugerauer, R. 1985: *Dwelling, place and environment: towards a phenomenology of person and world*. Dordrecht, The Netherlands: Martinus Nijhoff.

Tuan, Y.-F. 1977: *Space and place: the perspective of experience*. Minneapolis: University of Minnesota Press.

Suggested Reading

Agnew (1987).

Agnew, J. A. and Duncan, J. S. 1989: *The power of place: bring together geographical and sociological imaginations*. London: Unwin Hyman.

Entrikin (1991).

Johnston (1991).

Relph (1976).

place utility The measure of an individual's satisfaction with a given location. The term – derived from the concept of utility which is central to much of NEOCLASSICAL ECONOMICS – was introduced in studies of MIGRATION concerned with people's evaluations of the alternatives available to them (Wolpert, 1965), including their current homes. Having decided to investigate the possibility of a move, a household would search within its ACTION SPACE for available dwellings (cf. SEARCH BEHAVIOUR) and evaluate each against their criteria for assessing desirability (or utility). Such evaluations provide the measures of place utility which determine whether to move (the place utility of the existing home may be higher than that of any other identified) and, if a move is to occur, which of the potential destinations is the best.   RJJ

Reference

Wolpert, J. 1965: Behavioural aspects of the decision to migrate. *Pap. reg. Sci. Assoc.* 15, pp. 159–69.

Suggested Reading

Brown, L. A. and Moore, E. G. 1970: The intra-urban migration process: a perspective. *Geogr. Annlr.* 52B, pp. 1–13.

place-names As objects of philological study, the names of settlements, localities, fields, and features of natural and cultural landscapes may provide evidence of environmental, settlement and social conditions at the time a name was coined. This is possible because many place-names are composed of elements which have topographical, habitative or social meanings, and they can be approximately dated. Obviously, the utility of place-names is greatest for the periods in which names were coined, and when other sources of information are sparse.

In Western Europe, thousands of surviving place-names were coined in pre- or early medieval periods which are otherwise very poorly documented. For these periods, syntheses of place-name evidence with palaeo-environmental work underlie important work on the geography of settlements (e.g. Cameron, 1975), on woodland clearance and expanding agriculture (e.g. Hooke, 1989), on territorial organization (e.g. Fellows-Jensen, 1985) and on inter-settlement relations (e.g. Jones, 1990).

Geographical analysis of place-names faces four main problems. First, the earliest recording of a name may occur several centuries after its coining, and place-names were subject to prevailing linguistic transformations and developments (Fellows-Jensen, 1990). For example, many English place-names are first recorded in the *Domesday book*, but may have been coined as early as the sixth century (Cox, 1975). Their original form, the identification of their elements and hence their meaning, all have to be inferred from their later forms and known patterns of linguistic change.

Second, the interpretation of some place-name elements is disputed or uncertain. For example, it is often difficult to distinguish the habitative term 'ham' from the topographical term 'hamm' – yet they have different implications. Third, in dating the original coining of a place-name, it may be important to know whether the feature of LANDSCAPE or society to which the name relates is a long-run or an ephemeral one, the former being in general much more informative than the latter. Lastly, the name may not originally have been that of the settlement, field or feature which now bears it. The phenomenon of the 'mobile Dark Age hamlet' is now widely recognized (Taylor, 1983, 1989). If mobile settlements retained their previous names, they are no longer located at the place to which their names refer: a particular problem when dealing with topographical elements.

In areas settled much later, naming evidence relating to dominant cultural groups is much more accessible, and analysis centres on the cultural context and symbolism of naming. Particular attention has been paid to colonial contexts, where indigenous names have been lost with the deaths of native populations, or deliberately suppressed. Re-naming, along with new CARTOGRAPHY, formed part of European appropriations of native peoples' lands, and contributed to European portrayals of such land as 'empty' (Harley, 1988): a reminder of the political nature of the act of naming places.   PG

References

Cameron, K., ed. 1975: *Place-name evidence for the Anglo-Saxon invasion and Scandinavian settlements.* Nottingham: Place Name Society.

Cox, B. 1975: The place-names of the earliest English records. *Journal of the English Place-Names Society* 8, pp. 12–66.

Fellows-Jensen, G. 1985: Scandinavian settlement in England: the place-name evidence. In Bekker-Nielsen, H. and Frede-Nielsen, H., eds, *Vikingesymposium, Odense Universitet 1982.* Odense.

Fellows-Jensen, G. 1990: Place-names as a reflection of cultural interaction. *Anglo-Saxon England* 19, pp. 13–21.

Harley, J. B. 1988: Silences and secrecy: the hidden agenda of cartography in early modern Europe. *Imago Mundi* 40, pp. 111–30.

Hooke, D. 1989: Pre-conquest woodland: its distribution and usage. *Ag. hist. R.* 37, pp. 113–29.

Jones, G. R. J. 1990: Celts, Saxons and Scandinavians. In Dodgshon, R. and Butlin, R., eds, *An historical geography of England and Wales*, second edition. London: Academic Press, pp. 45–68.

Taylor, C. C. 1983: *Village and landscape: a history of rural settlement in England*. London: George Philip.

Taylor, C. C. 1989: Whittlesford: the study of a river-edge village. In Aston, M. et al., eds, *The rural settlements of medieval England: studies dedicated to Maurice Beresford and John Hurst*. Oxford: Blackwell, pp. 207–27.

Suggested Reading

Gelling, M. 1978: *Signposts to the past: place names and the history of England*. London: Dent.

Gelling, M. 1984: *Place-names in the landscape*. London: Dent.

Gelling, M. 1988: Towards a chronology for English place-names. In Hooke, D., *Anglo-Saxon settlements*. Oxford: Clarendon Press.

placelessness The existence of relatively homogeneous and standardized LANDSCAPES which diminish the local specificity and variety of PLACES that characterized preindustrial societies. This term is associated with HUMANISTIC GEOGRAPHY, particularly the work of Relph (1976) who, drawing upon Heidegger (1962), argues that in the modern world the loss of place diversity is symptomatic of a larger loss of meaning. The 'authentic' attitude which characterized preindustrial and handicraft cultures and produces 'SENSE OF PLACE' has largely been lost and replaced with an 'inauthentic' attitude. As examples of placelessness, and the 'inauthentic' attitude which produces them, Relph offers tourist landscapes, commercial strips, NEW TOWNS and SUBURBS, and the international style in architecture. Entrikin (1991) points out that while some meanings are indeed lost when places become increasingly homogenized, others are gained. To speak solely of loss, therefore, is to adopt the values of conservationists and preservationists who seek to preserve cultural artefacts and places (cf. CONSERVATION).   JD

References

Entrikin, J. N. 1991: *The betweenness of place: towards a geography of modernity*. Baltimore, MD: Johns Hopkins University Press.

Heidegger, M. 1962: *Being and time*. New York: Harper and Row.

Relph, E. 1976: *Place and placelessness*. London: Pion.

Suggested Reading

Entrikin (1991).

Porteous, J. D. 1988: Topicide: the annihilation of place. In Eyles, J. and Smith, D. J., eds, *Qualitative methods in human geography*. Cambridge: Polity Press, pp. 75–93.

Relph (1976).

Seamon, D. and Mugerauer, R., eds 1985: *Dwelling, place and environment: towards a phenomenology of person and world*. Dordrecht, The Netherlands: Martinus Nijhoff.

planning See CENTRAL PLANNING; URBAN AND REGIONAL PLANNING.

plantation The meaning of plantation has changed over time. Originally a plot of ground with trees, it came to mean a group of settlers or their political units during British overseas expansion (e.g. the Ulster Plantation). Later, plantation came to mean a large farm or landed estate, especially associated with tropical or subtropical production of 'classical' plantation crops such as sugar, coffee, tobacco, tea, cocoa, bananas, spices, cotton, sisal, rubber and palm oil (Thompson, 1983; see FARMING, TYPE OF). Most plantations combined an agricultural with an industrial process, but technologies, labour processes, property rights and infrastructure have varied enormously across space and time, making a generic definition of 'plantation' impossible (see AGRIBUSINESS). Plantations have witnessed historical transformations in labour relations between slave, feudal, migratory, indentured and free wage labour, and many plantations in Latin America operated on a mixture of these labour forms (see LABOUR PROCESS). All definitions of 'plantation' tend to differentiate it from other agricultural forms of production by size, authority structure, crop or labour-force characteristics (low skills, work gangs and various forms of servility). The theory of plantations has a long lineage that can be traced back to Ricardo and John Stuart Mill in the nineteenth century and to H. J. Nieboer and Edgar Thompson in the twentieth. An important distinction has been made between old- and new-style plantations in which the former (e.g. the hacienda in Central America) were essentially precapitalist with surpluses directed at conspicuous consumption, while the latter were capitalist enterprises driven by the rigours of capitalist accumulation (see FEUDALISM and CAPITALISM).

Recent work has seen plantations as 'totalizing institutions' the historical connections of which with RACISM and slavery have fundamentally shaped entire social and political structures (e.g. the Caribbean and the US South) but have also acted as powerful agents of UNDERDEVELOPMENT. Plantations and plantation economies and societies cannot be understood in terms of the narrow logic of production of the enterprise, however. The enormously diverse forms and circumstances in which the plantation has persisted and transformed itself must be rooted in the historical forms and rhythms of capitalist accumulation under specific land, labour and capital markets.   MW

References

Thompson, E. 1983: *The plantation: an international bibliography.* Boston: G. K. Hall.

plural society Coined by the British economist and colonial administrator J. S. Furnivall on the basis of his experience in South-East Asia, the term was applied to colonial societies in which an alien minority ruled over an indigenous majority. In his classic study of Burma and the Dutch East Indies, Furnivall used the term to describe those societies in which different sections of the community live side by side, but separately, within the same political unit: 'Each group holds by its own religion, its own culture and language, its own ideas and ways. As individuals they meet, but only in the market place, in buying and selling' (Furnivall, 1948, pp. 304–5). The term has since been applied to postcolonial societies in Africa and the Caribbean (Smith, 1965; Kuper and Smith, 1969). More recently its use has been extended by

other writers to societies such as Britain and the USA which, in Furnivall's terms, have plural elements but are not strictly plural societies. The concept has been criticized for implying a degree of equality between the different sections within such societies, denying the existence of structured inequalities between them.   PAJ

References

Furnivall, J. S. 1948: *Colonial policy and practice.* Cambridge: Cambridge University Press.
Kuper, L. and Smith, M. G., eds 1969: *Pluralism in Africa.* Berkeley: University of California Press.
Smith, M. G. 1965: *The plural society in the British West Indies.* Berkeley: University of California Press.

Suggested Reading

Clarke, C., Ley, D. and Peach, C., eds 1984: *Geography and ethnic pluralism.* London: Allen and Unwin.

pluralism A concept that has two distinct meanings.

1. A descriptive term signifying cultural diversity in a society (which may then be referred to as a PLURAL SOCIETY), the three most common criteria for division being RACE, LANGUAGE and RELIGION. Interest in plural societies is particularly strong among students of Third World countries where significant cultural diversity is almost endemic. Since cultural diversity is often associated with social conflict, Dahl terms this 'conflictual pluralism', which is a major theme in CULTURAL and SOCIAL GEOGRAPHY (Clarke et al., 1984) and POLITICAL GEOGRAPHY (Kliot and Waterman, 1983).

2. A theory of POWER in society associated with the work of Robert Dahl, which he has termed 'organizational pluralism'. The theory asserts that power is diffused and balanced in modern societies so that there is no one group or CLASS able to dominate DECISION-MAKING in government. A high degree of consensus is assumed such that 'conflicts' are not fundamental but can be dealt with pragmatically in the political marketplace. Decisions are ultimately legitimized through the electoral process. The institutions of the STATE take on the role of umpire,

adjudicating among competing interest groups. The theory was applied by Dahl (1961) to an urban area in order to disprove the conclusion of community power studies that American cities were run by local elites. The debate surrounding this study has been important for URBAN GEOGRAPHY, and is summarized in Saunders (1979) and Dunleavy (1980).

The major attempt to refute pluralism is still Miliband (1969), who argues that the theory takes as resolved the major questions concerning the nature of political power in capitalist society. He reasserts class domination of the state and sets out to show that pluralism 'far from providing a guide to reality, constitutes a profound obfuscation of it'. Lukes (1974) provides a theoretical discussion of POWER in which pluralism is designated a 'one-dimensional view' because it is limited to studying observable behaviour and the study of decision-making.   PJT

References

Clarke, C., Ley, D. and Peach, D., eds 1984: *Geography and ethnic pluralism*. London: Allen and Unwin.

Dahl, R. A. 1961: *Who governs?* New Haven: Yale University Press.

Dunleavy, P. 1980: *Urban political analysis*. London: Macmillan.

Kliot, N. and Waterman, S., eds 1983: *Pluralism and political geography*. London: Croom Helm/ New York: St. Martin's Press.

Lukes, S. 1974: *Power: a radical view*. London: Macmillan.

Miliband, R. 1969: *The state in capitalist society*. London: Quartet.

Saunders, P. 1979: *Urban politics: a sociological approach*. London: Hutchinson.

policing, geography of Policing is the mechanism that most societies use for preserving order, protecting people and property from illegal acts, and preventing crime. Human geography intersects with police studies in at least two key ways.

First, police practice feeds directly into the geography of CRIME. The official statistics which inform most geographies of deviance, patterns of offender behaviour and offence mapping, are themselves an index of police activity. The police discover relatively few crimes themselves, so that the statistics they compile are a reflection first of the public's reporting behaviour (which itself depends on relationships between the police and the public in different COMMUNITY settings), and, second, of bureaucratic recording procedures (which are partly a function of police culture).

Second, policing is part of the geography of SURVEILLANCE and social control: it has always been more about preserving public order than about preventing or managing crime. Studies of the policing of civil unrest and industrial disputes thus provide important clues about state strategies for the management of civil society. In this context, the debate on police accountability – on who should control the police – contributes to the wider project of POLITICAL GEOGRAPHY in monitoring the tension between central state and local democracy.

A fuller discussion of the links between police, space and society is provided by Fyfe (1991).   SJS

Reference

Fyfe, N. 1991: The police, space and society: the geography of policing. *Progr. hum. Geogr.* 15, pp. 249–67.

political economy A term first used in its contemporary sense in the late eighteenth and early nineteenth centuries, and associated with the English classical economists, who included Adam Smith and David Ricardo. Ricardo, in particular, emphasized two facets of economy and society that have remained pivotal in the definition of political economy: first, production and accumulation; and second, distribution of the 'surplus' so produced. It is the focus on distribution that really accounts for the political part of political economy; for questions of apportioning the surplus among the classes of society necessarily push inquiry beyond the purely economic, and into the spheres of the social and political.

Marx took up the issues of both production and distribution, but then wedded them to a theory of revolutionary change. In particular, maintaining political economy as a name, Marx argued for the method of DIALECTICAL MATERIALISM. From this perspective, he argued that the problem with the classical economists is that they treated concepts such as production and distribution as if they were eternal, failing to recognize that their forms are a product of a particular set of historical material circumstances. For this reason, we must always be aware of the historicity of our concepts but, even more importantly, be willing to challenge their current meanings in order to bring about progressive change.

After Marx, only the noun in political economy survived as NEOCLASSICAL ECONOMICS gained ascendancy from the late nineteenth century onwards. It was not until the 1960s that the original term was revived, and now consists of at least four different strains: fundamental Marxists, who keep to the letter of Marx (Farjoun and Machover, 1983); NEO-RICARDIANS, who provide a minimalist account of both politics and economics, following Sraffa (1960); ANALYTICAL MARXISTS, who employ RATIONAL CHOICE THEORY to scrutinize analytically and reconstruct logically Marx's essential insights (Roemer, 1988); and POST-MARXISTS, who draw upon a wide range of often POSTSTRUCTURAL writers (Resnick and Wolff, 1987).

Ironically, also during the 1960s the radical libertarian right from the University of Chicago appropriated the title 'political economy'. Focused on the problem of choosing among alternatives, the group examined all facets of human life – from deciding birth to deciding death – in terms of the tenets of rational choice theory. The nature of the STATE, and political choice and DECISION-MAKING are similarly examined by them, giving rise to PUBLIC CHOICE THEORY.

In human geography, political economy first emerged in the late 1960s with RADICAL GEOGRAPHY, and later with a full-blown Marxist approach assisted with, in particular, Harvey's (1973) and Castells's (1977) writings on URBANISM. Since the early 1980s, political economy has become both more diffuse and more pervasive. It has effectively set the agenda in five major debates over the past decade: on structure and agency, REALISM, LOCALITY studies, CULTURAL LANDSCAPES and POSTMODERNISM (see Peet and Thrift, 1989). Admittedly, it is difficult to find a common thread among the many uses of political economy within geography, but if it exists it is that in all practices the political and the economic are irrevocably linked; a sentiment not that distant from that proposed by the originators of the term.   TJB

References

Castells, M. 1977: *The urban question: a Marxist approach* (translated from the French by A. Sheridan). Cambridge, MA: MIT Press.

Farjoun, E. and Machover, M. 1983: *Laws of chaos: a probablistic approach to political economy.* London: Verso.

Harvey, D. 1973: *Social justice and the city.* London: Edward Arnold.

Peet, R. and Thrift, N. J. 1989: Political economy and human geography. In Peet, R. and Thrift, N. J., eds, *New models in geography, volume 1, The political-economy perspective.* London: Unwin Hyman, pp. 1–29.

Resnick, S. A. and Wolff, R. D. 1987: *Knowledge and class.* Chicago: University of Chicago Press.

Roemer J. 1988: *Free to lose: an introduction to Marxist economic philosophy.* Cambridge MA: Harvard University Press.

Sraffa, P. 1960: *Production of commodities by means of commodities.* Cambridge: Cambridge University Press.

Suggested Reading

Peet and Thrift (1989).

political geography It has become conventional to divide the subject matter of human geography into three subdisciplines dealing with economic, political and social events respectively. This is by no means original but merely mimics the standard division of modern social science into economics, political science and sociology. Hence, we may define what currently goes under the title of political geography as simply 'political studies carried out by geographers using the techniques and ideas associated with their spatial perspectives' (Burnett and Taylor, 1981, p. 4). Dear (1988, p. 270) argues that this tripartite division is more than a convention and reflects 'the three *primary processes* which structure the time–space fabric'. From this position he defines political geography more formally as 'the analysis of the systems of class/group conflict over time and space'. But the history of political geography is much more problematic than this contemporary division of human geography suggests.

Although it has recently been considered to be the weakest of the three divisions of human geography, political geography actually predates both ECONOMIC and SOCIAL GEOGRAPHY, and traditionally attracted some of the most prominent geographers to its subject matter. Before the emergence of modern geography as a generally accepted discipline, the term 'political geography' was applied generally to 'human' aspects of geography: physical geography was an adjunct of geology, political geography the equivalent adjunct of history (see Mackinder, 1887). With the establishment of geography in universities, human aspects of geography were given new names, indicating the creation of subdisciplines. In this way a 'new' political geography was created alongside colonial geography and COMMERCIAL GEOGRAPHY. This particularly trilogy of human geographical knowledge reflects the concerns of the late-nineteenth-century society in which the 'new' geography was being developed (see IMPERIALISM). Political geography was established as a subdiscipline by the publication in 1897 of Friedrich Ratzel's *Politische Geographie*. Ratzel is remembered today for his organic theory of the STATE and the concept of *LEBENSRAUM*, or 'living space', in which vigorous societies could expand. But Ratzel's political geography was much more than this. In keeping with the geography of his era he defined a broadly based environmental approach to political geography very different from the narrow 'political studies' currently in vogue (see ANTHROPOGEOGRAPHY).

The establishment of political geography cannot be discussed without mention of Sir Halford Mackinder's 'geographical pivot of history' (1904), which later developed into the HEARTLAND theory. This initiated a geostrategic tradition in political geography that continued to provide a framework for strategic thinking throughout the period of the Cold War in international relations. The first major opportunity for Mackinder to apply his ideas came with the First World War and its aftermath. Mackinder and many other geographers were government advisors at Versailles, where the task of redrawing the map of Europe brought geography and geographers into public view. This marks the heyday of traditional political geography both academically and in practice, epitomized by the publication in 1921 of *The new world: problems in political geography* by the chief geography advisor to the American government, Isaiah Bowman.

We now come to a very controversial episode in political geography: GEOPOLITIK, or German GEOPOLITICS, which has recently come under renewed scrutiny (see Sandner, 1989). Drawing on ideas from Ratzel, Mackinder and others, Karl Haushofer attempted to develop a special kind of political geography as a policy tool for the German state. His links with the Nazi leadership made him notorious during the Second World War. Some contemporary writers saw in Haushofer's work the blueprint for German conquests, and Allied geographers were very strong in their condemnation of this embarrassing skeleton in their cupboard. In hindsight it now seems improbable that Haushofer had as much influence as contemporary enemies imagined (Bassin, 1987; Heske, 1987); he was in effect a convenient and colourful bogeyman. Nevertheless, memories are long and the aftermath of *Geopolitik* has been hotly debated. It was obviously a negative factor for the image of political geography, so much so that it has often been blamed for the subsequent decline of the subdiscipline. Once again this position has now been revised, so that political geography's fortunes are seen to be based on much broader criteria than any one particular episode in its history (Claval, 1984).

In the immediate aftermath of the Second World War, political geography retreated into the safer realm of study at the scale of the individual STATE. Although publicly overshadowed by the more spectacular geostrategic studies, state-scale analyses had always been a major component of political geography, the most notable prewar example of this genre being Derwent Whittlesey's *The earth and the state* of 1939. By the early 1950s we see a quickening of the trend towards shedding some of the environmentalism baggage of political geography and making the sub-discipline more narrowly systematic in character. Four important papers of the period (Hartshorne, 1950; Gottmann, 1951, 1952; Jones, 1954) attempted to provide a new rigorous framework for analysing the geography of political areas and the modern state in particular. Basically, these amounted to a theory of the geographical integration of states as a balance of CENTRIFUGAL AND CENTRIPE-TAL FORCES. It was from this point until about 1970, just after Berry's (1969) oft-quoted remark about political geography being 'a moribund backwater', that the subdiscipline seemed to lose its way. As a 'logical' division of human geography it continued to be widely taught in univer-sities, but there was a dearth of research to back up the teaching. Just as human geography as a whole was going through the excitements of the QUANTITATIVE REVOLUTION, political geography was fail-ing to attract its share of the latest 'new' geographers. It seemed to many to be stodgy and old-fashioned. Textbooks con-sisted of the geography of different bits of politics – BOUNDARIES, capital cities, TER-RITORY, administrative areas, elections, geostrategy, etc. – but with no particular coordination of these parts. In shedding its environmental basis, traditional political geography would seem to have lost its coherence (Cox, 1979). It is this which is the real cause of its postwar demise (Claval, 1984).

Although political geography was in the doldrums in the 1960s, this was certainly not true of its related social science, political science. Hence the most obvious solution to political geography's problems seemed to be to follow the example of human geography's other subdisciplines and borrow heavily from the theories of the relevant social science. This approach was adopted in the most ambitious text-books of the period (Jackson, 1964; Kasperson and Minghi, 1969), but with-out the expected success. Quite simply, political science was not able to furnish any LOCATION THEORY equivalent to that available in economics and sociology. Furthermore, political geography's

continued emphasis at the scale of the state was out of step with the intra-state and largely urban concerns of the new human geography (Claval, 1984). Hence, even the most sophisticated application of systems theory to political geography (Cohen and Rosenthal, 1971), although briefly influen-tial, could not overcome the subdiscipline's handicaps. Systems theory became widely advocated but rarely applied in a construc-tive manner (Burnett and Taylor, 1981, p. 46), and in the end the subdiscipline's revival came about more because of external influences than the efforts of the political geographers themselves.

The momentous political events of the late 1960s in Europe and the USA – anti-Vietnam War demonstrations, city riots and student rebellions – had a profound effect on all social science. In human geography they brought the political di-mension to the fore. This was expressed in three distinctive ways. First, ECONOMIC and SOCIAL GEOGRAPHY included political variables in their analyses and interpreta-tions. Second, as geography became more politicized, RADICAL GEOGRAPHY was created, firmly establishing a MARXIST GEOGRAPHY. Third, there was the revival of political geography itself. The first two trends are important for understanding modern political geography because very often they covered subjects which were also dealt with in political geography; itself producing, as it were, 'Political Geogra-phers' and 'political Geographers'. The distinctions between the subdisciplines of human geography were becoming ex-tremely fuzzy in the wake of the criticism of POSITIVISM in geography.

Initially, two main areas of research came to dominate the growing political geogra-phy of the 1970s. First, urban conflicts became a very common topic in human geography generally and, in political geo-graphy, location of 'goods' and 'bads' with their respective EXTERNALITIES became an important part of a new urban political geography (Cox, 1973; Cox et al., 1974). This has developed into a WELFARE GEO-GRAPHY approach to political geography (Cox, 1979). The second growth was ELECTORAL GEOGRAPHY, in which the techniques of the quantitative revolution were, at last, comprehensively applied in political geography (Taylor and Johnston, 1979). But this research growth did not overcome the uncoordinated nature of political geography; if anything, it enhanced the lack of coherence. The general reaction was to order political geography information into three separate scales for teaching and research; international or global, national, and intranational or urban. This framework has become almost ubiquitous among political geographers of all persuasions.

There has been a remarkable resurgence in political geography since about 1980, reflected in the establishment of the journal *Political Geography Quarterly* in 1982. Reynolds and Knight (1989, p. 582) identify a ' "new" political geography' in which 'there now is a concern for SOCIAL THEORY and a readiness to examine afresh such central concepts as STATE, SOCIETY, NATIONALISM, PLACE and SPACE' (see Taylor, 1991). Renewal of interest at scales other than that of the state is reflected in both important work at local and international scales (Agnew, 1987; Dalby, 1990) and in attempts to devise frameworks that provide a coherence to analysis across scales. The latter has been attempted through a POLITICAL ECONOMY approach utilizing Marxist theories of IMPERIALISM, the STATE and the LOCAL STATE (Short, 1989) and through WORLD-SYSTEMS ANALYSIS, in which SCALE is integral to the analysis (Taylor, 1989) because geographical scale is itself political (Taylor, 1982). The next challenge for the subdiscipline is to incorporate new politicizations of human geography through resurgent CULTURAL GEOGRAPHY (the politics of the meanings and uses of culture) and FEMINIST GEOGRAPHY (the politics of 'public' and 'private'). PJT

References

Agnew, J. A. 1987: *Place and politics*. Boston: Allen and Unwin.

Bassin, M. 1987: Race contra space: the conflict between German *Geopolitik* and National Socialism. *Pol. Geogr. Q.* 6, pp. 115–34.

Berry, B. J. L. 1969: Review of Russett, B. M. *International regions and the international system*. *Geogrl. Rev.* 59, pp. 450–1.

Bowman, I. 1921: *The new world: problems in political geography*. New York: World Book.

Burnett, A. D. and Taylor, P. J., eds 1981: *Political studies from spatial perspectives*. Chichester: John Wiley.

Claval, P. 1984: The coherence of political geography: perspectives on its past evolution and its future relevance. In Taylor, P. J. and House, J. W., eds, *Political geography: recent advances and future directions*. London: Croom Helm/Totowa, NJ: Barnes and Noble, pp. 8–24.

Cohen, S. B. and Rosenthal, L. D. 1971: A geographical model for political systems analysis. *Geogrl. Rev.* 61, pp. 5–31.

Cox, K. R. 1973: *Conflict, power and politics in the city: a geographic view*. New York: McGraw-Hill.

Cox, K. R. 1979: *Location and public problems. A political geography of the contemporary world*. Chicago: Maaroufa/Oxford: Blackwell.

Cox, K. R., Reynolds, D. R. and Rokkan, S., eds 1974: *Locational approaches to power and conflict*. Beverly Hills, CA: Sage.

Dalby, S. 1990: *Creating the second cold war*. London: Frames Pinter/New York: Guilford.

Dear, M. J. 1988: The postmodern challenge: reconstructing human geography. *Trans. Inst. Br. Geogr.* n.s. 13, pp. 262–74.

Gottmann, J. 1951: Geography and international relations. *World Pol.* 3, pp. 153–73.

Gottmann, J. 1952: The political partitioning of our world. *World Pol.* 4, pp. 512–19.

Hartshorne, R. 1950: The functional approach to political geography. *Ann. Ass. Am. Geogr.* 40, pp. 95–130.

Heske, H. 1987: Karl Haushofer: his role in German geopolitics and Nazi politics. *Pol. Geogr. Q.* 6, pp. 135–44.

Jackson, W. A. D. 1964: *Politics and geographic relationships*. Englewood Cliffs, NJ: Prentice-Hall.

Jones, S. B. 1954: A unified field theory of political geography. *Ann. Ass. Am. Geogr.* 44, pp. 111–23.

Kasperson, R. E. and Minghi, J. V., eds 1969: *The structure of political geography*. Chicago: Aldine.

Mackinder, H. J. 1887: On the scope and methods of a geography. *Proc. roy. Geogr. Soc.* 3, pp. 141–61.

Mackinder, H. J. 1904: The geographical pivot of history. *Geogrl. J.* 23, pp. 421–42.

Ratzel, F. 1897: *Politsche Geographie*. Munich: Oldenburg.

Reynolds, D. R. and Knight, D. B. 1989: Political geography. In Gaile, D. L. and

Willmott, C. J., eds, *Geography in America*, Columbus, OH: Merrill.

Sandner, G., ed. 1989: Special issue: Historical studies of German political geography. *Pol. Geogr. Q.*, 8, pp. 311–403.

Short, J. R. 1989: *An introduction to political geography*, second edition. London: Routledge and Kegan Paul.

Taylor, P. J. 1982: A materialist framework for political geography. *Trans. Inst. Br. Geogr.* n.s. 7, pp. 15–34.

Taylor, P. J. 1989: *Political geography: world-economy, nation–state and locality*, second edition. London: Longman/New York: John Wiley.

Taylor, P. J. 1991: Political geography within world-systems analysis. *Review* 14, pp. 387–402.

Taylor, P. J. and Johnston, R. J., eds 1979: *Geography of elections*. London: Penguin.

Whittlesey, D. 1939: *The earth and the state: a study of political geography*. New York: Holt.

Suggested Reading

Busteed, M. 1983: The developing nature of political geography. In Busteed, M., ed., *Developments in political geography*. London: Academic Press, pp. 1–68.

Claval (1984).

Pacione, M. 1985: *Progress in political geography*. London: Croom Helm.

Reynolds and Knight (1989).

Short (1989).

Taylor (1989, 1991).

pollution The release of substances in the environment in the wrong place or the wrong quantity – wrong because they degrade or damage the environment, as defined by some chosen criteria. The assessment of substance releases as pollution may reflect awareness of consequences ranging from damage to health, through economic losses to aesthetic nuisance. A number of widely publicized episodes since the Second World War have been instrumental in widening the scope of ENVIRONMENTALISM from an earlier focus on resource depletion to incorporate pollution issues. More sporadic and localized concerns about pollution are far from new, however, as centuries of concern about London smoke pollution (Brimblecombe, 1987) and occupational health and nineteenth-century fears of 'miasma' indicate.

Pollutants of contemporary concern take a wide number of different forms, from the biological through the chemical to the physical and radioactive, affecting all of the principal environmental media (air, water, soil and biota). Attention once focused on concentrated point sources of pollution, usually representing production processes: the sometimes equal or greater importance of dispersed sources, often representing consumption emissions, is increasingly recognized, and such sources pose greater difficulties in detection and management. Pollutants operate at a variety of spatial and temporal scales. Some of them – chlorofluorocarbons (CFCs), which deplete stratospheric ozone, for example – are extremely long-lived and globally dispersed. Others – tropospheric ozone associated with urban smog, for instance – are highly reactive and thus short-lived and local in their impacts. Recognition of the importance of such continental- or global-scale pollutants as CFCs, carbon dioxide (contributing to GLOBAL WARMING), and ACID RAIN has been instrumental in the development of concern over issues of global environmental change that require international solutions.   JEm

Reference

Brimblecombe, P. 1987. *The big smoke: a history of air pollution in London since medieval times*. London: Routledge.

Suggested Reading

Brown, H. S., Kasperson, R. E. and Raymond, S. 1990. Trace pollutants. In Turner, B. L. II et al., eds, *The earth as transformed by human action*, pp. 437–54. Cambridge: Cambridge University Press.

Holdgate, M. 1979. *A perspective of environmental pollution*. Cambridge: Cambridge University Press.

population accounts An advanced form of spatial demographic analysis which takes fully into account MIGRATION between regions, FERTILITY and MORTALITY. In the past, population analysis and projections have typically been carried out for a single region only, connected via net MIGRATION to the outside world, but 'accounting' methods allow the building of population models for multiregional systems within which gross migration can be represented explicitly. The life histories of people are accounted for by demographic states. Accounting has great potential for integrating SPATIAL ANALYSIS and demography, thus serving as a vital part of models of urban and regional systems, as a basis for population projection, and as a basis for estimating demand for facilities of all kinds.   PEO

Suggested Reading

Rees, P. H. and Wilson, A. G. 1977: *Spatial population analysis.* London: Edward Arnold/ New York: Academic Press.

Woods, R. and Rees, P., eds 1986: *Population structures and models: developments in spatial demography.* London: Allen and Unwin.

population density The number of people in relation to the SPACE that they occupy. The simplest measure, the crude density of population, is the number of people per square kilometre or other unit area, and is most useful for small units such as counties or parishes rather than national states or continents, where internal environmental conditions vary markedly. More refined density measures may be calculated by relating numbers to cultivated or cultivable land or to other economic measures such as national income. Equally, for urban areas, measures such as persons per room or per house are useful refinements.   PEO

Suggested Reading

Clarke, J. I. 1972: *Population geography,* second edition. Oxford: Pergamon, ch. 4.

population geography The study of the ways in which spatial variations in the distribution, composition, MIGRATION and growth of population are related to the nature of places. A concern with spatial variation has been the geographer's distinctive contribution to population studies, and comparison is frequently made with demographers, who are much more interested in patterns of birth, death and marriage *per se*, neglecting the influence of migration and of spatial variations in general. Yet increasingly, and encouragingly, the boundaries between geography and other disciplines interested in population matters – economics, sociology, history, psychology and biology as well as

demography – are blurred. Thus, it is no longer accurate to think of population geographers as being concerned exclusively with distribution, since recent years have seen an interest in, for example, regional and national levels of FERTILITY and MORTALITY, detailed patterns of disease DIFFUSION and advanced modelling of interregional population growth (see Findlay and Graham, 1991). There is also a growing interest in the application of social theory to population geography. Nevertheless, there is still more concern with migration and spatial variation than with other matters. Within the wider discipline of geography, population study has always ranked prominently. Most university departments offer a separate course in population geography, while much research and teaching is also subsumed under URBAN, SOCIAL or HISTORICAL GEOGRAPHY.

FERTILITY, MORTALITY and MIGRATION are at the root of any studies of population growth and composition. So, for any area:

$$p^{t + n} = p^t + B^{t, t + n} - D^{t, t + n} + NM^{t, t + n},$$

where, given a population at time t (p^t), that population after a period of time from t to $t + n$ ($p^{t + n}$) will be the result of an increase due to births during the period ($B^{t, t + n}$), a decrease due to deaths ($D^{t, t + n}$) and either an increase or a decrease due to net migration ($NM^{t, t + n}$).

The study of overall population growth has concerned geographers working at a number of scales. Some have been interested in, for example, the history of world population growth and the relative prospects for both developing and developed countries; others have devoted attention to the experience of individual countries and regions. Patterns of growth through space and time (see DEMOGRAPHIC TRANSITION) have always been considered fundamental to the understanding of the wider geographical processes of URBANIZATION, INDUSTRIALIZATION and use of RESOURCES. Yet the element in the above equation to which geographers have given most attention is MIGRATION: estimating net and gross flows at all scales; looking at relationships of direction and distance (see DISTANCE DELAY); building models of interregional flows; and analysing economic and social causes and consequences. Studies of migration have included international movements, and rural–urban, urban–urban and intra-urban flows, as well as seasonal and diurnal movements. Migration has further been seen as an integral part of the study of the SOCIAL GEOGRAPHY of the city (see URBAN GEOGRAPHY). Geographers have also sought to make contributions to migration theory, although perhaps the most significant efforts have been devoted to relationships with distance and the recent development of POPULATION ACCOUNTS. They have naturally made use of myriad statistical sources, but their concern with recent and contemporary conditions has led them to rely mainly on, and make sophisticated use of, national CENSUSES.

The study of the other elements in the demographic equation, fertility and mortality, has not been neglected (see MEDICAL GEOGRAPHY). It is a fair judgement to say that geographers have neither made full use of, nor significantly contributed to, pure demographic method. Rather, attention has been devoted to highlighting the spatial dimension of patterns and their links with environmental or social conditions, e.g. the study of the spatial incidence of mortality and disease (see Howe, 1976). Geographers have also recently begun to take an interest in historical demography, reconstructing patterns of fertility and mortality, as well as household and family formation, through techniques such as FAMILY RECONSTITUTION.

The resultant patterns of population distribution and density have long been an object of geographical enquiry. Densities have been discussed in relation not only to general environmental conditions but also with respect to agriculture and economic potential. At a broad scale there has been concern with population growth, distribution and resources, e.g. in the countries of the THIRD WORLD, and increasingly with projections of these relationships. Population geography has also spread its net more widely to encompass population composition and structure. This ranges from studies of AGE AND SEX STRUCTURE and its implications for demographic and economic change to studies of marital status, occupation, education and religious beliefs. (See also OPTIMUM POPULATION, STABLE POPULATION.) PEO

References

Findlay, A. M. and Graham, E. 1991: The challenge facing population geography. *Progr. hum. Geogr.* 15, pp. 149–62.

Howe, G. M. 1976: *Man, environment and disease in Britain: a medical geography of Britain through the ages.* London: Penguin/New York: Barnes and Noble.

Suggested Reading

Alonso, W., ed. 1987: *Population in an interacting world.* Cambridge, MA: Harvard University Press.

Clarke, J. I., ed. 1984: *Geography and population – approaches and applications.* Oxford: Pergamon.

Jones, H. R. 1990: *Population geography,* second edition. London: Paul Chapman.

Lutz, W., ed. 1990: *Future demographic trends in Europe and North America.* London: Academic Press.

Woods, R. I. (1979): *Population analysis in geography.* London: Longman.

Woods, R. I. 1982: *Theoretical population geography.* London: Longman.

Woods, R. and Rees, P., eds 1986: *Population structures and models: developments in spatial demography.* London: Allen and Unwin.

population potential A measure of the nearness or ACCESSIBILITY of a given mass of people to a point. The term is derived from SOCIAL PHYSICS, and the concept is closely related to that of the GRAVITY MODEL, in that it relates mass (population) to distance, but whereas the gravity model deals with the separate relationships between pairs of points, population potential encompasses the influence of all other points on a particular one. The potential exerted on a point (V_i) is defined as:

$$V_i = \sum_{j=1}^{k} P_j / d_{ij}, \qquad j \neq i$$

where P_j is the population at the jth point, d_{ij} is the distance between points i and j, and summation is over all k points. (Most measures of potential include P_i and estimate d_{ij} where $i = j$.) The population potential at point i is thus the sum of the ratios of populations at all points to the distances to those points (d_{ij} may be raised to some power to incorporate the frictions of distance; see DISTANCE DECAY). Isopleth maps of population potentials have been produced at various scales, to indicate spatial variations in general accessibility. Population may be replaced by, for example, purchasing power (P_j becomes PP_j) to give a measure of the market potential – the accessibility to customers – at point i.   PEO

Suggested Reading
Stewart, J. Q. and Warntz, W. 1968: The physics of population distributions. In Berry, B. J. L. and Marble, D. F., eds, *Spatial analysis: a reader in statistical geography*. Englewood Cliffs, NJ: Prentice-Hall, pp. 130–46.

population projection An estimate of future population size or composition based on the extrapolation of past demographic trends. A distinction may be drawn between a projection and a FORECAST; the latter is the term used when demographic variables are set in a more general socioeconomic framework. The simplest form of projection is that based on extrapolation of the past growth of the total population, but modern projections tend to take into account detailed trends in FERTILITY, MORTALITY and MIGRATION.   PEO

Suggested Reading
Woods, R. I. 1979: *Population analysis in geography*. London: Longman, ch. 9.

population pyramid A diagrammatic representation of the AGE AND SEX STRUCTURE of a population (see the figure). Generally, the vertical axis represents age groups and the horizontal axis indicates the numerical or percentage distribution by sex. The population pyramid is a reflection of past and current demographic trends. A population whose pyramid has a broad base and narrows quickly upwards, for example, is young and

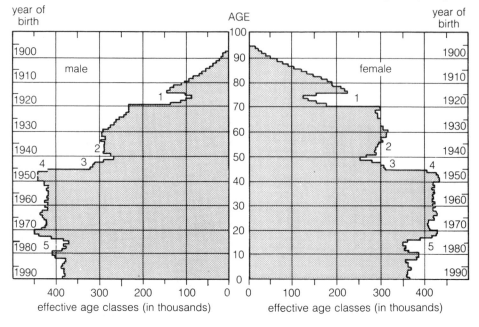

1   Shortfall in births due to the 1914–18 war (empty classes)
2   Passage of empty classes to age of fecundity
3   Shortfall in births due to the 1939–45 war
4   'baby boom'
5   Non-replacement of generations

population pyramid   *The population of France: provisional evaluation as of 1 January 1991 (Populations et Sociétés. 1991).*

highly fertile. The diagram for France is more typical of populations of the developed world. It shows the general influence of ageing which, because of lower male LIFE EXPECTANCY, produces a strong excess of women aged over 70. The recent decline in birth rates is also evident in the shortfall in those aged under 15. The demographic consequences of war are also apparent in the pyramid, e.g. the sharp decline in births during the First World War is reflected in the shortfall in the 70–75 age group. PEO

Reference

Populations et Sociétés 1991: No. 255, March, p. 3. INSEE.

Suggested Reading

Peterson, W. 1975: *Population,* third edition. New York: Collier-Macmillan. ch. 3.

pork barrel An American term for the unequal distribution of PUBLIC GOODS in order to promote a party's or a candidate's re-election prospects. Although not exclusively American, the activity is particularly common there because of the individual nature of much campaigning for Congressional office: the term is also applied more generally to describe any apparent government favouritism of a certain area. (The term's origin lies in the popular delicacy of the 'scrapings' of the barrels in which salted pork was preserved: to get the pork barrel scrapings was to get preferential treatment!) RJJ

Suggested Reading

Johnston, R. J. 1980: *The geography of federal spending in the United States.* Chichester: John Wiley.

positive discrimination A policy designed to favour disadvantaged groups within society and so to reduce, if not eliminate, inequalities. Some of these policies are targeted at particular areas (and are widely known as 'area-based policies'), either because the service is delivered on an areal basis (e.g. a NEIGHBOURHOOD school) or because it is the most effective way of reaching the group to benefit (e.g. defining those eligible for house improvement grants). Spatial targeting often means that some of the intended beneficiaries receive no advantage, because they live outside the defined areas, whereas residents of the targeted areas do benefit whether or not they are deserving cases. RJJ

positivism A philosophy of science originally proposed by Auguste Comte in the 1820s and 1830s, drawing upon the earlier ideas of Saint-Simon, the primary purpose of which was to distinguish *science* from metaphysics and religion. There are various versions of positivism, and its history in both philosophy and the (natural and social) sciences is complex (see Bryant, 1985; Kolakowski, 1972). In the most general terms, Comtean positivism determined the *scientific status* of its statements through five steps:

(1) Scientific statements were to be grounded in a direct, immediate and empirically accessible experience of the world, and observation statements were therefore privileged over theoretical ones (see EMPIRICISM): they were the leading particulars of scientific inquiry and could be made independently of any theoretical statements that might subsequently be constructed around them.

(2) Scientific observations had to be repeatable, and their generality was to be ensured by a unitary scientific method accepted and routinely drawn upon by the scientific community as a whole.

(3) Science would then advance through the formal construction of theories which, if empirically verified, would assume the status of scientific LAWS.

(4) Those scientific laws would have a strictly technical function, in that they would reveal the effectiveness or even the necessity – but emphatically not the desirability – of specific conjunctions of events: in other words, they had to take the form 'If A, then B' (laws of constant conjunction or 'Humean laws').

(5) Scientific laws would be progressively unified and integrated into a single and incontrovertible system of knowledge and truth (or, rather, absolute Truth).

The founders of the modern discipline of geography often relied on conceptions of science which were denied by positivism: Humboldt rejected the brute empiricism on which Comte's system was built, for example, and elaborated a sophisticated philosophical system in its place (Bowen, 1979). Yet much of the subsequent history of geography was dominated by the (often tacit) acceptance of some or all of these assumptions, so that when they were eventually formalized during the QUANTITATIVE REVOLUTION of the 1950s and 1960s the so-called 'New Geography' which resulted was 'less of a radical departure than a logical extension of ideas which were already generally accepted by many geographers' (Guelke, 1978; see also Gregory, 1978). In so far as these were in any sense philosophically novel, they derived their originality from a commitment to LOGICAL POSITIVISM.

The introduction of the prefix 'logical' signalled a break with the classical Comtean model, which had been made in the 1930s by the VIENNA CIRCLE. The basis of logical positivism was a distinction between the following:

(a) *Analytic statements*, i.e. *a priori* propositions the truth of which was guaranteed by their internal definitions and connections. These constituted the domain of the *formal sciences*, logic and mathematics, which (strictly speaking) seemed to have no place in a Comtean model which required all scientific statements to rely on empirical verification.

(b) *Synthetic statements*, i.e. propositions the truth of which still had to be established empirically through hypothesis testing. This 'principle of verification' was supposed to be the hallmark of the *factual sciences*, but it was soon challenged by Popper's principle of FALSIFICATION. Instead of making every effort to prove an HYPOTHESIS, Popper believed that the scientist's task was to try to disprove it: if it stood up, then the hypothesis could be accepted, but only for the time being (see CRITICAL RATIONALISM).

The revisions provided empirical inquiry with a more secure basis than the Comtean model, and the 'New Geography' was readily accommodated within their framework: the philosophical high point of this tradition was Harvey's *Explanation in geography* (1969). The major omission within this conception of geography was

the development of deductive–nomological explanation and a considered recognition of the importance of Popper's proposals for the business of hypothesis testing: certainly, much of the early work in SPATIAL SCIENCE depended on inductive–statistical rather than deductive–mathematical methods (Wilson, 1972). But the overriding concern with derivation, validation and integration of general theorems of spatial organization was an unequivocally positivist project (see LOCATION THEORY). The debate over EXCEPTIONALISM had established the legitimacy of a NOMOTHETIC conception of geography, and the search for models of SPATIAL STRUCTURE and methods of SPATIAL ANALYSIS was soon widened by the incorporation of models and techniques drawn from other sciences which were also predicated on positivism; for example, classical mechanics and NEO-CLASSICAL ECONOMICS. When research effort in human geography moved on from spatial form towards the study of generative PROCESS, much of its energy was still contained within the positivist tradition; for example, the development of BEHAVIOURAL GEOGRAPHY. But the discipline eventually broke through those bounds to confront a series of rival philosophical systems. The critique of positivism which followed was both fierce and decisive: 'almost every aspect of the prescribed method can be shown to be open to question' (Bowen, 1979; cf. Hay, 1979). This involved an assault on four main fronts of positivist EPISTEMOLOGY:

(a) Its *empiricism*: the relationship between observation statements and theoretical languages was shown to be much more problematic than positivism had allowed, so that alternative modes of statistical inference were required to allow for varying degrees of theoretical co-determination, such as Bayesian theory, and new philosophical and theoretical systems were used to provide a more incisive exposure of the structures of social life in time and space (see REALISM; STRUCTURAL MARXISM; STRUCTURALISM).

(b) Its *exclusivity*: the assumption that the 'objective' methods of the natural sciences could be extended into the domain of the humanities and the social sciences to provide a self-sufficient and unitary system of inquiry was challenged, and the application of essentially interpretative or QUALITATIVE METHODS showed the importance of recovering meanings, intentions and values as an essential moment in human geographical enquiry (see HERMENEUTICS; HUMANISTIC GEOGRAPHY; PHENOMENOLOGY). At the same time, those 'subjective' concerns were found to be important in the constitution of the natural sciences too, where enquiries also involved questions of meaning, interpretation and rhetoric (Woolgar, 1988).

(c) Its *autonomy*: it was no longer possible to claim that science was insulated from social life, offering 'neutral' and 'value-free' knowledge, and the embeddedness of scientific enquiry in social life was seen to require an explicit reflection on the ethics and politics of human geography: on its various 'regimes of truth' and the ways in which they are imbricated in wider relations of power and knowledge (see CRITICAL THEORY; DISCOURSE; IDEOLOGY; POSTCOLONIALISM; POSTSTRUCTURALISM).

(d) Its *universality*: even the natural sciences could be shown to be context-dependent in various ways, so that the extension and generalization of their findings becomes a precarious, negotiated *achievement* and not a given (Rouse, 1987). The same applied *a fortiori* to the humanities and the social sciences, and human geography has in consequence been obliged to recognize that explanations and understandings arrived at in one setting cannot be transferred to other settings without considerable scrutiny and often substantial reconstruction: in this sense human geographies, even when they address global concerns, are 'local knowledges' (cf. Barnes, 1989; see also ETHNOCENTRISM).

What these philosophical counter-claims amounted to was a reinstatement of the social foundations and responsibilities of intellectual enquiry and, more generally, a refusal to separate 'science' from DISCOURSE. While many human geographers no doubt continue to think of themselves as social *scientists*, many do not (the

connections between human geography and the humanities are now probably stronger than at any time since the Second World War). In either case, however, probably very few count themselves as positivists. The continued exploration of post-positivist geographies has: (a) dimmed the old enthusiasm for the unrestrained application of quantitative techniques as ends in themselves (although analytical methods continue to be important in many areas of non-positivist geography); (b) reinvigorated a number of areas which had hitherto been characterized by an unreflective positivism (notably LOCATION THEORY); and (c) helped to identify new avenues of enquiry throughout the discipline and beyond (e.g. FEMINIST GEOGRAPHY).   DG

References

Barnes, T. 1989: Place, space and theories of economic value: contextualism and essentialism in economic geography. *Trans. Inst. Br. Geogr.* n.s. 14, pp. 299–316.

Bowen, M. J. 1979: Scientific method – after positivism. *Aust. geogr. Stud.* 17, pp. 210–16.

Bryant, C. 1985: *Positivism in social theory and research.* London: Macmillan.

Gregory, D. 1978: *Ideology, science and human geography.* London: Hutchinson.

Guelke, L. 1978: Geography and logical positivism. In Herbert, D. and Johnston, R. J., eds, *Geography and the urban environment*, volume 1. New York: John Wiley, pp. 35–61.

Harvey, D. 1969: *Explanation in geography.* London: Edward Arnold.

Hay, A. 1979: Positivism in human geography: response to critics. In Herbert, D. and Johnston, R. J., eds, *Geography and the urban environment*, volume 2. New York: John Wiley, pp. 1–26.

Kolakowski, L. 1972: *Positivist philosophy: from Hume to the Vienna Circle.* London: Penguin.

Rouse, J. 1987: *Knowledge and power: toward a political philosophy of science.* Ithaca, NY: Cornell University Press.

Wilson, A. G. 1972: Theoretical geography: some speculations. *Trans Inst. Br. Geogr.* 57, pp. 31–44.

Woolgar, S. W. 1988: *Science: the very idea.* Andover, UK: Tavistock.

Suggested Reading

Bowen (1979).

Gregory (1978), chs 1 and 2.

Hay (1979).

possibilism The view that the physical environment provides the opportunity for a range of possible human responses and that people have considerable discretion to choose between them. Although elements of possibilism can be found in the work of many geographers (e.g. Bowman and Sauer) its formal enunciation is usually identified with the French school of human geography, and in particular with the encounter between Durkheim, Ratzel and Vidal de la Blache at the turn of the century. In effect, Vidal mediated between the two protagonists. He rejected Durkheim's proposed reduction of geography to social MORPHOLOGY by insisting that the human being 'joins in nature's game' and that the *milieu externe* was 'a partner not a slave of human activity'; and while he shared Ratzel's belief that society ought not to be left 'suspended in the air' he was quick to dispel any lingering determinism by insisting that 'nature is never more than an adviser' and that the *milieu interne* revealed the human being as 'at once both active and passive'. These mediations were doubly important because Vidal's scheme led neither to a radical possibilism nor to ENVIRONMENTAL DETERMINISM; rather, his was essentially a neo-Kantian philosophy (see KANTIANISM) which embraced 'the organizing freedom of [the human being], bounded by the realities of the mechanisms of the natural realm' (see Berdoulay, 1976: cf. Kirk's BEHAVIOURAL ENVIRONMENT and PHENOMENAL ENVIRONMENT). Vidal believed that whereas SOCIETY and NATURE were usually represented as 'two adversaries in a duel', the human being was in fact 'part of living creation' and 'its most active collaborator'. And it was this DIALECTIC which he subsumed in the concept of the *GENRE DE VIE*, wherein the moments of a recursive creativity could be both powerful *facteurs géographiques* and yet also vital *agents de formation humaine* (see Buttimer, 1971).

Vidal's programme was endorsed by the historian Lucien Febvre in a famous phrase: 'there are not necessities but everywhere possibilities; and man as master of these possibilities is the judge of their use' (Febvre, 1932). Febvre's intervention was the occasion of a sustained series of misrepresentations of the totality of Vidal's thought (Lacoste, 1985). And while Febvre's commentary enlarged Vidal's view of the power of HUMAN AGENCY – he had regarded geography as a natural rather than a social science – possibilism could still legitimately be regarded as a qualification rather than a negation of environmental determinism. Yet its doctrine became so distorted that by the 1950s it could be seen as a threat to the scientific status of geography as an autonomous discipline. First, the doctrine held science to depend on determinism and hence human geography required laws 'similar in stringency to those of physical science' (Martin, 1951); but this could be met by the recognition that the traditional emphasis on *contingence* and *probabilité* was consistent with modern physics (Jones, 1956; see also Lukermann, 1965). Second, the distinctiveness of geography was held to depend on (and be defined by) the relation between society and nature, in which the physical 'foundation must in large part control the superstructure': 'the logical end of possibilism is economic geography with a scatter of place-names' (Spate, 1957); but this was countered by a neo-determinism (PROBABILISM) and then overtaken by the QUANTITATIVE REVOLUTION and its redefinition of geography as SPATIAL SCIENCE.

More recently, this redefinition has itself been challenged by the supposed revivification of the Vidalian tradition through the rise of HUMANISTIC GEOGRAPHY; yet this often overlooks Vidal's materialism and relegates the physical environment to a secondary role in the society–nature relationship, rather than the equal role which possibilism originally envisaged (but see Pred, 1984). **DG**

References

Berdoulay, V. 1976: French possibilism as a form of neo-Kantian philosophy. *Proc. Ass. Am. Geogr.* 8, pp. 176–9.

Buttimer, A. 1971: *Society and milieu in the French geographic tradition.* Chicago: Rand McNally.

Febvre, L. 1932: *A geographical introduction to history.* London: Kegan Paul Trench Trübner.

Jones, E. 1956: Cause and effect in human geography. *Ann. Ass. Am. Geogr.* 46, pp. 369–77.

Lacoste, Y. 1985: *La géographie, ça sert, d'abord, à faire la guerre*, Paris: La Découverte.

Lukermann, F. 1965: The calcul des probabiliti̇és and the Ecole Française de Géographie. *Can. Geogr.* 9, pp. 128–37.

Martin, A. F. 1951: The necessity for determinism. *Trans. Inst. Br. Geogr.* 17, pp. 1–12.

Pred, A. 1984: Place as historically-contingent process: structuration and the time-geography of becoming places. *Ann. Ass. Am. Geogr.* 74, pp. 279–97.

Spate, O. H. K. 1957: How determined is possibilism? *Georgl. Stud.* 4, pp. 3–12.

Suggested Reading

Buttimer (1971).

Lukermann (1965).

Montefiore, A. G. and Williams, W. M. 1955: Determinism and possibilism: a search for clarification. *Geogrl. Stud.* 2, pp. 1–11.

post-Fordism A collection of workplace practices, modes of industrial organization and institutional forms identified with the period since the mid-1970s, following the era referred to as Fordist (see FORDISM). It is characterized by the application of production methods considered to be more flexible than those of the Fordist era. These may include more versatile, programmable machines, labour that is more flexibly deployed (in terms of both quantity and tasks performed), vertical disintegration of large corporations, greater use of inter-firm relations – such as subcontracting, strategic alliances and JUST-IN-TIME PRODUCTION – and a closer integration of product development, marketing and production. Accompanying these changes in production and industrial organization is a new set of enabling institutions to restructure labour–management relations, labour training, competition law and financial markets. Post-Fordism may also be conceived as a response to the crisis conditions that developed toward the end of the fordist period (a rupture of the postwar compromise between owners and workers, a breaking of the link between wages and productivity gains, and a lack of balance between the aggregate productive capabilities of the economy and the aggregate purchasing power of workers as consumers). Consequently, the classic

geographical pattern of economic activity associated with Fordist production (particularly the spatial separation of product development from the actual production of standardized goods) may be contrasted with a post-fordist geography characterized by strong AGGLOMERATION tendencies, to facilitate interaction between vertically disintegrated functions. (See also FLEXIBLE ACCUMULATION; PRODUCTION COMPLEX; TRANSACTIONAL ANALYSIS.)

MSG

Suggested Reading

Gertler, M. S. 1988: The limits to flexibility: comments on the post-Fordist vision of production and its geography. *Trans. Inst. Br. Geogr.* n.s. 13(4), pp. 419–32.

post-industrial city A city with an employment profile that favours growth of the quaternary sector; that is, jobs in the professions, management, administration and skilled technical areas (cf. INFORMATION CITY). The profile is reinforced by a downtown skyline of office towers and public institutions. Its middle-class ambience may be reflected in a distinctive politics charged with 'a responsible social ethos . . ., the demand for more amenities, for greater beauty and a better quality of life in the arrangement of our cities' (Bell, 1973, p. 367). Such a city is also characterized by a declining manufacturing workforce and, not infrequently, by a significant public-sector as well as a private-sector presence. Despite its middle-class ambience, income inequality is a serious problem, resulting from the dual labour market of a service economy, which includes a significant number of poorly paid service workers (cf. SEGMENTED LABOUR MARKET). The working poor and unemployed are particularly disadvantaged in a city geared to middle-class consumption, for example in the housing market, where an expanding downtown, GENTRIFICATION and inflating land values may contribute to serious problems of housing affordability. Research more recently has tended to emphasize the growing issue of social polarization in post-industrial cities, which has developed in tandem with neoconservative economic policy in the

1980s and early 1990s. (See also POST-INDUSTRIAL SOCIETY.)   DL

Reference

Bell, D. 1973: *The coming of post-industrial society.* New York: Basic Books.

Suggested Reading

Ley, D. 1980: Liberal ideology and the post-industrial city. *Ann. Ass. Am. Geogr.,* 70, pp. 238–58.

Mollenkopf, J. and Castells, M. eds 1991: *Dual city: restructuring New York.* New York: Russell Sage Foundation.

Savitch H. 1988: *Post-industrial cities: politics and planning in New York, Paris and London.* Princeton, NJ: Princeton University Press.

post-industrial society A widely used concept that, at its most general level, refers to an occupational transformation toward a white-collar, service-oriented workforce in advanced societies, with a pivotal role played by specialized knowledge in both the economy and in government. These propositions provide common ground for a number of more or less related theoretical departures. First, according to the French theorist Alaine Touraine (1971), the holders of theoretical knowledge become a class in ascendancy, a technocracy which extends its alienating control over ever-expanding domains of everyday life. Touraine's views have much in common with the antagonism towards the 'military–industrial complex' of government and corporations held by the student movement during the late 1960s. The critique of the rationalization of society also has links with his contemporaries, Habermas (1970) and Marcuse (1964), and with Weber's earlier portrait of the 'iron cage' of bureaucracy. A second theoretical departure is represented by a wide range of authors who emphasize the pervasive and central role played by the generation and transmission of specialized information in advanced societies. A third stream of work discusses the rise of a *new middle class* employed in the advanced services, and the implications of their growth in cultural and political fields (Gouldner, 1979; Ley, 1993).

The most influential writer on post-industrial society is Daniel Bell (1973) who, if he did not coin the term, is certainly responsible for its wide dissemination. In an ambitious synthesis, Bell attempted to describe the forward trajectory of advanced SOCIETIES (notably the USA) in terms of developments in social structure, CULTURE and politics. Bell posits theoretical knowledge to be the motive force in production in post-industrial society. As a result, the university is theoretically a more privileged institution than the factory. Moreover (and here Bell appears to be in accord with Habermas), a knowledge theory of value is stated to displace a labour theory of value (cf. CRITICAL THEORY). Consequently (and its most readily recognized characteristic) a post-industrial society shows a tendency towards service employment and the growth of a knowledge class in the favoured quaternary sector of the workforce. In politics, Bell sees a clear tendency towards the public household, with a managed economy and society. In culture, he is profoundly pessimistic of antinomian tendencies in both the arts and popular culture (Bell, 1976). Indeed, part of the complexity of his argument is a disjunction that he observes between a progressively more disciplined economy and a regressively less disciplined culture. This disjunction extends to his own normative position, as he describes himself to be a liberal in economics, a socialist in politics and a conservative in culture.

The breadth and influence of Bell's thesis has attracted considerable commentary. Despite his claim to hold a personal politics which varies by domain, he has often been portrayed as a leader of the intellectual avant-garde of neoconservatism (Habermas, 1989). This label may be substantiated in the realm of culture, but in politics the centralizing tendencies of neoconservatism in the 1980s and the assault upon the public household contradict both Bell's predictions and his predilections. If the post-industrial thesis contains more subtlety than is sometimes suggested, Bell's original statement, like all streams of SOCIAL THEORY, is also a child of its times. Published in the year in which the postwar boom ended, it is written from an optimistic middle-class and Western perspective, where CONFLICT and scarcity do not provide major problematics. Ironically, in these terms the thesis is not nearly sociological enough.

Nonetheless, the post-industrial thesis deserves respect both for its breadth and as a seminal source of subsequent research. Moreover, Bell's observations on the changing social structure and the centrality of science, technology and a knowledge class seem to fit empirical trends. Former critics now credit the post-industrial thesis with having greater predictive power than the competing deskilling argument of the 1970s in forecasting the development of the labour force in advanced societies over the past 20 years (Wright and Martin, 1987; Myles, 1988). As an heuristic, then, the thesis of post-industrial society throws a useful if partial light upon significant processes of social change. (See also POST-INDUSTRIAL CITY.)   DL

References

Bell, D. 1973: *The coming of post-industrial society.* New York: Basic Books.

Bell, D. 1976: *The cultural contradictions of capitalism.* New York: Basic Books.

Gouldner, A. 1979: *The future of intellectuals and the rise of the new class.* New York: Seabury Press.

Habermas, J. 1970: *Toward a rational society.* London: Heinemann.

Habermas, J. 1989: *The new conservatism.* Cambridge, MA: MIT Press.

Ley, D. 1993: *The new middle class and the remaking of the central city.* Oxford: Oxford University Press.

Marcuse, H. 1964: *One-dimensional man.* Boston: Beacon Press.

Myles, J. 1988: The expanding middle: some Canadian evidence on the deskilling debate. *Can. Rev. Sociol. Anthropol.* 25, pp. 335–64.

Touraine, A. 1971: *The post-industrial society.* New York: Random House.

Wright, E. and Martin, B. 1987: The transformation of the American class structure, 1960–1980. *Am. J. Soc.* 87, pp. 1–29.

Suggested Reading

Bell (1973).

post-Marxism Not so much a movement or a theoretical position as a reference point for the various efforts over the past two decades to overcome what are seen by some as the debilitating limitations of 'conventional', 'traditional' or 'classical' MARXISM as social theory, as politics and as practice. This 'crisis of Marxism' was thrown into stark relief by the waning role of organized revolutionary parties in continental Europe in the 1970s and by the rise of Eurocommunism, and more recently by the collapse of state SOCIALISMS in the Soviet Union and Eastern Europe. On a theoretical plane, various poststructuralisms associated with the work of Michel Foucault, Ernesto Laclau and Jacques Derrida – and more generally with the ascendancy of cultural studies and feminisms of many hues (Brantlinger, 1990) – have been critical of Marxism for its grand vision (its 'totalizing discourse'), for its crude economic determinism, and its class reductionism (see CLASS; DISCOURSE; EPISTEMOLOGY; POSTSTRUCTURALISM). In this sense, the identity politics and new social movements of the 1980s, the rise of discourse theory and what Perry Anderson (1983) called the absolutization of language, and the genesis of debates within the political Left over Marxist practice (reflected, for example, in the appearance of the journal *Marxism Today* in Britain and the debate over 'new times' and 'new true socialisms') are all part and parcel of what some see as post-Marxism, and hence of a crisis of Marxism itself.

Post-Marxism is a loose, portmanteau term typically used to refer to wide-ranging debates over causality, determinism, human agency and power from a variety of often incompatible theoretical positions (Laclau and Mouffe, 1985; Geras, 1987). A fundamental line of post-Marxist critique points to the inherent deficiencies of identifying CAPITALISM's logic or 'laws of motion'; it is, in short, a rationalist and evolutionary discourse steeped in late-nineteenth-century concepts and teleology. Marxism is thus mechanistic – history is simply a succession of stages and modes of production – and suffers from an enormous overdose of what Laclau and Mouffe (1985) call economism and class reduction. In this view, Marxism reduces the polity directly and unequivocably to the economy; Hindess and Hirst (1977) calls this the 'economic monist causality of

Marxism'. Booth (1985) and Corbridge (1989), for example, have launched similar critiques of Marxism and neo-Marxism as they have addressed THIRD WORLD development and DEVELOPMENT geography, emphasizing what they see as the pitfalls of capital-logic reasoning and of the epistemological weaknesses of 'rationalism and structural causality'. Efforts during the 1970s to upgrade Marxism theoretically – the project of Althusser and Balibar (1970), for example – are seen as interesting failures.

Post-Marxist theory has developed in several (non-unitary) directions. First came the efforts by John Roemer, John Elster, Adam Pzeworski, Pranab Bardhan and others (see Carling, 1986; Roemer, 1986) to make the philosophical and methodological basis of Marxism more rigorous scientifically (so-called ANALYTICAL MARXISM), a project which endeavours to fuse Marxism with RATIONAL CHOICE and METHODOLOGICAL INDIVIDUALISM. Second, Barry Hindess and Paul Hirst (1977), Ernesto Laclau and Chantal Mouffe (1985), Stuart Hall and others emphasize the fact that there is no necessary correspondence between economics and politics, and hence between the working class and socialism (see DISCOURSE; POSTSTRUCTURALISM). The relative autonomy of the political and ideological planes produces a concern with a multiplicity of popular struggles around universal human goals and an attendant concern with discourse and non-class practices (for example, identity politics – SEXUALITY and RACE). This post-Marxism rests, then, on a different notion of causality and on a presumption that capitalism requires conditions of existence that are not simply determined by the relations of production. A third approach is associated with the so-called REGULATION SCHOOL, which attempts to avoid teleology and essentialism by focusing on mesolevel concepts, and in particular on the historically specific institutional configurations of capital, labour and the state which give rise to distinctive, but unstable, regimes of accumulation (Lipietz, 1987).

Corbridge (1989) has, with a very substantial number of caveats, attempted to outline the lineaments of post-Marxism. It shares with classical Marxism a 'materialist ontology', a commitment to causal analysis and to a concept of determination. But it departs from this tradition in so far as it rejects the idea of exclusivism; in other words, that Marxism is epistemologically privileged and that primacy must be lent to the economic. Opposed to functionalist accounts of POWER, the STATE and CIVIL SOCIETY, post-Marxism draws insights from non-Marxism (FEMINISM, DISCOURSE theory and neo-Weberianism) and wishes to advance Marxism in terms of a compelling scientific methodology.

The 'crisis of Marxism' approach has naturally produced an enormous, wide-ranging and at times abusive debate. For Geras (1987), Anderson (1983) and Wood (1986), the post-Marxism of Laclau and Mouffe represents a vast misreading of the textured and open-ended tradition of Marxist theory, and instals in its a place a world of contingent discourses and slippery causality; in short, a social science without necessity or reason. A post-Marxist world rests, as Perry Anderson (1983) put it, on a foundation without a vantage point. In much of the acrimonious debate, there has often been a great deal of heat but little light, and a tendency vastly to simplify and caricature both classical and post-Marxisms. What needs to be emphasized is the following. First, the so-called crisis of Marxism, for better or worse (and in my opinion it is for the worse), is part of a larger intellectual landscape of the crisis of GRAND THEORY – 'a crisis of REPRESENTATION' – which speaks to the rise more generally of a postmodern sensibility (Harvey, 1989). The crisis of Marxism in this view, like other grand theories, is deeply flawed by its totalizing framework, its dogma and its canonical terminology (Marcus and Fischer, 1986). Second, to the extent that post-Marxism is a catch-all for the important debates, in and outside Marxism, over causality, EPISTEMOLOGY, determination and so on, one should be very wary of assuming that post-Marxism has any theoretical unity whatsoever (or, indeed, that it signifies the end of anything). Third, and most crucially, the 'crisis talk' is not a recent phenomenon in

Marxism but, as Althusser noted long ago, the very history of Marxism is a long succession of crises and transformations. Indeed, one of the strengths of Marxism is that it can be seen historically as a research enterprise which has expanded and deepened its core theoretical postulates through successive problem-solving innovations, driven by the anomalies and practical problems that it has been compelled to address. The tradition of theorizing from Marx to Luxemburg to Lenin to Trotsky to Gramsci represents a series of 'crises' in which post-Marxisms have arisen from the debates of specific historical conjunctures (Watts, 1988). Crisis does not mean collapse and death, but signals the liberation of something vital and alive.   MW

References

Althusser, L. and Balibar, E. 1970: *Reading Capital*. London: Verso.

Anderson, P. 1983: *In the tracks of historical materialism*. London: Verso.

Booth, D. 1985: Marxism and development sociology: interpreting the impasse. *World Development* 13, pp. 761–87.

Brantlinger, P. 1990: *Crusoe's footprints: cultural studies in Britain and America*. London: Routledge.

Carling, A. 1986: Rational choice Marxism. *New Left Rev.* 160, pp. 24–62.

Corbridge, S. 1989: Marxism, post-Marxism and the geography of development. In Peet, R. and Thrift, N., eds, *New models in geography*, Volume 1. London: Unwin Hyman, pp. 224–56.

Geras, N. 1987: Post-Marxism? *New Left Rev.* 163, pp. 40–82.

Harvey, D. 1989: *The condition of postmodernity*. Oxford: Blackwell.

Hindess, B. and Hirst, P. 1977: *Mode of production and social formation*. London: Macmillan.

Laclau, E. and Mouffe, C. 1985: *Hegemony and socialist strategy*. London: Verso.

Lipietz, A. 1987: *Mirages and miracles: the crisis of global fordism*. London: Verso.

Marcus, G. and Fischer, M. 1986: *Anthropology as cultural critique: an experimental moment in the human sciences*. Chicago: University of Chicago Press.

Roemer, J., ed. 1986: *Analytical Marxism*. Cambridge: Cambridge University Press.

Watts, M. 1988: Deconstructing determinism. *Antipode*, 20, pp. 142–68.

Wood, E. 1986: *The retreat from class: a new 'true' socialism*. London: Verso.

Suggested Reading

Callinicos, A. 1989: *Against postmodernism: a Marxist critique*. Cambridge: Polity Press.

Elliot, G. 1987: *Althusser: the detour of theory*. London: Verso.

Jameson, F. 1990: *Late Marxism*. London: Verso.

McCarney, J. 1990: *Social theory and the crisis of Marxism*. London: Verso.

Postan thesis   A theoretical explanation of economic and social change in medieval England, formulated and developed by the medievalist and economic historian Michael Postan (1966, 1973; Postan and Hatcher, 1978). Postan sought to replace earlier linear models of Western medieval economy that were based on the growth of international trade. Instead, he argued that medieval European societies needed to be analysed first and foremost in terms of their agrarian basis. He took the critical component of the agrarian base to be the ability of peasant households to produce sufficient to support themselves and their social superiors; in the case of the latter through rents, tithes and taxes.

While Postan's work involved comparative analysis of England and the continent, he drew mainly on empirical material from southern England, especially from large ecclesiastically-owned estates such as those of the Bishop of Winchester, for which extensive records survive. His chief inferences were based on evidence of population trends, land use, new colonization or abandonment of arable land, prices, wages, rents, grain yields and livestock numbers.

The Postan thesis holds that medieval England moved inexorably towards an agrarian crisis. Population growth during the eleventh, twelfth and thirteenth centuries put increasing strain on the ecological base of peasant production. Pasture, woodland and wasteland was converted to arable use, but scope for such expansion was finite, and peasant family landholdings became increasingly subdivided. The rate at which this impoverishment occurred varied between areas, according to their resource base, settlement history and population density. Eventually, population growth outstripped both the availability of new land to bring under arable cultivation, and the ability of farmers to maintain or increase productivity per cropped acre. Much arable land was abandoned (Baker, 1973). Land abandonment and falling yields precipitated chronic food crises, causing population to fall. Postan identified the early fourteenth century as a significant demographic turning point (Kershaw, 1973). Compared with earlier arguments, Postan played down the significance of the Black Death as a *turning point*, arguing that it accelerated a population decline that was already under way.

For Postan, the tendency towards ecological crisis built in to medieval agrarian society was twofold: 'People found that they had reached the limits of the land's productivity; not only because they were reclaiming new, poor soils but also because they had been cultivating old land for too long' (Postan, 1973, p. 15). Thus medieval husbandmen faced a double bind. Yields were falling on old-cultivated land (Titow, 1972), because the emphasis on arable was so extreme that diminished livestock populations could no longer provide sufficient dung to maintain soil fertility. On newly colonized areas of marginal land, yields were initially high but could not be maintained as accumulations of soil nutrient stores became depleted. (For analysis of the Postan thesis in terms of soil productivity, see Shiel, 1991; Clark, 1992.)

Among many areas of critical debate, five are of particular significance to historical geographers. First, many have argued that Postan underestimates the significance of feudal social relations as a cause of peasant hardship, and a constraint on agricultural technology (see BRENNER DEBATE; FEUDALISM). What is at issue here is not so much whether there was a general medieval agrarian crisis, but whether its ultimate causes were social rather than techno-ecological.

Others dispute the notion that the crisis was general and sustained (Hallam, 1972, 1988; Harvey, 1991), crediting at least some regional agrarian economies with a greater capacity to make technical innovations and increase productivity than does

Postan (Campbell, 1983a,b, 1991; Langdon, 1986). In part, it appears that the Postan thesis draws too heavily on evidence from atypically conservatively managed estates. However, even within the Winchester estates, later work has ascribed geographical variations in land productivity to differing levels of labour inputs (Thornton, 1991). Moreover, peasant agriculture may have been generally more dynamic than the seigneurial cultivation which provides most of the available evidence. For example, this seems to be the case in the use of horses and the cultivation of legumes (Langdon, 1986). Postan's focus on arable production also marginalizes pastoral agriculture, which Biddick (1989) sees as a dynamic sector.

Debates on all of these topics highlight geographical variations in rural life. So too has the growing realization of the extent of commercialization on patterns of agricultural production, especially around London. Whereas Glasscock wrote in 1963 that 'technology and exchange had not progressed far enough by the early fourteenth century to allow much [regional agricultural] specialisation', recent work identifies substantial spatial differentiation in agricultural systems, and ascribes this to widespread processes of commercialization (Campbell and Power, 1989).

Finally, Postan's concept of the geographical margin has been extended and refined. There were several senses in which land might be marginal; soil quality, climate, location, topography and tenure (Bailey, 1989; Dyer, 1989b). Postan conflated these senses, thereby oversimplifying the geography of expansion and contraction in settlement and cultivation. As Bailey observes with respect to the Norfolk and Suffolk Brecklands, 'the profitability of land depended as much upon its location, and upon institutional factors, as it did upon its quality' (1989, p. 320). The relationships between different dimensions of marginality were contingent rather than necessary, and the classic Postanian marginal decline was largely restricted to areas which were marginal in several respects simultaneously.

In all of these debates, much revision has taken the form of refining or elaborating the

Postan thesis, rather than rejecting it outright. There is no current uniformity of opinion as to whether geographical differences in agrarian systems are better understood as exceptions to (or disproofs of) the Postan thesis, or as different regional development trajectories within the same fundamental set of constraints. But whether we regard the Postan thesis as crumbling or as becoming more complicated, 'it is clear that a more comprehensive view of the medieval English economy is being developed' (Langdon, 1991, p. 209). PG

References

Bailey, M. 1989: *A marginal economy? East Anglian Breckland in the later middle ages.* Cambridge: Cambridge University Press.

Baker, A. R. H. 1973: Evidence in the '*Nonarum Inquisitiones*' of contracting arable land in England during the fourteenth century. *Econ. Hist. R.* 2nd series 19, pp. 518–32.

Biddick, K. 1989: *The other economy: pastoral husbandry on a medieval estate.* Berkeley, CA: University of California Press.

Campbell, B. M. S. 1983a: Agricultural progress in medieval England: some evidence from eastern Norfolk. *Econ. Hist. R.* 36, pp. 26–46.

Campbell, B. M. S. 1983b: Agricultural productivity in medieval England: some evidence from Norfolk. *J. econ. Hist.* 53, pp. 379–404.

Campbell, B. M. S. 1991: Land, labour, livestock, and productivity trends in English seigneurial agriculture, 1208–1450. In Campbell, B. M. S. and Overton, M., eds, *Land, labour and livestock: historical studies in European agricultural productivity.* Manchester: Manchester University Press, pp. 144–82.

Campbell, B. M. S. and Power, J. 1989: Mapping the agricultural geography of medieval England. *J. hist. Geogr.* 15, pp. 24–39.

Clark, G. 1992: The economics of exhaustion, the Postan thesis, and the agricultural revolution. *J. econ. Hist.* 52, pp. 61–84.

Dyer, C. 1989b: 'The retreat from marginal land': the growth and decline of medieval rural settlements. In Aston, M. et al., eds, *The rural settlements of medieval England: studies dedicated to Maurice Beresford and John Hurst.* Oxford: Blackwell, pp. 45–57.

Glasscock, R. E. 1963: The distribution of wealth in East Anglia in the early fourteenth century. *Trans. Inst. Br. Geogr.* 32, pp. 113–23.

Hallam, H. E. 1972: The Postan thesis. *Historical Studies* (Melbourne) 15.

Hallam, H. E., ed. 1988: *The agrarian history of England and Wales,* volume II, 1042–1350. Cambridge: Cambridge University Press.

Harvey, B. 1991: Introduction: the 'crisis' of the early fourteenth century. In Campbell, B. M. S., ed., *Before the Black Death: studies in the 'crisis' of the early fourteenth century.* Manchester: Manchester University Press, pp. 1–24. Kershaw, I. 1973: The agrarian crisis in England 1315–1322. *Past and Present* 59.

Langdon, J. 1986: *Horses, oxen and technological innovation: the use of draught animals in English farming from 1066–1500.* Cambridge: Cambridge University Press.

Langdon, J. 1991: Bringing it all together: medieval English economic history in transition. *J. Br. Stud.* 30, pp. 209–16.

Postan, M. M. 1966: Medieval agrarian society in its prime: England. In Postan, M. M., ed., *Cambridge economic history of Europe,* volume 1, *The agrarian life of the Middle Ages.* Cambridge: Cambridge University Press. pp. 549–632.

Postan, M. M. 1973: *Essays on medieval agriculture and general problems of the medieval economy.* Cambridge: Cambridge University Press.

Postan, M. M. and Hatcher, J. 1978: Population and class relations in feudal society. *Past and Present* 78, pp. 24–37.

Shiel, R. S. 1991: Improving soil productivity in the pre-fertilizer era. In Campbell, B. M. S. and Overton, M., eds, *Land, labour and livestock: historical studies in European agricultural productivity.* Manchester: Manchester University Press, pp. 51–77.

Thornton, C. 1991: The determinants of land productivity on the Bishop of Winchester's demesne of Rimpton, 1208–1403. In Campbell B. M. S. and Overton, M., eds, *Land, labour and livestock: historical studies in European agricultural productivity.* Manchester: Manchester University Press, pp. 183–210.

Titow, J. Z. 1972: *Winchester yields: a study in medieval agricultural productivity.* Cambridge: Cambridge University Press.

Suggested Reading

Clark (1992).
Postan (1966).

postcolonialism A movement among artists and intellectuals that challenges the impact of IMPERIALISM on non-Western cultures, aiming to 'decolonize the mind' (Thiong'o, 1986). Often allied stylistically with POSTMODERNISM, postcolonial writers such as Gabriel García Márquez, Luis Borges and Salman Rushdie oppose the ETHNOCENTRISM of the dominant (white, Anglo-Saxon) culture. Building on the work of anticolonialists such as Frantz Fanon and Paulo Freire, postcolonialism has developed a radical edge through political and literary critics such as Gayatri Chakravorty Spivak (1990) and the SUBALTERN STUDIES group. In turn, these authors have made important contributions to the enrichment of Western feminism (see FEMINIST GEOGRAPHY). Intersections with debates over NATIONALISM (Eagleton et al., 1990) and the prevalence of spatial, cartographic and territorial imagery (Huggan, 1989) suggest that postcolonialism will become an increasingly important aspect of the geographical imagination in future. Its connections (and tensions) with recent work in CULTURAL GEOGRAPHY (Barnes and Duncan, 1992) are already apparent. (See also CULTURAL GEOGRAPHY; ORIENTALISM; POSTSTRUCTURALISM.)   PAJ

References

Barnes, T. J. and Duncan, J. S., eds 1992: *Writing worlds: discourse, text and metaphor in the representation of landscape*. London: Routledge.

Eagleton, T., Jameson, F. and Said, E. 1990: *Nationalism, colonialism and literature*. Minneapolis: University of Minnesota Press.

Huggan, G. 1989: Decolonizing the map: postcolonialism, post-structuralism and the cartographic connection. *Ariel* 20, pp. 115–31.

Spivak, G. C. 1990: *The post-colonial critic: interviews, strategies, dialogues* (Harasym, S., ed.). London: Routledge.

Thiong'o, Ngugi wa 1986: *Decolonizing the mind*. London: James Currey.

Suggested Reading

Ashcroft, B., Griffiths, G. and Tiffin, H. 1989: *The Empire writes back: theory and practice in post-colonial literature*. London: Routledge.

Crush, J. 1993: Postcoloniality, decolonization, geography. In Godlewska, A. and Smith, N., eds, *Geography and empire*. Oxford: Blackwell.

Spivak (1990).

postmodernism A recent movement in philosophy, the arts and social sciences characterized by scepticism towards the grand claims and GRAND THEORY of the modern era, and their privileged vantage point, stressing in its place an openness to a range of voices in social enquiry, artistic experimentation and political empowerment. This much may be said by way of definition, but little else, as use of the term varies considerably both by discipline and by author (but see Hassan, 1985; Jencks, 1987). Indeed, in some fields the break between modern and postmodern genres is not at all clear; if collage, for example, is a quintessential feature of postmodernism as many assert (for example, citing the art of David Salle) it should not be forgotten that it was also part of the experimentation of the early modernism movement (Kern, 1983). So too the collision of disparate elements in postmodern pastiche projects the same strangeness to the familiar as was attempted by the modern tactic of defamiliarization.

Dear (1986) usefully classifies postmodernism into three components: postmodern style, postmodern method and a postmodern epoch. In *style*, architecture has become the paradigmatic art and is often a point of departure in the discussion of postmodernism more generally (e.g. Harvey, 1989). Such architecture has been criticized for its attention to facade variation, a diversity of colour, design elements and iconography which is no more than a superficial gift wrapping. However, this criticism is incomplete, for style is centrally implicated in the constitution of meaning and identity (Bourdieu, 1984). Styles may be either supportive of dominant ideologies, or offer a 'ritual of resistance' which are socially and politically oppositional to them (Hebdige, 1979), and the same is true of a postmodern built environment (Ley and Mills, 1992).

The issue of postmodern *method* has attracted enormous attention (see also POSTSTRUCTURALISM). Deconstruction is a principal strategy, a mode of critical interpretation which seeks to demonstrate how the (multiple) positioning of an author (or a reader) in terms of CULTURE, CLASS, GENDER, etc. has influenced the writing (and reading), of a TEXT. A text's range of meanings is, therefore, if not infinite at least considerable. Deconstruction is essentially a destabilizing method, throwing into doubt the authority claims of preceding traditions, and seeking to prise loose alternative readings of texts. In human geography, Olsson (1980) was the earliest exponent of deconstruction and remains its most innovative and skilful practitioner. But his work shows also the weaknesses of the position in a relativism which knows few limits. Moreover, given the uncertain (or at least contingent) grounds upon which the observer stands, the scholar's claims for an adequate interpretation of other people and places would seem to be modest indeed. This so-called crisis of representation has been a major theoretical concern in recent ETHNOGRAPHIC writing (Clifford and Marcus, 1986; Clifford, 1988). How is it possible to represent the other when the presuppositions of that representation are themselves so contaminated by the author's own position? (cf. Said, 1979).

Third, postmodernism may be thought of as an *epoch*, an historic era in which changes in culture and philosophy are themselves located in the evolution of a global economy and geopolitics. The strongest theoretical arguments have been advanced by materialists who see 'the postmodern condition' as caught up in, and ultimately propelled by, historic shifts in global CAPITALISM. Thus, for Jameson (1984) postmodernism is the culture of late capitalism, for Harvey (1989) the condition of postmodernity is an integral element of the new phase of post-Fordist FLEXIBLE ACCUMULATION. But these and other (Soja, 1989) interpretations are resolutely modern, maintaining a model of a mechanism in which art and culture are read off from economic logics. As such, they have been criticized for their totalizing character, for their claim to authority in an unreflected metanarrative, and for their inadequate portrayal of the experience and struggles of the other, the voices of marginalized social groups, and particularly the voices of women (Gregory, 1990; Deutsch, 1991; Massey, 1991).

Just as the notion of postmodernity as discontinuity is today less secure in art, so in discussions of the economy present writing is seeking to correct an unduly schismatic interpretation of change (Gertler,

1988). If these are indeed 'new times' they display important continuities with as well as departures from the geography of modernity. DL

References

Bourdieu, P. 1984: *Distinction: a social critique of the judgement of taste.* London: Routledge and Kegan Paul.

Clifford, J. 1988: *The predicament of culture.* Cambridge, MA: Harvard University Press.

Clifford, J. and Marcus, G., eds 1986: *Writing cultures: the poetics and the politics of ethnography.* Berkeley, CA: University of California Press.

Dear, M. 1986: Postmodernism and planning. *Environ. Plann. D: Society and Space* 4, pp. 367–84.

Deutsche, R. 1991: Boys town. *Environ. Plann. D:* Society and Space 9, pp. 5–30.

Gertler, M. 1988: The limits to flexibility. *Trans. Inst. Br. Geogr.* n.s. 13, pp. 419–32.

Gregory, D. 1990: *Chinatown* part three? Soja and the missing spaces of social theory. *Strategies* 3.

Harvey, D. 1989: *The condition of postmodernity.* Oxford: Blackwell.

Hassan, I. 1985: The culture of postmodernism. *Theory, Culture and Society* 2(3), pp. 119–32.

Hebdige, D. 1979: *Subculture: the meaning of style.* London: Methuen.

Jameson, F. 1984: Postmodernism, or the cultural logic of late capitalism. *New Left Rev.* 146, pp. 53–92.

Jencks, C. 1987: *What is postmodernism?* New York: St. Martin's Press.

Kern, S. 1983: *The culture of time and space 1880–1918.* Cambridge, MA: Harvard University Press.

Ley, D. and Mills, C. 1992: Can there be a postmodernism of resistance in the urban landscape? In Knox, P., ed., *The restless urban landscape.* Englewood Cliffs, NJ: Prentice Hall.

Massey, D. 1991: Flexible sexism. *Environ. Plann. D: Society and Space* 9, pp. 31–57.

Olsson G. 1980: *Birds in egg: eggs in bird.* London: Pion.

Said, E. 1979: *Orientalism.* New York: Vintage.

Soja, E. 1989: *Postmodern geographies: the reassertion of space in critical social theory.* London: Verso.

Suggested Reading

Barnes, T. J. and Duncan, J. S., eds 1991: *Writing worlds: discourses, texts and metaphors in the representation of landscape.* London: Routledge.

Best, S. and Kellner, D. 1991: *Postmodern theory: critical interrogations*. London: Macmillan.

Gregory, D. 1989: Areal differentiation and post-modern human geography. In Gregory, D. and Walford, R., eds, *Horizons in human geography*. London: Macmillan, pp. 67–96.

Harvey (1989).

Ley, D. 1989: Modernism, postmodernism and the struggle for place. In Agnew, J. and Duncan, J., eds, *The power of place*. London: Unwin Hyman, pp. 44–65.

poststructuralism (including **deconstruction**) A term used most commonly in English-speaking countries to refer to philsophical currents developed in France in the 1960s and since by 'theorists' such as Derrida, Lacan, Foucault and Kristeva. This chronological marker is complicated by the complex relationship between poststructuralist, prestructuralist (especially Hegel, Husserl, Heidegger, Freud, Marx and Nietzsche) and structuralist thought.

Poststructuralists draw on and extend some of the important insights of STRUCTURALISM, especially (a) Saussurian linguistics and (b) Althusser's critique of the subject.

(a) Language is seen as the medium for defining and contesting social organization and subjectivity. Saussure is credited with the understanding that meaning is produced within rather than reflected through language: language is therefore constitutive rather than reflective of social reality. He argued that there is no necessary fixed relation between a signifier (sound or written image) and a signified (meaning). The meaning of a signifer is derived from its difference from and relation to other signifiers – identity is created through difference. Poststructuralists have radicalized these views in several ways: Derrida insists that neither identity nor difference can be prioritized in theories of how meaning is produced (Saussure privileges the latter) and that the relations between signified and signifier are never fixed.

(b) Poststructuralists also absorbed the antihumanist critique of a unified, knowing and rational subject, instead interpreting SUBJECTIVITY as continually in process, as a site of disunity, conflict and contradictions, and hence potential political change.

They diverge from Althusser in seeing the production of subjectivity as a discursive rather than ideological effect. The distinction is an important one: while Althusser represented his critique of the subject as a scientific exposé, poststructuralist writers such as Foucault maintain that there is no extra discursive 'real' outside of cultural systems. The subject is thus rid of the last traces of essentialism: a real or essential CLASS consciousness is no longer anticipated on the basis of an individual's material conditions.

This points to another important break between structuralists and poststructuralists: while structuralists usually claim a scientific status for their theories, poststructuralists challenge the role and status of science as a DISCOURSE and are concerned to demonstrate the repressions and POWER relations that underlie scientific claims to truth rather than reproduce them.

Deconstruction is Derrida's method of destabilizing truth claims (Norris, 1982). Deconstruction is an attempt to undo claims to truth and coherence by uncovering the incoherences within TEXTS and tracking the traces of oppositional elements, each in the other. Deconstruction is sometimes seen as a two-step process: one first reverses and then displaces the oppositions (e.g. male/female, culture/nature or subject/object) that structure the text. Foucault pursues another, more empirical, route to unsettling truth claims, by tracing the history of DISCOURSES, the exclusions on which they rest, and the discursive contingency of truth claims.

Poststructuralism has immense implications for geography, as it has for all human sciences. Deutsche's (1991) critique of David Harvey's distanced and objectivist account of postmodern societies bears the influence of poststructuralism, as does the critical examination by FEMINIST GEOGRAPHERS of the gender dichotomies on which much of their analyses have rested (McDowell, 1991). Foucault's account of POWER, ascending from the disciplining of bodies through architecture and spatial sequestration, is inherently geographical (Foucault, 1977, 1980; Driver, 1985) and refocuses the theory and method of

POLITICAL, HISTORICAL and other strands of GEOGRAPHY. GP

References

Deutsche, R. 1991: Boys town. *Environ. Plann. D: Society and Space* 9, pp. 5–30.

Driver, F. 1985: Power, space and the body: a critical reassessment of Foucault's *Discipline and punish*. *Environ. Plann. D: Society and Space* 3, pp. 245–46.

Foucault, M. 1977: *Discipline and punish: the birth of the prison*, transl. A. M. Sheridan Smith. Andover, UK: Tavistock.

Foucault, M. 1980: *Power/knowledge: selected interviews and other writings*, C. Gordon, ed., transl. C. Gordon et al. Brighton, UK: Harvester.

McDowell, L. 1991: The baby and the bath water: diversity, deconstruction and feminist theory in geography. *Geoforum* 22, pp. 123–33.

Norris, C. 1982: *Deconstruction: theory and practice*. London: Methuen.

Further Reading

Sarup, M. 1989: *Post-structuralism and postmodernism*. Brighton, UK: Harvester/Athens, GA: University of Georgia Press.

power The ability to achieve certain ends. Strictly speaking, power is an absolute concept, but it is often treated as a synonym for *influence*, which may be either direct (the power to *do* something) or indirect (the power *over* something). The concept may refer to the relationship between an individual or group and the natural world (see NATURE), but it is more frequently used to characterize interpersonal and inter-group relationships, including those between STATES.

Power (other than power over nature, which is usually a technological relationship) can be achieved and sustained in a variety of ways, among which the most usual are: force (including psychic and physical – both violent and non-violent); manipulation; persuasion and the creation of consensus; and authority. It is most readily exercised if its source is recognized as legitimate by those subject to it (see SOVEREIGNTY): legitimation of a power relationship may be attained by appeal to tradition, by its institutionalization in societal structures, especially those of the STATE APPARATUS, or through the charisma of the powerful.

Power is exercized at all scales and levels of society, from within the individual household to the entire world-economy (see WORLD-SYSTEMS ANALYSIS). It is rarely symmetrical, so that x's power over y usually exceeds (often by many orders of magnitude) that of y over x. Such asymmetry is characteristic of many social structures – such as patrimony (see GENDER and GEOGRAPHY) – and most MODES OF PRODUCTION. Under CAPITALISM, for example, power is uneven because of the unequal distribution of ownership of the means of production, and thus of the ability to bargain over prices. Those with greatest power have greatest control over society's organization (including its spatial organization) of production, distribution and exchange, and over the allocation of the benefits that follow: this unequal power is reflected in the social relations between CLASSES and is the foundation of much social, economic and political CONFLICT. The more successful the legitimation of the resulting inequality is within a society (see HEGEMONY; IDEOLOGY), the less is the need for explicit coercion and the fewer the challenges to class power: where such legitimation is weak, however (see CRISIS), the greater are the demands on, and problems for, the state (Held, 1987; Johnston, 1992).

Much of the exercise of power in contemporary societies involves the state, and its infiltration and regulation of most aspects of economic and social life. In capitalist states, some of the bourgeoisie's power over labour is transferred to the state apparatus, in part to aid in its legitimation and in part to ensure the continued reproduction of the mode of production (Jessop, 1990): the state, for example, regulates a wide range of workplace practices in order to sustain profitability. The nature of this state power is theorized in a variety of ways (Alford and Friedland, 1985; Dunleavy and O'Leary, 1987). According to liberal theories of democracy, for example, power is equally distributed through the population, and can be exercised on its behalf only if those controlling the state have majority popular support (see PLURALISM). According to Marxian theories, on the other hand, state power is not independent of class power, although the state can act autonomously because of its particular status as a territorially defined institution (Mann, 1984). According to this view, the state exists to promote the capitalist mode of production and to advance the interests of the dominant forces in the local SOCIAL FORMATION (see also REGIONAL CLASS ALLIANCE): the interests of other groups within society are only advanced to the extent that this is perceived as in the whole society's, and thus the dominant class's, interests too. (Thus, for example, some states have granted liberal democratic participatory privileges through a universal franchise, as part of the ideological bulwark to legitimation of inequality: see Johnston, 1989.)

A major feature of the state's power is its territorial expression (Johnston, 1991a,b). A state's sovereignty involves it being recognized as the locus of authority within a defined – even if challenged – territory (see TERRITORIALITY), where it is usually the sole repository of coercive (military and police) force. Within that territory the state may, according to Mann, exercise either *despotic power* (actions taken without negotiation with the population, as under totalitarianism), or *infrastructural power*, whereby it infiltrates most aspects of life with (implicit) consent, as under capitalism. Under FEUDALISM, he argues, the state is relatively weak on both power dimensions.

Mann argues that a state is required for anything other than a primitive society (but see ANARCHISM), and that a state exercising a very wide range of infrastructural powers is necessary under capitalism. Furthermore, he argues that geography is crucial if the capitalist state is to be effective. State power is exercised from a central place over a unified territorial reach, and involves the mobilization of four types of power – economic, ideological, military and political. For each, the existence of a territory within which the power applies is fundamental. The interest groups associated with the four types of power all need to have their activities regulated over defined territories: for example, economic interests are provided with a single currency and a uniform set of laws of contract over that area; ideological interests are advanced through the association of the state and its society with a defined territory (see NATION; NATIONALISM); military interests are provided with clearly defined boundaries to defend; and political interests are given an arena within which to mobilize support and legitimation. Thus, as Mann expresses it, 'the state *is* merely and essentially an arena, a *place* . . .'.

The empirical analysis of state power reflects the adopted EPISTEMOLOGY. Much work set within the pluralist model of liberal democracy focuses on the competition for votes, for example, and is the subject of sophisticated mathematical analyses (Johnston, 1985): in the same context, the exercize of power is described behaviourally using indices such as military strength. Such work, most of it in the POSITIVIST mould, focuses on surficial appearances only. It fails to analyse the role of power as an integral part of any society's structure; nor does it, as in REALIST analyses, explore the crucial geographical components to the exercise of power which, as Sack's (1986) work on TERRITORIALITY shows, involves power over places of (cf. SURVEILLANCE).

Beyond the exercise of power in and through the state, societies encompass a wide range of other power relationships, in both the sphere of production (the workplace) and the sphere of consumption (see CIVIL SOCIETY). Most of these relationships are asymmetrical, and reflect the relative hegemony of certain groups over others (men over women, for example, and – in many countries – white over non-white ethnic groups). Many such unequal power relationships are legitimated by the state, because the powerful groups are able to dominate its apparatus.   RJJ

References

Alford, R. R. and Friedland, R. 1985: *Powers of theory: capitalism, the state and democracy.* Cambridge: Cambridge University Press.

Dunleavy, P. and O'Leary, B. 1987: *State theory: the politics of liberal democracy.* London: Macmillan.

Held, D. 1987: *Models of democracy.* Cambridge: Polity Press.

Jessop, B. 1990: *State theory: putting capitalist states in their place*. Cambridge: Polity Press.

Johnston, R. J. 1985: People, places and parliaments. *Geogr. J.* 151, pp. 327–38.

Johnston, R. J. 1989: Individual freedom in the world-economy. In Johnston, R. J. and Taylor, P. J., eds, *A world in crisis? geographical perspectives*, second edition. Oxford: Blackwell, pp. 200–28.

Johnston, R. J. 1991a: The territoriality of law: an exploration. *Urban Geogr.* 12, pp. 548–65.

Johnston, R. J. 1991b: *A question of place: exploring the practice of human geography*. Oxford: Blackwell.

Johnston, R. J. 1992: The internal operations of the state. In Taylor, P. J., ed., *The political geography of the twentieth century*. London: Belhaven Press, pp. 115–70.

Mann, M. 1984: The autonomous power of the state; its origins, mechanisms, and results. *Eur. J. Sociol.* 25, pp. 185–213.

Sack, R. D. 1986: *Human territoriality: its theory and history*. Cambridge: Cambridge University Press.

Suggested Reading

Claval, P. 1978: *Espace et pouvoir*. Paris: Presses Universitaires de France.

Giddens, A. 1984: *The constitution of society*. Cambridge: Polity Press.

Giddens, A. 1985: *The nation state and violence*. Cambridge: Polity Press.

poverty   See CYCLE OF POVERTY.

pragmatism   A philosophical perspective which is centrally concerned with the construction of meaning through the practical activity of human beings. Pragmatism had its origins in North America in the late nineteenth and early twentieth centuries, where it was identified with the diverse (and at times radically discrepant) writings of Charles Peirce (1839–1914), John Dewey (1859–1952) and William James (1842–1910). The differences between these authors make it difficult to characterize pragmatism with any great precision: and, indeed, a distrust of fixed and formal frameworks is one of the hallmarks of pragmatism. From a pragmatist perspective, knowledge is an essentially *fluid* and intrinsically *fallible* process of 'self-correcting inquiry':

Knowledge, as an abstract term, is a name for the product of competent inquiries . . . . The 'settlement' of a particular situation by a particular inquiry is no guarantee that *that* settled conclusion will always remain settled. The attainment of settled beliefs is a progressive matter; there is no belief so settled as not to be exposed to further inquiry' (Dewey, 1938).

Some commentators have seen elements of this view in Popper's CRITICAL RATIONALISM and even in Habermas's CRITICAL THEORY, but its (philosophical) implications are much more radical than either of these. For pragmatism calls into question the very possibility of philosophy as a 'foundational discipline' and rejects 'the notion that there is a permanent neutral framework whose "structure" philosophy can display' (Rorty, 1980; see also Rorty, 1982). In this sense, Rorty insists, pragmatism is not only distanced from but *opposed* to EPISTEMOLOGY; it is a critique of PHENOMENOLOGY – at least as Husserl envisioned it – POSITIVISM and REALISM. As Bernstein (1972) argued,

The shift of orientation from the foundation paradigm to that of inquiry as a continuous self-corrective process requires us to re-think almost every fundamental issue in philosophy . . . . [The human being] as inquirer, as a participant in a community of inquiry, is no longer viewed as "spectator" but rather as an active participant and experimenter. [The human being] as agent comes into the foreground here because human agency is the key for understanding all aspects of human life, including human inquiry and knowledge.

It is, however, largely through this focus on HUMAN AGENCY (rather than any wider claims about philosophy) that pragmatism has cast such a long shadow over liberal social theory: and particularly over the CHICAGO SCHOOL and SYMBOLIC INTERACTIONISM (see Lewis and Smith, 1980). For:

The dominance of the category of the practical, the emphasis on social categories for understanding [people] and the ways in which [people] function in a community, and even the understanding of [human] cognitive activities from the perspective of [human] practical activity, pervade the pragmatists' investigations (Bernstein, 1972).

Although 'the merits of pragmatism are as yet little exploited' in human geography, therefore, Jackson and Smith (1984) argue that pragmatism can be used to underwrite the importance of ETHNOGRAPHY and other 'participatory forms of research' for the construction of a genuinely HUMANISTIC GEOGRAPHY. And, certainly, pragmatism energises a deeply moral concern which distinguishes it from mere INSTRUMENTALISM: it makes reflection 'useful to those, in Foucault's phrase, "whose fight is located in the fine meshes of the webs of power" ' (Rorty, 1982). That fight does not privilege philosophy or social theory, however, and in his most recent writings Rorty (1989) makes much of the importance of imaginative literature for the political project of liberalism. His critics object that this does not provide for a sufficiently rigorous analysis of the materiality of power, but Barnes (1991) has drawn upon Rorty's ideas to offer an illuminating reflection on the power of metaphor in perhaps the most insistently material(ist) field of human geography, and one in which questions of language and meaning have rarely been debated.　DG

References

Barnes, T. 1991: Metaphors and conversations in economic geography: Richard Rorty and the gravity model. *Geogr. Annlr.* 73B, pp. 111–20.

Bernstein, R. 1972: *Praxis and action.* London: Duckworth.

Dewey, J. 1938: *Logic: the theory of inquiry.* New York: Holt.

Jackson, P. and Smith, S. 1984: *Exploring social geography.* London: Allen and Unwin.

Lewis, J. D. and Smith, R. L. 1980: *American sociology and pragmatism.* Chicago: University of Chicago Press.

Rorty, R. 1980: *Philosophy and the mirror of nature.* Oxford: Blackwell.

Rorty, R. 1982: *Consequences of pragmatism.* Minneapolis: University of Minnesota Press.

Rorty, R. 1989: *Contingency, irony, solidarity.* Cambridge: Cambridge University Press.

Suggested Reading

Bernstein (1972), part 3.

Jackson and Smith (1984), pp. 71–9.

Rorty (1982), ch. 11.

prediction The creation of an expected value, or estimate, for an observation involved in the generation of the estimating equation. (See also FORECAST.)　RJJ

preindustrial city All cities prior to the INDUSTRIAL REVOLUTION, plus those in non-industrialized regions today. The term reflects the theory, initially advocated by Gideon Sjoberg (see SJOBERG MODEL), that all preindustrial cities, regardless of their time, place or cultural backdrop, share similar reasons for existence, social hierarchies and internal spatial structures. Few now use the term, as the assumption of cross-cultural similarities in social and urban structure has become controversial.　DH

preservation The saving of relict features in the human landscape, typically in the built environment. It complements CONSERVATION, which is generally concerned with protecting features of the natural environment. The preservation of a feature involves its maintenance in a state of good repair: *restoration* aims to bring it back to its original condition, whereas *revival* reproduces past features.　RJJ

pricing policies The arrangements whereby the prices at which commodities are offered to consumers are determined. In spatial economic analysis the important distinguishing feature of pricing policies is the extent to which price varies with distance from the origin or source of the commodity. There are two major alternative policies. The first is known as the f.o.b. (free on board) price system, under which there is a basic price at origin, and the consumer pays the TRANSPORT COST involved in getting the commodity to the point of purchase. The second is the c.i.f. (cost, insurance, freight) price system, under which the producer adds insurance and shipping cost to the production cost and offers the commodity at a uniform delivered price irrespective of distance from origin. The distinction between these two policies is important, for commodities sold c.i.f. should have no bearing on COMPARATIVE locational ADVANTAGE for productive activities requiring them as inputs:

similarly, distance from origin should not affect the level of demand for goods offered on a c.i.f. basis (other things being equal). There is an increasing tendency for commodities to be sold at a uniform delivered price.

There are various alternative pricing policies that may be implemented. An f.o.b. system does not necessarily have minor incremental increases in price for small increases in distance; more often the prevailing FREIGHT RATES on which delivered price is based will be constant over broad zones. There may be forms of spatial price discrimination, under which customers in some areas are charged a high price (perhaps because the supplier has a local monopoly) so as to subsidize the price charged in a more competitive market. A well-known variant is the basing point price policy, whereby customers are charged as if the commodity originated at a certain (base) point; this can be used to protect producers in the basing point location, for commodities actually produced elsewhere will cost more. The operation of some pricing policies may involve collusion on the part of producers to maintain an artificially high price in the industry as a whole – an increasing tendency in the advanced capitalist world (see also MONOPOLY; OLIGOPOLY).

Under SOCIALISM, prices are determined centrally and there is less likelihood of spatial variation. The fact that such prices may be set without much regard for the actual cost of inputs involved (including transportation costs) carries efficiency implications from which the former socialist economies of Eastern Europe suffered.

DMS

Suggested Reading

Smith, D. M. 1981: *Industrial location: an economic geographical analysis*, second edition. New York: John Wiley.

primate city, law of the An empirical regularity in the relationship of the populations of a country's three largest cities, identified by Jefferson (1939). He noted that the ratio of the three populations in many cases approximated the sequence 100 : 30 : 20 (i.e. the third largest is one-fifth the size of the largest), which he attributed to the largest city's pre-eminence in economic, social and political affairs. The sequence that he identified is now largely ignored, but the concepts of *primacy* and a primate city are still widely referred to. Accounts usually relate a primate city's predominance to the small size of the country, the export orientation of its trade, and a recent colonial past. (See also CITY-SIZE DISTRIBUTION; MERCANTILIST MODEL; RANK–SIZE RULE.)

RJJ

Reference

Jefferson, M. 1939: The law of the primate city. *Geogrl. Rev.* 29, pp. 226–32.

principal components analysis (pca) A statistical procedure for transforming an (observations by variables) data matrix so that the variables in the new matrix are uncorrelated. Unlike FACTOR ANALYSIS, there are as many new variables (termed components) in the transformed as in the original matrix.

The components are extracted by an iterative averaging procedure. The first principal component occupies a position as close to (i.e. as highly correlated with) all of the original variables as possible. The second is as close as possible to the residual variation from the first, and so on until all have been extracted.

The output of a pca (which normally takes only a few seconds on modern computers, with many standard packages available) comprises three important sets of information. The *eigenvalues* are measures of the relative importance of each component (i.e. the proportion of the variation in the original variables accounted for by each); the greater the value of an eigenvalue, the greater the commonality among the original variables. The *component loadings* show the CORRELATIONS between the original variables and the new ones, thus identifying which groups of variables have common patterns. Finally, the *component scores* are values for the observations on each of the new variables.

Principal components analysis has been used by geographers: to identify groups of intercorrelated variables, in an inductive search for common patterns (as in FACTORIAL ECOLOGY); to simplify a data set by removing redundant information resulting from intercorrelated variables; to reorganize a data set by removing COLLINEARITY (see GENERAL LINEAR MODEL; REGRESSION;) and to test hypotheses.　　　RJJ

Suggested Reading
Johnston, R. J. 1978: *Multivariate statistical analysis in geography: a primer on the general linear model*. London: Longman.

prisoner's dilemma An application of GAME THEORY which illustrates the benefits of cooperative behaviour in certain situations.

In the classic example, two men are arrested on charges of car theft and armed robbery. The first offence is readily proven, but the other will not be unless at least one of the two confesses and implicates the other. The suspects know that if they both stay silent, each will be found guilty of the theft and sentenced to one year in jail; they also know that if both confess they will get eight years each for the armed robbery. They are interrogated separately, and not allowed to consult, let alone collude. Each is offered a deal: if you confess and as a result your accomplice is found guilty you will be freed and he will get ten years. The four possible outcomes to their separate decisions whether or not to confess are given in a pay-off matrix, in which the left-hand value in each cell indicates A's punishment at that outcome, and the right-hand value indicates B's punishment (thus if A does not confess and B does, A will get ten years and B will be released):

		Suspect B	
		Not confess	Confess
Suspect A	Not confess	1,1	10,0
	Confess	0,10	8,8

Each has to evaluate the possible consequence of each action, which can be done by rank-ordering the outcomes according to their relative desirability. (In this ranking, NC = not confess, and C = confess, so that the top left-hand cell of the matrix is [NC,NC]; > indicates 'is preferable to'.) For A the ordering (with A's decision first) is

$$[C,NC] > [NC,NC] > [C,C] > [NC,C]$$

and for B (also with A's decision first) it is

$$[NC,C] > [NC,NC] > [C,C] > [C,NC]$$

Each decides that confession is the best option, because if he does not and the other does, then the worst outcome will eventuate. Neither dare stay silent, for fear that the other will confess. So both confess, and both get eight years. If each could have been sure of the other (and sure that the other would not accept a police claim that he had already confessed) then both would have stayed silent and been given a one-year sentence. Because neither can guarantee the other's behaviour, however, they fail to select the optimal strategy, which they surely would have chosen had they been able to cooperate.

This dilemma has been used to illustrate how selfish behaviour may not be in the individual's best interest, and that it is also not in that person's interest to be unselfish unless everybody else is (cf. TRAGEDY OF THE COMMONS). In most cases, it is argued, unselfish behaviour by all can only be guaranteed if it is enforced by an external authority (i.e. the prisoners can collude), which is taken to provide a convincing case for the existence of the STATE to promote both the collective and the individual good. However, there are many other situations in which cooperation is sensible and promotes the general good without state involvement.　　　RJJ

Suggested Reading
Brams, S. J. 1975: *Game theory and politics*. New York: Free Press.

Laver, M. 1981: *The politics of private desires*. London: Penguin.

Taylor, M. 1987: *The possibility of cooperation*. Cambridge: Cambridge University Press.

private and public spheres Discursively constructed, contested categories that define boundaries between households, market economies, the STATE and political participation.

Habermas provides the most influential account of the interinstitutional relations among various spheres of public and private life in early and welfare state capitalist societies (see CAPITALISM). Early capitalist societies are organized into four institutional spheres: family–consumer (private), market economy (private), the state (public) and citizen–political

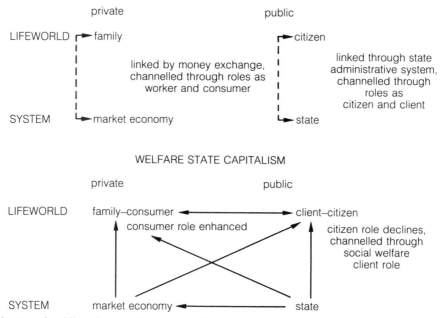

EARLY CAPITALISM

private   public

LIFEWORLD ┌─► family   ┌─► citizen
          │   │
          │   linked by money exchange, │   linked through state
          │   channelled through roles as│   administrative system,
          │   worker and consumer   │   channelled through
          │   │   roles as
          │   │   citizen and client
SYSTEM   └─► market economy   └─► state

WELFARE STATE CAPITALISM

private   public

LIFEWORLD   family–consumer ◄──────────► client–citizen
                    ▲ consumer role enhanced ▲
                     ╲   ╱   citizen role declines,
                      ╲   ╱   channelled through
                       ╲   ╱   social welfare
                        ╲   ╱   client role
                         ╲   ╱
SYSTEM   market economy ◄──────────── state

private and public spheres *Private and public spheres in early and welfare capitalist societies* (adapted from Fraser, 1989, and Habermas, 1987).

participation (public) (see the figure). In WELFARE STATE capitalist societies, the separation between the state and economy, public and private, dissolves and family–consumer and citizen roles are transformed, the latter declining in importance and changing form (from citizen to passive recipient of publicity and social welfare client). These distinctions were set out in Habermas's early work on *Legitimation crisis* (1975) and have since been developed more extensively in his *Theory of communicative action* (1987) (see CRITICAL THEORY). Habermas's account intersects with geography in a variety of ways as, for example, when he analyses LANDSCAPE changes that concretize and reinforce the decline in active public debate (Habermas, 1989). Gregory (1993) draws out the centrality of geographical context for Habermas's social theory.

Feminists are critical of theoretical accounts such as these that reproduce the conceptual separations between public and private spheres without tracing the gender subtext on which they are based (Fraser, 1989). Scholars of FEMINIST GEOGRAPHY

have argued that the conceptual separations between public and private underlie subdisciplinary boundaries between ECONOMIC and SOCIAL GEOGRAPHY (Hanson and Pratt, 1988) and account for strategic silences in POLITICAL GEOGRAPHY (Kofman and Peake, 1990). They have explored how urban SPATIAL STRUCTURE concretizes and rigidifies these conceptual and practical separations so as to sustain gender inequalities.   GP

References

Fraser, N. 1989: *Unruly practices: power, discourse and gender in contemporary social theory.* Minneapolis: University of Minnesota Press.

Gregory, D. 1993: *Geographical imaginations.* Oxford: Blackwell.

Habermas, J. 1975: *Legitimation crisis,* transl. T. McCarthy. Boston: Beacon Press.

Habermas, J. 1987: *The theory of communicative action,* volume 2, *Lifeworld and system: a critique of functionalist reason,* transl. T. McCarthy. Boston: Beacon Press.

Habermas, J. 1989: *The structural transformation of the public sphere: an inquiry into a category of bourgeois society*, transl. T. Burger. Cambridge: MIT Press.

Hanson, S. and Pratt, G. 1988: Reconceptualizing the links between home and work in urban geography. *Econ. Geogr.* 64, pp. 299–321.

Kofman, E. and Peake, L. 1990: Into the 1990s: a gendered agenda for political geography. *Pol. Geogr. Q.* 9, pp. 313–36.

privatization The sale or transfer of public assets to the private sector. This should not be confused with DEREGULATION, which concerns the reduction or elimination of state regulation on activities which may already be privately owned. The case for privatization is usually grounded in claims that EFFICIENCY will be increased, but the aim may also be to raise revenue for the STATE, to spread share ownership and to de-politicize decision-making. That private production is actually more efficient than state enterprise is hard to demonstrate, and depends crucially on the competitive process. Thus the privatization of state monopolies (such as Britain's telephone, gas and water services) carries no guarantee of greater efficiency passed on as benefits for the consumer, and may merely lead to high private profits.

Privatization is generally part of a broader political agenda intended to inculcate or strengthen positive attitudes towards the free enterprise system associated with CAPITALISM, as in Britain under the Thatcher governments and in post-socialist Eastern Europe. The term 'reprivatization' is used to describe the process of returning to the original private owners – or to their descendants – property expropriated by the state with the advent of socialism, as in Poland for example. DMS

probabilism The view that although the physical environment does not uniquely determine human actions, it does nevertheless make some responses more likely than others. The term was proposed for the terrain mid-way between a stark ENVIRONMENTAL DETERMINISM and a radical POSSIBILISM: human action was represented as 'not so much a matter of an all-or-nothing choice or compulsion, but a balance of probabilities' (Spate, 1957). This view was in fact perfectly compatible with the original Vidalian conception (see

Lukermann, 1964), but in any event it was not long before geographers sought 'to use the probability calculus as well as rely on its philosophical connotations', and probability theory came to be regarded as an essential component of geographical analysis since it provided 'a common mode of discourse' for 'scientific study of the landscape' (Curry, in House, 1966). DG

References

House, J. W., ed. 1966: *Northern geographical essays in honour of G. H. J. Daysh*. Newcastle upon Tyne: University of Newcastle upon Tyne, Department of Geography.

Lukermann, F. 1964: Geography as a formal intellectual discipline and the way in which it contributes to human knowledge. *Can. Geogr.* 8, pp. 167–72.

Spate, O. H. K. 1957: How determined is possibilism? *Geogrl. Stud.* 4, pp. 3–12.

Suggested Reading

Spate (1957).

probability map A map of data which are standardized according to a particular statistical distribution; an important form uses standard scores of the NORMAL DISTRIBUTION. When the values are mapped, analysis can be made of differences between observed and expected outcomes, e.g. normally distributed data would be expected to have only five per cent of values greater than ± 1.96 standard score units from the mean. Haggett et al. (1977) outline the use of Poisson probabilities for studying rare events, and Wrigley (1977) develops the concept of probability surface mapping, a TREND SURFACE model suitable for categorical data. In DIGITAL CARTOGRAPHY and REMOTE SENSING probability distribution maps are important in the classification of imagery. MJB

References

Haggett, P., Cliff, A. D. and Frey, A. E. 1977: *Locational analysis in human geography*, second edition. London: Edward Arnold/New York: John Wiley.

Wrigley, N. 1977: *Probability surface mapping: an introduction with examples and Fortran programs*. Concepts and techniques in modern geography 16. Norwich: Geo Books.

Suggested Reading
Davis, F. W. and Simonett, D. S. 1991: GIS and remote sensing. In Maguire, D. J., Goodchild, M. F. and Rhind, D. W., eds, *Geographical information systems: principles and applications*, volume 1. London: Longman, pp. 191–213.

problematic A framework which determines the ways in which problems are identified within a DISCOURSE, and which thereby 'appears' in the concepts and evidences through which they are realized. The term comes from Jacques Martin, but it gained prominence through Louis Althusser's 'symptomatic' reading of Marx, in which he tried to uncover the system of concepts at work behind the evident form of the various texts and, in particular, to identify an *epistemological break* in which Marx was supposed to have made the transition from IDEOLOGY to science (see STRUCTURAL MARXISM). As such, the concept owes much to modern STRUCTURALISM, so that while there are a number of superficial similarities between them it is in fact very different from the Kuhnian concept of a PARADIGM. Although the term is widely used as a convenient shorthand, particularly in Marxist theory, Althusser's particular usage has been subject to several criticisms, and most especially for a conflation of the *external* process, through which a discourse is produced, and its own *internal* structure of dependence and connection (see, e.g., Hindess, 1977).   DG

Reference
Hindess, B. 1977: *Philosophy and methodology in the social sciences*. Brighton, UK: Harvester/Atlantic Highlands, NJ: Humanities Press.

Suggested Reading
Glucksmann, M. 1974: *Structuralist analysis in contemporary social thought*. London: Routledge and Kegan Paul, pp. 3–10.

process A flow of events or actions which produces, reproduces or transforms a system or structure.

It was not until the 1960s that modern geography was alerted to the complexity of the concept of a process. Blaut (1961) insisted that the standard distinction between SPATIAL STRUCTURE and temporal process derived from a KANTIANISM which had been discredited by what he called 'the relativistic revolution'. It was now clear, so he claimed, that 'nothing in the physical world is purely spatial or temporal; everything is process ...'. In Blaut's view, therefore, 'structures of the real world' were simply 'slow processes of long duration'. Although most formalizations of geography as a SPATIAL SCIENCE appeared to accept such a claim – Golledge and Amedeo (1968) and Harvey (1969) endorsed the central importance of 'process laws' in their general accounts of explanation in geography (see POSITIVISM) – in practice many studies used distance as a surrogate for process (hence 'spatial processes') and thereby confirmed the geometric cast of much of LOCATIONAL ANALYSIS and SPATIAL ANALYSIS (see DISTANCE DECAY).

Many of these models depended upon *formal language systems*, i.e. language systems the elements of which have *unassigned meanings*. The xs and ys in their equations or the points and lines in their diagrams could thus refer to anything – they were empty of concrete content – and so analysis was governed by the relations between these abstract elements in the language system itself: by the laws of geometry, the calculus of probability theory or the mathematical theory of STOCHASTIC PROCESSES, rather than by 'the things we are talking *about*' (Olsson, 1974). These models were reviewed in Cliff and Ord (1981).

The past 20 years, however, have seen the resurgence of geographies based on *ordinary language systems*, the elements of which have assigned meanings. These have allowed much more *substantive* conceptions of process to be utilized, e.g. cognitive and DECISION-MAKING processes in BEHAVIOURAL GEOGRAPHY, the LABOUR PROCESS and the dynamics of capital ACCUMULATION in ECONOMIC GEOGRAPHY, and processes of STRUCTURATION in SOCIAL GEOGRAPHY, and this has in turn required a careful reworking of some of the most basic theorems of the other human and social sciences (see Gregory, 1985). For, as Harvey (1973) recognized: 'An understanding of space in all its complexity depends upon an appreciation of social

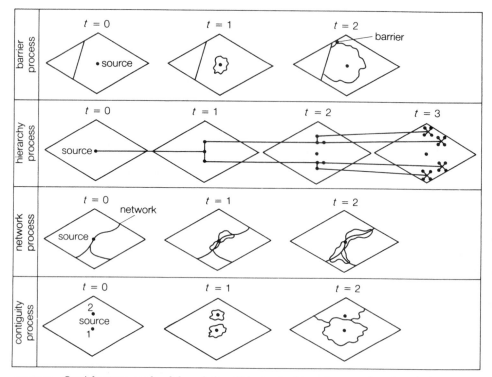

process   *Spatial patterns produced through time (t) by barrier, hierarchy, network and contiguity processes* (after Bennett, 1978).

processes . . . [and] an understanding of the social process in all its complexity depends upon an appreciation of spatial form'. One of his most pressing concerns was thus 'to heal the breach' between the 'sociological' and the 'GEOGRAPHICAL IMAGINATION'. (See also CONTEXTUAL THEORY.)

The distinction between 'formal' and 'substantive' definitions of process is cross-cut by a second distinction drawn by Hay and Johnston (1983) between the following:

(a) Process as *sequence* in space and/or time. This view of process is characteristic of the VERTICAL THEMES of traditional HISTORICAL GEOGRAPHY and of more modern SPACE-TIME FORECASTING models. In both cases, the account is usually descriptive: compare Darby's (1951) identification of the processes which changed the English landscape ('clearing the wood', 'draining the marsh', etc.) with Bennett's simple (1978) typology of

barrier, hierarchy, network and contiguity processes (see the figure).

(b) Process as *mechanism*. This view of process is most closely associated with SYSTEMS ANALYSIS, in which the 'central concept' of DIACHRONIC ANALYSIS is held to be 'that of process' (Langton, 1972, pp. 137–56), and more recently with those geographies which have been influenced by philosophies of REALISM, which requires the identification of the relations between the 'causal powers' of structures and their realizations (Sayer, 1984, pp. 94–107). In both cases, the account is *explanatory*: it seeks to show how – by what means – something happens.

Hay and Johnston (1983) integrate (a) and (b) as follows:

A process study seeks to identify the rules which govern spatio-temporal sequences, in such a form that the rules are interpretable in terms of the results of the sequence, in terms of the exogenous variables which influence the sequence, and in terms of the mechanisms by which exogenous and endogenous influences give rise to the results which the sequence itself records.

Although this formulation is explicitly restricted to quantitative studies in human geography, its emphasis on *interpretation* registers an important advance over most early spatial models (particularly those concerned with replication and SIMULATION) and it opens the door for *translations* between the two distinctions drawn above.

DG

References

Bennett, R. J. 1978: *Spatial time series: analysis, forecasting and control.* London: Pion.

Blaut, J. 1961: Space and process. *Prof. Geogr.* 13, pp. 1–7.

Cliff, A. D. and Ord, J. K. 1981: *Spatial processes: models and applications.* London: Pion.

Darby, H. C. 1951: The changing English landscape. *Geogrl. J.* 117, pp. 377–94.

Golledge, R. and Amedeo, D. 1968: On laws in geography. *Ann. Ass. Am. Geogr.* 58, pp. 760–74.

Gregory, D. 1985: People, places and practices: the future of human geography. In King, R., ed., *Geographical futures.* Sheffield: Geographical Association, pp. 56–75.

Harvey, D. 1969: *Explanation in geography.* London: Edward Arnold, pp. 419–32.

Harvey, D. 1973: *Social justice and the city.* London: Edward Arnold, pp. 22–49.

Hay, A. M. and Johnston, R. J. 1983: The study of process in quantitative human geography. *L'espace géogr.* 12, pp. 69–76.

Langton, J. 1972: Potentialities and problems of adopting a systems approach to the analysis of change in human geography. *Prog. Geog.* 4, pp. 125–79.

Olsson, G. 1974: The dialectics of spatial analysis. *Antipode* 6, pp. 50–62.

Sayer, A. 1984: *Method in social science: a realist approach.* London: Hutchinson.

Suggested Reading

Cliff and Ord (1981).

Harvey (1973).

Hay and Johnston (1983).

producer services Services which are supplied to businesses and government, rather than directly to individual users of CONSUMER SERVICES. Such services, which are often characterized as those which provide 'intermediate' inputs into the process of production, include economic activities as diverse as financial services, research and development, computer services, marketing and advertising, and certain kinds of transport and communication. Producer services have economically important and often quite distinctive geographies based upon the twin facts that the demand for these services and their supply need not be spatially coincident, and that they are often only partially dependent upon the level of economic activity in a city or region. The study of these geographies has become an increasing visible part of INDUSTRIAL GEOGRAPHY. They are also increasingly regarded as an important determinant in the formation of REGIONAL POLICY. (See also CONSUMER SERVICES; MONEY, GEOGRAPHY OF; SERVICES, GEOGRAPHY OF; CONSUMPTION, GEOGRAPHY OF.)

NJT

Suggested Reading

Daniels, P. W., ed. 1987: Special issue on producer services. *Environ. Plann.* A 19(5).

Daniels, P. W. ed. 1991: *Services and metropolitan development: international perspectives.* London: Routledge.

Marshall, J. N. ed. 1988: *Services and uneven development.* Oxford: Oxford University Press.

production See ASIATIC MODE OF PRODUCTION; FACTORS OF PRODUCTION; JUST-IN-TIME PRODUCTION; MODE OF PRODUCTION; PRODUCTION COMPLEX; RELATIONS OF PRODUCTION; TERRITORIAL PRODUCTION COMPLEX.

production complex A spatial cluster of specialized, interrelated economic activities bound together by the creation and exploitation of EXTERNAL ECONOMIES. Such clusters offer producers the ability to forge, and easily realign, transactional LINKAGES with other local buyers and suppliers, thereby encouraging the development and maintenance of a social division of labour (see JUST-IN-TIME PRODUCTION; TRANSACTIONAL ANALYSIS). They also provide a local labour market specialized to match the needs of local producers, and are further sustained by the existence of public and quasi-public institutions developed to support specialized

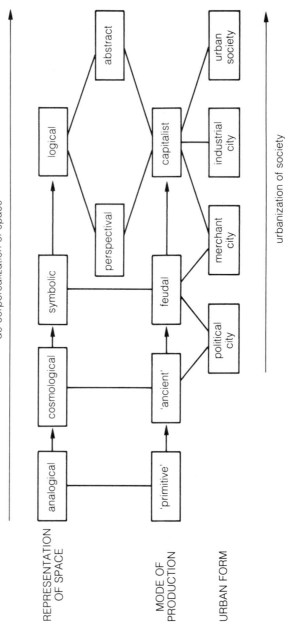

production of space 1: *The production of space* (Gregory, 1993; after Lefebvre).

local economic activity. (See also AGGLOMERATION.)   MSG

production of space The social production of the 'mental' and 'material' spaces within which social life takes place. The phrase derives from the French Marxist philosopher Henri Lefebvre (1901–91), who explored the social production of SPACE in a number of texts in the late 1960s and early 1970s (e.g., Lefebvre, 1970, 1972) and most notably in his *La production de l'espace* (1974; transl. 1991). This book represents probably the single most important source for understanding Lefebvre's ideas about social space. He was writing within a broadly humanist tradition of HISTORICAL MATERIALISM – one indebted to Hegel in several ways (see Poster, 1975; Soja, 1989) – which prompted him to be critical of POSTSTRUCTURALISM, STRUCTURALISM and STRUCTURAL MARXISM; he took particular exception to their use of spatial *metaphors* by means of which, so he said, 'the philosophico-epistemological notion of space is fetishized and the mental realm comes to envelop the social and physical one'. In place of these metaphors Lefebvre proposed a concept of socially produced space – of SPATIALITY – as a way of registering *both* 'mental space' *and* 'material space'.

Lefebvre's argument in *The production of space* was a complex one which drew on Marx, Hegel and Nietzsche. He provided a history of space which was, in effect, a (critical) history of 'the rise of the West': one that was particularly sensitive to the systematic *violence* involved in the formation and extension of CAPITALISM inside and outside Europe. But he saw this not simply in terms of CLASS struggle and capital accumulation - meat and drink to conventional Marxian accounts – but also as the inscription of masculine POWER ('phallic brutality') on social life and social space (see also PHALLOCENTRISM). In outline, Lefebvre sketched an historical series of representations of space, each connected to a specific MODE OF PRODUCTION, through which social space had been progressively 'de-corporealized': in other words, he argued that the advance of capitalism depended not only on a logic of accumulation but also on a *logic of visualization* through which human spatiality bore less and less relation to the

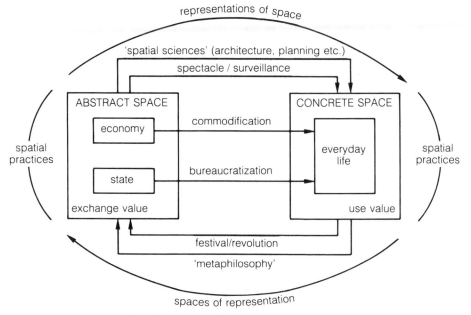

production of space   2: *The colonization of concrete space* (Gregory, 1993).

481

human body (see figure 1; see also Gregory, 1993). Lefebvre concluded that twentieth-century capitalism had successfully installed an *abstract space* – unevenly to be sure, but none the less globally – in which 'space had no social existence independently of an aggressive and repressive visualization'. He described this abstract space as a visual–geometric–phallic space' which was both symptomatic of and constitutive of MODERNITY and which had effectively *colonized* an older, historically sedimented *concrete space* (see also Lefebvre, 1971, 1992; cf. CRITICAL THEORY). As indicated in figure 2, Lefebvre suggested that this process of colonization had been effected through multiple *spatial practices* of bureaucratization and commodification, both of which relied on the imposition of spatial grids of POWER (e.g. TERRITORIALITY and ownership), and through *representations of space*, e.g. mainstream planning and SPATIAL SCIENCE, geographies of SPECTACLE and SURVEILLANCE. More recently, several commentators, drawing in some part on Lefebvre, have suggested that a new intensity of abstraction has been achieved within late-twentieth-century capitalism with the installation of the HYPERSPACE of POST-MODERNISM (Jameson, 1991).

Be that as it may, in the wake of the popular uprisings and student protests in France in May 1968 Lefebvre hoped that a counter-movement would emerge to resist the colonization of concrete space and to reclaim the spaces of everyday life. This would be informed by counter-discourses (*spaces of representation*): by his own 'metaphilosophy' and by critical practices in the arts, both of which would be involved in a series of spontaneous struggles ('festivals'). These spatial practices and spaces of representation had their origin in the concrete spaces of everyday life – in the memories and residues of an older, 'authentic' human existence inscribed within the TAKEN-FOR-GRANTED WORLD – and many of them depended on restoring an essential connective between human spatiality and the human body (see also Lefebvre, 1973, 1992).

Within Anglophone human geography Lefebvre's writings have been used to reflect on the relations between capitalism and urbanism (Harvey, 1973); to clarify general concepts of social space (Smith, 1990; Soja, 1989); and to illuminate the historical production of modern capitalist spatiality (Gregory, 1993; Harvey, 1989). His work remains indispensable to understanding the production and the politics of space.   DG

References

Gregory, D. 1993: *Geographical imaginations.* Oxford: Blackwell.

Harvey, D. 1973: *Social justice and the city.* London: Edward Arnold.

Harvey, D. 1989: *The condition of postmodernity: an enquiry into the origins of cultural change.* Oxford: Blackwell.

Jameson, F. 1991: *Postmodernism or, the cultural logic of late capitalism.* Duquesne: Duke University Press.

Lefebvre, H. 1970: *La révolution urbaine.* Paris: Gallimard.

Lefebvre, H. 1971: *Everyday life in the modern world.* New York: Harper.

Lefebvre, H. 1972: *Espace et politique.* Paris: Anthropos.

Lefebvre, H. 1973: *The survival of capitalism.* London: Allison and Busby.

Lefebvre, H. 1991: *The production of space.* Oxford: Blackwell.

Lefebvre, H. 1992: *Critique of everyday life.* London: Verso.

Poster, M. 1975: *Existential Marxism in post-war France.* Princeton, NJ: Princeton University Press.

Smith, N. 1990: *Uneven development.* Oxford: Blackwell, second edition.

Soja, E. 1989: *Postmodern geographies: the reassertion of space in critical social theory.* London: Verso.

Suggested Reading

Gregory (1993), ch. 6.

Lefebvre (1991), ch. 4.

productive forces The interaction of the means of production and labour, from which arises a society's capacity to produce. The means of production comprise the objects of labour and the means or instruments of labour. The objects of labour are all the things to which human labour is applied: they can be found as natural resources in the form of minerals, virgin timber, etc., or they can be objects to which some labour has already been applied, such as components and cultivated or harvested crops. The means of labour are the things that people use to transform the objects of labour. These can vary from a stick with which one may knock an apple from a tree to the complex plant used to produce pig iron from iron ore. The development of the LABOUR PROCESS and its capacity to generate a greater volume of output is crucially dependent on technological advances in the means of labour. Thus means of production created by human labour (such as machines) become steadily more important compared with natural objects of labour.

The means of production themselves cannot produce anything without the application of labour. The special status of labour in the productive forces is expressed in its capacity both to activate and to produce means of production. The advancement of labour skills and productivity contributes critically to the development of the productive forces.

The level of development of the productive forces is an indication of society's capacity to make use of NATURE. A territory that is well endowed with NATURAL RESOURCES will be able to generate things that are useful to people only to the extent that the other productive forces of human labour and the instruments at its disposal are also available. At any particular time and place, the further development of the productive forces may be crucially dependent on advances in either the means of labour or the capacity of labour itself, given the limits of natural resources, although these advances may themselves open up possibilities for using new resources. This emphasizes the importance of interdependence among the productive forces. (See also INFRASTRUCTURE; MODE OF PRODUCTION.)   DMS

productivity A measure of output relative to input. The term was initally developed in analyses of the EFFICIENCY of manufacturing industry, where it is equivalent to the *rate of surplus value* or *rate of exploitation* (cf. MARXIAN ECONOMICS). The higher the amount of value added in the production process relative to the costs incurred (of labour, materials and fixed capital), the greater is the productivity.

With the growth of SERVICE industries in advanced capitalist societies, attempts have been made to measure productivity in sectors other than manufacturing – such as higher education – although the concept of value added is not readily applied in many such situations.   RJJ

profit surface Spatial variations in the profit to be obtained from the sale of a good or service, depicted as a three-dimensional surface with distance along the two horizontal axes and profit in pecuniary units on the vertical axis. The profit surface is generated by the interaction of the appropriate COST SURFACE and REVENUE SURFACE. The technical assumptions and the quality of data required to identify a profit surface empirically are such as to make this exercise virtually impossible. However, the concept of the profit surface is of assistance in the development of certain theoretical approaches to industrial location. (See also VARIABLE COST ANALYSIS.)   DMS

projection In CARTOGRAPHY, a systematic two-dimensional transformation of the three dimensions of a sphere. Projection in its standard form is concerned with accurately representing the three dimensions of a sphere (Earth, Moon, planet, etc.) on a plane surace. Conventional instructions envisage a set of mathematical or geometrical transformations that attempt to retain one or more of the following spherical characteristics:

(a) *Area*: the area of a scaled unit on the projection is equivalent to its area on the original sphere – hence the equal-area or equivalent type.

(b) *distance*: the correct distance between two points is accurately retained – equidistant.

(c) *Direction*: a straight-line relationship which is the shortest route on the sphere (great circle) is also shown as such on the projection – azimuthal or zenithal.

(d) *Shape*: the shape of units is correctly shown (conformal), this being useful if the map is required for assessing angular relationships between points on the sphere.

An alternative classification is: (a) cylindrical, such as the Lambert and Mercator types (the latter is suitable for some navigational purposes); (b) conical; and (c) planar. Additionally, while many projections aim to show 'uninterrupted' images of the sphere, others use 'interrupted' styles; J. P. Good's projection of the world, for example, divides the Earth's land masses into 12 zones, each of which has a locally centred projection. More recently, the Peters Projection has caused controversy through its attempt to depict equal area and be 'fair to all peoples' (see Monmonier and Schnell, 1988). Although many aspects of this projection are not new, it has been widely adopted by agencies and pressure groups, indicating the geopolitical implications of projections.

The act of projection automatically incurs error, and thus one should choose a particular projection to suit the purpose of the MAP and to minimize the distortions that would inject 'noise' into the transmission of the message (see CARTOGRAPHY). (Distortion can be determined by measures such as Tissot's Indicatrix, which calculates the angular deformation occurring at points on projections.) This contrasts with traditional teaching which tends to stress construction, involving drafting a framework and interpolating the features onto that framework. The tedious nature of construction has been a major factor in a generally poor use of projection by geographers. All too often, a particular projection base is chosen not because it fits particular requirements of the message but because a preprepared base exists and is convenient to use. Robinson et al. (1985) noted that COMPUTER-ASSISTED CARTOGRAPHY allows a major change of emphasis, since 'the versatility of the computer and plotter have made it much easier to obtain a good match between map objective and projection'. In the same way that recent technology has absolved the map image from constraints of storage media, so the digital computer has alleviated computational and drafting problems of projection (Snyder, 1982). Thus human geographers require knowledge of basic spherical properties to be retained rather than any lengthy typographical classification. Indeed, it is often feasible to violate the strict objectives of projection and deliberately distort topology by using CARTOGRAMS.   MJB

References

Monmonier, M. S. and Schnell, G. A. 1988: *Map appreciation*. Englewood Cliffs, NJ: Prentice-Hall.

Robinson, A. H., Sale, R., Morrison, J. and Muehrcke, P. C. 1985: *Elements of cartography*, fifth edition. New York: John Wiley.

Snyder, J. P. 1982: *Map projections used by the U.S. Geological Survey*. Geological Survey Bulletin 1532. Washington, DC: US Department of the Interior.

Suggested Reading

Maling, D. H. 1991: Coordinate systems and map projections for GIS. In Maguire, D. J., Goodchild, M. F. and Rhind, D. W., eds, *Geographical information systems: principles and applications*, volume 1. London: Longman, pp. 135–46.

Snyder, J. P. 1987: *Map projections – a working manual*. US Geological Survey Professional Paper 1395. Washington, DC: US Government Printing Office.

protoindustrialization   A term coined by Mendels to describe 'the first phase' which 'preceded and prepared for' the INDUSTRIALIZATION of the capitalist space-economy through 'the rapid growth of traditionally organized but market-oriented, principally rural industry' (Mendels, 1972). The emergence of industries in the countryside was a commonplace of European HISTORICAL GEOGRAPHY, but since Mendels reopened the debate the process has been formalized in various ways which seek to contest conventional assumptions of a marked ('revolutionary') discontinuity between preindustrial and industrial economies and to elucidate the regional specificity of the transformation. Two main models have been proposed, and although their substantive connections have stimulated a series of cross-fertilizations, they can nevertheless be located within two distinctive theoretical traditions:

(a) *Ecological functionalist models.* These note that labour in an agrarian economy is intrinsically seasonal so that 'the adoption of industry by a growing number of PEASANTS . . . meant that labour previously unemployed or underemployed during a part of the year [could be] put to work on a more continuous basis' (Mendels, 1972). Such a logic would locate protoindustrialization in the arable regions, of course, whereas in her classic essay on 'Industries in the countryside' Thirsk (1961) drew attention to the importance of pastoral regions. Her argument was based on daily rather than seasonal 'time-budgets', however, and so there seems little reason to promote one logic over the other and to expect any simple relationship between protoindustrialization and the agrarian economy. Even so, many writers have accentuated the DIVISION OF LABOUR between the corn-growing arable regions and the cloth-making pastoral regions, and have explained its emergence in terms of 'COMPARATIVE ADVANTAGES' (Jones, 1968). This was achieved through the coordinating functions performed by merchants in the towns, who thus became foci of capital ACCUMULATION.

(b) *Economic structural models.* These suggest that the pace and pattern of protoindustrialization was determined by the relations between two basic circuits:

(1) *Petty commodity production*: at the microlevel, the artisan household strove to maintain a precarious balance between production and consumption and its labour discipline was thus oriented towards *use-values.* When prices fell, therefore, the system was peculiarly vulnerable because production was stepped up to boost the shortfall in receipts, thereby deepening and widening the recession.

(2) *Mercantile capitalism*: at the macrolevel, the products of the domestic labour process were consigned to distant (often overseas) markets by merchants who were oriented towards *exchange-values.* When prices rose, therefore, the system was peculiarly vulnerable because artisan households could satisfy their immediate needs most easily and production slowed down – at the very moments at which opportunities from mercantile profits were at their greatest.

The contradiction between (1) and (2) was supposedly resolved by merchants seizing hold of production and taking the first steps towards the mechanization of the LABOUR PROCESS and the formation of a factory system (see Kriedte et al., 1981, 1986).

One of the most serious weaknesses of both models is an unstated appeal to a transcendent logic of CAPITALISM. Thus:

. . . the major weakness of the comparative advantage model of regional specialization is its assumption of individual and social rationality in the various farming regions, and the implication that production will always adjust to comparative advantage in the long run. In reality, regional specialization was fundamentally affected by custom and tradition, embodied in the motivations and practices of economic actors, and in the variety of institutional environments (Berg et al., 1983).

The importance of 'custom' and 'tradition' is recognized by Medick and his collaborators, but usually confined to the artisan household where the pursuit of profit is hedged around by the precepts of a 'moral economy' (see Thompson, 1974). The merchant is reduced to the status of rational 'economic man', closed in the cloth-hall and the counting-house and the 'bearer' of the immanent logic of capitalist rationality. There is little room for the complex social and political affiliations which, in some instances, prompted merchants to set themselves *against* the incursions of the factory system (Wilson, 1971; Du Plessis and Howell, 1982; Gregory, 1982).

Both models also find common ground in their emphasis on the demographic consequences of protoindustrialization, and in particular on the creation of a labour-surplus economy (Levine, 1987; see also AGRICULTURAL INVOLUTION). Here too, however, the complexity of the situation belies the simplicity of most of the explanations which have been offered: the ways in which a labour-*surplus* economy 'prepared for' labour-*saving* technical change needs careful elucidation of the contingent features of the regional settings in which protoindustrialization took place (Hudson, 1981, 1983; see Berg, 1985). (See also INDUSTRIAL REVOLUTION.)   DG

References

Berg, M. 1985: *The age of manufacturers: industry, innovation and work in Britain, 1700–1820.* London: Fontana.

Berg, M., Hudson, P. and Sonenscher, M. 1983: Manufacture in town and country before the factory. In Berg, M., Hudson, P. and Sonenscher, M., eds, *Manufacture in town and country before the factory*. Cambridge: Cambridge University Press, pp. 1–32.

Du Plessis, R. and Howell, M. C. 1982: Reconsidering the early modern urban economy: the cases of Leiden and Lille. *Past and Present* 94, pp. 49–84.

Gregory, D. 1982: *Regional transformation and Industrial Revolution: a geography of the Yorkshire woollen industry*. London: Macmillan/Minneapolis: University of Minnesota Press.

Hudson, P. 1981: Proto-industrialisation: the case of the West Riding textile industry. *Hist. Workshop J.* 12, pp. 34–61.

Hudson, P. 1983: From manor to mill: the West Riding in transition. In Berg, M., Hudson, P. and Sonenscher, M., eds, *Manufacture in town and country before the factory*. Cambridge: Cambridge University Press, pp. 124–44.

Jones, E. L. 1968: The agricultural origins of industry. *Past and Present* 40, pp. 128–42.

Kriedte, P., Medick, H. and Schlumbohm, J. 1981: *Industrialization before industrialization: rural industry in the genesis of capitalism*. Cambridge: Cambridge University Press.

Kriedte, P., Medick, H. and Schlumbohm, J. 1986: Protoindustrialization on test with the guild of historians: response to some critics. *Econ. Societ.* 15, pp. 254–72.

Levine, D. 1987: *Reproducing families: the political economy of English population history*. Cambridge: Cambridge University Press.

Mendels, F. F. 1972: Proto-industrialization: the first phase of industrialization. *J. econ. Hist.* 32, pp. 241–61.

Thirsk, J. 1961: Industries in the countryside. In Fisher, F. J., ed., *Essays in the economic and social history of Tudor and Stuart England*. Cambridge: Cambridge University Press, pp. 70–88.

Thompson, E. P. 1974: Patrician society, plebeian culture. *J. soc. Hist.* 7, pp. 382–405.

Wilson, R. G. 1971: *Gentlemen merchants: the merchant community in Leeds, 1700–1830*. Manchester: Manchester University Press.

Suggested Reading

Houston, R. and Snell, K. D. M. 1984: Protoindustrialization? Cottage industry, social change and industrial revolution. *Hist. J.* 27, pp. 473–92.

Hudson (1981, 1983).

public administration, geography of Studies of spatial variations in the management of the STATE APPARATUS and of possible geographical contributions to that management.

Early works focused on the LOCATIONAL ANALYSIS approach, and what that PARADIGM could offer to understanding 'the influence of space and location on the provision of public services' (Massam, 1975). Massam's text concentrated on: (1) the size and shape of the administrative areas used in the delivery of public services; (2) interactions between those areas; and (3) the spatial allocation of public services among and within areas (see LOCATION-ALLOCATION MODELS; PUBLIC SERVICES, GEOGRAPHY OF). Later work has been more widely concerned with the administration of urban areas, especially those with fragmented local government structures (Barlow, 1991); and Bennett (1989) has argued for geographical involvement in determining what should be delivered as a public service, involving the transfer of resources from rich to poor (both people and areas) by the state, and what should be placed in the 'free market'. RJJ

References

Barlow, M. 1991: *Metropolitan government*. London: Routledge.

Bennett, R. J. 1989: Whither models and geography in a post-welfarist world? In Macmillan, B. ed., *Remodelling geography*. Oxford: Blackwell, pp. 273–90.

Massam, B. H. 1975: *Location and space in social administration*. London: Edward Arnold.

Suggested Reading

Bennett, R. J., ed., 1989: *Territory and administration in Europe*. London: Belhaven Press.

public choice theory Deriving from Duncan Black's (1958) pioneering work, public choice theory considers topics normally covered by political science, such as voting behaviour, the bureaucracy, party politics, and the theory of the STATE but examines them using the analytical techniques of NEOCLASSICAL ECONOMICS. In particular, it is assumed that all agents within the political sphere act out of a narrow self-interest, maximizing their own individual welfare through RATIONAL CHOICE. For example, politicians enact only those policies that will ensure their re-election, voters will remain deliberately ignorant because of the disproportionate costs of learning about election issues, and bureaucrats will do whatever is necessary to please their superiors in order to gain promotion. Within public choice theory three core theoretical concerns are recognizable: first, the problems attending aggregating individual choices in maximizing some social welfare function (following from Arrow's (1951) impossibility theorem); second, the difficulties stemming from the introduction of PUBLIC GOODS and market failure; and finally, the complexities entailed by treating PUBLIC FINANCE as a rational exchange among citizens. The last two areas are the ones that have been most explored by geographers (see, respectively, Cox and Johnston, 1982; Bennett, 1980). TJB

References

Arrow, K. J. 1951: *Social choice and individual values*. New York: John Wiley.

Bennett, R. J. 1980: *The geography of public finance*. London: Methuen.

Black, D. 1958: *The theory of committees and elections*. Cambridge: Cambridge University Press.

Cox, K. R. and Johnston, R. J., eds 1982: *Conflict, politics and the urban scene*. New York: St. Martin's Press.

Suggested Reading

Archer, J. C. 1981: Public choice paradigms in political geography. In Burnett, A. D. and Taylor, P. J., eds, *Political studies from spatial perspectives*. New York: John Wiley, pp. 73–90.

Dunleavy, P. J. 1990: *Democracy, bureaucracy and public choice*. Cambridge: Polity Press.

Mueller, D. C. 1979: *Public choice*. Cambridge: Cambridge University Press.

public finance, geography of

Studies of geographical variations in the incidence of public-sector income and expenditure. According to Bennett (1980), its particular focus is on the spatial imbalance between the geographies of revenue raising, on the one hand, and of public expenditure on the other, producing a subdiscipline concerned with:

. . . how burdens and expenditure incidence vary as a function of geographical location. Who gets what benefits, and bears what burdens

as a function of where they live: *who gets what, where, at what cost?* (p. ix).

Such a focus is needed within the broader study of public finance, Bennett argues, because needs, costs and preferences for various PUBLIC GOODS vary spatially, both among individuals and among the local governments which provide them (cf. COLLECTIVE CONSUMPTION), and if geographical redistribution is not undertaken to correct for such variations then spatial polarization of rich and poor (again, both individuals and local governments) will occur (cf. POSITIVE DISCRIMINATION). Bennett's detailed evaluation of the EQUITY issues involved in tackling such differentials, and his later (1985) empirical studies of British local government finance mechanisms, are countered by his recent arguments that equality in the distribution of public goods is unattainable, and that their provision by the STATE APPARATUS should be much reduced (Bennett, 1989). RJJ

References

Bennett, R. J. 1980: *The geography of public finance: welfare under fiscal federalism and local government finance*. London: Methuen.

Bennett, R. J. 1985: *Central grants for local governments*. Cambridge: Cambridge University Press.

Bennett, R. J. 1989: Whither models and geography in a post-welfarist world? In B. Macmillan, ed., *Remodelling geography*. Oxford: Blackwell, pp. 273–90.

public goods

Goods that are either freely available to all – such as unpolluted air – or those provided equally to all citizens of a defined TERRITORY. Public goods are generally provided by the STATE, and fall into three main categories:

(a) *Pure public goods*, which are freely and equally available to all people throughout a state's territory. Although, ideally, all public goods should fall within this category, few do because of difficulties – even impossibilities in many cases – in ensuring an equal provision. One of the few goods which does normally fall into this category is national defence.

(b) *Impure public goods*, which are services provided either at fixed locations (such as health centres and parks) or along fixed routes (such as public transport services). These are necessarily more accessible to some people than others, and because usage tends to decline with distance from a facility (cf. DISTANCE DECAY) then the closer people live to it the greater their (potential) benefit. As a consequence, there is likely to be social and political CONFLICT over the location of such facilities (cf. TURF POLITICS).

(c) *Pure public goods impurely distributed,* because of decisions to vary the density of provision. Many public services are provided by local governments, which may differ in their spending on a service (or even whether they provide it), thus producing a geography of uneven provision. Within one (local) government's territory, there may also be variations in the density of provision above a certain norm (cf. MERIT GOOD), perhaps reflecting political decisions on the greater 'need' of some areas relative to others (cf. PORK BARREL).

In NEOCLASSICAL ECONOMICS the rationale for the state provision of public goods is given by the impossibility of exclusion: because it is impossible to opt out of benefiting from national defence if you live within the national territory, for example, then defence should be paid for by all through public taxation. With regard to merit goods, public provision is defended on the grounds that unless people were required to consume a certain amount (as illustrated by a minimum school-leaving age, for example) they might 'underconsume', which would be in neither their individual nor society's collective long-term general interest.   RJJ

Suggested Reading
Bennett, R. J. 1980: *The geography of public finance.* London: Methuen.
Cox, K. R. and Johnston, R. J., eds 1982: *Conflict, politics and the urban scene.* London: Longman/New York: St. Martin's Press.
Pinch, S. P. 1985: *Cities and services: the geography of collective consumption.* London: Routledge and Kegan Paul.

public policy, geography and   Geographical study of and involvement in the creation, implementation, monitoring and evaluation of public policies. Work in this area (much of which could be termed APPLIED GEOGRAPHY) has increased in recent years in capitalist countries because of: the growing importance of the STATE in economic and social affairs, offering enhanced opportunities for such work; increased governmental recognition of environmental and spatial problems awaiting resolution; individual geographers' desire to contribute to the attack on such problems; and the perceived need for geographers to demonstrate the RELEVANCE of their field, and so earn protection of their discipline's resources within higher education institutions in an increasingly materialist situation.

Geographical analyses of public policies have largely been concerned with evaluation of the policies to address identified 'spatial problems of environment, economy and society' (House, 1983) and with assessment of their 'geographical impact and degree of effectiveness': in the volume of essays that he edited on *United States public policy,*

. . . Critique stops short of prescription but there is some attempt to look ahead and also, in some cases, to set the problems within a theoretical, as well as an operational, framework (pp. v–vi).

House saw the benefits of such work as twofold:

. . . to non-geographical academic or lay audiences . . . [it reflects] a particular set of perspectives on some urgent problems which face policymakers in our very critical times. To geographers in training, the relevance of applications of the discipline should be a major concern, whether to add practical purpose to their studies, or to point in the direction of possible professional careers outside the education field (p. vi).

The geographical perspectives identified as most valuable to public policy study were the discipline's technocratic skills and its practitioners' ability to synthesize the many component parts of a complex problem.

The nature of the applied contributions has been largely pragmatic, reflecting the available opportunities and the ability of geographers to capitalize on them with their technocratic skills – hence the current promotion of REMOTE SENSING and GEOGRAPHICAL INFORMATION SYSTEMS

(Openshaw, 1989). Whereas some geographers have promoted such involvement as necessary for the discipline's survival (Berry, 1970; Abler, 1992), others have queried this by pointing to the role of much public policy as sustaining, if not enhancing, the inequalities and exploitation that are inherent in CAPITALISM – hence Harvey's (1974) question 'What kind of geography for what kind of public policy?'.

In countries under SOCIALISM academics traditionally had much less freedom and most of their research was oriented towards public policy – at the direct requirement of the state (see Johnston and Claval, 1984)

RJJ

References

Abler, R. F. 1992: Desiderata for geography. In Johnston, R. J., ed., *The challenge for geography: a changing world; a changing discipline*. Oxford: Blackwell.

Berry, B. J. L. 1970: The geography of the US in the year 2000. *Trans. Inst. Br. Geogr.* 51, pp. 21–53.

Harvey, D. 1974: What kind of geography for what kind of public policy? *Trans. Inst. Br. Geogr.* 63, pp. 18–24.

House, J. W., ed., 1983: *United States public policy: a geographical view*. Oxford: Clarendon Press.

Johnston, R. J. and Claval, P., eds 1984: *Geography since the Second World War: an international survey*. London: Croom Helm/ Totowa NJ: Barnes and Noble.

Openshaw, S. 1989: Computer modelling in human geography. In Macmillan, B., ed., *Remodelling geography*. Oxford: Blackwell, pp. 273–90.

public services, geography of The study of geographical aspects of public services. Public services differ from non-public services (provided in the independent or 'private' sector) because they are part of the process of COLLECTIVE CONSUMPTION through which services are organized or managed by a STATE-operated system, financed at least partly through taxation, and are consumed by users according to non-market criteria, such as need for the services, rather than market criteria such as ability to pay. These services are often organized collectively because it would not be efficient, effective or equitable to leave their provision solely to the operation of commercial market forces or to the responsibility of charitable agencies. In a hypothetical sense, a public service would be considered as a *'pure'* PUBLIC GOOD if nobody in a society were excluded from using it and nobody could opt out of consuming it. Fluoridation of water supplies and defence might almost be considered to meet these criteria. However, few if any public services are actually consumed and benefitted from jointly by all members of a society, so that they are more properly considered as *impure public goods*. Various factors produce geographical differences in the ways in which public services are provided and used. These include geographical variations in population needs and demands for services, and local variation in political ideology. Other relevant spatial factors include the ways in which a country is divided into administrative areas for the organization of public services (*jurisdictional partitioning*), the flows of users between one administrative area and another, and the effect of distance from a facility on both the use made of it and the benefit gained from it by the population (see DISTANCE DECAY).

The public services that have been most widely studied by geographers are those which provide for individual welfare (e.g. state health care, state education, nonmedical caring services and public housing) and the major public utilities which contribute to a country's infrastructure (e.g. roads, railways and power systems).

Since the objective of public services is often to achieve what is considered to be a just distribution of resources and opportunities for all members of a society, EQUALITY and EQUITY are important themes in the geography of public services. From a geographical point of view, social justice is often interpreted in terms of *territorial justice* (a distribution of resources between areas which matches the population needs of those areas). Since societies generally wish to obtain the best return for their investment of resources in public services, questions of EFFICIENCY and effectiveness in the economy of welfare are also important. Therefore many studies in the geography of public services are concerned with the extent to which the distribution of public resources and the level of public-service provision, ACCESSIBILITY and use correspond to socially accepted definitions of need and eligibility. Questions of spatial, economic and social accessibility, and the availability of facilities such as hospitals, schools and state housing for populations needing to use them, are addressed by these studies. Issues of funding for public services, such as local taxation, are also examined. These studies are confronted by major theoretical and methodological questions concerning the definition and measurement of welfare service needs in the population, of the quantity and quality of services being provided and used, and of the outcomes of these services in terms of welfare.

The debate over the roles of the public and independent sectors in the provision of welfare services is also of major importance in this field. In many countries there have recently been important changes in policies for public services, sometimes referred to as a RESTRUCTURING of the welfare state, resulting in a shift away from collective consumption as a method of providing welfare services towards a greater reliance on market forces. This shift is often justified by claims that it will help to contain the cost of public expenditure and will lead to more efficient and effective services which are responsive to the demands of individual consumers. The debate also reflects different ideological perspectives on the extent to which societies should share responsibility for welfare or make it the responsibility of individual members of the society. Research in the geography of public services is often directed towards investigating the evidence for and against the different positions taken in this debate.

The influence of political ideology and processes is fundamental to any interpretation of the geography of public services, and especially to analysis of the role of the welfare state. The extent of the public sector and its spatial organization will vary from one country to another. Within countries, local political influences are also crucial in the geography of public services, and the relationship between central and local government control over public services is a further issue which is often addressed by geographers working in this field. There are thus important theoretical and substantive links between the geography of public services and POLITICAL GEOGRAPHY.

Although the public sector may therefore appear to be reduced in many countries, geographers examining public services still have many important questions to address concerning equity and efficiency and the relationship between public and non-public services. In poorer countries, public services are often in a more basic state of development, and the important issues are concerned with how limited state resources can be appropriately used and developed to protect and improve the welfare of the population. The geography of public services must be seen in the context of the wider social and economic structure of society, and explanations of the geography of public services are informed by theories concerning social processes, such as the mode of production, gender and race relations. SC

Suggested Reading

Bennett, R. 1980: *The geography of public finance: welfare under fiscal federalism and local government finance*. London: Methuen.

Bennett, R. 1982: *Central grants to local government*. Cambridge: Cambridge University Press.

Curtis, S. 1989: *The geography of public welfare provision*. London: Routledge.

Dunleavey, P. 1980: *Urban political analysis*, London: Macmillan.

Harvey, D. 1973: *Social justice and the city*. London: Edward Arnold.

Pahl, R. 1975: *Whose city?*, second edition. London: Penguin.

Pinch, S. 1980: *Cities and services*. London: Routledge and Kegan Paul.

Saunders, P. 1986: *Social theory and the urban question*, second edition. London: Hutchinson.

Q

---

quadrat A small area, usually square, used in sampling designs in the field and in the analysis of mapped patterns (hence the term 'quadrat analysis' for the study of point patterns within an arbitrary areal base). Quadrats are extensively used in ECOLOGY to assess the floral and/or faunal characteristics of an area.   RJJ

Suggested Reading

Thomas, R. W. 1977: *An introduction to quadrat analysis*. Concepts and techniques in modern geography 12. Norwich: Geo Books.

qualitative methods A set of tools developed to pursue the epistemological mandate of the philosophies of meaning (see EPISTEMOLOGY). They are a product of the advent of HUMANISTIC GEOGRA-PHY – a recognition of what Cloke et al. (1991) call the 'peopling of human geo-graphy'.

Qualitative methods range from passive observation and personal reflection, through routine participation to active intervention. The common theme is a preoccupation with systems of shared meaning: the common project, one of subjective understanding rather than statis-tical description; the primary goal, an ability to emphasize, communicate and (in some cases) emancipate, rather than to generalize, predict and control. To this end, qualitative research is organized in a variety of ways, from semi-structured interview schedules to the open-ended attempt to absorb the entirety of a LIFE-WORLD. Generally, there is a dynamic relationship between theory building and empirical enquiry: observable 'facts' are neither wholly independent of theory nor

wholly determined by it (see SYMBOLIC INTERACTIONISM).

Most qualitative approaches therefore depend on intensive empirical research: they assume that reality is (more or less) present in appearance, but usually recog-nize that there is no single 'real' world that exists independently of the relationships between observers and the observed. These relationships are a prerequisite for achiev-ing the intersubjectivity which leads to an appreciation of the constitution of social life. They also provide a basis for the appreciation, clarification and interpreta-tion of meaning, thus linking qualitative methods to the project of HERMENEUTICS. Nevertheless, there is some debate as to whether analysts should attempt to mini-mize their intrusion into the ACTIVITY SPACE of their subjects (emphasizing the role of onlooker that is implicit at one extreme of the strategy of PARTICIPANT OBSERVATION) or whether they should abandon any attempt to achieve this neutrality and instead engage more fully in a form of action research which allows them to translate their own, and their subject's, normative theories into experi-ence.

It has been argued that the distinction between observation and intervention is to an extent immaterial, because any changes resulting from current strategies of encoun-ter are likely to have less effect on the studied community than on the analyst's 'self' (Smith, 1988). This may mean that geographers should step beyond the philo-sophies of meaning towards the practice of psychoanalysis if they are fully to exploit the potential of qualitative research. Certainly, the study of 'self' is one of the least developed areas of human geography

(IBG Social and Cultural Geography Study Group, 1991). This is a serious oversight, given that an understanding of how 'selves' relate to 'others' is crucial to our handling of the 'double hermeneutic' which provides qualitative methods with their most formidable challenge (i.e. with the challenge of recognizing that the end-point of qualitative research is an analyst's construction of other people's constructions of the meaning systems within which they operate – a problem which is perhaps best, if rather unconventionally, illustrated by Mitchell, 1974).

Despite some common themes, the means and ends of the various approaches to qualitative human geography do vary. This is one consequence of the diverse philosophies that the field embraces (see EXISTENTIALISM; IDEALISM; PHENOMEN-OLOGY; PRAGMATISM). Idealism requires only observation and reflection and, in geography, is linked mainly to the project of reconstructing historical landscapes by rethinking the thoughts that built them. This approach is most often (although not uncontroversially) linked with the work of Leonard Guelke, but is equally applicable to much of the work of Carl Sauer, and can be seen as influential in a naively 'materialist' form of cultural geography (see CULTURAL LANDSCAPE). Existentialism and phenomenology (and their link through existential phenomenology) provide the underpinning for most qualitative research in geography, emphasizing the importance of understanding lived experience, and of reflecting on the meanings associated with everyday life.

Existential phenomenology thus requires participation as well as observation (see PARTICIPANT OBSERVATION), and demands an interpretation of the complex relationship between the (analyst's) self and the (studied) other(s). This provides the underpinning both of the descriptive ETH-NOGRAPHY (Jackson, 1985) and of a more rigorous case study method (Mitchell, 1983). Pragmatism stresses the inseparability of knowledge and action, and is more self-consciously interventionist than the other philosophies of meaning. This approach affords no privilege to the academic or analyst, and recognizes no distinction between our understanding of the world as it is, and our actions to achieve a world as it 'ought' to be. It is therefore more aligned with the project of action research than with that of participant observation (Smith, 1984).

Qualitative methods refer to more than the different ways of setting up a relationship between analysts and their subjects. Abstracting information through observation and experience is just one form of qualitative research. Another approach is through in-depth individual or group IN-TERVIEWING, which may be used to elicit personal life histories, community biographies and a range of information that is relevant to the understanding of human experience and aspiration. With the advent of software for coding, formalizing, summarizing and abstracting machine-readable interview transcripts, new methodological controversies can be expected concerning motivation and justification for objectifying and quantifying essentially qualitative data.

Qualitative research is not, of course, restricted to strategies of direct encounter. It is also informed by the analysis and interpretation of TEXT as inscribed in diaries, letters and other personal documents, in literature and film, and in the LANDSCAPE itself. This has turned qualitative geographers' attention to questions concerning the production and consumption of environmental meanings (Burgess, 1990), to the role of language in the making of place (Tuan, 1991), and to a range of new projects attempting to describe, experience and explain the resurgence of culture in a postmodern world.   SJS

References

Burgess, J. 1990: The production and consumption of environmental meanings in the mass media: a research agenda for the 1990s. *Trans. Inst. Br. Geogr.* n.s.15, pp. 139–61.

Cloke, P., Philo, C. and Sadler, D. 1991: *Approaching human geography*. London: Paul Chapman.

IBG Social and Cultural Geography Study Group 1991: *New words: new worlds: reconceptualising social and cultural geography*. Lampeter University, Geography Department.

Jackson, P. 1985: Urban ethnography. *Progr. hum. Geogr.* 9, pp. 157–76.

Mitchell, J. C. 1974: Perceptions of ethnicity and ethnic behaviour: an empirical exploration. In Cohen, A., ed., *Urban ethnicity*. London: Tavistock, pp. 1–35.

Mitchell, J. C. 1983: The logic of the analysis of social situations and cases. *Soc. Rev.* 31, pp. 187–211.

Smith, S. J. 1984: Practicing humanistic geography. *Ann. Ass. Am. Geogr.* 74, pp. 353–74.

Smith, S. J. 1988: Constructing local knowledge: the analysis of self in everyday life. In Eyles, J. and Smith, D. M., eds, *Qualitative methods in human geography*. Cambridge: Polity Press, pp. 17–38.

Tuan, Y.-F. 1991: Language and the making of place: a narrative–descriptive approach. *Ann. Ass. Am. Geogr.* 81, pp. 684–96.

Suggested Reading

Eyles, J., ed. 1988: *Research in human geography*. Oxford: Blackwell.

Eyles, J. and Smith, D. M., eds, 1988: *Qualitative methods in human geography*. Cambridge: Polity Press.

Jackson, P. 1989: *Maps of meaning*. London: Unwin Hyman.

Pickles, J. 1985: *Phenomenology, science and geography*. Cambridge: Cambridge University Press.

quality of life The state of SOCIAL WELL-BEING of an individual or group, either perceived or as identified by 'observable indicators'. Most studies of the quality of life concentrate on aspects of the human condition, either those revealed by observable indicators (in some cases, relative to defined norms) or those declared by the individuals concerned. Geographical studies of the concept have largely focused on the former, as revealed for the populations of defined areas (hence the potential for the ECOLOGICAL FALLACY to be committed). RJJ

quantitative methods The use of mathematical techniques, theorems and proofs in understanding geographical systems. Two main types of application exist: *statistical methods* which are employed in generating and testing hypotheses using empirical data; and pure *mathematical modelling*, which is employed when deriving formal models from a set of initial abstract assumptions. The two types come together in CALIBRATION: statistical methods are used to estimate, and test the significance of, various parameters associated with a given mathematical model, such as the FRICTION OF DISTANCE coefficient of the GRAVITY MODEL.

Statistical methods were first introduced into the discipline in the early 1950s (Burton, 1963). Consisting mainly of descriptive statistics, there was also some attempt at HYPOTHESIS testing, using, for example, CHI-SQUARE. Bivariate REGRESSION analysis followed shortly, but it was not until the 1960s that the GENERAL LINEAR MODEL was fully explored. Since then, much attention has been paid to a set of very sophisticated dynamic linear (e.g. SPACE–TIME FORECASTING MODELS) and non-linear (e.g. SPECTRAL ANALYSIS) statistical techniques, including those that bear peculiarly upon geographical problems (e.g. SPATIAL AUTOCORRELATION).

The inspiration for mathematical modelling came from at least two sources: first, SOCIAL PHYSICS, which focused initially on the GRAVITY MODEL, and later ENTROPY MAXIMIZATION; and, second, NEOCLASSICAL ECONOMICS which influenced geography principally through the REGIONAL SCIENCE movement and LOCATION THEORY. Associated with each were often different questions, and hence a different branch of mathematics. The typical preoccupation of social physics is the SPATIAL INTERACTION among a set of discrete geographical points (frequently, but not always, leading to the use of matrix algebra), while for neoclassical economics it is with OPTIMIZATION over continuous space (usually resulting in the use of differential calculus). Note, however, that this is a generalization: in fact, one of the reasons why spatial interaction theorists often confine themselves to discrete space is because of the very difficulty of the mathematics associated with spatial interaction over continuous space.

The evangelical fervour surrounding the widening use and application of quantitative methods during the 1960s produced a backlash in the 1970s, with both RADICAL (Harvey, 1973) and HUMANISTIC GEOGRAPHERS (Ley and Samuels, 1978) suggesting that geography's QUANTITATIVE REVOLUTION was itself ripe for overthrow.

Too many of the questions asked by human geographers, they argued, could not be answered using mathematics, and even those that could were not sensitively addressed using non-quantitative means. Perhaps a more considered judgement is that while quantitative methods are certainly important, they cannot be the intellectual foundation of the discipline (see Pratt, 1989). The questions posed by human geography are far too broad for such a narrow base.   TJB

References

Burton, I. 1963: The quantitative revolution and theoretical geography. *Can. Geogr.* 7, pp. 151–62.

Harvey, D. 1973: *Social justice and the city.* London: Edward Arnold.

Ley, D. and Samuels, M., eds 1978: *Humanistic geography: prospects and problems.* London: Croom Helm.

Pratt, G. 1989: Quantitative techniques and humanistic-historical materialist perspectives. In Kobayashi, A. and Mackenzie, S., eds, *Remaking human geography.* Boston: Unwin Hyman, pp. 101–15.

Suggested Reading

Burton (1963).

Pratt (1989).

Sayer, A. 1984: *Method in social science: a realist approach.* London: Hutchinson, ch. 6.

Wilson, A. G. and Bennett, R. J. 1985: *Mathematical methods in human geography and planning.* Chichester: John Wiley.

quantitative revolution The 'radical transformation of spirit and purpose' (Burton, 1963) which Anglo-American geography underwent in the 1950s and 1960s, replacing an earlier IDIOGRAPHIC concern with AREAL DIFFERENTIATION by a NOMOTHETIC search for models of SPATIAL STRUCTURE. Although a convenient and widely used shorthand, most commentators emphasize its limitations by prefacing it with the qualifying 'so-called'. It is, in fact, doubly misleading. First, it was not confined to the application of statistical and mathematical methods but also involved the conjoint construction of formal theories of spatial organization. Second, it was, in some senses at least, evolutionary rather than revolutionary (Chisholm, 1975), formalizing a longstanding but

ill-defined commitment to POSITIVISM. In more general terms, the phrase is clearly derived from Kuhn's concept of PARADIGM change and is susceptible to the same criticisms as that has received.   DG

References

Burton, I. 1963: The quantitative revolution and theoretical geography. *Can. Geogr.* 7, pp. 151–62.

Chisholm, M. 1975: *Human geography: evolution or revolution?* London: Penguin.

Suggested Reading

Billinge, M., Gregory, D. and Martin, R. L., eds 1984: *Recollections of a revolution: geography as spatial science.* London: Macmillan/New York: St. Martin's Press.

Johnston, R. J. 1991: *Geography and geographers: Anglo-American human geography since 1945,* fourth edition. London: Edward Arnold/New York: Halstead, ch. 3.

Taylor, P. J. 1976: An interpretation of the quantification debate in British geography. *Trans. Inst. Br. Geogr.* n.s. 1, pp. 129–42.

questionnaire An instrument used for the data collection segment of a SURVEY ANALYSIS. It comprises a carefully structured and ordered set of questions designed to obtain the needed information without either ambiguity or bias (and as such, according to some critics, it introduces an unequal power relationship between questioner and questioned). Every respondent answers the same questions, asked in the same way and in the same sequence, which contrasts with the more open-ended formats used in INTERVIEWS and other QUALITATIVE METHODS for obtaining information from individuals. The questionnaire may be administered by a trained person, either in a face-to-face meeting or by telephone, or it may be self-administered.

Questionnaires can be devised to obtain a variety of data. The simplest are the factual, ascertaining information such as age, place of birth, etc. The second type are the attitudinal, for which questions are designed (and carefully pre-tested and piloted to ensure their validity) to probe people's values, attitudes and opinions. Such data may be obtained through open-ended questions, with the 'free' responses recorded and later categorized, but the use of specially designed scaling instruments for measuring different types of attitude (personality, political ideology, etc.) is more common: some of these are generally applicable, but many are specifically designed for a particular study, to reflect the local cultural situation and context. (See also REPERTORY GRID ANALYSIS; SEMANTIC DIFFERENTIAL.)

The production of questionnaires is sometimes assumed to be a straightforward task and is undertaken in a rather cavalier manner. However, for collecting all but the simplest of factual information, great care is needed to ensure the absence of ambiguity (recalling that the questions may be asked of people from a wide range of backgrounds), so that all respondents will interpret them in the same way. (If a respondent has to ask what a question means, then the answer will potentially introduce bias, especially if not all puzzled respondents actually ask.) With a self-administered questionnaire, the problems of varying interpretations of an unclear question are very substantial, and may invalidate any analysis of the data obtained.

RJJ

Suggested Reading

Dixon, C. J. and Leach, B. 1976: *Questionnaires and interviews in geographical research.* Concepts and techniques in modern geography 18. Norwich: Geo Books.

R

race   Coming into English usage in the sixteenth century, this word took on its current problematic range of meanings in the nineteenth century, when writers such as Thomas de Gobineau began to confuse classifications of human beings based on physical criteria, such as skin colour, with value judgements about social status and moral worth. Further confusions followed from debates about SOCIAL DARWINISM in which the idea of human evolution as a competitive struggle was extended from the biological realm (where it referred to relations *between* species) to the sociological realm (where it referred to relations *within* species). Ideas of racial superiority (and their discriminatory consequences) quickly followed in association with Europe's imperial expansion overseas. The idea that human beings can be readily divided into a series of discrete 'races' is now widely regarded as fallacious: a political and social construction rather than a biological fact, the product of RACISM rather than of human genetics. Until recently (e.g. Jackson, 1989; Smith, 1989), geographical interest in 'race' has concentrated on the measurement and significance of residential SEGREGATION rather than on the social and spatial constitution of different racialized groups.

PAJ

References

Jackson, P. 1989: Geography, race, and racism, in Peet, R. and Thrift, N., eds, *New models in geography*, volume 2. London: Unwin Hyman, pp. 176–95.

Smith, S. J. 1989: *The politics of 'race' and residence*. Cambridge: Polity Press.

Suggested Reading

Banton, M. 1977: *The idea of race*. London: Tavistock.

Gould, S. J. 1984: *The mismeasure of man*. London: Penguin.

Rex, J. and Mason, D., eds 1986: *Theories of race and ethnic relations*. Cambridge: Cambridge University Press.

racism   An ideology of difference whereby social significance is attributed to culturally constructed categories of RACE. Expressed in more formal sociological language, racism is 'an ideology which ascribes negatively evaluated characteristics in a deterministic manner . . . to a group which is additionally identified as being in some way biologically . . . distinct' (Miles, 1982, p. 78). From such ideological distinctions, practical consequences inevitably follow, leading to racial discrimination and inequality. Recent geographical writings (e.g. Jackson, 1987) have highlighted the territorial basis of various forms of racism, including the institutionalization of racialized inequality in housing markets (cf. HOUSING CLASS).

PAJ

References

Jackson, P., ed. 1987: *Race and racism: essays in social geography*. London: Allen and Unwin.

Miles, R. 1982: *Racism and migrant labour*. London: Routledge and Kegan Paul.

Suggested Reading

Miles, R. 1989: *Racism*. London: Routledge.

Solomos, J. 1989: *Race and racism in contemporary Britain*. London: Macmillan.

radical geography   A term introduced in the 1970s to describe the increasing volume of geographical writing which was critical of SPATIAL SCIENCE, and also of POSITIVISM as the philosophy which dominated research trends in the discipline at that time. It began as a critique within the contemporary liberal concerns of society, but later coalesced around a belief in the power of Marxian analyses (see MARXIAN ECONOMICS; MARXIST GEOGRAPHY) and focused on the pages of *Antipode: A Radical Journal of Geography* (founded in 1969). By the late 1980s, what Walker (1989a, p. 620) termed 'left geography' had 'edged towards the mainstream' of the discipline's work: it can, he contends, 'claim a good deal of credit for broadening the intellectual respectability of the geographic enterprise outside the discipline in recent years, and can claim a measure of intellectual leadership and even hegemony within certain geographic subfields'.

The origins of the radical geography movement can be traced to concern in the late 1960s, especially in the US, with three contemporary political issues – the Vietnam war, civil rights (especially of American blacks) and the pervasive poverty and inequality suffered by residents of urban GHETTOS and deprived rural areas – all of which were generating increased social unrest. Out of these concerns grew a more general critique of capitalist society, which meant that radical geography, in Peet's (1977) words, developed largely as 'a negative reaction to the established discipline': this work also introduced the study of topics such as poverty, hunger, health and crime to human geographers, who had previously very largely ignored them. Led by Harvey (1973) and others, however, that critical stance was incorporated into a strong Marxist base, which sought, again to quote Peet, to create a 'radical science, which seeks to explain not only what is happening but also to prescribe revolutionary change': Marxism was the favoured theoretical structure (Harvey, 1982), and CLASS analysis the preferred approach to a wide range of topics covering virtually the whole of the discipline (as Walker's, 1989a, review shows).

With time, the critique of the mainstream human geography of the 1960s and 1970s became fairly widely accepted within the discipline, even if the radicals' revolutionary goals were not. And so, according to Peet and Thrift (1989), by the 1980s it had become less combative, for four reasons: Marxist thought itself was subject to powerful critiques; the failure of socialist-inspired states made the revolutionary goals less certain (intriguingly, radical geographers had done very little empirical work on the then-existing socialist states, including the USSR – but see Smith, 1979); the discipline had become more professional and less accepting of radicals; and a number of the 1960s–1970s radicals had joined the disciplinary 'establishment'.

By the end of the 1980s, various authors were relabelling radical geography – Peet and Thrift termed it 'the political-economy perspective', for example – whereas others (notably Harvey – see the 1987 debate in *Environment and Planning D, Society and Space* stimulated by his critique of British urban studies: Harvey, 1987; see also Walker, 1989a) pressed for a continued commitment to a Marxist perspective and theoretical foundation, which he, unlike many others, did not find antithetical to the criticisms of attempts to develop 'grand theory' coming from the adherents to POSTMODERNISM (on which see Harvey, 1989). The fall of the STATE APPARATUS practising socialism in the USSR and Eastern Europe at the end of the decade also caused some to reconsider (e.g. Walker, 1989b; Sayer and Folke, 1991): the latter conclude that whereas some people interpret the events of 1989–1991 as 'the final victory for capitalism', for them 'For decades all discussions in our part of the world about socialism have been marred by the bureaucratic and oppressive character of the "real, existing socialism". Now the slate is clean. Let us try a fresh start!'. (To most observers, the 'slate' left by the socialist governments in the USSR and Eastern Europe is far from clean, and capitalist development there will be substantially constrained by the inherited geography.) RJJ

References

Harvey, D. 1973: *Social justice and the city*. London: Edward Arnold.

Harvey, D. 1982: *The limits to capital*. Oxford: Blackwell.

Harvey, D. 1987: Three myths in search of a reality in urban studies. *Environ. Plann. D, Society and Space* 5, pp. 367–76.

Harvey, D. 1989: *The condition of postmodernity*. Oxford: Blackwell.

Peet, R. 1977: *Radical geography: alternative viewpoints on contemporary social issues*. Chicago: Maaroufa/London: Methuen.

Peet, R. and Thrift, N. J. 1989: Political economy and human geography. In Peet, R. and Thrift, N., eds, *New models in geography*, volume 1. London: Unwin Hyman, pp. 3–29.

Sayer, A. and Folke, S. 1991: What's left to do? Two views from Europe. *Antipode* 23, pp. 240–8.

Smith, D. M. 1979: *Where the grass is greener*. London: Penguin.

Walker, R. A. 1989a: Geography from the left. In Gaile, G. L. and Willmott, C. J., eds, *Geography in America*. Columbus, OH: Merrill, pp. 619–50.

Walker, R. A. 1989b: What's left to do? *Antipode* 21, pp. 133–65.

rank–size rule An empirical regularity in the CITY-SIZE DISTRIBUTIONS of countries and regions. In its most general form, if the cities are rank-ordered in terms of their populations from the largest (1) to the smallest (*n*), then the population of the city ranked *k* can be derived from

$$P_k = P_1/k$$

where P_k is the population of the city ranked *k* and P_1 is the population of the largest city. The form of the relationship between P_k and *k* is J-shaped, but is linear if both are transformed logarithmically (see TRANSFORMATION OF VARIABLES).

The precise relationship is usually identified empirically using REGRESSION analysis of the form:

$$\log P_k = \log P_1 - b \log k.$$

The larger the value of *b*, the steeper the slope is and thus the larger city P_1 relative to all others. (In the 'pure' formulation, *b* = 1.0.)

No convincing explanation for the existence of the relationship has been developed, despite the frequency with which it is observed. Nor are there convincing explanations for the varying size of *b*. (See also PRIMATE CITY, LAW OF THE.)   RJJ

Suggested Reading
Carroll, G. R. 1982: National city-size distributions: what do we know after 67 years of research? *Progr. hum. Geogr.* 16, pp. 1–43.

rational choice theory A NORMATIVE THEORY of individual DECISION-MAKING which claims that human action is based on getting the most for the least. On the one hand, individuals have an unlimited set of ends that provide utility but, on the other hand, they possess only a limited means to realize them. The role of the rationality postulate is to ensure that the best ends are chosen given the constraints. Often couched in terms of the mathematics of constrained maximization, the problem of making the best choices is formally shown to reduce to a set of consistency requirements with respect to choice: completeness, reflexivity, and transitivity (Hahn and Hollis, 1979). These three requirements define rationality, in the sense that if any one of them is contravened the choice is not rational.

The historical antecedents of rational choice theory are with the British classical economists, but it is now most closely associated with their successor, NEOCLASSICAL ECONOMICS, and even more recently with a maverick strain of Marxism (ANALYTICAL MARXISM). Not surprisingly, the use of rational choice theory is found most frequently in ECONOMIC GEOGRAPHY, and in particular in the formal location models associated with REGIONAL SCIENCE. Its role there is to impose a determinant order on spatial arrangements, one allowing the theorist to make scientific claims to precision, exact inference and predictability.

Criticisms of the rationality assumption are vast, and they frequently focus on the patently unrealistic characteristics attributed to a rational actor: perfect knowledge; egoism; independent preferences; the ability and desire to maximize utility (minimize costs); and pursuit of a single goal (see SATISFICING BEHAVIOUR). However, Barnes (1988) argues that such criticisms are often moot, because by its very construction the rationality postulate is empirically untestable and so charges of unrealism can never be sustained. More damaging is the rationality postulate's reliance on a supposedly foolproof EPIS-TEMOLOGY to justify its universalism. Of the four epistemologies that have been proposed – EMPIRICISM, INSTRUMENT-ALISM, *a priori* truths and IDEAL TYPES – none are convincing. For this reason it is better to see the historical rise of the rationality postulate not in terms of its ability to make truth claims, but rather in its sociological role – the power and prestige it afforded its users in an age of science (Mirowski, 1989).   TJB

References

Barnes, T. J. 1988: Rationality and relativism in economic geography: an interpretive review of the *Homo economicus* assumption. *Prog. hum. Geogr.* 12, pp. 473–96.

Hahn, F. and Hollis, M., eds 1979: Introduction. In *Philosophy and economic theory*. Oxford: Oxford University Press, pp. 1–17.

Mirowski, P. 1989: *More heat than light: economics as social physics: physics as nature's economics*. Cambridge: Cambridge University Press.

Suggested Reading

Barnes (1988).

Caldwell, B. 1982: *Beyond positivism: economic methodology in the twentieth century*. London: Allen and Unwin.

realism A philosophy of science based on the use of ABSTRACTION to identify the (necessary) *causal powers and liabilities* of specific *structures* which are realized under specific (contingent) *conditions*. If we 'unpack' this sentence – and the notion of 'unpacking' is an integral part of realism's conceptual vocabulary – then we must begin with a fundamental distinction between:

(a) the identification of *causal mechanisms*, typically the concern of 'INTENSIVE' RESEARCH – the key question here is 'how does something happen?'; and

(b) the identification of *empirical regularities*, typically the concern of 'EXTENSIVE' RESEARCH – the key question here is 'how widespread is something?'

The two need to be distinguished because, quite simply, 'what *causes* something to happen has nothing to do with the *number of times* it happens' (Sayer, 1985a). It is exactly this distinction which is erased in EMPIRICISM and POSITIVISM and,

inseeking to reinstate it, realism is not merely non-positivist, it is *anti-positivist* (Stockmann, 1983). During the QUANTITATIVE REVOLUTION, for example, much mainstream human geography was preoccupied with the identification of empirical regularities, a search for 'order' and 'pattern' which implicitly followed 'the guidelines proposed by positivism', and this tradition continues in the prediction of empirical regularities by SPACE–TIME FORECASTING MODELS. But, as Chouinard et al. (1984) emphasize, for these regularities to approach the status of the scientific LAWS required by positivism – *universal* statements which are sometimes called 'Humean laws' or laws of *constant conjunction* – then the configuration of the mechanism capable of generating them and the configuration of the conditions under which it in fact does so must *both be constant*. This kind of research strategy thus depends upon the existence, empirically or experimentally, of a *closed system*. Yet all of the cases with which human geography and the other human and social sciences are centrally concerned (and many of the natural sciences too) are *open systems*. Three points follow from this discussion:

(a) As Sayer (1984a) notes, 'the uneven success of [the identification and] prediction [of empirical regularities] across the "sciences" has plenty to do with the nature of their objects and little to do with their maturity'. Indeed, Williams (1981) concludes that, conceived in this way, the human and social sciences 'must be exclusively explanatory rather than predictive': a claim which cuts right through the symmetry between explanation and prediction assumed by positivism (and CRITICAL RATIONALISM).

(b) Realism offers a particular perspective on the nature of open systems. Its ONTOLOGY provides the basis for what Bhaskar (1975, 1979) calls a 'multi-tiered conception of reality' in contrast to the 'atomism' characteristic of both empiricism and positivism. What this means, rather more simply, is that empiricism and positivism typically assume that the world is made up of *events*: these are the 'empirical particulars' of science, the observation of which is usually accorded a special privilege as the leading edge of scientific discovery. Realism regards the world as differentiated and stratified, however, and made up not only of events but also of *mechanisms* and *structures*. The connection between the last two is straightfoward. 'Structures' are seen as sets of INTERNAL RELATIONS which have characteristic ways of acting, i.e. 'causal powers and liabilities' which they possess by virtue of what they are and which are thus 'necessary', and which are realized through 'mechanisms'. The task of a realist science is then to tease out causal chains which situate particular events within these 'deeper' mechanisms and structures. The technical term for this procedure is the recovery of *ontological depth*, so that whereas empiricism collapses the world into a singular plane pockmarked by the space–time incidence of events, realism seeks to recover the connective tissue between different dimensional domains. In doing so, it establishes relations of *natural necessity* rather than the relations of logical necessity which typify positivism and critical rationalism.

(c) Identification of mechanisms and structures is far from straightforward, however, because they are not immediately inscribed in the taken-for-granted categories which we draw upon in our everyday, 'commonsense' discourse. Their disclosure thus requires a research strategy in which theoretical categories inform (and are in turn informed by) empirical materials. It is for this reason, of course, that *abstraction* looms so large in what is sometimes called 'transcendental' or 'theoretical' realism. Hesse (1974) has formalized this strategy as a *network model* of scientific enquiry which, in its essentials, describes a hermeneutic circle (see HERMENEUTICS): a process of progressive and reflexive investigation (Gregory, 1978). (This in turn allows for the conjunction of realism and hermeneutics within some versions of CRITICAL THEORY.)

These three points can, in the main, be used to underpin both the natural sciences and the human and social sciences. Within the human and social sciences, realist perspectives have been opened up in history (e.g. McLennan, 1981), in

sociology (e.g. Keat and Urry, 1981) and in human geography (e.g. Williams, 1981; Sayer, 1982, 1985a; Chouinard et al. 1984). What is particularly noticeable, however, is that in all the examples cited here realism has been closely associated with HISTORICAL MATERIALISM, and the same relation – although by no means an exclusive one, as not all Marxists are realists and not all realists are Marxists – can be discerned in two of the most influential *philosophical* expositions of realism (and on which most of these examples draw, to a greater or lesser degree): R. Bhaskar's *A realist theory of science* (1975) and (especially) *The possibility of naturalism* (1979). Bhaskar's theses are open to objection, from within realism as well as from outside, partly because they are sustained 'by an unnecessarily restricted conception of the natural sciences' (Benton, 1985) and partly because 'a specific social ontology' does not follow directly from the more general ontology supposed by Bhaskar's transcendental realism (Keat and Urry, 1981). With these twin qualifications in mind, however, we can note that within the human and social sciences the 'mechanisms' which are the mainspring of realism usually refer to *systems of social practices* – Williams (1981) contends that 'in a fundamental sense the concept of practice lies at the heart of the realist account' – which, we may say, '*depend upon* knowledgeable and capable human subjects (although they are not reducible to them) and whose effects are to some substantial degree *determined* by contingent features of the settings in which they occur' (Gregory, 1985). Two further points then follow:

(d) The appeal to 'knowledgeable and capable human subjects' – to HUMAN AGENCY in its broadest sense – is intended to distance realism from 'essentialism' (the belief that there is an essential reality lying 'behind' the surface appearances and which is somehow more 'real') and from STRUCTURALISM (which displaces the human subject altogether). If we take this appeal seriously, then we must acknowledge that enquiry in the human and social sciences entails not the single hermeneutic described in (c) above but what Giddens

(1976) calls a *double hermeneutic*: unlike the natural sciences, the human and social sciences seek to understand a world which is *pre-interpreted*, and those pre-existing interpretations are of quite basic importance for any explanatory account. And yet, as Keat and Urry (1981) recognize, 'acceptance of the need for interpretive understanding in the [human and] social sciences' seems to 'undermine the possibility of a theoretical realist naturalism'. For the fact is that most of us most of the time *do not* make sense of the world through the clean and clinical abstractions demanded by realism; yet our 'lay' constructions *must not* be severed from the 'scientific' explanations provided by realism. As Sayer (1985b) has it:

In real life we live in conjunctures whose boundaries are arbitrary; they haphazardly cut across structures and causal relations, and unless we devote considerable energy to their understanding, we only disentangle such conjunctures sufficiently for us to cope with everyday tasks. As theorists, however, we seek to understand the world by making rational abstractions which isolate unified objects, structures or groups, and we try to conduct concrete research by starting from such abstraction.

Elsewhere, Sayer (1984b) argues that the separation of these two facets, which he calls the 'expressive' and the 'objective' respectively, has serious consequences for the social sciences and for social policy. Hence, realism needs to sustain substantive social theories capable of identifying 'the relations between different ontological domains at the same time as recognizing their integrity as differentiated features of social reality' (Layder, 1981): and it is for this reason that realism is often coupled with STRUCTURATION THEORY (see Gregory, 1982).

(e) The appeal to 'contingent features' of the 'settings' in which social practices occur, to their 'conditions', is intended to prise realism away from an unyielding determinism. In contrast to positivism, realism regards scientific 'laws' as statements of *necessity*, not universality. But consider gunpowder, says Sayer: it has the (necessary) causal power to explode, yet it does not do so anywhere and everywhere. Whether it does so 'depends on it being in

the right conditions – in the presence of a spark, etc. So although causal powers exist necessarily by virtue of the nature of the objects which possess them, it is contingent whether they are activated or exercised'. By extension, too, their effects 'depend on the presence of certain contingently related conditions'. What this means, Sayer concludes, is that in 'concrete research' – in the examination of the *exercise* and *effect* of causal powers – space (or, more correctly, spatial configuration) 'makes a difference'.

In closed system . . . science the contingencies of spatial form are either rendered constant or are a matter of indifference where they concern spatial relation between objects which do not causally interact . . . In social systems we have a continually changing jumble of spatial relations, not all of them involving objects which are causally indifferent to one another. So even though concrete studies may not be interested in spatial form *per se*, it must be taken into account if the contingencies of the concrete and the differences they make to outcomes are to be understood (Sayer, 1984a; see also Sayer, 1985b).

Important though this conclusion undoubtedly is – for the human and social sciences as a whole, not just for human geography, since it undermines the possibility of *any* aspatial science – some commentators would evidently regard it as the 'weak' version of a much 'stronger' thesis. This would claim that spatial configurations are important not only for concrete research but also for 'abstract research'. To use Sayer's own example: gunpowder is constituted as gunpowder and hence possesses its specific causal powers by virtue of the time–space relations which exist between its elements. Its constitution cannot be accounted for by *either* its time–space relations alone (the classical error of SPATIAL ANALYSIS) *or* its elements alone (the classical error of COMPOSITIONAL THEORY): they must be taken together. According to the 'strong' thesis, therefore, it is possible to generalize this example and to recognize, as a CONTEXTUAL THEORY such as structuration theory does, the *time–space constitution of social systems* (Giddens, 1981, 1984). Social structures possess spatial structures: they cannot be separated. Hence, as Urry (1985) concludes, 'the social world should be seen as comprised of space–time entities having causal powers which may or may not be realised depending on the patterns of spatial/temporal interdependence [between them]'. Sayer (1985b) has, in part, subsequently conceded the force of this argument, but he still regards abstract propositions about time–space relations as highly generalized:

While it is important for abstract theory to be aware of the existence of space, the claims that can be made about it are inevitably rather indifferent ones, such as Anthony Giddens's TIME–SPACE DISTANCIATION and 'time–space edges' . . . Concepts such as distanciation have a useful theoretical or meta-theoretical role but they do not and should not be expected to say much about concrete spatial forms.

What this seems to indicate, therefore, is not a rigid dividing line between 'abstract' and 'concrete' research, but rather the need for the careful delineation of a hierarchy of concepts in which time–space relations become ever more tightly specified.

Bhaskar has himself become increasingly interested in these questions – in the 'time–space dependence' of social practices and social structures (Bhaskar, 1986, pp. 129–31) – but these concerns extend beyond the philosophy of (social) science to raise a further series of questions about how accounts conducted under the sign of realism are to be *written*. Here one needs to remember that 'realism' refers not only to a philosophy; it also describes a mode of representation, in both literature and art, which was particularly important in nineteenth-century European culture. This is not to say that realist philosophies (in the first sense) require realist expression (in the second sense) – they almost certainly do not. But Sayer (1989) has provided an important discussion of textual strategies which are relevant to his politico-intellectual project. He argues in particular that the linear narratives which are typically used to encase and carry causal chains need to be interrupted and illuminated by irony, paradox and coincidence as a way of sparking off further critical reflection. In this sense, although not in most others, the philosophy of realism intersects with the interest in representation to be found in POSTMODERNISM.   DG

References

Benton, T. 1985: Realism and social science: some comments on Roy Bhaskar's 'The possibility of naturalism'. In Edgley, R. and Osborne, R., eds, *Radical philosophy reader*. London: Verso, pp. 174–92.

Bhaskar, R. 1975: *A realist theory of science*. Leeds: Leeds Books. (Reprinted 1978, Brighton, UK: Harvester.)

Bhaskar, R. 1979: *The possibility of naturalism: a philosophical critique of the contemporary human sciences*. Brighton, UK: Harvester.

Bhaskar, R. 1986: *Scientific realism and human emancipation*. London: Verso.

Chouinard, V., Fincher, R. and Webber, M. 1984: Empirical research in scientific human geography. *Prog. hum. Geogr.* 8, pp. 347–80.

Giddens, A. 1976: *New rules of sociological method: a positive critique of interpretative sociologies*. London: Hutchinson.

Giddens, A. 1981: *A contemporary critique of historical materialism*, volume 1, *Power, property and the state*. London: Macmillan.

Giddens, A. 1984: *The constitution of society*. Cambridge: Polity Press.

Gregory, D. 1978: *Ideology, science and human geography*. London: Hutchinson.

Gregory, D. 1982: A realist construction of the social. *Trans. Inst. Br. Geogr.* n.s. 7, pp. 254–6.

Gregory, D. 1985: People, places and practices: the future of human geography. In King, R., ed., *Geographical futures*. Sheffield: Geographical Association, pp. 56–76.

Hesse, M. 1974: *The structure of scientific inference*. London: Macmillan/Berkeley, CA: University of California Press.

Keat, R. and Urry, J. 1981: *Social theory as science*, second edition. London: Routledge and Kegan Paul.

Layder, D. 1981: *Structure, interaction and social theory*. London: Routledge and Kegan Paul.

McLennan, G. 1981: *Marxism and the methodologies of history*. London: Verso/New York: Schocken.

Sayer, A. 1982: Explanation in economic geography: abstraction versus generalization. *Progr. hum. Geogr.* 6, pp. 66–88.

Sayer, A. 1984a: *Method in social science: a realist approach*. London: Hutchinson. (Second edition 1992: London: Routledge.)

Sayer, A. 1984b: Defining the urban. *GeoJournal* 9, pp. 279–85.

Sayer, A. 1985a: Realism in geography. In Johnston, R. J., ed., *The future of geography*. London: Methuen, pp. 159–73.

Sayer, A. 1985b: The difference that space makes. In Gregory, D. and Urry, J., eds, *Social relations and spatial structures*. London: Macmillan, pp. 49–65.

Sayer, A. 1989: The 'new' regional geography and problems of narrative. *Environ. Plann. D, Society and Space* 7, pp. 253–76.

Stockmann, N. 1983: *Antipositivistic theories of the sciences: critical rationalism, critical theory and scientific realism*. Dordrecht: Reidel.

Urry, J. 1985: Social relations, space and time. In Gregory, D. and Urry, J., eds, *Social relations and spatial structures*. London: Macmillan, pp. 20–48.

Williams, S. 1981: Realism, Marxism and human geography. *Antipode* 13(2), pp. 31–8.

Suggested Reading

Cloke, P., Philo, C. and Sadler, D. 1991: *Approaching human geography: an introduction to contemporary theoretical debates*. London: Paul Chapman/New York: Guildford, ch. 5.

Lawson, V. and Staeheli, L. 1990: Realism and the practice of geography. *Prof. Geogr.* 42, pp. 13–19.

Outhwaite, W. 1987: *New philosophies of social science: realism, hermeneutics and critical theory*. London: Macmillan.

Pratt, A. 1991: Reflections on critical realism and geography. *Antipode* 23, pp. 248–55.

Sayer (1984a).

reciprocity A system of mutual exchange. In its most general form, reciprocity is closely associated with (STRUCTURAL) FUNCTIONALISM and especially with notions of SYSTEM (see Gouldner, 1975, pp. 190–259). More specifically, however, reciprocity was one of three FORMS OF ECONOMIC INTEGRATION identified by Karl Polanyi and linked with a characteristic spatial pattern: 'Reciprocity denotes movements between correlative points of symmetrical groupings' (in Dalton, 1968). This emphasis on symmetry was intended to distinguish reciprocity from other forms of exchange, notably REDISTRIBUTION, and was repeated by Harvey (1973) in his equation of reciprocity with *egalitarian* societies which were incapable of sustaining the concentration of a surplus required for the emergence of urbanism. But other versions of exchange theory have emphasized that reciprocity need not entail consensus (see Lebra, 1975), and indeed exchange theory – the modern development of which is usually attributed to Homans (1961) and Blau (1964) – has provided a much more elaborate typology of transactions than Polanyi's original sketches. Thus, for example, Sahlins (1974) distinguishes generalized, balanced and negative reciprocity and shows that in 'primitive' systems of exchange these variant forms are related to

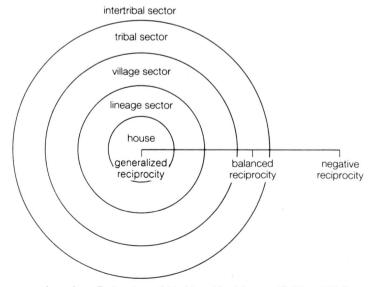

reciprocity *Reciprocity and kinship residential sectors* (Sahlins, 1974).

both kinship distance and rank: beyond the inner circles of some 'tribal societies' generalized and balanced reciprocity may give way to institutionalized raiding and stealing ('negative reciprocity') (see the figure; see also Smith, 1979).   DG

References

Blau, P. 1964: *Exchange and power in social life.* New York: John Wiley.

Dalton, G., ed. 1968: *Primitive, archaic and modern economics: essays of Karl Polanyi.* Boston: Beacon Press.

Gouldner, A. 1975: *For sociology.* London: Penguin.

Harvey, D. 1973: *Social justice and the city.* London: Edward Arnold/Baltimore, MD: Johns Hopkins University Press.

Homans, G. 1961: *Social behaviour: its elementary forms.* London: Routledge and Kegan Paul.

Lebra, T. 1975: An alternative approach to reciprocity. *Am. Anthr.* 77, pp. 550–65.

Sahlins, M. 1974: *Stone age economics.* London: Tavistock/Chicago: Aldine, ch. 5.

Smith, R. M. 1979: Kin and neighbours in a 13th century Suffolk community. *Journal of Family History* 4, pp. 219–56.

Suggested Reading

Ekeh, P. 1974: *Social exchange theory: the two traditions.* London: Heinemann.

Sahlins (1974).

Smith (1979).

recreation The generic term for lei-sure-time activities (cf. LEISURE, GEOGRA-PHY OF). Recreations are frequently indulged in away from home, and a major field of geographical research has been to model and explain the pattern of demand associated with recreational trips (Jackson and Burton, 1989). Demand is related to variables such as disposable income, leisure time, age, education and access to personal transport. However, there has been only limited success in constructing general predictive models, because a significant proportion of recreation demand is a direct response to the supply of resources and facilities, much of which is not market-driven (Pigram, 1983).

There have been several attempts to classify recreational activities, based on the degree to which they are passive or active, formal or informal, or resource- as opposed to user-orientated (Patmore 1983). User-orientated recreation depends on good accessibility for a large population and is characteristic of urban recreation or activity on the RURAL–URBAN FRINGE. Urban recreation has received far less attention from geographers than country-side recreation, the latter being more resource-based with some aspect of the land or LANDSCAPE, such as a national or state park, forming the recreational goal (President's Commission on Americans Outdoors, 1987).

Increases in rural recreation have height-ened a number of land-use CONFLICTS, including access to private and public land and the compatibility of recreation with other land uses, and has generated a general debate about the most appropriate landscape management strategies for mini-mizing ecological damage (Torkildsen, 1983). Notions of CARRYING CAPACITY, and the desirability of multiple land use, now play a large part in recreational planning, and attempts have been made to evaluate areas for their recreational poten-tial (Wall, 1989).   MB

References

Jackson, E. and Burton, T. L. 1989: *Understanding leisure and recreation.* Pennsylvania: Venture Publishing.

Patmore, J. A. 1983: *Recreation and resources. Leisure patterns and leisure places.* Oxford: Black-well.

Pigram, J. 1983: *Outdoor recreation and resource management.* London: Croom Helm.

President's Commission on Americans Outdoors 1987: *Americans Outdoors: the Legacy, the Challenge.* Washington, DC: Island Press.

Torkildsen, G. 1983: *Leisure and recreation management.* London: E. & F. N. Spon.

Wall, G. 1989: *Outdoor recreation in Canada.* New York: John Wiley.

Suggested Reading

Glyptis, S. 1991: *Countryside recreation.* London: Longman.

Jackson and Burton (1989).

Owens, P. 1984: Rural leisure and recreation research: a retrospective evaluation. *Progr. hum. Geogr.* 8, pp. 157–88.

Patmore (1983).

Pigram (1983).

Wall (1989).

recycling The re-use of resources, typically material or energy. Recycling may be undertaken to diminish demand for scarce resources or to lessen the emission of wastes; the motives may be strictly economic (if recycled materials cost less than raw ones) or broadly environmental. JEm

redistribution A system of transfer from one group or place to another, usually articulated by a mediating institution or group of institutions (e.g. the STATE). Redistribution is one of the general concerns of WELFARE GEOGRAPHY and its examination played a central role in Harvey's preliminary, so-called 'liberal' formulations of the relationships between social justice and spatial systems (Harvey, 1973, chapters 2 and 3). But as Harvey subsequently recognized in his 'socialist' reformulations (especially chapter 6), redistribution was, more specifically, one of three FORMS OF ECONOMIC INTEGRATION identified by Karl Polanyi and linked with a characteristic spatial pattern. Thus, 'redistribution designates appropriational movements toward a centre and out of it again' (Polanyi, in Dalton, 1968). These centrifugal and centripetal flows were supposed to be in marked contrast to other forms of exchange, notably RECIPROCITY, because they allowed for the concentration of a surplus. Hence, Harvey identified redistribution with hierarchical, *rank* societies and, following Wheatley (1971), claimed that 'the conditions that enabled the transformation from reciprocity to redistribution were crucial for the emergence of urbanism; they were instrumental in concentrating surplus product in a few hands and in a few places' (Harvey, 1973). Much of the debate over URBAN ORIGINS accepts the crucial importance of this transformation, but controversy continues over the nature of its 'conditions': Wheatley (1971) emphasizes the formative significance of religion, which Harvey regards as 'superstructural' and instead accentuates the classical Marxian 'base' in the economy itself (Harvey, 1973, p. 227; see also Harvey, 1972). But redistribution is not confined to the distant past and, returning to his original theme of social justice,

Harvey (1973, pp. 274–84) drew attention to reciprocity and redistribution as 'countervailing forces to market exchange in the contemporary metropolis'. He was writing before the rise of the New Right, however, and as he subsequently acknowledged, the 1970s and 1980s witnessed a 'political attack on redistributive politics' throughout the West and, eventually, the articulation of a 'post-welfare geography' (see Bennett, 1989): one of the most pervasive features of what he now described as the post-Keynesian transition was thus interurban *competition* for redistribution (Harvey, 1985, p. 218). (See also AID.) DG

References

Bennett, R. 1989: Whither models and geography in a post-welfarist world? In Macmillan, B., ed., *Remodelling geography*. Oxford: Blackwell, pp. 274–90.
Dalton, G., ed. 1968: *Primitive, archaic and modern economies: essays of Karl Polanyi*. Boston: Beacon Press.
Harvey, D. 1972: Review of Paul Wheatley's *Pivot of the four quarters. Ann. Ass. Am. Geogr.* 62, pp. 509–13.
Harvey, D. 1973: *Social justice and the city*. London: Edward Arnold/Baltimore, MD: Johns Hopkins University Press.
Harvey, D. 1985: *The urbanization of capital*. London: Blackwell.
Wheatley, P. 1971: *The pivot of the four quarters*. Edinburgh: Edinburgh University Press/Chicago: Aldine.

Suggested Reading

Harvey (1973), chs 2 and 6.
Wheatley, P. 1975: Satyantra in Suvarnadvipa: from reciprocity to redistribution in ancient S. E. Asia. In Sabloff, J. A. and Lamberg-Karlovsky, C. C., eds, *Ancient civilization and trade*. Albuquerque, NM: University of New Mexico Press, ch. 6.

redlining The delimitation by financial institutions of residential districts (by a red line) within a city as being in decline and thus not sensible areas for mortgage lending. By discriminating against potential borrowers who can only afford to live in certain low-cost areas, such policies also discriminate against low-income households. The existence of redlined districts is often denied by institutions; but map evidence has been produced, along with circumstantial evidence from a mapping of areas within which mortgage applications have been denied.   RJJ

Suggested Reading
Bassett, K. and Short, J. R. 1980: *Housing and residential structure: alternative approaches*. London: Routledge and Kegan Paul.
Dingemans, D. 1978: Redlining and mortgage lending in Sacramento. *Ann. Ass. Am. Geogr.* 68, pp. 225–39.

refugees Displacement, banishment and exodus are as old as human history, but the legal concept of refugee was not formulated until the inter-war period. Two basic statutes (the UN Convention relating to the Status of Refugees, 1951, and the UN Protocol, 1967) extend international protection to refugees, defined as persons who, owing to a well-founded fear of persecution for reasons of race, religion, nationality, membership of a particular social group or political opinion, are outside the country of their nationality and who are unable or unwilling to return. This broad definition encompasses refugees who are conventionally classified according to their desire or possibility of returning to their homeland (so-called majority-identified refugees, events-alienated refugees and self-alienated refugees). The Convention/Protocol definition does not however include internally displaced persons and victims of repressive military or economic policies, refugees who are often defined situationally (Harrell-Bond, 1986). At present, the African continent accounts for about half (five million) of the world's refugees.   MW

Reference
Harrell-Bond, B. 1986: *Imposing aid: emergency assistance to refugees*. Oxford: Oxford University Press.

regime of accumulation A concept from the REGULATION SCHOOL of political–economic theory, referring to an extended period of relative stability or growth within the capitalist economy. Adherents to the Regulation approach accept Marx's basic proposition that CAPITALISM is characterized by certain fundamental contradictions (such as the collective tendency

for capitalists to economize on workers' wages, thus ultimately reducing the effective demand for manufactured goods), and that these must be resolved, suppressed or controlled in order for successful ACCUMULATION to occur. Hence Regulation theorists contend that different solutions to this problem have been arrived at through time and across space. As a noted member of this school asserts, 'My central hypothesis is, in fact, that the overall reproduction of the system can take different forms. It then becomes essential to make a precise analysis of the *changes*, both qualitative and quantitative, that have been necessary for the maintenance of capitalist relations *in general* in the long run' (Boyer, 1990). Therefore Regulation theorists interpret capitalist history as consisting of a series of relatively stable periods, during which the organization of private productive activity is in some general state of balance with the organization of consumption (the level and stability of wages, and the distribution of purchasing power within society). Each regime ends in a CRISIS period of major instability or stagnation, and a new regime begins when new ways of organizing production are developed, supported by an appropriate new set of public and private institutions, and societal norms to structure labour markets and workplace practices. (See also FLEXIBLE ACCUMULATION; FORDISM; POST-FORDISM.)   MSG

Reference
Boyer, R. 1990: *The Regulation school: a critical introduction*. New York: Columbia University Press.

Suggested Reading
Lipietz, A. 1986: New tendencies in the international division of labor: regimes of accumulation and modes of regulation. In Scott, A. J. and Storper, M., eds, *Production, work, territory*. Boston: Allen and Unwin, pp. 16–40.

region 'A differentiated segment of earth-space' (D. Whittlesey, in James and Jones, 1954). As this implies, the study of regions was for a long time associated with a definition of geography as the study of AREAL DIFFERENTIATION, or CHOROLOGY. As this came under attack during the 1960s, so traditional conceptions of

REGIONAL GEOGRAPHY were displaced from the centre of the subject. But even those who were, in consequence, committed to geography as SPATIAL SCIENCE continued to regard the region as 'one of the most logical and satisfactory ways of organizing geographical information' (Haggett et al., 1977). Claims of this sort derived from and fed back into two related developments:

(a) A renewed recognition of the *purposive character* of region-building. This was part of both Hettner's and Hartshorne's influential discussions of the region: Hettner had made it clear that 'there is no universally-valid [regional] division which does justice to all the phenomena' (cited in Hartshorne, 1939). But its formal consequences remained undeveloped until Grigg (1965) argued that 'regionalization is similar to classification' and that any particular regional system 'is but one way of looking at the world'. In fact, Grigg's account of the logic of regional taxonomy provided the basis for a whole series of formal region-building algorithms in which regions were treated as combinatorial, assignment and districting problems (see Haggett et al. 1977, chapter 14; see also CLASSIFICATION AND REGIONALIZATION).

(b) A renewed recognition of the *practical importance* of functional regions. Many of the early studies in regional geography had been concerned with *formal regions*, identified on the basis of the presence or absence of particular distinguishing features, and while Hartshorne (1939) had prefigured the significance of the alternative concept of a *functional region*, the connections between the two were left largely unexplored until after the Second World War. Then, in his *City region and regionalism* (1947), Dickinson acknowledged the force of 'regional homogeneity' – which underpinned the identification of formal regions – but argued that its 'fullest measure' could be discovered only 'through the analysis of the character, intensity, extent and interrelations of [regional associations] and the ways in which they are interlocked and separated from each other in space'. This clearly reached back to Hartshorne, but what was novel about Dickinson's

formulation was its break from physical geography and the physical environment, and its provision of 'a central regionalizing principle that lies behind the spatial structure of a society'. This was the *city region*: 'an area of interrelated activities, kindred interests and common organizations, brought into being through the medium of the routes which bind it to the urban centres'. Dickinson's central concern with the human organization of space was reinforced ten years later by Philbrick (1957), for whom the task of any intellectually viable human geography was to 'analyse the areal structure of human occupance *independent of the natural environment*' (emphasis added), through an explication of 'the functional organization of human occupance in area'. He fashioned a set of theoretical constructs – focality, localization, interconnection and spatial discontinuity – which were supposed to provide a new framework for geographical enquiry. Both Dickinson and Philbrick had been greatly impressed by Christaller's CENTRAL PLACE THEORY, and together these three men fashioned a springboard for the eventual translation of functional regions into *spatial systems* (Berry, 1964): see also FUNCTIONALISM; SYSTEM).

These two developments found common ground through their importance for planning: in particular, through their role in the monitoring and explanation of patterns of *regional development* and in the formulation, implementation and evaluation of *regional policy*, both of which were major postwar concerns of governments in many countries (see Scott, 1982). Implicit within most of these discussions, and within regional geography more generally, was the identification of the region with a particular SCALE of analysis: somewhere between the local and the national/international. But little attention was paid to the historical and geographical variability of regional formations (except by those who had already dismissed the region as a concept that properly belonged to eighteenth-century Europe: see Kimble, 1951) or to the multiple contexts within which regional geography might be situated. This state of affairs has changed considerably in recent years, partly as a result of changes in the

SPACE-ECONOMY and partly through a critique of those previous formulations. The two are, of course, connected. Processes of RESTRUCTURING through the global economy have impacted on SPATIAL DIVISIONS OF LABOUR at a variety of national and regional scales, and these have been registered in dramatic shifts within the NEW INTERNATIONAL DIVISION OF LABOUR, while the heightened intensity of TIME–SPACE COMPRESSION within contemporary capitalism – an electronic gridding of the world-economy which has made many of these changes possible – has led some commentators to posit the emergence of a new global HYPERSPACE. As the ability or inclination of national governments to intervene in these developments changed, a shift which was often driven by the rise of neoconservatism and its commitment to unregulated MARKET EXCHANGE, so many liberal and radical geographers developed critiques which revolved around new understandings of regions, regional formation and regional transformation. Gilbert (1988) identified three critical conceptions of the region as follows:

(a) A 'local' response to the global dynamics of CAPITALISM produced through processes of UNEVEN DEVELOPMENT (see, e.g., Schoenberger, 1989; Smith, 1989). This perspective has been informed by political economy and a series of conceptual advances within MARXIST GEOGRAPHY; since it usually seeks to overcome the deeply sedimented divisions between different scales of analysis it also intersects, somewhat more informally, with ideas from WORLD-SYSTEMS ANALYSIS (see, e.g., Taylor 1991). Particular attention has been paid to the contemporary volatility of capital circulation – to changes within REGIMES OF ACCUMULATION that have, perhaps, installed a regime of FLEXIBLE ACCUMULATION – and to the dynamics of *territorial production complexes* within what Storper and Walker (1989) call 'the constant geography of capitalism'.

(b) A focus of cultural identification: a SENSE OF PLACE and, above all, of 'belonging' through the symbolic construction of PLACE. This perspective has been informed by HUMANISTIC GEOGRAPHY and, latterly, by the interest in cultural theory and cultural studies that has played a vital part in the renaissance of CULTURAL GEOGRAPHY. Particular attention has been paid to the analysis of symbolic landscapes, the constitution of regional political cultures, and struggles to secure local or regional identities in the face of extra-regional and often distant decisions and processes.

(c) A medium for social interaction. This perspective has been informed by STRUCTURATION THEORY, the principal architect of which claimed that:

Regionalization is a notion that should be seen as having a major role in social theory. Regionalization is best understood not as a wholly spatial concept but as one expressing the clustering of contexts in time–space. As such it is a phenomenon of quite decisive significance . . . on both a theoretical and an empirical level. No single concept helps more to redress the misleading divisions between 'micro' and 'macro-[scale]' research; no concept helps more to counter the assumption that a 'society' is always a clear-cut unity with precisely defined boundaries (Giddens, 1984).

So, for example, Thrift (1983) treated the region as 'the meeting place of human agency and social structure'. He saw the region as being made up of 'a number of different settings for interaction' – a particular intersection of different LOCALES – which help to structure 'the intricacies of interaction, the specificity of particular times and spaces, the sense of living as meeting'. These ideas have since been developed (and reworked) through two avenues of enquiry: a reading of EXISTENTIALISM which treats the production of social space as 'the opening and occupation of the "wheres" of human existence that automatically occurs along with interrelated lives' (Schatzki, 1991), and a reading of POSTSTRUCTURALISM which has prompted Thrift (1991) to connect the constitution of regions to 'a fully contextualized account of the human subject and a fully subjectified account of context' (see also CONTEXTUAL THEORY).

Whatever the differences between them, all these approaches imply that 'region' has a deep significance in the construction and conduct of social life (see ONTOLOGY), and they emphasize (a) the *contingency* of regional formations, which are supposed to be in constant motion and subject to major changes, partly through (b) the *contextuality* of regional formations, which may be accessed through an analysis of the 'local–global dialectic' installed through TIME–SPACE DISTANCIATION. DG

References

Berry, B. J. L. 1964: Approaches to regional analysis: a synthesis. *Ann. Ass. Am. Geogr.* 54, pp. 2–11.

Dickinson, R. E. 1947: *City region and regionalism: a geographical contribution to human ecology.* London: Kegan Paul Trench Trübner.

Giddens, A. 1984: *The constitution of society.* Cambridge: Polity Press.

Gilbert, A. 1988: The new regional geography in English and French speaking countries. *Progr. hum. Geogr.* 12, pp. 208–28.

Grigg, D. 1965: The logic of regional systems. *Ann. Ass. Am. Geogr.* 55, pp. 465–91.

Haggett, P., Cliff, A. and Frey, A. 1977: *Locational analysis in human geography.* London: Edward Arnold.

Hartshorne, R. 1939: *The nature of geography: a critical survey of current thought in the light of the past.* Lancaster, PA: Association of American Geographers.

James, P. E. and Jones, C. F., eds 1954: *American geography: inventory and prospect.* Syracuse, NY: Syracuse University Press.

Kimble, G. 1951: The inadequacy of the regional concept. In Stamp, L. D. and Wooldridge, S. W., eds, *London essays in geography.* London: Longman.

Philbrick, A. K. 1957: Principles of areal functional organization in regional human geography. *Econ. Geogr.* 33, pp. 299–336.

Schatzki, T. 1991: Spatial ontology and explanation. *Ann. Ass. Am. Geogr.* 81, pp. 650–70.

Schoenberger, E. 1989: New models of regional change. In Peet, R. and Thrift, N., eds, *New models in geography*, volume 1. London: Unwin Hyman, pp. 115–41.

Scott, A. 1982: The meaning and social origins of discourse on the spatial foundations of society. In Gould, P. and Olsson, G., eds, *A search for common ground.* London: Pion, pp. 141–55.

Smith, N. 1989: Uneven development and location theory: towards a synthesis. In Peet, R. and Thrift, N., eds, *New models in geography*, volume 1. London: Unwin Hyman, pp. 142–63.

Storper, M. and Walker, R. 1989: *The capitalist imperative: territory, technology and industrial growth.* Oxford: Blackwell.

Taylor, P. J. 1991: A theory and practice of regions: the case of Europe. *Environ. Plann. D, Society and Space* 9, pp. 183–96.

Thrift, N. J. 1983: On the determination of social action in space and time. *Environ. Plann. D, Society and Space* 1, pp. 23–57.

Thrift, N. J. 1991: For a new regional geography. *Progr. hum. Geogr.* 15, pp. 456–65.

Suggested Reading

Gilbert (1988).

Grigg, D. 1967: Regions, models and classes. In Chorley, R. J. and Haggett, P., eds, *Models in geography.* London: Methuen, ch. 12.

Thrift (1983).

regional alliance A treaty signed by a group of neighbouring STATES, agreeing to a system of collective security, whereby an attack on any one of them by an external aggressor is deemed to be an attack against them all (as with both NATO and the former Warsaw Pact). RJJ

Suggested Reading

Blacksell, M. 1981: *Post-war Europe: a political geography*, second edition. London: Hutchinson.

regional class alliance A coherent response by members of a region's different CLASSES (notably labour, capital and the local STATE APPARATUS) to economic problems there. Such a compromise is agreed by parties who otherwise might be in CONFLICT, in order both to promote profitability (for capital) and to ensure the continued availability of jobs (for labour) – and thereby also to sustain the state's legitimacy. According to Harvey (1985) such alliances are necessary to the continued reproduction of capitalism in a locality: 'if regional structures and class alliances did not already exist, then the processes at work under capitalism would necessarily create them'. (See also URBAN ENTREPRENEURIALISM.) RJJ

Reference

Harvey, D. 1985: The geopolitics of capitalism. In Gregory, D. and Urry, J., eds, *Social relations and spatial structures.* London: Macmillan, pp. 128–63.

regional convergence See CONVERGENCE, REGIONAL.

regional cycles Fluctuations or cyclical waves in the level of economic activity in a region, usually measured by industrial output or unemployment rates. Such fluctuations can be very long-term, as with KONDRATIEFF CYCLES, or shorter-term, reflecting both seasonal variations in the demand for labour and the regional impact of national business cycles of expansion and recession. Descriptive studies of regional cycles, measuring and comparing their average amplitudes, and the timings of peaks for different regions, were done in the early years of REGIONAL SCIENCE, but the major work was done in the 1970s and later.

There have been two main approaches. The first (mainly by economists) has involved building regional (e.g. the State of California) or multiregional (e.g. the States of the USA) econometric models. These relate macroeconomic variables of output, employment and expenditure at the regional level to each other, parallel to the development of national Keynesian econometric models, and also relate regional variables to national and other-region variables. Such models now exist for many countries and regions. The second approach (mainly by geographers) has focused on the statistical modelling of the magnitude and spatial DIFFUSION of regional cycles, mainly using unemployment rates, and comparing the timing and cyclical amplitude for different cities and regions. The regional and urban time series are related to each other using the REGRESSION methods of LEAD–LAG MODELS, SPACE–TIME FORECASTING and also SPECTRAL ANALYSIS to look separately at seasonal and business-cycle effects. Differences in magnitude and timing can then be linked to regional industrial structure and the hierarchical and spatial diffusion of the cycles. LWH

Suggested Reading
Glickman, N. J. 1977: *Econometric analysis of regional systems: explorations in model building and policy analysis.* London: Academic Press.

regional geography The study of the geography of REGIONS. Regional geography is often distinguished by its interest in 'a specific situation in a particular locality'

(Paterson, 1974) and has been hailed as 'the highest form of the geographer's art' (Hart, 1982), but these (supposedly disinterested) views obscure the political implications and interest written into regional geography. The classical approach was through CHOROLOGY, in which the study of regions was held to be of strategic importance for political and military leaders, as was the special geography that was promulgated in sixteenth-century Europe. When the modern discipline insisted on the centrality of regional geography, most particularly through the regional monographs of the French school, these were often associated with the politics of NATIONALISM. Vidal de la Blache's monograph on *France de l'Est*, for example, was written in the wake of the German occupation and annexation of Alsace-Lorraine, and was a determined attempt to show that the region was a distinctive *pays* indissolubly bound in France (Gregory, 1993).

However, these wider concerns were absent from Richard Hartshorne's *The nature of geography* (1939), even though (or perhaps because) it was based largely on an exegesis of the German tradition of regional geography (Elkins, 1989) and was written after the Nazi seizure of power and the annexation of Austria. It was through this text that regional geography received its modern imprimatur as the core of the modern discipline (see AREAL DIFFERENTIATION). During the Second World War regional geography still had a strategic function – such as the Admiralty Handbooks produced in Britain – but, following Hartshorne, most postwar practitioners of regional geography were more interested in the pedagogic than the political implications of their craft: to them, geography was essentially IDIOGRAPHIC and was articulated through the art of geographical description, a commitment to FIELDWORK, and the integration of physical geography and human geography within the study of a particular LANDSCAPE. However, in the 1950s and 1960s many of these assumptions came under critical scrutiny, and in the debate over EXCEPTIONALISM they were attacked on two main fronts:

(a) Regional geography was represented as being circumscribed by a debilitating parochialism. Kimble (in Stamp and Wooldridge, 1951) insisted that 'the region is an eighteenth-century concept' and that in the modern world 'it is the *links* in the landscapes . . . rather than the breaks that impress'. Schaefer (1953) went even further in his objections to the scientific sterility of what he took to be regional geography's contemplation of 'uniqueness' and urged instead a geography concerned with generalization. Against this, however, several commentators have argued that Hartshorne's view of geography as a 'correlative discipline' using map comparisons to disclose 'the functional integration of phenomena' over space in fact prepared the way for the development of a formal SPATIAL SCIENCE. Even so, this methodological continuity was masked by a change in objective, and in the 1960s the idiographic intentions of regional geography were overridden by the NOMOTHETIC aspirations of a more or less hegemonic SPATIAL SCIENCE.

(b) Outside the framework of the French school of human geography and its doctrine of POSSIBILISM, some critics objected that regional geography had reinstated a surreptitious ENVIRONMENTAL DETERMINISM in the movement of its descriptions from the 'physical landscape' to the 'cultural landscape'. Even where this was not the case, Wrigley (1965) argued that the presumed intimacy of these ecological bonds was 'admirably suited to the historical geography of Europe before the Industrial Revolution' but that 'with the final disappearance of the old, local, rural, largely self-sufficient way of life the centrality of regional work to geography has been permanently affected' (but cf. Langton, 1984).

These objections were profoundly Eurocentric, and they probably meant little to those (many) geographers who continued to believe in the practical and even moral importance of regional geography outside such narrowly Western horizons of meaning (see Farmer, 1973). In the 1970s and 1980s, however, there were attempts to overcome these twin objections through the following:

(a) The development of various versions of SYSTEMS ANALYSIS, which claimed to be capable of addressing both 'horizontal' (person-to-person) and 'vertical' (society–nature) relations within a coherent and nominally scientific framework: many of these constructs focused explicitly on regional systems and their interconnections with national and international systems, and the advance of WORLD-SYSTEMS ANALYSIS in particular placed a new emphasis on the production of (national) 'regions' within the capitalist world-economy (e.g. Agnew 1987; Dixon, 1991; Becker and Egler, 1992; for a general commentary, see Taylor, 1988).

(b) The emergence of MARXIST GEOGRAPHY, which was concerned with the differential (regional) geographies of capital accumulation: interest was directed towards successive LAYERS OF INVESTMENT and their impact on changing SPATIAL DIVISIONS OF LABOUR, and on the ways in which UNEVEN DEVELOPMENT could be traced back to its material base in the dialectic between society and nature (see, e.g. Massey, 1984; Soja, 1985).

(c) The renewed interest in CONTEXTUAL THEORY, which was concerned to elucidate the importance of place, space and landscape – often in regional configurations – to the constitution of human subjects and the conduct of social life, often informed by STRUCTURATION THEORY (see, e.g. Thrift, 1983; Pred, 1984).

It was the latter project that saw itself most explicitly as a 'reconstituted regional geography' (Thrift, 1983), but all three were much more concerned with PROCESS than with the lifeless tableaux and frozen patterns that preoccupied regional geographies à la Hartshorne, and they imbued their studies with a definite and deliberate *historicity* through a focus on processes of regional constitution and regional transformation (Gilbert, 1988).

As the 1980s have become the 1990s, so three axes of concern have animated the continuing debate:

(a) Traditional regional geography put a premium on description: on the art of regional geography. But for all the talk of aesthetic sensibility, Pudup (1988) complained, there was little attempt to reflect systematically on 'different ways of seeing', on the EPISTEMOLOGY of the gaze, and of the multiple modes of representation available: none of which, including 'realism', is an innocent genre. Any 'new' regional geography will be required to attend carefully to such concerns as an essential moment in its inquiries (cf. Lewis, 1985; Sayer, 1989).

(b) The reconstruction of regional geography has a theoretical accent that is far removed from the traditional canon: an interest in social structures, social practices and their implication in the constitution and reproduction of regional forms that promises to transform social theory as much as it does human geography (Agnew, 1989). But it is still far from clear how to achieve the necessary reciprocal movement between concept and evidence, and – most of all – how to use theoretical ideas to illuminate particular situations and, in turn, have those situations speak to and enlarge our understanding of wider concerns: 'Anyone trying to mesh theory with empirical description [in regional geography] soon learns that the movement among abstract concepts and empirical description is like performing ballet on a bed of quicksand' (Pudup, 1988: see also REALISM). For this reason, there have been objections that regional studies informed by structuration theory have been too abstract, and that contemporary LOCALITY studies have been too empirical.

(c) Both of these elements are being woven into a local–global dialectic in ways which challenge the view that MODERNITY erases difference and replaces it with homogeneity – so many traditional regional geographies were laments for lost worlds of pristine difference (cf. Entrikin, 1989) – but the complex webs of differeniation and integration that are being recovered in these new accounts raise questions about: (i) other modes of description, of what Jameson (1991) called modes of 'cognitive mapping' capable of figuring (in his terms) the late-twentieth-century world of HYPERSPACE and the culture of POSTMODERNISM or, less awkwardly, of ways of representing the new forms of dependence, hybridity and interconnection installed by TIME–SPACE COMPRESSION and TIME–SPACE DISTANCIATION (Appadurai, 1991); and (ii) the ETHNOCENTRISM of contemporary theory and whether, even as so-called 'travelling theory', it is adequate to the task of representing other voices and other cultures (Gregory, 1993: see also FEMINIST GEOGRAPHY; POSTCOLONIALISM).

What these formulations do, in related ways, is to revive the political dimensions of regional geography but in new, more subtle and perhaps even more demanding ways. The original, political salience of regional geography has not been diminished, as the explosion of movements around REGIONALISM and NATIONALISM in many parts of the world testifies; but much of the current discussion of regional geography connects these episodes to deep questions of ONTOLOGY: to the ways in which places, regions and landscapes are necessarily implicated in the ongoing constitution of subjectivities, identities and actions in time and space (cf. Thrift, 1991).   DG

References

Agnew, J. 1987: *The United States in the world-economy: a regional geography*. Cambridge: Cambridge University Press.

Agnew, J. 1989: The devaluation of place in social science. In Agnew, J. and Duncan, J. eds, *The power of place*. London: Unwin Hyman, pp. 9–29.

Appadurai, A. 1991: Global ethnoscapes: notes and queries for a transnational anthropology. In Fox, R., ed., *Recapturing anthropology: working in the present*. Santa Fe: School of American Research Press, pp. 191–210.

Becker, B. K. and Egler, C. 1992: *Brazil: a new regional power in the world-economy: a regional geography*. Cambridge: Cambridge University Press.

Dixon, C. 1991: *South-East Asia in the world-economy: a regional geography*. Cambridge: Cambridge University Press.

Elkins, T. H. 1989: Human and regional geography in the German-speaking lands in the first forty years of the twentieth century. In Entrikin, J. N. and Brunn, S. D., eds, *Reflections on Richard Hartshorne's The nature of geography*. Occasional Publications of the Association of American Geographers, 1, pp. 17–34.

Entrikin, J. N. 1989: Place, region and modernity. In Agnew, J. and Duncan, J., eds, *The power of place*. London: Unwin Hyman, pp. 30–43.

Farmer, B. H. 1973: Geography, area studies and the study of area. *Trans. Inst. Br. Geogr.* 60, pp. 1–16.

Gilbert, A. 1988: The new regional geography in English and French speaking countries. *Progr. hum. Geogr.* 12, pp. 208–28.

Gregory, D. 1993: *Geographical imaginations*. Oxford: Blackwell.

Hart, J. F. 1982: The highest form of the geographer's art. *Ann. Ass. Am. Geogr.* 72, pp. 1–29.

Hartshorne, R. 1939: *The nature of geography: a critical survey of current thought in the light of the past*. Lancaster, PA: Association of American Geographers.

Jameson, F. 1991: *Postmodernism, or the cultural logic of late capitalism*. Duquesne: Duke University Press.

Langton, J. 1984: The industrial revolution and the regional geography of England. *Trans. Inst. Br. Geogr.* n.s. 9, pp. 145–67.

Lewis, P. 1985: Beyond description. *Ann. Ass. Am. Geogr.* 75, pp. 465–78.

Massey, D. 1984: *Spatial divisions of labour*. London: Macmillan.

Paterson, J. H. 1974: Writing regional geography. In Board, C. et al., eds, *Progress in geography* 6. London: Edward Arnold, pp. 1–26.

Pred, A. 1984: Place as historically contingent process: structuration and the time-geography of becoming places. *Ann. Ass. Am. Geogr.* 74, pp. 279–97.

Pudup, M. B. 1988: Arguments within regional geography. *Progr. hum. Geogr.* 12, pp. 369–90.

Sayer, R. A. 1989: The 'new' regional geography and problems of narrative. *Environ. Plann. D, Society and Space* 7, pp. 253–76.

Schaefer, F. K. 1953: Exceptionalism in geography: a methodological examination. *Ann. Ass. Am. Geogr.* 43, pp. 226–49.

Soja, E. 1985: Regions in conflict: spatiality, periodicity and the historical geography of the regional question. *Environ. Plann. D, Society and Space* 3, pp. 175–90.

Stamp, L. D. and Wooldridge, S. W., eds 1951: *London essays in geography*. London: Longman.

Taylor, P. 1988: World-systems analysis and regional geography. *Prof. Geogr.* 40, pp. 259–65.

Thrift, N. J. 1983: On the determination of social action in space and time. *Environ. Plann. D, Society and Space* 1, pp. 23–57.

Thrift, N. J. 1991: For a new regional geography. *Progr. hum. Geogr.* 15, pp. 456–65.

Wrigley, E. A. 1965: Changes in the philosophy of geography. In Chorley, R. J. and Haggett, P., eds, *Frontiers in geographical teaching*. London: Methuen, pp. 3–24.

Suggested Reading

Farmer (1973).

Gilbert (1988).

Johnston, R. J., Hauer, J. and Hoekveld, G., eds 1990: *The challenge of regional geography*. London: Routledge.

Pudup (1988).

regional policy Policy directed explicitly at the problems of UNEVEN DEVELOPMENT between different regions. Although the area-based nature of regional policy sets it apart from other policies which may have pronounced regional effects, such as the Common Agricultural Policy of the EC or federal defence expenditure in the USA, the definition of what constitutes a *regional problem* (e.g. Massey, 1979) makes the precise specification of regional policy extremely difficult. An underlying reason for this difficulty is the complexity of the nature of regional differences (see Markusen, 1987).

'Regional problems' may derive from geographical unevenness in the distribution of income and welfare (see WELFARE GEOGRAPHY), in the conditions of effective production or in the level and effectiveness of regional cultural integrity or political representation. Whatever the origin of such unevenness, however, it becomes problematic when it begins to undermine economic, political or moral legitimacy (see CRISIS). Economic INTEGRATION may, for example, be responsible for helping to stimulate the growth of regional consciousness and the drive to regional separatism or even independence. Such has been the historical geography of the Basque province in northern Spain, since the inflow of capital and people associated with the development of heavy industry in an agricultural region as a result of the INDUSTRIAL REVOLUTION. The regional problem may be based in strongly felt and long-held cultural distinctions – as in the case of the Québecois in Canada. Although such distinctions may be long-dormant, they may be exploited for wider political objectives, as in the rapid rise of the right-wing Northern or Lombard Leagues in Italy.

Regional problems frequently originate in the process of regional RESTRUCTURING associated with the decline of basic industries having long-standing connections with their localities (see, e.g. Clark, 1986; Markusen, 1986). Indeed, Clark (1991) suggests that restructuring of this kind in the USA has precipitated an immanent crisis of regulation.

From the perspective of the STATE (see, e.g. Johnston, 1986), regional problems arise when uneven development threatens political stability and presents the possibility of the break-up of the state system (e.g. Nairn, 1977). Similarly, when looked at from the perspective of the economy as a whole, the regional problem arises when uneven development acts as a barrier to capital ACCUMULATION. Indeed, the 'regional' problem may simply be a geographical dimension of the wider problems of DEVELOPMENT (Massey, 1979).

Given the multifaceted nature and complex provenance of the regional problem, it is hardly surprising that regional policy has varied over time and space in terms of its determinants, formal content, relative significance and objectives. This variation reflects not only the policy perception of the problem but also the prevailing ideology of state involvement in the functioning of the economy or civil society. Thus regional policy may need to address the regional structure of the STATE APPARATUS itself in response to demands for greater self-government, autonomy or even dependence.

Within a given geography of the state apparatus, regional policy may be redistributive and directed at the amelioration of unevenness in levels of living. Such direct distributive intervention is normally aimed at individuals and groups and is undertaken through the WELFARE STATE at the national level, albeit with pronounced regional effects.

Alternatively, regional policy may be directed at improvements in the regional conditions of production through investment in INFRASTRUCTURE and social overhead capital or, as in the case of the NEW TOWNS built in the North-East of England, through the spatial recomposition of the labour force in more easily exploited geographical concentrations. The role of infrastructure in regional policy is contested, with one view suggesting that it provides the basis of development and another arguing that scarce resources should be allocated to the provision of infrastructure only when present provision is demonstrably overloaded and holding back accumulation (see Hirschmann, 1958).

Regional policy may attempt to influence the locational decisions of firms by offering inducements to investment in particular regions in the forms of tax incentives, grants, subsidies, purpose-built factories, regional employment premiums and so on. Sometimes, as in the case of Italian policy for the development of the Mezzogiorno, the STATE may direct the locational flow of investment. In the USA, Agnew (1987) points out that there is a long tradition of state-supported business enterprise, of which one of the more spectacular examples was the creation and subsequent activities of the Tennessee Valley Authority.

The problem of a restricted potential for accumulation may be addressed by regional policy through attempts to modernize and restructure the productive base of the economy by inducing a locational shift which corresponds to a more effective economic geography for production. Much of the rationale for regional policy in the UK advanced in the influential Barlow Report of 1940, for example, was of this kind, arguing in particular that the geographical concentration of the economy in and around London was not only economically inefficient but, under wartime conditions, strategically dangerous.

During the 1980s regional policy in the UK and the USA reflected the prevailing economic ideology and was redesigned (see, e.g. Brindley et al., 1989; Thornley, 1990). So-called 'market-led' policies were introduced in which the state provided basic infrastructure and some substantial inducements to investment, and reduced planning and labour market controls. The Urban Development Corporations in the UK were experiments of this sort, but rather than being 'market-led' they are more accurately described as 'state-pulled', in that they enable private capital to ensure substantial state support to try to secure profitable investment.

Regional policy is rarely, if ever, definable in purely economic terms (e.g. as a means of facilitating accumulation) or in purely political terms (e.g. as a means of buying-off regional political discontent; see REGIONAL ALLIANCE). The links between the geography of IDEOLOGY, accumulation, CLASS and politics in the evolution not only of the formal existence and content of regional policy but also of its determinants, objectives and measures of 'success' are extremely complex. In the USA for example, 'PORK BARREL politics' reflect the nature of the geography of political representation in the context of area-based policies. Nevertheless, regional policy cannot be reduced to a separate 'geographical' sphere of policy making and implementation. Like geography itself, regional policy is an intrinsic, although variable, part of the process of social reproduction.   RL

References and Suggested Reading

Agnew, J. 1987: *The United States in the world-economy*. Cambridge: Cambridge University Press.

Albrechts, L., Moulaert, F., Roberts, P. and Swyngedouw, E. 1989: *Regional policy at the crossroads: European perspectives*. London: Jessica Kingsley.

Brindley, T., Rydin, Y. and Stoker, G. 1989: *Remaking planning*. London: Unwin Hyman.

Clark, G. L. 1986: The crisis of the midwest auto industry. In Scott, A. J. and Storper, M., eds, 1986: *Production, work, territory: the geographical anatomy of industrial capitalism*. London: Allen and Unwin, pp. 127–48.

Clark, G. L. 1991: Regulating the restructuring of the US steel industry: chapter 11 of the Bankruptcy Code and Pension Obligations. *Reg. Stud.* 25(2), pp. 135–53.

Damesick, P. and Wood, P., eds 1987: *Regional problems, problem regions and public policy in the United Kingdom*. Oxford: Clarendon Press.

Hirschman, A. O. 1958: *The strategy of economic development*. New Haven: Yale University Press.

Johnston, R. J. 1986: The state, the region, and the division of labour. In Scott, A. J. and Storper, M., eds, *Production, work, territory: the geographical anatomy of industrial capitalism*. London: Allen and Unwin, pp. 265–80.

Knox, P. and Agnew, J. 1989: *The geography of the world-economy*. London: Edward Arnold.

Markusen, A. 1986: Neither ore, nor coal, nor markets: A policy-oriented view of steel sites in the USA. *Reg. Stud.* 20(5), pp. 449–61.

Markusen, A. 1987: *Regions: the economics and politics of territory*. Totowa, NJ: Rowman and Littlefield.

Massey, D. 1979: In what sense a regional problem? *Reg. Stud.* 13(2), pp. 233–43.

Massey, D. 1984: *Spatial divisions of labour*. London: Macmillan/New York: Methuen, ch. 6.

Nairn, T. 1981: *The break-up of Britain: crisis and neo-nationalism*. London: Verso.

Thornley, A. 1990: *Urban planning under Thatcherism*. London: Routledge.

regional science A hybrid discipline originating in the early 1950s which employs formal NEOCLASSICAL theory and rigorous statistical techniques to examine spatial issues in economics, geography and planning. The boundaries between regional science and the other related disciplinary concerns of LOCATION THEORY, regional economics and planning models are blurred. This lack of definition has meant that while regional science has become a convenient rubric under which to group methodologically similar pursuits, it has not obtained the disciplinary, and hence institutional, standing that its initial proponents perhaps envisaged.

Regional science was the vision of a single man, the American economist Walter Isard. Having published several papers during the 1940s that both lambasted the assumption of the pin-head economy found in economic theory, and provided an alternative reconstruction based upon the work of several German location theorists, Isard convened the first meeting of the Regional Science Association in Detroit in December 1954. In particular, by adding transportation inputs to neoclassical models, early regional scientists added a spatial plane to the hitherto 'wonderland of no dimensions'. In the formative years of the Association, the *Papers and Proceedings* (1954–present), and later the *Journal of Regional Science* (first published in the autumn of 1958), were the principal forums for debate and dissemination of research. Isard early on solidified the embryonic discipline with two major pieces of writing; *Location and space economy* (1956), and four years later the collective tome, *Methods of regional analysis* (1960). Using the literal translation of the German word *Raumwirstschaft* ('space economy') as his leitmotif, Isard (1956) in *Location and space economy* synthesized a number of disparate location theories into one general doctrine. Using the idea of a 'substitution framework' that applied to transportation inputs, Isard showed how each of the classical location theories could be restated, and hence integrated, in terms of the same fundamental logic. When scrutinized that logic was none other than neoclassical RATIONAL CHOICE theory, which in many ways continues to be the tie that binds within regional science. By 1960 Isard (1960, p. vii) had recognized that his earlier 'general theory of location was of little direct use in treating the concrete problems of reality', and so the second volume became a primer on all the operational techniques that a fully fledged regional scientiest would ever need to know when confronting the 'real' world. Together these two volumes provided the twin foundations for regional science; a combination of formal neoclassical theory and sophisticated techniques for manipulating empirical data.

Those foundations were secure enough for Isard to establish the first Department of Regional Science in 1958 at the University of Pennsylvania, subsequently followed by one at Cornell University. However, the growth of regional science departments has been slow since then. If it exists at all, regional science is typically an interdisciplinary programme rather than a department. The same disciplinary diversity also applies to the members and participants of the various Regional Science Congresses that occur around the world (for example, the European one that was first held in The Hague in 1961). They tend to be condensation points for researchers originating in very different disciplines, rather than those who are regional scientists *per se*. Certainly this promotes an exchange of ideas, but it makes defining the core of regional science problematic.

Regional science had a very important effect on human geography. During the 1960s it provided an umbrella under which the early quantifiers and spatial theorists in human geography could work. In particular, it exposed human geographers to the competitive equilibrium models of neoclassical economics and their associated techniques of optimization. For this reason some of the classic papers on, for example, CENTRAL PLACE THEORY, LINEAR PROGRAMMING, INPUT–OUTPUT modelling, the GRAVITY MODEL and urban RENT theory were published by geographers in regional science journals during this heyday of the QUANTITATIVE REVOLUTION. In addition, regional science was one of the vehicles by which the ideas of SOCIAL PHYSICS were brought to human geography. In fact, such was the blurred nature of boundaries that social physics' main popularizer, William Warntz, moved effortlessly among the trio of regional science, human geography and social physics during this period. Again this indicates that holding regional science together is not its subject matter but its methodology, one ultimately rooted in POSIVITISM and EMPIRICISM. In fact, this was the main attraction of regional science for some geographers. It provided a justification for prosecuting an extreme form of positivism and empiricism, tendencies that were admittedly always latent in human geography (see QUANTITATIVE REVOLUTION).

It was inevitable that, when those positivist and empiricist tendencies were criticized during the 1970s by both RADICAL and HUMANISTIC geographers, the influence of regional science on human geography waned. For radical geographers regional science failed because its vocabulary of equilibrium and optimization denied the social CONFLICT and injustice that they saw as endemic to capitalism, while for humanistic geographers the rational actor of regional science was only the palest reflection of a fully sentient and emotionally complex human being. Perhaps the strongest criticisms, however, were internal and came from those who turned regional science's creed against itself. Olsson (1980) brilliantly deconstructed the gravity model equation to illuminate the internal contradictions of regional science's broader methodology; Sack (1973) used the very language of science to show that spatial relations cannot have the properties ascribed to them by the models of regional science; and Holland (1976) undercut regional science's pretensions to realism by demonstrating the tenuous relation of their models to the 'real world' (Isard's work comes in for particular opprobrium). Most recently of all, regional science has been countered by some researchers from the political Left who use sophisticated mathematical models and statistical techniques; first, to demonstrate rigorously some of the errors of conventional regional science (see NEO-RICARDIANISM), and second, to reconstruct a formal POLITICAL ECONOMIC alternative (Sheppard and Barnes, 1990). Against this backdrop of two decades of critique, regional science has increasingly moved to the intellectual margins of human geography.   TJB

References

Holland, S. 1976: *Capital versus the region.* London: Macmillan.

Isard, W. 1956: *Location and space economy.* New York: John Wiley.

Isard, W. et al. 1960: *Methods of regional analysis: an introduction to regional science.* Cambridge, MA: MIT Press.

Olsson, G. 1980: *Birds in egg/eggs in bird.* London: Pion.

Sack, R. D. 1973: A concept of physical space in geography. *Geogr. Anal.* 5, pp. 16–34.

Sheppard, E. and Barnes, T. J. 1990: *The capitalist space economy: geographical analysis after Ricardo, Marx and Sraffa.* London: Unwin Hyman.

Selected Reading

Gore, C. G. 1984: *Regions in question: space, development theory and regional policy.* London: Methuen.

Gregory, D. 1978: *Ideology, science and human geography.* London: Hutchinson.

Isard (1960).

regionalism

A movement which seeks to politicize the territorial predicaments of its regions with the aim of protecting or furthering its regional interests. An important distinction should be drawn between *functional regionalism*, in which the state is responsible for regional demarcation, such as administrative and planning regions, and a *regional movement* with feelings of collective identity that are not rooted in an officially defined region but emanate from a grassroots identity, although its politicization can often be strengthened by such an arrangement (see REGIONAL ALLIANCE). Regionalism can also involve ethnic regions (see NATIONALISM), for all regionalisms have in common a counter-culture, aims of autonomy and local power, and a political rhetoric and self-assertiveness based on a deep-seated mistrust of an increasingly remote and interventionist state. Despite economic and social RESTRUCTURING, regional identities have proved highly malleable, although as a result of the pre-eminence of state-wide socio-economic cleavages over regionally based identities in many of today's industrial states, non-ethnic based regionalism has remained low on the political agenda.   GES

Suggested Reading

Bennett, R. J. 1985: Regional movements in Britain: a review of aims and status. *Environ. Plann. C, Government and Policy* 3(1), pp. 75–96.

Peet, R., 1989: World capitalism and the destruction of regional cultures. In Johnston, R. J. and Taylor, P. J. (eds), *A world in crisis? Geographical perspectives*, Oxford: Blackwell, pp. 175–99.

Smith, G. E. 1985: Nationalism, regionalism and the state. *Environ. Plann. C, Government and Policy* 3(1), pp. 3–9.

regionalization

See CLASSIFICATION AND REGIONALIZATION.

regression

A parametric statistical technique for identifying the relationship between a dependent variable and one or more independent variables. The data employed in regression analyses should normally be at the interval or ratio level of MEASUREMENT (although nominally measured independent variables, known as dummy variables, may be included in certain circumstances).

The technique fits a straight-line plane to the trend in a scatter of points in n dimensions (where n is the total number of variables being investigated). It can best be visualized in the two-dimensional case (i.e. with one independent variable only), in which the plane is represented by a straight line (see the figure), the parameters of which are determined by the formula

$$Y = a + bX \pm e$$

where X is the independent (or causal) variable, Y is the dependent (or effect) variable, b is the slope of the line (often termed the regression coefficient), a is its intercept (where the regression line crosses the vertical axis – i.e. the value of Y when $X = 0.0$) and e is the error term for the RESIDUALS (cf. SIGNIFICANCE TEST).

A multiple regression equation contains more than one independent variable and has the general form

$$Y = a + b_1X_1 + b_2X_2 \pm e$$

In this each value of b (termed the partial regression coefficient) indicates the change in the value of Y with a unit change in the value of the relevant X variable, assuming no change in the values of the other X (i.e. they are 'held constant', in the technical jargon). The intercept coefficient indicates the estimated value of Y when all values of the X variables are set to 0.0.

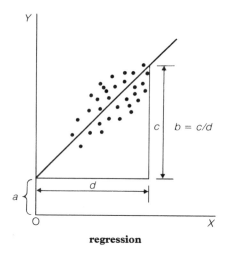

regression

The goodness-of-fit of a regression line (i.e. its closeness to all of the points in the scatter) is measured by a CORRELATION coefficient (R). The goodness-of-fit for each separate variable in a multiple regression is termed the partial correlation coefficient.

Regression analysis, like other techniques within the GENERAL LINEAR MODEL, makes a variety of assumptions about the data used. If these are not met in a data set being analysed, then the coefficients are likely to be either or both of inefficient and biased.

RJJ

Suggested Reading

Johnston, R. J. 1978: *Multivariate statistical analysis in geography: a primer on the general linear model.* London: Longman.

O'Brien, L. 1992: *Introducing quantitative geography: measurement, methods and generalised linear models.* London: Routledge.

Regulation school A group of French political–economic theories which explain the structure of capitalist economies and how these change over time. Born out of an explicit rejection of market equilibrium as the organizing force within CAPITALISM, the Regulation approach instead posits societal reproduction as the central imperative underlying capitalist dynamics. Such reproduction is said to be achieved through the 'mode of regulation' – a set of state and private institutional forms, social practices, habits and norms (such as those governing wage determination) which induce private individuals to act in the interests of achieving overall economic stability. Regulation theorists place particular importance on the balancing of national production and consumption (via the mode of regulation) in order to ensure the reproduction of capitalism. Distinctive historical periods of long-run expansion or relative stability (see REGIME OF ACCUMULATION) are seen to culminate in crisis (stagnation or instability) when such balance is no longer achieved by the existing mode of regulation. A new period of stability will arise only if successful ways of reorganizing production and/or consumption, or effective new institutions and social practices, are found. Modes of regulation will thus vary over time within the same national economy, and will also vary from country to country at any point in time. Because they are seen as being produced through active human struggle, many different modes of regulation can, in theory, support a given REGIME OF ACCUMULATION. Particular regimes, and the mode of regulation historically associated with them have, according to Scott (1988), each favoured a particular set of industries and production locations. (See also

FLEXIBLE ACCUMULATION; FORDISM; POST-FORDISM.) MSG

Reference

Scott, A. J. 1988: *New industrial spaces*. London: Pion.

Suggested Reading

Boyer, R. 1990: *The Regulation school: a critical introduction*. New York: Columbia University Press.

Reilly's law A method derived by a market researcher for estimating the relative flow of trade from a place to each of two towns (Reilly, 1931). Built on the same foundations as the GRAVITY MODEL, the law states that 'two cities attract trade from an intermediate town in the vicinity of the breaking point [the boundary between their HINTERLANDS] approximately in direct proportion to the populations of the two cities and in inverse proportion to the squares of the distances from these two cities to the intermediate town'. Algrebraically, this is expressed as

$$T_a/T_b = (P_a/P_b) \times (d_b/d_a)^2,$$

where T_a and T_b are the proportions of the trade (T) going to towns and a and b respectively, P_a and P_b are the populations of a and b respectively, and d_a and d_b are the distances from the place being considered to a and b. All other things being equal, more trade will go to the larger cities and to the closer places. (Note that in CENTRAL PLACE THEORY all trade goes to the closest centre, whatever its size.) RJJ

Reference

Reilly, W. J. 1931: *The law of retail gravitation*. New York: Knickerbocker Press.

relations of production The manner in which participants in the productive process relate to one another, sometimes referred to as the social relations of production. In MARXIAN ECONOMICS, relations of production correspond to a definite stage in the development of the PRODUCTIVE FORCES. the social relations of SLAVERY involved producers owning workers, and under FEUDALISM there existed rights whereby landowners could appropriate some of the production of others; these arrangements impeded the development of the productive forces, which was facilitated by the new social relations of CAPITALISM, whereby workers are free to sell their labour on the open market. The tension or contradiction between the forces of production and the social relations of production is held by Marxists to be a major force in history responsible for changes in the MODE OF PRODUCTION. (See also CLASS.) DMS

relevance In the 1970s, 'relevance' was used as a watchword to gauge the degree to which geographers made a contribution to the analysis and resolution of major economic, environmental and social problems. It was of great importance to the critique of geography as SPATIAL SCIENCE and its formulation of abstract models of SPATIAL STRUCTURE. For example, H. C. Prince (1971) noted that:

Many geographers were deeply frustrated by a sense of failure, conscious that the knowledge they already possessed was not being put to good use, that much had been learned about ways and means of reducing hunger, disease and poverty, but little had been achieved, that educated people had not been instrumental in stopping a barbarous war [in Vietnam] and that, within their own universities, they had failed to bring about overdue reforms (p. 152).

Put like this, there was perhaps little new in the movement other than its context: there was a distinguished tradition of work in APPLIED GEOGRAPHY, and its interface with planning had been given a much harder edge by a series of 'policy-relevant' developments and initiatives within model-based geography (Berry, 1972: Coppock, 1974). But for the most part these contributions were characterized by a firm commitment to a *technical* conception of science: science was considered to be constituted outside the social practices to which it had to be 'applied' or made 'relevant', and its purpose was to provide the *technical* means for the realization of objectives to be determined outside the (autonomous) domain of science (cf. CRITICAL THEORY; INSTRUMENTALISM). Against this, the 'relevance movement' of the late 1960s and early 1970s reached beyond the designs of social engineering to recognize the rootedness of science (and of knowledge more generally) in society and to construct concepts of social justice in explicitly political terms. Again, in itself this was not entirely novel – as the contributions of Kropotkin and Reclus testify (Stoddart, 1975) – but a definite turning-point for modern Anglophone geography was reached with the publication of David Harvey's *Social justice and the city* (1973). Harvey, one of the architects of spatial science, was now scathing about its achievements (and certainly more pessimistic than Prince about its power and promise):

The quantitative revolution has run its course, and diminishing marginal returns are setting in . . . There is a clear disparity between the sophisticated theoretical and methodological framework which we are using and our ability to say anything really meaningful about events as they unfold around us. There are too many anomalies between what we purport to manipulate and what actually happens. There is an ecological problem, an urban problem, an international trade problem, and yet we seem incapable of saying anything in depth or profundity about any of them (p. 129).

This clarion call led many to follow Harvey's lead and to join him in the development of a RADICAL GEOGRAPHY that drew on ANARCHISM and, most deeply of all, on HISTORICAL MATERIALISM; many others were drawn to the development of HUMANISTIC GEOGRAPHY and WELFARE GEOGRAPHY.

For all that, however, most critical discussions of *Social justice and the city* rapidly moved away from the first two words of the title and focused on the last two. Harvey's plea was followed closely by Buttimer in her spirited and in other ways quite different reflection on *Values in geography* (1974): and yet, for all the conceptual advances made by various forms of critical human geography in the late 1970s and through the 1980s, questions of political and moral philosophy were increasingly marginalized across the discipline as a whole (and beyond). This was, in part, the result of the rise of the New Right and its encroachments on the academy. 'Relevance' was now defined in quite different terms; academic enquiry was required to respond to rules and demands set by doctrinaire governments, corporate interests and the marketplace, and 'relevance' was often turned into a submissive compliance with (rather than critical and independent scrutiny of) public policy (Smith, 1985). But these developments were also symptomatic of a failure of imagination within the Left: although a series of major conceptual advances within MARXIST GEOGRAPHY had deepened and strengthened what Benhabib (1986) calls more generally its *explanatory–diagnostic* moment, there had been remarkably little attention to the other *anticipatory–utopian* moment that was supposed to be inscribed within the logic of critical inquiry. Put more simply, there was an incisive critique of CAPITALISM but virtually no discussion of the possible geography of a future SOCIALISM.

These concerns have been revived in the late 1980s and 1990s, although in ways which sometimes complement but often function as a critique of – and even out-flank – the concerns of an older Marxist geography: most particularly through the rise of FEMINIST GEOGRAPHY and a growing awareness of the practical implications of ETHNOCENTRISM (see POSTCOLONIALISM). These are intellectual issues, to be sure, and ones in which the necessity of the explanatory–diagnostic powers of theory are plain enough; but they are also issues which can be brought directly and immediately into the conduct of day-to-day life, inside the classroom and out. In this sense, perhaps, the horizons of a genuinely 'progressive human geography' (Lowe and Short, 1990) that can speak to (and learn from) the variety of the human condition in time and space are perhaps wider than ever before, and there is a real possibility that the *teaching* of a critical human geography will be valued as a means of democratic empowerment (Pickles, 1986).   DG

References

Benhabib, S. 1986: *Critique, norm and utopia: a study of the foundations of critical theory.* New York: Columbia University Press.

Berry, B. J. L. 1972: More on relevance and policy analysis. *Area* 4, pp. 77–80.

Buttimer, A. 1974: *Values in geography*. Washington, DC: Association of American Geographers.

Coppock, J. T. 1974: Geography and public policy: challenges, opportunities and implications. *Trans. Inst. Br. Geogr.* 63, pp. 1–16.

Harvey, D. 1973: *Social justice and the city*. London: Edward Arnold.

Lowe, M. and Short, J. R. 1990: Progressive human geography. *Progr. hum. Geogr.* 14, pp. 1–11.

Pickles, J. 1986: Geographic theory and educating for democracy. *Antipode* 18, pp. 136–54.

Prince, H. C. 1971: Questions of social relevance. *Area* 3, pp. 150–3.

Smith, D. 1985: The 'new blood' scheme and its application to geography. *Area* 17, pp. 237–43.

Stoddart, D. R. 1975: Kropotkin, Reclus and 'relevant' geography. *Area* 7, pp. 188–90.

Suggested Reading

Johnston, R. J. 1991: *Geography and geographers: Anglo-American human geography since 1945*. London: Edward Arnold, ch. 7.

Pickles (1986).

religion, geography of A subfield of CULTURAL GEOGRAPHY, variously concerned with the description and interpretation of the spatial relationships, landscapes and places of sacred phenomena and religious practices. The geography of religion is, consequently, most fully developed where cultural geography is itself strong, and notably in the USA and Germany.

Earlier reviews have noted both a 'lack of coherence' (Sopher, 1981) and that the subfield is 'in disarray' (Tuan, 1976). The earliest and still the largest number of studies are concerned with the patterning of religious phenomena, either as map distributions or as morphological features of the CULTURAL LANDSCAPE. The distribution of religious denominations, for example, has been taken as indicative of the boundaries of *cultural regions* (Zelinsky, 1961), while descriptive studies have itemized such visible landscape elements as cemeteries, sacred places, or the landscape of distinctive groups such as the Mormons. Much of this work is of a descriptive and IDIOGRAPHIC character, with limited explanation or theorization. Its concept of CULTURE is *superorganic*; that is, monolithic

and with a weak sense of HUMAN AGENCY. More analytical or interpretive studies of religious adherence (Doeppers, 1976), or in the case of Hannemann (1975), of a religious event, the Reformation, are indicative of more ambitious attempts to place religious phenomena in a broader explanatory context.

A second literature has assessed the role of religious belief and practice in the making of local geographies. A few geographers have examined the institutional role of the church as a landholder (Hamnett, 1987) or service provider (Pacione, 1990). More commonly, research has examined the practices of adherents as a group. A Catholic predisposition to wine-making, for example, has introduced marked variations in agricultural land use between adjacent Protestant and Catholic parishes in Germany (Geipel, 1978), whereas in Belfast the same indicators intimate the boundaries of mutually hostile ethnic territories (Boal, 1969). More generally, the role of religious variables in group formation is well known. In plural societies religious adherence often marks the divisions between more or less entitled citizens; the relative status of Jew and Arab (whether Muslim or Christian) in Israel is a case in point (Romann and Weingrod, 1991). A significant group of studies has traced the effect of religious beliefs on dietary practices and associated regimes of agriculture (Simoons, 1960, 1979). More specialized is work on the distinctive geography of sacred places, including Ben-Arieh's (1984) immense historical geography of Jerusalem. Using a variety of approaches (including the GRAVITY MODEL) other studies have examined pilgrimages as a special form of MIGRATION (Sopher, 1968).

An important question for cultural geographers who seek more than a descriptive approach to the geography of religion is knowledge of both the literature of religious studies and also familiarity with the nature of religious experience. Isaac (1961–2) was an early proponent of this view, as was the influential German scholar, Büttner (1980). Their persuasive argument is that for mature scholarship, interpretation or religious phenomena requires a prior contextual knowledge of religious process and precedent. Tuan (1976) has pressed the issue furthest, arguing for a PHE-NOMENOLOGY of religious experience, a humanistic perspective to which he has made important contributions (Tuan, 1978). Sharing this orientation is a detailed interpretation of the symbolic meaning of 36 landscape elements of Buddhist pilgrimage sites (Tanaka, 1977).

A related body of work has explored the relationship between religious cosmology or worldview and the meaning of the land. The cities of early civilizations were frequently laid out as a microcosm of a cosmological order, with the King's palace a mimetic representation of the centre of the universe (Wheatley, 1971; Duncan, 1990: cf. SACRED AND PROFANE SPACE). Cosmologies also provide a strong orientation to the land: the belief in the promised land, such a central tenet of the Jewish faith (Houston, 1978), has propelled the twentieth century re-invention of the Jewish state. Not least, and most controversial, has been the debate over the environmental implications of the Judaeo-Christian traditions. The earlier emphasis on dominion and its destructive consequences for environmental use, is now much tempered, as a countervailing argument has presented the evidence for an ethic of environmental stewardship from Biblical sources (Kay, 1989; see also Passmore, 1974). Discussions of this type are likely to increase in relevance with a growing normative interest in morality and ETHICS in human geography.

The turn of a new cultural geography towards cultural politics has led to several innovative studies. Harvey's (1979) materialist reading of the Basilica of Sacré-Couer in Paris identifies the building as a political symbol intended to restore a conservative politics following the insurrection of the Paris Commune. This attempt to establish cultural HEGEMONY through the built environment was resisted by republican Parisians, although the basilica was eventually completed. In a quite different cultural setting, with an alternative set of theoretical heuristics, Duncan (1990) has told much the same story. In pre-colonial Sri Lanka, the monarchy of the Kandyan

Kingdom sought to expand and legitimate its control in a series of ritualized building programmes. The new construction followed specific protocols laid out in religious texts. The designs were intended to rebuild the cosmological order in microcosm, with a detailed iconographic programme, but the larger political imperative was to legitimize the rule of the King. In a remarkable volume, Duncan has made several advances, and brought a new vitality to the conventional task of recording the presence of religious phenomena in the cultural landscape. Religious traits are not merely observed as visible forms, but are read as symbolic entries, authored by identifiable agents from a received tradition, and directed by them towards a broader political project. To accomplish this objective, the study includes a sophisticated knowledge of the religious texts themselves as well as a theoretical strategy of *intertextuality* that relates the holy books to the built landscape, itself conceived as a TEXT.

A final genre of work was labelled by Sopher (1981) as confessional, that is, it has offered geographical interpretations which are predicated upon a religious cosmology. While such an interpretation is most usually drawn from the tradition of a recognized religious worldview (Ley, 1974; Wallace, 1978), Sopher suggests that it may equally be derived from a secular cosmology, and he cites the conclusion of the interpretation of Sacré-Coeur, with Harvey (1979) 'coming forward, as it were, for Karl Marx'. While philosphically defensible, and illuminating in the context of the philosophy of geography, the expansion of the geography of religion to incorporate explicitly non-religious values and phenomena would further serve to dilute any distinctive character to the subfield.

Earlier anxieties that with global secularization the geography of religion would become increasingly an historical geography of relics and origins have been abruptly reversed by religious movements of the past decade. The rise of militant Islam, the role of the Roman Catholic Church in democracy movements in Latin America and elsewhere, and the development of a political ideology among conservative Christians in the USA, are all phenomena with geographies of their own, and which provide a significant constitutive force in the making and remaking of places.

A review of the geography of religion remains at present largely an inventory of eclectic, and mainly descriptive, empirical studies, interspersed with a smaller number of theoretically more ambitious works, and culminating in a handful of powerful research monographs, many of them addressing topics from the past. The global revitalization of religious belief and its consequences in the past decade provide the contemporary research problems around which a more theoretical and programmatic body of research in the geography of religion might yet develop. In the light of the salience of its subject matter and an incomplete intellectual development to date, there is certainly 'more room for geographical exploration (of religion) than has thus far been attempted' (Kong, 1990). DL

References

Ben-Arieh, Y. 1984: *Jerusalem in the nineteenth century: the old city*. New York: St. Martin's Press.

Boal, F. 1969: Territoriality on the Shankill-Falls divide, Belfast. *Irish Geography* 6, pp. 30–50.

Büttner, M. 1980: On the history and philosophy of the geography of religion in Germany. *Religion* 10, pp. 86–119.

Doeppers, D. 1976: The evolution of the geography of religious adherence in the Philippines before 1898. *J. hist. Geogr.* 2, pp. 95–110.

Duncan, J. 1990: *The city as text: the politics of landscape interpretation in the Kandyan Kingdom*. Cambridge: Cambridge University Press.

Geipel, R. 1978: The landscape indicators school in German geography. In Ley, D. and Samuels, M., eds, *Humanistic geography*. London: Croom Helm, pp. 155–72.

Hamnett, C. 1987: The church's many mansions: the changing structure of the Church Commissioners' land and property holdings, 1948–1977. *Trans. Inst. Br. Geogr* n.s. 12, pp. 465–81.

Hannemann, M. 1975: *The diffusion of the Reformation in southwestern Germany, 1518–1534*. Chicago: University of Chicago, Department of Geography, Research paper No. 167.

Harvey, D. 1979: Monument and myth. *Ann. Ass. Am. Geogr.* 69, pp. 362–81.

Houston, J. 1978: The concepts of 'place' and 'land' in the Judaeo-Christian tradition. In Ley, D. and Samuels, M., eds, *Humanistic geography*. London: Croom Helm, pp. 224–37.

Isaac, E. 1961–2: The act and the covenant: the impact of religion on the landscape. *Landscape* 11, pp. 12–17.

Kay, J. 1989: Human dominion over nature in the Hebrew Bible. *Ann. Ass. Am. Geogr.* 79, pp. 213–32.

Kong, L. 1990: Geography and religion: trends and prospects. *Progr. hum. Geogr.* 14, pp. 355–71.

Ley, D. 1974: The city and good and evil: reflections on Christian and Marxian interpretations. *Antipode* 6(1), pp. 66–74.

Pacione, M. 1990: The ecclesiastical community of interest as a response to urban poverty and deprivation. *Trans. Inst. Br. Geogr.* 15, pp. 193–204.

Passmore, J. 1974: *Man's responsibility to nature: ecological problems and Western traditions*. New York: Scribner's.

Romann, M. and Weingrod, A. 1991: *Living together separately: Arabs and Jews in contemporary Jerusalem*. Princeton, NJ: Princeton University Press.

Simoons, F. 1960: *Eat not this flesh*. Madison: University of Wisconsin Press.

Simoons, F. 1979: Questions in the sacred cow controversy. *Current Anthropology* 20, pp. 467–93.

Sopher, D. 1968: Pilgrim circulation in Gujarat. *Geogr. Rev.* 58, pp. 392–425.

Sopher, D. 1981: Geography and religions. *Prog. hum. Geogr.* 5, pp. 510–24.

Tanaka, H. 1977: Geographic expression of Buddhist pilgrim places in Shikoku Island, Japan. *Can. Geogr.* 21, pp. 111–32.

Tuan, Y.-F. 1976: Humanistic geography. *Ann. Ass. Am. Geogr.* 66, pp. 266–76.

Tuan, Y.-F. 1978: *Landscapes of fear*. Oxford: Blackwell.

Wallace, I. 1978: Towards a humanized conception of economic geography. In Ley, D. and Samuels, M., eds, *Humanistic geography*. London: Croom Helm, pp. 91–108.

Wheatley, P. 1971: *The pivot of the four quarters*. Chicago: Aldine.

Zelinsky, W. 1961: An approach to the religious geography of the United States: patterns of church membership in 1952. *Ann. Ass. Am. Geogr.* 51, pp. 139–93.

Suggested Reading

Kong (1990).

Social Compass: International Review of Sociology of Religion, 1992: The geography of religions. 39(4), whole issue.

Sopher, D. 1967: Geography of religions. Englewood Cliffs, NJ: Prentice-Hall.

remote sensing The acquisition of information about an object by a sensor that is not in direct physical contact with the object. The term was coined in the early 1960s by geographers at the US Office of Naval Research to describe the process of obtaining data using both photographic and non-photographic sensor systems (Colwell, 1983). Most remote sensing systems measure electromagnetic energy which is propagated by electromagnetic radiation (EMR) at a velocity of 3×10^8 m s^{-1} (the speed of light) from a source (usually the sun) through space, and which is then reflected or re-radiated from the object of interest back to the remote sensor. Upon detection by the remote sensor, changes in the amount and properties of the EMR become a valuable source of data about the object (Jensen et al., 1989).

Remote sensing is unique in that it can be used *to collect* data, unlike other techniques such as CARTOGRAPHY, GEOGRAPHIC INFORMATION SYSTEMS (GIS) and statistics, which rely on data already available. The most important types of remote sensors in use today include (Campbell, 1987): (1) metric aerial photography (primarily colour and colour-infrared); (2) visible, near-infrared and mid-infrared digital sensor systems (e.g. Landsat Thematic Mapper and SPOT data); (3) thermal infrared imaging radiometers (e.g. Daedalus DS-1268) which record the amount of heat energy emitted from the terrain; (4) active microwave (RADAR) systems which primarily record surface roughness characteristics; (5) passive microwave systems which record soil and vegetation brightness, temperatures and moisture conditions; (6) video remote sensing in the visible and near-infrared region; and (7) sonar systems which use sound energy to map bathymetry. Geographers use these sensors to obtain detailed spatial information about the Earth and human activities. Jensen et al. (1989) identified the major biophysical variables which can be remotely sensed, including:

an object's (x,y) location, elevation (height), colour, chlorophyll absorption characteristics, temperature, biomass, surface roughness (texture) and moisture content. The biophysical characteristics of an object can then be evaluated in conjunction with other data to yield hybrid information, such as vegetation stress, land use/cover information and socio-economic characteristics.

Fieldwork is usually performed to calibrate the remote sensor data. Once the fieldwork has been completed, the scientist interprets the imagery using analogue or digital image-processing techniques. Analogue techniques include visual monoscopic or stereoscopic analysis. Much of the analysis of urban areas continues to be performed using visual analysis. Digital image-processing techniques are applied to extract useful information when the imagery is in a digital format (Jensen, 1986). There are numerous public (NASA, VICAR, ELAS, Purdue Multi-Spec) and commercial digital image processing systems available today (ERDAS, IDRISI, INTERGRAPH) which are powerful and relatively easy to learn. Most systems require the use of a high-speed computer workstation (>33 MHz CPU), an arithmetic coprocessor, substantial mass storage (>300 MB), a high-resolution colour monitor and a graphics memory (capable of displaying 512×512 pixels with 16.7 million colours). To be of most value, the information derived from remote sensing is registered to a map PROJECTION and placed in a GIS, where it is analysed in conjunction with other spatial information (Lauer et al., 1991). It is becoming increasingly popular in geographical research to merge raster-based remotely sensed data with vector-based GIS thematic data in a single screen display.

Information derived from remote sensing is critical to the successful monitoring and modelling of natural (e.g. watershed runoff) and cultural (e.g. land-use conversion at the urban fringe) processes. Remotely sensed data can be acquired on multiple dates to identify (a) the location of change, (b) the rate of change, and (c) sometimes the agents of change. For example, remote sensing change detection studies have monitored: (1) the deforestation of the Amazon rain forest; (2) urban expansion onto prime farmland or in the coastal zone; (3) increased amounts of point and non-point source pollution into water bodies; (4) the expansion of the urban heat island; (5) urban infrastructure changes (especially transportation of utility systems); and (6) population expansion or contraction based on housing stock measurements.

The Earth Observing System (EOS) platforms to be placed in orbit from 1997 to 2010 will contain new remote sensing systems which will be of significance to human and physical geographers (EOS, 1987). These sensors will produce more than 1 terabyte of information per day. Geographers will have available high spatial, spectral and temporal resolution satellite remote sensor data covering essentially all areas of the globe. Improvements in artificial intelligence and expert systems in remote sensing will be required to use the data wisely. Similarly, the interface between remote sensing and GIS must continue to be simplified and strengthened. An integrating concept will be *telescience*, which allows a scientist to be networked to remote sensing space systems, data archives and other researchers. Telescience will allow geographers to perform interdisciplinary, multi-institutional, multinational research to understand environmental processes at SCALES ranging from local to global.   JRJ

References and Suggested Reading

Campbell, J. B. 1987: *Introduction to remote sensing*. New York: Guilford Press.

Colwell, R. N., ed. 1983: *Manual of remote sensing*. Falls Church, VA: American Society for Photogrammetry and Remote Sensing.

EOS Science Steering Committee 1987: *From pattern to process; the strategy of the Earth Observing System*. Washington, DC: NASA.

Jensen, J. R. 1986: *Introductory digital image processing: a remote sensing perspective*. Englewood Cliffs, NJ: Prentice-Hall.

Jensen, J. R., Campbell, J., Dozier, J., Estes, J., Hodgson, M., Lo., C., Lulla, K., Merchant, J., Smith, R., Stow, D., Strahler, A. and Welch, R. 1989: Remote sensing. In Gaile, G. L. and Willmott, C. J., eds, *Geography in America*. Columbus, OH: Merrill, pp. 746–75.

Lauer, D. T., Estes, J. E., Jensen, J. R. and Greenlee, D. D. 1991: Institutional issues affecting the integration and use of remotely sensed data and geographic information systems. *Photogramm. Eng. Remote Sensing* 57(6), pp. 647–54.

renewal   See URBAN RENEWAL.

rent   The payment to a FACTOR OF PRODUCTION over and above that necessary to keep it in its present occupation. Typically, in ECONOMIC GEOGRAPHY the use of the term is reserved for those cases in which the supply of a factor of production does not change in response to the price paid for it. The exemplar is land. Usually, the same fixed quantity of land is available regardless of the level of payment offered per unit. By definition, because landlords are potentially willing to lease the entire supply of land to users for even the most minimal payment, any actual payment above that level is equivalent to rent. The fact that land often achieves a price higher than that absolute minimum is because demand outstrips the fixed supply.

The case described above is one in which it is assumed that each unit of land is identical. However, not all land is the same, and in such circumstances differential rent arises. One source of differentiation is in terms of distance from some fixed point, such as a marketplace. This is best seen in VON THÜNEN'S MODEL of agricultural land use. Because agricultural goods are taken to market for sale, crops grown closer to that market make a saving in terms of transportation costs. Through a competitive process among farmers, that saving is in turn eventually bid away in the form of rent. Here, rent acts as a rationing device in ensuring that each plot of land is used in the best possible way, for only those farmers growing crops that make the best use of a given location (that is, maximize transportation savings) are able to outbid all others and capture the desired plot (Chisholm, 1962).

A second source of differentiation is with respect to the productivity of the land. Following the English classical economist David Ricardo (1772–1823), two forms of differential rent are recognized; extensive and intensive (Barnes, 1984). In order to calculate both, Ricardo needed to establish a marginal plot of land, one where its productivity is so low that the costs of production are equal to the market price of the agricultural good, and thereby leaving no room for the levying of rent. With the same amount of capital applied to every plot of land, extensive rent is equal to the difference between the cost of production on the intramarginal plot, and the cost on the marginal one. Intensive differential rent occurs where capital inputs are not equal. For example, a farmer on an intramarginal plot will probably invest more capital on her or his farm than the marginal farmer, because up to some finite maximum each unit of extra capital invested there yields a higher return. Intensive rent is then the sum of all the differences in capital productivity between the marginal and intramarginal farmers multiplied by the market price for the crop.

Marxists recognize differential rents I and II (the counterparts to extensive and intensive rents, respectively), and also introduce a form of land rent based upon the power of the landowner (Barnes, 1988). Two subtypes are recognizable. *Absolute rent* is the difference between the LABOUR VALUE of a crop and its price of production (see MARXIST ECONOMICS). Such a difference occurs because landowners as a class prevent new capital investment in agriculture; by keeping the capital:labour ratio artificially low, labour values and prices necessarily diverge, to the advantage of the landowner (Sheppard and Barnes, 1990, pp. 129–32). *Monopoly rent* occurs when landowners, because of their power, hold back land, not leasing it until they receive a positive return above some minimum threshold level (Harvey, 1974).   TJB

References

Barnes, T. J. 1984: Theories of agricultural rent within the surplus approach. *Int. reg. Sci. Rev.* 9, pp. 125–40.

Barnes, T. J. 1988: Scarcity and agricultural land rent in light of the capital controversy: three views. *Antipode* 20, pp. 207–38.

Chisholm, M. 1962: *Rural settlement and land use: an essay in location.* London: Hutchinson.

Harvey, D. 1974: Class monopoly rent, finance capital, and the urban revolution. *Reg. Stud.* 8, pp. 239–55.

Sheppard, E. and Barnes, T. J. 1990: *The capitalist space economy: geographical analysis after*

Ricardo, Marx and Sraffa. London: Unwin Hyman.

Suggested Reading

Ball, M. 1977: Differential rent and the role of landed property. *Int. J. urban and reg. Res.* 1, pp. 380–403.

Scott, A. J. 1976: Land and land rent: an interpretive review of the French literature. *Prog. Geog.* 9, pp. 101–46.

rent gap   The rent gap describes the discrepancy between actual rent attracted by a piece of land ('capitalized ground rent') and the rent that could be gleaned under a higher and better use ('potential ground rent'). The rent gap is a central element in explanations of GENTRIFICATION (Smith, 1979). To the extent that disinvestment in the built environment brings about a reciprocal decline in the value of the land on which structures sit, the rent gap enlarges and the opportunities for reinvestment increase. Geographically, the rent gap has emerged in inner-city areas where disinvestment was not sufficiently compensated by reinvestment, and a distinct valley in land values resulted (see the figure). Empirically, the rent gap has been identified from Sydney to Malmo to Toronto (Clark, 1987) as a precursor to gentrification. Theoretically, it has been

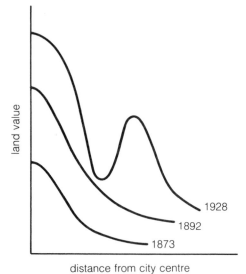

rent gap   *The evolution of land values in Chicago* (after Hoyt, 1933).

challenged as an incomplete explanation of gentrification, which gives short shrift to questions of individual preference (Hamnett, 1991; see also Smith, 1992).   NS

References

Clark, E. 1987: *The rent gap and urban change: case studies in Malmo, 1860–1985*. Lund: Lund University Press.

Hamnett, C. 1991: The blind men and the elephant: the explanation of gentrification. *Trans. Inst. Br. Geogr.* n.s. 16, pp. 173–89.

Hoyt, H. 1933: *One hundred years of land values in Chicago*. Chicago: Chicago University Press.

Smith, N. 1979: Toward a theory of gentrification: a back to the city movement by capital not people. *J. Am. Plann. Assoc.* 45, pp. 538–48.

Smith, N. 1992: Blind man's bluff, or Hamnett's philosophical individualism in search of gentrification. *Trans. Inst. Br. Geogr.* n.s. 17, 110–115.

repertory grid analysis A methodology used in BEHAVIOURAL GEOGRAPHY for the identification of people's attitudes and images. It was developed in psychotherapy and adapted for other social sciences. Most QUESTIONNAIRE studies of such phenomena define the categories which people must respond to, but personal construct theory allows them to define their own. This makes for problems of comparability, however, so that analysis of results depends greatly on the researcher's interpretative skills (see also SEMANTIC DIFFERENTIAL).
RJJ

Suggested Reading

Hudson, R. 1980: Personal construct theory, the repertory grid method and human geography. *Progr. hum. Geogr.* 14, pp. 346–59.

replacement rates Measures of the extent to which a given population is replacing itself. Natural increase, the simple balance of births over deaths, is too strongly influenced by age structures to give a real measure of replacement of generations. Three single-number indicators are frequently used instead; the total fertility rate, the gross reproduction rate and the net reproduction rate (see FERTILITY). The last of these (the NRR) is the most used. Devised by R. R. Kuczynski in the 1930s (see Kuczynski, 1935), it measures the average number of daughters

produced by a woman during her reproductive lifetime, taking into account mortality. If the NRR is less than 1 then the population will ultimately decline; if it equals 1 then the population is stationary.
PEO

Reference

Kuczynski, R. R. 1935: *The measurement of population growth: methods and results*. London: Sidgwick and Jackson/New York: Oxford University Press.

Suggested Reading

Woods, R. I. 1979: *Population analysis in geography*. London: Longman, ch. 5.

representation In ELECTORAL GEOGRAPHY, the translation of votes cast into seats in a legislature. The translation procedure is often assessed against the norm of proportional representation, in which a party's percentage of the seats allocated should be equal to its percentage of the votes cast: any deviation from this norm is termed electoral bias.   RJJ

Suggested Reading

Taagepera, R. and Shugart, M. S. 1989: *Seats and votes: the effects and determinants of electoral systems*. New Haven, CT: Yale University Press.

residual The difference between the estimated and actual value for an observation on the dependent variable in a REGRESSION equation: a positive residual is where the observed value exceeds the estimated; a negative value is where the latter has the larger value. The larger residuals indicate where the estimating equation has relatively failed, and Haggett (1965) suggested that advances in geographical research could be achieved by mapping the distribution of residual values in order to identify new causal variables. Maps of residuals can also be used to test for the presence of SPATIAL AUTOCORRELATION.   RJJ

Reference

Haggett, P. 1965: *Locational analysis in human geography*. London: Edward Arnold.

Suggested Reading
Johnston, R. J. 1978: *Multivariate statistical analysis in geography: a primer on the general linear model.* London: Longman.

resource A concept employed to denote sources of human satisfaction, wealth or strength. Labour, entrepreneurial skills, investment funds, fixed capital assets, technology and cultural and physical attributes may all be referred to as resources of a nation (or region, company or household).

In a RESOURCE MANAGEMENT context, the term is reserved for substances, organisms and properties of the physical environment (natural resources). Human beings evaluate natural systems, regarding as resources *only* those elements which they have the knowledge and technology to utilize and which provide desired goods and services. Natural attributes failing to meet these criteria remain unvalued, 'neutral stuff' (Zimmerman, 1951). Resources are therefore subjective, functional and dynamic. The perceived resource set alters markedly over time and space to reflect variations in knowledge, technology, social structures, economic conditions and political systems.

For minerals, the twentieth century has witnessed a marked reduction in the diversity of resource definitions over space with the development of modern communications systems and an increasingly interdependent global economy. Only when countries are isolated from the rest of the world economy can significant differences in resource definitions remain. Before the break-up of the Soviet bloc, for example, minerals self-sufficiency policies gave resource status to substances such as nepheline and alunite (non-bauxite sources of aluminium), which had little or no resource value elsewhere.

In the case of environmental resources, consensus over the resource definition is much less common. The cultural significance of landscapes, flora and fauna, and natural ECOSYSTEMS varies between countries, social groups and individuals (see ENVIRONMENTAL PERCEPTION). More fundamentally, there are many environmentalists who are ideologically opposed to the application of the resource concept for environmental systems. The resource notion is human centred, with the assumption that natural systems obtain '*instrument*' or 'use' value through the services they provide for human beings. However, writers such as Pedlar (1979) and Lovelock (1988) argue that humans are merely one component within an interdependent global ecosystem and that all elements within the ECOSYSTEM have '*intrinsic*' value quite separate from human needs and desires (see ENVIRONMENTALISM).

Natural resources are commonly divided into:

(a) *stock* resources (minerals and land), which have taken millions of years to form and – from a human perspective – are fixed in supply:

(b) *flow* (or renewable) resources, which naturally regenerate to provide new supply units within a human time-span.

The distinction between these categories is blurred, however, and it is more appropriate to think of a use–renewability continuum (see the figure). At one extreme, potential supplies are naturally determined, infinitely renewable and

resource *Continuum of natural resources* (Rees, 1989).

unrelated to current usage levels. At the other, utilization massively exceeds regeneration and use is consumptive, producing unusable forms of matter and energy. Between these extremes, renewability is dependent on human decisions, future supply availabilities being determined by usage rates and investment in artificial regeneration. All resources which reproduce biologically (including the capacity of the environment to biodegrade pollutants) can be 'mined' to exhaustion; soils only remain renewable if managed, and, since none of the element minerals are consumed by use, regeneration could theoretically occur through RECYCLING. However, given the laws of ENTROPY, infinite recycling may be impossible. JAR

References

Lovelock, J. 1988: *The ages of Gaia: a biography of our living Earth*. Oxford: Oxford University Press.

Pedlar, K. 1979: *The quest for Gaia*. London: Granada.

Rees, J. 1989: Natural resources, economy and society. In Gregory, D. and Walford, R. eds, *Horizons in human geography*. London: Macmillan, pp. 364–94.

Zimmerman, E. W. 1951: *World resources and industries*. New York: Harper and Brothers, ch. 1.

resource evaluation A generic term for assessments which attempt to determine either the value (expressed in physical, economic or perceptual terms) of a resource or the consequences and adequacy of resource-management strategies. Generalizing broadly, it has been applied to five distinct areas of work:

(a) Determination of the *quantity* of resource supplies. Even for *stock* RESOURCES, it is never easy to forecast what quantity will be available for human use. *Proven reserves* are those already discovered and known to be economically extractable under current demand, price and technological conditions; but new discoveries, changed technologies and altered socioeconomic and political circumstances will alter resource availabilities over time. For renewable and environmental resources even greater forecasting problems arise, since the quantity of new supplies is variable over time, depending on past use levels and investment or conservation decisions.

(b) Determination of the *capacity* of the global or individual ECOSYSTEMS to support human life and economic development over time (see SUSTAINABLE DEVELOPMENT). For land, soils and recreation resources the notion of CARRYING CAPACITY is employed, while the ability of environmental media to absorb waste products can be assessed by considering their absorptive or assimilative capacity (see POLLUTION).

(c) Determination of the *value* of a resource in social-welfare terms. There is no absolute measure of value and a host of alternative assessment bases have been employed; for example, market prices, opportunity costs, labour value, social indicators, energy accounting, public preferences and ecological (intrinsic) values (see ENVIRONMENTALISM; ENVIRONMENTAL PERCEPTION; WELFARE GEOGRAPHY). Where resource goods and services are *incorporated into the market-exchange system*, market prices are commonly taken as a value measure, but the identity between price and value only holds if: (i) the consumer is sovereign, with preferences unaffected by producer manipulation; (ii) markets are free and perfectly competitive; (iii) the 'ability to pay' problem is ignored (see NEOCLASSICAL ECONOMICS); and (iv) the price incorporates all the costs involved in supplying, using and, ultimately, discarding the resource product. This is rarely the case, since the costs of environmental degradation and of resource depletion are seldom added into the price. When resources are *common property and have no established market price*, attempts have been made to devise surrogate monetary measures (see Johansson, 1987; Pearce and Markandya, 1989). To obtain a full or total economic value of a resource, three elements need to be taken into account: (a) actual use value (the current benefits derived by individuals from using a resource, including the environment); (b) option value (the benefits from potential future use); and (c) the intrinsic or existence value (see ENVIRONMENTALISM). Inevitably, the whole question of resource valuation is highly complex, and there is considerable disagreement about the validity and reliability of the various methods used.

(d) Assessment of the likely consequences of resource programmes, projects, policies and administrative changes (see COST–BENEFIT ANALYSIS; ENVIRONMENTAL AUDIT; ENVIRONMENTAL IMPACT ASSESSMENT).

(e) Assessment of the adequacy or effectiveness of resource management strategies and policy implementation. The evaluation criteria chosen are crucial to the results of any assessment. Some assessments concentrate on the extent to which stated policy objectives are met: others use a variety of criteria – economic efficiency, distributive equity, sustainability, employment generation, etc.   JAR

References and Suggested Reading

Johansson, P.-O. 1987: *The economic theory and measurement of environmental benefits.* Cambridge: Cambridge University Press.

Mitchell, B. 1989: *Geography and resource analysis,* second edition. London: Longman.

Pearce, D. W. and Markandya, A. 1989: *The benefits of environmental policy.* Paris: OECD.

Pearce, D. W. and Turner, R. K. 1990: *Economics of natural resources and the environment.* London: Harvester Wheatsheaf.

resource management[1] A broad multidisciplinary area or programme of study concerned with the management of all NATURAL RESOURCES, renewable and non-renewable, whether managed by private enterprise or public-sector agencies. It seeks to:

(a) explain the processes (physical, socio-economic and political) involved in RESOURCE supply, exploitation and consumption;

(b) analyse the allocation of resource products and services over space and time;

(c) evaluate management systems, practices and policies;

(d) develop alternative management strategies and evaluatory tools.

Although academic research into resource questions has a long history, the establishment of degree courses (primarily in North America) in the subject and its recognition as a distinct area of enquiry have occurred largely since the 1960s. Its development mirrors the growth of the environmental movement and of public concern over declining environmental standards, ECOSYSTEM change, the EQUITY of resource allocations and the capacity of the Earth to sustain further increases in population and economic activity (see SUSTAINABLE DEVELOPMENT). Effective enquiry in the resources field cannot be confined to one discipline but must address the complex interrelationships that exist between the physical, social, economic and political systems. (See also ENVIRONMENTALISM.)   JAR

resource management[2] A process or system of decision-making whereby resource use, CONSERVATION or environmental policies and practices are devised and implemented. The decisions are basically concerned with the exploitation and allocation of resources over space and time, including investments in enhancing renewable resource flows, protecting environmental resources and ensuring SUSTAINABLE DEVELOPMENT. Resource management can involve the development or conservation of resources over different spatial scales, ranging from a single product or service (e.g. a forest or fishery) to the global ecosphere.

Rationalists have viewed resource management as a conscious logical process, or ends–means system. Given specific, clearly defined and non-conflicting objectives, the management task was to devise appropriate administrative structures, select and employ appropriate management tools, and create effective implementation strategies. However, it is well recognized that in reality decision systems diverge markedly from the ends–means model. Multiple, conflicting and shifting objectives are commonplace, many management decisions are habitual, and 'non-decisions' play a role in determining the practice of resource exploitation and allocation (see DECISION-MAKING). In addition, resource management takes place within the context of extant economic, social, political, legal and administrative conditions. It is rare for entirely new organizations, management tools or implementation practices to be devised that best address a specific resource problem; rather, conventional methods and already established organizations are employed.

The bulk of resource management decisions are made within the private sector, not only by large industrial conglomerates and financial institutions but also by individual farmers and householders. This dominance of private-sector choice is even greater today with the collapse of the planned economies in the former USSR and Eastern Europe, with the widely perceived failure of command and control systems (see COMMAND ECONOMY) and with worldwide moves towards PRIVATIZATION. Conventional theoretical assessments have assumed that profit or utility maximization are the management objectives of private decision-makers, and that in a perfectly working, competitive economy the result will be an economically efficient allocation of resources (see NEOCLASSICAL ECONOMICS; PARETO OPTIMALITY; UTILITY THEORY). Analysts have explored the reasons why efficient market conditions have not occurred (RISK and UNCERTAINTY, monopoly and government intervention), and have also evaluated the performance of resource sectors according to alternative (i.e. non-economic efficiency) criteria, such as distributive equity, employment generation, security or sustainability. During the 1970s and early 1980s, considerable attention was also paid to the structural limits inherent in the capitalist mode of exchange, and to the implications of these for trade and for the allocation of the wealth and welfare derived from resource exploitation.

At a completely different spatial SCALE studies have been conducted on the actual decision behaviour of individuals and organizations. Such work has laid stress on the way in which decision-makers are 'bounded' by their skills, knowledge and habitual modes of thought, the subjective and changing nature of management goals (reflecting individual, professional and societal value systems) and the impact of organizational structures and hierarchies on decision-making (see BEHAVIOURAL GEOGRAPHY; DECISION-MAKING).

Within the public sector, resource management involves two distinct sets of tasks:

(a) the introduction and implementation of measures to influence private resource decisions (laws, planning regulations, product or environmental standards, trade controls, taxation, subsidies, education, etc.); and

(b) the direct management of state-owned resources or resource-using industries.

Considerable debate has taken place over the legitimate role of government and over appropriate management goals. Analysts who take a free-market perspective argue that the STATE should concentrate on promoting competitive private-sector operations, controlling monopoly and correcting other forms of market failure (e.g. EXTERNALITIES). Others see it as vital that the state pursues resource policies which involve distributive justice, employment generation, security and long-term sustainability as management goals. Another controversial issue concerns the types of management tools to be used; the current trend is to reject regulation in favour of economic incentives.

Although resource management theory has been, and still largely is, dominated by economics, there is now a considerable literature which approaches resource issues from other disciplinary perspectives. Sociologists and social geographers have, for example, considered the cultural significance of resources and resource assemblages (see CULTURAL GEOGRAPHY), while international lawyers and students of international relations are currently exploring the role of transnational institutions in the development of resource policies for a sustainable future. Political scientists have also made a valuable contribution, particularly to our understanding of policy analysis and implementation. A key question is who has the power to make resource decisions (see DECISION-MAKING; POWER). An enormous ideological divide exists between those who see policy as an outcome of pluralistic competition between interest groups and those who take elitist, corporatist or structuralist perspectives (see MARXIST GEOGRAPHY; PLURALISM; STRUCTURALISM). JAR

Suggested Reading

Clark, W. and Munn, R. 1986: *Sustainable development of the biosphere*. Cambridge: Cambridge University Press.

Redclift, M. 1987: *Sustainable development*. London: Methuen.

Rees, J. 1990: *Natural resources, allocation, economics and policy*, second edition. London: Routledge.

Turner, R. K. 1988: *Sustainable environmental management*. London: Belhaven Press.

restructuring Change in and/or between the constituent parts of an economy, emanating from either the dynamics of economic DEVELOPMENT or the economy's conditions of existence. Within capitalist economies, the term frequently refers to changes in CAPITAL or the CIRCUIT OF CAPITAL. Such changes represent a response to changed conditions of ACCUMULATION induced, for example, by technical change or conflicts between labour and capital in the workplace, or transmitted through the competitive conditions endemic to CAPITALISM.

Restructuring may involve:

(a) sectoral switches of capital (e.g. DEINDUSTRIALIZATION);

(b) geographical change (see LAYERS OF INVESTMENT; NEW INTERNATIONAL DIVISION OF LABOUR; UNEVEN DEVELOPMENT);

(c) changes in the organization of production as a consequence of ECONOMIES OF SCALE, the concentration of centralized capital (see MARXIAN ECONOMICS) or transitions from one regime of accumulation to another (see REGULATION SCHOOL); and

(d) the development of flexibility in production based upon ECONOMIES OF SCOPE.

Restructuring has implications for, or may be undertaken through, changes in either the LABOUR PROCESS or the DIVISION OF LABOUR.

Restructuring is hardly a novel process in capitalist society. The inherently competitive relations of production under capitalism generate a permanent tendency to transformation, but the term has come to be more widely used since the end of the long boom in the late 1960s and early 1970s (see CRISIS; MODERNITY). For some

it is a process closely associated with the transition from one KONDRATIEFF CYCLE to another.

However, restructuring is not restricted to capitalist society. At the plenary meeting of the Central Committee of the Communist Party in April 1985, Mikhail Gorbachev announced a strategy for economic development in the former Soviet Union. This strategy was based upon restructuring, or *perestroika*. The parallels with capitalist restructuring are marked:

Perestroika is inevitable when existing economic conditions do not respond to . . . the needs of development of society and the demands of the future. Here it is necessary to change the economic system, to transform and renew it fundamentally. For this transformation restructuring is necessary not just of individual aspects and elements, but of the whole economic system (Aganbegyan, 1988, p. 6).

Such transformation included the transition to high levels of productivity through more intensive forms of production, increasing the provision of social INFRASTRUCTURE and level of COLLECTIVE CONSUMPTION, the reform of management, and the growth of decentralized control in production through the encouragement of co-operatives and self-employment. But this strategy for development also – and fatefully as it turned out – presumed *uskorenie*, an acceleration of economic growth, and *glasnost*, or openness, to be achieved by the spread of democracy and local self-management.

Although restructuring is a term applied mainly to economic transformation, it is clear from the above that it cannot be restricted to the economic sphere. If it is to be sustained, restructuring must be predicated upon responsiveness elsewhere in SOCIETY.   RL

References and Suggested Reading

Aganbegyan, A. 1988: *The challenge: economics of perestroika*. London: Hutchinson.

Agnew, J. 1987: *The United States in the world-economy: a regional geography*. Cambridge: Cambridge University Press.

Allen, J. and Massey, D. 1988: *The economy in question*. Newbury Park, CA: Sage.

Graham, J., Gibson, K., Horvarth, R. and Shakow, D. 1988: Restructuring in US manufacturing: the decline of monopoly capitalism. *Ann. Ass. Am. Geogr.* 78, pp. 473–90.

retailing, geography of Conventionally defined as the study of the interrelations between the spatial patterns of retail location and organization on the one hand, and the geography of retail consumer behaviour on the other (cf. Dawson, 1980; Potter, 1982; Jones and Simmons, 1990).

A well-established subdiscipline, mainstream retail geography has certain general characteristics. Broadly speaking, NEO-CLASSICAL ECONOMIC principles predominate, with considerable emphasis placed upon the structuring role of individual consumer decisions. This can be seen in the continuing influence of CENTRAL PLACE THEORY (Berry and Parr, 1988), the refinement of which played an important role in the QUANTITATIVE REVOLUTION of the 1960s. With strong links to marketing, retail geography is also applied in its emphases (see APPLIED GEOGRAPHY) (Davies, 1976), with an historically well-developed attention to the geographical concerns of retail management (Wrigley, 1988). Retail geography has conventionally adopted a specific spatial focus, with enquiry usually directed at the intra-urban and, occasionally, at the regional scale. The geographies of consumer behaviour and retail organization are also frequently theorized as some function of distance, actual or perceived (see DISTANCE DECAY; SPATIAL SCIENCE). Retail geography continues to develop – of special importance are recent developments in GEOGRAPHICAL INFORMATION SYSTEMS (GIS).

It is the geography of retail consumption that appears to be the most well developed subfield (see CONSUMPTION, GEOGRAPHY OF). One historically important perspective draws from general interaction theory, and its family of GRAVITY MODELS, to simulate and forecast consumer spatial behaviour. Spatial behaviour is assumed to be some response to distance minimization and utility maximization on the part of the consumer. From the 1960s, cognitive-behavioural perspectives were introduced, with consequent developments in consumer spatial cognition, perception and spatial learning (see REVEALED PREFERENCE ANALYSIS). This proved important to the wider field of BEHAVIOURAL GEOGRAPHY. More recently, important change has occurred in consumer modelling – with, for example, the development of DISCRETE CHOICE MODELS.

The emphasis on consumer demand accounts for the relatively limited attention given to the geography of retail capital. One important stream of analysis, however, drawn from the early pioneering work of Berry, has classified and analysed both the morphology of urban commercial structures and the central place hierarchy in line with principles derived from CENTRAL PLACE THEORY (Potter, 1982). Spatial changes in retailing – such as the relation between decentralized retail investment and traditional city centre retailing – have also received attention. Recent important developments include the importation of 'institutional' accounts of retail organization and spatial change (Brown, 1987). Again, the 'applied' focus of much research in this field is in evidence, as witnessed by the level of development of fields such as store location and MARKET AREA ANALYSIS.

The mainstream literature has many powerful insights. It can usefully be linked, for example, to the growing interest in the geography of SERVICES (Daniels, 1991). It is notable, however, that retail geography appears to have largely ignored – and been ignored by – the many turbulent theoretical debates of the wider discipline. Although the allied field of INDUSTRIAL GEOGRAPHY has been convulsed by dramatic intellectual shifts over the past 15 years, linked initially to the import of Marxist perspectives into spatial–economic analysis, mainstream retail geography has remained apparently unchanged. In part this reflects an institutional resistance to theoretical change within the subdiscipline, given the pragmatism of many of its practitioners. However, a widely scattered yet growing literature makes it increasingly possible to delineate an alternative model of retail geography. Such an alternative, although far from unified, offers very different interpretations of space and the retail economy, and claims to recover the full potential of retail geography from its overly focused orthodoxy.

Such an alternative reading of retail geography might begin with the analysis of Ducatel and Blomley (1990), who seek to retheorize retail capital itself. Rather than seeing it as either an unproblematic reflection of 'external' forces or as driven by its own unique institutional logic, retail capital is situated within a larger system of production, distribution and consumption. Retail capital is simultaneously understood as a vital component of this larger economic, social and political system, and as characterized by its own internal logic (see CAPITALISM).

Such an analysis helps in directing attention to the restructuring of retail capital, a process which seems to have intensified in the past decade (Lewis, 1985; Wrigley, 1988). Characteristic corporate tactics include changes in internal labour markets and work organization, the importation of new forms of sales and warehousing technology, and shifts in capital concentration and deployment. Moreover, spatial changes seem of vital importance, as witnessed by the construction of re-configured 'consumption spaces' (such as the 'mega-mall' – see Jones, 1991), and shifts in both the intra-urban and international location of retail capital (Wrigley, 1989; Findlay et al., 1990).

A retheorization of retail capital also directs attention to the importance of the wider social, cultural and economic context that is both expressed in, and shaped by, retailing and consumption. This expression and mediation appears to be spatial at several levels, and at several scales. One woefully underexplored topic, in this regard, is the way in which gender roles are formed in the 'retail spaces' such as the department store (Benson, 1986) and the suburban retail landscape (Bowlby, 1984; see GENDER AND GEOGRAPHY).

On this alternative reading, the question of the roles, functions and encodings of SPACE takes on a new urgency. Not only is space a critical concern for an understanding of the process of retail restructuring, but it also bears directly on the manner in which the relations between retail capital and other spheres of social, cultural and economic life are played out over time. However, rather than being seen as a passive surface upon which consumer decisions are inscribed, space is understood as strategic; as open to manipulation and production (see PRODUCTION OF SPACE). Considerable potential would seem to exist, for example, for the analysis of the production and contestation of space within the store, given its connection with class, consumption and gender (Miller, 1981; Williams, 1982: see CULTURAL GEOGRAPHY), labour (Sparks, 1981; Benson, 1986) and social mythology (Hopkins, 1990). Furthermore, the scale of enquiry can be extended up to the international level (Hallsworth, 1991), and down to the level of the store itself (Gardner and Sheppard, 1989).   NB

References

Benson, S. P. 1986: *Counter-cultures: saleswomen, managers and customers in American department stores 1880–1914.* Chicago: University of Illinois Press.

Berry, B. J. L. and Parr, J. 1988: *Market centers and retail location: theory and applications.* Englewood Cliffs, NJ: Prentice-Hall.

Bowlby, S. 1984: Planning for women to shop in post-war Britain. *Environ. Plann. D, Society and Space* 2, pp. 179–99.

Brown, S. 1987: Institutional change in retailing. *Prog. hum. Geogr.* 11(2), pp. 181–206.

Daniels, P. W. 1991: Some perspectives on the geography of services. *Progr. hum. Geogr.* 15(1), pp. 37–46.

Davies, R. L. 1976: *Marketing geography with special reference to retailing.* Retailing and Planning Associates, Corbridge.

Dawson, J. A., ed. 1980: *Retailing geography.* London: Croom Helm.

Ducatel, K. J. and Blomley, N. K. 1990: Rethinking retail capital. *Int. J. urban and reg. Res.* 14(2), pp. 207–27.

Findlay, A. M., Paddison, R. and Dawson, J. A., eds 1990: *Retailing environments in developing countries.* London: Routledge.

Gardner, C. and Sheppard, J. 1989: *Consuming passion: the rise of retail culture.* London: Unwin Hyman.

Hallsworth, A. H. 1991: The Campeau takeovers – the arbitrage economy in action. *Environ. Plann. A* 23, pp. 1217–23.

Hopkins, J. A. 1990: West Edmonton Mall: landscape of myths and elsewhereness. *Can. Geogr.* 34(1), pp. 2–17.

Jones, K. and Simmons, J. 1990: *Location, location, location: analyzing the retail environment.* Toronto: Methuen.

Jones, K. 1991: Mega-chaining, corporate concentration, and the mega-malls. *Can. Geogr.* 35(3), pp. 241–9.

Lewis, J. C. 1985: Technical change in retailing: its impact on employment and access. *Environ. Plann. D, Society and Space* 12, pp. 165–91.

Miller, M. B. 1981: *The Bon Marché: bourgeois culture and the department store 1868–1920.* Princeton, NJ: Princeton University Press.

Potter, R. 1982: *The urban retailing system.* Aldershot, UK: Gower.

Sparks, L. 1981: Female and part-time employment within superstore retailing. *Europ. J. Marketing* 16(7), pp. 16–29.

Williams, R. 1982: *Dream worlds: mass consumption in late nineteenth century France.* Berkeley, CA: University of California Press.

Wrigley, N. 1988: Retail restructuring and retail analysis. In Wrigley, N., ed., *Store choice, store location and market analysis.* London: Routledge, pp., 3–34.

Wrigley, N. 1989: The lure of the USA: further reflections on the internationalization of British grocery retailing capital. *Environ. Plann. A* 21, pp. 283–8.

Suggested Reading

Bowlby, R. 1985: *Just looking; consumer culture in Dreiser, Gissing and Zola.* New York: Methuen.

Noyelle, T. 1987: *Beyond industrial dualism.* Boulder, CO: Westview Press.

Williams (1982).

retroduction A mode of scientific inference used for explanation in REALISM: it involves postulating and identifying mechanisms which are capable of producing observed events. RJJ

Suggested Reading

Sayer, A. 1992: *Method in social science: a realist approach*, second edition. London: Routledge.

retrogressive approach A method of working towards an understanding of the past by an examination of the present (cf. RETROSPECTIVE APPROACH). The term gained its currency from Maitland's *Domesday Book and beyond* (1897) and achieved a wide circulation through the work of Marc Bloch. He insisted that the analysis of past landscapes required the prior analysis of the present LANDSCAPE, 'for it alone furnished

those comprehensive vistas without which it was impossible to begin'. Likening history to a film, Bloch argued that 'only the last picture remains quite clear' so that 'in order to reconstruct the faded features of others' it is first necessary 'to unwind the spool in the opposite direction from that in which the pictures were taken.' DG

Reference

Maitland, F. W. 1897: *Domesday Book and beyond.* Cambridge: Cambridge University Press.

Suggested Reading

Baker, A. R. H. 1968: A note on the retrogressive and retrospective approaches in historical geography. *Erdkunde* 22, pp. 243–4.

retrospective approach The study of the past for the light it throws on the present (cf. RETROGRESSIVE APPROACH). The approach would make HISTORICAL GEOGRAPHY a prerequisite – or, as Darby once claimed, an essential foundation – for contemporary geography. Its most explicit advocate was Roger Dion, who believed that a consideration of the present LANDSCAPE poses problems that can only be solved by a search for their origins; but the approach can evidently be extended beyond the analysis of the landscape and has much in common with 'genetic' or 'historical' explanations (cf. FUNCTIONALISM). DG

Suggested Reading

Gulley, J. L. M. 1961: The retrospective approach in historical geography. *Erdkunde* 15, pp. 306–9.

revealed preference analysis Statistical methods, many of them based on MULTIDIMENSIONAL SCALING, for deriving an aggregate set of decision rules from a series of individual decisions (e.g. in the choice of which shopping centre to patronize). The individual observed choices are termed *behaviour in space*; the general rules (unconstrained by any particular spatial arrangements of alternatives) are called the *rules of spatial behaviour* (Rushton, 1969). RJJ

Reference

Rushton, G. 1969: Analysis of spatial behavior by revealed space preference. *Ann. Ass. Am. Geogr.* 59, pp. 391–400.

revenue See VARIABLE REVENUE ANALYSIS.

revenue surface Spatial variations in the revenue to be derived from the sale of a given volume of output, depicted as a three-dimensional surface with distance along the two horizontal axes and revenue in pecuniary units on the vertical. Revenue surfaces are extremely difficult to identify empirically, and their value is more conceptual than practical. The revenue likely to be earned from alternative locations is normally estimated less directly, by using a MARKET POTENTIAL MODEL or MARKET AREA ANALYSIS. (See also COST SURFACE; SPATIAL MARGINS; VARIABLE REVENUE ANALYSIS.) DMS

rhetoric Originating in the fifth century BC with the sophists, rhetoric is the study of persuasive discourse. Rhetoricians suggest that researchers in *all* forms of enquiry employ a plethora of different stylistic devices (tropes) to convince others of the plausibility of their arguments. Metaphors, ironic asides, equations, jokes, citations and anecdotes are all part of the same attempt to establish authority and persuade one's audience. Rhetoric is often counterposed with EPISTEMOLOGY, which attempts to establish truth on the basis of a set of external, abstract criteria. For rhetoricians, however, truth emerges only within the hurly-burly of actual discourses on the ground. It is little use to focus on grand epistemologies because they only tell us what people ought to be doing. In contrast, it is what people actually do, and the strategies they use to convince others of what they have done, that is of prime concern to students of rhetoric. For example, POSITIVISTS would say that the DISTANCE DECAY effect is true because it was established using the most rigorous of statistical techniques. Yet most belief in the distance decay effect comes from other sources: from self-inspection (What would I do?), from thinking about others (What

would they do?), from authority (some eminent geographers believe in it), from analogy (if it works for planetary masses it should work for humans), and from a sense of parsimony (one equation explains everything). In short, what is persuasive is far wider than the official rhetoric admits, thereby casting doubt on the official rhetoric itself. TJB

Suggested Reading

Barnes, T. J. 1989: Rhetoric, metaphor, and mathematical modelling. *Environ. Plann. A* 21, pp. 1281–4.
Nelson, J. S., Megill, A. and McCloskey, D. 1987: *The rhetoric of the human sciences: language and argument in scholarship and public affairs.* Madison: University of Wisconsin Press.

ribbon development Urban SPRAWL along the main roads leading from a built-up area, which may generate the creation of a CONURBATION. Locations on such routes usually offer relatively cheap but accessible sites plus, for businesses, trade from passers-by. Within built-up areas, the term is often used to describe strings of commercial land uses along the main roads leading into major centres, with the same advantages. RJJ

risk The likelihood of a range of possible outcomes resulting from a decision or course of action. Strictly speaking, risk exists when known probabilities can be assigned to these outcomes. Risk is thus distinguished from UNCERTAINTY, under which probabilities cannot be established. Businesses tend to prefer working with risk to working with uncertainty, because of the calculable nature of risk. DMS

rural Areas which are dominated (either currently or recently) by extensive land uses such as agriculture or forestry, or by large open spaces of undeveloped land; which contain small, lower-order settlements demonstrating a strong relationship between buildings and surrounding extensive landscape, and which are perceived as rural by most residents; and which are thought to engender a way of life characterized by a cohesive identity based on respect for the environment, and behavioural qualities of living as part of an extensive landscape. In practice, rural areas vary considerably, from those which may still be defined functionally (by land use and geographical location) to those closer to urban centres where 'rural' is more of a socially constructed category.   PJC

Suggested Reading

Cloke, P. and Park, C. 1985: *Rural resource management*. London: Croom Helm, ch. 1.

Hoggart, K. 1990: Let's do away with rural. *J. Rural Stud.* 6, pp. 245–257.

rural community A collection of socially interacting people living in a rural area, and often sharing one or more common ties. As with rurality (see RURAL and RURAL GEOGRAPHY), COMMUNITY has been defined in widely different ways: G. A. Hillery's (1955) study revealed 94 specific definitions.

Geographers have leaned heavily on the work of anthropologists and sociologists in their evolving understanding of rural community. Early structural–functionist studies portrayed rural communities as resilient in the face of change (rural equilibrium concepts) and distinctively different from their urban counterparts. Tonnies' (1955) concept of *Gemeinschaft* was adopted to describe close kinship relations linked to a particular rural place leading to co-operative action for the common good (see RURAL–URBAN CONTINUUM). It was soon extended to cover actual social structures resulting in particular settlement forms, and this extension has been heavily criticized (see Harper, 1989).

More recently, two different strands of rural community study have been adopted. The first consists of new rural ethnographies which address the question of whether people are 'truly rural' in their lived worlds and whether there is an 'essence' in the emerging place of a village. A key theme here is *centredness* (Harper, 1987). It is argued that centred rural people will confine most of their physical, social and symbolic relationships to one rural place, and that centred rural places occur when the majority of their inhabitants are centred rural people. Truly rural communities will thus reflect centred people in centred places.

The second strand of study stresses the use of community as a mechanism for interpreting wider organizations and social relations. Fred Buttel in the USA and Howard Newby in the UK have both investigated the agricultural power relations which underlie changes in rural communities (Newby, 1977; Newby et al., 1978; Buttel et al., 1990). As in-migrant middle classes have exerted greater influence, so studies of the interelations between new CLASS fractions and rural communities have become increasingly important, as has the recognition of social groups who are being marginalized by wider economic and social changes.

There is still little common ground in the conceptualization of community in rural studies, and the term is still frequently used simply to denote a collection of people in a particular place. This is especially so when used in the context of RURAL PLANNING, in which the discourses of community analysis, community development and community renewal continue to infer the need for co-operative action for the common good.
          PJC

References

Buttel, F. H., Larson, O. F. and Gillespie, G. W. 1990: *The sociology of agriculture*. New York: Greenwood.

Harper, S. 1987: A humanistic approach to the study of rural populations. *J. Rural Stud.* 3, pp. 309–20.

Harper, S. 1989: The British rural community: an overview of perspectives. *J. Rural Stud.* 5, pp. 161–84.

Hillery, G. A. 1955: Definitions of community: areas of agreement, *Rural Sociol.* 20, pp. 111–23.

Newby, H. 1977: *The deferential worker*. London: Allen Lane.

Newby, H., Bell, C., Rose, D. and Saunders, P. 1978: *Property, paternalism and power*. London: Hutchinson.

Tonnies, F. 1955: *Community and society*. New York: Harper & Row (first published in 1887).

Suggested Reading

Cloke, P. and Thrift, N. 1987: Intra-class conflict in rural areas. *J. Rural Stud.* 3, pp. 321–34.

Cloke, P. and Thrift, N. 1990: Class change and conflict in rural areas. In Marsden, T., Lowe, P. and Whatmore, S., eds, *Rural restructuring: global processes and their responses.* London: David Fulton.

Lewis, G. J. 1979: *Rural communities: a social geography.* Newton Abbott, UK: David & Charles.

Swanson, B. E., Cohen, R. A. and Swanson, E. P. 1979: *Small towns and small towners.* Beverly Hills, CA: Sage.

rural geography The study of people, places and environments in RURAL areas, with special reference to society, economy, politics and culture in the developed world, although such study can also be applied to THIRD WORLD contexts. Rural geographers have widely differing interests, and are often closely associated with interdisciplinary research in rural areas with sociologists, economists and agricultural specialists. Indeed, in the USA there is little evidence of a specific subdiscipline called 'rural geography'.

Rural areas have traditionally been important to geography. The studies of rural settlement patterns by Paul Vidal de la Blache and Albert Demangeon, and the ensuing concern for agricultural land use and settlement systems, stemming in part from the classical models of von Thünen and Christaller, ensured that most human geographers would be familiar with aspects of rural space (see CHRISTALLER MODEL; VON THÜNEN MODEL). With the demise of regionalism, however, rural areas were relatively neglected in geography until a distinctly demarcated subject area of 'rural geography' emerged in the 1970s. Prompted by Hugh Clout's (1972) book *Rural geography: an introductory survey*, the agricultural focus of rural work was expanded to cover aspects of society, economy and land, and the literature of rural geography burgeoned in the 1970s and 1980s; covering, for example, ACCESSIBILITY, AGRICULTURE, EMPLOYMENT, HOUSING, LAND USE, RECREATION and RURAL PLANNING (see Cloke, 1980, 1985). Initially, there was a phase of resurgence for rural geography, particularly in parts of Europe, Canada and Australasia, but by the 1980s the bandwagon was again losing momentum. The general appetite for new information on the changing rural milieu had been satiated, and new challenges were required in order

to generate fresh energy. In particular, rural geographers were urged to be more policy-orientated and more theoretically informed.

During the early 1980s much of rural geography was characterized by a form of 'applied positivism' (Cloke and Moseley, 1990), a cobbled-together theoretical package which *both* acknowledged the virtues and discourses of political economy *and* permitted researchers to carry on with positivistic methods and results as before. In this way rural geographers began to tackle issues relating to problems of policy and planning in rural areas, and yet were unwilling to replace their technical role with one which engaged directly with politics and ideology. In some cases, rural geography was therefore seen to be 'broadly theory-free' (Gilg, 1985, p. 172), while others saw the subdiscipline as 'tinkering with existing socio-economic conditions in order to weaken the impress of malevolent trends [while failing] to recognise that the processes which brought about current maldistributions . . . are inherent in policy procedures' (Hoggart and Buller, 1987, p. 267).

This perceived bankruptcy of explanations of change grounded in NEOCLASSICAL ECONOMICS and POSITIVIST recording of trends provided a significant impulse to the wider acceptance of POLITICAL ECONOMIC concepts in the understanding of sociospatial phenomena. In the late 1980s and early 1990s, with the strong backing of progress being made by critical rural sociologists, there has been a greater willingness to develop a research agenda funded on a series of key themes: the role of *economic restructuring* in bringing about UNEVEN DEVELOPMENT; the recognition that RESTRUCTURING does not occur in a social vacuum and that *social recomposition* occurs both as a shaping mechanism for restructuring, and in response to it; the equally valid – yet less publicized – recognition that economic restructuring and social recomposition do not occur in an environmental vacuum, and that *environmental recomposition* is also relevant; and, the role of the STATE in mediating or organizing change (see Cloke, 1990). With this agenda, rural geographers have begun to inform several crucial questions: How attractive are particular areas to capital accumulation under contemporary modes of REGULATION? How and why are particular rural areas attractive to people seeking a 'rural experience', and how does the structuring and experience of rural lifestyle differ according to GENDER, age, ETHNICITY and localism? What public intervention is necessary for CONSERVATION purposes in processes of environmental recomposition? How and why does the state intervene to make rural places more attractive? These themes encompass both the traditional emphasis of rural geography on the AGRICULTURAL sector (dealing particularly with issues of pluriactivity, diversification, environmental and landscape impacts, the international food chain and policies of deregulation) and the broader task of bringing together a range of economic, social and political considerations in rural areas (including INDUSTRIALIZATION and the service sector, commodification, PRIVATIZATION, settlement rationalization, COUNTERURBANIZATION, GENTRIFICATION, poverty, ACCESSIBILITY and CITIZENSHIP).

Most recently, geographers have been seeking to clarify aspects of the dialectics of society–space and structure–agency as they occur in 'rural' areas. Rurality is being increasingly recognized as a social construct, and 'rural' may thus be increasingly interpreted as a world of social, moral and cultural values in which rural dwellers participate. Here the political economy emphases of the structuring of rural opportunities, places, landscapes and environments meet with the more humanistic concerns of interpreting different individual experiences and meanings associated with rurality. The task is to investigate the cultural arena so as to understand how different constructs of rurality are linked with power relations, social conflict, economic commodification, residential colonization, environmental recomposition and the many other key concerns of contemporary rural geographers. PJC

References

Cloke, P. 1980: New emphases for applied rural geography. *Progr. hum. Geogr.* 4, pp. 181–217.

Cloke, P. 1985: Whither rural studies? *J. Rural Stud.* 1, pp. 1–10.

Cloke, P. 1990: Rural geography and political economy, In Peet, R. and Thrift, N., eds, *New models in geography*, volume 1. London: Unwin Hyman.

Cloke, P. and Moseley, M. 1990: Rural geography in Britain, In Lowe, P. and Bodiguel, M., eds, *Rural studies in Britain and France*. London: Belhaven.

Clout, H. 1972: *Rural geography: an introductory survey*. Oxford: Pergamon.

Gilg, A. 1985: *An introduction to rural geography*. London: Edward Arnold.

Hoggart, K. and Buller, H. 1987: *Rural development: a geographical perspective*. London: Croom Helm.

Suggested Reading

Cloke, P. and Little, J. 1990: *The rural state? Limits to planning in rural society*. Oxford: Oxford University Press.

Friedland, W. H., Busch, L., Buttel, F. H. and Rudy, A. P., eds 1991: *Towards a new political economy of agriculture*. Boulder, CO: Westview Press.

Fuguitt, G. V., Brown, D. L. and Beale, C. L. 1989: *Rural and small town America*. New York: Russell Sage Foundation.

Marsden, T. K., Munton, R. J. C., Whatmore, S. J. and Little, J. K. 1986: Towards a political economy of capitalist agriculture: a British perspective. *Int. J. urban and reg. Res.* 10, pp. 498–520.

Robinson, G. 1990: *Conflict and change in the countryside*. London: Belhaven.

Short, J. R. 1991: *Imagined country: society, culture and environment*. London: Routledge.

rural planning The attempt to identify problems, organize resources and generate action in rural areas, often with the stated aims of diversifying the economic base, seeking a pluralistic social order and maintaining a healthy (and where necessary, conserved) environment. Policy-making and implementation occur at different scales of government and are often functionally discrete, such that it is possible for one arm of planning (e.g. agricultural improvement) to conflict with another (e.g. landscape conservation). Rural planning is usually studied in the developed world, although rural development strategies are also relevant in a THIRD WORLD context. Planning covers a wide diversity of land uses and socio-economic processes, including: agriculture and forestry, CONSERVATION, employment and training, ENERGY, HOUSING, RECREATION (e.g. HEALTH and EDUCATION; TOURISM; TRANSPORT.)

The geography of rural planning has focused particularly on attempts to bring a number of these planning functions together. This may reflect particular rural LOCALES, where the need is either to generate economic development to provide jobs, services and homes, or to control development or resource use so as to protect the character of the area. For example, key settlement policies (Cloke, 1979) have been used to concentrate resources into planned service centres, which can then serve the settlements in their rural hinterlands. Planning has also been integrated in particular rural areas (e.g. rural Wales and rural Scotland in the UK and Appalachia in the USA) where specific regional planning agencies have been established to deal with areas with special needs. More rarely, socio-economic land-use and landscape planning are all involved in specially designated zones such as NATIONAL PARKS.

There has been a widespread acceptance of *rational* concepts of planning in rural areas, such that until recently the place of planning in wider social and political relations has been little questioned. However, interest in the relative inability to implement policies with which to secure many planning aims in rural areas (see Cloke, 1987) has led some researchers to view planning as an activity in the wider context of the STATE. If planning is part of the STATE APPARATUS then it will also be subject to the constraints imposed by the form and function of the state. It may, for example, be better suited to aiding elements of production rather than consumption, and it may generate consistent biases in favour of dominant fractions of capital and class (Cloke and Little, 1990). Such a conceptual viewpoint allows an important understanding of the limitations of planning in rural societies.   PJC

References

Cloke, P. 1979: *Key settlements in rural areas.* London: Methuen.

Cloke, P. ed. 1987: *Rural planning: policy into action.* London: Harper and Row.

Cloke, P. and Little, J. 1990: *The rural state? Limits to planning in rural society.* Oxford: Oxford University Press.

Suggested Reading

Buller, H. and Wright, S., eds 1990: *Rural development: problems and practices.* Aldershot, UK: Avebury.

Cloke, P., ed. 1988: *Policies and plans for rural people.* London: Unwin Hyman.

Cloke, P., ed. 1989: *Rural land-use planning in developed nations.* London: Unwin Hyman.

Flora, C. B. and Christenson, J. A., eds 1991: *Rural policies for the 1990s.* Boulder, CO: Westview Press.

Lapping, M. B., Daniels, T. L. and Keller, J. W. 1989: *Rural planning and development in the United States.* New York: Guilford Press.

rural–urban continuum A continuous gradation of ways of life between the two poles of truly rural COMMUNITY and truly urban SOCIETY. The concept suggests that the way of life is best understood in terms of the type of settlement that people live in, and it has been used both to distinguish between URBAN and RURAL extremes and as a theory of social change which emphasizes the transformations from one pole to another. The characteristics of urban and rural polarities were drawn from Redfield's (1941) 'folk-urban continuum', Wirth's (1938) 'urbanism as a way of life' and Tonnies' (1955) differentiation between *Gemeinschaft* (the community built round kinship, attachment to place and co-operative action) and *Gesellschaft* (the association or society of industrialized populations, where impersonal relationships are founded on formal contract and exchange).

A series of studies (see Frankenberg, 1966, in the UK; also Fischer, 1976; Glenn and Hill, 1977, in the USA) have reflected the continuum concept in their descriptions of differences in economic, family, religious, political and social characteristics between rural community and urban society. Yet the question here is not whether such differences occur, but whether 'rural' or 'urban' are causal factors in these differences. The continuum has been heavily criticized not only for its Western ETHNOCENTRISM but also because studies clearly showed different elements of 'urban' and 'rural' in the same community (Gans, 1962). Thus the revelation of village communities in cities and urban societies in supposedly rural areas (Pahl, 1965) seriously undermined the concept. Indeed, Ray Pahl is commonly credited with demolishing the concept of a rural–urban continuum, finding its use simplistic and overgeneralized and, more crucially, arguing against the formulation of a sociological definition of any settlement type (Pahl, 1966). He preferred to describe the rural–urban relationship as 'a whole series of meshes of different textures superimposed on each other, together forming a process which is creating a much more complex pattern' (p. 321). More recently, attention has been focused on questions of HUMAN AGENCY, using HUMANISTIC approaches to discover the meanings of 'rural' in lifeworlds and places (see RURAL COMMUNITY) and questions of STRUCTURE, using POLITICAL ECONOMY approaches to map out the impacts in rural areas of wider social, economic and political changes.   PJC

References

Fischer, C. 1976: The metropolitan experience, In Hawley, A. H. and Rock, V., eds, *Metropolitan America in contemporary perspective*. New York: Halstead, pp. 201–34.

Frankenberg, R. 1966: *Communities in Britain*. London: Penguin.

Gans, H. 1962: *The urban villagers*. Glencoe, IL: Free Press.

Glenn, N. D. and Hill, L. 1977: Rural–urban differences in attitudes and behaviour in the United States. *Ann. Am. Acad. Po.. Soc. Sci.* 429, pp. 36–50.

Pahl, R. E. 1965: *Urbs in rure*. London: Weidenfeld and Nicolson.

Pahl, R. E. 1966: The rural–urban continuum. *Sociol. Rur.* 6, pp. 299–327.

Redfield, R. 1941: *The folk culture of Yucatan*. Chicago: University of Chicago Press.

Tonnies, F. 1955: *Community and society*. New York: Harper and Row (first published in 1887).

Wirth, L. 1938: Urbanism as a way of life. *Am. J. Soc.* 44, pp. 1–24.

rural–urban fringe A zone of transition between the continuously built-up URBAN and suburban areas of the central city and the rural hinterland (Pryor, 1968). This area displays a changing mix of land use, social and demographic characteristics, and is an arena in which issues of the siting of large-scale urban amenities (such as airports and sewage works), the problems of 'fringe' agriculture, the acquisitions of land banks for development, and the social integration of commuters have all been prominent. The idea of a fringe is problematic (see FRINGE BELT), both because particular mixes of characteristics may be sedimented in some places (for example, by strict planning controls on urban development – see GREEN BELT), and because views on the extent of the fringe vary from a tightly drawn girdle around a city to a much wider area containing socio-economic features of the fringe which have migrated away from a city-edge location.   PJC

Reference

Pryor, R. J. 1968: Defining the rural–urban fringe. *Social Forces* 47, pp. 202–15.

Suggested Reading

Bryant, C. R. and Johnston, J. R. R. 1992: *Agriculture in the city's countryside*. London: Frances Pinter.

Bryant, C. R., Russwurm, L. H. and McLellan, A. G. 1982: *The city's countryside: land and its management in the rural–urban fringe*. New York: Longman.

Herington, J. 1984: *The outer city*. London: Harper and Row.

S

sacred and profane space

A distinction which is drawn in the study and experience of religion between places and objects that are imbued with a transcendent spiritual quality and those that are not. In Eliade's terms, *sacred space* is oriented around a fixed point, a centre, while *profane space* is homogeneous and neutral. The symbolism of the cosmic centre is projected mimetically in the construction and consecration of sacred spaces; 'where the sacred manifests itself in space, *the real unveils itself* . . . [and] . . . communication with the transmundane is established' (Eliade, 1959). (See also RELIGION, GEOGRAPHY OF.)   DL

Reference

Eliade, M. 1959: *The sacred and the profane.* New York: Harcourt, Brace and World.

Suggested Reading

Duncan, J. 1990: *The city as text: the politics of landscape interpretation in the Kandyan Kingdom.* Cambridge: Cambridge University Press.

Eliade (1959).

Houston, J. 1978: The conceptions of 'place' and 'land' in the Judaeo-Christian tradition. In Ley, D. and Samuels, M., eds, *Humanistic geography.* Chicago: Maaroufa/London: Croom Helm, pp. 224–37.

Wheatley, P. 1971: *The pivot of the four quarters.* Chicago: Aldine.

sampling

The selection of a subset from a defined population of individuals to provide the information for a research study (as in a SURVEY ANALYSIS), used when the population is too large for a complete enumeration of all individuals, so that sampling is essential to contain the costs of the study: alternatively, the population may be infinitely large, or it may be of an unknown size.

Sampling theory has been developed by statisticians so that conclusions about the characteristics of a population can be derived from those of the selected sample – within error limits, the size of which are known from the theory. The selection procedure involved in taking the sample must follow certain rules if a valid INFERENCE regarding the population characteristics is to be made; if these rules are violated then the sample is likely to be biased and the conclusions drawn will be unreliable. In general, the larger the sample (in absolute terms, not as a percentage of the population) the more accurate it is likely to be as a representation of the population.

The commonest selection procedure is *random sampling*: the population is enumerated and a sample of predetermined size taken, usually employing a table of random numbers. To reduce effort, and also to counter problems if the size of the population is unknown, a *systematic sample* may be taken (e.g. of every tenth person entering a shopping centre). The investigator must be sure that this will not introduce bias because of some periodicity in the population (e.g. every tenth shopper is more likely to be a male than are the other nine!). *Stratified sampling* is used when the researcher wants to ensure a representative selection from two or more subgroups within the population. (If it is known that 20 per cent of all shoppers are male, for example, then to obtain an equal number of male and female respondents every fourth male and every sixteenth female entering the centre might be questioned.) A *quota sample* (commonly used in opinion polling)

542

is a variant on the stratified form: the investigator uses either random or systematic sampling procedures to obtain a set of respondents with a particular profile of characteristics and selection continues until the desired profile is achieved, with unneeded respondents discarded. (For example, in a sample of ten, six must be female, five aged under 40, seven in white-collar occupations, etc. Thus, once the sampling procedure delivers five persons aged under 40 in a survey of shoppers, that part of the profile will be complete. It will often be necessary to interview more than ten persons before all of the criteria are met, and it may be necessary to interview more aged under 40 in order to obtain a satisfactory sample on the other variables.)

In geographical studies, the standard procedures may be varied to ensure spatial coverage. Methods of random, systematic and stratified sampling of points on a map have been devised using co-ordinate systems, for example, as have methods of selecting transects (line samples) across an area.

Analyses of sample data seek to make statements about the population as a whole, using SIGNIFICANCE TESTS which are based on theoretical FREQUENCY DISTRIBUTIONS. They involve statements regarding the range of values around the sample statistic within which the population characteristic will probably be found (at a specified significance level). For example, the standard error around a sample mean may be four percentage points (cf. FREQUENCY DISTRIBUTION): thus if the observed percentage of shoppers purchasing shoes at a suburban centre is 23, then in 67 per cent of all samples the population value will lie between 19 and 27 per cent. The size of the range is a function of the sample size.   RJJ

Suggested Reading

Berry, B. J. L. and Baker, A. M. 1968: Methods of spatial sampling. In Berry, B. J. L. and Marble, D. F., eds, *Spatial analysis: a reader in statistical geography*. Englewood Cliffs, NJ: Prentice-Hall, pp. 91–100.

Dixon, C. J. and Leach, B. 1977: *Sampling methods for geographical research*. Concepts and techniques in modern geography 17. Norwich: Geo Books.

satisficing behaviour Originating with Herbert Simon (1956), satisficing was developed as an alternative to RATIONAL CHOICE THEORY and its presumption of optimization. In contrast to the optimizer, a satisficer chooses among alternatives only on the basis of whether they meet or exceed a certain threshold, and not whether the choices are the best or unique. There are two kinds of circumstances in which decision-makers opt to meet some minimum aspiration level: first, where it is either logically impossible to calculate an optimal solution, or where the costs and time necessary to make such a calculation are too great; and, second, where the very choices among which the individual chooses either are in conflict with one another (see PRISONER'S DILEMMA) or are incommensurable. In geography, the best known use of the satisficing concept is found in Allen Pred's (1969) behavioural matrix. (See also DECISION-MAKING.)   TJB

References

Pred, A. 1967, 1969: *Behavior and location: foundations for a geographic and dynamic location theory*, two volumes. Lund: C. W. K. Gleerup.

Simon, H. A. 1956: Rational choice and the structure of the environment. *Psych. Rev.* 63, pp. 129–38.

Suggested Reading

Simon, H. A. 1982: *Models of bounded rationality*. Cambridge, MA: MIT Press.

scale Technically, 'scale' refers to a level of representation (sometimes called a *resolution level*), but until the mid-twentieth century an explicit focus on scale in human geography was largely confined to cartography and regional geography. In CARTOGRAPHY, scale is defined as the relationship between distance on a MAP IMAGE and the corresponding distance in reality: thus 1:50 000 means that 1 cm on the map represents 50 000 cm (0.5 km). There has been considerable technical discussion of the effects of moving from one scale to another. In REGIONAL GEOGRAPHY there was a largely intuitive sensitivity to the scale problems in describing and characterizing areas – an awareness made explicit by Bird (1956) – but the historical and geographical specificity of the 'regional scale' was sometimes lost from view: the classical *pays* of French regional geography in the nineteenth century was a far cry from a region such as the Prairies in the twentieth century.

A more sharply focused but correspondingly more technical engagement with issues of scale in human geography emerged in the 1960s and 1970s, largely as a result of advances in spatial analysis and spatial science. Thus Haggett (1965) and Harvey (1969) identified three basic questions (see also Hudson, 1992):

(a) *Scale coverage*. There are evident difficulties in ensuring a regular and comprehensive monitoring of the world at all relevant scales, and these are partially overcome by the exploration, re-survey or continuous screening and sensing of particular domains (see SURVEILLANCE) and by the use of SAMPLING procedures.

(b) *Scale standardization*. It is often hard to obtain data from equivalent sampling frames, especially in comparative studies, and this problem is solved in part through various aggregation algorithms and in part through areal weighting procedures.

(c) *Scale linkage*. Three possible connections between scale levels can be envisaged: (i) same-level – a *comparative* relation; (ii) high to low level – a *contextual* relation; and (iii) low to high level – an *aggregative* relation. Inferential problems arise in the last two cases, so spatial analysts argued, because generalizations about patterns and processes at one level may not hold at another (see also ECOLOGICAL FALLACY). Indeed, the concept of 'emergence' which is intrinsic to most concepts of system in both the natural and the social sciences – 'the whole is greater than the sum of its parts' – makes this highly unlikely.

Physical geographers have been particularly sensitive to these problems, which Kennedy (1979) argued 'may point to the fundamental skeleton of the discipline which, if understood more clearly, might indicate the rules linking events and forms on different temporal and spatial scales'. In human geography, however, the call for a more creative response to 'the scale problem' (Watson, 1978) was first answered by Cliff and Ord (1981), who used spatial correlograms to assess the characteristic scale of 'spatial processes': theirs was still a largely technical response which conceived of PROCESS as a *descriptive sequence* rather than a *causal mechanism*.

Other, and usually more recent, discussions of scale have centred on substantive issues – on identifying causal mechanisms – many of which derive from the *globalization* of CAPITALISM and MODERNITY. These enquiries have raised acute questions of both theorization and representation which extend far beyond the domains of spatial science and analytical methods. So, for example, Taylor (1981) proposed a 'political economy of scale' which depended on specifying the characteristic scales of operation of substantive processes and exploring the ways in which they are articulated one with another. In a series of studies, Taylor (1981, 1982, 1985) distinguished between the modern world-economy, the NATION-STATE and the locality, and argued that the process of capital accumulation is *experienced* locally, *justified* nationally and *organized* globally.

Other geographers have also derived scales directly from the logic of capital accumulation. 'The differentiation of absolute spaces as particular scales of social activity is an inner necessity for capital', Smith (1984) argued, and so 'the origins, determination and inner coherence of each scale [is] already contained in the structure of capital'. But other writers have been reluctant to identify a single set of causal mechanisms: Giddens (1991) insists that the TIME–SPACE DISTANCIATION characteristic of the modern world cannot be reduced to the inner logic of capital, for example, and identifies other institutional dimensions of modernity – including industrialism, military power and SUR-VEILLANCE – all of which bear directly on the PRODUCTION OF SPACE at different scales, but none of which can be collapsed directly into capitalism. In his view, any account of the complex interconnections between 'local' and 'distant' events within this multidimensional totality must also be situated within a complex *local–global dialectic* in which events at one pole may have countervailing effects at another. This is a difficult enough analytical task; it is compounded by the problem of representation, which Jameson (1985) identifies as a dilemma that arises within POSTMODERNISM, and

involves our insertion as individual subjects into a multidimensional set of radically discontinuous realities, whose frames range from the still surviving spaces of bourgeois private life all the way to the unimaginable decentring of global capital itself. Not even Einsteinian relativity, or the multiple subjective worlds of the older modernists, is capable of giving any kind of adequate figuration to this process.

In the face of this call for a new 'cognitive mapping', therefore, one which resonates with the need to 'think globally, act locally', one might expect a renewed *and conjoint* interest in both the technical and the theoretical issues raised by the question of scale in human geography. (See also CONTEXTUAL THEORY.)   DG

References

Bird, J. 1956: Scale in regional study illustrated by brief comparisons between the western peninsulas of England and France. *Geography* 41, pp. 25–38.

Cliff, A. D. and Ord, J. K. 1981: *Spacial processes.* London: Pion.

Giddens, A. 1991: *The consequences of modernity.* Stanford, CA: Stanford University Press.

Haggett, P. 1965: Scale components in geographical problems. In Chorley, R. J. and Haggett, P., eds, *Frontiers in geographical teaching.* London: Methuen, pp. 164–85.

Harvey, D. 1969: *Explanation in geography.* London: Edward Arnold.

Hudson, J. 1992: Scale in space and time. In Abler, R. F., Marcus, M. G. and Olson, J. M., eds, *Geography's inner worlds: pervasive themes in contemporary American geography.* New Brunswick, NJ: Rutgers University Press, pp. 280–97.

Jameson, F. 1985: Cognitive mapping. In Grossberg, L. and Nelson, C., eds, *Marxism and the interpretation of culture.* London: Macmillan.

Kennedy, B. A. 1979: A question of scale? *Progr. phys. Geogr.* 1, pp. 154–7.

Smith, N. 1984: *Uneven development: nature, capital and the production of space.* Oxford: Blackwell.

Taylor, P. J. 1981: Geographical scales in the world systems approach. *Review* 5, pp. 3–11.

Taylor, P. J. 1982: A materialist framework for political geography. *Trans. Inst. Br. Geogr.* n.s. 7, pp. 15–34.

Taylor, P. J. 1985: *Political geography: world-economy, nation–state and locality.* London: Longman.

Watson, M. K. 1978: The scale problem in human geography. *Geogr. Annlr.* 60B, pp. 36–47.

Suggested Reading
Hudson (1992).

Meyer, W. B., Gregory, D., Turner, B. L. and McDowell, P. F. 1992: The local–global continuum. In Abler, R. F., Marcus, M. G. and Olson, J. M., eds, *Geography's inner worlds: pervasive themes in contemporary American geography.* New Brunswick, NJ: Rutgers University Press, pp. 255–79.

science park A particular form of GROWTH POLE established by property developers, usually in conjunction with a higher education institution and sometimes with local governments also, to promote *technology transfer* and investment in new industries. The goal is to capitalize on the available local scientific and technological expertise by ensuring that INNOVATIONS are followed by applications, generating jobs for the local economy and contributing to the higher education institution's costs. (See also SEED BED LOCATION.)   RJJ

Suggested Reading
Massey, D., Quintas, P. and Wield, D. 1991: *High-tech fantasies: science parks in society, science and space.* London: Routledge.

search behaviour The process of seeking out and evaluating alternatives in spatial decision-making, as in the selection of potential MIGRATION destinations. Search behaviour normally occurs within the constraints of an ACTION SPACE, that segment of all possible locations which are known to the searcher. (See also PLACE UTILITY.)   RJJ

secession The transfer of one part of a state's area and population to another new or existing STATE. There are many instances of groups that wish to secede and such movements are invariably very disruptive politically, leading to war or guerrilla conflicts. The establishment of the Irish Free State in Ireland in 1922 is an example of a successful secessionist movement, but most claims are frustrated by opposition from established states which stand to lose TERRITORY. Secessionist movements can take several forms: substate NATIONALISM, where a minority wishes to set up a separate independent state; unification nationalism, where minorities spread throughout a number of neighbouring states desire political unity; and IRREDENTISM, where the aim is to effect the transfer of territory from one state to another.   MB

Suggested Reading
Kidron, M. and Segal, R. 1984: *The new state of the world atlas.* London: Heinemann Educational and Pan.

second home A property owned or rented on a long lease as the occasional residence of a household that usually lives elsewhere. Second homes come in different shapes and sizes, from luxury houses to mobile homes and boats, and are more numerous in some nations than others: there are, for example, nearly one million 'dachas' located around Moscow. Although accurate data are difficult to construct, over 20 per cent of households in France and Sweden have access to a second home, whereas the equivalent figure in the USA, Canada and the UK is around 4 per cent. Second homes may bring economic advantages to a rural area, but they are sometimes viewed as a symbol of outsiders' involvement in the cultural and material takeover of local RURAL COMMUNITY. With trends of COUNTER-URBANIZATION some households now have their main residence in a rural area, and keep a 'second home' close to the urban workplace.   PJC

Suggested Reading
Coppock, J. T. 1977: *Second homes: curse or blessing?* Oxford: Pergamon.
Shucksmith, M. 1983: Second homes: a framework for policy. *Town Plan. Rev.* 54, pp. 174–93.

secondary data analysis The use of a data set for research projects other than that for which it was originally collected. Increasingly, data sets, such as those obtained through CENSUSES and SURVEY ANALYSIS, are stored in computer databases and housed in archives from which they are made available to other researchers. This further use of data involves ensuring that they are suitable for the new purposes; if they are it allows both efficiency in data collection and the conduct of comparative studies (across space and time) that otherwise would be impossible.   RJJ

Suggested Reading
Hakim, C. 1982: *Secondary analysis in social research: a guide to data, sources and methods with examples.* London: Allen and Unwin.

section A territorial division of a country associated with an electoral CLEAVAGE, brought about when a party mobilizes the majority of that area's population around a particular economic or social issue. The classic sectional cleavage occurred in the southern States of the former Confederation of the US for most of the century following the end of the American Civil War; the great majority of white voters were mobilized by the Democrat party to block the achievement of equality of civil rights granted to blacks constitutionally by the ending of SLAVERY.   RJJ

Suggested Reading
Archer, J. C. and Taylor, P. J. 1981: *Section and party: a political geography of American Presidential elections from Andrew Jackson to Ronald Reagan.* New York: John Wiley.

sectoral model A model of intra-urban land-use patterns developed by Homer Hoyt (1939) using housing (including rental and value) data. From observations of over 200 US cities in the 1930s, Hoyt argued that the common residential structure was for housing of different quality and value to be segregated into sectors radiating out along major routeways from the CENTRAL BUSINESS DISTRICT. The wealthy occupied the most desirable sector, which usually had the most attractive physical environment, and the lowest-income groups were to be found occupying land adjacent to the main industrial districts. Change in a district's characteristics was produced by the FILTERING process, with the affluent moving further out along their sector and releasing their former homes, closer to the city centre, for slightly lower-income groups.

Hoyt's model was presented as an alternative to Burgess's ZONAL MODEL, and was later incorporated with it in a MULTIPLE NUCLEI MODEL (see the figure for that entry). RJJ

Reference

Hoyt, H. 1939: *The structure and growth of residential neighborhoods in American cities.* Washington, DC: Federal Housing Administration.

Suggested Reading

Johnston, R. J. 1971: *Urban residential patterns: an introductory review.* London: George Bell.

sea See LAW OF THE SEA; TERRITORIAL SEA.

seed bed location An area the characteristics of which encourage the establishment and growth of new firms there. Initially, such areas were associated with the fringe of the CENTRAL BUSINESS DISTRICT, where relatively small, cheap and easily converted older properties offered favourable conditions for people wishing to set up their own businesses: in recent years, URBAN RENEWAL policies have restricted the availability of such properties. Various public policies have been experimented with to stimulate the development of new businesses in planned seed bed locations – as with ENTERPRISE ZONES and SCIENCE PARKS. RJJ

segmented labour market A LABOUR MARKET divided into two or more separate segments, between which movement is difficult. A dual labour market, for example, may comprise one segment for skilled labour and the other for unskilled, with people in the latter unable to compete for jobs in the former (which may itself be further divided according to the skills involved). Spatially, a country may be divided into a large number of separate labour markets, between which movement is difficult for at least some people because of the costs of MIGRATION. Such segmentation makes for particular difficulties during periods of RESTRUCTURING, when

the available labour supply does not match the demand. RJJ

Suggested Reading

Cooke, P. N. 1983: Labour market discontinuity and spatial development. *Progr. hum. Geogr.* 7, pp. 545–66.

segregation Deriving from the ecological ideas of the 'Chicago school' of urban sociology (Park and Burgess, 1925), the concept of segregation refers both to processes of social differentiation and to the spatial patterns that result from such processes. According to Park and his followers, ethnic groups in American cities went through a series of stages from contact and competition to conflict and eventual ASSIMILATION. Social geographers and 'spatial sociologists' (Peach, 1975) argued that patterns of residential segregation could be taken as an index of that process. INDICES OF SEGREGATION were calculated and refined, often with the implication that segregation was inherently undesirable and that some form of dispersal (voluntary or induced) was the most appropriate policy response. Many studies focused on the extreme case of segregation in America's black ghettos and their associated 'racial' violence (Morrill, 1965; Taeuber and Taeuber, 1965). After a period of debate about the balance of forces between 'choice' and 'constraint' (Jackson and Smith, 1981), attention turned to the potential role of residential segregation in class formation and the growth of COMMUNITY consciousness (Harris, 1984). Most recently, geographers have begun to acknowledge the political role of housing and residential segregation in the constitution of specific forms of RACISM (Smith, 1989). PAJ

References

Harris, R. 1984: Residential segregation and class formation in the capitalist city. *Prog. hum. Geogr.* 8, pp. 26–49.

Jackson, P. and Smith, S. J., eds 1981: *Social interaction and ethnic segregation.* London: Academic Press.

Morrill, R. L. 1965: The Negro ghetto: problems and alternatives. *Geogr. Rev.* 55, pp. 339–61.

Park, R. E. and Burgess, E. W. 1925: *The city.* Chicago: University of Chicago Press.

Peach, C., ed. 1975: *Urban social segregation.* London: Longman.

Smith, S. J. 1989: *The politics of 'race' and residence.* Cambridge: Polity Press.

Taeuber, K. E. and Taeuber, A. F. 1965: *Negroes in cities.* Chicago: Aldine.

Suggested Reading

Peach, C., Robinson, V. and Smith, S., eds 1981: *Ethnic segregation in cities.* London: Croom Helm.

self-determination The right of a group with a distinctive territorial identity to determine its own destiny (Knight, 1984). The concept, very similar to that of NATIONALISM, is generally applied to the claims of indigenous populations living within territories occupied by others (cf. COLONIALISM), such as American Indians and New Zealand Maori. These groups claim self-determination rights according to the statement in the United Nations' Charter that:

All people have the right to self-determination; by virtue of that right they may freely determine their political status and freely pursue their economic, social and cultural development.

RJJ

Reference

Knight, D. B. 1984: Geographical perspectives on 'self-determination' in Taylor, P. J. and House, J. W. eds, *Political geography: recent advances and future directions.* London: Croom Helm/Totowa, NJ: Barnes and Noble, pp. 139–47.

Suggested Reading

Johnston, R. J., Knight, D. B. and Kofman, E., eds 1988: *Nationalism, self-determination and political geography.* London: Croom Helm.

semantic differential A method for eliciting people's attitudes, opinions and values using QUESTIONNAIRES. Respondents are presented with a set of stimuli (e.g. places) and asked to assess each on a number of rating scales anchored by a pair of bipolar adjectives (e.g. dirty–clean or nice–nasty). The semantic differential differs from REPERTORY GRID ANALYSIS because the rating scales are chosen by the researcher in the former but by the individual respondent in the latter. RJJ

semiology (semiotics) Terms attributed to C. S. Peirce (semiotics) and F. de Saussure (semiology); they refer to theories of the ways in which signs are produced and/or given meanings. Geographers have been drawn to semiotics through the recognition that non-verbal behaviour, architecture and LANDSCAPES are also systems of signification.

Geographical analyses of these signifying systems reflect and parallel general developments within semiotics. Over the past 20 years semiotics has shifted from the classification of sign systems (and the basic units and levels of structural organization within them) to the study of the multiple ways in which signs and meanings are produced, interpreted and transformed through, as well as constitutive of, social and political practices. Jencks' (1969) attempt to develop a 'syntax' for architecture stands as an example of the earlier approach; Duncan's (1990) interpretation of the Kandyan landscape reflects the influence of the latter. Duncan explores how the landscape encodes information, including codes from other parts of the cultural system (see CULTURE), such as written TEXTS. He uses the concept of intertextuality to explore the relation between landscape and other texts. In line with a more dynamic socio-semiotic approach, he highlights the multiple ways in which a single landscape is read and how landscapes enter into the social and political process. The interpretation of landscape and culture as text is not without critics (Schneider, 1987). GP

References

Jencks, C. 1969: Semiology and architecture. In Jencks, C. and Baird, G., eds, *Meaning in architecture.* London: Barrie and Jenkins.

Duncan, J. 1990: *The city as text: the politics of landscape interpretation in the Kandyan kingdom.* Cambridge: Cambridge University Press.

Schneider, M. 1987: Culture-as-text in the work of Clifford Geertz. *Theory and Society* 16, pp. 803–39.

sense of place 1. The character intrinsic to a PLACE itself. 2. The attachments that people themselves have to a place. These are two distinct but interlocking perspectives.

In the first sense, certain places are regarded as distinctive or memorable through their unique physical characteristics or 'imagability', or through their association with significant events, real or mythical. Thus Ayers Rock, Jerusalem and Grand Canyon, and even Chernobyl and Bophal, may be said to possess a strong sense of place, a uniquely significant meaning for large numbers of people who may have no direct experience of the place.

In the second sense, in everyday life individuals and communities develop deep attachments to places through experience, memory and intention. The most obvious such attachments are to 'home', where above all one feels 'in place' (Eyles, 1985). Commonly, people give physical expression to their collective attachments to place through construction of symbolic structures (churches, monuments, etc.) that increase its more general distinctiveness.

In both cases, objective aspects of a place are conflated with subjective aspects of our experience of that place (whether direct or indirect), giving rise to the characteristic 'betweenness of place' identified by Entrikin (1991). In the past two decades conscious creation and promotion of place images has become a distinguishing feature of postmodern architecture and planning in consumption spaces (see POSTMODERNISM). The supposed 'authenticity' and 'heritage' value of former production spaces (docklands and textile mills, for example) is both emphasized by conserving their physical form and deployed to promote altered uses, while new places are created which draw upon references to 'other' places to enhance their own identity (Ley, 1989; Hopkins, 1990).   DEC

References

Entrikin, N. 1991: *The betweenness of place: towards a geography of modernity.* London: Macmillan.

Eyles, J. 1985: *Sense of place*, Warrington, UK: Silverbrook Press.

Hopkins, J. 1990: West Edmonton Mall: landscape of myths and elsewhereness. *Can. Geogr.* 34, pp. 2–17.

Ley, D. 1989: Modernism, post-modernism and the struggle for place. In Agnew, J. and Duncan, J., eds, *The power of place: bringing together the geographical and sociological imaginations.* London: Unwin Hyman, pp. 44–65.

sequent occupance 'The view of geography as a succession of stages of human occupance . . . which establishes the genetics of each stage in terms of its predecessor' (Whittlesey, 1929: cf. SETTLEMENT CONTINUITY). Whittlesey's scheme owed much to HUMAN ECOLOGY, but although he knew that 'the analogy between sequent occupance in chorology and plant succession in botany will be apparent to all', he insisted that his own conception was more 'intricate'. While 'human occupance of area, like other biotic phenomena, carries within itself the seed of its own transformation' (cf. DIALECTIC), such uninterrupted or 'normal' progressions were 'rare, perhaps only ideal, because extraneous forces are likely to interfere with the normal course, altering either its direction or rate, or both' and 'breaking or knotting the thread of sequent occupance'. These detailed qualifications were vital, but Whittlesey was also determined to distance himself from 'the physiographic cycle of erosion', an evolutionary scheme, with similar disclaimers – although few of those who followed in his wake displayed an equal caution or an equivalent subtlety (see Mikesell, 1975). The most successful applications of the concept (especially Broek, 1932) in fact departed from the series of stable CROSS-SECTIONS envisaged by Whittlesey and linked them with deliberately dynamic VERTICAL THEMES, so that his projected systematization of the 'relatively few sequence patterns that have ever existed' was never realized.   DG

References

Broek, J. O. M. 1932: *The Santa Clara Valley, California: a study in landscape changes.* Utrecht: Oosthock.

Mikesell, M. W. 1975: The rise and decline of sequent occupance. In Lowenthal, D. and Bowden, M., eds, *Geographies of the mind: essays in historical geosophy in honor of John Kirkland Wright.* New York: Oxford University Press.

Whittlesey, D. 1929: Sequent occupance. *Ann. Ass. Am. Geogr.* 19, pp. 162–6.

Suggested Reading

Mikesell (1975).

service class Professional, administrative and managerial workers who occupy the upper levels in a capitalist social hierarchy. Members of the 'service class' are not owners of capital (although they may have shares in it, both directly and – through pension funds and the like – indirectly); rather, they serve capital by providing it with specialist functions. Goldthorpe (1982) identifies three such functions: (1) *facilitating the use of labour* – as with research and development workers; (2) *controlling labour* – as with personnel managers; and (3) *orchestrating provision of services to labour* – as with health-care professionals. The disparate nature of the three means that the service class is not homogeneous (cf. CHAOTIC CONCEPTION), and members, political interests may be very different.

The service class has grown both relatively and absolutely during the recent DEINDUSTRIALIZATION and RESTRUCTURING trends in many 'advanced capitalist' societies: its success is now fundamental to the prosperity of most WORLD CITIES, for example.   RJJ

Reference

Goldthorpe, J. 1982: On the service class. In Giddens, A. and MacKenzie, G., eds, *Social class and the division of labour*. Cambridge: Cambridge University Press.

Suggested Reading

Lash, S. and Urry, J. 1987: *The end of organized capitalism*. Cambridge: Polity Press.

services, geography of The study of the geography of service industries. Services are usually defined as 'activities which are relatively detached from material production and which as a consequence do not directly involve the processing of physical materials. The main difference between manufacturing and service products seems to be that the expertise provided by services relies much more directly on work-force skills, experience, and knowledge than on physical techniques embodied in machinery or processes' (Marshall, 1988, p. 11). But general statements of this kind have proved very difficult to convert into clear working definitions of services and, in reality, the definition is often made by a process of exclusion; services are not agricultural, mining or industrial production. Only recently have complex and partly satisfactory definitions of services been made, usually on the basis of binary distinctions such as PRODUCER and CONSUMER SERVICES, public and private services, tradeable and non-tradeable services, office-based and non-office-based services, and so on (see Noyelle and Stanback, 1984; Marshall et al., 1987; Petit, 1986).

The study of services has clearly become a pressing task, as these industries have become an increasingly prominent part of all developed economies (in terms of both output and, more particularly, employment). As the absolute and proportional importance of services has become clear, so the debates over their actual economic importance have become more intense. On the one hand, there has been growing debate over whether service industries are dependent on manufacturing industry, for example, and over the apparently lower levels of productivity in many service industries (although measuring productivity in service industries is itself a vexed topic). On the other hand, some commentators (e.g. Sayer and Walker, 1992) have suggested that many of these problems only arise because service industries are seen as discrete entities rather than as links in extended production chains or '*filières*', and because it is too often forgotten that service industries themselves produce tangible, traded commodities (whether these are wills, pieces of software or instructional videotapes). Again, the success of manufacturing industry is often nowadays linked with intangible factors, many of which turn out to be associated with the quality of services provided from either within or outside the manufacturing firm (Marshall, 1989).

Given these problems, it is no surprise that the geography of services remains a somewhat confused area of research. Certain service industries (such as PRODUCER SERVICES) are comparatively well studied. Others, such as TOURISM and many PUBLIC SERVICES, are still comparatively neglected, given their undoubted economic, social and cultural importance

(Pinch, 1989). What seems certain is that there is no one geography of services: rather, there is a whole set of different geographies of services which vary according to the characteristics of the specific industry (Allen, 1988). It may still be possible to make some generalizations about the geography of services as a whole, because certain types of service industry are still concentrated in very large metropolitan centres, others are growing in intermediate cities, or major provincial cities, and others still are growing in small towns and rural areas, but whether the results repay the effort can be questioned.

There are five discernible tendencies in the study of the geography of services. The first is an increasing emphasis on large services firms as service industries have become increasingly centralized. The second tendency is a natural development of the first; service firms are becoming more and more international in scope. The past 20 years have seen the growth of the services MULTINATIONAL CORPORATION in industries as diverse as banking, RETAILING and tourism (Thrift, 1989; Daniels, 1991; Dicken, 1992).

The study of these large services multinational corporations involves research into many of the same strategies as those found in other sectors of the world economy, including franchising, strategic alliances, and the full range of flexible labour-force and production possibilities (see FLEXIBLE ACCUMULATION). The third tendency, one that is both counterposed and linked to the previous ones, is the growing interest in the role of small and medium-sized service firms. Small and medium-sized firms in the service industries have been relatively neglected in favour of their larger cousins. This exclusive emphasis has now begun to change as it has been increasingly realized that such firms can, under certain circumstances, become dynamic elements of urban and regional economies (Keeble et al., 1991). A fourth focus of study has been on the often vital role of advances in technology and communications, both in allowing services to internationalize and in making many services more tradeable. It is important to remember that without modern telecommunications many services

firms and products could not exist (Brunn and Leinbach, 1991). Finally, the nature of service industries' workforces is now seen as vital. In particular, much more attention has been paid to the exact role of managerial and professional workers, and especially their intense patterns of interaction, often at the world scale (Beaverstock, 1991). Because service industries are relatively more feminized than other industries, considerable attention has also been paid to issues of the social construction of gendered jobs in services, and the consequent struggles to redefine these jobs in terms of pay, conditions and status (Crompton and Jones, 1990). (See also GENDER AND GEOGRAPHY.)   NJT

References

Allen, J. 1988: The geographies of service. In Massey, D. and Allen, J., eds, *Uneven redevelopment: cities and regions in transition*. London: Hodder and Stoughton, pp. 124–41.

Beaverstock, J. 1991: Skilled international migration. *Environ. Plann. A* 23, pp. 1133–46.

Brunn, S. and Leinbach, T., eds 1991: *Collapsing space and time: geographic aspects of communication and information*. London: Harper Collins.

Crompton, R. and Jones, R. 1990: *Gendered jobs and social change*. London: Unwin Hyman.

Daniels, P. 1991: A world of services. *Geoforum* 22, pp. 359–76.

Dicken, P. 1992: *Global shift*, second edition. London: Paul Chapman.

Keeble, D., Bryson, J. and Wood, P. 1991: Small firms, business services growth and regional development in the UK. *Reg. Stud.* 25, pp. 439–54.

Marshall, J. N., ed. 1988: *Services and uneven development*. Oxford: Oxford University Press.

Marshall, J. N. 1989: Corporate reorganisation and the geography of services. *Reg. Stud.* 23, 139–50.

Marshall, J. N., Damesick, P. and Wood, P. 1987: Understanding the location and role of producer services in the UK. *Environ. Plann. A*, 19, pp. 575–95.

Noyelle, T. J., and Stanback, T. 1984: *The economic transformation of American cities*. Totowa, NJ: Rowman and Allanfeld, Osman.

Petit, D. 1986: *Slow growth and the service economy*. London: Frances Pinter.

Pinch, S. 1989: The restructuring thesis and the study of public services. *Environ. Plann. A*, 21, pp. 905–26.

Sayer, A. and Walker, R. A. 1992: *The new social economy: reworking the division of labour*. Oxford: Blackwell.

Thrift, N. J. 1989: The geography of international economic disorder. In Johnston, R. J. and Taylor, P. J., eds, *A world in crisis?*, second edition. Oxford: Blackwell, pp. 16–78.

Suggested Reading
Allen (1988).
Daniels (1991).

settlement See SQUATTER SETTLEMENT.

settlement continuity The maintenance of (typically rural) settlement sites, settlement systems and territorial structures across a period of major societal transformation (cf. SEQUENT OCCUPANCE). In Great Britain, a fundamental question of continuity arises over the fabric of rural settlement during the collapse of the Roman occupation and the beginnings of Anglo-Saxon colonization (*c*.AD 400–1110). The two extremes were posed by Finberg as 'Continuity or cataclysm?' (1964) and 'Revolution or evolution?' (1972). Within British HISTORICAL GEOGRAPHY, these two poles are conventionally represented by: Darby, who once wrote that 'As far as there ever is a new beginning in history, the coming of the Angles, Saxons and Jutes was such a beginning' (Darby, 1964) and that, even though 'the Anglo-Saxons did not come into an empty land, and . . . many contributions from pre-Saxon days have entered into the making of England', nevertheless 'with the coming of the Anglo-Saxons, a new chapter in the history of settlement and land utilisation was begun' (Darby, 1973); and Jones, for whom 'the roots of the Saxon settlements were planted while Britain was still part of the Roman Empire' (Jones, 1978). Jones proposed a *multiple estate model* to summarize his thesis. Multiple estates were groups of townships whose tenants 'were subject to the jurisdiction of the territorial lord and [who], in return for their lands, paid rents in cash or kind and performed various services on his behalf' (see FEUDALISM). 'A network of obligations linked even the most distant settlements on each estate to the lord's' (Jones, 1971). Multiple estates have been identified in Northumbria, Wales and South-East England and, so Jones claims, have a common pre-Saxon origin. He also argues that 'the multiple structure of these ancient estates appears to have conditioned the evolution of the constituent settlements', with some growing into villages or even market towns and the multiple structures breaking up or being re-sorted. Jones (1976) concludes that:

to arrive at an adequate understanding of the colonization of England it is essential to look beyond unitary settlements. Rather it is necessary to adopt as a model the multiple estate: for this provides the most meaningful of all frameworks for unravelling the complex interrelationships between society, economy and habitat involved in the process of colonization.

Whatever the rights and wrongs of Jones's specific thesis (see Gregson, 1985, for a commentary and Jones's response), most scholars would endorse his emphasis on the *complexity* of the situation – Roberts (1979) declares that the answer to Finberg's questions (above) 'is to be found, not only between the two extremes, but varying spatially across the complex and intricate landscape varieties within these small islands – and would probably, on balance, favour *continuity* rather than cataclysm (Fowler, 1976). For, as Jones (1978) notes, 'the chief sufferers from the Saxon conquest . . . were British kings and nobles'. As Taylor (1983) puts the matter:

the Saxons came not to a new and relatively untouched country but to a very old one, a country where most of the 'best' places had already been occupied not once but many times . . . . All this activity took place within clearly marked territories or estates, often grouped together under the control of large landowners.

When the Roman Empire began to collapse, all that happened was that the protection of the Imperial army was removed and the sophisticated central government system was taken away. But the great mass of the population stayed on, as they had to, in their homes and on their land, to face up to what were to be increasingly difficult times both socially and economically.   DG

References

Darby, H. C. 1964: Historical geography: from the coming of the Anglo-Saxons to the Industrial Revolution. In Wreford Watson, J., ed., *The British Isles: a systematic geography*. London: Nelson, pp. 198–220.

Darby, H. C. 1973: The Anglo-Scandinavian foundations. In Darby, H. C., ed., *A new historical geography of England*. Cambridge: Cambridge University Press, pp. 1–38.

Finberg, H. P. R. 1964: Continuity or cataclysm? In Finberg, H. P. R., ed., *Lucerna: studies of some problems in the early history of England*. London: pp. 1–20.

Finberg, H. P. R. 1972: Revolution or evolution? In Finberg, H. P. R., ed., *The agrarian history of England and Wales*, volumes I and II. Cambridge: Cambridge University Press, pp. 385–401.

Fowler, P. J. 1976: Agriculture and rural settlement. In Wilson, D. M., ed., *The archaeology of Anglo-Saxon England*. London: Methuen, pp. 23–48.

Gregson, N. 1985: The multiple estate model: some critical questions. *J. hist. Georgr.* 11, pp. 339–51.

Jones, G. R. J. 1971: The multiple estate as a model framework for tracing early stages in the evolution of rural settlements. In Dussart, F., ed., *L'Habitat et les paysages ruraux d'Europe*. Liège: University of Liège, pp. 255–62.

Jones, G. R. J. 1976: Multiple estates and early settlement. In Sawyer, P. H., ed., *Medieval settlement: continuity and change*. London: Edward Arnold, pp. 15–40.

Jones, G. R. J. 1978: Celts, Saxons and Scandinavians. In Dodgshon, R. A. and Butlin, R. A., eds, *An historical geography of England and Wales*. London: Academic Press, pp. 57–79.

Jones, G. R. J. 1985: Multiple estates perceived. *J. hist. Geogr.* 11, pp. 352–63.

Roberts, B. K. 1979: *Rural settlement in Britain*. London: Hutchinson.

Taylor, C. 1983: *Village and farmstead: a history of rural settlement in England*. London: George Philip.

Suggested Reading

Finberg (1972).

Gregson (1985).

Jones (1976).

sexuality and geography Studies of the sexualization of PLACE and SPACE and the SPATIALITY of the construction of sexual difference and identities. Three theoretical traditions have been particularly influential; the writings of Foucault, psychoanalysis, and feminist reinterpretations of the first two.

Foucault theorizes sexuality in relation to POWER and DISCOURSES. He argues that new types of internalized power relations developed in the nineteenth century and, increasingly, individuals have come to regulate both their own and the social body by means of self-surveillance and self-discipline. Foucault sees HUMAN SUBJECTIVITY as being produced discursively. He observes that a multiplicity of DISCOURSES of sexuality – medical, religious and state – developed in the nineteenth century. Through these discourses sexuality has become the central defining characteristic of subjectivity and a potent means of regulating individual and social bodies (Foucault, 1978). Although Foucault chooses not to interpret sexuality in gendered terms, feminists have adapted his ideas to analyse how feminine bodies and subjectivities are shaped and disciplined through a combination of self-surveillance and external domination. Several have written microgeographies of feminine bodily comportment, motility and spatiality (Bartky, 1988).

The tropes of distance and proximity are central to psychoanalytic accounts of psychosexual development and sexual differences. Freudian psychoanalysts argue that males' experiences of the Oedipus complex allow them to achieve a distance and separation from other individuals and objects that females never experience. The distance experienced by males also allows them to figure themselves as detached observers ('as eyes that see without being seen': Game, 1991, p. 42). Feminists have reinterpreted this account in many ways, for example, arguing against the singularity of the Oedipus complex as the only moment of separation during early psychosexual development, and re-reading Freud's account of femininity, not as lack, but in more positive terms. These psychoanalytical accounts, themselves inherently spatial, offer rich opportunities for geographical analyses. Deutsche's (1991) critique of Harvey's account of *The condition of postmodernity*, for example, draws on feminist criticisms of the PHALLOCENTRIC objectifying gaze. Pollock (1988) interprets modern urban spaces as sexualized places, where men gaze and act upon working-class women as objects.

Geographers are also recognizing the diversity of sexual identities, including homosexual ones, and the ways in which space and place enter into the constitution of them (Castells, 1983; Knopp, 1990). GP

References

Bartky, S. L. 1988: Foucault, femininity and the modernization of patriarchal power. In Diamond, I. and Quinby, L., eds, *Feminism and Foucault*. Boston: Northeastern University Press, pp. 61–86.

Castells, M. 1983: *The city and the grassroots*. London: Edward Arnold.

Deutsche, R. 1991: Boys town. *Environ. Plann. D, Society and Space* 9(1), pp. 5–30.

Foucault, M. 1978: *The history of sexuality*, volume one. *An introduction*, transl. R. Hurley. New York: Pantheon Books.

Game, A. 1991: *Undoing the social*. Toronto: University of Toronto Press.

Knopp, L. 1990: Some theoretical implications of gay involvement in an urban land market. *Pol. Geogr. Q.* 9, pp. 337–52.

Pollock, G. 1988: *Vision and difference*. London: Routledge.

sharecropping

sharecropping A form of land tenure in which the landlords' returns are produce rather than cash or farm rent. Many different systems of sharecropping occur around the world: most commonly, the landlord provides all the requisite fixed and movable capital and the sharecropper provides labour. The landlord receives a predetermined proportion of total production which is sometimes, as in France and Italy, laid down by law. Short-term leases are common in sharecropping, which discourages long-term land management. The system is often known by the French term *métayage*. (See also LAND TENURE.)

PEW/DBG

Suggested Reading

Barlowe, R. 1978: *Land resource economics*, third edition. Englewood Cliffs, NJ: Prentice-Hall, ch. 14.

Ransom, R. and Sutch, R. 1977: *One kind of freedom*. Cambridge: Cambridge University Press.

shift-share model A technique for assessing the relative importance of different components in regional employment growth or decline. Regional employment growth may be due to the REGION having a high concentration of industries that are growing (such as micro-electronics), or it may be due to locational shifts within industries or differential regional trends within an industry. Shift-share models try to disentangle and measure these effects using simple algebraic manipulation of growth rates.

Let E_{ij0} be the level of employment in industry i in region j in the initial time period 0, and let E_{ijt} be the level in the next period t. Then the total employment in region j at time 0 is

$$E_{j0} = \sum_i E_{ij0},$$

total national employment in industry i is

$$E_{i0} = \sum_j E_{ij0},$$

and total national employment is

$$E_0 = \sum_i \sum_j E_{ij0}.$$

The figures for time t are then obtained in the same way. The total shift (TS) is the difference between actual regional employment growth and that which would have occurred if the region had grown at the overall national rate:

$$TS = E_{jt} - E_{j0} \times (E_t/E_0).$$

This total shift can then be divided into a proportionality shift (or 'composition effect') and a differential shift. The *proportionality shift* (*PS*) measures change due to regional concentration in slow- or fast-growing sectors, and is calculated by applying to each industry a growth factor that is the difference between the actual industrial growth rate and the overall national rate. For industry i, this factor is:

$$G_i = E_{it}/E_{i0} - E_t/E_0$$

and the proportionality shift for region j is $PS = \sum_i G_i E_{ij0}$. The *differential shift* (*DS*) is the shift due to locational changes within industries and is obtained as $DS = TS - PS$.

The technique is purely descriptive, and does not explain why certain sectors are growing or declining or why locational shifts are taking place, but the data are easily obtained and it gives a useful starting point for further enquiry. The method is very dependent on the level of sector aggregation (more sectors produce lower differential shifts), and it takes no account of LINKAGES or MULTIPLIERS.   LWH

Suggested Reading

Armstrong, A. and Taylor, J. 1978: *Regional economic policy and its analysis*, second edition. Deddington, Oxford: Philip Allan, pp. 300–8.

shifting cultivation   Minimally, shifting cultivation is an agricultural system characterized by a rotation of fields rather than of crops, by discontinous cropping in which periods of fallowing are typically longer than periods of cropping, and by the clearing of fields (usually called swiddens) through the use of slash and burn techniques. Known by a variety of terms (including field-forest rotation, slash and burn, and swiddening), shifting cultivation is widespread throughout the humid tropics, but was also practised in temperate Europe (Conklin, 1962). It is estimated that there are over 250 million shifting cultivators worldwide, 100 million in Southeast Asia alone. Shifting cultivation is enormously heterogeneous, and subtypes can be distinguished according to crops raised, crop associations and successions, fallow lengths, climatic and edaphic conditions, field technologies, soil treatment and the mobility of settlement. Many distinguish between 'integral' (shifting cultivation as an integral part of SUBSISTENCE) and 'partial' (shifting cultivation as a technological expedient for cash cropping; see PEASANT) forms of shifting cultivation (Conklin, 1962). In all shifting cultivation systems the burning of cleared vegetation is critical to the release of nutrients, which ensures field productivity. By definition, shifting cultivation is land-extensive and is threatened by population growth and expanding land settlement (see CARRYING CAPACITY; INTENSIVE AGRICULTURE).

MW

Reference

Conklin, H. 1962: An ethnoecological approach to shifting cultivation. In Wagner, P. and Mikesell, M. eds, *Readings in cultural geography*. Chicago: University of Chicago Press, pp. 457–64

significance test   A statistical procedure for identifying the probability of an observed event having occurred by chance. Most statistics, such as CHI-SQUARE and the CORRELATION coefficient (r), have an associated sampling distribution of possible values with its own mean and standard error (the latter is equivalent to the standard deviation of a FREQUENCY DISTRIBUTION). For example, there is a large number of possible sets of cell values for a given set of row and column totals, each of which will produce a different value of chi-square when compared with the observed distribution (see also ENTROPY-MAXIMIZING MODELS). Because the frequency distribution of chi-square is known for every table size (i.e. numbers of rows and columns, the product of which – less one in each case – is the degrees of freedom for the test), then the probability of obtaining an observed value can be obtained readily from the relevant statistical table.

Significance tests are used in two ways. In CONFIRMATORY DATA ANALYSIS they assist in the testing of hypotheses about the characteristics of a population, from a study of a properly selected sample of that population only (see SAMPLING). For example, a chi-square test may be conducted to see whether the age structure of two counties varies (i.e. whether they are both samples of the same population). If, according to the frequency distribution, the observed value of chi-square would occur very frequently for samples of that size, given the degrees of freedom, then it is concluded that the two counties do not differ significantly. The usual criterion for 'very frequently' is more than one test in 20 (normally stated as at the 95 per cent or 0.05 level). If the observed value occurs only rarely in the frequency distribution, then it is unlikely that the observed value has occurred by chance, and it is concluded that the difference between the two samples is almost certainly present in the population from which they were drawn (i.e. the two county populations combined).

In EXPLORATORY DATA ANALYSIS the significance test is not used to draw a conclusion about a population from a sample, but rather to indicate the importance of an observed result. Again, the comparison is with what would happen if the only influences were random: if the observed value of the statistic falls in one of the tails (the extreme values) of the theoretical frequency distribution, then it is concluded that what has been observed is so unlikely to have occurred by chance that it must be 'real' and worthy of further investigation. RJJ

Suggested Reading

Hay, A. M. 1985: Statistical tests in the absence of sample: a note. *Prof. Geogr.* 37, pp. 334–8.

O'Brien, L. 1992: *Introducing quantitative geography: measurement, methods and generalised linear models.* London: Routledge.

simulation An heuristic device for solving theoretically intractable mathematical and statistical problems. Simulation is used either to model a 'real world' process or to create an empirical FREQUENCY DISTRIBUTION on which a SIGNIFICANCE TEST may be based.

Many simulation models use what are known as Monte Carlo procedures, involving the drawing of random numbers. These were the basis of Hägerstrand's original work on the DIFFUSION of INNOVATIONS, for example, using an empirically observed MEAN INFORMATION FIELD as the framework for allocation of the random numbers. (See also MICROSIMULATION; STOCHASTIC PROCESS.)

Other simulation methods include the construction of analogue models, as in the Varignon frame used in the WEBER MODEL for solving industrial location problems. RJJ

Suggested Reading

Board, C. 1967: Maps as models. In Chorley, R. J. and Haggett, P., eds, *Models in geography*. London: Methuen, pp. 671–726.

Morgan, M. A. 1967: Hardware models in geography. In Chorley, R. J. and Haggett, P., eds, *Models in geography*. London: Methuen, pp. 727–74.

Sjoberg model A model of social and spatial order of the PREINDUSTRIAL CITY, first expressed in Gideon Sjoberg's book of the same title. Sjoberg's model arose from his desire to provide a critique of, and alternative to, the concentric zonal model of the city offered by Ernest Burgess and, more generally, of HUMAN ECOLOGY as applied by prominent members of the CHICAGO SCHOOL. As such, Sjoberg's work was part of a larger project, initiated by Walter Firey, to replace human ecology with STRUCTURAL FUNCTIONALISM as the central PARADIGM of urban society. The major factors used to explain urban morphology in Sjoberg's model are social structure and technology.

Sjoberg begins by differentiating between non-urban, 'feudal' and industrial societies. He is concerned with the second of these, which he defines as societies that utilize animate sources of energy, and are literate and urbanized, including all world civilizations prior to the INDUSTRIAL REVOLUTION, as well as non-industrialized contemporary societies (but cf. FEUDALISM). He argues that such preindustrial societies everywhere, and through time, are characterized by similar technological achievements and by a three-tiered CLASS structure that includes a small ruling class, a large lower class and outcast groups. The ruling class, comprised of those in religious and administrative authority, establishes a social order that reproduces its control over succeeding generations; URBANIZATION is both the outcome of social stratification and a means whereby hegemony is perpetuated. The morphology of preindustrial cities reflects this interdependence between social and spatial order: power is consolidated by the ruling class through its residential location in the city centre, the most protected and most accessible district. Here residents forge a social solidarity based on their literacy, access to the surplus (which is stored in the central area of the city), and shared upper-class culture, which includes distinctive manners and patterns of speech. Elite clustering in the city centre is reinforced by the lack of rapid transportation.

The privileged central district is surrounded by haphazardly arranged neighbourhoods housing the lower class. Households in these areas are sorted by occupation or income (merchants near the centre, followed by minor bureaucrats, artisans and finally the unskilled), ethnic origin and extended family networks. Merchants are generally not accorded elite status, since power is achieved through religious and military control, while trade is viewed with suspicion. The model is less clear on the residential placement of outcast groups (typically slaves and other conquered peoples): some of these perform service roles and are intermingled with the rest of the urban population, while others live at the extreme periphery of the city – frequently beyond its walls.

In formulating this model, Sjoberg reverses the logic used by Burgess (see ZONAL MODEL), who placed commercial activities at the centre of the city, and a succession of poor to wealthy residential districts around it. Sjoberg notes that the Burgess model is applicable only to industrial cities, where production and commerce propel economic growth and where capitalists are accorded high social standing. Furthermore, he argues that human ecology incorrectly treats urbanization as an independent social force, when in reality urban growth should be seen as a 'dependent variable', as it depends on the distribution of social power and available technology. Empirical investigations of the Sjoberg model have been generally supportive, but caution that the model cannot account for the intricate details of urban development across different cultural contexts. Others have criticized the theoretical content of Sjoberg's work, especially his stress on the role of technology and his uncritical view of social power. However, Sjoberg's functionalist logic (which blurs distinctions between causes and consequences) remains largely unnoticed and unchallenged.   DH

Suggested Reading
Carter, H. 1983: *An introduction to urban historical geography*. London: Edward Arnold.
Firey, W. 1947: *Land use in central Boston*. Cambridge, MA: Harvard University Press.
Langton, J. 1975: Residential patterns in pre-industrial cities. *Trans. Inst. Br. Geogr.* 65, pp. 1–27.
Radford, J. P. 1979: Testing the model of the pre-industrial city. *Trans. Instit. Br. Geogr.* n.s. 4(3), pp. 392–410.
Sjoberg, G. 1960: *The pre-industrial city, past and present*. New York: The Free Press (two chapters are coauthored with Andrée F. Sjoberg).

skid row A run-down section of an urban area, usually close to the city centre, which houses a concentration of its transient population, notably those on the margins of economic survival (i.e. 'on the skids') and suffering from a variety of complaints, such as alcoholism. Skid rows are especially characteristic of North American cities, where they offer temporary homes in poor quality rental accommodation for transient male visitors – such as workers in logging and mining camps; they now also house permanent residents without access to conventional homes. In the ZONAL MODEL of urban residential structure, skid row occupies part of the zone in transition. (See also ANOMIE.)   RJJ

Suggested Reading
Rowley, G. 1978: Plus ça change . . . a Canadian skid row. *Can. Geogr.* 22, pp. 211–24.

slavery A MODE OF PRODUCTION in which labour is controlled through some form of non-economic compulsion. The individual slaves, plus other members of their households in many cases, are privately owned commodities who are denied any control over either their own labour or their own reproduction (i.e. there is no CIVIL SOCIETY under slavery). This complete control differentiates the slave from the condition of the serf under FEUDALISM. Slave-labour dominated in the Greek and Roman empires, which provided the paradigm exemplars of slavery, but many other societies have contained elements of it – not least the American South prior to the Civil War.   RJJ

Suggested Reading
Hindess, B. and Hirst, P. Q. 1975: *Pre-capitalist modes of production*. London: Routledge and Kegan Paul.

slum An area of overcrowded and dilapidated, usually old, housing, occupied by people who can afford only the cheapest dwellings available in the urban area, generally in or close to the INNER CITY. The term usually implies both a poverty-ridden population, an unhealthy environment, and a district rife with crime and vice (see also CYCLE OF POVERTY): it is also often associated with concentrations of people in certain ethnic groups (see ETHNICITY), although the terms GHETTO and slum should not be used as synonyms. RJJ

snowbelt See SUNBELT/SNOWBELT.

social area analysis A theory and technique developed by two American sociologists, Eshref Shevky and Wendell Bell (1955), to link changing urban social structure and residential patterns to the processes of economic DEVELOPMENT and URBANIZATION (which they termed the 'increasing scale' of society).

According to Shevky and Bell, increasing scale involved three interrelated trends:

(a) the *change in the range and intensity of social relations* consequent on the greater DIVISION OF LABOUR and its reflection in the distribution of skills and their rewards within society – Shevky identified this trend with the construct that he termed 'social rank', although Bell preferred the term 'economic status';

(b) the *increasing differentiation of functions within society and its constituent households*, which generates new lifestyles and household forms – a construct that Shevky termed 'urbanization' and Bell 'family status'; and

(c) the *concentration of people from different cultural backgrounds in cities* – producing 'SEGREGATION' for Shevky and 'ethnic status' (see ETHNICITY) for Bell.

This theory of changing urban society was linked to residential differentiation within urban areas although, as critics (e.g. Timms, 1971) pointed out, the link was far from clear. Shevky and Bell's empirical work illustrated that there were three dimensions to the residential differentiation of Los Angeles and San Francisco that were consistent with the three trends, although their adopted procedures involved the selection of variables to represent the three trends, suggesting that the theory may have been 'invented' inductively to account for their empirical mapping rather than as the source for a study of district socioeconomic differences.

Shevky and Bell's technique for analysing urban residential differentiation involved one of the first uses of CENSUS TRACT data for such work. Variables were selected to represent the three constructs: occupation and schooling for social rank; fertility, women at work and households in single-family dwelling units for urbanization; and population in certain ethnic and immigrant groups for segregation. These were combined to produce three standardized indices, which were then used to create residential area categories; such as high social rank, high urbanization and low segregation (i.e. tracts with many well-educated, white-collar workers living in apartments, with low fertility, and many adult women employed in the workforce, and with few members of ethnic groups).

Further work by Bell tested the validity of the constructs in other cities and used the categorization as a SAMPLING framework for investigating differences in social behaviour within cities (see Johnston, 1971). The technique was soon replaced by the more sophisticated inductive procedure of FACTORIAL ECOLOGY, and the absence of a clear theoretical base means that this initial stimulus to work in URBAN GEOGRAPHY soon became little more than an important historical reference. RJJ

References
Johnston, R. J. 1971: *Urban residential patterns: an introductory review*. London: George Bell.

Shevky, E. and Bell, W. 1955: *Social area analysis: theory, illustrative application and computational procedures*. Stanford, CA: Stanford University Press.

Timms, D. W. G. 1971: *The urban mosaic: towards a theory of residential differentiation*. Cambridge: Cambridge University Press.

Social Darwinism The application of Darwinian evolution to socio-economic and political affairs. Generally speaking, 'Social Darwinism' tends to be regarded as a 'pejorative tag' (Moore, 1986), and for this reason is typically used to label opponents. Yet this judgement has served to disguise how 'social' DARWINISM itself was from the start (Greene, 1959, 1977; Williams, 1973) and to permit a too comfortable critique of the doctrine as a 'distortion' of pure biology (Shapin and Barnes, 1979; La Vergata, 1985; Moore, 1991). Thus to conceive of Social Darwinism as an *extension* of Darwinism is likely to be a misconception.

It was under the influence of Richard Hofstadter's (1959) classic study that the term came to describe almost any evolutionary model of society – particularly if it was pernicious. Here the dangers of manufactured history assert themselves. For, as Donald Bellomy (1984) has shown, the *term* 'Social Darwinism' itself did not achieve currency in the English-speaking world until the early years of the twentieth century. Since then much debate about the issue has revolved around the question of definitions and labels. Moreover, the emphasis of figures such as Hofstadter tended to obscure alternative biological sources of social evolution, such as LAMARCKIANISM, and to ignore the substantial body of social evolutionary literature conceived quite independently of biology (Burrow, 1966). In its most vulgar form, social Darwinism is generally portrayed as an attempt 'to justify the competitive ethos of Victorian capitalism in terms of the struggle for existence' (Bowler, 1984).

In this vein, championed by Herbert Spencer and his disciples, social evolution could be used to justify *laissez-faire* economic policies, nationalistic aggression and ideas of racial supremacy. At the same time, as Jones has made clear, certain forms of 'Social Darwinism' were equally compatible with the traditional liberalism that sought to curb the power of the aristocracy which 'by awarding social status for reasons of birth rather than achievement, protected the idle and unproductive in society' (Jones, 1980). Opposition to the *laissez-faire* construal of

Social Darwinism was also forthcoming from those advocates of eugenics who felt that Darwinian evolution sanctioned a breeding programme for the human species in order to combat racial degeneration and to ensure the best eugenic mixtures (Haller, 1963; Mackenzie, 1982; Kevles, 1985). Besides this, the assumption that Social Darwinism was commonly embraced as an explicit economic philosophy has been questioned by Wyllie (1959) and Bannister (1979). At the same time, beyond the business community, the social implications of Lamarckian evolution became attractive to many. If organisms could adapt themselves to their environments and pass on the benefits to succeeding generations, then this model could give biological support to social interventionism, whether by educational initiatives or environmental improvement. It is not surprising, therefore, that it was its congruence with socialism that made Lamarckism attractive to so many reformers.

The strains of social evolutionary thought, whether derived from Darwinism or Lamarckism, are clearly detectable in the works of numerous geographers during the late nineteenth and early twentieth centuries (Livingstone, 1985, 1992). Ratzel's political geography, for example, with its attendant concept of the LEBENSRAUM, was grounded in the (Lamarckian) evolutionary outlook of figures such as Haeckel and Wagner (Stoddart, 1966; Bassin, 1987: see ANTHROPOGEOGRAPHY). The racialized geographies of Shaler, Gilman, Huntington, Taylor and Fleure all display various appropriations of evolutionary vocabulary. For some, as with Huntington and Taylor, climate, MIGRATION, and natural selection were the key ingredients (Livingstone, 1991) – an emphasis disclosing the geographical community's long-standing concern with questions to do with the role of acclimatization in imperial affairs (Livingstone, 1987). For others, as with Fleure, it was in the interplay of racial type, evolutionary mechanisms, anthropometric localization and psycho-social factors that was of central importance (Campbell, 1972). Again, the necessitarian cast of Mackinder's early geography *and* his later disquiet over a resigned *laissez-faire* show traces of social Lamarckism, as do the deterministic geographies of Brigham, Semple, Davis and Huntington (see ENVIRONMENTAL DETERMINISM). Socializing evolution, of course, was also to be found among geographers of a more radical outlook. Kropotkin, for instance, found in biological Lamarckism the grounds for championing collectivism, opposing Spencerian individualism, and connecting up the philosophy of natural science with ANARCHISM. Here we encounter a biologization of political categories akin to that of Patrick Geddes, who found in the same intellectual source inspiration for his planning and educational initiatives (Campbell and Livingstone, 1983).

Social evolutionary doctrines were thus used by geographers in a variety of ways: for some it was the idea of struggle that energized their geographical theorizing; for some it was a version of cultural evolution derived from anthropology that informed their writing of historical geography (Newson, 1976); for others, as Herbst (1961) puts it, 'environmental determinism . . . became the geographer's version of social Darwinism'; and for still others it was the idealist thrust of vitalistic evolution that undergirded a more possibilist outlook. Indeed, there is much to be said for the view that it was in a social evolutionary construal of the relations between nature and culture that the cognitive content of professional geography, within a specializing academy, was originally sought (Livingstone, 1992).

More recently, with the rise of sociobiology, the legitimacy of transferring biological categories to the social order has again become the subject of debate. Within the field of human geography, the issues raised by Social Darwinism are still in need of resolution. (See also HUMAN ECOLOGY.)   DNL

References

Bannister, R. C. 1979: *Social Darwinism: science and myth in Anglo-American social thought.* Philadelphia: Temple University Press.

Bassin, M. 1987: Friedrich Ratzel 1884–1904. *Geographers: Biobibliographical Studies* 11, pp. 123–32.

Bellomy, D. 1984: 'Social Darwinism' revisited. *Perspectives in American History.* n.s. 1, pp. 1–129.

Bowler, P. J. 1984: *Evolution: the history of an idea.* Berkeley, CA: University of California Press.

Burrow, J. W. 1966: *Evolution and society: a study in Victorian social theory.* Cambridge: Cambridge University Press.

Campbell, J. A. 1972: *Some sources of the humanism of H. J. Fleure.* School of Geography, University of Oxford, Research Paper No. 2.

Campbell, J. A. and Livingstone, D. N. 1983: Neo-Lamarckism and the development of geography in the United States and Great Britain. *Trans. Inst. Br. Geogr.* n.s. 8, pp. 267–94.

Greene, J. C. 1959: Biology and social theory in the nineteenth century: Auguste Comte and Herbert Spencer. In Clagett, M., ed., *Critical problems in the history of science.* Madison, WI: University of Wisconsin Press, pp. 419–46.

Greene, J. C. 1977: Darwin as a social evolutionist. *J. Hist. Biol.* 10, pp. 1–27.

Haller, M. H. 1963: *Eugenics: hereditarian attitudes in American social thought.* New Brunswick, NJ: Rutgers University Press.

Herbst, J. 1961: Social Darwinism and the history of American geography. *Proc. Am. Phil. Soc.* 105, pp. 538–44.

Hofstadter, R. 1959: *Social Darwinism in American thought,* revised edition. New York: George Braziller.

Jones, G. 1980: *Social Darwinism and English thought: the interaction between biological and social theory.* Brighton, UK: Harvester/Atlantic Highlands, NJ: Humanities Press.

Kevles, D. J. 1985: *In the name of eugenics: genetics and the uses of human heredity.* London: Penguin.

La Vergata, A. 1985: Images of Darwin: a historiographic overview. In D. Kohn, ed., *The Darwinian heritage.* Princeton, NJ: Princeton University Press, pp. 901–75.

Livingstone, D. N. 1985: Evolution, science and society: historical reflections on the geographical experiment. *Geoforum* 16, pp. 119–30.

Livingstone, D. N. 1987: Human acclimatization: perspectives on a contested field of inquiry in science, medicine and geography. *History of Science* 25, pp. 359–94.

Livingstone, D. N. 1991: The moral discourse of climate: historical considerations on race, place and virtue. *J. hist. Geogr.* 17, pp. 413–34.

Livingstone, D. N. 1992: *The geographical tradition: episodes in the history of a contested enterprise.* Oxford: Blackwell.

Mackenzie, D. 1982: *Statistics in Britain, 1865–1930: the social construction of scientific knowledge.* Edinburgh: Edinburgh University Press/New York: Columbia University Press.

Moore, J. R. 1986: Socializing Darwinism: historiography and the fortunes of a phrase. In Levidow, L., ed., *Science as politics*. London: Free Association Books, pp. 38–80.

Moore, J. R. 1991: Deconstructing Darwinism: the politics of evolution in the 1860s. *J. Hist. Biol.* 24, pp. 353–408.

Newson, L. 1976: Cultural evolution: a basic concept for human and historical geography. *J. hist. Geogr.* 2, pp. 239–55.

Shapin, S. and Barnes, B. 1979: Darwin and Social Darwinism: purity and history. In Barnes, B. and Shapin, S., eds, *Natural order: historical studies of scientific culture*. Beverly Hills, CA: Sage, pp. 125–42.

Stoddart, D. R. 1966: Darwin's impact on geography. *Ann. Ass. Am. Geogr.* 56, pp., 683–98.

Williams, R. 1973: Social Darwinism. In Benthall, J., ed., *The limits of human nature*. London: Allen Lane/New York: Dutton, pp. 115–30.

Wyllie, I. 1959: Social Darwinism and the businessman. *Proc. Am. Phil. Soc.* 103, pp. 629–35.

Suggested Reading
Bannister (1979).

Bellomy (1984).

Jones (1980).

Moore (1986).

social distance The separation of two or more social groups, by either mutual desire or discrimination by one or more against the others. Social distance is usually identified through the amount of interaction between the groups – as in rates of intermarriage: it is rarely complete (except in caste and similar societies: cf. APARTHEID) but is represented by a range of distances, from totally integrated groups at one extreme (see ASSIMILATION; INTEGRATION), to those which live almost entirely separate lives (usually within the same urban areas) at the other. The social distance between two groups is often related – both as cause and effect – to the spatial distance between them within an urban area, as argued in a classic paper by Park (1926: see CHICAGO SCHOOL): the greater the social distance between two groups the less they would be mixed together within the same residential area (see INDICES OF SEGREGATION). RJJ

Reference
Park, R. E. 1926: The urban community as a spatial pattern and a moral order. In Burgess, E. W., ed., *The urban community*. Chicago: University of Chicago Press.

social formation The specific combination of class relations, institutions and relations of social oppression within society at a particular time and place.

Whereas the MODE OF PRODUCTION specifies a society's class relations in the most general terms, identifying the central class relations involved in the production of surplus value, the concept of social formation refers to concrete forms of social relations at a specific conjuncture. It takes account of relict social relations and forms that survive and operate in later societies, as well as specific patterns of social oppression, whether based on RACE or ETHNICITY, gender or nationality (see NATIONALISM). The important question in discussions of any social formation is how these different specific experiences 'articulate' with the dominant class structure.

The concept of social formation was derived primarily by French STRUCTURALISTS, who sought to translate between the generalities of mode of production and the concreteness of everyday life (Poulantzas, 1973). 'Social formation' provides a middle-level conceptualization which aids in connecting the general economic rationale of the ACCUMULATION of CAPITAL with specific political and ideological cultural forms and relations, as well as STATE institutions.

More recently, 'social formation' has been used as a means of relating forms of consciousness to actual forms of social existence (Cosgrove, 1984). A social formation is thus similar to what Gramsci (1971) has termed an 'historic bloc'. In either usage, the idea of social formation calls attention to the need for a close material and conceptual analysis of social relations within a given place at a given time. NS

References
Cosgrove, D. E. 1984: *Social formation and symbolic landscape*. Totowa, NJ: Barnes and Noble.

Gramsci, A. 1971: *Selections from the prison notebooks* (edited and translated by Q. Hoare and G. Nowell Smith). London: Lawrence and Wishart/New York: International.

Poulantzas, N. 1973: *Political power and social classes*. London: New Left Books.

Suggested Reading

Cosgrove (1984).

Hindess, B. and Hirst, P. 1977: *Mode of production and social formation*. London: Macmillan.

social geography The study of social relations in space and the spatial structures that underpin those relations. According to some observers, social geography is suffering from an identity crisis (Cater and Jones, 1989, p. viii). The product of 1960s radicalism, social geography expanded dramatically in the 1970s until it was virtually synonymous with the whole field of human geography. Then, with the 'cultural turn' throughout the human sciences during the 1980s, social and CULTURAL GEOGRAPHY began to merge into what may now seem an even less coherent intellectual project.

Writing in the mid-1960s, the sociologist Ray Pahl declared that social geography was concerned with 'the theoretical location of social groups and social characteristics, often within an urban setting' (1965, p. 82). The emphasis on LOCATION THEORY is typical of geography's 'SPATIAL SCIENCE' phase, as also is its distinctly urban emphasis. But social geography's roots extend much deeper than this. The nineteenth-century French tradition of *la géographie humaine*, for example, is an important precursor of contemporary social geography. It represented a radical break with predominant forms of ENVIRONMENTAL DETERMINISM, reasserting the significance of HUMAN AGENCY against the claims of an all-constraining geographical environment. Similarly, there are important precedents for social geography's radical orientation in the anarchist tradition associated with Peter Kropotkin (1842–1921) and Elisee Reclus (1830–1905) (see ANARCHISM); continuities with the URBAN ECOLOGISTS of the 'CHICAGO SCHOOL'; and parallels with the development of the German 'landscape indicators' tradition.

An international perspective on social geography's disciplinary history is certainly overdue (Eyles, 1986).

Within Britain, Philo notes an early reference to social geography in a paper by G. W. Hoke concerning 'the localisation in space of . . . social phenomena' (Hoke, 1907; quoted in Philo, 1991, p. 5). That social geography's scientific agenda has rarely been divorced from its wider political context is suggested by Gilbert and Steel's (1945) confident assertion at the conclusion of the Second World War of social geography's continuing place in colonial studies. Despite passing references to the sociological aspects of geography during the 1950s, however, the real growth of social geography did not take place for another ten years.

The turbulent events of the 1960s saw the development of several new perspectives in social geography, stressing human welfare and social justice. Informed by current developments in Althusserian MARXISM and French sociology (Castells, 1977), a more politicized social geography developed rapidly. The emergence of a self-consciously HUMANISTIC GEOGRAPHY was signalled by a renewed concern with human subjectivity including an emphasis on 'understanding . . . the patterns which arise from the use social groups make of space as they see it, and . . . the processes involved in making and changing such patterns' (Jones, 1975, p. 7). For RADICAL GEOGRAPHERS, the emphasis was on spatially defined social inequalities and the analysis of 'social patterns and processes arising from the distribution of, and access to, scarce resources', where such distributions were acknowledged as being 'in large part economically determined' and governed by 'the distribution of POWER and inequality in society' (Eyles, 1975, pp. 29–30). As a result of these different pressures, social geography had become a thoroughly eclectic field by the late 1970s, encompassing a wide range of ideas, theories and empirical research including several different approaches to knowledge and understanding (Knox, 1982).

For a time in the early 1980s, social geography became rather narrowly focused on the measurement of ethnic SEGREGA-

TION, subsequently developing a more critical concern with the social construction of 'RACE' and the politics of RACISM. CLASS-based analyses of the spatial patterning of social inequality also began to be supplemented by studies of the geography of GENDER. More recently, social geography has been transformed by its encounter with social theory, including Anthony Giddens' concept of STRUCTURATION, a variety of FEMINIST perspectives and, most recently, theories of MODERNITY and POSTMODERNISM. Throughout this period, social geography has retained its emphasis on mapping and interpreting the spatial incidence of social problems, including the geographies of CRIME, HOUSING, health, EDUCATION, drug and alcohol abuse (Herbert and Smith, 1989). Rather than simply mapping spatial patterns, however, social geographers are increasingly insistent on asserting the importance of space in the constitution of social life and examining the spatial structures that underpin social relations as part of the more general reassertion of space in social theory (Soja, 1989).

A closer association between social and CULTURAL GEOGRAPHY is also taking place, with studies of the ICONOGRAPHY of LANDSCAPE and of CULTURAL POLITICS. These trends suggest that, in future, social geographers will increasingly focus on the politics of difference, examining the spatial constitution, symbolic expression and social significance of human diversity. As we begin to explore the complex ways in which RACE, CLASS and GENDER combine and intersect in specific places, at specific times, we shall also begin to explore the geographies of a range of other socially recognized groups, defined in terms of physical and mental disability, sexuality, age and generation. With its concern for the implications of human diversity, social geography will retain its critical edge, emphasizing not just how these differences are expressed in space but also how social inequalities are spatially structured. In this way, social geographers can begin to identify the weak points in various systems of oppression where resistances can be channelled most effectively and where their transformation is most likely to occur. PAJ

References

Castells, M. 1977: *The urban question*. London: Edward Arnold.

Cater, J. and Jones, T. 1989: *Social geography: an introduction to contemporary issues*. London: Edward Arnold.

Eyles, J. 1975: Social history and social geography. *Prog. Geog.* 6, pp. 27–87.

Eyles, J. ed. 1986: *Social geography: an international perspective*. London: Croom Helm.

Gilbert, E. W. and Steel, R. W. 1945: Social geography and its place in colonial studies. *Geogrl. J.* 106, 118–31.

Herbert, D. T. and Smith, D. M., eds, 1989: *Social problems and the city*, second edition. Oxford: Oxford University Press.

Jones, E., ed. 1975: *Readings in social geography*. Oxford: Oxford University Press.

Knox, P. 1982: *Urban social geography: an introduction*. London: Longman.

Pahl, R. E. 1965: Trends in social geography, in Chorley, R. J. and Haggett, P., eds, *Frontiers in geographical teaching*. London: Methuen, pp. 81–100.

Philo, C. ed. 1991: *New words, new worlds: reconceptualising social and cultural geography*. IBG Social and Cultural Geography Study Group.

Soja, E. W. 1989: *Postmodern geographies*. London: Verso.

Suggested Reading

Cater and Jones (1989).

Gregory, D. and Urry, J. eds. 1985: *Social relations and spatial structures*. London: Macmillan.

Harvey, D. 1973: *Social justice and the city*. London: Edward Arnold.

Jackson, P. and Smith, S. J. 1984: *Exploring social geography*. London: Allen and Unwin.

social indicator   See TERRITORIAL SOCIAL INDICATOR.

social justice   The distribution of society's benefits and burdens, and how this comes about. Social justice is the concern of various disciplines, in particular moral philosophy and political philosophy. The scope of the field, and the variety of perspectives adopted, is illustrated in a number of overviews; for example, by Arthur and Shaw (1991) and Kymlicka (1990, 1992). Geographical perspectives on social justice are informed by work in other disciplines, but there is also a specifically geographical interest in distribution among populations defined by the places in which they live, i.e. TERRITORIAL [social] JUSTICE.

In the first volume of his treatise on social justice, Brian Barry (1989, p. 3) states that 'a theory of social justice is a theory about the kind of social arrangements that can be defended'. While social justice is a very broad concept, attention is often focused on the distribution of income and other sources of need satisfaction on which the material conditions of a population depend. To echo Barry, it is *in*equality or *un*equal treatment that requires justification. People's common humanity and capacity for pleasure and pain is a plausible starting point for equalitarianism, with such individual differences as strength, skill, intellect, family, race or place of birth being regarded as fortuitous and hence morally irrelevant to the way in which people should be treated.

However, it does not follow that there are no grounds on which different and unequal treatment can be justified. Some people may be deemed to deserve more or less of what there is to distribute; for example, if they produce more than others or occupy positions of special responsibility. Greater or lesser contribution to the common good is often built in to the justification of unequal rewards in relation to quantity or quality of work performed. Need is another frequently invoked criterion for unequal treatment, some people being in greater need than others (e.g. for certain services).

A common point of entry into the question of what specific conditions justify unequal treatment is to try to identify an initial state of affairs which can be agreed to be just, and to argue that any outcome will be just provided that it arises from a just process. An example can be found in the libertarianism of Robert Nozick (1974). If peoples' holdings of property (such as land and natural resources) have been justly acquired, for example by settling land that belongs to no-one else or purchasing it by mutual agreement, and if they subsequently use this property justly to acquire further wealth, for example by free trade or mutually agreed employment of others,

then the distributional consequences can be justified no matter how unequal. In short, a distribution is just if it arises from a just prior distribution by just means: a process sometimes termed 'clean accumulation'. There is thus no particular pattern to which a just distribution should conform. Such an argument is sometimes used to justify the distribution generated by free-market forces, assumed to embody a just process, although the justice of the prior distribution (including how people actually acquired their property in the first place) may not be closely scrutinized.

An alternative starting point is to be found in social contract theory, the best known contribution to which is the work of John Rawls (1971). Although subject to extensive subsequent critique, Rawls' theory of justice is still extremely influential, and figures prominently in some recent texts on social justice (e.g. Barry, 1989) as well as in a persuasive attempt to sketch out a theory of human need (Doyal and Gough, 1991). The approach adopted by Rawls was to try to deduce the social contract to which people would subscribe in particular circumstances. He began with an 'original position', or 'state of nature', in which people would have to approve of institutions under a 'veil of ignorance' as to their social position; for example, whether they would belong to the rich or poor. Not knowing who, and where, they would be in society most people would be prepared to entertain only a narrow range of life chances, if any inequality at all, because they could end up among the worst off (although a few might be prepared to take the risk of ending up very poor for the sake of the chance of being very rich). Rawls' statement of principles runs as follows (Rawls, 1971, p. 302):

First Principle
Each person is to have an equal right to the most extensive total system of equal basic liberties compatible with a similar system of liberty to all.
Second Principle
Social and economic inequalities are to be arranged so that they are both:
(a) to the greatest benefit of the least advantaged, consistent with the just savings principle [required to respect the claims of future generations], and

(b) attached to offices and positions open to all under conditions of fair equality of opportunity.

The central distributional points here are that inequality can be justified, provided that society's poorest benefit from this, and that there are equal opportunities to acquire the positions of advantage. Rawls' formulation represents a strengthening of the familiar principle that contribution to the common good justifies favourable treatment: it is contribution to the well-being of the poorest that matters.

An interesting elaboration of Rawls' original theory has been provided by Peffer (1990), writing from a Marxian perspective. He departs from the position, common among Marxists, that morality and social justice are ideological constructs deployed by a ruling class to legitimate their position of privilege, in order to recover what he sees as the moral theory implicit (for the most part) in Marx's voluminous and occasionally contradictory writings. He concludes with a modification of Rawls' theory, which is claimed to entail Marx's moral principles but to be more complete and adequate. The main effect is to prioritize peoples' rights to security and subsistence, to make more specific certain liberties and opportunities which should prevail, and to further constrain the permissible degree of inequality by requiring that this should not exceed that which would seriously undermine equal worth of liberty or self-respect.

Despite the obvious significance of the subject, works which addressed social justice in geography with some rigour have been rare. By far the most influential early treatment was by Harvey (1973), who argued that a just territorial distribution of income (broadly defined) would be such that: the needs of the people of each territory would be met; resources would be allocated so as to maximize inter-territorial multiplier effects, thus rewarding contribution to national economic good; and extra resources would be allocated to help overcome special difficulties stemming from the physical and social environment, which could be considered as cases of merit. He also proposed that, in a just distribution justly arrived at, the prospects of the least advantaged territory

would be as great as possible – a clear echo from John Rawls. Smith (1977) subsequently reviewed a range of perspectives that might be applied to the task of judging distributions as better or worse.

Preoccupation with distribution characterizes much, if by no means all, of the discourse of social justice in moral philosophy as well as in geography. The implications are explained by Young (1990, p. 25) as follows:

The distributive paradigm implicitly assumes that social judgements are about what individual persons have, how much they have, and how that amount compares with what other persons have. This focus on possession tend to preclude thinking about what people are doing, according to what institutional rules, how their doings and havings are structured by institutionalized relations that constitute their positions, and how the combined effect of their doings has recursive effects on their lives.

To Young, social injustice concerns the domination and oppression of one group or groups in society by another, not merely the distributional outcomes. This involves not only formal institutions, but also the day-to-day practices whereby subordination and exclusion are realized and reproduced in the form of what is sometimes termed cultural IMPERIALISM. Democracy is central to social justice, but formal political rights conceived merely as 'one person: one vote' are not sufficient for the full democratization of society. With her mind on Rawls as well as on social reality, Young (1990, p. 16) asserts: 'Instead of a fictional contract, we require real participatory structures in which actual people, with their geographical, ethnic, gender, and occupational differences, assert their perspectives on social issues within institutions that encourage the representation of their distinct voices'.

While direct consideration of social justice in geography remained muted for much of the 1980s, interest in such issues as discrimination on grounds of RACE and GENDER raised relevant questions. However, at the beginning of the 1990s some geographers returned to the more explicit discussion of social justice. There was a call to examine moral geographies, or how people's codes of morality vary from place

565

to place, and to seek guidance from moral philosophy (Social and Cultural Geography Study Group Committee, 1991). Social change, for example in Eastern Europe and South Africa, has also provided a context for a return to issues of distributional justice (Smith, 1992a,b). Harvey (1992, 1993) has addressed the crucial question of the possibility of universal principles of social justice in a world where the relativist thinking characteristic of POSTMODERNISM tends to preclude such considerations: he makes particular use of the various forms of oppression discussed by Young (1990) as the basis for the specification of a just society. These and other relevant works, including a new book on the subject (Smith 1994), indicate that social justice is firmly back on the geographical agenda.   DMS

References

Arthur, J. and Shaw, W. H., eds 1991: *Justice and economic distribution*, second edition. Englewood Cliffs, NJ: Prentice-Hall.

Barry, B. 1989: *Theories of justice*. London: Harvester-Wheatsheaf.

Doyal, L. and Gough, I. 1991: *A theory of human need*. London: Macmillan.

Harvey, D. 1973: *Social justice and the city*. London: Edward Arnold.

Harvey, D. 1992: Social justice, postmodernism and the city. *Int. J. urban and reg. Res.* 16, pp. 588–601.

Harvey, D. 1993: Class relations, social justice, and the politics of difference. In Keith, M. and Pile, S., eds, *Place and the politics of identity*. London: Routledge.

Kymlicka, W. 1990: *Contemporary political philosophy: an introduction*. Oxford: Clarendon Press.

Kymlicka, W., ed. 1992: *Justice in Political Philosophy*, 2 volumes. Cheltenham: Edward Elgar.

Nozick, R. 1974: *Anarchy, state, and utopia*. New York: Basic Books.

Peffer, R. G. 1990: *Marxism, morality, and social justice*. Princeton, NJ: Princeton University Press.

Rawls, J. 1971: *A theory of justice*. Cambridge, MA: Harvard University Press.

Smith, D. M. 1977: *Human geography: a welfare approach*. London: Edward Arnold.

Smith, D. M., 1992a: Geography and social justice: some reflections on social change in Eastern Europe. *Geogr. Res. Forum*, 12, pp. 128–42.

Smith, D. M., 1992b: Redistribution after apartheid: who gets what where in the new South Africa. *Area* 24, pp. 350–8.

Smith, D. M., 1994: *Geography and social justice*. Oxford: Blackwell.

Social and Cultural Geography Study Group Committee 1991: De-limiting human geography: new social and cultural perspectives. In Philo, C. compiler, *New words, new worlds: reconceptualising social and cultural geography*. Lampeter, UK: Department of Geography, St David's College.

Young, I. M. 1990: *Justice and the politics of difference*. Princeton, NJ: Princeton University Press.

social movement The mobilization of people around a particular cause. According to Diani (1992, p. 13):

A social movement is a network of informal interactions between a plurality of individuals, groups and/or organizations, engaged in political or cultural conflict on the basis of a shared collective identity.

The 1960s and 1970s saw the birth of what were referred to as 'new social movements', when causes such as ENVIRONMENTALISM and feminism achieved political prominence. Some analysts argued that such mobilization was possible because the relative affluence of the 'advanced industrial countries' had resolved the problems of production and distribution, and had released political energies to focus on non-material issues. Within those countries, it was the affluent middle classes that were especially attracted to the movements (Inglehart, 1977). With the later recession in the world-economy, support for the movements should have declined (Inglehart, 1981), but many – including environmentalism and feminism – have remained high on political agenda. (See also CLEAVAGE; URBAN SOCIAL MOVEMENT.)   RJJ

References

Diani, M. 1992: The concept of social movement. *Soc. Rev.* 40, pp. 1–25.

Inglehart, R. 1977: *The silent revolution*. Princeton, NJ: Princeton University Press.

Inglehart, R. 1981: Post-materialism in an environment of insecurity. *Am. pol. Sc. Rev.* 75, pp. 880–99.

Suggested Reading

Lowe, S. 1986: *Urban social movements*. London: Macmillan.

social network The kin, neighbours and friends to whom an individual is tied socially, usually by shared values, attitudes and aspirations. Such networks may be spatially concentrated, as both cause and effect: members choose to live in the same place as others in their network, thereby maximizing the potential for contact and interaction; and people enter networks with their neighbours, reflecting the influence of DISTANCE DECAY on social interaction. (See also COMMUNITY.)   RJJ

Suggested Reading

Ley, D. 1983: *A social geography of the city*. New York: Harper and Row.

social physics An approach which suggests that aggregate human interaction over space can be explained and predicted using physical theories and laws. Implicit within such a view is theoretical monism, one where a single explanatory principle holds for both physical and social processes alike.

H. C. Carey (1858) first codified social physics when he proposed that use be made '. . . of the great law of molecular gravitation as the *indispensable* condition of . . . man [*sic*]', a suggestion that was subsequently empirically supported by E. G. Ravenstein's (1885) early work on MIGRATION. W. J. Reilly (1931) presented the first mathematical formulations in his study of retail trade areas (see REILLY'S LAW), but it was primarily J. Q. Stewart (1950), professor of astronomy and physics at Princeton University, who systematically worked through the analogy between interacting particles and interacting humans. During the late 1950s, Stewart, along with W. Warntz (1965), prosecuted social physics under the rubric of MACROGEOGRAPHY, a short-lived movement but one that paved the way for the subsequent success of scientism within human geography (exemplified by the QUANTITATIVE REVOLUTION and REGIONAL SCIENCE).

The GRAVITY MODEL remains the best exemplar of social physics. Drawing the analogy with Newton's law of gravitation, it is assumed that humans interact over space as heavenly bodies do in the celestial system. In this formulation, interaction between places is directly proportional to the product of their masses (usually measured by population size) and inversely proportional to some function of the distance between them. The gravity model, along with other social physical analogies such as potential, DIFFUSION and ENTROPY-MAXIMIZATION models, have been extensively tested. They often give good empirical fits, but are less satisfactory in their predictions – and even worse in providing explanations.

This lack of explanatory purchase, as Lukermann (1958) pointed out in a early critique of social physics, is because the assumptions made in the physical models are not met in the human realm: 'the lacuna is of the order of two worlds' (Lukerman, 1958, p. 2). There is nothing wrong with analogies *per se*, but for them to succeed there must be certain core similarities between the analogy and the analogized. However, for many critics of social physics the similarities between human and celestial movements are not just hard to find – they are simply not there to be found.   TJB

References

Carey, H. C. 1858: *Principles of social science*. Philadelphia: J. B. Lippincott.

Lukermann, F. 1958: Towards a more geographic economic geography. *Prof. Geogr.* 10, pp. 2–10.

Ravenstein, E. G. 1885: The laws of migration. *J. R. Statist. Soc.* 48, pp. 167–235.

Reilly, W. J. 1931: *The law of retail gravitation*. New York: W. J. Reiley.

Stewart, J. Q. 1950: The development of social physics. *American Journal of Physics* 18, pp. 239–53.

Warntz, W. 1965: *Macrogeography and income fronts*. Philadelphia, PA: Regional Science Research Institute.

Suggested Reading

Barnes, T. J. 1991: Conversations and metaphors in economic geography: Richard Rorty and the gravity model. *Geogr. Annlr. B* 73, pp. 111–20.

Lukermann, F. and Porter, P. W. 1960: Gravity and potential model in economic geography. *Ann. Ass. Am. Geogr.* 50, pp. 493–504.

Stewart (1950).

social reproduction Reproduction both of the social relations within which, and the material means by which, social life is premised (see ECONOMIC GEOGRAPHY; SOCIETY). Under CAPITALISM, for example, it involves not only the reproduction of the relations and forces of production but also the sustenance and development of hegemonic dominance (see HEGEMONY) and of the IDEOLOGIES which enable such sustenance. Subsumed within such a definition is biological reproduction. The existence and social significance of any distinction between these two notions of reproduction have been debated within FEMINIST GEOGRAPHY.

Without social reproduction, conflict may result, investment may be disrupted and DEVELOPMENT may be halted or reversed (see CRISIS; UNDERDEVELOPMENT). At the limit of the failure of social reproduction – a failure which is normally induced by social action, but rarely, if ever, without unintended consequences – social revolution occurs. The collapse of communism and the tortuous process of rebuilding societies in Eastern Europe and the former Soviet Union at the end of the 1980s and through the 1990s provides an example of the complexity of social reproduction and the causes of its breakdown as revealed in the consequences of its failure.
RL

social space Space as it is perceived and used by social groups. (Space as perceived and used by individuals is usually termed *personal space*.) As introduced by Buttimer (1969), the term closely approximated the definitions of both COMMUNITY and NATURAL AREA: a portion of an urban residential mosaic occupied by a homogeneous group whose members are identifiable not only by their socio-economic and demographic characteristics but also by their shared values and attitudes, leading to common behaviour patterns. Such spaces are defined and given meaning by the group, however, and so are

not readily identified from quantitative indicators alone, such as those used in SOCIAL AREA ANALYSES. (See also TERRITORIALITY; TERRITORY.)
RJJ

Reference

Buttimer, A. 1969: Social space in interdisciplinary perspective. *Geogrl. Rev.* 59, pp. 417–26.

social theory See CRITICAL THEORY; ETHNOMETHODOLOGY; EXISTENTIALISM; HISTORICAL MATERIALISM; HUMAN AGENCY; IDEALISM; PHENOMENOLOGY; PRAGMATISM; REALISM; STRUCTURAL FUNCTIONALISM; STRUCTURALISM; STRUCTURATION THEORY; SYMBOLIC INTERACTIONISM.

social well-being The degree to which the needs and wants of a population are being met. A well society is one in which all people have sufficient income to meet their basic needs, for example, where all are treated with equal dignity and have equal rights, where they have reasonable access to their needed range of services, and where their opinions are heard and respected. The quality of a society can be measured by its success on variables reflecting such desiderata, as can variations within a society.

Mapping the geography of social well-being was taken up in the 1970s, as part of a general acceptance of the need for TERRITORIAL SOCIAL INDICATORS with which to chart and understand spatial variations in the quality of life.
RJJ

Suggested Reading

Smith, D. M. 1973: *A geography of social well-being in the United States.* New York: McGraw-Hill.

socialism A term which refers to a body of writings, ideas and beliefs on social justice and EQUALITY which, in its most generally understood form, envisages a social system based on common ownership of the means of production and distribution. In communist writings, it is considered as a necessary precondition to achieving full COMMUNISM, from which it is also generally distinguished by an emphasis on the difference between common and STATE ownership. In many other socialist, writings, however, socialism is regarded as a system in which only a significant amount of the means of production is owned and run by the state.

As a response to nineteenth-century industrial CAPITALISM, nineteenth-century socialism encompassed a number of different socialist movements, the most important being utopian socialism, Marxian socialism and democratic socialism. All three share the following characteristics: (a) each contained an economic and social–humanist critique of the social and territorial injustices of the capitalism of its time; (b) each had a comprehensive and integrated programme based on a better organized and more just society; and (c) each was to change the human geography of state activity. But there are also vital differences between them.

Utopian socialists saw the self-contained small community as the ideal form for future society, based on the principle of co-operation. Land was to come under public ownership, while the daily economic and social life of the community was to be part of a well-planned and human distributive system in which basic needs would be met by the collective. Some utopians expressed in their ideas a yearning for the vanished past of rural life, while few had much faith in an impersonal urban society based on materialism and competition. Many of these ideas found expression in the communities founded by the early-nineteenth-century social reformer, Robert Owen, and in the later GARDEN CITY movement (see also KIBBUTZ).

Marxian socialism, however, saw such ideas as unrealizable and unscientific because they were not rooted in the historical realities of CLASS struggle and the structural necessities of capitalist production. According to Marx, social reforms cannot change the nature of society and the systems of property relations, for nothing short of an urban proletarian-led revolution could eradicate social injustices and the obstacles to the further development of productive forces (see MARXIAN ECONOMICS). It was only on the basis of collective ownership of the means of production, and through CENTRAL PLANNING, that town–country and other CLASS-based inequalities would be resolved. In contrast, *democratic socialists* contended that revolution was unnecessary, and that socialism could be achieved through the ballot box. For them, the bourgeois state of turn-of-the-century Great Britain and Germany did aid economic progress and had initiated social-welfare programmes for workers (see WELFARE STATE). On this basis, it was believed that democratic socialism could build and prosper through essentially reformist measures. Many of today's democratic socialists would argue that the experiences of post-1945 parliamentary industrial societies show that their path was right and Marx was wrong, for government could reform capitalism and was not simply the agent of a capitalist ruling class – as instrumental theories of the state contend: nor are all capitalist states the same, and politics simply an instrument of the prevailing mode of production.

State socialism is a term popularized in the West to describe societies the dominant values of which are those of Marxism–Leninism, with a character of society based on the determining influence of class forces operating through the laws of historical and dialectical materialism (cf. HISTORICAL MATERIALISM). The dominant institution is the Communist Party, the territorial power of which is assured through state control of the means of production. Central planning is also an important hallmark of state socialism. To varying degrees, such societies set themselves the task of ensuring that differences between town and country, state and collective forms of property, types of labour and ethnoregional distinctions would be overcome if not eradicated. However, the inability of modern-day state socialism to deliver living standards comparable to those offered by advanced capitalist societies, and to secure social justice and liberties for its peoples, led to popular revolutions between 1989 and 1991 throughout Eastern Europe and the former Soviet Union, a process also precipitated, at least initially, by the end of the Cold War. Rejection of state socialism has led to an acceptance of the market as the alternative to ensuring economic growth and the struggle for reincorporation into the capitalist world economy. GES

Suggested Reading
Bradshaw, M., ed. 1991: *The Soviet Union: a new regional geography?* London: Belhaven.
Callinicos, A. 1991: *The revenge of history: Marxism and the East European revolutions.* Oxford: Polity Press.
Forbes, D. and Thrift, N. 1987: *The socialist Third World: urban development and territorial planning.* Oxford: Blackwell.
Hankiss, E. 1980: *East European alternatives.* Oxford: Clarendon Press.
Linge, G. and Forbes, D. 1990: *China's spatial economy: recent developments and reforms.* Oxford: Oxford University Press.
Smith, G. E. 1989: *Planned development in the socialist world.* Cambridge: Cambridge University Press.
Smith, G. E. 1989: Privilege and place in Soviet society. In Gregory, D. and Walford, R., eds, *Horizons in human geography.* London: Macmillan, pp. 320–40.

societies See GEOGRAPHICAL SOCIETIES.

society Society is both a cluster of socially constructed institutions, relationships and forms of conduct that are reproduced and reconstructed across time and space, and the conditions under which such phenomena are formed. The stress here upon relationships, institutions and conduct underlines the point that societies are far more than the individuals which comprise them, but it does not imply that they are unitary totalities.

At least three levels of meaning may be ascribed to society: (a) human (or non-human) society in general; (b) historically distinct types of society – such as feudal society (see FEUDALISM), capitalist society (see CAPITALISM) – defined in terms of a particular set of social relations of production; and (c) particular instances of society, such as British society, Arabian society and Christian society. The relationship between these meanings is problematic and highly complex. (The notion of society as a particular interest group, e.g. the Royal Geographical Society, is not considered here.)

Human life is necessarily social in organization, if only for the most basic reason that it could not be reproduced outside society (Lee, 1989). Equally, human life is necessarily part of nature, and NATURE and society are conjoined in the LABOUR PROCESS (Gregory, 1978). But material production is rarely merely instinctive. It cannot somehow pre-date systems of meaning or significance. Systems of meaning direct and endow significance upon material practice. Even in the most desperate circumstances of material deprivation, human beings respond emotionally as well as physiologically to their plight, and try to make sense of, or protest at the nonsense of, their predicament. Social being certainly determines consciousness, but whether material production determines social being is another matter altogether (see ECONOMIC GEOGRAPHY).

Society is always in a process of becoming as a result of the conscious actions of human beings. Indeed, the term SOCIAL FORMATION carries with it the notion that society is an ever-changing process. Human actions are informed by society itself, by the understandings held of society and by the relationships between society and its knowledgeable participants. This means that the study of society cannot be reduced to the simplicities of natural or physical science. We cannot divorce subject and object, and alternative societies are always possible if we choose to construct them.

Human beings create societies at the same time as they are created by them, and they are knowledgeable participants in this double process of creation (see STRUCTURATION THEORY). Indeed, Godelier (1986, p. 1) argues that

human beings, in contrast to other social animals, do not just live in society, they *produce society in order to live.* In the course of their existence, they invent new ways of thinking and acting – both upon themselves and upon the nature which surrounds them. They therefore produce culture and create history . . . [italics in original]

and he should have added that the production of CULTURE and history is predicated upon the making of geography as an essential condition of human existence.

An alternative view (Mann, 1986, p. 14) of the relationship between people and society is that while human beings 'need to enter into social power relations, . . . they do not need social totalities'. Here the very notion of society as 'a bounded and patterned social totality' is questioned while, at the same time, the inherent sociability of human beings is acknowledged in the recognition of the inherency of social relations (Lee, 1989). Mann (1986, p. 5) describes the relationship between people and society thus:

Human goals require both intervention in nature – a material life in the widest sense – and social cooperation. It is difficult to imagine any of our pursuits or satisfactions occurring without these. Thus the characteristics of nature and the characteristics of social relations become relevant to, and may indeed structure, motivations. They have *emergent* properties of their own.

In their rejection of determinist and essentialist forms of analysis, Resnick and Wolff (1987) also shy away from the idea of a patterned social totality. Instead, they stress the multiple determinations involved in the complex of interactions between natural, economic, political and cultural processes, each of which may be subdivided into what they call class (production, appropriation and distribution of surplus production) and the wide (almost limitless) range of non-class processes (e.g. commodity exchange, friendship and social intercourse).

However, it would be a profound mistake to conclude from such arguments that human beings are not influenced in a quite fundamental fashion by the societies into which they are born and in which they live. Norms and VALUES, direction and purpose are social constructs, and the social relations which articulate such contrasts and enable individuals to engage with them, are inescapable for human involvement in society, even if they become nothing other than the object of opposition.

The systems of meanings to which people refer help to define the society to which they, in practice, belong. In one sense, societies are the means and the consequence of communication between human subjects. The breakdown of communication signals the breakdown of society in time and space, and so offers one means of defining particular societies. However, it follows that no pure form of society can exist, and that no clear social boundaries based upon a particular set of criteria may, realistically, be drawn (see TIME–SPACE DISTANCIATION).

Even societies defined in terms of production relations never exist in a pure state. They are always mixed with other forms of social relations (see SOCIAL FORMATION). And even within, say, capitalist societies there is great scope for cultural, political, moral and ideological differentiation. The struggle for HEGEMONY is, therefore, a fundamental driving force in human society. An alternative interpretation which assumes social determination and closure and treats society as a SYSTEM with clearly defined boundaries is associated with the writings of Talcott Parsons (see FUNCTIONALISM; STRUCTURAL FUNCTIONALISM).

Distinctions may be drawn between economy, state and society. The intention of so doing is to try to separate the idea of an association of free individuals from the coercion of economic imperatives or state power. Urry (1981), for example, refers to 'CIVIL SOCIETY', and defines it as 'that set of social practices outside the relations and forces of production in which agents are both constituted as subjects and which presuppose the actions of such subjects' in struggling to sustain their conditions of existence. This is a helpful concept because it recognizes the interdependence but extreme variability of social practices which both make up and transform society (Bauman, 1991).

Society remains a contested concept. Some fear the implication that to admit to society means to accept a form of social determinism, or at least the denial of individual responsibility in the making of geography and history. Others object to the possibility that society implies a form of totalizing discourse taking place, somehow, behind the backs of knowing subjects. As an example, Jackson (1989, p. 18) notes that Carl Sauer adopted a super-organic approach to culture which asserts that 'culture is an entity at a higher level than the individual, that it is governed by a logic of its own and that it actively constrains human behaviour'. Such an approach 'severely limits the questions that may be asked', as the answer is offered before the question is posed. Paradoxically, NEO-CLASSICAL ECONOMICS, that most asocial of social theories, makes massive assumptions about the sociability of people – communication is assumed to be perfect, instantaneous and unproblematic in the market economy. If ever there was a totalizing discourse which limits questioning, it is this doctrine so beloved of liberal champions of individual freedom.   RL

References

Bauman, Z. 1991: *Intimations of postmodernity.* London: Routledge.

Godelier, M. 1986: *The mental and the material.* London: Verso.

Gregory, D. 1978: *Ideology, science and human geography.* London: Hutchinson.

Jackson, P. 1989: *Maps of meaning.* London: Unwin Hyman.

Lee, R. 1989: Social relations and the geography of material life. In Gregory, D. and Walford, R., eds, *Horizons in human geography,* London: Macmillan/New York: St. Martin's Press, pp. 152–69.

Mann, M. 1986: *The sources of social power,* volume I, *A history of power from the beginning to A.D. 1760.* Cambridge: Cambridge University Press.

Resnick, S. A. and Wolff, R. D. 1987: *Knowledge and class: a Marxian critique of political economy.* Chicago: University of Chicago Press.

Urry, J. 1981: *The anatomy of capitalist societies.* London: Macmillan/Atlantic Highlands, NJ: Humanities Press.

Suggested Reading

Giddens, A. 1982: *Sociology: a brief but critical introduction.* London: Macmillan/New York: Harcourt Brace Jovanovich, ch. 1.

Giddens, A. 1989: *Sociology.* Oxford: Polity Press, ch. 2.

sovereignty A condition of final and absolute authority in a political community. In the modern world it is invested in the STATE, with its authority over the land and people in its TERRITORY. In a federal state sovereignty is divided, as specified in the constitution, between two territorial levels of state (see FEDERALISM).

The emergence of states based upon territorial sovereignty created an inter-state system, first in Europe and then worldwide, that is at the heart of POLITICAL GEO-GRAPHY (Taylor, 1989). This sovereignty implies two political processes. First, the happenings within the territory of a state are its formal exclusive concern: interference in the internal affairs of another country is usually viewed as the first offence of international law. Second, sovereignty cannot be simply proclaimed: it has to be reciprocated by other states. As such it acts as the ground rule for international relations, by defining who is and who is not a member of the inter-state system. For instance, the creation of black 'states' as part of South Africa's APART-HEID system failed to produce sovereign states, since no other state recognized the black political units as members of the inter-state system. Since 1945 the main way in which new states have confirmed their sovereignty has been by joining the United Nations.

Although an integral part of international law for providing an order to international relations, in practice state sovereignty has been a source of CONFLICT. Unlike earlier polities and their FRONTIERS, sovereign states are precisely delimited by BOUNDARIES. Disputes over boundaries have been the major cause of wars in the inter-state system since its firm establishment by the Treaty of Westphalia in 1648. Originally, such territorial claims by one state on another were mainly dynastic or simply opportunistic in character, but contemporary claims are usually based upon either historical–cultural arguments (national self-determination, e.g. Serbian claims on Croatian territory) or spatial integrity or proximity (e.g. Argentinian claims to the British colony of Malvinas/Falkland Islands) (Burghardt, 1973; Murphy, 1990).

Contemporary conflicts over claims to sovereignty are by no means limited to surface land areas. Theoretically, a state's sovereignty extends downwards to the centre of the Earth, defining a cone in which the state has claim to all subterranean resources. Similarly, sovereignty extends upwards, as a 1919 convention gave states the right to prevent their territory being overflown. The problem is defining the upper limit of this sovereignty; established practice is that the limit is defined by the operational ceiling of conventional aircraft, leaving everything above this level – satellites, for instance – free from sovereignty restrictions (therefore spy satellites are legal, spy planes are not).

Another important contemporary sovereignty conflict has concerned the extension of the sovereignty of coastal states over their adjacent seas (see LAW OF THE SEA). Originally a state's 'territorial waters' in which it claimed sovereignty were defined by security needs in terms of the threat of naval bombardment (a strip of water between the coast and a line 3 nautical miles or 5 km from the coast). State claims on the economic resources of the sea and sea bed beyond this distance led to the United Nations Conferences on the Law of the Sea, the third of which produced a new comprehensive convention in 1982 (Glassner, 1986). Territorial waters have been extended to 12 nautical miles (22 km), and a new exclusive economic zone of 200 nautical miles (370 km) has been established for each coastal state. In the latter zone states have the right to fishing and all seabed resources. Although now operating in practice, the new law of the sea is not universally accepted, the USA in particular refusing to ratify the 1982 agreements. PJT

References

Burghardt, A. F. 1973: The bases of territorial claims. *Geogrl. Rev.* 63, pp. 225–45.

Glassner, M. I., ed. 1986: Special issue: the new political geography of the law of the sea. *Pol. Geogr. Q* 5, pp. 5–72.

Murphy, A. B. 1990: Historical justifications of for territorial claims. *Ann. Ass. Am. Geogr.* 80, pp. 531–48.

Taylor, P. J. 1989: *Political geography: world-economy, nation–state and locality.* London: Longman.

Suggested Reading

Hinsley, F. A. 1986: *Sovereignty.* London: Watts.

James, A. 1984: Sovereignty: ground rule or gibberish? *Rev. int. Stud.* 10, pp. 1–18.

space Human geography has used absolute, relative and relational concepts of space.

Although Richard Hartshorne's seminal inquiry into *The nature of geography* (1939) concluded that geography should be defined as CHOROLOGY rather than as the 'science of distributions' and that studies in LOCATION THEORY required 'more training in economics than geography', conceptions of space nevertheless had a fundamental function in his thesis (see also Hartshorne, 1958). Indeed, it can be argued that his vision of geography as a 'correlative discipline' using map comparisons to disclose 'the functional integration of phenomena' over space prepared the way for the development of a formal SPATIAL SCIENCE (see REGIONAL GEOGRAPHY). But it was only in the late 1940s and early 1950s that conceptions of space became 'a recognizable tradition of inquiry' in modern geography (Pooler, 1977), when Schaefer objected to the manifest EXCEPTIONALISM of the Hartshornian tradition and declared that 'spatial relations are the ones that matter in geography and no others' (Schaefer, 1953).

Whittlesey (in James and Jones, 1954) proposed space as 'the basic organizing concept of the geographer', but this solved nothing; as Blaut (1961) was quick to point out, 'space is a treacherous philosophical word' and is certainly not a unitary concept. He distinguished *absolute* conceptions of space, in which space is 'a distinct, physical and eminently real or empirical entity in itself' and *relative* conceptions of space, in which space is 'merely a relation between events or an aspect of events, and thus bound to time and process'. The whole purpose of this distinction – itself of considerable significance to the development of general theorems of spatial organization, because 'if geography is to generalize it must be able to replicate cases and it has to use relative space' (Chapman, 1977) – was to attack another one. Blaut insisted that 'the distinction between spatial structure and process is essentially Kantian' (see KANTIANISM) and that it depends on an absolute conception of space, whereas in reality the two ought to be regarded as inseparable: 'structures of the real world are simply slow processes of long duration'. This was a significant challenge to those who, in the wake of the exchanges between Hartshorne and Schaefer, treated geography in essentially morphological terms (see especially Bunge, 1962) and perpetuated what Sack (1974) later identified, with splendid irony, as 'the spatial separatist theme' (see SPATIAL SEPARATISM). In fact several commentators had already noted that geography could not be reduced to geometry (see, e.g., Harris, 1971), and Sack himself observed that 'the usefulness of a geometry of location is not a matter of principle but of fact; for the physical sciences, and for the purely physical processes studied by geographers, the geometry of location is also the geometry of explanation', but 'the facts concerning the usefulness of the geometric properties of this space for the explanation of human behavior are not at all clear' (see DIFFUSION; DISTANCE DECAY). And it was at about this time that advances in the methods of SPATIAL ANALYSIS began to be disassociated from the models of spatial organization: many of the techniques provided for PATTERN recognition and eventually for SPACE–TIME FORECASTING and, as Gould (1970) had realized, these regularities were formally equivalent to AUTOCORRELATION structures; but any explanation of these structures had to be couched in non-geometric terms (see PROCESS). (Several geographers have noted that this entailed a move from POSITIVISM to REALISM; see, e.g., Johnston, 1980.) As Moss (1970) wrote:

Geometrical relationships must be assigned economic, social, physical or biological meaning before they can in any sense become explanatory . . . . Though geometries may be important tools in geographical study and research, they cannot be a source of theory since their analogy with geographical phenomena is simply through particular logical structures and not through explanatory deduction (p. 27).

To be sure, these logical structures are social constructions too, and Sack himself has provided an illuminating survey of *Conceptions of space in social thought* (1980); but the point, in the words of Harvey (1973), is that:

the problem of the poorer conceptualization of space is resolved through human practice with respect to it. In other words, there are no philosophical answers to philosophical questions that arise over the nature of space – the answers lie in human practice. The question 'what is space?' is therefore replaced by the question 'how is it that different human practices create and make use of distinctive conceptualizations of space?' (pp. 13–14).

This necessitates what Harvey calls a *relational* view of space, in which space is contained in objects in the sense that an object can be said to exist only insofar as it contains and represents within itself relationships to other objects. But to Schatzki (1991) such a formulation conflates two ONTOLOGIES which need to be distinguished: *objective space* and *social space*. In his view, any attempt to explore the social production of space and SPATIALITY needs to be grounded not in 'objects in space' ('objective space') but in the opening and occupation of sites for human existence within which social practice can *take* place ('social space'). By no means all of those interested in the PRODUCTION OF SPACE would accept Schatzki's Heideggerian reading, and many of them remain much closer to MARXISM (see Smith, 1984; Lefebvre, 1991). But, in any event, the analysis of social space has come to focus less on its abstract geometries and more on the relations of CLASS, RACE and GENDER which are inscribed in (and in part constituted through) its places, regions and landscapes (Gregory and Urry, 1985; Thrift and Williams, 1987; Gregory, 1993). In this sense, spatial analysis has indeed become social analysis, and vice versa. DG

References

Blaut, J. 1961: Space and process. *Prof. Geogr.* 13, pp. 1–7.

Bunge, W. 1962: *Theoretical geography*. Lund: C. W. K. Gleerup.

Chapman, G. P. 1977: *Human and environmental systems: a geographer's appraisal*. London: Academic Press.

Gould, P. 1970: Is *statistix inferens* the geographical name for a wild goose? *Econ. Geogr.* 46, pp. 439–48.

Gregory, D. 1993: *Geographical imaginations*. Oxford: Blackwell.

Gregory, D. and Urry, J., eds 1985: *Social relations and spatial structures*. London: Macmillan.

Harris, R. C. 1971: Theory and synthesis in historical geography. *Can. Geogr.* 15, pp. 157–72.

Hartshorne, R. 1939: *The nature of geography: a critical survey of current thought in the light of the past*. Lancaster, PA: Association of American Geographers.

Hartshorne, R. 1958: The concept of geography as a science of space, from Kant and Humboldt to Hettner. *Ann. Ass. Am. Geogr.* 48, pp. 97–108.

Harvey, D. 1973: *Social justice and the city*. London: Edward Arnold/Baltimore, MD: Johns Hopkins University Press.

James, P. E. and Jones, C. F., eds 1954: *American geography: inventory and prospect*. Syracuse, NY: Syracuse University Press.

Johnston, R. J. 1980: On the nature of explanation in human geography. *Trans. Inst. Br. Geogr.* n.s. 5, pp. 402–12.

Lefebvre, H. 1991: *The production of space*. Oxford: Blackwell.

Moss, R. P. 1970: Authority and charisma: criteria of validity in geographical method. *S. Afr. geogr. J.* 52, pp. 13–37.

Pooler, J. A. 1977: The origins of the spatial tradition in geography: an interpretation. *Ont. Geogr.* 11, pp. 56–83.

Sack, R. D. 1974: The spatial separatist theme in geography. *Econ. Geogr.* 50, pp. 1–19.

Sack, R. D. 1980: *Conceptions of space in social thought*. London: Macmillan/Minneapolis: University of Minnesota Press.

Schaefer, F. K. 1953: Exceptionalism in geography: a methodological examination. *Ann. Ass. Am. Geogr.* 43, pp. 226–49.

Schatzki, T. 1991: Spatial ontology and explanation. *Ann. Ass. Am. Geogr.* 81, pp. 650–70.

Smith, N. 1984: *Uneven development: nature, capital and the production of space*. Oxford: Blackwell.

Thrift, N. and Williams, P., eds 1987: *Class and space*. London: Routledge.

Suggested Reading

Harvey, D. 1969: *Explanation in geography*. London: Edward Arnold/New York: St. Martin's Press, ch. 14.

Harvey (1973), ch. 1 (see also introduction).

Lefebvre (1991).

Schatzki (1991).

Smith (1984), ch. 3.

space cost curve A plot of spatial variations in production cost along one distance dimension; in other words, a section through a cost SURFACE (see the figure illustrating SPATIAL MARGIN). This is the spatial analogy of the COST CURVE of conventional production theory in economics, which depicts the relationship between the cost of production and the volume of output. The space cost curve can portray single-input costs or total costs at a given scale. The form of the space cost curve – whether it is steep or shallow – can give some indication as to the degree of restriction likely to be imposed on locational choice if plant viability is to be achieved. (See also VARIABLE COST ANALYSIS.)   DMS

space revenue curve A plot of the revenue to be earned from a given volume of sales, in one distance dimension (i.e. a section through a REVENUE SURFACE; see the figure illustrating SPATIAL MARGIN). These are very difficult to identify empirically, but evidence or speculation as to their likely form can give a clue to the extent to which revenue, demand or market considerations are likely to impose constraints on locational choice. (See also VARIABLE REVENUE ANALYSIS.)   DMS

space-economy The SPATIAL STRUCTURE of an economy. The term is used to describe economic 'landscapes' at various scales, and geographers typically distinguish between the regional, national and international space-economy (see SCALE). These may be located and described in detail ('the space-economy of southern Ontario'); they may be thematized and stylized ('the space-economy of capitalism'); or they may be purely hypothetical ('the Löschian space-economy'). But they are all underwritten by theoretical assumptions.

Early usages represented the space-economy as the object of LOCATION THEORY; they were couched within the framework of NEOCLASSICAL ECONOMICS, and treated the space-economy as 'the spatial pattern of economic activities' which corresponds to a particular configuration of resources and to particular production

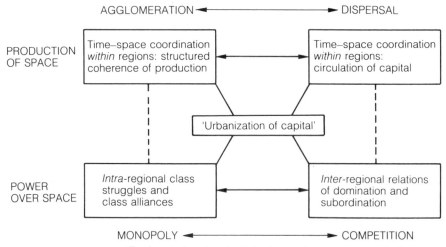

AGGLOMERATION ←——————————————→ DISPERSAL

PRODUCTION OF SPACE

| Time–space coordination *within* regions: structured coherence of production | ←——→ | Time–space coordination *within* regions: circulation of capital |

'Urbanization of capital'

POWER OVER SPACE

| *Intra*-regional class struggles and class alliances | ←——→ | *Inter*-regional relations of domination and subordination |

MONOPOLY ←——————————————→ COMPETITION

space economy *Fundamental tensions in the landscape of contemporary capitalism*

and transfer technologies. Because of its connections with general equilibrium theory (drawing on the pioneering work of Lösch), the original concept was a functionalist one (see FUNCTIONALISM) which could be treated in systems terms: 'not only are the mutual relations and interdependence of all economic elements, both in the aggregate and atomistically, of fundamental importance; but the spatial as well as the temporal (dynamic) character of the interrelated processes must enter the picture' (Isard, 1956). Hence for Isard a theory of the space-economy had to address 'the total spatial array of economic activities, with attention paid to the geographic distribution of inputs and outputs and the geographic variations in prices and costs'.

The concept was reformulated with the emergence of a critique drawn from Marxism: the autonomy of location theory was challenged and its interest in spatial organization integrated into a wider POLITICAL ECONOMY of CAPITALISM. Two main definitions were offered. One was drawn from STRUCTURAL MARXISM and identified different 'space–times' with the different economic, political and cultural-ideological levels of the SOCIAL FORMATION. For Lipietz (1977), for example, the space-economy was 'the material form of existence of the socio-economic relations which structure social formations', a formulation which drew attention to the hypothesized *determination* of an economy

within contemporary capitalism: the space-economy had a 'matrix role' within the social formation (see SPATIALITY). The other definition was drawn more specifically from MARXIAN ECONOMICS and theorized the capitalist space-economy as a landscape of capital accumulation and circulation. Harvey (1982, 1985) has argued that this landscape is riven by a fundamental contradiction between fixity and mobility – between agglomeration in place and dispersal over space – which is implicated in the constitution of CLASS alliances (see REGIONAL ALLIANCE) which are themselves caught between 'the stagnant swamp of monopoly controls fashioned out of the geopolitics of domination' and 'the fires of open and escalating competition with others' (see the figure). Harvey's claims have been given a substantially more analytical treatment by Sheppard and Barnes (1990), who focus on the connections between the location of economic activities, the production and circulation of commodities, and the dynamics of class formation and struggle over space.

DG

References

Harvey, D. 1982: *The limits to capital*. Oxford: Blackwell.

Harvey, D. 1985: *The urbanization of capital*. Oxford: Blackwell.

Isard, W. 1956: *Location and space-economy*. Cambridge, MA: MIT Press.

Lipietz, A. 1977: *Le capital et son espace*. Paris: Maspero.

Sheppard, E. and Barnes, T. 1990: *The capitalist space-economy: geographical analysis after Ricardo, Marx and Sraffa*. London: Unwin Hyman.

Suggested Reading
Harvey (1965), ch. 2.
Sheppard and Barnes (1990).

space–time forecasting models

Statistical models that attempt to forecast the evolution of variables over both time and space (sets of regions). These models are of the general REGRESSION form, and they forecast the value of a variable and an observation-unit in terms of (a) its own past values, (b) lagged spatial DIFFUSION effects, and (c) lagged exogenous or explanatory variables. The simplest form is (a), where a variable (such as population) in region j at time t is predicted by regression on its own earlier values (the 'autoregressive', or memory, effect) and also by its delayed response to the impact of random shocks e_{jt}, e_{jt-1} and e_{jt-2} (the moving average coefficients b_1 and b_2):

$$p_{jt} = a_1 p_{jt-1} + a_2 p_{jt-2} + e_{jt} + b_1 e_{jt-1} + b_2 e_{jt-2}.$$

This is the well-known time-series autoregressive-moving average (or ARMA) model. It is a 'black box' model in that it does not explain the population changes causally, but models and extrapolates them statistically. Such models can have quite good short-term forecasting ability.

Space–time forecasting models extend the single-region ARMA model to include (b), spatial diffusion between regions, so that p_{jt} is also dependent on population changes in nearby regions and hence trends in population change diffuse across the map. Defining the average (or weighted average) of population for regions adjacent to region j at time t as Lp_{jt}, the space–time ARMA model (STARMA) can be written (using only one-lag terms) as:

$$p_{jt} = a_1 p_{jt-1} + c_1 Lp_{jt-1} + e_{jt} + b_1 e_{jt-1} + d_1 Le_{jt-1}.$$

The final term allows random shocks to spill over between regions also. DISTANCE DECAY can also be built into the definition of weights L. The STARMA model is still a black box model, and the introduction of

(c), lagged exogenous variables (such as employment opportunities, *EMP*), is essential for a causal model:

$$p_{jt} = a_1 p_{jt-1} + c_1 Lp_{jt-1} + f_1 EMP_{jt-1} + g_1 LEMP_{jt-1} + \dots .$$

The exogenous variable *EMP* then has to be itself extrapolated (which is possible by STARMA) before population can be forecast more than one period ahead. However, STARMA models have not proved as useful as first hoped, mainly because of their purely black box structure, and modellers have found form (c) the most relevant, allowing conditional forecasts to be made based on different assumptions about the exogenous variables. LWH

Suggested Reading
Bennett, R. J. 1979: *Spatial time series*. London: Pion.

spatial analysis The quantitative procedures employed in LOCATIONAL ANALYSIS – the term is sometimes used as a synonym for that portion of the discipline. Unwin (1981), for example, presents spatial analysis as the study of the arrangements of points, lines, areas and surfaces on a MAP (see PATTERN). Whereas many geographers merely apply techniques derived from the GENERAL LINEAR MODEL to geographical examples, others have argued that spatial data analysis poses particular statistical problems (such as SPATIAL AUTOCORRELATION), which means developing procedures specifically designed to counter them (Haining, 1990). RJJ

References
Haining, R. P. 1990: *Spatial data analysis in the social and environmental sciences*. Cambridge: Cambridge University Press.
Unwin, D. J. 1981: *Introductory spatial analysis*. London: Methuen.

spatial autocorrelation

The presence of spatial PATTERN in a mapped variable due to geographical proximity. The most common form of spatial autocorrelation is where similar values for a variable (such as county income levels) tend to cluster together in adjacent observation-units or regions, so that on average across the map the values for neighbours are more similar than would occur if the allocation of values to observation-units were the result of a purely random mechanism. More general and complicated forms of autocorrelation can also be defined. The presence of spatial autocorrelation is very wide-spread, and violates a basic assumption (that the observations be 'independent' or non-autocorrelated) of many standard statistical tests. A variety of tests for spatial autocorrelation in raw data and regression residuals is available, and a group of techniques known as 'spatial econometrics' has been developed to allow the inclusion of autocorrelation in statistical models. (See also CORRELATION; REGRESSION.)   LWH

Suggested Reading
Haining, R. 1990: *Spatial data analysis in the social and environmental sciences*. Cambridge: Cambridge University Press.

spatial fetishism A term applied to LOCATIONAL ANALYSIS which, according to its critics, gives SPACE, and especially distance, causal powers – as in the so-called FRICTIONS OF DISTANCE. The critics contend that space *per se* is devoid of content and is only important when given status by human agents, as also occurs with NATURE. (See also SPATIAL SEPARATISM.)
                                    RJJ

Suggested Reading
Sayer, A. 1985: The difference that space makes. In Gregory, D. and Urry, J., eds, *Social relations and spatial structures*. London: Macmillan, pp. 49–66.

spatial interaction A term coined by E. L. Ullman (1980) to indicate interdependence between geographical areas. This interdependence was seen by Ullman as complementary to the people–environment interdependence within a single area; he therefore saw it as a major focus of geographical enquiry. It includes the movement of goods, people, money and information between places. The concept is similar to the 'geography of circulation' which was developed by French geographers at the beginning of the twentieth century.

The strength of Ullman's original concept is that many different forms of spatial interaction are themselves interdependent: for example, a flow of migrants will often stimulate subsequent flows (or backflows) of trade, tourists and information (see CHAIN MIGRATION). Furthermore, his bases of interaction, conceived originally as an explanation of commodity flow, may also be applied to the movement of people and ideas. This unity has been underlined by the application of similar models (especially GRAVITY MODELS) to commodity flow, telephone traffic, MIGRATION etc. Ullman clearly hoped that this unity of content would allow a wide appreciation of geography as spatial interaction, but this has not occurred: TRANSPORT GEOGRAPHY has become a separate subdiscipline, whereas migration studies have become part of POPULATION GEOGRAPHY, and the study of information DIFFUSION has been incorporated in CULTURAL GEOGRAPHY.

In recent years the term has been used in a more restricted sense for two types of study. First, some authors have restricted it to describing studies of spatial flow phenomena (especially GRAVITY MODELS). Second, a few have related it to sociological concepts of social interaction, and have therefore defined spatial interaction as the spatial dimension of social contacts.
                                    AMH

Reference
Ullman, E. L. 1980: *Geography as spatial interaction*. Seattle, WA: University of Washington Press.

Suggested Reading
Lowe, J. C. and Moryadas, S. 1975: *The geography of movement*. Boston: Houghton-Mifflin.
Ullman (1980).

spatial margin A locus of points of which the total cost of producing a given volume of output is equal to the total revenue obtainable from selling that output. This defines the area within which profitable operation is possible. The concept of the spatial margin to profitability was introduced by E. M. Rawstron (1958). It is one of the few really original

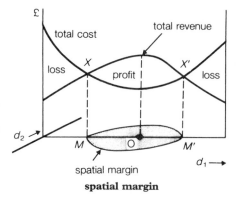

spatial margin

spatial–economic concepts devised by a geographer.

The derivation of the spatial margin to profitability is illustrated in the figure. A SPACE COST CURVE and a SPACE REVENUE CURVE are plotted along the horizontal distance dimensions d_1. The points X and X' show where total cost and total revenue are equal. When projected onto the distance axis, these identify points M and M' as the spatial margin to profitability; between these points total revenue is greater than total cost so some profit can be made, but beyond them total cost is greater than total revenue and the firm would operate at a loss. When a second distance dimension (d_2) is introduced, the spatial margin defines the area within which profitable operation is possible.

The conceptual significance of the concept of the spatial margin is that it permits the incorporation of suboptimal decisions into a theoretical framework previously directed towards searching for the single optimal profit-maximizing location (O in the figure). Anywhere within the margin offers some profit, so the firm would be able to exercise freedom of choice within these limits, trading off profits for personal considerations. Within the margin a firm can locate in total ignorance, yet still survive.

The shape and extent of the spatial margin will vary with the prevailing COST SURFACE and REVENUE SURFACE. Some industries will operate within wide margins, while others will be confined by tight and localized limits to viability. The margins can vary with the nature of the industrial organization – they may be wider for highly

skillful entrepreneurs than for the less able, for example.

The empirical identification of spatial margins is difficult, but not impossible. Even if the margin cannot be found in practice, speculation as to its extent and the degree of restriction imposed can be a useful aid to the interpretation of industrial location and change.   DMS

Reference

Rawstron, E. M. 1958: Three principles of industrial location. *Trans. Inst. Br. Geogr.* 25, pp. 132–42.

Suggested Reading

Smith, D. M. 1981: *Industrial location: an economic geographical analysis*, second edition. New York: John Wiley.

spatial monopoly Monopolistic control over a market by virtue of location. The usual meaning of 'monopoly' is that one firm or individual sells the entire output of some commodity or service. This is normally the final outcome of a competitive process taking place under capitalist market conditions, in which one supplier is able to produce and sell the commodity at a price favourable enough to consumers to force other suppliers out of business. Spatial monopoly is a special case, in which distance from competitors gives a producer monopolistic control over a section of the market.

Spatial monopoly can arise when a producer is distributing a commodity from its point of origin, and also when consumers travel to the point of origin. In the first case, the operation of an f.o.b. pricing policy, whereby the cost of transportation is passed on to the consumer (see PRICING POLICIES), will increase delivered price with distance from the production point, so that consumers close to the production point can purchase the commodity relatively cheaply; that is, more cheaply than from alternative suppliers. The greater the elasticity of demand, or the sensitivity of the consumer to price, the greater the likelihood of local monopoly.

The area within which monopoly control exists (assuming that consumers buy from the cheapest source) is bounded by a locus of points at which the delivered price from the supplier in question is equal to the price charged by a competitor (see MARKET AREA ANALYSIS). In the second case, consumers will tend to travel to the production point which is closest in time, effort or cost. In this case too, the area of monopoly control will be bounded by a locus of points of consumer indifference as to whether to purchase from one point to another.

Spatial monopoly can also rise from collusion between otherwise competing firms, who may agree to a 'carve-up' of the market among themselves. As in other situations of spatial monopoly, this will enable suppliers to raise prices and exact above-normal profits in the area over which they exert exclusive control. Distance provides no absolute protection of a market, however, for some consumers may choose to purchase from high-cost sources or to travel to more distant outlets out of preference, ignorance or other behavioural considerations.

In some instances, spatial monopoly may be a case of so-called natural monopoly, where the market in question is best served by a single firm because of the nature of the production process. Some public utilities, such as local water supply, are of this kind. Such public spatial monopoly may be turned into private monopoly by PRIVA-TIZATION.   DMS

Suggested Reading
Smith, D. M. 1981: *Industrial location: an economic geographical analysis*, second edition. New York: John Wiley.

spatial preference Individual or group evaluation of either the attractiveness of spatial phenomena or the desirability of spatial alternatives (e.g. residential attractiveness, MIGRATION strategies and LANDSCAPE predilections). (See also AC-TION SPACE; ACTIVITY SPACE; REVEALED PREFERENCE ANALYSIS; SATISFICING BE-HAVIOUR; UTILITY THEORY.)   DEC

spatial science The presentation of human geography as that component of the social sciences which focuses on the role of SPACE as a fundamental variable influencing both society's organization and operation and the behaviour of its individual members. It was formulated during the QUANTITATIVE REVOLUTION and is usually closely associated with the philosophy of POSITIVISM (cf. LOCATIONAL ANALYSIS).

The goal of such work was expressed as 'building accurate generalizations with predictive power by precise quantitative description of spatial distributions, SPA-TIAL STRUCTURE and organization, and spatial relationships' (Berry and Marble, 1968): according to Nystuen (1968) such generalizations could be based on just three fundamental spatial concepts – direction (or orientation), distance, and connection (or relative position).

Later criticisms of spatial science focused on its implicit spatial determinism, and the logical impossibility of defining spatial variables independent of the context within which they were supposed to operate. (See also SPATIAL FETISHISM; SPATIAL SEPARATISM.)   RJJ

References
Berry, B. J. L. and Marble, D. F. 1968: Introduction. In Berry, B. J. L. and Marble, D. F., eds, *Spatial analysis: a reader in statistical geography*. Englewood Cliffs, NJ: Prentice-Hall, pp. 1–9.
Nystuen, J. D. 1968: Identification of some fundamental spatial concepts. In Berry, B. J. L. and Marble, D. F., eds, *Spatial analysis: a reader in statistical geography*. Englewood Cliffs, NJ: Prentice-Hall, pp. 35–41.

Suggested Reading
Cox, K. R. 1976: American geography: social science emergent. *Soc. Sci. Q.* 57, pp. 182–207.
Eliot Hurst, M. E. 1985: Geography has neither existence nor future. In Johnston, R. J., ed., *The future of geography*. London: Methuen, pp. 59–91.

spatial separatism A term coined by Sack (1974) to describe the view – which he contested – that geography is the discipline which focuses on the independent role of space as an influence on human behaviour. He was explicitly criticizing Bunge's (1973) claim that geometry provided geography with a formal language with which spatial prediction was possible – as instanced by CENTRAL PLACE THEORY and the VON THÜNEN MODEL. Sack's (1972) position was that geometry could be used to describe but not to explain since it could not encapsulate human decision-making processes. (See also SPATIAL FETISHISM.)

RJJ

References

Bunge, W. 1973: Spatial prediction. *Ann. Ass. Am. Geogr.* 63, pp. 566–8.

Sack, R. D. 1972: Geography, geometry and explanation. *Ann. Ass. Am. Geogr.* 62, pp. 61–78.

Sack, R. D. 1974: The spatial separatist theme in geography. *Econ. Geogr.* 50, pp. 1–19.

spatial structure The mode in which SPACE is organized by and implicated in the operation and outcome of social and/or natural processes. It is possible to identify three main phases in the development of concepts of spatial structure in Anglophone human geography since the Second World War (see the figure).

(1) In the course of the postwar critique of REGIONAL GEOGRAPHY it was often claimed that 'spatial relations' were 'the only ones that matter' and that a properly scientific geography would necessarily be directed towards MORPHOLOGY and the search for an intrinsically *spatial order* defined in terms of 'morphological laws', or, more simply, PATTERN (Schaefer, 1953). Subsequently Bunge (1962) proposed a theoretical geography predicated on a dualism between *spatial process* and *spatial structure*: that is to say, between 'movements over the earth's surface' and 'the resulting arrangement of phenomena on the earth's surface'. In doing so, Bunge

strongly agreed with Schaefer that spatial structure could be defined 'most sharply by interpreting "structure" as "geometrical"', from which it followed, so he said, that 'the science of space [geography] finds the logic of space [geometry] a sharp tool'. The revival of this (classical) geometric tradition was a central feature of LOCATIONAL ANALYSIS in human geography and the constitution of geography as SPATIAL SCIENCE (see Haggett, 1965; Harvey, 1969). From this perspective, spatial structure was often translated into purely formal conceptions of 'spatial process': that is, into abstract sequences in mathematical spaces rather than concrete outcomes of causal mechanisms (see PROCESS).

(2) In the second phase, however, there was a movement towards the assignment of substantive rather than surrogate processes to the production and reproduction of particular spatial structures. But in the course of this intellectual transition – the critique of spatial science – spatial structure came to be seen as epiphenomenal: either as a 'codification' by the human subject or as a 'reflection' of human society. Explanations of spatial structure were typically sought within the primarily aspatial human and social sciences, most commonly psychology, cultural anthropology, political economy and sociology (see COMPOSITIONAL THEORY). Within human geography, therefore, the debates of most moment came to pivot around whether social life ought to be conceived in terms of *either* the human subject *or* the structures of society, a dualism which could be traced within and between HUMANISTIC GEOGRAPHY and

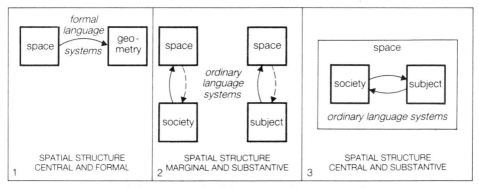

spatial structure *Spatial structure and human geography.*

MARXIST GEOGRAPHY. In general, and to simplify, the result was one geography preoccupied with intentions and meanings and another geography preoccupied with systems and structures. At best, spatial structuring was marginal to these exchanges; at worst, it was condemned as an irrelevant distraction that ran the risk of 'SPATIAL FETISHISM'.

(3) As the figure shows, however, more recently the interpenetration of these polar positions has made the substantive connections between social relations and spatial structures a central focus for inquiry across the whole spectrum of the social sciences (Gregory and Urry, 1985). The horizons of the GEOGRAPHICAL IMAGINATION have been widened through interests in CONTEXTUAL THEORY, in spatial ONTOLOGY, in the PRODUCTION OF SPACE and in concepts of SPATIALITY. But this has had another consequence: in the course of these explorations concepts of both 'subject' and 'society' have turned out to be highly unstable constructions – not unitary, homogeneous and coherent at all, but fractured, turbulent and in constant motion. (See also POST-MARXISM; POSTMODERNISM; POSTSTRUCTURALISM; REGIONAL GEOGRAPHY.)   DG

References

Bunge, W. 1962: *Theoretical geography*. Lund: C. W. K. Gleerup.

Gregory, D. and Urry, J., eds 1985: *Social relations and spatial structures*. London: Macmillan.

Haggett, P. 1965: *Locational analysis in human geography*. London: Edward Arnold.

Harvey, D. 1969: *Explanation in geography*. London: Edward Arnold.

Schaefer, F. K. 1953: Exceptionalism in geography: a methodological examination. *Ann. Ass. Am. Geogr.* 43, pp. 226–49.

Suggested Reading

Gregory, D. 1985: People, places and practices: the future of human geography. In King, R., ed., *Geographical futures*. Sheffield: Geographical Association.

spatiality There are four main senses in which 'spatiality' is used in human geography, all of which refer to the human and social implications of SPACE and each of which derives from a distinctive intellectual tradition.

(a) Drawing upon EXISTENTIALISM and PHENOMENOLOGY, and in particular the writings of Heidegger and Husserl, Pickles (1985) proposes human spatiality as the fundamental basis on which 'geographical inquiry as a human science of the world can be explicitly founded'. Pickles's primary concern is with ONTOLOGY: with understanding 'the universal structures characteristic of [human] spatiality as the precondition for any understanding of places and spaces as such'. In particular, Pickles objects to those views which regard 'the physical space of physics [as] the sole genuine space'; this sort of thinking is typical of spatial science but, in Pickles's view, is wholly inappropriate for a genuinely human geography. He urges in its place a recovery of our 'original experiences prior to their thematization by any scientific activity', in other words a rigorous exposure of the TAKEN-FOR-GRANTED WORLD assumed (but unexplicated) by SPATIAL SCIENCE. One of its essential characteristics is what Pickles calls 'the structural unity of the "in-order-to"'. Our most immediate experiences are not cognitive abstractions of separate objects, Pickles contends, but rather 'constellations of relations and meaning' which we encounter in our everyday activities – what Heidegger termed 'equipment' – and which are 'ready-to-hand'. Such a perspective reveals the human significance of *contextuality*. For human spatiality is related 'to several concurrent and nonconcurrent equipmental contexts' and 'cannot be understood independently of the beings that organise it'. Spatiality thus has the character of a 'situating' enterprise in which we 'make room' for and 'give space' to congeries of equipment. Put in this way, one can perhaps hear distant echoes of TIME-GEOGRAPHY, but Pickles is evoking an intellectual tradition antithetical to the physicalism of Hägerstrand's early writings and which fastens not on 'objective space' but on *social space* (see Schatzki 1991; cf. Hägerstrand, 1984).

(b) Drawing upon Althusser's STRUCTURAL MARXISM, a number of Francophone Marxists have suggested that

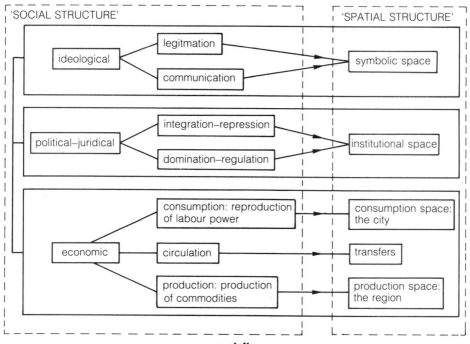

spatiality

concepts of spatiality serve to identify the connections and correspondences between social structures (MODES OF PRODUCTION or SOCIAL FORMATIONS) and SPATIAL STRUCTURES. Althusser had argued that different concepts and constructions of time ('temporalities') could be assigned to different levels of modes of production – 'economic time', 'political time' and 'ideological time' – and that they had to be constructed out of the concepts of these different social practices. But if, as Althusser claimed, the distinctions between these temporalities are essential for any properly theoretical ('scientific') history, then, as one historian reminded him, history is not only an interlacing of times but of spaces as well (Vilar, 1973). In much the same way, therefore, it was argued that different concepts of space (or 'spatialities') could also be assigned to the different levels. According to Lipietz (1977), for example, the concept of spatial structure is dependent on and so must be derived from a concept of social structure. From his perspective, spatiality consists of a correspondence between 'presence–absence' in space and 'participation–exclusion' in the

particular system of social practices contained within each level. Each of these correspondences is supposed to have its own topology, so that 'one can speak, for example, of the *economic* space of the capitalist mode of production . . . or of the *legal* space which is superimposed upon it'. Spatial structure then becomes the articulation of the spatialities of these different levels, at once a 'reflection' of different systems of social practices and a 'constraint' upon them. In his early writings, Castells (1977) presented the most detailed analysis of spatial structure in these terms (see the figure), but he concluded that it made more sense to theorize concepts of temporality and concepts of spatiality conjointly and to speak instead of *space–times*:

From the social point of view . . . there is no space (a physical quantity yet an abstract entity) . . . [only] an historically defined space–time, a space constructed, worked, practised by social relations . . . Socially speaking space, like time, is a conjuncture, that is to say, the articulation of concrete historical practices' (Castells, 1977).

(c) Drawing upon Lefebvre's vision of a critical Marxism, and in particular his account of the PRODUCTION OF SPACE, Soja (1985) has used the term spatiality 'to refer specifically to socially produced space, the created forms and relations of a broadly defined human geography'. 'All space is not socially produced', Soja continues, 'but all spatiality is'. In the course of his work as a whole Lefebvre provided critiques of existentialism and phenomenology and of structuralism and structural Marxism, and for this reason Soja insists that his 'materialist interpretation of spatiality' cannot be assimilated to either of the two traditions summarized above. For to speak of 'the production of space' in the spirit of Lefebvre (1991) is to accentuate spatiality as 'both the medium and the outcome' of situated HUMAN AGENCY and systems of social practices in a way which is, so Soja claims, broadly consonant with STRUC-TURATION THEORY. Hence:

Spatiality and temporality, human geography and human history, intersect in a complex social process which creates a constantly evolving sequence of spatialities, a spatio-temporal structuration of social life which gives form not only to the grand movements of social development but also to the recursive practices of day-to-day activity (Soja, 1985).

Transcending his earlier claims for a 'socio-spatial dialectic' (Soja, 1980), he concluded that 'spatiality is society, not as its definitional or logical equivalent, but as its concretisation, its formative *constitution*'. And it is precisely this realization, that is subsequently argued, that is characteristic of POSTMODERNISM and its reassertion of space – of spatiality – in critical social thought (Soja, 1989). Other writers have registered similar claims, though without the postmodern inflection. In his later writings, for example, Castells (1983) repudiated the monolithic structuralism of his previous formulations and declared that 'space is not a "reflection" of society, it is society'. Giddens (1984) also rejected the possibility of a distinctive social science of space predicted on the belief that 'space has its own intrinsic nature'. 'In human geography spatial forms are always social forms', he asserted, and 'spatial

configurations of social life' – spatialities – 'are just as much a matter of basic importance to social theory as are the dimensions of temporality'.

(d) Drawing upon POSTSTRUCTUR-ALISM, and in particular the work of Deleuze and Foucault, a number of writers use spatiality to indicate the ways in which constellations of power-knowledge are inscribed in space and through which particular subject-positions are constituted (Gregory, 1993).

For all the differences between these four traditions, they are united in their opposition to the conventional separations between 'space' and 'society' (which can be traced to a persistent KANTIANISM), and in this sense can be read as four moments in the movement towards an exploration of what Smith (1990) calls 'deep space': that is to say, 'quintessentially social space . . . physical extent fused through with social intent'.   DG

References

Castells, M. 1977: *The urban question*. London: Edward Arnold.

Castells, M. 1983: *The city and the grassroots*. London: Edward Arnold.

Giddens, A. 1984: *The constitution of society*. Cambridge: Polity Press.

Gregory, D. 1993: *Geographical imaginations*. Oxford: Blackwell.

Hägerstrand, T. 1984: Presence and absence: a look at conceptual choices and bodily necessities. *Reg. Stud.* 18, pp. 373–80.

Lefebvre, H. 1991: *The production of space*. Oxford: Blackwell.

Lipietz, A. 1977: *Le capital et son espace*. Paris: Maspero.

Pickles, J. 1985: *Phenomenology, science and geography: spatiality and the human sciences*. Cambridge: Cambridge University Press.

Schatzki, T. 1991: Spatial ontology and explanation. *Ann. Ass. Am. Geogr.* 81, pp. 650–70.

Smith, N. 1990: *Uneven development: nature, capital and the production of space*, second edition. Oxford: Blackwell.

Soja, E. 1980: The socio-spatial dialectic. *Ann. Ass. Am. Geogr.* 70, pp. 207–27.

Soja, E. 1985: The spatiality of social life: towards a transformative retheorisation. In Gregory, D. and Urry, J., eds, *Social relations and spatial structures*. London: Macmillan, pp. 90–122.

Soja, E. 1989: *Postmodern geographies: the reassertion of space in critical social theory.* London: Verso.

Vilar, P. 1973: Histoire marxiste, histoire en construction: essai de dialogue avec Althusser. *Annales: Economies, Sociétés, Civilisations* 28, pp. 165–98.

Suggested Reading
Pickles (1985).
Smith (1990), Afterword.
Soja (1989).

spectacle, geography of Geographical analysis of the most expressive examples of places and events of engineered mass leisure and mass consumption, such as sporting jamborees, world's fairs, theme parks and cultural festivals. While the notion of 'bread and circuses' as a strategy of social control by elites is long-established (Brantlinger, 1983), the concept of the spectacle as a form of cultural HEGEMONY has been revived in some recent interpretations of advanced Western societies (Debord, 1973; Harvey, 1987). Such an argument reopens the question of popular culture (Ley and Olds, 1988). To what extent is popular culture thrust upon an unwary public to secure compliance and profit; and to what extent is the public an active participant in constituting, appropriating and resisting cultural forms? DL

References
Brantlinger, P. 1983: *Bread and circuses: theories of mass culture as social decay.* Ithaca, NY: Cornell University Press.
Debord, G. 1973: *Society of the spectacle.* Detroit: Black and Red.
Harvey, D. 1987: Flexible accumulation through urbanization: reflections on 'postmodernism' in the American city. *Antipode* 19, pp. 260–86.
Ley, D. and Olds, K. 1988: Landscape as spectacle: world's fairs and the culture of heroic consumption. *Environ. Plann. D: Society and Space* 6, pp. 191–212.

spectral analysis A technique for examining the oscillations and patterns in a time series by calculating the relative importance of difference wavelengths, periodicities or 'frequency bands' (just as a prism analyses light in terms of colours of the spectrum). The method is an extension of classical Fourier analysis: it does not

analyse in terms of exact periodic waves (e.g. 12 months or 2.5 years), but uses frequency bands of specified width (e.g. 11–13 months and 2.25–2.75 years). This is more appropriate for socio-economic fluctuations, which are not exactly periodic. Major applications in human geography have been to REGIONAL CYCLES and LEAD–LAG MODELS of regional and urban unemployment, and to the geography of epidemics such as measles. Cross-spectral analysis between two or more time series allows the calculation of different CORRELATION and REGRESSION coefficients for each frequency band. Spectral analysis can also be applied to transects across space and to two-dimensional patterns, although examples are rare in human geography.
LWH

Suggested Reading
Bennett, R. J. 1979: *Spatial time series.* London: Pion.

spontaneous settlement A term, largely synonymous with SQUATTER SETTLEMENT, for unplanned, predominantly residential, developments in urban areas. The word 'spontaneous' implies that there is no forethought prior to the developments, but most such settlements are planned by their initial occupants, albeit often clandestinely. Such planning usually concentrates on occupation of land for dwellings only, however, and is unable to provide an urban INFRASTRUCTURE. RJJ

sport, geography of The study of spatial variations in the pursuit of various sports and of the impact of sporting activities on the landscape. Interest in these topics is growing, given the increased use of RECREATION and LEISURE in many societies, as evidenced by the launching of a specialized journal, *Sport Place*.

Bale (1989), the author of the first general text on the subject, identifies three main components to work on the geography of sport:

(a) study of the *changing spatial pattern of sports activity*, as, for example, with the DIFFUSION of a new sport from its origin and the study of sporting regions, areas identifying with particular sports (cf. LOCALITY);

(b) study of the *'sports landscape'* and how it changes, as in the design and visual impact of stadia and golf courses; and

(c) prescriptions for *changing the spatial organization* of sport and sporting landscapes.

Most studies have been of the first type – as in Rooney's (1974) work on various aspects of American sports.

Bale also argues that examples from sport, as with the study of the negative EXTERNALITIES generated by stadia, provide useful and readily accessible teaching materials for other fields of geography. RJJ

References

Bale, J. 1989: *Sports geography*. London: E. F. & N. Spon.

Rooney, J. F. 1974: *A geography of American sport: from Cabin Creek to Anaheim*. Reading, MA: Addison-Wesley.

sprawl A term, often used pejoratively, describing the unplanned extension of relatively low-density urban land uses into rural areas, usually alongside main roads (see RIBBON DEVELOPMENT). Sprawl implies little control of land subdivision (see ZONING), so that the conversion of plots for urban uses may create enclaves of agricultural land. Farmers in such areas may suffer negative EXTERNALITIES through the impact of neighbours on their land uses. Planning legislation, especially in heavily populated countries, often includes policies to reduce sprawl – as with GREEN BELTS. RJJ

squatter settlement An urban development, usually predominantly residential, on land neither owned nor rented by its occupants. Such settlements are mainly found in THIRD WORLD cities, where the conventional housing markets are unable to cope with the demands produced by rapid URBANIZATION. They are created when squatters illegally occupy land, either on the edge of a built-up area or in the interstices of existing development (as in deep gullies in Caracas and alongside railway lines in Mexico City). Such an occupation may be entirely unplanned (see SPONTANEOUS SETTLEMENT) and piecemeal, but most squatter settlements are the results of planned invasions of land which

neither private owners nor the STATE are likely to resist.

Squatter settlements – variously termed barrios, bidonvilles, bustees, favelas, kampongs and ranchos – are characteristic of most THIRD WORLD cities, in some of which they may form as much as three-quarters of the total residential area. They have grown especially rapidly in the past four decades.

Many squatter settlements lack a basic INFRASTRUCTURE – public utilities such as electricity, running water and sewerage and garbage removal – and much of the housing is of a poor quality. In an important paper, however, Stokes (1962) distinguished between those which were what he termed 'slums of despair' and those which were 'slums of hope'. The latter are characterized by strong self-help movements, which promote both improvements to individual dwellings and collective investment in the needed infrastructure so as to improve the residents' QUALITY OF LIFE.

For many governments, squatter settlements were for long seen as major irritants, creating not only substantial blots on the landscape and potential health hazards for the wider population but also possibly containing radical SOCIAL MOVEMENTS. From the 1960s on, however, some housing specialists argued that squatter settlements provide a sensible resolution of the housing problem in rapidly growing, relatively poor countries. The conventional housing market cannot cope with the explosion of demand, and scarce capital is better invested elsewhere in the economy. Thus squatter settlements provide a solution which works, allowing people to invest in housing and its improvement as their circumstances allow. In some countries, the squatter settlement movement has even been encouraged both by assisting groups in the search for land on which to establish their communities and by providing a basic infrastructure – a piped water system, a basic drainage network, and an electricity grid, for example. In some cases, even basic dwellings (core rooms – a kitchen and one bedroom, perhaps) are provided, which the occupants can extend when money is available. However, such policies are condemned by others as ways of ideologically sustaining CLASS differentials within divided societies (Burgess, 1981).   RJJ

References

Burgess, R. 1981: Ideology and urban residential theory in Latin America. In Herbert, D. T. and Johnston, R. J., eds, *Geography and the urban environment*, volume 4. Chichester: John Wiley, pp. 57–114.

Stokes, C. J. 1962: A theory of slums. *Land Economics* 38, pp. 127–37.

Suggested Reading

Hardoy, J. 1989: *Squatter citizen: life in the urban Third World*. London: Earthscan.

Lloyd, P. C. 1979: *Slums of hope: shanty towns in the Third World*. London: Penguin.

Ward, P. 1990: *Mexico City: the production and reproduction of an urban environment*. The World Cities Series. London: Belhaven Press.

squatting The illegal occupation of land and dwellings. In advanced industrial societies it is usually associated with the occupation of empty dwellings (possibly dilapidated and awaiting demolition) by individuals and groups who are either unable to afford (or who choose not to afford) homes through conventional market mechanisms, or are ineligible for the allocation of public housing: in some countries the laws give some security of occupation to such people – known as 'squatter's rights' – making their eviction difficult for the legal owners. Most squatting occurs in INNER-CITY areas, especially in districts characterized as SLUMS, although it is also common in some British cities where the allocation procedures for public housing are inefficient. (See also SQUATTER SETTLEMENT.)   RJJ

stable population A population in which age-specific FERTILITY and MORTALITY are assumed to be constant, and to and from which no MIGRATION takes place. The concept was first developed by Alfred Lotka and is much used in demographic analysis. He showed how such a population tends towards a constant age distribution which increases at a constant rate. A *stationary* population, a special case of a stable population, is one where fertility and mortality are equal, and the age distribution is the life table distribution.   PEO

Suggested Reading

Woods, R. I. 1979: *Population analysis in geography*. London: Longman, ch. 8.

stages of growth A five-stage sequence of economic and social DEVELOPMENT postulated by the American economic historian Walt W. Rostow (1971) through which, he argued, all societies may pass (see the figure). The stages represent an attempt to generalize 'the sweep of modern history'. Their elaboration in book form is described by its author as a 'non-communist manifesto', written in deliberate opposition to what were perceived to be Karl Marx's views on the relationships between economic and non-economic behaviour (see HISTORICAL MATERIALISM; MARXIAN ECONOMICS).

The model of economic development derived from the stages is both teleological (see TELEOLOGY) and mechanical: *teleological* in the sense that the end result (stage 5) is known at the outset (stage 1), and *mechanical* in that, despite the claim that the stages have an inner logic 'rooted in a dynamic theory of production', the underlying motor of change is not explained. As a result the stages become little more than a classificatory system. The model itself is based on data for 15 countries only, plus outline data for others (Healey and Ilbery, 1990).

The first of the five stages (the '*traditional society*') is characterized by 'primitive' technology, hierarchical social structures (the precise nature of which are not specified) and behaviour conditioned more by custom and accepted practice than by what Rostow takes to be 'rational' criteria. These characteristics combine to place a ceiling on production possibilities. Outside stimuli to change (including, for example, COLONIALISM and the expansion of CAPITALISM) are admitted in the transitional second stage (the '*preconditions for take-off*'). This stage emphasizes a rise in the rate of productive investment, a start on the provision of social and economic INFRASTRUCTURE, the emergence of a new, economically based elite and an effective centralized national STATE. Again, no specification of social relations

587

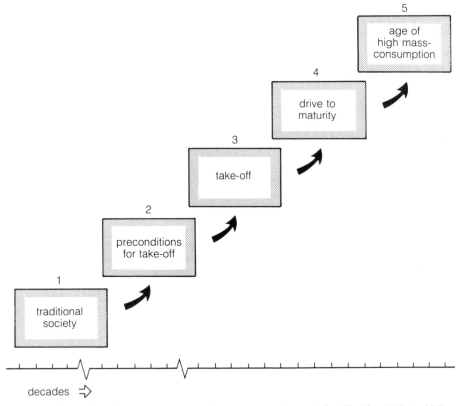

stages of growth *Rostow's stages theory of economic development* (after Keeble, 1967, p. 250).

is given. However, the opportunities for profitable investment presented by the preconditions for take-off are unlikely to be ignored by CAPITAL and they pave the way for the third stage: '*take-off into sustained growth.*' This is described by Rostow as 'the great watershed in the life of modern societies'. It is a period of around 10–30 years, during which growth dominates society, the economy and the political agenda (although the social relations which facilitate this dominance are not described) and investment rises, especially in the leading sectors of manufacturing industry. Self-sustaining growth results in the '*drive to maturity*' (stage 4), characterized by diversification as most sectors grow, imports fall and productive investment ranges between 10 and 20 per cent of national income. The increasing importance of consumer goods and services and the rise of the WELFARE STATE indicate that the final stage of the '*age of high mass*

consumption' has been reached (see POST-INDUSTRIAL SOCIETY).

The insistence within the model upon placing growth in a wider historical and social context and upon a disaggregated approach which reflects the UNEVEN nature of DEVELOPMENT marks a substantial advance upon abstracted and formal theories of economic growth. But at the same time these characteristics expose its socially universal and ahistoric features. The stages of growth are unrealistic, as they could apply to anywhere at any time – to China as well as to Brazil, to the former USSR as well as to the USA. However, the strategic implications are clear: following Rostow's logic, capitalist society is a necessary consequence of development (see CAPITALISM). All societies that are not currently capitalist in form will become so: 'there is no alternative'. State-socialist societies are simply in an arrested stage preceding the break-through to capitalism. Such underlying implications are not made explicit. By concealing the specific social relations of production of the stages – and most especially of the first and second stages – capitalist societies may be reproduced and extended by apparently neutral policies advocating apparently universal processes of growth. This is the true meaning of Rostow's subtitle. If it were to read 'a capitalist manifesto', its ideological objectives (see IDEOLOGY) would be revealed and their achievement limited or subverted.   RL

References

Healey, M. J. and Ilbery, B. W. 1990: *Location and change: perspectives on economic geography.* Oxford: Oxford University Press, ch. 14.

Keeble, D. E. 1967: Models of economic development. In Chorley, R. J. and Haggett, P., eds, *Models in geography*. London: Methuen, pp. 248–54.

Rostow, W. W. 1971: *The stages of economic growth: a non-communist manifesto,* second edition. Cambridge: Cambridge University Press.

Suggested Reading

Baran, P. A. and Hobsbawm, E. J. 1961: The stages of economic growth. *Kyklos* 14, pp. 324–42.

Foster-Carter, A. 1985: *The sociology of development.* Ormskirk, UK: Causeway.

Keeble (1967).

Rostow (1971).

staple A principal item of TRADE or consumption produced and/or consumed by a society. The potato was the staple commodity of consumption in Ireland before the famine of the 1840s. Production failures during the 1840s, coupled with the absence of alternative strategies as a consequence of the UNDERDEVELOPMENT of Irish agriculture, conditioned largely by its connections with the British economy and land ownership, led to widespread famine, emigration and the decimation of the rural population (but see MARXIST GEOGRAPHY). Rice is the staple foodstuff of many parts of Southeast Asia today in the sense that, like the potato in pre-famine Ireland, it forms the central contribution to diet.

Examples of heavy DEPENDENCE upon staple items of trade are many in the economies of the underdeveloped world. During the 1980s, in 48 out of the 55 countries in Africa the three leading commodity exports accounted for more than 50 per cent of total exports. Such dependence leaves economies vulnerable to fluctuations in demand and price, and to the long-term fall in demand for naturally produced products as they are replaced by industrial alternatives. Even in more diversified and industrialized economies, the process of UNEVEN DEVELOPMENT may lead to the emergence of a dominant staple commodity, with critical implications for sustained growth throughout the economy (see STAPLES THEORY). Conversely, staples of local consumption frequently face competition from more commercial, export-orientated users of land, with harmful consequences (such as those in Ethiopia during the 1980s and 1990s) for local food production and food supplies, as well as for the possibilities of SUSTAINABLE DEVELOPMENT.

Dependence upon staples is not restricted to the less economically developed countries. Cotton products accounted for over 50 per cent by value of British exports in 1830 (36 per cent in 1870). Such a heavy dependence serves to condition the possibilities of future development not only because alternatives are squeezed out but also because of the formative socio-economic influence of a distinctive DIVISION OF LABOUR. Even in highly developed economies such as that of Canada, where the production and export of resource-based staples are central to growth, they generate distinctive patterns and processes of development (Hayter and Barnes, 1990). (See STAPLES THEORY.)   RL

Reference

Hayter, R. and Barnes, T. 1990: Innis' staple theory, exports and recession: British Columbia, 1981–86. *Econ. Geogr.* 66, pp. 156–73.

staples theory A theory which suggests that national economic and social development is based upon the export of unprocessed or semi-processed primary resources (STAPLES). Although the theory has long historical antecedents, and different – frequently truncated – versions of it have been presented (e.g. export base theory), staples theory is most closely associated with the work of the Canadian economic historian Harold A. Innis (1894–1952).

In Mel Watkins' (1963, p. 144) classic exposition of Innis' staples model, exports of primary resources function as ' . . . the leading sector of the economy, and set the pace for economic growth'. In the optimistic version of the theory (particularly associated with NEOCLASSICAL ECONOMICS), this sector then stimulates diversification through its various linkages, eventually leading to full industrialization (Baldwin, 1956). In the pessimistic account, and one now associated with the so-called school of Canadian POLITICAL ECONOMY, the economy is ensnared in a staples trap (Williams, 1983); that is, diversification is blocked because of such reasons as an export mentality among producers, the domination of the economy by a few, large and often foreign-owned multinational corporations, and a truncated industrial branch-plant structure that minimizes the development of higher order control and research functions (Britton and Gilmour, 1971). The result, to use Innis's terminology, is that staples-producing regions become hinterland economies, the fates of which are strongly tied to events in more powerful foreign metropoles. Of these two different accounts, it has been the pessimistic version that has been most persuasive (Clement and Williams, 1989).

A principal task of those researchers supporting the pessimistic version has been to establish the causal relations between the nature of staples production, on the one hand, and the economic instability and dependency found within staples regions, on the other. Four principal connections have been noted. First, the market for staple commodities much more approximates perfect competition than does that for manufactured goods. As such, staples regions are price-takers in a market in which price volatility is the norm. In particular, the bulk and crude exports that are the basis of most staples regions tend to be very vulnerable to demand shifts in markets that are both highly competitive and price-elastic. Second, because domestic sales of staples are relatively small, international market volatility has direct and strong impacts, thereby producing the characteristic boom and bust economy of resource-producing regions. Third, for a variety of reasons (technological advances that reduce resource inputs for production, the growth of synthetic substitutes, and low long-run income elasticities of demand), the terms of trade for primary commodities are increasingly less favourable to staples-producing areas. Finally, resource production tends to be undertaken increasingly by large, often foreign-owned, multinational corporations. Spry (1981) argues that this is a direct consequence of the large capital expenditures and production indivisibilities associated with staples. However, the presence of foreign multinational firms in staples regions creates a number of potential problems including: appropriation of large economic rents because of the undervaluing of resources by the local STATE; the inhibition of resource upgrading prior to export, because the resource extraction subsidiaries are only one part of a vertically integrated corporation in which processing is often carried out elsewhere; very low levels of technological development; lack of local control; and, finally, a weakened ability to control trade through explicit policy because of the high degree of intra-corporate transfers.

In sum, there is very direct relationship between the type of trade in which a staples region engages, and its level of social and economic development. Note that this is not a connection that traditional (neoclassical) economic theory would ever make. It would say that a staples nation, such as Canada, must benefit from specializing and trading in those commodities for which it has the COMPARATIVE ADVANTAGE of primary resources. But in drawing upon this theory, as Innis (1956, p. 3) wrote some 60 years ago, orthodox economists ' . . . attempt to fit their analysis of new economic facts into . . . the economic theory of old countries . . . . The handicaps of this process are obvious, and there is evidence to show that [this is] . . . a new form of exploitation with dangerous consequences'.

To circumscribe such exploitation, Innis developed his staples theory in such a way that it was peculiarly suited to the 'new economic facts'. That theory brought together three types of concerns; geographical/ecological, institutional and technological. In turn, this triad became the basis for a theory of staples ACCUMULATION, one that begins with the metropole and the dominant technology found there in production, communications and transportation. That technology, in turn, determines the type of resources demanded by the metropole, and those sites within the periphery that are potentially exploitable. In fact, the centrality of technology to Innis's scheme has led some commentators to conclude that 'methodologically, [the] staple approach was more technological history writ large than a theory of economic growth in the conventional sense' (Watkins, 1963, p. 141). This cannot be entirely true because it is also necessary that the right kind of *geography* be present on which that technology can gain purchase. Unless, say, quantities of a resource are found at a location, or the site is accessible, no resource will be extracted regardless of the technology. As Innis (1946, p. 87) wrote: 'Geography provides the grooves which determine the course and to a large extent the character of economic life . . '. This is not geographical determinism, however, because geography and technology work together and, moreover, they can only work together provided that the third leg of the triad, an appropriate *institutional* structure, is also present. Investing in staples production in the periphery requires large amounts of capital expenditure because of the high ' . . . minimum indivisible cost[s] that must be met if production is to be undertaken at all . . .' (Spry, 1981, pp. 155–6). Only two institutional forms are capable of raising sufficient funds to cover such costs: the state, which provides basic infrastructure; and large corporations, often foreign-owned, that meet the immediate costs of plant and capital equipment.

When the right technology comes together with the right geography and the right institutional structure, the result is accumulation of 'cyclonic' frenzy. In this way virgin resource regions are transformed and enveloped within the produced spaces of the capitalist periphery. However, such intense accumulation never lasts, and because of the very instabilities of staples production, sooner rather than later investment shifts to yet other staples regions, leaving in its wake abandoned resource sites and communities. TJB

References

Baldwin, R. E. 1956: Patterns of development in newly settled regions. *Manchester Sch. Econ. Soc. Stud.* 24, pp. 161–79.

Britton, J. N. H. and Gilmour, J. M. 1971: *The weakest link: a technological perspective on Canadian industrial underdevelopment.* Background study 43. Ottawa: Science Council of Canada.

Clement, W. and Williams, G., eds 1989: *The new Canadian political economy.* Montreal and Kingston: McGill-Queen's University Press.

Innis, H. A. 1946: *Political economy in the modern state.* Toronto: Ryerson.

Innis, H. A. 1956: The teaching of economic history in Canada. In Innis, M. Q. ed., *Essays in Canadian economic history.* Toronto: University of Toronto Press, pp. 3–16.

Spry, I. M. 1981: Overhead costs, rigidities of productive capacity and the price system. In Melody, W. H., Salter, L. and Heyer, P., eds, *Culture, communication, and dependency: the tradition of H. A. Innis.* Norwood, NJ: Ablex, pp. 155–66.

Watkins, M. H. 1963: A staple theory of economic growth. *Can. J. Econ. pol. Sci.* 29, pp. 141–58.

Williams, G. 1983: *Not for export: towards a political economy of Canada's arrested industrialization.* Toronto: McClelland and Stewart.

Suggested Reading

Drache, D. 1982: Harold Innis and Canadian capitalist development. *Can. J. soc. pol. Theory,* 6, 25–60.

Hayter, R. and Barnes, T. J. 1990: Innis' staple theory, exports and recession: British Columbia 1981–86. *Econ. Geogr.,* 66, pp. 156–73.

Watkins (1963).

state Traditionally regarded as an area of land (or land and water) with relatively well defined, internationally recognized, political boundaries. Within this TERRITORY resides a people with an independent political identity, usually referred to as

NATIONALISM. This traditional use of the term is perhaps better confined to the notion of a NATION–STATE; another use of the term is common in the literature and refers to the *theory of the state*.

The nation–state has always been a major focus in POLITICAL GEOGRAPHY. The Greek philosopher Artistotle wrote about the ideal state in the third century BC, and its relevance in geography can be followed through the writings of C. Ritter and F. Ratzel in the nineteenth century. The evolution of the nation–state is usually traced through four broad phases: pre-agrarian, agrarian, industrial and post-industrial. In pre-agrarian societies, tribal loyalties predominated. Hunting and gathering bands were typically too small and isolated to allow for, or require, the existence of an independent political institution. In contrast, agrarian societies were mostly state-endowed. The emergence of literacy and a specialized clerical class made possible the centralized organization and storage of records, rules and culture. However, COMMUNITIES remained isolated, and the clerisy could not dominate beyond localized territories.

A crucial transitional phase in this conventional sequence was the absolutist state, in which a single monarchy displaced prior feudal arrangements of decentralized fiefdoms (see FEUDALISM), and created such key precursors of the modern nation–state as standing armies, uniform tax structures and bureaucracies. Industrial society permitted a specialized division of labour and the emergence of a high culture. In such a complex society, a centralized state agency takes over the roles of socialization, education and authority. In the POST-INDUSTRIAL SOCIETY, the state has grown to play a dominant role in social relations. A new world political organization is evidenced in the development of *supranation–states*, based on such things as trade and defence agreements (see COMMON MARKET). This has been paralleled by a resurgence of local NATIONALISMS, which have encouraged a splintering of nation–states into smaller units based on sentiments of ETHNICITY, RACE or local separatist nationalisms. The rise of both supranation–states and intense local nationalisms has brought into the question the continuing viability of existing nation–states. Needless to say, not all nation–states necessarily develop as a consequence of this four-stage model. Different patterns of nation–state evolution have been observed in, for example, the socialist states of Eastern Europe and the military/authoritarian states of South America.

More generally, a *theory of the state* focuses on the state as a set of institutions for the protection and maintenance of SOCIETY. These institutions include government, politics, the judiciary, armed forces, etc., and guarantee the reproduction of social relations in a way which is beyond the capability of any individual or single social group (cf. SOCIAL REPRODUCTION). The theory of the state is driven by a profoundly important question: Why is it necessary to constitute in society a separate agency called the state? Contemporary discussions of this question usually trace their roots back to Hobbes and Locke, through such liberal democrats as Mill and Bentham, to the social theories of Marx and Weber. These thinkers have touched on many enduring themes, including the design of a minimalist state, legitimacy and public accountability in a democracy, the potentially repressive nature of state control, and the bureaucratization of the state.

Current analyses of the state typically draw the distinction between state *form*, state *function* and state *apparatus*. The question of form examines how a specific state structure is constituted by, and evolves within, a given SOCIAL FORMATION. (A capitalist society should, in principle, give rise to a distinctively capitalist state.) The issue of function refers to those activities undertaken in the name of the state; in other words, what the state actually 'does'. Finally, STATE APPARATUS refers to the mechanisms through which these functions are executed.

Liberal political thought isolates four views of the state as: (a) supplier of PUBLIC GOODS and services; (b) regulator and facilitator of the economy; (c) social engineer with an agenda of its own; and (d) arbiter between the many groups which compose society (cf. PLURALISM).

Structuralist thought has focused on the links between the state elite and the ruling class. A popular view of the present-day state, which is common to theorists of many persuasions, is a view of the state as a 'crisis-manager'. According to this perspective, the state acts to contain the political repercussions of the socio-economic system, operating (in effect) as an input–output mechanism. State outputs consist of administrative decisions taken in the interest of diverse social groups; its inputs are constituent demands and mass loyalty. If the outputs do not satisfy the various constituencies, a 'rationality crisis' results, in which the viability of the state is brought into question. This could lead to a 'legitimation crisis' if mass loyalty to the state is withdrawn. (See also CRISIS; CRITICAL THEORY.)

The LOCAL STATE is key instrument of crisis management, as is the trend towards CORPORATISM, involving an institutionalized form of group or CLASS CONFLICT, in which formal avenues of conflict and compromise are established and maintained in order to minimize the risk of unpredictable crises. The expansion of the state apparatus is an important manifestation of contemporary corporatist relations.

The theory of the state is of vital importance in the rebirth of political geography. Some analysts question whether or not we need a theory of the state. Others claim that such a theory is of fundamental, central significance to a properly constituted political geography. Part of the difficulty in this latter task is the fact that state theory is a highly contested topic of scholarly debate. There are actually a great many *theories* of the state, each with a claim to privileged insight within its 'home domain'. But most contemporary theorists recognize the significance of territory/geography in the creation and re-creation of states.   MJD

Suggested Reading

Alford, R. R. and Friedland, R. 1985: *Powers of theory: capitalism, the state, and democracy*, New York: Cambridge University Press.

Clark, G. L. and Dear, M. J. 1984: *State apparatus: structures and language of legitimacy*. Boston: Allen and Unwin.

Gellner, E. 1983: *Nations and nationalism*. Oxford: Blackwell/Ithaca, NY: Cornell University Press.

Held, D. et al. 1983: *States and societies*. New York: New York University Press.

Mann, M. 1986: *The sources of social power*, volume 1, *A history of power from the beginning to A.D. 1760*. New York: Cambridge University Press.

Taylor, P. J. 1991: Political geography within world-systems analysis. *Review, Fernand Brandel Center* XIV, pp. 387–402.

state apparatus   The set of institutions and organizations through which STATE power is exercised. Analysis of the state apparatus is important because: (a) the apparatus is an imperfect, at times obsolescent, manifestation of changing social relations; (b) the apparatus acts as a medium through which the exercise of state POWER is 'filtered' and inevitably transformed; and (c) because it is manifest as a concrete set of institutions, the apparatus offers the potential for strategic intervention by powerful social groups.

The state apparatus consists of a number of sub-apparatus, as follows:

(a) *political*, the set of parties, elections, governments and constitutions;

(b) *legal*, the mechanisms which allow peaceful mediation between conflicting social groups;

(c) *repressive*, the mechanisms of internal (intranational) and external (international) enforcement of state power, including the civilian police and the armed forces;

(d) *production*, the range of state-manufactured and state-distributed goods and services;

(e) *provision*, whereby the state contracts with other agencies for the production and distribution of goods and services;

(f) *treasury*, fiscal and monetary arrangements for regulating internal and external economic relations;

(g) *health, education and welfare*, basic services for the promotion of population well-being;

(h) *information*, state-sponsored or state-controlled mechanisms for information dissemination;

(i) *communications and media*, licensed and regulated but usually relatively autonomous information-dissemination channels, including telecommunications and print;

(j) *administration*, a sub-apparatus designed to ensure the overall compatibility and operation of all the various state sub-apparatuses; and

(k) *regulatory agencies*, created to organize and extend state intervention into non-state activities, including family and industrial relations.

The various state apparatuses are vital in achieving the three functions of the modern capitalist state: (a) *to secure social consensus* by guaranteeing acceptance of the prevailing social contract by all groups in society; (b) *to secure the conditions of production* by regulating social investment to increase production in the public and private sectors, and social consumption to ensure the reproduction of labour force; and (c) *to secure social integration* by ensuring the welfare of all groups in society. The structure and practices of the state apparatus can alter dramatically according to the vicissitudes of the political climate (as, for example, in the PRIVATIZATION phenomenon). (See also LOCAL STATE.)   MJD

Suggested Reading

Clark, G. L. and Dear, M. J. 1984: *State apparatus: structures and language of legitimacy.* Boston: Allen and Unwin, ch. 3.

Kammerman, S. B. and Kahn, A. J., eds 1989: *Privatization and the welfare state.* Princeton, NJ: Princeton University Press.

Wolch, J. R. 1990: *The shadow state.* New York: The Foundation Center.

statistics   See NON-PARAMETRIC STATISTICS.

stochastic process   A mathematical–statistical model describing the sequence of outcomes from a series of trials in probability terms. Some authors distinguish between a probabilistic model in which the outcome of individual trials is predicted, and a stochastic model in which the development of a whole series of outcomes is modelled. A stochastic model may therefore include those situations in which the outcome of a specific trial is in some way dependent upon outcomes of preceding trials. It is a consequence of this that the same PROCESS can produce an infinite (or

at least very large) number of different realizations; for example, a sequence of 50 throws of a die produces many different sequences of the digits 1 to 6. It is therefore quite different from a deterministic model, which for one set of inputs can only yield one unique realization.

In applying this concept geographers have not only considered temporal sequences (e.g. yields of a crop, or prices of a commodity) but have also considered spatial sequences in one or more dimensions. The most recent uses have combined both time and space (e.g. in the study of prices or of epidemics). The underlying time scale may be discrete or continuous.

The stochastic or probabilistic element in these models may be included because the process is thought to have some purely random element, but more often the random element is thought to subsume a large number of (often minor) causal influences, the net effect of which is a quasi-random disturbance of the outcomes.

A common application of these ideas in geography is the proposal that a point pattern in geographical space (e.g. settlements or factories) may have resulted from a quasi-random process in which each geographical unit of a given size has an equal probability of receiving a point. This is modelled by the Poisson probability distribution (see FREQUENCY DISTRIBUTION), but if the receipt of one event changes the probability of receiving a further event (positively or negatively) then the process is stochastic and may be modelled accordingly; for example, by the negative binomial distribution.

In time series studies attention has been focused upon two main types of stochastic process: autoregressive and moving average models. In *autoregressive* models the value of the series at time t is highly correlated with the value at times $t - 1$, $t - 2$, etc., but includes a random component. *Moving average* models use a linear weighted sum of present and past random values. A third type of stochastic process is the MARKOV PROCESS.

In all these cases if the process evolves slowly (as is true, for example, in settlement) there are two problems. First, it may be necessary to infer the best-fitting process from a single cross-sectional pattern, or at best from a few points on the time scale. Second, most of the models assume stationarity – that the process is constant over time (temporal stationarity) and space (spatial stationarity). Where these assumptions are not met it may be possible to filter the data (e.g. to remove trends over time), but if this is not possible the results may be invalid. AMH

Suggested Reading

Bennett, R. J. 1979: *Spatial time series*. London: Pion.

Hoel, P. G., Port, S. C. and Stone, C. J. 1972: *Introduction to stochastic processes*. Boston: Houghton Mifflin.

structural functionalism A tradition of social theory usually associated with the writings of Talcott Parsons, whose central proposition is that the structure of any social SYSTEM cannot be derived from 'the actor's point of view' but must instead be explained by the ways in which four 'functional imperatives' necessary for the survival of the system are met

(see also FUNCTIONALISM). These functions are:

Adaptation [which] refers to the problem of obtaining enough resources or facilities from the system's external environment, and their subsequent distribution in the system.

Goal attainment [which] refers to the features of an action system which serve to establish its goals, and to motivate and mobilize effort and energy in the system towards their achievement.

Integration [which] refers to the problem of maintaining coherence or solidarity, and involves those elements which establish control, maintain co-ordination of subsystems and prevent major disruption in the system.

Latency [which] refers to the processes by which motivational energy is stored and distributed to the system, [and] involves two interlinked problems: *pattern-maintenance*, the supply of symbols, ideas, tastes and judgements from the cultural system, and *tension-management*, the resolution of internal strains and tensions of actors (Hamilton, 1983, p. 108).

The most detailed account of the schema is provided in Parsons's *The social system* (1951); perhaps the most comprehensive application of the model is Smelser's

ADAPTATION: procurement of capital		GOAL ATTAINMENT: control of production	
control of liquid funds	control of capital	budgeting	decisions to produce
valuation of capitalization	structural arrangements of capital	valuation of production	coordination of production
LATENCY: technical processes of production		INTEGRATION: control of industrial organization	
knowledge and skills	technical production processes	new techniques of production	control of improvement of products
valuation of implementation of production	managerial coordination	valuation of innovation	recombination of factors of production

structural functionalism *Functional dimensions* (after Smelser, 1959).

(1959) analysis of the structure of the Lancashire cotton industry (see the figure), which certainly shows why Craib (1984) says Parsons reminds him 'of a filing clerk who is too intelligent for his work'.

Parsons's 'A–G–I–L' schema is often contrasted with his early account of *The structure of social action* (1937), which is usually assumed to be 'voluntarist' in its overarching concern with developing an 'action theory' around the so-called 'unit act'. But there are some basic continuities between the two formulations, and Parsons himself subsequently rejected descriptions of his work as 'structural functionalism' and reinstated the earlier term 'action theory'. Whatever the merits of this manoeuvre, Parsons insisted that the analysis of any system requires the conjunction of both static ('structure') and dynamic ('function') components, and he constantly accentuated the need to grasp the *dynamics* of social systems. Hence he attributed crucial importance to the interchanges between the systems and subsystems and, in order to sharpen the focus still further, in his later formulations he developed a more formal *cybernetic* model of society. This drew upon biology and (GENERAL) SYSTEMS THEORY as much as it did upon classical social theory, and was primarily concerned with interchanges of information and energy and with modelling the evolution of societies 'as an extension of biological evolution' (Giddens, 1984, pp. 263–74; Parsons, 1971).

Although Parsons's views have been subjected to a sustained and at times devastating critique, his influence on modern social theory has been quite extraordinary. Not only has there been a series of striking developments of systems theory – including Alexander's (1983) vigorously constructive appraisal of Parsons's ideas, Luhmann's innovative extensions of Parsons's original schema (Luhmann, 1979, 1981), and Wallerstein's WORLD-SYSTEMS ANALYSIS, which Cooper (1981) calls 'Parsonianism on a world scale' (see Aronowitz, 1981) – but even those seemingly distant from Parsons have often made a series of critical

appropriations of his ideas (see, e.g., Giddens, 1977; Habermas, 1987).

For all this, however, Parsons's shadow over human geography has been much shorter. This is partly the result of the atheoretical cast of traditional SOCIAL GEOGRAPHY – Parsons described himself as 'an incurable theorist' – but even the more theoretical exercises in social geography that followed (where they addressed such issues at all) concerned themselves with general models of social systems rather than Parsons's specific formulations. Interestingly, however, many of the criticisms which were made of structural Marxism within human geography (e.g. Duncan and Ley, 1982) mimic exactly those objections which have been most frequently registered against structural functionalism (DiTomaso, 1982; Gregory, 1980: see also HUMAN AGENCY). More recently still, the interest in POSTMODERNISM, and in particular the scepticism with which totalizing claims to knowledge and so-called 'foundational' epistemologies have been greeted, make it unlikely that Parsons's version of GRAND THEORY will attract a sympathetic audience in the immediate future. A particular problem is the ETHNOCENTRISM of his work: many commentators have seen structural functionalism as another attempt to construct a general model of society out of what is in fact a highly particular reading of the United States of America.   DG

References

Alexander, J. 1983: *Theoretical logic in sociology*, volume 4, *The modern reconstruction of social thought: Talcott Parsons*. Berkeley, CA: University of California Press.

Aronowitz, S. 1981: A metatheoretical critique of Immanuel Wallerstein's The modern world-system. *Theory and society* 9, pp. 503–20.

Cooper, F. 1981: Africa and the world economy. *Afric. Stud. R.*, 14, pp. 1–86.

Craib, I. 1984: *Modern social theory: from Parsons to Habermas*. Brighton: Wheatsheaf/New York: St. Martin's Press.

DiTomaso, N. 1982: 'Sociological reductionism' from Parsons to Althusser: linking action and structure in social theory. *Am. Soc. R.* 47, pp. 14–28.

Duncan, J. and Ley, D. 1982: Structural Marxism and human geography: a critical assessment. *Ann. Ass. Am. Geogr.* 72, pp. 30–59.

Giddens, A. 1977: *Studies in social and political theory*. London: Hutchinson.

Giddens, A. 1984: *The constitution of society*. Cambridge: Polity Press.

Gregory, D. 1980: The ideology of control: systems theory and geography. *Tijdschr. econ. soc. Geogr.* 71, pp. 327–42.

Habermas, J. 1987: *The theory of communicative action*, volume 2; *Lifeworld and system: a critique of functionalist reason*. Cambridge: Polity Press.

Hamilton, P. 1983: *Talcott Parsons*. London: Tavistock.

Luhmann, N. 1979: *Trust and power*. New York: John Wiley.

Luhmann, N. 1981: *The differentiation of society*. New York: Columbia University Press.

Parsons, T. 1937: *The structure of social action*. New York: Free Press.

Parsons, T. 1951: *The social system*. London: Routledge and Kegan Paul.

Parsons, T. 1971: *The system of modern societies*. Englewood Cliffs, NJ: Prentice-Hall.

Smelser, N. 1959: *Social change in the Industrial Revolution*. London: Routledge and Kegan Paul/ Chicago: University of Chicago Press.

Suggested Reading

Alexander (1984).

Hamilton (1983).

structural Marxism   A modern school of HISTORICAL MATERIALISM, most closely associated with the work of the French philosopher Louis Althusser. His ideas went through a series of reformulations and autocritiques, but most critical attention has been focused on his work during the 1960s and 1970s (see Elliott, 1987). His project was ambitious and complex, but in general Althusser (1969) and Althusser and Balibar (1970) sought to distinguish between Marx's 'early' writings, which were supposedly still close enough to Kantian, and particularly Hegelian, philosophy to represent a 'humanism', and Marx's 'mature' writings which, they argued, broke so completely with Hegelian philosophy that they could be judged a 'science'. There are two issues woven together in these claims: on the one hand, the distinction between the work of the young Marx (1840–4) and the mature Marx (1857–83); and on the other hand, the opposition between an early humanism and a subsequent 'science'. Both claims

have been contested: even when separated by the 'transitional works' of 1845–57 (which include the *Grundrisse*, the notebooks composed in preparation for *Capital*), it is extremely difficult to divide Marx's thought into such distinct clinical stages; and Althusser's vision of Marxism as a science of MODES OF PRODUCTION which focuses on the structures of CAPITALISM, exposes the IDEOLOGY of humanism and seemingly evicts HUMAN AGENCY from historical eventuation has been attacked by critics who think Althusser was too heavily influenced by STRUCTURALISM.

The debate was particularly vigorous within Anglophone Marxism, particularly among social historians, where it was sparked off by Thompson's (1978) polemic against Althusser and by Johnston's (1978) survey of the limits of Thompson's own position. A barrage of exchanges then appeared in *History Workshop Journal* and the debate was eventually joined by, among others: Hirst (1979), who had collaborated with a number of others in a series of critical engagements with Althusser which went some considerable way beyond Althusser's own positions (Hindess and Hirst, 1975, 1977; Cutler et al., 1977); and Anderson (1980), who had played a large part in opening Anglophone Marxism to other traditions of Continental European Marxism and who had himself produced two distinguished Althusserian accounts of European history (Anderson, 1975, 1976). In Francophone circles, the main response to 'the rise and fall of structural Marxism' (Benton, 1984) was not a reinstatement of humanism but a move to POSTSTRUCTURALISM.

In human geography, the exchanges were more muted (Chouinard and Fincher, 1982; Duncan and Ley, 1982) – perhaps because Althusser's ideas never had the constituency that they enjoyed in other disciplines – and the interest in poststructuralism emerged correspondingly later. But the legacy of Althusser is much greater than this suggests, and includes the following:

(a) A critique of EMPIRICISM and a recognition of the basic importance of theoretical work (see also PROBLEMATIC).

In human geography this took the form of a critique of SPATIAL SCIENCE which depended, at least in part, on an engagement with structural Marxism (Gregory, 1978); it has since been developed most extensively within a different (but none the less connected) philosophy of science, namely REALISM.

(b) A much more complex view of the architectonics of capitalism than classical Marxism's base–superstructure model. Althusser distinguished between economic, political and ideological levels of a SOCIAL FORMATION, and argued that different levels would *dominate* different social formations (the political or ideological in feudalism, for example, and the economic in capitalism); the dominant level would in each case be *determined* by the economic level. This was intended to militate against a reductionism in which explanations are immediately and directly reduced to a single level: structural Marxism treated causality as a question of *overdetermination*. In human geography this sort of topography has now become something of a commonplace, although without the conceptual apparatus that accompanied it in Althusser's work: its most formal expression is probably found in those who have drawn on Jameson's (1991) account of POSTMODERNISM as the 'cultural dominant' in late-twentieth-century capitalism.

(c) The assignment of distinctive 'times' and 'spaces' to each of the levels of the social formation. Again, the social construction of these times and spaces was an important counter to spatial science, but the theoretical elaboration of SPATIALITY in this sense originally derived from work in urban sociology (Castells, 1977), political economy (Lipietz, 1977) and political philosophy (Poulantzas 1980; see Cooke, 1989). It has since fed into a more general interest in the PRODUCTION OF SPACE, where it has joined with work undertaken outside the framework of structural Marxism (Lefebvre, 1991).

(d) A recognition of the social constitution of the human subject: the autonomous, sovereign and 'centred' subject of humanism has been displaced from many human geographies, and Althusser's

concept of *interpellation* has proved to be of considerable importance in clarifying the different ways in which human subjects are constituted over space and through time, and in elaborating the concept of multiple and competing subject-positions in POST-MARXISM and POSTSTRUCTURALISM (see Smith, 1989).   DG

References

Althusser, L. 1969: *For Marx*. London: Verso.

Althusser, L. and Balibar, E. 1970: *Reading Capital*. London: New Left Books.

Anderson, P. 1975: *Passages from antiquity to feudalism*. London: New Left Books.

Anderson, P. 1976: *Lineages of the absolutist state*. London: New Left Books.

Anderson, P. 1980: *Arguments within English Marxism*. London: Verso.

Benton, T. 1984: *The rise and fall of structural Marxism: Althusser and his influence*. London: Macmillan.

Castells, M. 1977: *The urban question: a Marxist approach*. London: Edward Arnold.

Chouinard, V. and Fincher, R. 1983: A critique of 'Structural Marxism and human geography'. *Ann. Ass. Am. Geogr.* 73, pp. 137–46.

Cooke, P. 1989: Nation, space, modernity. In Peet, R., and Thrift, N., eds, *New models in geography*, volume 1. London: Unwin Hyman, pp. 267–91.

Cutler, A., Hindess, B, Hirst, P. Q. and Hussain, A. 1977: *Marx's Capital and capitalism today*. London: Routledge and Kegan Paul.

Duncan, J. and Ley, D. 1982: Structural Marxism and human geography. *Ann. Ass. Am. Geogr.* 72, pp. 30–59.

Elliott, G. 1987: *Althusser: the detour of theory*. London: Verso.

Gregory, D. 1978: *Ideology, science and human geography*. London: Hutchinson.

Hindess, B. and Hirst, P. Q. 1975: *Pre-capitalist modes of production*. London: Routledge and Kegan Paul.

Hindess, B. and Hirst, P. Q. 1977: *Mode of production and social formation*. London: Macmillan.

Hirst, P. 1979: The necessity of theory. *Econ. Societ.* 8, pp. 417–45.

Jameson, F. 1991: *Postmodernism, or the cultural logic of late capitalism*. Durham, NC: Duke University Press.

Johnston, R. 1978: Edward Thompson, Eugene Genovese and socialist–humanist history. *Hist. Workshop J.* 6, pp. 79–100.

Lefebvre, H. 1991: *The production of space.* Oxford: Blackwell.

Lipietz, A. 1977: *Le capital et son espace.* Paris: Maspero.

Poulantzas, N. 1980: *State, power, socialism.* London: Verso.

Smith, P. 1989: *Discerning the subject.* Minneapolis: University of Minnesota Press.

Thompson, E. P. 1978: *The poverty of theory and other essays.* London: Merlin.

Suggested Reading

Anderson (1980).

Benton (1984).

structuralism A set of principles and procedures, originally derived from linguistics and linguistic philosophy, which involve moving 'beneath' the visible and conscious designs of active human subjects in order to expose an essential logic which is supposed to bind these designs together in enduring and underlying *structures* that can be exposed through a series of purely intellectual operations. Structuralism was a dominant current in postwar French philosophy, where it owed much to the pioneering contributions of Roland Barthes in literary theory, Claude Lévi-Strauss in anthropology and Jean Piaget in psychology. It also had an important impact on the development of STRUCTURAL MARXISM (particularly the work of Louis Althusser and Etienne Balibar) and on the rise of POSTSTRUCTURALISM (including the work of Jacques Derrida and Michel Foucault); but it cannot be mapped directly onto either of these fields (see Merquior, 1986; Harland, 1987).

In the 1970s structuralism was extended, in a loose and for the most part programmatic fashion, into Anglophone human geography as part of the contemporary critique of EMPIRICISM and POSITIVISM that characterized modern SPATIAL SCIENCE (Tuan, 1972; Harvey, 1973; Marchand, 1974; Sayer, 1976; Gregory, 1978). In general, and in part in consequence, most human geographers came to recognize the importance of clarifying the theoretical status of the constructs with which they worked: there was a widespread acknowledgement that the 'facts' did not 'speak for themselves' and that all empirical enquiry required a keen theoretical

sensibility. That sensibility often entailed a suspicion about voluntarism – many geographers doubted that social life could be explained in terms of the unbounded capacities of HUMAN AGENCY – and this was given a political edge by those who believed that structures of various sorts constrained and shaped the outcomes of human actions over space. For this reason, many human geographers adopted various *depth models* of landscapes, space-economies and spatial systems, in order to look 'beneath' the taken-for-granted categories by means of which social life was usually comprehended. As the 1970s became the 1980s, however, these enquiries increasingly relied on the philosophy of REALISM rather than structuralism, and the most common theoretical tools used to dissect the surfaces of the social world were probably drawn from POLITICAL ECONOMY rather than literary theory, anthropology or psychology: and even within MARXIST GEOGRAPHY the influence of Althusser was never very pronounced and soon diminished. It was not until the end of the 1980s and the beginning of the 1990s that those three fields assumed a greater prominence, largely as a result of the rise of a FEMINIST GEOGRAPHY and the reinvigoration of a CULTURAL GEOGRAPHY, both of which have been theoretically informed by poststructuralism.   DG

References

Gregory, D. 1978: *Ideology, science and human geography.* London: Hutchinson, pp. 81–122.

Harland, R. 1987: *Superstructuralism: the philosophy of structuralism and post-structuralism.* New York: Methuen.

Harvey, D. 1973: *Social justice and the city.* London: Edward Arnold, pp. 286–314.

Marchand, B. 1974: Quantitative geography: revolution or counter-revolution? *Geoforum* 17, pp. 15–24.

Merquior, J. 1986: *From Prague to Paris: a critique of structuralist and post-structuralist thought.* London: Verso.

Sayer, R. A. 1976: A critique of urban modelling: from regional science to urban and regional political economy. *Progr. Plann.* 6(3).

Tuan, Y.-F. 1972: Structuralism, existentialism and environmental perception. *Environ. Behav.* 3, pp. 319–31.

Suggested Reading

Gregory (1978).
Merquior (1986).

structuration theory An approach to social theory concerned with the intersections between knowledgeable and capable *human agents* and the wider *social systems and structures* in which they are implicated. The dualism between 'agency' and 'structure' is focal to both social theory and social life:

People make their own history – but only under definite circumstances and conditions; we act through a world of rules which our action makes, breaks and renews – we are creatures of the rules, the rules are our creations; we make our own world – the world confronts us as an implacable order of social facts set over against us. The variations on the theme are innumerable; and the failures of the human sciences to work the theme to a satisfactory conclusion are inscribed on page after page of their literature. The estranged symbiosis of [agency] and structure is both a commonplace of everyday life and the persistent fulcrum of social analysis (Abrams, 1980).

In fact it is possible to distinguish 'two anthropologies', 'two sociologies', 'two human geographies' and the like, all produced by this basic dualism. Although some writers have identified a 'structurationist school' (Thrift, 1983), the attempt to develop structuration theory as a way of overcoming these dualisms is most closely associated with the work of the British sociologist Anthony Giddens (see Cohen, 1989; Craib, 1992). His project can be divided into two phases. For human geography, the first phase works in towards the discipline, so to speak, by mobilizing a critique of social theory to confront a problem which is common to all the humanities and the social sciences; the second phase, in contrast, threads out from the discipline to reveal the importance of time–space relations to all forms of social enquiry.

Phase I. Giddens's project is founded on a critique of major traditions of social theory, including broadly 'interpretative' traditions which have been concerned with questions of meaning and understanding (Giddens, 1976), and broadly 'structural' traditions which focus on the systems and structures that shape and constrain social life (Giddens, 1977). His conclusions may be summarized as follows:

(a) 'Social theory must incorporate a treatment of action as rationalized conduct ordered reflexively by human agents, and must grasp the significance of language as the practical medium whereby this is made

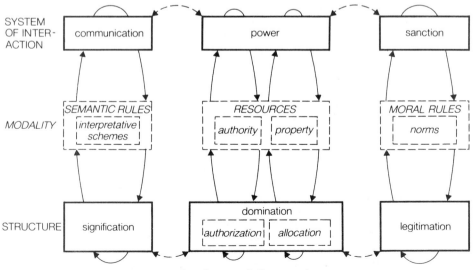

structuration theory *1: System and structure.*

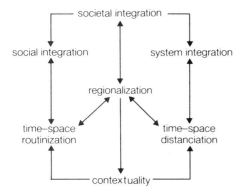

structuration theory *2: Time–space relations.*

possible'. In short, theory requires a concept of *reflexivity* through which the production and reproduction of social life is treated as a skilled accomplishment on the part of knowledgeable and capable subjects, rather than as an automatic response to some transcendental or trans-historical 'logic' or 'functional imperative'. A leading claim of structuration theory is thus that '*every social actor knows a great deal about the conditions of reproduction of the society of which he or she is a member*'.

(b) Social theory must incorporate a treatment of 'institutional organization, power and struggle as integral features of social life', and must therefore elucidate the ways in which social life goes forward under conditions that are neither 'wholly comprehended' nor 'wholly intended' by social actors, but which are nevertheless necessarily implicated in the production and reproduction of social life. In short, social theory requires a concept of *recursiveness* through which 'structural properties of social systems' are treated as both 'medium and outcome' of the social practices that constitute those systems. A second claim of structuration theory is thus that '*structure is not to be conceptualized as a barrier to action, but as essentially involved in its production*'.

These twin conclusions provide the framework for a *stratification model* (see HUMAN AGENCY) and for the model of the production and reproduction of social life set out in figure 1. This is the mainspring of structuration theory. Giddens's purpose is to replace the conventional dualism between 'agency' and 'structure' by a *duality*.

In order to do so, he makes a basic distinction between the 'outer' dimensions of (a) system and (b) structure:

(a) Social *systems* are systems of interaction, Giddens argues, the interdependencies of which can be analysed as recurrent social practices: as such, they involve *the situated activities of human subjects*.

(b) Social systems have *structures* which are characterized by *the absence of a subject*.

The 'inner' dimensions which bind systems and subjects to structures are made up of *rules and resources* which are instantiated in systems of social interaction by knowledgeable and capable human subjects, and which derive from the structures, which are in turn reconstituted through these recurrent social practices.

Three features of this model require emphasis:

(a) All systems of social interaction entail communication, POWER and sanction, and so depend upon structures of signification, domination and legitimation.

(b) The symmetry between the production of social practices and the reproduction of social structures ensures that 'the personal, transient encounters of daily life' are bound in to 'the long-term sedimentation or development of social institutions'.

(c) The production and reproduction of social life is contingent: 'the seeds of change are present in every moment of the constitution of social systems'. Of particular importance are *conflicts* between individuals or groups and *contradictions* between 'structural principles'.

These formulations have attracted three major criticisms. First, Giddens is charged with eclecticism. It is impossible, so many of his critics argue, to bring together such radically discrepant theoretical traditions and rework them into some new synthesis. Second, Giddens is supposed to have retained the very dualism he sought to transcend. According to Archer (1990), the theory of structuration 'oscillates between the two divergent images it bestrides, between (a) the hyperactivity of agency, whose corollary is the innate volatility of society, and (b) the rigid coherence of structural properties associated with the essential recursiveness of social life'. Indeed, throughout his work Giddens has consistently advocated a methodological *bracketing* which allows for either the analysis of strategic conduct or the analysis of institutions, and which transposes the dualism between 'agency' and 'structure' from the theoretical to the methodological level. Third, Giddens's conceptions of both 'agency' and 'structure' have been attacked; the former for collapsing agency into action, for tying agency too closely to everyday conduct understood as 'doing' (Dallmayr, 1982), and the latter for collapsing structure into rules and resources, and so driving the notion of structure back into the concrete and 'depriving it of autonomous [objective] properties which govern conduct quite independently of the creative and constituting capacities of actors' (Layder, 1981).

Phase II. The second phase of Giddens's work has been characterized by a critique of HISTORICAL MATERIALISM and by an interest in the time–space constitution of social life. In the first place, Giddens argues that historical materialism is irretrievably compromised by its FUNCTIONALISM, its evolutionary cast, and its view of the forces of production as the key to the history of human societies. He represents structuration theory, by contrast, as a non-functionalist, anti-evolutionary and multidimensional account of the constitution of (particularly modern) human societies. While most of his critics concede that his work represents a serious engagement with Marxism, they also object to the 'almost complete absence of any serious examination of the theory or history of Marxism after Marx' (Gane, 1983), and are often puzzled as to why his own account of social change, 'with its stress on changing modes of surplus-extraction', should be regarded 'as in any sense critical of or an alternative to Marxism' (Callinicos, 1985; Sayer, 1990). Indeed, Wright (1989) concludes that Giddens's propositions are 'largely compatible with most of the substantive claims of both classical and contemporary Marxism'.

In the second place, however, Giddens (1981, 1984, 1985) has departed substantially from both classical social theory and historical materialism in the centrality he accords to time–space relations. His basic schema is summarized in figure 2 (see Gregory, 1989; Saunders, 1989). Giddens now phrases the problem of 'agency' and 'structure' in terms of how societal integration is effected over time and space: how time and space are 'bound in' to the conduct of social life. He makes an analytical distinction between (a) social integration and (b) system integration:

(a) *Social integration*. Giddens argues that the continuity of day-to-day life depends, in part, on routinized interactions between actors who are typically *co-present* in time and/or space, so that a (reconstituted) version of Hägerstrand's TIME-GEOGRAPHY is, in principle, capable of clarifying the time–space constitution of these segments of recurrent social practices.

(b) *System integration*. In so far as regularized social practices are recognizably 'the same' over varying spans of time and space, Giddens argues that they flow from and fold back into structural relations which reach beyond the here and now to define interactions with others who are *absent* in time and/or space. A basic task of structuration theory is therefore to show how 'the limitations of individual "presence" are transcended by the "stretching" of social relations across time and space' through a process of TIME-SPACE DISTANCIATION.

The central pivot in the articulation of (a) and (b) – in the intermingling of *presence* and *absence* – is provided by the following:

(c) *Regionalization*. According to Giddens, the connections between social integration and system integration can be elucidated through the time–space organization of LOCALES, i.e. 'by examining the modes of regionalization which channel, and are channelled by, the time–space paths the members of a community or society follow in their day-to-day activities'. In so far as these are formed through a hierarchy of locales (cf. Hägerstrand's 'dominant projects' and domains), then such paths will be 'strongly influenced by, and also reproduce, basic institutional parameters of the social systems in which they are implicated' (Giddens, 1984).

In this way Giddens believes that it is possible to explicate the interconnection of routinized and repetitive conduct between actors or groups of actors with long-term, large-scale institutional development in a depth which is denied to both conventional social theory and historical materialism. But the status of his project is unclear. His critics object that there have been few detailed concrete studies of structuration as a process, and that there are considerable barriers in the way of translating these high-level ideas into empirical enquiry (Gregson, 1989). While there have been several attempts to explore the connections between structuration theory and REALISM, which would undoubtedly clarify the links between theoretical and empirical work, Giddens is plainly reluctant to see structuration theory 'applied' in any conventional way. He prefers to think of it not as a rigorous research programme but as a series of sensitizing devices, and he has used its propositions as a springboard from which to offer a series of provocative, but none the less highly general, characterizations of the contours of MODERNITY (Giddens, 1990, 1991).   DG

References

Abrams, P. 1980: History, sociology, historical sociology. *Past and Present* 87, pp. 3–16.

Archer, M. 1990: Human agency and social structure: a critique of Giddens. In Clark, J., Modgil C. and Modgil S., eds, *Anthony Giddens: consensus and controversy*. Brighton, UK: Falmer, pp. 73–84.

Callinicos, A. 1985: Anthony Giddens: a contemporary critique. *Theory and Society* 14, pp. 133–66.

Cohen, I. 1989: *Structuration theory: Anthony Giddens and the constitution of social life*. London: Macmillan.

Craib, I. 1992: *Anthony Giddens*. London: Routledge.

Dallmayr, F. 1982: The theory of structuration: a critique. In Giddens, A., *Profiles and critiques in social theory*. London: Macmillan, pp. 18–25.

Gane, M. 1983: Anthony Giddens and the crisis of social theory. *Econ. Societ.* 12, pp. 368–98.

Giddens, A. 1976: *New rules of sociological method*. London: Hutchinson.

Giddens, A. 1977: *Studies in social and political theory*. London: Hutchinson.

Giddens, A. 1981: *A contemporary critique of historical materialism*, volume 1, *Power, property and the state*. London: Macmillan.

Giddens, A. 1984: *The constitution of society*. Cambridge: Polity Press.

Giddens, A. 1985: *A contemporary critique of historical materialism*, volume 2; *The nation–state and violence*. Cambridge: Polity Press.

Giddens, A. 1990 *The consequences of modernity*. Stanford, CA: Stanford University Press.

Giddens,ʼ A. 1991: *Modernity and self-identity*. Cambridge: Polity Press.

Gregory, D. 1989: Presence and absences: time–space relations and structuration theory. In Held, D. and Thompson, J. B., eds, *Social theory of the modern societies: Anthony Giddens and his critics*. Cambridge: Cambridge University Press, pp. 185–214.

Gregson, N. 1989: On the (ir)relevance of structuration theory to empirical research. In Held, D. and Thompson, J. B., eds, *Social theory of the modern societies: Anthony Giddens and his critics*. Cambridge: Cambridge University Press, pp. 235–48.

Layder, D. 1981: *Structure, interaction and social theory*. London: Routledge.

Saunders, P. 1989: Space, urbanism and the created environment. In Held, D. and Thompson, J. B., eds, *Social theory of the modern societies: Anthony Giddens and his critics*. Cambridge: Cambridge University Press, pp. 215–34.

Sayer, D. 1990: Reinventing the wheel: Anthony Giddens, Karl Marx and social change. In Clark, J., Modgil C. and Modgil S., eds, *Anthony Giddens: consensus and controversy*. Brighton, UK: Falmer, pp. 235–50.

Thrift, N. 1983: On the determination of social action in space and time. *Environ. Plann. D, Society and Space* 1, pp. 23–57.

Wright, E. O. 1989: Models of historical trajectory: an assessment of Giddens's critique of Marxism. In Held, D. and Thompson, J. B., eds, *Social theory of the modern societies: Anthony Giddens and his critics*. Cambridge: Cambridge University Press, pp. 77–102.

Suggested Reading

Bryant, C. G. A. and Jary, D. 1991: *Giddens' theory of structuration: a critical appreciation*. London: Routledge, chs 4 and 5.

Cloke, P., Philo, C. and Sadler, D. 1991: *Approaching human geography: an introduction to contemporary theoretical debates*. London: Paul Chapman/New York: Guilford, ch. 4.

Giddens (1984).

subaltern studies   A school of literary and political criticism associated with the work of cultural theorist Gayatri Chakravorty Spivak. Her influential essay 'Can the subaltern speak?' (1985) considers the oppression of colonial subjects (especially women) and asks how their voices can be heard without distortion. Use of the military term 'subaltern' is a deliberate reference to the colonial context of women's subordination in India, although Spivak extends her analysis to the predicament of all thought and consciousness in a postcolonial world. Geographers have begun to explore this literature in the search for new, less oppressive ways of representing other cultures. (See also POSTCOLONIALISM.)   PAJ

Reference

Spivak, G. C. 1985: Can the subaltern speak? Reprinted in Nelson, C. and Grossberg, L., eds 1988: *Marxism and the interpretation of culture*. Urbana, IL: University of Illinois Press, pp. 271–313.

Suggested Reading

Guha, R. and Spivak, G. C. eds 1988: *Selected subaltern studies*. Oxford: Oxford University Press.

Spivak, G. C. 1987: *In other worlds: essays in cultural politics*. London: Methuen.

Young, R. 1990: Spivak: decolonization, deconstruction. In *White mythologies: writing history and the West*. London: Routledge, pp. 157–75.

subjectivity, human A concept that grounds our understanding of who we are, as well as our knowledge claims. All geography presumes some theory of subjectivity: even 'objective' SPATIAL SCIENCE rests on a theory of subjectivity as a foundation for 'objective' knowledge. Debates about the human subject lie at the heart of twentieth century philosophy: '[t]he critique of the subject is taken [as] the principal lesson of the philosophy of the second half of this century – and already, to a large extent, of the first half' (Henry, 1991). Many of the most self-reflective discussions have revolved around humanist and anti-humanist conceptions of subjectivity (Soper, 1986), and in geography these have been tied to questions of method, substantive focus and ethical responsibility.

Humanist/phenomenological versions (e.g. Ley and Samuels, 1978) take subjectivity as given in experience. Man (some feminists argue that the gendering of this term is by no means incidental; see

PHALLOCENTRISM) is at the centre of the world and, in order to be fully human, has the ethical responsibility to act autonomously, to claim his agency.

Anti-humanists interpret subjectivity as a regulatory idea, and question the capacity and the authority of individuals to direct their actions self-consciously and autonomously. In the most influential anti-humanist *structuralist* account of subjectivity, Althusser argues that subjectivity – especially notions of individuality and citizenship – is an ideological construct (see IDEOLOGY; STRUCTURALISM). In Foucault's *poststructuralist*, anti-humanist history of Western subjectivity, subject positions are seen to be constructed within and through DISCOURSES. He argues that, from the nineteenth century onwards, discourses of SEXUALITY and individual rights have altered our perceptions of subjectivity and society, and have acted as media of disciplinary control (see POST-STRUCTURALISM).

Anti-humanist accounts have been criticized for closing off the possibilities and responsibilities of agency, rights, ethics and politics. There is discussion surrounding the appropriateness of this criticism, and the necessity of scrutinizing and disentangling concepts of morality, ethics, agency, subjectivity, individuality, etc. (Rajchman, 1991): an interesting body of theory is being developed that attempts to do this without returning to the humanist subject (Smith, 1988).   GP

References

Henry, M. 1991: The critique of the subject. In Cadava, E., Connor, P. and Nancy, J.-L., eds, *Who comes after the subject?* New York: Routledge, pp. 157–66.

Ley, D. and Samuels, M., eds, 1978: *Humanistic geography: prospects and problems*. London: Croom Helm/Chicago: Maaroufa.

Rajchman, J. 1991: Foucault the philosopher: ethics and work. In his *Philosophical events: essays of the '80s*. New York: Columbia University Press, pp. 59–67.

Smith, P. 1988: *Discerning the subject*. Theory and History of Literature, volume 55. Minneapolis: University of Minnesota Press.

Soper, K. 1986: *Humanism and anti-humanism: problems in modern European thought*. London: Hutchinson.

subsistence agriculture A subsistence agricultural system is a complex of functionally related resources and human practices through which a group (a household, a village, a society) secures food for its reproduction through its own effort, typically by the direct exploitation of the environment (Nietschmann, 1973). The primary objective is food, whether from hunting, fishing, horticulture or agriculture. Subsistence normally refers to production for use (i.e. use values) as opposed to production for exchange, but food may circulate within social networks for ritual ceremonial and reciprocal exchange purposes, and some food may be sold on the open market (i.e. realize exchange values). Subsistence agriculture without market involvement of any sort is referred to as a tribal or 'primitive' economy, whereas household subsistence producers with some form of production for sale, and some degree of surplus production over needs, are PEASANTS. Subsistence agriculture is often seen as a form of cultural adaptation by which social groups adapt to and regulate the ecosystems of which they are part (see CULTURAL ECOLOGY). Self-sufficient, internally regulated subsistence systems are becoming rare in the modern world, as the expansion of the market and production for exchange erodes 'pure subsistence' and what is seen by many as the ecological stability and rational utilization of complex tropical ECOSYSTEMS.   MW

Reference

Nietschmann, B. 1973: *Between land and water: the subsistence ecology of the Miskito indians, eastern Nicaragua.* New York: Seminar Press.

suburb An outer district lying within the commuting zone of an urban area, often as a separate political jurisdiction. The concept has debatable utility, because it is used to describe a wide range of COMMUNITIES and LANDSCAPE forms.

Some of this variability reflects different stages of suburban development. In many industrialized countries construction of suburban elite residential environments, distanced from the crowding and pollution of industrial cities, began in the early nineteenth century. By the late nineteenth and early twentieth centuries,

suburbanization had become a mass phenomenon, as middle-class and skilled working-class families moved into residential communities located some distance from paid employment. After the Second World War, this trend was accentuated in many countries by freeway construction and governmental restructuring of mortgage financing, which put a single family house on a small plot of land within the reach of a larger number of households.

In a number of countries, including Canada, the US and Australia, the postwar suburb is conceived as a residential, privatized, automobile-oriented landscape, which houses a homogeneous grouping of white, middle-class households. In FEMINIST GEOGRAPHY both the representation and the reality of this suburban form have been contested: it has been argued that what is represented as a place of consumption is also a site of production and reproduction, and that the actual landscape form restricts women's access to services and paid employment (England, 1991). In MARXIST GEOGRAPHY the construction of the postwar suburban environment has been viewed as a means of staving off a crisis of overaccumulation, and as a mechanism of ideological incorporation (Walker, 1981). In HUMANISTIC GEOGRAPHY suburban landscapes have been criticized as placeless environments, devoid of authentic meaning and opportunities to invest identity in place (Relph, 1981; and see PLACELESSNESS).

It is clear that there is a considerable variability around this suburban model. In other national contexts, public, non-profit, as well as private, multifamily housing has been constructed in suburban contexts that are, in some cases, well served by public transport (see Popenoe, 1977, for a useful comparison of American and Swedish suburban environments). Strong-Boag (1991) doubts that Canadian postwar suburbs were ever as socially homogeneous as those portrayed in accounts of US suburbs. Certainly the model provides a poor description of many contemporary suburbs, including those in the USA, given the suburbanization of a variety of types of employment, the growing diversity of housing forms and the variety of age groups, household types, classes, and racial and ethnic groups living in them. In Muller's (1989, p. 43) view, the concept has little contemporary relevance: by 'the late 1980's, [the] outer city [was] no longer "sub" to the "urb" '.   GP

References

England, K. V. L. 1991: Gender relations and the spatial structure of the city. *Geoforum*, 22(2), pp. 135–47.

Muller, P. 1989: The transformation of bedroom suburbia into the outer city: an overview of metropolitan structural change since 1947. In Kelly, B., ed., *Suburbia re-examined*. New York: Greenwood Press, pp. 39–44.

Popenoe, D. 1977: *The suburban environment*. Chicago: University of Chicago Press.

Relph, E. 1981: *Rational landscapes and humanist geography*. London: Croom Helm.

Strong-Boag, V. 1991: Home dreams: women and the suburban experiment in Canada, 1945–60. *Can. hist. Rev.* 74(4), pp. 471–504.

Walker, R. A. 1981: A theory of suburbanization: capitalism and the construction of urban space in the United States. In Dear, M. J. and Scott, A. J., eds, *Urbanization and urban planning in capitalist society*. London: Methuen, pp. 383–429.

succession   See INVASION AND SUC-CESSION.

sunbelt/snowbelt   A popular term that polarizes the main growing and declining regions of the US economy in recent decades: the contrast is between the older industrial districts of the country's north-east (the snowbelt – sometimes termed either the frostbelt or the rustbelt) and the rapidly expanding parts of the south and west (the sunbelt). This major shift is usually accounted for by a combination of: (1) the increasing COMPARATIVE AD-VANTAGE of the sunbelt states, based on their agricultural and energy resources, relatively cheap and non-unionized la-bour, and attractive environments; (2) the processes of regional RESTRUCTURING involved in the creation of a new spatial DIVISION OF LABOUR to counter the low productivity in the traditional industries during economic recession; and (3) the substantial volume of federal investment in the southern states, reflecting the politics of the PORK BARREL. The major industries of

the sunbelt – aerospace, microprocessors etc. – are termed 'sunrise' industries.

The term is now frequently applied in other countries: the expanding industrial corridor along the M4 motorway to the west of London – including Reading, Swindon and Bristol – is sometimes referred to as Britain's sunbelt.   RJJ

Suggested Reading

Boddy, M., Lovering, J. and Bassett, K. 1986: *Sunbelt city: A study of economic change in Britain's M4 growth corridor*. Oxford: Clarendon Press.

Hall, P. G., Breheny, M., McQuaid, R. and Hart, D.A. 1987: *Western sunrise: the genesis and growth of Britain's major high-tech western corridor*. London: Allen and Unwin.

Markusen, A. R. 1987: *Regions: the economics and politics of territory*. Totowa, NJ: Rowman and Littlefield.

Massey, D. 1984: *Spatial divisions of labour: social structures and the geography of production*. London: Macmillan.

superstructure   An essentially rela-tional notion attempting to locate and signify ideational aspects of SOCIETY. In arguing for such a relational interpretation, Marx was, *contra* Hegel, attacking the view that politics and social practices are products simply of ideas and beliefs unrelated to the technical, productive and economic conditions in society. Marx (1968, p. 181) argues instead that 'a legal and political superstructure . . . to which correspond definite forms of social con-sciousness' rises on 'the real foundation' of the 'relations of production' which consti-tute the 'economic structure of society'.

A common reading of this argument is that immaterial social, political and cultural conditions are directly determined by the material – the social by the economic. Such a reading not only presupposes that there is an unproblematic distinction between the material (e.g. the economy) and the non-material (e.g. the law), despite the fact that both are based on ideas in practice and both must be produced and reproduced in material forms, but ignores the fact that Marx's suggestion is, in any case, more complex. It refers not only to the general question of material/non-material (infra-structure:superstructure) links and distinc-tions but also to the related links and distinctions between superstructure and consciousness.

However, the suggestion of a direct determinism seems to be given greater credence by Marx's (1968, p. 182) distinction between

the economic conditions of production, which can be determined with the precision of natural science, and the legal, political, religious, aesthetic or philosophic – in short, ideological forms

which together form 'the entire immense superstructure'.

Terrell Carver (1982, p. 29) argues that Marx

was not committed to the view that everything (including consciousness, ideas etc.) is ultimately material or is in principle explicable in wholly material terms, nor was he committed to a view that the realm of ideas is in some sense less real than material things . . .

The *existence* of material phenomena and consciousness and their combination in people does not presuppose a *dichotomy or dualism* between them. Carver suggests that the distinction being drawn by Marx was that between the *results* rather than the *constituents* of activity – goods and services as distinct from ideas, beliefs and opinions. But in a world in which the symbolic value of consumption is increasingly important, where the ownership of intellectual property is expensively contested, and where the commodification of medical care, religion and the arts becomes increasingly systematic, even this distinction is difficult to sustain (see MODERNISM; POSTMODERNISM). The question of the distinction between primacy of the material and/or the non-material then shifts back to that concerning the contested relationships between consciousness and matter.

However, it is important not to slip back into a dualistic position here. Marx's presupposition is a triune: living individuals, their activities and the material conditions that they find and hand on to others (Carver, 1982). In this context, the question of the abstract separation between superstructure and infrastructure is less important than their practical overlap and lack of distinction in social practice. This

CONFLICT and change in the 'infrastructure' are taken up in the 'superstructure' where 'men [sic] become conscious of this conflict and fight it out' (Marx, 1968, p. 182). Under such circumstances, any insistence on determination or complete distinction between infrastructure and superstructure is impossible to maintain. Individuals do not have two forms of consciousness corresponding to whether they are inside or outside the factory gate or office door. And it is in such a context of practice, with all the intended and unintended consequences which result from it, that the legal and political superstructure may be said to arise from the conditions of existence of the relations of production.

In this view, superstructure comes close to the concept of CIVIL SOCIETY derived from Gramsci (1971) and developed recently by John Urry (1981; see the figure in CIVIL SOCIETY). Civil society forms an integral part of capitalist SOCIAL FORMATIONS, overlapping both the economy and the state. It is connected to the former via circulation of capital and to the latter by the law. As well as providing the location for struggle, civil society also provides the location for the production and reproduction of labour. As such, civil society is the primary focus for state planning (see URBAN AND REGIONAL PLANNING), which attempts to cope with the dynamics of social conflict and to rationalize the landscape of production within and beyond the factory gate or office door (Cooke, 1983). But even this notion involves a kind of schematic dualism.

As E. P. Thompson (1968, p. 9) put it, 'We cannot have love without lovers, nor deference without squires and labourers'. Love and deference may be deep structures, but the relationship of love and deference 'must always be embodied in real people and in a real context'. The involvement of real people and real contexts is not insignificant because experience defines the meaning of love and deference which is, thereby, changed for others. The apparent dualism of infrastructure and superstructure is, in social practice, a duality in which both exist in dialectical relationship (see DIALECTIC). Social existence and practice is, therefore, a practice of multiple determinations through STRUCTURATION rather than a mere conflict between superstructure and infrastructure. It is in such a context that the correspondence between consciousness and superstructure may be grasped. The institutions of the law and formal politics help to sustain certain beliefs and desires and to suppress others – which do not, however, disappear.

Such a view may be exemplified within geography by Peter Jackson's (1989) arguments for a materialist CULTURAL GEOGRAPHY. The contested system of shared beliefs, social actions and material representations that constitute culture are grounded in materiality but not in a narrow or determinist fashion. Following Raymond Williams, Jackson suggests (p. 35) that 'the idea of "determination" as "the setting of limits" ' effectively restores 'an active conception of human agency but one which is subject to "very definite conditions" ' and is 'thoroughly appropriate for a reconstituted cultural geography'. The implication here is that the making of CULTURE may struggle to attempt to transcend those conditions in asserting that there are always political and ideological alternatives.

Such a reading insists that the superstructure is an integral part of social life – the place where consciousness is developed and struggles occur. It follows from this that the superstructure is neither a free-floating nor a determined and structured set of ideas, but rather a complex of practices conditioned (Marx's word) by the MODE OF PRODUCTION of material life. The distinction between infrastructure and superstructure is, then, an abstraction from rather than a reflection of reality. (See also INFRASTRUCTURE.)

RL

References and Suggested Reading

Carver, T. 1982: *Marx's social theory.* Oxford: Oxford University Press.

Cooke, P. 1983: *Theories of planning and spatial development.* London: Hutchinson.

Cosgrove, D. 1983: Towards a radical cultural geography: problems of theory. *Antipode* 15, pp. 1–11.

Cosgrove, D. 1984: *Social formation and symbolic landscape.* London: Croom Helm.

Gramsci, A. 1971: *Selections from the prison notebooks.* London: Lawrence and Wishart.

Jackson, P. 1989: *Maps of meaning.* London: Unwin Hyman.

Marx, K. 1968 Preface to *A contribution to the critique of political economy.* In Marx, K. and Engels, F. *Selected works.* London: Lawrence and Wishart (originally published 1859).

Thompson, E. P. 1968: *The making of the English working class.* London: Penguin.

Urry, J. 1981: *The anatomy of capitalist societies.* London: Macmillan.

Williams, R. 1973: Base and superstructure in Marxist cultural theory. *New Left Rev.* 82, pp. 3–16.

supply curve A plot of the level of supply of a product in relation to the price obtainable. A supply curve typically slopes upwards to the right, on a graph with supply on the horizontal axis and price on the vertical axis. This is because supply tends to increase as the price producers can expect increases. In conventional economic theory, the interaction of the supply curve with the DEMAND CURVE (which shows the relationship between volume of demand and price) determines the market price.

In the figure, the supply curve S (drawn as a straight line for simplicity of presentation) shows the relationship between price and quantity at a location L. The demand curve D intersects with S at X, indicating the market price P and the quantity produced Q. Introduction of another location L' allows the possibility of different supply and demand curves (S' and D'), arising from different local circumstances, and a different market equilibrium position (X'). Connecting these two locations along a distance axis illustrates three-dimensional supply and demand surfaces (shaded in the figure) and a spatial path of changing equilibrium position from X to X'.

DMS

Reference

Smith, D. M. 1981: *Industrial location: an economic geographical analysis*, second edition. New York: John Wiley, p. 29.

surface A generalized image depicting selected aspects of three-dimensional reality, which can be constructed conventionally (local fitting, using ISOLINES) or by techniques that consider every data point

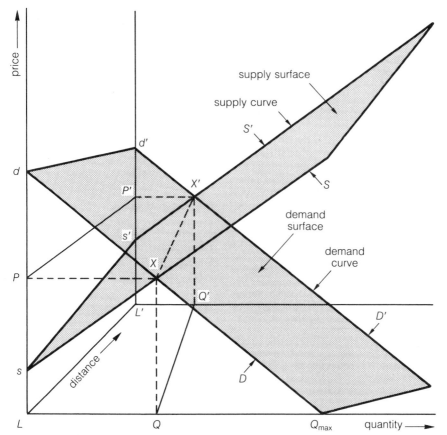

supply curve *The conventional analysis of the interaction of supply and demand, extended to incorporate distance in geographical space* (Smith, 1981).

(global fitting) by applying curve fitting, filtering or smoothing operations (see PROBABILITY MAP; SPECTRAL ANALYSIS; TREND SURFACE ANALYSIS) to generate mathematical functions that describe the surface's characteristics. Resulting generalized surfaces may be displayed conventionally (i.e. using a vertical viewpoint) or as oblique views (usually computer-produced) where consideration of the height above the surface, the viewing distance and the angle of viewing (azimuth) are important.   MJB

Suggested Reading

Raper, J. F. and Kelk, B. 1991: Three-dimensional GIS. In Maguire, D. J., Goodchild, M. F. and Rhind, D. W., eds, *Geographical information systems: principles and applications*, volume 1. London: Longman, pp. 299–317.

Weibel, R. and Heller, M. 1991: Digital terrain modelling. In Maguire, D. J., Goodchild, M. F. and Rhind, D. W. eds, *Geographical information systems: principles and applications*, volume 1. London: Longman, pp. 269–97.

surveillance The institutionalized monitoring of events and actions. It often relies upon a time–space grid, and for this reason modern human geography has become interested (and involved) in the process in two main ways:

(a) On the one hand, there has been a largely *technical* interest, expressed through the collection and analysis of official statistics, often sponsored by STATE or corporate institutions. This interest has been intensified by the development of GEOGRAPHICAL INFORMATION SYSTEMS (GIS), which have considerably enhanced the capacity of those powerful enough to have access to them to maintain routinized and often publically unaccountable surveillance (see Pickles, 1994).

(b) On the other hand, and mirroring those practices, has been a *critical* interest which has often been inspired by Foucault's *Discipline and punish* (1975, transl. 1977). This was ostensibly a history of the modern European prison, but Foucault used those materials to provide a much more ambitious genealogy of what he took to be the distinctively modern configuration of power and knowledge. In particular, Foucault argued that surveillance was indispensable to the formation of a modern *disciplinary society*:

Our society is one not of SPECTACLE but of surveillance; under the surface of images, one invests bodies in depth; behind the great abstraction of exchange, there continues the meticulous, concrete training of useful forces; the circuits of communication are the supports of an accumulation and centralization of knowledge; the play of signs defines the anchorages of power; it is not that the beautiful totality of the individual is amputated, repressed, altered by our social order, it is rather that the individual is carefully fabricated in it, according to a whole technique of forces and bodies.

These possibilities have been enlarged in the twentieth century with the installation of systems of electronic communication and surveillance, including GIS (Poster, 1990). Although human geographers have recently shown considerable interest in elucidating the connections between POWER, knowledge and SPATIALITY in the production of human subjects, and in disentangling the ways in which surveillance is deeply implicated in the process (Driver, 1985; Robinson, 1990; Sack, 1986; Philo, 1989), few of these analyses have yet reached far into the twentieth century.   DG

References

Driver, F. 1985: Power, space and the body: a critical assessment of Foucault's *Discipline and punish*. *Environ. Plann. D*, 3, pp. 425–46.

Foucault, M. 1977: *Discipline and punish: the birth of the prison*. London: Allen Lane.

Philo, C. 1989: Enough to drive one mad: the organisation of space in nineteenth-century lunatic asylums. In Wolch, J. and Dear, M.,
eds, *The power of geography*. London: Unwin Hyman, pp. 258–90.

Pickles, J. 1994: *Geography and GIS*. New York: Guilford Press.

Poster, M. 1990: *The mode of information: poststructuralism and social context*. Cambridge: Polity Press.

Robinson, J. 1990: 'A perfect system of control?' State power and native locations in South Africa. *Environ. Plann. D, Society and Space* 8, pp. 135–62.

Sack, R. D. 1986: *Human territoriality: its theory and history*. Cambridge: Cambridge University Press.

Suggested Reading

Dandeker, C. 1990: *Surveillance, power and modernity*. Cambridge: Polity Press.

Driver (1985).

Foucault (1977).

Pickles, forthcoming.

survey   See LAND-USE SURVEY.

survey analysis   The various research procedures involved in the collection and analysis of data from individuals. Surveys, almost invariably based on QUESTIONNAIRES, are undertaken to obtain data that is not available from other sources.

A survey involves several stages. The first is definition of the research problem, perhaps including the formulation of HYPOTHESES, and identification of the needed information. The second includes determining the population to be studied, which includes deciding whether SAMPLING will be necessary and, if so, how the sample will be taken. The next stage involves deciding how the hypotheses will be tested (including the analytical techniques to be employed), and is followed by the development (which will include pre-test stages and pilot investigations) of a questionnaire.

After administration of the questionnaires, which may be undertaken by the researchers themselves or contracted to a specialist market research or opinion poll company, the data are prepared for analysis: quantitative data are readily dealt with; qualitative data (such as reported occupations and responses to open-ended questions) have to be handled through the development of coding schemes, the application of which may call for special training of those involved. The data are then usually entered into a database for computer manipulation: they are checked for consistency ('cleaning' the data set) and the analyses are then conducted. (See also SECONDARY DATA ANALYSIS.) RJJ

Suggested Reading

Dixon, C. J. and Leach, B. 1978: *Questionnaires and interviews in geographical research*. Concepts and techniques in modern geography 18. Norwich: Geo Books.

Sheskin, I. M. 1985: *Survey research for geographers*. Washington, DC: Association of American Geographers.

surveying The process of gathering orderly data pertaining to the extent and features of chosen areas. The former manual techniques of data gathering on chain, plane-table and theodolite surveys, using baseline, traverse and triangulation, etc., are increasingly being replaced by computer-based technologies such as EDM (electronic distance measuring), GPS (Global Positioning System), high-quality imagery from aerial photographs and REMOTE SENSING. MJB

Suggested Reading

Dale, P. F. and McLaughlin, J. D. 1988: *Land information management – an introduction with special reference to cadastral problems in the Third World*. Oxford: Oxford Universty Press.

Goodchild, M. F. 1991: The technological setting of GIS. In Maguire, D. J., Goodchild, M. F. and Rhind, D. W., eds, *Geographical information systems: principles and applications*, volume 1. London: Longman, pp. 45–54.

sustainable development According to the World Commission on Environment and Development, which popularized the term in its 1987 report, sustainable development is the 'development that meets the needs of the present without compromising the ability of future generations to meet their own needs' (p. 43). The notion of sustainability has roots in utilitarian resource management, in the technocratic concept of sustained yield such renewable resources as forests and fisheries – the level of extraction that could be maintained without lessening future levels. The contemporary concept of sustainable development differs in its insistence on the complex interrelationship of the physical and the social. Yet some of the problems, in definition and in practice, with the idea of sustainable yield are also problems with the broader idea of globally sustainable development – particularly those posed by the continual redefinition and revaluation of resources by technological change. The idea has also come under attack from those who see ultimate LIMITS TO GROWTH making further development – as usually understood in terms of economic growth – and sustainability as being mutually exclusive. Others have criticized sustainable development as a convenient formula used to maintain the notion of growth and development as a way of avoiding or finessing intractable questions of distribution. If sustainable development has proven conceptually elusive, however, it has provided a focal point for discussion and debate in the chaotic realm of global change, and a reminder of the need to integrate questions of environmental CONSERVATION with those of livelihood, especially in the developing world. JEM

Reference

World Commission on Environment and Development 1987: *Our common future*. Oxford: Oxford University Press.

symbolic interactionism A diffuse tradition of SOCIAL THEORY which regards the social world as a social product, the meanings of which are constituted in and through social interaction. Craib (1984, p. 72) claims that symbolic interactionism conceives of social life as a conversation: 'the social world shows the same qualities of flow, development, creativity and change as we would experience in a conversation . . . [and] the world is made up of conversations, internal and external'. Other analogies can be equally salient, however, and Geertz (1983, chapter 1) speaks of a 'refiguration of social thought' around the interpretation of social life variously conceived as a game, as a drama and as a text. Whatever the difficulties of unambiguously characterizing symbolic interactionism – Rock (1979) speaks of its 'deliberately constructed vagueness' – most commentators agree that it had its orgins in the

CHICAGO SCHOOL of sociology in the 1920s (see PRAGMATISM). Contrary to the conventional wisdom of much mainstream URBAN GEOGRAPHY, the Chicago School was not uniquely concerned with the development of a HUMAN ECOLOGY based on brute Darwinian competition: Park and Thomas in particular treated *communication* as 'fundamental to the existence of society' (see Jackson and Smith, 1984, pp. 79–80). Important though these foundations were, however, the principal architect of symbolic interactionism is usually taken to be Mead. It was his *Mind, self and society*, composed posthumously from students' lecture notes and published in 1934, which was used – particularly by one of his students, Blumer, who coined the term 'symbolic interactionism', whereas Mead himself always referred to his 'social psychology' – to formalize its fundamental tenets. According to Craib (1984, p. 73; see also, Blumer, 1969), these are as follows:

1. Human beings act towards things on the basis of the meanings that the things have for them.
2. These meanings are the product of social interaction in human society.
3. These meanings are modified and handled through an interpretive process that is used by each individual in dealing with the signs each encounters.

Craib claims that these three postulates roughly correspond to the three sections of *Mind, self and society*, but that it is now clear that such a summary does considerable violence to the integrity of Mead's work. Joas (1985) has warned that:

[Symbolic interactionism] cannot be regarded as the authoritative interpretation of Mead's thought. For this theory's understanding both of social organization and of human needs, its reduction of the concept of action to that of interaction, its linguistic attenuation of the concept of meaning, and its lack of any consideration of evolution and history are enormous deviations from Mead's positions and, furthermore, achieved by means of an extremely fragmentary appropriation of Mead's work. Only those aspects of Mead's thought that are completely ignored by symbolic interactionism make it possible to correct this tradition's 'subjectivist' features' (pp. 6–7).

Within human geography, interactionist perspectives have opened up three progressively wider avenues of inquiry. First, a number of authors have continued the ethnographic tradition of the Chicago School to provide compelling accounts of the social construction of specific *milieux* (for a review, see Jackson, 1985; cf. ETHNOGRAPHY). Second, a more formal thematization of the social construction of PLACE has been proposed. Hence, for example, Ley (1981) identifies a major focus of HUMANISTIC GEOGRAPHY as a recovery of 'the relationship between landscape and identity'. In some part following Mead, Ley argues, its central argument is that: '[P]lace is a negotiated reality, a social construction by a purposeful set of actors. But the relationship is mutual, for places in turn develop and reinforce the identity of the social group that claims them'. Third, and spiralling away from propositions of this sort, is a series of more inclusive theorems about the constitution of society. *Elements* of interactionism can be found, in their most *general* form, in Schutz's constitutive PHENOMENOLOGY and in Giddens's STRUCTURATION THEORY, both of which have had a major impact on the development of post-positivist human geography, but it is undoubtedly Berger and Luckmann's *The social construction of reality* (1967) which has provided at once the most comprehensive and the most focused engagement of human geography with interactionism. Acutely critical of what elsewhere he calls the 'superorganic' (see Duncan, 1980), Duncan (1978) notes that:

Interactionism . . . posits no separation between the individual and society; individual selves are socially constructed. The self is largely a product of the opinions and actions of others as these are expressed in interaction with the developing self . . . . With interactionism there is no need for a transcendental object such as an abstract notion of culture [or] society . . . to mediate between the individual and society (p. 269).

(See also Ley, 1982; for a critique, see Gregory, 1982.)

These social constructions constitute a TAKEN-FOR-GRANTED WORLD, Duncan continues, and this is, at least in part, 'dependent on one's relation to a place and the persons associated with that place'. Although Berger and Luckmann said nothing about such relations, Duncan shows how such a place-specific perspective on 'the stranger' or 'the outsider' prompts a recognition of what he calls 'the social construction of *un*reality' (emphasis added). What Berger and Luckmann (1967) do acknowledge, however, is the importance of routinized and repetitive social conduct to the continuity of social life: 'The reality of everyday life maintains itself by being embodied in routines, which is the essence of institutionalization. Beyond this, however, the reality of everyday life is ongoingly reaffirmed in the individual's interaction with others' (p. 169). This makes it possible to rework their formulations to incorporate the time–space paths traced out in Hägerstrand's TIME-GEOGRAPHY. Although Berger and Luckmann regard the 'spatial structure' of everyday life as 'peripheral to our present considerations', therefore, Pred (1981, p. 7) regards this as a serious mistake:

[W]hat is wanting, among other things, in the Berger–Luckmann formulation is a spelling out of the detailed means whereby the everyday intersections of individual biographies with institutional activities, *at specific times and places*, are rooted in previous intersections, at specific times and places, yet simultaneously serve as the roots of future intersections between particular individuals and institutional activities . . . .

Using time-geography in this way, Pred claims, it is possible to expose 'the workings of society'. (See also PRAGMATISM.)

DG

References

Berger, P. and Luckmann, T. 1967: *The social construction of reality*. London: Doubleday/Garden City, NY: Anchor Books.

Blumer, H. 1969: *Symbolic interactionism: perspectives and method*. Englewood Cliffs, NJ: Prentice-Hall.

Craib, I. 1984: *Modern social theory: from Parsons to Habermas*. Brighton, UK: Wheatsheaf/New York: St. Martin's Press.

Duncan, J. S. 1978: The social construction of unreality: an interactionist approach to the tourist's cognition of environment. In Ley, D. and Samuels, M., eds, *Humanistic geography:*

prospects and problems. London: Croom Helm/Chicago: Maaroufa, pp. 269–82.

Duncan, J. S. 1980: The superorganic in American cultural geography. *Ann. Ass. Am. Geogr.* 70, pp. 181–98.

Geertz, C. 1983: *Local knowledge: further essays in interpretative anthropology*. New York: Basic Books.

Gregory, D. 1982: A realist construction of the social. *Trans. Inst. Br. Geogr.* n.s. 7, pp. 254–6.

Jackson, P. 1985: Urban ethnography. *Progr. hum. Geogr.* 9, pp. 157–76.

Jackson, P. and Smith, S. J. 1984: *Exploring social geography*. London: Allen and Unwin.

Joas, H. 1985: *G. H. Mead: a contemporary reexamination of his thought*. Cambridge: Polity Press; see especially ch. 5.

Ley, D. 1981: Behavioral geography and the philosophies of meaning. In Cox, K. R. and Golledge, R. G., eds, *Behavioral problems in geography revisited*. London: Methuen, pp. 209–30.

Ley, D. 1982: Rediscovering man's place. *Trans. Inst. Br. Geogr.* n.s. 7, pp. 248–53.

Mead, G. H. 1934: *Mind, self and society*. Chicago: Chicago University Press.

Pred, A. 1981: Social reproduction and the time-geography of everyday life. *Goegr. Annlr.* 63(B), pp. 5–22.

Rock, P. 1979: *The making of symbolic interactionism*. London: Macmillan/Totowa, NJ: Rowman and Littlefield.

Suggested Reading

Anderson, K. 1987: The idea of Chinatown: the power of place and institutional practice in the making of a racial category. *Ann. Ass. Am. Geogr.* 77, pp. 580–98.

Craib (1984), ch. 5.

Duncan (1978).

Jackson and Smith (1984), pp. 79–86.

symbolization The cartographic process for graphically encoding those spatial objects of data which have been selected for representation on a MAP. The processes of selection range from the scientific to the political. Scientific ones aim to select an optimum range of detail for a map, and are typified by the activities of major map agencies (see United States Geological Survey, 1986). Political processes involve propaganda and suppression of information (see Blakemore, 1992).

Selection is followed by graphic encoding, into point, line, area or three-dimensional map symbols, with associated legends (Aspaas and Lavon, 1989) and text (Zoraster, 1991, studies automated methods of placing text in COMPUTER-ASSISTED CARTOGRAPHY). The processes of generalization (Buttenfield and McMaster, 1991) reduce the detail so that it can fit within the confines of a MAP IMAGE.

Magnitude data utilize symbols where size is related to data value, and density data are depicted by area symbols (see CHOROPLETH MAP). Often, such symbols (see Bertin, 1983) are not directly identifiable by shape similarity with the data they represent (symbol–subject relationship), and there is the relationship of symbol size to data value plus associated perception problems. There is even some debate as to the best way of representing spatial statistics (Tufte 1983): Should the map be the dominant graphic, or just part of a statistical graphic?

TOPOGRAPHIC MAPS utilize symbols which mimic the objects that they represent, so returning a degree of realism. To improve visual recognition, moves have been made towards international standardization of map symbology as, for example, with signs at international airports. Muller and Zeshen (1990) develop computer-based rules for general symbol design, while Benjamin and Gaydos evaluate the interrelationship of spatial resolution and the representation of roads.

Finally, Campbell and Egbert (1990) note that most symbolization occurs for static paper-based maps, and that the development of such techniques as animated cartography has been limited.   MJB

References and Suggested Reading

Aspaas, M. R. and Lavon, S. J. 1989: Legend designs for unclassed, bivariate, choropleth maps. *Am. Cartogr* 16, pp. 257–68.

Benjamin, S. and Gaydos, L. 1990: Spatial resolution requirements for automated cartographic road extraction. *Photogramm. Engng Remote Sensing* 56(1), pp. 93–100.

Bertin, J. 1983: *Semiology of graphics: diagrams, networks, maps.* Madison, WI: University of Wisconsin Press.

Blakemore, M. 1992: Cartography. *Progr. hum. Geogr.* 16(1), pp. 75–87.

Buttenfield, B. P. and McMaster, R. B., eds 1991: *Map generalisation: making rules for knowledge representation.* London: Longman.

Campbell, C. S. and Egbert S. 1990: Animated cartography: thirty years of scratching the surface. *Cartographica* 27(2), pp. 24–6.

Muller, J.-C. and Zeshen, W. 1990: A knowledge based system for cartographic symbol design. *Cartogr. J.* 27(2), pp. 24–30.

Tufte, E. R. 1983: *The visual display of quantitative information.* Cheshire, CN: Graphics Press.

United States Geological Survey 1986: *Goals of the US Geological Survey.* USGS Circular 1010. Reston, VA: USGS.

Zoraster, S. 1991: Expert systems and the map label placement problem. *Cartographica* 28(1), pp. 1–9.

system   A group of elements organized in such a way that every element is to some degree interdependent (directly or indirectly) with every other element. Many authors also require that the system have some function, goal or purpose (if only the maintenance of the system itself), although this does not imply conscious goals or deliberate intention (see TELEOLOGY). In this latter respect, systems ideas are akin to those of FUNCTIONALISM. To identify a system it is necessary to delimit its boundaries, to identify its constituent elements, and to define its function. Although in some cases a system may have a clear objective existence (e.g. a domestic hot-water system) in most geographical cases it is a fairly arbitrary separation of part of the observed world in order to facilitate study, and may be small and simple or large and very complex (see ABSTRACTION; REALISM).

Studies of such systems often seek answers to a number of questions. First, it may be important to distinguish between *closed* and *open* systems. The former have no flows or links to or from their environment; whereas the latter, which are much more common in geography, have such flows and links. Second, it may be possible to identify *subsystems* – clusters of elements which have high levels of mutual interdependence but are weakly linked to the rest of the system. Third, it may be useful to identify the nature of the links between elements in the subsystem: some systems' models emphasize flows (e.g. people or money), others emphasize causal links, and yet others represent the relationships by a 'black box' (identifying the form of a response but not the causal mechanism). Fourth, it is possible to identify FEEDBACK loops: when positive feedback loops occur any change in an element is reinforced; when negative feedback loops occur any change in an element is reversed. Negative feedback is often seen as evidence of equilibrium-seeking behaviour (homeostasis). The time interval between a disturbance and the re-establishment of equilibrium is termed the *relaxation time*. In geography, the concept of a system may be used quite loosely to underline the interdependence of phenomena (e.g. in the terms ECOSYSTEM and regional economic system), but some authors (especially physical geographers) have used a complete SYSTEMS ANALYSIS methodology to examine geographical phenomena. (See also GENERAL SYSTEMS THEORY.)   AMH

Suggested Reading

Bennett, R. J. and Chorley, R. J. 1978: *Environmental systems: philosophy, analysis and control*. London: Methuen.

Chapman, G. P. 1977: *Human and environmental systems*. London: Academic Press.

Huggett, R. J. 1980: *Systems analysis in geography*. Oxford: Clarendon Press.

systems analysis A mathematical approach to the modelling of SYSTEMS which uses techniques developed in control engineering to investigate the behaviour of systems in response to external stimuli or inputs. In their simplest form these models consist of an input (X_t), an output (Y_{t+n}), and a transfer function S, such that

$$Y_{t+n} = SX_t.$$

The mathematics allow a systematic categorization of the nature of the inputs (transient shocks, a unit step, a ramp or linear function, periodic or stochastic) and of the form of the transfer function (e.g. summation, identity, multiplier, splitter, integrator, delay or cascade) to yield a set of output responses. There is an important distinction between those which refer to a continuous time scale and those in which the inputs and outputs occur, or are observed to occur, at discrete time intervals: attention is also paid to the time lags between an input and the output response. In most geographical applications the system is only observed at discrete time intervals, and time lags are usually present (see LEAD–LAG MODELS).

The mathematical models so derived can be used to examine the likely behaviour of systems, even where the transfer function is derived inductively without the precondition of any knowledge of the processes or mechanisms which underlie the function. An important exponent of this approach was Forrester (1969) who used it to examine urban dynamics, and later the global system, in order to establish LIMITS TO GROWTH. In geography the approach has been used not only to model temporal systems but also to examine spatial or spatio-temporal series.   AMH

Reference

Forrester, J. W. 1969: *Urban dynamics*. Cambridge, MA: MIT Press.

Suggested Reading

Bennett, R. J. and Chorley, R. J. 1978: *Environmental systems: philosophy, analysis and control*. London: Methuen.

T

taken-for-granted world Usually a synonym for LIFEWORLD, the term gained currency in contemporary human geography through an influential essay by Ley (1977), in which he argued for a recognition of the centrality of everyday, 'mundane experience' and in particular for the incorporation into HUMANISTIC GEOGRAPHY of the intersubjective meanings and intentions which gave shape and direction to 'the contours of the life-world'. Ley claimed that the appropriate methodology could be derived from PHENOMENOLOGY – 'the phenomenological method provides a logic for understanding the lifeworld' – and in this he followed, among others, Schutz and Merleau-Ponty. A common criticism of their work has been that it pays insufficient attention to the constellations of POWER which are involved in the production and reproduction of social life, and in order to meet these objections Warf (1986) extended Ley's ideas in the direction of STRUCTURATION THEORY. But the taken-for-granted assumed an even deeper significance in Husserl's (different) version of phenomenology, and Pickles (1985) used his writings to clarify 'the pre-theoretical character of the lifeworld and its pre-givenness in relation to all the sciences', in other words its *foundational* role, and thereby to offer an important corrective to those who would limit so-called 'geographical phenomenology' to 'a capturing of the everyday lifeworld as it is lived'.

Elucidation of the taken-for-granted world is not the unique preserve of phenomenology, however, and the French philosopher Henri Lefebvre has provided an important discussion of 'everyday life' which intersects with both of these traditions. Lefebvre treats the taken-for-grantedness of everyday life in the modern world as a product of its 'colonization by the abstract space of CAPITALISM, (see SPATIALITY); but he also sees the everyday as the site of resistance, as the source of an authentic (and in *this* sense 'foundational') mundanity that has remained untouched by the corrosions of capitalist modernity (Lefebvre 1991; see Gregory, 1993). Another important politico-intellectual reading of the taken-for-granted world and its spatiality is provided by Michel de Certeau (1984), who seeks to elucidate the everyday social practices – the myriad informal *tactics* – through which ordinary people are able to resist the encroachments and strategies of formal, institutionalized apparatuses of power. Neither of these contributions is phenomenological, but they join Ley in accentuating the creativity (rather than passivity) which inheres within everyday life and the supposedly taken-for-granted world. In this way, the concept is given a distinctly subversive cast.   DG

References

de Certeau, M. 1984: *The practice of everyday life.* Berkeley, CA: University of California Press.

Gregory, D. 1993: *Geographical imaginations.* Oxford: Blackwell.

Lefebvre, H. 1991: *Critique of everyday life.* London: Verso.

Ley, D. 1977: Social geography and the taken-for-granted world. *Trans. Inst. Br. Geogr.* n.s. 2, pp. 498–512.

Pickles, J. 1985: *Phenomenology, science and geography: spatiality and the human sciences.* Cambridge: Cambridge University Press.

Warf, B. 1986: Ideology, everyday life and emancipatory phenomenology. *Antipode* 18, pp. 268–83.

Suggested Reading
de Certeau (1984).
Ley (1977).
Pickles (1985), pp. 114–20.

tariff A tax on imported commodities. Tariffs are normally designed to regulate imports for a variety of reasons of STATE economic policy. These may include a concern for the balance of payments; the protection of infant industries, strategic sectors and sectors suffering from competition from imports; retaliation and protection from dumping. Tariffs may be preferential (favouring some importers over others) or non-discriminatory (extending the treatment of the most favoured nation to all trading partners).

Although it may be implemented on a bilateral basis, trade policy is set within the international context of the General Agreement on Tariffs and Trade (GATT). The objectives of the GATT are to reduce tariffs, to remove other non-tariff barriers (NTBs) to trade, and to eliminate trade restriction. Reciprocity and non-discrimination based upon the most favoured nation clause underpin the working of GATT, which since its formation in 1948 has set out to achieve its objectives via a series of eight negotiating rounds (the latest being the Uruguay Round, begun in 1986). While the average level of tariffs was around 40 per cent in 1940, the level in 1990 was about 5 per cent.   RL

Suggested Reading
Dicken, P. 1992: *Global shift: the internationalization of economic activity.* London: Paul Chapman, ch. 6.

Taylorism A set of workplace practices developed from the principles set out by Frederick W. Taylor (1911). Fundamental concepts include the fragmentation of production activities into their simplest constituent components, and the linking together of these fragmented activities into precisely coordinated and closely supervised sequences. Designed to enhance overall efficiency by reducing the scope of activity of individual workers, these practices (by their reliance on close supervision) also accentuate the separation of conception and execution of tasks in the workplace. The result is a distinctive occupational division of labour, in which unskilled or semi-skilled workers execute simple, repetitive shopfloor fabrication functions, while skilled technical and managerial workers perform functions related to research, product design, process control, coordination, finance and marketing. Large firms organized along Taylorist lines will often segregate skilled and unskilled functions in separate plants, producing a spatial DIVISION OF LABOUR. (See also FORDISM.)   MSG

Reference
Taylor, F. W. 1911: *The principles of scientific management.* New York: Harper and Brothers.

teleology A theory that events can only be accounted for as stages in the movement towards a pre-ordained end: the end may be determined by those involved in the event, as with various forms of planning, or it may be externally defined, as in many religions. (See also FUNCTIONALISM; STAGES OF GROWTH.)   RJJ

temporary urbanization A term sometimes used to describe a range of periodic or episodic events which swell the population of an urban centre for a short period. Examples include fairs, pilgrimages and periodic markets in traditional societies, and the complex of hallmark events (or urban SPECTACLES) in the contemporary city, which include sporting events and cultural festivals.   DL

Suggested Reading
Syme, G., Shaw, B., Fenton, M. and Mueller, W., eds 1989: *The planning and evaluation of hallmark events.* Aldershot, UK: Avebury.

terms of trade The ratio of the prices at which exports and imports are exchanged. Improvements in the terms of trade are said to occur when the price of exports rises relative to that of imports. Modifications may be made to the index to distinguish between price changes resulting from changes in costs and changes in demand, and to indicate the effect of the volume of trade upon national income.

The long-run terms of trade have tended to move against primary producers. During the 1980s – particularly after 1985 – there was a marked fall in the terms of trade of developing countries in Asia, Latin America and, most especially, Africa (see, e.g., Mathur, 1991). This is due in part to the fall in the price of non-oil commodity exports, which fell by almost 40 per cent between 1973 and 1990. Africa has been hit particularly hard by the fall in the prices of tropical beverages, as the international price-fixing agreements for cocoa and coffee have collapsed, and coffee prices reached a 15-year low in 1990.   RL

Reference

Mathur, P. N. 1991: *Why developing countries fail to develop*. London: Macmillan.

territorial justice   The application of principles of social justice (see WELFARE GEOGRAPHY) to territorial units. As such, it may be a principle of the application of area-based policies (see REGIONAL POLICY). But social justice must take account both of the conditions of production of wealth and SOCIAL WELL-BEING and of their distribution. It can, therefore, be given meaning only in the context of a particular set of social relations (see ECONOMIC GEOGRAPHY).

Need must be a primary variable in determining territorial justice and should be complemented by contribution to the common good. However, the problem of measuring such variables in the implementation of territorially based programmes of social justice is complicated by the ECOLOGICAL FALLACY and the appropriateness of the spatial definition of the territorial units. Furthermore, the achievement of territorial justice may exacerbate other forms of injustice. (See SOCIAL JUSTICE.)   RL

Suggested Reading

Herbert, D. T. and Smith, D. M., eds 1979: *Social problems and the city*. Oxford: Oxford University Press.

territorial production complex (TPC)   A concept originally applied to the planning of industrial development in the Soviet Union at a macro spatial scale. It was similar to the concept of the industrial complex in Anglo-American regional science. The TPC was part of the hierarchical structure of the centrally planned economy (see CENTRAL PLANNING). Mathematical models were used to determine the optimal production structure of a complex and to allocate the various activities to specific locations. The design of a TPC also extended into the settlement system and to the provision of goods and services required to maintain the population. Macroscale spatial planning of industrial development in the USSR began with the Ural–Kuznetz complex in the 1930s. The more recent development of the TPC concept was closely associated with the planned industrialization of parts of Siberia. (See also PRODUCTION COMPLEX.)
          DMS

territorial sea   The area of sea, beyond its coast and inland waters, over which a STATE claims exclusive jurisdiction. Coastal states have made such claims at least since the fifteenth century, but until the UN Convention on the Law of the Sea was signed in 1982 there was no definition of the extent of territorial seas. The Convention has still to be fully implemented, but it is the basis which most states now use to define their territorial seas. From the late eighteenth century most states claimed three nautical miles, sufficient for defence of the realm and for protecting exclusive access to inshore fisheries, but others laid claims to more extensive tracts. Following the lead of the USA, and later the USSR, more and more states began to lay claim to 12 nautical mile territorial seas in the first half of the twentieth century.

One of the main tasks of the third UN Convention on the Law of the Sea was to try to reach agreement on standardizing practice, and the result was an acceptance that states could claim territorial seas up to 12 nautical miles from their coasts and inland waters. The SOVEREIGNTY of a state extends to the airspace above its territorial seas, as well as to the sea bed and the subsoil below. Indeed, its jurisdiction is identical in all but one respect to that exercised over its land: the sole exception is the right of innocent passage through territorial seas that is granted to shipping.

Not all states have yet exercised their rights to claim territorial seas up to 12 nautical miles, while others still claim considerably more – up to 200 nautical miles – but there is a growing acceptance of the UN-brokered norm.   MB

Suggested Reading

Glassner, M. I. 1990: *Neptune's domain: a political geography of the sea.* Boston: Unwin Hyman.

territorial social indicator A measure of SOCIAL WELL-BEING in a defined territory, which may refer to either a broad concept or a specific condition – such as health status.

The social indicator movement developed during the 1960s, initially in the USA, as a response to growing concern over a wide range of social problems. It was argued that social indicators should be collected and published by governments to chart trends in society's social health, to go alongside the well-established economic indicators. Within this movement, geographers argued that territorial social indicators should be developed, so that spatial trends in the country's well-being could be assessed and, if necessary, spatial policies developed to counter identified disparities.

Within the United States, the seminal work was that of Smith (1973; but see Lewis, 1968, who extended the related concept of a 'level of living' index developed by rural sociologists). Smith selected seven sets of indicators representing different aspects of social well-being: income, wealth and employment; the living environment, including housing; physical and mental health; education; social order; social belonging; and recreation and leisure. Available numerical indicators were collated and analysed (using PRINCIPAL COMPONENTS ANALYSIS) to identify the extent and nature of spatial variations between states, between metropolitan areas, and between residential areas within cities. Similar work was reported for England and Wales by Knox (1974, 1975), and later studies sought to account for the observed spatial variations at a variety of scales (e.g. Coates et al. 1977; Smith, 1977, 1979).

Although the approach has been subject to a number of criticisms, on the selection and nature of the data used and the problems of the ECOLOGICAL FALLACY in analysis of spatially aggregated data about individuals, for example, the case for mapping spatial variations in social welfare has been widely accepted as a desirable monitoring tool – as indicated by the 'booming towns studies' undertaken at the University of Newcastle upon Tyne (Green and Champion, 1991). A wider range of variables has been investigated in later studies than those used by Smith and Knox (e.g. Jones and Kodras, 1991), and subjective perceptions of the quality of life in different places have also been investigated (Knox and MacLaren, 1978; Rogerson et al., 1989).

The social indicators movement has in large part fulfilled its original mission – and has established its own literature, as with the journal *Quantitative Social Indicators* – and the case for territorial disaggregation has similarly largely been accepted: mapping spatial variations in social well-being is now a standard activity, and increased attention is being addressed to understanding their causes and consequences (as in Herbert and Smith, 1989) and to developing a rigorous theoretical framework for understanding spatial variations in *welfare* (Smith, 1977).   RJJ

References

Coates, B. E., Johnston, R. J. and Knox, P. L. 1977: *Geography and inequality.* Oxford: Oxford University Press.

Green, A. E. and Champion, A. G. 1991: The 'booming towns' studies: methodological issues. *Environ. Plann. A* 23, pp. 1393–408.

Herbert, D. T. and Smith, D. M., eds 1989: *Social problems and the city: New perspectives.* Oxford: Oxford University Press.

Jones, J. P. and Kodras, J. E., eds 1991: *Geographic dimensions of United States social policy.* London: Edward Arnold.

Knox, P. L. 1974: Spatial variations in levels of living in England and Wales. *Trans. Inst. Br. Geogr.* 62, pp. 1–24.

Knox, P. L. 1975: *Social well-being: a spatial perspective.* Oxford: Clarendon Press.

Knox, P. L. and MacLaran, A. 1978: Values and perceptions in descriptive approaches to urban social geography. In Herbert, D. T. and Johnston, R. J., eds, *Geography and the urban environment: progress in research and applications*, volume 1. Chichester: John Wiley, pp. 197–248.

Lewis, G. M. 1968: Levels of living in the northeastern United States *c*.1960: a new approach to regional geography. *Trans. Inst. Br. Geogr.* 45, pp. 11–37.

Rogerson, R. J., Findlay, A. M., Morris, A. S. and Coombes, M. G. 1989: Indicators of quality of life: some methodological issues. *Environ. Plann. A* 21, pp. 1655–66.

Smith, D. M. 1973: *A geography of social wellbeing in the United States*. New York: McGraw-Hill.

Smith, D. M. 1977: *Human geography: a welfare approach*. London: Edward Arnold.

Smith, D. M. 1979: *Where the grass is greener: living in an unequal world*. London: Penguin.

territoriality The spatial organization of persons and social groups through the demarcation of boundaries. Some works drawing from the literature on animal behaviour see the need for TERRITORY as a universal drive or instinct. More typically, however, human territoriality is seen as the strategy whereby individuals and groups exercize control over a given portion of space. This can range from the bubble of personal space established by the individual person to the space associated with group membership, through patterns of territorial regionalism (as in FEDERALISM) to the division of the world into territorial NATION-STATES.

In different types of SOCIETY and in different historical periods the characteristic patterns of behaviour and systems of symbols of different groups produce different forms of territoriality. Thus, for example, the average size of personal space differs between contemporary Mediterranean and Scandinavian societies, and the emergence of the transnational corporation has given rise to a new global territoriality of business organization, with a central HQ and widely scattered production locations.

Territoriality is put into practice through: (1) popular acceptance of *classifications* of space (e.g. 'ours' versus 'yours'); (2) *communication* of a SENSE OF PLACE (where markers and BOUNDARY have meaning); and (3) *enforcing control* over space (be means of SURVEILLANCE, POLICING and legitimation). The mixture of consent and coercion in strategies of territoriality is often referred to as HEGEMONY.   JAA

Suggested Reading

Agnew, J. A. 1987: *Place and politics: the geographical mediation of state and society*. London: Allen and Unwin.

Sack, R. D. 1986: *Human territoriality: its theory and history*. Cambridge: Cambridge University Press.

territory A general term used to describe a portion of space occupied by a person, group or STATE. When associated with the state the term has two specific connotations. The first is one of territorial SOVEREIGNTY, whereby a state claims exclusive legitimate control over a given area defined by clear boundaries. The second is that of an area not fully incorporated into the political life of a state, as with a 'colonial' territory or the 'Northern Territory' of Australia.

In more social geographical usage, territory refers to the bounded SOCIAL SPACE occupied and used by different social groups as a consequence of their practice of TERRITORIALITY or the field of POWER exercized over space by dominant institutions. From this point of view, territory can be used as an equivalent to such spatial concepts as PLACE and REGION (Ericksen, 1980). It also finds increasing popularity as a metaphor; as, for instance, in the 'territory' of the geographer, when referring to the academic division of labour, or the 'territory' of the imagination, to symbolize both a psychological terrain and personal ownership of it. This latter metaphor betrays the origins of the term, in the definition of private property rights associated with the modern territorial state and the modern 'self' owning or investing exclusively in its territory (Wikse, 1977).
                                    JAA

References and Suggested Reading

Ericksen, E. G. 1980: *The territorial experience: human ecology as symbolic interaction*. Austin, TX: University of Texas Press.

Wikse, J. R. 1977: *About possession: the self as private property.* University Park, PA: Penn State Press.

text A set of signifying practices commonly associated with the written page, but over the past several decades increasingly broadened to include other types of cultural production such as LANDSCAPES, maps and paintings as well as economic, political and social institutions (Cosgrove and Daniels, 1988; Duncan and Duncan, 1988; Harley, 1991). Since the nineteenth century textual analysis has been associated with the HERMENEUTIC method of Wilhelm Dilthey and others (Rose, 1981). According to this method, an interpretation is produced which results from the interaction between the text being studied and the intellectual framework of the interpreter. Throughout the twentieth century, competing methods of textual analysis have been put forward, such as STRUCTURALISM, which would include semiotics, POSTSTRUCTURALISM, which includes DISCOURSE analysis, and DECONSTRUCTION. These textual analyses, once overwhelmingly confined to fields such as literature, religion and history within the humanities, have diffused as part of the 'linguistic turn' within the social sciences. An important consequence of this DIFFUSION is that the humanities have become an important source of method and theory for the social sciences and, as a consequence, the oft-noted divide between the social sciences and the humanities has become blurred.

Once the notion of text has been expanded to include types of cultural production other than writing, then the assumption is made that these productions, whether they be landscapes or political institutions, have a text-like quality. Ricoeur (1971) attempts to demonstrate that this assumption has merit. By first posing two questions – 'Is the model of the text a good PARADIGM for social science?' and 'Is the textual method of interpretation relevant?' – he offers four reasons why the answer to both should be affirmative. First, he argues that the principal characteristics of written discourse also describe social life. For example, as meaning in written discourse is concretized through inscription, so recurrent behaviour in the built environment becomes concretized. Second, just as within written works an author's intentions and the meaning of the text often cease to coincide, similarly institutionalized patterns of action are frequently detached from their collective agents. Third, as written texts are reinterpreted in the light of changing circumstances, so social events are subject to continual reinterpretation. Fourth, while the meaning of a text is unstable due to its dependence upon the interpretations of its different readers, so social action and institutions are open to a range of interpretations.

It is probably within anthropology that we find the most developed notion of social action as text. Geertz (1973, 1988) was the first anthropologist systematically to develop the notion that CULTURE is a text. He interprets culture as a text to be read by an ethnographer as one might read written material. He further argues that it is not simply ethnographers who read cultures; rather, such reading is practised by all those who live within a culture. Hermeneutic and postcultural notions of text have served to problematize the notion of REPRESENTATION in ETHNOGRAPHY and geography (Marcus and Fischer, 1986; Gregory, 1989; Pred, 1990; Barnes and Duncan, 1991). The question of representation has both epistemological and ethical implications, for it simultaneously poses the question of the translatability of cultural difference, while raising the question of the morality of speaking for others (Clifford, 1988).

Another concept of increasing importance is intertextuality, the textual context of a literary work (Eagleton, 1983). Tyler (1987) has argued that although most empirical work is portrayed as objectivist it can be better described as intertextual; that is, mediated by a traditional corpus of monographs and theories. Furthermore, it is not simply academic accounts of the world which are intertextual; the world itself is intertextual. PLACES are intertextual sites because texts and discursive practices based upon texts are (re)inscribed in social practices, institutions and landscapes (Duncan, 1990).   JD

References

Barnes, T. and Duncan, J., eds 1991: *Writing worlds: discourse, text and metaphor in the representation of landscape*. London: Routledge.

Clifford, J. 1988: *The predicament of culture: twentieth century ethnography, literature and art*. Cambridge: Cambridge University Press.

Cosgrove, D. and Daniels, S., eds 1988: *The iconography of landscape: essays on the symbolic representation, design and use of past environments*. Cambridge: Cambridge University Press.

Duncan, J. 1990: *The city as text: the politics of landscape interpretation in the Kandyan kingdom*. Cambridge: Cambridge University Press.

Duncan, J. and Duncan, N. 1988: (Re)reading the landscape. *Environ. Plann. D, Society and Space* 6, pp. 117–26.

Eagleton, T. 1983: *Literary theory: an introduction*. Minneapolis: University of Minnesota Press.

Geertz, C. 1973: *The interpretation of cultures*. New York: Basic Books.

Geertz, C. 1988: *Works and lives: the anthropologist as author*. Cambridge: Polity Press.

Gregory, D. 1989: Areal differentiation and postmodern human geography. In Gregory, D. and Walford, R., eds, *New horizons in human geography*. London: Macmillan, pp. 67–96.

Harley, B. 1991: Deconstructing the map. In Barnes, T. and Duncan, J. eds, *Writing worlds: discourse, text and metaphor in the representation of landscape*. London: Routledge, pp. 231–47.

Marcus, G. E. and Fischer, M. M. J. 1986: *Anthropology as cultural critique: an experimental moment in the human sciences*. Chicago: Chicago University Press.

Pred, A. 1990: *Lost words and lost worlds: modernity and the language of everyday life in late nineteenth century Sweden*. Cambridge: Cambridge University Press.

Ricoeur, P. 1971: The model of the text: meaningful action considered as text. *Social Res.* 38, pp. 529–62.

Rose, C. 1981: Wilhelm Dilthey's philosophy of historical understanding: a neglected heritage of contemporary humanistic geography. In Stoddart, D. R., ed., *Geography, ideology and social concern*. Oxford: Blackwell, pp. 99–113.

Tyler, S. 1987: *The unspeakable: discourse, dialogue and rhetoric in the postmodern world*. Madison: University of Wisconsin Press.

Suggested Reading

Barnes and Duncan (1991).

Duncan (1990).

Ricoeur (1971).

Rose (1981).

thematic map A map that depicts statistical variations of objects in space. (See SYMBOLIZATION.)   MJB

Suggested Reading

Mersey, J. E. 1990: *Colour and thematic map design: the role of colour scheme and map complexity in choropleth map communication*. *Cartographica* 27(3), Monograph 41.

Petchenik, B. B. 1979: From place to space: the psychological achievement of thematic mapping. *Am. Cartogr.* 6, pp. 5–12.

Robinson, A. H. 1981: *Early thematic mapping in the history of cartography*. Chicago: University of Chicago Press.

theory A set of connected statements used in the process of explanation. The nature and status of theories differs among philosophies of social science (cf. EPISTEMOLOGY).

Within POSITIVISM, a theory comprises a set of hypotheses and constraining conditions which, if validated empirically, assume the status of LAWS, so that the theory structures understanding of the relevant portion of the empirical world through its system of interrelated laws. These linked coherent statements then provide the stimuli for future research: deduction and speculation from the known (the validated theory) to the unknown (the HYPOTHESIS) guide the production of future knowledge.

Whereas within positivism a theory is assumed to be universal in its application, within IDEALISM, on the other hand, there are no universals – only the individual theories resident in each individual's mind – which are used to guide action and which may be refined, and even changed, according to the outcome of the action (see also PRAGMATISM). In this context, human action is directed by personal theories, not external ones.

In REALISM a theory is a means of conceptualizing reality, and thus provides a mental framework for its apprehension: the test of a theory is not its validation against empirical evidence but, rather, its coherence and, especially, its practical adequacy. For the individual, a theory is adequate if the understanding that it provides is sufficient as a basis for a satisfactory personal life: for the social scientist, it must provide a basis for understanding and, potentially, changing society. Realists argue that because societies are open systems in which the same conditions are rarely reproduced, theories cannot, as positivists contend, predict the future; they can only illuminate the past and the present, and provide guidance to an appreciation of the future.   RJJ

Suggested Reading

Harvey, D. 1969: *Explanation in geography.* London: Edward Arnold.

Keat, R. and Urry, J. R. 1981: *Social theory as science,* second edition. London: Routledge and Kegan Paul.

Sayer, A. 1992: *Method in social science: a realist approach,* second edition. London: Routledge.

thick description A term coined by the philosopher Ryle and introduced into social science by Geertz (1973), referring to interpretations which engage in intensive interrogation of informants' actions and interpretations in order to sort out 'the structures of signification' of these events. Thick description, which is usually associated with the ethnographic method, is contrasted by Geertz to 'thin description', such as that based upon the tenets of behaviourism or upon SURVEY RESEARCH, where a detailed description of the informants' meaning system and social context is not collected. Thick description is a type of HERMENEUTIC rather than phenomenological method in that it represents the researchers interpretation of her or his informants' interpretations. (See also PHENOMENOLOGY).   JD

Reference

Geertz, C. 1973: *The interpretation of cultures.* New York: Basic Books.

Thiessen polygon A framework constructed around points, often as an alternative to QUADRAT ANALYSIS (also called a Voroni polygon). The polygons are formed by drawing straight lines between each point and all of its adjacent points, and bisecting these with new lines at right angles. The latter intersect to form polygons. The technique assumes that each point dominates the area defined by its polygon, but often discards important detail about relative location.   MJB

Suggested Reading

Boots, B. and Getis, A. 1988: *Point pattern analysis.* Sage Scientific Geography Series no. 8. London: Sage.

Haggett, P., Cliff, A. D. and Frey, A. E. 1977: *Locational analysis in human geography,* second edition. London: Edward Arnold/New York: John Wiley, pp. 55–62 and 436–9.

Third World Those nations apparently outside the first (advanced capitalist) and second (state-socialist) worlds. 'Third World' is a loose term which is frequently used even more loosely to denote underdeveloped countries in general (see UNDERDEVELOPMENT) – especially those in Africa and Asia. Most of the countries of the Third World are in Latin America, Africa and Asia and they contain over 70 per cent of the population of the world. At one extreme are the members of OPEC and at the other are countries such as Kampuchea, Bangladesh, Lao PDR, Bhutan and Ethiopia – the poorest of the poor. By contrast, a 'mere ten countries produce more than two thirds of all manufacturing output in the Third World' (Dicken, 1992, p. 441). And the diversity within countries of the Third World, especially the contrasts between urban and rural areas, tends to be much greater than that within the advanced capitalist world.

The United Nations has abstracted the 25 least developed countries as a separate group. Today this group is rapidly becoming known as the 'Fourth World' or, if the OPEC group is also considered separately, as the 'Fifth World'. The World Bank distinguishes between low-income countries, lower and upper middle-income countries – including the dozen or so Newly Industrializing Countries (see NEW INTERNATIONAL DIVISION OF LABOUR), high-income industrialized countries, capital-surplus oil exporters and the former centrally planned economies. The average per capita income of the low-income countries is 50 times less than that of the high-income industrialized countries.

The notion of the worlds is misleading (see, e.g., Crush and Riddell, 1980) in that it implies a degree of separation between them. Under the global conditions of INTERDEPENDENCE, IMPERIALISM and NEOCOLONIALISM, such a separation is never found in practice – despite the increasing importance of links between the advanced economies of the world at the expense of the Third World, and their highly selective contacts within the latter. (See also DEPENDENCE; WORLD-SYSTEMS ANALYSIS.) RL

References

Crush, J. S. and Riddell, J. B. 1980: Third World misunderstanding? *Area* 12 (3), pp. 204–6.

Dicken, P. 1992: *Global shift: the internationalization of economic activity.* London Paul Chapman.

Krugman, P. R. 1989: Developing countries in the world economy. *Daedalus* 118, pp. 183–203.

Suggested Reading

Crow, B., Thomas, A., Jenkins, R. and Kimble, J. 1983: *Third World atlas.* Milton Keynes, UK: Open University Press.

Worsley, P. 1984: *The three worlds: culture and world development.* London: Weidenfeld and Nicolson.

Tiebout model An argument for a large number of local government units offering would-be residents a range of choice of 'service-taxation packages'. According to Tiebout (1956), large local governments are inefficient because they cannot react to the great diversity of demand for locally provided public services (see PUBLIC GOODS) and the willingness to pay for them. Fragmentation of local government is thus more efficient, because each unit can tailor its service provision and tax requirements to meet a particular set of demands, and the consumers (householders and other land users) can choose to locate in that unit which is closest to their preferences. Consumer mobility will then ensure that provision and preferences are matched (see FISCAL MIGRATION), and a local government unit that fails to attract residents will have to change its service-tax package in order to ensure viability.

Tiebout's model provides a theoretical justification for local government, and an underpinning for aspects of the 'consumer sovereignty' arguments promoted strongly during the 1980s by the 'New Right'. However, it is based on strong assumptions regarding consumer information and mobility, and its validity as a guide to policy

has been questioned by those who point to the constraints on mobility which many people suffer. Thus the fragmented local government system in most US metropolitan areas is seen not as a paradigm example of the model in action, but rather as a device for the affluent and powerful in society to create 'tax havens' from which, through exclusionary ZONING practices, those less well-off than themselves are excluded. RJJ

Reference

Tiebout, C. M. 1956: A pure theory of local expenditures. *Jnl. Polit. Econ.* 64, pp. 416–24.

Suggested Reading

Johnston, R. J. 1984: *Residential segregation, the state and constitutional conflict in American urban areas.* London: Academic Press.

Whiteman, J. 1983: Deconstructuring the Tiebout hypothesis. *Environ. Plann. D, Society and Space* 1, pp. 339–54.

Zodrow, G. R., ed. 1983: *Local provision of public services: the Tiebout model after twenty-five years.* New York: Academic Press.

time-geography An approach to CONTEXTUAL THEORY originally developed by the Swedish geographer Torsten Hägerstrand and his associates at the University of Lund ('the Lund School'), which conceives of time and space as providers of 'room' for *collateral processes.* The latter term is of fundamental importance to Hägerstrand's approach: in contrast to COMPOSITIONAL THEORY, time-geography emphasizes the *continuity* and *connectedness* of sequences of events which necessarily take place in *situations* bounded in time and space, and the outcomes of which are thereby mutually modified by their common *localization* (Hägerstrand, 1976, 1984). This perspective 'on human geography is analogous to Kant's view of history and geography as the architects of 'physical' rather than 'logical' classifications (see KANTIANISM), although in other respects time-geography departs fundamentally from Kant's original prospectus. It is also one which, in more informal terms, can be traced back to early-twentieth-century writers such as Walter Benjamin and Georg Simmel, who wrote of webs of social interaction in time and space in be represented as a web model (see the figure), spun across four basal propositions:

(a) Space and time are *resources* on which individuals have to draw in order to realize *projects*.

(b) The realization of any project is subject to three *constraints:*

(i) *Capability constraints*, which limit the activities of individuals through their own physical capabilities and/or the facilities which they can command. They derive in large measure from the individual's *livelihood position* (Hägerstrand, 1970; Hoppe and Langton, 1988) and define the individual's *prism*, which contains a set of feasible time–space *paths* flowing through a constellation of accessible *stations*, e.g. farms, factories, schools and shops.

(ii) *Coupling constraints*, which define where, when and for how long an individual has to join with other individuals, tools and materials in order to produce, transact or consume. Coupling constraints define time–space *bundles.*

(iii) *authority or 'steering' constraints*, which impose conditions of access to and modes of conduct within particular time–space *domains.*

(c) These constraints are interactive rather than additive, and together they delineate a series of *possibility boundaries* which mark out the paths available for individuals or groups to fulfil particular projects. These boundaries correspond to an underlying and evolving 'logic' or 'structure' (Carlstein, 1982), the disclosure of which requires a way of 'dealing with POWER in space–time terms of considerable conceptual precision' (Hägerstrand, 1973).

(d) Within these structural templates, *competition* between projects for 'free paths' and 'open space–times' is the 'central problem for analysis' and is mediated by specific *institutions* which seek to maintain an essential time–space coherence (Hägerstrand, 1973, 1975).

These claims can be read in several different ways. A number of writers, including Hägerstrand himself, have attributed a profound NATURALISM to time-geography. Certainly, Hägerstrand's (1973) belief that the human being can be considered 'a central elementary particle'

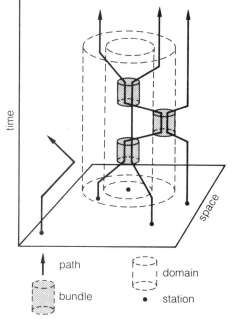

time
space

path

bundle

domain

station

time-geography *Hägerstrand's web model*

ways which, on the surface at least, resemble Hägerstrand's ideas (see Gregory, 1989, 1991). But time-geography represents an important advance over those previous formulations because it provides a *notation* which resonates with both theoretical and nethodological implications.

Although the first formal discussions of time-geography appeared in the 1960s, it had its origins in an investigation of what Hägerstrand called the 'population archaeology' of Asby in central southern Sweden. It was then that he thought of depicting individual biographies as paths in time and space; but he was unable to devise a notation capable of describing the intricacies of a 'forest' of time–space paths and so turned instead to the exploration of generalized social networks. It was this investigation which culminated in his models of spatial DIFFUSION and, in particular, in the concept of the MEAN INFORMATION FIELD (Gregory, 1985). But Hägerstrand soon returned to his original problem, and eventually developed an elementary time–space notation from standard Lexis–Becker diagrams used in demography. His basic framework can and that human geography can, in consequence, be reconstructed around the systematic time–space recording of events in a landscape something like 'the bubble-chamber of the physicist' reveals a deliberate *physicalism* (cf. Hägerstrand, 1983); and his debt to the biological sciences is disclosed in his own description of time-geography as a 'situational ecology' concerned 'to incorporate certain essential biotic and ecological predicates' within human geography and the social sciences more generally. Other writers have represented time-geography as a version of STRUCTURALISM: the distinction between a repertoire of *possible* time–space paths and a concrete configuration of trajectories *realized* within these structural templates is supposed to be formally equivalent to Saussure's distinction between *langue* (language) and *parole* (speech) (Carlstein, 1982). Certainly, structuralism seeks to displace the human subject from its formulations, and one of the most consistent criticisms of Hägerstrand's model has been its relegation of HUMAN AGENCY in the broadest of senses. Hägerstrand describes the realization of projects with compelling originality, but he says little about their constitution or accomplishment by knowledgeable and skilled actors (Buttimer, 1976). The relegation of the human subject in this way reduces social life to a form of what Sartre called *seriality*, in which subjects regard themselves and others as *objects* (Gregory, 1985), and this effectively limits Hägerstrand's spatial ONTOLOGY to *objective* rather than social space (Schatzki, 1991).

Hägerstrand has both acknowledged and anticipated the salience of these objections:

The fact that a human path in the time-geographic notation seems to represent nothing more than a point on the move should not lead us to forget that at its tip – as it were – in the persistent present stands a living body subject, endowed with memories, feelings, knowledge, imagination and goals – in other words capabilities too rich for any conceivable kind of symbolic representation but decisive for the direction of paths (Hägerstrand, 1982). And, like several other writers, Hägerstrand has noted the immanent convergence between time-geography and STRUCTURATION THEORY, which is concerned to promote a *recovery* of the subject

without lapsing into subjectivism. Time-geography is supposed to be 'absolutely central' to structuration theory, because its graphical representations enable us to see the 'material logic' of structuration: the 'cement' binding individuals and institutions into a coherent matrix (Carlstein, 1981, Pred, 1981). But the essential contribution of time-geography to structuration theory is, in Giddens's view, primarily methodological. He regards Hägerstrand's formulations as conceptually primitive – he has substantial reservations about Hägerstrand's conceptions of human agency, institutional formation and transformation, and power – but methodologically quite sophisticated (Giddens, 1984).

In fact, one of the most common claims about time-geography has been its methodological potency. And yet, as Hoppe and Langton (1988) note, most of the empirical work carried out under its aegis has been illustrative and confined to the small-scale, short-term and essentially *individual* level (see Pred, 1990). Furthermore, many time-geographic studies have focused on the time–space intersections of individual paths and institutional projects, with little regard for the changing *structural templates* and station configurations that make them possible (Gregory, 1985). These restrictions are not necessary ones, of course, but it is clear that what Pred (1977) once called 'the choreography of existence' *cannot* be understood 'unless the stations are considered as more than points on a plane, and unless the social rules [and resources] which constrain and permit behaviour of different kinds by different people are fully and explicitly introduced into the analytical scheme, (Hoppe and Langton, 1988; cf. Pred, 1986). This presumably requires the integration of time-geography with an historically sensitive LOCATION THEORY. But the *existential* dimension of Pred's 'choreography' needs to be emphasized too: if time-geography is indeed to register the significance of flows and encounters in *social space* for the constitution of 'social reality' (cf. Schatzki, 1991), then it is also necessary to treat the social construction of space as inherently involved in the construction of social meaning. Here a series of important advances have been made within FEMINIST GEOGRAPHY. Rose (1991) is troubled by what she sees as time-geography's masculinist ontology of power over space, and contrasts this vision of freedom with the constraints which most women experience in their everyday lives. In one sense, clearly, time-geography was devised precisely to disclose the operation of such constraints but, in an exceptionally important study of the time-geography of 'mothering', Dyck (1990) argues that time–space configurations may also be enabling. She shows that the bundle of activities around which many mothers condense their social activities is shaped by various constraints, but that the configurations that result are also enabling, even empowering, because it is through those regular relationships with other women in a diversity of LOCALES that conceptions of identity, of self-esteem and of mothering are constructed and negotiated. 'Women' and 'motherhood' thus emerge from her study as categories the meanings of which are situationally defined, and the social construction of space is shown to be important not simply as a logistical exercise – time–space budgets, time–space packing and the like – but also as an essential component of the construction of social meaning. DG

References

Buttimer, A. 1976: Grasping the dynamism of the life-world. *Ann. Ass. Am. Geogr.* 66, pp. 277–92.

Carlstein, T. 1981: The sociology of structuration in time and space: a time-geographic assessment of Giddens's theory. *Swedish Geographical Yearbook.* Lund: Swedish Geographical Society.

Carlstein, T. 1982: *Time resources, society and ecology*, volume 1. London: Allen and Unwin.

Dyck, I. 1990: Space, time and renegotiating motherhood: an exploration of the domestic workplace. *Environ. Plann. D*, pp. 459–83.

Giddens, A. 1984: *The constitution of society*. Cambridge: Polity Press.

Gregory, D. 1985: Suspended animation: the stasis of diffusion theory. In Gregory D, and Urry, J., eds, *Social relations and spatial structures*. London: Macmillan, pp. 296–336.

Gregory, D. 1989: Presences and absences: time–space relations and structuration theory. In Held D. and Thompson J. B., eds, *Social theory of modern societies: Anthony Giddens and his critics*. Cambridge: Cambridge University Press, pp. 185–214.

Gregory, D. 1991: Interventions in the historical geography of modernity: social theory, spatiality and the politics of representation. *Geogr. Annlr.* 73B, pp. 17–44.

Hägerstrand, T. 1970: What about people in regional science? *Pap. reg. Sci. Assoc.* 24, pp. 7–21.

Hägerstrand, T. 1973: The domain of human geography. In Chorley, R. J., ed., *Directions in geography*. London: Methuen, pp. 67–87.

Hägerstrand, T. 1975: Space, time and human conditions. In Karlqvist, A., Lunqvist L. and Snickars, F., eds, *Dynamic allocation of urban space*. Farnborough, UK: Saxon House, pp. 3–14.

Hägerstrand, T. 1976: Geography and the study of interaction between society and nature. *Geoforum* 7, pp. 329–34.

Hägerstrand, T. 1978: Survival and arena: on the life-history of individuals in relation to their geographical environment. In Carlstein, T., Parkes, D. and Thrift, N., eds, *Timing space and spacing time*, volume 2, *Human activity and time-geography*. London: Edward Arnold, pp. 122–45.

Hägerstrand, T. 1982: Diorama, path and project. *Tijdschr. econ. soc. Geogr.* 73, pp. 323–56.

Hägerstrand, T. 1983: In search for the sources of concepts. In Buttimer, A., ed., *The practice of geography*. Harlow: Longman, pp. 238–56.

Hägerstrand, T. 1984: Presence and absence: a look at conceptual choices and bodily necessities. *Reg. Stud.* 18, pp. 373–80.

Hoppe, G. and Langton, J. 1988: Time-geography and economic development: the changing structure of livelihood positions on farms in nineteenth-century Sweden. *Geogr. Annlr.* 68B, pp. 115–37.

Pred, A. 1977: The choreography of existence: some comments on Hägerstrand's time-geography and its effectiveness. *Econ. Geogr.* 53, pp. 207–21.

Pred, A. 1981: Social reproduction and the time-geography of everyday life. *Geogr. Annlr.* 63B, pp. 5–22.

Pred, A. 1986: *Place, practice and structure: space and society in Southern Sweden 1750–1850*. Cambridge: Polity Press.

Pred, A. 1990: *Lost words and lost worlds: modernity and the language of everyday life in late nineteenth-century Stockholm*. Cambridge: Cambridge University Press.

Rose, G. 1991: On being ambivalent: women and feminisms in geography. In Philo, C., ed., *New words, new worlds: reconceptualising social and cultural geography*. Aberystwyth: Social and Cultural Geography Study Group, Institute of British Geographers, pp. 156–63.

Schatzki, T. 1991: Spatial ontology and explanation. *Ann. Ass. Am. Geogr.* 81, pp. 650–70.

Suggested Reading

Dyck (1990).

Hägerstrand (1973, 1982).

Hoppe and Langton (1988).

Pred, A. 1990: *Making histories and constructing human geographies*. Boulder, CO: Westview Press

time–space compression 'Processes that so revolutionize the objective qualities of space and time that we are forced to alter, sometimes in quite radical ways, how we represent the world to ourselves' (Harvey, 1989). Consistent with his version of MARXIST GEOGRAPHY, Harvey treats time–space compression primarily as the product of the compulsion to 'annihilate space by time' under CAPITALISM, shaped by the rules of commodity production and capital accumulation. 'I use the word "compression"', he explains, 'because a strong case can be made that the history of capitalism has been characterized by speed-up in the pace of life, while so overcoming barriers that the world sometimes seems to collapse in upon us'. As this suggests, the concept of time–space compression is intended to have an *experiential* dimension that is missing from the concepts of TIME–SPACE CONVERGENCE or TIME–SPACE DISTANCIATION. Harvey pays particular attention to the ways in which time–space compression dislocates the HABITUS which gives social life its (precarious) coherence: implicated in a CRISIS of representation, therefore, its consequences are alarming, disturbing and threatening; a 'maelstrom' and a 'tiger', it induces 'foreboding', 'shock', a 'sense of collapse' and, ultimately, 'terror' (Harvey, 1989, 1990). This reading owes something to D. Bell's *The cultural consequences of capitalism* (1978), which provides a parallel critique of MODERNISM: not only was 'physical distance compressed' by new systems of transportation and communication at the end of the nineteenth and beginning of the twentieth centuries, Bell argues, but aesthetic distance was suppressed by modernism's stress on 'immediacy, impact, sensation and simultaneity'. In effect, therefore, Harvey radicalizes Bell's argument to suggest that

POSTMODERNISM can be attributed to the heightened intensity of a new round of time–space compression. In making these claims, however, the multiple and compound *geographies* of the process often seem to disappear from his account: time–space compression concentrates its furious energies on individuals and points to such a degree that its differential impacts are lost from view (see Gregory, 1993).   DG

References

Bell, D. 1978: *The cultural consequences of capitalism*. New York: Basic Books.

Gregory, D. 1993: *Geographical imaginations*. Oxford: Blackwell.

Harvey, D. 1989: *The condition of postmodernity: an enquiry into the origins of cultural change*. Oxford: Blackwell.

Harvey, D. 1990: Between space and time: reflections on the geographical imagination. *Ann. Ass. Am. Geogr.* 80, pp. 418–34.

Suggested Reading

Harvey (1989), chs 15–17.

time–space convergence A decrease in the FRICTION OF DISTANCE between places (see also DISTANCE DECAY). The concept was first formulated by Janelle (1968), who defined the *convergence rate* between two places as the average rate at which the time needed to travel between them decreases over time; the measure was supposed to be 'mathematically analogous to velocity as defined by the physicist'. Time–space convergence was attributed to technological change: 'as a result of transport innovations, places approach each other in time–space' (Janelle, 1969). Janelle showed that time–space convergence is usually discontinuous in time – hence the convergence curve in figure 1 is not smooth but jagged – and uneven over space: 'any transport improvement will tend to be of greatest advantage to the highest-ordered centre that it connects' (Janelle, 1968). Forer (1974) noted that the converse is also true – that time–space convergence is partly a function of CENTRAL PLACE structure – and that Janelle's (1969) model of 'spatial reorganization' thus entailed 'cyclic causality' in which 'places define spaces' and spaces in turn progressively 'redefine' places.

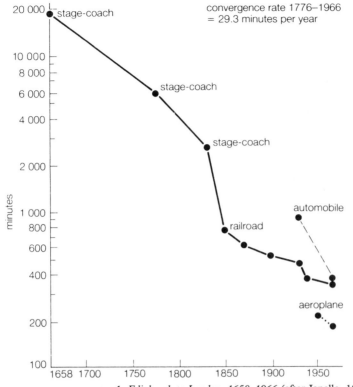

time–space convergence *1: Edinburgh to London, 1658–1966* (after Janelle, 1968).

The concept was extended by Abler (1971), who distinguished Janelle's original *distance-convergence* from an equally important *cost-covergence* (see figure 2): taken together, these were supposed to be 'two basic determinants of human spatial behaviour'. Although *time–space divergence* is theoretically possible, Abler identified a pervasive tendency, in the modern world at least, for the friction of distance to decrease. And since the friction of distance is a fundamental postulate of conventional LOCATION THEORY, CENTRAL PLACE THEORY and DIFFUSION THEORY – it is what makes the identification of regular PATTERN possible – then time–space convergence 'scrambles' and 'plays havoc' with these standard spatial models (see also Falk and Abler, 1980). Hence, time–space convergence has been connected with the concept of *plastic space*: 'a space defined by separation in time or cost terms, a space which the progressions and regressions of

technology make one of continuous flux' (Forer, 1978).

Forer (1978) also noted a 'lack of response to Janelle's ideas', and attributed this (in part) to their links with 'the large canvas of economic history and the long-term development of society'. Since Forer wrote, however, it is precisely those links which have been forged into the wider conceptual chains of TIME–SPACE COMPRESSION and TIME–SPACE DISTANCIATION. Thus, 'the shifting nature of the relations between the expansion of interaction over space and its contraction over time is obviously part and parcel of the "time–space convergence" so prominent in the development of the contemporary social world' (Giddens, 1981). As the global geography of capitalist MODERNITY becomes ever more important – and ever more intrusive – so one might expect a renewed interest in the changing geographies of time–space convergence (see Janelle, 1991).   DG

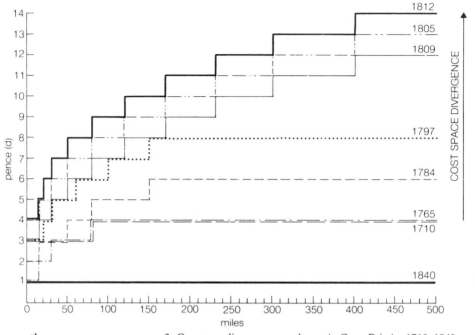

time–space convergence *2: Cost-space divergence: postal rates in Great Britain, 1710–1840.*

References

Alber, R. F. 1971: Distance, intercommunications and geography. *Proc. Ass. Am. Geogr.* 3, pp. 1–4.

Falk, T. and Abler, R. 1980: Intercommunications, distance and geographical theory. *Geogr. Annlr.* 62B, pp. 59–67.

Forer, P. 1974: Space through time. In Cripps, E. L., ed., *Space–time concepts in urban and regional models*. London: Pion, pp. 22–45.

Forer, P. 1978: A place for plastic space? *Progr. hum. Geogr.* 2, pp. 230–67.

Giddens, A. 1981: *A contemporary critique of historical materialism*, volume 1, *Power, property and the state*. London: Macmillan/Berkeley, CA: University of California Press.

Janelle, D. G. 1968: Central place development in a time–space framework. *Prof. Geogr.* 20, pp. 5–10.

Janelle, D. G. 1969: Spatial reorganization: a model and concept. *Ann. Ass. Am. Geogr.* 59, pp. 348–64.

Janelle, D. G. 1991: 'Global interdependence and its consequences', in Brunn, S. D. and Leinbach, T., eds, *Collapsing space and time: geographic aspects of communications and information*. London: Harper Collins, pp. 49–81.

Suggested Reading

Forer (1978).
Janelle (1968, 1991).

time–space distanciation 'The stretching of social systems across time–space' (Giddens, 1984). The concept of distanciation derives from Ricoeur's description of the process through which writing 'distances' a discourse from the immediate circumstances of its production. Giddens uses it to describe a wider series of societal transformations to do with what he calls *system integration*, i.e. interaction with people who are absent in time or space, and which (historically) has entailed 'the expansion of interaction over space and its contraction over time' (Giddens, 1981: see also TIME–SPACE COMPRESSION; TIME–SPACE CONVERGENCE).

Time–space distanciation is of fundamental importance to Giddens's STRUCTURATION THEORY, in which it has both (a) a *general* and (b) a *specific* purpose:

(a) One of the main features of structuration theory is that 'the extension and "closure" of societies across space and time is regarded as problematic'

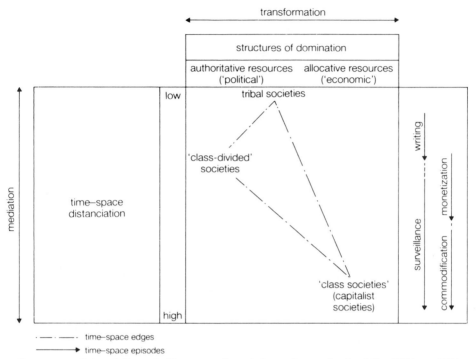

time–space distanciation   *1: Time–space distanciation and types of society* (after Giddens, 1981, 1984: Gregory, 1993).

(Giddens, 1984). Conventional social theory, like human geography, has been strongly influenced by a FUNCTIONALISM which assumes that societies are coherent and bounded systems, and by endogenous models of social change which presume that the basic structural dimenions of societies are internal to those systems. Giddens rejects these propositions and insists that 'the nexus of relations –

TYPES OF SOCIETY ──────▶ INTERSOCIETAL SYSTEMS

tribal societies   } 'prehistorical' and fragmentary systems

class-divided societies
tribal societies   } imperial world systems

capitalist societies
class-divided societies   } early capitalist world economy
tribal societies

capitalist societies
state-socialist societies

'developing countries'   contemporary capitalist world economy
                                (world nation–state system)
class-divided societies
tribal societies

time–space distanciation   *2: Intersocietal systems* (after Giddens, 1981). *Note that, to date, Giddens has said little about 'state-socialist societies' and has provided no characterization of 'developing countries' in terms congruent with figure 1.*

political, economic or military – in which a society exists with others – is usually integral to the very nature of that society' and, indeed, 'to what "societies" are conceived to be' (Giddens, 1981). At the limit, Giddens seems to suggest, the time–space constitution of societies dislocates most of the 'totalizing' ambitions of conventional social theory (cf. Mann, 1986; see also Gregory, 1990).

(b) More specifically, Giddens proposes that time–space distanciation is articulated with the *production of power* and the *reproduction of structures of domination*. As shown in figure 1, structures of domination are supposed to be constituted through *authoritative resources* that sustain relations of (roughly) 'political' POWER, and *allocative resources* that sustain relations of (roughly) 'economic' power. These resources are not constant, Giddens argues, and connect in different ways in different types of societies. This is not so very different from some of the claims of contemporary Marxism (see Wright, 1989), but in speaking of power in this way Giddens means to signal that its exercise is a chronic feature of social life: in other words, it is not inherently repressive but is bound in to the transformative capacities of HUMAN AGENCY. *Transformation*, in this sense of practical intervention, the capability to make a difference, links directly with *mediation* – with 'the variety of ways in which interaction is made possible across space and time' – because, according to Giddens, 'any co-ordination of social systems across time and space involves a definite combination of these two types of resource'. Authorization and allocation are thus also media of time–space distanciation.

This argument makes it possible to cross-cut transformation and mediation to produce a series of analytical distinctions among what Giddens calls *tribal societies*, *class-divided societies* and *class societies*. Thus, for example, authorization is the mainspring of class-divided societies such as FEUDALISM, but their degree of regularized interaction over space and time is much lower than that of CLASS societies such as CAPITALISM, where allocation is the key to their constitution.

Giddens intends this typology to clarify some of the distinctive features of MODERNITY, but he evidently accentuates the centrality of class and fails to accord (for example) PATRIARCHY the same constitutive importance. One could press such a feminist critique still further: when Giddens treats space as a gap to be overcome and describes how time–space is 'bound in' to the conduct of social life, so space as barrier and as void is transcended, incorporated and subjugated. The process is, tacitly, one in which phallocratic power is inscribed on a feminized SPACE (see Gregory, 1993; see also PHALLO-CENTRISM). Giddens identifies a number of *time–space episodes* which have been structurally implicated in the constitution of modernity and the 'disembedding' of spheres of social life from the immediacies of the here and now. In his early writings, which focus on the genealogy of modernity, Giddens (1981, 1984) pays particular attention to (a) writing and SURVEILLANCE and (b) monetization and commodification, and suggests that the modern world has been shaped by the intimacy of the connections between them. In his later writings, which focus on modernity itself, Giddens (1990, 1991) distinguishes between (i) *expert systems*, which 'bracket time and space through deploying modes of technical knowledge which have validity independent of the practitioners and clients who make use of them' and (ii) *symbolic tokens*, which are 'media of exchange which have standard value and thus are interchangeable across a plurality of contexts'. Together these constitute *abstract systems* which penetrate all aspects of everyday life, and in doing so undermine local practices and local knowledges; they dissolve the ties that once held the conditions of daily life in place and recombine them across much larger tracts of space. These proposals invite a comparison with Lefebvre's (1991) discussion of abstract space and concrete space (see PRODUCTION OF SPACE). Although Giddens (1985) is as sensitive as Lefebvre to the violence involved in the constitution of modern societies, he is much less attentive to the significance of constellations of phallocratic and colonial power. Indeed, Hirst (1982) has objected to the ETHNOCENTRISM of Giddens's treatment of time–space distanciation, 'which harbours an idea of the immediate and intimate and our movement away from them'. 'This is a myth,' Hirst claims, 'if we take the categories of non-Western societies seriously'. But in drawing attention to ways in which time–space distanciation opens out interaction and stretches social systems across time and space, Giddens does at least recognize the importance of *time–space edges* which denote forms of contact and connection 'between different types of society' and which are supposed to be axes of immanent social change. In his most recent writings, however, Giddens (1991) argues that *globalization* has become so pervasive, 'connect[ing] individuals to large-scale systems as part of complex dialectics of change at both local and global poles', that we now inhabit a world in which 'there are no "others" '. DG

References

Giddens, A. 1981: *A contemporary critique of historical materialism*, volume 1, *Power, property and the state*. London: Macmillan.

Giddens, A. 1984: *The constitution of society*. Cambridge: Polity Press.

Giddens, A. 1985: *A contemporary critique of historical materialism*, volume 2, *The nation–state and violence*. Cambridge: Polity Press.

Giddens, A. 1990: *The consequences of modernity*. Stanford, CA: Stanford University Press.

Giddens, A. 1991: *Modernity and self-identity*. Cambridge: Polity Press.

Gregory, D. 1990: 'Grand maps of history': structuration theory and social change, in Clark, J., Modgil, C. and Modgil, S. eds, *Anthony Giddens: consensus and controversy*. Brighton, UK: Falmer, pp. 217–33.

Gregory, D. 1993: *Geographical imaginations*. Oxford: Blackwell.

Hirst, P. 1982: The social theory of Anthony Giddens: a new syncretism? *Theory, Culture and Society* 1(2), pp. 78–82.

Lefebvre, H. 1991: *The production of space*. Oxford: Blackwell.

Mann, M. 1986: *The sources of social power*, Volume 1, *A history of power from the beginning to AD 1760*. Cambridge: Cambridge University Press.

Wright, E. O. 1989: Models of historical trajectory: an assessment of Giddens's critique of Marxism. In Held, D. and Thompson, J. B.,

eds, *Social theory of modern societies: Anthony Giddens and his critics*. Cambridge: Cambridge University Press, pp. 77–102.

Suggested Reading

Giddens (1984, chs 4 and 5; 1991).

Kilminster, R. 1991: Structuration theory as world view. In Bryant, C. G. A. and Jary, D., eds *Giddens' theory of structuration: a critical appreciation*. London: Routledge, pp. 74–115.

Wright (1989).

topographic map A map that represents the form of the Earth's surface, giving the horizontal and vertical positions of those features depicted (see SYMBOLIZATION). Increasingly, topographic map data are being provided in digital formats (United States Geological Survey, 1990) with the possible goals of scale-free map databases (Guptill, 1989). Topographic and environmental data are important components of the developments in global environmental databases (Clark, et al., 1991). MJB

References and Suggested Reading

Clark, D. M., Hastings, D. A. and Kineman, J. J. 1991: Global databases and their implications for GIS. In Maguire, D. J., Goodchild, M. F. and Rhind, D. W., eds, *Geographical information systems: principles and applications*, volume 2 London: Longman, pp. 217–31.

Guptill, S. 1989: Speculations on seamless, scaleless cartographic databases. *Proceedings, Auto Carto 9*, pp. 436–43. Falls Church, VA: ASPRS/ACSM.

United States Geological Survey 1990: *Digital line graphs for 1 : 24,000 scale maps*. USGS Data Users Guide 1. Reston, VA: USGS.

topophilia Literally, love of PLACE. The term was introduced into geography by Yi-Fu Tuan (1961) from its original use by the French phenomenologist Gaston Bachelard in *La poetique de l'espace* (1958), who coined it with reference to the sense of poetic reverie stimulated by our affective ties to the elemental world and emotionally charged places. Tuan's original usage, which referred to the flood of sentiment experienced in our surroundings when we relax more analytic attention to them, was extended in his 1974 text to encompass the entire range of imaginative experiences that relate individuals and groups to geographical environments significant to them. For Tuan, and for many humanistic geographers (see HUMANISTIC GEOGRAPHY), topophilia is foundational to the geographical imagination, stimulating geography's traditions of both exploration of place and LANDSCAPE representation in MAPS, TEXTS and pictures. Topophilia gestures towards aesthetic, sensual, nostalgic and utopian aspects of geographical awareness and investigation. It is thus an important dimension of the symbolic significance of places and landscapes. Although topophilia refers primarily to positive emotions about the world, the concept encompasses the entire range of feelings about places, landscapes and environments, including fear, dread and loathing (topophobia; see Tuan, 1979)DEC

References

Bachelard, G. 1958: *La poetique de l'espace*. Paris: Presses Universitaires de France. (English translation, *The poetics of space*. Boston: Beacon Press, 1969.)

Tuan, Y.-F. 1961: Topophilia, or sudden encounter with landscape. *Landscape* 11, pp. 28–32.

Tuan, Y.-F. 1974: *Topophilia: a study of environmental perception, attitudes and values*. Englewood Cliffs, NJ: Prentice-Hall.

Tuan, Y.-F. 1979: *Landscapes of fear*. Oxford: Blackwell.

Suggested Reading

Bunske, E. 1990: St Exupery's geography lesson: art and science in the creation and cultivation of landscape values. *Ann. Ass. Am. Geogr.* 80, pp. 96–108.

Cosgrove, D. E. 1989: Geography is everywhere: culture and symbolism in human landscapes. In Gregory, D. and Walford, R., eds, *Horizons in human geography*. London: Macmillan, pp. 118–35.

tourism, geography of The study of the geography of tourism. According to some sources, tourism is now the largest industry in the world: one study found that in 1987 the industry had sales of $2 trillion worldwide and employed 6.3 per cent of the global workforce (*The Economist*, 1991). Even more importantly, perhaps, tourism frames massive and continuous flows of people to more and more places all around the globe (*Theory, Culture and Society*, 1990).

In recent years, tourism has undergone several major shifts. The first has been one of industrial organization; the industry has not only grown rapidly but it has also increasingly become the domain of large, and often multinational, corporations, many of which have not only become horizontally but also vertically integrated, spilling from one part of the industry into others. This is especially the case in the package holiday market, where corporations have become progressively involved in all parts of the tourist market, from retail outlets through transportation to hotels. However, it should not be forgotten that much of the tourist industry is, and no doubt will continue to be, reliant on numerous small businesses (see, e.g., Williams et al., 1989).

Another major shift has been in the technology of tourism. The growth of modern tourism would not have been possible without several technological innovations; in particular, the means to transport people in bulk to far-off places has increased rapidly, and the increase in the size and range of jet aircraft has led to the creation of a long-haul package holiday market (for example, to Thailand) that hardly existed a decade ago. Similarly, the enormous advances in computerized booking systems have been vital in allowing travel and reservations to be organized and linked.

A third shift has been in the nature of the tourist gaze (Urry, 1990). It is quite clear that different tourists (identified by nationality, class, gender and so on) have quite different ways of seeing and evaluating tourist sites. These ways of seeing have changed over time, with the result that certain sites have become more or less popular as places to visit. For example, in their home country British tourists are now more attracted to rural, cultural and heritage sites, and less attracted than they were to seaside resorts. But this example may in turn be part of a more general shift in Western society: tourists (and especially middle-class tourists) seem to have become more inclined to seek out 'authenticity' while, at the same time, being more aware of how inauthentic much that is 'authentic' actually is. The growth of a 'heritage' tourist industry, fixed on historic places, and on cultural experiences of various kinds, such as museums, is testimony to this. At the same time it is also a testimony to other changes, and especially to the increasing number of links between the tourist gaze and the mass media. Most especially, the images and signs attached to tourist places by the mass media have become a crucial determinant of how those places are seen and why these places are visited. In other words, images and signs associated with tourist sites become another layer of reality (see COMMODITY; POSTMODERNISM).

The mention of tourist places and the heritage industry unlocks a fourth major shift in the practices of tourism – in the nature of the tourist places themselves. Tourist places have, of course, played to tourists for hundreds of years, as exemplified by a massive archive of travel writing, by both men and women, on which geographers have only just begun to draw in detail (Domosh, 1991). What is different now is the conscious drive to play on a place's past, to play up its unique features, or simply to play with the place in an attempt to create something spectacular and so worth visiting. This is a direct result of the increasing confusion between 'tourism', as it is conventionally understood, and a whole host of other social practices – especially shopping and watching television or films, but also sports, leisure and education.

This impulse is particularly noticeable in major tourist theme parks such as Disneyland, Disneyworld and Espace Eurodisney, in carefully manicured heritage centres such as Bath, in Japanese 'honeymoon' resorts in Australia (Rimmer, 1992), and in the larger, themed shopping malls such as the West Edmonton Mall in Canada (Shields, 1989). In each of these cases, these tourist SPECTACLES have been developed by coalitions of developers, retailers, image constructors and planners, who are willing routinely to cross the dividing line between economic and the cultural in the pursuit of profit (see CONSUMPTION).

Another major shift has been an increasing awareness of the economic, social and cultural impacts of tourism. These impacts can be favourable or detrimental. Thus the tourist industry may create much-needed employment and income in a locality but, equally, it can threaten the integrity of a locality's society and culture. Even worse, in some cases the sheer weight of tourists may begin to threaten the locality's character as a tourist destination – it no longer counts as an exotic place to visit. But the most serious impact of tourism is undoubtedly environmental, whether in the form of pollution, loss of habitat or erosion.

These different impacts explain the final major shifts in the character of tourism: the steadily increasing involvement of government. More and more STATES have developed strategies to promote and control tourism. States can encourage tourism, for example, through investments in infrastructure. They can also regulate it, for example, by concentrating tourism in certain designated areas to minimize environmental and cultural danger. Certainly, the uncomfortable fact is that tourism is now so all-pervasive that some are beginning to ask whether the world can be saved from it. NJT

References

Domosh, M. 1991: Toward a feminist historigraphy of geography. *Trans. Inst. Br. Geogr.* n.s. 16, pp. 95–104.

Rimmer, P. J. 1992: Japanese resort archipelago. *Environ. Plann. A* 24, pp. 1599–626.

Shields, R. 1989: Social spatialisation and the built environment: the West Edmonton Mall. *Environ. Plann. D, Society and Space* 7, pp. 147–64.

The Economist 1991: Broadening the mind: a survey of world travel and tourism. 23 March, special supplement.

Theory, Culture and Society 1990: Special issue on global culture, 7(2–3).

Urry, J. 1990: *The Tourist Gaze*. London: Sage.

Williams, A., Shaw, G. and Greenwood, P. 1989: From tourist to tourism entrepreneur. *Environ. Plann A* 21, pp. 1639–53.

Suggested Reading

Britton, S. 1991: Tourism, capital and place: towards a critical geography of tourism. *Environ. Plann. D, Society and Space* 9, pp. 451–70.

town A general name for an urban place, usually a settlement exceeding a prescribed minimum population threshold. No specific size range is generally accepted to distinguish a town from either a CITY or a village, however, and local practices differ significantly. In some countries, a town occupies a particular position in the hierarchy of local government, as in several American states, where the town is generally a small settlement – and in the UK would probably be termed a village. (See also NEW TOWN.) RJJ

townscape A central concept in an approach to URBAN GEOGRAPHY which emphasizes description and classification of the principal visual features of urban form. In its early development, urban geography was primarily a study of the MORPHOLOGY and MORPHOGENESIS of historic phases of land-use development. Together, study of the town plan, its land-use units and architectural forms provided an appreciation of the townscape (Carter, 1981, p. 8). This approach has been developed in Britain in the work of Conzen (1969), Whitehand (1984) and their students. In recent years it has also considered the respective roles of the agents and institutions who are the makers of the townscape, including owners, developers, architects and planners (Larkham, 1988; Whitehand, 1990).

Outside Britain similar urban research has been conducted by students of the CULTURAL LANDSCAPE, notably in Germany and the US. But the concept of the LANDSCAPE is itself undergoing a reappraisal. Influenced by a literature in social and cultural theory, some see the urban landscape as a TEXT to be read to reveal the ideas, practices, interests and contexts of the society that created it (Ley, 1987; Knox, 1991). Moreover, such landscapes may themselves be constitutive in the ongoing reproduction of society (Duncan, 1990). DL

References

Carter, H. 1981: *The study of urban geography*, third edition. London: Edward Arnold.

Conzen, M. R. G. 1969: *Alnwick, Northumberland: a study in townplan analysis*. London:

Institute of British Geographers, Publication No. 27.

Duncan, J. 1990: *The city as text: the politics of landscape interpretation in the Kandyan kingdom*. Cambridge: Cambridge University Press.

Knox, P. 1991: The restless urban landscape: economic and sociocultural change and the transformation of metropolitan Washington, D.C. *Ann. Ass. Am. Geogr.* 81, pp. 181–209.

Larkham, P. 1988: Agents and types of change in the conserved townscape. *Trans. Inst. Br. Geogr.* n.s. 13, pp. 148–64.

Ley, D. 1987: Styles of the times: liberal and neoconservative landscapes in inner Vancouver, 1968–1986. *J. hist. Geogr.* 13, pp. 40–56.

Whitehand, J. 1984: Commercial townscapes in the making. *J. hist. Geogr.* 10, pp. 174–200.

Whitehand, J. 1990: Makers of the residential landscape: conflict and change in Outer London. *Trans. Inst. Br. Geogr.* n.s. 15, pp. 87–101.

Suggested Reading

Conzen (1969).

Whitehand (1990).

trade A flow of commodities from producers to consumers. In terms of the CIRCUIT OF CAPITAL, trade represents the conversion of capital as commodities back into its money form, and it involves the realization of surplus value (see ECONOMIC GEOGRAPHY; MARXIAN ECONOMICS). Conventionally, trade is considered as an aggregate set of flows of one or more commodities between one or more urban, regional, national or international economies – hence the distinction between intra- and inter-urban, intra- and inter-regional, and intra- and international trade.

Two schools of thought exist on the reasons for trade. First, following the classical analysis of David Ricardo, are those who start from pre-existing natural or historically created differences between areas. Trade is then explained in terms of the law of COMPARATIVE ADVANTAGE, which suggests that only a relative advantage, measured in terms of opportunity costs, is necessary to make trade of benefit to all participants and thereby to the economic system as a whole. The exploitation of relative advantage may help to shift the PRODUCTIVE FORCES from higher to lower cost activities and hence to increase total productivity. Such a consequence is explicit in the explanation of comparative advangage advanced by the *Heckscher–Ohlin principle*. This states that comparative advantage stems from geographical variations in the endowment of FACTORS OF PRODUCTION between places. Given the (unrealistic) assumption of invariant production functions (the quantitative relationship between inputs and outputs in production) between places, trade will enable its participants to export commodities which are intensive in factors in which they are well endowed, and to import commodities intensive in those factors in which they are less well endowed.

Second, there are those who explain trade in terms of the exchange relationships within and between MODES OF PRODUCTION. Thus the limited amount of trade under FEUDALISM – limited, that is, in relation to the value of total feudal production – was made possible and encouraged by the profits to be made by merchants who were able to exploit the spatially parcellized SOVEREIGNTY of feudal society by buying commodities cheaply and selling them elsewhere at much higher prices. By contrast, the emergence of CAPITALISM increased the total value and volume of production and reduced its unit price through large-scale production, thereby expanding the market for the commodities. In addition, the inherently competitive social relations of capitalism constantly drive it to seek new markets for the realization of surplus value and sources of supply. Thus the volume and extent of trade was greatly increased both between capitalist economies and between pre-capitalist and capitalist economies. In the same way, the restrictions on trade initially imposed by the emergence of state-socialist economies were soon penetrated by the internal and external pressure of demands for inputs and outlets.

These two schools of thought come together as the integrated system of production and exchange embodied within modes of production is projected upon a network of national economies. Differences between countries in the level of DEVELOPMENT or capital intensity of the productive forces, and in the availability and unionization of labour, may enable a larger surplus to be appropriated in developed economies by exchanging goods at prices above their value for goods priced below value. The latter originate in economies having inferior productive facilities and large, unorganized labour reserves which help to keep prices low. Such a process of *unequal exchange* may be intensified by a dependence upon a limited number of commodities or a limited number of markets, or both. Unequal exchange may help to maintain a permanent inability to gain from trade by the systematic extraction of value from underdeveloped economies and by the development of a permanent technology gap. This may not only result in the increased penetration of imports into the developed economies, but may also undermine traditional modes of production and intensify technological DEPENDENCE in the underdeveloped economies. However, this is only one aspect of the more general condition of social dependence which results from the penetration of traditional economies by developed ones.

In fact, the majority of world trade flows between the developed economies, as a result of the technologically induced division of labour between them. However, the realization of surplus value through sale and exchange remains a problem – hence the long-standing and increasing interest in developing the underdeveloped countries to serve not merely as a market for consumer goods but also as a market for capital goods. Similarly, food, raw materials and energy are still produced in large quantities by the underdeveloped countries, and so it is vital for the reproduction of developed economies that they maintain a hold upon supplies by strategic and commercial means (see NEOCOLONIALISM).

The flow of commodities across international frontiers enables its regulation by national and international agencies. Such regulation is made increasingly difficult, however, when trade takes place between different branches of the same MULTINATIONAL CORPORATION. During the present century two periods, the first between 1929 and 1933 and the second during the period of reconstruction after the Second World War, have witnessed the erection of barriers to trade. TARIFFS, import quotas and more covert measures such as marginal adjustments to national standards may be used singly or together as barriers to trade. The General Agreement on Tariffs and Trade (GATT), which began operations in 1948 and has met regularly ever since, was one response to the postwar period of protectionism. The United Nations Conference on Trade and Development (UNCTAD) was first convened in 1964, with the objectives of reorganizing the institutional arrangements affecting world trade and of prompting the redesign of trade policies in the developed economies in order to encourage trade with and development of the underdeveloped world, through a generalized system of preferences within GATT. Control is also exerted by international agreement on particular commodities such as sugar and fibres. Regionally based organizations such as the EC, LAFTA (Latin American Free Trade Association) and ASEAN (Association of South-East Asian Nations) have been established, in part to encourage the growth of trade between their members. In so far as economic growth is stimulated by such arrangements, external trade may also be encouraged. But the erection of external tariffs around such free trade areas, customs unions or common markets may have the effect of reducing world trade. In practice, however, little more than 30 per cent of US and Japanese trade is with the rest of the Americas and the ASEAN group respectively, despite recent moves to establish free trade areas in both regions. Furthermore, only 17 per cent of US GDP and 18 per cent of Japanese GDP is traded. By contrast, nearly three-quarters of the trade of the member countries of the EC is within Europe, while the average proportion of GDP accounted for by trade in the member states of the EC is nearly 50 per cent. The external trade of the EC as a whole amounts to less than 19 per cent of its total Community GNP.

The volume of world trade at any moment in time reflects the global level of output and production and the restrictions – social, geographical and institutional – upon the exchange of this output. The emergence of capitalist social relations both stimulated output and reduced barriers to trade. This stimulus has been intensified during the present century by the rapid development of state-socialist economies, and their consequently increased capacity for trade within and beyond COMECON (Council for Mutual Economic Aid). The collapse of communism in Eastern Europe and the former USSR has led to dramatic declines in the trade of the region and rapid increases in the negative balance of its international trade.

One of the most characteristic features of the postwar development of the world economy has been the rapid growth of output, especially from the 1950s, and the even faster growth of trade in almost every year. The implication of this relationship is not only that the world economy has become more integrated but that production anywhere is subjected to more intense competition from around the world economy. Although manufacturing drives this growth of output and trade, such growth implies the rapid growth of global service activity within the sphere of circulation in the circuit of capital. However, data on trade in services remains scanty.

Participation in trade remains uneven: almost four-fifths of all manufactured exports are generated by the developed market economies of the world economy and nearly 60 per cent of such exports are to other developed market economies. One effect of the growth of international trade has been a systematic decline of the share of underdeveloped economies in world trade, most especially from Africa (with a very low proportion of exports accounted for by manufactures) and Latin America. To some extent this has been compensated for by the increasing share in manufactured exports from developing market economies, but this emanates largely from South-east Asia (with very high shares of manufactured exports in total exports) and is due mainly to the newly industrializing countries. Western Europe, Asia (especially Japan) and North America dominate world trade in tradable services.

To understand and explain international trade, it is necessary both to understand the differential capacity of modes of production for trade and the uneven implications of their articulation with a historically produced world division of labour based upon the existence of particular social formations.   RL

Suggested Reading
Corbridge, S. and Agnew, J. 1991: The US trade and budget deficits in global perspective: an essay in geopolitical-economy. *Environ. Plann. D, Society and Space*, 9, pp. 71–90.
Dicken, P. 1992: *Global shift: the internationalization of economic activity*, second edition. London: Paul Chapman, chs 2 and 6.
Harvey, D. 1975: The geography of capitalist accumulation. *Antipode* 2, pp. 9–21.
Moore, L. 1985: *The growth and structure of international trade since the Second World War*. Brighton, UK: Wheatsheaf.

tragedy of the commons A metaphor used to illustrate and account for situations in which the depletion of natural resources occurs because individual and collective interests do not coincide, and no institution has the power to ensure that they do.

Hardin's (1968) classic paper defining the metaphor gives the example of graziers using common land and continually adding to their herds for so long as the marginal return from the additional animal is positive, even though this means that the resource is being depleted and the average return per animal is falling. Indeed, he argues that graziers will be impelled to follow the example of all others and add to their herds in order to maintain overall returns, given the fall in average yield that follows the addition of every further animal. Efficient use of the resource requires its rationing through limitations on herd size. However, individuals will not altruistically limit their herd sizes unless they know that all others will also (see PRISONER'S DILEMMA), and to ensure that all do requires an external organization (such as the STATE) with the power to enforce optimal use and to ensure the best interests of both the individuals and the collective.

Hardin's metaphor has been extended to a wide range of other situations, beyond the issue of the use of destructible natural resource use: for example, he used it to develop a case for population control (Hardin, 1974). Others have argued that

the metaphor's applicability depends on the resource in question. Laver (1984, 1986) has identified three possible solutions: (1) *privatization* of the commons, with private owners acting to protect the natural resource in ways that collective owners could not; (2) the conclusion of *collective agreements* among the users, which they enforce without the need for external power (as illustrated by Ostrom, 1990); and (3) *regulation by an external body*. The extent to which the first two are viable strategies for the long-term conservation of the Earth's natural resources is doubted by many (Johnston, 1992).   RJJ

References
Hardin, G. 1968: The tragedy of the commons: the population problem has no technical solution; it requires a fundamental extension in morality. *Science* 162, pp. 1243–8.
Hardin, G. 1974: Living on a lifeboat. *Bioscience* 24, pp. 561–8.
Johnston, R. J. 1992: Laws, states and superstates: international law and the environment. *Appl. Geogr.* 12, pp. 211–28.
Laver, M. 1984: The politics of inner space: tragedies of three commons. *Europ. J. pol. Res.* 12, pp. 59–71.
Laver, M. 1986: Public, private and common in outer space. *Pol. Stud.* 34, pp. 359–73.
Ostrom, E. 1990: *Governing the commons: the evolution of institutions for collective action*. Cambridge: Cambridge University Press.

transactional analysis An approach to understanding how the number of firms in an industry, and the nature of exchanges between such firms, are determined. It is based on the fundamental proposition 'that the economic institutions of capitalism have the main purpose and effect of economizing on transaction costs' (Williamson, 1985, p. 17). To this end, a firm may judge it cheaper to administer the production of a commodity within its internal organizational hierarchy (perhaps to exploit internal ECONOMIES OF SCOPE or to reap internal ECONOMIES OF SCALE). Alternatively, the firm may judge it cheaper to acquire the same commodity through an external transaction (e.g. market purchase or subcontracting), the cost of making this transaction perhaps having been reduced by the clustering of suppliers near to the

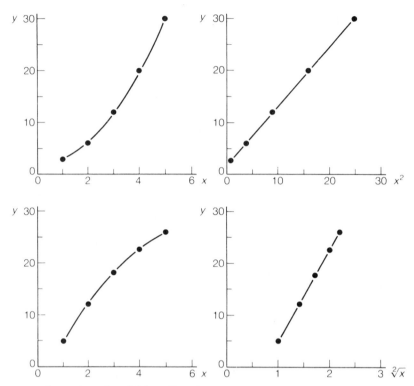

transformation of variables   *Transformation from non-linear to linear relationships.*

firm. This type of analysis illuminates one of the forces said to propel the AGGLOMERATION of productive activities in urban centres. (See also LOCATION THEORY; PRODUCTION COMPLEX.)   MSG

Reference

Williamson, O. E. 1985: *The economic institutions of capitalism.* New York: The Free Press.

transferability   One of the bases of SPATIAL INTERACTION identified by E. L. Ullman. It covers (a) the TRANSPORT COSTS, which in turn reflect characteristics of the commodity and the transport system, and (b) the ability of goods to bear transport costs. Precious metals, for example, have high transferability because they are easy to handle and transport costs are small in proportion to their monetary value, but plate glass has low transferability because it is difficult to handle and has relatively low value. The general concept and the term are often used without specific reference to Ullman's work.   AMH

transformation   See CARTOGRAM.

transformation of variables   A set of procedures used in parametric statistical analysis, whereby one set of numbers is replaced by another which is some function of the first (e.g. their logarithms or their square roots).

In EXPLORATORY DATA ANALYSIS transformations are used to improve the descriptive accuracy of statements – usually statements of relationships. The GENERAL LINEAR MODEL assumes that relationships between pairs of variables are linear, for example, so that fitting a straight line into a curvilinear relationship describes it inefficiently. Transformation of either or both of the independent and the dependent variable may 'linearize' the relationship, however, and thus justify the use of, say, REGRESSION analysis on the data set.

The figure shows two examples of a transformation. In the first, a curvilinear relationship is linearized by transforming the *X* variable – on the horizontal axis – to

X^2. In the second, the X variable is transformed into its square root.

In CONFIRMATORY DATA ANALYSIS, used in the testing of HYPOTHESES according to the rules of statistical INFERENCE, transformations are needed to ensure that the requirements of the general linear model are met. If this is not done, the estimated coefficients are inefficient, and valid inferences cannot be drawn from the sample analysed.

A common transformation, which does not alter either the form of the FREQUENCY DISTRIBUTION for a variable or the shape of a relationship between two variables, but puts the data into a universal metric, involves expressing each value in a data set as a Z-score, where

$$Z_i = (X_i - \bar{x})/\text{s.d.}_x$$

so that the original value (X_i) is expressed as its distance from the mean for all values of $X(\bar{x})$, divided by the standard deviation (s.d.) of that mean. With a NORMAL DISTRIBUTION, the location of each individual value of the data set can then be identified, relative to the location for the same observation on a different variable with its own mean and standard deviation. (For example, we may have data for the percentage voting Labour in a set of Parliamentary constituencies – mean 30.0, s.d. 15.0 – and the percentage of households in each living in rented dwellings – mean 35.0, s.d. 8.0. A constituency with 45 per cent voting Labour and 39.0 per cent living in rented dwellings would have Z-scores of +1.0 for the first variable [(45 − 30)/15] and +0.5 [(39 − 35)/8] for the second.) Such transformations are central to the computational work involved in the techniques grouped under the rubric of the general linear model. RJJ

Suggested Reading
Johnston, R. J. 1978: *Multivariate statistical analysis in geography: a primer on the general linear model.* London: Longman.

O'Brien, L. 1992: *Introducing quantitative geography: measurements, methods and generalised linear models.* London: Routledge.

transhumance The practice by some pastoralists and pastoral farmers of moving herds of animals seasonally or periodically to exploit locally specific ECOSYSTEMS, typically seasonal pastures (see MIXED FARMING). Transhumance was first used in a precise sense to describe the spatially limited patterns of animal movement in Alpine Europe, among people who were primarily agrarian and who identified with a permanent settlement rather than a pastoral encampment (Johnson, 1969). Farmers who normally occupy permanent dwellings in one ecotype typically move animals, and often a proportion of household members, *vertically* from mountain to valley pastures between summer and winter months. Pastoral nomads who are periodically sedentary (for example, around dry-season water holes) but who rely primarily upon animal products, may also engage in seasonal patterns of movements of animals and people, typically a *horizontal* search for pasture associated with spatial variation in monsoonal rainfall. MW

Reference
Johnson, D. 1969: *The nature of nomadism.* Chicago: University of Chicago, Department of Geography, Research Paper No. 118.

transnational corporation See MULTINATIONAL CORPORATION.

transport costs The total cost of moving goods, which includes the FREIGHT RATE but also costs of documentation, packaging, insurance and inventory costs. Transport costs were seen by classical LOCATION THEORY as a primary determinant of agricultural location (see VON THÜNEN MODEL) and industrial location, but even if they were important in the nineteenth century they have become less important in the twentieth due to technological changes in freight transport (e.g. containerization, pipelines and bulk carriers). AMH

Suggested Reading
Lowe, J. C. and Moryadas, S. 1975: *The geography of movement.* Boston: Houghton Mifflin, ch. 3.

transport geography The study of the role of transport in geography, including the provision of transport systems, the use of those systems for the movement of people and goods, and the relationships between transport and other geographical phenomena.

Nineteenth-century geographers (e.g. F. Ratzel and A. Hettner) recognized the importance of transport as providing features of the landscape and as an agent of geographical change. In the early twentieth century leading French geographers (P. Vidal de la Blache and J. Brunhes) developed transport geography as part of what they called the 'geography of circulation', which studied not only the permanent landscape features but also the transient movements of goods and people. The subdiscipline developed little until the 1950s, when studies of individual transport modes (ports, airports and railways) were initiated. Then, in the 1960s, North American geographers, led by E. L. Ullman, W. L. Garrison, E. J. Taaffe and others, demonstrated the applicability of quantitative techniques. As a consequence there was a rapid expansion of studies in transport geography (often with direct or indirect planning application). Since 1970 the dominance of POSITIVISM in transport geography has been criticized, because it is thought to inhibit a critical study of transport systems.

The first and most persistent feature of transport geography has been the study of transport phenomena in their own right. Five categories of work can be identified:

(a) NETWORK studies attempt to describe and explain the geographical pattern of transport networks (roads, railways and canals). In their description use is made of GRAPH THEORY and similar techniques. Explanation is focused upon the spatial association between the form of networks and other geographic phenomena.

(b) Studies of transport terminals have concentrated mainly on ports and airports, describing not only the morphology of individual facilities and their evolution over time, but also of whole systems of competing ports or airports. Some authors have attempted to construct ideal–typical sequences of port and port system evolution.

(c) Studies of the provision of scheduled services (by train, bus and air) complement the study of networks and terminals. Some of the descriptive studies use the same techniques as network analysis in an attempt to measure the ACCESSIBILITY provided by such services, but more successful measures include some reference to frequency in time as well as density in space. Recent studies have focused especially upon the changes in scheduled services occasioned by the trend towards national and international DEREGULATION. In all of these studies, attention is increasingly being paid to inequalities in mobility between those who are car owners and the relatively disadvantaged who are dependent upon public transport (usually scheduled services).

(d) studies of the movement of commodities make use of descriptive techniques such as *transaction flow analysis* and FACTOR ANALYSIS. Explanations in terms of the geographical character of places have often used Ullman's bases for SPATIAL INTERACTION; operational models have been based upon LINEAR PROGRAMMING, INPUT–OUTPUT and especially GRAVITY MODELS. Attention is also given to the issue of MODAL SPLIT. Recent studies have increasingly emphasized the role of firms as the initiators and agents of commodity flow.

(e) The movement of people is studied at all geographical scales (within cities, between cities, interregionally and internationally). Early descriptive studies have been replaced by explanatory studies which seek to account, first, for the number of trips originating or terminating within a geographical area; second, for the flows between areas; and third, for the allocation of this traffic between competing modes. Earlier studies used AGGREGATE TRAVEL MODELS, the most successful of which has been the GRAVITY MODEL (see also ENTROPY-MAXIMIZING MODELS), but other models including INTERVENING OPPORTUNITY have their champions. More recently, the aggregate and deterministic nature of these models has led to increased interest in DISAGGREGATE TRAVEL DEMAND MODELS in which the trip-making behaviour of individuals is related to the perceived utility of alternative destinations (see DISCRETE CHOICE MODELS). TIME-

GEOGRAPHY, with its emphasis on household time–space budgets, has presented an alternative disaggregate approach.

A second common theme is the role of transport as an agent of geographical change. The geographical pattern of transport networks can often be correlated with urban growth, and the geography of manufacturing and service industry. Such spatial associations are used as causal evidence that transport innovations induce geographical change. But attempts to verify this hypothesis stumble over two problems. The first is one of circular causation; in other words, although transport may lead to urban growth, urban growth itself may be the cause of transport expansion. The second is that the transport-induced effects may be difficult to distinguish from concurrent changes induced by other causes.

The third area of interest has only recently come into prominence. It is evident that the transport sector is a major source of atmospheric pollution, especially from the internal combustion engine. The emission of hydrocarbons, additives, and the products of combustion (oxides of nitrogen and carbon dioxide) has raised two questions: First, if the use of transport has to be restrained for environmental reasons, what new geographical patterns will emerge? Conversely, what new geographical patterns would contribute to such a restraint?

All of these concerns of transport geography have potential importance for planning the provision of transport services and facilities. Transport geography has therefore forged close links with transport planning and traffic engineering.   AMH

Suggested Reading

Eliot Hurst, M. E., ed. 1974: *Transportation geography: comments and readings.* New York: McGraw-Hill.

Hanson, S. ed. 1986: *The geography of urban transportation.* New York: Guilford Press.

Hoyle, B. S. and Knowles, R. D. 1992: *Modern transport geography.* London: Belhaven.

Lowe, J. C. and Moryadas, S. 1975: *The geography of movement.* Boston: Houghton Mifflin.

McKinnon, A. C. 1989: *Physical distribution systems.* London: Routledge.

Taaffe, E. J. and Gauthier, H. L. 1973: *Geography of transportation.* Englewood Cliffs, NJ: Prentice-Hall.

transportation problem A special case in LINEAR PROGRAMMING, dealing with the least-cost supply of goods from N origins to M destinations. If the amounts available at the N origins, the amounts needed at the M destinations, and the costs of movement between each origin and each destination are known, it is possible to determine the least-cost pattern of flows between the origins and the destinations. (The costs may be expressed in terms of transport effort, e.g. tonne–kilometres, or in terms of monetary costs.)

The method of solution is iterative, starting from a feasible solution and converging upon an optimum (if there is more than one optimum it converges upon one of the optimal solutions). The method involves the establishment of relative prices at origins and at destinations, such that whenever goods are allocated to an origin–destination pair, the price difference between origin and destination exactly equals the cost of transport between them. These are termed shadow prices: as iteration proceeds, these also converge upon an optimal set of prices. The transportation problem may therefore be considered in two ways: (a) as a *primal* problem, to establish the optimal pattern of flows which minimizes system costs; and (b) as a *dual* problem, to establish a pattern of prices which maximizes the value added in transportation.

The basic procedure can be adapted to more complex situations: a capacitated network may restrict the maximum flow on particular links, and a dummy or dump region can be used in the solution of problems where amounts available exceed requirements (in which case the primal problem may be defined to minimize the joint costs of production and transport). Furthermore, some problems which have no transport element can be approached in this way: for example, the allocation of M plots of agricultural land to produce amounts of N crops with a minimum expenditure of labour or fertilizer.

The application of this technique in geography may take two forms. It may be an attempt to explain patterns of flow or of production and flow. It is seldom successful in this, as the observed patterns of flow typically have many more used links than the optimal solution. Second, it may be an attempt to measure the relative efficiency of reality. Both types of application raise a number of questions: Over what time period should the system be optimized? Is the good indeed so homogeneous that destinations are indifferent as to the origin from which supplies are drawn? Are all the constraints faced in reality represented in the problem as specified?   AMH

Suggested Reading

Hay, A. M. 1977: *Linear programming: elementary geographical applications of the transportation problem*. Concepts and techniques in modern geography 11. Norwich: Geo Books.

Taaffe, E. J. and Gauthier, H. L. 1973: *Geography of transportation*. Englewood Cliffs, NJ: Prentice-Hall, ch. 6.

travel   See AGGREGATE TRAVEL MODEL; DISAGGREGATE TRAVEL DEMAND MODELLING.

trend surface analysis   A technique used to fit a statistical SURFACE to the spatial distribution of a data-set, using a mathematical power function which is an extension of REGRESSION analysis. The observations of the dependent variable refer to a series of sample points on a map; the independent variables are the co-ordinates of those points. Haining (1990) develops the trend surface model, noting that the main problem areas include boundary effects (points near to boundaries may have neighbours beyond the boundary which are not included in the model), sensitivity to outliers (extreme values in a skewed distribution), and SPATIAL AUTOCORRELATION of residuals.   MJB

Suggested Reading

Haining, R. 1990: *Spatial data analysis in the social and environmental sciences*. Cambridge: Cambridge University Press.

turf politics   Political activity by a NEIGHBOURHOOD'S residents, in resisting proposed changes to their locality. Most of such activity is very local in scale and involves responses to changes in either the built environment (e.g. a new road through a suburb) or an area's socio-economic characteristics. (See also INVASION AND SUCCESSION.)   RJJ

Suggested Reading

Cox, K. R. 1989: The politics of turf and the question of class. In Wolch, J. and Dear, M. J., eds, *The power of geography: how territory shapes social life*. Boston: Unwin Hyman, pp. 61–90.

Cox, K. R. and Johnston, R. J., eds 1982: *Conflict, politics and the urban scene*. London: Longman.

U

uncertainty The possibility of more than one outcome resulting from a particular course of action, the form of each possible outcome being known, but the chance or probability of one particular outcome being unknown. Uncertainty differs from RISK, in that under conditions of risk it is possible to know the probability of a particular outcome. For example, in tossing a coin the probability of heads coming up is 50 per cent, so betting on the toss of a coin is a risk. Playing Russian roulette is a risk (also 'risky') if the pistol is known to be loaded; with a bullet in one of the six chambers there is a one-in-six probability of death with any shot. However, if it were not known whether the gun were loaded, this would be a situation of uncertainty.

Uncertainty is part of the environment within which location (and other) decisions are made. This greatly limits the practical value of theories and models that assume perfect knowledge. For example, the firm setting up a new factory or service outlet in a new territory cannot know what the reaction of competitors is likely to be. They may follow suit with new facilities of their own, they may find an alternative competitive strategy, or they may choose not to compete – there is no way of calculating the probability of each alternative. Similarly, residential choice is made under conditions of uncertainty – for example, with respect to the stability of the NEIGHBOURHOOD or the sociability of the neighbours.

How uncertainty actually affects DECISION-MAKING has attracted much attention in geography, but it is questionable whether these efforts have made much progress towards predicting response to the unpredictable. (See also GAME THEORY.)   DMS

underclass Multiply deprived individuals who experience a form of poverty from which there is virtually no escape. Those facing long-term poverty typically lack basic education, skills and any apparent means of achieving upward mobility. Their problems are compounded by various forms of discrimination, and members of visible minorities, women and children in single-parent families comprise the majority of the underclass. The size of the underclass appears to be growing in North America and the UK as governments reduce the scope and universality of social programmes, and as mental health patients are deinstitutionalized.

While liberal and radical analysts emphasize the structural causes of poverty (the nature of CAPITALISM, PATRIARCHY and RACISM), conservative authors concentrate on the personal characteristics and lifestyles of the disadvantaged. This latter view usually draws upon the 'culture of poverty' thesis outlined by Oscar Lewis in his anthropological studies of Latin American slums during the 1950s and 1960s. Lewis argued that the very poor share behavioural patterns that on the one hand allow them to cope with poverty, but on the other hand reproduce their disadvantage (e.g. a sceptical attitude towards education that is passed on to children). Public policy tends to oscillate between liberal/radical and conservative views, sometimes targeting structural problems (the 'war on poverty' of the 1970s in the USA), while at other times attempting to change the behaviour of the poor by reducing welfare payments and/or providing additional funds to those who are entrepreneurially inclined.   DH

Suggested Reading

Auletta, K. 1982: *The underclass.* New York: Random House.

Lewis, O. 1959: *Five families: Mexican case studies in the culture of poverty.* New York: Basic Books.

Wilson, W. J. 1987: *The truly disadvantaged: the inner city, the underclass, and public policy.* Chicago: University of Chicago Press.

underconsumption A concept of particular importance in MARXIAN ECONOMICS, where it refers to a persistent shortfall in demand, frequently explained in terms of inadequate purchasing power.

From this perspective there is a basic contradiction in capitalist societies (see CAPITALISM). The consumption of goods by labour forms an important component of aggregate demand for the total output of the economy. But, at the same time, the consumption of labour is, in part, merely a moment in the process of production as labour power must be reproduced. Wages must, therefore, be set sufficiently high to enable a level of effective demand that will ensure the reproduction of labour. However, competition between capitalists as measured by the rate of profit tends to force down the level of wages paid and so reduces demand. The STATE may respond to this contradiction through the provision of the means of COLLECTIVE CONSUMPTION. Equally, advertising can shape consumption by labour in both quantitative and qualitative terms and so help to make consumption rather more rational with respect to the ongoing process of ACCUMULATION.

Strictly speaking, underconsumption refers only to consumption goods. But there are other, related, components of demand in the economy. The consumption of constant capital is more directly under the control of capital than is the consumption of variable capital. However, when constant capital is particularly lumpy or characterized by substantial externalities, investment is frequently undertaken by the state. This does not mean that the state can solve the problem of underconsumption, for it, too, is dependent upon the capitalist economy for resources. However, the state can help to annihilate time by borrowing, and so may contribute to the management of demand.

There remains the problem of where the demand for the surplus value produced, but not yet realized through exchange, comes from. The capacity of luxury consumption as a solution to this problem is self-limiting. Another solution is the geographical expansion of the market, a process closely connected with IMPERIALISM. Again, clearly, there are limits to this possibility. However, it is not so much the expansion of markets that is served by geographical extension as the conversion of money into capital through the further exploitation of labour power (see ACCUMULATION). Thus, the solution to the problem of the realization of surplus value through exchange is resolved by the further exploitation of labour power in production (Harvey, 1982, p. 95). Perpetual accumulation provides the solution and so, of course, simply intensifies the problem. RL

Reference

Harvey, D. 1982: *The limits of capital.* Oxford: Blackwell.

underdevelopment A barrier to or subversion of DEVELOPMENT and a consequently distorted, limited and increasingly marginal state of human existence or process of becoming. Underdevelopment may thus be defined both by the lack of a creative force or dynamic (or the presence of destructive forces) and by the underdeveloped social conditions which result.

The use of indicators (of production and levels of SOCIAL WELL-BEING) to describe the state of underdevelopment is subject to criticisms similar to those made of their use in defining development, and the representations transmitted by descriptions of the THIRD WORLD are far from unproblematic (Forbes, 1990). However, in so far as they may be used to demonstrate the massive inequality in the conditions likely to promote development and in conditions of life, such indicators may be politically useful in raising the level of political consciousness of the existence of such inequalities, and of movements designed to remove their causes (Harrison, 1981).

Nevertheless, in labelling the victims as the problem they miss the underlying cause of underdevelopment: the disempowerment of people in their struggle to make a living (Friedmann, 1992). The ability to make a living involves adequate access to natural RESOURCES and to the knowledge and techniques needed for productive consumption and production. People must be mentally and physically capable of productive work – a preparedness which, whatever else it may involve, involves prior consumption.

However, the capacity to make a living is not reducible merely to physical access to the means of consumption; it involves the access to and the manipulation of three kinds of power. *Social power* concerns access to the means to make a living; *political power* involves control over decisions shaping the struggle to make a living; and *psychological power* refers to a sense of individual potency. Barriers to these sources of power constitute both a condition and a process of underdevelopment. The condition of underdevelopment may then be understood not merely as poverty but as a lack of social power; in other words, a lack of the means to make a living and the process of underdevelopment understood as disempowerment.

A number of conditions of existence are necessary to enable people to make a living (Friedmann, 1992):

- access to *defensible life space* in the home and immediate locality
- *availability of time* beyond that spent in the struggle to keep alive
- access to *knowledge and skills*
- links to *appropriate information* about effective means of social reproduction
- membership and involvement in *social organizations* for information, mutual support and collective action
- attachment to *social networks* both horizontal among family, friends and neighbours and vertical through a social hierarchy
- availability of, or access to, the *forces of production* (most importantly, healthy *labour power* or the ability to perform labour, to work) and the *means of production* for domestic and informal work (e.g. household goods, bicycles

and sewing machines) as well as for formal work beyond the household or locality
- availability of, or access to, *financial resources and formal and informal credit.*

These conditions of existence are effectively denied to the two-thirds of the world's population whose income is less than 10 per cent of the per capita income of the US, and who are rendered largely superfluous to the contemporary global process of social reproduction enjoyed (unequally) by the remaining fortunate one-third. And this superfluity is apparent throughout the world economy. Even in the US, the so-called UNDERCLASS – those people living well below culturally defined levels of subsistence and able to make only minimal contributions to officially measured economic output of GNP – amount to 10 per cent of the population. How is it that these conditions exist during a phase of development of the world economy which, since the beginning of the nineteenth century, has experienced previously unheard of rates of growth of GDP per head, literally hundreds of times greater than those of earlier epochs (Maddison, 1982), and in the face of claims (e.g. Beenstock, 1984, p. 226) that increasing integration within the world economy will lead to 'the inexorable spread of economic development over the next hundred years'?

It is possible to distinguish between *underdevelopment in general* and *uneven underdevelopment*. The former refers to an actual or potential breakdown of social reproduction at the global level. Such a breakdown, or potential breakdown, may be the consequence of internal contradictions within a MODE OF PRODUCTION which may lead to its transformation or extinction. By this definition the contemporary world is in a stage of *underdevelopment in general*, facing a range of contradictions in NATURE and SOCIETY which have the potential for social destruction. *Uneven underdevelopment* refers to a socially or spatially restricted process or state of underdevelopment.

The most important influence upon the contemporary state of uneven underdevelopment has undoubtedly been the emergence and rapid spread of the materially (but unevenly) successful and revolutionary set of social relations associated with CAPITALISM. The social relations of capitalism have been responsible for the revolutionary development of the PRODUCTIVE FORCES and have enabled the creation of an expansionary (Brenner, 1986) worldwide economy (Thrift, 1989). The exploitative and unequal relations of power within society and nature and between people under capitalism embody some profound social and environmental contradictions (Peet, 1991). Capitalism is based upon the highly flexible exploitation of labour by CAPITAL and its single-minded objective, structured through its social relations (Brenner, 1986), is ACCUMULATION.

With such perspectives a powerful analysis of uneven underdevelopment may be constructed (Corbridge, 1989). But the potential power of such an explanation – based, as it is, in an understanding of the power of capitalism – should not obscure the ECONOMIC GEOGRAPHY of capitalism. The spread of capitalism across the world did not take place across an isotropic plain, nor did it encounter an undifferentiated or politically unstructured social vacuum; rather, it was confronted with a geographically diverse range of more or less well developed sets of social and environmental relations, the distinctions between which served to differentiate social formations. So the response to the spread of capitalism was by no means uniform (Larrain, 1989), and the paths from uneven underdevelopment towards development must be equally diverse – notwithstanding the universal need to escape from capitalist accumulation as the highly dangerous and amoral arbiter of development.

Such transformations may be enabled only through social struggle which – as is increasingly apparent – must take place from below (Friedmann, 1992). Unless people can succeed in creating humane conditions of existence, underdevelopment must remain the normal human condition (see also WORLD-SYSTEMS ANALYSIS). But, as Corbridge (1989, 1991) has pointed out (see also Hettne, 1990), it is one thing to mount a critique of an exploitative system based upon the crucial recognition of inequalities in relations of power, and

quite another to imagine an alternative (or, more appropriately, a geographically diverse range of alternatives) based upon rights and participation as well as upon needs and equality. RL

References

Beenstock, M. 1984: *The world economy in transition*. London: Allen and Unwin.

Brenner, R. 1986: The social basis of economic development. In Roemer, J. ed., *Analytical Marxism*. Cambridge: Cambridge University Press/Paris: Editions de la Maison des Sciences et de l'Homme, ch. 2, pp. 23–53.

Corbridge, S. 1986: *Capitalist world development*. London: Macmillan.

Corbridge, S. 1989: Marxism, post-Marxism and the geography of development. In Peet, R. and Thrift, N., eds, *New models in geography*, volume 1 London: Unwin Hyman, ch. 9, pp. 224–54.

Corbridge, S. 1991: Third world development *Prog. hum. Geogr.* 15(3), pp. 311–21.

Forbes, D. 1990: Geography and development practice: a postmodern challenge. *Environ. Plann. D, Society and Space* 8, pp. 131–3.

Friedmann, J. 1992: *Empowerment: the politics of alternative development*. New York: Oxford University Press.

Harrison, P. 1981: *Inside the Third World: an anatomy of poverty*. London: Penguin.

Hettne, B. 1990: *Development theory and the three worlds*. London: Longman.

Larrain, J. 1989: *Theories of development*. Cambridge: Polity Press.

Maddison, A. 1982: *Phases of capitalist development*. Oxford: Oxford University Press.

Peet, R. 1991: *Global capitalism: theories of societal development*. London: Routledge.

Thrift, N. 1989: The geography of international economic disorder. In Johnston, R. J. and Taylor, P. J., eds, *A world in crisis?* Oxford: Blackwell.

Suggested Reading

Corbridge (1989).
Friedmann (1992).
Thrift (1989).

uneven development A systematic process of economic and social development that is uneven in space and time, and endemic to CAPITALISM. Uneven development is a basic geographical hallmark of the capitalist MODE OF PRODUCTION. It reflects far more than simply the lack of geographical evenness in capitalist growth; rather, it comprises an integral aspect of capitalist development, combining the opposed but connected processes of DE-VELOPMENT and UNDERDEVELOPMENT.

Marx argued that 'capital grows in one place to a huge mass in a single hand because it has in another place been lost by many' (1987 edn, p. 586). More broadly, this implies that underdevelopment is not simply the result of neglect but is actively produced (Frank, 1967), and that uneven development is closely bound up with the logic of capital ACCUMULATION. There is a geographical as much as an economic logic to capitalist development and underdevelopment, and this is captured in theories of uneven development. Uneven development takes place at different geographical scales, and indeed the same processes of CENTRALIZATION and development, and DECENTRALIZATION and underdevelopment that create geographically uneven development are also largely responsible for producing geographical scale in the first place (Smith, 1990).

At the global scale, capitalist development has been concentrated in the so-called 'First World' of Europe and North America, while the Third World has been underdeveloped. The former contains the majority of the world's industrial production and accounts for most of its consumption, while the latter has become a supplier of cheap raw materials and labour power. While the developed world enjoys a balanced, self-centred mode of ACCUMULATION, the Third World is continually dependent on the First World for markets, capital and technology (Amin, 1976). This same pattern of development and underdevelopment is repeated at other scales, as capital is agglomerated in one place in favour of another (Webber, 1982). Within Britain, the rapid development of the South-East contasts sharply with the underdevelopment of the Scottish Highlands and Islands; in India the development of Bengal contrasts just as sharply with the underdevelopment of South India. Suburban growth and inner-city decline, especially in the USA, represent a parallel contrast of development and underdevelopment at the urban scale.

Uneven development is highly dynamic, however, and the patterns of unevenness are continually transformed as the mode of production itself evolves. At the global scale, the economies of Japan and the German-led EC are threatening to supercede the power of the USA, much as the USA superceded the UK in the early decades of the twentieth century. In addition, a NEW INTERNATIONAL DIVISION OF LABOUR (NIDL; see Fröbel, et al., 1980) has led to the partial industrialization of the newly industrializing countries (NICs) such as Taiwan, South Korea and Malaysia, which were previously underdeveloped, while sub-Saharan Africa is virtually REDLINED in the global economy and is experiencing the most intensely debilitating effects of uneven development. At the regional scale, some previously developed regions, such as Northern England or the Upper Midwest of the USA, have experienced rapid DEINDUSTRIALIZATION, while other long deindustrialized regions have experienced significant economic redevelopment associated with a new regime of FLEXIBLE ACCUMULATION (e.g. Central Scotland and New England). At the urban scale, the relative underdevelopment of the central and inner cities of the First World is partially offset by GENTRIFICATION and RESTRUCTURING, while the suburbs are experiencing the growth of integrated urban functions. At each of these scales, different political economic variables, such as the price and productivity of labour, the availability and cost of infrastructure, political stability, and ground rent, mediate the geographical mobility of capital between different places.

From these empirical trends, as well as from Marx's general theory of capital ACCUMULATION, it is possible to derive a theory of uneven development which describes the geography of development and underdevelopment under capitalism. In the process of developing a particular place or region, capital creates some of the very conditions that can mitigate against future development: wages and ground rent levels rise, while the agglomeration of large numbers of labourers working under similar conditions encourages political organization in opposition to the social relations of capitalism. By contrast, under-development produces the conditions that are likely to encourage development: lowered wage rates and ground rent levels, unemployment, and defeated working-class organizations. In so far as under-development creates the conditions for its opposite, and vice versa, there is a tendency for CAPITAL to oscillate geographically from places of development to those of underdevelopment and back again. This see-saw movement can be observed in recent patterns of uneven development, especially at the sub-national scale, but can also be derived theoretically as the geography of capital accumulation (Smith, 1990).

Marx grasped only some of the importance of uneven development. He expected that the world market would largely homogenize global levels and conditions of development, a position furthered by Rosa Luxemburg (1968 edn) who expected that when the capitalist system had expanded into every geographical corner of the Earth its expansion would necessarily end and SOCIALISM would follow. That geographical expansion of capital was effectively ended by the beginning of the twentieth century – the end of colonial expansion, the end of frontier – was recognized by geographers such as Alexander Supan in Germany, Halford Mackinder in Britain and Isaiah Bowman in the USA, as well as by Cecil Rhodes, the British imperialist, who argued the importance of the colonies as a safety valve for political discontent at home. It was Lenin, however, who most explicitly recognized the advent of uneven development proper when he argued that, henceforth, economic expansion would not take place in consort with territorial expansion (COLONIALISM), but as an internal redifferentiation of an already conquered world (Lenin, 1975 edn). The spatial constitution of global capitalism was definitively altered.

From the early part of the twentieth century, uneven development came to characterize the geography of capitalism. This dramatic shift in the spatial constitution of capitalism, from continued external expansion to internal uneven development, came at the same time that concepts of space and time were being revolutionized in art and physics (Kern, 1983). However, the recognition of the importance of uneven development was stunted. First, the Russian revolution of 1917 put more immediate political issues on the agenda. Second, rather than deal with the radical implications of the recognition of uneven development, orthodox geographers veered away from such global issues and either focused on local and regional questions or took a technocratic approach to geographical problems. In the 1920s Leon Trotsky proposed a 'law of uneven and combined development', which explored the political possibilities and constraints of constructing SOCIALISM directly out of FEUDAL society (Trotsky, 1969 edn; Löwy, 1981). The rediscovery of uneven development in its geographical and economic as well as political guise took place in the 1970s in connection with a resurgence of interest in Marxist theory (see MARXIST GEOGRAPHY), but also as a result of the evident RESTRUCTURING of the geography of capitalism at all spatial scales that began at the same time. The contours of uneven development are again changing rapidly, as part of the protracted crisis of capital accumalation (and responses to it) that has emerged since the late 1960s.　　NS

References

Amin, S. 1976: *Unequal development*. New York: Monthly Review Press.

Frank, A. 1967: *Capitalism and underdevelopment in Latin America*. New York: Monthly Review Press.

Fröbel, F., Kreye, O., and Heinrichs, J.; 1980: *The new international division of labour*. Cambridge: Cambridge University Press.

Kern, S. 1983: *The culture of time and space 1880–1918*. London: Weidenfeld and Nicolson.

Lenin, V. 1975 edn: *Imperialism, the highest stage of capitalism*. Bejing: Foreign Languages Press.

Löwy, M. 1981: *The politics of combined and uneven development*. London: Verso.

Luxemburg, R. 1968 edn: *The accumulation of capital*. New York: Monthly Review Press.

Marx, K. 1987 edn: *Capital*, volume 1. New York: International.

Smith, N. 1990: *Uneven development: nature, capital and the production of space*, second edn. Oxford: Blackwell.

Trotsky, L. 1969 edn. *Permanent revolution: results and prospects*. New York: Pathfinder Press.

Webber, M. 1982: Aglomeration and the regional question. *Antipode* 14(2), pp. 1–11.

Suggested Reading

Harris, N. 1983: *Of bread and guns: The world economy in crisis*. London: Penguin.

Löwy (1981).

Smith (1990).

urban Relating to TOWNS and CITIES. If URBANIZATION is regarded as a demographic phenomenon only, then urban places are those which exceed the thresholds of population size and/or density which are frequently used in CENSUS definitions of urban places. However, if urbanization is also considered to be both a structural and a behavioural process, then urban places are those above a certain size and density, containing particular economic functions within the spatial division of labour, and with their own particular lifestyles.

The study of urban places has long been central to many of the social sciences, including geography, because of their importance not only in the distribution of population within countries but also in the organization of economic production, distribution and exchange, in the structuring of social reproduction and cultural life, and in the exercise of political power. Various subfields of the different social science disciplines – such as urban anthropology, economics, geography, politics and sociology – were established in the decades after the Second World War to study these separate components. It was only several decades later that attempts were made to pull these together under the umbrella title of urban studies.

According to such arguments, urban and RURAL places are distinct in a number of ways, therefore, a distinction which was formalized by scholars in the concept of an RURAL-URBAN CONTINUUM, which suggested that as the size of a place changed so did its characteristics: Wirth's (1938) classic paper on URBANISM defined those characteristics, and there was a strong tradition, extending back to Jefferson's anti-urban and pro-rural sentiments in the United States, of promoting the 'idyllic rural' myth and denigrating the urban. More recently, however, the association of particular lifestyles with different settlement sizes has been substantially criticized: 'rural-like' COMMUNITIES have been 'discovered' in INNER CITIES (cf URBAN VILLAGE) while the concept of COUNTERURBANIZATION has carried the urban way of life into the remotest rural fastnesses. In this sense, the concept of urban appears to have become redundant because it cannot be negated: wherever we live, we are all urban now (Saunders, 1986). In socialist countries, such as the former Soviet Union, anti-urban policies sought to restrict the growth of such places to the minimum necessary for their CENTRAL PLANNING.

These arguments over the concept of a separate urban realm are not entirely new, however: in the nineteenth century, for example, both Durkheim and Marx argued that whereas towns and cities may have played a distinct role in the transition from FEUDALISM to CAPITALISM, they then became a part of that universal mode of organization with no independent identity or function. To study urban places separately was thus, in modern language, to draw upon CHAOTIC CONCEPTIONS.

A major stimulus to re-interpreting the nature of the urban was provided in the 1970s by the appearance of David Harvey's (1973) *Social justice and the city* and Manuel Castells's (1977) *The urban question* (cf. SPATIALITY). Harvey set out, in the longest chapter of his book, on what he thought was the impossible task of constructing a general urban theory, and concluded that urbanism has a separate structure with its own dynamic set within the larger forces of capitalism (p. 311). His later essays continue the attempt: *The limits to capital* (1982) is introduced as his reworking of Marxist economic theory en route to a 'theory of urbanization' (p. xiii); the essays in *The urbanization of capital* (1985a) explore how capitalism creates a 'physical landscape of roads, houses, factories, schools, shops and so forth' as part of the process of creating space (see also Lefebvre, 1991); and in *Consciousness and the urban experience* (1985b) he focuses on the experience of living in such places and the social relations and forms of political consciousness that result. He concludes the last of those volumes with the emancipatory case (see APPLIED GEOGRAPHY) that 'If the urbanization of capital and of consciousness is so central to the perpetuation and experience of capitalism, . . . then we have no option but to put the urbanization of revolution at the center of our political strategies' (p. 276).

Castells's book was also presented as an attempt to reinterpret what was already known – 'in order to detect the distorting ideological mechanisms and to reread in a new light the empirical discoveries made' (p. viii). He argued, as did Harvey, that social science was unable to provide an understanding of the 'urban problems' then increasingly besetting the world, because of ideological blinkers which prevented the development of a theory that could inform practice. This was because of the widespread belief in a separate urban realm, which Castells sought to show was a wrong ABSTRACTION of a part from a whole – urban problems are problems of societies, not of particular types of place, however defined: thus (p. 454),

. . . there is no cultural system linked to a given form of spatial organization; . . . the social history of humanity is not determined by the type of development of the territorial collectivities; and the spatial environment is not the root of a specificity of behaviour and representation.

The processes that characterize late capitalism are general: its economic forms are as apparent in AGRIBUSINESSES as in city-based manufacturing industries, and ideologies and attitudes are shared by people in similar socio-economic positions, whatever their home location. Nevertheless, Castells did argue that in a capitalist system, urban places were the spatial units within which COLLECTIVE CONSUMPTION, the processes of reproducing labour power and social relations, was grounded: indeed, he suggests that this is their *raison d'être*.

These two books were part of a major trend in social science from the 1970s on, which sought to redefine 'urban' in other than empirical terms (and thus to end its treatment as a form of SPATIAL FETISHISM), and to create a theory of the role of

urban places in capitalist society – a theory that would not only advance understanding but would also inform political practice and lead to a restructuring of society.

The concept of a separate urban realm is still widely used in general language and much social science, however, and as such urban places are still popular topics for study. Two areas have been advanced in which this is particularly valid: (1) in historical investigations, which illustrate the role of urban places as the motor for capitalist development (Sutcliffe, 1983); and (2) in parts of the world where capitalism has not fully penetrated all areas and aspects of life, so that urban and rural stand out as unique in certain respects. Nevertheless, the relative decline of URBAN GEOGRAPHY in recent years in North America and the UK may be associated with the critiques launched by Harvey and Castells.   RJJ

References

Castells, M. 1977: *The urban question: a Marxist approach*. London: Edward Arnold/Cambridge, MA: MIT press.

Harvey, D. 1973: *Social justice and the city*. London: Edward Arnold.

Harvey, D. 1982: *The limits to capital*. Oxford: Blackwell/Baltimore, MD: Johns Hopkins University Press.

Harvey, D. 1985a: *The urbanization of capital*. Oxford: Blackwell.

Harvey, D. 1985b: *Consciousness and the urban experience*. Oxford: Blackwell.

Lefebvre, H. 1991: *The production of space*. Oxford: Blackwell.

Saunders, P. 1986: *Social theory and the urban question*, second edition. London: Hutchinson.

Sutcliffe, A. R. 1983: In search of the urban variable: Britain in the later nineteenth century. In Fraser, D. and Sutcliffe, A. R. eds, *The study of urban history*. London: Edward Arnold, pp. 234–63.

Wirth, L. 1938: Urbanism as a way of life. *Am. J. Soc.* 44, pp. 1–24.

Suggested Reading

Pahl, R. E. 1983: Concepts in context: pursuing the urban of 'urban' sociology. In Fraser, D, and Sutcliffe, A. R., eds, *The study of urban history*. London: Edward Arnold, pp. 371–87.

Saunders, P. 1985: Space, the city, and urban sociology. In Gregory, D. and Urry, J., eds,

Social relations and spatial structures. London: Macmillan, pp. 67–89.

Smith, M. P. 1979: *The city and social theory.* Oxford: Blackwell/New York: St. Martin's Press.

Smith, M. P. 1988: *City, state and market: the political economy of urban society.* Oxford: Blackwell.

urban and regional planning At a purely technical level, the meaning of urban and regional planning is quite straightforward. Peter Hall (1974) considers planning first as 'a general activity . . . the making of an orderly sequence of action that will lead to the achievement of a stated goal or goals'. In this view, planning is an ahistoric, universal process common to all thinking beings and it is essentially technical: its 'main techniques', Hall goes on, 'will be written statements, supplemented as appropriate by statistical projections, mathematical representations, quantified evaluations and diagrams illustrating relationships between different parts of the plan. It may, but need not necessarily, include exact physical blueprints of objects'. From this perspective, urban and regional planning is simply 'a special case of general planning' which incorporates 'spatial representation' (Hall, 1974).

Thus urban and regional planning may be understood as a rational process of forethought set in motion by the need to resolve urban and regional problems. Hall (1974), for example, finds the origins of urban planning in Great Britain in the nature of urban growth from 1800 to 1940. It was first carried out by 'practical men dealing with practical matters' who were, nevertheless, infuenced by 'thinkers about the urban problem'. Similarly, regional planning arose, according to Hall, in the regional economic problem of the 1930s. Postwar planning was quite different, being dominated by the creation of the 'post war planning system' which was strongly influenced in its formation by follow-up studies to the Barlow Report of 1940, which 'brought together the urban and regional economic elements as two aspects of a single problem'.

However, this view of urban and regional planning as a set of ideas, procedures and responses fails to address the relationship between planning and the society being planned. Urban and regional planning is seen in technical terms as a rational response to a set of problems. The objectives or goals of planning – the definition of what is 'rational' – seem to be unproblematic, as does the definition of the nature of the problems themselves. Even the nature of the institutions carrying out urban and regional planning is left unexplored.

Allen Scott's (1980, p. 238) comments on this state of affairs, coming at the end of his own attempt to connect the dynamics of capitalist production, the urban land nexus and the state in a critique of planning and planning theory, are especially pertinent:

Mainstream planning theory presents itself to the world as a system of ideas that is no doubt internally coherent and logical. However, it fails dramatically to reflect and explain an underlying historical reality. On the contrary, it interposes identifiable barriers to a global understanding of the real universe of urbanization and urban planning. It is, in the fullest sense of the term, an ideology.

Planning law is introduced by the STATE, and agencies of the state are primarily responsible for its implementation. But the state is an integral part of the wider society (see Held, 1983), and planning both grows out of and contributes towards socially distinctive processes of SOCIAL production and REPRODUCTION (see SOCIETY). Looked at in this way, urban and regional planning becomes a material, political and economic activity rather than a mere technical process (Ambrose, 1986). It is, according to Cooke (1983), part of the 'civilizing process, performed by the state through the medium of the law . . . not only to rationalize the external physical configuration of production, but to sustain the . . . forms of social relations that have developed' (see CAPITALISM; SOCIAL REPRODUCTION).

Thus, urban and regional planning cannot be understood merely on the basis of its content; rather, it must connect with the processes of physical, social and economic development characteristic of the particular societies in which planning is being carried out (Ambrose, 1986). Thus, the involvement of the state in urban and regional planning may arise out of the conflict between capital and labour. The resolution of this conflict may involve the RESTRUCTURING of capital, with consequent effects upon the territorial DIVISION OF LABOUR.

Under these circumstances, urban and regional planning might address the sphere of circulation, with the provision, for example, of social security. Equally, the state may be active in the sphere of the reproduction of labour, via the production of state housing and education, for example, or in the collection and spatial ordering of labour in settlement systems, such as those represented in the network of new towns in Great Britain and in the *metropoles d'équilibres* in France, more in tune with the spatial requirements of production in advanced capitalism. Capital may be offered a variety of direct (e.g. participation in urban redevelopment schemes) or indirect opportunities to extend the possibilities for accumulation or to resolve the crises of restructuring (e.g. via grants, subsidies or the provision of physical infrastructure and the means of production). Under conditions of advanced capitalism in Great Britain during the postwar years, the dominant concern of the urban and regional planning system was with the reproduction of labour power. But since the onset of the economic crisis in the early 1970s, the emphasis has shifted towards a more direct concern with the reproduction and circulation of capital (Cooke, 1983).

Allen Scott (1980, p. 184) insists on greater precision in his analysis of the nature of urban and regional planning within the state apparatus:

. . . . urban planning itself cannot be derived in a simple *a priori* manner out of a globalized description of the functions of the state . . . before urban planning can be adequately conceptualized, it is essential to unravel the complex logic that governs the spatiotemporal development of the urban land nexus . . . . Urban planning . . . is society's way of dealing with the historical imperative of controlling the crisis-ridden land-contingent logic that constitutes the urbanization process in capitalism. As such, planning . . . is imbued with spatially determinate social conflicts that cut across strictly class lines of demarcation.

Urban and regional planning does not simply serve capital; it works within the SUPERSTRUCTURE and so is subject to the struggles which take place within civil society, struggles which may themselves be geographically distinctive as a result of the regional characteristics and social and political consequences of previous LAYERS OF INVESTMENT. Thus, the increased effectiveness of political struggle in opposition to regionally differentiated unemployment in Great Britain in the 1930s may help to explain why regional planning emerged as late as the interwar period, despite at least five prior decades of marked regional inequalities (Southall, 1983). But the significance of planning goes beyond the immediate material or political concern.

Within the UK, for example (Robson, 1988), spatial targeting, as represented in the increasingly tight boundaries around areas eligible for regional assistance and in the creation of Enterprise Zones and Garden Festivals, the formation of central–local and public–private partnerships, and the introduction of new agencies such as Urban Development Corporations, City Action Teams and Task Forces, not only indicate an increased concern for cities but present an ideological message about the belief in the power of the market to rectify problems of UNEVEN DEVELOPMENT (see, e.g. Mohan and Lee, 1989). Needless to say, however, the message is not ideologically pure (Thornley, 1990; Brindley et al., 1989) as the scale of state subsidy and market-induced disruption of redevelopment in, for example, the London Docklands makes clear (e.g. Lee, 1992). (See also URBAN ENTREPRENEURIALISM.)

The existence and activities of urban and regional planning prompt some profoundly geographical questions about the nature of the dynamics of society, the role of UNEVEN DEVELOPMENT and the relations, central and local, between the political and the economic. In consequence, this poses some crucial issues concerned not merely with the acceptability or otherwise of the techniques of implementation (which, for the people affected by them, are of signal importance) but with the role and potential of the state and planning in developing alternatives in urban and regional development. (See also REGIONAL POLICY.)   RL

References and Suggested Reading

Ambrose, P. 1986: *Whatever happened to planning?* London: Methuen.

Brindley, T., Rydin, Y. and Stoker, G., eds 1989: *Remaking planning: the politics of urban change in the Thatcher years.* London: Harper Collins.

Cooke, P. 1983: *Theories of planning and spatial development.* London: Hutchinson.

Hall, P. 1974: *Urban and regional planning.* London: Penguin.

Held, D. 1983: Central perspectives on the modern state. In Held, D. et al., eds, *States and societies.* Oxford: Martin Robertson.

Lee, R. 1992: 'London Docklands: the exceptional place'? An economic geography of inter-urban competition. In Ogden P. E., ed., *London Docklands: the challenge of change.* Cambridge: Cambridge University Press.

Mohan, J. and Lee, R. 1989: Unbalanced growth? Public services and labour shortages in a European core region. In Breheny, M. and Congdon, P., eds, *Growth and change in a core region: the case of South-East England.* London: Pion, pp. 33–54.

Robson, B. 1988: *Those inner cities: reconciling the economic and social aims of urban policy.* Oxford: Oxford University Press.

Scott, A. J. 1980: *The urban land nexus and the state.* London: Pion.

Southall, H. 1983: Long-run trends in unemployment. *Area* 15, pp. 238–42.

Thornley, A. 1990: *Urban planning under Thatcherism: the challenge of the market.* London: Routledge.

Urry, J. 1981: *The anatomy of capitalist societies.* London: Macmillan/Atlantic Highlands, NJ: Humanities Press, ch. 7.

urban ecology A term applied by later adherents of the CHICAGO SCHOOL of sociologists to their study of the social and spatial organization of urban society. Although urban ecologists have paid some attention to URBAN SYSTEMS at national and regional scales, most of their attention has been focused on the internal structure of large cities.

Berry and Kasarda (1977) suggest that traditional urban ecology, as represented by Hawley's classic (1950) text, concentrated on three areas of study: (1) application of concepts obtained from the study of animal and plant ECOLOGY to the human COMMUNITY – which was characteristic of the Chicago School (as in work on, for example, INVASION AND SUCCESSION); (2) detailed descriptions of the NATURAL AREAS of cities; and (3) investigations of the geography of social problems (such as CRIME and vice) in the context of those natural areas – hence the validity of the term 'ecology', since the individual elements were being looked at in the context of the societal whole. Since the 1960s, they argue, the focus has been a concern with 'how a population organizes itself in adapting to a constantly changing yet restricting environment'.

This contemporary urban ecological approach assumes that urban societies are constantly seeking to re-establish an equilibrium following a shock to the previous arrangement, and such equilibrium encompasses the functional, demographic and spatial structures of the community under investigation. Theorists such as Duncan (1959) and Schnore (1965) identified what they termed the *ecological complex* comprising four interrelated variables which characterize the urban realm: (1) *population*, a functionally integrated and structured collectivity; (2) *organization*, the system of relationships which allows a population to sustain itself within its physical and built environment; (3) *environment*, identified by Berry and Kasarda as 'the least well conceptualized of the variables . . . It has been broadly defined as all phenomena, including other social systems, that are external to and have influence upon the population under study'; and (4) *technology*, comprising the artefacts and techniques developed by the community to assist in its sustenance. All four are interdependent, so a change in any one will have an impact on the other three: urban ecology thus differs from URBAN GEOGRAPHY, which focuses much more exclusively on spatial arrangement as both a causal and a dependent variable in the study of evolving social systems.

Berry and Kasarda note that all of the programmatic statements for contemporary urban ecology were written during the late 1950s and early 1960s, and that none had appeared since because 'their raison d'etre no longer prevails'. Sociologists had moved from macro- to micro-concerns, and so the purpose of their 1977 book was to remind the 'sociological audience' that not 'all principles of sociological organization could be reduced to individualistic concepts' (see HOLISM). The four variables in the ecological complex are necessary to the understanding of patterns and processes of social and spatial organization, which they illustrate with a SYSTEMS ANALYSIS approach.

Although work continues to be done in the ecological tradition, focusing especially on patterns of population change (such as DECENTRALIZATION and suburbanization within METROPOLITAN AREAS), the area is not in the mainstream of contemporary urban sociology. RJJ

References

Berry, B. J. L. and Kasarda, J. D. 1977: *Contemporary urban ecology*. London: Macmillan.

Duncan, O. D. 1959: Human ecology and population studies. In Hauser, P. M. and Duncan, O. D., eds, *The study of population*. Chicago: University of Chicago Press/ Cambridge: Cambridge University Press, pp. 678–716.

Hawley, A. H. 1950: *Human ecology: a theory of community structure*. New York: Ronald Press.

Schnore, L. F. 1965: On the spatial structure of cities in the two Americas. In Hauser, P. M. and Schnore, L. F., eds, *The study of urbanization*. London: John Wiley, pp. 347–98.

urban entrepreneurialism The promotion of local economic development by urban governments, in alliance with private capital and trades unions (cf. REGIONAL CLASS ALLIANCE). Urban area governments have typically (although more so in the UK than the USA, for example) been restricted in their role in the promotion of their local economy to the provision of physical INFRASTRUCTURE and small amounts of advertising. With the shift from FORDISM to FLEXIBLE ACCUMULATION in the crisis of the 1970s and 1980s, however, local governments have been impelled to extend away from their managerial role (cf. URBAN MANAGERS AND GATEKEEPERS) and to adopt 'more initiatory and "entrepreneurial" forms of action' (Harvey, 1989, p. 4), a trend which he finds common throughout the advanced capitalist world.

Central to urban entrepreneurialism has been the concept of 'public–private partnerships', through which public money has been used as leverage to attract private investment to an area. This process has been encouraged by national governments, as with the Development Corporations established in the UK to promote economic regeneration in depressed areas (such as the Liverpool and London Dockland Development Areas) – although outside local government control – and the City Challenge programme, which offers central government money to local governments promoting similar schemes of urban regeneration involving much larger sums of private than of public money. As Harvey points out, this often involves the public sector taking the risks, and the private sector reaping the benefits.

This era of urban entrepreneurialism (often termed 'urban boosterism' in the USA) involves local governments of urban areas – but not necessarily only those in urban areas – in substantial competition for economic growth. To promote the COMPARATIVE ADVANTAGES of their cities, many such governments become involved in major image-development and image-enhancement strategies, a number of which have been based on major investments in leisure facilities and 'world events', such as the Seville World Fair and the Barcelona Olympic Games in 1992 (see SPECTACLE, GEOGRAPHY OF): these are often promoted initially as potential profit-making activities (as with the 1984 Olympic Games in Los Angeles), but they usually turn out to be loss-making, and leave the local population with large long-term debt repayments to be met from local taxes (as with the 1991 Universiade in Sheffield). As more cities invest in such facilities and events, so the competitive edge that they gain is increasingly transitory, and the public debt grows while mobile capital rapidly moves on to reap the advantages of new partnerships elsewhere. RJJ

Reference

Harvey, D. 1989: From managerialism to entrepreneurialism: the transformation in urban governance in late capitalism. *Geogr. Annlr.* 71B, pp. 3–17.

Suggested Reading

Bennett, R. J. ed., 1990: *Decentralization, local government and markets: towards a post-welfare agenda.* Oxford: Clarendon Press.

Cox, K. R. and Mair, A. J. 1988: Locality and community in the politics of local economic development. *Ann. Ass. Am. Geogr.* 78, pp. 307–25.

Logan, J. R. and Molotch, H. L. 1987: *Urban fortunes: the political economy of place.* Berkeley, CA: University of California Press.

Marston, S. A., ed., Review symposium. *Urban Geogr.* 11, pp. 176–208.

Mawson, J. and Miller, D. 1986: Interventionist approaches to local employment and economic development. In Hausner, V. A., ed., *Critical issues in urban economic development* volume 1. Oxford: Clarendon Press, pp. 89–144.

Mills, L. and Young, K. 1986: Local authorities and economic development: a preliminary analysis. In Hausner, V. A., ed., *Critical issues in urban economic development,* volume 1. Oxford: Clarendon Press, pp. 89–144.

Seyd, P. 1990: Radical Sheffield: from socialism to entrepreneurialism. *Pol. Stud.* 38, pp. 325–44.

urban geography The geographical study of URBAN areas. Until the 1940s, the literature on urban geography in English was small, with the first general text appearing in 1946. The subsequent decades saw a major surge of interest, and during the 1960s and 1970s scholars who termed themselves urban geographers were at the forefront of the discipline's QUANTITATIVE REVOLUTION.

Early studies were typical of the currently dominant PARADIGM. With the importance of ENVIRONMENTAL DETERMINISM in the 1920s and 1920s, for example, the focus of urban studies was on the role of physical features – site and situation – as determinants of urban foundations and growth, and with the growth of REGIONAL GEOGRAPHY in the 1930s attention switched to the regional relations of towns and the existence of morphological regions within them – see MORPHOLOGY and TOWNSCAPE. (All of these topics are illustrated in Taylor's (1946) pioneering text, and in Dickinson's (1947) seminal work on urban ecology, the latter influenced by both German and North American sources.)

These regional interests were maintained and extended in the 1950s, 1960s and 1970s by the growing number of urban geographers who were attracted to, and led developments in, LOCATION THEORY and LOCATIONAL ANALYSIS. (The programmatic essay of Berry (1964) indicates the continued importance of defining formal and functional REGIONS to the expanding subdiscipline.)

Urban geographers' adoption of locational analysis, the philosophy of POSITIVISM, and the methodology and goals of SPATIAL SCIENCE was characterized by two main strands of work in the late 1950s and early 1960s, much of it stimulated by the pioneering studies by Berry and others at the University of Washington, Seattle (Johnston, 1991). The first, which was initially predominant, concentrated on the pattern of urban settlement in a country or region, thereby treating towns and cities as points on a map; the second, which grew in importance during the 1960s and which predominated in the 1970s, focused on the internal structure of cities, thereby treating them as areas rather than as points. In both, the goal was to identify the laws which, it was believed, governed the observed spatial arrangements.

In the study of URBAN SYSTEMS, much attention was given to testing the applicability of CENTRAL PLACE THEORY, especially the work of Walther Christaller. The town as a central place within a spatially structured hierarchy attracted many empirical investigations, and the concepts were also applied to the study of shopping centres within urban areas – as exemplified in Berry's (1967; see also Berry and Parr, 1988) classic text. Linked to studies of the functional structure and spatial arrangements of central places were investigations of shopping behaviour, to see whether people adhered to the distance-minimizing principles which underpinned the entire theory (cf. RETAILING, GEOGRAPHY OF).

For the study of the internal structure of urban areas, attention increasingly shifted away from the commercial districts to the residential areas. The main stimuli for this came from the literature on URBAN ECOLOGY, especially the works of the CHICAGO SCHOOL on models of land-use patterns (see ZONAL MODEL). These suggested not only that various social groups lived in separate residential areas, but also that those areas were arranged in a particular spatial order. Geographers set about testing the validity of those hypotheses, using their recently adopted statistical procedures for the analysis of CENSUS TRACT data (as in the widely cited paper by Berry and Rees, 1969: see FACTORIAL ECOLOGY; SOCIAL AREA ANALYSIS).

By the late 1960s many empirical studies, both inter-urban and intra-urban, had identified disparities between the observed and expected patterns: the models did not appear to be working well, although they continued to provide the base for further exploration. The assumptions on which the models were built, especially those concerning spatial behaviour (see SPATIAL PREFERENCE), came under close scrutiny, and behaviourist approaches were introduced as an alternative – and much more inductive – foundation for empirical work.

Research in this new field of BEHAVIOURAL GEOGRAPHY at that time was not critical of the positivist philosophy, and shared the goal of theory development premised on the existence of laws of spatial behaviour (as illustrated in a later text; King and Golledge, 1978). It involved collecting data on the DECISION-MAKING which underpins the creation of the observed patterns of central places and residential segregation: initially, the data described the outcomes of such decisions only (as with work on intra-urban MIGRATION) but, increasingly, with stimuli from social psychology, it explored the actual choice decisions themselves.

During this period, the study of urban geography was closely linked to that of URBAN AND REGIONAL PLANNING, for the latter was built on the premise that well-ordered and efficient cities and regions could be created through the application of the uncovered laws of spatial behaviour and organization. By the end of the 1960s, however, the failure of planners to resolve many of the pressing social issues of the day – such as poverty, deprivation and inequality – led to a questioning of that apparently rational process. Urban geographers were

drawn into this. Initially, they refocused their work onto the roles of URBAN MANAGERS AND GATEKEEPERS as controllers of the spatial structuring of urban areas; in this way, it was realized that the decisions studied in the behavioural geography mould were made in contexts and not in vacuums, and that constraints were as important as choices in determining where, for example, people migrated to.

This broadening of empirical studies was followed by further realization that those who managed urban areas, and thereby constrained choices were themselves operating in a constrained context within which their degrees of freedom were limited. Thus attention shifted to the nature of those wider contexts, and urban geographers were led by the writings of Harvey (1973), Castells (1977) and others into the field of POLITICAL ECONOMY, especially those parts of it dominated by Marxian thought (see also MARXIST GEOGRAPHY; RADICAL GEOGRAPHY; URBAN). Although many accepted part at least of the thrust of these writings – in particular that the nature of urban areas and of the choices that people exercise within them reflects the dominant characteristics of the MODE OF PRODUCTION – they nevertheless wished to continue with empirical studies. Thus some suggested a hierarchical, or layered, approach to urban geography (e.g. Herbert, 1979), which separated out studies of the general processes from those of their particular outcomes.

From the mid-1970s on, the position of urban geography at the vanguard of innovative work within the discipline declined. Many still call themselves urban geographers, as illustrated by the size of the relevant groups within the main GEOGRAPHICAL SOCIETIES: there is a thriving journal of *Urban Geography*, and the subdiscipline is still widely taught. But many of the concerns that were formerly encapsulated within urban geography are now studied under different banners: the revival of POLITICAL GEOGRAPHY and the expansion of both SOCIAL GEOGRAPHY and CULTURAL GEOGRAPHY have all attracted workers whose empirical focus is mainly urban (intriguingly, RURAL GEOGRAPHY has prospered during the same period), and studies of topics such as COUNTER-URBANIZATION are now as likely to be found under the title of POPULATION GEOGRAPHY as of urban geography. Thus, to some extent, urban geographers now respond to trends elsewhere in the discipline, refashioning their investigations of particular areas, as well as reacting to new urban issues identified by society at large. Leitner (1992), for example, reviews recent work by urban geographers which responds to the challenges of either 'new urban problems' (such as RACISM) or 'new developments in social theory' (such as POSTSTRUCTURALISM and POST-MODERNISM).

Part of the reason for this apparent decline in the vitality of urban geography is shown by a review of the subdiscipline in the recent conspectus of *Geography in America*. The relevant chapter is entitled 'The urban problematic' (Marston et al., 1989), which begins by noting that 'Over three-quarters of the American population is now urban (employing standard definitions), and almost any empirical analysis, and much theoretical conjecture, must in some way touch upon the realities of urban life' (p. 651). The authors see the subdiscipline as suffering from a 'crippling historical legacy' of outmoded approaches, but argue that it is now 'developing a historical consciousness, has sophisticated analytical skills, and is moving into new and challenging areas of substantive research' (p. 669). Whether a major commitment to urban geography will characterize the 1990s remains to be seen, however; which is not to doubt that urban areas will continue to be the focus of much geographical study, and that geographers will continue to be major interpreters of the individual components of the urban realm (as in Ward, 1990; Cybriwsky, 1991; Enyedi and Szirmai, 1992).

As in so much Anglo-American geography, the predominant focus of empirical work in urban geography has been on the towns and cities of the First World. The THIRD WORLD has received some attention, as in the initial work of McGee (1971) and later volumes such as that edited by Gilbert and Gugler (1992; see also Gugler, 1988). The Second World of the now ex-socialist

states has been even more ignored – with a few exceptions, such as the volumes edited by French and Hamilton (1979) and by Forbes and Thrift (1987; see also Thrift and Forbes, 1986). More generally, however, these areas have been debated by other urban scholars, notably in the pages of the *International Journal of Urban and Regional Research*. RJJ

References

Berry, B. J. L. 1964: Approaches to regional analysis: a synthesis. *Ann. Ass. Am. Geogr.* 54, pp. 2–11.

Berry, B. J. L. 1967: *The geography of market centers and retail distribution.* Englewood Cliffs, NJ: Prentice-Hall.

Berry, B. J. L. and Parr, J. L. 1988: *The geography of market centers and retail distribution,* second edition. Englewood Cliffs, NJ: Prentice-Hall.

Berry, B. J. L. and Rees, P. H. 1969: The factorial ecology of Calcutta. *Am. J. Soc.* 74, pp. 445–91.

Castells, M. 1977: *The urban question: a Marxist approach.* London: Edward Arnold/Cambridge, MA: MIT Press.

Cybriwsky, R. 1991: *Tokyo.* The World Cities Series. London: Belhaven Press.

Dickinson, R. E. 1947: *City, region and regionalism.* London: Routledge and Kegan Paul.

Enyedi, G. and Szirmai, Y. 1992: *Budapest.* The World Cities Series. London: Belhaven Press.

Forbes, D. and Thrift, N. J., eds 1987: *The socialist Third World: urban development and territorial planning.* Oxford: Blackwell.

French, R. A. and Hamilton, F. E. I., eds 1979: *The socialist city: spatial structure and urban policy.* Chichester: John Wiley.

Gilbert, A. G. and Gugler, J., eds 1992: *Cities, poverty and development: urbanization in the Third World,* second edition. Oxford: Clarendon Press.

Gugler, J. 1988: *The urbanization of the Third World.* Oxford: Clarendon Press.

Harvey, D. 1973: *Social justice and the city.* London: Edward Arnold/Baltimore, MD: Johns Hopkins University Press.

Herbert, D. T. 1979: Introduction: geographical perspectives and urban problems. In Herbert, D. T. and Smith, D. M., eds, *Social problems and the city: geographical perspectives.* Oxford: Oxford University Press, pp. 1–10.

Johnston, R. J. 1991: *Geography and geographers: Anglo-American human geography since 1945,* fourth edition. London: Edward Arnold.

King, L. J. and Golledge, R. G. 1978: *Cities, space and behavior: the elements of urban geography*. Englewood Cliffs, NJ: Prentice-Hall.

Leitner, H. A. 1992: Urban geography: responding to new challenges. *Progr. hum. Geogr.* 16, pp. 105–18.

McGee, T. G. 1971: *The urbanization process in the Third World: explorations in search of a theory*. London: George Bell.

Marston, S. A., Towers, G., Cadwallader, M. and Kirby, A. 1989: The urban problematic. In Gaile, G. L. and Willmott, C. J. eds, *Geography in America*. Columbus, OH: Merrill, pp. 651–72.

Taylor, T. G. 1946: *Urban geography*. New York: E. P. Dutton.

Thrift, N. J. and Forbes, D. N. 1986: *The price of war: urbanization in Vietnam, 1954–1985*. London: Allen and Unwin.

Ward, P. M. 1990: *Mexico City*. The World Cities Series. London: Belhaven Press.

Suggested Reading

Carter, H. 1988: *The study of urban geography*, fourth edition. London: Edward Arnold/New York: John Wiley.

Hartshorn, T. A. 1991: *Interpreting the city: an urban geography*, second edition. New York: John Wiley.

Johnston, R. J. 1984: *City and society: an outline for urban geography*. London: Hutchinson.

urban managers and gatekeepers
Professionals and bureaucrats who make decisions that influence the internal spatial structure of urban areas through their control of, for example, access to public housing and the allocation of mortgages. Bureaucrats who work in parts of the STATE APPARATUS are normally termed *urban managers*, whereas professionals engaged in the private sector (such as real estate agents) are called *gatekeepers*.

Identification of the important role of managers and gatekeepers in the structuring of urban areas is generally associated with the works of Pahl (1975) and Rex (1968; cf. HOUSING CLASS), who demonstrated the importance of such individuals in constructing and operating the constraints to choice in access to key resources, such as housing. Their writing stimulated considerable research by urban geographers in the 1970s (as in the special issue of the *Transactions, Institute of British Geographers* published in 1976; e.g. Boddy, 1976), but later developments in RADICAL

GEOGRAPHY directed attention away from the managers and their operations towards the constraints on their activities posed by the demands of the capitalist political economy (Williams, 1982; cf. URBAN). RJJ

References

Boddy, M. J. 1976: The structure of mortgage finance: building societies and the British social formation. *Trans. Inst. Br. Geogr.* n.s. 1, pp. 58–71.

Pahl, R. E. 1975: *Whose city? and further essays on urban society*. London: Penguin.

Rex, J. 1968: The sociology of a zone in transition. In Pahl, R. E., ed., *Readings in urban sociology*. Oxford: Pergamon Press, pp. 211–31.

Williams, P. R. 1982: Restructuring urban managerialism. *Envir. Plann. A* 14, pp. 95–105.

Suggested Reading

Saunders, P. 1986: *Social theory and the urban question*, second edition. London: Hutchinson.

urban origins The origins of UR-BANISM are as problematic as its definition, but four broad explanations have been proposed:

(a) *Ecological models*, which typically associate urbanism with the production and concentration of a 'surplus' of some kind through, in particular, the construction of large-scale irrigation schemes: see HYDRAULIC SOCIETY.

(b) *Economic models*, which, although they typically focus on changing FORMS OF ECONOMIC INTEGRATION and, in particular, on the transition from RECIPROCITY to REDISTRIBUTION, are especially concerned with the ways in which such systems of exchange are 'embedded' in non-economic institutions. Most of these models are indebted to Polanyi's substantivist anthropology but Harvey (1973) has attempted to give them a Marxian gloss and to elucidate the concentration of a socially designated surplus product, defined via the labour theory of value, 'in a few hands and in a few places'. In his view, urbanism *may* arise with the emergence of redistribution, *necessarily* arises with the emergence of MARKET EXCHANGE, and in both cases is causally connected to the ALIENATION of the surplus.

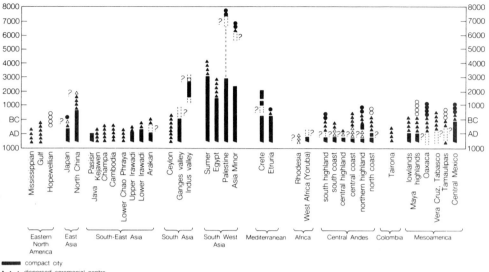

urban origins *1: Urban genesis in space and time* (after Wheatley, 1971: Carter, 1983).

(c) *Cultural models*, which typically examine the formative influence of religion on urban genesis. 'The religious component is almost alone', Wheatley (1971) argued, 'in having left in several of the realms of nuclear urbanism [see figure 1] a more or less continuous success of surviving material traces through . . . to fully evolved urban life'. In his view, 'the earliest foci of power and authority took the form of ceremonial centres, with religious symbolism imprinted deeply on their physiognomy and their operation in the hands of organized priesthoods'. Wheatley made much of the cosmo-magical symbolism or ICONOGRAPHY of the ancient city, which 'projected images of the cosmic order on to the plane of human experience, where they could provide a framework for [and legitimation of] social action' (see figure 2; and see also Sack, 1980).

(d) *Politico-military models*, which typically conceive of the first cities as both fortresses and refuges. Many of these models are, of course, compatible with the arguments of the previous paragraphs – the supposed conjunction between 'hydraulic society' and 'Oriental despotism', for example, or the centring of 'political and military power . . . first in theocratic and

later in monarchical control' (Giddens, 1981; see also Giddens, 1985) – but they usually go beyond those claims to emphasize the decisive importance of military power exercised through a grid of cities for the creation of empires.

Most modern debates, at least in geography, have fastened on the relations between (b) and (c), but the relations between urbanism and the origins of the STATE also mark out (d) as an arena of considerable interest. DG

References

Carter, H. 1983: *An introduction to urban historical geography.* London: Edward Arnold, pp. 1–17.

Giddens, A. 1981: *A contemporary critique of historical materialism*, volume 1, *Power, property and the state.* London: Macmillan.

Giddens, A. 1985: *A contemporary critique of historical materialism.* volume 2, *The nation-state and violence.* Cambridge: Polity Press.

Harvey, D. 1973: *Social justice and the city.* London: Edward Arnold/Baltimore, MD: Johns Hopkins University Press.

Sack, R. D. 1980: *Conceptions of space in social thought: a geographic perspective.* London: Macmillan/Minneapolis: University of Minnesota Press.

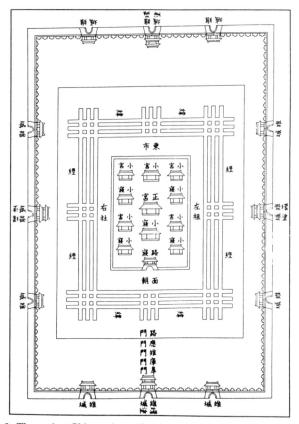

urban origins   *2: The ancient Chinese city as the pivot of the four quarters* (after Wheatley, 1971).

Wheatley, P. 1971: *The pivot of the four quarters: a preliminary inquiry into the origins and character of the ancient Chinese city.* Edinburgh: Edinburgh University Press/Chicago: Aldine.

Suggested Reading

Adams, R. Mc. C. 1966: *The evolution of urban society.* Chicago: Chicago University Press.

Carter, H. 1977: Urban origins: a review. *Progr. hum. Geogr.* 1, pp. 12–32.

Carter (1983).

Kostof, S. 1985: *A history of architecture: settings and rituals.* New York: Oxford University Press, chs 3–5.

Wheatley (1971), part two.

Wheatley, P. 1972: Proleptic observations on the origins of urbanism. In Steel, R. W. and Lawton, R., eds, *Liverpool essays in geography.* London: Longman, pp. 315–45.

urban renewal   In its broadest sense, this represents any upgrading of part of an urban area. More commonly and narrowly, it refers to the rehabilitation, usually by or under the stimulation of a public authority, of urban districts below prevailing levels of public acceptability. Such rehabilitation depends upon appropriate motivation and resources among those with the necessary authority and, where implemented, the improvements and the agencies of change can take many forms.

The most frequent focus for renewal are INNER-CITY districts. Unlike central business areas, which are easier to upgrade by market processes, public authorities are necessary to grapple with typical inner-city problems: to consolidate the mosaic of small urban lots and land holdings and afford the land prices required for renewal programmes; to implement necessary regulations and compulsory purchases and by-pass obstructive red tape; and to provide suitable accommodation and facilities for low-income residents, commercially unattractive to private capital.

On both sides of the Atlantic the form of urban renewal has changed significantly over time. Early emphasis on inner-city SLUM clearance in the UK led to the removal of some two million homes (and five million residents) since the 1930s, but at a cost in social displacement and loss of COMMUNITY. Wartime bombing contributed its share of demolition, and ensuing postwar renewal, stimulated by new urban planning thinking, encouraged local authorities to identify Comprehensive Development Areas for integrated development of housing, facilities and amenities. Where *in situ*, on cleared sites, this was at lower densities than hitherto and so was accompanied by planned DECENTRALIZATION of homes and jobs, as to the NEW TOWNS.

In the 1970s the emphasis shifted again to improvement grants for existing housing, accompanied by delimitation of General Improvement and Housing Action Areas as the focus of rehabilitation, although these excluded equally deserving but more scattered areas of decline. Some districts have benefited from a reversal of fortunes, with a GENTRIFICATION-led upward spiral of vitality and environmental quality (and house prices).

The stabilization of loss of employment, seen by the 1980s as a major trigger to inner-city decline, became important in both the USA, through Urban Development Action Grants (1979) and in the UK, following the Inner Urban Areas Act (1978). Subsequent designation in both countries of some inner-city ENTERPRISE ZONES typifies such job-stimulation. Later, under their non-elected management bodies, the UK's Urban Development Corporations also became concerned with residential quality and quantity, thereby spawning very different residential compositions in some inner cities. Another feature of the 1980s was the 'leverage' by 'New Right' administrations of private-sector investment into urban renewal by initial public expenditure, a trend reinforced by recent economic downturns and cuts in public expenditure (Barnikov et al., 1989). In the UK, housing associations provided some 10 per cent of publicly funded

residential rehabilitation by 1981, while in the USA neighbourhood housing services represent partnerships of local government, residents' groups and financial institutions.

Cooperation between public and private sectors and extensive public participation in local community involvement are important themes in contemporary urban renewal, as are such special opportunities offered for historical heritage enhancement and by urban waterfronts, as in the London Docklands and Baltimore. (See also INNER CITY; URBAN ENTREPRENEURIALISM).

AGH

Reference
Barnikov, T., Boyle, R. and Rich, D. 1989: *Privatism and urban policy in Britain and the United States.* Oxford: Oxford University Press.

Suggested Reading
Gibson, M. S. and Langstaff, M. J. 1982: *An introduction to urban renewal.* London: Hutchinson.

urban social movement A form of protest challenging the STATE provision of urban social services and/or environmental regulation, such as popular movements against expressways, to preserve NEIGHBOURHOODS threatened by redevelopment, or squatters' rights movements. The term originates in the work of Manuel Castells, who linked the definition of urban social movements to his conception of the city and its place within CAPITALISM. Critical of all previous theories of the city, especially the legacy of the CHICAGO SCHOOL, Castells argued that urban sociologists should embrace a Marxist approach according to which the city is seen as a spatial expression of a unit of labour power that must be continuously reproduced for capitalism to survive. Basic social services, such as education and public transporation, must be provided by the state, because corporations find these activities unprofitable. However, it is virtually impossible for the state to deliver collective goods and services evenly across an entire urban population; moreover, in recent decades local states have found it difficult to maintain the level of service provision achieved in the 1960s. Also, in a society geared to profit maximization the capacity of the state to protect urban environments is limited. Conflicts over the provision of public services, or to strengthen environmental regulations, are therefore inevitable. In his early work, Castells argued that these struggles should be classified as urban social movements only when they have the potential to improve the class position of workers *vis-à-vis* the bourgeoisie. He asserted that the escalation of these movements, in conjunction with other forms of conflict (e.g. labour–capital), will lead to a 'ruptual unity' and transform capitalism. In later work, Castells broadened his definition of urban social movements to include struggles to maintain cultural identity, and to achieve more decentralized urban government, as well as conflicts over public services. In the process he has begun to recognize the importance of feminism as a social movement and, more generally, the need to understand the motivations and beliefs of actors involved in protest movements.

Subsequent research has explored the nature of urban social movements in a variety of national contexts; much of this is reported in *The International Journal of Urban and Regional Research*. Key issues are the identification of factors that encourage or impede the mobilization process, state responses to urban social movements, and cross-cultural comparisons of these movements. Critical appraisals of the concept focus on the imputed linkages between social structure and political behaviour. Pahl (1989), among others, believes that theorists of urban social movements have yet to reveal how people acquire a consciousness of structured inequities, and how they transform this consciousness into political action. (See also COLLECTIVE CONSUMPTION; NIMBY.)   DH

Reference

Pahl, R. E. 1989: Is the emperor naked? Some questions on the adequacy of sociological theory in urban and regional research. *International Journal of Urban and Regional Research* 13(4), pp. 709–20.

Suggested Reading

Castells, M. 1977: *The urban question: a Marxist approach*. London: Edward Arnold.

Castells, M. 1978: *City, class and power*. London: Macmillan.

Castells, M. 1983: *The city and the grassroots*. London: Edward Arnold.

Lowe, S. 1986: *Urban social movements: the city after Castells*. New York: St. Martin's Press.

urban system   A set of interdependent urban places. The term was introduced by Berry (1964) as part of his application of SYSTEMS ANALYSIS and GENERAL SYSTEMS THEORY to the study of CENTRAL PLACE THEORY.

The concept of an urban system is that national territories are organized as a set of urban-centred regions – towns and cities plus their hinterlands – which together exhaust the land area, and are articulated into a working system through networks along which goods, services, ideas, capital and labour flow. Economic functions are distributed among these regions such that each urban centre and its associated hinterland has a prescribed set of roles within the parts (i.e. within the functional DIVISION OF LABOUR): over time those roles will change and the relative functions of places will vacillate. In the now ex-socialist countries of the Second World, such as the former USSR, the planning of a balanced urban system was a major aspiration.

Full description of the organization, operation and change in a system usually involves much data analysis (as in FUNCTIONAL CLASSIFICATION OF CITIES), but empirical studies have not been matched by theoretical advances which have shown the value of the terminology and concepts of systems theory, other than as very general descriptive devices.

With the increasing integration of the capitalist world-economy (cf. WORLD-SYSTEMS ANALYSIS), urban systems are developing which transgress national boundaries, as implied by the concept of a WORLD CITY.   RJJ

Reference

Berry, B. J. L. 1964: Cities as systems within systems of cities. *Pap. Proc. reg. Sci. Assoc.* 13, pp. 147–63.

urban village   A residential district, usually in the INNER CITY or the zone in transition of the ZONAL MODEL, and comprising a clustering of people with a common cultural background and forming a COMMUNITY. Early studies in URBAN ECOLOGY (cf. CHICAGO SCHOOL) suggested that cities were characterized by weak community ties, in contrast to rural areas (cf. RURAL–URBAN CONTINUUM) – by *Gesellschaft* (association) rather than *Gemeinschaft* (community), in Tonnies's classic dualism – although Wirth's classic study of the urban GHETTO contradicted this claim (cf. URBANISM). The identification of urban villages is often associated with Gans's (1962) detailed PARTICIPANT OBSERVATION of an area of inner Boston, where he found an Italian community brought together there through CHAIN MIGRATION and remaining there to assist with assimilation into the host society, to defend the migrants' culture, and to make possible the provision of services – such as food shops – oriented to their market alone.

RJJ

Reference

Gans, H. J. 1962: *The urban villagers: group and class in the life of Italian-Americans.* New York: Free Press of Glencoe.

Suggested Reading

Johnston, R. J. 1988: Living in America. In Knox, P. L., Bohland, J., Holcomb, B., Johnston, R. J. and Bartels, E. H., *The United States: a contemporary human geography.* London: Longman, pp. 237–59.
Ley, D. F. 1974: *The black inner city as frontier outpost.* Washington, DC: Association of American Geographers.

urbanism A way of life associated with residence in an urban area. The concept was introduced in the 1930s in a classic essay by a sociologist of the CHICAGO SCHOOL, Louis Wirth (1938), who was concerned with moral issues relating to observed urban social problems; he identified URBANIZATION as a process leading to the erosion of the moral order of society because of the concomitant decline of COMMUNITY. The complexity of social and economic organization and the fineness of the DIVISION OF LABOUR in urban areas fragments the individual's life: much social interaction is thus transitory and superficial with 'unknown' others, in con-

trast to the situation of strong extended family ties and communities in rural areas and small settlements. Thus, to Wirth, the social disorganization of cities stems from their size, their density and their heterogeneity, his three criteria for distinguishing urban places (cf. RURAL–URBAN CONTINUUM).

Wirth's thesis was typical of work that identified the URBAN as a separate spatial realm with its own environmental influences on individuals. However, it contradicted much of the other work of the Chicago School (including Wirth's own on the GHETTO), which identified strong communities within urban areas (cf. URBAN VILLAGE), and it failed to locate the processes of URBANIZATION within the wider political economy of CAPITALISM. RJJ

Reference

Wirth, L. 1938: Urbanism as a way of life. *Am. J. Soc.* 44, pp. 1–24.

Suggested Reading

Smith, M. P. 1979: *The city and social theory.* Oxford: Blackwell/New York: St. Martin's Press.

urbanization The process of becoming urban. In general usage, urbanization refers to the relative concentration of a territory's population in towns and cities (i.e. relative urban growth).

As a *demographic process*, which is the commonest use of the term, urbanization is presented as a process whereby towns and cities grow in relative importance within a space-economy through, first, an increasing proportion of the population living in all urban places and, second, the growing concentration of those people in the larger urban settlements. The end of the sequence is thus an almost completely urbanized society, with the great majority of its population living in just a few large urban places (but see COUNTERURBANIZATION).

Linked to these demographic processes (of which MIGRATION is usually the main contributor to urban growth) are the *structural changes* in society consequent upon the development of industrial CAPITALISM. Cities are the foci of the production, distribution and exchange processes that lie at the heart of this mode of production, because of the ECONOMIES

OF SCALE and the benefits of concentration and centralization of ownership (see AGGLOMERATION), and so urbanization is seen as a necessary component of INDUSTRIALIZATION and DEVELOPMENT (but see OVERURBANIZATION).

Finally, there is what is termed *behavioural urbanization*. Urban areas, especially the larger ones, are presented as the centres of social change: values, attitudes and behaviour patterns are modified in the urban milieux (cf URBANISM), and new forms are then spread to the rest of the territory by DIFFUSION processes operating through the URBAN SYSTEM.

This three-part model of urbanization sees demographic change as a dependent variable within a process driven by structural imperatives. However, it is a model particularly suited to analysis of capitalist systems. It has been demonstrated, for example, that substantial urban growth and urbanization occurred in other parts of the world, notably Asia, long before the INDUSTRIAL REVOLUTION and rapid urbanization of the North Atlantic area in the nineteenth and twentieth centuries: city growth is not a feature of industrial societies alone, and large settlements have been characteristic of other FORMS OF ECONOMIC INTEGRATION: similarly, rapid urban growth is occurring in many parts of the contemporary THIRD WORLD, as migrants flock to SQUATTER SETTLEMENTS, with aspirations for better economic and social conditions than found in smaller places. Thus, as the arguments on counterurbanization and overurbanization also show, demographic urbanization can come about in a variety of contexts, and there is no reason to suppose that what is typical of one time and place will necessarily be typical of others.   RJJ

Suggested Reading

Johnston, R. J. 1989: *City and society: an outline for urban geography*. London: Unwin Hyman.

Taylor, P. J. 1989: The error of developmentalism in human geography. In Gregory, D. and Walford, R., eds, *New horizons in human geography*. London: Macmillan, pp. 303–19.

utility   See PLACE UTILITY.

utility theory   The basis of NEOCLASSICAL ECONOMICS, which rests on the doctrine of consumer sovereignty and an ideological belief in both individualism and libertarianism – that individuals are the best judges of their own needs (cf. MERIT GOODS). The theory identifies a consumer's utility function based on (either assumed or revealed) preferences and predicts choices, constrained by the available budget (cf. REVEALED PREFERENCE ANALYSIS). Utility theory has provided the base for much work on travel behaviour and the choice of which shopping centre to patronize, referring to destination, MODAL SPLIT (choice of travel mode) and choice of route (cf. DISCRETE CHOICE MODEL).   RJJ

Suggested Reading

Golledge R. G. and Timmermans, H. 1990: Applications of behavioural research on spatial problems. I. Cognition. II. Preference and choice. *Progr. hum. Geogr.* 14, pp. 57–100 and 311–44.

V

values A set of beliefs and ideas which inform our assessments of worthiness.

Values are socially specific; they are derived from the concepts that we use to legitimate SOCIETY. To take values seriously implies far more than the liberal manoeuvre of presenting different points of view about the same set of circumstances – for example, whether nuclear power is good or bad – or even of evaluating between alternative sets of circumstances – for example, whether this distributive outcome is better or worse than that one. Rather, the issue is to relate these assessments, which are perfectly valid in their own right, to the wider social framework which sets the parameters – such as profitability and human needs – within which measures of worth are defined.

For example, in pointing to fundamentals, the expression 'the bottom line' is both offensive and realistic. It is *offensive* in its assumption that values measured in a particular form of market economy are somehow elemental; but it is *realistic* if it represents a response to the imperatives of capitalist society (see CAPITALISM). However, it is *particularly offensive* when the latter usage is simply assumed as unproblematic and beyond debate – most especially in a context in which critical thought might be a reasonable expectation.

Consider the diminution of geography implied in the following assertions:

The need for theory still exists but only to the extent that it will be used if it can be shown to deliver 'better' working models or is otherwise useful . . . . . if geographers are not prepared to meet these emerging needs . . . . [they] will be left with no other course of action other than to become social theorists in the style of Harvey and Scott (Openshaw, 1989, p. 74).

Usefulness is here contrasted with knowledge, categorized as 'useless' if

the questions being asked relate to the pursuit of knowledge rather than more pressing [*sic*!] applied matters of contemporary relevance and public concern (Openshaw, 1986, p. 143).

However, there is some compensation for looking at the world from such a narrow perspective; it opens up a more 'valuable' alternative:

There are vast potential new markets if geographers are able to sell themselves, merchandise their products, and adopt a less [*sic*!] restrictive *modus operandi* (Openshaw, 1989, p. 88).

Again, it is one thing to make the legitimate, if value-laden, claim that the 'key aspect' for the future health of geography as an academic discipline 'is a better understanding of the structure of economic incentives and rights, rather than class' (Bennett, 1989, p. 289). But it is quite another if this is taken to mean that a concern for 'CLASS' is not relevant to issues such as ' "choice" conceptions of rights which promote autonomy, freedom, self-determination, and human development' (Bennett, 1989, p. 289) on the grounds that

capitalism has become seen as the means of creating and distributing the good things of life . . . [as] . . . . the spirit of market freedom of individuals has heralded a consumer and service economy which has offered the release from the least attractive toils and labours, and has seemed to offer the potential to satisfy many of people's most avaricious dreams (p. 286).

Not only does the conclusion (that issues such as class are no longer relevant to geography) not follow from the premise (capitalism produces and generates the good things of life – a view which is, in any case, hotly contested) but – and much more importantly from the point of view of this discussion – there is an unquestioned assumption that 'the bottom line' may be *unproblematically* defined in terms of 'avaricious dreams'. The assumption of a particular measure of value could hardly be more clear.

One of the major contributions of RADICAL GEOGRAPHY was its demonstration of the social construction of value and, by implication, the possibility of changing values. In parallel fashion, HUMANISTIC GEOGRAPHY pointed to the often contested and limiting prior definitions of the objects of research implied in particular methodologies – notably those such as EMPIRICISM – which rest upon a limited perception and narrow definition of 'facts' (Buttimer, 1974).

Unless it is literally true that 'facts' are both unproblematic and, always and everywhere, speak for themselves, a value-free geography is impossible. How, for example, do we value the environment: in monetary terms? That would be a socially relative, and geographically and historically uncertain measure if ever there was one. In ecological terms – but then what about the social construction of science? Or in political terms which recognize that human beings are part of NATURE, but are social (and socially constructed) entities too, and so actively contest the meaning of the environment and their engagement with it? (See ECONOMIC GEOGRAPHY.)

If we accept the need for the political resolution of such problems (and it is difficult to see how we may proceed without doing so, despite the fact that the formal practice of politics itself is far from unproblematic) then we must accept that nature itself is a social construct and so reject in no uncertain terms the notion that geography is nothing more than an uncontested 'space–time data model' or 'huge integrated GIS' (Openshaw, 1991, pp. 622 and 627). And we must go further, for geographers cannot merely *contemplate*

alternative social constructions of values, for they are themselves *participants* in the process of the production and reproduction of values. The question of ETHICS goes well beyond the important matter of *conducting* and *reporting* research. It asks questions about the *moral purposes* of research. But it can never be enough merely to assert

a moral duty to help society and the world to unlock and understand the key patterns and relationships that may exist encrypted in . . . [GIS] . . . data bases. (Openshaw, 1991, p. 625)

It is not enough because, despite the phenomenal but geographically highly uneven power of GISs to generate data, the very processes of *unlocking, understanding* and *identifying key* patterns and relationships implies a set of values which cannot be assumed away or ignored.

Values and ethics force geographers to reconsider questions of, for example, social justice as well as 'economic incentives and rights', not merely as states to be measured or defined but as the basis for the purpose of their labours. RL

References and Suggested Reading

Bennett, R. J. 1989: Whither models and geography in a post-welfarist world? In Macmillan, B., ed., *Remodelling geography*. Oxford: Blackwell, pp. 273–90.

Buttimer, A. 1974: *Values in geography*. Association of American Geographers, Commission on College Geography, Resource Paper number 24. Washington, DC.

Openshaw, S. 1986: Modelling relevance. *Environ. Plann. A* 18, pp. 143–7.

Openshaw, S. 1989: Computer modelling in geography. In Macmillan, B, ed., *Remodelling geography*. Oxford: Blackwell, pp. 70–88.

Openshaw, S. 1991: A view of the GIS crisis in geography, or, using GIS to put Humpty-Dumpty back together again. *Environ. Plann. A*, 23, pp. 621–8.

variable cost analysis An approach to industrial location (or the location of facilities in general), concerned with spatial variations in production costs. This is one of two major alternative approaches to INDUSTRIAL LOCATION THEORY in ANALYSIS.

In its simplest form, the variable cost model may be expressed as follows:

$$TC_i = \sum_{j=1}^{n} Q_j U_{ij},$$

where TC_i is the total cost of producing a given volume of output at location i, Q_j is the input coefficient or required quantity of input j, and U_{ij} is the unit cost of the input in question at location i. The total cost is simply the summation over n inputs of the product of required quantity and unit cost.

As the above expression shows, total cost (for a given output) depends on two major considerations; the input coefficients and spatial variations in input cost. The input coefficients arise from the technique adopted in manufacturing the goods in question. Input coefficients can vary from place to place, within technical constraints that may require certain minimum quantities, as the quantity of a particular input used increases where its cost is low relative to that of other inputs. The capacity to substitute among inputs, along with the fact that input combinations may also vary with scale of output, greatly increases the complexity of variable cost analysis in both theory and practice.

The unit cost of the required input will vary in geographical space in obvious ways. For many materials these will be a reflection of TRANSPORT COSTS, but for other inputs all manner of complications can arise to influence the spatial cost pattern. For example, the cost of labour per unit of output can vary with actual wage rates, fringe benefits paid, training costs and welfare facilities provided by the firm, as well as with the productivity of labour. The intricacy of modern systems of INPUT-OUTPUT linkages, as manufacturing processes become more sophisticated technically, is a major complication in calculating input costs. Added to this is the difficulty of incorporating more general EXTERNAL ECONOMIES and advantages arising from AGGLOMERATION.

Variable cost analysis proceeds under one or other of two assumptions concerning the incidence of alternative locations: that they are discrete points, or that a continuous surface exists. The assumption of relatively few discrete points is the more realistic, in the sense that actual location practice generally involves the evaluation of a small number of alternatives. This is the usual framework for COMPARATIVE COST ANALYSIS. However, industrial location theory often proceeds on the implicit assumption that those locations actually considered and costed are selected from an infinite number of possible locations. Total cost is thus conceived of as a continuous spatial variable.

The concept of a continuous COST SURFACE is central to variable cost analysis as an approach to industrial location theory. The cost surface reveals, in effect, the topography of cost of production, any section through which can be depicted as a SPACE COST CURVE. With appropriate assumptions as to the form of the REVENUE SURFACE, an optimal or profit maximizing location can be identified, along with the SPATIAL MARGINS to profitability constraining freedom of choice of location.

If revenue is assumed to be a spatial constant, then the optimal location for the profit-maximizing firm will be where total cost is minimized; in other words, at the lowest point on the total cost surface. How this point arises and how it may be identified are the problems around which Alfred Weber (1929) built his classical approach to industrial location theory. Weber used the LOCATIONAL TRIANGLE to show how the point of least transport cost would arise in a simple situation, using the device of the ISODAPANE to identify spatial cost variations. The empirical identification of the point of least cost (or minimum aggregate travel) in an n-cornered locational figure has been a major operational problem in the subsequent development of the WEBER MODEL.

Much of the work of later exponents of the variable cost approach, such as T. Palander (1935) and E. M. Hoover (1948), was greatly influenced by Weber's theory. For almost half a century the variable cost model constituted the core of industrial location theory, but its lack of realism resulted in a broadening perspective with more attention given to revenue and decision-making considerations. Nevertheless, variable cost analysis is still highly relevant to actual location practice, from the small unit of production to the

MULTINATIONAL form. The cost of production is still very important to locational viability. And in the field of industrial development planning, variable cost analysis still provides a useful framework for the design of spatial strategy.   DMS

References

Hoover, E. M. 1948: *The location of economic activity.* New York: McGraw-Hill.

Palander, T. 1935: *Beitrage zur Strandortstheorie.* Uppsala: Almqvist and Wiksell.

Weber, A. 1929: *Alfred Weber's theory of the location of industries,* transl. C. J. Friedrich. Chicago: University of Chicago Press. (Reprinted 1971, New York: Russell and Russell; first German edition 1909.)

Suggested Reading

Smith, D. M. 1981: *Industrial location: an economic geographical analysis,* second edition. New York: John Wiley.

Smith, D. M. 1987: Neoclassical location theory. In Lever, W., ed., *Industrial change in the United Kingdom.* London: Longman, pp. 23–37.

variable revenue analysis An approach to INDUSTRIAL LOCATION THEORY concerned with spatial variations in revenue. It concentrates on the demand side of the industrial location problem, as opposed to the cost side addressed in VARIABLE COST ANALYSIS.

Total revenue may be defined as the product of the quantity of goods sold and the price obtainable for them. Revenue in alternative locations is thus:

$$TR_i = \sum_{j=1}^{n} Q_j P_j,$$

where TR_i is the revenue that can be earned by a plant located at i, Q_j is the quantity of goods that can be sold in market j, and P_j is the price at j. This expression is a first step to opening up the various determinants of revenue, operating through quantity sold and price charged respectively.

On the quantity (demand) side, sales expectations in any market j will be influenced by a number of variables. The most obvious is population: the more people, the greater the demand, other things being equal. Among those other things (which seldom, if ever, are equal) are the incomes of the people and their tastes or preferences, which influence the propensity to consume. Demand generally rises with income, but it can fall (which is the case for the so-called inferior goods that people tend to buy in smaller quantities as they become better off). Tastes may vary with income, but they are also subject to spatial variations in accordance with culture, custom and so on. Another influence on the local level of demand for a good is the availability and price of substitutes.

The other variable in the above expression – price – is discussed under PRICING POLICIES. There are various ways in which goods can be priced, and this choice will determine whether price varies from place to place and the pattern that such variations might take. As price falls, more of a good should be consumed, subject to limits on capacity to consume and on the ability of some goods to attract additional sales as price rises; for example, goods where status is gained by the purchase of things that are expensive. Price and quantity are thus related to each other in determining volume of revenue.

MARKET AREA ANALYSIS forms an important component of the variable revenue approach. The revenue that a firm can earn may be proportional to the market size or areal extent of the territory over which control can be exerted. However, the same area may yield different levels of revenue, because of the operation of the variables described above relating to the nature of the local population and its demand characteristics.

The analysis of market areas is closely bound up with LOCATIONAL INTERDEPENDENCE. The location of one unit of production is seen as dependent on the strategy of competitors, as they seek SPATIAL MONOPOLY or control over market areas. Specific analyses of how firms locate in competition with one another under variable revenue conditions include the HOTELLING MODEL and its extensions, which incorporate alternative assumptions as to the elasticity of demand. The variable revenue approach has arisen as much from the development of the theory of imperfect competition in economics as from the realization that the effect of the market on plant location goes further than the cost of distribution (as approached via the AGGRE-GATE TRAVEL MODEL).

The variable revenue approach is prone to both conceptual and practical difficulties. Although cost variations among alternative locations need not be disregarded completely (for example, they can be built into delivered price from alternative suppliers), the reciprocal relationship of unit cost to price via ECONOMIES OF SCALE is extremely difficult to handle. If unit cost varies with volume of sales, and this is dependent on price, which, in its turn, is influenced by unit costs, then the problem of the capital location is impossible to resolve. This is why industrial location theory makes such stringent assumptions on either the cost or the demand side.

At a practical level the variable revenue approach is more difficult to apply than variable cost analysis, because it is hard to identify consumer demand schedules: hence the adoption of alternatives, notably the MARKET POTENTIAL MODEL. Further complications arise from the actual practice of decision-making under the conditions of UNCERTAINTY that characterize real market competition. The unpredictability of consumer behaviour in choosing which outlet to patronize is a further complication.　　　　　　　　　　　　　　DMS

Suggested Reading
Smith, D. M. 1981: *Industrial location: an economic geographical analysis*, second edition. New York: John Wiley.
Smith, D. M. 1987: Neoclassical location theory. In Lever, W., ed., *Industrial change in the United Kingdom*. London: Longman, pp. 23–37.

vertical theme The testing out and tracing through of a distinctive PROCESS operating in a society and (particularly) its LANDSCAPE over time. The establishment of vertical themes is characteristic of studies of landscape change in classical HISTORICAL GEOGRAPHY (see MORPHOGENESIS; cf. CROSS-SECTION). Within that tradition, the model is usually taken to be Darby's (1951) account of the changing English landscape, which identified six themes: clearing the wood, draining the marsh, reclaiming the heath, the changing arable, the landscape garden, and urban–industrial growth. These themes are described in

conventional narrative form and often summarized as a progressive sequence of thematic maps. Darby reaffirmed his belief in such a procedure some ten years later, as an attempt to deal with the problem of combining historical and geographical description (Darby, 1962), and the schema has been adopted by a number of his students and others (see, e.g., Williams, 1974).　　　　　　　　　　　　　　DG

References
Darby, H. C. 1951: The changing English landscape. *Geogrl. J.*, 117, pp. 377–98.
Darby, H. C. 1962: The problem of geographical description. *Trans. Inst. Br. Geogr.* 30, pp. 1–14.
Williams, M. 1974: *The making of the South Australian landscape: a study in the historical geography of Australia*. London: Academic Press.

Vienna Circle (*Wiener Kreis*) A group of philosophers, mathematicians and natural scientists originally formed around Moritz Schlick, Professor in the Philosophy of the Inductive Sciences, at the University of Vienna in the 1920s and 1930s (see Kraft, 1953). The group first met in 1923, and in 1929 published its manifesto, 'The scientific conception of the world: the Vienna Circle' (translated in Neurath, 1973), which formalized the tenets of LOGICAL POSITIVISM. There were three basic claims:

(a) 'The scientific conception of the world knows only *empirical* statements about things of all kinds and *analytical* statements of logic and mathematics' (Neurath, 1973; emphasis added): hence Habermas's discussion of the 'empirical–analytical sciences' in his formulation of CRITICAL THEORY. But where Habermas also discussed the 'historical–hermeneutic sciences concerned with the clarification of meaning, the Vienna Circle had insisted that:

(b) 'The meaning of a proposition is identical with its *verification*' (Schlick, 1959; emphasis added): hence metaphysics was dismissed as meaningless.

(c) For some members of the Circle, the particulars of science were 'publicly accessible events', that is 'physical events locatable within a single set of space and time co-ordinates', and this principle of *physicalism* made possible the vision of a *unified* science which all members of the Circle endorsed (Bryant, 1985).

The Circle included Gustav Bergmann, who subsequently directly influenced Schaefer's critique of EXCEPTIONALISM in geography, and there were also close personal and intellectual connections with the artists and architects of the *Bauhaus*, and their conception of a systematic PRODUCTION OF SPACE under the sign of MODERNISM (Galison, 1990). Other members of the Circle included Rudolf Carnap, Kurt Gödel and Otto Neurath. Although Karl Popper and Ludwig Wittgenstein maintained critical links with the Circle they were not members; Popper's CRITICAL RATIONALISM was formulated, at least in part, as a *critique* of logical positivism, and he was especially scathing about (b) and (c) above.   DG

References

Bryant, C. G. A. 1985: *Positivism in social theory and research.* London: Macmillan.

Galison, P. 1990: Aufbau/Bauhaus: logical positivism and architectural modernism. *Critical Inquiry* 16, pp. 709–752.

Kraft, V. 1953: *The Vienna Circle: the origins of neo-positivism.* New York: Philosophical Library.

Neurath, O. 1973: *Empiricism and sociology.* Dordrecht: Reidel.

Schlick, M. 1959: Positivism and realism. In Ayer, A. J., ed, *Logical positivism.* London: Allen and Unwin, pp. 82–107.

Suggested Reading

Feigl, H. 1969: The origin and spirit of logical positivism. In Achinstein, P. and Barker, S., eds, *The legacy of logical positivism.* Baltimore, MD: Johns Hopkins University Press.

Galison (1990).

village   See URBAN VILLAGE.

von Thünen model   A model for analysing agricultural location patterns, based on the pioneering work of a Prussian landowner, Johann Heinrich von Thünen (see 1966 edn). The aim of his first volume was to explain variations in farm product prices and the way in which such variations influenced the use of agricultural land in any location. He envisaged a single market for the products and, by simplifying his analysis to a small number of variables

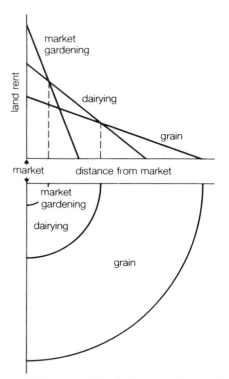

von Thünen model   *Land rent variations and land-use patterns.*

only, suggested that distance from the market would be a prime determinant of agricultural land use. Thus his model was a statement of what the contemporary distribution of land uses should be, given certain assumptions, and it has been widely used as a norm against which actual patterns are compared – thereby accepting that the assumptions are largely valid (Chisholm, 1979).

The model is constructed around the concept of RENT, and assumes that all farmers will produce on their land that commodity which yields the 'highest' rent, and so will maximize their net profits. This net profit is termed land rent (L), and its value is controlled by the production costs per unit of the commodity (a), its market price (P), the yield per unit of land (E), and the distance from the market to the production point (k). These are combined to give (Dunn, 1954):

$$L = E(p - a) - Efk.$$

In this context, land rent differs from economic rent in that it takes no account of OPPORTUNITY COSTS and so ignores what might be earned from alternative uses of the land.

In the simplest applications of the model, which have attracted geographers for several decades, transport costs are taken as the only variable (i.e. prices, production costs and yields are held constant for each commodity): rates per unit of distance vary, being highest for bulky and/or perishable items such as dairy products and timber. Thus land rent can be shown to decline away from the market point (cf. DISTANCE DECAY), but the rate of decline differs by commodity. The market price for each commodity determines the maximum rent, at the market point, and the result is differing land rent slopes, as shown for three commodities in the figure. If those distance decay curves are translated from one- to two-dimensional space, they suggest a zonal pattern of land-use organization around the market point.

Although geographers have focused on the distance variable in von Thünen's model, each of the others can also be allowed to vary, thereby producing idealized land-use patterns which reflect differences in land productivity, as von Thünen himself did, for example. Similarly, price changes and/or changes in production costs can be introduced, to illustrate how the zonal pattern might change as a consequence – on the assumption that farmers respond rationally to those changes (cf. RATIONAL CHOICE).

Geographers were particularly attracted to the zonal component of von Thünen's model, having 'discovered' it during the period in which LOCATIONAL ANALYSIS was a dominant paradigm, and its validity has been evaluated with considerable success at a range of spatial scales from the global (Peet, 1969) to the individual village and farm holding (Blaikie, 1971; Chisholm, 1979): the model also stimulated the modelling of zonal patterns of intra-urban land use in the same way (cf.

ALONSO MODEL). This concentration on the spatial factors has led to less recognition of the role of environmental factors as determinants of land-use patterns: von Thünen provided an analytical framework for geographers, only part of which was widely adopted, whereas the remainder was considered the source of a 'deviation' from the basic principles of LOCATIONAL ANALYSIS.

As with many economic models, von Thünen's simplifies the 'real world' in order to understand it, in ways that some find unacceptable. The processes of DECISION-MAKING by farmers are considerably oversimplified, for example, and the elements of RISK and UNCERTAINTY are ignored (see GAME THEORY and Wolpert, 1964). Its spatial component is thus no more than an IDEAL TYPE, therefore, whereas its analytical framework has much wider applicability.   RJJ

References

Blaikie, P. M. 1971: Spatial organization of agriculture in some north Indian villages. *Trans. Inst. Br. Geogr.* 52, pp. 1–40; 53, pp. 15–30.

Chisholm, M. 1979: *Rural settlement and location*, third edition. London: Hutchinson/Atlantic Highlands NJ: Humanities Press.

Dunn, E. S. 1954: *The location of agricultural production*. Gainesville, FL: University of Florida Press.

Peet, J. R. 1969: The spatial expansion of commercial agriculture in the nineteenth century: a von Thünen explanation. *Econ. Geogr.* 45, pp. 283–301.

von Thünen, J. H. 1966: *Isolated state, an English translation of 'Der isolierte staat' by C. M. Wartenberg*, ed. P. Hall. Oxford: Pergamon Press (originally published in 1826).

Wolpert, J. 1964: The decision process in spatial context. *Ann. Ass. Am. Geogr.* 54, pp. 337–58.

Suggested Reading

Grigg, D. B. 1984: *An introduction to agricultural geography*. London: Hutchinson.

Grotewold, A. A. 1959: Von Thünen in retrospect. *Econ. Geogr.* 35, pp. 346–55.

W

Weber model A device for analysing the location of industry, originated by Alfred Weber and elaborated as the LO-CATIONAL TRIANGLE. The Weber model provided the foundations for the VARIABLE COST ANALYSIS, which dominated the study of industrial location for many years. The emphasis on TRANSPORT COSTS and access to materials in the Weber model, as well as its outdated assumptions about industrial organization, limit its value in understanding the contemporary industrial world, although it can still be used to solve problems of locational optimality in conditions conforming to the broad structure of the model. Weber himself was critical of his preliminary formulations, however, and later sharply questioned the possibility of an autonomous LOCATION THEORY – and certainly of one which failed to acknowledge the importance of historical specificity (Gregory, 1981).   DMS

Reference

Gregory, D. 1981: Alfred Weber and location theory. In Stoddart, D. R., ed., *Geography, ideology and social concern*. Oxford: Blackwell, pp. 165–85.

Suggested Reading

Smith, D. M. 1981: *Industrial location: an economic geographical analysis*, second edition. New York: John Wiley.

welfare geography An approach to human geography that emphasizes questions of inequality and social justice. The welfare approach emerged from the radical reaction to the quantitative and model-building preoccupations of the 1960s, which were thought to be insufficiently concerned with contemporary social issues

(see RADICAL GEOGRAPHY). The 1970s saw a major redirection of human geography towards such welfare problems as poverty, hunger, CRIME, racial discrimination (see RACISM) and access to public services (e.g. health care and education). This corresponded to a major shift in societal concern, from narrow economic criteria of development or progress to broader aspects of the 'quality of life'.

Distributional issues have assumed additional importance in the current era of slow (or no) economic growth, for in these conditions policies of redistribution in favour of the poor or socially deprived can be implemented only at the expense of the rich or better-off members of a society (see PARETO OPTIMALITY). Dramatic political and social change, of the kind taking place in Eastern Europe and South Africa (see APARTHEID), also highlight distributional issues with a spatial dimension that raise questions of social justice (Smith, 1992). For example, the PRIVATIZATION of state assets such as housing and industrial enterprises in Eastern Europe is generating new forms of inequality, as some people in some places are better able than others elsewhere to benefit from post-socialist society.

The basic focus of the welfare approach is on who gets what, where and how. The 'who' refers to the population of the area under review (a city, region or nation, or even the entire world), subdivided into groups on the basis of CLASS, RACE, gender or other relevant characteristics. The 'what' refers to the various goods (and bads) enjoyed or endured by the population, in the form of commodities, services, environmental quality, social relationships and so on. The 'where' reflects the fact that living standards differ according to area of residence. The 'how' refers to the process whereby the observed differences arise.

The initial task posed by the welfare approach is descriptive. The present state of society, with respect to who gets what where, may be represented by extension of the abstract formulations of welfare economics, and the practical objective is to give these empirical substance. In a spatially disaggregated society, the general level of welfare may be written as:

$$W = f(S_1 \ldots S_n),$$

where S is the level of living or social well-being in a set of n territorial subdivisions. In other words, welfare is some function of the distribution of goods and bads among groups of the population defined by area of residence. Social well-being may be defined in terms of what the people actually get, as follows:

$$S = f(X_1 \ldots X_m),$$

where X represents the quantity of the m goods and bads consumed or experienced. Social well-being may also be expressed in terms of the distribution within the area in question:

$$S = f(U_1 \ldots U_k),$$

where U is the level of well-being, satisfaction or 'utility' of each of the k population subgroups. In all of the above expressions, the terms may be weighted differentially and combined according to any function, to represent the combination of territorial levels of well-being, goods and bads or group well-being that maximizes the objective function (W or S).

The empirical identification of inequality in any territorial distribution involves developing social indicators. These may combine particular elements of social well-being in a composite measure. Conditions that might be included are income, wealth, employment, housing, environmental quality, health, education, social order (i.e. absence of crime, deviancy and other threats to social stability and security), social participation, recreation and leisure. Alternatively, the focus may be on individual aspects of social well-being, such as inequalities in access to health care or the differential experience of a nuisance such as noise, air pollution and so on.

Descriptive research of this kind was initially justified on the grounds that it provided information on aspects of life hitherto neglected in geography. It also provides a basis for evaluation, whereby the existing state is judged against an alternative (past, predicted or planned) according to some criterion of welfare improvement. Thus the impact of alternative plans for facility location or closure (e.g. of hospitals) could be judged by the criterion of which would most equally (or least unequally) distribute the benefits (such as access to health care) among the populations of various subdivisions of the area under review. This raises the question of rules of distributive justice and the manner in which they are actually applied (explicitly or otherwise) in the political process.

The early preoccupation with descriptive research in welfare geography subsequently gave way to more process-oriented work on the question of how inequality arises. The abstract formulation of welfare problems based in NEOCLASSICAL ECONOMICS was found impotent as a basis for explanatory analysis, and alternatives such as MARXIAN ECONOMICS have become useful sources of guidance. Explanation tends to be sought at two different levels:

(a) The first involves understanding the operation of the economic–social–political system as an integrated whole, in order to reveal its general tendencies (see MODE OF PRODUCTION; SOCIAL FORMATION). Thus a broad examination of CAPITALISM shows that the generation of inequality is inevitable because it is endemic to the system: UNEVEN DEVELOPMENT is its spatial consequence. SOCIALISM as actually practised may have its own in-built tendencies towards inequality, apparently similar in spatial expression to some of those observed under capitalism, but with different origins and probably with less extreme manifestations among regions and within the city.

(b) The second level of explanation is concerned with details of how specific elements of an economic–social–political system operate. Examples might be the differential distribution of public services in a city, how the location of health-care facilities benefits some people in some places and disadvantages others elsewhere, or how the housing market (under capitalism) or administrative allocation process (under socialism) differentially bestows shelter according to who and where people are.

Although originally proposed as an alternative framework for human geography (Smith, 1977), the welfare approach soon merged with other lines of enquiry within geography directed towards the fundamental problem of inequality. The issues in question extend beyond the limits of a single discipline, and in fact render disciplinary boundaries increasingly irrelevant. The welfare approach logically requires an holistic social science perspective, including economic, social and political factors, and also consideration of the moral philosophy which underpins conceptions of social justice. In this rapidly changing world, where new political and economic institutional arrangements can benefit populations unequally, there is renewed interest in the issues raised by the welfare approach. (See also EQUALITY; EQUITY; INEQUALITY, GEOGRAPHY OF.)   DMS

References

Smith, D. M. 1977: *Human geography: a welfare approach*. London: Edward Arnold/New York: St. Martin's Press.

Smith, D. M. 1992: Geography and social justice: some reflections on social change in Eastern Europe. *Geogr. Res. Forum* 12, pp. 1–15.

Suggested Reading

Herbert, D. T. and Smith, D. M., eds 1989: *Social problems and the city: new perspectives*. Oxford: Oxford University Press.

Smith, D. M. 1979: *Where the grass is greener; living in an unequal world*. London: Penguin/Baltimore, MD: Johns Hopkins University Press. (Also published as *Geographical perspectives on inequality*. New York: Barnes and Noble.)

Smith, D. M. 1988: *Geography, inequality and society*. Cambridge: Cambridge University Press.

Smith, D. M. 1988: A welfare approach to human geography. In Eyles, J., ed., *Research in human geography: problem, tactics and opportunities*. Oxford: Blackwell, pp. 139–54.

Smith, D. M. 1989: *Urban inequality under socialism: case studies from Eastern Europe*. Update Series. Cambridge: Cambridge University Press.

Smith, D. M. and Pile, S. J. 1992: Inequality in the American city: some evidence from the South. *Geogr. Pol.*.

welfare state   A general term for those parts of the STATE APPARATUS involved in the provision of public services and benefits. It is generally assumed that the welfare state redistributes income and wealth in favour of the poorer groups within society, although empirical analyses have suggested that in at least some countries the more affluent benefit most from at least some public services (such as education and health care). The growth of the welfare state was especially rapid in the countries of the First World after the depression of the 1930s (see KONDRATIEFF CYCLES). Its size and extent have been under considerable attack (at the level of rhetoric in particular) from the 'New Right' in its formulation of policies to counter the recessions of the 1970s–1990s.   RJJ

Suggested Reading

Johnston, R. J. 1992: The rise and decline of the corporate-welfare state. In P. J. Taylor, ed., *The political geography of the twentieth century*. London: Belhaven Press, pp. 115–70.

well-being   See SOCIAL WELL-BEING.

wilderness   The United States Wilderness Act of 1964 defines wilderness as a landscape that 'generally appears to have been affected primarily by the forces of nature, with the imprint of man's [*sic*] works substantially unnoticeable'. The word derives from the Anglo-Saxon *wildeor*, denoting wild or savage beasts; in its early European sense, wilderness meant places (especially forests) in a savage condition, untamed by humankind. The Biblical meanings for which the word was adopted referred to different physical landscapes – such as deserts – but equally uncultivated and unhumanized ones. Wilderness in its early meaning thus carried strongly negative connotations, as an area to be feared and avoided if it could not be conquered and transformed. Such were the perceptions brought by early European settlers to the Americas. The early signs of a positive revaluation of wilderness in the USA are usually traced to the writings of the explorer and painter George Catlin and the naturalist Henry David Thoreau. Concern for protecting the remaining wilderness areas of North America spread rapidly, leading to the creation of the first NATIONAL PARKS and, more recently, National Wilderness Areas.   JEm

Suggested Reading
Nash, R. 1975: *Wilderness and the American mind.* New Haven: Yale University Press.
Oelschlaeger, M. 1991: *The idea of wilderness.* New Haven: Yale University Press.

world city A term coined by Patrick Geddes (1915) for 'certain great cities in which a quite disproportionate part of the world's most important business is conducted' (Hall, 1984, p. 1). Hall identified eight such cities, suggesting that they were centres of both economic and political power (although he later referred to them as 'giant metropolises'), but most writing has focused on their economic functions.

With the increasing global organization of the capitalist world-economy, the concept of a world city as a major focus of that organization has become increasingly commonplace.   RJJ

References
Geddes, P. 1915: *Cities in evolution.* London: Benn.
Hall, P. 1984: *The world cities*, third edition. London: Weidenfeld and Nicolson.

Suggested Reading
Chase-Dunn, C. 1985: The system of world cities. A.D. 800–1975. In M. Timberlake, ed., *Urbanization in the world economy.* New York: Academic Press, pp. 269–92.
Thrift, N. J. 1989: The geography of international economic disorder. In Johnston, R. J. and Taylor, P. J., eds, *A world in crisis? Geographical perspectives*, second edition. Oxford: Blackwell, pp. 16–78.

world-systems analysis A materialist approach to the study of social change developed by Immanuel Wallerstein (1974, 1979, 1980, 1983, 1984a). The approach builds upon three research traditions: the study of DEPENDENCE; the ANNALES SCHOOL; and Marxist theory and practice (see HISTORICAL MATERIALISM). The product is a unidisciplinary study of society combining economic, political and social aspects with history in an holistic historical social science.

Wallerstein argues that historically there have only been three basic ways in which societies have been organized to sustain production and reproduction, what he terms MODES OF PRODUCTION, but which derive more from Polanyi (1944) than from Marx. The *reciprocal-lineage* mode describes a society in which production is largely differentiated by age and gender, and exchange is simply reciprocal. The *redistributive-tributary* mode occurs when a society is class-based, with production carried on by a large majority of agriculturalists who pay tribute to a small ruling class. The *capitalist* mode of production is also class-based, but the distinguishing characteristic is ceaseless capital accumulation, operating through a market logic where prices and wages are set through supply and demand mechanisms (see CAPITALISM).

To discover which mode prevails in any society one must first define the real bounds of that society, as indicated by the DIVISION OF LABOUR in production. There are, therefore, just three types of society: *mini-systems* encompassing the reciprocal-lineage mode; *world-empires* defined by the redistributive-tributary mode; and *world-economies* which are capitalist (see FORM OF ECONOMIC INTEGRATION; SCALE). The latter two describe societies whose divisions of labour are larger than any one local grouping and so are designated 'world-systems'. There have been 'countless' mini-systems in the evolution of humankind and numerous world-empires since the Neolithic Revolution, but only one successful capital-expanding world-economy, which originated in Europe after 1450 and spread to cover the whole world by about 1900. Recent work on pre-capitalist systems has attempted to be historically more specific (Abu-Lughod, 1989; Chase-Dunn, 1990; Frank, 1990; Amin, 1991) but most studies using this approach focus on the capitalist world-economy.

World-systems analysis of the current situation treats the world as a single entity, the *capitalist world-economy*. The primary message of this approach is, therefore, that any meaningful study of social change cannot proceed country by country, but must incorporate the whole world-system. This is the single-society assumption which replaces the multiple-society assumption of most social science (Taylor, 1989). In world-systems terms the latter commit the fundamental error of DEVELOPMENTALISM (Taylor, 1989, 1992). Wallerstein identifies this error as being dominant in liberal studies of DEVELOPMENT and in orthodox Marxist analyses, both of which envisage individual countries progressing through stages.

The capitalist world-economy has three fundamental structural features. First, there is one world market, the logic of which permeates economic decisions throughout the system. Second, there is a multiple-state system in which no one state is able to dominate totally; it is this political competition which gives economic decision-makers room for manoeuvre that is not available in unitary world-empires. Finally, there is a three-tier structure of stratification throughout the system, which prevents polarization by the existence of middle groupings between the extremes. One representation of this structure is to be found in the spatial organization of the world-economy, where Wallerstein adds a '*semi-periphery*' category between the commonly recognized '*core*' and '*periphery*'. The semi-periphery is political in nature, as a stabilizing force between the economic–geographical extremes. It plays a key role in the dynamics of the world-economy, since it is in the semi-periphery where the most acute CLASS struggle occurs, particularly when it becomes the focus of periodic restructuring, as illustrated by Latin America and Eastern Europe in the 1980s. In Wallerstein's scheme, core and periphery are not geographically static, but are continually changing, with selected countries moving up and down through the semi-periphery. Furthermore, this process does not occur at a constant rate. Wallerstein recognizes that the goal of ceaseless accumulation produces consecutive

periods of stagnation and growth. Long waves (KONDRATIEFF CYCLES, logistic curves) are interpreted as the basic rhythm of the world-system (Wallerstein, 1984b), with the stagnation providing the necessary conditions for restructuring the world-economy, heavily involving the semi-periphery.

The capitalist world-economy is defined concretely by its integrated and hierarchical DIVISION OF LABOUR. This is expressed through myriad interlocking COMMODITY chains connecting extraction of raw materials to points of final consumption. Every chain is made up of numerous nodes of production, where value is added to the commodity on its way up the chain (Taylor, 1992). The social relations at each node will vary depending on the roles of the four basic institutions of the system at the node (Wallerstein, 1984a). These institutions are households, classes, peoples and states, which reproduce labour, capital, consent and order respectively (Taylor, 1991). The operation of these institutions varies immensely over the zones of the world-economy to reproduce UNEVEN DEVELOPMENT.

Wallerstein (1979) claims to be following 'the spirit of Marx if not the letter', so it is important to identify his differences with orthodox Marxism. As well as the error of developmentalism, there are two other key differences. First, in terms of MODE OF PRODUCTION Wallerstein uses a broader definition, resulting in his identification of capitalism not being reliant on the existence of 'free labour'. Hence, both 'feudal-like' social relations in parts of the 'third-world' and 'socialist-like' relations in what was the 'second world' are all part of a single division of labour which is the capitalist world-system. Second, Wallerstein proposes an alternative 'meta-history' which is also related to his identification of fewer modes of production. Orthodox Marxists share with liberals a progressive theory of history so that, for instance, the transition from FEUDALISM to capitalism is interpreted by both as a victory of 'advanced' bourgeois forces over 'traditional' feudal forces. Wallerstein identifies this transition as a regression, in that capitalism was the European, feudal ruling classes' solution to the crisis of their world-system – feudal Europe. The ruling class remained largely intact as the mode of production changed to provide new means of exploitation. This interpretation is important for understanding the current situation. The rhythm of the system is accompanied by secular trends which are asymptotic and, as these run their course, so the world-economy enters its CRISIS phase. The next transition will either be towards a more egalitarian system, which we may term socialism, or a new mode of production will again be invented to perpetuate inequalities. World-systems analysis is a contribution towards making the former more likely, but the future remains to be won.   PJT

References

Abu-Lughod, J. 1989: *Before European hegemony: the world system A.D.1250–1350*. New York: Oxford University Press.

Amin, S. 1991: The ancient world-system versus the modern capitalist world-system. *Review* 14, pp. 349–86.

Chase-Dunn, C. 1990: World-state formation: historical processes and emergent necessity. *Pol. Geogr. Q.* 9, pp. 108–30.

Frank, A. G. 1990: A theoretical introduction to 5,000 years of world system history. *Review* 8, pp. 155–248.

Polanyi, K. 1944: *The great transformation*. Boston: Beacon Press.

Taylor, P. J. 1989: The error of developmentalism in human geography. In Walford, R. and Gregory, D., eds, *New horizons in human geography*. London: Macmillan.

Taylor, P. J. 1991: The legacy of imperialism. In Dixon, C. and Heffernan, M., eds, *Colonialism and development in the contemporary world*. London: Mansell.

Taylor, P. J. 1992: Understanding global inequalities: a world-systems approach. *Geogr.* 77, pp. 1–11.

Wallerstein, I. 1974: *The modern world system: capitalist agriculture and the origins of the European world-economy in the sixteenth century*. New York: Academic Press.

Wallerstein, I. 1979: *The capitalist world-economy*. Cambridge: Cambridge University Press.

Wallerstein, I. 1980: *The modern world system II: mercantilism and the consolidation of the European world-economy, 1600–1750*. New York: Academic Press.

Wallerstein, I. 1983: *Historical capitalism*. London: Verso.

Wallerstein, I. 1984a: *The politics of the world-economy*. Cambridge: Cambridge University Press.

Wallerstein, I. 1984b: Long waves as capitalist process. *Review* VII(4), pp. 559–76.

Suggested Reading

Amin, S., Arrighi, G., Frank, A. G. and Wallerstein, I. 1982: *Dynamics of global crisis*. New York: Monthly Review Press.

Chase-Dunn, C. 1988: *Global formation*. Oxford: Blackwell.

Foster-Carter, A. 1978: The modes of production controversy. *New Left Rev.* 107. pp. 47–77.

Goldstein, J. 1988: *Long cycles*. New Haven: Yale University Press.

Hopkins, T. K. and Wallerstein, I. 1982: *World-systems analysis*. Beverly Hills, CA: Sage.

Taylor, P. J. 1989: The world-systems project. In Johnston, R. J. and Taylor, P. J., eds, *A world in crisis? Geographical perspectives*, second edition. Oxford: Blackwell.

Taylor, (1992).

Thompson, W. R., ed. 1983: *Contending approaches to world system analysis*. Beverly Hills, CA: Sage.

Wallerstein (1979, 1983, 1984a, b).

Wallerstein, I. 1991a: *Geopolitics and geoculture*. Cambridge: University Press.

Wallerstein, I. 1991b: *Unthinking social science: the limits of nineteenth century paradigms*. Cambridge: Polity Press.

Z

zero population growth (ZPG)

The tendency of a population to become stationary (see STABLE POPULATION). The likelihood of achieving ZPG, and its advantages and disadvantages, have been discussed increasingly both as a result of the marked decline in FERTILITY in many developed countries and as a possible long-term aim for the developing world. ZPG has direct implications in the short term for age structure and economic and social policy, but long-term relationships, especially with economic growth, are problematical. PEO

Suggested Reading

Spengler, J. J. 1978: *Facing zero population growth: reactions and interpretations, past and present.* Durham, NC: Duke University Press.

zone

See CHICAGO SCHOOL; CONTIGUOUS ZONE; ENTERPRISE ZONE; ZONAL MODEL; ZONING.

zonal model

A model of urban spatial organization developed by E. W. Burgess (1924, 1927), one of the sociologists of the CHICAGO SCHOOL. Burgess's main research interest was the determinants of urban social problems, such as vice and crime, and his mapping of their occurrence within Chicago indicated a concentration in certain type areas only. To appreciate the nature of these areas, he developed a model of the sociospatial organization of the entire city, which consisted of five major zones (see the figure).

The dominant feature of this zonal structure is the positive correlation between the socio-economic status of residential areas and their distance from the CENTRAL BUSINESS DISTRICT: the most affluent urban residents live in the outer suburbs, a finding which Burgess's followers generalized from Chicago to all American cities (see Schnore, 1965). Growth within the city was propelled from the centre through the process of INVASION AND SUCCESSION, whereby new in-migrants occupied the lowest-quality homes in the zone in transition, and pressed longer-established groups to migrate outwards towards the suburbs.

Burgess's model has been tested empirically many times, and has been subjected to a variety of criticisms. Hoyt, for example, proposed an alternative SECTORAL MODEL, and Harris and Ullman combined the two into their MULTIPLE NUCLEI MODEL. In addition, invasion and succession was presented as a special case of the FILTERING process which underpinned Hoyt's model. These models were popular with urban geographers in the 1960s and 1970s (Johnston, 1971) but are now widely considered as obsolete. RJJ

References

Burgess, E. W. 1924: The growth of the city: an introduction to a research project. *Publ. Am. Sociol. Soc.* 18, pp. 85–97.

Burgess, E. W. 1927: The determination of gradients in the growth of the city. *Publ. Am. Sociol. Soc.* 21, pp. 178–84.

Johnston, R. J. 1971: *Urban residential patterns: an introductory review.* London: George Bell.

Park, R. E., Burgess, E. W. and Mackenzie, R. T. 1925: *The city.* Chicago: University of Chicago Press.

Schnore, L. F. 1965: On the spatial structure of cities in the two Americas. In Hauser, P. M. and Schnore, L. F. eds, *The study of urbanization.* New York: John Wiley, pp. 347–98.

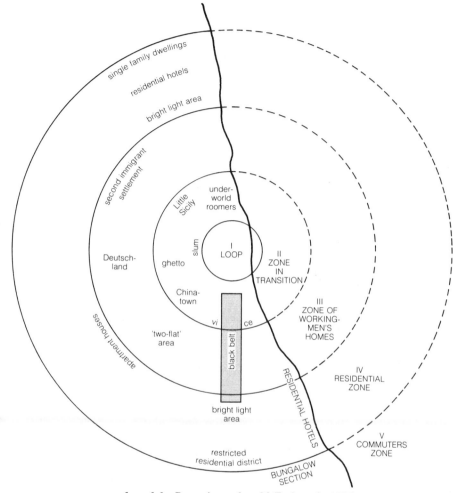

zonal model *Burgess's zonal model* (Park et al., 1925).

Suggested Reading

Burgess, E. W. and Bogue, D. J., eds 1965: *Urban sociology.* Chicago: University of Chicago Press.

zone of dependence The spatial clustering or 'ghettoization' of service-dependent groups and facilities designed to assist them in the core areas of cities (also referred to as the service-dependent population GHETTO). The most prominent force for present-day ghettoization is the trend towards deinstitutionalization, whereby many disabled people, such as the mentally retarded and the physically disabled, are discharged from institution-based care to care in the community.

The deinstitutionalization of ex-psychiatric patients is typical of the experience of many service-dependent groups. Their ghettoization following discharge is the result of a complex process. For instance, the INNER CITY is the place where there are: large properties available for conversion to community facilities; an established supply of cheap rental accommodation; and established support networks, both personal and those associated with service facilities. The ex-patients have gravitated towards core areas in search of housing opportunities. Such movement has often occurred over large distances, and includes rural–urban MIGRATION. Ex-patients have also been referred by professionals to core-area housing and service opportunities. The market operations of supply and demand have been complicated by two other factors. First, there has sometimes been an extensive community opposition, which has excluded ex-patients from many residential areas, especially suburban neighbourhoods. Second, planners have typically attempted to avoid community conflicts over locational decisions by seeking out non-controversial sites for community-based facilities. These have typically been found in the inner city.

The ex-psychiatric patients have been joined in the service-dependent ghetto by a host of other deinstitutionalized populations, including the dependent elderly, the mentally retarded, the physically disabled, former prisoners and substance abusers (alcoholics and drug addicts). The past two decades have witnessed an unprecedented concentration of these populations in the inner-city zone of dependence, partly as a consequence of the current crisis of HOMELESSNESS.

As an urban phenomenon, the service-dependent ghetto represents a significant component of inner-city morphology. As a social-welfare phenomenon, the ghetto acts as a reservoir of potential clients and as a reception area for discharged individuals. For them, the inner city has become a coping mechanism. As more and more deinstitutionalized individuals arrive in the ghetto, so increasing numbers of services are needed to care for them. The new services themselves act as a catalyst to attract more clients, and so a self-reinforcing cycle of ghettoization is established.

MJD

Suggested Reading

Dear, M. and Wolch, J. R. 1986: *Landscapes of despair*. Princeton, NJ: Princeton University Press.

Rowe, S. and Wolch, J. 1990: Social networks in time and space: homeless women in skid row, Los Angeles. *Ann. Ass. Am. Geogr.* 80(2), pp. 184–204.

Wolch, J. R. and Dear, M. 1993: *Inside outside: homelessness in Los Angeles*. San Francisco: Jossey-Bass.

zoning The general process of sub-dividing geographical space for some purpose, especially for implementing public space-use policy. While usually applied to land designations, zoning can also relate to water bodies and to reconcile the competing demands of various commercial and recreational uses. Whatever the context, individual tracts, or zones, are identified with some preferred uses(s) either by positive designation (for example, low-cost housing or community recreation) or, by precluding undesirable ones, through negative, exclusionary, zoning.

In Britain land-use policy is primarily based on judging planning applications on their merits, with regard to previously agreed planning strategies, but in North America, where the term zoning is most widely applied today, decisions on what is allowed where in a municipality are taken in advance of particular applications, through zoning ordinances. In the USA it is 'the most influential public technique for controlling private land use . . . in the 20th century' (Ervin, 1977, p. 6). Its first appearance in Boston in about 1904 was followed by the first zoning ordinance for an entire community, in New York City in 1916. A landmark decision in the US Supreme Court a decade later upheld the constitutional basis of zoning regulations, since when they have extended to specifying the height, density and size of urban construction, as well as permitted uses.

Zoning's proponents point to its offering protection against undesirable EXTERNALITIES (for example, polluting, noisy or otherwise dangerous activities), the constraining of costs of supplying municipal services, and the efficient provision of PUBLIC GOODS. Its opponents emphasize the essentially negative effect of slowing or preventing developments and maintaining the status quo, by eliminating undesirable activities (for example, low-income housing for blacks, or obnoxious industry). Thwarted developers can challenge zoning ordinances through the Courts. Generation of zoning regulations is very much part and parcel of LOCAL STATE politics within US municipalities (Allensworth,

1980). Most, although not all, operate zoning practices under the aegis of state enabling legislation, which allows for a variety of municipality-level responses. Houston has developed with no zoning regulations at all. AGH

References

Allensworth, D. 1980: *City planning politics*. New York: Praeger.

Ervin, D. E. et al. 1977: *Land use control: evaluation economic and political effects*. Cambridge, MA: Ballinger.

INDEX

resistance to cultural hegemony,
244
subjectivity, human, **604**
poststructural view of, 468, 604
and science, 457
and sexuality, 553
in social geography, 562
and value-free research, 171
subsistence agriculture, 6, **605**
adaptation to local environment,
111
exchange not part of, 78
intensification, 7, 35–6
suburbs, **605–6**
decentralization to, 121
invasion and succession, 14,
62–3, 680
Marxist analysis, 366–7, 605
women's isolation in, 194, 605
succession
vegetation, 155
see also invasion and succession
sunbelt, **606**
migration to, 99
sunrise industries, 606
superstructure, 289, 361, **606–8**
and planning, 654
see also infrastructure
Suppe, F., 350–1
supply
in equilibrium with demand,
169–70, 411–12
supply curves, 124, **608–9**
supranation-states, 592
surfaces, 608–9
see also cost surfaces; revenue
surfaces; trend surface analysis
surplus
extraction under feudalism, 198,
199
neo-Ricardian analysis, 417
political economy emphasis on,
446–7
surplus labour, 485
surplus value
alienation, 12; and urban origins,
660
and development of dependence,
126
expropriation by capitalists, 312,
362–3
neoclassical economics'
interpretation, 312
as productivity measure, 483
underconsumption, 646
surveillance, **609–10**
and modernity, 389–90
police role, 446
see also data collection;
geographical information
systems
survey analysis, **610–11**
in industrial location studies, 122
interview data in, 298
in medical geography, 242
questionnaires in, 200, 298,
494–5, 610–11
thin description in, 623

see also sampling
surveying, 45, **611**
and GIS, 219
surveys
land-use, 6, 21–2, **315–16**
national: map series related to, 51
promoted by le Play Society, 328
sustainable development, **611**
global policy and planning
guided by, 232
not limited to environmental
relations, 148
see also resource management
Sweden, second homes in, 546
swidden, 555
Switzerland, consociationalism in,
88
symbolic interactionism, **611–13**
in humanistic geography, 264
symbolization, 45, 46, **613–14**
synthetic statements, 350, 456
systematic samples, 542, 543
systems, **614–15**
abstract, 632
chaotic conception of, 61
equilibrium, 192, 615
feedback in, 192, 396–7, 615
functionalism, 209, 210, 614
information in, 288
interdependence within, 614–15;
and bifurcation, 34–5
isomorphisms among, 216
open, 614; realist approach to,
499–500
social, 595–6, 601
structural functionalist approach
to, 595–6
urban, *see* urban systems
see also general systems theory
systems analysis, 396–7, **615**
and functionalism, 210
process in, 478
regional, 511
of space-economy, 576
in urban ecology, 656
see also lead–lag models; world-
systems analysis

taken-for-granted worlds, 582,
616–17
and discourse, 136
and geographical imagination,
218
ideal types in, 269
spaces of representation in, 482
and symbolic interactionism,
612–13
Tansley, A.G., 155
tariffs, **617**, 638
in common markets, 79
taxation
avoided in informal economy,
287
and fiscal crisis, 202
and migration, 202
and public service provision, 624
taxation policy
input–output analysis of, 291

Taylor, C., 552
Taylor, E.G.R., 224, 559
Taylor, F.W., 617
Taylor, G.T., 163
Taylor, P.J., 23, 86, 544
Taylor, T.G., 657
Taylorism, 311, **617**
technical division of labour, 139
technological change
and flexible production, 152, 311
and Kondratieff cycles, 305–7
and labour process, 311
and leisure, 330
technological risks, 241
technology
and staple production, 591
transfer of, 545
telecommunications
and service industries, 551
teleology, **617**
in stages-of-growth model, 587
telescience, 525
tenancy, 314
tenants
feudal, 198
sharecropping, 554
tenure, *see* housing tenure; land
tenure
terms of trade, 617–18
territorial justice, 565, **618**
and public service provision,
489–90
territorial production complex, 618
territorial seas, 326, 573, **618–19**
see also contiguous zones
territorial social indicators, 568,
619–20, 675
territoriality, 36, **620**
and crime prevention, 100
dynamic: and boundaries, 26
and geopiety, 227
territory, **620–1**
and community, 80–1
state: defence of, 86; enclaves
within, 158–9, 299; exclaves,
175–6; secession, 546;
sovereignty over, *see*
sovereignty; struggles for, 18
see also place; regions
texts, **621–2**
culture as, 116, 621
deconstruction, 466–7, 468
hermeneutic approach to, 244–6,
621
landscape as, 317, 636
and qualitative methods, 492
thematic apperception test, 31
thematic maps, 622
see also choropleth map
theories, **622–3**
falsification, 104, 187, 268
fragmentation associated with,
233
historical geography's
contribution to, 248
in humanistic geography, 264–5
and hypotheses, 267
and laws, 320–1, 622

Index compiled by Ann Barham